SIXTH EDITION

ESSENTIALS OF PSYCHOLOGY

SIXTH EDITION

ESSENTIALS OF PSYCHOLOGY

SPENCER A. RATHUS

MONTCLAIR STATE UNIVERSITY

HARCOURT COLLEGE PUBLISHERS

FORT WORTH   PHILADELPHIA   SAN DIEGO   NEW YORK   ORLANDO   AUSTIN   SAN ANTONIO
TORONTO   MONTREAL   LONDON   SYDNEY   TOKYO

Publisher	Earl McPeek
Acquisitions Editor	Brad Potthoff
Market Strategist	Katie Matthews
Project Editor	Michele Tomiak
Art Director	Carol Kincaid
Production Manager	Cynthia Young

ISBN: 0-15-508065-2
Library of Congress Catalog Card Number: 00-105868

Address for Domestic Orders
Harcourt College Publishers, 6277 Sea Harbor Drive, Orlando, FL 32887-6777
800-782-4479

Address for International Orders
International Customer Service
Harcourt, Inc., 6277 Sea Harbor Drive, Orlando, FL 32887-6777
407-345-3800
(fax) 407-345-4060
(e-mail) hbintl@harcourt.com

Address for Editorial Correspondence
Harcourt College Publishers, 301 Commerce Street, Suite 3700, Fort Worth, TX 76102

Web Site Address
http://www.harcourtcollege.com

Harcourt College Publishers will provide complimentary supplements or supplement packages to those adopters qualified under our adoption policy. Please contact your sales representative to learn how you qualify. If as an adopter or potential user you receive supplements you do not need, please return them to your sales representative or send them to: Attn: Returns Department, Troy Warehouse, 465 South Lincoln Drive, Troy, MO 63379.

Printed in the United States of America

0 1 2 3 4 5 6 7 8 9   048   9 8 7 6 5 4 3 2 1

Harcourt College Publishers

Voltaire, the French man of letters, apologized to a friend for writing a long letter. He had not the time, he lamented, to write a brief one. Similarly, writing *Essentials of Psychology* has posed a special challenge for me. The book has had three key goals that have brought it to the present day.

GOALS FOR ESSENTIALS OF PSYCHOLOGY

The first goal is to provide concise yet accurate coverage of the science of psychology. The second is the presentation of a complete learning package, one that includes a built-in Study Guide and application of the PQ4R method of learning and studying. The third is to stimulate critical thinking in students so that they can distinguish between science and superstition and continue to educate themselves for a lifetime.

Concise, Accurate Coverage of the Science of Psychology

I have striven to be concise, yet to cover the common core of subject matter that psychology professors will agree is essential. Conciseness is needed so that students can cover the course within the framework of a college term. As this book enters its sixth edition, however, it has been brought home to me repeatedly that finding the "essential" material in psychology is no less daunting a task than finding, say, the one true psychological theory of learning or personality. To put it another way, no such agreement is possible. Most (but not all!) psychologists would agree that such a book should cover research methods, biology and behavior, human growth and development, sensation and perception, learning, memory, thinking (cognition), intelligence, motivation and emotion, personality, psychological disorders and their treatment, and social psychology. Yet some editions of this textbook have not had a chapter on health psychology (labeled "Stress and Health" in the current edition), and many professors have let me know in no uncertain way that they consider the topic to be essential. Similarly, the previous edition of the text did not have a chapter on gender and sexual behavior, and so many professors said that they considered to topic to be essential that the current edition has full-chapter coverage of "Gender and Sexuality." On the other hand, some professors over the years have told me that chapters such as "Sensation and Perception," "Consciousness," "Personality," "Social Psychology," and others are not essential to them. I have already ripped out most of my hair, so I have little left to give. But let me note that the current edition addresses the areas mentioned above and also has chapters on "Stress and Health" and "Gender and Sexuality." Yet it manages to be more concise than the previous edition—it contains 15 chapters instead of 16.

A Complete Learning Package

The second key goal is to provide a complete learning package in the textbook. To this end the pedagogy has been fine-tuned and amplified to include the PQ4R method and more—much more. Each chapter has a built-in Study Guide, which includes a summary in question-and-answer format *(new feature)*, exercises, Bridging the Gap—Language and Culture sections that acquaint students with the English idioms and cultural references used in the chapter, a 20-item multiple-choice quiz, and Recite sections that provide students with the opportunity to respond to the questions raised in the chapter *(new feature)*.

Critical Thinking

The third key goal in the text is to stimulate critical thinking in the student. Critical thinking involves development of skepticism about explanations and conclusions, the ability to inquire about causes and effects, refinement of curiosity about behavior, knowledge of research methods, and the ability to critically analyze arguments. The focus on critical thinking reflects my view that a college education is intended to do more than provide students with a data bank of knowledge or occupational skills. It is also meant to provide students with the intellectual tools that will allow them to learn from and analyze information independently. With these tools, they can educate themselves for the rest of their lives.

Critical thinking is addressed both through features and through the subject matter of the text. "Truth or Fiction" features found at the beginning of each chapter encourage students to challenge folklore and common sense. "Reflect" features found throughout the text (*new feature*) encourage students to think deeply about what they are reading and to relate the subject matter to their own lives. Chapter 1 has a section on research methods that begins by defining the scientific attitude of skepticism and explains how psychologists know what they know. Theories and research are analyzed and criticized throughout the text so that students learn to analyze arguments for themselves and, when necessary, challenge the views of authority figures.

WHAT'S NEW IN THIS EDITION

The sixth edition of *Essentials of Psychology* contains several advances over earlier editions, including two new chapters and enhanced pedagogy.

New Chapters

The new chapters cover "Thinking and Intelligence" and "Gender and Sexuality."

Chapter 8: Thinking and Intelligence This concise but complete chapter covers the topics of thinking, concepts and concept formation, methods of problem solving, the role of creativity in problem solving, reasoning, judgment and decision making, the linguistic relativity hypothesis, definitions and theories of intelligence, the measurement of intelligence, socioeconomic and ethnic differences in intelligence, the issue of bias in intelligence testing, and the genetic and environmental determinants of intelligence.

Chapter 15: Gender and Sexuality This new chapter defines gender and discusses its impact on attitudes and behavior. It covers the topics of gender polarization (how people are polarized according to their gender and the costs of polarization for all of us), research findings on psychological gender differences, theories and research on gender-typing (on how we develop mental processes and behaviors that are considered stereotypical of women or men), the psychology of interpersonal attraction (including the topics of love and sexual orientation—that is, why people are attracted to people of the other gender or of their own gender), sexual response and sexual dysfunctions, and sexual coercion (rape and sexual harassment).

Enhanced Pedagogy

The sixth edition of *Essentials of Psychology* makes full use of the PQ4R method of learning and studying. The PQ4R method promotes active learning; students are encouraged to become proactive rather than reactive. *PQ4R* stands for *Preview, Question, Read, Reflect, Recite, and Review,* a method that is based on the work of educational psychologist Francis P. Robinson.

Previewing the Material With *Truth or Fiction?* **Features and Chapter** *Previews*
Previewing the material fine-tunes students' expectations. It helps them create mental templates or "advance organizers" into which they fit the material. The sixth edition of *Essentials of Psychology* has two features at the beginnings of chapters that help students preview the material: Truth or Fiction? items and a chapter Preview. The Truth or Fiction? items were found in previous editions and are intended to challenge common knowledge (which often has a way of being common ignorance). They stimulate students to delve into the subject matter to see whether their preconceptions are supported by the evidence. The *new* Preview feature outlines the sections in each chapter and tells students what each section does.

Phrasing and Answering Questions about the Material   Devising questions about the subject matter, before reading it in detail, is another feature of the PQ4R method. Writing questions gives students goals: They attend class or *read* the text *in order to answer the questions.* (Reading is the first "R" in PQ4R.) *New* to this edition: Students are helped to use the PQ4R method because they will find questions phrased in **blue** as they read along. When they see a question, they have the opportunity to read the following material in order to answer it. They can write the questions and answers in their notebooks, or they can use the *new* Recite feature in the built-in Study Guide at the end of each chapter.

Following are the first five questions in the Recite feature for Chapter 2—Biology and Behavior:

1. What are neurons?

2. What are the parts of neurons?

3. What is the neural impulse?

4. What is a synapse?

5. What are neurotransmitters?

Note that each question is followed by a number of lines where students can write out a complete answer or jot down key words that will help them recall a complete answer when they review the chapter.

Reflecting on the Material With New *Reflect* Features   Students learn more effectively when they *reflect* (the second "R" in PQ4R is for "Reflect") on what they are learning. In Chapter 7 ("Memory") we see that psychologists refer to reflection on subject matter as *elaborative rehearsal*. One way of reflecting on a subject is to relate it to things students already know about, whether it be academic material or events in their own lives (Willoughby et al., 1994[1]). Reflecting makes the material meaningful and easier to remember (Woloshyn et al., 1994[2]). It also makes it more likely that students will be able to *apply* the information to their own lives (Kintsch, 1994[3]). Through effective reflection, students may embed material firmly in their memory so that rote repetition is unnecessary.

Because of the value of reflection, *new* Reflect features have been placed in the margins. Some of them ask students to compare what they are reading with the ideas they had before they took the course. For example, the first Reflect feature reads "How would you have defined psychology before you began this course or opened your book? How does the true scientific nature of psychology differ from your expectations?" A Reflect feature in the chapter on "Developmental Psychology" reads "Why do you think that parents are so concerned about *when* their infants sit up or crawl or walk?"

Reciting and Reviewing the Material With New *Section Reviews, Summaries,* and *Recite* Sections   The PQ4R method recommends that once students have taken notes in question-and-answer format, they recite each answer aloud. Reciting answers aloud helps students remember them by means of repetition, by stimulating students to produce concepts and ideas they have learned, and by associating them with spoken words and gestures.

Each chapter of the text contains features that help students recite and review the material. These include Section Reviews, and, in the Study Guide at the end of each chapter, Summaries and Recite features.

The *new* Section Reviews are written in a format that prompts students to fill in missing material. For example, the first Section Review in the chapter on "Biology and Behavior" begins as follows: "The nervous system contains billions of cells called (1) _____ons. Neurons transmit messages to other neurons by means of chemical substances called (2) _____mitters." The blank spaces are numbered, and the answers (1—Neurons, 2—Neurotransmitters, etc.) are found at the ends of the chapters. Part of the missing words is provided to prompt recall.

The *new* Summaries review the material in question-and-answer format. To provide a sense of closure, the summaries repeat the questions found within the chapters, again in blue. The answers are concise but include most of the key terms found in the text.

The *new* Recite sections repeat the questions posed in the chapter, again in blue, and leave space for students to write answers in sentence form, or key words that will telegraph the answers to them when they return to study the section. The head of the section repeats the word *Recite,* and the word grows larger with each repetition. This is to suggest that students' knowledge of the material grows progressively stronger as they recite and review it.

---

[1] Willoughby, T., Wood, E., & Khan, M. (1994). Isolating variables that impact on or detract from the effectiveness of elaboration strategies. *Journal of Educational Research, 86,* 279–289.

[2] Woloshyn, V. E., Paivio, A., & Pressley, M. (1994). Use of elaborative interrogation to help students acquire information consistent with prior knowledge and information inconsistent with prior knowledge. *Journal of Educational Psychology, 86,* 79–89.

[3] Kintsch, W. (1994). Text comprehension, memory, and learning. *American Psychologist, 49,* 294–303.

TRADITIONAL ELEMENTS

The sixth edition of *Essentials of Psychology* retains a number of elements that have met the needs of students and professors in earlier editions. One of these is extensive coverage of human diversity. Another is tried and true pedagogy.

Coverage of Human Diversity

Coverage of human diversity is essential to the study of psychology. Although the profession of psychology focuses mainly on the individual, students cannot understand people's behavior and mental processes without reference to their diversity in terms of ethnicity, gender, and sexual orientation. Awareness of human diversity helps students understand how cultural beliefs, values, and attitudes affect behavior and mental processes.

Essentials of Psychology therefore continues to address the study of human diversity and its contribution to psychology. However, coverage of diversity is not segregated from the text in boxed format. It is integrated fully into the flow of the text, in topics as follows:

- The Sociocultural Perspective (Chapter 1)
- Gender, Ethnicity, and the Profession of Psychology (Chapter 1)
- Samples and Populations: Representing Human Diversity (Chapter 1)
- The Endocrine System and Human Diversity: Cross-Cultural Perspectives on Menstruation (*new*—Chapter 2)
- Language Development and Human Diversity: Ebonics (*new*—Chapter 3)
- Moral Development and Gender: Are There Gender Differences in Moral Development? (*new*—Chapter 3)
- Identity Formation, Gender, and Ethnicity (Chapter 3)
- Late Adulthood, Gender, and Ethnicity: Different Patterns of Aging (*new*—Chapter 3)
- Personality Development and Gender: Gender Differences (*new*—Chapter 3)
- Deafness, Sign Language, and Human Diversity: The Signs of the Times Are Changing (Chapter 4)
- Alcoholism, Gender, and Ethnicity (Chapter 5)
- Human Diversity and Smoking (Chapter 5)
- Cognitive Learning and Diversity: Culture, Ethnicity, and Learning (*new*—Chapter 6)
- Long-Term Memory and Human Diversity: The Role of Prejudice in the Reconstruction of Memories (*new*—Chapter 7)
- Intelligence and Diversity: Socioeconomic and Ethnic Differences in Intelligence (Chapter 8)
- Cultural Bias in Intelligence Testing (Chapter 8)
- Intelligence and Diversity: Stereotype Vulnerability (*new*—Chapter 8)
- Obesity and Diversity: Sociocultural Factors in Obesity (*new*—Chapter 9)
- Aggression and Diversity: The Sociocultural Perspective on Aggression (Chapter 9)
- Personality and Diversity: The Sociocultural Perspective (Chapter 10)
- The Effects of Individualistic and Collectivistic Societies on Personality (Chapter 10)
- The Effects of Sociocultural Factors on the Self-Concept (Chapter 10)
- The Effects of Acculturation on Self-Esteem (Chapter 10)
- Factors in Health and Diversity: The Roles of Ethnicity, Gender, and Socioeconomic Status (Chapter 11)
- Mood Disorders and Diversity: The Case of Women and Depression (*new*—Chapter 12)

- Suicide and Diversity: Who Commits Suicide? (Chapter 12)
- Psychotherapy and Diversity: Issues of Ethnicity, Gender, and Sexual Orientation (*new*—Chapter 13)
- Attitudes and Diversity: The Problem of Prejudice (Chapter 14)
- Gender, Helping Behavior, and Personal Space (Chapter 14)
- Gender Polarization (*new*—Chapter 15)
- Psychological Gender Differences (Chapter 15)
- Gender-Typing (Chapter 15)
- Sexual Coercion (*new*—Chapter 15)
- Attraction and Diversity: Gender Differences in the Importance of Physical Attractiveness (*new*—Chapter 15)
- The Matching Hypothesis: Do "Opposites Attract" or Do "Birds of a Feather Flock Together"? (Chapter 15)
- Sexual Orientation and Diversity: A Matter of Belonging (Chapter 15)

Tried and True Pedagogy

The learning aids in this book, as noted, contain the PQ4R method and more. Let us talk about the "more." The book also contains tried and true pedagogy that has helped students in previous editions: Truth or Fiction Revisited features, a running glossary, and in the Study Guide, exercises, Bridging the Gap features, and quizzes.

Truth or Fiction Revisited Features   Truth or Fiction Revisited features are found in the text where discussions of Truth or Fiction? topics take place. In this way, students are intermittently prompted to reflect on their answers to the Truth or Fiction? items at the beginning of each chapter. They help motivate students to continue to compare their preconceptions with scientific knowledge.

Running Glossary   Research shows that most students do not use a glossary at the end of a book. Switching back and forth between the text and an end-of-book glossary interrupts concentration and slows the learning process. With the text's running glossary, key terms are **boldfaced** in the text and defined nearby in the margin. As part of their review process, students can also read through the running glossary and check the text when they find that they need to learn how the key terms are used.

Exercises   At least one exercise is found in the Study Guide at the end of each chapter. These vary quite a bit. In the chapters on "Biology and Behavior" and "Sensation and Perception," students are shown diagrams of anatomical features such as the brain and the eye and asked to label the parts. Other exercises ask students to complete information in tabular form or to connect the names of theories with statements about behavior. The answers are found at the end of the Study Guide.

Bridging the Gap—Language and Culture Sections   These Study Guide sections are intended to provide common ground for all students. For example, many introductory psychology students have spoken languages other than English in the home. Some have only recently immigrated to the United States and have been speaking English for only a few years (and in some cases, few months) before entering college. The Bridging the Gap—Language and Culture sections highlight and explain idioms in the English language, cultural references to life in the United States, and phrases and expressions whose meanings are not obvious to speakers of foreign languages. Many U.S.-born native English-speaking students are also unfamiliar with some American usages of language and cultural references. Many students will find it helpful to review this section before reading the chapter.

Quizzes   Each Study Guide section contains a 20-item multiple-choice quiz along with the answer key. Most instructors use multiple-choice questions in their assessment of students' progress. These quizzes thus give students the opportunity not only to measure their mastery of the subject matter, but also to predict their performance on their instructor's tests.

THE ANCILLARIES

For the Student

The following supplementary materials are available for purchase by students. Please contact your local college bookstore for prices and ordering information.

Web Site   The *Essentials of Psychology* Web site provides resources for both students and instructors. Students can test themselves with our self-assessment quizzes or learn more about introductory psychology concepts with our Web activities, shockwave animations, and guide to psychology research. Instructors will find an electronic version of the Instructor's Manual, the Harcourt guide to using films in teaching introductory psychology concepts, overhead transparencies to print out, and teaching strategies. Instructors should contact their Harcourt sales representative for the password to the instructor's materials. (http://www.harcortcollege.com/psych/essentials)

Thinking and Writing About Psychology

SPENCER A. RATHUS, MONTCLAIR STATE UNIVERSITY

Thinking and Writing About Psychology is designed to promote two aspects of contemporary college education: critical thinking and writing across the curriculum. To this end, the ancillary contains a discussion of what critical thinking is, a comprehensive guide to writing about psychology using the APA's latest recommendations, and dozens of writing exercises. Writing exercises may be assigned as a way of providing an opportunity for class participation and, perhaps, as a way of earning part of the grade for the course.
ISBN: 0-15-547460-1

Applying Psychology to Everyday Life   This unique ancillary shows students how psychological principles can be applied to important areas in students' lives. It contains 16 chapters that can be grouped into four major areas: Using Psychology to Enhance Your Academic Life; Using Psychology to Enhance Your Physical Health; Using Psychology to Enhance Your Psychological Health; and Using Psychology to Enhance Your Life as an Adult.

Primary Sources in Psychology   Contains a total of 43 original readings, which are divided into the following sections: Biology and Behavior; Sensation, Perception, and Consciousness; Learning and Cognition; Motivation and Emotion; Personality and Psychotherapy; Developmental Psychology; and Social and Environmental Psychology.

PowerPsych CD-ROM   PowerPsych offers students an opportunity to learn the core concepts in psychology in an interactive and fun environment. It contains exciting graphics, tutorials, and even a "Check Mastery" self-test section to accompany each major feature. Use of virtual reality technology and 3D-rendered animations and simulations enables students to view and manipulate structures. For example, they may view the brain to study functions such as ion movement during the action potential, and to review concepts such as classical conditioning and systematic desensitization. This is all possible from different perspectives, at their pace, and under their control. Professors may show animations in class from the PowerPoint Slide Set or from PowerPsych. The CD-ROM provides students with access to the same animations plus the ability to interact with them. Some modules encourage students to engage in active problem solving by requiring them to type in their steps toward problem solution; PowerPsych provides feedback based on their responses. To check mastery of the material, both drag-and-drop puzzles and multiple-choice quizzes are provided. Students can immediately return to the PowerPysch module where correct answers can be found and reviewed. Page references to the textbook are also immediately available from the quiz and all other segments of PowerPsych as well. Chapter quiz results can be sent by e-mail to instructors. In addition, student responses to PowerPsych simulations, such as the Gambler's Fallacy module or the Owl and Lark questionnaire, can be posted to the Internet, where they are compiled with other student responses for comparison. PowerPsych provides students with compelling and engaging presentations and simulations covering select key psychological concepts in a rich, appealing, and unique format.

For the Instructor

Harcourt College Publishers may provide complimentary instructional aids and supplements or supplement packages to those adopters qualified under our adoption policy. Please contact your sales representative for more information. If, as an adopter or potential user, you receive textbooks or supplements you do not need, please return them to your sales representative or send them to:

> Attn: Returns Department
> Troy Warehouse
> 465 South Lincoln Drive
> Troy, MO 63379

Instructor's Manual With Video Instructor's Guide

AMY BALDWIN, LOS ANGELES CITY COLLEGE

Thoroughly revised to include the use of PQ4R from the text into the instructor's reference. The Instructor's Manual for *Essentials of Psychology,* sixth edition, includes chapter outlines and a list of teaching strategies and objectives. The new PQ4R activities are an addition to the other class activities, including reproducible handouts and a list of references and films, with videodisc information.

Test Bank

JOHN BRENNECKE, MT. SAN ANTONIO COLLEGE

The Test Bank has been revised to maintain over 100 multiple-choice items for each chapter. Careful attention to accuracy has been paid by the author to ensure that answers are correct and that information covered in the text is covered in the Test Bank. Test items appear in the order of presentation in the textbook and are keyed to learning objectives and coded in terms of correct answer and textbook page reference.

EXAMaster+ Computerized Test Banks: Mac and Windows Versions   Offers easy-to-use options for test creation:

- *EasyTest* creates a test from a single screen in just a few easy steps. Instructors choose parameters and then select questions from the databases or let *EasyTest* randomly select them.
- *FullTest* offers a range of options that includes selecting, editing, adding, or linking questions or graphics; random selection of questions form a wide range of criteria; creating criteria; blocking questions; and printing up to 99 different versions of the same test and answer sheet.
- *Online Testing* allows instructors to create a test in *EXAMaster,* save it to the OLT subdirectory or diskette, and administer the test online. The results of the test can then be imported to ESAGrade.
- *ESAGrade* can be used to set up new classes, to record grades from tests or assignments utilizing Scantron, and to analyze grades and produce class and individual statistics. *ESAGrade* comes packaged with *EXAMaster+*.
  Macintosh ISBN: 0-15-5065663-7
  MS Windows ISBN: 0-15-506555-6
- *RequesTest* is a service for instructors without access to a computer. A software specialist will compile questions according to the instructor's criteria and mail or fax the test master within 48 hours!
- *The Software Support Hotline* is available to answer questions Monday through Friday, 9 a.m. to 4 p.m. Central Time.

(1-800 telephone numbers for these services are provided in the Preface to the printed Test Bank.)

Introductory Psychology Overhead Transparencies   This set of more than 130 acetates covers the full range of topics typical to an introductory psychology course.

The Harcourt Psychology and Human Development Multimedia Library   Consisting of a variety of videos and videodiscs for classroom presentation, this library's selections include materials created exclusively for Harcourt College Publishers as well as videos from Films for the Humanities and Sciences, Pyramid Films, PBS Video, and other sources. Please contact your sales representative for adoption requirements and other details.

The Whole Psychology Catalog: Instructional Resources To Enhance Student Learning, 1997   Written by Michael B. Reiner, Kennesaw State College, this book provides instructors with experimental exercises, questionnaires, lecture outlines, visual aids, and Internet and World Wide Web guides. These resources can be used to supplement course work and other assignments.

Harcourt Psychology Instructor's Resources on the Web   Come visit us at www.harcourtcollge.com/psych

WebCT General Psychology Course   Includes all major topics covered in introductory psychology and is designed to help you to build a sophisticated Web-based learning environment for your students. Student features include:

- Course content aligned specifically to *Essentials,* organized by chapter
- Online self-quizzing and testing
- Psychology glossary
- Communications tools — mail, bulletin board, chat, and white board

WebCT also includes Instructor Course Management tools. You can build course calendars, provide online testing and grading, and track your students' progress—all available at the click of a button. Try it for yourself with a live demonstration! Go to http://webct.harcoutcollege.com/public/genpsychdemo/

Dynamic Concepts in Psychology II   A highly successful videodisc developed by John Mitterer (Brock University) covers every major concept of introductory psychology. Media include animated sequences, video footage, still images, and demonstrations of well-known experiments. A modular format allows instructors to tailor the program to their course. LectureActive presentation software (Windows, Macintosh) accompanies Dynamic Concepts in Psychology II. This software gives instructors the ability to preprogram classroom presentations as well as to import material from other multimedia sources, such as other videodiscs, CD-ROMs, or instructors' own hard drives.

Psychology MediaActive™   A CD-ROM–based psychology image bank to be used with commercially available presentation packages like PowerPoint™ 2.0 for Windows and Macintosh.

ACKNOWLEDGMENTS

I am grateful to my professional colleagues for suggesting topics I had omitted, the deletion of extraneous stuff, and various fine-tunings of language and expression. Given that they are afforded the supreme pleasure of an advance look at the book, it seems surprising that they would be concerned about being paid so little. Nevertheless, my deep appreciation to: Winfield Brown, Florence Darling Technical College; Tony Fowler, Florence Darling Technical College; Charles McMullen, Tompkins Cortland Community College; John Tucker, John Tyler Community College; Margaret Longenecker, Antelope Valley Community College; David Murphy, Waubonsee Community College; Norma Caltagirone, Hillsborough Community College–Ybor City; Paul Stegner, Canada College; Charles Greene, Florida Community College; Carol Pandey, L. A. Pierce College; Mary Coplen, Hutchinson Community College; Tom Oswarld, North Iowa Area Community College; Deborah Podwika, Kankakee Community College; Nick Siciliano, Fisher College; Frank Hager, Allegany Community College; David Wolfe, Ocean County College, Mark Kelland, Lansing Community College; Kevin Keating, Broward Community College; Stan Gilbert, Community College of Philadelphia; Dixon Bramblett, Lindenwood University; Rosa Preciado, Mount San Antonio College.

Let me once more thank the fine group of publishing professionals at Harcourt who helped me create the current edition of this textbook. First is Brad Potthoff, acquisitions editor, who is new to Harcourt but an old friend from a former professional "life." (Nothing supernatural, just geographical.) Ingrid Mount, the developmental editor, carried out her task from the mountains of suburban Chicago. Glenna Stanfield, development support specialist, coordinated the work of the freelance developmental editor; Glenna pulled it all together, moving the manuscript into production, supervising meetings, and several "what-nots." Katie Matthews, the executive market strategist, is responsible for getting this textbook into your hands and pointing out how it excels in a crowded marketplace (it does excel, of course). Caroline Robbins is the photo acquisitions/permissions editor, who arranged for me to empty my life savings by leasing the photos in the textbook. Cindy Young is the production manager, who broadly oversees the process by which words typed on printer paper become converted into the book you are holding in your hands. Carol Kincaid, art director, created the splendid colorful design of the text and its "today" cover. David Day assisted Carol in much of the day-to-day design work that allowed us to actually fit the text and the visuals into the overall design. David's a great guy (I am assured) and jumped in and filled the void for Carol after she suffered an automobile accident. (Get well, Carol!) Michele Tomiak has once again been the most able project editor on the planet (I can't speak for other planets). Despite her failure to have enough "L's" in her name, Michele is the one I called from day to day to ask what was going on, whether I needed to actually do something to help get the book into its final form, and whether she got the latest jokes on my PG-13 on-line joke list. Last and most, thanks to Ted Buchholz, Chris Klein, and Earl McPeek, the "brass" at Harcourt; if I don't thank them here, I may not be able to ask them for favors in the future. Guys, I would like to say it's been a pleasure. ("It's been a pleasure.")

Psychology has been a great source of illumination and pleasure to me, and this book is my opportunity to share that illumination and pleasure with you. Psychology is right in the thick of things. It is a hard laboratory science and a source of inspiration for the imagination. It addresses our consciousness and our individual sense of self, and it addresses how we are part of a vast social fabric. It is about "public" events like behavior—the things we observe people doing—and it is about the intimate thoughts and feelings that are known to us alone. It is about people and about lower animals. It is about the things we hold closest and dearest—our bodies, which make it possible to perceive the world and act on the world; our consciousness; learning, remembering, and thinking; basic drives like hunger and sex; health and wellness; psychological problems and what we can do about them; and our behavior as members of groups and of the human species. It is about processes as basic as our ability to think about thinking. It is science; it is challenging; it is fun.

It is no surprise that psychology is popular on campus. In fact, psychology is the second most popular undergraduate major, just behind business administration. Business and other popular majors lead to jobs in the chosen field, but most psychology majors choose it for the intellectual pleasure it provides and general knowledge of the world. Only a minority go on to become psychologists. But the great majority profit from the experience of studying psychology. Welcome.

This objective of this book is to present the story of psychology as a concise but complete learning package. One of the core topics in psychology is learning—what it is, how it happens, how we can enhance it. This book uses what we know of the psychology of learning to help you learn about psychology. This knowledge is put to use in the book's built-in Study Guide. The Study Guide is based on the PQ4R method, but it contains more, as we will see.

PQ4R

This textbook is designed to help you use psychology to take charge of this course. By following the PQ4R method, you can become an active student rather than a reactive student. *PQ4R* stands for *Preview, Question, Read, Reflect, Recite, and Review,* a method that is based on the work of educational psychologist Francis P. Robinson. Let us take these steps one by one.

Preview

Previewing material fine-tunes your expectations. It helps set up mental compartments into which you fit the material. This textbook has two features at the beginnings of chapters that will help you preview the material: "Truth or Fiction?" items and a chapter Preview. The ***Truth or Fiction?*** items are intended to challenge common knowledge (which is sometimes common *ignorance*). They will stimulate you to delve into the subject matter to see whether your preconceptions are supported by the evidence.

The ***Preview*** outlines the sections in each chapter and tells you what each section does.

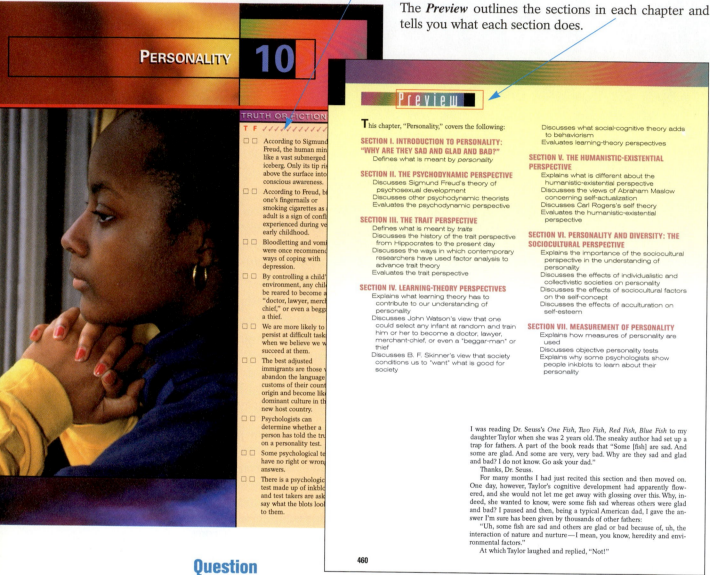

PERSONALITY 10

TRUTH OR FICTION

T F

☐ ☐ According to Sigmund Freud, the human min... like a vast submerged iceberg. Only its tip ris... above the surface into conscious awareness.

☐ ☐ According to Freud, bi... one's fingernails or smoking cigarettes as adult is a sign of confl... experienced during ve... early childhood.

☐ ☐ Bloodletting and vomi... were once recommend... ways of coping with depression.

☐ ☐ By controlling a child'... environment, any chil... be reared to become a "doctor, lawyer, merch... chief," or even a begga... a thief.

☐ ☐ We are more likely to persist at difficult task... when we believe we w... succeed at them.

☐ ☐ The best adjusted immigrants are those abandon the language customs of their count... origin and become like dominant culture in th... new host country.

☐ ☐ Psychologists can determine whether a person has told the tr... on a personality test.

☐ ☐ Some psychological te... have no right or wron... answers.

☐ ☐ There is a psychologic... test made up of inkbl... and test takers are ask... say what the blots loo... to them.

Preview

This chapter, "Personality," covers the following:

SECTION I. INTRODUCTION TO PERSONALITY: "WHY ARE THEY SAD AND GLAD AND BAD?"
 Defines what is meant by *personality*

SECTION II. THE PSYCHODYNAMIC PERSPECTIVE
 Discusses Sigmund Freud's theory of psychosexual development
 Discusses other psychodynamic theorists
 Evaluates the psychodynamic perspective

SECTION III. THE TRAIT PERSPECTIVE
 Defines what is meant by *traits*
 Discusses the history of the trait perspective from Hippocrates to the present day
 Discusses the ways in which contemporary researchers have used factor analysis to advance trait theory
 Evaluates the trait perspective

SECTION IV. LEARNING-THEORY PERSPECTIVES
 Explains what learning theory has to contribute to our understanding of personality
 Discusses John Watson's view that one could select any infant at random and train him or her to become a doctor, lawyer, merchant-chief, or even a "beggar-man" or thief
 Discusses B. F. Skinner's view that society conditions us to "want" what is good for society

 Discusses what social-cognitive theory adds to behaviorism
 Evaluates learning-theory perspectives

SECTION V. THE HUMANISTIC-EXISTENTIAL PERSPECTIVE
 Explains what is different about the humanistic-existential perspective
 Discusses the views of Abraham Maslow concerning self-actualization
 Discusses Carl Rogers's self theory
 Evaluates the humanistic-existential perspective

SECTION VI. PERSONALITY AND DIVERSITY: THE SOCIOCULTURAL PERSPECTIVE
 Explains the importance of the sociocultural perspective in the understanding of personality
 Discusses the effects of individualistic and collectivistic societies on personality
 Discusses the effects of sociocultural factors on the self-concept
 Discusses the effects of acculturation on self-esteem

SECTION VII. MEASUREMENT OF PERSONALITY
 Explains how measures of personality are used
 Discusses objective personality tests
 Explains why some psychologists show people inkblots to learn about their personality

I was reading Dr. Seuss's *One Fish, Two Fish, Red Fish, Blue Fish* to my daughter Taylor when she was 2 years old. The sneaky author had set up a trap for fathers. A part of the book reads that "Some [fish] are sad. And some are glad. And some are very, very bad. Why are they sad and glad and bad? I do not know. Go ask your dad."

Thanks, Dr. Seuss.

For many months I had just recited this section and then moved on. One day, however, Taylor's cognitive development had apparently flowered, and she would not let me get away with glossing over this. Why, indeed, she wanted to know, were some fish sad whereas others were glad and bad? I paused and, being a typical American dad, I gave the answer I'm sure has been given by thousands of other fathers:

"Uh, some fish are sad and others are glad or bad because of, uh, the interaction of nature and nurture—I mean, you know, heredity and environmental factors."

At which Taylor laughed and replied, "Not!"

460

Question

A key feature of the PQ4R method is making up questions about the subject matter before you get into it. Making up questions gives you goals: You attend class or read the text *in order to answer questions* you have phrased. This textbook helps you by phrasing ***Questions*** in **blue** as you read along. When you see a question, you can read the following material in order to answer it.

The Peripheral Nervous System: The Body's Peripheral Devices

Question: What are the divisions and functions of the peripheral nervous system? The peripheral nervous system consists of sensory and motor neurons that transmit messages to and from the central nervous system. Without the peripheral nervous system, our brains would be like isolated CPUs. There would be no keyboards, mouses, diskettes, or other ways of inputting information. There would be no monitors, printers, modems, or other ways of displaying or transmitting information. We would be detached from the world: We would not be able to perceive it; we would not be able to act on it. The two main divisions of the peripheral nervous system are the *somatic nervous system* and the *autonomic nervous system.*

The **somatic nervous system** contains sensory (afferent) and motor (efferent) neurons. It transmits messages about sights, sounds, smells, temperature, body positions, and so on, to the central nervous system. As a result, we can experience the beauties and the horrors of the world, its physical ecstasies and agonies. Messages transmitted from the brain

SOMATIC NERVOUS SYSTEM The division of the peripheral nervous system that connects the central nervous system with sensory receptors, skeletal muscles, and the surface of the body.

AUTONOMIC NERVOUS SYSTEM (ANS) The division of the peripheral nervous system that regulates glands and activities such as heartbeat, respiration, digestion, and dilation of the pupils.

Read

Once you have phrased questions, in the PQ4R method, read the material in the chapter in order to answer the questions. This method creates a sense of purpose that will help you focus on the key points of the subject matter. You can keep notes as you do so and write answers to each question. These answers need not be complete. It is probably better to jot down some key words in your notebook instead. In that way you will be less slowed down by your note-taking. Nevertheless, the key words or terms will stimulate your recollection of the answer later on when you are reciting and reviewing the material.

Reflect

Psychologists and educators have shown that you learn more effectively when you *reflect* on what you are learning. Reflecting on a subject means *relating* it to things you already know about. Reflecting makes the material meaningful and easier to remember, and it makes it more likely that you will be able to *apply* the information to your own life.

It takes time to reflect—to sit back and relate what you have been reading to your own life—but it's a worthwhile investment. Through effective reflection, you may embed the material so firmly in your memory that you retain it on the basis of one or just a few reviews.

Each chapter has many ***Reflect*** features in the margins. Many of them ask you to compare what you are reading with the ideas you had before you opened the book. For example, the first Reflect feature reads "How would you have defined psychology before you began this course or opened your book? How does the true scientific nature of psychology differ from your expectations?" A Reflect feature in the chapter on Lifespan Development reads "Why do you think that parents are so concerned about *when* their infants sit up or crawl or walk?"

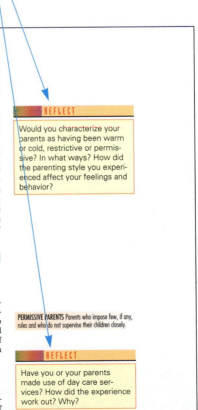

view, and they may be cold and rejecting. When their children ask them why they should behave in a certain way, authoritarian parents often answer, "Because I say so!"

3. *Permissive parents.* **Permissive parents** are generally easygoing with their children. As a result, the children do pretty much whatever they wish. Permissive parents are warm and supportive, but poor at communicating.

Research evidence shows that warmth is superior to coldness in rearing children. Children of warm parents are more likely to be socially and emotionally well-adjusted and to internalize moral standards—that is, to develop a conscience (MacDonald, 1992; Miller et al., 1993).

Strictness also appears to pay off, provided it is tempered with reason and warmth. Children of authoritative parents have greater self-reliance, self-esteem, social competence, and achievement motivation than other children (Baumrind, 1991; Putallaz & Hefflin, 1990). Children of authoritarian parents are often withdrawn or aggressive, and they usually do not do as well in school as children of authoritative parents (Olson et al., 1992; Westerman, 1990). Children of permissive parents seem to be the least mature. They are frequently impulsive, moody, and aggressive. In adolescence, lack of parental monitoring is often linked to delinquency and poor academic performance.

✓ **Truth or Fiction Revisited**

It is true that children with strict parents are most likely to be successful. This is especially so when the parents also reason with their children and are loving and supportive.

Let us now consider two other important areas that involve the connections between parental behavior and the social and personality development of children. The first of these, day care, considers what happens to young children's social and personality development when they spend their days in the care of people *other than* family members. The second of these, child abuse, considers the causes of child abuse and its effects on the development of the child.

Day Care

As we cross over into the new millennium, only a small percentage of U.S. families fit the traditional model in which the husband is the breadwinner

REFLECT

Would you characterize your parents as having been warm or cold, restrictive or permissive? In what ways? How did the parenting style you experienced affect your feelings and behavior?

PERMISSIVE PARENTS Parents who impose few, if any, rules and who do not supervise their children closely.

REFLECT

Have you or your parents made use of day care services? How did the experience work out? Why?

Recite

The PQ4R method recommends that once you have read a section and taken notes, you recite each answer—aloud, if possible. Reciting answers helps you remember them because you repeat your study of the material, and repetition fosters retention. You also *produce* the concepts and ideas you have taken in. In this way, you associate them with spoken words and gestures.

This textbook helps you recite the material by means of two features found in the **Built-in Study Guide.** These include the Summaries and Recite sections.

The **Summaries** are written in question-and-answer format. To help reveal the structure of the material, the questions are repeated from the body of the text, again in **blue.** They are followed by answers I have written. These answers may be identical to the ones in your notes. They may not be. Comparing my answers to yours will help you embed the material in memory.

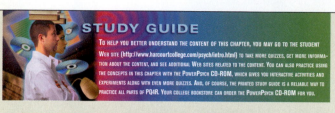

STUDY GUIDE

To help you better understand the content of this chapter, you may go to the student Web site (http://www.harcourtcollege.com/psych/intro.html) to take more quizzes, get more information about the content, and see additional Web sites related to the content. You can also practice using the concepts in this chapter with the PowerPsych CD-ROM, which gives you interactive activities and experiments along with even more quizzes. And, of course, the printed study guide is a reliable way to practice all parts of PQ4R. Your college bookstore can order the PowerPsych CD-ROM for you.

SUMMARY

1. **What are sensation and perception?** Sensation is a mechanical process that involves the stimulation of sensory receptors (neurons) and the transmission of sensory information to the central nervous system. Perception is not mechanical. Perception is the active organization of sensations into a representation of the outside world, and it reflects learning and expectations.

2. **How do we know when something is there? How do we know when it has changed?** We know something is there when the intensity of the stimulus, such as a light, exceeds the absolute threshold for that stimulus. The absolute threshold is the lowest intensity at which the stimulus can be detected. We know that something has changed when the change in intensity exceeds the difference threshold. The difference threshold is the minimum difference in intensity that can be discriminated. Difference thresholds are expressed in Weber's constants.

3. **What is signal-detection theory?** Signal-detection theory explains the ways in which stimulus characteristics and psychological factors—for example, motivation, familiarity with a stimulus, and attention—interact to influence whether a stimulus will be detected.

4. **What are feature detectors?** Feature detectors are neurons that fire in response to specific features of sensed stimuli. For example, detectors in the visual cortex fire in response to particular features of visual input, such as lines sensed at various angles or specific colors.

5. **How do our sensory systems adapt to a changing environment?** We become more sensitive to stimuli of low magnitude and less sensitive to stimuli that remain the same (such as the background noises outside the window). Growing more sensitive to stimulation is termed sensitization, or positive adaptation. Growing less sensitive to continuous stimulation is called desensitization, or negative adaptation.

6. **Just what is this stuff called light?** Visible light triggers visual sensations and is part of the spectrum of electromagnetic energy. Light is made up of waves of energy; the color violet has the shortest wave-

length, and red has the longest. White sunlight can be broken down into the colors of the rainbow by means of a prism.

7. **How does the eye work?** The eye senses and transmits visual stimulation to the occipital lobe of the cerebral cortex. After light passes through the cornea, the size of the pupil determines the amount that can pass through the lens. The lens focuses light onto the retina, which is composed of photoreceptors (neurons) called rods and cones. Cones permit perception of color. Rods permit sensations of light and dark only. Light is transmitted from the retina to the brain via the optic nerve, which is made up of the axons of retinal ganglion cells. Visual acuity is connected with the shape of the eye and age. As we age the lenses grow brittle, making it difficult to focus; the condition is called presbyopia. Rods are more sensitive than cones to lowered lighting and continue to adapt to darkness once cones have reached their peak adaptation.

8. **How do we perceive color?** There are two theories as to how we perceive color. According to trichromatic theory, there are three types of cones—some sensitive to red, others to green, and still others to blue-violet. The opponent-process theory proposes three types of color receptors: red-green, blue-yellow, and light-dark; it is supported by the appearance of afterimages.

9. **What is color blindness? Why are some people color blind?** People with normal color vision are called trichromats. Monochromats see no color, and dichromats are blind to some parts of the spectrum. Partial color blindness is a sex-linked trait that impairs the working of cones sensitive to red or green.

10. **How do we organize bits of information like perceptions into meaningful wholes?** Perceptual organization involves recognizing patterns and processing information about relationships between parts and the whole. Gestalt rules of perceptual organization involve figure-ground relationships, proximity, similarity, continuity, common fate, and closure. Perception of a whole followed by perception of parts is termed top-down processing.

To help you understand the structure of the material, the **Recite** sections also repeat the questions in **blue.** They are followed by lines on which

Recite Recite Recite Recite Recite

1. What are sensation and perception?

2. How do we know when something is there? How do we know when it has changed?

3. What is signal-detection theory?

4. What are feature detectors?

5. How do our sensory systems adapt to a changing environment?

6. Just what is this stuff called light?

7. How does the eye work?

8. How do we perceive color?

9. What is color blindness? Why are some people color blind?

10. How do we organize bits of information like perceptions into meaningful wholes?

you can jot down answers or key words that will help you remember answers. You will notice that the feature title—"Recite"—is repeated several times and grows larger with each repetition. This is done to suggest that your mastery of the subject matter will grow stronger each time you recite the material.

Review

One way to foster retention is to relate subject matter to things you already know. Another is to repeat or review it according to a reasonably regular schedule, such as once weekly.

Psychologists and educators recognize that after you read or learn new material, there is a strong initial drop-off in memory. Therefore, it is helpful to review the material soon after you have read or learned about it. This textbook includes frequent *Section Reviews* that encourage you to produce new material soon after you have learned it. These section reviews are written in fill-in-the-blanks format, which stimulate you to produce the new material. Parts of words are written in as prompts. The prompts are intended to guide you through the new material in such a way that you produce it in an error-free manner. But do not be concerned if you have to search for the answer in the body of the text; this activity will help you learn.

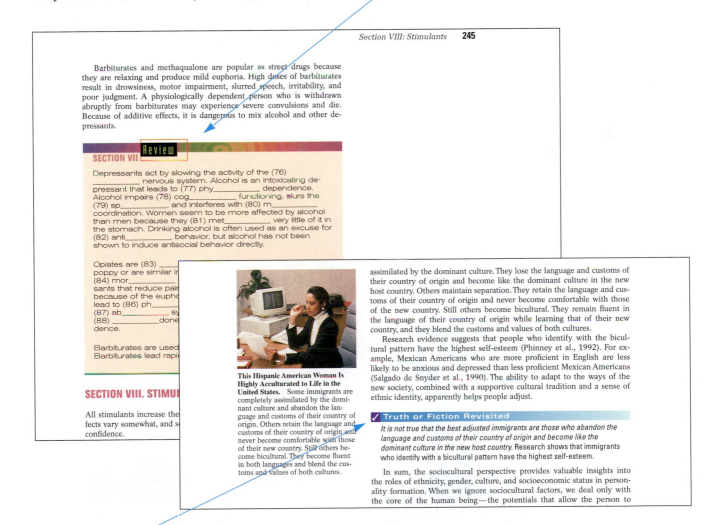

Additional Helpful Features

The text also includes a number of additional features that will help you understand and remember the material. These include Truth or Fiction Revisited features, a running glossary, and—in the built-in Study Guide—Exercises, Bridging the Gap features, and Quizzes.

Truth or Fiction Revisited features are found in the text where discussions of Truth or Fiction? topics take place. They encourage you to reconsider your answers to the Truth or Fiction? items at the beginning of the chapter. In this way, they motivate you to compare your preconceptions with scientific knowledge.

Many students do not use a glossary at the end of a book. Switching back and forth between the text and an end-of-book glossary interrupts concentration and slows the learning process. This text's *Running Glossary* **boldfaces** key terms in the text and defines them nearby in the margin. Therefore, the flow of the text is not interrupted.

One or more *Exercises* are found in the Built-in Study Guide at the end of each chapter. The exercises vary quite a bit. In the chapters on "Biology and Behavior" and "Sensation and Perception," you are shown diagrams of anatomical features such as the brain and the eye and asked to label the parts. Other exercises ask you to complete information found in tables, to connect the names of psychologists with theories, or with statements about behavior, and so on. The answers are found at the end of the Study Guide.

option of answering "none of the above." Forced-choice formats are frequently used in interest inventories, which help predict whether the person would function well in a certain occupation. The following item is similar to those found in occupational interest inventories:

I would rather

   a. be a forest ranger.

   b. work in a busy office.

   c. play a musical instrument.

The Minnesota Multiphasic Personality Inventory (MMPI) contains hundreds of items presented in a true–false format. The MMPI is designed to be used by clinical and counseling psychologists to help diagnose psychological disorders. Accurate measurement of an individual's problems should point to appropriate treatment. The MMPI is the most widely used psychological test in clinical work (Watkins et al., 1995). It is also the most widely used instrument for personality measurement in psychological research.

Psychologists can score tests by hand, send them to computerized scoring services, or have them scored by on-site computers. Computers

Is This Test Taker Telling the Truth?
How can psychologists determine whether or not people answer test items honestly? What are the validity scales of the MMPI?

BEHAVIOR-RATING SCALE A systematic means for recording the frequency with which target behaviors occur.

OBJECTIVE TESTS Tests whose items must be answered in a specified, limited manner. Tests whose items have concrete answers that are considered correct.

STANDARDIZED TEST A test given to a large number of respondents so that data concerning the typical responses can be accumulated and analyzed.

FORCED-CHOICE FORMAT A method of presenting test questions that requires a respondent to select one of a number of possible answers.

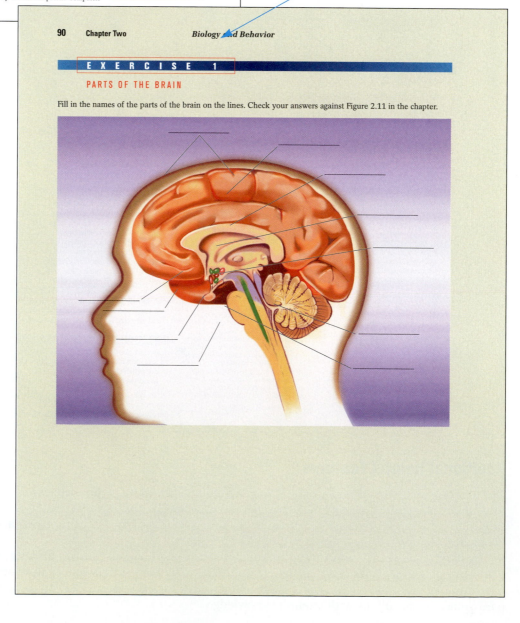

90   **Chapter Two**   *Biology and Behavior*

E X E R C I S E   1

PARTS OF THE BRAIN

Fill in the names of the parts of the brain on the lines. Check your answers against Figure 2.11 in the chapter.

BRIDGING THE GAP

LANGUAGE AND CULTURE

to abbreviate (59)   *to shorten*

abnormal behavior (65)   *not a typical or ordinary manner of acting*

above average (64)   *better than ordinary*

to accelerate (57)   *to increase in frequency or rate*

an adolescent (76)   *a young person who has passed puberty but is not yet an adult*

adoptee (87)   *a person who has been adopted, taken into a family as if the child were born as a member of the family*

adoptive parent (80)   *person who assumes the role and responsibility of rearing a child*

aesthetic response (73)   *reaction to beauty*

affliction (54)   *damage, disease*

amateur sports (79)   *not professional athletic events (such as school sports)*

aphasia (76)   *loss of speech caused by brain damage*

archaeological site (66)   *place of investigation*

to arouse (78)   *to excite, to awaken*

association areas (72)   *parts of the brain that are not the primary part involved in an action but that are*

buffeted (54)   *influenced, hit*

butterfly pattern (63)   *symmetrical shape like a butterfly*

to button (75)   *to close with buttons*

calorie (83)   *unit of heat, energy unit from food*

capacity (79)   *potential, limit*

carbohydrate metabolism (80)   *burning of starch and sugars of foods for body use*

caste (81)   *rigid social grouping*

central processing unit (60)   *the "brain" of a computer*

cerebellum (67)   *part of the brain, part of the hindbrain*

cerebral cortex (67)   *gray matter on the outside of the brain*

characterized by (78)   *typical of*

cognitive (69)   *mental, intellectual, thinking-related*

coming out of left field (74)   *being unexpected or difficult to understand*

committed relationship (82)   *marriage or family*

to confine (74)   *(here) to limit*

Bridging the Gap—Language and Culture sections are intended to provide common ground for all students. Some students have spoken languages other than English in the home. Some have only recently immigrated to the United States and have been speaking English for only a few years (and in some cases, a few months) before entering college. The Bridging the Gap—Language and Culture sections highlight and explain idioms in the English language, cultural references to life in the United States, and phrases and expressions whose meanings are not obvious to speakers of foreign languages. Many U.S.-born native English-speaking students are also unfamiliar with some American usages of language and cultural references and will find it helpful to review this section.

Each built-in Study Guide section contains a 20-item multiple-choice *Quiz* along with an answer key. Most instructors use multiple-choice questions in their assessment of students' progress. Therefore, these quizzes not only give you the opportunity to measure your mastery of the subject matter, but also to predict your performance on your instructor's tests.

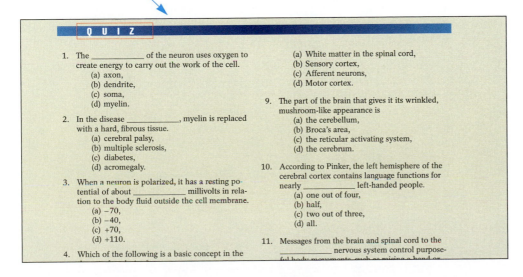

QUIZ

1. The _____ of the neuron uses oxygen to create energy to carry out the work of the cell.
   (a) axon,
   (b) dendrite,
   (c) soma,
   (d) myelin.

2. In the disease _____, myelin is replaced with a hard, fibrous tissue.
   (a) cerebral palsy,
   (b) multiple sclerosis,
   (c) diabetes,
   (d) acromegaly.

3. When a neuron is polarized, it has a resting potential of about _____ millivolts in relation to the body fluid outside the cell membrane.
   (a) −70,
   (b) −40,
   (c) +70,
   (d) +110.

4. Which of the following is a basic concept in the

   (a) White matter in the spinal cord,
   (b) Sensory cortex,
   (c) Afferent neurons,
   (d) Motor cortex.

9. The part of the brain that gives it its wrinkled, mushroom-like appearance is
   (a) the cerebellum,
   (b) Broca's area,
   (c) the reticular activating system,
   (d) the cerebrum.

10. According to Pinker, the left hemisphere of the cerebral cortex contains language functions for nearly _____ left-handed people.
   (a) one out of four,
   (b) half,
   (c) two out of three,
   (d) all.

11. Messages from the brain and spinal cord to the _____ nervous system control purpose-

These are the features of the text that will help you understand and enjoy the subject matter. Now you have the pleasure of diving into psychology for the first time. I envy you.

Dedicated with affection to Lois,
whose support makes these volumes possible

CONTENTS IN BRIEF

CONTENTS

10   Personality   459

12 Psychological Disorders 549

TRUTH OR FICTION?

T F ✓✓✓✓✓✓✓✓✓✓✓✓

☐ ☐ A book on psychology, whose contents are similar to those of the book you are now holding, was written by Aristotle more than 2,000 years ago.

☐ ☐ The ancient Greek philosopher Socrates suggested a research method that is still used in psychology.

☐ ☐ Even though she had worked to complete all the degree requirements, the first female president of the American Psychological Association turned down the doctoral degree that was offered to her.

☐ ☐ Men receive the majority of doctoral degrees in psychology.

☐ ☐ You could survey 20 million voters and still not predict the outcome of a presidential election accurately.

☐ ☐ In many experiments, neither the subjects nor the researchers know who is receiving the real treatment and who is not.

☐ ☐ Psychologists would not be able to carry out many kinds of studies without deceiving subjects as to the purposes and methods of the studies.

This chapter, "What Is Psychology?", covers the following:

"What a piece of work is man," wrote William Shakespeare. He was writing about you: "How noble in reason! How infinite in faculty! In form and moving how express and admirable! In action how like an angel! In apprehension how like a god! The beauty of the world! The paragon of animals!"

You probably had no trouble recognizing yourself in this portrait— "noble in reason," "admirable," godlike in understanding, head and shoulders above other animals. That's you to a *tee*, isn't it? Consider some of the noble and admirable features of human behavior:

- The human abilities to think and solve problems have allowed us to build cathedrals and computers and to scan the interior of the body without surgery. Yet, just what is thinking? How do we solve problems?

- The human ability to create led to the writing of great works of literature and the composition of music from opera to rap. Yet, what exactly is creativity?

- Human generosity and charity have encouraged us to care for older people, people who are ill, and people who are less advantaged than we are—even to sacrifice ourselves for those we love. Why do we care for others? What motivates us to care for our children and protect our families?

Some human behavior is not as noble or admirable as these examples suggest. In fact, human behavior varies greatly, and some of it is downright puzzling. Consider some more examples:

- Although people can be generous, most adults on crowded city streets will not stop to help a person lying on the sidewalk. Why?
- Most people who overeat or smoke cigarettes know they are jeopardizing their health. Yet they continue their bad habits. Why?
- A person claims to have raped, killed, or mutilated a victim because of insanity. The person was overcome by an irresistible impulse, or by "another personality" that took control. What is insanity? What is an irresistible impulse?

Human behavior has always fascinated people. Sometimes we are even surprised at ourselves. We have thoughts or impulses that seem to be out of character, or we cannot recall something that seems to be hovering on the "tip of the tongue." Psychologists, like other people, are also intrigued by the mysteries of behavior, but for them the scientific study of behavior is their life's work. Question: What is psychology?

"What a piece of work is man," wrote William Shakespeare. "How noble in reason! How infinite in faculty!" Chinese American artist Hung Liu, seen here with one of her paintings, illustrates the creativity that humans are capable of. Psychologists are interested in all aspects of human behavior and mental processes.

SECTION I. PSYCHOLOGY AS A SCIENCE

Psychology is the scientific study of behavior and mental processes. Topics of interest to psychologists include the nervous system, sensation and perception, learning and memory, intelligence, language, thought, growth and development, personality, stress and health, psychological disorders, ways of treating those disorders, sexual behavior, and the behavior of people in social settings such as groups and organizations.

Sciences have certain goals. Question: What are the goals of psychology? Psychology, like other sciences, seeks to describe, explain, predict, and control the events it studies. Psychology thus seeks to describe, explain, predict, and control behavior and mental processes.

When possible, descriptive terms and concepts are interwoven into **theories.** Theories are formulations of apparent relationships among observed events. They allow us to derive explanations and predictions. Many psychological theories combine statements about behavior (such as eating or aggression), mental processes (such as attitudes and mental images), and biological processes. For instance, many of our responses to drugs such as alcohol and marijuana can be measured as overt behavior, and they are presumed to reflect the biochemical actions of these drugs and our (mental) expectations about their effects.

A satisfactory psychological theory allows us to predict behavior. For instance, a theory of hunger should allow us to predict when people will or will not eat. If our observations cannot be adequately explained by, or predicted from, a given theory, we should consider revising or replacing it.

What do we mean by "controlling" behavior and mental processes? Some people erroneously think that psychologists seek ways to make people do their bidding, like puppets on strings. This is not so. Psychologists are committed to a belief in the dignity of human beings, and human dignity demands that people be free to make their own decisions and choose their own behavior. Psychologists are learning more about the influences on human behavior all the time, but they implement this knowledge only on request and in order to help people clarify and meet their own goals.

The remainder of this chapter presents an overview of psychology as a science. You will see that psychologists have diverse interests and fields of

PSYCHOLOGY The science that studies behavior and mental processes.

THEORY A formulation of relationships underlying observed events.

specialization. We discuss the history of psychology and the major perspectives from which today's psychologists view behavior. Finally, we consider the research methods psychologists use to study behavior and mental processes.

Review

SECTION I

Psychology is defined as the study of (1) b_____ and mental processes. Psychology seeks to describe, explain, (2) _____dict, and (3) c_____ behavior.

Behavior is explained through psychological (4) _____ries, which are sets of statements that involve assumptions about behavior. Explanations and (5) pre_____ are derived from theories.

SECTION II. WHAT PSYCHOLOGISTS DO

Psychologists share a keen interest in behavior, but in other ways, they may differ markedly. Question: Just what do psychologists do? Psychologists engage in research, practice, and teaching. Some researchers engage primarily in basic, or **pure, research.** Pure research has no immediate application to personal or social problems and therefore has been characterized as research for its own sake. Others engage in **applied research,** which is designed to find solutions to specific personal or social problems. Although pure research is sparked by curiosity and the desire to know and understand, today's pure research frequently enhances tomorrow's way of life (Leibowitz, 1996; Miller, 1995). For example, pure research on learning and motivation in lower animals done early in the 20th century has found widespread applications in today's school systems. Pure research into the workings of the nervous system has enhanced knowledge of disorders such as epilepsy, Parkinson's disease, and Alzheimer's disease.

Many psychologists do not conduct research. Instead, they *practice* psychology by applying psychological knowledge to help people change their behavior so that they can meet their own goals more effectively. Still other psychologists engage primarily in teaching. They share psychological knowledge in classrooms, seminars, and workshops. Some psychologists engage in all three: research, practice, and teaching.

Let us describe the different fields of psychology and then bring psychologists back together again as we describe an approach to behavior and mental processes that is shared by all of them—critical thinking.

Fields of Psychology

Psychologists are found in a number of different specialties. Although some psychologists wear more than one hat, most of them carry out their functions in the following fields.

Clinical psychologists help people with psychological disorders adjust to the demands of life. People's problems may range from anxiety and depression to sexual dysfunctions to loss of goals. Clinical psychologists evaluate these problems through interviews and psychological tests. They help their clients resolve their problems and change self-defeating behavior. Clinical psychologists are the largest subgroup of psychologists (see

PURE RESEARCH Research conducted without concern for immediate applications.

APPLIED RESEARCH Research conducted in an effort to find solutions to particular problems.

Figure 1.1). These psychologists differ from psychiatrists in that *psychiatrists* are *medical* doctors who specialize in the study and treatment of psychological disorders.

Counseling psychologists, like clinical psychologists, use interviews and tests to define their clients' problems. Their clients typically have adjustment problems but not serious psychological disorders. Clients may have trouble making academic or vocational decisions or making friends in college. They may experience marital or family conflicts, have physical disabilities, or have adjustment problems such as those encountered by people who lose their jobs because of mergers or downsizing. Counseling psychologists advise clients to help them clarify their goals and overcome obstacles. Counseling psychologists are often employed in college and university counseling and testing centers. As suggested by Figure 1.1, more than half of psychologists are clinical or counseling psychologists.

School psychologists are employed by school systems to identify and assist students who have problems that interfere with learning. Such problems range from social and family problems to emotional disturbances and learning disorders. They help schools make decisions about the placement of students in special classes.

Educational psychologists, like school psychologists, attempt to facilitate learning. But they usually focus on course planning and instructional methods for a school system rather than on individual children. Educational psychologists research theoretical issues related to learning, measurement, and child development. For example, they study how learning is affected by psychological factors such as motivation and intelligence, sociocultural factors such as poverty and acculturation, and teacher behavior. Some educational psychologists prepare standardized tests such as the Scholastic Assessment Tests (SATs).

Developmental psychologists study the changes—physical, emotional, cognitive, and social—that occur throughout the life span. They attempt to sort out the influences of heredity (nature) and the environment

REFLECT

If a friend had a problem, would you advise him or her to see a psychologist? What kind of psychologist?

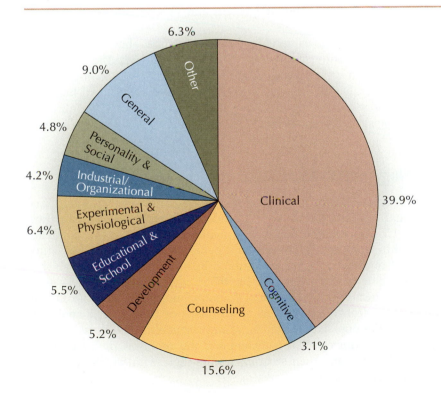

FIGURE 1.1

RECIPIENTS OF DOCTORATES IN THE VARIOUS SUBFIELDS OF PSYCHOLOGY

NEARLY 40% OF THE DOCTORATES IN PSYCHOLOGY ARE AWARDED IN CLINICAL PSYCHOLOGY. THE NEXT MOST POPULAR SUBFIELD IS COUNSELING PSYCHOLOGY.

Source: Office of Demographic, Employment, and Educational Research (1994). Table WO4846, Summary report doctorate recipients from United States universities. Washington, D.C.: American Psychological Association.

Environmental Psychology.
Environmental psychologists focus on the ways in which people affect and are affected by their physical environment. How are city dwellers affected by crowding and "stimulus overload"?

(nurture) on development. Developmental psychologists conduct research on issues such as the effects of maternal use of drugs on an embryo, the outcomes of various patterns of child rearing, children's concepts of space and time, conflicts during adolescence, and problems of adjustment among older people.

Personality psychologists attempt to define human traits; to determine influences on human thought processes, feelings, and behavior; and to explain psychological disorders. They are particularly concerned with issues such as anxiety, aggression, and gender roles.

Social psychologists are primarily concerned with the nature and causes of individuals' thoughts, feelings, and behavior in social situations. Whereas personality psychologists tend to look within the person for explanations of behavior, social psychologists tend to focus on external or social influences.

Environmental psychologists focus on the ways in which behavior influences, and is influenced by, the physical environment. They are concerned with how buildings and cities serve, or fail to serve, human needs. They investigate the effects of temperature, noise, and air pollution on behavior and mental processes.

Psychologists in all specialties may conduct experiments. However, those called *experimental psychologists* specialize in basic processes such as the nervous system, sensation and perception, learning and memory, thought, motivation, and emotion.

Industrial psychology and organizational psychology are closely related fields. *Industrial psychologists* focus on the relationships between people and work. *Organizational psychologists* study the behavior of people in organizations such as businesses. *Human factors psychologists* make technical systems such as automobile dashboards and computer keyboards more user-friendly. *Consumer psychologists* study the behavior of shoppers in an effort to predict and influence their behavior. They advise store managers how to lay out the aisles of a supermarket in ways that boost impulse buying, how to arrange window displays to attract customers, and how to make newspaper ads and TV commercials more persuasive.

Health psychologists examine the ways in which behavior and mental processes such as attitudes are related to physical health. They study the effects of stress on health problems such as headaches, cardiovascular disease, and cancer. Health psychologists also guide clients toward healthier behavior patterns—such as exercising and quitting smoking—and diets.

Psychologists continue to apply their knowledge and skills in new areas.

Psychology and Critical Thinking

Regardless of their area of specialization, psychologists are scientists, and one hallmark of science is **critical thinking.** Question: What is critical thinking? Critical thinking has many meanings. On one level, it means taking nothing for granted. It means not believing things just because they are in print or because they were uttered by authority figures or celebrities. It means not necessarily believing that it is healthful to express all of your feelings just because a friend in "therapy" urges you to do so. On another level, critical thinking refers to a process of thoughtfully analyzing and probing the questions, statements, and arguments of others. It means examining definitions of terms, examining the premises or assumptions behind arguments, and then scrutinizing the logic with which arguments are developed.

CRITICAL THINKING An approach to thinking characterized by skepticism and thoughtful analysis of statements and arguments — for example, probing arguments' premises and the definitions of terms.

A group of psychologists (McGovern, 1989) defined the goals of critical thinking as fostering the following thinking skills:

- Development of skepticism about explanations and conclusions
- The ability to inquire about causes and effects
- Increased curiosity about behavior
- Knowledge of research methods
- The ability to analyze arguments critically

Let us consider some principles of critical thinking that can be of help to you in college and beyond:

1. *Be skeptical.* Keep an open mind. Politicians and advertisers try to persuade you. Even research reported in the media or in textbooks may take a certain slant. Extend this principle to yourself. Perhaps some of your own attitudes and beliefs are superficial or unfounded. Accept nothing as true until you have examined the evidence.

2. *Examine definitions of terms.* Some statements are true when a term is defined in one way but not when it is defined in another way. Consider the statement "Head Start programs have raised children's IQs." The correctness of the statement depends on the definition of "IQ." (You will see later in the text that *IQ* has a specific meaning and is not exactly the same as *intelligence.*)

3. *Examine the assumptions or premises of arguments.* Consider the statement that one cannot learn about human beings by engaging in research with animals. One premise in the statement seems to be that human beings are not animals. We are, of course. (Would you rather be a plant?)

4. *Be cautious in drawing conclusions from evidence.* For many years studies had shown that most clients who receive psychotherapy improve. It was therefore generally assumed that psychotherapy worked. Some 40 years ago, however, a psychologist named Hans Eysenck pointed out that most psychologically troubled people who did *not* receive psychotherapy also improved! The question thus becomes whether people receiving psychotherapy are *more* likely to improve than those who do not. Current research on the effectiveness of psychotherapy therefore carefully compares the benefits of therapy techniques to the benefits of other techniques or of no treatment at all. Be skeptical, moreover, when a friend swears by the effectiveness of megavitamin therapy for colds. What is the nature of the "evidence"? Is it convincing?

5. *Consider alternative interpretations of research evidence.* Does alcohol cause aggression? Is the assertion that it does so truth or fiction? Later in the chapter we see that evidence shows a clear *connection,* or "correlation," between alcohol and aggression. That is, many people who commit violent crimes have been drinking. Does the evidence show that this connection is *causal,* however? Could other factors, such as gender, age, or willingness to take risks, account for both drinking and aggressive behavior?

6. *Do not oversimplify.* Most human behavior involves complex interactions of genetic and environmental influences. Also consider the issue of whether psychotherapy helps people with psychological problems. A broad answer to this question—a simple yes or no—might be oversimplifying. It is more worthwhile to ask, What *type* of

REFLECT

Do you think it is important to be a critical thinker? Are you a critical thinker? (Are you sure?)

psychotherapy, practiced by *whom,* is most helpful for *what kind of problem?*

7. *Do not overgeneralize.* Consider the statement that one cannot learn about human beings by engaging in research with animals. Is the truth of the matter an all-or-nothing issue? Are there certain kinds of information we can obtain about people from research with animals? What kinds of things are you likely to be able to learn only through research with people?

8. *Apply critical thinking to all areas of life.* A skeptical attitude and a demand for evidence are not simply of use in college. They are of value in all areas of life. Be skeptical when you are bombarded by TV commercials, when political causes try to sweep you up, when you see the latest cover stories about Elvis and UFOs in supermarket tabloids. How many times have you heard the claim "Studies have shown that . . ."? Perhaps such claims sound convincing, but ask yourself: Who ran the studies? Were the researchers neutral scientists, or were they biased toward obtaining certain results?

These are the kinds of principles that guide psychologists' thinking as they observe behavior, engage in research, or advise clients as to how to improve the quality of their lives. Perhaps these principles will help you improve the quality of your own life.

REFLECT

Why is learning to think critically a key part of higher education? How might critical thinking protect the individual from dictators, advertisers, and other tyrants of the mind?

Review

SECTION II

Some psychologists engage in basic, or (6) p_____, research, which has no immediate applications. Other psychologists engage in (7) ap_____ research, which seeks solutions to specific problems. In addition to research, many psychologists are found in (8) _____tice and teaching.

The largest number of psychologists are (9) _____al psychologists. Clinical psychologists help people resolve problems through (10) _____therapy. (11) Co_____ psychologists work with individuals who have adjustment problems but do not show seriously abnormal behavior.

School psychologists assist students with problems that interfere with (12) _____ing. (13) Ed_____ psychologists are more concerned with theoretical issues concerning human learning.

(14) _____mental psychologists study the changes that occur throughout the life span. They attempt to sort out the relative influences of nature and (15) n_____ on development. Personality psychologists seek to define and explain the origins of human

(16) _____its. (17) _____ial psychologists study the nature and causes of our thoughts, feelings, and behavior in social situations. Environmental psychologists study the ways in which behavior influences and is influenced by the (18) p_____ environment.

(19) Ex_____ psychologists conduct research into basic psychological processes, such as sensation and perception, learning and memory, and motivation and emotion. Experimental psychologists who seek to understand the relationships between biological changes and psychological events are called (20) b_____ psychologists.

Industrial psychologists focus on the relationships between people and (21) w_____. (22) _____nal psychologists study the behavior of people in organizations.

As scientists, psychologists engage in (23) cri_____ thinking, which is characterized by an attitude of skepticism. When they evaluate arguments, critical thinkers examine the definitions of (24) _____ms and the assumptions or (25) _____mises of arguments.

SECTION III. WHERE PSYCHOLOGY COMES FROM: A HISTORY

Know then thyself, presume not God to scan,
The proper study of mankind is man. . . .
Created half to rise, and half to fall,
Great lord of all things, and yet a prey to all;
Sole judge of truth, in endless error hurled;
The glory, jest, and riddle of the world!

FROM "AN ESSAY ON MAN," ALEXANDER POPE

The English poet Alexander Pope advised "Know then thyself" in the 1700s. He was not the first. The ancient Greek philosopher Socrates, writing more than 2,000 years earlier, also advised "Know thyself." Psychology, which is in large part the endeavor to know ourselves, is as old as history and as modern as today. Knowledge of the history of psychology allows us to appreciate its theoretical conflicts, its place among the sciences, the evolution of its methods, and its social and political roles (McGovern et al., 1991).

Question: Who were some of the ancient contributors to psychology? One of them is the ancient Greek philosopher Aristotle. Did you know that the outline for this textbook could have been written by Aristotle? One of Aristotle's works is *Peri Psyches,* which translates as "About the Psyche." Like this book, *Peri Psyches* begins with a history of psychological thought and historical perspectives on the nature of the mind and behavior. Aristotle argued that human behavior, like the movements of the stars and the seas, is subject to rules and laws. Then he delved into his subject matter topic by topic: personality, sensation and perception, thought, intelligence, needs and motives, feelings and emotion, and memory. This book presents these topics in a different order, but each is here.

✓ Truth or Fiction Revisited

It is true that a book on psychology, whose contents are similar to those of the book you are now holding, was written by Aristotle more than 2,000 years ago. Its title is Peri Psyches.

Aristotle also declared that people are motivated to seek pleasure and avoid pain. This view remains as current today as it was in ancient Greece.

Other ancient Greek philosophers also contributed to psychology. Around 400 B.C., Democritus suggested that we could think of behavior in terms of a body and a mind. (Contemporary psychologists still talk about the interaction of biological and mental processes.) He pointed out that our behavior is influenced by external stimulation. Democritus was one of the first to raise the question of whether there is free will or choice. Putting it another way, where do the influences of others end and our "real selves" begin?

Plato (ca. 427–347 B.C.) was a disciple of the great philosopher Socrates. He recorded Socrates' advice to "Know thyself," which has remained a motto of psychology ever since. Socrates claimed that we could not attain reliable self-knowledge through our senses because the senses do not mirror reality exactly. Because the senses provide imperfect knowledge, Socrates suggested that we should rely on processes such as rational thought and **introspection**—careful examination of one's own thoughts and emotions—to achieve self-knowledge. He also pointed out that people are social creatures who influence one another.

REFLECT

Do you think it is useful for this book to talk about topics like the history of psychology? Would you prefer it if the book just listed the 100 or 200 "facts" you need to know for the final exam? Why or why not?

INTROSPECTION Deliberate looking into one's own mind to examine one's own thoughts and feelings.

Wilhelm Wundt

William James

REFLECT

William James visited Helen Keller when she was a child and brought a gift of an ostrich feather. Why do you think he did that?

✓ **Truth or Fiction Revisited**

It is true that the ancient Greek philosopher Socrates suggested a research method that is still used in psychology. That method is introspection.

Had we room enough and time, we could trace psychology's roots to thinkers even farther back in time than the ancient Greeks, and we could trace its development through the great thinkers of the Renaissance. As it is, we must move on to the development of psychology as a laboratory science during the second half of the 19th century. Some historians set the marker date at 1860. It was then that Gustav Theodor Fechner (1801–1887) published his landmark book *Elements of Psychophysics,* which showed how physical events (such as lights and sounds) are related to psychological sensation and perception. Fechner also showed how we can scientifically measure the effect of these events. Most historians set the debut of modern psychology as a laboratory science in the year 1879, when Wilhelm Wundt established the first psychological laboratory in Leipzig, Germany.

Structuralism

Like Aristotle, Wilhelm Wundt saw the mind as a natural event that could be studied scientifically, like light, heat, and the flow of blood. Wundt used introspection to try to discover the basic elements of experience. When presented with various sights and sounds, he and his colleagues tried to look inward as objectively as possible to describe their sensations and feelings.

Wundt and his students founded the school of psychology called **structuralism.** Question: What is structuralism? Structuralism attempted to break conscious experience down into *objective* sensations, such as sight or taste, and *subjective* feelings, such as emotional responses, will, and mental images like memories or dreams. Structuralists believed that the mind functions by combining objective and subjective elements of experience.

Functionalism

I wished, by treating Psychology like a natural science, to help her become one.

WILLIAM JAMES

Toward the end of the 19th century, William James was a major figure in the development of psychology in the United States. James adopted a broad view of psychology that focused on the relation between conscious experience and behavior. He argued, for example, that the stream of consciousness is fluid and continuous. Introspection convinced him that experience cannot be broken down into objective sensations and subjective feelings as the structuralists maintained.

James was a founder of the school of **functionalism.** Question: What is functionalism? The school of functionalism dealt with behavior as well as consciousness. Functionalism addressed the ways in which experience permits us to function more adaptively in our environments—for example, how the development of habits allows us to cope with commonly occurring situations. It used behavioral observation in the laboratory to supplement introspection. The structuralists tended to ask, "What are the pieces that make up thinking and experience?" The functionalists tended to ask, "What are the *purposes* (functions) of behavior and mental processes? What difference do they make?"

James was influenced by Charles Darwin's theory of evolution. Earlier in the 19th century, Darwin had argued that organisms with adaptive features—that is, the "fittest"—survive and reproduce. Functionalists adapted Darwin's theory in the study of behavior and proposed that adaptive behavior patterns are learned and maintained. Maladaptive behavior patterns tend to drop out. They are discontinued, and the "fittest" behavior patterns survive. Adaptive actions tend to be repeated and become habits. James wrote that "habit is the enormous flywheel of society." Habit keeps civilization going from day to day.

The formation of habits is seen in acts such as lifting a fork to our mouth and turning a doorknob. At first, these acts require our full attention. If you are in doubt, stand by with paper towels and watch a baby's first efforts at self-feeding. Through repetition, the acts that make up self-feeding become automatic, or habitual. The multiple acts involved in learning to drive a car also become routine through repetition. We can then perform them without much attention, freeing ourselves to focus on other matters such as our clever conversation and the CD player. The idea of learning by repetition is also basic to the behavioral tradition in psychology.

Behaviorism

Imagine you have placed a hungry rat in a maze. It meanders down a pathway that ends in a T. It can then turn left or right. If you consistently reward the rat with food for turning right at this choice point, it will learn to turn right when it arrives there, at least when it is hungry. But what does the rat *think* when it is learning to turn right? "Hmm, last time I was in this situation and turned to the right, I was given some food. Think I'll try that again"?

Does it seem absurd to try to place yourself in the "mind" of a rat? So it seemed to John Broadus Watson (1878–1958), the founder of American behaviorism. Question: What is behaviorism? We will define behaviorism in a minute, but first let us note that Watson was asked to consider the same question as one of the requirements for his doctoral degree, which he received from the University of Chicago in 1903. Functionalism was the dominant view of psychology at the University of Chicago, and functionalists were concerned with the stream of consciousness as well as observable behavior. But Watson (1913) believed that if psychology was to be a natural science, like physics or chemistry, it must limit itself to observable, measurable events—that is, to behavior—hence, **behavior***ism.* Observable behavior includes activities such as pressing a lever; turning left or right; eating and mating; even involuntary body functions such as heart rate, dilation of the pupils of the eyes, blood pressure, and emission of brain waves. These behaviors are *public.* They can be measured by simple observation or by laboratory instruments, and different observers would readily agree about their existence and features. Behaviorists, by the way, define psychology as the scientific study of *behavior,* not of *behavior and mental processes.*

Harvard University psychologist B. F. Skinner (1904–1990) was another major contributor to behaviorism. Organisms, he believed, learn to behave in certain ways because they have been **reinforced** for doing so—that is, their behavior has had a positive outcome. He demonstrated that laboratory animals carry out behaviors, both simple and complex, because of reinforcement. They peck buttons (Figure 1.2), turn in circles, climb ladders, and push toys across the floor. Many psychologists adopted the view that, in principle, one could explain complex human behavior in terms of thousands of instances of learning through reinforcement.

REFLECT

Why do behaviorists object to schools of psychology that use introspection? Do you agree with the behaviorist point of view? Why or why not?

BEHAVIORISM The school of psychology that defines psychology as the study of observable behavior and studies relationships between stimuli and responses.

REINFORCEMENT A stimulus that follows a response and increases the frequency of the response.

FIGURE 1.2

EXAMPLES OF THE POWER OF REINFORCEMENT   IN THE PHOTO ON THE LEFT, WE SEE HOW OUR FEATHERED GIFT TO CITY LIFE HAS EARNED ITS KEEP IN EXPERIMENTS ON REINFORCEMENT. HERE, THE PIGEON PECKS THE BLUE BUTTON BECAUSE PECKING IT HAS BEEN FOLLOWED (REINFORCED) WITH FOOD. IN THE PHOTO ON THE RIGHT, "AIR RACCOON" SHOOTS A BASKET. BEHAVIORISTS TEACH ANIMALS COMPLEX BEHAVIORS SUCH AS SHOOTING BASKETS BY FIRST REINFORCING APPROXIMATIONS TO THE GOAL (OR TARGET BEHAVIOR). AS TIME PROGRESSES, CLOSER APPROXIMATIONS ARE DEMANDED BEFORE REINFORCEMENT IS GIVEN.

Gestalt Psychology

In the 1920s, another school of psychology—**Gestalt psychology**—was prominent in Germany. In the 1930s, the three founders of the school— Max Wertheimer (1880–1943), Kurt Koffka (1886–1941), and Wolfgang Köhler (1887–1967)—left Europe to escape the Nazi threat. They carried on their work in the United States, giving further impetus to the growing American ascendance in psychology.

Question: What is Gestalt psychology? Wertheimer and other Gestalt psychologists focused on perception and on how perception influences thinking and problem solving. In contrast to the behaviorists, Gestalt psychologists argued that we cannot hope to understand human nature by focusing only on overt behavior. In contrast to the structuralists, they claimed that we cannot explain human perceptions, emotions, or thought processes in terms of basic units. Perceptions are *more* than the sums of their parts: Gestalt psychologists saw our perceptions as wholes that give meaning to parts.

Gestalt psychologists illustrated how we tend to perceive separate pieces of information as integrated wholes, including the contexts in which they occur. Consider Figure 1.3. The dots in the centers of the configurations at the left are the same size, yet we may perceive them as being of different sizes because of the contexts in which they appear. The inner squares in the central figure are equally bright, but they may look different because of their contrasting backgrounds. The second symbol in each line at the right is identical, but in the top row we may perceive it as a B and in the bottom row as the number 13. The symbol has not changed, only the context in which it appears. There are many examples of this in literature and everyday life. In *The Prince and the Pauper*, Mark Twain dressed a peasant boy as a prince, and the kingdom bowed to him. Do clothes sometimes make the man or woman? Try wearing cutoffs for a job interview!

GESTALT PSYCHOLOGY The school of psychology that emphasizes the tendency to organize perceptions into wholes and to integrate separate stimuli into meaningful patterns.

A. Are the dots in the center of the configurations the same size? Why not take a ruler and measure them?

B. Is the second symbol in each line the letter B or the number 13?

C. Which one of the gray squares is brighter?

FIGURE 1.3

THE IMPORTANCE OF CONTEXT   GESTALT PSYCHOLOGISTS HAVE SHOWN THAT OUR PERCEPTIONS DEPEND NOT ONLY ON OUR SENSORY IMPRESSIONS BUT ALSO ON THE CONTEXT OF OUR IMPRESSIONS. YOU WILL INTERPRET A MAN RUNNING TOWARD YOU VERY DIFFERENTLY DEPENDING ON WHETHER YOU ARE ON A DESERTED STREET AT NIGHT OR AT A TRACK IN THE MORNING.

Gestalt psychologists believed that learning could be active and purposeful, not merely responsive and mechanical as in Skinner's experiments. Wolfgang Köhler and the others demonstrated that much learning, especially in learning to solve problems, is accomplished by **insight,** not by mechanical repetition. Köhler was marooned during World War I on one of the Canary Islands, where the Prussian Academy of Science kept a colony of apes, and his research while there gave him, well, insight into the process of learning by insight.

Have you ever pondered a problem for quite a while and then, suddenly, seen the solution? Did the solution seem to come out of nowhere? In a "flash"? Consider the chimpanzee in Figure 1.4. At first, it is unsuccessful in reaching for bananas suspended from the ceiling. Then it suddenly stacks the boxes and climbs up to reach the bananas. It seems the chimp has experienced a sudden reorganization of the mental elements of the problem—that is, it has had a "flash of insight." Köhler's findings suggest that we often manipulate the elements of problems until we group them in such a way that we believe we will be able to reach a goal. The manipulations may take quite some time as mental trial and error proceeds. Once the proper grouping has been found, however, we seem to perceive it all at once.

Psychoanalysis

Psychoanalysis, the school of psychology founded by Sigmund Freud, is very different from the other schools in both background and approach. Freud's theory has invaded popular culture, and you may be familiar with a number of its concepts. For example, on at least one TV crime show each season, an unstable person goes on a killing spree. At the end of the show, a psychiatrist explains that the killer was "unconsciously" doing away with his own mother or father. Or perhaps a friend has tried to "interpret" a slip of the tongue you made or has asked you what you thought might be the symbolic meaning of an especially vivid dream.

INSIGHT In Gestalt psychology, the sudden reorganization of perceptions, allowing the sudden solution of a problem.

PSYCHOANALYSIS The school of psychology that emphasizes the importance of unconscious motives and conflicts as determinants of human behavior.

FIGURE 1.4
SOME INSIGHT INTO INSIGHT   AT FIRST, THE CHIMPANZEE CANNOT REACH THE BANANAS HANGING FROM THE CEILING. AFTER SOME TIME HAS PASSED, IT HAS AN APPARENT "FLASH OF INSIGHT" AND PILES THE BOXES ON TOP OF ONE ANOTHER TO REACH THE FRUIT.

REFLECT

Had you heard of Sigmund Freud before you began this course? What had you heard? Were your impressions accurate? Why or why not?

PSYCHODYNAMIC Referring to Freud's theory, which proposes that the motion of underlying forces of personality determines our thoughts, feelings, and behavior.

Question: What is psychoanalysis? The notions that people are driven by hidden impulses and that verbal slips and dreams represent unconscious wishes lie at the heart of the school of psychology known as psychoanalysis. These ideas largely reflect the influence of Freud (1856–1939), a Viennese physician who fled to England in the 1930s to escape the Nazi tyranny. While academic psychologists were conducting their research in the laboratory, Freud gained his understanding of people by working with patients. He was astounded at how little insight his patients seemed to have into their motives. Some patients justified, or rationalized, the most abominable behavior with absurd explanations. Others seized the opportunity to blame themselves for nearly every misfortune that had befallen the human species.

Freud came to believe that unconscious processes, especially sexual and aggressive impulses, are more influential than conscious thought in determining human behavior. He thought that most of the mind is unconscious—a seething cauldron of conflicting impulses, urges, and wishes. People are motivated to gratify these impulses, ugly as some of them are. But at the same time, people are motivated to see themselves as decent, and hence may delude themselves about their true motives. Because Freud proposed that the motion of underlying forces of personality determines our thoughts, feelings, and behavior, his theory is referred to as **psychodynamic.**

Freud devised a method of psychotherapy called psychoanalysis. Psychoanalysis aims to help patients gain insight into many of their deep-seated conflicts and find socially acceptable ways of expressing wishes and gratifying needs. It can extend for years.

Today we no longer find psychologists who describe themselves as structuralists or functionalists. Although the school of Gestalt psychology gave birth to current research approaches in perception and problem solving, few would consider themselves Gestalt psychologists. The numbers of orthodox behaviorists and psychoanalysts have also been declining. Many contemporary psychologists in the behaviorist tradition look on themselves as social-cognitive[1] theorists, and many psychoanalysts consider themselves neoanalysts rather than traditional Freudians. They have influenced or become part of contemporary perspectives in psychology.

Review

SECTION III

The Greek philosopher (26) A_____ was among the first to argue that human behavior is subject to rules and laws. Socrates proclaimed "Know thyself" and suggested the use of (27) _____tion to gain self-knowledge.

Wilhelm (28) W_____ is usually credited with establishing the first psychological laboratory in 1879. Wundt founded the school of (29) _____alism and used introspection to study the objective and subjective elements of experience.

William James founded the school of (30) _____alism. Functionalism dealt with behavior, as well as conscious experience, and focused on the importance of (31) h_____, which James referred to as "the enormous flywheel of society."

John B. Watson founded the school of (32) b_____. Behaviorists argue that psychology must limit itself to (33) ob_____ behavior and forgo excursions into subjective consciousness. B. F. Skinner introduced the concept of (34) _____ment as an explanation of how learning occurs.

Gestalt psychology focused on (35) per_____. Gestalt psychologists saw our perceptions as (36) _____oles that give meaning to parts. They argued that learning can be active and (37) _____ful, not merely responsive and (38) _____nical, as the behaviorists believed.

Sigmund Freud founded the school of (39) p_____. According to Freud, people are driven by hidden impulses and distort reality in order to protect themselves from (40) an_____.

SECTION IV. HOW TODAY'S PSYCHOLOGISTS VIEW BEHAVIOR AND MENTAL PROCESSES

The history of psychological thought has taken many turns, and contemporary psychologists differ in their approaches. Today there are six broad, influential perspectives in psychology: the biological, cognitive, humanistic-existential, psychodynamic, learning, and sociocultural perspectives. Each emphasizes different topics of investigation. Each tends to approach its topics in its own ways.

The Biological Perspective

Psychologists assume that our thoughts, fantasies, and dreams are made possible by the nervous system and especially by the brain. Question: What is the biological perspective? Psychologists with a biological perspective seek the links between events in the brain—such as the activity of brain cells—and mental processes. They use techniques such as CAT scans and PET scans to show what parts of the brain are involved in

REFLECT

Did you think that psychologists would be interested in biology? Why or why not?

REFLECT

How would you define the *mind?* Why do some psychologists argue that it is fruitless to talk about people's minds?

---

[1]Formerly termed social-learning theorists.

A

B

The Biological Perspective. Psychologists with a biological perspective investigate the connections among biological processes, behavior, and mental processes. They use methods such as brain electrical activity mapping (BEAM), in which electrodes measure the electrical activity of parts of the brain while people are exposed to various stimuli (photo A). The left-hand column of photo B shows the average level of electrical activity of the brains of 10 normal people at four time intervals. The right-hand column shows the average activity of 10 people diagnosed with schizophrenia, a severe psychological disorder. The more intense the activity, the brighter the color (white is most intense). The bottom diagram summarizes similarities and differences between people not diagnosed with schizophrenia and people diagnosed with schizophrenia: Areas in blue reflect smaller differences; white areas reflect larger differences.

activities like language, mathematical problem solving, and music. We have learned how natural chemical substances in the brain are involved in the formation of memories. Among some lower animals, electrical stimulation of parts of the brain prompts the expression of innate, or built-in, sexual and aggressive behaviors.

Biological psychologists are also concerned with the influences of hormones (naturally occurring chemicals that are released into the bloodstream and regulate behavior) and heredity. In people, for instance, the hormone prolactin stimulates production of milk. In rats, however, prolactin also gives rise to maternal behavior. In lower animals, sex hormones determine whether mating behavior will follow stereotypical masculine or feminine behavior patterns. In people, hormones play a subtler role.

Psychologists are interested in the role of heredity in behavior and mental processes such as psychological disorders, criminal behavior, and thinking. Generally speaking, our heredity provides a broad range of behavioral and mental possibilities. Environmental factors interact with inherited factors to determine specific behavior and mental processes.

EVOLUTIONARY PSYCHOLOGY **Evolutionary psychologists** study the evolution of behavior and mental processes. Charles Darwin argued that in the age-old struggle for survival, only the "fittest" organisms manage to reach maturity and reproduce. For example, fish that swim faster or people who are naturally immune to certain diseases are more likely to transmit their **genes** to future generations. Their species are therefore likely to evolve in these adaptive directions. Evolutionary psychologists suggest that much human social behavior, such as tendencies toward aggression and mating patterns, also has a hereditary basis. People might also be influenced by social rules, cultural factors, and the capacity for personal choice, but evolutionary psychologists believe that inherited tendencies sort of whisper in people's ears and tend to move them in certain directions.

The Cognitive Perspective

Question: What is the cognitive perspective? Psychologists with a **cognitive** perspective venture into the realm of mental processes to understand human nature (Sperry, 1993). They investigate the ways in which we perceive and mentally represent the world, how we learn, remember the past, plan for the future, solve problems, form judgments, make decisions, and use language (Basic Behavioral Science Task Force, 1996a). Cognitive psychologists, in short, study all the things that we refer to as the *mind*.

The cognitive tradition has roots in Socrates' advice to "Know thyself" and in his suggested method of introspection. We also find cognitive psychology's roots in structuralism, functionalism, and Gestalt psychology, each of which, in its own way, addressed issues that are of interest to cognitive psychologists.

The Humanistic-Existential Perspective

The humanistic-existential perspective is related to Gestalt psychology and is cognitive in flavor. Question: What is the humanistic-existential perspective? Let us consider each of the parts of this perspective: *humanism* and *existentialism*. **Humanism** stresses the human capacity for self-fulfillment and the central roles of consciousness, self-awareness, and decision making. Humanistic psychology considers personal, or subjective, experience to be the most important event in psychology. Humanists believe that self-awareness, experience, and choice permit us, to a large extent, to "invent ourselves" and our ways of relating to the world as we progress through life. Consciousness—our sense of being in the world—is seen as the force that unifies our personalities. **Existentialism** views people as free to choose and be responsible for choosing ethical conduct.

Humanistic-existential psychologists stress the importance of subjective experience and assert that people have the freedom to make choices.

The Psychodynamic Perspective

In the 1940s and 1950s, Freud's psychodynamic theory dominated the practice of psychotherapy and was influential in scientific psychology and the arts. Most psychotherapists were psychodynamically oriented. Many renowned artists and writers consulted psychodynamic therapists as a way to liberate the expression of their unconscious ideas. Freud's influence continues to be felt, although it no longer dominates methods of psychotherapy. Some psychologists even argue that Freud's ideas are of no more than historic interest.

Question: What is the role of psychoanalysis today? Contemporary psychologists who follow Freud are likely to call themselves *neoanalysts*. Neoanalysts such as Karen Horney and Erik Erikson focus less on unconscious processes and more on conscious choice and self-direction.

Many Freudian ideas are retained in watered-down form by the population at large. For example, sometimes we have ideas or desires that seem atypical to us. We may say that it seems as if something is trying to get the better of us. In the Middle Ages, such thoughts and impulses were usually attributed to the devil or to demons. Dreams, likewise, were thought to enter us magically from the spirit world. Today, in part because of the influence of Sigmund Freud, many people ascribe dreams and atypical ideas or desires to unconscious processes within themselves.

Learning Perspectives

Many psychologists study the effects of experience on behavior. Learning, to them, is the essential factor in describing, explaining, predicting, and controlling behavior. The term *learning* has different meanings to psychologists of different persuasions, however. Some students of learning find roles for consciousness and insight. Others do not. This distinction is found among those who adhere to the behavioral and social-cognitive perspectives. Question: What are the learning perspectives?

For John B. Watson, behaviorism was an approach to life as well as a broad guideline for psychological research. Not only did Watson despair of measuring consciousness and mental processes in the laboratory, he also applied behavioral analysis to virtually all situations in his daily life. He viewed people as doing things because of their learning histories, their situations, and rewards rather than because of conscious choice.

Behaviorists emphasize environmental influences and the learning of habits through repetition and reinforcement. **Social-cognitive theorists** (previously termed *social-learning theorists*), in contrast, suggest that people can modify or create their environments. Since the 1960s, social-cognitive theorists have gained influence in the areas of personality development, psychological disorders, and methods of therapy. Theorists such as Albert Bandura, Julian Rotter, and Walter Mischel see themselves as part of the behaviorist tradition because of their focus on the importance of learning. Yet they also grant cognition a key role. They note that

EVOLUTIONARY PSYCHOLOGY The field of psychology that studies the evolution of behavior and mental processes. It is based on the principle of natural selection — that only the "fittest" organisms reach maturity and reproduce, thereby transmitting their genes to future generations and enabling their species to evolve in adaptive directions.

GENES The basic building blocks of heredity.

COGNITIVE Having to do with mental processes such as sensation and perception, memory, intelligence, language, thought, and problem solving.

HUMANISM The philosophy and school of psychology that asserts that people are conscious, self-aware, and capable of free choice, self-fulfillment, and ethical behavior.

EXISTENTIALISM The view that people are free and responsible for their own behavior.

SOCIAL-COGNITIVE THEORY A school of psychology in the behaviorist tradition that includes cognitive factors in the explanation and prediction of behavior. Formerly termed *social-learning theory*.

REFLECT

Do you learn by observing others? Is your learning intentional? How would you know?

people also engage in intentional learning by observing others. Through observational learning, we acquire a storehouse of responses to life's situations.

The Sociocultural Perspective

The profession of psychology focuses mainly on the individual and is committed to the dignity of the individual. However, psychology students cannot understand people's behavior and mental processes without reference to their diversity (Basic Behavioral Science Task Force, 1996b). Studying perspectives other than their own helps students understand the role of a culture's beliefs, values, and attitudes in behavior and mental processes. It helps students perceive why people from diverse cultures behave and think in different ways, and how the science of psychology is enriched by addressing those differences (Denmark, 1994; Reid, 1994).

Question: What is the sociocultural perspective? The **sociocultural perspective** addresses many of the ways in which people differ from one another. It studies the influences of ethnicity, gender, culture, and socioeconomic status on behavior and mental processes (Allen, 1993; Lewis-Fernández & Kleinman, 1994). For example, what is often seen as healthful, self-assertive, outspoken behavior by most U.S. women may be interpreted as brazen behavior in Hispanic American or Asian American communities (Lopez & Hernandez, 1986).

ETHNICITY One kind of diversity involves people's ethnicity. Members of an **ethnic group** are united by their cultural heritage, race, language, and common history. The experiences of various ethnic groups in the United States highlight the impact of social, political, and economic factors on human behavior and development (Basic Behavioral Science Task Force, 1996b; Phinney, 1996).

The probing of human diversity enables students to appreciate the cultural heritages and historical problems of various ethnic groups. This textbook considers many psychological issues related to ethnicity, such as the representation of ethnic minority groups in psychological research studies, substance abuse among adolescents from various ethnic minority groups, bilingualism, ethnic differences in intelligence test scores, the prevalence of suicide among members of different ethnic groups, ethnic differences in vulnerability to physical problems and disorders ranging from obesity to hypertension and cancer, multicultural issues in the practice of psychotherapy, and prejudice.

GENDER **Gender** is the state of being male or being female. Gender is not simply a matter of anatomic sex. It involves a complex web of cultural expectations and social roles that affect people's self-concepts and hopes and dreams as well as their behavior. How can sciences such as psychology and medicine hope to understand the particular viewpoints, qualities, and problems of women if most research is conducted with men and by men (Matthews et al., 1997)?

Just as members of ethnic minority groups have experienced prejudice, so, too, have women. Even much of the scientific research on gender roles and gender differences assumes that male behavior represents the norm (Ader & Johnson, 1994).

Our discussion of the sociocultural perspective naturally leads us to reflect on the roles of women and people from various racial and ethnic backgrounds in psychology.

REFLECT

How does the sociocultural perspective help us understand behavior and mental processes? Why is knowledge of human diversity important to the dignity of the individual?

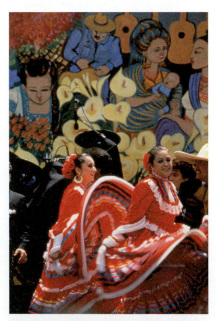

The Sociocultural Perspective. How can psychologists understand the hopes and problems of people from a particular ethnic group without understanding that group's history and cultural heritage? The sociocultural perspective helps us understand and appreciate the scope of behavior and mental processes.

SECTION IV   `Review`

Biologically oriented psychologists study the links between behavior and biological events, such as the firing of cells in the (41) b_____ and the release of hormones. (42) _____nary psychologists study the evolution of behavior and mental processes. According to evolutionary theory, only the (43) _____test organisms reach maturity and reproduce. Therefore, the fittest organisms are likely to transmit their (44) _____s to future generations, causing species to evolve in adaptive directions.

Cognitive psychologists study the ways in which we perceive and mentally (45) rep_____ the world. Humanistic-existential psychologists stress the importance of (46) self-_____ness and people's freedom to make responsible (47) ch_____. Many contemporary psychoanalysts consider themselves to be (48) _____analysts. Although they generally follow Freud's views,

they focus less on the roles of (49) un_____ sexual and aggressive impulses and see people as more capable of making conscious choices.

Watson and his followers are referred to as (50) _____ists. Social-cognitive theorists are in the behaviorist tradition because of their strong focus on the role of (51) _____ing in human behavior. Social-cognitive theorists also find roles for (52) ob_____ learning, expectations, and values in explaining human behavior.

The sociocultural perspective fosters the consideration of matters of ethnicity, gender, culture, and (53) socio_____ status in psychology. People's (54) _____nic groups are defined by features such as their common cultural heritage, race, language, and history. (55) _____er is defined as the state of being male or being female.

SECTION V. GENDER, ETHNICITY, AND THE PROFESSION OF PSYCHOLOGY

Although the overwhelming majority of psychologists in the 1800s were White males, women and people from various racial and ethnic backgrounds have made key contributions to the science of psychology in the past century. Let's consider some of the women.

Women in Psychology

Women have traditionally been channeled into domestic pursuits, regardless of their wishes as individuals. Not until relatively modern times were women generally considered suitable for higher education (and in many parts of the world, women are still considered unsuited to education!). Women have attended college in the United States only since 1833, when Oberlin College opened its doors to women. Today, however, more than half (54.5%) of U.S. postsecondary students are women. Women receive more than 50% of the doctoral degrees in psychology (Pion et al., 1996).

Question: What contributions have women made to psychology? There are interesting stories of particular women in psychology. Christine Ladd-Franklin (1847–1930) was born during an era in American history in which women were expected to remain at home and were excluded from careers in science (Furumoto, 1992). She nevertheless pursued a career in psychology, taught at Johns Hopkins and Columbia Universities, and formulated a theory of color vision. Margaret Floy Washburn (1871–1939) was the first woman to receive a Ph.D. in psychology. Washburn also wrote *The Animal Mind*, a work that contained many ideas that would later become part of behaviorism.

Mary Whiton Calkins (1863–1930) became the first female president of the American Psychological Association in 1905. Calkins studied

SOCIOCULTURAL PERSPECTIVE The view that focuses on the roles of ethnicity, gender, culture, and socioeconomic status in behavior and mental processes.

ETHNIC GROUP A group characterized by common features such as cultural heritage, history, race, and language.

GENDER The state of being female or being male.

Mary Whiton Calkins

psychology with William James at Harvard University, but as a "guest student." Harvard was not yet admitting women. When she completed her degree requirements, Harvard would not award her the degree because of her gender (*APA Monitor,* 1999). Instead, Harvard offered to grant her a doctorate from its sister school, Radcliffe. Calkins declined the offer because accepting it would help perpetuate discrimination against women. Even without a doctorate, Calkins pioneered research in memory at Wellesley College, where she founded a psychology laboratory in 1891. She introduced a number of methods for studying memory and other mental processes.

✓ Truth or Fiction Revisited

It is true that the first female president of the American Psychological Association turned down the doctoral degree that was offered to her. She had earned it at Harvard, but the degree was offered from Radcliffe because Harvard was not yet accepting women students.

Ethnicity and Psychology

Question: What contributions to psychology have been made by people from various racial and ethnic groups? Numerous early psychologists came from different ethnic backgrounds. Back in 1901, Gilbert Haven Jones, an African American, received his Ph.D. in psychology in Germany. J. Henry Alston engaged in research on perception of heat and cold and was the first African American psychologist to be published in a major psychology journal (the year was 1920).

In the 1940s, African American psychologist Kenneth B. Clark and his wife, psychologist Mamie Phipps Clark, conducted research showing the negative effects of school segregation on African American children. In one such study, African American children were shown white and brown dolls and asked to "Give me the pretty doll," or "Give me the doll that looks bad." Most children's choices showed that they preferred the white dolls over the brown ones. The Clarks concluded that the children had swallowed the larger society's preference for White people. The Clarks' research was cited by the Supreme Court when it overturned the "separate but equal" schools doctrine in 1954.

Kenneth B. Clark

Today African Americans continue to have a powerful impact on the profession of psychology. For example, as we see in Chapter 3, psychologist Robert Williams—sometimes referred to as the "father of Ebonics"—has offered us insight into language differences that are often found between European Americans and African Americans. Psychologist Claude Steele has shown that many African Americans self-destruct on intelligence tests because of *stereotype vulnerability.* That is, rather than focus on the test items, they worry about the stereotype, or widespread belief, that African Americans are not as bright as European Americans, and thereby hurt their own performance.

Hispanic American and Asian American psychologists have also made their mark. Jorge Sanchez, for example, was among the first to show how intelligence tests are culturally biased—to the disadvantage of Mexican American children. Asian American psychologist Stanley Sue has shown how discrimination may be connected with racial differences in intelligence and academic achievement.

REFLECT

Why do you think that increasing numbers of women have been drawn to the study of psychology?

Today more than half of the Ph.D.s in psychology are awarded to women. African Americans and Hispanic Americans each receive 3% to 4% of the Ph.D.s awarded in psychology (ODEER, 1994). This percentage is far below their representation in the general population, unfortunately. In a recent year, only one tenth of 1% of the 65,000 members of the

American Psychological Association were Native Americans (DeAngelis, 1993). Even so, fewer than two psychology Ph.D.s in five are now awarded to White males. Psychology, like the societies in which it flourishes, is becoming increasingly diverse.

✓ **Truth or Fiction Revisited**

It is not true that men receive the majority of degrees in psychology. Women actually receive the majority of Ph.D.s in psychology today.

Put it another way: Psychology belongs to everyone.

Review

SECTION V

Women and people from various ethnic groups have made key contributions to psychology. Christine (56) Ladd-F_____ formulated a theory of color vision. Mary Whiton (57) C_____ introduced the method of paired associates and discovered the primacy and recency effects. Calkins refused the doctorate offered her by Radcliffe because she had completed her graduate work at (58) _____. Margaret Floy (59) W_____ wrote *The Animal Mind.*

The African American psychologist J. Henry (60) A_____ engaged in research in the perception of heat and cold. Kenneth B. (61) C_____ influenced a key Supreme Court decision on desegregation. Robert (62) _____ms is referred to as the father of Ebonics. Claude Steele heightened our awareness of (63) _____ vulnerability as a reason that many African Americans perform below their ability levels on intelligence tests. Jorge (64) S_____ was among the first to show how intelligence tests are culturally biased.

Today the majority of doctoral degrees in psychology are awarded to (65: Women or Men?).

Psychology is the scientific study of behavior and mental processes. By now we have a sense of the various fields of psychology, the history of psychology, and the ways in which today's psychologists look at behavior and mental processes. Like other scientists, psychologists rely on research to seek answers to the questions that interest them. The next section follows through on some questions of interest to psychologists to demonstrate how research is conducted.

SECTION VI. HOW PSYCHOLOGISTS STUDY BEHAVIOR AND MENTAL PROCESSES

Consider some questions of interest to psychologists: Do only humans use tools? Does alcohol cause aggression? Why do some people hardly ever think of food, whereas others are obsessed with it and snack all day long? Why do some unhappy people attempt suicide, whereas others seek ways of coping with their problems? Does having people of different ethnic backgrounds collaborate in their work serve to decrease or increase feelings of prejudice?

Many of us have expressed opinions on questions like these at one time or another. Different psychological theories also suggest a number of possible answers. Psychology is an *empirical* science, however. In an empirical science, assumptions about the behavior of cosmic rays, chemical compounds, cells, or people must be supported by evidence. Strong arguments, reference to authority figures, even tightly knit theories are not adequate as scientific evidence. Psychologists make it their business—literally and figuratively—to be skeptical.

Psychologists use research to study behavior and mental processes empirically. To undertake our study of research methods, let us recount some famous research undertaken at Yale University more than 30 years ago.

People are capable of boundless generosity and of hideous atrocities. Throughout history, people have sacrificed themselves for the welfare of their families, friends, and nations. Throughout history, people have maimed and destroyed other people to vent their rage or please their superiors.

Let us follow up on the negative side. Soldiers have killed civilians and raped women in occupied areas to obey the orders of their superiors or to win the approval of their comrades. Millions of Native Americans, Armenians, Muslims, and Jews have been slaughtered by people who were obeying the orders of officers.

How susceptible are people—how susceptible are you and I—to the demands of authority figures such as military officers? Is there something unusual or abnormal about people who follow orders and inflict pain and suffering on their fellow human beings? Are they very much unlike you and me? Or *are* they you and me?

It is easy to imagine that something must be terribly wrong with people who would hurt a stranger without provocation. There must be something abnormal about people who would slaughter innocents. But these are assumptions, and scientists are skeptical of assumptions. Psychologist Stanley Milgram wondered whether normal people would comply with authority figures who made immoral demands. But rather than speculate on the issue, he undertook a series of classic experiments at Yale University that have become known as the Milgram studies on obedience.

In an early phase of his work, Milgram (1963) placed ads in New Haven (Connecticut) newspapers for people who would be willing to participate in studies on learning and memory. He enlisted 40 people ranging in age from 20 to 50—teachers, engineers, laborers, salespeople, people who had not completed elementary school, people with graduate degrees.

Let's suppose that you have answered the ad. You show up at the university in exchange for a reasonable fee ($4.50, which in the early 1960s might easily fill your gas tank) and to satisfy your own curiosity. You may be impressed. After all, Yale is a venerable institution that dominates the city. You are no less impressed by the elegant labs, where you meet a distinguished behavioral scientist dressed in a white coat and another person who has responded to the ad. The scientist explains that the purpose of the experiment is to study the *effects of punishment on learning*. The experiment requires a "teacher" and a "learner." By chance, you are appointed the teacher and the other recruit the learner.

You, the scientist, and the learner enter a laboratory room containing a threatening chair with dangling straps. The scientist straps the learner in. The learner expresses some concern, but this is, after all, for the sake of science. And this is Yale University, isn't it? What could happen to a person at Yale?

You follow the scientist to an adjacent room, from which you are to do your "teaching." This teaching promises to have an impact. You are to punish the learner's errors by pressing levers marked from 15 to 450 volts on a fearsome-looking console (see Figure 1.5). Labels describe 28 of the 30 levers as running the gamut from "Slight Shock" to "Danger: Severe Shock." The last two levers are simply labeled "XXX." Just in case you have no idea what electric shock feels like, the scientist gives you a sample 45-volt shock. It stings. You pity the person who might receive more.

Your learner is expected to learn pairs of words, which are to be read from a list. After hearing the list once, the learner is to produce the word that pairs with the stimulus word from a list of four alternatives. This is done by pressing a switch that lights one of four panels in your room. If it is the correct panel, you proceed to the next stimulus word. If not, you are to deliver an electric shock. With each error, you are to increase the voltage of the shock (Figure 1.6).

You probably have some misgivings. Electrodes have been strapped to the learner's wrists, and the scientist has applied electrode paste "to avoid blisters and burns." You have also been told that the shocks will cause "no permanent tissue damage," although they might be extremely painful. Still, the learner is going along. And after all, this is Yale.

The learner answers some items correctly and then makes some errors. With mild concern you press the levers up through 45 volts. You've tolerated that much yourself. Then a few more mistakes are made. You press the 60-volt lever, then 75. The learner makes another mistake. You pause and look at the scientist, who is reassuring: "Although the shocks may be painful, there is no permanent tissue damage, so please go on." The learner makes more errors, and soon you are up to a shock of 300 volts. But now the learner is pounding on the other side of the wall! Your chest tightens and you begin to perspire. 'Damn science and the $4.50!' you think. You hesitate and the scientist says, "The experiment requires that you continue." After the delivery of the next stimulus word, the learner chooses no answer at all. What are you to do? "Wait for 5 to 10 seconds," the scientist instructs, "and then treat no answer as a wrong answer." But after the next

FIGURE 1.5

THE "AGGRESSION MACHINE"   IN THE MILGRAM STUDIES ON OBEDIENCE TO AUTHORITY, PRESSING LEVERS ON THE "AGGRESSION MACHINE" WAS THE OPERATIONAL DEFINITION OF AGGRESSION.

FIGURE 1.6

THE EXPERIMENTAL SET-UP IN THE MILGRAM STUDIES   WHEN THE "LEARNER" MAKES AN ERROR, THE EXPERIMENTER PRODS THE "TEACHER" TO DELIVER A PAINFUL ELECTRIC SHOCK.

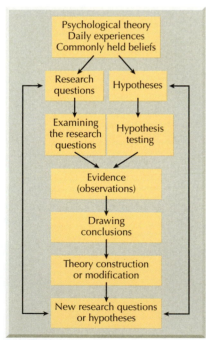

FIGURE 1.7

THE SCIENTIFIC METHOD

THE SCIENTIFIC METHOD IS A SYSTEMATIC WAY OF ORGANIZING AND EXPANDING SCIENTIFIC KNOWLEDGE. DAILY EXPERIENCES, COMMON BELIEFS, AND SCIENTIFIC OBSERVATIONS ALL CONTRIBUTE TO THE DEVELOPMENT OF THEORIES. PSYCHOLOGICAL THEORIES EXPLAIN OBSERVATIONS AND LEAD TO HYPOTHESES ABOUT BEHAVIOR AND MENTAL PROCESSES. OBSERVATIONS CONFIRM THE THEORY OR LEAD TO ITS REFINEMENT OR ABANDONMENT.

shock the pounding on the wall resumes! Now your heart is racing, and you are convinced you are causing extreme pain and discomfort. Is it possible that no lasting damage is being done? Is the experiment that important, after all? What to do? You hesitate again, and the scientist says, "It is absolutely essential that you continue." His voice is very convincing. "You have no other choice," he says, "you *must* go on." You can barely think straight, and for some unaccountable reason you feel laughter rising in your throat. Your finger shakes above the lever. *What are you to do?*

Milgram (1963, 1974) found out what most people in his sample would do. The sample was a cross-section of the male population of New Haven. Of the 40 men in this phase of his research, only 5 refused to go beyond the 300-volt level, the level at which the learner first pounded the wall. Nine other "teachers" defied the scientist within the 300-volt range. But 65% of the subjects complied with the scientist throughout the series, believing they were delivering 450-volt, XXX-rated shocks.

Were these subjects unfeeling? Not at all. Milgram was impressed by their signs of stress. They trembled, they stuttered, they bit their lips. They groaned, they sweated, they dug their fingernails into their flesh. Some had fits of laughter, although laughter was inappropriate. One salesperson's laughter was so convulsive that he could not continue with the experiment.

We return to the Milgram studies later in the chapter. They are a rich mine of information about human nature. They are also useful for our discussions of research issues such as replication, the experimental method, and ethics.

The Scientific Method: Putting Ideas to the Test

Question: What is the scientific method? The scientific method is an organized way of using experience and testing ideas in order to expand and refine knowledge. Psychologists do not necessarily follow the steps of the scientific method as we might follow a cookbook recipe. However, their research endeavors are guided by certain principles.

Psychologists usually begin by *formulating a research question.* Research questions can have many sources. Our daily experiences, psychological theory, even folklore all help generate questions for research. Consider some questions that may arise from daily experience. Daily experience in using day-care centers may motivate us to conduct research on whether day care influences the development of social skills or the bonds of attachment between children and mothers.

Or consider questions that might arise from psychological theory (see Figure 1.7). Social-cognitive principles of observational learning may prompt research on the effects of TV violence. Sigmund Freud's psychoanalytic theory may prompt research on whether the verbal expression of feelings of anger helps relieve feelings of depression.

Research questions may also arise from common knowledge. Consider familiar adages such as "Misery loves company," "Opposites attract," and "Beauty is in the eye of the beholder." Psychologists may ask, *Does* misery love company? *Do* opposites attract? *Is* beauty in the eye of the beholder?

A research question may be studied as a question or reworded as a hypothesis (see Figure 1.7). A **hypothesis** is a specific statement about behavior or mental processes that is tested through research. One hypothesis about day care might be that preschoolers who are placed in day care will acquire greater social skills in relating to peers than preschoolers who are cared for in the home. A hypothesis about TV violence might be that elementary school children who watch more violent TV shows tend to behave more aggressively toward their peers. A hypothesis that addresses Freudian theory might be that verbally expressing feelings of anger will decrease feelings of depression.

Psychologists next examine the research question or *test the hypothesis* through controlled methods such as the experiment. For example, we could introduce children who are in day care and children who are not to a new child in a college child-research center and observe how children in each group interact with the new acquaintance.

Psychologists draw conclusions about their research questions or the accuracy of their hypotheses on the basis of their observations or findings. When their observations do not bear out their hypotheses, they may modify the theories from which the hypotheses were derived (see Figure 1.7). Research findings often suggest refinements to psychological theories and, consequently, new avenues of research.

In our research on day care, we would probably find that children in day care show greater social skills than children who are cared for in the home (Clarke-Stewart, 1991). We would probably also find that more aggressive children spend more time watching TV violence. Research on the effectiveness of psychoanalytic forms of therapy is usually based on case studies.

As psychologists draw conclusions from research evidence, they are guided by principles of critical thinking. For example, they try not to confuse correlations between findings with cause and effect. Although more aggressive children apparently spend more time watching violent TV shows, it may be erroneous to conclude from this kind of evidence that TV violence *causes* aggressive behavior. Perhaps a **selection factor** is at work—because the children studied choose (select) for themselves what they will watch. Perhaps more aggressive children are more likely than less aggressive children to tune into violent TV shows.

To better understand the effects of the selection factor, consider a study on the relationship between exercise and health. Imagine that we were to compare a group of people who exercised regularly with a group of people who did not. We might find that the exercisers were physically healthier than the couch potatoes. But could we conclude that exercise is a causal factor in good health? Perhaps not. The selection factor—the fact that one group chose to exercise and the other did not—could also explain the results. Perhaps healthy people are more likely to *choose* to exercise.

Some psychologists include publication of research reports in professional journals as a crucial part of the scientific method. Researchers are obligated to provide enough details of their work that others will be able to repeat or **replicate** it to see whether the findings hold up over time and with different subjects. Publication of research also permits the scientific community at large to evaluate the methods and conclusions of other scientists.

Samples and Populations: Representing Human Diversity

Consider a piece of history that never quite happened: The Republican candidate Alf Landon defeated the incumbent president, Franklin D. Roosevelt, in 1936. Or at least Landon did so in a poll conducted by a popular magazine of the day, the *Literary Digest*. In the actual election, however, Roosevelt routed Landon by a landslide of 11 million votes. How, then, could the *Digest* predict a Landon victory? How was so great a discrepancy possible?

The *Digest*, you see, had surveyed voters by phone. Today telephone sampling is a widely practiced and reasonably legitimate polling

REFLECT

Have you heard the expressions "Misery loves company," "Opposites attract," or "Beauty is in the eye of the beholder"? Is there evidence for them? Is the evidence scientific? Why or why not?

REFLECT

People who exercise are generally healthier than people who do not. Does this fact show that exercise is a causal factor in good health? Why or why not?

HYPOTHESIS In psychology, a specific statement about behavior or mental processes that is tested through research.

SELECTION FACTOR A source of bias that may occur in research findings when subjects are allowed to choose for themselves a certain treatment in a scientific study.

REPLICATE Repeat, reproduce, copy.

technique. But the *Digest* poll was taken during the Great Depression, when people who had telephones were much wealthier than those who did not. People at higher income levels are also more likely to vote Republican. No surprise, then, that the overwhelming majority of those sampled said they would vote for Landon.

Question: How do psychologists use samples to represent populations? The *Digest* poll failed because of its method of sampling. Samples must be drawn so that they accurately *represent* the population they are intended to reflect. Only representative samples allow us to **generalize**—or *extend* our findings—from research samples to populations.

✓ Truth or Fiction Revisited

It is true that you could survey 20 million voters and still not predict the outcome of a presidential election accurately. Sample size alone does not guarantee that a sample will accurately represent the population from which it was drawn.

In surveys such as that conducted by the *Literary Digest,* and in other research methods, the individuals who are studied are referred to as a **sample.** A sample is a segment of a **population** (the group that is targeted for study). Psychologists and other scientists need to ensure that the people they observe *represent* their target population, such as U.S. voters, and not subgroups such as southern Californians or non-Hispanic White members of the middle class.

PROBLEMS IN GENERALIZING FROM PSYCHOLOGICAL RESEARCH

All generalizations are dangerous, even this one.

ALEXANDRE DUMAS

Many factors must be considered in interpreting the accuracy of the results of scientific research. One is the nature of the research sample.

Milgram's initial research on obedience was limited to a sample of New Haven men. Could he generalize his findings to other men or to women? Would college students, who are considered to be independent thinkers, show more defiance? A replication of Milgram's study with a sample of Yale men yielded similar results. What about women, who are supposedly less aggressive than men? In subsequent research, women, too, administered shocks to the learners. All this took place in a nation that values independence and free will.

Later in the chapter we consider research in which the subjects were drawn from a population of college men who were social drinkers. That is, they tended to drink at social gatherings but not when alone. Who do college men represent, other than themselves? To whom can we extend, or generalize, the results? For one thing, the results may not extend to women, not even to college women. In the chapter on consciousness, for example, we will learn that alcohol goes more quickly to women's heads than to men's.

College men also tend to be younger and more intelligent than the general adult population. We cannot be certain that the findings extend to older men of average intelligence, although it seems reasonable to assume they do. Social drinkers may also differ biologically and psychologically from alcoholics, who have difficulty controlling their drinking. Nor can we be certain that college social drinkers represent people who do not drink at all.

By and large, we must also question whether findings of research with men can be generalized to women (Ader & Johnson, 1994), and whether

---

REFLECT

Are you surprised that women in the Milgram study obeyed orders and shocked "learners" just as men did? Why or why not?

GENERALIZE To extend from the particular to the general; to apply observations based on a sample to a population.

SAMPLE Part of a population.

POPULATION A complete group of organisms or events.

research with White men can be extended to members of ethnic minority groups. For example, personality tests completed by non-Hispanic White Americans and by African Americans may need to be interpreted in diverse ways if accurate conclusions are to be drawn. The well-known Kinsey studies on sexual behavior (Kinsey et al., 1948, 1953) did not adequately represent African Americans, poor people, older people, and numerous other groups.

RANDOM AND STRATIFIED SAMPLING One way to achieve a representative sample is by means of **random sampling.** In a random sample, each member of a population has an equal chance of being selected to participate. Researchers can also use a **stratified sample,** which is selected so that identified subgroups in the population are represented proportionately in the sample. For instance, 12% of the American population is African American. A stratified sample would thus be 12% African American. As a practical matter, a large randomly selected sample will show reasonably accurate stratification. A random sample of 1,500 people will represent the general U.S. population reasonably well. A haphazardly drawn sample of 20 million, however, might not.

Large-scale magazine surveys of sexual behavior have asked readers to fill out and return questionnaires. Although many thousands of readers completed the questionnaires and sent them in, did they represent the general U.S. population? Probably not. These studies and similar ones may have been influenced by **volunteer bias.** People who offer or volunteer to participate in research studies differ systematically from people who do not. In the case of research on sexual behavior, volunteers may represent subgroups of the population—or of readers of the magazines in question—who are willing to disclose intimate information (Rathus et al., 2000). Volunteers may also be more interested in research than nonvolunteers, as well as have more spare time. How might such volunteers differ from the population at large? How might such differences slant or bias the research outcomes?

Methods of Observation: The Better to See You With

Many people consider themselves experts on behavior and mental processes. How many times, for example, have grandparents told us what they have seen in their lives and what it means about human nature?

Indeed we see much during our lifetimes. Our personal observations tend to be fleeting and uncontrolled, however. We sift through experience for the things that interest us. We often ignore the obvious because it does not fit our assumptions about the way things ought to be. Scientists, however, have devised more controlled ways of observing others. *Question: What methods of observation are used by psychologists?* In this section we consider three methods of observation widely used by psychologists and other behavioral scientists: the case study, survey, and naturalistic observation methods.

CASE STUDY We begin with the case study method because our own informal ideas about human nature tend to be based on **case studies,** or information we collect about individuals and small groups. But most of us gather our information haphazardly. We often see only what we want to see. Unscientific accounts of people's behavior are referred to as *anecdotes.* Psychologists attempt to gather information about individuals more carefully.

RANDOM SAMPLE A sample drawn so that each member of a population has an equal chance of being selected to participate.

STRATIFIED SAMPLE A sample drawn so that identified subgroups in the population are represented proportionately in the sample. How can stratified sampling be carried out to ensure that a sample represents the ethnic diversity we find in the population at large?

VOLUNTEER BIAS A source of bias or error in research reflecting the prospect that people who offer to participate in research studies differ systematically from people who do not.

CASE STUDY A carefully drawn biography that may be obtained through interviews, questionnaires, and psychological tests.

Sigmund Freud developed psychodynamic theory largely on the basis of case studies. He studied the people who sought his help in great depth, seeking the factors that seemed to contribute to certain patterns of behavior. He followed some people for many years, meeting with them several times a week.

Case studies are also often used to investigate rare occurrences, as in the case of "Eve." Eve was an example of a person with multiple personalities (technically termed *dissociative identity disorder*). "Eve White" was a mousy, well-intentioned woman who had two other "personalities" living inside her. One of them was "Eve Black," a promiscuous personality who emerged now and then to take control of her behavior.

Case studies can provide compelling portraits of individuals, but they also have some sources of inaccuracy. For example, there are gaps and factual inaccuracies in people's memories (Azar, 1997; Brewin et al., 1993). People may also distort their pasts to please the interviewer or because they want to remember things in certain ways. Interviewers may also have certain expectations and may subtly encourage subjects to fill in gaps in ways that are consistent with these expectations. Bandura (1986) notes, for example, that psychoanalysts have been criticized for guiding people who seek their help into viewing their own lives from the psychodynamic perspective. No wonder, then, that many people provide "evidence" that is consistent with psychodynamic theory. However, interviewers and other kinds of researchers who hold *any* theoretical viewpoint run the risk of indirectly prodding people into saying what they want to hear.

THE SURVEY In the good old days, we had to wait until the wee hours of the morning to learn the results of local and national elections. Throughout the evening and early morning hours, suspense would build as ballots from distant neighborhoods and states were tallied. Nowadays, we are barely settled with an after-dinner cup of coffee on election night when reporters announce that a computer has examined the ballots of a "scientifically selected sample" and predicted the next president of the United States. All this may occur with less than 1% of the vote tallied.

Just as computers and pollsters predict election results and report national opinion on the basis of scientifically selected samples, psychologists conduct **surveys** to learn about behavior and mental processes that cannot be observed in the natural setting or studied experimentally. Psychologists conducting surveys may employ questionnaires and interviews or examine public records. One of the great advantages of the survey is that by distributing questionnaires and analyzing answers with a computer, psychologists can study many thousands of people at a time.

Alfred Kinsey of Indiana University and his colleagues published two surveys of sexual behavior, based on interviews, that shocked the nation. These were *Sexual Behavior in the Human Male* (1948) and *Sexual Behavior in the Human Female* (1953). Kinsey reported that masturbation was virtually universal in his sample of men at a time when masturbation was still widely thought to impair health. He also reported that about 1 woman in 3 who was still single at age 25 had engaged in premarital intercourse.

Surveys, like case studies, have various sources of inaccuracy. People may recall their behavior inaccurately or purposefully misrepresent it. Some people try to ingratiate themselves with their interviewers by answering in what they perceive to be the socially desirable direction. The Kinsey studies all relied on male interviewers, for example. It has been speculated that female interviewees might have been more open and honest with female interviewers. Similar problems may occur when interview-

---

REFLECT

What methods of observation do you use when you try to "figure out" other people? Are your methods scientific? Why or why not?

REFLECT

Have you read the results of a survey or a poll in a popular magazine or online? Were they representative of the general population? Why or why not?

SURVEY A method of scientific investigation in which a large sample of people answer questions about their attitudes or behavior.

ers and the people surveyed are from different ethnic or socioeconomic backgrounds. Other people may falsify their attitudes and exaggerate their problems in order to draw attention to themselves or intentionally foul up the results.

Consider some examples of survey measurement errors caused by inaccurate self-reports of behavior (Barringer, 1993). If people brushed their teeth as often as they claimed, and used the amount of toothpaste they indicated, three times as much toothpaste would be sold in the United States as is actually sold. People also appear to overreport church attendance and to underreport abortions (Barringer, 1993). Why do you think this is so?

NATURALISTIC OBSERVATION You use **naturalistic observation**— that is, you observe people in their natural habitats—every day. So do psychologists. The next time you opt for a fast-food burger lunch, look around. Pick out slender people and overweight people and observe whether they eat their burgers and fries differently. Do the overweight people eat more rapidly? Chew less frequently? Leave less food on their plates? Psychologists have used this method to study the eating habits of normal weight and overweight people. In fact, while you're at McDonald's, if you notice people peering over sunglasses and occasionally tapping the head of a partly concealed microphone, perhaps they are recording their observations of other people's eating habits.

Naturalistic observation has the advantage of allowing psychologists and other scientists to observe behavior where it happens, or "in the field." In doing so, researchers use *unobtrusive* measures to avoid interfering with the behaviors they are observing. For example, Jane Goodall has observed the behavior of chimpanzees in their natural environment to learn about their social behavior, sexual behavior, use of tools, and other facts of chimp life (see Figure 1.8). Her observations have shown us that (1) we were incorrect to think that only humans use tools; and (2) kissing, as a greeting, is apparently used by chimpanzees as well as by humans.

NATURALISTIC OBSERVATION A scientific method in which organisms are observed in their natural environments.

FIGURE 1.8

THE NATURALISTIC-OBSERVATION METHOD JANE GOODALL HAS OBSERVED THE BEHAVIOR OF CHIMPANZEES IN THE FIELD, "WHERE IT HAPPENS." SHE HAS FOUND THAT CHIMPS USE STICKS TO GRUB FOR FOOD AND THAT THEY APPARENTLY KISS EACH OTHER AS A SOCIAL GREETING. SCIENTISTS WHO USE THIS METHOD TRY NOT TO INTERFERE WITH THE ANIMALS OR PEOPLE THEY OBSERVE, EVEN THOUGH THIS SOMETIMES MEANS ALLOWING AN ANIMAL TO BE MISTREATED BY OTHER ANIMALS OR TO DIE FROM A CURABLE ILLNESS.

REFLECT

What kinds of correlations (positive or negative) would you expect to find among behavior patterns such as churchgoing and crime? Language ability and musical ability? Level of education and incidence of teenage pregnancy? Grades in school and delinquency? Why?

Correlation

Are people with higher intelligence more likely to do well in school? Are people with a stronger need for achievement likely to climb higher up the corporate ladder? What is the relationship between stress and health?

Such questions are often answered by means of the correlational method. Question: What is the correlational method? Correlation follows observation. By using the correlational method, psychologists investigate whether observed behavior or a measured trait is related to, or correlated with, another. Consider the variables of intelligence and academic performance. These variables are assigned numbers such as intelligence test scores and academic averages. Then the numbers are mathematically related and expressed as a **correlation coefficient.** A correlation coefficient is a number that varies between +1.00 and −1.00.

Studies report **positive correlations** between intelligence test scores and academic achievement, as measured, for example, by grade point averages. Generally speaking, the higher people score on intelligence tests,

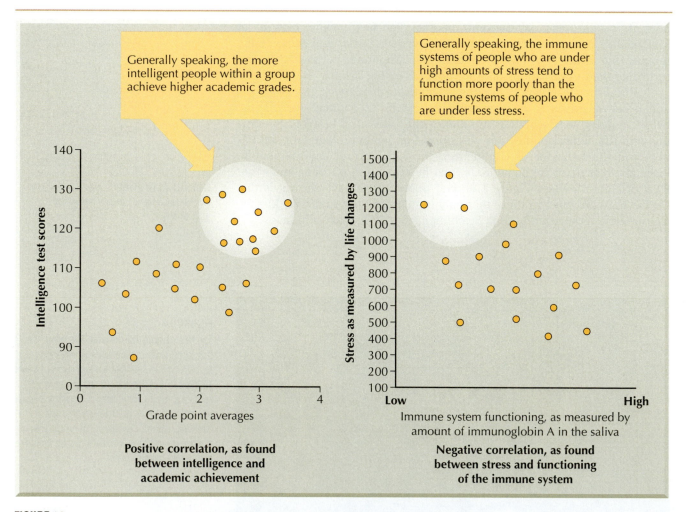

Generally speaking, the more intelligent people within a group achieve higher academic grades.

Generally speaking, the immune systems of people who are under high amounts of stress tend to function more poorly than the immune systems of people who are under less stress.

Positive correlation, as found between intelligence and academic achievement

Negative correlation, as found between stress and functioning of the immune system

FIGURE 1.9

POSITIVE AND NEGATIVE CORRELATIONS   WHEN THERE IS A POSITIVE CORRELATION BETWEEN VARIABLES, AS THERE IS BETWEEN INTELLIGENCE AND ACHIEVEMENT, ONE INCREASES AS THE OTHER INCREASES. BY AND LARGE, THE HIGHER PEOPLE SCORE ON INTELLIGENCE TESTS, THE BETTER THEIR ACADEMIC PERFORMANCE IS LIKELY TO BE, AS IN THE DIAGRAM TO THE LEFT. (EACH DOT REPRESENTS AN INDIVIDUAL'S INTELLIGENCE TEST SCORE AND GRADE POINT AVERAGE.) BUT THERE IS A NEGATIVE CORRELATION BETWEEN STRESS AND HEALTH. AS THE AMOUNT OF STRESS WE EXPERIENCE INCREASES, THE FUNCTIONING OF OUR IMMUNE SYSTEM TENDS TO DECREASE. CORRELATIONAL RESEARCH MAY SUGGEST BUT DOES NOT DEMONSTRATE CAUSE AND EFFECT.

the better their academic performance is likely to be. The scores attained on intelligence tests tend to be positively correlated (about +0.60 to +0.70) with academic achievement (see Figure 1.9). But factors *other* than performance on intelligence tests also contribute to academic success. These include achievement motivation, adjustment, and common sense (Collier, 1994; Sternberg et al., 1995).

There is a **negative correlation** between stress and health. As the amount of stress affecting us increases, the functioning of our immune system decreases. Under high levels of stress, many people show poorer health.

Correlational research may suggest but does not prove cause and effect. For instance, it may seem logical to assume that high intelligence makes it possible for children to profit from education. Research has also shown, however, that education contributes to higher scores on intelligence tests. Preschoolers who are placed in stimulating Head Start programs later attain higher scores on intelligence tests than age-mates who did not have this experience. The relationship between intelligence and academic performance may not be as simple as you might think. What of the link between stress and health? Does stress impair health, or is it possible that people in poorer health encounter more stress? (See Figure 1.10.)

The Experimental Method: Trying Things Out

The people who signed up for the Milgram studies participated in an elaborate experiment. Question: What is the experimental method? In an experiment, the subjects received a treatment. Milgram's subjects received an intricate *treatment*—one that involved a well-equipped research laboratory. The experiment also involved deception. Milgram had even foreseen subjects' objections to the procedure. He had therefore conceived standardized statements that his assistants would use when subjects balked—for example: "Although the shocks may be painful, there is no permanent tissue damage, so please go on." "The experiment requires that you continue." "It is absolutely essential that you continue." "You have no other choice, you *must* go on." These statements, the bogus "aggression machine," the use of the "learner" (who was actually a confederate of the experimenter)—all these were part of the experimental treatment.

Intelligence and Achievement. Correlations between intelligence test scores and academic achievement—as measured by school grades and achievement tests—tend to be positive and strong. Does the correlational method allow us to say that intelligence *causes* or *is responsible for* academic achievements? Why or why not?

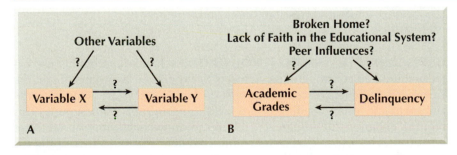

FIGURE 1.10

CORRELATIONAL RELATIONSHIPS, CAUSE, AND EFFECT CORRELATIONAL RELATIONSHIPS MAY SUGGEST BUT DO NOT DEMONSTRATE CAUSE AND EFFECT. IN PART A, THERE IS A CORRELATION BETWEEN VARIABLES X AND Y. DOES THIS MEAN THAT EITHER VARIABLE X CAUSES VARIABLE Y OR THAT VARIABLE Y CAUSES VARIABLE X? NOT NECESSARILY. OTHER FACTORS COULD AFFECT BOTH VARIABLES X AND Y. CONSIDER THE EXAMPLES OF ACADEMIC GRADES (VARIABLE X) AND JUVENILE DELINQUENCY (VARIABLE Y) IN PART B. THERE IS A NEGATIVE CORRELATION BETWEEN THE TWO. DOES THIS MEAN THAT POOR GRADES CONTRIBUTE TO DELINQUENCY? PERHAPS. DOES IT MEAN THAT DELINQUENCY CONTRIBUTES TO POOR GRADES? AGAIN, PERHAPS. BUT THERE COULD ALSO BE OTHER VARIABLES—SUCH AS A BROKEN HOME, LACK OF FAITH IN THE EDUCATIONAL SYSTEM, OR PEER INFLUENCES—THAT CONTRIBUTE BOTH TO POOR GRADES AND DELINQUENCY.

CORRELATION COEFFICIENT A number from +1.00 to −1.00 that expresses the strength and direction (positive or negative) of the relationship between two variables.

POSITIVE CORRELATION A relationship between variables in which one variable increases as the other also increases.

NEGATIVE CORRELATION A relationship between variables in which one variable increases as the other decreases.

Although we can raise many questions about the Milgram studies, most psychologists agree that the preferred method for answering questions about cause and effect is the experiment. In an **experiment,** a group of subjects obtains a **treatment,** such as a dose of alcohol, a change in room temperature, perhaps an injection of a drug. The subjects are then observed carefully to determine whether the treatment makes a difference in their behavior. Does alcohol alter the ability to take tests, for example? What about differences in room temperatures and level of background noise?

Experiments are used whenever possible because they allow psychologists to control the experiences of subjects and draw conclusions about cause and effect. A psychologist may theorize that alcohol leads to aggression because it reduces fear of consequences or because it energizes the activity levels of drinkers. She or he may then hypothesize that a treatment in which subjects receive a specified dosage of alcohol will lead to increases in aggression. Let us follow the example of the effects of alcohol on aggression to further our understanding of the experimental method.

What Are the Effects of Alcohol? Psychologists have conducted numerous studies to determine the effects of alcohol. Questions have been raised about the soundness of research in which people *know* that they have drunk alcohol. Why is this research questioned?

INDEPENDENT AND DEPENDENT VARIABLES In an experiment to determine whether alcohol causes aggression, subjects would be given an amount of alcohol and its effects would be measured. In this case, alcohol is an **independent variable.** The presence of an independent variable is manipulated by the experimenters so that its effects may be determined. The independent variable of alcohol may be administered at different levels, or doses, from none or very little to enough to cause intoxication or drunkenness.

The measured results, or outcomes, in an experiment are called **dependent variables.** The presence of dependent variables presumably depends on the independent variables. In an experiment to determine whether alcohol influences aggression, aggressive behavior would be a dependent variable. Other dependent variables of interest might include sexual arousal, visual-motor coordination, and performance on intellectual tasks such as defining words or doing numerical computations.

In an experiment on the relationships between temperature and aggression, temperature would be an independent variable and aggressive behavior would be a dependent variable. We could set temperatures from below freezing to blistering hot and study its effects. We could also use a second independent variable such as social provocation. That is, we could insult some subjects but not others. This method would allow us to study the ways in which two independent variables—temperature and social provocation—affect aggression, singly and together.

EXPERIMENT A scientific method that seeks to confirm cause-and-effect relationships by introducing independent variables and observing their effects on dependent variables.

TREATMENT In experiments, a condition received by subjects so that its effects may be observed.

INDEPENDENT VARIABLE A condition in a scientific study that is manipulated so that its effects may be observed.

DEPENDENT VARIABLE A measure of an assumed effect of an independent variable.

EXPERIMENTAL GROUPS In experiments, groups whose members obtain the treatment.

CONTROL GROUPS In experiments, groups whose members do not obtain the treatment, while other conditions are held constant.

EXPERIMENTAL AND CONTROL GROUPS Ideal experiments use experimental and control groups. Subjects in **experimental groups** obtain the treatment. Members of **control groups** do not. Every effort is made to ensure that all other conditions are held constant for both groups. This method enhances the researchers' ability to draw conclusions about cause and effect. The researchers can be more confident that outcomes of the experiment are caused by the treatments and not by chance factors or chance fluctuations in behavior.

In an experiment on the effects of alcohol on aggression, members of the experimental group would ingest alcohol and members of the control group would not. In a complex experiment, different experimental groups might ingest different dosages of alcohol and be exposed to different types of social provocations.

BLINDS AND DOUBLE BLINDS One experiment on the effects of alcohol on aggression (Boyatzis, 1974) reported that men at parties where beer and liquor were served acted more aggressively than men at parties where only soft drinks were served. But subjects in the experimental group *knew* they had drunk alcohol, and those in the control group *knew* they had not. Aggression that appeared to result from alcohol might not have reflected drinking per se. Instead, it might have reflected the subjects' *expectations* about the effects of alcohol. People tend to act in stereotypical ways when they believe they have been drinking alcohol. For instance, men tend to become less anxious in social situations, more aggressive, and more sexually aroused.

A **placebo,** or "sugar pill," often results in the kind of behavior that people expect. Physicians sometimes give placebos to demanding, but healthy, people, many of whom then report that they feel better. When subjects in psychological experiments are given placebos—such as tonic water—but think they have drunk alcohol, we can conclude that changes in their behavior stem from their beliefs about alcohol, not from the alcohol itself.

Well-designed experiments control for the effects of expectations by creating conditions under which subjects are unaware of, or **blind** to, the treatment. Yet researchers may also have expectations. They may, in effect, be "rooting for" a certain treatment. For instance, tobacco company executives may wish to show that cigarette smoking is harmless. In such cases, it is useful if the people measuring the experimental outcomes are unaware of which subjects have received the treatment. Studies in which neither the subjects nor the experimenters know who has obtained the treatment are called **double-blind studies.**

The Food and Drug Administration requires double-blind studies before it allows the marketing of new drugs. The drug and the placebo look and taste alike. Experimenters assign the drug or placebo to subjects at random. Neither the subjects nor the observers know who is taking the drug and who is taking the placebo. After the final measurements have been made, a neutral panel (a group of people who have no personal stake in the outcome of the study) judges whether the effects of the drug differed from those of the placebo.

> ✓ **Truth or Fiction Revisited**
>
> *It is true that in many experiments, neither the subjects nor the researchers know who is receiving the real treatment and who is receiving a placebo ("sugar pill"). Such double-blind studies control for the effects of subjects' and researchers' expectations.*

In one double-blind study on the effects of alcohol, Alan Lang and his colleagues (1975) pretested a highball of vodka and tonic water to determine that it could not be discriminated by taste from tonic water alone. They recruited college men who described themselves as social drinkers to participate in the study. Some of the men drank vodka and tonic water. Others drank tonic water only. Of the men who drank vodka, half were misled into believing they had drunk tonic water only (Figure 1.11). Of those who drank tonic water only, half were misled into believing their drink contained vodka. Thus, half the subjects were blind to their treatment. Experimenters who measured the men's aggressive responses were also blind concerning which subjects had drunk vodka.

The research team found that men who believed that they had drunk vodka responded more aggressively to a provocation than men who believed that they had drunk tonic water only. The actual content of the

PLACEBO A bogus treatment that has the appearance of being genuine.

BLIND In experimental terminology, unaware of whether or not one has received a treatment.

DOUBLE-BLIND STUDY A study in which neither the subjects nor the observers know who has received the treatment.

REFLECT

Can you devise a method in which researchers would use placebos and double blinds to investigate the effects of a new drug on the urge to smoke cigarettes?

FIGURE 1.11

THE EXPERIMENTAL CONDITIONS IN THE LANG STUDY

THE TASTE OF VODKA CANNOT BE DISCERNED WHEN VODKA IS MIXED WITH TONIC WATER. FOR THIS REASON, IT WAS POSSIBLE FOR SUBJECTS IN THE LANG STUDY ON THE EFFECTS OF ALCOHOL TO BE KEPT "BLIND" AS TO WHETHER OR NOT THEY HAD ACTUALLY DRUNK ALCOHOL. BLIND STUDIES ALLOW PSYCHOLOGISTS TO CONTROL FOR THE EFFECTS OF SUBJECTS' EXPECTATIONS.

drink was immaterial. That is, men who had actually drunk alcohol acted no more aggressively than men who had drunk tonic water only. The results of the Lang study differ dramatically from those reported by Boyatzis, perhaps because the Boyatzis study did not control for the effects of expectations or beliefs about alcohol.

Review

SECTION VI

The (66) _____fic method is an organized way of going about expanding and refining knowledge. Psychologists usually begin by formulating a (67) re_____ question. A research question may be reworded as a (68) _____sis, which is a specific statement about behavior or mental processes that is tested through research. Research findings often suggest refinements to psychological (69) _____ries and new avenues of research.

Samples must accurately (70) rep_____ the populations they are intended to reflect. Otherwise, we cannot (71) _____lize from research samples to populations. In a (72) _____dom sample, each member of a population has an equal chance of being selected to participate. Researchers can also use a (73) _____fied sample, which is drawn so that identified subgroups in the population are represented proportionately in the sample. The concept behind (74) _____-teer bias is that people who offer to participate in research studies differ systematically from people who do not.

Sigmund (75) _____d developed psychodynamic theory largely on the basis of case studies. Problems with the case study include gaps in (76) m_____ and purposeful distortion of the past. Interviewers may also subtly guide people to fill in gaps in ways that are (77: Consistent or Inconsistent?) with their theoretical perspectives.

Psychologists conduct surveys to learn about behavior and mental processes that cannot be observed in the natural setting or studied

(78) ex_____ally. Psychologists making surveys may employ questionnaires and interviews or examine public (79) re_____s. In responding to surveys, people may inaccurately recall their behavior or purposefully (80) mis-_____ it. Some people try to ingratiate themselves with their interviewers by answering in what they perceive to be the (81) _____ally desirable direction. Other people may falsify attitudes and exagerate problems to draw (82) at_____ to themselves or try to foul up the results.

The (83) _____-observation method observes individuals in their natural habitats. Psychologists and other scientists try to avoid interfering with the behaviors they are observing by using (84) _____sive measures. Jane (85) _____ has extensively observed the behavior of chimpanzees in their natural environment.

Psychologists use the correlational method to investigate whether one observed behavior or measured trait is related to, or (86) _____-lated with, another. A number called the correlation (87) co_____ indicates the direction and the magnitude of a correlation between variables. A correlation coefficient can vary between +1.00 and (88) _____. When variables are (89) _____ly correlated, one increases as the other increases. When variables are (90) _____ly correlated, one increases as the other decreases. Studies report (91) _____tive correlations between intelligence and achievement. Correlational research does not show cause and (92) _____.

An (93) _____ment is considered the best research method for answering questions concerning cause and effect. In an experiment, a group of subjects receives a (94) _____ment, such as a dose of alcohol. The subjects are then observed to determine whether the treatment has an effect.

The (95) _____dent variable is manipulated by the experimenters so that its effects may be determined. The measured results, or outcomes, in an experiment are called (96) _____dent variables. The presence of (97) _____dent variables presumably depends on the (98) _____dent variables.

Ideal experiments use experimental and (99) con_____ groups. Individuals in (100) _____tal groups receive the treatment, whereas individuals in control groups do

not. Every effort is made to ensure that all other (101) _____tions are held constant for experimental and control groups. In this way, researchers can have confidence that the experimental outcomes reflect the (102) _____ments and not chance factors or chance fluctuations in behavior.

A (103) p_____, or "sugar pill," often results in the behavior that people expect. When people in experiments are given placebos but think that they have received the real treatment, we can conclude that changes in behavior and mental processes stem from their (104) _____tations about the treatment and not from the treatment itself. Well-designed experiments control for the effects of expectations by creating conditions under which subjects are unaware of, or (105) _____ to, the treatment they have received.

SECTION VII. ETHICAL ISSUES IN PSYCHOLOGICAL RESEARCH AND PRACTICE

It is in the area of ethics that we raise the most serious questions about the Milgram studies. The Milgram studies on obedience made key contributions to our understanding of the limits of human nature. In fact, it is difficult for professional psychologists to imagine a history of psychology without the knowledge provided by such studies. But the subjects experienced severe psychological anguish. Were the Milgram studies **ethical?**

Question: What are the ethical issues that concern psychological research and practice with humans? Psychologists adhere to a number of ethical standards that are intended to promote individual dignity, human welfare, and scientific integrity (McGovern et al., 1991). They are also intended to ensure that psychologists do not undertake research methods or treatments that are harmful to subjects or clients (American Psychological Association, 1992a). Let us first look at these ethical standards as they apply to psychological research and practice with humans.

Research With Humans

Lang and his colleagues (1975) gave small doses of alcohol to college students who were social drinkers. Other researchers, however, have paid alcoholics—people who have difficulty limiting their alcohol consumption—to drink in the laboratory so that they could study their reactions and those of family members (e.g., Jacob et al., 1991). Practices such as these raise ethical questions. For example, paying the alcoholics to drink in the laboratory, and providing the alcohol, could be viewed as encouraging them to engage in self-destructive behavior (Koocher, 1991).

Recall the signs of stress shown by the subjects in the Milgram studies on obedience. They trembled, stuttered, groaned, sweated, bit their lips, and dug their fingernails into their flesh. In fact, if Milgram had attempted to run his experiments in the 1990s rather than in the 1960s, he might have been denied permission to do so by a university ethics review committee. In virtually all institutional settings, including colleges, hospitals, and research foundations, **ethics review committees** help researchers

ETHICAL Moral; referring to one's system of deriving standards for determining what is moral.

ETHICS REVIEW COMMITTEE A group found in an institutional setting that helps researchers consider the potential harm of their methods and reviews proposed studies according to ethical guidelines.

REFLECT

The Milgram studies were conducted prior to the advent of ethics review committees. If you were on such a committee, would you approve Milgram's proposed research? Why or why not?

consider the potential harm of their methods and review proposed studies according to ethical guidelines. When such committees find that proposed research might be unacceptably harmful to subjects, they may withhold approval until the proposal has been modified. Ethics review committees also weigh the potential benefits of research against the potential harm.

Today individuals must provide **informed consent** before they participate in research. Having a general overview of the research and the opportunity to choose not to participate apparently gives them a sense of control and decreases the stress of participating (Dill et al., 1982). Is there a way in which subjects in the Milgram studies could have provided informed consent? What do you think?

Psychologists treat the records of research subjects and clients as confidential. This is because they respect people's privacy and also because people are more likely to express their true thoughts and feelings when researchers or therapists keep their disclosures confidential. Sometimes conflicts of interest arise, however, for example, when a client threatens a third party and the psychologist feels an obligation to warn that person.

Ethics limit the types of research that psychologists may conduct. For example, how can we determine whether early separation from one's mother impairs social development? One way would be to observe the development of children who have been separated from their mothers at an early age. It is difficult to draw conclusions from such research, however, because of the selection factor. That is, the same factors that led to the separation—such as family tragedy or irresponsible parents—and *not* the separation, may have led to the outcome. Scientifically, it would be more sound to run experiments in which researchers separate children from their mothers at an early age and compare their development with that of other children. But psychologists would not undertake such research because of the ethical issues they pose. Yet, they run experiments with lower animals in which infants are separated from mothers.

Many psychological experiments cannot be run without deceiving the people who participate. However, the use of deception raises ethical issues. You are probably skeptical enough to wonder whether the "teachers" in the Milgram studies actually shocked the "learners" when the teachers pressed the levers on the console. They didn't. The only real shock in this experiment was the 45-volt sample given to the teachers. Its purpose was to make the procedure believable.

The learners in the experiment were actually confederates of the experimenter. They had not answered the newspaper ads but were in on the truth from the start. The "teachers" were the only real subjects. They were led to believe they had been chosen at random for the teacher role, but the choosing was rigged so that newspaper recruits would always become teachers.

As you can imagine, psychologists have debated the ethics of deceiving subjects in the Milgram studies (Fisher & Fyrberg, 1994). According to the American Psychological Association's (1992a) *Ethical Principles of Psychologists and Code of Conduct*, psychologists may use deception only when they believe the benefits of the research outweigh its potential harm, they believe the individuals might have been willing to participate if they had understood the benefits of the research, and subjects are **debriefed**. Debriefing means that the purposes and methods of the research are explained afterward. Milgram provided subjects with detailed explanations of his experiment after they participated. He emphasized the fact that they had not actually harmed anyone.

Return to the Lang (Lang et al., 1975) study on alcohol and aggression. In this study, the researchers (1) misinformed subjects about the beverage they were drinking and (2) misled them into believing they were giving other subjects electric shock when they, like the subjects in the

INFORMED CONSENT The term used by psychologists to indicate that a person has agreed to participate in research after receiving information about the purposes of the study and the nature of the treatments.

DEBRIEF To elicit information about a completed procedure.

Milgram studies, were actually only pressing switches on a dead control board. (*Aggression* was defined as pressing these switches in the study.) In the Lang study, students who believed they had drunk vodka were "more aggressive"—that is, selected higher levels of shock—than students who believed they had not. The actual content of the beverages was immaterial.

Ethics and Animal Research. Is it ethical for researchers to harm animals in order to obtain knowledge that may benefit humans?

✓ Truth or Fiction Revisited

It is true that psychologists would not be able to carry out certain kinds of research without deceiving subjects as to the purposes and methods of the studies.

Research With Animals

Psychologists and other scientists frequently use animals to conduct research that cannot be carried out with humans. For example, experiments on the effects of early separation from the mother have been done with monkeys and other animals. Such research has helped psychologists investigate the formation of attachment bonds between parent and child.

Question: What are the ethical issues that concern research with animals? Experiments with infant monkeys highlight some of the ethical issues faced by psychologists and other scientists who contemplate potentially harmful research. Psychologists and biologists who study the workings of the brain destroy sections of the brains of laboratory animals to learn how they influence behavior. For instance, a **lesion** in one part of a brain structure causes a rat to overeat. A lesion elsewhere causes the rat to go on a crash diet. Psychologists generalize to humans from experiments such as these in the hope of finding solutions to problems such as eating disorders. Proponents of the use of animals in research argue that major advances in medicine and psychology could not have taken place without them (Fowler, 1992).

The majority of psychologists disapprove of research in which animals are exposed to pain or killed (Plous, 1996). According to the ethical guidelines of the American Psychological Association (1992b), animals may be harmed only when there is no alternative and when researchers believe that the benefits of the research justify the harm.

REFLECT

Is it ethical to harm lower animals in conducting research when the results may be beneficial to humans? Why or why not?

LESION An injury that results in impaired behavior or loss of a function.

Review

SECTION VII

Psychologists adhere to a number of (106) _____cal standards that are intended to promote the dignity of the individual, foster human welfare, and maintain scientific integrity. They also protect subjects or clients from harm.

In order to help avoid harm, human subjects must provide (107) _____consent. Psychologists treat the records of research subjects and clients as (108) _____tial because they respect people's privacy and because people are more likely to express their true thoughts and feelings when researchers or therapists keep their disclosures confidential. In institutional settings, (109) ethics _____ committees help researchers consider the potential harm of their methods. (110) E_____ _____view committees may also recommend ways of decreasing the harm that comes to subjects.

Many experiments, like the Lang study on the effects of alcohol, cannot be run without (111) de_____ing people. Psychological ethics require that research subjects who are deceived be (112) _____fed afterward to help eliminate misconceptions and anxieties about the research and to leave them with their dignity intact.

Psychologists and other scientists frequently turn to (113) _____mals to conduct harmful or potentially harmful research that cannot be carried out with humans. Psychologists still face the (114) eth_____ dilemma of subjecting animals to harm. As with people, psychologists follow the principle that animals should be subjected to (115) h_____ only when there is no alternative and they believe that the benefits of the research justify the harm.

STUDY GUIDE

SUMMARY

1. **What is psychology?** Psychology is the scientific study of behavior and mental processes.

2. **What are the goals of psychology?** Psychology seeks to describe, explain, predict, and control behavior and mental processes. Behavior and mental processes are explained through psychological theories, which are sets of statements that involve assumptions about behavior. Explanations and predictions are derived from theories. Theories are revised, as needed, to accommodate new observations.

3. **Just what do psychologists do?** Psychologists engage in research and practice. Research can be pure or applied. Basic or pure research has no immediate applications. Applied research seeks solutions to specific problems. Psychologists also specialize in various fields. Clinical psychologists help people with psychological disorders adjust to the demands of life. Counseling psychologists work with people with adjustment problems. School psychologists assist students with problems that interfere with learning. Developmental psychologists study the changes that occur throughout the life span. Personality psychologists study influences on our thought processes, feelings, and behavior. Social psychologists focus on the nature and causes of behavior in social situations. Experimental psychologists conduct research into basic psychological processes such as sensation and perception, learning and memory, and motivation and emotion. Industrial psychologists focus on the relationships between people and work. Health psychologists study the ways in which behavior and mental processes such as attitudes are related to physical health.

4. **What is critical thinking?** Critical thinking is a hallmark of psychologists and of scientists in general. Critical thinking is associated with skepticism. It involves thoughtfully analyzing the questions, statements, and arguments of others. It means examining the definitions of terms, examining the premises or assumptions behind arguments, and scrutinizing the logic with which arguments are developed. Critical thinking also refers to the ability to inquire about causes and effects, as well as knowledge of research methods. Critical thinkers are cautious in drawing conclusions from evidence. They do not oversimplify or overgeneralize.

5. **Who were some of the ancient contributors to psychology?** The ancient Greek philosopher Aristotle declared that people are motivated to seek pleasure and avoid pain. Another Greek, Democritus, suggested that we could think of behavior in terms of a body and a mind and raised the question of whether there is free will or choice. Plato recorded Socrates' advice to "Know thyself," primarily by means of introspection.

6. **What is structuralism?** Structuralism, founded by Wilhelm Wundt, used introspection to study the objective and subjective elements of experience. Wundt also established the first psychological laboratory in Leipzig, Germany, in 1879.

7. **What is functionalism?** Functionalism is the school founded by William James. It dealt with observable behavior as well as conscious experience and focused on the importance of habit.

8. **What is behaviorism?** Behaviorism, founded by John B. Watson, argues that psychology must limit itself to observable behavior and not attempt to deal with subjective consciousness. Behaviorism focuses on learning by conditioning, and B. F. Skinner introduced the concept of reinforcement as an explanation of how learning occurs.

9. **What is Gestalt psychology?** Gestalt psychology is the school of psychology founded by Wertheimer, Koffka, and Köhler. It is concerned with perception and argues that the wholeness of human experience is more than the sum of its parts.

10. **What is psychoanalysis?** Psychoanalysis was founded by Sigmund Freud. The school asserts that people are driven by hidden impulses and that they distort reality to protect themselves from anxiety.

11. **What is the biological perspective?** The biological perspective views the links between behavior and biological structures and events such as the brain, hormones, and heredity. Evolutionary psychology is based on the work of Charles Darwin, who argued that in the age-old struggle for survival, only the "fittest" organisms reach maturity and reproduce,

thereby transmitting the traits that enable them to survive to their offspring. Evolutionary psychologists suggest that aggressive and mating behaviors have a hereditary basis.

12. **What is the cognitive perspective?** The cognitive perspective is concerned with the ways in which we mentally represent the world and process information. Cognitive psychologists study how we learn, remember the past, plan for the future, solve problems, form judgments, make decisions, and use language.

13. **What is the humanistic-existential perspective?** Humanistic-existential psychologists stress the importance of subjective experience and assert that people have the freedom to make choices.

14. **What is the role of psychoanalysis today?** Contemporary psychoanalysts often call themselves *neoanalysts* because they focus less on unconscious processes and more on conscious choice and self-direction. Psychoanalysis remains popular in the culture at large.

15. **What are the learning perspectives?** There are two learning perspectives: the behavioral perspective and the social-cognitive perspective. Behaviorism — the historic view of Watson — focuses on environmental influences on learning. Social-cognitive theory argues that psychologists can address thought processes and that people are free to modify and create environments.

16. **What is the sociocultural perspective?** The sociocultural perspective focuses on the roles of ethnicity, gender, culture, and socioeconomic status in behavior and mental processes.

17. **What contributions have women made to psychology?** Women have made major contributions to psychology in the United States for more than a century, despite the fact that many entered the field when it was still widely believed that "a woman's place" was in the home. Ladd-Franklin formulated a theory of color vision. Washburn's views presaged behaviorism. Calkins studied memory and heightened awareness of prejudice against women.

18. **What contributions to psychology have been made by people from various racial and ethnic groups?** People from ethnic minority groups have contributed to all areas of psychology, but some, like Kenneth Clark and Robert Williams, have heightened awareness of issues concerning their groups, such as prejudice and Ebonics.

19. **What is the scientific method?** The scientific method is an organized way of going about expanding and refining knowledge. Psychologists usually begin by formulating a research question, which may be re-

worded as a hypothesis. They reach conclusions about their research questions or the accuracy of their hypotheses on the basis of their research observations or findings.

20. **How do psychologists use samples to represent populations?** The individuals who participate in research are referred to as a sample. A sample is a segment of a population. Samples must accurately represent the population they are intended to reflect. In a *random sample,* each member of a population has an equal chance of being selected to participate. Researchers can also use a *stratified sample,* which is selected so that identified subgroups in the population are represented proportionately in the sample.

21. **What methods of observation are used by psychologists?** The methods used include the case study, the survey, and naturalistic observation. Case studies gather information about the lives of individuals or small groups. The survey method uses interviews, questionnaires, or public records to gather information about behavior that cannot be observed directly. The naturalistic observation method observes behavior where it happens — "in the field."

22. **What is the correlational method?** The correlational method reveals relationships between variables but does not determine cause and effect. In a positive correlation, variables increase simultaneously. In a negative correlation, one variable increases while the other decreases.

23. **What is the experimental method?** Experiments are used to discover cause and effect — that is, the effects of independent variables on dependent variables. Experimental groups receive a specific treatment, whereas control groups do not. Blinds and double blinds may be used to control for the effects of the expectations of the subjects and the researchers. Results can be generalized only to populations that have been adequately represented in the research samples.

24. **What are the ethical issues that concern psychological research and practice with humans?** The ethical standards of psychologists are intended to protect subjects in research and clients in practice from harm. Records of human behavior are kept confidential. Ethics review committees judge the harmfulness of proposed research and help make it less harmful. Human subjects are required to give informed consent prior to participating in research and are debriefed following participation.

25. **What are the ethical issues that concern research with animals?** Some research can be conducted only with animals. Ethical standards require that animals may be harmed only if there is no alternative and the benefits justify the harm.

E X E R C I S E   1

MATCHING—NAMES TO KNOW

The names of people who are important to psychology are in the first column. Schools of psychology and other identifying information are in the second column. Place the letter of the item that is best associated with the person in the blank space to the left of the person's name. Answers are given below.

____ 1. Aristotle	A. Found cultural bias in intelligence tests
____ 2. Wolfgang Köhler	B. Behaviorism
____ 3. Gustav Theodor Fechner	C. Gestalt psychology
____ 4. Erik Erikson	D. Studied ethnicity and influenced a Supreme Court decision on desegregation
____ 5. Margaret Floy Washburn	E. Psychodynamic perspective
____ 6. B. F. Skinner	F. Author, *Elements of Psychophysics*
____ 7. Mary Whiton Calkins	G. Structuralism
____ 8. Robert Williams	H. First female president of American Psychological Association
____ 9. Socrates	I. Introspection
____ 10. John B. Watson	J. Formulated a theory of color vision
____ 11. Wilhelm Wundt	K. Functionalism
____ 12. Claude Steele	L. Author, *The Animal Mind*
____ 13. Max Wertheimer	M. Author, *Peri Psyches*
____ 14. Jorge Sanchez	N. Said "Know thyself"
____ 15. Kurt Koffka	O. Introduced the method of paired associates and discovered the primacy and recency effects
____ 16. Sigmund Freud	P. "Father" of Ebonics
____ 17. Karen Horney	Q. Studied "stereotype vulnerability"
____ 18. Kenneth B. Clark	
____ 19. William James	
____ 20. Christine Ladd-Franklin	

E X E R C I S E   2

TRUE OR FALSE

Circle the T or F for each of the following, to indicate whether the item is true or false. Check your answers in the key given below. It is more important at this time for you to understand why each item is true or false than to get them all right.

T F   1. In the scientific method, participants are randomly selected and assigned to experimental groups or control groups.

T F   2. A hypothesis is a formulation of the relationships and principles that underlie observed events that allows us to explain and predict behavior.

T F   3. A hypothesis is a specific statement about behavior or mental processes that is tested through research.

T F   4. In the Lang study on the effects of alcohol on aggression, aggression was operationally defined as selection of a level of shock to deliver to another person.

T F   5. The most important factor about a sample is that it is very large.

T F   6. If a sample is not randomly selected, the results of the study are inaccurate.

T F   7. A random sample is selected by picking out telephone numbers in a directory by chance.

T F   8. People who volunteer to participate in research studies differ from people who refuse to participate.

T F   9. There is a positive correlation between intelligence and academic achievement.

T F   10. There is a negative correlation between two variables. We can conclude that increasing one variable causes the other to decrease.

T F   11. Researchers attempt to use unobtrusive measures in the naturalistic-observation method so that they do not influence the behavior they are observing.

T F   12. Experimental blinds aim at controlling for the effects of expectations.

T F   13. Case studies differ from surveys in the numbers of individuals studied.

T F   14. It is unethical for a psychologist to breach confidentiality with a client, even when the client states that she or he is going to kill a third party.

BRIDGING THE GAP

LANGUAGE AND CULTURE

abominable (14) *hateful, contemptible, physically or emotionally injurious*

absurd (14) *foolish*

academic average (30) *grades at school relative to others' performance*

acculturation (5) *learned adjustment to a new culture*

adage (24) *common saying, cliche*

adaptive features (11) *aspects that change to suit the environment*

admirable (3) *worthy of notice and imitation*

age-old (16) *very old, historical*

apprehension (2) *mental grasp, understanding*

ascendance (12) *growing position of prestige and influence*

back in (+ a year) (20) *as long ago as (+ year)*

to bear out (25) *to prove, to demonstrate the truth of something*

biased (8) *prejudiced, having a strong extreme opinion*

blistering hot (32) *hot enough to burn the skin*

bogus (30) *false, phony*

to be bombarded (81) *to be overwhelmed (by)*

brazen behavior (18) *inappropriately loud and aggressive way of acting*

cause and effect (30) *reason and result*

chance factor (32) *accidental influence*

to climb higher on the corporate ladder (30) *to advance in the importance of position or job*

confederate (30) *accomplice, someone who secretly cooperates*

a conflict of interest (36) *a situation in which a person's loyalty is divided*

context (13) *situation, frame*

to control for (33) *to make allowances for, to manipulate an experimental situation so as to be able to focus on one aspect*

convulsive (24) *uncontrolled*

a couch potato (25) *a person who does not exercise, chronic television watcher*

a crash diet (37) *a fast weight-loss plan*

cultural heritage (18) *distinctive traditions of one ethnic group (celebrations, values, costumes, etc.)*

cutoffs (12) *blue jeans that are shortened to the knee*

do their bidding (3) *obey them*

debut (10) *(here) beginning*

to delve into (9) *to dig into, to investigate*

downright puzzling (3) *extremely difficult to understand*

downsizing (5) *reducing (the number of people in an organization)*

to drop out (11) *(here) to disappear*

to earn its keep (12) *to contribute according to what it costs, to pay for itself*

Ebonics (20) *African-American dialect of English, a language with some special characteristics that are different from standard English*

ethical question (35) *question about whether it is appropriate to act in a certain way*

an ethnic minority group (27) *collectively, the people who share language and cultural background, like Hispanic Americans*

express (2) *great, wonderful, clear*

facilitate (5) *help, promote, encourage, make (it) easy*

faculty (2) *ability, capacity*

fantasy (15) *imagined scenes and sounds or results (as opposed to remembered scenes and sounds)*

flywheel (11) *heavy machine-driving wheel that maintains and evens out the speed*

for the sake of science (22) *in the interest of learning*

to foster (7) *to help (someone) develop*

to foul up (29)   *to confuse, to mix up*

founder of a school (11)   *person who started a system of understanding to which others also contributed, someone who first stated a philosophical position in an area of study*

to give birth to (15)   *to start, to be the beginning of*

to go to one's head (26)   *to affect or influence the thinking of one*

hallmark (6)   *distinctive feature*

to have a stake in something (33)   *to be interested in (the outcome of) something because of personal interest*

Head Start programs (30)   *planned educational experiences for young children to prepare them for school*

immaterial (37)   *valueless, insignificant*

infinite (2)   *boundless, extremely great*

in the field (29)   *in a naturally occurring environment*

intrigued by (3)   *interested in*

IQ (7)   *measure of a person's ability to function intellectually*

(an) irresistible impulse (31)   *a desire (to do something) that is impossible to stop*

to jeopardize (31)   *to put into danger, to risk the safety of something*

a killing spree (13)   *a wild, uncontrolled series of murders, a rampage*

laboratory science (10)   *area of study in which experiments are done under controlled conditions to learn techniques and to investigate the unknowns*

landmark (10)   *(said of something that is a classic, something that changes the direction of thought in a particular area of study) important, influential*

led to believe (36)   *told a story to change (someone's) opinion*

literally and figuratively (22)   *both in practice and in theory*

to look inward (10)   *to reflect on one's actions and thoughts*

to make a mark (20)   *to contribute something significant*

maladaptive (11)   *not fitting in well*

Mark Twain (12)   *famous American writer; he lived in the 1800s, and he wrote many amusing and insightful works*

a maze (11)   *(here) a box with dividers into which an experimental animal is put, the dividers of which define different paths that an animal can use in reaching a goal*

to meander (11)   *to wonder, to go without a goal*

measurement (5)   *(in psychology) assessment of the level of some mental quality, trait, or capacity*

merger (5)   *(the) combining of two groups, like two companies*

to mirror reality (9)   *to reflect what is real*

motto (9)   *saying, statement of belief*

mousy (28)   *plain, mouselike, ordinary, unassertive*

the Nazi threat (12)   *the danger of the right-wing Germans in the 1930s and 1940s*

neoanalyst (17)   *"new" analyst (said of someone starting in a new direction of thought)*

neutral (8)   *unbiased, not taking sides*

(to) nurture (5)   *to care for a child, to aid a child in growing up*

on the tip of the tongue (3)   *almost ready to be said, but not quite remembered*

organisms (11)   *living creatures*

paragon (2)   *model, perfect example, ideal*

placebo (33)   *harmless pill or treatment given to humor or satisfy a patient (who is given no real medicine at all)*

popular culture (13)   *commonly shared values among a group of people (their music, decorations, fashions, etc.)*

to play a role (15)   *to have an effect or influence (on someone or something)*

probing (18)   *closely examining, digging into*

proper grouping (13)   *appropriate context, right frame*

psychological disorders (3)   *problems with emotional or thought processes*

to put it another way (21)   *to say it in other words, to define it*

reinforcement (11)   *reward for proper or desired behavior*

SATs (5)   *scores on a standardized test that measures readiness for university work*

to scan (2)   *to survey, to scrutinize, to examine*

the Scholastic Assessment Test (5)   *a standardized test, (the SAT) which measures readiness for university work*

to scrutinize (6)   *to examine carefully*

(a) seething cauldron (14)   *a potentially explosive mixture (a symbol of mixed and confusing thoughts)*

skeptical (7)   *doubting, critical, questioning*

(to) slaughter innocents (22)   *to murder children*

slip of the tongue (13)   *a verbal mistake (usually one that reveals what a person is thinking about)*

social drinker (26)   *person who drinks alcohol only in partylike situations*

something is trying to get the better of us (17)   *an outside force is attempting to influence us* spare time (27)   *period of time during which one is free to do as he or she wishes*

sparked by curiosity (4)   *caused, begun with interest*

stream of consciousness (11)   *flow of thoughts in a person's mind, a chronological record of thought*

supermarket tabloids (8)   *sensationalistic newspapers*

to swallow (20)   *(here) to accept as truth*

to take something for granted (6)   *to assume that something is true without explanation or proof*

technical systems (6)   *practical applications of technology*

that's you to a tee (2)   *that describes you exactly*

to trace (something's) roots (10)   *to search back in history to understand (something)*

to try to sweep you up (8)   *to try to convince you, to win you over*

user-friendly (6)   *easily learned*

a venerable institution (22)   *a well-respected organization*

to vent rage (22)   *to express great anger*

to venture into (16)   *to begin or enter investigation*

violent crimes (7)   *misdeeds that hurt or threaten other people (such as murder, assault, mugging)*

watered-down (17)   *weak, less well defined*

way of life (4)   *lifestyle*

the wee hours of the morning (28)   *one or two o'clock in the morning, after midnight*

to wear more than one kind of hat (4)   *to work in more than one field, to play different roles*

a work (19)   *an example of an artist's or writer's production, a piece*

your heart is racing (24)   *the pulse of your heart is going faster—too fast*

QUIZ

1. Applied research is best described as research undertaken
   - (a) with human beings,
   - (b) with lower animals,
   - (c) to find solutions to specific problems,
   - (d) for its own sake.

2. If you knew someone who was having an adjustment problem, you would be best advised to refer that person to a(n) _____ psychologist.
   - (a) educational,
   - (b) developmental,
   - (c) personality,
   - (d) counseling.

3. If you were to read an article comparing the values of breast-feeding and bottle-feeding, it would probably report research that had been carried out by _____ psychologists.
   - (a) social,
   - (b) personality,
   - (c) developmental,
   - (d) school.

4. _____ psychologists are most directly concerned with the investigation of issues related to anxiety, aggression, and gender roles.
   - (a) Personality,
   - (b) Developmental,
   - (c) Organizational,
   - (d) School.

5. The first author of a book about psychology was
   - (a) Democritus,
   - (b) Darwin,
   - (c) Sophocles,
   - (d) Aristotle.

6. Which of the following schools of psychology originated in Germany?
   - (a) Functionalism,
   - (b) Structuralism,
   - (c) Behaviorism,
   - (d) Psychoanalysis.

7. _____ is a neoanalyst.
   - (a) Christine Ladd-Franklin,
   - (b) Erik Erikson,
   - (c) Democritus,
   - (d) Sigmund Freud.

8. Social-cognitive theorists differ from behaviorists in that social-cognitive theorists focus on the role of _____ in behavior.
   - (a) unconscious processes,
   - (b) cognition,
   - (c) reinforcement,
   - (d) learning.

9. Who introduced the method of paired associates?
   - (a) Margaret Floy Washburn,
   - (b) Elizabeth Loftus,
   - (c) Christine Ladd-Franklin,
   - (d) Mary Whiton Calkins.

10. Which of the following psychologists influenced a key Supreme Court decision on desegregation?
    (a) B. F. Skinner,
    (b) J. Henry Alston,
    (c) Jorge Sanchez,
    (d) Kenneth B. Clark.

11. Unobtrusively observing diners at a fast-food restaurant in order to determine how frequently they take bites is an example of the
    (a) experimental method,
    (b) case-study method,
    (c) survey method,
    (d) naturalistic-observation method.

12. If you were to run an experiment on the effects of temperature on aggressive behavior, aggressive behavior would be the
    (a) hypothesis,
    (b) dependent variable,
    (c) treatment,
    (d) correlation coefficient.

13. In the Lang experiment on alcohol and aggression, the condition that led to the most aggressive behavior was
    (a) drinking tonic water only,
    (b) drinking vodka and tonic water,
    (c) belief that one had drunk tonic water only,
    (d) belief that one had drunk vodka and tonic water.

14. A _____ sample is one in which every member of a population has an equal chance of being selected.
    (a) biased,
    (b) chance,
    (c) random,
    (d) stratified.

15. The development of psychodynamic theory relied largely on the
    (a) case-study method,
    (b) naturalistic-observation method,
    (c) survey method,
    (d) psychological testing method.

16. Psychologists generally agree that the best research method for determining cause and effect is the
    (a) naturalistic-observation method,
    (b) case-study method,
    (c) correlational method,
    (d) experimental method.

17. A _____ is defined as a specific statement about behavior or mental processes that is tested through research.
    (a) research question,
    (b) hypothesis,
    (c) theory,
    (d) scientific principle.

18. Psychologists have observed that more-aggressive children spend more time watching TV violence than less-aggressive children. What can we conclude from this observation?
    (a) TV violence causes aggression,
    (b) Aggressive behavior causes the watching of violent TV shows,
    (c) There is a correlation between aggression and watching TV violence,
    (d) None of the above conclusions is possible.

19. The concept behind _____ is that people who offer to participate in research studies differ systematically from people who do not.
    (a) the selection factor,
    (b) blinds and double blinds,
    (c) the use of placebos,
    (d) volunteer bias.

20. Which of the following is apparently an effect of providing informed consent in psychological research?
    (a) A sense of control,
    (b) Volunteer bias,
    (c) Selection factor,
    (d) Violation of ethical principles.

1. What is psychology?

_____
_____
_____
_____
_____

2. What are the goals of
   psychology?

_____
_____
_____
_____

3. Just what do psychologists
   do?

_____
_____
_____
_____

4. What is critical thinking?

_____
_____
_____
_____
_____

5. Who were some of the
   ancient contributors to
   psychology?

_____
_____
_____
_____

6. What is structuralism?

_____
_____
_____
_____

7. What is functionalism?

_____
_____
_____
_____

8. What is behaviorism?

_____
_____
_____
_____

9. What is Gestalt psychology?

_____
_____
_____
_____

10. What is psychoanalysis?

_____
_____
_____
_____

11. What is the biological
    perspective?

    _____
    _____
    _____
    _____
    _____

12. What is the cognitive
    perspective?

    _____
    _____
    _____
    _____
    _____

13. What is the humanistic-
    existential perspective?

    _____
    _____
    _____
    _____

14. What is the role of psycho-
    analysis today?

    _____
    _____
    _____
    _____
    _____

15. What are the learning
    perspectives?

    _____
    _____
    _____
    _____
    _____

16. What is the sociocultural
    perspective?

    _____
    _____
    _____
    _____
    _____

17. What contributions have
    women made to psychology?

    _____
    _____
    _____

18. What contributions to psy-
    chology have been made by
    people from various racial
    and ethnic groups?

    _____
    _____
    _____

19. What is the scientific
    method?

    _____
    _____
    _____
    _____

20. How do psychologists use
    samples to represent
    populations?

    _____
    _____
    _____
    _____

21. What methods of observa-
    tion are used by psycholo-
    gists?

    _____
    _____
    _____
    _____

22. What is the correlational method?

_____
_____
_____
_____
_____

23. What is the experimental method?

_____
_____
_____
_____

24. What are the ethical issues that concern psychological research and practice with humans?

_____
_____
_____
_____

25. What are the ethical issues that concern research with animals?

_____
_____
_____
_____
_____

ANSWERS TO SECTION REVIEWS

1. Behavior
2. Predict
3. Control
4. Theories
5. Predictions
6. Pure
7. Applied
8. Practice
9. Clinical
10. Psychotherapy
11. Counseling
12. Learning
13. Educational
14. Developmental
15. Nurture
16. Traits
17. Social
18. Physical
19. Experimental
20. Biological
21. Work
22. Organizational
23. Critical
24. Terms
25. Premises
26. Aristotle
27. Introspection
28. Wundt
29. Structuralism
30. Functionalism
31. Habit
32. Behaviorism
33. Observable
34. Reinforcement
35. Perception
36. Wholes
37. Purposeful
38. Mechanical
39. Psychoanalysis
40. Anxiety
41. Brain
42. Evolutionary
43. Fittest
44. Genes
45. Represent
46. Self-awareness
47. Choices
48. Neoanalysts (or ego analysts)
49. Unconscious
50. Behaviorists
51. Learning
52. Observational
53. Socioeconomic
54. Ethnic
55. Gender
56. Ladd-Franklin
57. Calkins
58. Harvard
59. Washburn
60. Alston
61. Clark
62. Williams
63. Stereotype
64. Sanchez
65. Women
66. Scientific
67. Research
68. Hypothesis
69. Theories
70. Represent
71. Generalize
72. Random
73. Stratified
74. Volunteer
75. Freud
76. Memory
77. Consistent
78. Experimentally
79. Records
80. Misrepresent
81. Socially
82. Attention
83. Naturalistic
84. Unobtrusive
85. Goodall
86. Correlated
87. Coefficient
88. -1.00
89. Positively
90. Negatively
91. Positive
92. Effect
93. Experiment
94. Treatment
95. Independent
96. Dependent
97. Dependent
98. Independent
99. Control
100. Experimental
101. Conditions
102. Treatments
103. Placebo
104. Expectations
105. Blind
106. Ethical
107. Informed
108. Confidential
109. Review
110. Ethics Review
111. Deceiving
112. Debriefed
113. Animals
114. Ethical
115. Harm

ANSWER KEY TO EXERCISE 1

1. M	6. B	11. G, I	16. E
2. C	7. H	12. Q	17. E
3. F	8. A, P	13. C	18. D
4. E	9. I, N	14. A	19. K
5. L	10. B	15. C	20. J

ANSWER KEY TO EXERCISE 2

1. F   This statement describes an experiment. The scientific method is a way of obtaining scientific evidence in which research questions or hypotheses are formulated and tested.

2. F   The statement defines a theory, not a hypothesis.

3. T

4. T   The operational definition of a variable is defined in terms of the methods used to create or measure that variable.

5. F   The most important factor about a sample is that it represent the targeted population.

6. F   The results of the study may be accurate enough for the sample in the study. The results may not be able to be generalized to a target population, however.

7. F   A random sample is defined as a sample that is drawn so that each member of a population has an equal chance of being selected to participate. Telephone numbers may be used in random sampling but are not essential to the definition of random sampling.

8. T   Sure they do. They may be more willing to help other people, more interested in research, or simply have more time. In the case of sex surveys, they may also be more willing to disclose intimate information. Factors such as these may introduce volunteer bias into the results of a study.

9. T   That is, people who are more intelligent also tend to obtain better grades in school. Such a correlation does not delve into matters of cause and effect, however.

10. F   We can assume that as one variable increases, the other is *likely* to decrease. Correlation does not demonstrate cause and effect, however.

11. T

12. T   Double-blind studies, which are the standard for demonstrating the effectiveness of new drugs, attempt to control for the expectations of both study participants and researchers.

13. T   Case studies usually address an individual or a small group, whereas surveys may address thousands of people. Ways of acquiring information may be similar, however, including interviews and questionnaires.

14. F   As pointed out in the chapter, such situations create ethical dilemmas, but many psychologists—and many states—require that a psychologist warn the threatened party of the danger.

ANSWER KEY TO QUIZ

1. C	6. B	11. D	16. D
2. D	7. B	12. B	17. B
3. C	8. B	13. D	18. C
4. A	9. D	14. C	19. D
5. D	10. D	15. A	20. A

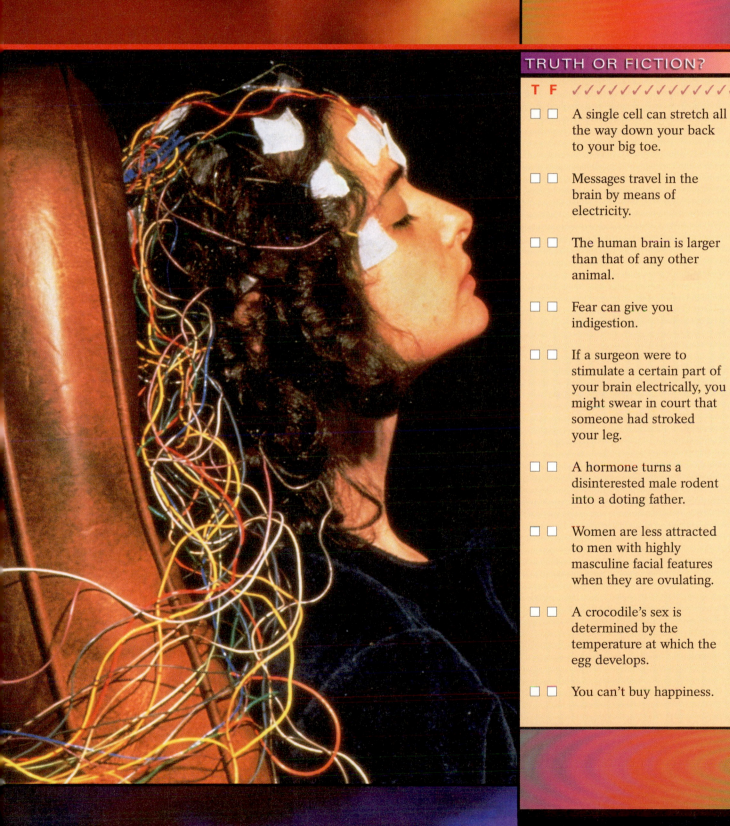

BIOLOGY AND BEHAVIOR

2

This chapter, "Biology and Behavior," covers the following:

He almost missed the boat. Literally. The British naturalist Charles Darwin volunteered to serve as the scientist for an expedition by the HMS *Beagle,* but the captain, Robert Fitz-Roy, objected to Darwin at first because of the shape of his nose. Fitz-Roy believed that you could judge a person's character by the outline of his facial features, and Darwin's nose didn't fit the . . . bill. But Fitz-Roy relented, and in the 1830s, Darwin undertook the historic voyage that led to the development of his theory of evolution.

In one of history's coincidences, Darwin was born on the same day as Abraham Lincoln (February 12, 1809). Darwin's father was a well-known physician and his mother was Susannah Wedgwood, of the chinaware family. His cousin was Sir Francis Galton, who made many innovations in psychological measurement. Darwin did so poorly in school that his father predicted that he would disgrace himself and the family. Nevertheless, Darwin went on to become a key figure in modern thought.

Darwin enjoyed collecting and classifying plants, minerals, and animals. He tried medical school, entered Cambridge University to become an Anglican priest, and eventually graduated with a degree in science. Independently wealthy, Darwin undertook the unpaid five-year position aboard the *Beagle.* The ship stopped at the Galápagos Islands, where Darwin noticed how species of lizards, tortoises, and plants differed somewhat on different islands. Although Darwin undertook his voyage as a believer in the *Book of Genesis* account of creation, his observations convinced him that the organisms he observed shared common ancestors but had *evolved* in different directions.

In midlife Darwin almost missed the boat again. When he returned from his voyage, he initially did not want his theory of evolution to be published until after his death. He feared it would be immensely unpopular because it contradicted religious views, and that it would bring scorn on his family. He shared his ideas with a few fellow scientists, but he published them more broadly 20 years later because he learned that other scientists, including Alfred Russel Wallace, were about to present similar ideas on evolution. Needless to say, Darwin's views became better known. (Have you ever heard of Wallace's theory of evolution?)

At the core of the theory of evolution is the concept of a *struggle for survival.* Since the beginning of time, the universe has been changing. For billions of years, microscopic particles have been forming immense gas clouds in space. Galaxies and solar systems have been condensing from the clouds, sparkling for some eons, and then winking out.

Change has brought life and death and countless challenges to survival. As described by evolutionary theory, some creatures have adapted successfully to these challenges and their numbers have increased. Others have not met the challenges and have fallen back into the distant mists of time. The species which prosper and those which fade away are thus determined by *natural selection.*

When humans first appeared on Earth, our survival required a different sort of struggle than it does today. We fought predators such as leopards. We foraged across parched lands for food. We might have warred with creatures very much like ourselves—creatures who have since become extinct. Because of the evolution of our intellect, not fangs or wings or claws, we prevailed. Our numbers have increased. We continue to transmit the traits that led to our selection down through the generations by means of genetic material whose chemical codes are only now being cracked.

Just what is handed down through the generations? The answer is biological, or physiological, structures and processes. Our biology serves as the material base for our behaviors, emotions, and cognitions (our thoughts, images, and plans). Biology gives rise to specific behavioral tendencies in some organisms, such as the chick's instinctive fear of the shadow of the hawk (Knight, 1994). But human behavior is flexible and affected by learning and choice as well as by heredity.

Biological psychologists work at the interface of psychology and biology. They study the ways in which our mental processes and behaviors are linked to biological structures and processes. In recent years, biological psychologists have been exploring these links in several areas:

1. *Neurons.* Neurons are the building blocks of the nervous system. There are billions of neurons in the body—perhaps as many as the stars in the Milky Way galaxy. Biological psychologists are showing how neurons communicate with one another and how millions, perhaps billions, of such communications make up our mental images and thoughts.

2. *The nervous system.* Neurons combine to form the structures of the nervous system. The nervous system has branches that are responsible for muscle movement, perception, automatic functions such as breathing and the secretion of hormones, and psychological events such as thoughts and feelings.

3. *The cerebral cortex.* The cerebral cortex is the large, wrinkled mass inside your head that you think of as your brain. Actually, it is only one part of the brain—the part that is the most characteristically human.

REFLECT

Do you imagine that people could ever become extinct? If so, how? Why did powerful animals like dinosaurs become extinct?

Psychology is the study of behavior and mental processes. Why, then, are psychologists interested in biological matters such as the nervous system, the endocrine system, and heredity?

4. *The endocrine system.* Through secretion of hormones, the endocrine system controls functions ranging from growth in children to production of milk in nursing women.

5. *Heredity.* Within every cell of your body there are about 140,000 genes. These chemical substances determine what type of creature you are, from the color of your hair to your body temperature to the fact that you have arms and legs rather than wings or fins.

SECTION I. NEURONS: INTO THE FABULOUS FOREST

Let us begin our journey in a fabulous forest of nerve cells, or **neurons.** Question: What are neurons? Neurons are cells that can be visualized as having branches, trunks, and roots—something like trees. As in other forests, many nerve cells lie alongside one another like a thicket of trees. Neurons can also lie end to end, however, with their "roots" intertwined with the "branches" of the neurons that lie below. Trees receive sunlight, water, and nutrients from the soil. Neurons receive "messages" from a number of sources such as light, other neurons, and pressure on the skin, and they can pass these messages along.

Neurons communicate by means of chemicals called **neurotransmitters.** They release neurotransmitters, which are taken up by other neurons, muscles, and glands. Neurotransmitters cause chemical changes in the receiving neuron so that the message can travel along its "trunk," be translated back into neurotransmitters in its "branches," and then travel through the small spaces between neurons to be received by the "roots" of yet other neurons. Each neuron transmits and coordinates messages in the form of neural impulses.

We are born with more than 100 billion neurons. Most of them are found in the brain. The nervous system also contains **glial cells.** Glial cells remove dead neurons and waste products from the nervous system, nourish and insulate neurons, and direct their growth (Zheng et al., 1996). But neurons occupy center stage in the nervous system. The messages transmitted by neurons somehow account for phenomena ranging from the perception of an itch from a mosquito bite to the coordination of a skier's vision and muscles to the composition of a concerto to the solution of an algebraic equation.

What does it mean to say that a cell "communicates" or "sends a message"? Is it the same thing as people communicating or sending messages to one another? Explain.

The Makeup of Neurons

Neurons vary according to their functions and their location. Some neurons in the brain are only a fraction of an inch in length, whereas others in the legs are several feet long. Every neuron is a single nerve cell with a cell body, dendrites, and an axon (see Figure 2.1). The cell body contains the core or *nucleus* of the cell. The nucleus uses oxygen and nutrients to generate the energy needed to carry out the work of the cell. Anywhere from a few to several hundred short fibers, or **dendrites,** extend like roots from the cell body to receive incoming messages from thousands of adjoining neurons. Each neuron has one **axon** that extends like a trunk from the cell body. Axons are very thin, but those that carry messages from the toes to the spinal cord extend for several feet.

NEURON A nerve cell.

NEUROTRANSMITTERS Chemical substances involved in the transmission of neural impulses from one neuron to another.

GLIAL CELLS Cells that nourish and insulate neurons, direct their growth, and remove waste products from the nervous system.

DENDRITES Rootlike structures, attached to the cell body of a neuron, that receive impulses from other neurons.

AXON A long, thin part of a neuron that transmits impulses to other neurons from branching structures called *terminals.*

✓ **Truth or Fiction Revisited**

It is true that a single cell can stretch all the way down your back to your big toe. These cells are neurons. How do you think it is possible that cells this long are "microscopic"?

FIGURE 2.1
THE ANATOMY OF A NEURON   "MESSAGES" ENTER NEURONS THROUGH DENDRITES, ARE TRANSMITTED ALONG THE TRUNKLIKE AXON, AND THEN ARE SENT FROM AXON TERMINALS TO MUSCLES, GLANDS, AND OTHER NEURONS. AXON TERMINALS CONTAIN SACS OF CHEMICALS CALLED *NEUROTRANSMITTERS.* NEUROTRANSMITTERS ARE RELEASED INTO THE SYNAPTIC CLEFT, WHERE MANY OF THEM ARE TAKEN UP BY RECEPTOR SITES ON THE DENDRITES OF RECEIVING NEURON. DOZENS OF NEURO-TRANSMITTERS HAVE BEEN IDENTIFIED.

Like tree trunks, axons can divide and extend in different directions. Axons end in small bulb-shaped structures, aptly named *terminals.* Neurons carry messages in one direction only: from the dendrites or cell body through the axon to the axon terminals. The messages are then transmitted from the terminals to the dendrites or cell bodies of other neurons.

As a child matures, the axons of neurons become longer and the dendrites and terminals proliferate, creating vast interconnected networks for the transmission of complex messages. The number of glial cells also increases as the nervous system develops, contributing to its dense appearance.

MYELIN A fatty substance that encases and insulates axons, facilitating transmission of neural impulses.

MYELIN The axons of many neurons are wrapped tightly with white, fatty **myelin** that makes them look like strings of sausages under the microscope (bratwurst, actually). The fat insulates the axon from electrically charged atoms, or ions, found in the fluids that surround the nervous system. The myelin sheath minimizes leakage of the electrical current being carried along the axon, thereby allowing messages to be conducted more efficiently.

Myelination is part of the maturation process that leads to a child's ability to crawl and walk during the first year. Infants are not physiologically "ready" to engage in visual-motor coordination and other activities until the coating process reaches certain levels. In people with the disease multiple sclerosis, myelin is replaced with a hard fibrous tissue that throws

REFLECT

Why do authors describe unfamiliar things, like neurons, in familiar terms? Why would an author compare a neuron to a tree, or a myelin sheath with bratwurst (hold the mustard)?

off the timing of nerve impulses and disrupts muscular control. Affliction of the neurons that control breathing can result in suffocation.

AFFERENT AND EFFERENT NEURONS If someone steps on your toes, the sensation is registered by receptors or sensory neurons near the surface of your skin. Then it is transmitted to the spinal cord and brain through **afferent neurons,** which are perhaps 2 to 3 feet long. In the brain, subsequent messages might be buffeted by associative neurons that are only a few thousandths of an inch long. You experience pain through this process and perhaps entertain some rather nasty thoughts about the perpetrator, who is now apologizing and begging for understanding. Long before you arrive at any logical conclusions, however, motor neurons (**efferent neurons**) send messages to your foot so that you withdraw it and begin an impressive hopping routine. Other efferent neurons stimulate glands so that your heart is beating more rapidly, you are sweating, and the hair on the back of your arms has become erect! Being a good sport, you say, "Oh, it's nothing." But considering all the neurons involved, it really is something, isn't it?

In case you think that afferent and efferent neurons will be hard to distinguish because they sound pretty much the SAME to you, remember that they *are* the "SAME." That is, *S*ensory = *A*fferent, and *M*otor = *E*fferent. But don't tell your professor I let you in on this secret.

The Neural Impulse: Let Us "Sing the Body Electric"[1]

In the 18th century, the Italian physiologist Luigi Galvani (1737–1798) conducted a shocking experiment in a rainstorm. While his neighbors had the sense to remain indoors, Galvani and his wife were out on the porch connecting lightning rods to the heads of dissected frogs whose legs were connected by wires to a well of water. When lightning blazed above, the frogs' muscles contracted. This is not a recommended way to prepare frogs' legs. Galvani was demonstrating that the messages (**neural impulses**) that travel along neurons are electrochemical in nature.

Question: What are neural impulses? Neural impulses are messages that travel within neurons at somewhere between 2 (in nonmyelinated neurons) and 225 miles an hour (in myelinated neurons). This speed is not impressive when compared with that of an electric current in a toaster oven or a lamp, which can travel at the speed of light—over 186,000 miles per second. Distances in the body are short, however, and a message will travel from a toe to the brain in perhaps 1/50th of a second.

AN ELECTROCHEMICAL PROCESS The process by which neural impulses travel is electrochemical. Chemical changes take place within neurons that cause an electrical charge to be transmitted along their lengths. Neurons and body fluids contain ions—positively or negatively charged atoms. In a resting state—that is, when a neuron is not being stimulated by its neighbors—negatively charged chloride ($Cl-$) ions are plentiful within the neuron, giving it an overall negative charge in relation to the outside. The difference in electrical charge **polarizes** the neuron with a negative **resting potential** of about –70 millivolts in relation to the body fluid outside the cell membrane.

AFFERENT NEURONS Neurons that transmit messages from sensory receptors to the spinal cord and brain. Also called *sensory neurons.*

EFFERENT NEURONS Neurons that transmit messages from the brain or spinal cord to muscles and glands. Also called *motor neurons.*

NEURAL IMPULSE The electrochemical discharge of a nerve cell, or neuron.

POLARIZE To ready a neuron for firing by creating an internal negative charge in relation to the body fluid outside the cell membrane.

RESTING POTENTIAL The electrical potential across the neural membrane when it is not responding to other neurons.

---

[1] From a poem by Walt Whitman.

When an area on the surface of the resting neuron is adequately stimulated by other neurons, the cell membrane in the area changes its permeability to allow positively charged sodium ions to enter. Thus the area of entry becomes positively charged, or **depolarized,** with respect to the outside (Figure 2.2). The permeability of the cell membrane then changes again, allowing no more sodium ions to enter.

The inside of the cell at the disturbed area has an **action potential** of 110 millivolts. This action potential, added to the −70 millivolts that characterize the resting potential, brings the membrane voltage to a positive charge of about +40 millivolts. This inner change causes the next section of the cell to become permeable to sodium ions. At the same time, other positively charged (potassium) ions are being pumped out of the area of the cell that was previously affected, which returns the area to its resting potential. In this way, the neural impulse is transmitted continuously along an axon. Because the impulse is created anew as it progresses, its strength does not change.

✓ Truth or Fiction Revisited

It is true that messages travel in the brain by means of electricity. However, this is not the whole story. Messages also travel from neurons to other neurons, muscles, or glands via chemical messengers termed *neurotransmitters.*

FIRING The conduction of the neural impulse along the length of a neuron is what is meant by "firing." When a rifle fires, it sends a bullet speeding through its barrel and discharges it at more than 1,000 feet per second. Question: What happens when a neuron fires? Neurons also fire, but instead of a barrel, a neuron has an axon. Instead of discharging a bullet, it releases neurotransmitters.

Some neurons fire in less than 1/1,000 of a second. In firing, neurons attempt to transmit messages to other neurons, muscles, or glands. However, other neurons will not fire unless the incoming messages combine to reach an adequate *threshold*. A weak message may cause a temporary shift in electrical charge at some point along a neuron's cell membrane, but this charge will dissipate if the neuron is not stimulated to its threshold.

DEPOLARIZE To reduce the resting potential of a cell membrane from about −70 millivolts toward zero.

ACTION POTENTIAL The electrical impulse that provides the basis for the conduction of a neural impulse along an axon of a neuron.

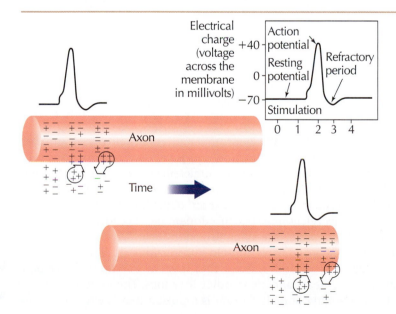

FIGURE 2.2

THE NEURAL IMPULSE

WHEN A SECTION OF A NEURON IS STIMULATED BY OTHER NEURONS, THE CELL MEMBRANE BECOMES PERMEABLE TO SODIUM IONS SO THAT AN ACTION POTENTIAL OF ABOUT 40 MILLIVOLTS IS INDUCED. THIS ACTION POTENTIAL IS TRANSMITTED ALONG THE AXON. THE NEURON FIRES ACCORDING TO THE ALL-OR-NONE PRINCIPLE.

A neuron may transmit several hundred messages in a second. Yet, in accordance with the **all-or-none principle,** each time a neuron fires, it transmits an impulse of the same strength. Neurons fire more frequently when they have been stimulated by larger numbers of other neurons. Stronger stimuli cause more frequent firing.

For a few thousandths of a second after firing, a neuron is insensitive to messages from other neurons and will not fire. It is said to be in a **refractory period.** This period is a time of recovery during which sodium is prevented from passing through the neuronal membrane. When we realize that such periods of recovery might take place hundreds of times per second, it seems a rapid recovery and a short rest indeed.

The Synapse: On Being Well-Connected

A neuron relays its message to another neuron across a junction called a **synapse.** Question: What is a synapse? A synapse consists of a "branch," or an axon terminal from the transmitting neuron; a dendrite ("root"), or the body of a receiving neuron; and a fluid-filled gap between the two that is called the *synaptic cleft* (see Figure 2.1). Although the neural impulse is electrical, it does not jump across the synaptic cleft like a spark. Instead, when a nerve impulse reaches a synapse, axon terminals release chemicals into the synaptic cleft like myriad ships being cast into the sea.

Neurotransmitters: The Chemical Keys to Communication

Sacs called synaptic vesicles in the axon terminals contain neurotransmitters. When a neural impulse reaches the axon terminal, the vesicles release varying amounts of neurotransmitters—the chemical keys to communication—into the synaptic cleft. From there, they influence the receiving neuron. Questions: Which neurotransmitters are of interest to psychologists? What do they do?

Dozens of neurotransmitters have been identified. Each has its own chemical structure, and each can fit into a specifically tailored harbor, or **receptor site,** on the receiving cell. The analogy of a key fitting into a lock is often used to describe this process. Once released, not all molecules of a neurotransmitter find their way into receptor sites of other neurons. "Loose" neurotransmitters are usually either broken down or reabsorbed by the axon terminal (a process called *reuptake*).

Some neurotransmitters act to *excite* other neurons—that is, to cause other neurons to fire. Other neurotransmitters act to *inhibit* receiving neurons. That is, they prevent them from firing. The sum of the stimulation—excitatory and inhibitory—determines whether a neuron will fire and, if so, which neurotransmitters will be released.

SOME KEY CHEMICAL KEYS Neurotransmitters are involved in physical processes such as muscle contraction and psychological processes such as thoughts and emotions. Excesses or deficiencies of neurotransmitters have been linked to psychological disorders such as depression and schizophrenia. Let us consider the effects of some neurotransmitters of interest to psychologists: acetylcholine (ACh), dopamine, noradrenaline, serotonin, and endorphins, which are summarized in Table 2.1.

Acetylcholine (ACh) controls muscle contractions. It is excitatory at synapses between nerves and muscles that involve voluntary movement but inhibitory at the heart and some other locations. The effects of curare highlight the functioning of ACh. Curare is a poison that is extracted from

ALL-OR-NONE PRINCIPLE The fact that a neuron fires an impulse of the same strength whenever its action potential is triggered.

REFRACTORY PERIOD A phase following firing during which a neuron is less sensitive to messages from other neurons and will not fire.

SYNAPSE A junction between the axon terminals of one neuron and the dendrites or cell body of another neuron.

RECEPTOR SITE A location on a dendrite of a receiving neuron tailored to receive a neurotransmitter.

ACETYLCHOLINE A neurotransmitter that controls muscle contractions. Abbreviated *ACh.*

TABLE 2.1	SOME KEY NEUROTRANSMITTERS AND THEIR FUNCTIONS	
NEUROTRANSMITTER	**FUNCTIONS**	**ABOUT . . .**
Acetylcholine (ACh)	Causes muscle contractions and is involved in formation of memories	Found at synapses between motor neurons and muscles. Deficiencies are linked with paralysis and Alzheimer's disease.
Dopamine	Is involved in muscle contraction, learning and memory, and emotional response	Tremors of Parkinson's disease are linked with low levels of dopamine. People with schizophrenia may *overutilize* dopamine.
Noradrenaline	Accelerates the heart rate, affects eating, and is linked with activity levels, learning, and remembering	Imbalances are linked with mood disorders such as depression and bipolar disorder.
Serotonin	Is involved in behavior patterns and psychological problems, including obesity, depression, insomnia, alcoholism, and aggression	Drugs that block the reuptake of serotonin are helpful in the treatment of depression.
Endorphins	Inhibit pain by locking pain-causing chemicals out of their receptor sites	Endorphins may be connected with some people's indifference to pain, the pain-killing effects of acupuncture, and the "runner's high" experienced by many long-distance runners.

plants by South American Indians and used in hunting. If an arrow tipped with curare pierces the skin and the poison enters the body, it prevents ACh from lodging within receptor sites in neurons. Because ACh helps muscles move, curare causes paralysis. The victim is prevented from contracting the muscles used in breathing and therefore dies from suffocation. Botulism, a disease that stems from food poisoning, prevents the release of ACh and has the same effect as curare.

ACh is also normally prevalent in a part of the brain called the **hippocampus,** a structure involved in the formation of memories. When the amount of ACh available to the brain decreases, memory formation is impaired, as in Alzheimer's disease.

Dopamine is primarily an inhibitory neurotransmitter. It is involved in voluntary movements, learning and memory, and emotional arousal. Deficiencies of dopamine are linked to Parkinson's disease, in which people progressively lose control over their muscles. They develop muscle tremors and jerky, uncoordinated movements. The drug L-dopa, a substance that stimulates the brain to produce dopamine, helps slow the progress of Parkinson's disease.

The psychological disorder *schizophrenia* is characterized by confusion and false perceptions, and it has been linked to dopamine. People with schizophrenia may have more receptor sites for dopamine in an area of the brain that is involved in emotional responding. For this reason, they may *overutilize* the dopamine available in the brain. This leads to hallucinations and disturbances of thought and emotion. The phenothiazines, a group of drugs used in the treatment of schizophrenia, block the action of dopamine by locking some dopamine out of these receptor sites (Carpenter & Buchanan, 1994). Because of their action, phenothiazines may have Parkinson-like side effects, which are usually treated by lowering the dose, prescribing additional drugs, or switching to another drug.

Noradrenaline is produced largely by neurons in the brain stem. It acts both as a neurotransmitter and as a hormone. It is an excitatory neurotransmitter that speeds up the heartbeat and other body processes and is

HIPPOCAMPUS A part of the limbic system of the brain that is involved in memory formation.

DOPAMINE A neurotransmitter that is involved in Parkinson's disease and that appears to play a role in schizophrenia.

NORADRENALINE A neurotransmitter whose action is similar to that of the hormone adrenaline and that may play a role in depression.

Runner's High? Why have thousands of people taken up long-distance running? Running promotes cardiovascular conditioning, muscle strength, and weight control. But many long-distance runners also experience a "runner's high" that appears to be connected with the release of endorphins. Endorphins are naturally occurring substances that are similar in function to the narcotic morphine.

SEROTONIN A neurotransmitter, deficiencies of which have been linked to affective disorders, anxiety, and insomnia.

ENDORPHINS Neurotransmitters that are composed of amino acids and that are functionally similar to morphine.

involved in general arousal, learning and memory, and eating. Excesses and deficiencies of noradrenaline have been linked to mood disorders.

The stimulants cocaine and amphetamines ("speed") facilitate the release of noradrenaline and also prevent its reabsorption by the releasing synaptic vesicles—that is, reuptake. As a result, there are excesses of noradrenaline in the nervous system, increasing the firing of neurons and leading to persistent arousal.

Also primarily an inhibitory transmitter, **serotonin** is involved in emotional arousal and sleep. Deficiencies of serotonin have been linked to overeating, alcoholism, depression, aggression, and insomnia (Azar, 1997). The drug LSD decreases the action of serotonin and may also influence the utilization of dopamine. With LSD, "two no's make a yes." By inhibiting an inhibitor, it increases brain activity, in this case frequently producing hallucinations.

Endorphins are inhibitory neurotransmitters. The word *endorphin* is the contraction of *endogenous morphine. Endogenous* means "developing from within." Endorphins occur naturally in the brain and in the bloodstream and are similar to the narcotic morphine in their functions and effects. They lock into receptor sites for chemicals that transmit pain messages to the brain. Once the endorphin "key" is in the "lock," the pain-causing chemicals are locked out. Endorphins may also increase our sense of competence and be connected with the pleasurable "runner's high" reported by many long-distance runners (Grady, 1997).

There you have it—a fabulous forest of neurons in which billions upon billions of vesicles are pouring neurotransmitters into synaptic clefts at any given time: when you are involved in strenuous activity, now as you are reading this page, even as you are passively watching television. This microscopic picture is repeated several hundred times every second. The combined activity of all these neurotransmitters determines which messages will be transmitted and which ones will not. You experience your sensations, your thoughts, and your control over your body as psychological events, but the psychological events somehow result from many billions of electrochemical events (Greenfield, 1995).

Review

SECTION I

The nervous system contains billions of cells called (1) _____ons. Neurons transmit messages to other neurons by means of chemical substances called (2) _____mitters. Neurons have a cell body, or (3) s_____; (4) d_____, which receive "messages"; and (5) a_____ which extend trunklike from the cell body.

The axons of many neurons have a fatty sheath made of a fatty substance called (6) m_____. Myelin (7) _____lates the axon from chemically charged atoms called (8) _____ns found in the fluids that surround the nervous system, thereby allowing messages to be conducted more efficiently.

Sensory or (9) _____ent neurons transmit sensory messages to the central nervous system. Motor or (10) _____ent neurons conduct messages from the central nervous system that stimulate glands or cause muscles to contract.

Neural transmission is an (11) _____ical process. An electrical charge is conducted along an axon through a process that allows (12) _____ium ions into the cell and then pumps them out. The neuron has a (13) _____ing potential of −70 millivolts in relation to the body fluid outside the cell membrane and an (14) _____tion potential of +110 millivolts. The conduction of the neural impulse along the length of the neuron is what is meant by (15) _____ing.

Neurons (16) f_____ according to an all-or-none principle. Neurons may fire (17:

Dozens or Hundreds?) of times per second. Firing is first followed by a (18) _____tory period, during which neurons are less sensitive to further stimulation.

A synapse consists of an axon (19) _____al from the transmitting neuron, a (20) _____ite of a receiving neuron, and a small fluid-filled gap between them that is called the synaptic (21) c_____. (22) _____tory synapses stimulate neurons to fire. (23) _____tory synapses influence neurons in the direction of not firing.

Neurotransmitters are contained within synaptic (24) _____cles. These vesicles are found in axon (25) _____als. Each neurotransmitter can fit into a specific (26) _____tor site on the receiving neuron.

(27) Ace_____ (abbreviated ACh) is the neurotransmitter that controls muscle contractions. ACh is normally prevalent in a brain structure essential to the formation of memories: the (28) _____pus. The neurotransmitter (29) _____ine is involved in learning and memory and in emotional arousal. Deficiencies of dopamine are linked to (30) _____son's disease. It is also theorized that schizophrenic individuals (31) over_____ dopamine because of a greater-than-normal number of receptor (32) _____s. Imbalances in noradrenaline have been linked to (33) _____ disorders. Deficiencies of (34) _____nin are linked to anxiety, depression, and insomnia. "Runner's high" may be caused by the release of chains of amino acids called (35) _____ns.

SECTION II. THE NERVOUS SYSTEM

As a child, I did not think it was a good thing to have a "nervous" system. After all, if your system were not so nervous, you might be less likely to jump at strange noises.

Question: Just what is the nervous system? Later I learned that a nervous system is not a system that is nervous. It is a system of nerves involved in thought processes, heartbeat, visual–motor coordination, and so on. (A **nerve** is a bundle of axons and dendrites.) I also learned that the human nervous system is more complex than that of any other animal and that our brains are larger than those of any other animal. Now, this last piece of business is not quite true. A human brain weighs about 3 pounds, but the brains of elephants and whales may be four times as heavy. Still, our brains account for a greater part of our body weight than do those of elephants or whales. Our brains weigh about 1/60 of our body weight. Elephant brains weigh about 1/1,000 of their total weight, and whale brains are a paltry 1/10,000 of their weight. So, humans win the brain-as-a-percentage-of-body-weight contest.

✓ Truth or Fiction Revisited

It is not true that the human brain is larger than that of any other animal. Elephants and whales have larger brains.

The brain is only one part of the nervous system. The nervous system consists of the brain, the spinal cord, and the nerves linking them to the sensory organs, muscles, and glands. As shown in Figure 2.3, the brain and spinal cord make up the **central nervous system.** If you compared your nervous system with a computer, your central nervous system would be your central processing unit (CPU).

The sensory (afferent) neurons, which receive and transmit messages to the brain and spinal cord, and the motor (efferent) neurons, which transmit messages from the brain or spinal cord to the muscles and glands, make up the **peripheral nervous system.** In the comparison of the nervous

REFLECT

Before taking this course, had you heard of "nerves?" How do the definitions of *neurons* and *nerves* agree with your earlier ideas?

NERVE A bundle of axons and dendrites from many neurons.

CENTRAL NERVOUS SYSTEM The brain and spinal cord.

PERIPHERAL NERVOUS SYSTEM The part of the nervous system consisting of the somatic nervous system and the autonomic nervous system.

REFLECT

Before taking this course, did you have any ideas about what makes the human brain special? What were they?

FIGURE 2.3

THE DIVISIONS OF THE NERVOUS SYSTEM

THE NERVOUS SYSTEM CONTAINS TWO MAIN DIVISIONS: THE CENTRAL NERVOUS SYSTEM AND THE PERIPHERAL NERVOUS SYSTEM. THE CENTRAL NERVOUS SYSTEM CONSISTS OF THE BRAIN AND SPINAL CORD. THE PERIPHERAL NERVOUS SYSTEM CONTAINS THE SOMATIC AND AUTONOMIC SYSTEMS. IN TURN, THE AUTONOMIC NERVOUS SYSTEM HAS SYMPATHETIC AND PARASYMPATHETIC DIVISIONS.

system with a computer, the peripheral nervous system makes up the nervous system's peripheral devices—keyboard, mouse, diskettes, and so on. You would not be able to feed information to your computer's central processing unit without these *peripheral* devices. Other peripheral devices, such as your monitor and printer, allow you to follow what is happening inside your CPU and to see what it has accomplished.

The Peripheral Nervous System: The Body's Peripheral Devices

Question: What are the divisions and functions of the peripheral nervous system? The peripheral nervous system consists of sensory and motor neurons that transmit messages to and from the central nervous system. Without the peripheral nervous system, our brains would be like isolated CPUs. There would be no keyboards, mouses, diskettes, or other ways of inputting information. There would be no monitors, printers, modems, or other ways of displaying or transmitting information. We would be detached from the world: We would not be able to perceive it; we would not be able to act on it. The two main divisions of the peripheral nervous system are the *somatic nervous system* and the *autonomic nervous system.*

The **somatic nervous system** contains sensory (afferent) and motor (efferent) neurons. It transmits messages about sights, sounds, smells, temperature, body positions, and so on, to the central nervous system. As a result, we can experience the beauties and the horrors of the world, its physical ecstasies and agonies. Messages transmitted from the brain and spinal cord to the somatic nervous system control purposeful body movements such as raising a hand, winking, or running, as well as the tiny, almost imperceptible movements that maintain our balance and posture.

Autonomic means "automatic." The **autonomic nervous system** (ANS) regulates the glands and the muscles of internal organs. Thus, the ANS controls activities such as heartbeat, respiration, digestion, and dilation of the pupils of the eyes. These activities can occur automatically, while we

SOMATIC NERVOUS SYSTEM The division of the peripheral nervous system that connects the central nervous system with sensory receptors, skeletal muscles, and the surface of the body.

AUTONOMIC NERVOUS SYSTEM (ANS) The division of the peripheral nervous system that regulates glands and activities such as heartbeat, respiration, digestion, and dilation of the pupils.

REFLECT

Is breathing voluntary or involuntary (autonomic, automatic)? Could it be both? Explain.

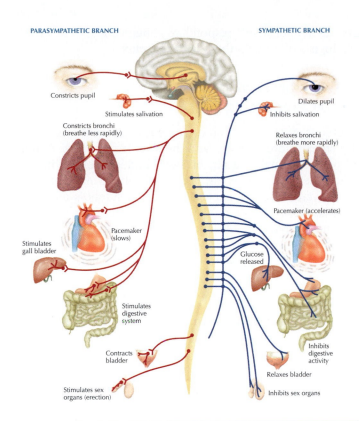

PARASYMPATHETIC BRANCH   SYMPATHETIC BRANCH

Constricts pupil   Dilates pupil

Stimulates salivation   Inhibits salivation

Constricts bronchi   Relaxes bronchi
(breathe less rapidly)   (breathe more rapidly)

Pacemaker (accelerates)

Stimulates   Pacemaker
gall bladder   (slows)

                    Glucose   Glucose
                    released   released

Stimulates
digestive
system   Inhibits
                                          digestive
                                          activity
Contracts
bladder   Relaxes bladder

Stimulates sex   Inhibits sex organs
organs (erection)

FIGURE 2.4

THE BRANCHES OF THE AUTONOMIC NERVOUS SYSTEM (ANS)   THE PARASYMPATHETIC BRANCH OF THE ANS GENERALLY ACTS TO REPLENISH STORES OF ENERGY IN THE BODY. THE SYMPATHETIC BRANCH IS MOST ACTIVE DURING ACTIVITIES THAT EXPEND ENERGY. THE TWO BRANCHES OF THE ANS FREQUENTLY HAVE ANTAGONISTIC EFFECTS ON THE ORGANS THEY SERVICE.

are asleep. But some of them can be overridden by conscious control. You can breathe at a purposeful pace, for example. Methods like biofeedback and yoga also help people gain voluntary control of functions such as heart rate and blood pressure.

The ANS also has two branches, or divisions: **sympathetic** and **parasympathetic.** These branches have largely opposing effects. Many organs and glands are stimulated by both branches of the ANS (Figure 2.4). When organs and glands are simultaneously stimulated by both divisions, their effects can average out to some degree. In general, the sympathetic division is most active during processes that involve spending body energy from stored reserves, such as a fight-or-flight response to a predator or when you find out that your rent is going to be raised. The parasympathetic division is most active during processes that replenish reserves of energy, such as eating. When we are afraid, the sympathetic division of the ANS accelerates the heart rate. When we relax, the parasympathetic division decelerates the heart rate. The parasympathetic division stimulates digestive processes, but the sympathetic branch inhibits digestion. Because the sympathetic division predominates when we feel fear or anxiety, these feelings can cause indigestion.

✓ Truth or Fiction Revisited

It is true that fear can give you indigestion. Fear predominantly involves sympathetic ANS activity, whereas digestive processes involve parasympathetic activity. Because sympathetic activity can inhibit parasympathetic activity, fear can prevent digestion.

The ANS is of particular interest to psychologists because its activities are linked to various emotions such as anxiety and love. Some people seem to have overly reactive sympathetic nervous systems. In the absence

REFLECT

Have you ever lost your appetite or thrown up because of anxiety or fear? What biological processes caused fear to produce indigestion?

SYMPATHETIC The branch of the ANS that is most active during emotional responses such as fear and anxiety that spend the body's reserves of energy.

PARASYMPATHETIC The branch of the ANS that is most active during processes such as digestion that restore the body's reserves of energy.

of external threats, their bodies still respond as though they were faced with danger. Psychologists often help them learn to relax.

The Central Nervous System: The Body's Central Processing Unit

It is your central nervous system that makes you so special. Other species see more sharply, smell more keenly, and hear more acutely. Other species run faster, or fly through the air, or swim underwater—without the benefit of artificial devices such as airplanes and submarines. But it is your central nervous system which enables you to use symbols and language, the abilities that allow people not only to adapt to their environment but to create new environments and give them names (Deacon, 1997). Question: What are the divisions and functions of the central nervous system? The central nervous system consists of the spinal cord and the brain.

THE SPINAL CORD The **spinal cord** is a true "information highway"—a column of nerves about as thick as a thumb. It transmits messages from sensory receptors to the brain, and from the brain to muscles and glands throughout the body. The spinal cord is also capable of some "local government." That is, it controls some responses to external stimulation through **spinal reflexes.** A spinal reflex is an unlearned response to a stimulus that may involve only two neurons—a sensory (afferent) neuron and a motor (efferent) neuron (Figure 2.5). In some reflexes, a third neuron, called an **interneuron,** transmits the neural impulse from the sensory neuron through the spinal cord to the motor neuron.

We have many reflexes. We blink in response to a puff of air in our faces. We swallow when food accumulates in the mouth. A physician may tap the leg below the knee to elicit the knee-jerk reflex, a sign that the nervous system is operating adequately. Urinating and defecating are reflexes that occur in response to pressure in the bladder and the rectum. Parents typically spend weeks or months toilet-training infants—in other

SPINAL CORD A column of nerves within the spine that transmits messages from sensory receptors to the brain and from the brain to muscles and glands throughout the body.

SPINAL REFLEX A simple, unlearned response to a stimulus that may involve only two neurons.

INTERNEURON A neuron that transmits a neural impulse from a sensory neuron to a motor neuron.

FIGURE 2.5

THE REFLEX ARC A CROSS-SECTION OF THE SPINAL CORD, SHOWING A SENSORY NEURON AND A MOTOR NEURON, WHICH ARE INVOLVED IN THE KNEE-JERK REFLEX. IN SOME REFLEXES, INTERNEURONS LINK SENSORY AND MOTOR NEURONS.

words, teaching them to involve their brains in the process of elimination. Learning to inhibit these reflexes makes civilization possible.

Sexual response also involves many reflexes. Stimulation of the genital organs leads to erection in the male, vaginal lubrication in the female (both are reflexes that make sexual intercourse possible), and the involuntary muscle contractions of orgasm. As reflexes, these processes need not involve the brain, but most often they do. Feelings of passion, memories of an enjoyable sexual encounter, and sexual fantasies usually contribute to sexual response by transmitting messages from the brain to the genitals through the spinal cord (Rathus et al., 2000).

The spinal cord (and the brain) consists of gray matter and white matter. The **gray matter** is composed of nonmyelinated neurons. Some of these are involved in spinal reflexes. Others send their axons to the brain. The **white matter** is composed of bundles of longer, myelinated (and thus whitish) axons that carry messages to and from the brain. As you can see in Figure 2.5, a cross-section of the spinal cord shows that the gray matter, which includes cell bodies, is distributed in a butterfly pattern.

> **REFLECT**
>
> Does it seem possible that sexual responses like erection and orgasm are reflexive? Why or why not?

GRAY MATTER In the spinal cord, the grayish neurons and neural segments that are involved in spinal reflexes.

WHITE MATTER In the spinal cord, axon bundles that carry messages from and to the brain.

Review

SECTION II

A nerve is composed of a bundle of (36) _____ns of neurons. The first major division of the nervous system is into the (37) _____al and central nervous systems. The peripheral nervous system is further divided into the (38) _____ic and autonomic nervous systems. The somatic nervous system transmits sensory information about muscles, skin, and joints to the (39) c_____ nervous system. Messages transmitted from the central nervous system to the somatic nervous system control voluntary movements such as raising a hand or running.

The autonomic nervous system (ANS) is subdivided into sympathetic and (40) _____tic branches. The ANS regulates the glands and (41) in_____ activities such as heartbeat, digestion, and dilation of the pupils. The (42) _____tic division of the ANS dominates in responses that spend bodily resources, such as feeling anxious or

fleeing a predator. The (43) _____tic division dominates during restorative processes such as eating.

The (44) _____al cord and brain compose the central nervous system. A spinal (45) re_____ is an unlearned response to a stimulus that does not involve the brain. A spinal reflex may involve as few as two neurons: a sensory or (46) _____ent neuron, and a motor or (47) _____ent neuron. A third kind of neuron, an (48) _____ron, may transmit the neural impulse from the sensory neuron through the spinal cord to the motor neuron.

In the spinal cord, (49: Gray or White?) matter consists of small, nonmyelinated neurons that are involved in reflexes. (50: Gray or White?) matter is composed of bundles of longer, myelinated axons that carry messages back and forth to and from the brain.

SECTION III. THE BRAIN

Every show has a star, and the brain is the undisputed star of the human nervous system. The size and shape of your brain are responsible for your large, delightfully rounded head. In all the animal kingdom, you (and about 6 billion other people) are unique because of the capacities for learning and thinking residing in the human brain.

The brains of men are about 15% larger than those of women on average (Blum, 1997), which, feminists might argue, shows that bigger is not necessarily better. In the human brain it may be that how well-connected one is (in terms of synapses) is more important than size. (After all, Albert Einstein's brain was only average in size [Witelson et al., 1999].)

> **REFLECT**
>
> Does it matter that men's brains, on average, are larger than women's? Why or why not?

Moreover, women's brains "run hotter" than men's. Women metabolize more glucose and appear to use more of their brains on a given task (Blum, 1997). In fact, columnist Maureen Dowd (1997) suggests, tongue in cheek, that men squander many of their neurons in preoccupation with things like seduction techniques, sexual fantasies, thinning hair, stock tips, Web sites, and better gear (like cross-training socks).

The French Surgeon Paul Broca (1824–1880) was one of those who believed that the size of the brain was connected with intelligence. Yet upon Broca's death, his own brain was found to be only slightly above average in size. Nevertheless, Broca made a major contribution to neuroscience. It happened in 1861, when a 51-year-old patient at the Paris asylum known as La Bicêtre was admitted to Broca's surgical ward because of gangrene in the leg. The patient, Leborgne, could understand what he heard, but he himself could apparently only enunciate a meaningless sound ("tan"), although, when he was particularly frustrated, he would sometimes shout, "Sacred name of God!" in French.

Leborgne died a few days after he was admitted to the surgical ward, and Broca conducted an autopsy. He found that an egg-shaped part of the left side of Leborgne's brain had degenerated. Broca concluded that this area of the brain, which is now known as *Broca's area* (see Figure 2.14) was essential to speech. Broca was the first scientist to connect a specific part of the brain with a particular behavior problem—in this case, loss of speech. Question: How do researchers learn about the functions of the brain?

Methods of Probing the Brain

People have noted the effects of various kinds of damage to the brain throughout history, although not with the precision of Broca. Broca's discovery was the result of careful clinical observation of a natural occurrence. Leborgne's brain had deteriorated, resulting in loss of speech, and an autopsy revealed the part of the brain that was apparently connected with the loss of function.

It has been known for about two centuries that damage to the left side of the brain is connected with loss of sensation or movement on the right side of the body, and vice versa. Thus it has been assumed that the brain's control mechanisms must cross over from right to left, and vice versa, as they descend into the body.

FIGURE 2.6
PHINEAS GAGE'S SKULL
THE TRAJECTORY OF THE TAMPING ROD THAT INJURED GAGE APPEARS TO HAVE BYPASSED AREAS OF THE FRONTAL LOBES THAT ARE CONNECTED WITH LANGUAGE AND MOVEMENT, BUT TO HAVE AFFECTED HIS PERSONALITY.

THE CASE OF PHINEAS GAGE "Gage is no longer Gage," said those who had known him before the accident. Phineas Gage was a promising young railroad worker, admired by his friends and coworkers. All that changed one day in 1848. While he was tamping down the blasting powder for a dynamite charge, Gage accidentally set the powder off. The inch-thick metal tamping rod shot upward through his cheek and brain and out the top of his head.

Gage fell back in a heap, but he was miraculously alive. His coworkers watched in shock as he stood up a few moments later and spoke. As the local doctor marveled at the hole through Gage's head, Gage asked when he'd be able to return to work. Two months later, Gage's external wounds had healed, but the psychological aspects of the wound were now obvious. Gage had become undependable, foul-mouthed, and ill-mannered.

Generations of researchers have wondered how the changes in Gage's personality might have been caused by the damage to his brain. Perhaps the trajectory of the rod spared parts of the frontal lobes that are involved in language and movement but damaged areas connected with personality (Figure 2.6).

Many accidents, such as that which befell Phineas Gage, have taught us about the brain. From injuries to the head—some of them minimal, some horrendous—we have learned that brain damage can impair consciousness and awareness. Brain damage can result in loss of vision and hearing, confusion, or loss of memory. In some cases, the loss of large portions of the brain may result in little loss of function. Ironically, the loss of smaller portions in particularly sensitive locations can result in language problems, memory loss, or death.

Accidents provide unplanned and uncontrolled opportunities of studying the brain. Scientists have learned more about the brain, however, through methods like experimentation, use of the electroencephalograph, and brain scans.

EXPERIMENTING WITH THE BRAIN The results of disease (as in the case of Leborgne) and accidents (as in the case of Gage) have shown us how injury to some parts of the brain is connected with changes in behavior and mental processes. Scientists have also purposefully experimented with the brain to observe the results. For example, damaging—creating a **lesion** in—one part of the brain's limbic system causes monkeys to exhibit a so-called rage response at the slightest provocation. Damaging another area of this system causes rats and monkeys to behave gently. Damaging part of the brain region called the hypothalamus causes rats to overeat. Damaging another part of the hypothalamus causes them to stop eating. It is as if parts of the brain contain on–off switches for certain kinds of behavior, at least in lower animals.

Surgeon Wilder Penfield (1969) stimulated parts of the brain with electrical probes, and as a result his patients reported the occurrence of certain kinds of memories. Similar experiments in electrical stimulation of the brain have found that parts of the brain are connected with specific kinds of sensations (as of light or sound) or motor activities (such as movement of an arm or leg).

THE ELECTROENCEPHALOGRAPH Penfield stimulated parts of the brain with an electric current and asked people to report what they experienced as a result. Researchers have also used the **electroencephalograph (EEG)** to record the natural electrical activity of the brain.

When I was an undergraduate psychology student, I first heard that psychologists studied sleep by "connecting" people to the EEG. I had a gruesome image of people somehow being plugged in. Not so. As suggested in Figure 2.7, electrodes are simply attached to the scalp with tape or paste. Once the brain activity under study has been recorded, the electrodes are removed. A bit of soap and water and you're as good as new.

The EEG detects minute amounts of electrical activity—called brain waves—that pass between the electrodes. Certain brain waves are associated with feelings of relaxation and with various stages of sleep. Researchers and physicians use the EEG to locate the areas of the brain that respond to certain stimuli, such as lights or sounds, and to diagnose some kinds of abnormal behavior. The EEG also helps locate tumors.

BRAIN-IMAGING TECHNIQUES At the time when Phineas Gage had his fabled accident, the only ways to look into the brain were to drill holes

LESION (LEE-shun). An injury that results in impaired behavior or loss of a function.

ELECTROENCEPHALOGRAPH (el-eck-trow-en-SEFF-uh-lo-graf). An instrument that measures electrical activity of the brain. Abbreviated *EEG*. ("Cephalo-" derives from the Greek *kephale,* meaning "head.")

FIGURE 2.7
THE ELECTROENCEPHALOGRAPH (EEG)
IN THIS METHOD, BRAIN WAVES ARE DETECTED BY PLACING ELECTRODES ON THE SCALP AND MEASURING THE CURRENT THAT PASSES BETWEEN THEM.

REFLECT

Do you know of anyone who has had a "brain scan?" What kind of scan? For what purpose? What was the outcome?

FIGURE 2.8

THE COMPUTERIZED AXIAL TOMOGRAPH (CAT) SCAN
IN THE CAT SCAN, AN X-RAY IS PASSED THROUGH THE HEAD AND THE AMOUNT OF RADIATION THAT PASSES THROUGH IS MEASURED FROM VARIOUS ANGLES. THE COMPUTER INTEGRATES THE MEASUREMENTS INTO A VIEW OF THE BRAIN.

FIGURE 2.9

THE POSITRON EMISSION TOMOGRAPH (PET) SCAN   THESE PET SCANS OF THE BRAINS OF NORMAL, SCHIZOPHRENIC, AND DEPRESSED INDIVIDUALS ARE COMPUTER-GENERATED IMAGES OF NEURAL ACTIVITY AS INDICATED BY THE AMOUNT OF GLUCOSE METABOLIZED BY PARTS OF THEIR BRAINS. MORE ACTIVE PARTS METABOLIZE MORE GLUCOSE. METABOLIC ACTIVITY RANGES FROM LOW (BLUE) TO HIGH (RED).

REFLECT

What is meant by the "old" versus the "new" parts of your brain? (After all, your brain was all born at the same time, wasn't it?)

or crack it open, neither of which would have contributed to the well-being of the subject. But in the latter years of the 20th century, researchers tapped the computer's capacity to generate images of the parts of the brain from sources of radiation to develop imaging techniques that have been useful to researchers and physicians (Goleman, 1995; Posner & Raichle, 1994).

The CAT (computerized axial tomograph) scan passes a narrow X-ray beam through the head and measures the structures that reflect the X-rays from various angles, generating a three-dimensional image of the brain (Figure 2.8). The CAT scan reveals deformities in shape and structure that are connected with blood clots, tumors, and other health problems.

A second method, positron emission tomography (PET scan), forms a computer-generated image of the activity of parts of the brain by tracing the amount of glucose used (or metabolized) by these parts. More glucose is metabolized in more active parts of the brain. To trace the metabolism of glucose, a harmless amount of a radioactive compound, called a *tracer,* is mixed with glucose and injected into the bloodstream. When the glucose reaches the brain, the patterns of activity are revealed by measurement of the positrons—positively charged particles—that are given off by the tracer. The PET scan has been used by researchers to see which parts of the brain are most active when we are, for example, listening to music, working out a math problem, using language, or playing chess ("Pinpointing Chess Moves," 1994; Sarter et al., 1996). As shown in Figure 2.9, patterns of activity in the brains of people diagnosed with schizophrenia appear to differ from patterns of other people. Researchers are exploring the meanings and potential applications of these differences.

A third imaging technique is magnetic resonance imaging (MRI). In MRI, the person lies in a powerful magnetic field and is exposed to radio waves that cause parts of the brain to emit signals, which are measured from multiple angles. MRI relies on subtle shifts in blood flow. (More blood flows to more active parts of the brain, supplying them with oxygen.) If Broca had had these imaging techniques available, he would not have had to wait until Leborgne died to study his brain.

A Tour of the Brain

Your brain is a fascinating archaeological site. It reveals much of what is so special about you. It also holds a record of your connectedness with other animals that have walked, swum, and flown the Earth for hundreds of millions of years. In fact, some parts of your brain—those that we meet first on our tour—are not all that different from the corresponding parts of the brains of rats, cats, and monkeys. They even bear some resemblance to the brains of birds and fish (Figure 2.10). The "older" parts of your brain, evolutionarily speaking—those that are found beneath your rounded skull—also have functions very similar to those of these other species. They are involved in basic survival functions such as breathing, feeding, and the regulation of cycles of sleeping and waking. Question: What are the structures and functions of the brain?

Let us now begin our tour of the brain (Figure 2.11). We begin with the oldest part of our "archaeological dig"—the hindbrain, where the spinal cord rises to meet the brain. The hindbrain consists of three major structures: the medulla, the pons, and the cerebellum. Many pathways that connect the spinal cord to higher levels of the brain pass through the **medulla.** The medulla regulates vital functions such as heart rate, blood pressure, and respiration. It also plays a role in sleeping, sneezing, and coughing. The **pons** is a bulge in the hindbrain that lies forward of the

☐ **Cerebral cortex**
☐ **Cerebellum**
☐ **Medulla**

Bass   Pigeon   Cat   Chimpanzee   Human

FIGURE 2.10

COMPARISON OF THE HUMAN BRAIN TO THE BRAINS OF OTHER SPECIES

SOME PARTS OF THE HUMAN BRAIN, ESPECIALLY THE OLDER PARTS, ARE QUITE SIMILAR TO THE CORRESPONDING PARTS OF THE BRAINS OF OTHER MAMMALS. THEY ARE EVEN SOMEWHAT SIMILAR TO THOSE OF BIRDS AND FISH, AND ARE INVOLVED IN SURVIVAL FUNCTIONS SUCH AS BREATHING, FEEDING, AND THE REGULATION OF THE SLEEPING-WAKING CYCLE. HOWEVER, THE CEREBRUMS, WHICH ARE INVOLVED IN COGNITIVE PROCESSES, ARE QUITE DIFFERENT.

medulla. *Pons* is the Latin word for "bridge." The pons is so named because of the bundles of nerves that pass through it. The pons transmits information about body movement and is involved in functions related to attention, sleep and alertness, and respiration.

Behind the pons lies the **cerebellum** ("little brain" in Latin). The cerebellum has two hemispheres that are involved in maintaining balance and in controlling motor (muscle) behavior. Injury to the cerebellum may lead to lack of motor coordination, stumbling, and loss of muscle tone.

The **reticular activating system** (RAS) begins in the hindbrain and ascends through the midbrain into the lower part of the forebrain. It is vital in the functions of attention, sleep, and arousal. Injury to the RAS may result in a coma. Stimulation of the RAS causes it to send messages to the cerebral cortex (the large wrinkled mass that you think of as your

MEDULLA An oblong area of the hindbrain involved in regulation of heartbeat and respiration.

PONS A structure of the hindbrain involved in respiration, attention, and sleep and dreaming.

CEREBELLUM A part of the hindbrain involved in muscle coordination and balance.

RETICULAR ACTIVATING SYSTEM A part of the brain involved in attention, sleep, and arousal.

Cerebrum

Fissure

Corpus callosum

Thalamus

Midbrain

Hypothalamus

Pituitary gland

Pons

Cerebellum

Medulla

Reticular activating system

FIGURE 2.11

THE PARTS OF THE HUMAN BRAIN   THIS VIEW OF THE BRAIN, SPLIT TOP TO BOTTOM, SHOWS SOME OF THE MOST IMPORTANT STRUCTURES.

brain), making us more alert to sensory information. In classic neurological research, Guiseppe Moruzzi and Horace Magoun (1949) discovered that electrical stimulation of the reticular formation of a sleeping cat caused it to awaken at once. But when the reticular formation was severed from higher parts of the brain, the animal fell into a coma from which it would not awaken. Drugs known as central nervous system depressants, such as alcohol, are thought to work, in part, by lowering RAS activity.

Sudden loud noises stimulate the RAS and awaken a sleeping animal or person. But the RAS may become selective through learning. That is, it comes to play a filtering role. It may allow some messages to filter through to higher brain levels and awareness while screening others out. For example, the parent who has primary responsibility for child care may be awakened by the stirring sounds of an infant, while the sounds of traffic or street noise are filtered out, even though they are louder. The other parent, in contrast, may sleep through loud crying by the infant. If the first parent must be away for several days, however, the second parent's RAS may quickly become sensitive to noises produced by the child. This sensitivity may rapidly fade again when the first parent returns.

Also located in the midbrain are areas involved in vision and hearing. These include the area that controls eye reflexes such as dilation of the pupils and eye movements.

Key areas of the forward-most part of the brain, or forebrain, are the thalamus, the hypothalamus, the limbic system, and the cerebrum (see Figures 2.11 and 2.12). The **thalamus** is located near the center of the brain. It consists of two joined egg- or football-shaped structures. The thalamus serves as a relay station for sensory stimulation. Nerve fibers from the sensory systems enter from below; the information carried by them is then transmitted to the cerebral cortex by way of fibers that exit from above. For instance, the thalamus relays sensory input from the eyes to the visual areas of the cerebral cortex. The thalamus is also involved in controlling sleep and attention in coordination with other brain structures, including the RAS.

The **hypothalamus** lies beneath the thalamus and above the pituitary gland. It weighs only 4 grams, yet it is vital in the regulation of body temperature, concentration of fluids, storage of nutrients, and various aspects of motivation and emotion. Experimenters learn many of the functions of the hypothalamus by implanting electrodes in parts of it and observing the ef-

THALAMUS An area near the center of the brain involved in the relay of sensory information to the cortex and in the functions of sleep and attention.

HYPOTHALAMUS A bundle of nuclei below the thalamus involved in body temperature, motivation, and emotion.

FIGURE 2.12
THE LIMBIC SYSTEM

Thalamus

Cingulate Gyrus

Fornix

Septum

Septal Nucleus

Hypothalamus

Olfactory Bulb

Pituitary Gland

Amygdala

Hippocampus

fects of an electrical current. They have found that the hypothalamus is involved in hunger, thirst, sexual behavior, caring for offspring, and aggression. Among lower animals, stimulation of various areas of the hypothalamus can trigger instinctual behaviors such as fighting, mating, or even nest building.

Canadian psychologists James Olds and Peter Milner (1954) made a wonderful mistake in the 1950s. They were attempting to implant an electrode in a rat's reticular formation to see how stimulation of the area might affect learning. Olds, however, was primarily a social psychologist and not a biological psychologist. He missed his target and found a part of the animal's hypothalamus instead. Olds and Milner dubbed this area the "pleasure center" because the animal would repeat whatever it was doing when the area was stimulated. The term *pleasure center* is not used too frequently, because it appears to attribute human emotions to rats. Yet the "pleasure centers" must be doing something right, because rats stimulate themselves in these centers by pressing a pedal several thousand times an hour, until they are exhausted (Olds, 1969).

The hypothalamus is just as important to humans as it is to lower animals. Unfortunately (or fortunately), our "pleasure centers" are not as clearly defined as those of the rat. Then, too, our responses to messages from the hypothalamus are less automatic and relatively more influenced by higher brain functions—that is, cognitive factors such as thought, choice, and value systems. It is all a part of being human.

The **limbic system** is made up of several structures, including the amygdala, hippocampus, and parts of the hypothalamus (Figure 2.12). The limbic system lies along the inner edge of the cerebrum and is fully evolved only in mammals. It is involved in memory and emotion, and in the drives of hunger, sex, and aggression. People in whom operations have damaged the hippocampus can retrieve old memories but cannot permanently store new information. As a result, they may reread the same newspaper day in and day out without recalling that they read it before. Or they may have to be perpetually reintroduced to people they have met just hours earlier (Squire, 1996).

The **amygdala** looks like two little almonds. Studies using lesioning and electrical stimulation show that the amygdala is connected with aggressive behavior in monkeys, cats, and other animals. Early in the 20th century Heinrich Klüver and Paul Bucy (1939) lesioned part of the amygdala of a rhesus monkey. Rhesus monkeys are normally a scrappy lot and try to bite or grab at intruders, but destruction of this animal's amygdala made it docile. No longer did it react aggressively to people. It even allowed people to poke and pinch it. Electrical stimulation of the part of the amygdala that Klüver and Bucy had destroyed, however, triggers a so-called rage response. For example, it causes a cat to hiss and arch its back in preparation for an attack. Yet, if you electrically stimulate another part of the amygdala, the cat cringes in fear when you cage it with a mouse. Not very tigerlike.

The **cerebrum** is the crowning glory of the brain. Only in human beings does the cerebrum account for such a large proportion of the brain (Figure 2.11). The cerebrum is responsible for the cognitive abilities of thinking and language. The surface of the cerebrum is wrinkled, or convoluted, with ridges and valleys. This surface is termed the **cerebral cortex.** The convolutions allow a great deal of surface area to be packed into the brain—and surface area is apparently connected with human cognitive ability.

Valleys in the cortex are called *fissures.* A key fissure almost divides the cerebrum in half, creating two hemispheres with something of the shape of a walnut. The hemispheres are connected by the **corpus callosum** (Latin for "thick body" or "hard body"), a bundle of some 200 million nerve fibers.

REFLECT

If your brain had a pleasure center, would you like to have your finger on the switch that turns it on or off? Might religious leaders be concerned? Why or why not?

LIMBIC SYSTEM A group of structures involved in memory, motivation, and emotion that forms a fringe along the inner edge of the cerebrum.

AMYGDALA A part of the limbic system that apparently facilitates stereotypical aggressive responses.

CEREBRUM The large mass of the forebrain, which consists of two hemispheres.

CEREBRAL CORTEX The wrinkled surface area (gray matter) of the cerebrum.

CORPUS CALLOSUM A thick fiber bundle that connects the hemispheres of the cortex.

Over the centuries, most discoveries about the brain have been made by (51) _____dent, as in the case of Phineas Gage. Penfield used (52) _____cal probes to learn the effects of stimulating parts of the brain. The (53) _____lograph records the electrical activity of the brain. Computerized (54) _____ _____ passes a narrow X-ray beam through the head and measures the structures that reflect the rays from various angles. Positron (55) _____ _____ forms an image of brain activity from measuring the amount of glucose metabolized by parts of the brain. In magnetic (56) _____ imaging, radio waves cause parts of the brain to emit signals that are integrated into an image of the brain.

The hindbrain includes the (57) m_____, which is vital in heartbeat, blood pressure, and respiration. The pons transmits information concerning movement and is also involved in attention and respiration. The (58) _____lum is involved in balance and co-ordination. The (59) _____ar activating system (RAS) begins in the hindbrain and continues through the midbrain into the fore-brain and is vital in the functions of attention, sleep, and arousal.

Key parts of the forebrain include the thala-mus, hypothalamus, limbic system, and cere-brum. The (60) _____mus serves as a relay station for sensory stimulation. The (61) _____us is involved in body tempera-ture, motivation, and emotion. Olds and Milner discovered a (62) "_____ center" in the hypothalamus by accident. The (63) _____ic system is involved in memory and in the drives of hunger, sex, and aggres-sion. Klüver and Bucy demonstrated that the (64) _____ala is connected with aggres-sion in monkeys. The hemispheres of the cerebrum are connected by the (65) _____ _____sum.

SECTION IV. THE CEREBRAL CORTEX

The cerebral cortex is the part of the brain that you usually think of as your brain. *Cortex* is a Latin word meaning "bark," as in the bark of a tree. Just as the bark is the outer coating of a tree, the cerebral cortex is the outer coating of the cerebrum. It is only about one-eighth of an inch thick.

The cerebral cortex is involved in almost every bodily activity, includ-ing most sensations and most responses. It is also the part of the brain that frees people from the tyranny of genetic dictates and instinct. It is the seat of thinking and language, and it enables humans to think deeply about the world outside and to make decisions. Other organisms run faster than we do, are stronger, or bite more sharply. Yet humans think faster, are intellec-tually "stronger," and, we might add, have a "biting" wit—all of which is made possible by the cerebral cortex. Question: What are the parts of the cerebral cortex?

The cerebral cortex has two hemispheres, left and right. Each of the hemispheres is divided into four lobes, as shown in Figure 2.13. The **frontal lobe** lies in front of the central fissure and the **parietal lobe** behind it. The **temporal lobe** lies below the side, or lateral, fissure—across from the frontal and parietal lobes. The **occipital lobe** lies behind the temporal lobe and behind and below the parietal lobe.

When light strikes the eyes, neurons in the occipital lobe fire, and as a result, we "see" (that is, the image is projected in the brain). Direct artifi-cial stimulation of the occipital lobe also produces visual sensations. If neurons in the occipital region of the cortex were stimulated with electric-ity, you would "see" flashes of light even if it were pitch black or your eyes were covered. The hearing or auditory area of the cortex lies in the temporal lobe along the lateral fissure. Sounds cause structures in the ear to vibrate. Messages are relayed from those structures to the auditory area of the cortex, and when you hear a noise, neurons in this area are firing.

FRONTAL LOBE The lobe of the cerebral cortex that lies to the front of the central fissure.

PARIETAL LOBE The lobe that lies just behind the central fissure.

TEMPORAL LOBE The lobe that lies below the lateral fissure, near the temples of the head.

OCCIPITAL LOBE The lobe that lies behind and below the parietal lobe and behind the temporal lobe.

FIGURE 2.13
THE GEOGRAPHY OF THE CEREBRAL CORTEX THE CORTEX IS DIVIDED INTO FOUR LOBES: FRONTAL, PARIETAL, TEMPORAL, AND OCCIPITAL. THE VISUAL AREA OF THE CORTEX IS LOCATED IN THE OCCIPITAL LOBE. THE HEARING OR AUDITORY CORTEX LIES IN THE TEMPORAL LOBE. THE SENSORY AND MOTOR AREAS FACE EACH OTHER ACROSS THE CENTRAL FISSURE. WHAT HAPPENS WHEN A SURGEON STIMULATES AREAS OF THE SENSORY OR MOTOR CORTEX DURING AN OPERATION?

Just behind the central fissure in the parietal lobe lies an area called the **somatosensory cortex,** which receives messages from skin senses all over the body. These sensations include warmth and cold, touch, pain, and movement. Neurons in different parts of the sensory cortex fire, depending on whether you wiggle your finger or raise your leg. If a brain surgeon were to stimulate the proper area of your somatosensory cortex with an electric probe, it might seem as if someone were touching your arm or leg.

✓ Truth or Fiction Revisited

It is true that if a surgeon were to stimulate a certain part of your brain electrically, you might swear in court that someone had stroked your leg.

Figure 2.13 suggests that our face and head are overrepresented (too big) on the cortex compared with, say, our trunk and legs. This overrepresentation is one of the reasons that our face and head are more sensitive to touch than other parts of the body.

Many years ago it was discovered that patients with injuries to one hemisphere of the brain would show sensory or motor deficits on the opposite side of the body below the head. This led to the recognition that sensory and motor nerves cross in the brain and elsewhere. The left hemisphere controls acts on, and receives inputs from, the right side of the body. The right hemisphere controls acts on, and receives inputs from, the left side of the body.

How do you make a monkey smile? One way is by inserting an electrical probe in its motor cortex and giving it a burst of electricity. Let us see what we mean by this.

The **motor cortex** lies in the frontal lobe, just across the valley of the central fissure from the somatosensory cortex. Neurons firing in the motor cor-

SOMATOSENSORY CORTEX The section of cortex in which sensory stimulation is projected. It lies just behind the central fissure in the parietal lobe.

MOTOR CORTEX The section of cortex that lies in the frontal lobe, just across the central fissure from the sensory cortex. Neural impulses in the motor cortex are linked to muscular responses throughout the body.

tex cause parts of our body to move. More than 100 years ago, German scientists electrically stimulated the motor cortex in dogs and observed that muscles contracted in response (Fritsch & Hitzig, 1870/1960). Since then, neuroscientists have mapped the motor cortex in people and lower animals by inserting electrical probes and seeing which muscles contract. For example, José Delgado (1969) caused one patient to make a fist even though he tried to prevent his hand from closing. The patient said, "I guess, doctor, that your electricity is stronger than my will" (Delgado, 1969, p. 114). Delgado also made a monkey smile in this manner, many thousands of times in a row. If a surgeon were to stimulate a certain area of the right hemisphere of the motor cortex with an electric probe, you would raise your left leg. This action would be sensed in the somatosensory cortex, and you might have a devil of a time trying to figure out whether you had intended to raise that leg!

Thinking, Language, and the Cortex

Areas of the cerebral cortex that are not primarily involved in sensation or motor activity are called *association areas*. They make possible the breadth and depth of human learning, thought, memory, and language. Question: What parts of the cerebral cortex are involved in thinking and language? The association areas in the frontal lobes, near the forehead, could be called the brain's executive center. It appears to be where we make plans and decisions (Goldman-Rakic, 1992).

Areas in the frontal lobes are also involved in the memory functions required for problem solving and decision making (Goldman-Rakic, 1992). These areas are connected with different sensory areas and therefore tap different kinds of sensory information. They retrieve visual, auditory, and other kinds of memories and manipulate them—similar to the way in which a computer retrieves information from files in storage and manipulates it in working memory.

Certain neurons in the visual area of the occipital lobe fire in response to the visual presentation of vertical lines. Others fire in response to presentation of horizontal lines. Although one group of cells may respond to one aspect of the visual field and another group of cells may respond to another, association areas put it all together. As a result, we see a box or an automobile or a road map and not a confusing array of verticals and horizontals.

LANGUAGE FUNCTIONS   In some ways, the left and right hemispheres of the brain duplicate each other's functions. In other ways, they are very different. The left hemisphere contains language functions for nearly all right-handed people and for 2 out of 3 left-handed people (Pinker, 1994). However, the brain remains "plastic," or changeable, through about the age of 13. As a result, children who lose the left hemisphere of the brain because of surgery to control **epilepsy** usually transfer speech functions to the right hemisphere (Zuger, 1997).

Two key language areas lie within the hemisphere of the cortex that contains language functions (usually the left hemisphere): Broca's area and Wernicke's area (see Figure 2.14). Damage to either area is likely to cause an **aphasia**—that is, a disruption of the ability to understand or produce language.

Wernicke's area lies in the temporal lobe near the auditory cortex. It responds mainly to auditory information. As you are reading this page, however, the visual information is registered in the visual cortex of your occipital lobe. It is then recoded as auditory information as it travels to

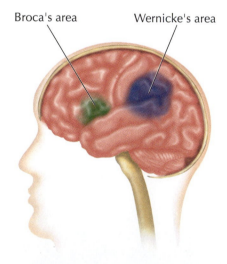

Broca's area   Wernicke's area

FIGURE 2.14
BROCA'S AND WERNICKE'S AREAS OF THE CEREBRAL CORTEX   THE AREAS THAT ARE MOST INVOLVED IN SPEECH ARE BROCA'S AREA AND WERNICKE'S AREA. DAMAGE TO EITHER AREA CAN PRODUCE AN *APHASIA*—A DISRUPTION OF THE ABILITY TO UNDERSTAND OR PRODUCE LANGUAGE.

EPILEPSY Temporary disturbances of brain functions that involve sudden neural discharges.

APHASIA A disruption in the ability to understand or produce language.

Wernicke's area. Broca's area is located in the frontal lobe, near the section of the motor cortex that controls the muscles of the tongue, throat, and other areas of the face used when speaking (Pinker, 1994; Raichle, 1994). Broca's area processes the information and relays it to the motor cortex. The motor cortex sends the signals that cause muscles in your throat and mouth to contract. If you are "subvocalizing"—saying what you are reading "under your breath"—that is because Wernicke's area transmits information to Broca's area via nerve fibers.

People with damage to Wernicke's area may show **Wernicke's aphasia,** which impairs their abilities to comprehend speech and to think of the proper words to express their own thoughts. Ironically, they usually speak freely and with proper syntax. Wernicke's area is essential to understanding the relationships between words and their meanings. When Broca's area is damaged, people usually understand language well enough but speak slowly and laboriously, in simple sentences. This pattern is termed **Broca's aphasia.**

A part of the brain called the *angular gyrus* lies between the visual cortex and Wernicke's area. The angular gyrus "translates" visual information, as in perceiving written words, into auditory information (sounds) and sends it on to Wernicke's area. It appears that problems in the angular gyrus can give rise to *dyslexia,* or serious impairment in reading, because it becomes difficult for the reader to segment words into sounds (Shaywitz, 1998).

Left Brain, Right Brain?

We often hear of being "left-brained" or "right-brained." Question: What would it mean to be "left-brained" or "right-brained"? The notion is that the hemispheres of the brain are involved in very different kinds of intellectual and emotional functions and responses. According to this view, left-brained people would be primarily logical and intellectual. Right-brained people would be intuitive, creative, and emotional. Those of us who are fortunate enough to have our brains "in balance" would presumably have the best of it—the capacity for logic combined with emotional richness.

Like so many other popular ideas, the left-brain–right-brain notion is at best exaggerated. Research does suggest that in right-handed individuals, the left hemisphere is relatively more involved in intellectual undertakings that require logical analysis and problem solving, language, and mathematical computation (Gazzaniga, 1995). The other hemisphere (usually the right hemisphere) is usually superior in visual-spatial functions (it's better at putting puzzles together), recognition of faces, discrimination of colors, aesthetic and emotional responses, understanding metaphors, and creative mathematical reasoning.

Despite these differences, it would be erroneous to think that the hemispheres of the brain act independently—that some people are truly left-brained and others right-brained (Gazzaniga, 1995). The functions of the left and right hemispheres overlap to some degree, and the hemispheres tend to respond simultaneously as we focus our attention on one thing or another. The hemispheres are aided in their "cooperation" by the corpus callosum, the bundle of 200 million axons that connects them.

Now let us consider another issue involving sidedness: left-handedness. People who are left-handed are different from people who are right-handed in terms of the way they write, throw a ball, and so on. But there are interesting questions as to whether people who are left-handed are psychologically different from "righties."

REFLECT

As you read the words on this page, neurons in your brain are firing. Where are the neurons whose firing results in your seeing the words? If you "hear" the words inside your head, what neurons are making that possible?

REFLECT

Do you think of yourself as predominantly "left-brained" or "right-brained"? Why?

WERNICKE'S APHASIA A language disorder characterized by difficulty comprehending the meaning of spoken language.

BROCA'S APHASIA A language disorder characterized by slow, laborious speech.

Handedness: Is It Gauche or Sinister to Be Left-Handed?

What do Michelangelo, Leonardo da Vinci, Pablo Picasso, and Steve Young all have in common? No, they are not all artists. Only one is a football player. But they are all left-handed. Questions: Does it matter if one is left-handed? Why are people right-handed or left-handed?

Being a "lefty" is often regarded as a deficiency. The language swarms with slurs on lefties. We speak of "left-handed compliments," of having "two left feet," of strange events as "coming out of left field." The word *sinister* means "left-hand or unlucky side" in Latin. *Gauche* is a French word that literally means "left," though in English it is used to mean awkward or ill-mannered. Compare these usages with the positive phrases "being righteous" or "being on one's right side."

Yet, 8% to 10% of us are lefties. Left-handedness is more common in boys than girls. We are usually labeled right-handed or left-handed on the basis of our handwriting preferences, yet some people write with one hand and pass a football with the other. Some people even swing a tennis racket and pitch a baseball with different hands.

Being left-handed may not be gauche or sinister, but it may matter in that it appears to be connected with learning disabilities (especially in reading) and health problems such as migraine headaches and allergies (Geschwind & Galaburda, 1987). On the other hand, there may be some advantages to being left-handed. According to a British study, left-handed people are twice as likely as right-handed people to be numbered among the ranks of artists, musicians, and mathematicians (Kilshaw & Annett, 1983).

The origins of handedness are likely to have a genetic component. If both of your parents are right-handed, your chances of being left-handed are about 1 in 50. If one of your parents is left-handed, your chances of being left-handed are about 1 in 6. And if both of your parents are left-handed, your chances of also being left-handed are about 1 in 2 (Springer & Deutsch, 1993). In any event, handedness comes early. A study employing ultrasound found that about 95% of fetuses suck their right thumbs rather than their left (Hepper et al., 1990).

Whether we are talking about language functions, being "left-brained" or "right-brained," or handedness, we are talking about people whose hemispheres of the cerebral cortex communicate back and forth. Now let us see what happens when the major avenue of communication between the hemispheres shuts down.

Split-Brain Experiments: When Hemispheres Stop Communicating

A number of people with severe cases of epilepsy have split-brain operations in which much of the corpus callosum is severed (Engel, 1996). The purpose of the operation is to confine seizures to one hemisphere of the cerebral cortex rather than allowing a neural tempest to reverberate. Split-brain operations do seem to help people with epilepsy. Question: What happens when the brain is split in two?

People who have undergone split-brain operations can be thought of as winding up with two brains, yet under most circumstances their behavior remains ordinary enough. Still, some aspects of hemispheres that have stopped talking to each other are intriguing.

As reported by pioneering brain surgeon Joseph Bogen (1969), each hemisphere may have a "mind of its own." One split-brain patient reported that her hemispheres frequently disagreed on what she should be

REFLECT

Do you know anyone who was "changed" from a lefty to a righty? Why was the change made? How was it done? Was it completely successful? Explain.

wearing. What she meant was that one hand might undo her blouse as rapidly as the other was buttoning it. A man reported that one hemisphere (the left hemisphere, which contained language functions) liked reading but the other one did not. If he shifted a book from his right hand to his left hand, his left hand would put it down. The left hand is connected with the right hemisphere of the cerebral cortex, which in most people—including this patient—does not contain language functions.

Michael Gazzaniga (1995) showed that people with split brains whose eyes are closed may be able to verbally describe an object such as a key when they hold it in one hand, but not when they hold it in the other hand. As shown in Figure 2.15, if a person with a split brain handles a key with his left hand behind a screen, tactile impressions of the key are projected into the right hemisphere, which has little or no language ability. Thus, he will not be able to describe the key. If he holds it in his right hand, he will have no trouble describing it because sensory impressions are projected into the left hemisphere of the cortex, which contains language functions. To further confound matters, if the word *ring* is projected into the left hemisphere while the person is asked what he is handling, he will say "ring," not "key."

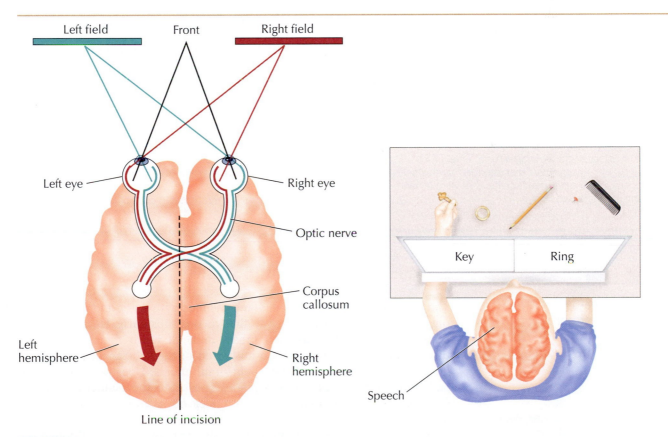

FIGURE 2.15

A DIVIDED-BRAIN EXPERIMENT IN THE DRAWING ON THE LEFT, WE SEE THAT VISUAL SENSATIONS IN THE LEFT VISUAL FIELD ARE PROJECTED IN THE OCCIPITAL CORTEX OF THE RIGHT HEMISPHERE. VISUAL SENSATIONS FROM THE RIGHT VISUAL FIELD ARE PROJECTED IN THE OCCIPITAL CORTEX OF THE LEFT HEMISPHERE. IN THE DIVIDED-BRAIN EXPERIMENT DIAGRAMED ON THE RIGHT, A PERSON WITH A SEVERED CORPUS CALLOSUM HANDLES A KEY WITH HIS LEFT HAND AND PERCEIVES THE WRITTEN WORD *KEY* IN HIS LEFT VISUAL FIELD. THE WORD *KEY* IS PROJECTED IN THE RIGHT HEMISPHERE. SPEECH, HOWEVER, IS USUALLY A FUNCTION OF THE LEFT HEMISPHERE. THE WRITTEN WORD *RING*, PERCEIVED BY THE RIGHT VISUAL FIELD, IS PROJECTED IN THE LEFT HEMISPHERE. SO, WHEN ASKED WHAT HE IS HANDLING, THE DIVIDED-BRAIN SUBJECT REPORTS "RING," NOT "KEY."

However, this discrepancy between what is felt and what is said occurs only in people with split brains. Most of the time the two hemispheres work together, even when we are playing the piano or solving math problems.

In our discussion of the nervous system, we have described naturally occurring chemical substances—neurotransmitters—that facilitate or inhibit the transmission of neural messages. Let us now turn our attention to other naturally occurring chemical substances that influence behavior: hormones. We shall see that some hormones also function as neurotransmitters.

Review

SECTION IV

The cerebral cortex is divided into two hemispheres and (66) _____ lobes. The lobes include frontal, parietal, (67) _____ral, and occipital lobes. The visual cortex is in the (68) _____al lobe, and the auditory cortex is in the (69) _____al lobe. The sensory cortex lies behind the central fissure in the (70) _____al lobe. The motor cortex lies in the (71) _____al lobe, across the (72) _____al fissure from the sensory cortex.

(73) A_____ areas of the cortex are involved in learning, thought, memory, and language. The language areas of the cortex are usually found in the (74: Left or Right?) hemisphere. (75) _____'s aphasia impairs the ability to understand speech. In (76) _____'s aphasia, people speak slowly and laboriously, in simple sentences. In (76) _____'s aphasia, the ability to understand language is impaired. The (77) _____ gyrus "translates" written words into sounds and transmits the information to Wernicke's area.

Although the hemispheres of the brain tend to work together, the left hemisphere is relatively more involved in (78) _____cal analysis and problem solving. The right hemisphere is usually superior in (79) visual-_____ functions, face recognition, color discrimination, aesthetic and emotional responses, and creative math.

About (80) _____ % of people are left-handed. Being left-handed appears to be connected with (81) _____ing disabilities and some health problems. Left-handed people are (82: More or Less?) likely than right-handed people to be artists, musicians, and mathematicians. Handedness appears (83: To have or Not to have?) a genetic component.

Some people have split-brain operations that sever much of the corpus callosum in order to control severe cases of (84) _____. Gazzaniga showed that people with split brains whose eyes are covered are usually able to verbally describe an object such as a key when it is held in (85: Only one or Either?) hand.

GLAND An organ that secretes one or more chemical substances such as hormones, saliva, or milk.

ENDOCRINE SYSTEM The body's system of ductless glands that secrete hormones and release them directly into the bloodstream.

HORMONE A substance secreted by an endocrine gland that regulates various body functions.

PITUITARY GLAND The gland that secretes growth hormone, prolactin, antidiuretic hormone, and other hormones.

SECTION V. THE ENDOCRINE SYSTEM

The body contains two types of **glands:** glands with ducts and glands without ducts. A *duct* is a passageway that carries substances to specific locations. Saliva, sweat, tears, and breast milk all reach their destinations through ducts. Psychologists are interested in the substances secreted by ductless glands because of their behavioral effects. Question: What is the endocrine system? The ductless glands constitute the **endocrine system,** and they secrete **hormones** (from the Greek *horman*, meaning "to stimulate" or "to excite").

Hormones are released into the bloodstream and circulate through the body. Like neurotransmitters, hormones have specific receptor sites. That is, they act only on receptors in certain locations. Some hormones that are released by the hypothalamus influence only the **pituitary gland.** Other hormones released by the pituitary influence the adrenal cortex; still others influence the testes and ovaries; and so on.

Question: What functions of hormones are of interest to psychologists? Much hormonal action helps the body maintain steady states, as in fluid levels, blood sugar levels, and so on. Bodily mechanisms measure current levels, and when these levels deviate from optimal, they signal glands to release hormones. The maintenance of steady states requires feedback of bodily information to glands. This type of system is referred to as a *negative feedback loop*. That is, when enough of a hormone has been secreted, the gland is signaled to stop.

The hypothalamus secretes a number of releasing hormones, or factors, that influence the pituitary gland to secrete corresponding hormones. For example, growth hormone-releasing factor (hGRF) causes the pituitary to produce growth hormone. A dense network of blood vessels between the hypothalamus and the pituitary gland provides a direct route of influence for these factors.

The pituitary gland lies just below the hypothalamus (see Figure 2.16). Although it is only about the size of a pea, it is so central to the body's functioning that it has been referred to as the "master gland." Despite this designation, today we know that the hypothalamus regulates much pituitary activity. The anterior (front) and posterior (back) lobes of the pituitary gland secrete many hormones. **Growth hormone** regulates the growth of muscles, bones, and glands. Children whose growth patterns are abnormally slow may catch up to their age-mates when they obtain growth hormone. **Prolactin** largely regulates maternal behavior in lower mammals such as rats and stimulates production of milk in women. As a water conservation measure, **antidiuretic hormone** (ADH) inhibits production of urine when fluid levels in the body are low. ADH is also connected with stereotypical paternal behavior patterns in some mammals. For example, it transforms an unconcerned male prairie vole (a mouselike rodent) into an affectionate and protective mate and father.

GROWTH HORMONE A pituitary hormone that regulates growth.

PROLACTIN A pituitary hormone that regulates production of milk and, in lower animals, maternal behavior.

ANTIDIURETIC HORMONE A pituitary hormone that conserves body fluids by increasing reabsorption of urine and is connected with paternal behavior in some mammals. Also called *vasopressin*.

FIGURE 2.16

MAJOR GLANDS OF THE ENDOCRINE SYSTEM THE ENDOCRINE SYSTEM CONSISTS OF DUCTLESS GLANDS THAT RELEASE HORMONES DIRECTLY INTO THE BLOODSTREAM. BUT HORMONES ARE TAKEN UP ONLY BY PARTS OF THE BODY THAT HAVE APPROPRIATE RECEPTOR SITES.

Oxytocin stimulates labor in pregnant women and is connected with maternal behavior (cuddling and caring for young) in some mammals. Obstetricians may induce labor by injecting pregnant women with oxytocin. During nursing, stimulation of nerve endings in and around the nipples sends messages to the brain that cause oxytocin to be secreted. Oxytocin then causes the breasts to eject milk.

The pineal gland secretes the hormone **melatonin,** which helps regulate the sleep-wake cycle and may affect the onset of puberty. Some researchers speculate that melatonin is also connected with aging.

Thyroxin is produced by the thyroid gland. It affects the body's *metabolism*—that is, the rate at which the body uses oxygen and produces energy. Some people are overweight because of *hypothyroidism,* a condition that results from too little thyroxin. Thyroxin deficiency in children can lead to *cretinism,* a condition characterized by stunted growth and mental retardation. Adults who secrete too little thyroxin may feel tired and sluggish and may put on weight. People who produce too much thyroxin may develop *hyperthyroidism,* which is characterized by excitability, insomnia, and weight loss.

The adrenal glands, located above the kidneys, have an outer layer, or cortex, and an inner core, or medulla. The adrenal cortex is regulated by pituitary ACTH. It secretes hormones known as **corticosteroids,** or cortical steroids. These hormones increase resistance to stress; promote muscle development; and cause the liver to release stored sugar, making more energy available in emergencies, as when you see another car veering toward your own.

Adrenaline and noradrenaline are secreted by the adrenal medulla. **Adrenaline,** also known as epinephrine, is manufactured exclusively by the adrenal glands, but noradrenaline (norepinephrine) is also produced elsewhere in the body. The sympathetic branch of the autonomic nervous system causes the adrenal medulla to release a mixture of adrenaline and noradrenaline that helps arouse the body to cope with threats and stress. Adrenaline is of interest to psychologists because it has emotional as well as physical effects. It intensifies most emotions and is crucial to the experience of fear and anxiety. Noradrenaline raises blood pressure and acts as a neurotransmitter in the nervous system.

If it were not for the secretion of the male sex hormone **testosterone** about 6 weeks after conception, we would all develop into females. Testosterone is produced by the testes and, in smaller amounts, by the ovaries and adrenal glands. A few weeks after conception, testosterone causes the male sex organs to develop. (The amount produced by the ovaries and adrenal glands is normally not enough to foster development of male sex organs.)

During puberty, testosterone stokes the growth of muscle and bone and the development of primary and secondary sex characteristics. *Primary sex characteristics* such as the increased size of the penis and the sperm-producing ability of the testes are directly involved in reproduction. *Secondary sex characteristics* such as presence of a beard and a deeper voice differentiate males from females but are not directly involved in reproduction.

Anabolic steroids (synthetic versions of the male sex hormone testosterone) have been used, sometimes in tandem with growth hormone, to enhance athletic prowess. Steroids increase muscle mass, heighten resistance to stress, and increase the body's energy supply by signaling the

---

REFLECT

Have you heard anything about melatonin or other hormones that are supposedly connected with aging? Are there any dangers connected with using them?

OXYTOCIN A pituitary hormone that stimulates labor and lactation.

MELATONIN A pineal hormone that helps regulate the sleep-wake cycle and may affect the onset of puberty.

THYROXIN The thyroid hormone that increases metabolic rate.

CORTICOSTEROIDS Steroids produced by the adrenal cortex that regulate carbohydrate metabolism and increase resistance to stress by fighting inflammation and allergic reactions. Also called *cortical steroids.*

ADRENALINE A hormone produced by the adrenal medulla that stimulates sympathetic ANS activity. Also called *epinephrine.*

TESTOSTERONE A male sex hormone produced by the testes that promotes growth of male sexual characteristics and sperm.

REFLECT

Do you know of any athletes who have used steroids? What are the advantages and dangers of using steroids?

liver to release sugar into the bloodstream. Steroids may also spur the sex drive and raise self-esteem. Steroids are generally outlawed in amateur and professional sports. The lure of steroids is understandable. Sometimes the difference between an acceptable athletic performance and a great one is rather small. Thousands of athletes try to make it in the big leagues, and the "edge" offered by steroids—even if minor—can spell the difference between a fumbling attempt and a smashing success. If steroids help, why the fuss? Some of it is related to the ethics of competition—the notion that athletes should "play fair." Part of it is related to the fact that steroid use is linked to liver damage and other health problems.

The ovaries produce **estrogen** and **progesterone.** Estrogen is also produced in smaller amounts by the testes. Estrogen fosters female reproductive capacity and secondary sex characteristics such as accumulation of fat in the breasts and hips. Progesterone stimulates growth of the female reproductive organs and prepares the uterus to maintain pregnancy.

Whereas testosterone levels remain fairly stable, estrogen and progesterone levels vary markedly and regulate the woman's menstrual cycle. Following menstruation—the monthly sloughing off of the inner lining of the uterus—estrogen levels increase, leading to the ripening of an ovum (egg cell) and the growth of the lining of the uterus. Ovulation (release of the ovum by an ovary) occurs when estrogens reach peak blood levels. Then the lining of the uterus thickens in response to the secretion of progesterone, gaining the capacity to support an embryo if fertilization should occur. If the ovum is not fertilized, estrogen and progesterone levels drop suddenly, triggering menstruation once more.

Estrogen appears to have psychological effects as well as biological effects. For one thing, higher levels of estrogen seem to be connected with cognitive functioning and feelings of well-being among women (Sourander, 1994). Women are also more interested in sexual activity when estrogen levels are high, particularly during ovulation, when they are fertile. Estrogen even affects women's perceptions of who is attractive. Research shows that women in Britain and Japan prefer feminized male faces, as shown in Figure 2.17(b), during most phases of the menstrual cycle (Penton-Voak, 1999). Women apparently associate such facial features with personality traits like warmth and honesty. However, they prefer the masculinized faces, as shown in Figure 2.17(a), when they are ovulating. Perhaps they interpret such features as indicative of reproductive

---

REFLECT

What hormones are involved in reproductive behavior? Has anyone you know been given any of these hormones by a physician? For what reason? Does it disturb you or anyone you know when scientists "interfere with nature?" Why?

ESTROGEN A generic term for several female sex hormones that promote growth of female sex characteristics and regulate the menstrual cycle.

PROGESTERONE A female sex hormone that promotes growth of the sex organs and helps maintain pregnancy.

FIGURE 2.17
WHICH ONE IS MR. RIGHT?
THE ANSWER MAY DEPEND ON THE PHASE OF THE WOMAN'S MENSTRUAL CYCLE. WOMEN ARE APPARENTLY MORE ATTRACTED TO MEN WITH MASCULINIZED FEATURES WHEN THEY ARE CAPABLE OF CONCEIVING (LEFT), AND MEN WITH MORE FEMINIZED FEATURES (RIGHT) WHEN THEY ARE NOT.

TABLE 2.2	THE ENDOCRINE SYSTEM	
GLAND	**HORMONE**	**FUNCTIONS**
Hypothalamus	Releasing hormones, or factors (e.g., Growth-hormone releasing factor, corticotrophin-releasing hormone)	Influences the pituitary gland to secrete corresponding hormones (e.g., growth hormone, adrenocorticotrophic hormone)
Pituitary		
Anterior Lobe	Growth hormone	Causes growth of muscles, bones, and glands
	Adrenocorticotrophic hormone (ACTH)	Regulates adrenal cortex
	Thyrotrophin	Causes thyroid gland to secrete thyroxin
	Follicle-stimulating hormone	Causes formation of sperm and egg cells
	Luteinizing hormone	Causes ovulation, maturation of sperm and egg cells
	Prolactin	Stimulates production of milk
Posterior Lobe	Antidiuretic hormone (ADH)	Inhibits production of urine
	Oxytocin	Stimulates uterine contractions during delivery and ejection of milk during nursing
Pineal	Melatonin	Involved in regulation of sleep-wake cycle; possibly connected with aging
Pancreas	Insulin	Enables body to metabolize sugar; regulates storage of fats
Thyroid	Thyroxin	Increases metabolic rate
Adrenal		
Cortex	Corticosteroids	Increase resistance to stress; regulate carbohydrate metabolism
Medulla	Adrenaline (epinephrine)	Increases metabolic activity (heart and respiration rates, blood sugar level, etc.)
	Noradrenaline (norepinephrine)	Raises blood pressure; acts as neurotransmitter
Testes	Testosterone	Promotes development of male sex characteristics
Ovaries	Estrogen	Regulates menstrual cycle; promotes development of female sex characteristics
	Progesterone	Promotes development of the uterine lining to maintain pregnancy

capacity—that is, they see these men as likely to father children but more "feminine" men as likely to be nurturant and friendly.

✓ Truth or Fiction Revisited

Women are actually more attracted to men with highly masculine facial features when they are ovulating. Estrogen peaks during the menstrual phase when women ovulate and are fertile, perhaps increasing their interest in men who seem more capable of impregnating them.

The glands and functions of the endocrine system are summarized in Table 2.2.

The Endocrine System and Human Diversity: Cross-Cultural Perspectives on Menstruation

In Peru, they speak of a "visit from Uncle Pepé." In Samoa, menstruation is referred to as "the boogie man." One of the more common epithets given to the menstrual period throughout history is "the curse." The Fulani of Burkina Faso in Africa use a term for it that translates as "to see dirt." Some nations even blame "the curse" on their historic enemies. The French once referred to menstruation as "the English" and to its onset as "the English are coming." Iranians used to say, "The Indians have attacked" to announce menstrual bleeding. Question: What prejudices do we find against menstruating women throughout the world?

A common folk belief in preliterate societies is that menstrual blood is tainted (Rathus et al., 2000). Men avoid contact with menstruating women for fear of their lives. To avoid contamination, menstruating women are sent to special huts on the fringe of the village. In the traditional Navajo

REFLECT

Were people with your cultural background reared with any negative attitudes toward menstruation? What were they? Do you personally believe in them? Explain.

culture, for instance, menstruating women would be consigned to huts that were set apart from other living quarters.

The Old Testament (Leviticus 15:19) warns against physical contact with a menstruating woman—including of course, sexual contact: "And if a woman have an issue, and her issue in her flesh be blood, she shall be put apart seven days; and whosoever toucheth her shall be unclean." Orthodox Jews still abstain from sex during menstruation and the week afterward. Prior to resuming sexual relations, the woman must attend a *mikvah*—a ritual cleansing.

Fears of contamination by menstruating women are nearly universal and persist today (Rathus et al., 2000). As late as the 1950s, women were not allowed in some European breweries for fear that the beer would turn sour. Some Indian castes still teach that a man who touches a woman during her period is contaminated and must be purified by a priest.

We might laugh off these misconceptions as folly were it not for their profound effect on women. Women who suffer from premenstrual syndrome may be responding to negative cultural attitudes toward menstruation as well as to menstrual symptoms. The traditional view of menstruation as a time of pollution may make women highly sensitive to internal sensations at certain times of the month as well as concerned about how to dispose of the menstrual flow discreetly.

Review

SECTION V

The endocrine system consists of (86) _____less glands that secrete hormones. The (87) _____mus secretes a number of hormones that regulate the functions of other glands. The pituitary gland secretes (88) _____in, which regulates maternal behavior in lower animals and stimulates production of (89) m_____ in women. ADH increases the reabsorption of (90) _____ to conserve fluid. ADH also makes a male rodent into an (91: Attentive or Inattentive?) father. (92) _____in stimulates labor in pregnant women.

(93) _____nin is secreted by the pineal gland and helps regulate the sleep-wake cycle and the onset of puberty. The thyroid gland secretes (94) _____xin, which affects the metabolism. Deficiency in thyroxin can cause (95) _____ism in children. The adrenal cortex produces (96) _____oids, which promote development of muscle mass and increase resistance to stress and activity level. The adrenal medulla secretes (97) _____ine (also called epinephrine), which increases the metabolic rate and is involved in general emotional arousal.

Sex hormones secreted by the testes and (98) _____-es are responsible for prenatal sexual differentiation. Female sex hormones also regulate the (99) _____al cycle. Women are (100: More or Less?) attracted to men with masculinized facial features when they are ovulating.

SECTION VI. EVOLUTION AND HEREDITY: THE NATURE OF NATURE

Let us return to Charles Darwin's voyage on the *Beagle*. From his observations of sea lions and tortoises and insects and plants, he was ready to formulate his theory of evolution upon his return. Reading Thomas Malthus's

Essay of the Principle of Population, which had been written back in 1798, also helped. Malthus pointed out that the Earth's food supply was increasingly mathematically (1, 2, 3, 4, 5, 6, etc.) while population was increasing geometrically (1, 2, 4, 8, 16, 32, etc). Therefore, the world's population would outstrip the world's ability to feed it, except for tragic events such as war, famine, and plague. Darwin applied Malthus's ideas to all species:

> In October 1838 . . . I happened to read for amusement Malthus on *Population,* and being well prepared to appreciate the struggle for existence which everywhere goes on from long-continued observation of the habits of animals and plants, it at once struck me that under these circumstances favourable variations would tend to be preserved and unfavourable ones to be destroyed. The result of this would be the formation of new species. Here, then, I had at last got a theory by which to work; but I was so anxious to avoid prejudice, that I determined not for some time to write even the briefest sketch of it. (F. Darwin, 1892/1958, pp. 42–43.)

Question: What are the basics of the theory of evolution? According to the theory of evolution, there is a struggle for survival as various species and individuals compete for the same territories. Organisms who are better adapted to their environments are more likely to survive (that is, to be "naturally selected"), to reproduce, and to transmit their features or traits to the next generation. Organisms evolve into more adaptive and complex creatures over time as those that are better adapted are selected and pool their genes. *Adaptation* and *natural selection* are key concepts in **evolutionary psychology.** This field of psychology studies the ways in which adaptation and natural selection—the core concepts in evolutionary theory—are connected with mental processes and behavior (Buss et al., 1998). Human evolution has given rise to such diverse activities as language, art, committed relationships, and warfare.

But because of fear of "prejudice," Darwin delayed publication of his theory by more than 20 years. In fact, he might not have permitted it to be published until after his death except that he learned that a scientist who had worked in the Amazon, Alfred Russel Wallace, was about to publish his own views, which were very similar to Darwin's. Papers by both theorists were read at the Linnaean Society, and Darwin's *On the Origin of Species by Natural Selection* (1959) was published shortly thereafter. The public's interest in evolutionary theory had been aroused, and the first printing sold out on the first day.

In 1871 Darwin published *The Descent of Man,* which made the case that humans, like other species, were a product of evolution. He argued that the great apes (chimpanzees, gorillas, and so on) and humans shared a common primate ancestor. Many ridiculed Darwin's views because they were displeased with the notion that they might have much in common with apes. Darwin's theory also contradicted the Book of Genesis, which stated that humans had been created in one day in the image of God.

One of the fascinating concepts of today's evolutionary psychologists is that not only physical traits but also social behavior evolves and is transmitted from generation to generation. In other words, some of the behavior patterns that help an organism to survive and reproduce are transmitted to the next generation. Such behaviors are believed to include aggression, strategies of mate selection, even altruism (that is, self-sacrifice of the individual to help the perpetuation of the family grouping) (Archer, 1996). Such behavior patterns are termed *instinctive* or *species-specific* because they evolved within certain species.

REFLECT

Why was Darwin reluctant to publish his theory of evolution? Do you believe that this textbook, and other textbooks, should present the theory of evolution? Why or why not?

EVOLUTIONARY PSYCHOLOGY The field of psychology that studies the ways in which adaptation and natural selection are connected with behavior and mental processes.

Consider some examples of instinctive behavior. If you place an egg from the nest of a goose a few inches in front of her, she will roll it back to the nest with her beak. If you raise a white-crowned sparrow in isolation from other sparrows, it will still sing a recognizable species-specific song when it matures. The male stickleback fish instinctively attacks fish (or pieces of painted wood) with the kinds of red bellies that are characteristic of other male sticklebacks. Linguist Steven Pinker (1994) and a number of psychologists characterize language as an instinct among humans. Psychologists are trying to determine what kinds of behavior in humans may be instinctive. However, even instinctive behavior can be modified by learning, and most psychologists agree that human behavior owes its complexity to learning ability.

Transmission of Traits From Generation to Generation

Consider some facts of life:

- People cannot breathe underwater (without special equipment).
- People cannot fly (again, without rather special equipment).
- Fish cannot learn to speak French or do an Irish jig even if you rear them in enriched environments and send them to finishing school.
- Chimpanzees and gorillas can use sign language but cannot speak.

People cannot breathe underwater or fly (without oxygen tanks, airplanes, or other devices) because of their **heredity.** Question: What is meant by heredity? Heredity defines one's nature—which is based on one's biological structures and processes. Heredity transmits traits that have evolved from generation to generation. Fish are limited in other ways by their natural traits. Chimpanzees and gorillas can understand many spoken words and express some concepts through nonverbal symbol systems such as American Sign Language. However, apes cannot speak. They have probably failed to inherit the humanlike speech areas of the cerebral cortex. Their nature differs from ours. Our speech mechanisms have evolved differently.

Heredity is basic to the transmission of physical traits such as height, hair texture, and eye color. Animals can be selectively bred to enhance desired physical and psychological traits. We breed cattle and chickens to be bigger and fatter so that they provide more food calories for less feed. We breed animals to enhance psychological traits such as aggressiveness and intelligence. For example, poodles are relatively intelligent. Golden retrievers are gentle and patient with children. Border collies show a strong herding instinct. Even as puppies, Border collies attempt to corral people who are out for a stroll.

Heredity both makes behaviors possible and places limits on them. The subfield of biology that studies heredity is called **genetics. Behavioral genetics** bridges the sciences of psychology and biology. It is concerned with the genetic transmission of traits that give rise to patterns of behavior.

Heredity is involved in almost all human traits and behavior (Rutter, 1997). Examples include sociability, shyness, social dominance, aggressiveness, leadership, thrill seeking, effectiveness as a parent or a therapist, even interest in arts and crafts (Carey & DiLalla, 1994; Lykken et al., 1992). Genetic influences are also involved in most behavioral problems, including anxiety and depression, schizophrenia, bipolar disorder, alcoholism, even criminal behavior (DiLalla et al., 1996; Plomin et al., 1997). However, most behavior patterns also reflect life experiences and personal choice (Rose, 1995).

Heredity occurs by means of genes and chromosomes. Question: What are the roles of genes and chromosomes in heredity?

REFLECT

Have you known any family pets that have engaged in instinctive behavior? What was the behavior? Why do you believe it was instinctive?

REFLECT

Which family members seem to be like you physically or psychologically? Which seem to be very different? How do you explain the similarities and differences?

HEREDITY The transmission of traits from one generation to another through genes.

GENETICS The branch of biology that studies heredity.

BEHAVIORAL GENETICS The study of the genetic transmission of structures and traits that give rise to behavior.

Adenine   Cytosine

Thymine   Guanine

S = Sugar   P = Phosphate

FIGURE 2.18
THE DOUBLE HELIX OF DNA
SEGMENTS OF DNA ARE MADE UP OF GENES THAT DETERMINE
PHYSICAL TRAITS SUCH AS HEIGHT, EYE COLOR, AND WHETHER
PIGS HAVE WINGS (NO, BECAUSE OF THEIR GENETIC MAKEUP,
THEY DON'T). PSYCHOLOGISTS DEBATE THE EXTENT TO WHICH
GENES INFLUENCE PSYCHOLOGICAL TRAITS SUCH AS INTELLI-
GENCE, AGGRESSIVENESS, AND HAPPINESS, AND THE APPEAR-
ANCE OF PSYCHOLOGICAL DISORDERS SUCH AS SCHIZOPHRENIA.

REFLECT

Do you know anyone with
Down syndrome? What is the
person like?

Genes and Chromosomes

Genes are the building blocks of heredity. They are the biochemical materials that regulate the development of specific traits. Some traits, such as
blood type, are controlled by a single pair of genes. (One gene is derived
from each parent.) Other traits are determined by combinations of genes.
The inherited component of complex psychological traits, such as intelligence, is believed to be determined by combinations of genes. We have
about 100,000 genes in every cell in our bodies.

Genes are segments of **chromosomes,** each of which consists of more
than 1,000 genes. Each cell in the body contains 46 chromosomes
arranged in 23 pairs. Chromosomes are large complex molecules of deoxyribonucleic acid, which has several chemical components. (You can
breathe a sigh of relief, for this acid is usually referred to simply as DNA.)
The tightly wound structure of DNA was first demonstrated in the 1950s
by James Watson and Francis Crick. It takes the form of a double helix—a
twisting ladder (see Figure 2.18). In all living things, the sides of the ladder consist of alternating segments of phosphate (P) and a kind of sugar
(S). The "rungs" of the ladder are attached to the sugars and consist of one
of two pairs of bases, either *adenine* with *thymine* (A with T) or *cytosine*
with *guanine* (C with G). A single gene can contain hundreds of thousands
of base pairs. The sequence of the rungs is the *genetic code* that will cause
the unfolding organism to grow arms or wings, skin or scales.

We normally receive 23 chromosomes from our father's sperm cell and
23 chromosomes from our mother's egg cell (ovum). When a sperm cell
fertilizes an ovum, the chromosomes form 23 pairs (Figure 2.19). The 23rd
pair consists of **sex chromosomes,** which determine whether we are female or male. We all receive an X sex chromosome (so called because of
the X shape) from our mother. If we also receive an X sex chromosome
from our father, we develop into a female. If we receive a Y sex chromosome (named after the Y shape) from our father, we develop into a male.

Gender is not determined by sex chromosomes throughout the animal
kingdom. Reptiles such as crocodiles, for example, do not have sex chromosomes. The crocodile's sex is determined by the temperature at which
the egg develops (Crews, 1994). Some like it hot. That is, hatchlings are
usually male when the eggs develop at temperatures in the mid-90s
Fahrenheit or above. Some like it . . . well, not cold perhaps, but certainly
cooler. When crocodile eggs develop at temperatures below the mid-80s
Fahrenheit, the hatchlings are usually female.[2]

✓ Truth or Fiction Revisited

*It is true that a crocodile's sex is determined by the temperature at which
the egg develops.* This is a rather intriguing departure from chromosomal
determination of sex.

When people do not have the normal complement of 46 chromosomes,
physical and behavioral abnormalities may result. The risk of these abnormalities rises with the age of the parents. Most persons with Down
syndrome, for example, have an extra, or third, chromosome on the 21st
pair. The extra chromosome is usually contributed by the mother, and the
condition becomes increasingly likely as the mother's age at the time of
pregnancy increases (Rathus et al., 2000). Persons with Down syndrome
have a downward-sloping fold of skin at the inner corners of the eyes, a
round face, a protruding tongue, and a broad, flat nose. They are men-

---

[2] This does not mean that male crocodiles are hot-blooded. Reptiles are cold-
blooded animals.

Female   Male

FIGURE 2.19

THE 23 PAIRS OF HUMAN CHROMOSOMES   PEOPLE NORMALLY HAVE 23 PAIRS OF CHROMOSOMES. WHETHER ONE IS FEMALE OR MALE IS DETERMINED BY THE 23RD PAIR OF CHROMOSOMES. FEMALES HAVE TWO X SEX CHROMOSOMES (LEFT), WHEREAS MALES HAVE AN X AND A Y SEX CHROMOSOME (RIGHT).

tally retarded and usually have physical problems that cause death by middle age.

Behavior geneticists are attempting to sort out the relative importance of **nature** (heredity) and **nurture** (environmental influences) in the origins of behavior. Psychologists are especially interested in the roles of nature and nurture in intelligence and psychological disorders. Organisms inherit physical features that set the stage for certain behaviors. But none of us is the result of heredity alone. Environmental factors such as nutrition, learning opportunities, cultural influences, exercise, and (unfortunately) accident and illness also determine whether genetically possible behaviors will be displayed. Behavior thus represents the interaction of nature and nurture. A potential Shakespeare who is reared in poverty and never taught to read or write will not create a *Hamlet*.

GENES The biochemical materials that regulate the development of specific traits.

CHROMOSOMES Structures consisting of genes that are found in the nuclei of the body's cells.

SEX CHROMOSOMES The 23rd pair of chromosomes, which determine whether the child will be male or female.

NATURE In behavior genetics, heredity.

NURTURE In behavior genetics, environmental influences on behavior, such as nutrition, culture, socioeconomic status, and learning.

A Person With Down Syndrome.
Down syndrome is caused by an extra chromosome on the 21st pair and becomes more likely to occur as the mother's age at the time of pregnancy increases. Persons with Down syndrome have characteristic facial features including downward-sloping fold of skin at the inner corners of the eyes, are mentally retarded, and usually have health problems that lead to death by middle age.

Kinship Studies

The more *closely* people are related, the more *genes* they have in common. Parents and children have a 50% overlap in their genetic endowments, and so do siblings (brothers and sisters). Aunts and uncles related by blood have a 25% overlap with nieces and nephews. First cousins share 12.5% of their genetic endowment. If genes are involved in a trait or behavior pattern, people who are more closely related should be more likely to show similar traits or behavior.

Question: What are kinship studies? **Kinship studies** are ways in which psychologists compare the presence of traits and behavior patterns in people who are biologically related or unrelated to help determine the role of genetic factors in their occurrence. Psychologists are especially interested in running kinship studies with twins and adopted individuals.

TWIN STUDIES The fertilized egg cell (ovum) that carries genetic messages from both parents is called a *zygote*. Now and then, a zygote divides into two cells that separate, so that instead of developing into a single person, it develops into two people with the same genetic makeup. Such people are identical, or **monozygotic (MZ), twins.** If the woman releases two ova in the same month and they are both fertilized, they develop into fraternal, or **dizygotic (DZ), twins.** DZ twins are related in the same way that other siblings are. They share 50% of their genes. MZ twins are important in the study of the relative influences of nature (heredity) and nurture (the environment) because differences between MZ twins are the result of nurture. (They cannot differ in heredity or nature because their genetic makeup is identical.)

Twin studies compare the presence of traits and behavior patterns in MZ twins, DZ twins, and other people to help determine the role of genetic factors in their occurrence. For example, twin studies show that genetic factors have a strong influence on physical features. MZ twins are more likely to look alike and to be similar in height, even to have more similar cholesterol levels than DZ twins (Heller et al., 1993). Psychologically speaking, MZ twins resemble one another more strongly than DZ twins and other siblings in the following ways:

1. Personality traits—for example, shyness, activity levels, irritability, sociability, even happiness (Adler, 1993; Goleman, 1996). Twin studies carried out by psychologist David Lykken at the University of Minnesota suggest that people inherit a tendency toward a certain level of happiness (Goleman, 1996). Despite the ups and downs of experience, people tend to drift back to their usual levels of cheerfulness or grumpiness. Factors such as availability of money, level of education, and marital status are much less influential than heredity when it comes to human happiness.

✓ **Truth or Fiction Revisited**

It is apparently true that you can't buy happiness. Heredity is a more important determinant of happiness than money and other social factors.

2. Developmental factors such as cognitive functioning, autism, and early signs of attachment—smiling, cuddling, and expression of fear of strangers (DeFries et al., 1987; DiLalla et al., 1996; Scarr & Kidd, 1983).

3. Presence of psychological disorders such as anxiety, substance dependence, and schizophrenia (DiLalla et al., 1996).

REFLECT

Do you know sets of twins? Monozygotic or dizygotic? How are they alike? How do they differ?

KINSHIP STUDIES Studies that compare the presence of traits and behavior patterns in people who are biologically related or unrelated in order to help determine the role of genetic factors in their occurrence.

MONOZYGOTIC (MZ) TWINS Identical twins. Twins who develop from a single zygote, thus carrying the same genetic instructions.

DIZYGOTIC (DZ) TWINS Fraternal twins. Twins who develop from separate zygotes.

REFLECT

If there is an inherited component in psychological disorders, should we try to prevent or treat them? Explain.

ADOPTEE STUDIES The interpretation of kinship studies can be confused when relatives share similar environments as well as genes. This is especially true of identical twins, who may be dressed identically and encouraged to follow similar interests. Adoptee studies which compare children who have been separated from their parents at an early age (or in which identical twins are separated at an early age) and reared in different environments provide special opportunities for sorting out nature and nurture. Psychologists look for similarities between children and their adoptive and natural parents. When children reared by adoptive parents are more similar to their natural parents in a particular trait, strong evidence exists for a genetic role in the appearance of that trait.

Review

SECTION VI

According to the theory of evolution, there is a struggle for (101) _____val as various species compete for territories. Organisms who are better (102) _____ted are more likely to survive and transmit their traits to the next generation. Organisms (103) e_____ into more adaptive and complex creatures. (104) Evolutionary _____logy studies the ways in which adaptation and natural selection are connected with mental processes and behavior. In his 1871 book, *The (105) _____ of Man,* Darwin argued that humans are a product of evolution.

Evolutionary psychologists believe that not only physical traits but also (106) _____al behavior evolves and is transmitted from generation to generation. Such behaviors are believed to include aggression, strategies of mate selection, and altruism. Evolved behavior patterns are termed instinctive or (107) _____-specific.

(108) _____s are the basic building blocks of heredity. Genes consist of (109) _____ _____, which is abbreviated DNA. A large number of genes make up each (110) _____ome. People normally have (111: How many?) _____ chromosomes, receiving 23 from the father and 23 from the mother.

Psychologists use kinship studies to sort out the effects of heredity and the (112) _____ment. There is reason to believe that heredity is a factor in the development of the trait when people who are (113: More or Less?) similar in kinship exhibit the trait. A fertilized egg cell is called a (114) _____e. Identical twins are formed from one zygote and are termed (115) _____zygotic. Fraternal twins are formed from (116: One or Two?) zygote(s) and are termed (117) _____zygotic. It is assumed that all differences between (118: Monozygotic or Dizygotic?) twins are determined by environmental factors.

(119) _____tee studies compare children who have been separated from their parents at an early age and reared in different environments. When adopted children are more similar to their (120: Adoptive or Natural?) parents in a trait, there is strong evidence for a genetic role in the appearance of that trait.

There are thus important connections between biological factors and psychological events. Thoughts and mental images may seem like intangible pictures that float in our heads, but they have substance. They involve billions of brain cells (neurons) and the transmission of thousands of chemicals from one brain cell to another—repeated perhaps many times per second. These countless bits and pieces of microscopic activity give rise to feelings, plans, computation, art and music, and all the cognitive activities that characterize being human. We pour chemicals called hormones into our own bloodstreams, and they affect our activity levels, our anxiety levels, even our sex drives. We inherit traits that make us human, that enable us to think more deeply and act more cleverly than any other organism (after all, we write the textbooks). We also inherit unique dispositions as individuals—dispositions that affect our personalities, our patterns of development, and our psychological stability. An understanding of biology helps us grasp many psychological events that might otherwise seem elusive and without substance.

STUDY GUIDE

TO HELP YOU BETTER UNDERSTAND THE CONTENT OF THIS CHAPTER, YOU MAY GO TO THE STUDENT WEB SITE (HTTP://WWW.HARCOURTCOLLEGE.COM/PSYCH/INTRO.HTML) TO TAKE MORE QUIZZES, GET MORE INFORMATION ABOUT THE CONTENT, AND SEE ADDITIONAL WEB SITES RELATED TO THE CONTENT. YOU CAN ALSO PRACTICE USING THE CONCEPTS IN THIS CHAPTER WITH THE POWERPSYCH CD-ROM, WHICH GIVES YOU INTERACTIVE ACTIVITIES AND EXPERIMENTS ALONG WITH EVEN MORE QUIZZES. AND, OF COURSE, THE PRINTED STUDY GUIDE IS A RELIABLE WAY TO PRACTICE ALL PARTS OF PQ4R. YOUR COLLEGE BOOKSTORE CAN ORDER THE POWERPSYCH CD-ROM FOR YOU.

SUMMARY

1. **What are neurons?** The nervous system consists of neurons, which are cells that transmit information through neural impulses, and glial cells, which mainly serve support functions. Neurons have a cell body; dendrites, which receive messages; and trunk-like axons, which conduct and then transmit messages to other cells by means of chemicals called neurotransmitters. Many neurons have a myelin coating that insulates their axons, allowing for more efficient conduction of messages. Afferent neurons transmit sensory messages to the central nervous system. Efferent neurons conduct messages from the central nervous system that stimulate glands or cause muscles to contract.

2. **What are neural impulses?** Neural transmission is electrochemical. An electrical charge is conducted along an axon through a process that allows sodium ions to enter the cell and then pumps them out. The neuron has a resting potential of −70 millivolts and an action potential of about +40 millivolts.

3. **What happens when a neuron fires?** Neurons fire by releasing neurotransmitters. They fire according to an all-or-none principle, up to hundreds of times per second. Each firing is followed by a refractory period, during which neurons are insensitive to messages from other neurons.

4. **What is a synapse?** Neurons fire across synapses, which consist of an axon terminal from the transmitting neuron; a dendrite or the body of a receiving neuron; and a fluid-filled synaptic cleft between the two.

5. **Which neurotransmitters are of interest to psychologists? What do they do?** These include acetylcholine, which is involved in muscle contractions and Alzheimer's disease; dopamine, imbalances of which have been linked to Parkinson's disease and schizophrenia; noradrenaline, which accelerates the heartbeat and other body processes; serotonin, which is involved in eating, sleep, and emotional arousal; and endorphins, which are naturally occurring painkillers.

6. **Just what is the nervous system?** A nerve is a bundle of axons and dendrites. The nervous system is one of the systems that regulates the body. It is involved in thought processes, emotional responses, heartbeat, motor activity, and so on.

7. **What are the divisions and functions of the peripheral nervous system?** The peripheral nervous system has two main divisions: somatic and autonomic. The somatic nervous system transmits sensory information about skeletal muscles, skin, and joints to the central nervous system. It also controls skeletal muscular activity. The autonomic nervous system (ANS) regulates the glands and activities such as heartbeat, digestion, and dilation of the pupils. The sympathetic division of the ANS helps expend the body's resources, such as when fleeing from a predator, and the parasympathetic division helps build the body's reserves.

8. **What are the divisions and functions of the central nervous system?** The central nervous system consists of the brain and spinal cord. Reflexes involve the spinal cord but not the brain. The central nervous system has gray matter, which is composed of nonmyelinated neurons, and white matter, which is composed of bundles of myelinated (and thus whitish) axons.

9. **How do researchers learn about the functions of the brain?** Researchers historically learned about the brain by studying the effects of accidents. They have also studied the effects of purposeful damage to the brain, made by lesions. They have seen how animals and people respond to electrical stimulations of certain parts of the brain. They have studied the waves emitted by the brain with the electroencephalograph. Contemporary brain scans such as the CAT scan, PET scan, and MRI are made possible by computer-generated images that are generally made possible by passing radiation of some sort through the brain.

10. **What are the structures and functions of the brain?** The hindbrain includes the medulla, which regulates the heart rate, blood pressure, and respiration; the pons, which is involved in movement, attention, and respiration; and the cerebellum, which is involved in balance and coordination. The reticular activating system, which is involved in wakefulness and sleep, begins in the hindbrain and continues through the

midbrain into the forebrain. Important structures of the forebrain include the thalamus, which serves as a relay station for sensory stimulation; the hypothalamus, which regulates body temperature and various aspects of motivation and emotion, such as eating and sexual behavior; the limbic system, which is involved in memory, emotion, and motivation; and the cerebrum, which is the brain's center of thinking and language.

11. **What are the parts of the cerebral cortex?** The outer fringe of the cerebrum is the cerebral cortex, which is divided into two hemispheres and four lobes: frontal, parietal, temporal, and occipital. The visual cortex is in the occipital lobe, and the auditory cortex is in the temporal lobe. The somatosensory cortex lies behind the central fissure in the parietal lobe, and the motor cortex lies in the frontal lobe, across the central fissure from the somatosensory cortex.

12. **What parts of the cerebral cortex are involved in thinking and language?** Language areas of the cortex usually lie in the left hemisphere, near the intersection of the frontal, temporal, and parietal lobes. Wernicke's area in the temporal lobe responds mainly to auditory information. Broca's area is located in the frontal lobe and is mainly responsible for speech. Damage to either area can result in an aphasia—a problem in understanding (Wernicke's aphasia) or producing (Broca's aphasia) language.

13. **What would it mean to be "left-brained" or "right-brained"?** The left hemisphere is usually relatively more involved in cognitive functions involving logical analysis and problem solving, whereas the right hemisphere is usually superior in visual-spatial functions, aesthetic and emotional responses, and creative mathematical reasoning. But the notion that some people are "left-brained" (that is, only logical and lacking completely in functions involving visual-spatial responses, etc.) and others are "right-brained" is exaggerated.

14. **Does it matter if one is left-handed? Why are people right-handed or left-handed?** About 1 person in 10 is left-handed. Learning disabilities are somewhat more common among left-handed people, but so is creativity, as shown in the arts. Handedness appears to have a genetic component.

15. **What happens when the brain is split in two?** For the most part, the behavior of people who have had split-brain operations (which sever most of the corpus callosum) is perfectly normal. However, although they may verbally be able to describe a screened-off object such as a pencil held in the hand connected to the hemisphere that contains language functions, they cannot do so when the object is held in the other hand.

16. **What is the endocrine system?** The endocrine system consists of ductless glands that secrete hormones.

17. **What functions of hormones are of interest to psychologists?** The pituitary gland secretes growth hormone; prolactin, which regulates maternal behavior in lower animals and stimulates production of milk in women; and oxytocin, which stimulates labor in pregnant women. The pineal hormone melatonin is connected with the sleep-wake cycle and the onset of puberty. Thyroxin affects the body's metabolism, and deficiency in childhood is connected with mental retardation. The adrenal cortex produces steroids, which promote the development of muscle mass and increase activity level. The adrenal medulla secretes adrenaline (epinephrine), which increases the metabolic rate and is involved in general emotional arousal. The sex hormones are responsible for prenatal sexual differentiation, and female sex hormones regulate the menstrual cycle.

18. **What prejudices do we find against menstruating women throughout the world?** Despite the fact that the menstrual flow is harmless, most cultures have viewed menstruation as a time of pollution.

19. **What are the basics of the theory of evolution?** In nature there is a struggle for survival. Species that are adaptive manage to survive (they are said to be naturally selected); their numbers increase and they transmit their traits to future generations. Species that do not adapt dwindle in numbers and may become extinct.

20. **What is meant by heredity?** Heredity is the transmission of traits from generation to generation by means of genes and chromosomes ("nature," not nurture).

21. **What are the roles of genes and chromosomes in heredity?** Genes, which consist of DNA, are the basic building blocks of heredity. A thousand or more genes make up each chromosome. People normally have 46 chromosomes arranged in 23 pairs in each cell in the body. They receive 23 chromosomes from the father and 23 from the mother.

22. **What are kinship studies?** These are studies of the distribution of traits or behavior patterns among related people. When certain behaviors are shared by close relatives, such as identical twins, they may have a genetic component. This is especially so when the behaviors are shared by close blood relatives (parents and children, or identical twins) who have been separated early and thus influenced by different environments.

EXERCISE 1

PARTS OF THE BRAIN

Fill in the names of the parts of the brain on the lines. Check your answers against Figure 2.11 in the chapter.

EXERCISE 2

MAJOR GLANDS OF THE ENDOCRINE SYSTEM

Fill in the names of the glands of the endocrine system. Can you list the important hormones secreted by each gland and explain their functions? Check your answers against Figure 2.16 in the chapter.

LANGUAGE AND CULTURE

to abbreviate (59)   *to shorten*

abnormal behavior   (65) *not a typical or ordinary manner of acting*

above average (64)   *better than ordinary*

to accelerate (57)   *to increase in frequency or rate*

an adolescent (76)   *a young person who has passed puberty but is not yet an adult*

adoptee (87)   *a person who has been adopted, taken into a family as if the child were born as a member of the family*

adoptive parent (80)   *person who assumes the role and responsibility of rearing a child*

aesthetic response (73)   *reaction to beauty*

affliction (54)   *damage, disease*

amateur sports (79)   *not professional athletic events (such as school sports)*

aphasia (76)   *loss of speech caused by brain damage*

archaeological site (66)   *place of investigation*

to arouse (78)   *to excite, to awaken*

association areas (72)   *parts of the brain that are not the primary part involved in an action but that are somewhat involved or related*

associative (54)   *related, close by*

autonomic (60)   *automatic, said of something that works by itself*

auditory (71)   *hearing*

awkward (74)   *clumsy, not graceful*

being on one's right side (74)   *being in favor, being fortunate*

being righteous (74)   *having right moral standards*

bellies (83)   *undersides (of fish)*

in the big leagues (79)   *in professional athletics play*

bipolar disorder (83)   *mental disorder of feeling very happy and energetic one moment and depressed soon thereafter*

biting wit (70)   *sharp and injurious sense of humor*

to block the action (56)   *to reduce or stop the effect*

blood sugar level (76)   *relative amount of sucrose in the blood*

the boogie man (80)   *the scary one*

brain scan (65)   *electronic method of determining the internal structure of the brain*

to bridge (83)   *to connect, to span, to cover the area between two things*

buffeted (54)   *influenced, hit*

butterfly pattern (63)   *symmetrical shape like a butterfly*

to button (75)   *to close with buttons*

calorie (83)   *unit of heat, energy unit from food*

capacity (79)   *potential, limit*

carbohydrate metabolism (80)   *burning of starch and sugars of foods for body use*

caste (81)   *rigid social grouping*

central processing unit (60)   *the "brain" of a computer*

cerebellum (67)   *part of the brain, part of the hindbrain*

cerebral cortex (67)   *gray matter on the outside of the brain*

characterized by (78)   *typical of*

cognitive (69)   *mental, intellectual, thinking-related*

coming out of left field (74)   *being unexpected or difficult to understand*

committed relationship (82)   *marriage or family*

to confine (74)   *(here) to limit*

to confound matters (75)   *to make the situation more puzzling*

connectedness (66)   *relationship*

consciousness (65)   *awareness, awakeness*

conservation measure (77)   *attempt to save or limit use of*

contamination (80)   *pollution, being affected negatively*

to contradict (51)   *to say with evidence against, to challenge*

convoluted (69)   *wrinkled, folded, complex in structure*

to cope with (78)   *to manage*

to corral people (83)   *to make the people gather in close quarters*

CPU (60)   *central processing unit or "brain" of a computer*

to create (82)   *to make out of nothing, to imagine*

cuddling someone (78)   *being gently loving in touch toward someone*

the curse (80)   *the evil thing that is wished on someone*

to decelerate (61)   *to decrease in speed*

deficiency (74)   *shortfall (not having enough of something)* to degenerate (64)   *to break down into its parts, to decompose*

delightfully (63)   *beautifully, pleasingly*

designation (77)   *(here) name*

to deviate (77)   *(here) to be different from (the expected)*

a devil of a time (72)   *a challenging or difficult attempt (to do something)*

diagramed (75)   *shown as in a picture*

to differentiate (78)   *to distinguish, to tell apart*

digestive processes (61)   *internal food processing*

disability (76)   *handicap*

discrepancy (76)   *difference from the expected*

discrimination (73)   *distinguishing, separating for purpose of identification*

disposition (87)   *temperament, nature*

diverse (82)   *varied*

do an Irish jig (83)   *dance in the manner of a folkdance from Ireland*

doting (50)   *loving, attentive, caring*

edge (79)   *(here) advantage*

to eject (78)   *to throw out or off*

electrode (65)   *end-point of a wire connected to an electrical device, terminal (that conducts electrical signals to or from a point)*

electroencephalograph (EEG) (65)   *device that measures brain activity*

enriched (83)   *specially adapted*

to enunciate (64)   *to say clearly*

epilepsy (74)   *disease or brain disorder that causes seizures or convulsions*

epinephrine (78)   *adrenaline*

essential to (64)   *necessary for, required for*

ethics of competition (79)   *rules of what is considered right in sports*

evolution (81)   *theory of adaptive change over many generations, changes from heredity*

evolutionarily speaking (66)   *referring to the theory of adaptive change*

excitability (78)   *restlessness*

executive center (72)   *administration or regulation point*

extinct (51)   *(said of a plant or animal that no longer exists) died out*

feminized male faces (79)   *faces of men that have been changed to look softer and more like women's faces*

fertile (79)   *able to conceive a child*

fertilization (79)   *conception of a child*

fetus (74)   *unborn human child, creature in utero*

fibrous (53)   *stringy, muscle-like*

fight-or-flight response (61)   *reaction of choosing whether to run away or stay to defend*

to filter (67)   *to separate selectively, to remove some parts and not others*

finishing school (83)   *place where social skills are learned*

fissure (69)   *crack, cut, split*

to fit the bill (50)   *to be right for the job (note, "bill" also refers to a person's nose)*

folly (81)   *foolishness*

to formulate (81)   *to state in formal terms*

fringe (80)   *outer edge*

genetic dictate (70)   *predetermined force of inherited characteristics, predisposition*

hallucination (57)   *vision of imagined or drug-induced origin*

handwriting preference (74)   *writing with right or left hand*

hatchling (84)   *newly born baby (from an egg)*

to have in common (82)   *to share*

to heighten (78)   *to make taller or more prominent*

hemisphere (67)   *half of a ball-shape*

hindbrain (60)   *brain part that sits in the back of the head on top of the spinal cord*

horrendous (65)   *appalling, major, awful*

hypothalamus (65)   *part of the brain (regulates basic body functions)*

imaging technique (65)   *method of visualizing an internal structure*

imperceptible (60)   *invisible, inaudible*

to impregnate (80)   *to fertilize*

incoming messages (55)   *received pieces of information*

indigestion (50)   *upset stomach*

to induce labor (78)   *to cause the birth process to begin*

inhibit (56)   *preclude, decrease, prevent*

insomnia (78)   *sleeplessness, inability to sleep*

intangible (87)   *vague, abstract*

interface (51)   *connecting point*

interneuron (62)   *nerve between motor and sensory neurons*

in relation to the outside (54)   *in comparing inside with outside parts*

instinct (70)   *inborn or natural reaction or desire to do something*

instinctive fear (51)   *genetically based alarm (related to a specific cause)* to insulate (52)   *to protect*

in tandem with (78)   *together with*

in the image of God (82)   *like God, in the way God is made*

intuitive (73)   *insightful*

issue (81)   *(here) child, baby*

key concepts (82)   *main ideas*

key figure (in) (50)   *major contributor (to)*

kinship (86)   *family relationship, fact of being members of an extended family*

left-handed (73)   *using the left hand in preference to the right hand, not right-handed (which is more common)*

left-handed compliment (74)   *insincere or indirect statement about an attribute of another person*

lefty (74)   *(a) person who uses the left hand in preference to the right hand*

lesion (65)   *scar, surface mark of an injury*

to let someone in on a secret (54)   *to share private unknown information*

living quarters (80)   *house*

male sex hormones (78)   *testosterone, androgen*

to manipulate (72)   *to handle, to manage, to adjust for use*

markedly (79)   *considerably*

masculinized faces (79)   *faces of normal men that have been changed to look even more like stereotypical men's faces*

maternal (77)   *motherly*

to mature (83)   *to become adult*

medulla (66)   *part of the hindbrain*

membrane (58)   *tough and thin body tissue that holds cell material inside*

menstruation (50)   *female hormone cycle*

to metabolize (66)   *to burn as fuel, to use as fuel in the body*

midlife (51)   *(at age) 40 to 50 years*

migraine headache (74)   *sick headache that lasts for several days*

(to have a) mind of its own (74)   *to act or think independently*

misconception (81)   *wrong idea, misunderstanding*

to miss the boat (51)   *to be late, to miss an opportunity*

the mists of time (51)   *the unknown periods in time, some vague and undetermined way*

neuroscientist (72)   *brain expert*

notion (79)   *idea*

nutrient (52)   *essential valuable food part*

nurturant (80)   *caring, helping to develop*

to occupy center stage (52)   *to be the major focus*

onset (78)   *beginning*

optimal (77)   *best condition*

organisms (50)   *plants and animals*

to outstrip (82)   *to surpass, to exceed*

to overutilize (57)   *to use too much, to deplete as a result of using too much*

ovulating (79)   *during the time when the woman is producing an ovum, or egg*

parched (51)   *dry, waterless*

Parkinson-like side effects (56)   *effects like those of Parkinson's disease*

paternal (77)   *fatherly*

peak (80)   *high point*

peak blood levels (79)   *the time at which the blood contains the most (of some substance)*

to perceive (73)   *to recognize, to become aware of, to see*

peripheral (60)   *(said of something that is) added-on or on the outside*

permeability (55)   *capacity for allowing a membrane to act like a filter*

perpetrator (54)   *doer, person responsible*

perpetuation (82)   *continuation*

persistent (58)   *continuing, not giving up*

perspective (50)   *point of view, opinion*

phase (79)   *time periods*

phenomenon (52)   *event, incident*

pioneering (74)   *being the first of its kind, early in experimenting*

pons (66)   *part of the hindbrain*

portion (65)   *section, part*

to predominate (61)   *to be the most important influence*

prejudice (82)   *bias, feeling of prejudgment*

preliterate societies (80)   *cultures in which reading and writing do not yet exist*

preoccupation (64)   *concentration of thinking, daydreaming*

to preserve (82)   *to save, to keep unchanged*

to prevail (51)   *to survive (opposite of become extinct)*

primate (82)   *ape family*

projected (75)   *placed, shown, as in a movie on a screen*

to protrude (84)   *to stick out*

prowess (78)   *ability*

puberty (78)   *point of sexual maturity*

to rear (a child) (83)   *to raise and nurture the child, to help a child develop over time*

receptor site (77)   *site or place where something is absorbed or received*

to replenish (61)   *to restore, to fill up again*

restorative (63)   *replenishing, rebuilding*

reticular activating system (67)   *brain part that regulates attention, alertness (bundle of nerves)*

to reverberate (74)   *to echo, to repeat its action*

richness (73)   *depth, range of experience*

righty (73)   *a person who uses the right hand in preference to the left hand*

to ripen (79)   *to become mature or to cause to become mature*

ritual (81)   *ceremonial*

to run hotter (64)   *to work at a higher temperature*

sac (56)   *sack-like container (of neurotransmitters)*

to screen (67)   *to remove some parts, as with a filter*

screen (75)   *partition (something that hides what is behind it)*

to secrete (76)   *to produce, to discharge*

seduction techniques (64)   *ways of enticing a person into intimacy*

selection (51)   *(here) survival (in the sense of Darwin)*

self-esteem (79)   *feeling of being worthy*

to set apart (81)   *to be put into a separate place*

sheath (53)   *covering, casing*

to shift (75)   *to change position*

shocking (54)   *(pun) surprising (also lightning shocks)*

shyness (83)   *unwillingness to interact with people who are not known to one, reserve*

side effects (56)   *results in addition to the intended results*

simultaneous (73)   *same-time, coincidental*

sketch (82)   *outline, simple picture*

sloughing off (79)   *losing, shedding*

sluggish (78)   *slow-moving*

slur (74)   *put-down, negative statement about someone or something*

smashing success (79)   *widely acclaimed positive outcome*

social dominance (83)   *ability to have great influence among a group of people*

to squander (64)   *to waste, to spend without getting something useful*

stability (87)   *balance, evenness*

to stoke (78)   *to give fuel to, to feed*

stroll (83)   *walk*

stunted (78)   *inhibited, slowed*

to support (79)   *(here) to feed, to maintain*

to swarm (74)   *to abound, to have a large and moving number (of something) acting together*

synaptic cleft (56)   *space between the bulb of an axon terminal and a dendrite*

syndrome (81)   *set of symptoms*

tactile (75)   *(related to sense of touch)*

tainted (80)   *dirty*

to tamp down (64)   *to pat firmly down by a series of strikes or blows, to hammer down*

to tap (72)   *to access, to use as a source*

tempest (74)   *storm, internal turmoil*

tendency (51)   *predisposition, likeliness to show some trait*

testes (76)   *male sex hormone-producing organ*

there you have it (58)   *That is the explanation.*

three-dimensional image (66)   *picture with height, width, and depth*

threshold (55)   *critical level, level necessary for*

thrill seeking (83)   *desiring to risk to feel the effects of adrenaline produced by risk taking*

tomograph (66)   *X-ray picture of layer or cross-section, computer-generated single-level scan*

tongue in cheek (64)   *meaning to be amusing*

to translate (73)   *to interpret, to represent*

transmission (76)   *passing on from one person to another*

triggering (79)   *causing to start*

to turn sour (81)   *to spoil*

(to have) two left feet (74)   *to be clumsy or awkward*

two no's make a yes (58)   *the result of one thing canceling out the other*

to undergo (74)   *to experience, to endure*

undertaking (73)   *project, attempt*

to veer (78)   *to change direction*

vesicle (56)   *tiny container (in a body)*

view (82)   *(here) opinion*

to wind up with (74)   *to have in the end*

Q U I Z

1. The _____ of the neuron uses oxygen to create energy to carry out the work of the cell.
   - (a) axon,
   - (b) dendrite,
   - (c) soma,
   - (d) myelin.

2. In the disease _____, myelin is replaced with a hard, fibrous tissue.
   - (a) cerebral palsy,
   - (b) multiple sclerosis,
   - (c) diabetes,
   - (d) acromegaly.

3. When a neuron is polarized, it has a resting potential of about _____ millivolts in relation to the body fluid outside the cell membrane.
   - (a) –70,
   - (b) –40,
   - (c) +70,
   - (d) +110.

4. Which of the following is a basic concept in the theory of evolution?
   - (a) The all-or-none principle,
   - (b) Struggle for survival,
   - (c) DNA,
   - (d) Sexual orientation.

5. Receptor sites for neurotransmitters are mainly found on the _____ of receiving neurons.
   - (a) dendrites,
   - (b) synaptic vesicles,
   - (c) clefts,
   - (d) axon terminals.

6. People normally have _____ chromosomes.
   - (a) 21,
   - (b) 23,
   - (c) 46,
   - (d) 47.

7. _____ increase(s) the release of noradrenaline and also impede(s) its reabsorption after neurons have fired.
   - (a) Phenothiazines,
   - (b) LSD,
   - (c) Amphetamines,
   - (d) Endorphins.

8. You sit and cross your legs, and a physician taps your leg just below the knee. As a result, you kick reflexively. Which of the following is involved in your reflexive response?
   - (a) White matter in the spinal cord,
   - (b) Sensory cortex,
   - (c) Afferent neurons,
   - (d) Motor cortex.

9. The part of the brain that gives it its wrinkled, mushroom-like appearance is
   - (a) the cerebellum,
   - (b) Broca's area,
   - (c) the reticular activating system,
   - (d) the cerebrum.

10. According to Pinker, the left hemisphere of the cerebral cortex contains language functions for nearly _____ left-handed people.
    - (a) one out of four,
    - (b) half,
    - (c) two out of three,
    - (d) all.

11. Messages from the brain and spinal cord to the _____ nervous system control purposeful body movements, such as raising a hand or running.
    - (a) autonomic,
    - (b) somatic,
    - (c) sympathetic,
    - (d) parasympathetic.

12. The parasympathetic division of the autonomic nervous system stimulates
    - (a) digestive processes,
    - (b) the fight-or-flight response,
    - (c) the heart rate,
    - (d) ejaculation.

13. People with damage to _____ area of the brain may have problems understanding speech and thinking or the right words to express their thoughts, even though they usually speak freely and with proper grammar.
    - (a) Broca's,
    - (b) Gage's,
    - (c) Wernicke's,
    - (d) Gazzaniga's.

14. Concerning the left brain–right brain controversy, it is most accurate to conclude that
    - (a) the sounds of speech evoke a response in the left hemisphere only,
    - (b) the sounds of speech evoke a response in the right hemisphere only,
    - (c) creativity and intuition are confined to the right hemisphere,

(d) the hemispheres are similar enough so that each can function quite well independently, but not as well as they function in normal combined usage.

15. Which of the following is referred to as the "master gland"?
    (a) The hypothalamus,
    (b) The pancreas,
    (c) The pineal,
    (d) The pituitary gland.

16. In women, prolactin
    (a) regulates maternal behavior,
    (b) causes uterine contractions,
    (c) stimulates production of milk,
    (d) maintains pregnancy.

17. Psychologists conduct kinship studies to
    (a) learn of the origins of physical traits such as eye color and height,
    (b) help determine the role of genetic factors in behavior patterns and mental processes,
    (c) sort out the effects of cultural beliefs and personal attitudes on behavior,
    (d) learn how to correct abnormalities in the endocrine system.

18. Psychologists primarily engage in adoptee studies because

(a) there are no other ways to determine the effects of selective breeding in rats and other laboratory animals,
(b) they are easier to conduct than physiologically based studies,
(c) adopted siblings share 50% of their inheritance,
(d) results of kinship studies may be confused by the fact that relatives usually share common backgrounds as well as genes.

19. According to the text, hormones secreted by the _____ increase resistance to stress.
    (a) Adrenal cortex,
    (b) Adrenal medulla,
    (c) Anterior lobe of the pituitary,
    (d) Posterior lobe of the pituitary.

20. The relationship between genetics and behavior, as expressed in the text, is that
    (a) genetics determines all of the behavior of rats but not of primates,
    (b) genetics determines all of the behavior of lower mammals, including lower primates, but not of humans,
    (c) genetics completely determines the level of aggressiveness but not of intelligence in mammalian species,
    (d) genetics makes behaviors possible and also sets limits on them.

Recite Recite Recite Recite **Recite**

1. What are neurons?

_____
_____
_____
_____
_____

2. What are neural impulses?

_____
_____
_____
_____
_____

3. What happens when a neuron fires?

_____
_____
_____
_____
_____

4. What is a synapse?

_____
_____
_____
_____
_____
_____

5. Which neurotransmitters are of interest to psychologists? What do they do?

_____
_____
_____
_____
_____

6. Just what is the nervous system?

_____
_____
_____
_____
_____

7. What are the divisions and functions of the peripheral nervous system?

_____
_____
_____
_____
_____

8. What are the divisions and functions of the central nervous system?

_____
_____
_____
_____

9. How do researchers learn about the functions of the brain?

_____
_____
_____
_____

10. What are the structures and functions of the brain?

_____
_____
_____
_____

11. What are the parts of the cerebral cortex?

12. What parts of the cerebral cortex are involved in thinking and language?

13. What would it mean to be "left-brained" or "right-brained"?

14. Does it matter if one is left-handed? Why are people right-handed or left-handed?

15. What happens when the brain is split in two?

16. What is the endocrine system?

17. What functions of hormones are of interest to psychologists?

18. What prejudices do we find against menstruating women throughout the world?

19. What are the basics of the theory of evolution?

20. What is meant by heredity?

21. What are the roles of genes
    and chromosomes in
    heredity?

    _____
    _____
    _____
    _____
    _____
    _____

22. What are kinship studies?

    _____
    _____
    _____
    _____
    _____
    _____
    _____

ANSWERS TO SECTION REVIEWS

1. Neurons
2. Neurotransmitters
3. Soma
4. Dendrites
5. Axons
6. Myelin
7. Insulates
8. Ions
9. Afferent
10. Efferent
11. Electrochemical
12. Sodium
13. Resting
14. Action
15. Firing
16. Fire
17. Hundreds
18. Refractory
19. Terminal
20. Dendrite
21. Cleft
22. Excitatory
23. Inhibitory
24. Vesicles
25. Terminals
26. Receptor
27. Acetylcholine
28. Hippocampus
29. Dopamine
30. Parkinson's
31. Overutilize

32. Sites
33. Mood
34. Serotonin
35. Endorphins
36. Axons
37. Peripheral
38. Somatic
39. Central
40. Parasympathetic
41. Involuntary
42. Sympathetic
43. Parasympathetic
44. Spinal
45. Reflex
46. Afferent
47. Efferent
48. Interneuron
49. Gray
50. White
51. Accident
52. Electrical
53. Electroencephalo-
    graph
54. Axial tomography
55. Emission tomog-
    raphy
56. Resonance
57. Medulla
58. Cerebellum
59. Reticular
60. Thalamus

61. Hypothalamus
62. Pleasure
63. Limbic
64. Amygdala
65. Corpus callosum
66. Four
67. Temporal
68. Occipital
69. Temporal
70. Parietal
71. Frontal
72. Central
73. Association
74. Left
75. Wernicke's
76. Broca's
77. Angular
78. Logical
79. Spatial
80. 8 to 10
81. Learning
82. More
83. To have
84. Epilepsy
85. Only one
86. Ductless
87. Hypothalamus
88. Prolactin
89. Milk
90. Urine
91. Attentive

92. Oxytocin
93. Melatonin
94. Thyroxin
95. Cretinism
96. Corticosteroids
97. Adrenaline
98. Ovaries
99. Menstrual
100. More
101. Survival
102. Adapted
103. Evolve
104. Psychology
105. *Descent*
106. Social
107. Species
108. Genes
109. Deoxyribonucleic
     acid
110. Chromosome
111. 46
112. Environment
113. More
114. Zygote
115. Monozygotic
116. Two
117. Dizygotic
118. Monozygotic
119. Adoptee
120. Natural

ANSWERS TO QUIZ

1. C
2. B
3. A
4. B
5. A

6. C
7. C
8. C
9. D
10. C

11. B
12. A
13. C
14. D
15. D

16. C
17. B
18. D
19. A
20. D

DEVELOPMENTAL PSYCHOLOGY

3

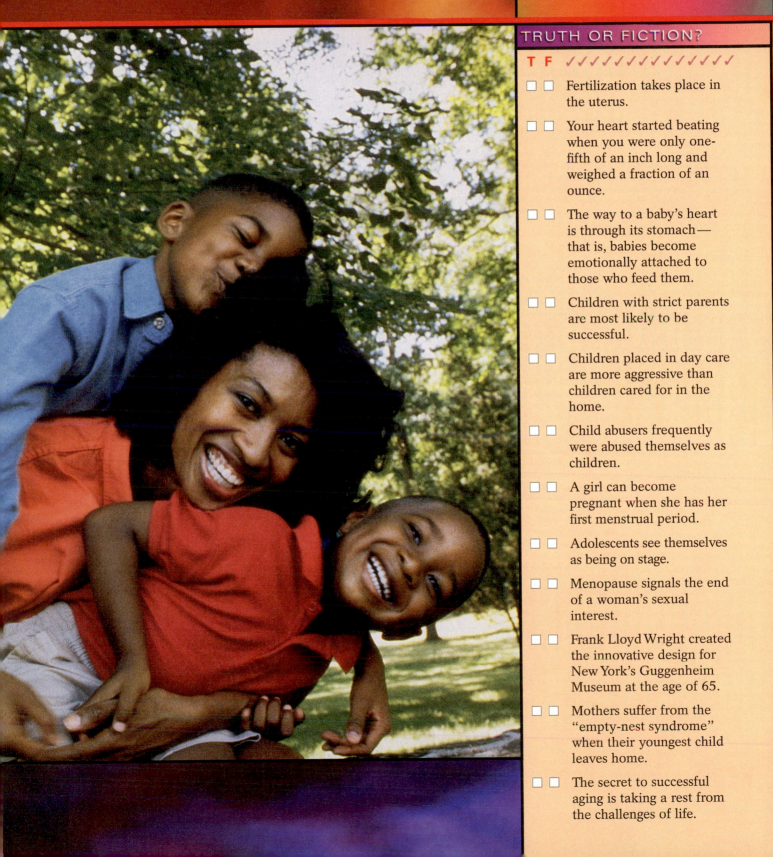

This chapter, "Developmental Psychology," covers the following:

SECTION I. PRENATAL DEVELOPMENT: THE BEGINNING OF OUR LIFE STORY

Describes the developments that occur from conception through birth

SECTION II. CHILDHOOD: PHYSICAL DEVELOPMENT

Describes the physical developments that occur during childhood

SECTION III. CHILDHOOD: COGNITIVE DEVELOPMENT

Describes Piaget's views of cognitive development

Describes language development

Describes the ways in which developing children reason about what is right and wrong

SECTION IV. CHILDHOOD: SOCIAL AND PERSONALITY DEVELOPMENT

Describes Erikson's views of psychosocial development

Describes the development of feelings of attachment

Discusses the parenting styles that are connected with self-esteem, achievement motivation, and independence in children

SECTION V. ADOLESCENCE: PHYSICAL DEVELOPMENT

Describes the physical developments that occur during adolescence

SECTION VI. ADOLESCENCE: COGNITIVE DEVELOPMENT

Describes the cognitive developments during adolescence

SECTION VII. ADOLESCENCE: SOCIAL AND PERSONALITY DEVELOPMENT

Describes the social and personality developments that occur during adolescence

SECTION VIII. ADULTHOOD: PHYSICAL DEVELOPMENT

Describes the physical developments that occur during adulthood

Discusses theories of aging

SECTION IX. ADULTHOOD: COGNITIVE DEVELOPMENT

Describes the cognitive developments that occur during adulthood

SECTION X. ADULTHOOD: SOCIAL AND PERSONALITY DEVELOPMENT

Describes the social and personality developments that occur during young adulthood

Describes the social and personality developments that occur during middle adulthood

Describes the social and personality developments that occur during late adulthood

Describes psychological perspectives on death and dying

SECTION XI. CONTROVERSIES IN DEVELOPMENTAL PSYCHOLOGY

Discusses the relative influences of nature and nurture on development

Applies the nature-nurture controversy to language development

Discusses whether development occurs gradually or in stages

There is no cure for birth or death save to enjoy the interval.

GEORGE SANTAYANA

We have a story to tell. An important story. A fascinating story. It is your story. It is about the remarkable journey you have already taken through childhood and adolescence. It is about the unfolding of your adult life. Billions have made this journey before. You have much in common with them. Yet you are unique, and things will happen to you, and because of you, that have never happened before.

Let us watch as Ling and Patrick Chang begin such a story by conceiving a child. On a summerlike day in October, Ling and Patrick rush to their jobs as usual. While Ling, a trial attorney, is preparing a case to present in court, a very different drama is unfolding in her body. Hormones are causing a follicle (egg container) in one of her ovaries to ovulate—that is, to rupture and release an egg cell, or ovum. Ling, like other women, possessed from birth all the egg cells she will ever have. How this particular ovum was selected to ripen and be released this month is unknown. But in any case, Ling will be capable of becoming pregnant for only a couple of days following ovulation.

When it is released, the ovum begins a slow journey down a 4-inch-long fallopian tube to the uterus. It is within this tube that one of Patrick's sperm cells will unite with the egg. The fertilized ovum, or zygote, is 1/175th of an inch across—a tiny stage for the drama that is about to unfold.

✓ Truth or Fiction Revisited

It is not true that fertilization takes place in the uterus. Fertilization normally occurs in a fallopian tube.

Developmental psychologists are interested in studying the development of Patrick and Ling's new child from the time of conception until death for several reasons. The discovery of early influences and developmental sequences helps psychologists understand adults. Psychologists are also interested in the effects of genetic factors, early interactions with parents and siblings (brothers and sisters), and the school and community on traits such as aggressiveness and intelligence.

Developmental psychologists seek to learn the causes of developmental abnormalities. For instance, should pregnant women abstain from smoking and drinking? (Yes.) Is it safe for a pregnant woman to take aspirin for a headache or tetracycline to ward off a bacterial invasion? (Perhaps not. Ask your obstetrician.) What factors contribute to child abuse? Some developmental psychologists focus on adult development. For example, what conflicts and disillusionments can we expect as we journey through our 30s, 40s, and 50s? The information acquired by developmental psychologists can help us make decisions about how we rear our children and lead our own lives.

Let us now turn to prenatal developments—the changes that occur between conception and birth. Although they may be literally "out of sight," the most dramatic biological changes occur within the short span of 9 months.

SECTION I. PRENATAL DEVELOPMENT: THE BEGINNING OF OUR LIFE STORY

The most dramatic gains in height and weight occur during prenatal development. Question: What developments occur from conception through birth? Within 9 months a child develops from a nearly microscopic cell to a **neonate** (newborn) about 20 inches long. Its weight increases a billionfold.

During the months following conception, the single cell formed by the union of sperm and egg—the **zygote**—multiplies, becoming two, then four, then eight, and so on. By the time the infant is ready to be born, it contains trillions of cells.

The zygote divides repeatedly as it proceeds on its 3- to 4-day journey to the uterus. The ball-like mass of multiplying cells wanders about the uterus for another 3 to 4 days before beginning to implant in the uterine wall. Implantation takes another week or so. The period from conception to implantation is called the **germinal stage, or the period of the ovum.**

The **embryonic stage** lasts from implantation until about the eighth week of development. During this stage, the major body organ systems take form. As you can see from the relatively large heads of embryos (see Figure 3.1), the growth of the head precedes that of other parts of the

FIGURE 3.1

EMBRYOS AND FETUSES AT VARIOUS INTERVALS OF PRENATAL DEVELOPMENT

NEONATE A newly born child.

ZYGOTE A fertilized ovum (egg cell).

GERMINAL STAGE The first stage of prenatal development, during which the dividing mass of cells has not become implanted in the uterine wall.

PERIOD OF THE OVUM Another term for the *germinal stage.*

EMBRYONIC STAGE The baby from the third through the eighth weeks following conception, during which time the major organ systems undergo rapid differentiation.

An Exercise Class for Pregnant Women. Years ago pregnant women were not expected to exert themselves. Today, it is recognized that exercise is healthful for pregnant women because it promotes fitness, which is beneficial during childbirth as well as at other times.

REFLECT

How can you use knowledge of prenatal development in your own life?

ANDROGENS Male sex hormones.

AMNIOTIC SAC A sac within the uterus that contains the embryo or fetus.

PLACENTA A membrane that permits the exchange of nutrients and waste products between the mother and her developing child but does not allow the maternal and fetal bloodstreams to mix.

UMBILICAL CORD A tube between the mother and her developing child through which nutrients and waste products are conducted.

FETAL STAGE The baby from the third month following conception through childbirth, during which time there is maturation of organ systems and dramatic gains in length and weight.

body. The growth of the organs—heart, lungs, and so on—also precedes the growth of the extremities. The relatively early maturation of the brain and the organ systems allows them to participate in the nourishment and further development of the embryo. During the fourth week, a primitive heart begins to beat and pump blood—in an organism that is one-fifth of an inch long. The heart will continue to beat without rest every minute of every day for perhaps 80 or 90 years.

✓ **Truth or Fiction Revisited**

It is true that your heart started beating when you were only one-fifth of an inch long and weighed a fraction of an ounce. It started about 3 weeks after conception.

By the end of the second month, the head has become rounded and the facial features distinct—all in an embryo that is about 1 inch long and weighs 1/30th of an ounce. During the second month, the nervous system begins to transmit messages. By 5 to 6 weeks, the embryo is only a quarter to half an inch long, yet nondescript sex organs have formed. By about the seventh week, the genetic code (XY or XX) begins to assert itself, causing the sex organs to differentiate. If a Y sex chromosome is present, testes form and begin to produce **androgens** (male sex hormones), which further masculinize the sex organs. In the absence of these hormones, the embryo develops female sex organs.

As it develops, the embryo is suspended within a protective **amniotic sac** in the mother's uterus. The sac is surrounded by a clear membrane and contains amniotic fluid. The fluid is a sort of natural air bag, allowing the child to move or even jerk around without injury. It also helps maintain an even temperature.

From now until birth, the embryo exchanges nutrients and wastes with the mother through a pancake-shaped organ called the **placenta.** The embryo is connected to the placenta by the **umbilical cord.** The placenta is connected to the mother by the system of blood vessels in the uterine wall.

The circulatory systems of the mother and baby do not mix. A membrane in the placenta permits only certain substances to pass through. Oxygen and nutrients are passed from the mother to the embryo. Carbon dioxide and other wastes are passed from the child to the mother, where they are removed by the mother's lungs and kidneys. Unfortunately, a number of other substances can pass through the placenta. They include some microscopic disease organisms—such as those that cause syphilis and German measles—and some chemical agents, including acne drugs, aspirin, narcotics, alcohol, and tranquilizers. Because these and other agents may be harmful to the baby, pregnant women are advised to consult their physicians before using any drugs, even those sold over the counter.

The **fetal stage** lasts from the beginning of the third month until birth. By the end of the third month, the major organ systems and the fingers and toes have formed. In the middle of the fourth month, the mother usually detects the first fetal movements. By the end of the sixth month, the fetus moves its limbs so vigorously that mothers often feel that they are being kicked. The fetus opens and shuts its eyes, sucks its thumb, alternates between periods of being awake and sleeping, and perceives light. It also turns somersaults, which can be perceived clearly by the mother. The umbilical cord is composed so that it will not break or become dangerously wrapped around the fetus, no matter how many acrobatic feats the fetus performs.

During the last 3 months, the organ systems of the fetus continue to mature. The heart and lungs become increasingly capable of sustaining independent life. The fetus gains about 5 1/2 pounds and doubles in length. Newborn boys average about 7 1/2 pounds and newborn girls about 7 pounds.

Review

SECTION I

It is possible to become pregnant for a day or so following (1) _____tion. Ovulation is defined as the releasing of an (2) _____ from an ovary. A person begins to grow and develop when a sperm cell combines with an ovum to become a (3) z_____.

Prenatal development is divided into (4: How many?) _____ stages or periods. These are the (5) _____nal stage (approximately the first 2 weeks), the (6) em_____ stage (which lasts from 2 weeks to about 2 months after conception), and the (7) f_____ stage. During the germinal stage, the zygote divides repeatedly as it travels through the (8) f_____ tube and then within the uterus. Then the zygote becomes implanted in the wall of the (9) u_____. During the embryonic period, the major (10) o_____ systems of the unborn child undergo rapid development.

SECTION II. CHILDHOOD: PHYSICAL DEVELOPMENT

Childhood begins with birth. When my children are enjoying themselves, I kid them and say, "Stop having fun. You're a child, and childhood is the worst time of life." I get a laugh because they know that childhood is supposed to be the best time of life—a time for play and learning and endless possibilities. For many children it is that, but other children suffer from problems such as malnutrition, low self-esteem, and child abuse.

Let us chronicle the events of childhood. The most obvious aspects of child development are physical. Let us therefore begin with physical development. However, we will see that cognitive development and social and personality development are also essential.

Physical development includes gains in height and weight; maturation of the nervous system; and development of bones, muscles, and organs. Question: What physical developments occur during childhood?

During infancy—the first two years of childhood—dramatic gains in height and weight continue. Babies usually double their birth weight in about 5 months and triple it by their first birthday. Their height increases by about 10 inches in the first year. Children grow another 4 to 6 inches during the second year and gain some 4 to 7 pounds. After that, they gain about 2 to 3 inches a year until they reach the adolescent growth spurt. Weight gains also remain fairly even at about 4 to 6 pounds per year until the spurt begins.

Let us now consider other aspects of physical development in childhood: reflexes, perceptual development, and motor development.

Reflexes

Soon after you were born, a doctor or nurse probably pressed her fingers against the palms of your hands. Although you would have had no idea what to do in response, most likely you grasped the fingers firmly—so firmly that you could have been lifted from your cradle! Grasping at birth is inborn. It is one of the neonate's many **reflexes**—simple, unlearned, stereotypical responses elicited by specific stimuli. Reflexes are essential to survival and do not involve higher brain

REFLECT

Why do you think that babies are born with reflexes?

REFLEX A simple, unlearned response to a stimulus.

functions. They occur automatically—that is, without thinking about them.

Newborn children do not know that it is necessary to eat to survive. Fortunately, they have rooting and sucking reflexes that cause them to eat. They turn their head toward stimuli that prod or stroke the cheek, chin, or corner of the mouth. This is termed **rooting.** They suck objects that touch their lips.

Neonates have numerous other reflexes that aid in survival. They withdraw from painful stimuli. This is known as the withdrawal reflex. They draw up their legs and arch their backs in response to sudden noises, bumps, or loss of support while being held. This is the startle, or Moro, reflex. They grasp objects that press against the palms of their hands (the grasp, or palmar, reflex). They fan their toes when the soles of their feet are stimulated (the Babinski reflex). Pediatricians assess babies' neural functioning by testing these reflexes.

Babies also breathe, sneeze, cough, yawn, and blink reflexively. And it is guaranteed that you will learn about the sphincter (anal muscle) reflex if you put on your best clothes and hold an undiapered neonate on your lap for a while.

Perceptual Development

Newborn children spend about 16 hours a day sleeping and do not have much opportunity to learn about the world. Yet they are capable of perceiving the world reasonably well soon after birth.

Within a couple of days, infants can follow, or track, a moving light with their eyes (Kellman & von Hofsten, 1992). By the age of 3 months, they can discriminate most colors (Banks & Shannon, 1993; Teller & Lindsey, 1993). Neonates are nearsighted but by about the age of 4 months, infants seem able to focus on distant objects about as well as adults can.

The visual preferences of infants are measured by the amount of time, termed **fixation time,** they spend looking at one stimulus instead of another. In classic research by Robert Fantz (1961), 2-month-old infants preferred visual stimuli that resembled the human face to newsprint, a bull's-eye, and featureless red, white, and yellow disks. At this age the complexity of facelike patterns may be more important than their content. For example, babies have been shown facelike patterns that differ either in the number of elements they contain or the degree to which they are organized to match the human face. Five- to 10-week-old babies fixate longer on patterns with high numbers of elements. The organization of the elements—that is, the degree to which they resemble the face—is less important. By 15 to 20 weeks, the organization of the pattern also matters. At that age babies dwell longer on facelike patterns (e.g., Haaf et al., 1983).

Infants thus seem to have an inborn preference for complex visual stimuli. However, preference for faces as opposed to other equally complex stimuli may not emerge until infants have had experience with people.

Classic research has shown that infants tend to respond to cues for depth by the time they are able to crawl (at about 6 to 8 months). Most also have the good sense to avoid crawling off ledges and table tops into open space (Campos et al., 1978). Note the setup (Figure 3.2) in the classic "visual cliff" experiment run by Walk and Gibson (1961). An 8-month-old infant crawls freely above the portion of the glass with a checkerboard pattern immediately beneath it but hesitates to crawl over the portion of

FIGURE 3.2
THE CLASSIC VISUAL CLIFF EXPERIMENT
THIS YOUNG EXPLORER HAS THE GOOD SENSE NOT TO CRAWL OUT ONTO AN APPARENTLY UNSUPPORTED SURFACE, EVEN WHEN MOTHER BECKONS FROM THE OTHER SIDE. RATS, PUPS, KITTENS, AND CHICKS ALSO WILL NOT TRY TO WALK ACROSS TO THE OTHER SIDE. (SO DON'T BOTHER ASKING WHY THE CHICKEN CROSSED THE VISUAL CLIFF.)

ROOTING The turning of an infant's head toward a touch, such as by the mother's nipple.

FIXATION TIME The amount of time spent looking at a visual stimulus.

the glass beneath which the checkerboard has been dropped a few feet. Because the glass would support the infant, this is a "visual cliff," not an actual cliff.

Normal neonates hear well unless their middle ears are clogged with amniotic fluid. In such cases, hearing improves rapidly after the ears are opened up. Most neonates reflexively turn their heads toward unusual sounds, suspending other activities as they do so. This finding, along with findings about visual tracking, suggests that infants are preprogrammed to survey their environments. Speaking or singing softly in a low-pitched tone soothes infants. This is why some parents use lullabies to get infants to fall asleep.

Three-day-old babies prefer their mother's voice to those of other women, but they do not show a similar preference for their father's voice (DeCasper & Prescott, 1984; Freeman et al., 1993). By birth, of course, babies have had many months of "experience" in the uterus. For at least 2 or 3 months before birth, babies have been capable of hearing sounds. Because they are predominantly exposed to sounds produced by their mother, learning may contribute to neonatal preferences.

The nasal preferences of babies are similar to those of adults. Newborn infants spit, stick out their tongue, and literally wrinkle their nose at the odor of rotten eggs. They smile and make licking motions in response to chocolate, strawberry, vanilla, and honey. The sense of smell, like the sense of hearing, may provide a vehicle for mother–infant recognition. Within the first week, nursing infants prefer to turn to look at their mother's nursing pads (which can be discriminated only by smell) rather than those of strange women (Macfarlane, 1975). By 15 days, nursing infants prefer their mother's underarm odor to those of other women (Porter et al., 1992). Bottle-fed babies do not show this preference.

Shortly after birth, infants can discriminate tastes. They suck liquid solutions of sugar and milk but grimace and refuse to suck salty or bitter solutions.

Newborn babies are sensitive to touch. Many reflexes (including rooting and sucking) are activated by pressure against the skin. Newborns are relatively insensitive to pain, however. This may be adaptive, considering the squeezing that occurs during the birth process. Sensitivity to pain increases within a few days.

The sense of touch is an extremely important avenue of learning and communication for babies. Sensations of skin against skin appear to provide feelings of comfort and security that may contribute to the formation of affectionate bonds between infants and their caregivers.

Motor Development

Motor development provides some of the most fascinating changes in infants, in part because so much seems to happen so quickly—and so much of it during the first year. Children gain the capacity to move about through a sequence of activities that includes rolling over, sitting up, crawling, creeping, walking, and running. There is a great deal of variation in the ages at which infants first engage in these activities, but the sequence generally remains the same (see Figure 3.3). A number of children will skip a step, however. For example, an infant may creep without ever having crawled.

Let us now consider cognitive developments during childhood. Physical development is not possible without the participation of the brain, and the brain is also the seat of cognition.

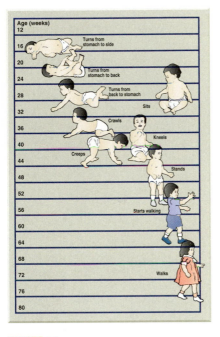

FIGURE 3.3
MOTOR DEVELOPMENT
AT BIRTH, INFANTS APPEAR TO BE BUNDLES OF AIMLESS "NERVOUS ENERGY." THEY HAVE REFLEXES BUT ALSO ENGAGE IN RANDOM MOVEMENTS THAT ARE REPLACED BY PURPOSEFUL ACTIVITY AS THEY MATURE. MOTOR DEVELOPMENT PROCEEDS IN AN ORDERLY SEQUENCE. PRACTICE PROMPTS SENSORIMOTOR COORDINATION, BUT MATURATION IS ESSENTIAL. THE TIMES IN THE FIGURE ARE APPROXIMATE: AN INFANT WHO IS A BIT BEHIND MAY DEVELOP WITH NO PROBLEMS AT ALL, AND A PRECOCIOUS INFANT WILL NOT NECESSARILY BECOME A ROCKET SCIENTIST (OR GYMNAST).

REFLECT

Why do you think that parents are so concerned about *when* their infants sit up or crawl or walk?

SECTION II Review

SECTION II Review

Infants usually double their birth weight in about (11: How many?) _____ months and triple it by the (12: Which?) birthday. Following the gains of infancy, children gain about (13: How many?) _____ to 3 inches a year and (14: How many?) _____ to 6 pounds a year until they reach the adolescent growth spurt.

Infants are born with a number of reflexes, which are (15) _____ typical responses elicited by specific stimuli. In the (16) _____ing reflex, infants turn their heads toward stimuli that touch the cheek. In the (17) _____ing reflex, infants suck objects that touch the lips. In the (18) s_____, or Moro reflex, infants arch their backs and draw up their legs in response to sudden noises and bumps. In the grasp, or (19) _____r reflex, infants grasp objects pressed against the palms of the hands. In the (20) B_____ reflex, they spread their toes when the soles of the feet are stimulated.

Infants are generally capable of depth perception, as measured by behavior on the visual cliff, by the time they are able to (21) c_____. Most newborns (22) _____xively turn their heads toward unusual sounds. Newborns prefer their (23) _____rs' voices to those of other women but do not show similar preferences for the voices of their fathers. The nasal and taste preferences of babies (24: Are or Are not?) similar to those of adults. Newborns are sensitive to touch but relatively insensitive to (25) p_____.

SECTION III. CHILDHOOD: COGNITIVE DEVELOPMENT

The ways in which children mentally represent and think about the world—that is, their *cognitive development*—are explored in this section. Because cognitive functioning develops over many years, young children have ideas about the world that differ considerably from those of adults. Many of these ideas are charming but illogical—at least to adults. Question: What are Jean Piaget's views of cognitive development?

Jean Piaget's Cognitive-Developmental Theory

The Swiss biologist and psychologist Jean Piaget contributed significantly to our understanding of children's cognitive development. He hypothesized that children's cognitive processes develop in an orderly sequence of stages. Although some children may be more advanced than others at particular ages, the developmental sequence remains the same. Piaget (1963) identified four major stages of cognitive development: sensorimotor, preoperational, concrete operational, and formal operational (see Table 3.1).

ASSIMILATION According to Piaget, the inclusion of a new event into an existing scheme.

SCHEME According to Piaget, a hypothetical mental structure that permits the classification and organization of new information.

REFLECT

Can you provide some examples of assimilation and accommodation in your own learning about psychology?

ASSIMILATION AND ACCOMMODATION Piaget described human thought, or intelligence, in terms of two basic concepts: assimilation and accommodation. **Assimilation** means responding to a new stimulus through a reflex or existing habit. Infants, for example, usually try to place new objects in their mouth to suck, feel, or explore. Piaget would say that the child is assimilating a new toy to the sucking scheme. A **scheme** is a pattern of action or a mental structure involved in acquiring or organizing knowledge.

TABLE 3.1	PIAGET'S STAGES OF COGNITIVE DEVELOPMENT	
Stage	**Approximate Age**	**Description**
Sensorimotor	Birth–2 years	At first, the child lacks language and does not use symbols or mental representations of objects. In time, reflexive responding ends and intentional behavior begins. The child develops the object concept and acquires the basics of language.
Preoperational	2–7 years	The child begins to represent the world mentally, but thought is egocentric. The child does not focus on two aspects of a situation at once and therefore lacks conservation. The child shows animism, artificialism, and objective responsibility for wrongdoing.
Concrete operational	7–12 years	The child develops conservation concepts, can adopt the viewpoint of others, can classify objects in series, and shows comprehension of basic relational concepts (such as one object being larger or heavier than another).
Formal operational	12 years and above	Mature, adult thought emerges. Thinking is characterized by deductive logic, consideration of various possibilities (mental trial and error), abstract thought, and the formation and testing of hypotheses.

Piaget regarded children as natural physicists who seek to learn about and control their world. In the Piagetian view, children who squish their food and laugh enthusiastically are often acting as budding scientists. In addition to enjoying the responses of their parents, they are studying the texture and consistency of their food. (Parents, of course, often wish their children would practice these experiments in the laboratory, not the dining room.)

Accommodation is the creation of new ways of responding to objects or looking at the world. In accommodation, children transform existing schemes—action patterns or ways of organizing knowledge—to incorporate new events. Children (and adults) accommodate to objects and situations that cannot be integrated into existing schemes. (For example, children who study biology learn that whales cannot be assimilated into the "fish" scheme. They accommodate by constructing new schemes, such as "mammals without legs that live in the sea.") The ability to accommodate to novel stimuli advances as a result of maturation and experience.

Most of the time, newborn children assimilate environmental stimuli according to reflexive schemes, although adjusting the mouth to contain the nipple is a primitive kind of accommodation. Reflexive behavior, to Piaget, is not "true" intelligence. True intelligence involves adapting to the world through a smooth, fluid balancing of the processes of assimilation and accommodation. Let us now apply these concepts to the stages of cognitive development.

THE SENSORIMOTOR STAGE The newborn infant is capable of assimilating novel stimuli only to existing reflexes (or ready-made schemes) such as the rooting and sucking reflexes. But by the time an infant reaches the age of 1 month, it already shows purposeful behavior by repeating behavior patterns that are pleasurable, such as sucking its hand. During the first month or so, an infant apparently does not connect stimuli perceived through different senses. Reflexive turning toward sources of auditory and olfactory stimulation cannot be considered purposeful searching. But within the first few months the infant begins to coordinate vision with grasping so that it looks at what it is holding or touching.

A 3- or 4-month-old infant may be fascinated by its own hands and legs. It may become absorbed in watching itself open and close its fists.

ACCOMMODATION According to Piaget, the modification of schemes so that information inconsistent with existing schemes can be integrated or understood.

The infant becomes increasingly interested in acting on the environment to make interesting results (such as the sound of a rattle) last longer or occur again. Behavior becomes increasingly intentional and purposeful. Between 4 and 8 months of age, the infant explores cause-and-effect relationships such as the thump that can be made by tossing an object or the way kicking can cause a hanging toy to bounce.

Prior to the age of 6 months or so, out of sight is literally out of mind. Objects are not yet represented mentally. For this reason, as you can see in Figure 3.4, a child makes no effort to search for an object that has been removed or placed behind a screen. By the age of 8 to 12 months, however, infants realize that objects removed from sight still exist and attempt to find them. In this way, they show what is known as **object permanence,** thereby making it possible to play peek-a-boo.

Between 1 and 2 years of age, children begin to show interest in how things are constructed. It may be for this reason that they persistently touch and finger their parents' faces and their own. Toward the end of the second year, children begin to engage in mental trial and error before they try out overt behaviors. For instance, when they look for an object you have removed, they will no longer begin their search in the last place they saw it. Rather, they may follow you, assuming you are carrying the object even though it is not visible. It is as though they are anticipating failure in searching for the object in the place where they last saw it.

Because the first stage of development is dominated by learning to coordinate perception of the self and of the environment with motor (muscular) activity, Piaget termed it the **sensorimotor stage.** This stage comes to a close with the acquisition of the basics of language at about age 2.

THE PREOPERATIONAL STAGE The **preoperational stage** is characterized by the use of words and symbols to represent objects and relationships among them. But be warned—any resemblance between the logic of children between the ages of 2 and 7 and your own logic very often is purely coincidental. Children may use the same words that adults do, but this does not mean their views of the world are similar to adults'. A major

OBJECT PERMANENCE Recognition that objects removed from sight still exist, as demonstrated in young children by continued pursuit.

SENSORIMOTOR STAGE The first of Piaget's stages of cognitive development, characterized by coordination of sensory information and motor activity, early exploration of the environment, and lack of language.

PREOPERATIONAL STAGE The second of Piaget's stages, characterized by illogical use of words and symbols, spotty logic, and egocentrism.

limit on preoperational children's thinking is that it tends to be one-dimensional—to focus on one aspect of a problem or situation at a time.

One consequence of one-dimensional thinking is **egocentrism.** Preoperational children cannot understand that other people do not see things the same way they do. When Allyn was 2½, I asked her to tell me about a trip to the store with her mother. "You tell me," she replied. Upon questioning, it seemed she did not understand that I could not see the world through her eyes.

To egocentric preoperational children, all the world's a stage that has been erected to meet their needs and amuse them. When asked, "Why does the sun shine?" they may say, "To keep me warm." If asked, "Why is the sky blue?" they may respond, "'Cause blue's my favorite color." Preoperational children also show **animism.** They attribute life and consciousness to physical objects like the sun and the moon. They also show **artificialism.** They believe that environmental events like rain and thunder are human inventions. Asked why the sky is blue, 4-year-olds may answer, "'Cause Mommy painted it." Examples of egocentrism, animism, and artificialism are shown in Table 3.2.

To gain further insight into preoperational thinking, consider these problems:

1. Imagine that you pour water from a tall, thin glass into a low, wide glass. Now, does the low, wide glass contain more, less, or the same amount of water that was in the tall, thin glass? I won't keep you in suspense. If you said the same amount of water (with possible minor exceptions for spillage and evaporation), you were correct. Now that you're on a roll, go on to the next problem.

2. If you flatten a ball of clay into a pancake, do you wind up with more, less, or the same amount of clay? If you said the same amount of clay, you are correct once more.

REFLECT

Can you think of examples of adults using egocentrism, animism, or artificialism in their own thinking? Why do you imagine that they do?

TABLE 3.2	EXAMPLES OF PREOPERATIONAL THOUGHT	
Type of Thought	**Sample Questions**	**Typical Answers**
Egocentrism	Why does it get dark out? Why does the sun shine? Why is there snow? Why is grass green? What are TV sets for?	So I can go to sleep. To keep me warm. For me to play in. Because that's my favorite color. To watch my favorite shows and cartoons.
Animism (attributing life and consciousness to physical objects)	Why do trees have leaves? Why do stars twinkle? Why does the sun move in the sky? Where do boats go at night?	To keep them warm. Because they're happy and cheerful. To follow children and hear what they say. They sleep like we do.
Artificialism (assuming that environmental events are human inventions)	What makes it rain? Why is the sky blue? What is the wind? What causes thunder? How does a baby get in Mommy's tummy?	Someone emptying a watering can. Somebody painted it. A man blowing. A man grumbling. Just make it first. (How?) You put some eyes on it, then put on the head.

EGOCENTRISM According to Piaget, assuming that others view the world as one does oneself.

ANIMISM The belief that inanimate objects move because of will or spirit.

ARTIFICIALISM The belief that natural objects have been created by human beings..

FIGURE 3.5

CONSERVATION

THE BOY IN THESE PHOTOGRAPHS AGREED THAT THE AMOUNT OF JUICE IN TWO IDENTICAL CONTAINERS IS EQUAL. HE THEN WATCHED AS JUICE FROM ONE CONTAINER WAS POURED INTO A TALL, THIN CONTAINER. IN THE MIDDLE PHOTOGRAPH, HE IS EXAMINING ONE OF THE ORIGINAL CONTAINERS AND THE NEW CONTAINER. WHEN ASKED WHETHER HE THINKS THE AMOUNTS OF JUICE IN THE TWO CONTAINERS ARE NOW THE SAME, HE SAYS NO. APPARENTLY, HE IS IMPRESSED BY THE HEIGHT OF THE NEW CONTAINER, AND, PRIOR TO THE DEVELOPMENT OF CONSERVATION, HE FOCUSES ON ONLY ONE DIMENSION OF THE SITUATION AT A TIME—IN THIS CASE, THE HEIGHT OF THE NEW CONTAINER.

REFLECT

Is reliance on objective responsibility limited to children? Can you think of situations in which adults you know have shown objective responsibility in their thinking?

To arrive at the correct answers to these questions, you must understand the law of **conservation.** This law holds that basic properties of substances such as mass, weight, and volume remain the same—that is, are *conserved*—when you change superficial properties such as their shape or arrangement.

Conservation requires the ability to think about, or **center** on, two aspects of a situation at once, such as height and width. Conserving the mass, weight, or volume of a substance requires the recognition that a change in one dimension can compensate for a change in another. But the preoperational boy in Figure 3.5 focuses on only one dimension at a time. First he is shown two glasses of juice and agrees that they contain the same amount of juice. Then, while he watches, juice is poured from one glass into a tall, thin glass. Now he is asked which glass contains more juice. After mulling over the problem, he points to the tall glass. Why? Because when he looks at the glasses he is "overwhelmed" by the fact that the thinner glass is taller. The preoperational child focuses on the most apparent dimension of the situation—in this case, the greater height of the thinner glass. He does not realize that the increased width of the squat glass compensates for the decreased height. By the way, if you ask him whether any juice has been added or taken away in the pouring process, he readily says no. But if you then repeat the question about which glass contains *more* juice, he again points to the taller glass.

If all this sounds rather illogical, that is because it is illogical—or, in Piaget's terms, preoperational.

After you have tried the experiment with the water, try the following. Make two rows of five pennies each. In the first row, place the pennies about half an inch apart. In the second row, place the pennies 2 to 3 inches apart. Ask a 4- to 5-year-old child which row has more pennies. What do you think the child will say? Why?

Piaget (1997) found that the moral judgment of preoperational children is also one-dimensional. Five-year-olds are slaves to rules and authority. When you ask them why something should be done in a certain way, they may insist, "Because that's the way to do it!" or, "Because my Mommy says so!" Right is right and wrong is wrong. Why? "Because!"—that's why.

According to most older children and adults, an act is a crime only when there is criminal intent. Accidents may be hurtful, but the perpetrators are usually seen as blameless. But in the court of the one-dimensional, preoperational child, there is **objective responsibility.** People are sentenced (and harshly!) on the basis of the amount of damage they have done, not their motives or intentions.

To demonstrate objective responsibility, Piaget would tell children stories and ask them which character was naughtier and why. John, for instance, accidentally breaks 15 cups when he opens a door. Henry breaks 1 cup when he sneaks into a kitchen cabinet to find forbidden jam. The preoperational child usually judges John to be naughtier. Why? Because he broke more cups.

THE CONCRETE-OPERATIONAL STAGE By about age 7, the typical child is entering the stage of **concrete operations.** In this stage, which lasts until about age 12, children show the beginnings of the capacity for adult logic. However, their logical thoughts, or *operations,* generally involve tangible objects rather than abstract ideas. Concrete operational children are capable of **decentration;** they can center on two dimensions of a problem at once. This attainment has implications for moral judgments, conservation, and other intellectual undertakings.

Children now become **subjective** in their moral judgments. When assigning guilt, they center on the motives of wrongdoers as well as on the amount of damage done. Concrete-operational children judge Henry more harshly than John because John's misdeed was an accident.

Concrete-operational children understand the laws of conservation. The boy in Figure 3.5, now a few years older, would say that the squat glass still contains the same amount of juice. If asked why, he might reply, "Because you can pour it back into the other one." Such an answer also suggests awareness of the concept of **reversibility**—the recognition that many processes can be reversed or undone so that things are restored to their previous condition. Centering simultaneously on the height and the width of the glasses, the boy recognizes that the loss in height compensates for the gain in width.

Concrete-operational children can conserve *number* as well as weight and mass. They recognize that the number of pennies in each of the rows described earlier is the same, even though one row may be spread out to look longer than the other.

Children in this stage are less egocentric. They are able to take on the roles of others and to view the world, and themselves, from other people's perspectives. They recognize that people see things in different ways because of different situations and different sets of values.

During the concrete-operational stage, children's own sets of values begin to emerge and acquire stability. Children come to understand that feelings of love between them and their parents can endure even when someone feels angry or disappointed at a particular moment.

We discuss the formal-operational stage and evaluate Piaget's theory in the section on adolescence.

Language Development

Language is the communication of thoughts and feelings through symbols that are arranged according to rules of grammar. Language makes it possible for one person to communicate knowledge to another and for one generation to record information for another. Language allows people to learn more than they could from direct experience. It enables parents to give children advice, which now and then they heed. Language also provides many of the basic units of thinking, which is at the core of cognition.

Question: How does language develop?

Piaget theorized that children's cognitive development follows a specific sequence of steps. Such sequencing also applies to language development, beginning with the *prelinguistic* vocalizations of crying, cooing, and babbling. These sounds are not symbols. That is, they do not represent objects or events. Therefore, they are *prelinguistic*, not linguistic.

As parents are well aware, newborn children have one inborn, highly effective form of verbal expression: crying—and more crying. During the second month, babies begin *cooing*. Babies use their tongues when they coo, so coos are more articulated than cries. Coos are often vowel-like and resemble "oohs" and "ahs." Cooing appears to be linked to feelings of pleasure. Babies do not coo when they are hungry, tired, or in pain. Parents soon learn that different cries and coos can indicate different things: hunger, gas pains, or pleasure at being held or rocked.

By the fifth or sixth month, children begin to *babble*. Babbling sort of sounds like speech. Children babble sounds that occur in many languages, including the throaty German *ch*, the clicks of certain African languages, and rolling *r*'s. In babbling, babies frequently combine consonants and

CONSERVATION According to Piaget, recognition that basic properties of substances such as weight and mass remain the same when superficial features change.

CENTER According to Piaget, to focus one's attention

OBJECTIVE RESPONSIBILITY According to Piaget, the assignment of blame according to the amount of damage done rather than the motives of the actor.

CONCRETE-OPERATIONAL STAGE Piaget's third stage, characterized by logical thought concerning tangible objects, conservation, and subjective morality.

DECENTRATION Simultaneous focusing on more than one dimension of a problem, so that flexible, reversible thought becomes possible.

SUBJECTIVE MORAL JUDGMENT According to Piaget, moral judgments that are based on the motives of the perpetrator.

REVERSIBILITY According to Piaget, recognition that processes can be undone, that things can be made as they were.

REFLECT

Some people have pets, like dogs, who communicate very clearly what they want at times. How do they do so without language?

vowels, as in "ba," "ga," and, sometimes, the much valued "dada." "Dada" at first is purely coincidental (sorry, dads), despite the family's delight over its appearance.

Babbling, like crying and cooing, is inborn. Children from cultures whose languages sound very different all seem to babble the same sounds, including many they could not have heard (Gleason & Ratner, 1993). But children single out the sounds used in the home within a few months. By the age of 9 or 10 months they repeat them regularly, and foreign sounds begin to drop out.

Babbling, like crying and cooing, is prelinguistic. Yet infants usually understand much of what others are saying well before they utter their first words. Understanding precedes the production of language, and infants show what they understand by their actions.

DEVELOPMENT OF VOCABULARY Ah, that long-awaited first word! What a thrill! What a milestone! Children tend to utter their first word at about 1 year of age, but many parents miss it, often because it is not pronounced clearly or because pronunciation varies from one usage to the next. *Ball* may be pronounced "ba," "bee," or even "pah." The majority of an infant's early words are names of things (Nelson et al., 1993).

The growth of vocabulary is slow at first. It may take children 3 to 4 months to achieve a 10-word vocabulary after they have spoken their first word (Nelson, 1973). By about 18 months, children are producing nearly two dozen words. Reading to children increases their vocabulary, so parents do well to stock up on story books (Arnold et al., 1994; Robbins & Ehri, 1994).

Children try to talk about more objects than they have words for. As a result, they often extend use of a word to refer to other things and actions for which they do not yet have words. This phenomenon is termed **overextension.** At some point, for example, many children refer to horses as *doggies*. At age 6, my daughter Allyn counted by tens as follows: sixty, seventy, eighty, ninety, *tenty*.

DEVELOPMENT OF GRAMMAR Children's first linguistic utterances are single words, but they may express complex meanings. When they do, they are called **holophrases.** For example, *mama* may be used by the child to signify meanings as varied as "There goes Mama," "Come here, Mama," and "You are my Mama." Similarly, *poo-cat* can signify "There is a pussycat," "That stuffed animal looks just like my pussycat," or "I want you to give me my pussycat right now!" Most children readily teach their parents what they intend by augmenting their holophrases with gestures, intonations, and reinforcers. That is, they act delighted when parents do as requested and howl when they do not.

Toward the end of the second year, children begin to speak two-word sentences. These sentences are termed *telegraphic speech* because they resemble telegrams. Telegrams cut out the "unnecessary" words. "Home Tuesday" might stand for "I expect to be home on Tuesday." Similarly, only essential words are used in children's telegraphic speech—in particular, nouns, verbs, and some modifiers. When a child says "That ball," the words *is* and *a* are implied.

Two-word utterances seem to appear at about the same time in the development of all languages (Slobin, 1983). Although two-word utterances are brief, they show understanding of grammar. The child says, "Sit chair" to tell a parent to sit in a chair, not "Chair sit." The child says, "My shoe," not "Shoe my," to show possession. "Mommy go" means Mommy is leav-

OVEREXTENSION Overgeneralizing the use of words to objects and situations to which they do not apply — a normal characteristic of the speech of young children.

HOLOPHRASE A single word used to express complex meanings.

ing. "Go Mommy" expresses the wish for Mommy to go away. (For this reason, "Go Mommy" is not heard often.)

There are different kinds of two-word utterances. Some, for example, contain nouns or pronouns and verbs ("Daddy sit"). Others contain verbs and objects ("Hit ball"). The sequence of emergence of the various kinds of two-word utterances is apparently the same in all languages—languages diverse as English, Luo (an African tongue), German, Russian, and Turkish (Slobin, 1983). The invariance of this sequence has implications for theories of language development, as we see later in the chapter.

Between the ages of 2 and 3, children's sentence structure usually expands to include the missing words in telegraphic speech. Children add articles (*a, an, the*), conjunctions (*and, but, or*), possessive and demonstrative adjectives (*your, her, that*), pronouns (*she, him, one*), and prepositions (*in, on, over, around, under,* and *through*) to their utterances. Their grasp of grammar is shown in linguistic oddities such as *your one* instead of simply *yours,* and *his one* instead of *his.*

OVERREGULARIZATION One intriguing language development is **overregularization.** To understand children's use of overregularization, consider the formation of the past tense and of plurals in English. We add *d* or *ed* to make the past tense of regular verbs and *s* or *z* sounds to make regular nouns plural. Thus, *walk* becomes *walked* and *look* becomes *looked. Pussycat* becomes *pussycats* and *doggy* becomes *doggies.* There are also irregular verbs and nouns. For example, *see* becomes *saw, sit* becomes *sat,* and *go* becomes *went. Sheep* remains *sheep* (plural) and *child* becomes *children.*

At first children learn a small number of these irregular verbs by imitating their parents. Two-year-olds tend to form them correctly—at first! Then they become aware of the grammatical rules for forming the past tense and plurals. As a result, they tend to make charming errors (Pinker, 1994). Some 3- to 5-year-olds, for example, are more likely to say "I seed it" than "I saw it" and to say "Mommy sitted down" than "Mommy sat down." They are likely to talk about the "gooses" and "sheeps" they "seed" on the farm and about all the "childs" they ran into at the playground. This tendency to regularize the irregular is what is meant by overregularization.

Some parents recognize that at one point their children were forming the past tense of irregular verbs correctly and that they later began to make errors. The thing to remember is that overregularization reflects knowledge of grammar, not faulty language development. In another year or two, *mouses* will be boringly transformed into *mice,* and Mommy will no longer have *sitted* down. Parents might as well enjoy overregularization while they can.

TOWARD MORE COMPLEX LANGUAGE As language develops beyond the third year, children show increasing facility in their use of pronouns (such as *it* and *she*) and prepositions (such as *in, before,* or *on*) that represent physical or temporal relationships among objects and events. Children's first questions are telegraphic and characterized by a rising pitch (which signifies a question mark) at the end. "More milky?" for example, can be translated into "May I have more milk?" or "Would you like more milk?" or "Is there more milk?"—depending on the context.

Wh questions usually appear after age 2. Consistent with the child's general cognitive development, certain *wh* questions (*what, who,* and *where*) appear earlier than others (*why, when, which,* and *how*) (Bloom

REFLECT

Can you think of examples of overextension or overregularization in your own experience?

OVERREGULARIZATION The application of regular grammatical rules for forming inflections (e.g., past tense and plurals) to irregular verbs and nouns.

et al., 1982). *Why* is usually too philosophical for the 2-year-old, and *how* is too involved. Two-year-olds are also likely to be now-oriented, so *when* is of less than immediate concern. By the fourth year, however, most children are asking *why, when,* and *how* questions—and frequently their parents despair as to how to answer them.

By the fourth year, children are also taking turns talking and engaging in lengthy conversations. By the age of 6, their vocabularies have expanded to 10,000 words, give or take a few thousand. By age 7 to 9, most children realize that words can have more than one meaning, and they are entertained by riddles and jokes that require some sophistication with language ("What's black and white, but read all over?").

Between the elementary school and high school years, language becomes still more complex, and vocabulary continues to grow rapidly. Vocabulary, in fact, can grow for a lifetime, especially in one's fields of specialization and interest.

Language Development and Human Diversity: Ebonics

The term *Ebonics* is derived from the words *ebony* and *phonics*. It was coined by the African American psychologist Robert Williams (Burnette, 1997). Ebonics was previously called Black English or Black Dialect (Pinker, 1994). Williams explains that a group of African American scholars convened "to name our language, which had always been named by White scholars in the past" (Burnette, 1997, p. 12).

According to linguists, Ebonics is rooted in the remnants of the West African dialects used by slaves. It reflects attempts by the slaves, who were denied formal education, to imitate the speech of the dominant White culture. Some observers believe that Ebonics uses verbs haphazardly, downgrading standard English. As a result, some school systems react to the concept of Ebonics with contempt—which is hurtful to the child who speaks Ebonics. Other observers say that Ebonics has different grammatical rules than standard English, but that the rules are consistent and allow for complex thought (Pinker, 1994). In 1996 the Oakland, California, school board recognized Ebonics as the primary language of African American students, just as Spanish had been recognized as the primary language of Hispanic American students. "I was honored," said Williams. "And truthfully, I was shocked. It was like the truth that had been covered up in the ground for so long just exploded one day" (Burnette, 1997, p. 12).

"TO BE OR NOT TO BE": USE OF VERBS IN EBONICS There are differences between Ebonics and standard English in the use of verbs. For example, the Ebonics usage "She-ah touch us" corresponds to the standard English "She will touch us." The Ebonics "He be gone" is the equivalent of the standard English "He has been gone for a long while." "He gone" is the same as "He is not here right now" in standard English.

Consider the rules in Ebonics that govern the use of the verb *to be*. In standard English, *be* is part of the infinitive form of the verb and is used to form the future tense, as in "I'll be angry tomorrow." Thus, "I *be* angry" is incorrect. But in Ebonics *be* refers to a continuing state of being. The Ebonics sentence "I be angry" is the same as the standard English "I have been angry for a while" and is grammatically correct.

Ebonics leaves out *to be* in cases in which standard English would use a contraction. For example, the standard "She's the one I'm talking about" could be "*She* the one *I* talking about" in Ebonics. Ebonics also often drops *ed* from the past tense and lacks the possessive *'s*.

REFLECT

How do you feel when people correct your English? Why?

"NOT TO BE OR NOT TO BE NOTHING": NEGATION IN EBONICS
Consider the sentence "I don't want no trouble," which is, of course, commendable. Middle-class White children would be corrected for using double negation (do*n't* along with *no*) and would be encouraged to say "I don't want *any* trouble." Yet double negation is acceptable in Ebonics (Pinker, 1994). Nevertheless, many teachers who use standard English have demeaned African American children who speak this way.

Some African American children are bicultural and bilingual. They function competently within the dominant culture in the United States and among groups of people from their own ethnic background. They use standard English in a conference with their teacher or in a job interview, but switch to Ebonics among their friends. Other children cannot switch back and forth. The decision by the Oakland school board was intended in part to help children maintain their self-esteem and stay in school.

Lawrence Kohlberg's Theory of Moral Development

Another aspect of cognitive development has to do with the ways in which people arrive at judgments of right or wrong. Question: How do children reason about what is right and wrong? Cognitive-developmental theorist Lawrence Kohlberg (1981) used the following tale in his research into children's moral reasoning. Before going on, why not read the tale yourself?

> In Europe a woman was near death from a special kind of cancer. There was one drug that the doctors thought might save her. It was a form of radium that a druggist in the same town had recently discovered. The drug was expensive to make, but the druggist was charging ten times what the drug cost him to make. He paid $200 for the radium and charged $2,000 for a small dose of the drug. The sick woman's husband, Heinz, went to everyone he knew to borrow the money, but he could only get together about $1,000, which was half of what it cost. He told the druggist that his wife was dying and asked him to sell it cheaper or let him pay later. But the druggist said: "No, I discovered the drug and I'm going to make money from it." So Heinz got desperate and broke into the man's store to steal the drug for his wife. (Kohlberg, 1969)

Heinz is caught in a moral dilemma in which a legal or social rule (in this case, the law forbidding stealing) is pitted against a strong human need (his desire to save his wife). According to Kohlberg's theory, children and adults arrive at yes or no answers for different reasons. These reasons can be classified according to the level of moral development they reflect.

As a stage theorist, Kohlberg argues that the stages of moral reasoning follow a specific sequence (see Table 3.3). Children progress at different rates, and not all children (or adults) reach the highest stage. But the sequence is always the same: Children must go through stage 1 before they enter stage 2, and so on. According to Kohlberg, there are three levels of moral development and two stages within each level.

When it comes to the dilemma of Heinz, Kohlberg believed that people could justify Heinz's stealing of the drug or his decision not to steal it by the reasoning of any level or stage of moral development. In other words, Kohlberg was not as interested in the eventual "yes" or "no" as he was in *how a person reasoned* to arrive at a yes or no answer.

REFLECT

What do you think? Should Heinz have tried to steal the drug? Was he right or wrong? Is the answer more complicated than a simple yes or no?

TABLE 3.3	KOHLBERG'S LEVELS AND STAGES OF MORAL DEVELOPMENT	
Stage of Development	**Examples of Moral Reasoning That Support Heinz's Stealing the Drug**	**Examples of Moral Reasoning That Oppose Heinz's Stealing the Drug**
LEVEL I: PRECONVENTIONAL		
STAGE 1: Judgments guided by obedience and the prospect of punishment (the consequences of the behavior).	It isn't wrong to take the drug. Heinz did try to pay the druggist for it, and it's only worth $200, not $2,000.	Taking things without paying is wrong because it's against the law. Heinz will get caught and go to jail.
STAGE 2: Naively, egoistic, instrumental orientation (Things are right when they satisfy people's needs.)	Heinz ought to take the drug because his wife really needs it. He can always pay the druggist back.	Heinz shouldn't take the drug. If he gets caught and winds up in jail, it won't do his wife any good.
LEVEL II: CONVENTIONAL		
STAGE 3: Good-boy orientation (Moral behavior helps others and is socially approved.)	Stealing is a crime, so it's bad, but Heinz should take the drug to save his wife or else people would blame him for letting her die.	Stealing is a crime. Heinz shouldn't just take the drug because his family will be dishonored and they will blame him.
STAGE 4: Law-and-order orientation (Moral behavior is doing one's duty and showing respect for authority.)	Heinz must take the drug to do his duty to save his wife. Eventually, he has to pay the druggist for it, however.	If everyone took the law into his own hands, civilization would fall apart, so Heinz shouldn't steal the drug.
LEVEL III: POSTCONVENTIONAL		
STAGE 5: Contractual, legalistic orientation (One must weigh pressing human needs against society's need to maintain social order.)	This thing is complicated because society has a right to maintain law and order, but Heinz has to take the drug to save his wife.	I can see why Heinz feels he has to take the drug, but laws exist for the benefit of society as a whole and can't simply be cast aside.
STAGE 6: Universal ethical principles orientation (People must follow universal ethical principles and their own conscience, even if it means breaking the law.)	In this case, the law comes into conflict with the principle of the sanctity of human life. Heinz must take the drug because his wife's life is more important than the law.	If Heinz truly believes that stealing the drug is worse than letting his wife die, he should not take it. People have to make sacrifices to do what they think is right.

THE PRECONVENTIONAL LEVEL The **preconventional level** applies to most children through about the age of 9. Children at this level base their moral judgments on the consequences of behavior. For instance, stage 1 is oriented toward obedience and punishment. Good behavior is obedient and allows one to avoid punishment. However, a child in stage 1 can decide that Heinz should or should not steal the drug, as shown in Table 3.3.

In stage 2, good behavior allows people to satisfy their needs and those of others. (Heinz's wife needs the drug; therefore, stealing the drug—the only way of obtaining it—is not wrong.)

THE CONVENTIONAL LEVEL In the **conventional level** of moral reasoning, right and wrong are judged by conformity to conventional (familial, religious, societal) standards of right and wrong. According to the stage 3 "good-boy orientation," moral behavior is that which meets the needs and expectations of others. Moral behavior is what is "normal"—what the majority does. (Heinz should steal the drug because that is what a "good husband" would do. It is "natural" or "normal" to try to help one's wife. *Or,* Heinz should *not* steal the drug because "good people do not steal.")

In stage 4, moral judgments are based on rules that maintain the social order. Showing respect for authority and doing one's duty are valued highly. (Heinz *must* steal the drug; it would be his fault if he let his wife

PRECONVENTIONAL LEVEL According to Kohlberg, a period during which moral judgments are based largely on expectation of rewards or punishments.

CONVENTIONAL LEVEL According to Kohlberg, a period during which moral judgments largely reflect social conventions. A "law and order" approach to morality.

die. He would pay the druggist later, when he had the money.) Many people do not mature beyond the conventional level.

THE POSTCONVENTIONAL LEVEL Postconventional moral reasoning is more complex and focuses on dilemmas in which individual needs are pitted against the need to maintain the social order and on personal conscience. We discuss the postconventional level of moral reasoning in the section on adolescence.

SECTION III Review

Piaget saw children as budding (26) _____ists who strive to understand the world. Piaget referred to action patterns and mental structures that are involved in acquiring or organizing knowledge as (27) _____mes. He saw intelligence as including the processes of (28) _____tion—that is, responding to events according to existing schemes, and (29) _____tion—that is, changing schemes to incorporate new events.

Piaget hypothesizes that there are (30: How many?) stages or periods of cognitive development. First is the (31) _____or period, which occurs prior to use of symbols and language. During the sensorimotor period, the child comes to mentally represent objects and thus develops object (32) per_____. Second is the (33) _____tional period, which is characterized by egocentrism, animism, artificialism, inability to (34) _____ter on more than one aspect of a problem at a time, and (35: Objective or Subjective?) moral judgments. Third is the (36) _____-operational period, which is characterized by conservation, reversibility, and (37: Objective or Subjective?) moral judgments. The fourth period is the (38) _____-operational period, which is characterized by capacity for abstract logic.

Children cry at birth and begin to (39) c_____ by about 2 months. Cooing appears associated with feelings of (40) _____sure. (41) _____ling is the first vocalization that has the sound of speech. Crying, cooing, and babbling are all (42) pre_____tic events.

Children speak their first words at about (43) _____. Children may talk about more objects than they have words for, so they often (44) over_____ the meanings of words. One-word utterances that have the meanings of complete sentences are called (45) _____ases. Two-word telegraphic utterances appear toward the end of the (46) _____ year. Children also use (47) over_____ations, as in "I seed it" and "Mommy sitted down." The "errors" made in overregularizing (48: Do or Do not?) indicate a grasp of grammar.

Kohlberg's theory focuses on (49) _____-al reasoning. Kohlberg hypothesizes that moral reasoning develops through (50: How many?) _____ "levels" and two stages within each level. In the (51) _____tional level, judgments are based on expectation of rewards or punishments. Stage 1 is oriented toward obedience and (52) _____ment. In stage 2, "good" behavior allows people to satisfy their (53) _____ds. Conventional-level moral judgments reflect the need to conform to conventional standards of right or wrong. According to the stage 3 (54) "_____ orientation," it is good to meet the needs and expectations of others. In stage 4, moral judgments are based on rules that maintain the (55) _____ order.

SECTION IV. CHILDHOOD: SOCIAL AND PERSONALITY DEVELOPMENT

Social relationships are crucial to us as children. When we are infants, our very survival depends on them. Later in life, they contribute to our feelings of happiness and satisfaction. In this section we discuss many aspects of social development, including Erikson's theory of psychosocial development, attachment, styles of parenting, and the effects of day care and child abuse.

Erik Erikson's Stages of Psychosocial Development

According to Erik Erikson, we undergo several stages of psychosocial development (see Table 3.4). Question: What are Erikson's stages of psychosocial development? During Erikson's first stage, **trust versus mistrust,** we depend on our primary caregivers (usually our parents) and come to expect that our environments will—or will not—meet our needs. During early childhood and the preschool years, we begin to explore the environment more actively and try new things. At this time, our relationships with our parents and friends can encourage us to develop either **autonomy** (self-direction) and initiative, or feelings of shame and guilt. During the elementary school years, friends and teachers take on more importance, encouraging us to become industrious or to develop feelings of inferiority.

Attachment: Ties That Bind

At the age of 2, my daughter Allyn almost succeeded in preventing me from finishing a book. When I locked myself into my study, she positioned herself outside the door and called, "Daddy, oh Daddy." At other times, she would bang on the door or cry outside. When I would give in (several

TRUST VERSUS MISTRUST Erikson's first stage of psychosexual development, during which children do — or do not — come to trust that primary caregivers and the environment will meet their needs.

AUTONOMY Self-direction.

TABLE 3.4	ERIKSON'S STAGES OF PSYCHOSOCIAL DEVELOPMENT	
Time Period	**Life Crisis**	**The Developmental Task**
Infancy (0–1)	Trust versus mistrust	Coming to trust the mother and the environment—to associate surroundings with feelings of inner goodness
Early childhood (1–3)	Autonomy versus shame and doubt	Developing the wish to make choices and the self-control to exercise choice
Preschool years (4–5)	Initiative versus guilt	Adding planning and "attacking" to choice, becoming active and on the move
Elementary school years (6–12)	Industry versus inferiority	Becoming eagerly absorbed in skills, tasks, and productivity; mastering the fundamentals of technology
Adolescence	Identity versus role diffusion	Connecting skills and social roles to formation of career objectives; developing a sense of who one is and what one stands for
Young adulthood	Intimacy versus isolation	Committing the self to another; engaging in sexual love
Middle adulthood	Generativity versus stagnation	Needing to be needed; guiding and encouraging the younger generation; being creative
Late adulthood	Integrity versus despair	Accepting the time and place of one's life cycle; achieving wisdom and dignity

Source: Erikson, 1963, pp. 247–269.

times a day) and open the door, she would run in and say, "I want you to pick up me" and hold out her arms or climb into my lap. Although we were separate human beings, it was as though she were very much *attached* to me. Questions: How do feelings of attachment develop? What kinds of experiences affect attachment?

Psychologist Mary D. Salter Ainsworth defines **attachment** as an emotional tie that is formed between one animal or person and another specific individual. Attachment keeps organisms together—it is vital to the survival of the infant—and it tends to endure.

The behaviors that define attachment include (1) attempts to maintain contact or nearness and (2) shows of anxiety when separated. Babies and children try to maintain contact with caregivers to whom they are attached. They engage in eye contact, pull and tug at them, ask to be picked up, and may even jump in front of them in such a way that they will be "run over" if they are not picked up!

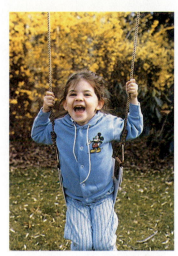

Allyn. At the age of 2 the author's daughter Allyn nearly succeeded in preventing the publication of a book by continually pulling him away from the computer when he was at work. Because of their mutual attachment, separation was painful.

THE STRANGE SITUATION AND PATTERNS OF ATTACHMENT

The ways in which infants behave in strange situations are connected with their bonds of attachment with their caregivers. Given this fact, Ainsworth and her colleagues (1978) innovated the *strange situation method* to measure attachment in infants. The method involves a series of separations and reunions with a caregiver (usually the mother) and a stranger. Infants are led through episodes involving the mother and a stranger in a laboratory room. For example, the mother carries the infant into the room and puts him or her down. A stranger enters and talks with the mother. The stranger then approaches the infant with a toy and the mother leaves the room. The mother and stranger take turns interacting with the infant in the room, and the infant's behavior is observed in each case.

Using the strange situation, Ainsworth and her colleagues (1978) identified three major types of attachment—secure attachment and two types of insecure attachment:

1. *Secure attachment.* Securely attached infants mildly protest their mother's departure, seek interaction upon reunion, and are readily comforted by her.

2. *Avoidant attachment.* Infants who show avoidant attachment are least distressed by their mother's departure. They play by themselves without fuss and ignore their mothers when they return.

3. *Ambivalent/resistant attachment.* Infants with ambivalent/resistant attachment are the most emotional. They show severe signs of distress when their mother leaves and show ambivalence upon reunion by alternately clinging to and pushing their mother away when she returns.

Attachment is connected with the quality of care that infants receive. The parents of securely attached children are more likely to be affectionate and reliable caregivers (Cox et al., 1992; Isabella, 1993). A wealth of research literature speaks of the benefits of secure attachment. For example, securely attached children are happier, more sociable, and more cooperative than insecurely attached children (Belsky et al., 1991; Thompson, 1991a). Securely attached preschoolers have longer attention spans, are less impulsive, and are better at solving problems (Frankel & Bates, 1990; Lederberg & Mobley, 1990). At ages 5 and 6, securely attached children are liked better by their peers and teachers, are more competent, and have fewer behavior problems than insecurely attached children (Lyons-Ruth et al., 1993; Youngblade & Belsky, 1992).

ATTACHMENT The enduring affectional tie that binds one person to another.

Yet some research questions whether infant attachment as measured by means of the strange situation predicts adjustment later on. For example, Michael Lewis (1997) located 84 high school seniors who had been evaluated by the strange situation method at age 1. Extensive interviews showed that of the 49 who had been considered securely attached at age 1, 43% were currently maladjusted. Of the 35 who had been considered insecurely attached in infancy, only 26% were rated as currently maladjusted. Lewis (1998) suggests that childhood events such as accidents, parental divorce, and illness can be more powerful influences on adolescents' security than the quality of parenting during the first year. But most developmental psychologists continue to endorse the strange situation as a predictor of adjustment later in life (Blakeslee, 1998). For example, Alan Sroufe (1998) found that insecure attachment at the age of 1 year predicted psychological disorders at the age of 17.

INDISCRIMINATE ATTACHMENT Showing attachment behaviors toward any person.

INITIAL-PREATTACHMENT PHASE The first phase in forming bonds of attachment, characterized by indiscriminate attachment.

ATTACHMENT-IN-THE-MAKING PHASE The second phase in forming bonds of attachment, characterized by preference for familiar figures.

CLEAR-CUT-ATTACHMENT PHASE The third phase in forming bonds of attachment, characterized by intensified dependence on the primary caregiver.

CONTACT COMFORT A hypothesized primary drive to seek physical comfort through contact with another.

CRITICAL PERIOD A period of time when an instinctive response can be elicited by a particular stimulus.

IMPRINTING A process occurring during a critical period in the development of an organism, in which that organism responds to a stimulus in a manner that will afterward be difficult to modify.

REFLECT

Have you had experience with a child who showed fear of strangers? How did he or she act in their presence?

STAGES OF ATTACHMENT Ainsworth also studied phases in the development of attachment. She and her colleagues observed infants in many societies, including the African country of Uganda. She noted the efforts of infants to maintain contact with the mother, their protests when separated from her, and their use of her as a base for exploring their environment. At first, infants show **indiscriminate attachment.** That is, they prefer being held or being with someone to being alone, but they show no preferences for particular people. Specific attachment to the mother begins to develop at about 4 months of age and becomes intense by about 7 months of age. Fear of strangers, which develops in some but not all children, follows 1 or 2 months later.

From studies such as these, Ainsworth identified three stages of attachment:

1. The **initial-preattachment phase,** which lasts from birth to about 3 months and is characterized by indiscriminate attachment
2. The **attachment-in-the-making phase,** which occurs at about 3 or 4 months and is characterized by preference for familiar figures
3. The **clear-cut-attachment phase,** which occurs at about 6 or 7 months and is characterized by intensified dependence on the primary caregiver

John Bowlby (1988), a colleague of Mary Ainsworth, believes that attachment is also characterized by fear of strangers ("stranger anxiety"). That is, at about 8 to 10 months of age, children may cry and cling to their parents when strangers try to befriend them. But not all children develop fear of strangers. It therefore does not seem necessary to include fear of strangers as an essential part of the process of attachment.

THEORETICAL VIEWS OF ATTACHMENT Early in the century, behaviorists argued that attachment behaviors are learned through experience. Caregivers feed their infants and tend to their other physiological needs. Thus, infants associate their caregivers with gratification of needs and learn to approach them to meet their needs. The feelings of gratification associated with the meeting of basic needs generalize into feelings of security when the caregiver is present.

Classic research by psychologist Harry F. Harlow suggests that skin contact may be more important than learning experiences. Harlow noted that infant rhesus monkeys reared without mothers or companions became attached to pieces of cloth in their cages. They maintained contact

FIGURE 3.6

ATTACHMENT IN INFANT MONKEYS

ALTHOUGH THIS RHESUS MONKEY INFANT IS FED BY THE WIRE "MOTHER," IT SPENDS MOST OF ITS TIME CLINGING TO THE SOFT, CUDDLY TERRYCLOTH "MOTHER." IT KNOWS WHERE TO GET A MEAL, BUT CONTACT COMFORT IS APPARENTLY MORE IMPORTANT THAN FOOD IN THE DEVELOPMENT OF ATTACHMENT IN INFANT MONKEYS (AND INFANT HUMANS?).

with them and showed distress when separated from them. Harlow conducted a series of experiments to find out why (Harlow, 1959).

In one study, Harlow placed infant rhesus monkeys in cages with two surrogate mothers, as shown in Figure 3.6. One "mother" was made of wire mesh from which a baby bottle was extended. The other surrogate mother was made of soft, cuddly terrycloth. The infant monkeys spent most of their time clinging to the cloth mother, even though "she" did not gratify their need for food. Harlow concluded that monkeys—and perhaps humans—have an inborn need for **contact comfort** that is as basic as the need for food. Gratification of the need for contact comfort, rather than food, might be why infant monkeys (and humans) cling to their mothers.

✓ Truth or Fiction Revisited

It is not true that the way to a baby's heart is through its stomach. Babies do not necessarily become attached to the people who feed them. Contact comfort may be a stronger wellspring of attachment. The path to a baby's heart may lie through its skin, not its stomach.

Harlow and Zimmerman (1959) found that a surrogate mother made of terrycloth could also serve as a comforting base from which an infant monkey could explore its environment. Toys such as stuffed bears (see Figure 3.7) and oversized wooden insects were placed in cages with infant rhesus monkeys and their surrogate mothers. When the infants were alone or had wire surrogate mothers for companions, they cowered in fear as long as the "bear monster" or "insect monster" was present. But when the terrycloth mothers were present, the infants clung to them for a while and then explored the intruding "monster." With human infants, too, the bonds of mother–infant attachment appear to provide a secure base from which infants feel encouraged to express their curiosity.

Other researchers, such as ethologist Konrad Lorenz, note that for many animals, attachment is an instinct—inborn. Attachment, like other instincts, is theorized to occur in the presence of a specific stimulus and during a **critical period** of life—that is, a period during which the animal is sensitive to the stimulus.

Some animals become attached to the first moving object they encounter. The unwritten rule seems to be, "If it moves, it must be Mother." It is as if the image of the moving object becomes "imprinted" on the young animal. The formation of an attachment in this manner is therefore called **imprinting.**

FIGURE 3.7

SECURITY

WITH ITS TERRYCLOTH SURROGATE MOTHER NEARBY, THIS INFANT RHESUS MONKEY APPARENTLY FEELS SECURE ENOUGH TO EXPLORE THE "BEAR MONSTER" PLACED IN ITS CAGE. BUT INFANTS WITH WIRE SURROGATE MOTHERS OR NO MOTHERS AT ALL COWER IN A CORNER WHEN SUCH "MONSTERS" ARE INTRODUCED.

FIGURE 3.8
IMPRINTING

QUITE A FOLLOWING? KONRAD LORENZ MAY NOT LOOK LIKE MOMMY TO YOU, BUT THESE GOSLINGS BECAME ATTACHED TO HIM BECAUSE HE WAS THE FIRST MOVING OBJECT THEY PERCEIVED AND FOLLOWED. THIS TYPE OF ATTACHMENT PROCESS IS REFERRED TO AS *IMPRINTING*.

Lorenz (1981) became well known when pictures of his "family" of goslings were made public (see Figure 3.8). How did Lorenz acquire his following? He was present when the goslings hatched and during their critical period, and he allowed them to follow him. The critical period for geese and some other animals is bounded, at the younger end, by the age at which they first walk and, at the older end, by the age at which they develop fear of strangers. The goslings followed Lorenz persistently, ran to him when they were frightened, honked with distress at his departure, and tried to overcome barriers between them. If you substitute crying for honking, it all sounds rather human.

Ainsworth and Bowlby (1991) consider attachment to be instinctive in humans. However, the process would not be quite the same as with ducks and geese. The upper limit for waterbirds is the age at which they develop fear of strangers, but not all children develop this fear. When children do develop fear of strangers, they do so at about 6 to 8 months of age—*prior to* independent locomotion, or crawling, which usually occurs 1 or 2 months later. Moreover, the critical period with humans would be quite extended.

Another issue in social and personality development is parenting styles. Parental behavior contributes not only to the development of attachment, but also to the development of self-esteem, self-reliance, achievement motivation, and competence.

Parenting Styles

Many psychologists have been concerned about the relationships between parenting styles and the personality development of the child. Question: What types of parental behavior are connected with variables such as self-esteem, achievement motivation, and independence in children? Diana Baumrind and her colleagues (1973; Lamb & Baumrind, 1978) have been particularly interested in the connections between parental behavior and the development of **instrumental competence** in their children. (*Instrumental competence* refers to the ability to manipulate the environment to achieve one's goals.) Baumrind has largely focused on four aspects of parental behavior: (1) strictness; (2) demands for the child to achieve intellectual, emotional, and social maturity; (3) communication ability; and (4) warmth and involvement. She labeled the three most important parenting styles the *authoritative, authoritarian,* and *permissive* styles.

1. *Authoritative parents.* The parents of the most competent children rate high in all four areas of behavior (see Table 3.5). They are strict (restrictive) and demand mature behavior. However, they temper their strictness and demands with willingness to reason with their children, and with love and support. They expect a lot, but they explain why and offer help. Baumrind labeled these parents **authoritative parents** to suggest that they know what they want but are also loving and respectful of their children.

2. *Authoritarian parents.* **Authoritarian parents** view obedience as a virtue to be pursued for its own sake. They have strict guidelines about what is right and wrong, and they demand that their children adhere to those guidelines. Both authoritative and authoritarian parents adhere to strict standards of conduct. However, authoritative parents explain their demands and are supportive, whereas authoritarian parents rely on force and communicate poorly with their children. Authoritarian parents do not respect their children's points of

INSTRUMENTAL COMPETENCE Ability to manipulate one's environment to achieve one's goals.

AUTHORITATIVE PARENTS Parents who are strict and warm. Authoritative parents demand mature behavior but use reason rather than force in discipline.

AUTHORITARIAN PARENTS Parents who are rigid in their rules and who demand obedience for the sake of obedience.

TABLE 3.5	PARENTING STYLES			
	PARENTAL BEHAVIOR			
Style of Parenting	**Restrictiveness**	**Demands for Mature Behavior**	**Communication Ability**	**Warmth and Support**
Authoritative	High (use of reasoning)	High	High	High
Authoritarian	High (use of force)	Moderate	Low	Low
Permissive	Low (easygoing)	Low	Low	High

Note: According to Baumrind, the children of authoritative parents are most competent. The children of permissive parents are the least mature.

view, and they may be cold and rejecting. When their children ask them why they should behave in a certain way, authoritarian parents often answer, "Because I say so!"

3. *Permissive parents.* **Permissive parents** are generally easygoing with their children. As a result, the children do pretty much whatever they wish. Permissive parents are warm and supportive, but poor at communicating.

Research evidence shows that warmth is superior to coldness in rearing children. Children of warm parents are more likely to be socially and emotionally well-adjusted and to internalize moral standards—that is, to develop a conscience (MacDonald, 1992; Miller et al., 1993).

Strictness also appears to pay off, provided it is tempered with reason and warmth. Children of authoritative parents have greater self-reliance, self-esteem, social competence, and achievement motivation than other children (Baumrind, 1991; Putallaz & Hefflin, 1990). Children of authori*tarian* parents are often withdrawn or aggressive, and they usually do not do as well in school as children of authoritative parents (Olson et al., 1992; Westerman, 1990). Children of permissive parents seem to be the least mature. They are frequently impulsive, moody, and aggressive. In adolescence, lack of parental monitoring is often linked to delinquency and poor academic performance.

✓ Truth or Fiction Revisited

It is true that children with strict parents are most likely to be successful. This is especially so when the parents also reason with their children and are loving and supportive.

Let us now consider two other important areas that involve the connections between parental behavior and the social and personality development of children. The first of these, day care, considers what happens to young children's social and personality development when they spend their days in the care of people *other than* family members. The second of these, child abuse, considers the causes of child abuse and its effects on the development of the child.

Day Care

As we cross over into the new millennium, only a small percentage of U.S. families fit the traditional model in which the husband is the breadwinner

REFLECT

Would you characterize your parents as having been warm or cold, restrictive or permissive? In what ways? How did the parenting style you experienced affect your feelings and behavior?

PERMISSIVE PARENTS Parents who impose few, if any, rules and who do not supervise their children closely.

REFLECT

Have you or your parents made use of day care services? How did the experience work out? Why?

and the wife is a full-time homemaker. Most mothers, including more than half of mothers of children younger than 1 year of age, work outside the home (U.S. Bureau of the Census, 1998). As a consequence, millions of American preschoolers are placed in day care. Parents and psychologists are concerned about what happens to children in day care. What, for example, are the effects of day care on cognitive development and social development?

In part, the answer depends on the quality of the day care center. A large-scale study funded by the National Institute on Child Health and Human Development found that children in high-quality day care—for example, children who have learning resources, a low children-to-caregiver ratio, and individual attention—did as well on cognitive and language tests as children who remained in the home with their mother (Azar, 1997). Children whose day care providers spent time talking to them and asking them questions also achieved the highest scores on tests of cognitive and language ability. A Swedish study found that children in high-quality day care outperformed children who remained in the home on tests of math and language skills (Broberg et al., 1997).

Studies of the effects of day care on parent–child attachment yield mixed results. Children in full-time day care show less distress when their mothers leave them and are less likely to seek out their mothers when they return. Some psychologists suggest that this distancing from the mother could signify insecure (avoidant) attachment (Belsky, 1990). Others suggest, however, that the children are adapting to repeated separations from, and reunions with, their mother (Field, 1991; Lamb et al., 1992; Thompson, 1991b).

Day care seems to have both positive and negative influences on children's social development. First, the positive: Children in day care are more likely to share their toys and be independent, self-confident, and outgoing (Clarke-Stewart, 1991; Field, 1991). However, some studies have found that children in day care are less compliant and more aggressive than are other children (Vandell & Corasaniti, 1990). Perhaps some children in day care do not receive the individual attention or resources they need. When placed in a competitive situation, they become more aggressive in an attempt to meet their needs. Clarke-Stewart (1990), however, interprets the

Day Care.   Because most parents in the United States are in the workforce, day care is a major influence on the lives of millions of children.

greater noncompliance and aggressiveness of children placed in day care as signs of greater independence rather than social maladjustment.

✓ Truth or Fiction Revisited

It is true that children placed in day care are more aggressive than children cared for in the home. Perhaps they are so because they have become more independent.

Child Abuse

Nearly 3 million children in the United States are neglected or abused by their parents or other caregivers each year (Fein, 1998). More than half a million of these suffer serious injuries. Nearly 1,000 die (Fein, 1998).

Many factors contribute to child abuse: stress, a history of child abuse in at least one of the parents' families of origin, acceptance of violence as a way of coping with stress, failure to become attached to the children, substance abuse, and rigid attitudes toward child rearing (Belsky, 1993; Kaplan, 1991). Unemployment and low socioeconomic status are common stressors that lead to abuse (Lewin, 1995; Trickett et al., 1991).

Children who are abused are quite likely to develop personal and social problems and psychological disorders. They are less likely than other children to venture out to explore the world (Aber & Allen, 1987). They are more likely to have psychological problems such as anxiety, depression, and low self-esteem (Wagner, 1997). They are less likely to be intimate with their peers and more likely to be aggressive (DeAngelis, 1997; Parker & Herrera, 1996; Rothbart & Ahadi, 1994). As adults, they are more likely to be violent toward their dates and spouses (Malinosky-Rummell & Hansen, 1993).

Child abuse runs in families to some degree (Simons et al., 1991). That is, child abusers are more likely to have been abused than is true for the general population. Even so, *the majority of children who are abused do not abuse their own children as adults* (Kaufman & Zigler, 1989).

Why does abuse run in families? There are several hypotheses (Belsky, 1993). One is that parents serve as role models. According to Murray Strauss (1995), "Spanking teaches kids that when someone is doing something you don't like and they won't stop doing it, you hit them." Another is that children adopt parents' strict philosophies about discipline. Exposure to violence in their own home leads some children to view abuse as normal. A third is that being abused can create feelings of hostility that are then expressed against others, including one's own children.

REFLECT

Do you know anyone who was abused as a child? Do you think that the person has been affected by the experience? How?

✓ Truth or Fiction Revisited

It is true that child abusers have frequently been abused as children. However, the majority of victims of abuse do not abuse their own children.

The years of childhood may seem to pass rapidly, but a great deal occurs during them in terms of physical, cognitive, and social and personality development. Following childhood is the period of adolescence, which is for many a period of passage to adulthood. For many adolescents, and for their parents, the goals of adolescence and the behaviors deemed acceptable loom as huge question marks. Because of these questions, psychologists have focused a great deal of attention on adolescence, as we see next.

Erik Erikson presents a(n) (56: How many?) stage theory of psychosocial development. Each stage centers around a life (57) _____. During the first stage, trust versus (58) _____, we depend on our primary caregivers and come to expect that our environments will—or will not—meet our needs.

Ainsworth defines attachment as an (59) _____tional tie that binds organisms together. She developed the (60) _____ situation method to study attachment. There are three major types of attachment: (61) _____, avoidant, and (62) ambivalent/re_____. The caregivers of (63) _____ly attached children are likely to be affectionate and reliable.

Ainsworth identified three stages of attachment: The (64) _____-_____chment phase lasts from birth to about 3 months and is characterized by indiscriminate attachment. The (65) attachment-in-the-_____ing phase occurs at about 3 or 4 months and is characterized by preference for familiar figures. The (66) c_____-cut-attachment phase occurs at 6 or 7 months and is characterized by greater dependence on the primary caregiver. Bowlby finds a role for (67) _____ of strangers in the development of attachment.

Behaviorists argue that children become attached to mothers through (68) _____ning, because their mothers feed them and attend to other basic needs. The Harlow studies with monkeys suggest that (69) _____ comfort is more important than conditioning in the development of attachment. Harlow's infant monkeys spent more time on soft terrycloth (70) _____gate "mothers" than on wire "mothers," even when their feeding bottles protruded from the wire mothers. Ethologists argue that attachment is an (71) in_____ that occurs during a (72) c_____ period. During this critical period, young animals such as ducks and geese become (73) _____ted on the first moving objects they encounter. Attachment in these animals is bounded at the early end by the age at which they first engage in (74) _____otion and, at the upper end, by the development of (75) _____ of strangers.

Baumrind and her colleagues have studied the connections between parental behavior and (76) _____tal competence in children. Baumrind has focused on four aspects of parental behavior: (77) _____ness, demands for maturity, communication ability, and warmth and involvement. She labeled the three most important parenting styles (78) _____tative, authoritarian, and permissive. Authoritative parents are strict and (79: Warm or Cold?).

Children in day care are (80: More or Less?) independent and (81: More or Less?) aggressive than children reared in the home. Much of the effects of day care has to do with the (82) _____ity of the day care center.

Stressors that are commonly connected with child abuse include (83) _____ment. Children who are abused are (84: More or Less?) likely to be adventuresome. Child abusers are (85: More or Less?) likely than other parents to have been abused themselves.

SECTION V. ADOLESCENCE: PHYSICAL DEVELOPMENT

Adolescence is a time of transition from childhood to adulthood. In our society, adolescents often feel that they are "neither fish nor fowl," as the saying goes—neither children nor adults. Although adolescents may be old enough to have children and are as large as their parents, they are often treated quite differently than adults. They may not be eligible for a driver's license until they are 16 or 17. They cannot attend R-rated films unless they are accompanied by an adult. They are prevented from working long hours. They are usually required to remain in school through age 16 and may not marry until they reach the "age of consent." Let us consider the physical, cognitive, and social and personality changes of adolescence.

Following infancy, children grow about 2 to 3 inches a year. Weight gains also remain fairly even at about 4 to 6 pounds per year. Question:

ADOLESCENCE The period of life bounded by puberty and the assumption of adult responsibilities.

What physical developments occur during adolescence? One of the most noticeable physical developments of adolescence is a growth spurt. The adolescent growth spurt lasts for 2 to 3 years and ends the stable patterns of growth in height and weight that characterize most of childhood. Within this short span of years, adolescents grow some 8 to 12 inches. Most boys wind up taller and heavier than most girls.

In boys, the weight of the muscle mass increases notably. The width of the shoulders and circumference of the chest also increase. Adolescents may eat enormous quantities of food to fuel their growth spurt. Adults fighting the "battle of the bulge" stare at them in wonder as they wolf down french fries and shakes at the fast-food counter and later go out for pizza.

Puberty

Puberty is the period during which the body becomes sexually mature. It heralds the onset of adolescence. Puberty begins with the appearance of **secondary sex characteristics** such as body hair, deepening of the voice in males, and rounding of the breasts and hips in females. In boys, pituitary hormones stimulate the testes to increase the output of testosterone, which in turn causes enlargement of the penis and testes and the appearance of bodily hair. By the early teens, erections become common, and boys may ejaculate. Ejaculatory ability usually precedes the presence of mature sperm by at least a year. Ejaculation thus is not evidence of reproductive capacity.

In girls, a critical body weight in the neighborhood of 100 pounds is thought to trigger a cascade of hormonal secretions in the brain that cause the ovaries to secrete higher levels of the female sex hormone, estrogen (Frisch, 1997). Estrogen stimulates the growth of breast tissue and fatty and supportive tissue in the hips and buttocks. Thus the pelvis widens, rounding the hips. Small amounts of androgens produced by the adrenal glands, along with estrogen, spur the growth of pubic and underarm hair. Estrogen and androgens together stimulate the development of female sex organs. Estrogen production becomes cyclical during puberty and regulates the menstrual cycle. The beginning of menstruation, or **menarche,** usually occurs between the ages of 11 and 14. Girls cannot become pregnant until they begin to ovulate, however, and this may occur as much as two years after menarche.

✔ Truth or Fiction Revisited

It is not usually true that girls are capable of becoming pregnant when they have their first menstrual period. Menarche can precede ovulation by a year or more.

REFLECT

Did you undergo puberty early or late compared with your peers? How did your experience with puberty affect your popularity and your self-esteem?

PUBERTY The period of physical development during which sexual reproduction first becomes possible.

SECONDARY SEX CHARACTERISTICS Characteristics that distinguish the sexes, such as distribution of body hair and depth of voice, but that are not directly involved in reproduction.

MENARCHE The beginning of menstruation.

Review

SECTION V

During adolescence a growth (86) sp_____ occurs. Puberty begins with the appearance of (87) _____ary sex characteristics, such as the growth of bodily hair, deepening of the voice in males, and rounding of the breasts and hips in females. The changes of puberty are stimulated by (88) _____rone in the male and by estrogen and androgens in the female. (89) _____gen regulates the menstrual cycle. First menstruation is termed (90) _____che.

Jean Piaget

SECTION VI. ADOLESCENCE: COGNITIVE DEVELOPMENT

I am a college student of extremely modest means. Some crazy psychologist interested in something called "formal operational thought" has just promised to pay me $20 if I can make a coherent logical argument for the proposition that the federal government should under no circumstances ever give or lend more to needy college students. Now what could people who believe *that* possibly say by way of supporting argument? Well, I suppose they *could* offer this line of reasoning . . . (Adapted from Flavell et al., 1993, p. 140)

The adolescent thinker approaches problems very differently from the elementary school child. Question: What cognitive developments occur during adolescence? Let us begin to answer this question by comparing the child's thought processes to that of the adolescent. The child sticks to the facts, to concrete reality. Speculating about abstract possibilities and what might be is very difficult. The adolescent, on the other hand, is able to deal with the abstract and the hypothetical. As shown in the above example, adolescents realize that one does not have to believe in the truth or justice of something in order to argue for it (Flavell et al., 1993). In this section we explore some of the cognitive developments of adolescence by referring to the theories of Jean Piaget and Lawrence Kohlberg.

The Formal Operational Stage

According to Piaget, children typically undergo three stages of cognitive development prior to adolescence: sensorimotor, preoperational, and concrete operational. They develop from infants who respond automatically to their environment to older children who can focus on various aspects of a situation at once and solve complex problems. The stage of **formal operations** is the final stage in Jean Piaget's theory of cognitive development, and it represents cognitive maturity. For many children in Western societies, formal operational thought begins at about the beginning of adolescence—the age of 11 or 12. However, not all individuals enter this stage at this time, and some individuals never reach it.

The major achievements of the stage of formal operations involve classification, logical thought, and the ability to hypothesize. Central features are the ability to think about ideas as well as objects and to group and classify ideas—symbols, statements, entire theories. The flexibility and reversibility of operations, when applied to statements and theories, allow adolescents to follow arguments from premises to conclusions and back again.

Several features of formal-operational thought give the adolescent a generally greater capacity to manipulate and appreciate the outer environment and the world of the imagination: hypothetical thinking, the ability to use symbols to stand for symbols, and deductive reasoning.

Formal-operational adolescents (and adults) think abstractly. They become capable of solving geometric problems about circles and squares without reference to what the circles and squares may represent in the real world. Adolescents in this stage derive rules for behavior from general principles and can focus, or center, on many aspects of a situation at once in arriving at judgments and solving problems.

In a sense, it is during the stage of formal operations that adolescents tend to emerge as theoretical scientists—even though they may see themselves as having little or no interest in science. They become capable of

FORMAL-OPERATIONAL STAGE Piaget's fourth stage, characterized by abstract logical thought; deduction from principles.

dealing with hypothetical situations. They realize that situations can have different outcomes, and they think ahead, experimenting with different possibilities. Adolescents also conduct experiments to determine whether their hypotheses are correct. These experiments are not conducted in the laboratory. Rather, adolescents may try out different tones of voice, ways of carrying themselves, and ways of treating others to see what works best for them.

ADOLESCENT EGOCENTRISM: "YOU JUST DON'T UNDER-STAND!" Adolescents in the formal-operational stage can reason deductively, or draw conclusions about specific objects or people once they have been classified accurately. Adolescents can be somewhat proud of their new logical abilities, and so a new sort of egocentrism can develop in which adolescents emotionally press for acceptance of their logic without recognizing the exceptions or practical problems that are often considered by adults. Consider this example: "It is wrong to hurt people. Company A occasionally hurts people" (perhaps through pollution or economic pressures). "Therefore, Company A must be severely punished or shut down." This thinking is logical. By impatiently pressing for immediate major changes or severe penalties, however, one may not fully consider various practical problems such as the thousands of workers who would be laid off if the company were shut down. Adults frequently have undergone life experiences that lead them to see shades of gray in situations, rather than just black or white.

The thought of preschoolers is characterized by egocentrism in which they cannot take another's point of view. Adolescent thought is marked by another sort of egocentrism, in which they can understand the thoughts of others but still have trouble separating things that are of concern to others and those that are of concern only to themselves (Elkind, 1967, 1985). Adolescent egocentrism gives rise to two interesting cognitive developments: *the imaginary audience* and the *personal fable.*

The concept of the **imaginary audience** refers to the belief that other people are as concerned with our thoughts and behavior as we are. As a result, adolescents see themselves as the center of attention and assume that other people are about as preoccupied with their appearance and behavior as they are (Lapsley, 1991; Milstead et al., 1993). Adolescents may feel they are on stage and all eyes are focused on them.

The concept of the imaginary audience may fuel the intense adolescent desire for privacy. It helps explain why adolescents are so self-conscious about their appearance, why they worry about every facial blemish and spend long hours grooming. Self-consciousness seems to peak at about the age of 13 and then decline. Girls tend to be more self-conscious than boys (Elkind & Bowen, 1979).

✓ Truth or Fiction Revisited

It is true that adolescents tend to see themselves as being on stage. This is a manifestation of adolescent egocentrism and fuels the adolescent desires for privacy and physical perfection.

The **personal fable** is the belief that our feelings and ideas are special, even unique, and that we are invulnerable. The personal fable seems to underlie various adolescent behavior patterns, such as showing off and taking risks (Arnett, 1992; Cohn et al., 1995; Lapsley, 1990, 1991; Milstead et al., 1993). Some adolescents adopt an "it can't happen to me" attitude—assuming that they can smoke without risk of cancer or engage in

REFLECT

Did you have an intense need for privacy as an adolescent? How do you explain that need in terms of Piaget's theory?

IMAGINARY AUDIENCE An aspect of adolescent egocentrism; the belief that other people are as concerned with our thoughts and behaviors as we are.

PERSONAL FABLE Another aspect of adolescent egocentrism; the belief that our feelings and ideas are special and unique and that we are invulnerable.

REFLECT

Do you know adolescents who act as if they believe they will live forever? Why do adolescents think like this?

sexual activity without risk of sexually transmitted infections or pregnancy. Another aspect of the personal fable is the idea that no one has ever experienced or could understand the "unique" feelings one is experiencing, such as needing independence or being in love. Perhaps the personal fable is the basis for the common teenage lament, "You just don't understand me!"

EVALUATION OF PIAGET'S THEORY A number of questions have been raised concerning the accuracy of Piaget's views. Among them are these:

1. *Was Piaget's timing accurate?* Some critics argue that Piaget's methods led him to underestimate children's abilities (Bjorklund, 1995; Meltzoff & Gopnik, 1997). Other researchers using different methods have found, for example, that preschoolers are less egocentric and that children are capable of conservation at earlier ages than Piaget thought.

2. *Does cognitive development occur in stages?* Cognitive events such as egocentrism and conservation appear to develop more continuously than Piaget thought—that is, they may not occur in stages (Bjorklund, 1995; Flavell et al., 1993). Although cognitive developments appear to build on previous cognitive developments, the process may be more gradual than stagelike.

3. *Are developmental sequences always the same?* Here, Piaget's views have fared better. It seems there is no variation in the sequence in which cognitive developments occur.

In sum, Piaget's theoretical edifice has been rocked, but it has not been reduced to rubble. Psychologist Andrew Meltzoff believes that "Piaget's theories were critical for getting the field of [cognitive development] off the ground, . . . but it's time to move on" (1997, p. 9). Some psychologists are moving on to *information processing.* That is, they view children (and adults) as akin to computer systems. Children, like computers, obtain information (receive "input") from their environment, store it, retrieve it, manipulate it (think about it), and then respond to it overtly in terms of their behavior (produce "output") (Harnishfeger & Bjorklund, 1990). One goal of the information-processing approach is to learn just how children do these things, how their "mental programs" develop. Critical issues involve children's capacity for memory and their use of cognitive strategies, such as the ways in which they focus their attention (Bjorklund, 1995; Case, 1992; Kail & Salthouse, 1994). The future of cognitive development remains to be written.

The Postconventional Level of Moral Reasoning

REFLECT

Can you think of situations—historic or current—in which people have had to break the law in order to do the right thing? Can you think of situations in which people have done the wrong thing by following the law?

Lawrence Kohlberg's theory of moral reasoning involves three levels: preconventional, conventional, and postconventional. Individuals can arrive at the same decision—for example, as to whether or not Heinz should save his wife by taking the drug without paying for it—but they would be doing so for a different kind of reason. (Deciding not to take the drug for fear of punishment is cognitively less complex than not taking the drug because of the belief that doing so could have negative consequences for the social order.)

None of Kohlberg's levels is tied precisely to a person's age. Although postconventional reasoning is the highest level, for example, most adolescents and adults reason conventionally. However, when postconventional reasoning does emerge, it usually does so in adolescence. Kohlberg's (1969) research showed that postconventional moral judgments were clearly absent among the 7- to 10-year-olds. But by age 16, stage 5 reasoning is shown by about 20% of adolescents, and stage 6 reasoning is shown by about 5% of adolescents.

At the **postconventional level,** moral reasoning is based on the person's own moral standards. In each instance, moral judgments are derived from personal values, not from conventional standards or authority figures. In the contractual, legalistic orientation characteristic of stage 5, it is recognized that laws stem from agreed-upon procedures and that the rule of law is in general good for society; therefore, laws should not be violated. But under exceptional circumstances laws cannot bind the individual. (Although it is illegal for Heinz to steal the drug, in this case it is the right thing to do.)

Stage 6 moral reasoning demands adherence to supposed universal ethical principles such as the sanctity of human life, individual dignity, justice, and the Golden Rule ("Do unto others as you would have them do unto you"). If a law is unjust or contradicts the rights of the individual, it is wrong to obey it.

People at the postconventional level look to their conscience as the highest moral authority. This point has created confusion. To some it suggests that it is right to break the law when it is convenient. But this interpretation is incorrect. Kohlberg means that people at this level of moral reasoning must do what they believe is right even if this action runs counter to social rules or laws or requires personal sacrifice.

EVALUATION OF KOHLBERG'S THEORY Consistent with Kohlberg's theory, research suggests that moral reasoning does follow a developmental sequence (Snarey, 1985), even though most people do not reach the level of postconventional thought. Postconventional thought, when found, first occurs during adolescence. It also seems that Piaget's stage of formal operations is a prerequisite for postconventional reasoning, which requires the capacities to understand abstract moral principles and to empathize with the attitudes and emotional responses of other people (Flavell et al., 1993).

Also consistent with Kohlberg's theory, children do not appear to skip stages as they progress (Flavell et al., 1993). When children are exposed to adult models who exhibit a lower stage of moral reasoning, they can be enticed to follow along (Bandura & McDonald, 1963). Children who are exposed to examples of moral reasoning above and below their own stage generally prefer the higher stage, however (Rest, 1983). The thrust of moral development would therefore appear to be from lower to higher in terms of Kohlberg's levels and stages, even if children can be influenced by the opinions of others.

POSTCONVENTIONAL LEVEL According to Kohlberg, a period during which moral judgments are derived from moral principles and people look to themselves to set moral standards.

MORAL DEVELOPMENT AND GENDER: ARE THERE GENDER DIFFERENCES IN MORAL DEVELOPMENT? Some studies using Heinz's dilemma have found that boys reason at higher levels of moral development than girls. However, Carol Gilligan (1982; Gilligan et al., 1989) argues that this gender difference is illusory and reflects different patterns of socialization for boys and girls.

Gilligan makes her point through two examples of responses to Heinz's dilemma. Eleven-year-old Jake views the dilemma as a math problem. He sets up an equation showing that life has greater value than property. Heinz is thus obligated to steal the drug. Eleven-year-old Amy

REFLECT

In your own experience, would you say that adolescent boys or girls are more "moral"? On what do you base your judgment? Does your experience coincide with Kohlberg's views?

vacillates. She notes that stealing the drug and letting Heinz's wife die would both be wrong. Amy searches for alternatives, such as getting a loan, stating that it would profit Heinz's wife little if he went to jail and were no longer around to help her.

According to Gilligan, Amy's reasoning is as sophisticated as Jake's, yet she would be rated as showing a lower level of moral development. Gilligan asserts that Amy, like other girls, has been socialized to focus on the needs of others and forgo simplistic judgments of right and wrong. As a consequence, Amy is more likely to exhibit stage 3 reasoning, which focuses in part on empathy for others. Jake, by contrast, has been socialized to make judgments based purely on logic. To him, clear-cut conclusions are derived from a set of premises. Amy was aware of the logical considerations that influenced Jake, but she saw them as one source of information—not as the only source. It is ironic that Amy's empathy, a trait that has "defined the 'goodness' of women," marks Amy "as deficient in moral development" (Gilligan, 1982, p. 18). Prior to his death, Kohlberg had begun to correct the sexism in his scoring system.

Review

SECTION VI

Not everyone shows formal-operational thinking, but those who do usually begin to do so in (91) _____scence. Formal operational thought is characterized by (92) hypo_____ thinking and deductive reasoning. Adolescents' pride in their cognitive abilities leads to a new sort of (93) ego_____. Adolescent egocentrism gives rise to the (94) _____ audience and the personal fable. The imaginary audience refers to the belief that other people are concerned with our thoughts and behavior, so adolescents may see themselves as the center of (95) _____tion and develop an intense desire for (96) pri_____. The personal fable is the belief that one's feelings and ideas are (97) _____cial and that one is invulnerable. The personal fable apparently underlies adolescent showing off and (98) _____-taking.

Piaget's methodology apparently led him to (99: Overestimate or Underestimate?) the ages at which children can carry out certain kinds of tasks. Also, egocentrism and conservation may develop (100: More or Less?) continuously than Piaget thought. It does seem that the sequences of development are (101: Variant or Invariant?), as Piaget believed.

When Kohlberg's (102) _____tional reasoning emerges, it usually does so in adolescence. In stage 5's (103) co_____, legalistic orientation, it is recognized that laws stem from agreed-upon procedures and that existing laws cannot bind the individual's behavior in unusual circumstances. In stage 6, people consider behavior that is consistent with (104) _____sal ethical standards as right. Kohlberg's scoring system has led to the misimpression that (105: Males or Females?) operate at a higher level of moral reasoning.

SECTION VII. ADOLESCENCE: SOCIAL AND PERSONALITY DEVELOPMENT

Adolescents also differ markedly from children in their social and personality development. Question: What social and personality developments occur during adolescence? In terms of social and personality development, adolescence has been associated with turbulence. In the 19th century, psychologist G. Stanley Hall described adolescence as a time of *Sturm und Drang*—storm and stress. Certainly, many American teenagers abuse drugs, get pregnant, contract sexually transmitted infections, become involved in violence, fail in school, and even attempt suicide (Garland & Zigler, 1993; Gentry & Eron, 1993; Kazdin, 1993). Each year nearly 1 in 10 adolescent girls becomes pregnant. Nearly 10% of teenage boys and 20% of teenage girls attempt suicide. Alcohol-related incidents are the overall leading cause of death among adolescents.

Hall attributed the conflicts and distress of adolescence to biological changes. Research evidence does suggest that hormonal changes affect the activity levels, mood swings, and aggressive tendencies of many adolescents (Buchanan et al., 1992). Overall, however, it would appear that sociocultural influences have a greater impact than hormones (Buchanan et al., 1992).

Adolescents do try to become more independent from their parents, which often leads to some bickering (Smetana et al., 1991). They usually bicker about issues such as homework, chores, money, appearance, curfews, and dating (Galambos & Almeida, 1992; Smetana et al., 1991). Arguments are common when adolescents want to make their own choices about matters such as clothes and friends (Smetana et al., 1991).

The striving for independence is also characterized by withdrawal from family life, at least relative to prior involvement. In one study, children ranging in age from 9 to 15 carried electronic pagers for a week so that they could report what they were doing and whom they were with when signaled (Larson & Richards, 1991). The amount of time spent with family members decreased dramatically with greater age. The 15-year-olds spent only half as much time with their families as the 9-year-olds. Yet this change does not mean that most adolescents spend their time on the streets. For 15-year-old boys in the study, time with the family tended to be replaced by time spent alone. For older girls, this time was divided between friends and solitude.

Adolescents and parents are often in conflict because adolescents experiment with many things that can be harmful to their health. Yet—apparently because of the personal fable—adolescents often do not perceive such activities to be as risky as their parents see them as being. Lawrence Cohn and his colleagues (1995) found, for example, that parents perceived drinking, smoking, failure to use seat belts, drag racing, and a number of other activities to be riskier than their teenagers saw them as being.

Some distancing from parents is beneficial for adolescents (Galambos, 1992). After all, they do have to form relationships outside the family. But greater independence does not necessarily mean that adolescents become emotionally detached from their parents or fall completely under the influence of their peers. Most adolescents continue to feel love, respect, and loyalty toward their parents (Montemayor & Flannery, 1991). Adolescents who feel close to their parents actually show greater self-reliance and independence than do those who are distant from their parents. Adolescents who retain close ties with their parents also fare better in school and have fewer adjustment problems (Davey, 1993; Papini & Roggman, 1992; Steinberg, 1996).

Despite parent–adolescent conflict over issues of control, parents and adolescents tend to share social, political, religious, and economic views (Paikoff & Collins, 1991). In sum, there are frequent differences between parents and adolescents on issues of personal control. However, there apparently is no "generation gap" on broader matters.

Ego Identity Versus Role Diffusion

According to Erik Erikson, individuals undergo eight stages of psychosocial development, each of which is characterized by a certain kind of "crisis." Four of these stages, beginning with the stage of trust versus mistrust, occur during the years of childhood. The fifth stage, that of *ego identity versus role diffusion*, occurs during adolescence. The major challenge of

REFLECT

Consider the stereotype of adolescence as a time of "storm and stress." Does this stereotype fit your own experiences as an adolescent? How or how not?

Adolescents. In our culture adolescents are "neither fish nor fowl." Although they may be old enough to reproduce and may be as large as their parents, they are often treated like children.

REFLECT

Have you formed your own ego identity? If so, what was the process like? If not, are you concerned? Why or why not?

adolescence is the creation of an adult identity. Identity is achieved mainly by committing oneself to a particular occupation or a role in life. But identity also extends to sexual, political, and religious beliefs and commitments.

Erikson (1963) theorized that adolescents experience a life crisis of *ego identity versus role diffusion*. **Ego identity** is a firm sense of who one is and what one stands for. It can carry one through difficult times and give meaning to one's achievements. Adolescents who do not develop ego identity may experience **role diffusion.** They spread themselves too thin, running down one blind alley after another and placing themselves at the mercy of leaders who promise to give them the sense of identity that they cannot find for themselves.

IDENTITY FORMATION, GENDER, AND ETHNICITY Erik Erikson's views of the development of identity were intended to apply primarily to males (Archer, 1992; Patterson et al., 1992). In Erikson's theory, the stage of identity development includes embracing a philosophy of life and commitment to a career. It is in the next stage that people develop the capacity to form intimate relationships. Erikson believed that the development of interpersonal relationships was more important to women's identity than occupational and ideological issues because women's identities were intimately connected with women's roles as wives and mothers. Men's identities did not depend on their roles as husbands and fathers.

But research shows that in the United States, young women's identities are also strongly connected with occupational issues (Archer, 1992). The economic realities of life in the United States call for full participation of women in the workplace. Thus adolescent girls today voice about equal concern with boys about their occupational plans. But girls also express concern about how to balance the needs of a career and a family in their daily lives (Archer, 1992). Although most women will be full-time workers, they still usually bear the primary responsibility for rearing the children and maintaining the home. (When is the last time you heard a man wonder how he will balance the demands of a career and a family?)

Identity formation is more complicated for adolescents from ethnic minority groups (Markstrom-Adams, 1992). These adolescents may be faced with two sets of cultural values: those of their ethnic group and those of the dominant culture (Phinney & Rosenthal, 1992). When these values are in conflict, the minority adolescent needs to reconcile the differences and, frequently, decide where she or he stands. Maha Alkhateeb, a Muslim adolescent, talks about why she skipped the prom: "At the time of the prom, I was sad, but just about everyone I knew had sex that night, which I think was immoral. Now, I like saying that I didn't go. I didn't go there just because it was a cool thing to do" ("Muslim Women," 1993, p. B9).

Biracial adolescents whose parents are of different religions wrestle with yet another issue as to what constitutes their own dominant cultural heritage (Gibbs, 1992). Parents from different ethnic groups may decide to spend their lives together, but their values sometimes do not dwell contentedly side by side in the minds of their children.

A key aspect of identity is sexual identity—how the adolescent perceives himself or herself as a sexual being. The sex organs of adolescents undergo rapid maturation, and adolescents develop the capacity for reproduction. As we see next, many of them do reproduce before they are socially, emotionally, and financially ready to do so.

EGO IDENTITY Erikson's term for a firm sense of who one is and what one stands for.

ROLE DIFFUSION Erikson's term for lack of clarity in one's life roles (due to failure to develop ego identity).

Adolescent Sexuality

My first sexual experience occurred in a car after the high school junior prom. We were both virgins, very uncertain but very much in love. We had been going together since eighth grade. The experience was somewhat painful. I remember wondering if I would look different to my mother the next day. I guess I didn't because nothing was said. (Adapted from Morrison et al., 1980, p. 108)

Although adolescents may not form enduring romantic relationships or be able to support themselves, the changes of puberty ready their bodies for sexual activity. High hormone levels also stir interest in sex. Adolescents therefore wrestle with issues of how and when to express their awakening sexuality. To complicate matters, Western culture sends mixed messages about sex. Teenagers may be advised to wait until they have married or at least entered into meaningful relationships, but they are also bombarded by sexual messages in films, TV and radio commercials, print advertising, and virtually every other medium (Rathus et al., 2000).

Adolescent girls by and large obtain little advice at home or in school about how to resist sexual advances. Nor do most of them have ready access to effective contraception. According to the Alan Guttmacher Institute (1998), fewer than half of the adolescents who are sexually active report using contraceptives consistently. As a result, about 10% of American adolescent girls—about 1 million teenage girls—get pregnant each year (Meckler, 1998). This rate is higher than that for teens in other Western nations. For example, the U.S. rate is twice as high as the comparable rate in England and Canada. More than 200,000 American teenage girls have abortions (Shalala, 1998). Nearly 3 million teenagers in the United States also contract a sexually transmitted infection each year.

Why is teenage pregnancy so common? Some teenage girls become pregnant as a way of eliciting a commitment from their partner or rebelling against their parents. But most become pregnant because they misunderstand reproduction and contraception or miscalculate the odds of conception. Even those who are well-informed about contraception often do not use it consistently (Rathus et al., 2000). Peers also play an important role in determining the sexual behavior of adolescents. When 1,000 teenagers were asked why they had not waited to have sexual intercourse until they were older, the top reason given was peer pressure, cited by 34% of girls and 26% of boys (Kelley & Byrne, 1992).

The medical, social, and economic costs of unplanned teenage pregnancies are enormous to teenage mothers and their children. Teenage mothers are more likely to have medical complications during pregnancy and to have prolonged labor. Their babies are more likely to be born prematurely and to have low birth weight. It appears that these medical problems are largely due not to the young age of the mother, but to the inadequate prenatal care and poor nutrition obtained by teenage mothers living in poverty (Etaugh & Rathus, 1995).

Teenage mothers are also less likely to graduate from high school or attend college. Their lack of educational achievement leads to a lower standard of living and a greater need for public assistance (Center for the Study of Social Policy, 1993). Few receive consistent financial or emotional help from the fathers, who generally are unable to support themselves, let alone a family (Klein, 1993).

REFLECT

How important a part of your adolescence (or that of your peers) was sexuality? Did any of your peers experience problems related to their sexuality during adolescence? Did they resolve these problems? If so, how?

Still, there is some encouraging news. The final decade of the 20th century saw a decline in the teenage pregnancy rate because of increased use of contraception as well as the leveling off of sexual activity among teenagers (Kolbe, 1998; Meckler, 1998). Perhaps sex-education programs and the increased availability of contraceptives are making inroads.

Review

SECTION VII

Psychologist G. Stanley Hall described adolescence as a time of *Sturm und Drang*—(106) st_____ and st_____. Each year nearly 1 in (107: How many?) adolescent girls become pregnant. (108) AI_____ is the leading cause of death among adolescents. Hall attributed the storm and stress of adolescence to (109) _____gical changes. Research evidence suggests that (110) _____ural influences have a greater impact than hormones.

Adolescents strive to become (111: More or Less?) independent from parents, which often leads to bickering. Striving for independence is characterized by (112: Greater or Lesser?) involvement in family life. Adolescents and parents are often in conflict because adolescents see experimentation with cars, drugs, and sex as (113: More or Less?) risky than their parents do. Greater independence (114: Does or Does not?) mean that adolescents become emotionally detached from their parents. Parents and adolescents tend to (115: Agree or Disagree?) on social, political, religious, and economic issues.

According to Erik Erikson, the stage of ego (116) _____ versus role (117) _____ occurs during adolescence. Research shows that in the United States young women's identities (118: Are or Are not?) strongly connected with occupational issues. (119: More or Fewer?) than half of the adolescents who are sexually active report using contraceptives consistently. Teenage mothers are (120: More or Less?) likely to graduate from high school or go to college.

SECTION VIII. ADULTHOOD: PHYSICAL DEVELOPMENT

Development continues throughout the lifespan. Many theorists believe that adult concerns and involvements follow observable patterns, so that we can speak of "stages" of adult development. Others argue that there may no longer be a standard life cycle with predictable stages or phases (Sheehy, 1995, 1998). Age now has an "elastic quality" (Butler, 1998). People are living longer than ever before and are freer than ever to choose their own destiny.

The most obvious aspects of development during adulthood are physical. Question: What physical developments occur during adulthood? In the following section we consider the physical developments that take place in young, or early, adulthood, which covers the period between the ages of 20 and 40; middle adulthood, which spans the ages of about 45 to 65; and late adulthood, which begins at 65.

Young Adulthood

Physical development peaks in young adulthood. Most people are at their height of sensory sharpness, strength, reaction time, and cardiovascular fitness. Women gymnasts find themselves going downhill in their early 20s because they accumulate body fat and lose suppleness and flexibility. Other athletes are more likely to experience a decline in their 30s. Most athletes retire before they reach 40.

Sexually speaking, most people in early adulthood become readily aroused. They tend to attain and maintain erections as desired, and to lubricate readily. A man in his 20s is more likely to be concerned about ejaculating too quickly than about whether or not he will be able to obtain an erection (Rathus et al., 2000).

Middle Adulthood

As we enter our middle years, we are unlikely to possess the strength, coordination, and stamina that we had during our 20s and 30s. The decline is most obvious in the professional sports ranks, where peak performance is at a premium. Gordie Howe still played hockey at 50 and George Blanda was still kicking field goals at that age, but most professionals at those ages can no longer keep up with the "kids."

But the years between 40 and 60 are reasonably stable. There is gradual physical decline, but it is minor and only likely to be of concern if we insist on competing with young adults—or with idealized memories of ourselves. And many of us first make time to develop our physical potentials during middle adulthood. The 20-year-old couch potato occasionally becomes the 50-year-old marathoner. By any reasonable standard, we can maintain excellent cardiorespiratory condition throughout middle adulthood.

Because the physical decline in middle adulthood is gradual, people who begin to eat more nutritious diets (e.g., decrease intake of fats and increase intake of fruits and vegetables) and to exercise during this stage of life may find themselves looking and feeling better than they did in young adulthood. Sedentary people in young adulthood may gasp for air if they rush half a block to catch a bus, whereas fit people in middle adulthood—even in late adulthood—may run for miles before they feel fatigued.

MENOPAUSE **Menopause,** or cessation of menstruation, usually occurs during the late 40s or early 50s, although there are wide variations in the age at which it occurs. Menopause is the final stage of a broader female experience, the *climacteric,* which is caused by a falling off in the secretion of the hormones estrogen and progesterone, and during which many changes occur that are related to the gradual loss of reproductive ability. At this time ovulation also draws to an end. There is some loss of breast tissue and of elasticity in the skin. There can also be a loss of bone density that leads to osteoporosis (a condition in which the bones break easily) in late adulthood.

During the climacteric, many women encounter symptoms such as hot flashes (uncomfortable sensations characterized by heat and perspiration) and loss of sleep. Loss of estrogen can be accompanied be feelings of anxiety and depression, but women appear to be more likely to experience serious depression prior to menopause, when they may feel overwhelmed by the combined demands of the workplace, child rearing, and homemaking (Brody, 1993). Most women get through the mood changes that can accompany menopause without great difficulty. According to psychologist Karen Matthews, who followed a sample of hundreds of women through menopause, "The vast majority [of women] have no problem at all getting through the menopausal transition" (Matthews, 1994, p. 25).

Menopause does not signal the end of a woman's sexual interests (Brody, 1993). Many women find the separation of sex from reproduction to be sexually liberating. Some of the physical problems that may stem from the fall-off in hormone production may be alleviated by hormone replacement therapy (Grodstein et al., 1997). A more important issue may be what menopause means to the individual. Women who equate

REFLECT

Do you know anyone who has undergone menopause? What was the experience like for her?

MENOPAUSE The cessation of menstruation.

menopause with loss of femininity are likely to encounter more distress than those who do not (Rathus et al., 2000).

✓ Truth or Fiction Revisited

It is not true that menopause signals the end of a woman's sexual interests. Many women find the separation of sex from reproduction to be sexually liberating.

MANOPAUSE (*MANOPAUSE?*) Men cannot experience menopause, of course. Yet now and then we hear the term *male menopause,* or "manopause." Middle-aged or older men may be loosely alluded to as menopausal. This epithet is doubly offensive: It reinforces the negative, harmful stereotypes of aging people, especially aging women, as crotchety and irritable. Nor is the label consistent with the biology or psychology of aging. Alternate terms are *andropause* (referring to a drop-off in androgens, or male sex hormones) and *viropause* (referring to the end of virility) (Cowley, 1996).

For women, menopause is a time of relatively acute age-related declines in sex hormones and fertility. In men, however, the decline in the production of male sex hormones and fertility is more gradual (Sheehy, 1998b). It therefore is not surprising to find a man in his 70s or older fathering a child. Moreover, some viable sperm are produced even in late adulthood. However, many men in their 50s and 60s experience intermittent problems in achieving and maintaining erections (Laumann et al., 1994), which may or may not have to do with hormone production.

Sexual performance is only one part of the story, however. Between the ages of 40 and 70, the typical American male loses 12 to 20 pounds of muscle, about 2 inches in height, and 15% of his bone mass. (Men as well as women are at risk for osteoporosis [Brody, 1996].) The amount of fat in the body nearly doubles. The eardrums thicken, as do the lenses of the eyes, resulting in some loss of hearing and vision. There is also loss of endurance as the cardiovascular system and lungs become less capable of responding effectively to exertion.

Some of these changes can be slowed or even reversed. Exercise helps maintain muscle tone and keep the growth of fatty tissue in check. A diet rich in calcium and vitamin D can help ward off bone loss in men as well as in women. Hormone replacement may also help, but is controversial. Although testosterone replacement appears to boost strength, energy, and the sex drive, it is connected with increased risks of prostate cancer and cardiovascular disease (Cowley, 1996). Erection is made possible by the flow of blood into the caverns within the penis (vasocongestion), which then stiffens as does a balloon when air or water is pumped in. The drug Viagra, which was first marketed in 1998, facilitates erection by relaxing the muscles that surround the caverns, enabling blood vessels in the region to dilate.

Even though sexual interest and performance decline, men can remain sexually active and father children at advanced ages (Sheehy, 1998b). For both genders, attitudes toward the biological changes of aging—along with general happiness—may affect sexual behavior as much as biological changes do.

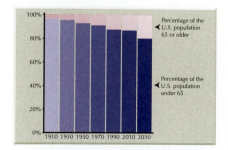

FIGURE 3.9
LIVING LONGER

AS WE ENTER THE NEW MILLENNIUM, MORE PEOPLE IN THE UNITED STATES ARE LIVING TO BE AGE 65 OR ABOVE.

Late Adulthood

Did you know that an *agequake* is coming? With improved health care and knowledge of the importance of diet and exercise, more Americans than ever before are 65 or older (Abeles, 1997a). In 1900, only 1 American in 30 was over 65, compared with 1 in 9 in 1970. By 2030, 1 American in 5 will be 65 or older ("Longer, healthier, better," 1997; see Figure 3.9).

Various changes—some of them troublesome—do occur during the later years (Figure 3.10). Changes in calcium metabolism lead to increased

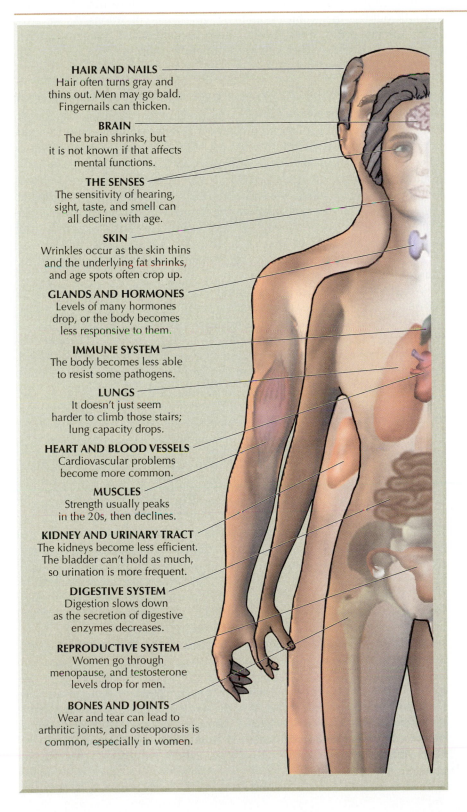

HAIR AND NAILS
Hair often turns gray and thins out. Men may go bald. Fingernails can thicken.

BRAIN
The brain shrinks, but it is not known if that affects mental functions.

THE SENSES
The sensitivity of hearing, sight, taste, and smell can all decline with age.

SKIN
Wrinkles occur as the skin thins and the underlying fat shrinks, and age spots often crop up.

GLANDS AND HORMONES
Levels of many hormones drop, or the body becomes less responsive to them.

IMMUNE SYSTEM
The body becomes less able to resist some pathogens.

LUNGS
It doesn't just seem harder to climb those stairs; lung capacity drops.

HEART AND BLOOD VESSELS
Cardiovascular problems become more common.

MUSCLES
Strength usually peaks in the 20s, then declines.

KIDNEY AND URINARY TRACT
The kidneys become less efficient. The bladder can't hold as much, so urination is more frequent.

DIGESTIVE SYSTEM
Digestion slows down as the secretion of digestive enzymes decreases.

REPRODUCTIVE SYSTEM
Women go through menopause, and testosterone levels drop for men.

BONES AND JOINTS
Wear and tear can lead to arthritic joints, and osteoporosis is common, especially in women.

FIGURE 3.10
THE RELENTLESS MARCH OF TIME
A NUMBER OF PHYSICAL CHANGES OCCUR DURING THE LATER YEARS. HOWEVER, THE REASONS FOR AGING ARE NOT YET COMPLETELY UNDERSTOOD. PEOPLE CAN ALSO AFFECT THE PACE OF THEIR AGING BY EATING PROPERLY, EXERCISING, MAINTAINING A POSITIVE OUTLOOK, AND FINDING AND MEETING CHALLENGES THAT ARE CONSISTENT WITH THEIR ABILITIES.

brittleness in the bones and heightened risk of breaks due to accidents such as falls. The skin becomes less elastic and subject to wrinkles and folds.

The senses are also affected. Older people see and hear less acutely. Because of a decline in the sense of smell, they may use more spice to flavor their food. Older people need more time (called **reaction time**) to respond to stimuli. Older drivers, for example, need more time to respond to traffic lights, other vehicles, and changing road conditions. As we grow older, our immune system also functions less effectively, leaving us more vulnerable to disease. These changes ultimately result in death.

LATE ADULTHOOD, GENDER, AND ETHNICITY: DIFFERENT PATTERNS OF AGING Although Americans in general are living longer, there are gender and ethnic differences in life expectancy. For example, women in our society tend to live longer, but older men tend to live *better* ("Longer, healthier, better," 1997). White Americans from European backgrounds live longer on the average than do Hispanic Americans, African Americans, and Native Americans. Life expectancy for Hispanic Americans falls somewhere between the figures for African Americans and White Americans. The longevity of Asian Americans falls closer to that of White Americans than to that of African Americans. Native Americans have the lowest average longevity of the major racial/ethnic groups in the United States (Nevid et al., 1998).

Women in the United States outlive men by six to seven years. Why? For one thing, heart disease, the nation's leading killer, typically develops later in women than in men. Men are also more likely to die because of accidents, cirrhosis of the liver, strokes, suicide, homicide, AIDS, and cancer (excepting cancers of the female sex organs) (Nevid et al., 1998). Many deaths from these causes are the result of unhealthy habits more typical of men, such as excessive drinking and reckless behavior.

Many men are also reluctant to have regular physical exams or to talk to their doctors about their health problems. "In their 20's, [men are] too strong to need a doctor; in their 30's, they're too busy, and in their 40's, too scared" ("Doctors tie male mentality," 1995). Women are much more likely to examine themselves for signs of breast cancer than men are even to recognize the early signs of prostate cancer.

Although women tend to outlive men, their prospects for a happy and healthy old age are dimmer. Men who beat the statistical odds by living beyond their 70s are far less likely than their female counterparts to live alone, suffer from chronic disabling conditions, or be poor. Older women are more likely than men to live alone largely because they are more likely to be widowed. One reason that older women are more likely to be poor is that women who are now age 65 or older were less likely to hold jobs. If they had jobs, they were paid far less than men and received smaller pensions and other retirement benefits.

Socioeconomic differences play a role in ethnic differences in life expectancy. Members of ethnic minority groups in our society are more likely to be poor, and poor people tend to eat less nutritious diets, encounter more stress, and have less access to health care. There is a seven-year difference in life expectancy between people in the highest income brackets and those in the lowest. Yet other factors, such as cultural differences in diet and lifestyle, the stress of coping with discrimination, and genetic differences, may partly account for ethnic group differences in life expectancy.

REFLECT

How do older people you know cope with the physical changes that occur in late adulthood?

REACTION TIME The amount of time required to respond to a stimulus.

Theories of Aging

Although it may be hard to believe it will happen to us, every person who has walked the Earth so far has aged—which may not be a bad fate, considering the alternative. Question: Why do we age? Various factors, some of which are theoretical, apparently contribute to aging.

The theory of **programmed senescence** sees aging as determined by a biological clock that ticks at a rate governed by instructions in the genes. Just as genes program children to grow and reach sexual maturation, they program people to deteriorate and die. There is evidence to support a role for genes in aging. Longevity runs in families. People whose parents and grandparents lived into their 80s and 90s have a better chance of reaching these ages themselves.

The **wear-and-tear theory** does not suggest that people are programmed to self-destruct. Instead, environmental factors such as pollution, disease, and ultraviolet light are assumed to contribute to wear and tear of the body over time. The body is like a machine whose parts wear out through use. Cells lose the ability to regenerate themselves, and vital organs are worn down by the ravages of time.

Our behavior also influences our aging. People who exercise regularly seem to live longer. Cigarette smoking, overeating, and stress can contribute to an early death. Fortunately, we can exert control over some of these factors.

PROGRAMMED SENESCENCE The view that aging is determined by a biological clock that ticks at a rate governed by genes.

WEAR-AND-TEAR THEORY The view that factors such as pollution, disease, and ultraviolet light contribute to wear and tear on the body, so that the body loses the ability to repair itself.

Review

SECTION VIII

In young adulthood, most people are at their height of (121) _____ory sharpness, strength, reaction time, and (122) _____-vascular fitness. In middle adulthood, there is usually a (123: Sharp or Gradual?) physical decline. Cessation of menstruation, termed (124) _____, usually occurs during the late 40s or early 50s. Menopause is part of a broader female experience, the (125) _____teric, which is caused by a fall-off in female sex hormones. During the climacteric, many women have (126) _____ flashes. Loss of (127) _____gen can be accompanied be feelings of anxiety and depression. Most women get through the mood changes that can accompany menopause (128: With or Without?) great difficulty. The word (128) "_____pause" is not a technical term, but we hear it used to refer to the changes that can accompany decline in the production of male sex hormones, such as problems in maintaining erections.

In late adulthood, changes in (129) _____ium metabolism lead to increased brittleness in the bones. The senses become (130: More or Less?) acute, so older people tend to spice their food more heavily. The time required to respond to stimuli—that is, (131) _____ion time—increases. Women tend to live (132: Longer or Shorter?) lives than men, and African Americans tend to live (133: Longer or Shorter?) lives than White Americans.

According to the (134) pro_____ _____scence theory of aging, aging is determined by a genetic biological clock. According to the (135) _____-and-tear theory, cells lose the ability to regenerate because of environmental factors such as pollution, disease, and ultraviolet light.

SECTION IX. ADULTHOOD: COGNITIVE DEVELOPMENT

Question: What cognitive developments occur during adulthood? As is the case with physical development, people are also at the height of their cognitive powers during early adulthood. Many professionals show the broadest knowledge of their fields at about the time they are graduating from college or graduate school. At this time their course work is freshest. They may have just recently studied for comprehensive examinations. Once they enter their fields, they often specialize. As a result, knowledge deepens in certain areas, but understanding of related areas may grow relatively superficial.

Cognitive development in adulthood has many aspects—creativity, memory functioning, and intelligence. People can be creative for a lifetime. Picasso was painting in his 90s. Grandma Moses did not even begin painting until she was 78 years old. The architect Frank Lloyd Wright designed New York's spiral-shaped Guggenheim Museum when he was 89 years old.

✓ Truth or Fiction Revisited

It is not true that Frank Lloyd Wright created the innovative design for the Guggenheim Museum at the age of 65. But the reason is that he created the New York City museum at the age of 89!

Memory functioning declines with age. It is common enough for older people to have trouble recalling the names of common objects or people they know. Memory lapses can be embarrassing, and older people sometimes lose confidence in their memories, which then lowers their motivation to remember things (Cavanaugh & Green, 1990). But declines in memory are not usually as large as people assume (Abeles, 1997b). Memory tests usually measure ability to recall meaningless information. Older people show better memory functioning in areas in which they can apply their experience, especially in their areas of specialization, to new challenges (Graf, 1990). For example, who would do a better job of learning and remembering how to solve problems in chemistry—a college history major or a retired professor of chemistry?

People also obtain the highest intelligence test scores in young adulthood (Baltes, 1997). Yet people tend to retain their verbal skills, as demonstrated by their vocabularies and general knowledge, into advanced old age. It is their performance on tasks that require speed and visual-spatial skills, such as putting puzzles together, that tends to fall off (Lindenberger et al., 1993; Schaie, 1994).

Crystallized Versus Fluid Intelligence

Consider the difference between *crystallized intelligence* and *fluid intelligence*. **Crystallized intelligence** represents one's lifetime of intellectual attainments, as shown by vocabulary and accumulated facts about world affairs. Therefore, crystallized intelligence generally increases over the decades. **Fluid intelligence** is defined as mental flexibility, demonstrated by the ability to process information rapidly, as in learning and solving problems in new areas of endeavor.

In terms of people's worth to their employers, familiarity in solving the kinds of problems found on the job (their crystallized intelligence) may be more important than their fluid intelligence. Experience on the job enhances people's specialized vocabularies and their knowledge of the area. People draw on fluid intelligence when the usual solutions no longer work, but experience is often more valuable than fluid intelligence.

REFLECT

Can you apply the concepts of crystallized intelligence and fluid intelligence to older people in your own life?

CRYSTALLIZED INTELLIGENCE One's lifetime of intellectual achievement, as shown largely through vocabulary and knowledge of world affairs.

FLUID INTELLIGENCE Mental flexibility as shown in learning rapidly to solve new kinds of problems.

Review

SECTION IX

People are at the height of their cognitive powers during (136)_____ adulthood. People (137: Can or Cannot?) be creative for a lifetime. Memory functioning (138: Remains stable or Declines?) with age. Older people show (139: Better or Worse?) memory functioning in areas in which they can apply their experience. People tend to retain (140: Verbal skills or Performance on tasks that require speed and visual-spatial skills?) into advanced old age.

(141) _____lized intelligence refers to one's lifetime of intellectual achievement, as shown by vocabulary and general knowledge. (142) _____ intelligence is mental flexibility, as shown by the ability to solve new kinds of problems. (143: Crystallized or Fluid?) intelligence generally increases over the decades. In terms of people's worth to employers, (144: Crystallized or Fluid?) intelligence is usually more important. People draw on (145: Crystallized or Fluid?) intelligence when the usual solutions no longer work.

SECTION X. ADULTHOOD: SOCIAL AND PERSONALITY DEVELOPMENT

Changes in social and personality development during adulthood are probably the most "elastic" or fluid. Question: What changes in social and personality development occur during adulthood? These changes are clearly affected by cultural expectations and individual behavior patterns. As a result, there is so much variety that it can be misleading to expect that any individual will follow a particular pattern. Nevertheless, many developmental theorists suggest that there are enough commonalities that we can speak of trends. One trend that will become obvious, however, is that the outlook for older people has become much more optimistic over the past generation—not only because of medical advances but also because the behavior and mental processes of many older people are remaining younger than at any other time in history.

Young Adulthood

Many theorists suggest that young adulthood is the period of life during which people tend to establish themselves as independent members of society. Many adults in their 20s are fueled by ambition. Journalist Gail Sheehy (1976) labeled the 20s the **Trying 20s**—a period during which people basically strive to advance their careers. They are concerned about establishing their pathway in life. They are generally responsible for their own support, make their own choices, and are largely free from parental influences. Many young adults adopt what theorist Daniel Levinson and his colleagues (1978) call the **dream**—the drive to "become" someone, to leave their mark on history—which serves as a tentative blueprint for their life.

During young adulthood, people also tend to leave their families of origin and to create families of their own. Erik Erikson (1963) characterized young adulthood as the stage of **intimacy versus isolation.** Erikson saw the establishment of intimate relationships as central to young

TRYING 20S Sheehy's term for the third decade of life, when people are frequently occupied with advancement in the career

DREAM In this usage, Levinson's term for the overriding drive of youth to become someone important, to leave one's mark on history.

INTIMACY VERSUS ISOLATION Erikson's life crisis of young adulthood, which is characterized by the task of developing abiding intimate relationships.

Establishing Intimate Relationships.
According to Erik Erikson, establishing intimate relationships is a central task of young adulthood.

adulthood. Young adults who have evolved a firm sense of identity during adolescence are ready to "fuse" their identities with those of other people through marriage and abiding friendships. People who do not reach out to develop intimate relationships risk retreating into isolation and loneliness.

Erikson warned that we may not be able to commit ourselves to others until we have achieved ego identity—that is, established stable life roles. Achieving ego identity is the central task of adolescence. Lack of personal stability is connected with the high divorce rate for teenage marriages.

PERSONALITY DEVELOPMENT AND GENDER: GENDER DIFFERENCES Most Western men consider separation and individuation to be key goals of personality development during young adulthood (Guisinger & Blatt, 1994). For women, however, the establishment and maintenance of social relationships are also of primary importance (Gilligan et al., 1990, 1991). Women, as Gilligan (1982) has pointed out, are likely to undergo a transition from being cared for by others to caring for others. In becoming adults, men are more likely to undergo a transition from being restricted by others to autonomy and perhaps control of other people.

Although there are differences in the development of women and men, between the ages of 21 and 27 college women also develop in terms of individuation and autonomy (Helson & Moane, 1987). Women, like men, assert increasing control over their own lives. College women, on average, are relatively liberated and career-oriented compared with their less-well-educated peers.

THE THIRTIES Levinson labeled the ages of 28 to 33 the **age-30 transition.** For men and women, the late 20s and early 30s are commonly characterized by reassessment: "Where is my life going?" "Why am I doing this?" Sheehy (1976) labeled this period the **Catch 30s** because of this tendency toward reassessment. During our 30s, we often find that the lifestyles we adopted during our 20s do not fit as comfortably as we had expected. One response to the disillusionments of the 30s, according to Sheehy,

> is the tearing up of the life we have spent most of our 20s putting together. It may mean striking out on a secondary road toward a

Where do you fit into the chronicle of the adult years? Do events in your own life fit with any of the research findings or theories presented in this chapter?

AGE-30 TRANSITION Levinson's term for the ages from 28 to 33, which are characterized by reassessment of the goals and values of the

CATCH 30S Sheehy's term for the fourth decade of life, when many people undergo major reassessments of their accomplishments and goals.

new vision or converting a dream of "running for president" into a more realistic goal. The single person feels a push to find a partner. The woman who was previously content at home with children chafes to venture into the world. The childless couple reconsiders children. And almost everybody who is married . . . feels a discontent. (1976, p. 34)

Many psychologists find that the later 30s are characterized by settling down or planting roots. Many young adults feel a need to make a financial and emotional investment in their home. Their concerns become more focused on promotion or tenure, career advancement, and long-term mortgages.

Middle Adulthood

There are also a number of key changes in social and personality development that tend to occur during middle adulthood. Consider Erikson's views on the middle years.

GENERATIVITY VERSUS STAGNATION Erikson (1963) labeled the life crisis of the middle years **generativity versus stagnation.** Generativity involves doing things that we believe are worthwhile, such as rearing children or producing on the job. Generativity enhances and maintains self-esteem. Generativity also involves helping to shape the new generation. This shaping may involve rearing our own children or making the world a better place, for example, through joining church or civic groups. Stagnation means treading water, as in keeping the same job at the same pay for 30 years, or even moving backward, as in moving into a less responsible and poorer paying job or removing oneself from rearing one's children. Stagnation has powerful destructive effects on self-esteem.

MIDLIFE TRANSITION According to Levinson (1978), whose research involved case studies of 40 men, there is a **midlife transition** at about age 40 to 45 characterized by a shift in psychological perspective. Previously, men had thought of their age in terms of the number of years that had elapsed since birth. Now they begin to think of their age in terms of the number of years they have left. Men in their 30s still think of themselves as older brothers to "kids" in their 20s. At about age 40 to 45, however, some marker event—illness, a change of job, the death of a friend or parent, or being beaten at tennis by their son—leads men to realize that they are a full generation older. Suddenly there seems to be more to look back on than forward to. It dawns on men that they will never be president or chairperson of the board. They will never play shortstop for the Dodgers. They mourn the passing of their own youth and begin to adjust to the specter of old age and the finality of death.

There are gender differences. Research suggests that women may undergo a midlife transition a number of years earlier than men do (e.g., Reinke et al., 1985). Sheehy (1976) writes that women enter midlife about 5 years earlier than men, at about age 35 instead of 40. Why? Much of it has to do with the winding down of the "biological clock"—that is, the abilities to conceive and bear children. For example, once they turn 35, women are usually advised to have their fetuses routinely tested for Down syndrome and other chromosomal disorders. At age 35, women also enter higher risk categories for side effects from birth control pills. Yet

REFLECT

Have you made "false starts" in life? Have you reassessed your life's paths? Are your experiences of value to you? Explain.

Midlife Crisis or "Middlescence?" According to Gail Sheehy, many middle-aged people undergo a second quest for identity (the first occurs during adolescence). They are trying to decide what they will do with their "second adulthoods"—the three to four healthy decades they may have left.

GENERATIVITY VERSUS STAGNATION Erikson's term for the crisis of middle adulthood, characterized by the task of being productive and contributing to younger generations.

MIDLIFE TRANSITION Levinson's term for the ages from 40 to 45, which are characterized by a shift in psychological perspective from viewing ourselves in terms of years lived to viewing ourselves in terms of the years we have left.

many women today are having children in their 40s and, occasionally, even later (Clay, 1996; Matus, 1996).

THE MIDLIFE CRISIS According to Levinson, the midlife transition may trigger a crisis—the **midlife crisis.** The middle-level, middle-aged businessperson looking ahead to another 10 to 20 years of grinding out accounts in a Wall Street cubbyhole may encounter severe depression. The housewife with two teenagers, an empty house from 8:00 A.M. to 4:00 P.M., and a 40th birthday on the way may feel that she is coming apart at the seams. Both feel a sense of entrapment and loss of purpose. Some people are propelled into extramarital affairs by the desire to prove to themselves that they are still attractive.

REFLECT

Do you see your future as open-ended or as quite limited? Why?

MASTERY Sheehy (1995) is much more optimistic than Levinson. She terms the years from 45 to 65 the "Age of Mastery." Rather than viewing them as years of decline, her interviews suggest that many Americans find that these years present opportunities for new direction and fulfillment. Many people are at the height of their productive powers during this period. Sheehy believes that the key task for people aged 45 to 55 is to decide what they will do with their "second adulthoods"—the 30 to 40 healthy years that may be left for them once they reach 50. She believes that both men and women can experience great success and joy if they identify meaningful goals and pursue them wholeheartedly.

"MIDDLESCENCE" Yet people need to define themselves and their goals. Sheehy coined the term **middlescence** to describe a period of searching that is in some ways similar to adolescence. Both are times of transition. Middlescence involves a search for a new identity: "Turning backward, going around in circles, feeling lost in a buzz of confusion and unable to make decisions—all this is predictable and, for many people, a necessary precursor to making the passage into midlife" (Sheehy, 1995).

Women frequently experience a renewed sense of self in their 40s and 50s as they emerge from "middlescence" (Apter, 1995; Sheehy, 1995). Many women in their early 40s are already emerging from some of the fears and uncertainties that are first confronting men. For example, Helson and Moane (1987) found that women at age 43 are more likely than women in their early 30s to feel confident; to exert an influence on their community; to feel secure and committed; to feel productive, effective, and powerful; and to extend their interests beyond their family.

THE EMPTY-NEST SYNDROME In earlier decades, psychologists placed great emphasis on a concept referred to as the **empty-nest syndrome.** This concept was applied most often to women. It was assumed that women experience a profound sense of loss when their youngest child goes off to college, gets married, or moves out of the home. Research findings paint a more optimistic picture, however. Certainly there can be problems, and these apply to both parents. Perhaps the largest of these is letting go of one's children after so many years of mutual dependence.

Many mothers report increased marital satisfaction and personal changes such as greater mellowness, self-confidence, and stability after their children have left home (Reinke et al., 1985). Middle-aged women show increased dominance and assertiveness, an orientation toward achievement, and greater influence in the worlds of politics and work. It is as if they are cut free from traditional shackles by the knowledge that their childbearing years are behind them.

MIDLIFE CRISIS A crisis experienced by many people during the midlife transition when they realize that life may be more than halfway over and reassess their achievements in terms of their dreams.

MIDDLESCENCE Sheehy's term for a stage of life, from 45 to 55, when people seek new identity and are frequently "lost in a buzz of confusion."

EMPTY-NEST SYNDROME A sense of depression and loss of purpose felt by some parents when the youngest child leaves home.

✓ Truth or Fiction Revisited

It is not true that mothers in general suffer from the "empty-nest syndrome" when their youngest child leaves home. Most mothers (and fathers) do *not* suffer when their youngest child leaves home.

Late Adulthood

It's never too late to be what you might have been.

GEORGE ELIOT

According to Erikson, late adulthood is the stage of **ego integrity versus despair.** The basic challenge is to maintain the belief that life is meaningful and worthwhile in the face of the inevitability of death. Ego integrity derives from wisdom, as well as from the acceptance of one's lifespan as occurring at a certain point in the sweep of history and as being limited. We spend most of our lives accumulating objects and relationships. Erikson also argues that adjustment in the later years requires the ability to let go. Other views of late adulthood stress the importance of creating new challenges; however, biological and social realities may require older people to become more selective in their pursuits.

SUCCESSFUL AGING The later years were once seen mainly as a prelude to dying. Older people were viewed as crotchety and irritable. It was assumed that they reaped little pleasure from life. *No more.* Many stereotypes about aging are becoming less prevalent. Despite the changes that accompany aging, most people in their 70s report being generally satisfied with their lives (Margoshes, 1995). Americans are eating more wisely and exercising at later ages, so many older people are robust.

Sheehy (1995) coined the term *middlescence* to highlight her finding that people whom she interviewed in their 50s were thinking about what they would do with their *second adulthood*—the 30 to 40 healthy years they had left! Developmental psychologists are using another new term: *successful aging* (Margoshes, 1995). The term is not just meant to put a positive spin on the inevitable. "Successful agers" have a number of

EGO INTEGRITY VERSUS DESPAIR Erikson's term for the crisis of late adulthood, characterized by the task of maintaining one's sense of identity despite physical deterioration.

"Successful Aging"? The later years were once seen mainly as a prelude to dying. As we cross into the new millennium, however, many older people—termed "successful agers"—are seeking new challenges.

characteristics that can inspire all of us to lead more enjoyable and productive lives. There are three components of successful aging:

1. *Reshaping one's life to concentrate on what one finds to be important and meaningful.* Laura Carstensen's (1997) research on people aged 70 and above reveals that successful agers form emotional goals that bring them satisfaction. For example, rather than cast about in multiple directions, they may focus on their family and friends. Successful agers may have less time left than those of us in earlier stages of adulthood, but they tend to spend it more wisely (Garfinkel, 1995).

Researchers (Baltes, 1997; Schulz & Heckhausen, 1996) use terms such as "selective optimization and compensation" to describe the manner in which successful agers lead their lives. That is, successful agers no longer seek to compete in arenas best left to younger people—such as certain kinds of athletic or business activities. Rather, they focus on matters that allow them to maintain a sense of control over their own actions. Moreover, they use available resources to make up for losses. If their memory is not quite what it once was, they make notes or other reminders. For example, if their senses are no longer as acute, they use devices such as hearing aids or allow themselves more time to take in information. There are also some ingenious individual strategies. The great pianist Arthur Rubinstein performed into his 80s, even after he had lost much of his pianistic speed. In his later years, he would slow down before playing faster passages in order to enhance the impression of speed during those passages.

2. *A positive outlook.* For example, some older people attribute occasional health problems such as aches and pains to *specific* and *unstable* factors like a cold or jogging too long. Others attribute aches and pains to *global* and *stable* factors such as aging itself. Not surprisingly, those who attribute these problems to specific, unstable factors are more optimistic about surmounting them. They thus have a more positive outlook or attitude. Of particular interest here is research conducted by William Rakowski (1995). Rakowski followed 1,400 people aged 70 or older with nonlethal health problems such as aches and pains. He found that those who blamed the problems on aging itself were significantly more likely to die in the near future than those who blamed the problems on specific, unstable factors.

3. *Self-challenge.* Many people look forward to late adulthood as a time when they can rest from life's challenges. But sitting back and allowing the world to pass by is a prescription for vegetating, not for living life to its fullest. Consider an experiment conducted by Curt Sandman and Francis Crinella (1995) with 175 people whose average age was 72. They randomly assigned subjects either to a foster grandparent program with neurologically impaired children or to a control group, and followed both groups for 10 years. The foster grandparents carried out various physical challenges, such as walking a few miles each day, and also engaged in new kinds of social interactions. Those in the control group did not engage in these activities. When they were assessed by the experimenters, the foster grandparents showed improved overall cognitive functioning, including memory functioning, and better sleep patterns. Moreover, the foster grandparents showed superior functioning in these areas compared with people assigned to the control group.

REFLECT

Some people age faster than others, physically, cognitively, and socially. Considering the older people in your own experience, how do you account for the differences?

✓ **Truth or Fiction Revisited**

Actually, one of the "secrets" to successful aging is taking on new challenges, not avoiding challenge.

On Death and Dying

Death is the last great taboo. Psychiatrist Elisabeth Kübler-Ross commented on our denial of death in her landmark book *On Death and Dying:* "We use euphemisms, we make the dead look as if they were asleep, we ship the children off to protect them from the anxiety and turmoil around the house if the [person] is fortunate enough to die at home, [and] we don't allow children to visit their dying parents in the hospital" (1969, p. 8). Question: What are psychological perspectives on death and dying?

In her work with terminally ill patients, Kübler-Ross found some common responses to news of impending death. She identified five stages of dying through which many patients pass, and she suggested that older people who suspect that death is approaching may undergo similar stages:

1. *Denial.* In the denial stage, people feel that "it can't be happening to me. The diagnosis must be wrong."

2. *Anger.* Denial usually gives way to anger and resentment toward the young and healthy and, sometimes, toward the medical establishment—"It's unfair. Why me?"

3. *Bargaining.* Next, people may try to bargain with God to postpone their death, promising, for example, to do good deeds if they are given another six months, another year to live.

4. *Depression.* With depression come feelings of loss and hopelessness—grief at the inevitability of leaving loved ones and life itself.

5. *Final acceptance.* Ultimately, an inner peace may come, a quiet acceptance of the inevitable. Such "peace" does not resemble contentment. It is nearly devoid of feeling.

Psychologist Edwin Shneidman, who has specialized in the concerns of suicidal and dying individuals, acknowledges the presence of feelings such as those identified by Kübler-Ross, but he does not perceive them to be linked in a sequence like the one just described. Instead, he suggests that dying people show a variety of emotional and cognitive responses that tend to be fleeting or relatively stable, to ebb and flow, and to reflect pain and bewilderment. He also points out that the kinds of responses shown by individuals reflect their personality traits and their philosophies of life.

REFLECT

Erik Erikson wrote that one aspect of wisdom is the ability to visualize one's role in the march of history and to accept one's own death. Do you believe that acceptance of death is a sign of wisdom? Why or why not?

"LYING DOWN TO PLEASANT DREAMS . . ." The American poet William Cullen Bryant is best known for his poem "Thanatopsis," which he composed at the age of 18. "Thanatopsis" expresses Erik Erikson's goal of ego integrity—optimism that we can maintain a sense of trust through life. By meeting squarely the challenges of our adult lives, perhaps we can take our leave with dignity. When our time comes to "join the innumerable caravan"—the billions who have died before us—perhaps we can depart life with integrity.

Live, wrote the poet, so that

. . . when thy summons comes to join
The innumerable caravan that moves
To that mysterious realm, where each shall take
His chamber in the silent halls of death,
Thou go not, like the quarry-slave at night,
Scourged to his dungeon, but, sustained and soothed
By an unfaltering trust, approach thy grave
Like one that wraps the drapery of his couch
About him, and lies down to pleasant dreams.

Bryant, of course, wrote "Thanatopsis" at age 18, not at 85, the age at which he died. At that advanced age, his feelings—and his verse—might have differed. But literature and poetry, unlike science, need not reflect reality. They can serve to inspire and warm us.

Review

SECTION X

According to Sheehy, (146) _____ adulthood is generally fueled by ambition. Erikson considers the development of (147) _____ate relationships a central task of young adulthood. Erikson labels young adulthood the stage of intimacy versus (148) _____tion. According to Levinson, young adults often adopt a (149) _____, which serves as a tentative blueprint for their lives and is characterized by the drive to "become" someone, to leave their mark on history.

During the late 20s and 30s, many women encounter a crisis involving concerns about nearing the end of the (150) _____tile years, closing opportunities, and heightened responsibilities. Sheehy labels the 30s the (151) _____ 30s because many adults encounter disillusionment and reassess their lives at this time.

Many middle-aged people encounter feelings of entrapment and loss of purpose that are termed the (152) mid_____ _____. Erikson labels middle age the

stage of (153) _____ versus stagnation. Sheehy coins the term (154) "mid_____" to describe a period of searching for identity during the middle years. It was once thought that middle-aged women experience the (155) "_____-nest syndrome" when the youngest child leaves home, but research does not support this view. During middle adulthood, many women show (156: Increased or Decreased?) dominance and assertiveness.

Erikson terms late adulthood the stage of ego (156) _____ versus despair. "Successful aging" is characterized by reshaping one's life to focus on what is meaningful, a positive outlook, and (157) self-_____.

Kübler-Ross identifies five stages of dying among the terminally ill: (158) de_____, anger, bargaining, depression, and final (159) _____ance. Research by other investigators finds that psychological reactions to approaching death are (160: More or Less?) varied than Kübler-Ross suggests.

SECTION XI. CONTROVERSIES IN DEVELOPMENTAL PSYCHOLOGY

Now that we have traced development through the lifespan, we are ready to consider some controversies in developmental psychology. These have to do with the relative importance of nature and nurture in development, and with whether development is continuous or occurs in stages (that is, is discontinuous).

Does Development Reflect Nature or Nurture?

REFLECT

Which aspects of your own development seem to be most influenced by nature or nurture? Explain.

Question: What is the nature-nurture controversy about? The nature-nurture controversy reflects the effort to sort out the relative influences of nature and nurture on development. Our nature concerns those aspects of behavior that originate in our genes and are biologically "programmed" to unfold as long as minimal needs for nutrition and social experience are met. The effects of nurture concern those aspects of behavior that largely reflect environmental influences such as nutrition and learning.

Psychologists seek to understand the influences of nature in our genetic heritage, in the functioning of the nervous system, and in the process of **maturation** (that is, the unfolding of traits, as determined by the genetic code). Psychologists look for the influences of nurture in our nutrition, cultural and family backgrounds, and opportunities for learning, including early mental stimulation and formal education. The American psychologist Arnold Gesell (1880–1961) leaned heavily toward natural explanations of development. He argued that all areas of development are self-regulated by the unfolding of natural plans and processes. John Watson and other behaviorists, in contrast, leaned heavily toward environmental explanations. Let us consider the relative influences of nature and nurture in language development.

NATURE AND NURTURE IN LANGUAGE DEVELOPMENT

Since all normal humans talk but no house pets or house plants do, no matter how pampered, heredity must be involved in language. But since a child growing up in Japan speaks Japanese whereas the same child brought up in California would speak English, the environment is also crucial. Thus, there is no question about whether heredity or environment is involved in language, or even whether one or the other is "more important." Instead, . . . our best hope [might be] finding out how they interact.

STEVEN PINKER

Billions of children have acquired the languages spoken by their parents and passed them down, with minor changes, from generation to generation. Language development, like many other areas of development, apparently reflects the interactions between the influences of heredity (nature) and the environment (nurture). Question: How is the nature-nurture controversy applied to language development?

Learning theorists see language as developing according to laws of learning (Gleason & Ratner, 1993). They usually refer to the concepts of imitation and reinforcement. From a social-cognitive perspective, parents serve as *models*. Children learn language, at least in part, through observation and imitation. It seems likely that many words, especially nouns and verbs (including irregular verbs), are learned by imitation.

At first children accurately repeat the irregular verb forms they observe. This repetition can probably be explained in terms of modeling, but modeling does not explain all the events involved in learning. Children later begin to overregularize irregular verb forms *because of* their knowledge of rules of grammar, not through imitation. Nor does imitative learning explain how children come to utter phrases and sentences that they have *not* observed. Parents, for example, are unlikely to model utterances such as "bye-bye sock" and "allgone Daddy," but children do say them.

Learning theory cannot account for the unchanging sequence of language development and the spurts in children's language acquisition. Even the types of two-word utterances emerge in a consistent pattern in diverse cultures. Although timing differs from one child to another, the types of questions used, passive versus active sentences, and so on, all emerge in the same order.

The nativist theory of language development holds that innate or inborn factors—which make up children's *nature*—cause children to attend to and acquire language in certain ways. From this perspective, children bring a certain neurological "prewiring" to language learning (Newport, 1998; Pinker, 1994).

MATURATION The orderly unfolding of traits, as regulated by the genetic code.

According to **psycholinguistic theory,** language acquisition involves the interaction of environmental influences—such as exposure to parental speech and reinforcement—and an inborn tendency to acquire language. Noam Chomsky (1980, 1991) refers to the inborn tendency as a **language acquisition device (LAD).** Evidence for an LAD is found in the universality of human language abilities and in the specific sequence of language development.

The LAD prepares the nervous system to learn grammar. On the surface, languages differ a great deal. However, the LAD serves children all over the world because languages share what Chomsky refers to as a "universal grammar"—an underlying set of rules for turning ideas into sentences (Pinker, 1994). Consider an analogy with computers: According to psycholinguistic theory, the universal grammar that resides in the LAD is the same as a computer's basic operating system. The particular language that a child learns to use is the same as a word-processing program.

Today, most researchers would agree that both nature and nurture affect most areas of development. We can argue as to which is more prominent in a given area of development, but as in the case of language development, they are both essential.

Is Development Continuous or Discontinuous?

Do developmental changes tend to occur gradually (continuously)? Or do they tend to occur in major leaps (discontinuously) that dramatically alter our bodies and behavior? Question: Does development occur gradually or in stages?

Watson and other behaviorists viewed development as a mainly continuous process in which the effects of learning mount gradually, with no major sudden changes. Maturational theorists, however, argue that people are prewired or preset to change dramatically at certain times of life. Rapid qualitative changes can be ushered in during new stages of development. They point out that the environment, even when enriched, profits us little until we are ready, or mature enough, to develop in a certain direction. For example, newborn babies do not imitate their parents' speech, even when the parents speak clearly and deliberately. Nor does aided practice in "walking" during the first few months after birth significantly accelerate the date at which the child can walk on her own.

Stage theorists, such as Sigmund Freud and Jean Piaget, saw development as discontinuous. Both theorists saw biological changes as providing the potential for psychological changes. Freud focused on the ways in which sexual development might provide the basis for personality development. Piaget's research centered on the ways in which maturation of the nervous system permits cognitive advances.

Certain aspects of physical development do occur in stages. For example, from the age of 2 to the onset of puberty (the period of development during which reproduction becomes possible), children gradually grow larger. Then the adolescent growth spurt occurs. It is ushered in by hormones and characterized by rapid changes in structure and function (as in the development of the sex organs) as well as in size. Thus a new stage of life has begun. Psychologists disagree more strongly on whether aspects of development such as cognitive development, attachment, and gender typing occur in stages.

REFLECT

Which aspects of your own development have clearly occurred in stages? Which seem to be more gradual? Why?

PSYCHOLINGUISTIC THEORY The view that language learning involves an interaction between environmental factors and an inborn tendency to acquire language.

LANGUAGE ACQUISITION DEVICE (LAD) In psycholinguistic theory, neural "prewiring" that facilitates the child's learning of grammar.

SECTION XI `Review`

Aspects of behavior that originate in our genes and unfold as long as minimal environmental support is provided are referred to as our (161) _____ure. Aspects of behavior that can be largely traced to environmental influences such as nutrition and learning are said to reflect our (162) _____-ure. Psychologist Arnold (163) G_____ endorsed natural explanations of development. Gesell argued that development is self-regulated by the unfolding of natural plans and processes, or by (164) _____ation. John Watson and other behaviorists leaned heavily toward (165) ___ mental explanations.

(166) _____ing theorists see parents as models for usage of language. They argue that children learn language by (167) obser_____ and imitation. But learning theory does not explain children's (168) _____ization of regular nouns and verbs. The (169) _____ist view holds that inborn factors cause children to develop language in certain ways. According to (170) _____istic theory, language development involves the interaction of nurture, such as parental speech, and an inborn tendency to acquire language. This inborn tendency has been labeled the (171) _____ _____tion device (LAD). Chomsky argues that the LAD allows children to understand a (172) "uni_____ grammar."

Psychologists debate whether developmental changes occur gradually—that is, (173) _____ously, or in major qualitative leaps—that is, discontinuously. Stage theorists see development as (174) _____uous. Watson and other learning theorists see development as mainly (175) _____uous.

Development is a process that continues for a lifetime. If we include the formation of the genetic codes and the sperm and ova that gave rise to us and that give rise to our children, development becomes a continuous process that chronicles the existence of humans on planet Earth and possibly, as we move farther into the new millennium, our existence on other orbs. Development stems from the interaction of the unfolding of genetically directed processes and the effects of the environments into which we are plunged at birth. But then we grow aware of those environments and learn how to change them to better meet our needs. Learning and wisdom are as much a part of development as prenatal differentiation and the exciting changes of puberty.

STUDY GUIDE

To help you better understand the content of this chapter, you may go to the student Web site (http://www.harcourtcollege.com/psych/intro.html) to take more quizzes, get more information about the content, and see additional Web sites related to the content. You can also practice using the concepts in this chapter with the PowerPsych CD-ROM, which gives you interactive activities and experiments along with even more quizzes. And, of course, the printed study guide is a reliable way to practice all parts of PQ4R. Your college bookstore can order the PowerPsych CD-ROM for you.

SUMMARY

1. **What developments occur from conception through birth?** Prenatal development occurs in stages: the germinal, embryonic, and fetal stages. During the germinal stage, the zygote divides as it travels through the fallopian tube and becomes implanted in the uterine wall. The major organ systems are formed during the embryonic stage, and the fetal stage is characterized by maturation and gains in size.

2. **What physical developments occur during childhood?** Early physical development—prenatal and infant—occurs the most rapidly. Reflexes are inborn responses to stimuli that in many cases are essential to the survival of the infant. Examples include sucking and swallowing. Newborn babies can see quite well and show greater interest in complex visual stimuli than in simple ones. Infants are capable of depth perception by the time they can crawl. Newborns can normally hear and show a preference for their mother's voice. Newborns show preferences for pleasant odors and sweet foods. Motor development usually proceeds in a particular sequence in which infants roll over and sit before they stand and walk.

3. **What are Jean Piaget's views of cognitive development?** Piaget saw children as budding scientists who actively strive to make sense of the perceptual world. He defined intelligence as involving the processes of assimilation (responding to events according to existing schemes) and accommodation (changing schemes to permit effective responses to new events). Piaget's view of cognitive development includes four stages: sensorimotor (prior to the use of symbols and language); preoperational (characterized by egocentric thought, animism, artificialism, and inability to center on more than one aspect of a situation); concrete operational (characterized by conservation, less egocentrism, reversibility, and subjective moral judgments); and formal operational (characterized by abstract logic).

4. **How does language develop?** Children make the prelinguistic sounds of crying, cooing, and babbling before true language develops. Single-word utterances occur at about 1 year of age; two-word utterances, by the age of 2. Early language is characterized by overextension of familiar words and concepts to unfamiliar objects (calling horses *doggies*) and by overregularization of verbs ("She *sitted* down"). As time passes, vocabulary grows larger, and sentence structure grows more complex.

5. **How do children reason about what is right and wrong?** Lawrence Kohlberg hypothesized that children's sense of moral reasoning develops through three levels, each of which consists of two stages. Moral decisions develop from being based on pain and pleasure ("preconventional") through necessity to maintain the social order ("conventional") to reliance on one's own conscience ("postconventional"). Not all individuals reach the postconventional level.

6. **What are Erikson's stages of psychosocial development?** Erikson hypothesizes that there are eight stages of psychosocial development. Each represents a life crisis. The first of these is "trust versus mistrust," during which the crisis centers on the child's learning that the world is a good place that can meet its needs.

7. **How do feelings of attachment develop? What kinds of experiences affect attachment?** Mary Ainsworth developed the strange situation method to study attachment. According to Ainsworth, there are three stages of attachment: the initial-preattachment phase, which is characterized by indiscriminate attachment; the attachment-in-the-making phase, which is characterized by preference for familiar figures; and the clear-cut-attachment phase, which is characterized by intensified dependence on the primary caregiver. Bowlby adds fear of strangers as a factor in attachment. Behaviorists have argued that children become attached to their mothers through conditioning because their mothers feed them and attend to their other needs. Harlow's studies with rhesus monkeys suggest that an innate motive, contact comfort, may be more important than conditioning in the development of attachment. There are critical developmental periods during which animals such as geese and ducks will become attached instinctively to (or imprinted on) an object that they follow.

8. **What types of parental behavior are connected with variables such as self-esteem, achievement motivation, and independence in children?** Styles of parental behavior include the authoritative, authoritarian, and permissive styles. The children of authoritative parents are the most achievement-oriented and well-adjusted.

9. **What physical developments occur during adolescence?** Adolescence is a period of life that begins at puberty and ends with assumption of adult responsibilities. Changes that lead to reproductive capacity and secondary sex characteristics are stimulated by increased levels of testosterone in the male and of estrogen and androgens in the female. During the adolescent growth spurt, young people may grow 6 or more inches in a year.

10. **What cognitive developments occur during adolescence?** Formal-operational thinking appears in adolescence, but not everyone reaches this stage. Two consequences of adolescent egocentrism are the imaginary audience and the personal fable. The imaginary audience refers to the adolescent beliefs that they are the center of attention and that other people are as concerned with their appearance and behavior as they are. The personal fable refers to the adolescent belief that one's feelings and ideas are special, even unique, and that one is invulnerable.

11. **What social and personality developments occur during adolescence?** Adolescents and parents are often in conflict because adolescents desire more independence and may experiment with things that can jeopardize their health. Despite bickering, most adolescents continue to love and respect their parents. According to Erikson, adolescents strive to forge an ego identity—a sense of who they are and what they stand for. The changes of puberty prepare the body for sexual activity, and high hormone levels also stir interest in sex. But most sexually active adolescents do not use contraceptives reliably. Thus about 1 teenage girl in 10 gets pregnant each year.

12. **What physical developments occur during adulthood?** People are usually at the height of their physical powers during young adulthood. Middle adulthood is characterized by a gradual decline in strength. Menopause has been thought to depress many women, but research suggests that most women go through this passage without great difficulty. Older people show less sensory acuity, and their reaction time lengthens. The immune system weakens, and changes occur that eventually result in death.

13. **Why do we age?** Heredity plays a role in longevity. One theory (programmed senescence) suggests that aging and death are determined by our genes.

Another theory (wear-and-tear theory) holds that factors such as pollution, disease, and ultraviolet light weaken the body so that it loses the ability to repair itself. Lifestyle factors such as exercise, proper nutrition, and *not* smoking also contribute to longevity.

14. **What cognitive developments occur during adulthood?** People are usually at the height of their cognitive powers during early adulthood, but people can be creative for a lifetime. Memory functioning declines with age, but memory deficits are not usually as large as people assume. People tend to retain verbal ability, as shown by vocabulary and general knowledge, into advanced old age. Crystallized intelligence—one's vocabulary and accumulated knowledge—generally increases with age. Fluid intelligence—the ability to process information rapidly—declines more rapidly, but workers' familiarity with solving specific kinds of problems is often more important than their fluid intelligence.

15. **What social and personality developments occur during young adulthood?** Young adulthood is generally characterized by efforts to advance in the business world and the development of intimate ties. Many young adults reassess the directions of their lives during the "age-30 transition."

16. **What social and personality developments occur during middle adulthood?** Many theorists view middle adulthood as a time of crisis (the "midlife crisis") and further reassessment. Many adults try to come to terms with the discrepancies between their achievements and the dreams of their youth during middle adulthood. Some middle-aged adults become depressed when their youngest child leaves home (the so-called empty-nest syndrome), but many report increased satisfaction, stability, and self-confidence. On a more positive note, many people in middle adulthood experience "middlescence"—a phase during which they redefine themselves and their goals for the 30 to 40 healthy years they expect lie ahead of them.

17. **What social and personality developments occur during late adulthood?** Erikson characterizes late adulthood as the stage of ego integrity versus despair. He saw the basic challenge as maintaining the belief that life is worthwhile in the face of physical deterioration. However, many stereotypes about aging are growing less prevalent. Most older Americans report being generally satisfied with their lives. Those who experience "successful aging" reshape their lives to focus on what they find to be important, maintain a positive outlook, and find new challenges.

18. **What are psychological perspectives on death and dying?** Kübler-Ross has identified five stages of

dying among people who are terminally ill: denial, anger, bargaining, depression, and final acceptance. However, other investigators find that psychological reactions to approaching death are more varied than Kübler-Ross suggests.

19. **What is the nature-nurture controversy about?** The nature-nurture controversy concerns the relative influences of heredity (nature) and nurture (environmental influences) on development. Development appears to reflect an interaction between nature (genetic factors) and nurture (environmental influences). Maturational theorists focus on the influences of nature, whereas learning theorists focus on environmental influences.

20. **How is the nature-nurture controversy applied to language development?** The two main theories of language development are learning theories and nativist theories. Learning theories focus on the roles of reinforcement and imitation. Nativist theories assume that innate factors cause children to attend to and perceive language in certain ways.

21. **Does development occur gradually or in stages?** Stage theorists like Freud and Piaget view development as discontinuous. According to them, people go through distinct periods of development that differ in quality and follow an orderly sequence. Learning theorists, in contrast, tend to view psychological development as a more continuous process.

EXERCISE 1

PIAGET'S STAGES OF COGNITIVE DEVELOPMENT

Fill in the blanks.

Stage	Approximate Age	Description
(1) _____motor	Birth–2 years	At first, the child lacks language and does not use (2) _____bols or mentally represent objects. In time, reflexive responding ends and intentional behavior begins. The child develops the (3) ob_____ concept (understands that objects continue to exist even if they are out of sight) and basics of language.
Preoperational	2–7 years	The child begins to represent the world mentally, but thought is (4) _____centric. The child does not focus on two aspects of a situation at once and therefore lacks (5) con_____. The child shows animism, artificialism, and (6) _____ responsibility for wrongdoing.
(7) _____ operational	7–12 years	The child develops conservation concepts, can adopt the viewpoint of others, can classify objects in series, and shows comprehension of basic relational concepts (such as one object being larger or heavier than another).
(8) _____ operational	12 years and above	Mature, adult thought emerges. Thinking is characterized by deductive logic, mental (9) _____ and error, abstract thought, and the formation and testing of (10) _____ses.

E X E R C I S E   2

KOHLBERG'S LEVELS AND STAGES OF MORAL DEVELOPMENT

Fill in the blanks.

STAGE OF DEVELOPMENT	Examples of Moral Reasoning That Support Heinz's Stealing the Drug	Examples of Moral Reasoning That Oppose Heinz's Stealing the Drug
LEVEL I: PRECONVENTIONAL		
STAGE 1: Judgments guided by (1) obe_____ and the prospect of (2) _____ment (the consequences of behavior.)	It isn't wrong to take the drug. Heinz did try to pay the druggist for it, and it's only worth $200, not $2,000.	Taking things without paying is wrong because it's against the law. Heinz will get caught and go to jail.
STAGE 2: Naively (3) _____tic, instrumental orientation; things are right when they satisfy people's needs.	Heinz ought to take the drug because his wife really needs it. He can always pay the druggist back.	Heinz shouldn't take the drug. If he gets caught and winds up in jail, it won't do his wife any good.
LEVEL II: CONVENTIONAL		
STAGE 3: (4) _____-boy orientation; moral behavior helps others and is socially approved.	Stealing is a crime, so it's bad, but Heinz should take the drug to save his wife or else people would blame him for letting her die.	Stealing is a crime. Heinz shouldn't just take the drug because his family will be dishonored and they will blame him.
STAGE 4: Law-and-(5) _____ orientation; moral behavior is doing one's duty and showing respect for (6) _____ity.	Heinz must take the drug to do his duty to save his wife. Eventually, he has to pay the druggist for it, however.	If everyone took the law into their own hands, civilization would fall apart, so Heinz shouldn't steal the drug.
LEVEL III: (7) _____TIONAL		
STAGE 5: (8) Con_____, legalistic orientation; one must weigh pressing human needs against society's need to maintain (9) so_____ order.	This thing is complicated because society has a right to maintain law and order, but Heinz has to take the drug to save his wife.	I can see why Heinz feels he has to take the drug, but laws exist for the benefit of society as a whole and can't simply be cast aside.
STAGE 6: (1) _____sal ethical principles orientation; people must follow universal ethical principles and their own conscience, even if it means breaking the law.	In this case, the law comes into conflict with the principle of the sanctity of human life. Heinz must take the drug because his wife's life is more important than the law.	If Heinz truly believes that stealing the drug is worse than letting his wife die, he should not take it. People have to make sacrifices to do what they think is right.

E X E R C I S E   3

PARENTING STYLES

Fill in the blanks with either "High" or "Low."

PARENTAL BEHAVIOR				
Style of Parenting	Restrictiveness	Demands for Mature Behavior	Communication Ability	Warmth and Support
Authoritarian	(1) _____ (use of force)	Moderate	(2) _____	(3) _____
Authoritative	(4) _____ (use of reasoning)	(5) _____	(6) _____	(7) _____
Permissive	(8) _____ (easygoing)	(9) _____	Low	(10) _____

LANGUAGE AND CULTURE

to accommodate (109)   *(here) to adjust to a situation*

agent (104)   *(here) chemical substances*

aided practice (154)   *assistance while learning*

all the world's a stage (111)   *the environment is free for (the child) to play on*

the alternative (143)   *(here) death*

autonomy (146)   *independence, self-rule*

battle of the bulge (129)   *fight against weight gain (pun on an important World War II battle)*

to be on a roll (111)   *to be doing something well and therefore continuing*

biracial (136)   *of mixed race (such as both Asian and Caucasian)*

blueprint (145)   *plan*

to be bombarded by (137)   *to be surrounded by and influenced by*

to chafe to (147)   *to be eager to do something that one is not being permitted to do*

child abuse (103)   *bad treatment of children, hurtful actions toward children*

to cling to (122)   *to hold onto with*

to coin a term (148)   *to make up a new expression or word*

to come apart at the seams (148)   *to fall apart figuratively, to lose one's sense of control*

by conformity to (118)   *by following*

contraception (137)   *prevention of pregnancy*

cooing (113)   *happy baby sounds*

to cower in fear (123)   *try to hide themselves to stay away from danger, to hide out of fear*

a critical body weight (129)   *body weight necessary to cause a change*

crotchety (140)   *ill-tempered, disagreeable*

curfew (135)   *hour at which a person must be back at home, time limit*

to dawn on (147)   *to occur as a thought to*

to derive rules (130)   *to infer the governing principles*

discontent (147)   *(a) sense of unhappiness about something*

double negation (117)   *two "no" words used in one sentence*

druggist (117)   *pharmacist*

to do one's duty (118)   *to perform as society says one should, to do what is expected of one*

to dwell longer on (106)   *to remain attentive to, to hold one's eyes on (something)*

ego identity (146)   *knowledge and security of self, stable life role*

the elementary school years (120)   *years in school between ages 6 and 11*

epithet (140)   *label, name*

excepting (142)   *except for, not counting*

exertion (140)   *hard work, exercise*

the extremities (104)   *the fingers and toes, hands and feet, arms and legs*

to fare better (135)   *to have a better chance of success*

to give in (120)   *to allow oneself to be manipulated, to agree to do something against one's better judgment*

to go downhill (138)   *to deteriorate, to lose one's strength*

gosling (124)   *baby goose*

gratification of needs (122)   *satisfaction of hunger and comfort*

growth spurt (105)   *acceleration of growing over a limited amount of time*

to herald (129)   *to signal, to welcome*

haphazardly (116)   *randomly, without plan or order*

to howl (114)   *to cry, to protest*

illusory (133)   *imaginary, deceptive, not real*

individuation (146)   *development of personal identity*

the "kids" (139)   *those who are younger than one*

longevity (142)   *long life, length of life*

a low children-to-caregiver ratio (126)   *a small number of children under the care of each caregiver*

to make inroads (138)   *to make changes, to bring about improvements*

malnutrition (105)   *circumstances in which a person does not get good food that contains what the body needs to be healthy*

marathoner (139)   *person who runs marathons, athlete*

to meet something squarely (151)   *to deal with a problem, not to try to avoid*

mood swing (135)   *change in feeling (from happiness to sadness)*

moral dilemma (117)   *problem of what is right and what is wrong*

moral judgment (112)   *ability to distinguish between right and wrong* neither fish nor fowl (135)   *(here) neither adult nor child*

nondescript (104)   *unclear, not describable, shapeless, formless*

nonlethal (150)   *not capable of killing, not dangerous to life*

novel (109)   *new, different*

to be now-oriented (116)   *to be settled or comfortable in the here and now, to live in the present*

occupational issues (136)   *job-related matters*

out of sight . . . out of mind (110)   *what is not seen is not part of the conscious thinking*

peer pressure (137)   *the opinion of others in one's age group*

to play peek-a-boo (110)   *to amuse a child by hiding one's face behind one's hands and then looking out from behind the hands at a child, and saying, "peek-a-boo"*

to be plunged into (155)   *to be immersed, to be suddenly involved with*

precocious (107)   *advanced, intelligent*

prelinguistic vocalization (113)   *baby sounds that come before speech*

preprogrammed to (107)   *naturally ready to (act in a specific way)*

prerequisite (133)   *condition that must exist (before something can happen), conditional aspect for*

to profit (134)   *to benefit*

prolonged labor (137)   *difficulty in giving birth*

prom (136)   *formal high school dance and party*

to put a positive spin on (149)   *to interpret positively*

rattle (110)   *child's toy that makes noise*

the ravages of time (143)   *the aging process, the effects of getting older*

robust (149)   *healthy, strong*

the sanctity of human life (133)   *the value of life for human beings*

sedentary (139)   *inactive*

sexually transmitted infection (137)   *disease caused by sexual contact*

to single out (114)   *to separate (from background noise)*

to skip (136)   *not to attend*

socialized (134)   *trained*

somersault (104)   *head-over-heels roll*

specter (147)   *spirit, ghost*

squat (112)   *short and fat*

to squish food (109)   *to turn food into mush, to crush and squeeze food into pudding*

stagelike (132)   *occurring in steps or stages*

stagnation (147)   *state without no change*

the startle reflex (106)   *the natural reaction to a loud noise*

to stick to the facts (130)   *to say only what is true and not explain*

suppleness (138)   *stretchiness, elasticity, bend-ability*

to surmount (150)   *to conquer, to overcome*

to switch (117)   *to change back and forth*

to temper (124)   *to soften, to modify, to adjust*

to usher in (154)   *to guide, to accompany*

to vacillate (134)   *(here) to be unable to decide yes or no*

vegetating (150)   *just sitting or lying down, not doing anything*

viable (140)   *living, able to live*

Wall Street cubbyhole (148)   *tiny office in the business center*

ways of carrying oneself (131)   *posture, body language*

wellspring (123)   *source*

to be widowed (142)   *to lose one's husband or wife to death*

without fuss (121)   *without objection, happily*

to wolf down (129)   *to eat voraciously (fast and wildly) like a hungry wolf*

to be in the work force (126)   *to be working outside of the home*

1. Conception normally takes place in the
   - (a) uterus,
   - (b) fallopian tube,
   - (c) ovary,
   - (d) vagina.

2. Development tends to be continuous, according to the views of
   - (a) Sigmund Freud,
   - (b) Erik Erikson,
   - (c) John Watson,
   - (d) Jean Piaget.

3. The embryonic period lasts from _____ until about the eighth week of prenatal development.
   - (a) implantation,
   - (b) conception,
   - (c) ovulation,
   - (d) the time the zygote reaches the uterus.

4. There is a sudden noise in the nursery, and a newborn baby draws up his legs and arches his back in response. This response is an example of the _____ reflex.
   - (a) Babinski,
   - (b) palmar,
   - (c) sphincter,
   - (d) Moro.

5. Piaget explains adolescent risk taking in terms of
   - (a) puberty,
   - (b) the personal fable,
   - (c) storm and stress,
   - (d) the imaginary audience.

6. Mary Ainsworth devised the strange situation method to study
   - (a) parenting styles,
   - (b) adolescent development,
   - (c) fluid intelligence,
   - (d) attachment.

7. In Harlow's experiments, infant rhesus monkeys showed preference for surrogate mothers
   - (a) of their own species,
   - (b) that were made from soft material,
   - (c) that fed them,
   - (d) that were present when they wanted to explore the environment.

8. According to Piaget, children first show object permanence during the
   - (a) sensorimotor period,
   - (b) preoperational period,
   - (c) concrete-operational period,
   - (d) formal-operational period.

9. According to Piaget, children first center on the motives of wrongdoers, as well as the amount of damage done, during the
   - (a) sensorimotor period,
   - (b) preoperational period,
   - (c) concrete-operational period,
   - (d) formal-operational period.

10. The nativist view of language development is supported by the research finding that
    - (a) prelinguistic verbalizations precede linguistic verbalizations,
    - (b) children overextend the meanings of words,
    - (c) two-word utterances develop in the same sequence among speakers of various languages,
    - (d) reinforcement affects language development.

11. Which of the following stages of moral development comes earliest, according to Kohlberg?
    - (a) Good-boy orientation,
    - (b) Contractual, legalistic orientation,
    - (c) Naively egoistic orientation,
    - (d) Obedience-and-punishment orientation.

12. According to Kohlberg, stage _____ moral judgments are characterized by respect for authority and social order.
    - (a) 1,
    - (b) 2,
    - (c) 3,
    - (d) 4.

13. Carstensen's research on people aged 70 and above reveals that successful agers
    - (a) do not experience menopause or manopause,
    - (b) are fixated in the stage of middlescence,
    - (c) compete with younger people,
    - (d) find challenges that bring them satisfaction.

14. The period of adolescence is defined by
    - (a) biological changes only,
    - (b) psychosocial changes only,
    - (c) both biological and psychosocial changes,
    - (d) neither biological nor psychosocial changes.

15. Sheehy uses the term "middlescence" to suggest that
    - (a) adolescence occurs in the middle of life,
    - (b) many middle-aged people seek to redefine themselves,
    - (c) psychologists take a scientific approach to the study of middle age,

(d) there is a stage of life between childhood and adolescence.

16. Menarche is defined as
    (a) the beginning of puberty in girls,
    (b) the appearance of secondary sex characteristics in girls,
    (c) the complete maturation of secondary sex characteristics in girls,
    (d) first menstruation.

17. According to Erikson, adolescence is characterized by the crisis of
    (a) ego identity versus role diffusion,
    (b) intimacy versus isolation,
    (c) autonomy versus doubt,
    (d) ego integrity versus despair.

18. Which of the following is characterized by one's vocabulary and accumulated knowledge?

    (a) Performance IQ,
    (b) Fluid intelligence,
    (c) Wechsler Adult Intelligence Scale IQ,
    (d) Crystallized intelligence.

19. Research shows that middle-aged women
    (a) frequently show increased dominance and assertiveness,
    (b) most often report decreased marital satisfaction,
    (c) cannot make the transition from motherhood to socially useful occupations,
    (d) come under the influence of the dream.

20. Which of the following groups has the greatest longevity?
    (a) African American men,
    (b) African American women,
    (c) White men,
    (d) White women.

1. What developments occur from conception through birth?

_____
_____
_____
_____
_____

2. What physical developments occur during childhood?

_____
_____
_____
_____
_____
_____

3. What are Jean Piaget's views of cognitive development?

_____
_____
_____
_____
_____

4. How does language develop?

_____
_____
_____
_____
_____

5. How do children reason about what is right and wrong?

_____
_____
_____
_____
_____

6. What are Erikson's stages of psychosocial development?

_____
_____
_____
_____
_____

7. How do feelings of attachment develop? What kinds of experiences affect attachment?

_____
_____
_____
_____

8. What types of parental behavior are connected with variables such as self-esteem, achievement motivation, and independence in children?

_____
_____
_____

9. What physical developments occur during adolescence?

_____
_____
_____
_____

10. What cognitive developments occur during adolescence?

_____
_____
_____
_____

11. What social and personality developments occur during adolescence?

12. What physical developments occur during adulthood?

13. Why do we age?

14. What cognitive developments occur during adulthood?

15. What social and personality developments occur during young adulthood?

16. What social and personality developments occur during middle adulthood?

17. What social and personality developments occur during late adulthood?

18. What are psychological perspectives on death and dying?

19. What is the nature-nurture controversy about?

20. How is the nature-nurture controversy applied to language development?

21. Does development occur gradually or in stages?

ANSWERS TO CHAPTER REVIEW

1. Ovulation
2. Ovum
3. Zygote
4. Three
5. Germinal
6. Embryonic
7. Fetal
8. Fallopian
9. Uterus
10. Organ
11. 5
12. First
13. 2
14. 4
15. Stereotypical
16. Rooting
17. Sucking
18. Startle
19. Palmar
20. Babinski
21. Crawl
22. Reflexively
23. Mothers'
24. Are
25. Pain
26. Scientists or Physicists
27. Schemes
28. Assimilation
29. Accommodation
30. Four
31. Sensorimotor
32. Permanence
33. Preoperational
34. Center
35. Objective
36. Concrete
37. Subjective
38. Formal
39. Coo
40. Pleasure
41. Babbling
42. Prelinguistic
43. 1 year (12 months)
44. Overextend

45. Holophrases
46. Second
47. Overregularizations
48. Do
49. Moral
50. Three
51. Preconventional
52. Punishment
53. Needs
54. Good-boy
55. Social
56. Eight
57. Crisis
58. Mistrust
59. Emotional or Affectional
60. Strange
61. Secure
62. Ambivalent/resistant
63. Securely
64. Initial preattachment
65. Making
66. Clear
67. Fear
68. Conditioning
69. Contact
70. Surrogate
71. Instinct
72. Critical
73. Imprinted
74. Locomotion
75. Fear
76. Instrumental
77. Strictness
78. Authoritative
79. Warm
80. More
81. More
82. Quality
83. Unemployment
84. Less
85. More
86. Spurt
87. Secondary
88. Testosterone

89. Estrogen
90. Menarche
91. Adolescence
92. Hypothetical
93. Egocentrism
94. Imaginary
95. Attention
96. Privacy
97. Special
98. Risk
99. Underestimate
100. More
101. Invariant
102. Postconventional
103. Contractual
104. Universal
105. Males
106. Storm and stress
107. 10 (ten)
108. Alcohol
109. Biological or physiological
110. Sociocultural
111. More
112. Lesser
113. Less
114. Does not
115. Agree
116. Identity
117. Diffusion
118. Are
119. Fewer
120. Less
121. Sensory
122. Cardiovascular
123. Gradual
124. Menopause
125. Climacteric
126. Hot
127. Estrogen
128. Without
129. Calcium
130. Less
131. Reaction
132. Longer

133. Shorter
134. Programmed senescence
135. Wear
136. Young or Early
137. Can
138. Declines
139. Better
140. Verbal Skills
141. Crystallized
142. Fluid
143. Crystallized
144. Crystallized
145. Fluid
146. Early or Young
147. Intimate
148. Isolation
149. Dream
150. Fertile
151. Catch
152. Midlife crisis
153. Generativity
154. Middlescence
155. Empty
156. Increased
157. Challenge
158. Denial
159. Acceptance
160. Varied
161. Nature
162. Nurture
163. Gesell
164. Maturation
165. Environmental
166. Learning
167. Observation
168. Overregularization
169. Nativist
170. Psycholinguistic
171. Language acquisition
172. Universal
173. Continuously
174. Discontinuous
175. Continuous

ANSWERS TO EXERCISE 1

1. Sensorimotor
2. Symbols
3. Object
4. Egocentric
5. Conservation
6. Objective
7. Concrete
8. Formal
9. Trial
10. Hypotheses

ANSWERS TO EXERCISE 2

1. Obedience	4. Good	7. Conventional	9. Social
2. Punishment	5. Order	8. Contractual	10. Universal
3. Egoistic	6. Authority		

ANSWERS TO EXERCISE 3

1. High	4. High	7. High	9. Low
2. Low	5. High	8. Low	10. High
3. Low	6. High		

ANSWERS TO QUIZ

1. B	6. D	11. D	16. D
2. C	7. B	12. D	17. A
3. A	8. A	13. D	18. D
4. D	9. C	14. C	19. A
5. B	10. C	15. B	20. D

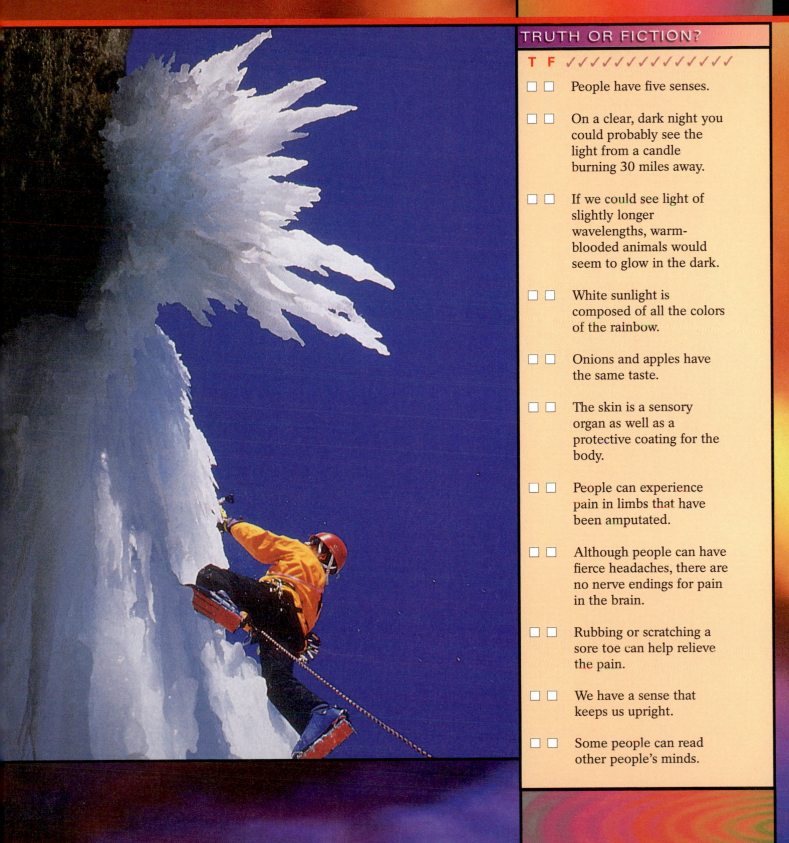

SENSATION AND PERCEPTION

4

TRUTH OR FICTION?

T F ✓✓✓✓✓✓✓✓✓✓✓✓✓

☐ ☐ People have five senses.

☐ ☐ On a clear, dark night you could probably see the light from a candle burning 30 miles away.

☐ ☐ If we could see light of slightly longer wavelengths, warm-blooded animals would seem to glow in the dark.

☐ ☐ White sunlight is composed of all the colors of the rainbow.

☐ ☐ Onions and apples have the same taste.

☐ ☐ The skin is a sensory organ as well as a protective coating for the body.

☐ ☐ People can experience pain in limbs that have been amputated.

☐ ☐ Although people can have fierce headaches, there are no nerve endings for pain in the brain.

☐ ☐ Rubbing or scratching a sore toe can help relieve the pain.

☐ ☐ We have a sense that keeps us upright.

☐ ☐ Some people can read other people's minds.

This chapter, "Sensation and Perception," covers the following:

Five thousand years ago in China, give or take a day or two, an arrow was shot into the air. Where did it land? Ancient records tell us precisely where: in the hand of a fierce warrior and master of the martial arts. As the story was told to me, the warrior had grown so fierce because of a chronic toothache. Incessant pain had ruined his disposition.

One fateful day, our hero watched as invading hordes assembled on surrounding hills. His troops were trembling in the face of the enemy's great numbers, and he raised his arms to boost their morale. A slender wooden shaft lifted into the air from a nearby rise, arced, and then descended—right into the warrior's palm. His troops cringed and muttered among themselves, but our hero said nothing. Although he saw the arrow pass through his palm, he did not scream. He did not run. He did not even complain. He was astounded. His toothache had vanished. In fact, his whole jaw was numb.

Meanwhile the invaders looked on, horrified. They, too, muttered among themselves. What sort of warrior could watch an arrow pierce his hand with such indifference? Even with a smile? If this was the caliber of the local warriors, the invaders would be better off traveling west and looking for a brawl in Sumer or in Egypt. They sounded the retreat and withdrew.

Back in town, our warrior received a hero's welcome. A physician offered to remove the arrow without a fee—a tribute to bravery. But the warrior would have none of it. The arrow had worked wonders for his toothache, and he would brook no meddling. He had already discovered that if the pain threatened to return, he need only twirl the arrow and it would recede once more.

But all was not well on the home front. His wife was thrilled to find him jovial once more, but the arrow put a crimp in their romance. When he put his arm around her, she was in danger of being stabbed. Finally, she gave him an ultimatum: The arrow must go, or she would.

Placed in deep conflict, our warrior consulted a psychologist, who then huddled with the physician and the village elders. After much to-do, they asked the warrior to participate in an experiment. They would remove the arrow and replace it with a pin that the warrior could twirl as needed.

To the warrior's wife's relief, the pin worked. And here, in ancient China, lay the origins of the art of *acupuncture*—the use of needles to relieve pain and treat assorted ills.

I confess that this tale is not entirely accurate. To my knowledge, there were no psychologists in ancient China (their loss). Moreover, the part about the warrior's wife is fictitious. It is claimed, however, that acupuncture as a means of dealing with pain originated in ancient China when a soldier was, in fact, wounded in the hand by an arrow and discovered that a chronic toothache had disappeared. Historians say the Chinese then set out to map the body by sticking pins into various parts of it to learn how the pins would influence the perception of pain.

Control of pain is just one of the many issues that interest psychologists who study the closely related concepts of sensation and perception. Question: What are sensation and perception? **Sensation** is the stimulation of sensory receptors and the transmission of sensory information to the central nervous system (the spinal cord or brain). Sensory receptors are located in sensory organs such as the eyes and ears and, as we will see, in the skin and elsewhere in the body. Stimulation of the senses is an automatic process. It results from sources of energy like light and sound or from the presence of chemicals, as in smell and taste.

Perception is not automatic. Perception is an active process in which sensations are organized and interpreted to form an inner representation of the world. Perception may begin with sensation, but it also reflects our experiences and expectations as it makes sense of sensory stimuli. A human shape and a 12-inch ruler may look to be equally tall; whether we interpret the shape to be a foot-long doll or a full-grown person 15 feet away is a matter of perception that depends on our experience with dolls and people.

In this chapter you will see that your personal map of reality—your ticket of admission to a world of changing sights, sounds, and other sources of sensory input—depends largely on the so-called five senses: vision, hearing, smell, taste, and touch. We will see, however, that touch is just one of several "skin senses," which also include pressure, warmth, cold, and pain. There are also senses that alert you to your own body position without your having to watch every step you take. As we explore the nature of each of these senses, we will find that similar sensations may lead to different perceptions in different people—or within the same person in different situations.

Sensory Thresholds. How much stimulation is necessary before a person can detect a stimulus? How bright must the beacon from the lighthouse be to enable you to see it through the fog from several miles offshore?

✓ **Truth or Fiction Revisited**

It is not true that people have five senses. People have more, as we will see.

SENSATION The stimulation of sensory receptors and the transmission of sensory information to the central nervous system.

PERCEPTION The process by which sensations are organized into an inner representation of the world.

SECTION I. SENSATION AND PERCEPTION: YOUR TICKET OF ADMISSION TO THE WORLD OUTSIDE

Before we begin our journey through the senses, let us consider a number of concepts that apply to all of them: absolute threshold, difference threshold, signal-detection theory, and sensory adaptation. In doing so, we will learn why we might be able to dim the lights gradually to near darkness without other people becoming aware that we are doing so. We will also learn why we might grow unaware of the savory aromas of delightful dinners. Questions: How do we know when something is there? How do we know when it has changed?

Absolute Threshold: Is It There or Isn't It?

Gustav Fechner used the term **absolute threshold** to refer to the weakest amount of a stimulus that can be distinguished from no stimulus at all. For example, the amount of physical energy required to activate the visual sensory system is the absolute threshold for light.

Psychophysicists conduct experiments to determine the absolute thresholds of the senses. These involve exposing subjects to stimuli of progressively greater intensity. In the **method of constant stimuli,** researchers present sets of stimuli with magnitudes close to the expected threshold. Subjects say yes if they detect a stimulus and no if they do not. The stimuli are presented repeatedly in random order. An individual's absolute threshold for a stimulus is the lowest magnitude of the stimulus that he or she reports detecting 50% of the time. Weaker stimuli are detected less than 50% of the time and stronger stimuli more than 50% of the time.

The relationship between the intensity of a stimulus (a physical event) and its perception (a psychological event) is considered to be *psychophysical.* It bridges psychological and physical events.

Absolute thresholds have been determined for the senses of vision, hearing, taste, smell, and touch. They are approximately as follows:

- For vision, the equivalent of a candle flame viewed from a distance of about 30 miles on a clear, dark night
- For hearing, the equivalent of the ticking of a watch from about 20 feet away in a quiet room
- For taste, the equivalent of about 1 teaspoon of sugar dissolved in 2 gallons of water
- For smell, the equivalent of about one drop of perfume diffused throughout a small house (1 part in 500 million)
- For touch, the equivalent of the pressure of the wing of a fly falling on a cheek from a distance of about 0.4 inch

There are individual differences in absolute thresholds. That is, some people are more sensitive to sensory stimuli than others. The same person may also differ somewhat in sensitivity from one day to the next or from one occasion to another.

If the absolute thresholds for the human senses differed significantly, our daily experiences would be unrecognizable. Our ears are particularly sensitive, especially to sounds that are low in **pitch.** If they were any more sensitive, we might hear the collisions among molecules of air. Light consists of waves of energy, and if our eyes were sensitive to light with slightly longer wavelengths, we would sense infrared light waves. Heat generates infrared light. Thus animals that are warm-blooded and give off heat—including our mates—would literally glow in the dark.

REFLECT

What is the dimmest light you can see? The softest sound you can hear? How do psychophysicists answer such questions?

ABSOLUTE THRESHOLD The minimal amount of energy that can produce a sensation.

PSYCHOPHYSICIST A person who studies the relationships between physical stimuli (such as light or sound) and their perception.

METHOD OF CONSTANT STIMULI A psychophysical method for determining thresholds in which the researcher presents stimuli of various magnitudes and asks the person to report detection.

PITCH The highness or lowness of a sound, as determined by the frequency of the sound waves.

It is true that on a clear, dark night you could probably see the light from a candle burning 30 miles away. This figure is in keeping with the absolute threshold for light. *It is also true that if we could see light with slightly longer wavelengths, warm-blooded animals would seem to glow in the dark.*

Difference Threshold: Is It the Same or Is It Different?

How much of a difference in intensity between two lights is required before you will detect one as being brighter than the other? The minimum difference in magnitude of two stimuli required to tell them apart is their **difference threshold.** As with the absolute threshold, psychologists have agreed to the criterion of a difference in magnitudes that can be detected 50% of the time.

Psychophysicist Ernst Weber discovered through laboratory research that the threshold for perceiving differences in the intensity of light is about 2% (actually closer to 1/60) of their intensity. This fraction, 1/60, is known as **Weber's constant** for light. A closely related concept is the **just noticeable difference** (jnd), the minimal amount by which a source of energy must be increased or decreased so that a difference in intensity will be perceived. In the case of light, people can perceive a difference in intensity 50% of the time when the brightness of a light is increased or decreased by 1/60. Weber's constant for light holds whether we are comparing two quite bright lights or two rather dull lights. However, it becomes inaccurate when we compare extremely bright or extremely dull lights.

Weber's constant for noticing differences in lifted weight is 1/53. (Round it off to 1/50.) That means that one would probably have to increase the weight on a 100-pound barbell by about 2 pounds before the lifter would notice the difference. Now think of the 1-pound dumbbells used by many runners. Increasing the weight of each dumbbell by 2 pounds would be readily apparent to almost anyone because the increase would be threefold, not a small fraction. Yet the increase is still "only" 2 pounds. Return to our power lifter. When he is pressing 400 pounds, a 2-pound difference is less likely to be noticeable than when he is pressing 100 pounds. This is because 2 pounds is only 1/200 of 400 pounds.

People are most sensitive to changes in the pitch (frequency) of sounds. The constant for pitch is 1/333, meaning that on average, people can tell when a tone rises or falls in pitch by one-third of 1%. (Singers have to be right on pitch. The smallest error makes them sound sharp or flat.) The sense of taste is much less sensitive. On average, people cannot detect differences in saltiness of less than 20%.

Signal-Detection Theory: Is Being Bright Enough?

Does our discussion so far strike you as "inhuman"? We have written about perception of sensory stimuli as if people are simply switched on by certain amounts of stimulation. This is not quite so. People are influenced by psychological factors as well as by external changes. **Signal-detection theory** considers the human aspects of sensation and perception. Question: What is signal-detection theory?

According to signal-detection theory, the intensity of the signal is just one factor that determines whether people will perceive sensory stimuli (signals) or a difference between signals. Another is the degree to which the signal can be distinguished from background noise. It is easier to hear

Can you think of a personal example of a just noticeable difference? How much weight do you have to gain or lose to notice a difference? How much harder would you have to work to make a noticeable difference in your grades?

DIFFERENCE THRESHOLD The minimal difference in intensity required between two sources of energy so that they will be perceived as being different.

WEBER'S CONSTANT The fraction of the intensity by which a source of physical energy must be increased or decreased so that a difference in intensity will be perceived.

JUST NOTICEABLE DIFFERENCE The minimal amount by which a source of energy must be increased or decreased so that a difference in intensity will be perceived.

SIGNAL-DETECTION THEORY The view that the perception of sensory stimuli involves the interaction of physical, biological, and psychological factors.

a friend in a quiet room than in a room in which people are talking loudly and clinking glasses. The sharpness or acuteness of a person's biological sensory system is still another factor. Is sensory capacity fully developed? Is it diminished by advanced age?

Signal-detection theory also considers psychological factors such as motivation, expectations, and learning. For example, the place in which you are reading this book may be abuzz with signals. If you are outside, perhaps a breeze is blowing against your face. Perhaps the shadows of passing clouds darken the scene now and then. If you are inside, perhaps there are the occasional clanks and hums emitted by a heating system. Perhaps the aromas of dinner are hanging in the air, or the voices from a TV set suggest a crowd in another room. Yet, you are focusing your attention on this page (I hope). Thus, the other signals recede into the background of your consciousness. One psychological factor in signal detection is the focusing or narrowing of attention to signals that the person deems important.

Consider some examples. One parent may sleep through a baby's crying while the other parent is awakened. This is not necessarily because one parent is innately more sensitive to the sounds of crying (although some fathers may conveniently assume that mothers are). Instead, it may be because one parent has been assigned the task of caring for the baby through the night and is therefore more motivated to attend to the sounds. Because of training, an artist might notice the use of line or subtle colors that would go undetected by another person looking at the same painting.

The relationship between a physical stimulus and a sensory response is more than mechanical or mathematical. People's ability to detect stimuli such as meaningful blips on a radar screen depends not only on the intensity of the blips themselves but also on the people's training (learning), motivation (desire to perceive meaningful blips), and psychological states such as fatigue or alertness.

Feature Detectors

Imagine that you are standing by the curb of a busy street as a bus approaches. When neurons in your sensory organs—in this case, your eyes—are stimulated by the approach of the bus, they relay information to the sensory cortex in the brain. Nobel prize winners David Hubel and Torsten Wiesel (1979) discovered that various neurons in the visual cortex fire in response to particular features of the visual input. Question: What are feature detectors? Many cells, for example, detect (fire in response to) lines presented at various angles—vertical, horizontal, and in between. Other cells fire in response to specific colors.

Because they respond to different aspects or features of a scene, these cells are termed **feature detectors.** In the example of the bus, visual feature detectors respond to the bus's edges, depth, contours, textures, shadows, speed, and kinds of motion (up, down, forward, and back). There are also feature detectors for other senses. Auditory feature detectors, for example, respond to the pitch, loudness, and other aspects of the sounds of the bus.

Sensory Adaptation: Where Did It Go?

Our sensory systems are admirably suited to a changing environment. Question: How do our sensory systems adapt to a changing environment? We become more sensitive to stimuli of low magnitude and less sensitive to stimuli that remain the same (such as the background noises outside the window). **Sensory adaptation** refers to these processes of adjustment.

Consider how the visual sense adapts to lower intensities of light. When we first walk into a darkened movie theater, we see little but the

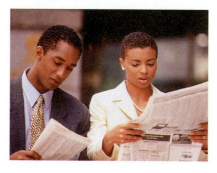

Signal Detection. The detection of signals is determined not only by the physical characteristics of the signals but also by psychological factors such as motivation and attention. The people in this photo are tuned into their newspapers for the moment, and not to each other.

FEATURE DETECTORS Neurons in the sensory cortex that fire in response to specific features of sensory information such as lines or edges of objects.

SENSORY ADAPTATION The processes by which organisms become more sensitive to stimuli that are low in magnitude and less sensitive to stimuli that are constant or ongoing in magnitude.

images on the screen. As time goes by, however, we become increasingly sensitive to the faces of those around us and to the features of the theater. The process of becoming more sensitive to stimulation is referred to as **sensitization,** or positive adaptation.

But we become less sensitive to constant stimulation. Sources of light appear to grow dimmer as we adapt to them. In fact, if you could keep an image completely stable on the retinas of your eyes—which is virtually impossible to accomplish without a motionless image and stabilizing equipment—the image would fade within a few seconds and be very difficult to see. Similarly, at the beach we soon become less aware of the lapping of the waves. When we live in a city, we become desensitized to traffic sounds except for the occasional backfire or siren. And as you may have noticed from experiences with freshly painted rooms, sensitivity to disagreeable odors fades quite rapidly. The process of becoming less sensitive to stimulation is referred to as **desensitization,** or negative adaptation.

Review

SECTION I

Sensation is a mechanical process that involves the stimulation of sensory (1) _____tors and the transmission of sensory information to the (2) _____ nervous system. (3) Per_____ is the active organization of sensations into an inner representation of the world. (4) _____tion reflects learning and expectations, as well as sensations.

The (5) _____ threshold for a stimulus, such as light, is the lowest intensity at which it can be detected. A person's absolute threshold for light is the lowest intensity of light that he or she can see 50% of the time, according to the method of (6) _____ stimuli. The minimum difference in intensity that can be discriminated is the (7) _____ threshold. Difference thresholds are expressed in fractions called (8) _____'s constants.

According to (9) _____-detection theory, many factors determine whether a person will perceive a stimulus. The detection of a signal is determined by the sensory stimuli themselves, the biological (10) _____sory system of the person, and (11) _____logical factors, such as motivation and attention. Receptors called (12) _____ detectors respond to specific kinds of stimulation, such as contours and kinds of motion.

Sensory (13) _____tion refers to our growing more sensitive to stimuli that are low in magnitude and less sensitive to stimuli that are relatively constant in magnitude. Becoming more sensitive to stimulation is referred to as (14) _____tion, or positive adaptation. The process of becoming less sensitive to stimulation is referred to as desensitization, or (15) _____tive adaptation.

SECTION II. VISION: LETTING THE SUN SHINE IN

Our eyes are our "windows on the world." More than half of the cerebral cortex is devoted to visual functions (Basic Behavioral Science Task Force, 1996). Because vision is our dominant sense, we consider blindness the most debilitating type of sensory loss (Moore, 1995). To understand vision, we need to begin with the nature of light.

SENSITIZATION The type of sensory adaptation in which we become more sensitive to stimuli that are low in magnitude. Also called *positive adaptation.*

DESENSITIZATION The type of sensory adaptation in which we become less sensitive to constant stimuli. Also called *negative adaptation.*

Light: What Is This Stuff?

In almost all cultures, light is a symbol of goodness and knowledge. We describe capable people as being "bright" or "brilliant." If we are not being complimentary, we label them as "dull." People who aren't in the know are said to be "in the dark." Question: Just what is this stuff called light?

Visible light is the stuff that triggers visual sensations. It is just one small part of a spectrum of electromagnetic energy (see Figure 4.1). All forms of electromagnetic energy move in waves. Different kinds of electromagnetic energy have different wavelengths. Cosmic rays have extremely short wavelengths, only a few trillionths of an inch long. But some radio waves extend for miles. Although visible light seems to move in a steady stream, it also consists of waves of energy. Different colors have different wavelengths, with violet the shortest and red the longest. Radar, microwaves, and X-rays are also forms of electromagnetic energy.

You have probably seen rainbows or light that has been broken down into several colors as it filtered through your windows. Sir Isaac Newton, the British scientist, discovered that sunlight could be broken down into different colors by means of a triangular solid of glass called a *prism* (Figure 4.1). When I took introductory psychology, I was taught to remember the colors of the spectrum, from longest to shortest wavelengths, by using the mnemonic device *Roy G. Biv* (red, orange, yellow, green, blue, indigo, violet). I must have been a backward student because I found it easier to recall them in reverse order, using the meaningless acronym *vibgyor*.

✓ **Truth or Fiction Revisited**

It is true that white sunlight is actually composed of all the colors of the rainbow.

REFLECT

Have you ever seen a rainbow? How do you account for the colors in it?

VISIBLE LIGHT The part of the electromagnetic spectrum that stimulates the eye and produces visual sensations.

FIGURE 4.1

THE VISIBLE SPECTRUM   BY PASSING A SOURCE OF WHITE LIGHT, SUCH AS SUNLIGHT, THROUGH A PRISM, WE BREAK IT DOWN INTO THE COLORS OF THE VISIBLE SPECTRUM. THE VISIBLE SPECTRUM IS JUST A NARROW SEGMENT OF THE ELECTROMAGNETIC SPECTRUM. THE ELECTROMAGNETIC SPECTRUM ALSO INCLUDES RADIO WAVES, MICROWAVES, X-RAYS, COSMIC RAYS, AND MANY OTHERS. DIFFERENT FORMS OF ELECTROMAGNETIC ENERGY HAVE WAVELENGTHS WHICH VARY FROM A FEW TRILLIONTHS OF A METER TO THOUSANDS OF MILES. VISIBLE LIGHT VARIES IN WAVELENGTH FROM ABOUT 400 TO 700 *BILLIONTHS* OF A METER. (A METER = 39.37 INCHES.)

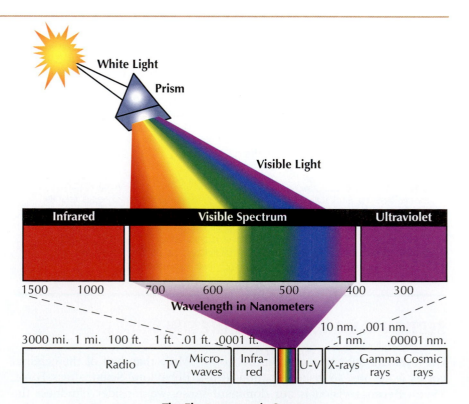

The Electromagnetic Spectrum

The wavelength of visible light determines its color, or **hue.** The wavelength for red is longer than the wavelength for orange, and so on through the spectrum.

The Eye: The Better to See You With

Consider that magnificent invention called the camera, which records visual experiences. In traditional cameras, light enters an opening and is focused onto a sensitive surface, or film. Chemicals on film create a lasting impression of the image that entered the camera.

Question: How does the eye work? The eye—our living camera—is no less remarkable. Look at its major parts, as shown in Figure 4.2. As with a film or TV camera, light enters through a narrow opening and is projected onto a sensitive surface. Light first passes through the transparent **cornea,** which covers the front of the eye's surface. (The "white" of the eye, or *sclera,* is composed of hard protective tissue.) The amount of light that passes through the cornea is determined by the size of the opening of the muscle called the **iris,** which is the colored part of the eye. The opening in the iris is the **pupil.** The size of the pupil adjusts automatically to the amount of light present. You do not have to try purposefully to open your

HUE The color of light, as determined by its wavelength.

CORNEA Transparent tissue forming the outer surface of the eyeball.

IRIS A muscular membrane whose dilation regulates the amount of light that enters the eye.

PUPIL The apparently black opening in the center of the iris, through which light enters the eye.

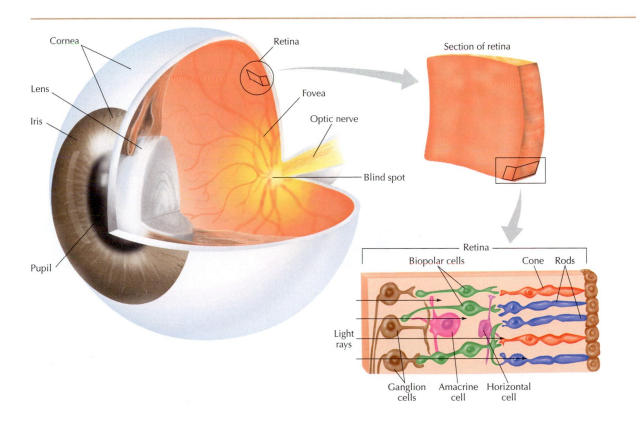

FIGURE 4.2

THE EYE   IN BOTH THE EYE AND A CAMERA, LIGHT ENTERS THROUGH A NARROW OPENING AND IS PROJECTED ONTO A SENSITIVE SURFACE. IN THE EYE, THE PHOTOSENSITIVE SURFACE IS CALLED THE RETINA, AND INFORMATION CONCERNING THE CHANGING IMAGES ON THE RETINA IS TRANSMITTED TO THE BRAIN. THE RETINA CONTAINS PHOTORECEPTORS CALLED RODS AND CONES. RODS AND CONES TRANSMIT SENSORY INPUT BACK THROUGH THE BIPOLAR NEURONS TO THE GANGLION NEURONS. THE AXONS OF THE GANGLION NEURONS FORM THE OPTIC NERVE, WHICH TRANSMITS SENSORY STIMULATION THROUGH THE BRAIN TO THE VISUAL CORTEX OF THE OCCIPITAL LOBE.

eyes further to see better in low lighting conditions. The more intense the light, the smaller the opening. In a similar fashion, we adjust the amount of light allowed into a camera according to its brightness. Pupil size is also sensitive to emotional response: We can literally be "wide-eyed with fear."

Once light passes through the iris, it encounters the **lens.** The lens adjusts or accommodates to the image by changing its thickness. Changes in thickness permit a clear image of the object to be projected onto the retina. These changes focus the light according to the distance of the object from the viewer. If you hold a finger at arm's length and slowly bring it toward your nose, you will feel tension in the eye as the thickness of the lens accommodates to keep the retinal image in focus. When people squint to bring an object into focus, they are adjusting the thickness of the lens. The lens in a camera does not accommodate to the distance of objects. Instead, to focus the light that is projected onto the film, the camera lens is moved farther from the film or closer to it, as in a zoom lens.

The **retina** is like the film or image surface of the camera. However, the retina consists of cells called **photoreceptors** that are sensitive to light (photosensitive). There are two types of photoreceptors: *rods* and *cones.* The retina (see Figure 4.2) contains several layers of cells: the rods and cones, **bipolar cells,** and **ganglion cells.** All of these cells are neurons. Light travels past the ganglion cells and bipolar cells and stimulates the rods and cones. The rods and cones then send neural messages through the bipolar cells to the ganglion cells. The axons of the million or so ganglion cells in our retinae form the **optic nerve.** The optic nerve conducts sensory input to the brain, where it is relayed to the visual area of the occipital lobe. Other neurons in the retina—amacrine cells and horizontal cells—make sideways connections at a level near the receptor cells and at another level near the ganglion cells. As a result of these lateral connections, many rods and cones funnel visual information into one bipolar cell, and many bipolar cells funnel information to one ganglion cell. Receptors outnumber ganglion cells by more than 100 to 1.

LENS A transparent body behind the iris that focuses an image on the retina.

RETINA The area of the inner surface of the eye that contains rods and cones.

PHOTORECEPTORS Cells that respond to light.

BIPOLAR CELLS Neurons that conduct neural impulses from rods and cones to ganglion cells.

GANGLION CELLS Neurons whose axons form the optic nerve.

OPTIC NERVE The nerve that transmits sensory information from the eye to the brain.

FIGURE 4.3

LOCATING THE BLIND SPOTS IN YOUR EYES   TO TRY A "DISAPPEARING ACT," FIRST LOOK AT DRAWING 1. CLOSE YOUR RIGHT EYE. THEN MOVE THE BOOK BACK AND FORTH ABOUT 1 FOOT FROM YOUR LEFT EYE WHILE YOU STARE AT THE PLUS SIGN. YOU WILL NOTICE THE CIRCLE DISAPPEAR. WHEN THE CIRCLE DISAPPEARS, IT IS BEING PROJECTED ONTO THE BLIND SPOT OF YOUR RETINA, THE POINT AT WHICH THE AXONS OF GANGLION NEURONS COLLECT TO FORM THE OPTIC NERVE. THEN CLOSE YOUR LEFT EYE. STARE AT THE CIRCLE WITH YOUR RIGHT EYE AND MOVE THE BOOK BACK AND FORTH. WHEN THE PLUS SIGN DISAPPEARS, IT IS BEING PROJECTED ONTO THE BLIND SPOT OF YOUR RIGHT EYE. NOW LOOK AT DRAWING 2. YOU CAN MAKE THIS FIGURE DISAPPEAR AND "SEE" THE BLACK LINE CONTINUE THROUGH THE SPOT WHERE IT WAS BY CLOSING YOUR RIGHT EYE AND STARING AT THE PLUS SIGN WITH YOUR LEFT. WHEN THIS FIGURE IS PROJECTED ONTO YOUR BLIND SPOT, YOUR BRAIN "FILLS IN" THE LINE, WHICH IS ONE REASON THAT YOU'RE NOT USUALLY AWARE THAT YOU HAVE BLIND SPOTS.

The **fovea** is the most sensitive area of the retina (see Figure 4.2). Receptors there are more densely packed. The **blind spot,** in contrast, is insensitive to visual stimulation. It is the part of the retina where the axons of the ganglion cells collect to form the optic nerve (Figure 4.3).

Visual acuity (sharpness of vision) is connected with the shape of the eye. People who have to be unusually close to an object to discriminate its details are *nearsighted.* People who see distant objects unusually clearly but have difficulty focusing on nearby objects are *farsighted.* Nearsightedness can result when the eyeball is elongated so that the images of distant objects are focused in front of the retina. When the eyeball is too short, the images of nearby objects are focused behind the retina, causing farsightedness. Eyeglasses or contact lenses can be used to help nearsighted people focus distant objects on their retinas. Farsighted people usually see well enough without eyeglasses until they reach their middle years, when they may need glasses for reading.

Beginning in the late 30s to the mid-40s, the lenses grow brittle, making it difficult to accommodate to, or focus on, objects. This condition is called **presbyopia,** from the Greek words for "old man" and "eyes," but presbyopia occurs by middle adulthood, not late adulthood. Presbyopia makes it difficult to perceive nearby visual stimuli. People who had normal visual acuity in their youth often require corrective lenses to read in middle adulthood and beyond.

RODS AND CONES **Rods** and **cones** are the photoreceptors in the retina. About 125 million rods and 6.5 million cones are distributed across the retina. The fovea is composed almost exclusively of cones. Cones become more sparsely distributed as you work forward from the fovea toward the lens. Rods, in contrast, are nearly absent at the fovea but are distributed more densely as you approach the lens.

Rods are sensitive only to the intensity of light. They allow us to see in black and white. Cones provide color vision. In low lighting, it is possible to photograph a clearer image with black-and-white film than with color film. Similarly, rods are more sensitive to light than cones. Therefore, as the illumination grows dim, as during the evening and nighttime hours, objects appear to lose their color well before their outlines fade from view.

LIGHT ADAPTATION Immediately after we enter it, a movie theater may seem too dark to allow us to find seats readily. But as time goes on we begin to see the seats and other people clearly. The process of adjusting to lower lighting conditions is called **dark adaptation.**

Figure 4.4 shows the amount of light needed for detection as a function of the amount of time spent in the dark. The cones and rods adapt at different rates. The cones, which permit perception of color, reach their maximum adaptation to darkness in about 10 minutes. The rods, which allow perception of light and dark only, are more sensitive and continue to adapt to darkness for up to about 45 minutes.

Adaptation to brighter lighting conditions takes place much more rapidly. When you emerge from the theater into the brilliance of the afternoon, you may at first be painfully surprised by the featureless blaze around you. The visual experience is not unlike turning the brightness of the TV set to its maximum setting, at which the edges of objects seem to dissolve into light. Within a minute or so of entering the street, however, the brightness of the scene dims, and objects regain their edges.

FOVEA An area near the center of the retina that is dense with cones and where vision is consequently most acute.

BLIND SPOT The area of the retina where axons from ganglion cells meet to form the optic nerve.

VISUAL ACUITY Sharpness of vision.

PRESBYOPIA A condition characterized by brittleness of the lens.

RODS Rod-shaped photoreceptors that are sensitive only to the intensity of light.

CONES Cone-shaped photoreceptors that transmit sensations of color.

DARK ADAPTATION The process of adjusting to conditions of lower lighting by increasing the sensitivity of rods and cones.

FIGURE 4.4

DARK ADAPTATION THIS ILLUSTRATION SHOWS THE AMOUNT OF LIGHT NECESSARY FOR DETECTION AS A FUNCTION OF THE AMOUNT OF TIME SPENT IN THE DARK. CONES AND RODS ADAPT AT DIFFERENT RATES. CONES, WHICH PERMIT PERCEPTION OF COLOR, REACH MAXIMUM DARK ADAPTATION IN ABOUT 10 MINUTES. RODS, WHICH PERMIT PERCEPTION OF DARK AND LIGHT ONLY, ARE MORE SENSITIVE THAN CONES. RODS CONTINUE TO ADAPT FOR UP TO ABOUT 45 MINUTES.

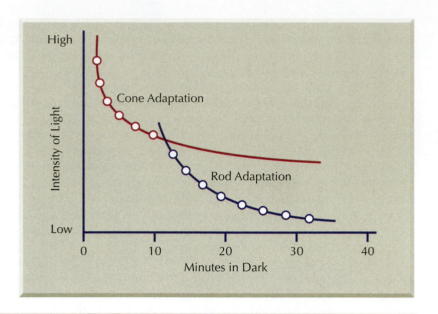

Color Vision: Creating an Inner World of Color

For most of us, the world is a place of brilliant colors—the blue-greens of the ocean, the red-oranges of the setting sun, the deepened greens of June, the glories of rhododendron and hibiscus. Color is an emotional and aesthetic part of our everyday lives. Question: How do we perceive color? In this section we examine theories about how we convert different wavelengths of light into perceptions of color.

Adults with normal color vision can discriminate among hundreds of colors across the visible spectrum. Different colors have different wavelengths. Although we can vary the physical wavelengths of light in a continuous manner from shorter to longer, many changes in color are *dis*continuous. For example, our perception of a color shifts suddenly from blue to green, even though the change in wavelength may be smaller than that between two blues.

Our ability to perceive color depends on the eye's transmission of different messages to the brain when lights with different wavelengths stimulate the cones in the retina. Let us consider two theories of how lights with different wavelengths are perceived as different colors: the *trichromatic theory* and the *opponent-process theory*.

THE TRICHROMATIC THEORY **Trichromatic theory** is based on an experiment conducted by the British scientist Thomas Young in the early 1800s. As in Figure 4.5, Young projected three lights of different colors onto a screen so that they partly overlapped. He found that he could create any color from the visible spectrum simply by varying the intensities of the lights. When all three lights fell on the same spot, they created white light, or the appearance of no color at all. The three lights manipulated by Young were red, green, and blue-violet.

The German physiologist Hermann von Helmholtz saw in Young's discovery an explanation of color vision. Von Helmholtz suggested that the eye must have three different types of photoreceptors or cones. Some must be sensitive to red light, some to green, and some to blue. We see other colors when two different types of color receptors are stimulated. The perception of yellow, for example, would result from the simultaneous

TRICHROMATIC THEORY The theory that color vision is made possible by three types of cones, some of which respond to red light, some to green, and some to blue.

FIGURE 4.5

ADDITIVE AND SUBTRACTIVE COLOR MIXTURES PRODUCED BY LIGHTS AND PIGMENTS THOMAS YOUNG DISCOVERED THAT WHITE LIGHT AND ALL THE COLORS OF THE SPECTRUM COULD BE PRODUCED BY ADDING COMBINATIONS OF LIGHTS OF RED, GREEN, AND VIOLET-BLUE AND VARYING THEIR INTENSITIES (SEE PART A). PART B SHOWS SUBTRACTIVE COLOR MIXTURES, WHICH ARE FORMED BY MIXING PIGMENTS, NOT LIGHT.

stimulation of receptors for red and green. The trichromatic theory is also known as the Young-Helmholtz theory.

THE OPPONENT-PROCESS THEORY Before reading on, why don't you try a brief experiment? Look at the strangely colored American flag in Figure 4.6 for at least half a minute. Then look at a sheet of white or gray paper. What has happened to the flag? If your color vision is working properly, and if you looked at the miscolored flag long enough, you should see a flag composed of the familiar red, white, and blue. The flag you perceive on the white sheet of paper is an **afterimage** of the first. (If you didn't look at the green, black, and yellow flag long enough the first time, try it again. It will work any number of times.) The phenomenon of afterimages has contributed to another theory of color vision.

In 1870, Ewald Hering proposed the **opponent-process theory** of color vision: There are three types of color receptors, but they are not sensitive to the simple hues of red, green, and blue. Hering suggested instead that afterimages are made possible by three types of color receptors: red-green, blue-yellow, and a type that perceives differences in brightness. A red-green cone could not transmit messages for red and green at the same time. According to Hering, staring at the green, black, and yellow flag for 30 seconds would disturb the balance of neural activity. The afterimage of red, white, and blue would represent the eye's attempt to reestablish a balance.

Research suggests that both theories of color vision are partly correct. For example, it shows that some cones are sensitive to blue, some to

AFTERIMAGE The lingering visual impression made by a stimulus that has been removed.

OPPONENT-PROCESS THEORY The theory that color vision is made possible by three types of cones, some of which respond to red or green light, some to blue or yellow light, and some only to the intensity of light.

FIGURE 4.6

THREE CHEERS FOR THE . . . GREEN, BLACK, AND YELLOW? DON'T BE CONCERNED. WE CAN READILY RESTORE OLD GLORY TO ITS FAMILIAR HUES. PLACE A SHEET OF WHITE PAPER BENEATH THE BOOK, AND STARE AT THE CENTER OF THE FLAG FOR 30 SECONDS. THEN REMOVE THE BOOK. THE AFTERIMAGE ON THE PAPER BENEATH WILL LOOK FAMILIAR.

green, and some to red parts of the spectrum. But studies of the bipolar and ganglion neurons suggest that messages from cones are transmitted to the brain and relayed by the thalamus to the occipital lobe in an opponent-process fashion (DeValois & Jacobs, 1984). Some opponent-process cells that transmit messages to the visual centers in the brain are excited ("turned on") by green light but inhibited ("turned off") by red light. Others can be excited by red light but are inhibited by green light. A second set of opponent-process cells responds in an opposite manner to blue and yellow. A third set responds in an opposite manner to light and dark.

A neural rebound effect apparently helps explain the occurrence of afterimages. That is, a green-sensitive ganglion that had been excited by green light for half a minute or so might switch briefly to inhibitory activity when the light is shut off. The effect would be to perceive red even though no red light is present.

These theoretical updates allow for the afterimage effects with the green, black, and yellow flag and are also consistent with Young's experiments in mixing lights of different colors.

Color Blindness

If you can discriminate among the colors of the visible spectrum, you have normal color vision and are labeled a **trichromat.** This means you are sensitive to red-green, blue-yellow, and light-dark. Questions: What is color blindness? Why are some people color blind? People who are totally color blind, called **monochromats,** are sensitive only to lightness and darkness. Total color blindness is rare. Fully color blind individuals see the world as trichromats would on a black-and-white TV set or in a black-and-white movie.

Partial color blindness is more common than total color blindness. Partial color blindness is a sex-linked trait that affects mostly males and impairs the functioning of cones that are sensitive to red or green. People with this problem are called **dichromats,** and they find it difficult to tell red and green apart. For this reason, a dichromat might put on one red sock and one green sock but would not mix red and blue socks. Monochromats might put on socks of any color. They would not notice a difference as long as the socks' colors did not differ in brightness.

REFLECT

How do you imagine that color blind people know when to stop at a traffic light and when to proceed?

TRICHROMAT A person with normal color vision.

MONOCHROMAT A person who is sensitive to black and white only and hence color blind.

DICHROMAT A person who is insensitive to the colors of red and green and hence partially color blind.

Review

SECTION II

Visible light is part of a spectrum of (16) _____netic energy. Electromagnetic energy moves in (17) _____s. The color of visible light is determined by its (18) _____gth. White light can be broken down into the colors of the rainbow by a (19) p_____.

Light enters the eye through the transparent (20) c_____. The muscle called the (21) _____ determines the amount of light that is allowed in. The opening in the iris is called the (22) p_____. Light then passes through the (23) _____s, which accommodates to the image by changing thickness. Accommodation of the lens focuses light onto the (24) r_____. The

retina is made up of (25) photo_____s called rods and cones. These photoreceptors send neural messages through the (26) _____ar cells to ganglion cells. The axons of the ganglion cells make up the (27) _____ic nerve, which conducts visual input to the brain.

The (28) f_____ is the most sensitive part of the retina. The blind spot is the part of the retina where the axons of (29) _____ion cells collect to form the optic nerve. The fovea is made up of nearly all (30) _____s, which permit perception of color. Rods are densest near the (31) _____s and transmit only sensations of light and (32) d_____. Rods are (33:

More or Less?) sensitive than cones to light. Rods continue to (34) a_____ to darkness once cones have reached peak adaptation.

According to the (35) _____ theory of color vision, there are three types of cones. Some cones are sensitive to red, some to blue, and some to green light. Opponent-process theory proposes three types of color receptors: red-green, (36) _____, and light-dark. (37) _____ theory better accounts for afterimages.

People with normal color vision are called (38) _____mats. Color-blind people who can see light and dark only are called (39) _____mats. Dichromats usually find it difficult to tell red and (40) _____ apart.

SECTION III. VISUAL PERCEPTION: GETTING IT TOGETHER

Perception is the process by which we organize or make sense of our sensory impressions. Although visual sensations are caused by electromagnetic energy, visual perception also relies on our knowledge, expectations, and motivations. Whereas sensation may be thought of as a mechanical process, perception is an active process through which we interpret the world around us.

For example, just what do you see in Figure 4.7? Do you see random splotches of ink or a rider on horseback? If you perceive a horse and rider, it is not just because of the visual sensations provided by the drawing. Each of the blobs is meaningless in and of itself, and the pattern they form is also less than clear. Despite the lack of clarity, however, you may still perceive a horse and rider. Question: How do we organize bits of information like perceptions into meaningful wholes? The answer has something to do with your general knowledge and your desire to fit incoming bits and pieces of information into familiar patterns.

In the case of the horse and rider, your integration of disconnected pieces of information into a meaningful whole also reflects what Gestalt psychologists refer to as the principle of **closure,** or the tendency to perceive a complete or whole figure even when there are gaps in the sensory input. Put another way, in perception the whole can be very much more than the mere sum of the parts. A collection of parts can be meaningless. It is their configuration that matters.

FIGURE 4.7

Closure   Meaningless splotches of ink or a horse and rider? This figure illustrates the Gestalt principle of closure.

Perceptual Organization

Early in the 20th century, Gestalt psychologists noted certain consistencies in the way we integrate bits and pieces of sensory stimulation into meaningful wholes. They attempted to identify the rules that govern these processes. Max Wertheimer, in particular, discovered many such rules. As a group, these rules are referred to as the laws of *perceptual organization.* We examine several of them, beginning with those concerning figure-ground perception. Then we consider top-down and bottom-up processing.

FIGURE-GROUND PERCEPTION If you look out your window, you may see people, buildings, cars, and streets, or perhaps grass, trees, birds, and clouds. All these objects tend to be perceived as figures against backgrounds. Cars seen against the background of the street are easier to pick out than cars seen piled on top of one another in a junkyard. Birds seen against the sky are more likely to be perceived than birds seen "in the bush."

CLOSURE The tendency to perceive a broken figure as being complete or whole.

REFLECT

Why is it easier to spot a friend walking alone than in a crowd?

FIGURE 4.8

FIGURE AND GROUND   HOW MANY ANIMALS AND DEMONS CAN YOU FIND IN THIS ESCHER PRINT? DO WE HAVE WHITE FIGURES ON A BLACK BACKGROUND OR BLACK FIGURES ON A WHITE BACKGROUND? FIGURE-GROUND PERCEPTION IS THE TENDENCY TO PERCEIVE GEOMETRIC FORMS AGAINST A BACKGROUND.

When figure-ground relationships are ambiguous, or capable of being interpreted in various ways, our perceptions tend to be unstable, to shift back and forth. As an example, look for a while at Figure 4.8. How many people, objects, and animals can you find? If your eye is drawn back and forth, so that sometimes you are perceiving light figures on a dark background and at other time dark figures on a light background, you are experiencing figure-ground reversals. In other words, a shift is occurring in your perception of what is figure and what is ground, or background. The artist was able to have some fun with us because of our tendency to try to isolate geometric patterns or figures from a background. However, in this case the "background" is as meaningful and detailed as the "figure." Therefore, our perceptions shift back and forth.

The vase in Figure 4.9 is one of psychologists' favorite illustrations of figure-ground relationships. The figure-ground relationship in part A of the figure is ambiguous. There are no cues that suggest which area must be the figure. For this reason, our perception may shift from seeing the vase as the figure to seeing two profiles as the figure. There is no such problem in part B. Because it seems that a white vase has been brought forward against a colored background, we are more likely to perceive the vase than the profiles. In part C, we are more likely to perceive the profiles than the vase because the profiles are whole and the vase is broken against the background. Of course, if we wish to, we can still perceive the vase in part C, because experience has shown us where it is. Why not have some fun with friends by covering up parts B and C and asking them what they see? (They'll catch on quickly if they can see all three drawings at once.)

OTHER GESTALT RULES FOR ORGANIZATION In addition to the law of closure, Gestalt psychologists have noted that our perceptions

FIGURE 4.9
THE RUBIN VASE   A FAVORITE DRAWING USED BY PSYCHOLOGISTS TO DEMONSTRATE FIGURE-GROUND PERCEPTION. PART A IS AMBIGUOUS, WITH NEITHER THE VASE NOR THE PROFILES CLEARLY THE FIGURE OR THE GROUND. IN PART B, THE VASE IS THE FIGURE; IN PART C, THE PROFILES ARE.

are guided by rules or laws of *proximity, similarity, continuity,* and *common fate.*

Without reading further, describe part A of Figure 4.10. Did you say it consists of six lines or of three groups of two parallel lines? If you said three sets of lines, you were influenced by the **proximity,** or nearness, of some of the lines. There is no other reason for perceiving them in pairs or subgroups: All of the lines are parallel and of equal length.

Now describe part B of the figure. Did you perceive the figure as a 6 × 6 grid, or as three columns of *x*'s and three columns of *o*'s? According to the law of **similarity,** we perceive similar objects as belonging together. For this reason, you may have been more likely to describe part B in terms of columns than in terms of rows or a grid.

What about part C? Is it a circle with two lines stemming from it, or is it a (broken) line that goes through a circle? If you saw it as a single (broken) line, you were probably organizing your perceptions according to the

PROXIMITY Nearness. The perceptual tendency to group together objects that are near one another.

SIMILARITY The perceptual tendency to group together objects that are similar in appearance.

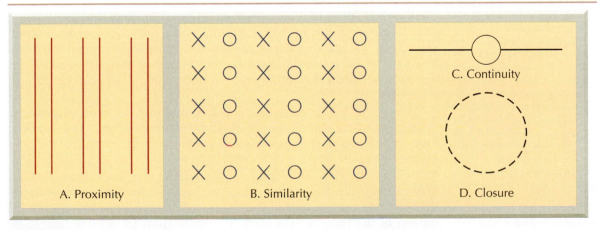

A. Proximity

B. Similarity

C. Continuity

D. Closure

FIGURE 4.10
SOME GESTALT LAWS OF PERCEPTUAL ORGANIZATION   THESE DRAWINGS ILLUSTRATE THE GESTALT LAWS OF PROXIMITY, SIMILARITY, CONTINUITY, AND CLOSURE.

REFLECT

Have you ever seen two people walking next to each other and then been surprised to see them split up without saying anything? Why did you assume that they knew each other?

rule of **continuity.** That is, we perceive a series of points or a broken line as having unity.

According to the law of **common fate,** elements seen moving together are perceived as belonging together. A group of people running in the same direction appears unified in purpose. Birds that flock together seem to be of a feather. (Did I get that right?)

Part D of Figure 4.10 provides another example of the law of closure. The arcs tend to be perceived as a circle (or circle with gaps) rather than as just a series of arcs.

TOP-DOWN VERSUS BOTTOM-UP PROCESSING Imagine that you are trying to put together a thousand-piece puzzle—a task I usually avoid, despite the cajoling of my children. Now imagine that you are trying to accomplish it after someone has walked off with the box showing the picture formed by the completed puzzle.

When you have the box—when you know what the "big picture" or pattern looks like—cognitive psychologists refer to the task of assembling the pieces as **top-down processing.** The "top" of the visual system refers to the image of the pattern in the brain, and the top-down strategy for putting the puzzle together implies that you use the pattern to guide subordinate perceptual motor tasks such as hunting for particular pieces. Without knowledge of the pattern, the assembly process is referred to as **bottom-up processing.** You begin with bits and pieces of information and become aware of the pattern formed by the assembled pieces only after you have worked at it for a while.

Perception of Movement

REFLECT

Have you had the experience of being in a train and not knowing whether your train or one on the next track was moving? How do you explain your confusion? How did you figure out which one was really moving?

Moving objects—whether they are other people, animals, cars, or boulders plummeting down a hillside—are vital sources of sensory information. Moving objects even capture the attention of newborn infants. Question: How do we perceive movement?

To understand how we perceive movement, recall what it is like to be on a train that has begun to pull out of the station while the train on the adjacent track remains stationary. If your own train does not lurch as it accelerates, you might think at first that the other train is moving. Or you might not be certain whether your train is moving forward or the other train is moving backward.

The visual perception of movement is based on change of position relative to other objects. To early scientists, whose only tool for visual observation was the naked eye, it seemed logical that the sun circled the earth. You have to be able to imagine the movement of the earth around the sun as seen from a theoretical point in outer space—you cannot observe it directly.

How, then, do you determine which train is moving when your train is pulling out of the station (or the other train is pulling in)? One way is to look for objects that you know are stable, such as platform columns, houses, signs, or trees. If you are stationary in relation to them, your train is not moving. Observing people walking on the station platform may not provide the answer, however, because they are also changing their position relative to stationary objects. You might also try to sense the motion of the train in your body. You know from experience how to do these things quite well, although it may be difficult to find words to explain them.

We have been considering the perception of real movement. Psychologists have also studied several types of apparent movement, or

CONTINUITY The tendency to perceive a series of points or lines as having unity.

COMMON FATE The tendency to perceive elements that move together as belonging together.

TOP-DOWN PROCESSING The use of contextual information or knowledge of a pattern in order to organize parts of the pattern.

BOTTOM-UP PROCESSING The organization of the parts of a pattern to recognize, or form an image of, the pattern they compose.

FIGURE 4.11
STROBOSCOPIC MOTION   IN A MOTION PICTURE, VIEWING A SERIES OF STATIONARY IMAGES AT THE RATE OF ABOUT 16 TO 22 FRAMES PER SECOND PROVIDES AN ILLUSION OF MOVEMENT TERMED *STROBOSCOPIC MOTION.*

illusions of movement. These include *stroboscopic motion* and the *phi phenomenon.*

Stroboscopic motion makes motion pictures possible. In **stroboscopic motion,** the illusion of movement is provided by the presentation of a rapid progression of images of stationary objects. So-called motion pictures do not really consist of images that move. Rather, the audience is shown 16 to 22 pictures, or *frames,* per second. Each is slightly different from the one before (see Figure 4.11). Showing the frames in rapid succession provides the illusion of movement.

At the rate of at least 16 frames per second, the "motion" in a film seems smooth and natural. With fewer than 16 or so frames per second, the movement looks jumpy and unnatural. That is why slow motion is achieved by filming perhaps 100 or more frames per second. When they are played back at about 22 frames per second, the movement seems slowed down, yet still smooth and natural.

Have you seen news headlines spelled out in lights that rapidly wrap around a building? Have you seen an electronic scoreboard in a baseball or football stadium? When the home team scores, some scoreboards suggest explosions of fireworks. What actually happens is that a row of lights is switched on and then off. As the first row is switched off, a second row is switched on, and so on for dozens, perhaps hundreds of rows. When the switching occurs rapidly, the **phi phenomenon** occurs: The on-off process is perceived as movement (Figure 4.12).

Like stroboscopic motion, the phi phenomenon is an example of apparent motion. Both appear to occur because of the law of continuity. We tend to perceive a series of points as having unity, so each series of lights (points) is perceived as a moving line.

FIGURE 4. 12
THE PHI PHENOMENON   THE PHI PHENOMENON IS AN ILLUSION OF MOVEMENT THAT IS PRODUCED BY LIGHTS BLINKING ON AND OFF IN SEQUENCE, AS WITH THIS NEW YORK STOCK EXCHANGE ELECTRONIC "TICKER."

Depth Perception

Think of the problems you might have if you could not judge depth or distance. You might bump into other people, believing them to be farther away. An outfielder might not be able to judge whether to run toward the infield or the fence to catch a fly ball. You might give your front bumper a workout in stop-and-go traffic. Question: How do we perceive depth? It happens that *monocular and binocular cues* both help us perceive the depth of objects—that is, their distance from us.

MONOCULAR CUES   Now that you have considered how difficult it would be to navigate through life without depth perception, ponder the problems of the artist who attempts to portray three-dimensional objects on a two-dimensional surface. Artists use **monocular cues**—also termed pictorial cues—to create an illusion of depth. These are cues that can be perceived by one eye (*mono-* means "one"). They include perspective, relative size, clearness, interposition, shadows, and texture gradient, and they cause certain objects to appear more distant from the viewer than others.

Distant objects stimulate smaller areas on the retina than nearby ones. The amount of sensory input from them is smaller, even though they may be the same size. The distances between far-off objects also appear to be smaller than equivalent distances between nearby objects. For this reason, the phenomenon known as **perspective** occurs. That is, we tend to perceive parallel lines as coming closer together, or converging, as they recede from us. However, as we will see when we discuss *size constancy*, experience teaches us that distant objects that look small are larger when they are close. In this way, their relative size also becomes a cue to their distance.

The two engravings in Figure 4.13 represent impossible scenes in which the artists use principles of perspective to fool the viewer. In the one on the left, *Waterfall*, note that the water appears to be flowing away from the viewer in a zigzag because the stream gradually becomes narrower (that is, lines we assume to be parallel are shown to be converging) and the stone sides of the aqueduct appear to be stepping down. However, given that the water arrives at the top of the fall, it must actually be flowing upward somehow. However, the spot from which it falls is no farther from the viewer than the collection point from which it appears to (but does not) begin its flow backward.

Artists normally use *relative size*—the fact that distant objects look smaller than nearby objects of the same size—to suggest depth in their works. The paradoxes in the engraving on the right, *False Perspective*, are

PERSPECTIVE A monocular cue for depth based on the convergence (coming together) of parallel lines as they recede into the distance.

FRONTISPIECE TO KERBY.

FIGURE 4.13

WHAT IS WRONG WITH THESE PICTURES?   IN *WATERFALL*, TO THE LEFT, HOW DOES DUTCH ARTIST M. C. ESCHER SUGGEST THAT FALLEN WATER FLOWS BACK UPWARD, ONLY TO FALL AGAIN? IN *FALSE PERSPECTIVE*, TO THE RIGHT, HOW DOES ENGLISH ARTIST WILLIAM HOGARTH USE MONOCULAR CUES FOR DEPTH PERCEPTION TO DECEIVE THE VIEWER?

made possible because more distant objects are *not* necessarily depicted as smaller than nearby objects. Thus, what at first seems to be background suddenly becomes foreground, and vice versa.

The *clearness* of an object also suggests its distance. Experience teaches us that we sense more details of nearby objects. For this reason, artists can suggest that objects are closer to the viewer by depicting them in greater detail. Note that the "distant" hill in the Hogarth engraving (Figure 4.13) is given less detail than the nearby plants at the bottom of the picture. Our perceptions are mocked when a man "on" the distant hill in the background is shown conversing with a woman leaning out a window in the middle ground.

We also learn that nearby objects can block our view of more-distant objects. Overlapping, or **interposition,** is the placing of one object in front of another. Experience teaches us that partly covered objects are farther away than the objects that obscure them (Figure 4.14). In the Hogarth engraving (Figure 4.13), which looks closer: the trees in the background (background?) or the moon sign hanging from the building (or is it buildings?) to the right? How does the artist use interposition to confuse the viewer?

Additional information about depth is provided by **shadowing** and is based on the fact that opaque objects block light and produce shadows. Shadows and highlights give us information about an object's three-dimensional shape and its relationship to the source of light. For example, the left part of Figure 4.15 is perceived as a two-dimensional circle, but the right part tends to be perceived as a three-dimensional sphere because of the highlight on its surface and the shadow underneath. In the "sphere," the highlighted central area is perceived as closest to us, with the surface receding to the edges.

Another monocular cue is **texture gradient.** (A gradient is a progressive change.) Closer objects are perceived as having rougher textures. In the Hogarth engraving (Figure 4.13), the building just behind the large fisherman's head has a rougher texture and therefore seems to be closer than the building with the window from which the woman is leaning. Our surprise is heightened when the moon sign is seen as hanging from both buildings. Cues for depth perception are summarized in Table 4.1.

MOTION CUES Motion cues are another kind of monocular cue. If you have ever driven in the country, you have probably noticed that distant objects such as mountains and stars appear to move along with you. Objects at an intermediate distance seem to be stationary, but nearby objects such as roadside markers, rocks, and trees seem to go by quite rapidly. The tendency of objects to seem to move backward or forward as a function of their distance is known as **motion parallax.** We learn to perceive objects that appear to move with us as being at greater distances.

Earlier we noted that nearby objects cause the lens of the eye to accommodate or bend more in order to bring them into focus. The sensations of tension in the eye muscles also provide a monocular cue to depth, especially when we are within about 4 feet of the objects.

BINOCULAR CUES Binocular cues, or cues that involve both eyes, also help us perceive depth. Two binocular cues are *retinal disparity* and *convergence.*

Try an experiment. Hold your index finger at arm's length. Now, gradually bring it closer until it almost touches your nose. If you keep your eyes relaxed as you do so, you will see two fingers. An image of the finger will be projected onto the retina of each eye, and each image will be

FIGURE 4.14

THE EFFECTS OF INTERPOSITION THE FOUR CIRCLES ARE ALL THE SAME SIZE. WHICH CIRCLES SEEM CLOSER? THE COMPLETE CIRCLES OR THE CIRCLES WITH CHUNKS BITTEN OUT OF THEM?

FIGURE 4.15

SHADOWING AS A CUE FOR DEPTH SHADOWING MAKES THE CIRCLE ON THE RIGHT LOOK THREE-DIMENSIONAL.

REFLECT

Have you ever driven in the country and perceived the stars or distant hills to be moving along with you? How do you explain the phenomenon?

INTERPOSITION A monocular cue for depth based on the fact that a nearby object obscures a more distant object behind it.

SHADOWING A monocular cue for depth based on the fact that opaque objects block light and produce shadows.

TEXTURE GRADIENT A monocular cue for depth based on the perception that closer objects appear to have rougher (more detailed) surfaces.

MOTION PARALLAX A monocular cue for depth based on the perception that nearby objects appear to move more rapidly in relation to our own motion.

BINOCULAR CUES Stimuli suggestive of depth that involve simultaneous perception by both eyes.

TABLE 4.1		CUES FOR DEPTH PERCEPTION
MONOCULAR CUES		
Pictorial cues*	Perspective	Perceiving parallel lines as coming closer to-gether, or converging, as they recede from us
	Relative size	Perceiving larger objects as being closer to us
	Clearness	Perceiving objects with greater detail as being closer to us
	Interposition	Perceiving objects that block our view of other objects as being closer to us (also called *over-lapping*)
	Shadowing	Perceiving shadows and highlights as giving depth to two-dimensional objects
	Texture gradient	Perceiving objects with rougher textures as be-ing closer
Motion cues	Motion parallax	Perceiving objects that seem to move forward with us as distant and objects that seem to move backward as nearby
BINOCULAR CUES		
Retinal disparity		Perceiving objects that cast more greatly differing images on the retinas of the eyes as being closer
Convergence		Perceiving objects for whom focusing requires greater inward movement of the eyes (and therefore greater feelings of tension in the eyes) as being closer

*These cues are commonly used by artists to create the impression of depth (a third dimension) in two-dimensional works such as drawings and paintings.

slightly different because the finger will be seen from different angles. The difference between the projected images is referred to as **retinal disparity** and serves as a binocular cue for depth perception (see Figure 4.16). Note that the closer your finger comes, the farther apart the "two fingers" appear to be. Closer objects have greater retinal disparity.

If we try to maintain a single image of the nearing finger, our eyes must turn inward, or converge on it, making us cross-eyed. **Convergence** causes feelings of tension in the eye muscles and provides another binocular cue for depth. (After convergence occurs, try looking at the finger first with one eye closed, then the other. You will readily see how different the images are in each eye.) The binocular cues of retinal disparity and convergence are strongest when objects are close.

Perceptual Constancies

The world is a constantly shifting display of visual sensations. Think how confusing it would be if you believed that a door was a trapezoid and not a rectangle because it is ajar (Figure 4.17). Or what if we perceived a doorway to be a different doorway when seen from 6 feet away compared with 4 feet. As we neared it, we might think it was larger than the door we were seeking, and become lost. Or consider the problems of the pet owner who recognizes his dog from the side but not from above because its shape is different when seen from above. Fortunately, these problems tend not to occur—at least with familiar objects—because perceptual constancies enable us to recognize objects even when their apparent shape or size differs. Questions: What are perceptual constancies? Why do we perceive a door to be a rectangle even when it is ajar?

FIGURE 4.16
RETINAL DISPARITY AND CONVERGENCE AS CUES FOR DEPTH   AS AN OBJECT NEARS YOUR EYES, YOU BEGIN TO SEE TWO IMAGES OF IT BECAUSE OF RETINAL DISPARITY. TO MAINTAIN PERCEPTION OF A SINGLE IMAGE, YOUR EYES MUST CONVERGE ON THE OBJECT.

RETINAL DISPARITY A binocular cue for depth based on the difference in the image cast by an object on the retinas of the eyes as the object moves closer or farther away.

CONVERGENCE A binocular cue for depth based on the inward movement of the eyes as they attempt to focus on an object that is drawing nearer.

FIGURE 4.17
SHAPE CONSTANCY WHEN CLOSED, THIS DOOR IS A RECTANGLE. WHEN OPEN, THE RETINAL IMAGE IS TRAPEZOIDAL. BUT BECAUSE OF SHAPE CONSTANCY, WE STILL PERCEIVE IT AS RECTANGULAR.

SIZE CONSTANCY There are a number of perceptual constancies, including that of **size constancy.** We may say that people "look like ants" when viewed from the top of a tall building, but because of size constancy, we know they remain people even if the details of their forms are lost in the distance. We can thus say that we *perceive* people to be the same size, even when viewed from different distances.

The image of a dog seen from 20 feet away occupies about the same amount of space on your retina as an inch-long insect crawling on your hand. Yet you do not perceive the dog to be as small as the insect. Through your visual experiences you have acquired size constancy—that is, the tendency to perceive an object as the same size even though the size of its image on your retina varies as a function of its distance. Experience teaches us about perspective—that the same object seen at a distance appears to be smaller than when it is nearby.

COLOR CONSTANCY We also have **color constancy**—the tendency to perceive objects as retaining their color even though lighting conditions may alter their appearance. Your bright yellow car may edge toward gray as the hours wend their way through twilight to nighttime. But when you finally locate the car in the parking lot, you may still think of it as yellow. You expect to find a yellow car and still judge it to be "more yellow" than the (faded) red and green cars on either side of it.

BRIGHTNESS CONSTANCY Similar to color constancy is **brightness constancy.** Consider Figure 4.18. The orange squares within the blue squares are equally bright, yet the one within the dark blue square is perceived as brighter. Why? Again, consider the role of experience. If it were nighttime, we would expect orange to fade to gray. The fact that the orange within the dark square stimulates the eye with equal intensity suggests that it must be much brighter than the orange within the lighter square.

SHAPE CONSTANCY We also perceive objects as maintaining their shape, even if we look at them from different angles so that the shape of their image on the retina changes dramatically. This ability is called **shape constancy.** You perceive the top of a coffee cup or a glass to be a circle

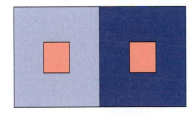

FIGURE 4.18
BRIGHTNESS CONSTANCY THE ORANGE SQUARES WITHIN THE BLUE SQUARES ARE EQUALLY BRIGHT, YET THE ORANGE WITHIN THE DARK BLUE SQUARE IS PERCEIVED AS BRIGHTER. WHY?

SIZE CONSTANCY The tendency to perceive an object as being the same size even as the size of its retinal image changes according to the object's distance.

COLOR CONSTANCY The tendency to perceive an object as being the same color even though lighting conditions change its appearance.

BRIGHTNESS CONSTANCY The tendency to perceive an object as being just as bright even though lighting conditions change its intensity.

SHAPE CONSTANCY The tendency to perceive an object as being the same shape although the retinal image varies in shape as it rotates.

even though it is a circle only when seen from above. When seen from an angle, it is an ellipse. When the cup or glass is seen on edge, its retinal image is the same as that of a straight line. So why do you still describe the rim of the cup or glass as a circle? Perhaps for two reasons: First, experience has taught you that the cup will look circular when seen from above. Second, you may have labeled the cup as circular or round. Experience and labels help make the world a stable place. Can you imagine the chaos that would prevail if we described objects as they appear as they stimulate our sensory organs with each changing moment, rather than according to stable conditions?

Let us return to the door that "changes shape" when it is ajar. The door is a rectangle only when viewed straight on (Figure 4.17). When we move to the side or open it, the left or right edge comes closer and appears to be larger, changing the retinal image to a trapezoid. Yet we continue to think of doors as rectangles.

Visual Illusions

The principles of perceptual organization make it possible for our eyes to "play tricks on us." Psychologists, like magicians, enjoy pulling a rabbit out of a hat now and then. Let me demonstrate how the perceptual constancies trick the eye through *visual illusions.*

The Hering-Helmholtz and Müller-Lyer illusions (Figure 4.19, part A) are named after the people who devised them. In the Hering-Helmholtz illusion, the horizontal lines are straight and parallel. However, the radiating lines cause them to appear to be bent outward near the center. The two lines in the Müller-Lyer illusion are the same length, but the line on the left, with its reversed arrowheads, looks longer. Question: How can principles of visual perception be used to trick the eye?

Let us try to explain these illusions. Because of our experience and lifelong use of perceptual cues, we tend to perceive the Hering-Helmholtz drawing as three-dimensional. Because of our tendency to perceive bits of sensory information as figures against grounds, we perceive the white area in the center as a circle in front of a series of radiating lines, all of which lie in front of a white ground. Next, because of our experience with per-

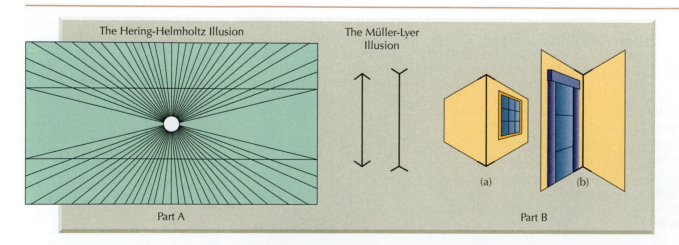

FIGURE 4.19

THE HERING-HELMHOLTZ AND MÜLLER-LYER ILLUSIONS   IN THE HERING-HELMHOLTZ ILLUSION, ARE THE HORIZONTAL LINES STRAIGHT OR CURVED? IN THE MÜLLER-LYER ILLUSION, ARE THE VERTICAL LINES EQUAL IN LENGTH?

spective, we perceive the radiating lines as parallel. We perceive the two horizontal lines as intersecting the "receding" lines, and we know that they would have to appear bent out at the center if they were to be equidistant at all points from the center of the circle.

Experience probably compels us to perceive the vertical lines in the Müller-Lyer illusion as the corners of a room as seen from inside a house, at left, and from outside a house, at right (see Figure 4.19, part B). In such an example, the reverse arrowheads to the left are lines where the walls meet the ceiling and the floor. We perceive such lines as extending toward us. They push the corner away from us. The arrowheads to the right are lines where exterior walls meet the roof and foundation. We perceive them as receding from us. They push the corner toward us. The vertical line to the left therefore is perceived as being farther away. Because both vertical lines stimulate equal expanses across the retina, the principle of size constancy encourages us to perceive the line to the left as longer.

Figure 4.20 is known as the Ponzo illusion. In this illusion, the two horizontal lines are the same length. However, do you perceive the top line as longer? The rule of size constancy may give us some insight into this illusion as well. Perhaps the converging lines again strike us as being lines receding into the distance, like the train tracks in the drawing above. If so, we assume from experience that the horizontal line at the top is farther down the track—that is, farther away from us. And again, the rule of size constancy tells us that if two objects appear to be the same size and one is farther away, the farther object must be larger. So we perceive the top line as larger.

FIGURE 4.20

THE PONZO ILLUSION   THE HORIZONTAL LINES IN THIS DRAWING ARE EQUAL IN LENGTH, BUT THE TOP LINE IS PERCEIVED AS BEING LONGER. CAN YOU USE THE PRINCIPLE OF SIZE CONSTANCY TO EXPLAIN WHY?

Review

SECTION III

Perceptual organization has been studied extensively by (41) G_____ psychologists. Perceptual organization concerns the grouping of bits of sensory stimulation into meaningful (42) _____s. Rules of perceptual organization address (43) _____-ground relationships, proximity, similarity, continuity, common fate, and closure. Our perceptions may be unstable when figure-ground relationships are (44) _____ous. When we are putting puzzle pieces together, a picture of the result enables us to engage in (45) _____-_____ processing; otherwise, we must solve the puzzle by bottom-up processing.

We perceive actual movement by sensing (46) m_____ across the retina, and by sensing change of (47) p_____ of an object in relation to other objects. (48) _____opic motion, used in films, is an illusion of motion caused by the rapid presentation of a series of still images.

Depth perception involves monocular and (49) _____lar cues. Monocular cues include perspective, in which we tend to perceive (50) p_____ lines as converging as they recede from us; clearness, in which (51: Nearby or Distant)? objects are perceived as clearer; interposition; shadowing; texture gradient; motion (52) p_____; and accommodation. According to motion parallax, distant objects appear to move more (53: Rapidly or Slowly?) than nearby objects. Binocular cues include retinal (54) _____ and convergence of the eyes. Closer objects have (55: Greater or Lesser?) retinal disparity and require more convergence.

Because of size (56) _____, objects are perceived as being the same size despite their distance from us. Because of (57) _____ constancy, a door may be perceived to be a rectangle even when it is ajar. Perceptual constancies help make the world a(n) (58: Stable or Unstable?) place.

When principles of visual perception are used to trick the eye, they can give rise to visual (59) _____ions. The effects of the Müller-Lyer and Ponzo illusions can probably be explained by using the principle of (60) _____ constancy.

SECTION IV. HEARING: MAKING SENSE OF SOUND

Consider the advertising slogan for the science fiction film *Alien:* "In space, no one can hear you scream." It's true. Space is an almost perfect vacuum. Hearing requires a medium through which sound can travel, such as air or water. Question: What is sound?

Sound, or *auditory* stimulation, travels through the air like waves. Sound is caused by changes in air pressure that result from vibrations. These vibrations, in turn, can be created by a tuning fork, your vocal cords, guitar strings, or the slam of a book thrown down on a desk.

Figure 4.21 suggests how a tuning fork creates sound waves. During a vibration back and forth, the right prong of the tuning fork moves to the right. In doing so, it pushes together, or compresses, the molecules of air immediately to the right. Then the prong moves back to the left, and the air molecules to the right expand. By vibrating back and forth, the tuning fork actually sends air waves in many directions. A cycle of compression and expansion is one wave of sound. Sound waves can occur many times in 1 second. The human ear is sensitive to sound waves that vary in frequency from 20 to 20,000 cycles per second.

Pitch and Loudness

Pitch and loudness are two psychological dimensions of sound. The pitch of a sound is determined by its frequency, or the number of cycles per second as expressed in the unit **hertz** (Hz). One cycle per second is 1 Hz. The greater the number of cycles per second (Hz), the higher the pitch of the sound. The pitch of women's voices is usually higher than that of men's voices because women's vocal cords are usually shorter and therefore vibrate at a greater frequency. The strings of a violin are shorter than those of a viola or bass viol. They vibrate at greater frequencies, and we perceive them as higher in pitch. Pitch detectors in the brain allow us to tell the difference (Blakeslee, 1995).

The loudness of a sound is determined by the height, or amplitude, of sound waves. The higher the amplitude of the wave, the louder the sound. Frequency and amplitude are independent. Both high- and low-pitched sounds can be either high or low in loudness.

HERTZ A unit expressing the frequency of sound waves. One Hertz, or *1 Hz,* equals one cycle per second.

FIGURE 4.21
CREATION OF SOUND WAVES THE VIBRATION OF THE PRONGS OF A TUNING FORK ALTERNATELY COMPRESSES AND EXPANDS AIR MOLECULES, SENDING FORTH WAVES OF SOUND.

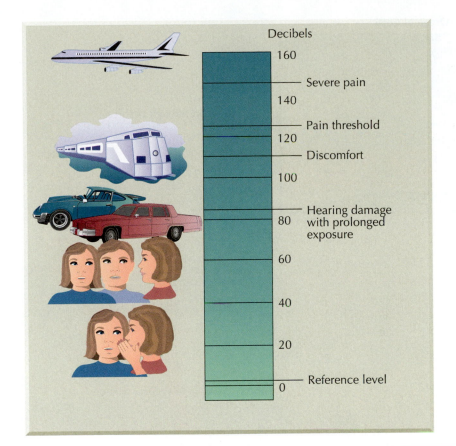

FIGURE 4.22
DECIBEL RATINGS OF FAMILIAR SOUNDS   ZERO DB
IS THE THRESHOLD OF HEARING. YOU MAY SUFFER HEARING
LOSS IF YOU INCUR PROLONGED EXPOSURE TO SOUNDS OF
85–90 DB.

The loudness of a sound is usually expressed in **decibels** (dB). Zero dB is equivalent to the threshold of hearing—the lowest sound that the typical person can hear. How loud is that? It's about as loud as the ticking of a watch 20 feet away in a very quiet room.

The decibel equivalents of many familiar sounds are shown in Figure 4.22. Twenty dB is equivalent in loudness to a whisper at 5 feet. Thirty dB is roughly the limit of loudness at which your librarian would like to keep your college library. You may suffer hearing damage if you are exposed to sounds of 85 to 90 dB for very long periods.

Now let us turn our attention to the human ear—the marvelous instrument that senses all these different "vibes."

The Ear: The Better to Hear You With

The human ear is good for lots of things—including catching dust, combing your hair around, hanging jewelry from, and nibbling. It is also admirably suited for sensing sounds. Question: How does the ear work? The ear is shaped and structured so as to capture sound waves, vibrate in sympathy with them, and transmit them to centers in the brain. In this way, you not only hear something, you can also figure out what it is. The ear has three parts: the outer ear, middle ear, and inner ear (see Figure 4.23).

THE OUTER EAR   The outer ear is shaped to funnel sound waves to the **eardrum,** a thin membrane that vibrates in response to sound waves and thereby transmits them to the middle and inner ears.

DECIBEL A unit expressing the loudness of a sound. Abbreviated *dB.*

EARDRUM A thin membrane that vibrates in response to sound waves, transmitting the waves to the middle and inner ears.

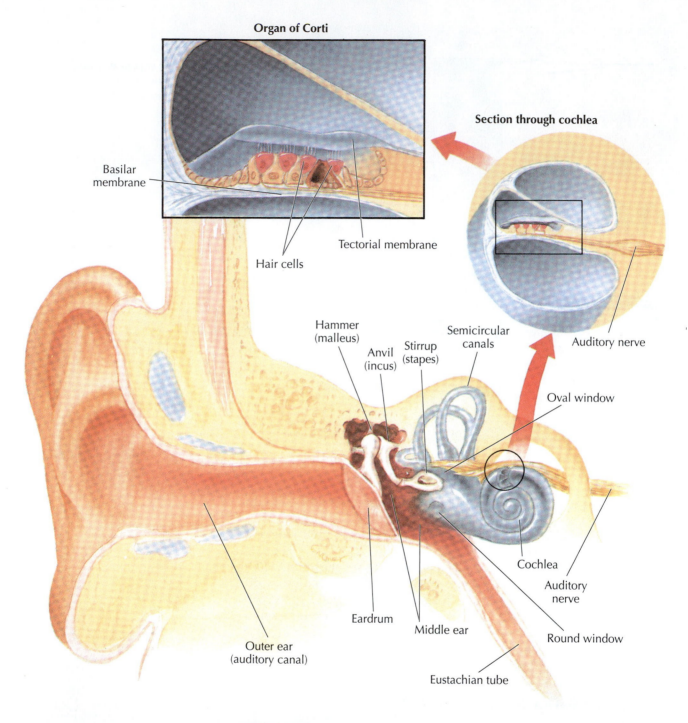

Organ of Corti

Basilar membrane

Section through cochlea

Tectorial membrane

Hair cells

Auditory nerve

Hammer (malleus)

Anvil (incus)

Stirrup (stapes)

Semicircular canals

Oval window

Eardrum

Middle ear

Outer ear (auditory canal)

Cochlea

Auditory nerve

Round window

Eustachian tube

FIGURE 4.23

THE EAR   THE OUTER EAR FUNNELS SOUND TO THE EARDRUM. INSIDE THE EARDRUM, VIBRATIONS OF THE HAMMER, ANVIL, AND STIRRUP TRANSMIT SOUND TO THE INNER EAR. VIBRATIONS IN THE COCHLEA TRANSMIT THE SOUND TO THE AUDITORY NERVE BY WAY OF THE BASILAR MEMBRANE AND THE ORGAN OF CORTI.

THE MIDDLE EAR The middle ear contains the eardrum and three small bones—the hammer, the anvil, and the stirrup—which also transmit sound by vibrating. These bones were given their names (actually the Latin *malleus, incus,* and *stapes* [pronounced STAY-peas], which translate as hammer, anvil, and stirrup) because of their shapes. The middle ear functions as an amplifier: It increases the pressure of the air entering the ear.

The stirrup is attached to another vibrating membrane, the *oval window.* The *round* window shown in Figure 4.23 balances the pressure in the inner ear. It pushes outward when the oval window pushes in, and it is pulled inward when the oval window vibrates outward.

THE INNER EAR The oval window transmits vibrations into the inner ear, the bony tube called the **cochlea** (from the Greek word for "snail"). The cochlea, which is shaped like a snail shell, contains two longitudinal membranes that divide it into three fluid-filled chambers. One of the membranes that lies coiled within the cochlea is called the **basilar membrane.** Vibrations in the fluids within the chambers of the inner ear press against the basilar membrane.

The **organ of Corti,** sometimes referred to as the "command post" of hearing, is attached to the basilar membrane. Hair cells (receptor cells that project like hair from the organ of Corti) "dance" in response to the vibrations of the basilar membrane. Their up-and-down movements generate neural impulses, which are transmitted to the brain via the 31,000 neurons that form the **auditory nerve.** Auditory input is then projected onto the hearing areas of the temporal lobes of the cerebral cortex.

Locating Sounds

How do you balance the loudness of a stereo set? You sit between the speakers and adjust the volume until the sound seems to be equally loud in each ear. If the sound to the right is louder, the musical instruments are perceived as being toward the right rather than straight ahead.

Question: How do we locate sounds? There is a resemblance between balancing a stereo set and locating sounds. A sound that is louder in the right ear is perceived as coming from the right. A sound coming from the right also reaches the right ear first. Both loudness and the sequence in which the sounds reach the ears provide directional cues.

But it may not be easy to locate a sound coming from directly in front or in back of you or overhead. Such sounds are equally distant from each ear and equally loud. So what do we do? Simple—usually we turn our head slightly to determine in which ear the sound increases. If you turn your head a few degrees to the right and the loudness increases in your left ear, the sound must be coming from in front of you. Of course, we also use vision and general knowledge in locating the source of sounds. If you hear the roar of jet engines, most of the time you can bet that the airplane is overhead.

Perception of Loudness and Pitch

Sounds are heard because they cause vibration in parts of the ear and information about these vibrations is transmitted to the brain. Question: How do we perceive loudness and pitch?

The loudness and pitch of sounds appear to be related to the number of receptor neurons on the organ of Corti that fire and how often they fire. Psychologists generally agree that sounds are perceived as louder when more of these sensory neurons fire.

It takes two processes to explain perception of color: *trichromatic theory* and *opponent-process theory.* Similarly, it takes at least two processes to explain pitch perception—that is, perception of sound waves with frequencies that vary from 20 to 20,000 cycles per second: *place theory* and *frequency theory.*

REFLECT

Have you ever been unsure where a sound was coming from? How did you locate the source of the sound?

COCHLEA The inner ear; the bony tube that contains the basilar membrane and the organ of Corti.

BASILAR MEMBRANE A membrane that lies coiled within the cochlea.

ORGAN OF CORTI The receptor for hearing that lies on the basilar membrane in the cochlea.

AUDITORY NERVE The axon bundle that transmits neural impulses from the organ of Corti to the brain.

Hermann von Helmholtz helped develop the place theory of pitch discrimination as well as the Young-Helmholtz (trichromatic) theory of color vision. **Place theory** holds that the pitch of a sound is sensed according to the place along the basilar membrane that vibrates in response to it. In classic research with guinea pigs and cadavers that led to the award of a Nobel prize, Georg von Békésy (1957) found evidence for place theory. He determined that receptors at different sites along the membrane fire in response to tones of differing frequencies. Receptor neurons appear to be lined up along the basilar membrane like piano keys (Azar, 1996). The higher the pitch of a sound, the closer the responsive neurons lie to the oval window. However, place theory appears to apply only to sound higher in pitch than 4,000 Hz, and people sense pitches as low as 20 Hz.

Frequency theory accounts for pitches at the lower end of the range. **Frequency theory** notes that pitch perception depends on the stimulation of neural impulses that match the frequency of the sound waves. That is, in response to low pitches—pitches of about 20 to 1,000 cycles per second—hair cells on the basilar membrane fire at the same frequencies as the sound waves. However, neurons cannot fire more than 1,000 times per second. Therefore, frequency theory can account only for perception of pitches between 20 and 1,000 cycles per second. In actuality, frequency theory appears to account only for pitch perception between 20 and a few hundred cycles per second.

I noted that it takes *at least two processes* to explain how people perceive pitch. The *volley principle* is the third, and it accounts for pitch discrimination between a few hundred and 4,000 cycles per second (Matlin & Foley, 1995). In response to sound waves of these frequencies, groups of neurons take turns firing, in the way that one row of soldiers used to fire rifles while another row knelt to reload. Alternating firing—that is, volleying—appears to transmit sensory information about pitches in the intermediate range.

Unfortunately, not everyone perceives sound, and many of us do not perceive sounds of certain frequencies. Let us now consider the health problem of deafness.

Deafness

Perhaps 30 million Americans have difficulty hearing. Two million of them are deaf (Nadol, 1993). They are thus deprived of a key source of information about the world around them. In recent years, however, society has made greater efforts to bring them into the mainstream of sensory experience. People are usually on hand to convert political and other speeches into hand signs (such as those of American Sign Language) for hearing-impaired members of the audience. Many TV shows are "closed captioned" so that they can be understood by people with hearing problems. Special decoders render the captions visible. Questions: What is deafness? What can we do about it?

There are two major types of deafness: conductive deafness and sensorineural deafness. **Conductive deafness** is a result of damage to the structures of the middle ear—either to the eardrum or to the three bones that conduct (and amplify) sound waves from the outer ear to the inner ear (Nadol, 1993). This is the type of hearing impairment often found among older people. People with conductive deafness often profit from hearing aids, which provide the amplification that the middle ear does not.

Sensorineural deafness usually stems from damage to the structures of the inner ear, most often the loss of hair cells, which will not regenerate. Sensorineural deafness can also stem from damage to the auditory nerve,

PLACE THEORY The theory that the pitch of a sound is determined by the section of the basilar membrane that vibrates in response to the sound.

FREQUENCY THEORY The theory that the pitch of a sound is reflected in the frequency of the neural impulses that are generated in response to the sound.

CONDUCTIVE DEAFNESS The forms of deafness in which there is loss of conduction of sound through the middle ear.

SENSORINEURAL DEAFNESS The forms of deafness that result from damage to hair cells or the auditory nerve.

REFLECT

Do you know anyone with hearing problems? What is the source of the impairment? How does the person cope with the impairment?

for example, because of disease or because of acoustic trauma (prolonged exposure to very loud sounds). In sensorineural deafness, people tend to be more sensitive to some pitches than to others. In Hunter's notch, hearing impairment is limited to particular frequencies—in this case, the frequencies of the sound waves generated by a gun firing. Prolonged exposure to 85 dB can cause hearing loss. People who attend rock concerts, where sounds may reach 140 dB, risk damaging their ears, as do workers who run pneumatic drills or drive noisy vehicles. The ringing sensation that often follows exposure to loud sounds probably means that hair cells in the inner ear have been damaged. If you find yourself suddenly exposed to loud sounds, remember that your fingertips serve as good emergency ear protectors.

Cochlear implants, or "artificial ears," contain microphones that sense sounds and electronic equipment that transmits sounds past damaged hair cells to stimulate the auditory nerve directly. Such implants have helped many people with sensorineural deafness. However, they cannot assume the functions of damaged auditory nerves.

DEAFNESS, SIGN LANGUAGE, AND HUMAN DIVERSITY: THE SIGNS OF THE TIMES ARE CHANGING As recently as 1990, a deaf person might make the sign meaning *Japanese person* by twisting the little finger next to the eye (see Figure 4.24). Today, many people who use American Sign Language have discarded this sign because it refers to the stereotypical physical feature of slanted eyes. Instead, they are adopting Japanese people's own sign for themselves: They press the thumb and index finger of both hands together and then pull them apart to sculpt the outline of Japan in the air.

"In American Sign Language, politically incorrect terms are often a visual representation of the ugly metaphors we have about people," notes psycholinguist Elissa Newport (1994). As with the sign for *Japanese*, the signs for *Chinese* and *Korean*, which are made by forming the letters *C*

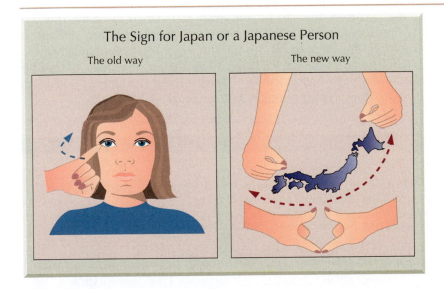

FIGURE 4.24
OLD AND NEW SIGNS FOR JAPAN OR A JAPANESE PERSON IN AMERICAN SIGN LANGUAGE THE OLD SIGN FOR JAPANESE IS NOW CONSIDERED OFFENSIVE BECAUSE IT REFERS TO THE STEREOTYPICAL PHYSICAL FEATURE OF SLANTED EYES. THE NEW SIGN OUTLINES THE ISLAND OF JAPAN.

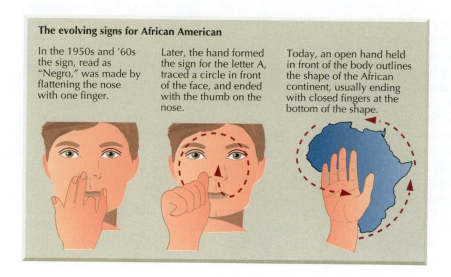

The evolving signs for African American

In the 1950s and '60s the sign, read as "Negro," was made by flattening the nose with one finger.

Later, the hand formed the sign for the letter A, traced a circle in front of the face, and ended with the thumb on the nose.

Today, an open hand held in front of the body outlines the shape of the African continent, usually ending with closed fingers at the bottom of the shape.

FIGURE 4.25

OLD AND NEW SIGNS FOR AFRICAN AMERICANS IN AMERICAN SIGN LANGUAGE   THE OLD SIGNS FOR AFRICAN AMERICANS WERE CONSIDERED OFFENSIVE BECAUSE THEY REFERRED TO THE SHAPE OR LOCATION OF THE NOSE. THE NEW SIGN OUTLINES THE AFRICAN CONTINENT.

and *K* around the eye, are also changing. There is also a new sign for *African American.* This population group was once indicated by flattening the nose. That sign was replaced by signs for the color black—the index finger either placed by the eyebrow or wiped across the forehead. The current sign for *African American* is still centered on the nose, however, and therefore is being replaced by a sign that outlines Africa (see Figure 4.25).

The old sign for *gay male* was an offensive swish of the wrist. Now it is more widely acceptable to simply spell out words like *homosexual, gay male,* or *lesbian* with the hands.

Politically correct changes in American Sign Language have thus far caught on mainly among highly educated deaf people in urban settings. It is taking longer for them to catch on in the wider deaf community and to appear in dictionaries of sign language. Nevertheless, the clear trend is for the deaf—who have been victims of stereotyping themselves—to learn how to avoid stereotyping others in sign language.

Review

SECTION IV

(61) _____tory stimulation, or sound waves, require a medium such as air or water for transmission. Sound waves alternately (62) _____press and expand molecules of the medium.

The human ear can hear sounds varying in frequency from 20 to (63) _____ cycles per second (Hz). Sound waves with greater frequencies are perceived as (64: Lower or Higher?) in pitch. The loudness of a sound is measured in (65) _____els, abbreviated *dB.*

The outer ear funnels sound waves to a membrane called the (66) _____, which then transmits the auditory information to the middle ear. The middle ear contains the three bones—the "hammer," (67) "_____," and "stirrup." These bones vibrate and transmit sound waves to another membrane called the (68) _____ window. The oval window transmits sound waves to the bony tube of the inner ear called the (69) _____a. The cochlea contains fluids that vibrate against the (70) _____ membrane. The "command post" of hearing, called the organ of (71)

C_____, is attached to the basilar membrane. Sound waves travel from the organ of Corti to the brain by the (72) _____ nerve.

Sounds are perceived as louder when more sensory neurons on the organ of (73) _____ fire. According to place theory, the pitch of a sound is determined by the segment of the (74) _____ _____ne that vibrates in response to it. According to frequency theory, the frequency with which sensory neurons fire corresponds to the

(75) _____ of the sound. Place theory accounts for perception of (76: High or Low?) pitches. Frequency theory accounts for perception of (77: High or Low?) pitches. The (78) _____ principle accounts for the perception of intermediate pitches.

(79) _____tive deafness occurs because of damage to the middle ear, which conducts and amplifies sound waves from the outer ear to the inner ear. (80) _____ral deafness stems from damage to the inner ear or the auditory nerve.

SECTION V. THE CHEMICAL SENSES: SMELL AND TASTE

Smell and taste are the chemical senses. In the cases of vision and hearing, physical energy strikes our sensory receptors. With smell and taste, we sample molecules of the substances being sensed.

Smell

You could say that we are underprivileged when it comes to the sense of smell. Dogs, for instance, devote about seven times as much of the cerebral cortex as we do to the sense of smell. Male dogs sniff in order to determine where the boundaries of other dogs' territories leave off and whether female dogs are sexually receptive. Some dogs even make a living sniffing out illegal drugs in closed packages and suitcases for law enforcement agencies.

Still, smell has an important role in human behavior. It makes a crucial contribution to the flavor of foods, for example (Bartoshuk & Beauchamp, 1994). If you did not have a sense of smell, an onion and an apple would taste the same to you! People's sense of smell may be deficient when we compare them with those of a dog, but we can detect the odor of 1 one-millionth of a milligram of vanilla in a liter of air.

✓ **Truth or Fiction Revisited**

It is true that onions and apples have the same taste (as sensed by taste buds). Their *flavors,* however, which also reflect their odors and other qualities, are quite different.

Question: How does the sense of smell work? Smell is the sense that senses odors. An *odor* is a sample of the substance being sensed. Odors are detected by sites on receptor neurons in the *olfactory membrane* high in each nostril. Receptor neurons fire when a few molecules of the substance in gaseous form come into contact with them. Their firing transmits information about odors to the brain via the **olfactory nerve.** That is how the substance is smelled.

It is unclear how many basic kinds of odors there are. In any event, olfactory receptors may respond to more than one kind of odor. Mixtures of smell sensations also help produce the broad range of odors that we can perceive.

The sense of smell adapts rapidly to odors, such that you lose awareness of them, even obnoxious ones. This might be fortunate if you are in a

REFLECT

Has food ever seemed to lose its flavor when you had a cold or an allergy attack? Why?

OLFACTORY NERVE The nerve that transmits information concerning odors from olfactory receptors to the brain.

REFLECT

Have you had the experience of growing accustomed to a noxious odor so that you have lost awareness of it?

Sensational? The flavors of foods are determined not only by their taste, but also by their odor, texture, and temperature.

TASTE CELLS Receptor cells that are sensitive to taste.

TASTE BUDS The sensory organs for taste. They contain taste cells and are located on the tongue.

REFLECT

Why do older people tend to spice their food heavily?

locker room or an outhouse. It might not be so fortunate if you are exposed to paint fumes or secondhand smoke, because you may lose awareness of them while danger remains. One odor can mask another, which is how air fresheners work.

Taste

Your cocker spaniel may jump at the chance to finish off your ice cream cone, but your Siamese cat may turn up her nose at the opportunity. Why? Dogs can perceive the taste quality of sweetness, as can pigs, but cats cannot.

Question: How does the sense of taste work? There are four primary taste qualities: sweet, sour, salty, and bitter. The *flavor* of a food involves its taste but is more complex. Although apples and onions are similar in taste, their flavors differ greatly. After all, you wouldn't chomp into a nice cold onion on a warm day, would you? The flavor of a food depends on its odor, texture, and temperature as well as on its taste. If it were not for odor, heated tenderized shoe leather might pass for steak.

Taste is sensed through **taste cells**—receptor neurons located on **taste buds.** You have about 10,000 taste buds, most of which are located near the edges and back of your tongue. Taste buds tend to specialize a bit. Some, for example, are more responsive to sweetness, whereas others react to several tastes. Other taste receptors are found in the roof, sides, and back of the mouth, even in the throat.

We live in different taste worlds. Those of us with low sensitivity for the sweet taste may require twice the sugar to sweeten our food as others who are more sensitive to sweetness. Those of us who claim to enjoy very bitter foods may actually be taste blind to them. Sensitivities to different tastes apparently have a strong genetic component.

By eating hot foods and scraping your tongue, you regularly kill off many taste cells. But you need not be alarmed at this inadvertent oral aggression. Taste cells are the rabbits of the sense receptors. They reproduce rapidly enough to completely renew themselves about once a week.

Although older people often complain that their food has little or no "taste," they are more likely to experience a decline in the sense of smell. Because the flavor of a food represents both its tastes and its odors or aromas, older people experience loss in the *flavor* of their food. Older people often spice their food heavily to enhance its flavor.

Review

SECTION V

Smell and (81) _____ are the chemical senses. An odor is a sample of a number of (82) _____ules of the substance being smelled. Odors are detected by the (83) _____ membrane in each nostril. The sense of smell adapts (84: Rapidly or Slowly?) to odors.

There are four primary taste qualities: sweet, sour, (85) _____, and (86) _____. Flavor involves not only the taste of food, but also its (87) _____, texture, and temperature. The receptor neurons for taste are called (88) _____ cells. Taste cells are located in (89) _____ _____s on the tongue. The "taste loss" found among older people is probably mainly due to a decline in the sense of (90) _____.

SECTION VI. THE SKIN SENSES (YES, IT DOES)

The skin is much more than a protective coating for your body. As you may know from lying on the sand beneath a broiling sun, and perhaps from touching the person lying next to you, the skin also discriminates among many kinds of sensations. Questions: What are the skin senses? How do they work? The skin senses include touch, pressure, warmth, cold, and pain. We have distinct sensory receptors for pressure, temperature, and pain, but some nerve endings may receive more than one type of sensory input.

✓ Truth or Fiction Revisited

It is true that the skin is a sensory organ as well as a protective coating for the body. The skin senses touch, pressure, temperature, and pain.

Touch and Pressure

Sensory receptors located around the roots of hair cells appear to fire when the surface of the skin is touched. You may have noticed that if you are trying to "get the feel of" a fabric or the texture of a friend's hair, you must move your hand over it. Otherwise, the sensations quickly fade. If you pass your hand over the fabric or hair and then hold it still, again the sensations of touching will fade. This sort of "active touching" involves reception of information concerning not only touch per se but also pressure, temperature, and feedback from the muscles involved in movements of our hands.

Other structures beneath the skin are sensitive to pressure. Different parts of the body are more sensitive to touch and pressure than others. Psychophysicists use methods such as the **two-point threshold** to assess sensitivity to pressure. This method determines the smallest distance by which two rods touching the skin must be separated before the (blindfolded) individual reports that there are two rods rather than one. With this method, psychophysicists have found that our fingertips, lips, noses, and cheeks are more sensitive than our shoulders, thighs, and calves. That is, the rods can be closer together but perceived as distinct when they touch the lips more than when they touch the shoulders. Why the difference in sensitivity? First, nerve endings are more densely packed in the fingertips and face than in other locations. Second, more sensory cortex is devoted to the perception of sensations in the fingertips and face.

The sense of pressure, like the sense of touch, undergoes rapid adaptation. For example, you may have undertaken several minutes of strategic movements to wind up with your hand on the arm or leg of your date, only to discover that adaptation to this delightful source of pressure reduces the sensation you experience.

Temperature

The receptors for temperature are neurons located just beneath the skin. When skin temperature increases, the receptors for warmth fire. Decreases in skin temperature cause receptors for cold to fire.

Sensations of temperature are relative. When we are at normal body temperature, we might perceive another person's skin as warm. When we are feverish, though, the other person's skin might seem cool. We also

REFLECT

Can you think of instances of active touching in your own life?

TWO-POINT THRESHOLD The least distance by which two rods touching the skin must be separated before the person will report that there are two rods, not one, on 50% of occasions.

REFLECT

How can a drink that is 70° F be either warming or cooling, depending on the weather?

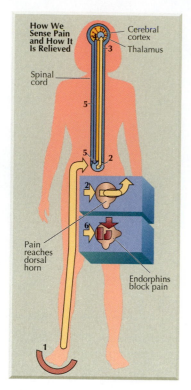

FIGURE 4.26
PERCEPTION OF PAIN   PAIN ORIGINATES AT THE POINT OF CONTACT, AND THE PAIN MESSAGE TO THE BRAIN IS INITIATED BY THE RELEASE OF PROSTAGLANDINS, BRADYKININ, AND SUBSTANCE *P*.

REFLECT

Have you ever experienced intense pain? How did you cope with it?

REFLECT

How do you think it is possible for someone to "feel" pain in a missing limb?

adapt to differences in temperature. When we walk out of an air-conditioned house into the July sun, we feel intense heat at first. Then the sensations of heat tend to fade (although we may still be uncomfortable because of high humidity). Similarly, when we first enter a swimming pool, the water may seem cool or cold because it is below our body temperature. Yet after a few moments an 80° F pool may seem quite warm. In fact, we may chide a newcomer for not jumping right in.

Pain: The Often Unwanted Message

Headaches, backaches, toothaches—these are only a few of the types of pain that most of us encounter from time to time. Some of us also experience bouts of pain caused by arthritis, digestive disorders, cancer, or wounds. Questions: What is pain? What can we do about it?

Pain means something is wrong in the body. It is adaptive in the sense that it motivates us to do something about it. For some of us, however, chronic pain—pain that lasts once injuries or illnesses have cleared—saps our vitality and interferes with the pleasures of everyday life (Karoly & Ruehlman, 1996).

We can sense pain throughout most of the body, but pain is usually sharpest where nerve endings are densely packed, as in the fingers and face. Pain can also be felt deep within the body, as in the cases of abdominal pain and back pain. Even though headaches may seem to originate deep inside the head, there are no nerve endings for pain in the brain. Brain surgery can be done with a local anesthetic that prevents the patient from feeling the drilling of a small hole through the skull. Can it be that the lack of nerve endings in the brain is evolution's way of saying that normally speaking, when someone has a reason to experience pain deep inside the brain, it might be too late to do anything about it?

✓ Truth or Fiction Revisited

It is true that there are no nerve endings for pain in the brain, even though people can have fierce headaches. The pain actually originates elsewhere in the head.

Pain usually originates at the point of contact, as with a stubbed toe (see Figure 4.26). The pain message to the brain is initiated by the release of chemicals, including prostaglandins, bradykinin, and a chemical called *P* (yes, *P* stands for "pain"). Prostaglandins facilitate transmission of the pain message to the brain and heighten circulation to the injured area, causing the redness and swelling that we call inflammation. Inflammation serves the biological function of attracting infection-fighting blood cells to the affected area to protect it against invading germs. Analgesic drugs such as aspirin and ibuprofen work by inhibiting the production of prostaglandins.

The pain message is relayed from the spinal cord to the thalamus and then projected to the cerebral cortex, making us aware of the location and intensity of the damage.

PHANTOM LIMB PAIN   One of the more fascinating phenomena of psychology is the fact that many people experience pain in limbs that are no longer there (Sherman, 1997). About 2 out of 3 combat veterans with amputated limbs report feeling pain in missing, or "phantom," limbs (Kimble, 1992). In such cases, the pain occurs in the absence of (present) tissue damage, but the pain itself is real enough. It sometimes involves activation of nerves in the stump of the missing limb, but local anesthesia does not always eliminate the pain. Therefore, the pain must also reflect activation of neural circuits that have stored memories connected with the missing limb (Melzack, 1997).

✔ **Truth or Fiction Revisited**

It is true that many amputees experience pain in limbs that have been removed. The pain apparently reflects activation of neural circuits that have stored memories connected with the missing limbs.

GATE THEORY Simple remedies like rubbing and scratching an injured toe frequently help relieve pain. Why? One possible answer lies in the *gate theory* of pain originated by Melzack (1980). From this perspective, the nervous system can process only a limited amount of stimulation at a time. Rubbing or scratching the toe transmits sensations to the brain that, in a sense, compete for the attention of neurons. Many nerves are thus prevented from transmitting pain messages to the brain. The mechanism is analogous to shutting down a "gate" in the spinal cord. It is like a switchboard being flooded with calls. The flooding prevents any of the calls from getting through.

✔ **Truth or Fiction Revisited**

It is true that rubbing or scratching a sore toe is often an effective way of relieving pain. Rubbing or scratching may "flood" the nervous system with messages so that news of the pain does not get through to the brain.

ACUPUNCTURE Thousands of years ago, the Chinese began mapping the body to learn where pins might be placed to deaden pain. Acupuncture remained largely unknown in the West, even though Western powers occupied much of China during the 1800s. But in the 1970s *New York Times* columnist James Reston underwent an appendectomy in China, with acupuncture his primary anesthetic. He reported no discomfort. More recently, TV journalist Bill Moyers (1993) reported on current usage of acupuncture in China. For example, one woman underwent brain surgery to remove a tumor after receiving anesthesia that consisted of a mild sedative, a small dose of narcotics, and six needles placed in her forehead, calves, and ankles. The surgery itself and the use of a guiding CAT scan were consistent with contemporary U.S. practices.

Some of the effects of acupuncture may be due to the release of *endorphins*—naturally occurring chemical messengers that are similar in effect to the narcotic morphine (Richardson & Vincent, 1986). Evidence to support this suggestion is found in the fact that the drug *naloxone* blocks the painkilling effects of morphine. The analgesic effects of acupuncture are also blocked by naloxone (Kimble, 1992). Therefore, it may well be that the analgesic effects of acupuncture can be linked to the morphinelike endorphins.

THE PLACEBO EFFECT Some scientists have also credited endorphins with the so-called *placebo effect,* in which the expectation of relief sometimes leads to relief from pain and other problems. They speculate that a positive attitude may lead to release of endorphins.

KINESTHESIS The sense that informs us about the positions and motion of parts of our bodies.

VESTIBULAR SENSE The sense that informs us about our bodies' positions relative to gravity.

REFLECT

Can you touch your nose with your finger when you close your eyes? How do you manage to find your nose?

Kinesthesis. This young acrobat receives information about the position and movement of the parts of his body through the sense of kinesthesis. Information is fed to his brain from sensory organs in the joints, tendons, and muscles. This allows him to follow his own movements without looking at himself.

SECTION VII. KINESTHESIS AND THE VESTIBULAR SENSE

Try a brief experiment. Close your eyes, and then touch your nose with your finger. If you weren't right on target, I'm sure you came close. But how? You didn't see your hand moving, and you didn't hear your arm swishing through the air.

Kinesthesis

Question: What is kinesthesis? **Kinesthesis** is the sense that informs you about the position and motion of parts of the body. The term is derived from the ancient Greek words for "motion" (*kinesis*) and "perception" (*aisthesis*). In kinesthesis, sensory information is fed back to the brain from sensory organs in the joints, tendons, and muscles. You were able to bring your finger to your nose by employing your kinesthetic sense. When you make a muscle in your arm, the sensations of tightness and hardness are also provided by kinesthesis.

Imagine going for a walk without kinesthesis. You would have to watch the forward motion of each leg to be certain you had raised it high enough to clear the curb. And if you had tried our brief experiment without the kinesthetic sense, you would have had no sensory feedback until you felt the pressure of your finger against your nose (or cheek, or eye, or forehead), and you probably would have missed dozens of times.

Are you in the mood for another experiment? Close your eyes again. Then "make a muscle" in your right arm. Could you sense the muscle without looking at it or feeling it with your left hand? Of course you could. Kinesthesis also provides information about muscle contractions.

The Vestibular Sense: On Being Upright

Your **vestibular sense** tells you whether you are upright (physically, not morally). Question: How does the vestibular sense work? Sensory organs located in the semicircular canals and elsewhere in the ears monitor your body's motion and position in relation to gravity. They tell you whether

TABLE 4.2	THE SENSES		
Sense	**What Is Sensed**	**Receptor Organs**	**Nature of Sensory Receptors**
Vision	Visible light (part of the spectrum of electromagnetic energy; different colors have different wavelengths)	Eyes	Photoreceptors in the retinas (*rods,* which are sensitive to the intensity of light, and *cones,* which are sensitive to color)
Hearing	Changes in air pressure (or in another medium, such as water) that result from vibrations called *sound waves*	Ears	"Hair cells" in the organ of Corti, which is attached to a membrane (the *basilar membrane*) within the inner ear (the *cochlea*)
Smell	Molecules of the substance	Nose	Receptor neurons in the olfactory membrane high in each nostril
Taste	Molecules of the substance	Tongue	Taste cells located on taste buds on the tongue
Touch, pressure	Pushing or pulling of the surface of the body	Skin	Nerve endings in the skin, some of which are located around the hair follicles
Kinesthesis	Muscle contractions	Sensory organs in joints, tendons, and muscles	Receptor cells in joints, tendons, and muscles
Vestibular sense	Movement and position in relation to gravity	Sensory organs in the ears (e.g., in the *semicircular canals*)	Receptor cells in the ears

you are falling and provide cues to whether your body is changing speed, such as when you are in an accelerating airplane or automobile.

✓ Truth or Fiction Revisited

It is true that we have a sense that keeps us upright. The sense—the vestibular sense—keeps us physically upright. It apparently takes more than the vestibular sense to keep us morally upright. Information on the senses is summarized in Table 4.2.

Review

SECTION VII

Kinesthesis is the sensing of bodily (101) p_____ and movement. Kinesthesis relies on sensory organs in the joints, (102) t_____, and (103) _____s.

The vestibular sense informs us as to whether we are in an (104) _____ position or changing speeds. The vestibular sense is housed primarily in the (105) s_____ _____ of the ears.

SECTION VIII. EXTRASENSORY PERCEPTION: IS PERCEPTION POSSIBLE WITHOUT SENSATION?

Imagine the wealth you could amass if you had *precognition,* that is, if you were able to perceive future events in advance. Perhaps you would check the next week's stock market reports and know what to buy or sell. Or you could bet with confidence on who would win the next Superbowl or World Series.

Or think of the power you would have if you were capable of *psychokinesis,* that is, of mentally manipulating or moving objects. You may have gotten a glimpse of the possibilities in films like *Carrie, The Sixth Sense,* and *Star Wars.*

Precognition and psychokinesis are two concepts associated with *extrasensory perception* (ESP) or psi communication. ESP by definition refers to the perception of objects or events through means other than sensory organs. Psi communication refers to the transfer of information through an irregular or unusual process—not through the usual senses. Two other theoretical forms of ESP are *telepathy,* or direct transmission of thoughts or ideas from one person to another, and *clairvoyance,* or the perception of objects that do not stimulate the sensory organs. An example of clairvoyance is "seeing" what card will be dealt next, even though it is still in the deck and unseen even by the dealer. Question: Is there really such a thing as extrasensory perception (ESP)?

Many psychologists do not believe that ESP is an appropriate area for scientific inquiry. Scientists study natural events, but ESP smacks of the supernatural, even the occult. ESP also has the flavor of a nightclub act in which a blindfolded "clairvoyant" calls out the contents of an audience member's pocketbook. Other psychologists, however, believe that there is nothing wrong with investigating ESP. The issue for them is not whether ESP is sensationalistic but whether its existence can be demonstrated in the laboratory.

Perhaps the best known of the respected ESP researchers was the late Joseph Banks Rhine of Duke University. Rhine studied ESP for several decades, beginning in the late 1920s. In a typical experiment in clairvoyance, Rhine would use a pack of 25 Zener cards, which contained 5 sets of the 5 cards shown in Figure 4.27. Pigeons pecking patterns at random to indicate which one was about to be turned up would select the correct one 20% of the time. Rhine found that some people guessed correctly significantly more often than the 20% chance rate. He concluded that these individuals may have had some degree of ESP.

A preferred contemporary method for studying telepathy is the Ganzfeld procedure. In this method, one subject acts as a "sender" and the other as a "receiver." The sender views randomly selected visual stimuli such as photographs of videotapes, while the receiver, who is in another room and whose eyes and ears are covered, tries to mentally tune in to the sender. After a session, the receiver is shown four visual stimuli and

REFLECT

Do you believe in ESP? Why or why not?

FIGURE 4.27

ZENER CARDS   ZENER CARDS HAVE BEEN USED IN RESEARCH ON CLAIRVOYANCE. SUBJECTS ARE ASKED TO PREDICT WHICH CARD WILL BE TURNED UP.

asked to select the one that was transmitted by the sender. A person guessing which stimulus was "transmitted" would be correct 25% of the time (1 time in 4) by chance alone. An analysis of 28 experiments using the Ganzfeld procedure, however, found that receivers correctly identified the visual stimulus 38% of the time (Honorton, 1985), a percentage highly unlikely to be due to chance. A series of 11 more studies by Honorton and his colleagues using the Ganzfeld procedure obtained comparable results (Bem & Honorton, 1994; Honorton et al., 1990).

Overall, however, there are many reasons for skepticism of ESP. One is the *file-drawer problem*. Buyers of supermarket magazines tend to forget "psychics'" predictions when they fail to come true (they "file" them away) (Tavris, 1998). Similarly, ESP researchers are less likely to report research results that show failure. Therefore, we would expect unusual findings (for example, a subject with a high success rate at psi-communication tasks over a period of several days) to appear in the research literature. In other words, if you flip a coin indefinitely, eventually you will flip 10 heads in a row. The odds against this are high, but if you report your eventual success and do not report the weeks of failure, you give the impression that you have unique coin-flipping ability. (You may even fool yourself.)

Then, too, it has not been easy to replicate experiments in ESP. Hyman (1994) acknowledges that the studies reported by Honorton are the most tightly controlled studies conducted to date. However, he argues that the studies need to be replicated by other researchers before they are granted credibility. People who have "demonstrated" ESP with one researcher have failed to do so with another researcher or have refused to participate in other studies. Let's make this point a bit more strongly: From all of these studies, *not one person has emerged who can reliably show psi communication from one occasion to another and from one researcher to another.* Science, in other words, has not identified a single indisputable telepath or clairvoyant.

In any event, most psychologists do not grant ESP research much credibility. They prefer to study perception that involves sensation. After all, what is life without sensation?

REFLECT

Do you believe that some people are "psychics"? What is the evidence for their supposed abilities? Is it scientific? Explain.

✓ Truth or Fiction Revisited

It is not true that some people can read other people's minds. Of course, we can make educated guesses about the feelings of people whom we know well. We may also be able to interpret other people's smiles and frowns. But it has not been shown that we can directly read other people's minds.

Review

SECTION VIII

Extrasensory perception or (106) _____ communication is a controversial issue that refers to perception of objects or events through means other than sensory organs. Joseph Banks (107) _____ used Zener cards to study clairvoyance. The (108) G_____ procedure is currently used to study telepathy. One reason for skepticism about ESP is the (109) _____-drawer problem, that is, ESP researchers are less likely to report research results that show failure. It has also been difficult to (110) _____cate positive results.

STUDY GUIDE

TO HELP YOU BETTER UNDERSTAND THE CONTENT OF THIS CHAPTER, YOU MAY GO TO THE STUDENT WEB SITE (http://www.harcourtcollege.com/psych/intro.html) TO TAKE MORE QUIZZES, GET MORE INFORMATION ABOUT THE CONTENT, AND SEE ADDITIONAL WEB SITES RELATED TO THE CONTENT. YOU CAN ALSO PRACTICE USING THE CONCEPTS IN THIS CHAPTER WITH THE POWERPSYCH CD-ROM, WHICH GIVES YOU INTERACTIVE ACTIVITIES AND EXPERIMENTS ALONG WITH EVEN MORE QUIZZES. AND, OF COURSE, THE PRINTED STUDY GUIDE IS A RELIABLE WAY TO PRACTICE ALL PARTS OF PQ4R. YOUR COLLEGE BOOKSTORE CAN ORDER THE POWERPSYCH CD-ROM FOR YOU.

SUMMARY

1. **What are sensation and perception?** Sensation is a mechanical process that involves the stimulation of sensory receptors (neurons) and the transmission of sensory information to the central nervous system. Perception is not mechanical. Perception is the active organization of sensations into a representation of the outside world, and it reflects learning and expectations.

2. **How do we know when something is there? How do we know when it has changed?** We know something is there when the intensity of the stimulus, such as a light, exceeds the absolute threshold for that stimulus. The absolute threshold is the lowest intensity at which the stimulus can be detected. We know that something has changed when the change in intensity exceeds the difference threshold. The difference threshold is the minimum difference in intensity that can be discriminated. Difference thresholds are expressed in Weber's constants.

3. **What is signal-detection theory?** Signal-detection theory explains the ways in which stimulus characteristics and psychological factors—for example, motivation, familiarity with a stimulus, and attention—interact to influence whether a stimulus will be detected.

4. **What are feature detectors?** Feature detectors are neurons that fire in response to specific features of sensed stimuli. For example, detectors in the visual cortex fire in response to particular features of visual input, such as lines sensed at various angles or specific colors.

5. **How do our sensory systems adapt to a changing environment?** We become more sensitive to stimuli of low magnitude and less sensitive to stimuli that remain the same (such as the background noises outside the window). Growing more sensitive to stimulation is termed sensitization, or positive adaptation. Growing less sensitive to continuous stimulation is called desensitization, or negative adaptation.

6. **Just what is this stuff called light?** Visible light triggers visual sensations and is part of the spectrum of electromagnetic energy. Light is made up of waves of energy; the color violet has the shortest wavelength, and red has the longest. White sunlight can be broken down into the colors of the rainbow by means of a prism.

7. **How does the eye work?** The eye senses and transmits visual stimulation to the occipital lobe of the cerebral cortex. After light passes through the cornea, the size of the pupil determines the amount that can pass through the lens. The lens focuses light onto the retina, which is composed of photoreceptors (neurons) called rods and cones. Cones permit perception of color. Rods transmit sensations of light and dark only. Light is transmitted from the retina to the brain via the optic nerve, which is made up of the axons of retinal ganglion cells. Visual acuity is connected with the shape of the eye and age. As we age the lenses grow brittle, making it difficult to focus; the condition is called presbyopia. Rods are more sensitive than cones to lowered lighting and continue to adapt to darkness once cones have reached their peak adaptation.

8. **How do we perceive color?** There are two theories as to how we perceive color. According to the trichromatic theory, there are three types of cones—some sensitive to red, others to green, and still others to blue-violet. The opponent-process theory proposes three types of color receptors: red-green, blue-yellow, and light-dark; it is supported by the appearance of afterimages.

9. **What is color blindness? Why are some people color blind?** People with normal color vision are called trichromats. Monochromats see no color, and dichromats are blind to some parts of the spectrum. Partial color blindness is a sex-linked trait that impairs the working of cones sensitive to red-green.

10. **How do we organize bits of information like perceptions into meaningful wholes?** Perceptual organization involves recognizing patterns and processing information about relationships between parts and the whole. Gestalt rules of perceptual organization involve figure-ground relationships, proximity, similarity, continuity, common fate, and closure. Perception of a whole followed by perception of parts is termed top-down processing.

Perception of the parts that leads to perception of a whole is termed bottom-up processing.

11. **How do we perceive movement?** We visually perceive movement when the light reflected by moving objects moves across the retina, and also when objects shift in relation to one another. Distant objects appear to move more slowly than nearby objects, and objects in the middle ground may give the illusion of moving backward. Stroboscopic motion, responsible for the illusion of motion pictures, occurs through the presentation of a rapid progression of images of stationary objects (frames).

12. **How do we perceive depth?** Depth perception involves monocular and binocular cues. Monocular cues include perspective, clearness, interposition, shadows, texture gradient, motion parallax, and accommodation. Binocular cues include retinal disparity and convergence.

13. **What are perceptual constancies? Why do we perceive a door to be a rectangle even when it is ajar?** Perceptual constancies are acquired through experience and make the world a stable place. For example, we learn to assume that objects retain their size, shape, brightness, and color despite their distance from us, their position, or changes in lighting conditions.

14. **How can principles of visual perception be used to trick the eye?** Visual illusions such as the Hering-Helmholtz and Müller-Lyer illusions tend to trick the eye because they play with perceptual constancies.

15. **What is sound?** Sound waves, also called auditory stimulation, require a medium such as air or water in order to be transmitted. Sound waves alternately compress and expand molecules of the medium, creating vibrations. The human ear can hear sounds varying in frequency from 20 to 20,000 cycles per second (Hz). The greater the frequency, the higher the sound's pitch. The loudness of a sound corresponds to the amplitude of sound waves as measured in decibels (dB). We can experience hearing loss if we are exposed to protracted sounds of 85 to 90 dB or more.

16. **How does the ear work?** The ear captures sound waves, vibrates in sympathy with them, and transmits auditory information to the brain. The outer ear funnels sound waves to the eardrum, which vibrates in sympathy with them and transmits the auditory information through the bones of the middle ear to the cochlea of the inner ear. The basilar membrane of the cochlea transmits those stimuli to the organ of Corti. From there, sound travels to the brain via the auditory nerve.

17. **How do we locate sounds?** We locate sounds by determining in which ear they are louder. We may turn our heads to pin down that information.

18. **How do we perceive loudness and pitch?** Sounds are perceived as louder when more sensory neurons fire. The place theory of pitch perception holds that the pitch of a sound is sensed according to the place along the basilar membrane that vibrates in response to it; it accounts for sounds whose frequencies exceed 4,000 Hz. Frequency theory states that pitch perception depends on the stimulation of neural impulses that match the frequency of the sound waves, and accounts for frequencies of 20 to 1,000 Hz. The volley principle accounts for pitch discrimination between a few hundred and 4,000 cycles per second

19. **What is deafness? What can we do about it?** Conductive deafness—common among older people—is caused by damage to the middle ear and is often ameliorated by hearing aids, which amplify sounds. Sensorineural deafness is usually caused by damage to neurons in the inner ear, and can sometimes be corrected by cochlear implants.

20. **How does the sense of smell work?** The sense of smell is chemical. It samples molecules of substances called odors through the olfactory membrane in each nostril. Smell makes a key contribution to the flavor of foods.

21. **How does the sense of taste work?** There are four primary taste qualities: sweet, sour, salty, and bitter. Flavor involves the odor, texture, and temperature of food, as well as its taste. Taste is sensed through taste cells, which are located in taste buds on the tongue.

22. **What are the skin senses? How do they work?** The skin senses include touch, pressure, warmth, cold, and pain. Touches and pressure are sensed by receptors located around the roots of hair cells below the surface of the skin. We have separate receptors for warmth and cold beneath the skin.

23. **What is pain? What can we do about it?** Pain originates at the point of contact and is transmitted to the brain by various chemicals, including prostaglandins, bradykinin, and *P*. Amputees often experience pain in "phantom" limbs. Rubbing or scratching painful areas can decrease perception of pain by transmitting additional messages that have the effect of shutting down a "gate" in the spinal cord. Acupuncture may decrease pain by causing release of endorphins.

24. **What is kinesthesis?** Kinesthesis is the sensation of body position and movement. It relies on sensory organs in the joints, tendons, and muscles.

25. **How does the vestibular sense work?** The vestibular sense is housed primarily in the semicircular canals of the ears and tells us whether we are in an upright position.

26. **Is there really such a thing as extrasensory perception (ESP)?** ESP, or psi communication, refers to the perception of objects or events through means other than sensory organs. Many psychologists do not believe that ESP is an appropriate area for scientific inquiry. The Ganzfeld procedure studies telepathy by having one person (the sender) try to mentally transmit visual information to a receiver in another room. Because of the file-drawer problem and poor replication of positive results, reliable evidence for the existence of ESP has not emerged.

EXERCISE 1

PARTS OF THE EYE

Below is a drawing of the human eye. Can you label its parts and explain the function of each part? Check your answers against Figure 4.2 in the chapter.

Section of

EXERCISE 2

PARTS OF THE EAR

Below is a drawing of the human ear. Can you label its parts and explain the function of each part? Check your answers against Figure 4.23 in the chapter.

LANGUAGE AND CULTURE

to accommodate to (179)   *to adjust to*

absolute thresholds (177)   *minimal recognition level*

advertising slogan (194)   *jingle or motto for selling something, words that people will associate with a product*

background noise (173)   *indistinguishable sounds caused by unimportant elements in the environment*

birds of a feather (186)   *people in similar circumstances*

blips on a radar screen (174)   *irregular marks from radar indicating the presence of an object or something to be measured*

blob (183)   *shapeless form*

brawl (170)   *battle, fight*

to brook no meddling (171)   *to tolerate no interference*

to bump into (187)   *to meet by accident*

cajoling (186)   *trying to convince*

caliber (170)   *quality, size*

to chomp into (202)   *to bite into as if to eat*

chronic (170)   *repeating over time, never ending*

clank (174)   *sound of metal falling onto a hard surface*

cocker spaniel (202)   *kind of dog*

credibility (209)   *trustworthiness*

debilitating (175)   *handicapping*

to deem (174)   *to consider, to value*

to diffuse (172)   *to spread, to scatter*

to dim the lights (172)   *to decrease the amount of light*

disappearing act (178)   *like a magician's act; something you know is there seems to disappear*

dumbbells (173)   *exercise equipment held in the hands; weights for exercise with a bar and two weights on the two ends*

featureless blaze (179)   *brightness (as in fire) without shape or form in it*

to funnel (178)   *to guide, to channel*

to glow in the dark (172)   *to give off light that can be seen in the dark*

hibiscus (180)   *kind of flower*

hum (174)   *sound of a motor*

to impair (182)   *to affect negatively*

inner representation (171)   *personal picture, image in one's own head*

in random order (172)   *without purpose or planning in the sequence*

in the bush (183)   *in among leaves*

lapping (175)   *the sound of waves*

lateral (178)   *(to the) side*

to look like ants (191)   *(from a distance) they appear like ants on an anthill*

make a muscle (206)   *flex your arm muscles so that the muscles can be seen and felt by another person*

martial arts (170)   *oriental military or fighting arts such as judo, taekwando, aikido, or karate*

miscolored flag (181)   *flag that has the wrong colors on it*

mnemonic device (176)   *memory helper*

much to-do (171)   *a great deal of talking and negotiating*

nibbling (195)   *using the teeth to bite on food (or here, an ear) with tiny bites*

photoreceptors (177)   *light receivers*

to plummet (186)   *to fall quickly*

pneumatic drill (199)   *tool for making holes that uses air power and makes a lot of noise; tool used for drilling holes in roads*

politically incorrect (199)   *unfashionable in political ideas*

progressively (172)   *increasingly*

pulling a rabbit out of a hat (192)   *surprising people with a magic trick*

rebound (182)   *echo effect, reaction*

rhododendren (180)   *a kind of flowering bush*

to sap (204)   *to detract, to pull away energy*

secondhand smoke (202)   *smoke from the cigarette or pipe that another person is smoking (firsthand)*

Siamese cat (202)   *brown and tan cat with blue eyes; a variety of cat*

sideways connections (178)   *connections that are not straight; lateral connections*

to squint (178)   *to look with eyes that are partially closed as if against bright light*

stop-and-go traffic (187)   *city traffic regulated by traffic lights in which drivers start and stop many times in a short distance* subtractive color mixtures (181)   *blends of color pigment, not light, from which separate pigments can be removed*

Superbowl (208)   *the biggest football game in the United States in a season*

swish of the wrist (200)   *quick (somewhat feminine) movement or gesture of the wrist*

ticket of admission (172)   *(here) perception, idea, ability to see*

trapezoid (190)   *figure of four sides, with two acute angles*

to be tuned into (174)   *to be aware of*

tuning fork (194)   *tool for adjusting a musical instrument to the tones of other instruments*

ultimatum (171)   *order (follow this order or else there will be serious consequences)*

the underprivileged (201)   *those people who do not have all the privileges or rights of the rich or educated*

vibes (195)   *vibrations*

to give something a workout (187)   *to use a lot*

World Series (208)   *the set of games of baseball at the end of the season that determine who the world champions are*

a zoom lens (178)   *a camera lens that allows the photographer to quickly move in closer to take a photograph; a special telescopic lens*

QUIZ

1. Of the following colors, _____ has the shortest wavelength.
   - (a) violet,
   - (b) red,
   - (c) green,
   - (d) yellow.

2. Weber's constant for the pitch of a tone is closest to
   - (a) 1/7,
   - (b) 1/53,
   - (c) 1/333,
   - (d) 1/20,000.

3. You look at a lamp 10 feet away and it is clearly in focus. As you walk toward it, the lamp remains in focus. The lamp remains in focus because the _____ of your eyes are accommodating to the image of the lamp by changing their thickness.
   - (a) corneas,
   - (b) irises,
   - (c) lenses,
   - (d) pupils.

4. The cones reach their maximum adaptation to darkness in about _____ minutes.
   - (a) 5,
   - (b) 10,
   - (c) 30,
   - (d) 45.

5. The Ganzfeld procedure is used in research on
   - (a) visual perception,
   - (b) perceptual organization,
   - (c) touch and pressure,
   - (d) psi communication

6. _____ suggested that the eye must have three different types of cones, some sensitive to red, some to green, and some to blue.
   - (a) Thomas Young,
   - (b) Sir Isaac Newton,
   - (c) Hermann von Helmholtz,
   - (d) Ewald Hering.

7. Which of the following is found in the middle ear?
   - (a) Anvil,
   - (b) Cochlea,
   - (c) Olfactory nerve,
   - (d) Basilar membrane.

8. You attend a motion picture, and it seems to you as if the people and objects being projected onto the screen are moving. Actually, your impression that the people and objects are moving is made possible by
   - (a) the phi phenomenon,
   - (b) stroboscopic motion,
   - (c) the autokinetic effect,
   - (d) motion parallax.

9. When we are driving along a dark road at night, the moon may appear to move along with us. This is an example of
    (a) the autokinetic effect,
    (b) perspective,
    (c) motion parallax,
    (d) the phi phenomenon.

10. The unit for expressing the loudness of a sound is named after
    (a) Bell,
    (b) Hertz,
    (c) Helmholtz,
    (d) Newton.

11. Sensorineural deafness is usually caused by damage to the
    (a) eardrum,
    (b) outer ear,
    (c) inner ear,
    (d) stapes.

12. Hairlike receptor cells on the organ of Corti bend in response to vibrations of the
    (a) eardrum,
    (b) oval window,
    (c) stirrup,
    (d) basilar membrane.

13. Within the ears are found organs for
    (a) vision,
    (b) kinesthesis,
    (c) the vestibular sense,
    (d) extrasensory perception.

14. The volley principle is used to explain perception of pitch at the frequency of
    (a) 20 Hz,
    (b) 2,000 Hz,
    (c) 12,000 Hz,
    (d) 20,000 Hz.

15. Which of the following is a chemical sense?
    (a) Smell,
    (b) Touch,
    (c) Kinesthesis,
    (d) Temperature.

16. People have about _____ taste buds.
    (a) 100,
    (b) 1,000,
    (c) 10,000,
    (d) 100,000.

17. Sensory receptors located _____ appear to fire in response to touching the surface of the skin.
    (a) on the surface of the skin,
    (b) around the roots of hair cells,
    (c) at the tips of hair cells,
    (d) in tendons, joints, and muscles.

18. Psychophysicists use the two-point threshold to measure sensitivity to
    (a) body position,
    (b) sound waves of low frequencies,
    (c) pressure,
    (d) movement.

19. The view that pain messages may not get through to the brain when the "switchboard" that transmits pain messages becomes "flooded" is termed
    (a) gate theory,
    (b) opponent-process theory,
    (c) volley principle,
    (d) acupuncture.

20. Organs in the _____ alert you as to whether your body is changing speeds.
    (a) joints,
    (b) tendons,
    (c) ears,
    (d) olfactory membrane.

1. What are sensation and perception?

2. How do we know when something is there? How do we know when it has changed?

3. What is signal-detection theory?

4. What are feature detectors?

5. How do our sensory systems adapt to a changing environment?

6. Just what is this stuff called light?

7. How does the eye work?

8. How do we perceive color?

9. What is color blindness? Why are some people color blind?

10. How do we organize bits of information like perceptions into meaningful wholes?

11. How do we perceive movement?

12. How do we perceive depth?

13. What are perceptual constancies? Why do we perceive a door to be a rectangle even when it is ajar?

14. How can principles of visual perception be used to trick the eye?

15. What is sound?

16. How does the ear work?

17. How do we locate sounds?

18. How do we perceive loudness and pitch?

19. What is deafness? What can we do about it?

20. How does the sense of smell work?

21. How does the sense of taste work?

22. What are the skin senses? How do they work?

_____
_____
_____
_____
_____

23. What is pain? What can we do about it?

_____
_____
_____
_____
_____

24. What is kinesthesis?

_____
_____
_____
_____
_____

25. How does the vestibular sense work?

_____
_____
_____
_____
_____

26. Is there really such a thing as extrasensory perception (ESP)?

_____
_____
_____
_____
_____

ANSWERS TO SECTION REVIEWS

1. Receptors
2. Central
3. Perception
4. Perception
5. Absolute
6. Constant
7. Difference
8. Weber's
9. Signal
10. Sensory
11. Psychological
12. Feature
13. Adaptation
14. Sensitization
15. Negative
16. Electromagnetic
17. Waves
18. Wavelength
19. Prism
20. Cornea
21. Iris
22. Pupil
23. Lens
24. Retina
25. Photoreceptors
26. Bipolar
27. Optic
28. Fovea
29. Ganglion
30. Cones
31. Lens
32. Dark
33. More
34. Adapt
35. Trichromatic
36. Blue-yellow
37. Opponent-process
38. Trichromats
39. Monochromats
40. Green
41. Gestalt
42. Wholes
43. Figure
44. Ambiguous
45. Top-down
46. Movement or Motion
47. Position
48. Stroboscopic
49. Binocular
50. Parallel
51. Nearby
52. Parallax
53. Slowly
54. Disparity
55. Greater
56. Constancy
57. Shape
58. Stable
59. Illusions
60. Size
61. Auditory
62. Compress
63. 20,000
64. Higher
65. Decibels
66. Eardrum
67. "Anvil"
68. Oval
69. Cochlea
70. Basilar
71. Corti
72. Auditory
73. Corti
74. Basilar membrane
75. Frequency
76. High
77. Low
78. Volley
79. Conductive
80. Sensorineural
81. Taste
82. Molecules
83. Olfactory
84. Rapidly
85. Salty or Bitter
86. Bitter or Salty
87. Odor
88. Taste
89. Taste buds
90. Smell
91. Cold or Pain
92. Pain or Cold
93. Two-point
94. Roots
95. Temperature

96. Prostaglandins
97. Phantom
98. Gate
99. Spinal

100. Endorphins
101. Position
102. Tendons
103. Muscles

104. Upright
105. Semicircular canals
106. Psi
107. Rhine

108. Ganzfeld
109. File
110. Replicate

ANSWERS TO QUIZ

1. A
2. C
3. C
4. B
5. D

6. C
7. A
8. B
9. C
10. A

11. C
12. D
13. C
14. B
15. A

16. C
17. B
18. C
19. A
20. C

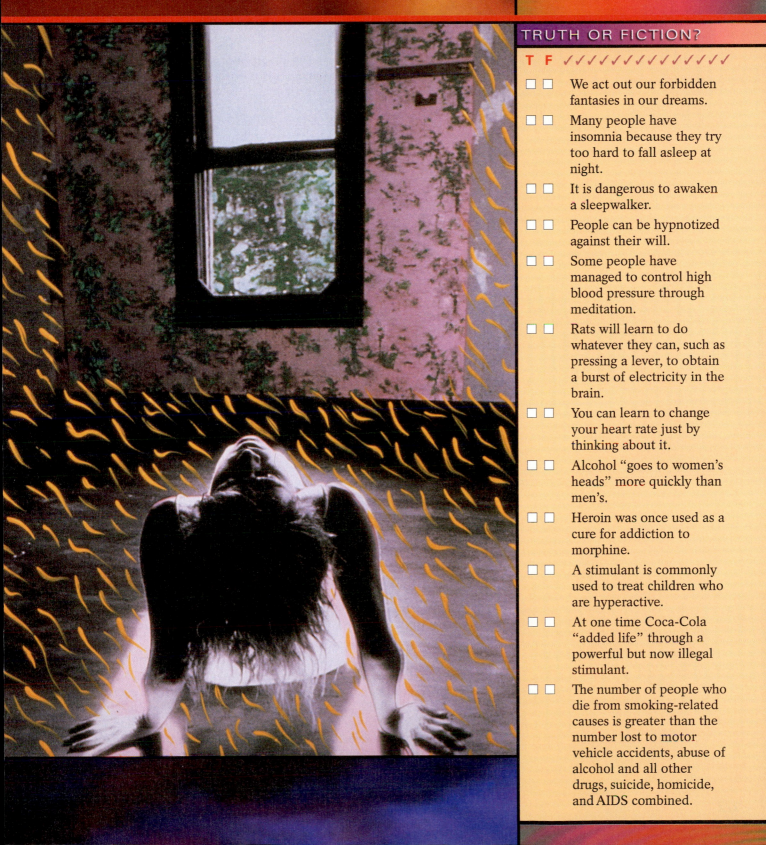

TRUTH OR FICTION?

T F ✓✓✓✓✓✓✓✓✓✓✓✓✓

☐ ☐ We act out our forbidden fantasies in our dreams.

☐ ☐ Many people have insomnia because they try too hard to fall asleep at night.

☐ ☐ It is dangerous to awaken a sleepwalker.

☐ ☐ People can be hypnotized against their will.

☐ ☐ Some people have managed to control high blood pressure through meditation.

☐ ☐ Rats will learn to do whatever they can, such as pressing a lever, to obtain a burst of electricity in the brain.

☐ ☐ You can learn to change your heart rate just by thinking about it.

☐ ☐ Alcohol "goes to women's heads" more quickly than men's.

☐ ☐ Heroin was once used as a cure for addiction to morphine.

☐ ☐ A stimulant is commonly used to treat children who are hyperactive.

☐ ☐ At one time Coca-Cola "added life" through a powerful but now illegal stimulant.

☐ ☐ The number of people who die from smoking-related causes is greater than the number lost to motor vehicle accidents, abuse of alcohol and all other drugs, suicide, homicide, and AIDS combined.

REFLECT

Are *you* conscious, or aware, of yourself and the world around you? How do you know whether you are?

When you talk to yourself, who talks, and who listens?

This is the type of question posed by philosophers and scientists who study consciousness. Although it might seem that psychologists, who study the brain and mental processes, are also well-equipped to look into consciousness, consciousness has not always been an acceptable topic in psychology (Crick & Koch, 1997). In 1904, for example, William James wrote an article with the intriguing title "Does Consciousness Exist?" James did not think that consciousness was a proper area of study for psychologists because no scientific method could directly observe or measure another person's consciousness.

John Watson, the "father of modern behaviorism," agreed. Watson insisted that only observable, measurable behavior is the province of psychology: "The time seems to have come when psychology must discard all references to consciousness" (1913, p. 163). In 1914 Watson was elected president of the American Psychological Association. This honor further cemented his ideas in the minds of many psychologists.

Today, however, many psychologists believe that we cannot capture the richness of the human experience without referring to consciousness (Rychlak, 1997). Studies on consciousness have turned from a stream into a flood (Gorman, 1997). Psychologists, neuroscientists, philosophers, physicists, even computer scientists are searching for the elusive marvel of consciousness. Most assume that consciousness dwells within the brain. Some, like Michael Gazzaniga (1997), suggest that the biological basis for consciousness can be found in specific sites in the brain. Question: What is consciousness?

SECTION I. JUST WHAT *IS* CONSCIOUSNESS?

Consciousness is a mental concept that cannot be directly seen or touched. Yet it is real enough to most people. Mental concepts such as consciousness acquire scientific status from being tied to behavior (Kimble, 1994).

CONSCIOUSNESS AS SENSORY AWARENESS One meaning of consciousness is *sensory awareness* of the environment. The sense of vision enables us to see, or be *conscious* of, the sun gleaming on the snow. The sense of hearing allows us to hear, or be conscious of, a concert.

CONSCIOUSNESS AS THE SELECTIVE ASPECT OF ATTENTION
Sometimes we are not aware of sensory stimulation. We may be unaware, or unconscious, of sensory stimulation when we do not pay attention to it. The world is abuzz with signals, yet you are conscious of, or focusing on, only the words on this page (I hope).

Focusing one's consciousness on a particular stimulus is referred to as **selective attention.** The concept of selective attention is important to self-control. To pay attention in class, you must screen out the pleasant aroma of the cologne or perfume wafting toward you from the person in the next seat. To keep your car on the road, you must pay more attention to driving conditions than to your hunger pangs or your feelings about an argument with a friend. If you are out in the woods at night, attending to rustling sounds in the brush nearby may be crucial to your survival.

Adaptation to our environment involves learning which stimuli must be attended to and which ones can be safely ignored. Selective attention makes our senses keener (Basic Behavioral Science Task Force, 1996). This is why we can pick out the speech of a single person across a room at a cocktail party, a phenomenon suitably termed the *cocktail party effect*.

Although we can decide where and when we will focus our attention, various kinds of stimuli also tend to capture attention. Among them are these:

- Sudden changes, as when a cool breeze enters a sweltering room or we receive a particularly high or low grade on an exam,
- Novel stimuli, as when a dog enters the classroom or a person shows up with an unusual hairdo,
- Intense stimuli, such as bright colors, loud noises, or sharp pain,
- Repetitive stimuli, as when the same TV commercial is played a dozen times throughout the course of a football game.

How do advertisers of Nike, Microsoft, or cologne use these facts to get "into" our consciousness and, they hope, into our pocketbooks?

CONSCIOUSNESS AS DIRECT INNER AWARENESS Close your eyes and imagine spilling a can of bright red paint across a black tabletop. Watch it spread across the black, shiny surface and then spill onto the floor. Although this image may be vivid, you did not "see" it literally. Neither your eyes nor any other sensory organs were involved. You were *conscious* of the image through **direct inner awareness.**

SELECTIVE ATTENTION The focus of one's consciousness on a particular stimulus.

DIRECT INNER AWARENESS Knowledge of one's own thoughts, feelings, and memories without use of sensory organs.

We are conscious of—or have direct inner awareness of—thoughts, images, emotions, and memories. We may not be able to measure direct inner awareness scientifically. Nevertheless, many psychologists argue, "It is detectable to anyone that has it" (Miller, 1992, p. 180). These psychological processes are connected with the firings of myriads of neurons. We do not consciously experience the firing of individual neurons, but consciousness reflects the total of these millions or billions of neural events.

Sigmund Freud, the founder of psychoanalysis, differentiated among the thoughts and feelings we are conscious, or aware, of and those that are preconscious and unconscious. **Preconscious** material is not currently in awareness but is readily available. For example, if you answer the following questions, you will summon up "preconscious" information: What did you eat for dinner yesterday? About what time did you wake up this morning? What is your phone number? You can make these preconscious bits of information conscious by directing your inner awareness, or attention, to them.

According to Freud, still other mental events are **unconscious**. This means that they are unavailable to awareness under most circumstances. Freud believed that some painful memories and sexual and aggressive impulses are unacceptable to us, so we *automatically* (unconsciously) eject them from our awareness. In other words, we *repress* them. **Repression** of these memories and impulses allows us to avoid feelings of anxiety, guilt, or shame.

People can also *choose* to stop thinking about unacceptable ideas or distractions. When we consciously eject unwanted mental events from awareness, we are engaging in **suppression**. We may, for example, suppress thoughts of a date when we need to study for a test. We may also try to suppress thoughts of a test while we are on a date!

Some bodily processes, such as the firings of neurons, are **nonconscious**. They cannot be experienced through sensory awareness or direct inner awareness. The growing of hair and the carrying of oxygen in the blood are nonconscious. We can see that our hair has grown, but we have no sense receptors that give us sensations of growing. We can feel the need to breathe but do not directly experience the exchange of carbon dioxide and oxygen.

CONSCIOUSNESS AS PERSONAL UNITY: THE SENSE OF SELF
As we develop, we differentiate ourselves from that which is not us. We develop a sense of being persons, individuals. There is a totality to our impressions, thoughts, and feelings that makes up our conscious existence—our continuing sense of self in a changing world. That self forms intentions and guides its own behavior (Rychlak, 1997). In this usage of the word, consciousness *is* self.

CONSCIOUSNESS AS THE WAKING STATE
The word *conscious* also refers to the waking state as opposed, for example, to sleep. From this perspective, sleep, meditation, the hypnotic "trance," and the distorted perceptions that can accompany use of consciousness-altering drugs are considered *altered states of consciousness*.

In the remainder of this chapter, we explore various types of altered states of consciousness. They include sleep and dreams, hypnosis, meditation, biofeedback, and finally, the effects of various kinds of psychoactive drugs.

REFLECT

Do you think people have an "unconscious" mind? If so, what do you think happens within it?

PRECONSCIOUS In psychodynamic theory, descriptive of material that is not in awareness but can be brought into awareness by focusing one's attention.

UNCONSCIOUS In psychodynamic theory, descriptive of ideas and feelings that are not available to awareness.

REPRESSION In psychodynamic theory, the automatic (unconscious) ejection of anxiety-evoking ideas, impulses, or images from awareness.

SUPPRESSION The deliberate, or conscious, placing of certain ideas, impulses, or images out of awareness.

NONCONSCIOUS Descriptive of bodily processes such as the growing of hair, of which we cannot become conscious. We may "recognize" that our hair is growing but cannot directly experience the biological process.

SECTION I **Review**

In 1904, William (1) _____ wrote an article, "Does Consciousness Exist?" John (2) _____, the father of modern behaviorism, argued that only observable (3) b_____ should be studied by psychologists. However, (4) cog_____ psychologists believe that we cannot discuss meaningful human behavior without referring to consciousness.

Consciousness has several meanings, including sensory awareness; the selective aspect of attention; direct (5) _____r awareness of cognitive processes; personal (6) _____y, or the sense of self; and the waking state. Sensory (7) _____ness refers to consciousness of the environment. (8) D_____ inner awareness refers to consciousness of thoughts, images, emotions, and memories.

Sigmund Freud differentiated among ideas that are conscious; (9) _____scious, that is, available to awareness by focusing on them; and (10) _____scious, that is, unavailable to awareness under ordinary circumstances.

SECTION II. SLEEP AND DREAMS

Sleep is a fascinating topic. After all, we spend about one-third of our adult lives asleep. Most adults need 8 to 9 hours of sleep, but one survey found they typically get only 7 (National Sleep Foundation, 1998). About one-third get 6 hours or less of sleep a night during the work week. One-third admitted that lack of sleep impaired their ability to function during the day, and nearly 1 in 4 admitted to falling asleep at the wheel at some time within the past year.

Our alternating periods of wakefulness and sleep provide an example of an internally generated **circadian rhythm.** Question: What is a circadian rhythm? A circadian rhythm is a cycle that is connected with the 24-hour period of the earth's rotation. A cycle of wakefulness and sleep is normally 24 hours long. However, when people are removed from cues that signal day or night, a cycle tends to become extended to about 25 hours, and people sleep nearly 10 of them (National Sleep Foundation, 1998). Why? We do not know.

Why do we sleep? Why do we dream? Next we explore the nature of sleep, dreams, and sleep disorders.

The Stages of Sleep

A major tool of sleep researchers is the electroencephalograph, or EEG. The EEG measures the electrical activity of the brain, or brain waves. Figure 5.1 shows EEG patterns that reflect the frequency and strength of brain waves that occur during the waking state, when we are relaxed, and when we are in the various stages of sleep. Question: What occurs during sleep?

Brain waves, like other waves, are cyclical. During the various stages of sleep, the brain emits waves with different *frequencies* (numbers of waves per second) and *amplitudes* (heights—an index of strength). The printouts

CIRCADIAN RHYTHM Referring to cycles that are connected with the 24-hour period of the earth's rotation.

FIGURE 5.1

THE STAGES OF SLEEP   THIS FIGURE ILLUSTRATES TYPI-
CAL EEG PATTERNS FOR THE STAGES OF SLEEP. DURING REM
SLEEP, EEG PATTERNS RESEMBLE THOSE OF THE LIGHTEST
STAGE OF SLEEP, STAGE 1 SLEEP. FOR THIS REASON, REM
SLEEP IS OFTEN TERMED *PARADOXICAL SLEEP*. AS SLEEP PRO-
GRESSES FROM STAGE 1 TO STAGE 4, BRAIN WAVES BECOME
SLOWER AND THEIR AMPLITUDE INCREASES. DREAMS, INCLUD-
ING NORMAL NIGHTMARES, ARE MOST VIVID DURING REM
SLEEP. MORE DISTURBING SLEEP TERRORS TEND TO OCCUR
DURING DEEP STAGE 4 SLEEP.

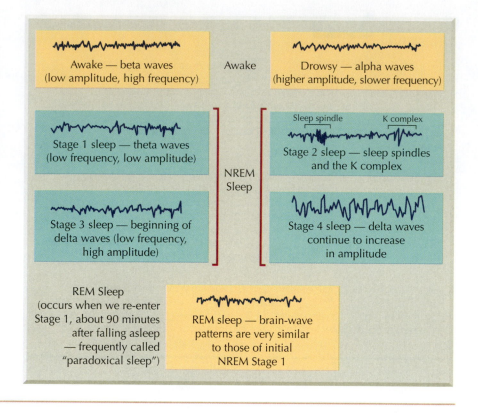

NON-RAPID-EYE-MOVEMENT SLEEP Stages of sleep, 1
through 4. Abbreviated *NREM* sleep.

RAPID-EYE-MOVEMENT SLEEP A stage of sleep
characterized by rapid eye movements, which have been
linked to dreaming. Abbreviated *REM* sleep.

ALPHA WAVES Rapid low-amplitude brain waves that
have been linked to feelings of relaxation.

THETA WAVES Slow brain waves produced during the
hypnagogic state.

HYPNAGOGIC STATE The drowsy interval between
waking and sleeping, characterized by brief,
hallucinatory, dreamlike experiences.

DELTA WAVES Strong, slow brain waves usually emitted
during stage 4 sleep.

in Figure 5.1 show what happens during a period of 15 seconds or so.
Brain waves that are high in frequency are associated with wakefulness.
The amplitude of brain waves reflects their strength. The strength or en-
ergy of brain waves is expressed in volts (an electrical unit).

Figure 5.1 shows five stages of sleep: four stages of **non-rapid-eye-
movement** (NREM) **sleep** and one stage of **rapid-eye-movement** (REM)
sleep. When we close our eyes and begin to relax before going to sleep,
our brains emit many **alpha waves.** Alpha waves are low-amplitude brain
waves of about 8 to 13 cycles per second.

As we enter stage 1 sleep, our brain waves slow down from the alpha
rhythm and enter a pattern of **theta waves.** Theta waves, with a frequency
of about 6 to 8 cycles per second, are accompanied by slow, rolling eye
movements. The transition from alpha waves to theta waves may be accompanied by a **hypnagogic state** during which we may experience brief
dreamlike images that resemble vivid photographs. Stage 1 sleep is the
lightest stage of sleep. If we are awakened from stage 1 sleep, we may feel
that we have not slept at all.

After 30 to 40 minutes of stage 1 sleep, we undergo a rather steep descent into stages 2, 3, and 4 (see Figure 5.2). During stage 2, brain waves
are medium in amplitude with a frequency of about 4 to 7 cycles per second, but these are punctuated by *sleep spindles.* Sleep spindles have a frequency of 12 to 16 cycles per second and represent brief bursts of rapid
brain activity.

During deep sleep stages 3 and 4, our brains produce slower **delta
waves.** During stage 3, the delta waves have a frequency of 1 to 3 cycles
per second. Delta waves reach relatively great amplitude compared with
other brain waves. Stage 4 is the deepest stage of sleep, from which it is
the most difficult to be awakened. During stage 4 sleep, the delta waves
slow to about 0.5 to 2 cycles per second, and their amplitude is greatest.

FIGURE 5.2
SLEEP CYCLES THIS FIGURE ILLUSTRATES THE ALTERNATION OF REM AND NON-REM SLEEP FOR THE TYPICAL SLEEPER. THERE ARE ABOUT FIVE PERIODS OF REM SLEEP DURING AN EIGHT-HOUR NIGHT. SLEEP IS DEEPER EARLIER IN THE NIGHT, AND REM SLEEP TENDS TO BECOME PROLONGED TOWARD MORNING.

After perhaps half an hour of deep stage 4 sleep, we begin a relatively rapid journey back upward through the stages until we enter REM sleep (Figure 5.2). REM sleep derives its name from the *rapid eye movements*, observable beneath the closed eyelids, that characterize this stage. During REM sleep we produce relatively rapid, low-amplitude brain waves that resemble those of light stage 1 sleep. REM sleep is also called *paradoxical sleep* because the EEG patterns observed suggest a level of arousal similar to that of the waking state (Figure 5.1). However, it is difficult to awaken a person during REM sleep. When people are awakened during REM sleep, as is the practice in sleep research, about 80% of the time they report that they have been dreaming. (We also dream during NREM sleep, but less frequently. People report dreaming only about 20% of the time when awakened during NREM sleep.)

Each night we tend to undergo five trips through the stages of sleep (see Figure 5.2). These trips include about five periods of REM sleep. Our first journey through stage 4 sleep is usually longest. Sleep tends to become lighter as the night wears on. Our periods of REM sleep tend to become longer, and toward morning our last period of REM sleep may last close to half an hour.

Now that we have some idea of what sleep is like, let us examine the question of *why* we sleep.

Functions of Sleep

Question: Why do we sleep? Researchers do not have all the answers as to why we sleep. One hypothesis is that sleep helps rejuvenate a tired body. Most of us have had the experience of going without sleep for a night and feeling "wrecked" or "out of it" the following day. Perhaps the next evening we went to bed early in order to "catch up on our sleep." What happens to you if you do not sleep for one night? For several nights?

Compare people who are highly sleep-deprived with people who have been drinking heavily. Sleepless people's abilities to concentrate and perform may be seriously impaired, but they may be the last ones to recognize their limitations (Adler, 1993).

Most students can pull successful "all-nighters" (Webb, 1993). They can cram for a test through the night and then perform reasonably well the following day. When we are deprived of sleep for several nights, however, aspects of psychological functioning such as attention, learning, and

REFLECT

How much sleep do you need? (How do you know?) Did you ever "pull an all-nighter"? What were the effects?

memory deteriorate notably (Maas, 1998). The National Highway Traffic Safety Administration (1998) estimates that sleep deprivation is connected with 100,000 crashes and 1,500 vehicular deaths each year. Many people sleep late or nap on their days off (Webb, 1993). Perhaps they suffer from mild sleep deprivation during the week and catch up on the weekend.

The amount of sleep we need seems to be in part genetically determined (Webb, 1993). People also tend to need more sleep during periods of stress, such as a change of job, an increase in work load, or an episode of depression (Maas, 1998). Sleep seems to help us recover from stress.

Newborn babies may sleep 16 hours a day, and teenagers often sleep around the clock. It is widely believed that older people need less sleep than younger adults do. However, sleep in older people is often interrupted by physical discomfort or the need to go to the bathroom. Older people often sleep more during the day to make up for sleep lost at night.

DEPRIVATION OF REM SLEEP In some studies, animals or people have been deprived of REM sleep. Under these conditions animals and people learn more slowly and forget what they have learned more rapidly (Adler, 1993). Fetuses have periods of waking and sleeping, and REM sleep may foster the development of the brain before birth (McCarley, 1992). REM sleep may also help maintain neurons in adults by "exercising" them at night. Deprivation of REM sleep is accomplished by monitoring EEG records and eye movements and waking the person during REM sleep. There is too much individual variation to conclude that people who are deprived of REM sleep learn more poorly than they otherwise would. It does seem, though, that such deprivation interferes with memory—that is, retrieval of information that has been learned previously. In any event, people and other animals that are deprived of REM sleep tend to show *REM rebound.* They spend more time in REM sleep during subsequent sleep periods. In other words, they catch up.

It is during REM sleep that we tend to dream. Let us now turn our attention to dreams, a mystery about which philosophers, poets, and scientists have theorized for centuries.

Dreams

To quote from Shakespeare's *The Tempest,* Just what is the "stuff"[1] of dreams? What are they "made on"? Question: What are dreams and why do we dream what we dream? Like memories and fantasies, dreams involve imagery in the absence of external stimulation. Some dreams seem very real. In college I often had "anxiety dreams" the night before a test. I dreamed repeatedly that I had taken the test and it was all over. (Imagine the disappointment when I awakened and realized that the test still lay before me!)

Dreams are most likely to contain vivid imagery during REM sleep. Images are vaguer and more fleeting during NREM sleep. You may dream every time you are in REM sleep. Therefore, if you sleep for eight hours and undergo five sleep cycles, you may have five dreams. Upon waking, you may think that time seemed to expand or contract during your dream, so that during 10 or 15 minutes of actual time, the content of your dream ranged over days or weeks. But dreams actually tend to take place in "real time." Fifteen minutes of events fills about 15 minutes of dream-

---

[1] The phrase "such stuff as dreams are made on" comes from Shakespeare's *The Tempest.*

Dream Images?   In *Winter Night in Vitebsk,* Marc Chagall seems to depict images born in dreams.

ing. Your dream theater is quite flexible. You can dream in black and white or in full color.

THEORIES OF THE CONTENT OF DREAMS You may recall dreams involving fantastic adventures, but most dreams involve memories of the activities and problems of the day (Wade, 1998). If we are preoccupied with illness or death, sexual or aggressive urges, or moral dilemmas, we are likely to dream about them. The characters in our dreams are more likely to be friends and neighbors than spies, monsters, and princes.

"A dream is a wish your heart makes" is a song lyric from the Disney film *Cinderella.* Freud theorized that dreams reflect unconscious wishes and urges. He argued that through dreams we can express impulses we would censor during the day. Moreover, he said that the content of dreams is symbolic of unconscious fantasized objects such as the genitals. A key part of Freud's method of psychoanalysis involved interpretation of his clients' dreams. Freud also believed that dreams "protect sleep" by providing imagery that helps keep disturbing, repressed thoughts out of awareness.

The theory that dreams protect sleep has been challenged by the observation that disturbing events tend to be followed by disturbing dreams on the same theme—not by protective imagery (Reiser, 1992). Our behavior in dreams is also generally consistent with our waking behavior. Most dreams, then, are unlikely candidates for the expression of repressed urges (even disguised). A person who leads a moral life tends to dream moral dreams.

✓ Truth or Fiction Revisited

It is not true that we act out our forbidden fantasies in our dreams. Most dreams are humdrum.

There are also biological views of the "meanings" of dreams. According to the **activation-synthesis model,** acetylcholine (a

ACTIVATION-SYNTHESIS MODEL The view that dreams reflect activation of cognitive activity by the reticular activating system and synthesis of this activity into a pattern by the cerebral cortex.

neurotransmitter) and the pons (a structure in the lower part of the brain) stimulate responses that lead to dreaming (Hobson & McCarley, 1977). One is *activation* of the reticular activating system (RAS), which arouses us, but not to waking. During the waking state, firing of these cells in the reticular formation is linked to movement, particularly the movements involved in walking, running, and other physical acts. During REM sleep, however, neurotransmitters generally inhibit activity, so we usually do not thrash about as we dream. In this way, we save ourselves (and our bed partners) some wear and tear. The eye muscles are stimulated and thus show the rapid eye movement associated with dreaming. The RAS also stimulates neural activity in the parts of the cortex involved in memory. The cortex then *synthesizes,* or puts together, these sources of stimulation to some degree to yield the stuff of dreams. Yet research with the PET scan shows that the frontal lobes of the brain, which make sense of experience, are pretty much shut down during sleep (Wade, 1998). Dreams are therefore more likely to be emotionally gripping than coherent in plot.

Another view of dreams is that with the brain cut off from the world outside, memories are replayed and consolidated during sleep (Wade, 1998). Another possibility is that REM activity is a way of testing whether the individual has benefitted from the restorative functions of sleep (Wade, 1998). When restoration is adequate, the brain awakens. According to this view, dreams are just the by-products of the testing.

NIGHTMARES Have you ever dreamed that something heavy was sitting on your chest and watching you as you breathed? Or that you were trying to run away from a terrible threat but couldn't gain your footing or coordinate your leg muscles?

Nightmares, like most pleasant dreams, are generally products of REM sleep. College students report an average of two nightmares a month in dream logs (Wood & Bootzin, 1990). Traumatic events can spawn nightmares, as reported in a study of survivors of the San Francisco earthquake of 1989 (Wood et al., 1992). People who suffer frequent nightmares are more likely than other people to also suffer from anxieties, depression, and other kinds of psychological discomfort (Berquier & Ashton, 1992).

Sleep Disorders

There are a number of sleep disorders. Some, like insomnia, are all too familiar. Question: What types of problems or sleep disorders can we encounter as we sleep? In this section we discuss insomnia and the deep-sleep disorders—sleep terrors, bed-wetting, and sleepwalking.

INSOMNIA According to the National Sleep Foundation (1999), more than half of American adults are affected by insomnia in any given year. Women complain of insomnia more often than men do (Kupfer & Reynolds, 1997). People who experience insomnia show greater restlessness and muscle tension than those who do not (Lacks & Morin, 1992). People with insomnia are also more likely to worry and report "racing thoughts" at bedtime (White & Nicassio, 1990). Insomnia comes and goes with many people, increasing during periods of stress (Kupfer & Reynolds, 1997).

People with insomnia tend to compound their sleep problems when they try to force themselves to fall asleep (Bootzin et al., 1991). Their concern heightens autonomic activity and muscle tension. You cannot force or will yourself to go to sleep. You can only set the stage for sleep by lying down and relaxing when you are tired. If you focus on sleep too closely, it

The *Scream.* The Norwegian artist Edvard Munch's well-known painting contains the kind of imagery that we might find in a nightmare.

Insomnia. "You know I can't sleep at night" goes the 1960s song by the Mamas and the Papas. Why are women more likely than men to have insomnia? What can people do about insomnia?

will elude you. Yet millions of people go to bed each night dreading the possibility of insomnia.

✓ **Truth or Fiction Revisited**

It is true that many people have insomnia because they try too hard to fall asleep at night. Trying to go to sleep heightens tension and anxiety, both of which counter the feelings of relaxation that help induce sleep.

DEEP-SLEEP DISORDERS: SLEEP TERRORS, BED-WETTING, AND SLEEPWALKING Sleep terrors, bed-wetting, and sleepwalking all occur during deep (stage 3 or 4) sleep, are more common among children, and may reflect immaturity of the nervous system.

Sleep terrors are similar to, but more severe than, nightmares. They usually occur during deep sleep, whereas nightmares take place during REM sleep. Sleep terrors occur during the first couple of sleep cycles; nightmares are more likely to occur later on. Experiencing a surge in the heart and respiration rates, the dreamer may suddenly sit up, talk incoherently, and move about wildly. The dreamer is never fully awake, returns to sleep, and may recall a vague image, as of someone pressing on his or her chest. (Memories of nightmares tend to be more vivid.) Sleep terrors are often decreased by taking a minor tranquilizer at bedtime. The drug reduces the amount of time spent in stage 4 sleep.

Bed-wetting is often seen as a stigma that reflects parental harshness or the child's attempt to punish the parents, but this disorder, too, may stem from immaturity of the nervous system. In most cases it resolves itself before adolescence, often by age 8. Behavior therapy methods that condition children to awaken when they are about to urinate have been helpful. The drug imipramine often helps, although the reason is not fully known. Sometimes all that is needed is reassurance that no one is to blame for bed-wetting and that most children "outgrow" it.

Perhaps half of all children occasionally talk in their sleep. Nearly 15% walk in their sleep (Mindell, 1993). Sleepwalkers may roam about almost nightly while their parents fret about the accidents that could befall them. Sleepwalkers typically do not remember their excursions,

SLEEP TERRORS Frightening dreamlike experiences that occur during the deepest stage of NREM sleep. Nightmares, in contrast, occur during REM sleep.

although they may respond to questions while they are up and about. Contrary to myth, there is no evidence that sleepwalkers become violent if they are awakened, although they may be confused and upset. Mild tranquilizers and maturity typically put an end to sleepwalking.

> ### ✓ Truth or Fiction Revisited
>
> *It is not true that it is dangerous to awaken a sleepwalker.* Sleepwalkers may be confused and startled when awakened, but they are not usually violent.

The Greek word for "sleep" is *hypnos,* which raises the question as to whether there are connections between the state of consciousness we call sleep and another one we call hypnosis. Although many people are hypnotized by being told that they are "going to sleep," we now see many differences between sleep and hypnosis.

Review

SECTION II

(11) Electro_____ (EEG) records show different stages of sleep. Different stages of sleep are characterized by different (12) b_____ waves. We have four stages of (13) non_____ (NREM) sleep. Stage (14) _____ sleep is lightest, and stage (15) _____ sleep is deepest.

The strength of brain waves is measured in the unit (16) _____s. When we close our eyes and relax before going to sleep, our brains emit (17) _____a waves. As we enter stage 1 sleep, we enter a pattern of (18) _____a waves. The transition from alpha to theta waves may be accompanied by brief hallucinatory, dreamlike images referred to as the (19) _____gic state. We emit slow, strong (20) _____a waves during stages 3 and 4 sleep.

After a half hour or so of stage (21) _____ sleep, we journey upward through the stages until we enter REM sleep. REM sleep is characterized by rapid (22) _____ movements beneath closed lids and by the emission of brain waves that resemble those of light stage (23) _____ sleep. Because EEG patterns during REM sleep resemble those of the waking state, REM sleep is also referred to as (24) _____ical sleep. During REM sleep we dream about (25) _____% of the time.

During a typical 8-hour night, we undergo about (26: How many?) _____ trips through the different stages of sleep. Our first journey through stage 4 sleep is usually (27: Longest or Shortest?). Sleep tends to become (28: Lighter or Deeper?) as the night progresses. Periods of REM sleep tend to become (29: Longer or Shorter?) toward morning. People deprived of REM sleep show (30) REM-_____nd during subsequent sleep periods.

Dreams are most vivid during (31: REM or NREM?) sleep. Freud theorized that dreams reflect (32) _____scious wishes and "protect" sleep. According to the activation-synthesis model, dreams reflect activation by the (33) _____s and automatic integration of resultant neural activity by the (34) cerebral co_____. The content of most dreams is an extension of the events or concerns of the day.

Nightmares generally occur during (35: REM or NREM?) sleep. (36: More or Fewer?) than half of American adults are affected by insomnia in a given year. People with insomnia are (37: More or Less?) likely to worry at bedtime. Sleep terrors, bed-wetting, and sleepwalking all occur during (38) d_____ sleep. Bed-wetting may stem from immaturity of the (39) n_____ system. There (40: Is or Is not?) evidence that sleepwalkers become violent if they are awakened.

SECTION III. HYPNOSIS: ON BEING ENTRANCED

Perhaps you have seen films in which Count Dracula hypnotized resistant victims into a stupor. Then he could give them a bite in the neck with no further nonsense. Perhaps you have watched a fellow student try to place a friend in a "trance" after reading a book on hypnosis. Or perhaps you have seen an audience member hypnotized in a nightclub act. If so, chances are the person acted as if he or she had returned to childhood, imagined that a snake was about to have a nip, or lay rigid between two chairs for a while. Question: What is hypnosis?

Hypnosis, a term derived from the Greek word for sleep, is an altered state of consciousness in which people appear to be highly suggestible and behave as though they are in a trance. Hypnosis has only recently become a respectable subject for psychological inquiry. Modern hypnosis seems to have begun with the ideas of Franz Mesmer in the 18th century. Mesmer asserted that everything in the universe was connected by forms of magnetism—which actually may not be far from the mark. He claimed that people, too, could be drawn to one another by "animal magnetism." (No bull's-eye here.) Mesmer used bizarre props to bring people under his "spell." He did manage a respectable cure rate for minor ailments. But scientists attribute his successes to the placebo effect, not to animal magnetism.

Today hypnotism retains its popularity in nightclubs, but it is also used as an anesthetic in dentistry, childbirth, and even surgery. Some psychologists use hypnosis to teach clients how to reduce anxiety, manage pain, or overcome fears. Research shows that hypnosis is a useful supplement to other forms of therapy, especially in helping obese people lose weight (Kirsch et al., 1995). Police also use hypnosis to prompt the memories of witnesses.

The state of consciousness called the *hypnotic trance* has traditionally been induced by asking people to narrow their attention to a small light, a spot on the wall, an object held by the hypnotist, or the hypnotist's voice. The hypnotist usually suggests that the person's limbs are becoming warm, heavy, and relaxed. People may also be told that they are becoming sleepy or falling asleep. Hypnosis is *not* sleep, however. This is shown by differences between EEG recordings for the hypnotic trance and the stages of sleep. But the word *sleep* is understood by subjects to suggest a hypnotic trance.

It is also possible to induce hypnosis through instructions that direct subjects to remain active and alert (Miller et al., 1991). So the effects of hypnosis probably cannot be attributed to relaxation.

People who are readily hypnotized are said to have *hypnotic suggestibility*. Part of "suggestibility" is knowledge of what is expected during the "trance state." Generally speaking, suggestible people have positive attitudes toward hypnosis. They *want* to be hypnotized. Moreover, they attend closely to the hypnotist's instructions (Crawford et al., 1993). It is therefore extremely unlikely that someone could be hypnotized against his or her will.

REFLECT

Had you heard of hypnosis or hypnotic trance before taking this course? How does the information presented here correspond to what you had heard?

Hypnosis. Hypnotized people become passive and follow the suggestions of the hypnotist. Only recently has hypnosis become a respectable subject for psychological inquiry.

REFLECT

Do you believe it's true that you can be hypnotized only if you want to be hypnotized? Why or why not?

✓ Truth or Fiction Revisited

There is no evidence that people can be hypnotized against their will. People who are readily hypnotized desire the experience and cooperate with the hypnotist.

HYPNOSIS A condition in which people appear to be highly suggestible and behave as though they are in a trance.

Changes in Consciousness Brought About by Hypnosis

Question: What changes in consciousness are induced by hypnosis? Hypnotists and people who have been hypnotized report that hypnosis can bring about the following changes in consciousness. As you read about them, bear in mind that changes in "consciousness" are inferred from changes in observable behavior and self-reports.

- *Passivity.* When being hypnotized or in a trance, people await instructions and appear to suspend planning.

- *Narrowed attention.* People focus on the hypnotist's voice or on a spot of light and avoid attending to background noise or intruding thoughts.

- *Pseudomemories and hypermnesia.* People may be instructed to report pseudomemories (false memories), or **hypermnesia.** In police investigations, for example, hypnotists attempt to heighten witnesses' memories by instructing them to focus on details of a crime and then reconstruct the scene. Studies suggest, however, that although people may report recalling more information when they are hypnotized, such information is often incorrect (Weekes et al., 1992).

- *Suggestibility.* People may respond to suggestions that an arm is becoming lighter and will rise or that the eyelids are becoming heavier and must close. They may act as though they cannot unlock hands clasped by the hypnotist or bend an arm "made rigid" by the hypnotist. Hypnotized individuals serving as witnesses may incorporate ideas presented by interviewers into their "memories" and report them as facts (Loftus, 1994).

- *Playing unusual roles.* Most people expect to play sleepy, relaxed roles, but they may also be able to play roles calling for increased strength or alertness, such as riding a bicycle with less fatigue than usual. In **age regression,** people may play themselves as infants or children. Research shows that many supposed childhood memories and characteristics are played inaccurately. Nonetheless, some people show excellent recall of such details as hairstyle or speech pattern. A person may speak a language forgotten since childhood.

- *Perceptual distortions.* Hypnotized people may act as though hypnotically induced **hallucinations** and delusions are real. In the "thirst hallucination," for example, people act as if they are parched, even if they have just had a drink. People may behave as though they cannot hear loud noises, smell odors, or feel pain (Miller & Bowers, 1993).

- *Posthypnotic amnesia.* Many people apparently cannot recall events that take place under hypnosis (Bowers & Woody, 1996) or, if so directed, that they were hypnotized at all. However, if they are hypnotized again, they can usually recall what occurred when instructed by the hypnotist to do so.

- *Posthypnotic suggestion.* People who have been hypnotized may later follow instructions given in prearranged cues of which they are supposedly unaware. For instance, during hypnosis a subject may be directed to fall into a deep trance later upon the single command, "Sleep!" Smokers frequently seek the help of hypnotists to break their habit, and they may be given the suggestion that upon "waking" they will find cigarette smoke aversive.

HYPERMNESIA Greatly enhanced or heightened memory.

AGE REGRESSION In hypnosis, taking on the role of childhood, commonly accompanied by vivid recollections of one's past.

HALLUCINATIONS Perceptions in the absence of sensation.

Theories of Hypnosis

Question: How can we explain the effects of hypnosis? Hypnotism is no longer explained in terms of animal magnetism, but psychodynamic and learning theorists have offered explanations. According to Freud, the hypnotic trance represents **regression.** Hypnotized adults suspend "ego functioning," or conscious control of their behavior. They permit themselves to return to childish modes of responding that emphasize fantasy and impulse rather than fact and logic.

ROLE THEORY Theodore Sarbin offers a **role theory** view of hypnosis (Sarbin & Coe, 1972). He points out that the changes in behavior attributed to the hypnotic trance can be successfully imitated when people are instructed to behave *as though* they were hypnotized. For example, people can lie rigid between two chairs whether they are hypnotized or not. Also, people cannot be hypnotized unless they are familiar with the hypnotic "role"—the behavior that constitutes the trance. Sarbin is not saying that subjects *fake* the hypnotic role. Research evidence suggests that most people who are hypnotized are not faking (Kinnunen et al., 1994). Instead, Sarbin is suggesting that people *allow* themselves to enact this role under the hypnotist's directions.

DISSOCIATION Runners frequently get through the pain and tedium of long-distance races by *dissociating*—by imagining themselves elsewhere, doing other things. (My students inform me that they manage the pain and tedium of *other* instructors' classes in the same way.) Ernest Hilgard (1994) similarly explains hypnotic phenomena through **neodissociation theory.** This is the view that we can selectively focus our attention on one thing (like hypnotic suggestions) and dissociate ourselves from the things going on around us.

In one experiment related to neodissociation theory, subjects were hypnotized and instructed to submerge their arms in ice water—causing "cold pressor pain" (Miller et al., 1991). Subjects were given suggestions to the effect that they were not in pain, however. Highly hypnotizable people reported dissociative experiences that allowed them to avoid the perception of pain, such as imagining that they were at the beach or that their limbs were floating in air above the icewater.

Although hypnotized people may be focusing on the hypnotist's suggestions and perhaps imagining themselves to be somewhere else, they still tend to perceive their actual surroundings peripherally. In a sense, we do this all the time. We are not fully conscious, or aware, of everything going on about us. Rather, at any given moment we selectively focus on events such as tests, dates, or television shows that seem important or relevant. Yet, while taking a test we may be peripherally aware of the color of the wall or the sound of rain.

Role theory and neodissociation theory do not suggest that the phenomena of hypnosis are phony. Instead, they suggest that we do not need to explain these events through an altered state of awareness called a trance. Hypnosis may not be special at all. Rather, it is *we* who are special—through our imagination, our role-playing ability, and our capacity to divide our consciousness—concentrating now on one event that we deem important, and concentrating on another event later.

Let us now consider two other states of consciousness that involve different ways of focusing our attention: meditation and biofeedback.

REGRESSION Return to a form of behavior characteristic of an earlier stage of development.

ROLE THEORY A theory that explains hypnotic events in terms of the person's ability to act *as though* he or she were hypnotized. Role theory differs from faking in that subjects cooperate and focus on hypnotic suggestions instead of pretending to be hypnotized.

NEODISSOCIATION THEORY A theory of hypnotic events as the splitting of consciousness.

Review

SECTION III

Hypnosis in its modern form was originated by Franz (41) M_____. Mesmer explained the hypnotic "trance" through his concept of animal (42) _____ism. Many psychologists today use hypnosis to help clients relax, (43) _____ine vivid imagery, and manage (44) p_____. Police use hypnosis to prompt the (45) m_____ of witnesses. People who are easily hypnotized are said to have hypnotic (46) _____lity. Suggestible people have (47: Positive or Negative?) attitudes toward hypnosis.

Hypnosis typically brings about the following changes in consciousness: passivity, narrowed (48) _____tion, (49) _____sia (heightened memory), suggestibility, assumption of unusual roles, perceptual distortions, (50) post_____ amnesia, and posthypnotic suggestion.

According to Freud's psychoanalytic theory, the hypnotic trance represents (51) _____sion. Current theories of hypnosis do not rely on the existence of a special (52) t_____ state. According to role theory, hypnotized subjects enact the (53) _____ of being in a hypnotic trance. In order to enact this role, they must be aware of the (54) _____iors that constitute the trance and motivated to imitate them. According to (55) neo_____ theory, we can selectively focus on one thing (like hypnotic suggestions) and dissociate ourselves from the things going on around us.

SECTION IV. MEDITATION: LETTING THE WORLD FADE AWAY

Question: What is meditation? The dictionary defines *meditation* as the act or process of thinking. But the concept usually suggests thinking deeply about the universe or about one's place in the world, often within a spiritual context. As the term is commonly used by psychologists, however, meditation refers to various ways of focusing one's consciousness to alter one's relationship to the world. As used by psychologists, ironically, *meditation* can also refer to a process in which people seem to suspend thinking and allow the world to fade away.

The kinds of meditation that psychologists and other kinds of helping professionals speak of are *not* the first definition you find in the dictionary. Rather, they tend to refer to rituals, exercises, and even passive observation—activities that alter the normal relationship between the person and her or his environment. They are various methods of suspending problem solving, planning, worries, and awareness of the events of the day. These methods alter consciousness—that is, the normal focus of attention—and help people cope with stress by inducing feelings of relaxation.

Let us consider one common form of meditation in more detail. **Transcendental meditation (TM)** is a simplified form of Far Eastern meditation that was brought to the United States by the Maharishi Mahesh Yogi in 1959. Hundreds of thousands of Americans practice TM by repeating and concentrating on *mantras*—words or sounds that are

TRANSCENDENTAL MEDITATION (TM) The simplified form of meditation brought to the United States by the Maharishi Mahesh Yogi and used as a method for coping with stress.

REFLECT

Do you know anyone who has tried meditation? What was the purpose? Were the effects consistent with what is reported in this text? Why or why not?

claimed to help the person achieve an altered state of consciousness. TM has a number of spiritual goals, such as expanding consciousness so that it encompasses spiritual kinds of experiences, but there are also more worldly goals, such as reducing anxiety and normalizing blood pressure.

Question: What are the effects of meditation? In early research, Herbert Benson (1975) found no scientific evidence that TM expands consciousness (how do you measure spiritual experience with earthly instruments?), despite the claims of many of its practitioners. However, TM lowered the heart and respiration rates—changes that can be measured through commonly used medical instruments—and also produced what Benson labeled a *relaxation response*. The blood pressure of people with hypertension decreased. In fact, people who meditated twice daily tended to show more normal blood pressure through the day. Meditators produced more frequent alpha waves—brain waves associated with feelings of relaxation.

Meditation. People use many forms of meditation to try to expand their inner awareness and experience inner harmony. The effects of meditation, like those of drugs, reflect both the bodily changes induced by meditation *and* the meditator's expectations.

✓ Truth or Fiction Revisited

It is true that people have managed to bring high blood pressure under control through meditation.

Other researchers agree that TM lowers a person's level of arousal, as measured by heart rate, respiration rate, and blood pressure, but they argue that the same relaxing effects can be achieved in other ways, such as by resting quietly (Holmes, 1984). The issue is not whether meditation helps, but whether this particular approach to meditation—TM—has special measurable effects as compared with a break from a tense routine.

SECTION IV Review

In meditation, one focuses "passively" on an object or a (56) m_____ in order to alter the normal person–environment relationship. In this way, (57) _____ness (that is, the normal focuses of attention) is altered and a (58) re_____ response is often induced. (59) Tr_____ meditation (TM) and other forms of meditation appear to normalize the blood pressure and produce relaxation. There is controversy as to whether meditation is more relaxing or effective in reducing high (60) b_____ pressure than quiet sitting or resting.

SECTION V. BIOFEEDBACK: GETTING IN TOUCH WITH THE UNTOUCHABLE

Let us begin our discussion of biofeedback by recounting some remarkable experiments in which psychologist Neal E. Miller (1969) trained laboratory rats to increase or decrease their heart rates. His procedure was simple but ingenious. As discovered by psychologists James Olds and Peter Milner, there is a "pleasure center" in the rat's hypothalamus. A small burst of electricity in this center is strongly reinforcing: Rats learn to do what they can, such as pressing a lever, to obtain this shock.

Biofeedback. Biofeedback is a system that provides, or "feeds back," information about a bodily function to an organism. Through biofeedback training, people have learned to gain voluntary control over a number of functions that are normally automatic, such as heart rate and blood pressure.

It is true that rats will learn to do what they can to obtain a burst of electricity in the brain —when the electricity stimulates the so-called pleasure centers of their brains.

Miller implanted electrodes in the rats' pleasure centers. Then some rats were given an electric shock whenever their heart rate happened to increase. Other rats received a shock when their heart rate went lower. In other words, one group of rats was consistently "rewarded" (that is, shocked) when their heart rate showed an increase. The other group was consistently rewarded for a decrease in heart rate. After a single 90-minute training session, the rats learned to alter their heart rates by as much as 20% in the direction for which they had been rewarded.

Miller's research was an early example of **biofeedback training (BFT).** What is biofeedback training? Biofeedback is a system that provides, or "feeds back," information about a bodily function. Miller used electrical stimulation of the brain to feed back information to rats when they had engaged in a targeted bodily response (in this case, raised or lowered their heart rates). Somehow the rats then used this information to raise or lower their heart rates voluntarily.

Similarly, people have learned to change various bodily functions voluntarily, including heart rate, that were once considered to be beyond their control.

It is true that you can learn to change your heart rate just by thinking about it —particularly when "thinking about it" involves biofeedback training.

However, electrodes are not implanted in people's brains. Rather, people hear a "blip" or observe some other signal that informs them when the targeted response is being displayed.

Question: How is biofeedback training used? BFT has been used in many ways, including helping people combat stress, tension, and anxiety. For example, people can learn to emit alpha waves (and feel somewhat more relaxed) through feedback from an EEG. A blip may increase in frequency whenever alpha waves are being emitted. The psychologist's instructions are simply to "make the blip go faster." An **electromyograph (EMG),** which monitors muscle tension, is commonly used to help people become more aware of muscle tension in the forehead and elsewhere and to learn to lower the tension. Through the use of other instruments, people have learned to lower their heart rate, their blood pressure, and the amount of sweat in the palm of the hand. All of these changes are relaxing. Biofeedback is widely used by sports psychologists to teach athletes how to relax muscle groups that are unessential to the task at hand so that they can control anxiety and tension.

People have also learned to elevate the temperature of a finger. Why bother, you ask? It happens that limbs become subjectively warmer when more blood flows into them. Increasing the temperature of a finger—that is, altering patterns of blood flow in the body—helps some people control migraine headaches, which may be caused by dysfunctional circulatory patterns.

Sleep, hypnosis, meditation, and biofeedback training all involve "natural" ways of deploying our attention or consciousness. Some altered states depend on the ingestion of psychoactive chemical substances we call "drugs." Let us now deploy our attention to the effects of alcohol and other drugs.

REFLECT

How do you think that a rat manages to elevate or decrease its heart rate? Does it seem pointless to speculate on an answer? Why or why not?

BIOFEEDBACK TRAINING (BFT) The systematic feeding back to an organism information about a bodily function so that the organism can gain control of that function.

ELECTROMYOGRAPH (EMG) An instrument that measures muscle tension.

Review

SECTION V

Biofeedback is a system that (61) _____s back information about a bodily function to an organism. Neal Miller taught rats to increase or decrease their (62) _____ rates by giving them an electric shock in their "pleasure centers" when they performed the targeted response. Through biofeedback training, people and lower animals have learned to control automatic functions like the heart rate (63: Voluntarily or Involuntarily?). People use (64) _____graph (EMG) biofeedback to lessen muscle tension. Some people use BFT to learn to raise the (65) _____ture of a finger in order to lessen migraine headaches.

SECTION VI. ALTERING CONSCIOUSNESS THROUGH DRUGS

The world is a supermarket of **psychoactive substances,** or drugs. The United States is flooded with drugs that distort perceptions and change mood—drugs that take you up, let you down, and move you across town. Some people use drugs because their friends do or because their parents tell them not to. Some are seeking pleasure; others are seeking inner truth or escape.

For better or worse, drugs are part of American life. Young people often become involved with drugs that impair their ability to learn at school and are connected with reckless behavior (Basen-Engquist et al., 1996). Alcohol is the most popular drug on high school and college campuses (Johnston et al., 1996). More than 40% of college students have tried marijuana, and 1 in 6 or 7 smokes it regularly. St. Louis Cardinal Mark McGwire slugged his way through the 1998 baseball season to a new home run record "with a little help from [his] friends" (Johnson, 1998). His "friends"? Androstenedione pills. Androstenedione is converted to the male sex hormone testosterone in the body and helps pump up muscle mass.

Many Americans take **depressants** to get to sleep at night and **stimulants** to get going in the morning. Karl Marx charged that "religion . . . is the opium of the people," but heroin is the real "opium of the people." Cocaine was, until recently, a toy of the well-to-do, but price breaks have brought it into the lockers of high school students.

Substance Abuse and Dependence

Where does drug use end and abuse begin? Question: What are substance abuse and dependence? The American Psychiatric Association (1994) defines **substance abuse** as repeated use of a substance despite the fact that it is causing or compounding social, occupational, psychological, or physical problems. If you are missing school or work because you are drunk or "sleeping it off," you are abusing alcohol. The amount you drink is not as crucial as the fact that your pattern of use disrupts your life.

Dependence is more severe than abuse. Dependence has both behavioral and biological aspects (American Psychiatric Association, 1994). Behaviorally, dependence is often characterized by loss of control over one's use of the substance. Dependent people may organize their lives around getting and using a substance. Biological or physiological dependence is typified by tolerance, withdrawal symptoms, or both. **Tolerance** is the body's habituation to a substance so that with regular usage, higher

PSYCHOACTIVE SUBSTANCES Drugs that have psychological effects such as stimulation or distortion of perceptions.

DEPRESSANT A drug that lessens activity of the nervous system.

STIMULANT A drug that increases activity of the nervous system.

SUBSTANCE ABUSE Persistent use of a substance even though it is causing or compounding problems in meeting the demands of life.

TOLERANCE Habituation to a drug, with the result that increasingly higher doses of the drug are needed to achieve similar effects.

doses are required to achieve similar effects. There are characteristic withdrawal symptoms, or an **abstinence syndrome,** when the level of usage suddenly drops off. The abstinence syndrome for alcohol includes anxiety, tremors, restlessness, weakness, rapid pulse, and high blood pressure.

When doing without a drug, people who are *psychologically* dependent show signs of anxiety (such as shakiness, rapid pulse, and sweating) that may be similar to abstinence syndromes. Because of these signs, they may believe that they are physiologically dependent on a drug when they are actually psychologically dependent. But symptoms of abstinence from some drugs are unmistakably physiological. One is **delirium tremens** ("the DTs"), experienced by some chronic alcoholics when they suddenly lower their intake of alcohol. The DTs are characterized by heavy sweating, restlessness, general disorientation, and terrifying hallucinations—often of crawling animals.

Causal Factors in Substance Abuse and Dependence

Question: What are the causes of substance use and dependence? Substance abuse and dependence usually begin with experimental use (Petraitis et al., 1995). Why do people experiment with drugs? Reasons include curiosity, conformity to peer pressure, parental use, rebelliousness, and escape from boredom or pressure (Chassin et al., 1996; Curran et al., 1997). Let us have a deeper look at some psychological and biological theories of substance abuse.

PSYCHOLOGICAL VIEWS Psychodynamic explanations of substance abuse propose that drugs help people control or express unconscious needs and impulses. Alcoholism, for example, is sometimes interpreted as reflecting the need to remain dependent on an overprotective mother. The idea here is that drinking alcohol is an "oral" activity. Within psychodynamic theory, dependence is considered an "oral" trait that develops from experiences during infancy.

Social-cognitive theorists suggest that people commonly try tranquilizing agents such as Valium (the trade name for diazepam) and alcohol on the basis of a recommendation or observation of others. Cognitive psychologists note that expectations about the effects of a substance are powerful predictors of its use (Sher et al., 1996). Use may be reinforced by the drug's positive effects on mood and its reduction of unpleasant sensations such as anxiety, fear, and tension. For people who are physiologically dependent, avoidance of withdrawal symptoms is also reinforcing. Carrying a supply of the substance is reinforcing because one need not worry about doing without it. Some people, for example, do not leave home without taking along some Valium.

Parents who use drugs may increase their children's knowledge of drugs. They also, in effect, show their children when to use them—for example, when drinking alcohol to reduce tension or to "lubricate" social interactions (Stacy et al., 1991).

BIOLOGICAL VIEWS Certain people may have a genetic predisposition toward physiological dependence on various substances, including alcohol, cocaine, and nicotine (Azar, 1999; Haney et al., 1994; Pihl et al., 1990; Pomerleau et al., 1993). For example, the biological children of alcoholics who are reared by adoptive parents seem more likely to develop alcohol-related problems than the natural children of the adoptive parents. An inherited tendency toward alcoholism may involve greater sensi-

REFLECT

Do you know anyone who has a problem with substance abuse or dependence? Does he or she admit to the problem or deny it? What can be done about the problem?

ABSTINENCE SYNDROME A characteristic cluster of symptoms that results from sudden decrease in an addictive drug's level of usage.

DELIRIUM TREMENS A condition characterized by sweating, restlessness, disorientation, and hallucinations. The DTs occur in some chronic alcohol users when there is a sudden decrease in usage.

tivity to alcohol (that is, greater enjoyment of it) and greater tolerance of it (Pihl et al., 1990). College students with alcoholic parents exhibit better muscular control and visual-motor coordination when they drink than do college students whose parents are not alcoholics. They also feel less intoxicated when they drink (Pihl et al., 1990).

There are many kinds of psychoactive drugs. Some are depressants, others stimulants, and still others hallucinogenics. Let us consider the effects of these drugs on consciousness.

Review

SECTION VI

Substance use is considered abuse when it causes or compounds social, (66) oc_____, psychological, or (67) ph_____ problems. The (68) am_____ of the substance used is not the crucial factor. Substance dependence is characterized by loss of (69) c_____ over the substance and by (70) _____cal dependence. Physiological dependence is evidenced by tolerance or by an (71) ab_____ syndrome upon withdrawal.

People often first (72) _____iment with drugs because of curiosity or a friend's recommendation, but usage can be reinforced by reduction of (73) _____ty and elevation of the mood. People are also motivated to avoid (74) _____wal symptoms once they become physiologically dependent. Some people may have (75) gen_____ predispositions to become physiologically dependent on certain substances.

SECTION VII. DEPRESSANTS

Depressant drugs generally act by slowing the activity of the central nervous system. There are also effects that are specific to each depressant drug. In this section we consider the effects of alcohol, opiates, barbiturates, and methaqualone.

Alcohol

No drug has meant so much to so many as alcohol. Alcohol is our dinnertime relaxant, our bedtime sedative, our cocktail party social facilitator. We use alcohol to celebrate holy days, applaud our accomplishments, and express joyous wishes. The young assert their maturity with alcohol. It is used at least occasionally by 8 to 9 of every 10 high school students (Johnston et al., 1996). Older people use alcohol to stimulate circulation in peripheral areas of the body. Alcohol even kills germs on surface wounds.

Alcohol is the tranquilizer you can buy without prescription. It is the relief from anxiety you can swallow in public without criticism or stigma. A man who takes a Valium tablet may look weak. A man who downs a bottle of beer may be perceived as "macho."

No drug has been so abused as alcohol. Ten million to 20 million Americans are alcoholics. In contrast, 750,000 to 1 million use heroin regularly, and about 800,000 use cocaine regularly (O'Brien, 1996). Excessive drinking has been linked to lower productivity, loss of employment, and downward movement in social status. Yet half of all Americans use

Why Does Alcohol Affect Women More Quickly Than Men?   Alcohol "goes to women's heads" more quickly, even when we control for body weight.

Do you believe that people can be held responsible for their behavior when they have been drinking? Why or why not?

alcohol. Despite widespread marijuana use, alcohol is the drug of choice among adolescents.

ALCOHOLISM, GENDER, AND ETHNICITY   Men are more likely than women to become alcoholics. Why? A cultural explanation is that tighter social constraints are usually placed on women. A biological explanation is that alcohol hits women harder. If, for example, you have the impression that alcohol "goes to women's heads" more quickly than to men's, you are probably correct. Women seem to be more affected by alcohol because they metabolize very little of it in the stomach. Women have less of an enzyme that metabolizes alcohol in the stomach than men do (Lieber, 1990). Thus alcohol reaches women's bloodstream and brain relatively intact. Women metabolize alcohol mainly in the liver. According to one health professional, for women "drinking alcohol has the same effect as injecting it intravenously" (Lieber, 1990). Strong stuff indeed.

✓ Truth or Fiction Revisited

It is true that alcohol goes to women's heads more quickly than to men's. Women are less likely to metabolize alcohol before it affects psychological functioning.

Ethnicity is connected with alcohol abuse. Native Americans and Irish Americans have the highest rates of alcoholism in the United States (Nevid et al., 2000). Jewish Americans have relatively low rates of alcoholism, a fact for which a cultural explanation is usually offered. Jewish Americans tend to expose children to alcohol (wine) early in life, but they do so within a strong family or religious context. Wine is offered in small quantities, with consequent low blood alcohol levels. Alcohol therefore is not connected with rebellion, aggression, or failure in Jewish culture.

There are also biological explanations for low levels of drinking among some ethnic groups (e.g., Asian Americans). Asians are more likely than White people to show a "flushing response" to alcohol, as evidenced by redness of the face, rapid heart rate, dizziness, and headaches (Ellickson et al., 1992). Such sensitivity to alcohol may inhibit immoderate drinking among Asian Americans as it may among women.

EFFECTS OF ALCOHOL   Question: What are the effects of alcohol? The effects of alcohol vary with the dose and the duration of use. Low doses of alcohol may be stimulating. Higher doses of alcohol have a sedative effect, which is why alcohol is classified as a depressant. Alcohol relaxes people and deadens minor aches and pains. Alcohol also intoxicates: It impairs cognitive functioning, slurs the speech, and reduces motor coordination. Alcohol is involved in about half of the fatal automobile accidents in the United States.

Alcohol consumption is connected with a drop-off in sexual activity (Leigh, 1993). Yet, some drinkers may do things they would not do if they were sober, such as engage in sexual activity on the first date or engage in unprotected sex (Cooper & Orcutt, 1997). Why? Perhaps alcohol impairs the thought processes needed to inhibit impulses (Steele & Josephs, 1990). When drunk, people may be less able to foresee the consequences of their behavior. They may also be less likely to summon up their moral beliefs. Then, too, alcohol induces feelings of elation and euphoria that may wash away doubts. Alcohol is also associated with a liberated social role in our culture. Drinkers may place the blame on alcohol ("It's the alcohol, not me"), even though they choose to drink.

As a food, alcohol is fattening. Even so, chronic drinkers may be malnourished. Although it is high in calories, alcohol does not contain nutrients such as vitamins and proteins. Moreover, it can interfere with the body's absorption of vitamins, particularly thiamine, a B vitamin. Thus chronic drinking can lead to a number of disorders such as **cirrhosis of the liver,** which has been linked to protein deficiency, and **Wernicke–Korsakoff syndrome,** which has been linked to vitamin B deficiency. On the other hand, there is some evidence that light to moderate drinking can be beneficial. Light to moderate drinking increases levels of high-density lipoprotein (HDL, or "good" cholesterol) in the bloodstream and thus decreases the risk of cardiovascular disorders (Gaziano et al., 1993). Moreover, there is the danger that people who drink lightly or moderately to raise their blood levels of HDL may run into problems with self-control. Chronic heavy drinking has been linked to cardiovascular disorders and cancer. In particular, heavy drinking places women at risk for breast cancer (McTiernan, 1997). Drinking by a pregnant woman may also harm the embryo.

Adolescent involvement with alcohol has repeatedly been linked to poor school grades and other stressors (Wills et al., 1996). Drinking can, of course, contribute to poor grades and other problems, but adolescents may drink to reduce academic and other stresses.

Regardless of how or why one starts drinking, regular drinking can lead to physiological dependence, which then motivates people to drink to avoid withdrawal symptoms. Still, even when alcoholics have "dried out"—withdrawn from alcohol—many return to drinking (Schuckit, 1996). Perhaps they still want to use alcohol as a way of coping with stress or as an excuse for failure.

TREATING ALCOHOLISM Alcoholics Anonymous (AA) is the most widely used program to treat alcoholism, yet research suggests that other approaches work as well for most people (Ouimette et al., 1997; "Tailoring treatments," 1997). The National Institute on Alcohol Abuse and Alcoholism funded an 8-year study in which more than 1,700 problem drinkers were randomly assigned to AA's 12-step program, cognitive-behavioral therapy, or "motivational-enhancement therapy." The cognitive-behavioral treatment taught problem drinkers how to cope with temptations and how to refuse offers of drinks. Motivational enhancement was designed to enhance drinkers' desires to help themselves. The treatments worked equally well for most people with some exceptions. For example, people with psychological problems fared somewhat better with cognitive-behavioral therapy.

Research is also under way on the use of medicines in treating problem drinking. Disulfiram (Antabuse), for example, cannot be mixed with alcohol. People who take disulfiram experience symptoms such as nausea and vomiting if they drink (Schuckit, 1996).

Opiates

Opiates are a group of **narcotics** that are derived from the opium poppy, from which they obtain their name. **Opioids** are similar in chemical structure but are synthesized in a laboratory. The ancient Sumerians gave the opium poppy its name: It means "plant of joy." Opiates include morphine, heroin, codeine, Demerol, and similar drugs. Question: What are the effects of opiates? The major medical application of this group of drugs is relief from pain.

CIRRHOSIS OF THE LIVER A disease caused by protein deficiency in which connective fibers replace active liver cells, impeding circulation of the blood. Alcohol does not contain protein; therefore, persons who drink excessively may be prone to this disease.

WERNICKE–KORSAKOFF SYNDROME A cluster of symptoms associated with chronic alcohol abuse and characterized by confusion, memory impairment, and filling in gaps in memory with false information (confabulation).

OPIATES A group of narcotics derived from the opium poppy that provide a euphoric rush and depress the nervous system.

NARCOTICS Drugs used to relieve pain and induce sleep. The term is usually reserved for opiates.

OPIOIDS Chemicals that act on opiate receptors but are not derived from the opium poppy.

Morphine was introduced in the United States in the 1860s, at about the time of the Civil War, and in Europe during the Franco-Prussian War. It was used liberally to deaden pain from wounds. Physiological dependence on morphine therefore became known as the "soldier's disease." Little stigma was attached to dependence before morphine became a legally restricted substance.

Heroin was so named because it made people feel "heroic." It was also hailed as the "hero" that would cure physiological dependence on morphine.

✓ Truth or Fiction Revisited

It is true that heroin was once used as a cure for addiction to morphine. Today an opioid, methadone, is used to help addicts avert the symptoms caused by withdrawal from heroin.

Heroin can provide a powerful euphoric "rush." Users of heroin claim that it is so pleasurable it can eradicate any thought of food or sex. Although regular users develop tolerance for heroin, high doses can cause drowsiness, stupor, altered time perception, and impaired judgment.

Heroin is illegal. Because the penalties for possession or sale are high, it is also expensive. For this reason, many physiologically dependent people support their habit through dealing (selling heroin), prostitution, or selling stolen goods.

Methadone is a synthetic opioid. It has been used to treat physiological dependence on heroin in the same way that heroin was once used to treat physiological dependence on morphine. Methadone is slower acting than heroin and does not provide the thrilling rush. Some people must be maintained on methadone for many years before they can be gradually withdrawn from it (O'Brien, 1996). Some must be maintained on methadone indefinitely because they are unwilling to undergo any withdrawal symptoms.

Narcotics can have distressing withdrawal syndromes, especially when used in high doses. Such syndromes may begin with flu-like symptoms and progress through tremors, cramps, chills alternating with sweating, rapid pulse, high blood pressure, insomnia, vomiting, and diarrhea. However, these syndromes are variable from one person to another.

Many people who obtain prescriptions for opiates for pain relief neither experience a euphoric rush nor become psychologically dependent on them (Lang & Patt, 1994). If they no longer need opiates for pain but have become physiologically dependent on them, they can usually quit with few, if any, side effects by gradually decreasing their dosage (Rosenthal, 1993). Thus difficulty or ease of withdrawal may be connected with one's motives for using psychoactive drugs. Those who are seeking habitual relief from psychological pain seem to become more dependent on them than people who are seeking time-limited relief from physical pain.

Barbiturates and Methaqualone

Question: What are the effects of barbiturates and methaqualone?
Barbiturates (e.g., phenobarbital, secobarbital) are depressants with a number of medical uses, including relief of anxiety and tension, deadening of pain, and treatment of epilepsy, high blood pressure, and insomnia. Barbiturates lead rapidly to physiological and psychological dependence. **Methaqualone** is a depressant whose effects are similar to those of barbiturates. Methaqualone also leads to physiological dependence and is quite dangerous.

REFLECT

Do you think that cocaine and narcotics such as heroin are the most dangerous psychoactive drugs? Why or why not?

BARBITURATE An addictive depressant used to relieve anxiety or induce sleep.

METHAQUALONE An addictive depressant. Often called "ludes."

Barbiturates and methaqualone are popular as street drugs because they are relaxing and produce mild euphoria. High doses of barbiturates result in drowsiness, motor impairment, slurred speech, irritability, and poor judgment. A physiologically dependent person who is withdrawn abruptly from barbiturates may experience severe convulsions and die. Because of additive effects, it is dangerous to mix alcohol and other depressants.

Review

SECTION VII

Depressants act by slowing the activity of the (76) _____ nervous system. Alcohol is an intoxicating depressant that leads to (77) phy_____ dependence. Alcohol impairs (78) cog_____ functioning, slurs the (79) sp_____, and interferes with (80) m_____ coordination. Women seem to be more affected by alcohol than men because they (81) met_____ very little of it in the stomach. Drinking alcohol is often used as an excuse for (82) anti_____ behavior, but alcohol has not been shown to induce antisocial behavior directly.

Opiates are (83) _____tics derived from the opium poppy or are similar in chemical structure. The opiates (84) mor_____ and (85) he_____ are depressants that reduce pain, but they are also bought on the street because of the euphoric rush they provide. Opiates can lead to (86) ph_____ dependence and distressing (87) ab_____ syndromes. The synthetic narcotic (88) _____done has been used to treat heroin dependence.

Barbiturates are used medically to treat (89) _____epsy. Barbiturates lead rapidly to (90) phy_____ dependence.

SECTION VIII. STIMULANTS

All stimulants increase the activity of the nervous system. Their other effects vary somewhat, and some contribute to feelings of euphoria and self-confidence.

Amphetamines

Question: What are the effects of amphetamines? **Amphetamines** are a group of stimulants that were first used by soldiers during World War II to help them remain alert through the night. Truck drivers have used them to stay awake all night. Amphetamines have become perhaps more widely known through students, who have used them for all-night cram sessions, and through dieters, who use them because they reduce hunger.

Called speed, uppers, bennies (for Benzedrine), and dexies (for Dexedrine), these drugs are often used for the euphoric rush they can produce, especially in high doses. Some people swallow amphetamines in pill form or inject liquid methedrine, the strongest form, into their veins. They may stay awake and high for days on end. Such highs must come to an end. People who have been on prolonged highs sometimes "crash," or fall into a deep sleep or depression. Some people commit suicide when crashing.

AMPHETAMINES Stimulants derived from *alpha-methyl-beta-phenyl-ethyl-amine,* a colorless liquid consisting of carbon, hydrogen, and nitrogen.

Snorting Cocaine. Cocaine is a powerful stimulant. Health professionals have become concerned about some of its effects, including sudden rises in blood pressure, constriction of blood vessels, and acceleration of heart rate. Several athletes have died from cocaine overdoses.

A related stimulant, methylphenidate (Ritalin), is widely used to treat **attention-deficit/hyperactivity disorder** in children. Although critics believe that Ritalin is prescribed too freely (Pear, 2000), Ritalin has been shown to increase attention span, decrease aggressive and disruptive behavior, and lead to academic gains (Klorman et al., 1994). Why should Ritalin, a stimulant, calm children? Hyperactivity may be connected with immaturity of the cerebral cortex, and Ritalin may stimulate the cortex to exercise control over more primitive centers in the lower brain.

✓ **Truth or Fiction Revisited**

It is true that a stimulant is commonly used to treat children who are hyperactive. That stimulant is methylphenidate, or Ritalin.

High doses of amphetamines may cause restlessness, insomnia, loss of appetite, hallucinations, paranoid delusions (e.g., false ideas that others are eavesdropping or intend to harm them), and irritability.

Cocaine

Do you recall the commercials claiming that "Coke adds life"? Given its caffeine and sugar content, "Coke"—Coca-Cola, that is—should provide quite a lift. But Coca-Cola hasn't been "the real thing" since 1906, when the company discontinued the use of cocaine in its formula. Cocaine is derived from coca leaves—the plant from which the soft drink took its name.

✓ **Truth or Fiction Revisited**

It is true that Coca-Cola once "added life" through a powerful but now illegal stimulant. That stimulant is cocaine.

Question: What are the effects of cocaine? Cocaine is a stimulant that produces euphoria, reduces hunger, deadens pain, and bolsters self-confidence. Cocaine's popularity with college students seems to have peaked in the mid-1980s (Johnston et al., 1996). The majority of high school students now believe that use of cocaine is harmful (Johnston et al., 1996).

Cocaine may be brewed from coca leaves as a "tea," "snorted" in powder form, or injected in liquid form. Repeated snorting constricts blood vessels in the nose, drying the skin and sometimes exposing cartilage and perforating the nasal septum. These problems require cosmetic surgery. The potent cocaine derivatives known as "crack" and "bazooka" are inexpensive because they are unrefined.

Biologically speaking, cocaine stimulates sudden rises in blood pressure, constricts the coronary arteries and thickens the blood (both of which decrease the oxygen supply to the heart), and quickens the heart rate (Kaufman et al., 1998). These events occasionally result in respiratory and cardiovascular collapse (Moliterno et al., 1994; Tang, 1999). The sudden deaths of a number of athletes have been caused in this way. Overdoses can lead to restlessness and insomnia, tremors, headaches, nausea, convulsions, hallucinations, and delusions. Use of crack has been connected with strokes.

Cocaine—also called *snow* and *coke,* like the slang term for the soft drink—has been used as a local anesthetic since the early 1800s. In 1884 it came to the attention of a young Viennese neurologist named Sigmund Freud, who used it to fight his own depression and published an article about it titled "Song of Praise." Freud's early ardor was tempered when he learned that cocaine is habit-forming and can cause hallucinations and delusions. Cocaine causes physiological as well as psychological dependence (Tang, 1999).

ATTENTION-DEFICIT/HYPERACTIVITY DISORDER A disorder that begins in childhood and is characterized by a persistent pattern of lack of attention, with or without hyperactivity and impulsive behavior.

Cigarettes (Nicotine)

Smoking: a "custome lothesome to the Eye, hatefull to the Nose, harmefull to the Braine, dangerous to the Lungs."

KING JAMES I, 1604

Nicotine is the stimulant in cigarettes. Question: What are the effects of nicotine? Nicotine stimulates discharge of the hormone adrenaline and the release of many neurotransmitters, including dopamine and acetylcholine. Adrenaline creates a burst of autonomic activity that accelerates the heart rate and pours sugar into the blood. Acetylcholine is vital in memory formation, and nicotine appears to enhance memory and attention, improve performance on simple, repetitive tasks (Kinnunen et al., 1996; O'Brien, 1996), and enhance mood. Yet it also appears to relax people and reduce stress (O'Brien, 1996).

Nicotine depresses the appetite and raises the metabolic rate (Meyers et al., 1997). Thus some people smoke in order to control their weight. People also tend to eat more when they stop smoking (Klesges et al., 1997), causing some to return to the habit.

Nicotine is the agent that creates physiological dependence on cigarettes (Kessler, 1995). Regular smokers adjust their smoking to maintain fairly even levels of nicotine in their bloodstream (Shiffman et al., 1997). Symptoms of withdrawal from nicotine include nervousness, drowsiness, loss of energy, headaches, irregular bowel movements, lightheadedness, insomnia, dizziness, cramps, palpitations, tremors, and sweating. Because many of these symptoms resemble those of anxiety, it was once thought that they might reflect the anxiety of attempting to quit smoking, rather than addiction.

THE PERILS OF SMOKING It's no secret. Cigarette packs sold in the United States carry messages like "Warning: The Surgeon General Has Determined That Cigarette Smoking Is Dangerous to Your Health." Cigarette advertising has been banned on radio and television. Nearly 420,000 Americans die from smoking-related illnesses each year (Rosenblatt, 1994). This is the equivalent of two jumbo jets colliding in midair each day with all passengers lost. It is higher than the number of people who die from motor vehicle accidents, alcohol and drug abuse, suicide, homicide, and AIDS *combined* (Rosenblatt, 1994).

✓ Truth or Fiction Revisited

It is true that the number of people who die from smoking-related causes is greater than the total number lost to motor vehicle accidents, abuse of alcohol and all other drugs, suicide, homicide, and AIDS.

The percentage of American adults who smoke overall declined from more than 40% in the mid-1960s to about 25% in recent years, but there have been increases among women, African Americans, and 8th to 12th graders (Feder, 1997). The incidence of smoking is connected with gender, age, ethnicity, level of education, and socioeconomic status (see Table 5.1). Better-educated people are less likely to smoke. They are also more likely to quit smoking (Rose et al., 1996).

Every cigarette smoked steals about 7 minutes of a person's life. The carbon monoxide in cigarette smoke impairs the blood's ability to carry oxygen, causing shortness of breath. It is apparently the **hydrocarbons** ("tars") in cigarette smoke that lead to lung cancer. Heavy smokers are about 10 times as likely as nonsmokers to die of lung cancer (Nevid et al.,

Cigarettes: Smoking Guns?   The perils of cigarette smoking are widely known today. One Surgeon General declared that cigarette smoking is the chief preventable cause of death in the United States. The number of Americans who die from smoking is comparable to the number of lives that would be lost if two jumbo jets crashed *every day*. If flying were that unsafe, would the government ground all flights? Would the public continue to make airline reservations?

HYDROCARBONS Chemical compounds consisting of hydrogen and carbon.

REFLECT

Do you think that researchers have exaggerated the dangers of smoking? Why or why not?

TABLE 5.1	HUMAN DIVERSITY AND SMOKING	
FACTOR	**GROUP**	**PERCENT WHO SMOKE**
Gender	Women	23.5
	Men	28.1
Age	18–24	22.9
	25–44	30.4
	45–64	26.9
	65–74	16.5
	75 and above	8.4
Ethnic Group	African American	29.2
	Asian American/Pacific Islander	16.0
	Hispanic American	20.2
	Native American	31.4
	Non-Hispanic White American	25.5
Level of Education (in years)	Fewer than 12 years	32.0
	12	30.0
	13–15	23.4
	16 and above	13.6
Socioeconomic Status (SES)	Below poverty level	33.3
	At poverty level or above	24.7

Note: From Office of Smoking and Health, Centers for Disease Control (1993).

1998). Cigarette smoking is also linked to death from heart disease, chronic lung and respiratory diseases, and other health problems. Women who smoke show reduced bone density, significantly increasing the risk of fracture of the hip and back (Hopper & Seeman, 1994). Pregnant women who smoke risk miscarriage, premature birth, and birth defects.

Passive smoking is also connected with respiratory illnesses, asthma, and other health problems and accounts for more than 50,000 deaths per year (Nevid et al., 1998). Because of the noxious effects of secondhand smoke, smoking has been banished from many public places such as airplanes, restaurants, and elevators.

Why, then, do people smoke? For many reasons—such as the desire to look sophisticated (although these days smokers may be more likely to be judged foolish than sophisticated), to have something to do with their hands, and—of course—to take in nicotine.

Review

SECTION VIII

Stimulants act by (91: Increasing or Decreasing?) the activity of the nervous system. (92) _____mines are stimulants that produce feelings of euphoria when taken in high doses. But high doses of amphetamines may also cause restlessness, insomnia, psychotic symptoms, and a "crash" upon (93) _____wal. A related stimulant, Ritalin, is widely used to treat (94) att_____-deficit/hyperactivity disorder in children.

The stimulant (95) c_____ was used in Coca-Cola prior to 1906. Now it is an illegal drug that provides feelings of (96) eu_____ and bolsters self-confidence. As with the

PASSIVE SMOKING Inhaling of smoke from the tobacco products and exhalations of other people; also called *secondhand smoking.*

amphetamines, overdoses can lead to (97) _____ness, (98) ins_____, and psychotic reactions. Cocaine also triggers sudden rises in (99) _____ pressure, constricts the coronary (100) _____ries, and quickens the heart rate, which may lead to cardiovascular collapse.

Cigarette smoke contains carbon (101) _____ide, hydrocarbons, and the stimulant (102) _____ine. Regular smokers adjust their smoking to maintain a consistent blood level of nicotine, suggestive of (103) _____cal dependence. About (104) _____ percent of adults in the United States smoke today. People (105: Above or Below?) the poverty level are more likely to smoke.

SECTION IX. HALLUCINOGENICS

Hallucinogenic drugs are so named because they produce hallucinations—that is, sensations and perceptions in the absence of external stimulation. But hallucinogenic drugs may also have additional effects such as relaxation, euphoria, or, in some cases, panic.

Marijuana

Marijuana is a substance that is produced from the *Cannabis sativa* plant, which grows wild in many parts of the world. Question: What are the effects of marijuana? Marijuana helps some people relax and can elevate their mood. It also sometimes produces mild hallucinations, which is why it is classified as a **psychedelic,** or hallucinogenic, drug. The major psychedelic substance in marijuana is delta-9-tetrahydrocannabinol, or THC. THC is found in the branches and leaves of the plant, but it is highly concentrated in the sticky resin. **Hashish,** or "hash," is derived from the resin. Hashish is more potent than marijuana.

In the 19th century marijuana was used much as aspirin is used today for headaches and minor aches and pains. It could be bought without a prescription in any drugstore. Today marijuana use and possession are illegal in most states. Marijuana also carries a number of health risks. For example, it impairs motor coordination and perceptual functions used in driving and operating machines. It impairs short-term memory and slows learning. Although it causes positive mood changes in many people, there are also disturbing instances of anxiety and confusion and occasional reports of psychotic reactions. Marijuana increases the heart rate to 140–150 beats per minute and, in some people, raises blood pressure. This higher demand on the heart and circulation poses a threat to people with hypertension and cardiovascular disorders. Moreover, marijuana smoke contains more carcinogenic hydrocarbons than tobacco smoke.

PSYCHOLOGICAL EFFECTS OF MARIJUANA Some people report that marijuana helps them socialize at parties. Moderate to strong intoxication is linked to reports of heightened perceptions and increases in self-insight, creative thinking, and empathy for the feelings of others. Time seems to pass more slowly for people who are strongly intoxicated. A song might seem to last an hour rather than a few minutes. There is increased awareness of bodily sensations such as heartbeat. Marijuana smokers also

HALLUCINOGENIC Giving rise to hallucinations.

MARIJUANA The dried vegetable matter of the *Cannabis sativa* plant.

PSYCHEDELIC Causing hallucinations, delusions, or heightened perceptions.

HASHISH A drug derived from the resin of *Cannabis sativa*. Often called "hash."

LSD Lysergic acid diethylamide. A hallucinogenic drug.

FLASHBACKS Distorted perceptions or hallucinations that occur days or weeks after LSD usage but mimic the LSD experience.

MESCALINE A hallucinogenic drug derived from the mescal (peyote) cactus.

PHENCYCLIDINE Another hallucinogenic drug whose name is an acronym for its chemical structure. Abbreviated *PCP*.

REFLECT

Do you know people who smoke marijuana? Do you believe that researchers exaggerate the dangers of marijuana just to discourage people from using it? Why or why not?

An LSD Trip? This hallucinogenic drug can give rise to a vivid parade of colors and visual distortions. Some users claim to have achieved great insights while "tripping," but typically they have been unable to recall or apply them afterward.

report that strong intoxication heightens sexual sensations. Visual hallucinations are not uncommon. Strong intoxication may cause smokers to experience disorientation. If the smoker's mood is euphoric, loss of a sense of personal identity may be interpreted as being in harmony with the universe.

Some marijuana smokers have negative experiences. An accelerated heart rate and heightened awareness of bodily sensations leads some smokers to fear that their heart will "run away" with them. Some smokers find disorientation threatening and are afraid that they will not regain their identity. Strong intoxication sometimes causes nausea and vomiting.

People can become psychologically dependent on marijuana, but it is not known to cause physiological dependence. Tolerance of a drug is a sign of physiological dependence. With marijuana, however, regular usage is often associated with the need for *less,* not *more,* to achieve the same effects.

Marijuana has been used to treat health problems, including glaucoma and the nausea experienced by cancer patients undergoing chemotherapy ("More research needed," 1997). However, in most cases other drugs are available for these purposes (Kolata, 1994).

LSD and Other Hallucinogenics

LSD is the abbreviation for lysergic acid diethylamide, a synthetic hallucinogenic drug. Question: What are the effects of LSD and other kinds of hallucinogenic drugs? Users of "acid" claim that it "expands consciousness" and opens up new worlds to them. Sometimes people believe they have achieved great insights while using LSD, but when it wears off they often cannot apply or recall these discoveries. As a powerful hallucinogenic, LSD produces vivid and colorful hallucinations.

Some LSD users have **flashbacks**—distorted perceptions or hallucinations that mimic the LSD "trip" but occur days, weeks, or longer after usage. Some researchers have speculated that flashbacks stem from chemical changes in the brain produced by LSD. Others suggest psychological explanations for flashbacks. Matefy (1980) found that LSD users who have flashbacks can become engrossed in role playing. Perhaps flashbacks involve enacting the role of being on a trip. This does not mean that people who claim to have flashbacks are lying. They may be more willing to surrender personal control in their quest for psychedelic experiences. Users who do not have flashbacks prefer to be more in charge of their thought processes and choose to focus on the demands of daily life.

Other hallucinogenic drugs include **mescaline** (derived from the peyote cactus) and **phencyclidine** (PCP). Regular use of hallucinogenics may lead to tolerance and psychological dependence. But hallucinogenics are not known to lead to physiological dependence. High doses may induce frightening hallucinations, impaired coordination, poor judgment, mood changes, and paranoid delusions.

The effects of various kinds of drugs are summarized in Table 5.2.

TABLE 5.2	**PSYCHOACTIVE DRUGS AND THEIR EFFECTS**					
DRUG	**TYPE**	**HOW TAKEN**	**DESIRED EFFECTS**	**TOLERANCE**	**ABSTINENCE SYNDROME**	**SIDE EFFECTS**
Alcohol	Depressant	By mouth	Relaxation, euphoria, lowered inhibitions	Yes	Yes	Impaired coordination, poor judgment, hangover
Opiates	Depressants	Injected, smoked, by mouth	Relaxation, euphoria, relief from anxiety and pain	Yes	Yes	Impaired coordination and mental functioning, drowsiness, lethargy
Barbiturates and Methaqualone	Depressants	By mouth, injected	Relaxation, sleep, euphoria, lowered inhibitions	Yes	Yes	Impaired coordination and mental functioning, drowsiness, lethargy
Amphetamines	Stimulants	By mouth, injected	Alertness, euphoria	Yes	?	Restlessness, loss of appetite, psychotic symptoms
Cocaine	Stimulant	By mouth, snorted, injected	Euphoria, self-confidence	Yes	Yes	Restlessness, loss of appetite, convulsions, strokes, psychotic symptoms
Nicotine	Stimulant	By tobacco (smoked, chewed, or sniffed)	Relaxation, stimulation, weight control	Yes	Yes	Cancer, heart disease, lung and respiratory diseases
Marijuana	Hallucinogenic	Smoked, by mouth	Relaxation, perceptual distortions, enhancement of experience	No	No	Impaired coordination, respiratory problems, panic
LSD, Mescaline, PCP	Hallucinogenics	By mouth	Perceptual distortions, vivid hallucinations	Yes	No	Impaired coordination, psychotic symptoms, panic

SECTION IX Review

Hallucinogenic substances distort (106) _____tions and perceptions. Marijuana often produces feelings of relaxation and (107) emp_____, the feeling that time is (108: Speeding up or Slowing down?), and reports of new insights. However, it raises the (109) h_____ rate, and the (110) s_____ can be harmful.

LSD produces vivid (111) _____tions. So-called LSD (112) _____cks may reflect psychological rather than physiological factors. Regular use of hallucinogenics may lead to psychological (113) _____dence and to (114) tol_____. However, hallucinogenics are not known to lead to (115) phy_____ dependence.

Consciousness is that precious thing that enables us to observe and make sense of our environment and to act on our environment. Most conscious activity occurs in what we call the "normal" waking state, but we apparently need rest from this state through sleep. Being creative, humans have also experimented with many ways of altering consciousness, often as a way of enhancing the nature of everyday experience or gaining special insight. The widespread use of alcohol indicates that some methods of altering consciousness have become an integral part of our culture. However, as noted in this chapter, many ways of altering consciousness—including the use of alcohol—carry certain risks. Rather than focusing on ways of altering consciousness, most of us can probably do a great deal more to appreciate the normal waking state—perhaps by listening to music, exploring hobbies, getting involved in exercise, visiting museums, and thinking about our philosophies of life. It's a big universe out there, filled with endless potential, and our consciousness is our way of connecting to it.

STUDY GUIDE

SUMMARY

1. **What is consciousness?** The term *consciousness* has several meanings, including (1) sensory awareness, (2) direct inner awareness of cognitive processes, (3) personal unity or the sense of self, and (4) the waking state.

2. **What is a circadian rhythm?** A circadian rhythm is a cycle that is connected with the 24-hour period of the earth's rotation, such as the sleep-wake cycle.

3. **What occurs during sleep?** We undergo several stages of sleep. According to electroencephalograph (EEG) records, each stage of sleep is characterized by a different type of brain wave. There are four stages of non-rapid-eye-movement (NREM) sleep and one stage of REM sleep. Stage 1 sleep is the lightest, and stage 4 is the deepest.

4. **Why do we sleep?** Sleep apparently serves a restorative function, but we do not know exactly how sleep restores us or how much sleep we need. Animals and people who have been deprived of REM sleep learn more slowly and forget what they have learned more rapidly.

5. **What are dreams and why do we dream what we dream?** Dreams are a form of cognitive activity that occurs mostly while we are sleeping. Most dreaming occurs during REM sleep. Freud believed that dreams reflected unconscious wishes and "protected sleep" by keeping unacceptable ideas out of awareness. The activation-synthesis hypothesis suggests that dreams largely reflect automatic biological activity by the pons and the synthesis of subsequent sensory stimulation by the frontal part of the brain. The content of most dreams is an extension of the events of the previous day. Nightmares are also dreams that occur during REM sleep.

6. **What types of problems or sleep disorders can we encounter as we sleep?** A common sleep disorder is insomnia, which is most often encountered by people who are anxious and tense. Deep sleep disorders include sleep terrors, bed-wetting, and sleepwalking.

7. **What is hypnosis?** Hypnosis is an altered state of consciousness in which people are suggestible and behave as though they are in a trance.

8. **What changes in consciousness are induced by hypnosis?** People who are hypnotized may show passivity, narrowed attention, hypermnesia (heightened memory), suggestibility, assumption of unusual roles, perceptual distortions, posthypnotic amnesia, and posthypnotic suggestion.

9. **How can we explain the effects of hypnosis?** Current theories of hypnosis deny the existence of a special trance state. Rather, they emphasize people's ability to role-play the "trance" and to divide consciousness as directed by the hypnotist.

10. **What is meditation?** In meditation, one focuses "passively" on an object or a mantra in order to alter the normal relationship between oneself and the environment. In this way, consciousness (that is, the normal focuses of attention) is altered.

11. **What are the effects of meditation?** Meditation often has the effect of inducing relaxation. TM appears to normalize the blood pressure.

12. **What is biofeedback training?** Biofeedback is a method for increasing consciousness of bodily functions. In biofeedback, the organism is continuously provided with information about a targeted biological response such as heart rate or emission of alpha waves.

13. **How is biofeedback training used?** People and lower animals can learn to control involuntary functions such as heart rate, blood pressure, and even the emission of certain brain waves through biofeedback training.

14. **What are substance abuse and dependence?** Substance abuse is use that persists even though it impairs one's functioning. Dependence has behavioral and physiological aspects. It may be characterized by organizing one's life around getting and using the substance and by the development of tolerance, withdrawal symptoms, or both.

15. **What are the causes of substance abuse and dependence?** People usually try drugs out of curiosity, but usage can be reinforced by anxiety reduction, feelings of euphoria, and other positive sensations. People are also motivated to avoid withdrawal symptoms once they become physiologically dependent on a drug. Some people may have genetic

predispositions to become physiologically dependent on certain substances.

16. **What are the effects of alcohol?** Alcohol, the most widely used drug, is a depressant. It belongs to the group of substances that act by slowing the activity of the central nervous system. Alcohol is also intoxicating and can lead to physiological dependence. It provides an excuse for failure or for antisocial behavior, but it has not been shown to induce such behavior directly.

17. **What are the effects of opiates?** The opiates morphine and heroin are depressants that reduce pain, but they are also bought on the street because of the euphoric "rush" they provide. Opiate use can lead to physiological dependence.

18. **What are the effects of barbiturates and methaqualone?** Barbiturates and a similar drug, methaqualone, are depressants. Barbiturates have medical uses, including relaxation, pain management, and treatment of epilepsy, high blood pressure, and insomnia. Barbiturates lead rapidly to physiological and psychological dependence.

19. **What are the effects of amphetamines?** Stimulants are substances that act by increasing the activity of the nervous system. Amphetamines are stimulants that produce feelings of euphoria when taken in high doses. But high doses may also cause restlessness, insomnia, psychotic symptoms, and a "crash" upon withdrawal. Amphetamines and a related

stimulant, Ritalin, are commonly used to treat hyperactive children.

20. **What are the effects of cocaine?** Psychologically speaking, the stimulant cocaine provides feelings of euphoria and bolsters self-confidence. Physically, it causes sudden rises in blood pressure and constricts blood vessels. Overdoses can lead to restlessness, insomnia, psychotic reactions, and cardiorespiratory collapse.

21. **What are the effects of nicotine?** Nicotine is an addictive stimulant that can paradoxically help people relax. Nicotine is the drug found in cigarette smoke, but cigarette smoke also contains carbon monoxide and hydrocarbons. Cigarette smoking has been linked to death from heart disease and cancer and to other health problems.

22. **What are the effects of marijuana?** Hallucinogenic substances produce distorted sensations and perceptions. Marijuana is a hallucinogenic substance whose active ingredients, including THC, often produce relaxation, heightened and distorted perceptions, feelings of empathy, and reports of new insights. Hallucinations may occur. The long-term effects of marijuana use are not fully known, although it appears that marijuana smoke itself is harmful.

23. **What are the effects of LSD and other kinds of hallucinogenic drugs?** LSD is a hallucinogenic drug that produces vivid hallucinations. Some LSD users have "flashbacks" to earlier experiences.

E X E R C I S E   1

TYPES OF DRUGS

Below are the names of several types of drugs that are discussed in the text. Indicate whether each drug is a depressant (D), stimulant (S), or hallucinogenic (H) by writing the appropriate letter—D, S, or H—in the blank space to the left of the drug.

____ 1. Codeine
____ 2. Benzedrine
____ 3. Lysergic acid (LSD)
____ 4. Cocaine
____ 5. Demerol
____ 6. Nicotine
____ 7. Mescaline
____ 8. Methadone
____ 9. Methaqualone
____ 10. Ritalin

____ 11. Phenobarbital
____ 12. Valium
____ 13. Dexedrine
____ 14. Alcohol
____ 15. Marijuana
____ 16. Morphine
____ 17. Phencyclidine (PCP)
____ 18. Heroin
____ 19. Secobarbital
____ 20. Methedrine

EXERCISE 2

PSYCHOACTIVE DRUGS AND THEIR EFFECTS

Fill in the missing information.

DRUG	TYPE	HOW TAKEN	DESIRED EFFECTS	TOLERANCE	ABSTINENCE SYNDROME	SIDE EFFECTS
Alcohol	Depressant	By mouth	Relaxation, euphoria, lowered inhibitions	1. _____	2. _____	Impaired coordination, poor judgment, hangover
Opiates	3. _____	Injected, smoked, by mouth	Relaxation, euphoria, relief from anxiety and pain	Yes	4. _____	Impaired coordination and mental functioning, drowsiness, lethargy
Barbiturates and Methaqualone	5. _____	By mouth, injected	Relaxation, sleep, euphoria, lowered inhibitions	6. _____	Yes	Impaired coordination and mental functioning, drowsiness, lethargy
Amphetamines	7. _____	By mouth, injected	Alertness, euphoria	8. _____	?	Restlessness, loss of appetite, psychotic symptoms
Cocaine	9. _____	By mouth, snorted, injected	Euphoria, self-confidence	Yes	10. _____	Restlessness, loss of appetite, convulsions, strokes, psychotic symptoms
Nicotine	Stimulant	By tobacco (smoked, chewed, or sniffed)	Relaxation, stimulation, weight control	11. _____	12. _____	Cancer, heart disease, lung and respiratory diseases
Marijuana	Hallucinogenic	Smoked, by mouth	Relaxation, perceptual distortions, enhancement of experience	13. _____	14. _____	Impaired coordination, respiratory problems, panic
LSD, Mescaline, PCP	15. _____	By mouth	Perceptual distortions, vivid hallucinations	Yes	16. _____	Impaired coordination, psychotic symptoms, panic

BRIDGING THE GAP

LANGUAGE AND CULTURE

additive effect (245)   *results of putting two chemicals together*

alternation (227)   *cyclical off and on*

attention span (246)   *length of time a person can stay focused on one topic*

ardor (246)   *goodwill, interest*

around the clock (228)   *24 hours a day*

blip (238)   *radio signal*

bull's eye (233)   *target to hit*

to catch up on sleep (227)   *to attempt to sleep after being without sleep to restore balance*

to cement (222)   *to make firm*

to censor (229)   *to screen out, to monitor*

childish mode (235)   *way of acting as a child*

to compound (230)   *to add to, to make worse*

consciousness-altering drugs (224)   *medicines that change one's awareness*

cosmetic surgery (246)   *plastic surgery, operation to change the appearance of something*

to cram (227)   *to study hard at the last minute before a test*

cyclical (225)   *repeating, up and down*

for days on end (245)   *for more than one day, for a long time*

deadening of pain (244)   *decrease in feelings of discomfort*

to deploy (238)   *to put into action*

to depress (247)   *to cause to decrease*

diarrhea (244)   *sickness of the bowels*

distraction (224)   *unrelated thought*

to dread (231)   *to be fearful of*

drop-off (242)   *decrease*

dysfunctional (238)   *improperly working*

to emit (225)   *to send out*

to enhance (247)   *to add to, to improve*

enzyme (242)   *body chemical for digestion*

euphoria (242)   *good feeling, a high*

excursion (231)   *trip, traveling*

to fake (235)   *to pretend*

to foresee (242)   *to predict*

to gain your footing (230)   *to be able to run*

to get into (223)   *to enter, to become part of*

gleaming (223)   *shining*

to go to someone's head (242)   *to affect one's thinking*

hairdo (223)   *style of wearing one's hair*

harshness (231)   *anger, hostility*

to have a nip (233)   *(here) to bite*

humdrum (229)   *ordinary, not special*

impaired judgment (244)   *loss of good sense*

to implant (238)   *put in through surgery*

incoherently (231)   *confused, without order or sense*

ingenious (237)   *clever*

insomnia (230)   *inability to sleep*

intravenously (242)   *into the vein, directly into the bloodstream*

jumbo jet (247)   *huge airplane*

to lubricate (240)   *to oil, to make work more smoothly*

lyric (229)   *words to a song*

to mean so much to so many (241)   *to have been so popular and well-liked by many people*

to metabolize (242)   *to use as food*

in midair (247)   *in the air*

to move you across town (239)   *to change your perspective greatly*

normalizing (237)   *returning to normal, reducing or increasing to normal*

noxious (248)   *poisonous*

obese (233)   *fat, overweight*

to be out of it (227)   *to be disoriented because of lack of sleep*

paradoxical (226)   *opposite of what it seems to be, strange, curious*

passive observation (236)   *watching, not participating*

peripherally (235)   *not in main focus, but on the side*

period (225)   *length of time*

phony (235)   *false, pretending*

preconscious (224)   *not yet in the awareness*

price break (239)   *bargain*

province (222)   *(here) scope, area to be studied*

psychoactive drug (224)   *medicine that changes the way the brain works*

to pull an all-nighter (227)   *not to sleep at all during a night, to work through a night and continue through the day*

to pump up (239)   *to build up, to increase*

racing thoughts (230)   *rapid series of unrelated worries that pass through one's mind* to recount (237)   *to retell*

to rejuvenate (227)   *to become young again, to give new energy to*

repressed (229)   *hidden from ourselves*

to run away with them (250)   *escape*

rush (244)   *sudden feeling*

sleep disorder (225)   *inability to sleep, restlessness, insomnia, unnatural sleep*

to sleep it off (239)   *to recover from a bad experience by sleeping until the body recovers*

to slug (239)   *to hit with a bat*

to snort (246)   *to sniff into the nose*

social facilitator (241)   *that which makes a party fun*

to speculate (250)   *to guess*

to spawn (230)   *to cause*

stigma (244)   *mark, prejudice, stain, taint*

stupor (244)   *extreme sleepiness, insensibility*

to suspend (236)   *to hold back for a while*

sweltering (223)   *hot*

to talk to yourself (222)   *to reflect on your own ideas*

tedium (235)   *boredom*

to temper (246)   *to modify, to soften*

trance (224)   *state of suggestibility under hypnosis*

to be an unlikely candidate (229)   *usually not to be considered as possible*

unprotected sex (242)   *sexual intercourse without a device to prevent pregnancy and sexually transmitted infections*

unrefined (246)   *not purified*

untouchable (237)   *that which cannot be reached*

vaguer (228)   *less clear*

to waft (223)   *to travel on the air*

wear and tear (230)   *effects of normal use*

wrecked (227)   *in bad shape*

QUIZ

1. Sigmund Freud labeled mental events that are unavailable to awareness under most circumstances as
   (a) preconscious,
   (b) unconscious,
   (c) repressed,
   (d) dissociated.

2. According to the text, the least controversial meaning of the word *consciousness* refers to
   (a) direct inner awareness,
   (b) sensory awareness,
   (c) the normal waking state,
   (d) the sense of self.

3. Brain waves are measured by means of the
   (a) electrocardiogram,
   (b) electroencephalograph,
   (c) electromyograph,
   (d) thermistor.

4. During stage 4 sleep, the brain emits _____ waves.
   (a) alpha,
   (b) beta,
   (c) delta,
   (d) theta.

5. Sleep spindles appear during stage _____ sleep.
   (a) 1,
   (b) 2,
   (c) 3,
   (d) 4.

6. Jim usually sleeps 8 hours a night. About how many dreams is he likely to have during the night?
   (a) None,
   (b) 1,
   (c) 5,
   (d) 25 or more.

7. Freud believed that dreams "protected sleep" by
   (a) causing us to emit alpha waves,
   (b) inhibiting the reticular activating system,
   (c) producing rapid eye movements,
   (d) keeping disturbing ideas out of awareness.

8. When they drink, the college-age children of alcoholics _____ than the children of nonalcoholics.
   (a) show lower tolerance,
   (b) develop withdrawal symptoms more rapidly,
   (c) show better visual-motor coordination,
   (d) are more likely to become ill.

9. In terms of its action on the body, cocaine is correctly categorized as a
   (a) depressant,
   (b) hallucinogenic,
   (c) narcotic,
   (d) stimulant.

10. The most widely used drug on college campuses is
    (a) cocaine,
    (b) marijuana,
    (c) LSD,
    (d) alcohol.

11. Neal E. Miller is known for his contribution to the history of
    (a) the activation-synthesis hypothesis,
    (b) biofeedback training,
    (c) the electroencephalograph,
    (d) meditation.

12. Which of the following is *not* part of the abstinence syndrome for alcohol?
    (a) Rapid pulse,
    (b) Low blood pressure,
    (c) Anxiety,
    (d) Tremors.

13. Methaqualone is a(n) _____ drug.
    (a) depressant,
    (b) stimulant,
    (c) antidepressant,
    (d) hallucinogenic.

14. Which of the following is least likely to cause physiological dependence?
    (a) Barbiturates,
    (b) LSD,
    (c) Methaqualone,
    (d) Methadone.

15. TM was introduced by
    (a) Maharishi Mahesh Yogi,
    (b) Franz Mesmer,
    (c) Herbert Benson,
    (d) Neal Miller.

16. Biofeedback is defined as a system that feeds back information about _____ to an organism.
    (a) autonomic functions,
    (b) heart rate,
    (c) voluntary functions,
    (d) a body function.

17. A friend tells you that he has learned how to raise the temperature in a finger through biofeedback training. Your friend probably acquired this skill in order to
    (a) relax the muscles of the forehead,
    (b) control headaches,
    (c) lower acid secretion in the gastrointestinal tract,
    (d) emit alpha waves.

18. According to neodissociation theory,
    (a) hypnotized subjects are aware of many things going on around them, even though they are focusing primarily on the hypnotist,
    (b) the trance state is induced by age regression,
    (c) only subjects who are highly motivated to be hypnotized can be hypnotized,
    (d) one cannot enter a hypnotic trance unless one is suggestible.

19. Franz Mesmer explained hypnosis in terms of
    (a) regression,
    (b) neodissociation theory,
    (c) animal magnetism,
    (d) role theory.

20. Arnold knows that you are taking a psychology course and asks you whether you think he would be a "good subject" for hypnosis. You point out that research suggests that hypnosis is most successful with people who
    (a) understand what is expected of them during the "trance state,"
    (b) are seeking the approval of the hypnotist,
    (c) are unfamiliar with hypnosis,
    (d) are below average in intelligence.

1. What is consciousness?

2. What is a circadian rhythm?

3. What occurs during sleep?

4. Why do we sleep?

5. What are dreams and why do we dream what we dream?

6. What types of problems or sleep disorders can we encounter as we sleep?

7. What is hypnosis?

8. What changes in consciousness are induced by hypnosis?

9. How can we explain the effects of hypnosis?

10. What is meditation?

11. What are the effects of meditation?

_____
_____
_____
_____
_____
_____

12. What is biofeedback training?

_____
_____
_____
_____
_____

13. How is biofeedback training used?

_____
_____
_____
_____
_____

14. What are substance abuse and dependence?

_____
_____
_____
_____
_____

15. What are the causes of substance use and dependence?

_____
_____
_____
_____
_____

16. What are the effects of alcohol?

_____
_____
_____
_____
_____

17. What are the effects of opiates?

_____
_____
_____
_____

18. What are the effects of barbiturates and methaqualone?

_____
_____
_____
_____

19. What are the effects of amphetamines?

_____
_____
_____
_____

20. What are the effects of cocaine?

_____
_____
_____
_____

21. What are the effects of nicotine?

_____
_____
_____
_____

22. What are the effects of marijuana?

_____
_____
_____
_____
_____
_____

23. What are the effects of LSD and other kinds of hallucinogenic drugs?

_____
_____
_____
_____
_____

ANSWERS TO SECTION REVIEWS

1. James
2. Watson
3. Behavior
4. Cognitive
5. Inner
6. Unity
7. Awareness
8. Direct
9. Preconscious
10. Unconscious
11. Electroencephalograph
12. Brain
13. Non-rapid-eye-movement
14. 1
15. 4
16. Volts
17. Alpha
18. Theta
19. Hypnagogic
20. Delta
21. 4
22. Eye
23. 1
24. Paradoxical
25. 80
26. Five
27. Longest
28. Lighter

29. Longer
30. REM-rebound
31. REM
32. Unconscious
33. Pons
34. Cortex
35. REM
36. More
37. More
38. Deep
39. Nervous
40. Is not
41. Mesmer
42. Magnetism
43. Imagine
44. Pain
45. Memory
46. Suggestibility
47. Positive
48. Attention
49. Hypermnesia
50. Posthypnotic
51. Regression
52. Trance
53. Role
54. Behaviors
55. Neodissociation
56. Mantra
57. Consciousness
58. Relaxation

59. Transcendental
60. Blood
61. Feeds
62. Heart
63. Voluntarily
64. Electromyograph
65. Temperature
66. Occupational
67. Physical
68. Amount
69. Control
70. Biological or Physiological
71. Abstinence
72. Experiment
73. Anxiety
74. Withdrawal
75. Genetic
76. Central
77. Physiological
78. Cognitive
79. Speech
80. Motor
81. Metabolize
82. Antisocial
83. Narcotics
84. Morphine
85. Heroin
86. Physiological
87. Abstinence

88. Methadone
89. Epilepsy
90. Physiological
91. Increasing
92. Amphetamines
93. Withdrawal
94. Attention
95. Cocaine
96. Euphoria
97. Restlessness
98. Insomnia
99. Blood
100. Arteries
101. Monoxide
102. Nicotine
103. Physiological
104. 25
105. Below
106. Sensations
107. Empathy
108. Slowing down
109. Heart
110. Smoke
111. Hallucinations
112. Flashbacks
113. Dependence
114. Tolerance
115. Physiological

ANSWERS TO EXERCISE 1

1. D
2. S
3. H
4. S
5. D
6. S
7. H
8. D
9. D
10. S
11. D
12. D
13. S
14. D
15. H
16. D
17. H
18. D
19. D
20. S

ANSWERS TO EXERCISE 2

1. Yes	5. Depressants	9. Stimulant	13. No
2. Yes	6. Yes	10. Yes	14. No
3. Depressants	7. Stimulants	11. Yes	15. Hallucinogenics
4. Yes	8. Yes	12. Yes	16. No

ANSWERS TO QUIZ

1. B	6. C	11. B	16. D
2. A	7. D	12. B	17. B
3. B	8. C	13. A	18. A
4. C	9. D	14. B	19. C
5. B	10. D	15. A	20. A

T F ✓✓✓✓✓✓✓✓✓✓✓✓✓✓

☐ ☐ Dogs can be trained to salivate when a bell is sounded.

☐ ☐ One nauseating meal can give rise to a food aversion that persists for years.

☐ ☐ Psychologists helped a young boy overcome his fear of rabbits by having him eat cookies while a rabbit was brought progressively nearer to him.

☐ ☐ During World War II, a psychologist devised a plan for training pigeons to guide missiles to their targets.

☐ ☐ Punishment does not work.

☐ ☐ Rats can be trained to climb a ramp, cross a bridge, climb a ladder, pedal a toy car, and do several other tasks—all in sequence.

☐ ☐ Psychologists fashioned a method to teach an emaciated 9-month-old infant to stop throwing up.

☐ ☐ We must make mistakes if we are to learn.

☐ ☐ Despite all the media hoopla, no scientific connection has been established between violence viewed on TV and aggressive behavior in real life.

☐ ☐ One third of high school students in the United States say their parents do not know how well they are doing in school.

I was teaching my new dog, Phoebe, to fetch. I bought a soft yellow ball for her that squeaked when she bit into it. She enjoyed playing with it, and I assumed she would want to run after it. (Wrong!) I waved it under her nose. She sniffed at it, barked, and wagged her tail excitedly.

Then, as Phoebe watched, I tossed the ball about 20 feet away. "Fetch!" I said as the ball bounced invitingly in the grass.

"People say, 'Take it!'" my teenage daughter Allyn said.

Perhaps Allyn was right. Phoebe watched the ball but didn't run after it. Instead, she barked at me and snapped softly at my legs.

"Okay," I said (to both of them). I ran after the ball, picked it up, and waved it under Phoebe's nose again. She barked and wagged her tail rapidly like a reed in a brisk wind.

"Take it!" I said and tossed the ball into the air again.

Again Phoebe refused to run after it. She barked and snapped at my legs again. "This is ridiculous," I muttered, and I went to get the ball. As I brought it back to Phoebe, Allyn said, "Don't you see what's happening?"

"What?"

"Phoebe's teaching you to fetch," Allyn laughed.

"Don't you mean to 'take it'?" I said.

SECTION I. LEARNING

Yes, Phoebe was teaching me to fetch. Somehow she got me to run after the ball. When I brought it back to her, she responded to my behavior with a show of excitement and (apparent) glee. One could say that Phoebe was teaching me what to do by showing excitement when I did the "right" thing. I was learning. One of the key areas in psychology is that of learning. Question: What is learning?

It is not possible to offer a simple definition of learning to which all psychologists will agree. From the behaviorist perspective, **learning** is defined as a relatively permanent change in behavior that arises from experience. But changes in behavior also arise from maturation and physical changes; such changes do not reflect learning. For example, frogs hatch as tadpoles that swim. After they develop legs, they hop on land. The behaviorist defines learning in terms of the changes in behavior by which it is known. From the behaviorist perspective, I learned to fetch the ball (a change in behavior) because Phoebe reinforced me for doing so.

From the cognitive perspective, learning is a mental change that may or may not be displayed in terms of behavior. Cognitive psychologists see learning in terms of experience changing the way that organisms mentally represent the environment. Changes in mental representation may affect, but do not directly cause, changes in behavior. From the cognitive perspective, learning is *demonstrated* by changes in behavior, but learning itself is a mental process. From the cognitive perspective, Phoebe's reinforcement of my fetching of the ball did not make me fetch. Rather, it gave me information. It showed me that Phoebe wanted me to repeat the act. But my continued fetching was not mechanical or automatic. (At least I don't think it was.)

In lower organisms, much behavior is unlearned. It is labeled instinctive, or inborn. Fish (and tadpoles) are born "knowing" how to swim. Salmon instinctively use the sense of smell to find and return to spawn in the stream where they were hatched after they have spent years roaming the seas. Robins instinctively know how to sing the song of their species and to build nests. Rats instinctively mate and rear their young. Among humans, however, the variety and complexity of behavior patterns are largely products of experience. Experience is essential to learning to walk and acquiring the language of our parents and community. We learn to read, to compute numbers, and to surf the Net. We learn to seek out the foods that are valued in our culture when we are hungry. We get into the habit of starting our day with coffee, tea, or other beverages. We learn which behavior patterns are deemed socially acceptable and which are considered wrong. And, of course, our families and communities use verbal guidance, set examples, and apply rewards and punishments to try to teach us to stick to the straight and narrow.

Sometimes our learning experiences are direct, like Phoebe's reinforcement of my fetching the ball. But we can also learn from the experiences of others. For example, I warn my children against the perils of jumping from high places and running wild in the house. (Occasionally they heed me.) But from books and visual media, we learn about the past, about other peoples, and about how to put things together. And we learn as we invent ways of doing things that have never been done before.

In this chapter we will consider various kinds of learning. These include the simple forms of learning called classical and operant conditioning, and kinds of learning in which cognition plays a more central role. We will see that learning is crucial to the adaptation and survival of organisms, and that we humans engage in many different kinds of learning, which makes us the most adaptive organisms on planet Earth.

LEARNING (1) According to behaviorists, a relatively permanent change in behavior that results from experience. (2) According to cognitive theorists, the process by which organisms make relatively permanent changes in the way they represent the environment because of experience. These changes influence the organism's behavior but do not fully determine it.

> **REFLECT**
>
> Are you more sympathetic to the behaviorist or the cognitive definition of learning? Why?

> **REFLECT**
>
> What is the difference between instinctive behavior and learned behavior? What does it mean to say that fish "know" how to swim when they are born?

How Do We Learn How to Play Chess? Games like chess are learned, but how? Can we explain playing chess as the summation of myriad instances of conditioning, or must we explain it in terms of mental representations and cognitive maps? What developments in the nervous system make us "ready" to learn the right moves? What biological changes register the memories of games played in the past?

Ivan Pavlov. Pavlov, his assistants, and a professional salivator (the dog) in Russia early in the 20th century.

SECTION II. CLASSICAL CONDITIONING

On the next day, I showed Phoebe the ball again. She became excited and barked at the door of the family room, apparently because she had learned to associate the ball with the fun we had had the day before. Such learning by association is an example of classical conditioning. Question: What is classical conditioning?

Classical conditioning is a simple form of associative learning that enables organisms to anticipate events. Classical conditioning involves some of the ways in which we learn to associate events with other events. Consider: We have a distinct preference for a grade of A rather than F. We are also (usually) more likely to stop for a red light than for a green light. Why? We are not born with instinctive attitudes toward the letters *A* and *F*. Nor are we born knowing that red means stop and green means go. We learn the meanings of these symbols because they are associated with other events. A's are associated with instructor approval and the likelihood of getting into graduate school. Red lights are associated with avoiding accidents and traffic citations.

Ivan Pavlov Rings a Bell

Lower animals also learn relationships among events, as the Russian physiologist Ivan Pavlov (1927) discovered in research with dogs. Question: What is the contribution of Ivan Pavlov to the psychology of learning? Ivan Pavlov made his contribution to the psychology of learning by accident. Pavlov was actually attempting to identify neural receptors in the mouth that triggered a response from the salivary glands. But his efforts were hampered by the dogs' salivating at undesired times, such as when a laboratory assistant inadvertently clanged a food tray.

Because of its biological makeup, a dog salivates if meat powder is placed on its tongue. Salivation in response to meat powder is a **reflex.** Reflexes are simple unlearned responses to stimuli. Reflexes are evoked by stimuli. A **stimulus** is an environmental condition that evokes a response from an organism, such as meat on the tongue or tapping the leg just below the knee. Ivan Pavlov discovered that reflexes (involuntary responses) can also be learned, or *conditioned,* through association. His dogs began salivating in response to clinking food trays because in the past this noise had repeatedly been paired with the arrival of food. The dogs would also salivate when an assistant entered the laboratory. Why? In the past, the assistant had brought food.

When we are faced with novel events, we sometimes have no immediate way of knowing whether they are important. When we are striving for concrete goals, for example, we often ignore the unexpected, even when the unexpected is just as important, or more important, than the goal. So

CLASSICAL CONDITIONING A simple form of learning in which an organism comes to associate or anticipate events. A neutral stimulus comes to evoke the response usually evoked by another stimulus by being paired repeatedly with the other stimulus. (Cognitive theorists view classical conditioning as the learning of relationships among events so as to allow an organism to represent its environment.) Also referred to as *respondent conditioning* or *Pavlovian conditioning.*

REFLEX A simple, unlearned response to a stimulus.

STIMULUS An environmental condition that elicits a response.

FIGURE 6.1

<small>PAVLOV'S DEMONSTRATION OF CONDITIONED REFLEXES IN LABORATORY DOGS</small>

<small>FROM BEHIND THE TWO-WAY MIRROR AT THE LEFT, A LABORATORY ASSISTANT RINGS A BELL AND THEN PLACES MEAT ON THE DOG'S TONGUE. AFTER SEVERAL PAIRINGS, THE DOG SALIVATES IN RESPONSE TO THE BELL ALONE. A TUBE COLLECTS SALIVA AND PASSES IT TO A VIAL. THE QUANTITY OF SALIVA IS TAKEN AS A MEASURE OF THE STRENGTH OF THE ANIMAL'S RESPONSE.</small>

it was that Pavlov at first viewed the uncalled-for canine salivation as an annoyance, a hindrance to his research. But in 1901 he decided that his "problem" was worth looking into. He set about to show that he could train, or condition, his dogs to salivate when he wished and in response to any stimulus he chose.

Pavlov termed these trained salivary responses "conditional reflexes." They were *conditional* upon the repeated pairing of a previously neutral stimulus (such as the clinking of a food tray) and a stimulus (in this case, food) that predictably elicited the target response (in this case, salivation). Today, conditional reflexes are more generally referred to as **conditioned responses (CRs).** They are responses to previously neutral stimuli that have been learned, or conditioned.

Pavlov demonstrated conditioned responses by strapping a dog into a harness like the one shown in Figure 6.1. When meat powder was placed on the dog's tongue, the dog salivated. Pavlov repeated the process several times, with one difference. He preceded the meat powder by half a second or so with the sounding of a bell on each occasion. After several pairings of meat powder and bell, Pavlov sounded the bell but did *not* follow the bell with the meat powder. Still the dog salivated. It had learned to salivate in response to the bell.

✓ Truth or Fiction Revisited

It is true that dogs can be trained to salivate when a bell is sounded. The training is accomplished by means of the classical conditioning method of pairing the sound of the bell with the delivery of food.

Why did the dog learn to salivate in response to the bell? Behaviorists and cognitive psychologists explain the learning process in very different ways. Put on your critical thinking cap: Would behaviorists say that after a few pairings of bell and food a dog "knows" that the bell "means" food is on its way? Why or why not?

Behaviorists explain the outcome of this process, termed *classical conditioning,* in terms of the publicly observable conditions of learning. They define classical conditioning as a simple form of learning in which one stimulus comes to evoke the response usually evoked by a second stimulus by being paired repeatedly with the second stimulus. In Pavlov's demonstration, the dog learned to salivate in response to the bell *because* the sounding of the bell had been paired with meat powder. That is, in classical conditioning, the organism forms associations between stimuli because the stimuli are *contiguous*—that is, they occur at about the same

CONDITIONED RESPONSE (CR) In classical conditioning, a learned response to a conditioned stimulus.

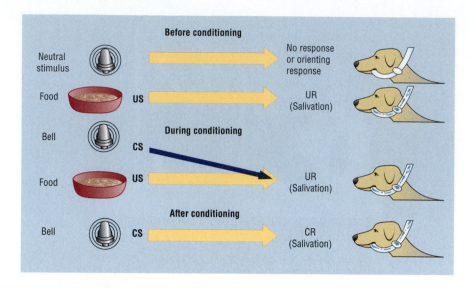

FIGURE 6.2

A SCHEMATIC REPRESENTATION OF CLASSICAL CONDITIONING

PRIOR TO CONDITIONING, FOOD ELICITS SALIVATION. THE BELL, A NEUTRAL STIMULUS, ELICITS EITHER NO RESPONSE OR AN ORIENTING RESPONSE. DURING CONDITIONING, THE BELL IS RUNG JUST BEFORE MEAT IS PLACED ON THE DOG'S TONGUE. AFTER SEVERAL REPETITIONS, THE BELL, NOW A CS, ELICITS SALIVATION, THE CR.

time. Behaviorists do *not* say that the dog "knew" food was on the way. They argue that we cannot speak meaningfully about what a dog "knows." We can only outline the conditions under which targeted behaviors reliably occur.

Cognitive psychologists view classical conditioning as the learning of relationships among events. The relationships allow organisms to mentally represent their environments and make predictions (Rescorla, 1988). In Pavlov's demonstration, the dog salivated in response to the bell because the bell—from the cognitive perspective—became mentally connected with the meat powder. The cognitive focus is on *the information gained by the organism.* Organisms are viewed as seekers of information that generate and test rules about the relationships among events (Weiner, 1991).

Stimuli and Responses in Classical Conditioning

In the demonstration just described, the meat powder is an unlearned or **unconditioned stimulus (US).** Salivation in response to the meat powder is an unlearned or **unconditioned response (UR).** The bell was at first a meaningless or neutral stimulus. It might have produced an *orienting reflex* in the dog because of its distinctness. That is, the animal might have oriented itself toward the bell by turning toward it. But the bell was not yet associated with food. Then, through repeated association with the meat powder, the bell became a learned, or **conditioned stimulus (CS)** for the salivation response. Salivation in response to the bell (or CS) is a learned or conditioned response (CR). A conditioned response is a response similar to an unconditioned response, but the response evoked by the conditioned stimulus is defined as a conditioned response, not an unconditioned response (see Figure 6.2).

Types of Classical Conditioning

The Pavlovian experiments we have described so far involve one kind of classical conditioning. Question: What are the various types of classical conditioning? We have described the most efficient type of classical conditioning, which tends to occur when the conditioned stimulus (CS) is pre-

UNCONDITIONED STIMULUS (US) A stimulus that elicits a response from an organism prior to conditioning.

UNCONDITIONED RESPONSE (UR) An unlearned response to an unconditioned stimulus.

CONDITIONED STIMULUS (CS) A previously neutral stimulus that elicits a conditioned response because it has been paired repeatedly with a stimulus that already elicited that response.

FIGURE 6.3
TYPES OF CLASSICAL CONDITIONING
IN DELAYED CONDITIONING (PART A), THE CS IS PRESENTED BEFORE THE US. IN SIMULTANEOUS CONDITIONING (PART B), THE CS AND US ARE PRESENTED TOGETHER. IN TRACE CONDITIONING (PART C), THE CS IS PRESENTED AND REMOVED PRIOR TO THE US. THUS ONLY THE MEMORY TRACE OF THE CS REMAINS WHEN THE US IS PRESENTED. IN BACKWARD CONDITIONING (PART D), THE US IS PRESENTED BEFORE THE CS. DELAYED CONDITIONING IS MOST EFFICIENT, PERHAPS BECAUSE IT ALLOWS ORGANISMS TO MAKE PREDICTIONS ABOUT THEIR ENVIRONMENTS.

sented about 0.5 second before the unconditioned stimulus (US) and is continued until the learner responds to the US. This is an example of **delayed conditioning**, in which the conditioned stimulus (for example, a light) can be presented anywhere from a fraction of a second to several seconds before the unconditioned stimulus (in this case, meat powder) and is left on until the response (salivation) is shown (see Figure 6.3).

Conditioning can also take place via **simultaneous conditioning**. In simultaneous conditioning, a conditioned stimulus, such as a light, is presented along with an unconditioned stimulus, such as meat powder. In **trace conditioning**, the conditioned stimulus (for example, a light) is presented and then removed (or turned off) prior to presentation of the unconditioned stimulus (meat powder). Therefore, only the memory trace of the conditioned stimulus (light) remains to be conditioned to the unconditioned stimulus.

Conditioning may occur most effectively in delayed conditioning because it is most adaptive. That is, in delayed conditioning, the occurrence of the conditioned stimulus signals the consequent appearance of the unconditioned stimulus. As a result, organisms can learn to make predictions about their environment. Predictability is adaptive because it allows the organism to prepare for future events. Learning is inefficient and may not take place at all when the unconditioned stimulus is presented before the conditioned stimulus—a sequence referred to as **backward conditioning**. Why? Perhaps because backward conditioning may not permit an organism to make predictions about its environment.

DELAYED CONDITIONING A classical conditioning procedure in which the CS is presented before the US and remains in place until the response occurs.

SIMULTANEOUS CONDITIONING A classical conditioning procedure in which the CS and US are presented at the same time.

TRACE CONDITIONING A classical conditioning procedure in which the CS is presented and then removed before the US is presented.

BACKWARD CONDITIONING A classical conditioning procedure in which the unconditioned stimulus is presented prior to the conditioned stimulus.

Taste Aversion

When I was a child in The Bronx, my friends and I would go to the movies on Saturday mornings. There would be a serial followed by a feature film, and the price of admission was a quarter. We would also eat candy (I loved Nonpareils and Raisinets) and popcorn. One morning my friends dared me to eat two huge containers of buttered popcorn by myself. I rose to the challenge: Down went an enormous container of buttered popcorn. More slowly—much more slowly—I stuffed down the second container. Predictably, I felt bloated and nauseated. The taste of the butter, corn, and salt lingered in my mouth and nose, and my head spun. It was obvious to

REFLECT

Do you have any taste aversions? If so, do you know how you acquired them?

Formation of a Taste Aversion? Taste aversions may be acquired as a result of only one association of the US and the CS. Most kinds of classical conditioning require that the US and CS be contiguous, but in a taste aversion the US (nausea) can occur hours after the CS (flavor of food).

me that I would have no more popcorn that day. However, I was surprised that I could not face buttered popcorn again for a year.

Years later I learned that psychologists refer to my response to buttered popcorn as a *taste aversion*. Questions: What are taste aversions? Why are they of special interest to psychologists? Many decades have now passed (how many is *my* business), and the odor of buttered popcorn still turns my stomach. Such is the power of taste aversions.

✓ Truth or Fiction Revisited

It is true that one nauseating meal can give rise to a food aversion that persists for years.

Taste aversions are fascinating examples of classical conditioning. Taste aversions are adaptive because they motivate organisms to avoid potentially harmful foods. Although taste aversions are acquired by association, they are of special interest because they differ from other kinds of classical conditioning in a couple of ways. First, only one association may be required. I did not have to go back for seconds at the movies to develop my aversion for buttered popcorn! Second, whereas most kinds of classical conditioning require that the unconditioned stimulus (US) and conditioned stimulus (CS) be contiguous, in taste aversion the unconditioned stimulus (the US—in this case, nausea) can occur hours after the conditioned stimulus (the CS—in this case, the flavor of food).

Research on taste aversion also challenges the behaviorist view that organisms learn to associate any stimuli that are contiguous. In reality, not all stimuli are created equal. Instead, it seems that organisms are biologically predisposed to develop aversions that are adaptive in their environmental settings (Garcia et al., 1989). In a classic study, Garcia and Koelling (1966) conditioned two groups of rats. Each group was exposed to the same three-part conditioned stimulus (CS): a taste of sweetened water, a light, and a clicker. Afterward, one group was presented with an unconditioned stimulus (US) of nausea (induced by poison or radiation), and the other group was presented with an unconditioned stimulus (US) of electric shock.

After conditioning, the rats who had been nauseated showed an aversion for sweetened water but not to the light or clicker. Although all three stimuli had been presented at the same time, *the rats had acquired only the taste aversion*. After conditioning, the rats that had been shocked avoided both the light and the clicker, *but they did not show a taste aversion to the sweetened water*. For each group of rats, the conditioning that took place was adaptive. In the natural scheme of things, nausea is more likely to stem from poisoned food than from lights or sounds. So, for nauseated rats, acquiring the taste aversion was appropriate. Sharp pain, in contrast, is more likely to stem from natural events involving lights (fire, lightning) and sharp sounds (twigs snapping, things falling). Therefore, it was more appropriate for the shocked animals to develop an aversion to the light and the clicker than to the sweetened water.

This finding fits my experience as well. My nausea led to a taste aversion to buttered popcorn—but not to an aversion to the serials I watched (which, in retrospect, were more deserving of nausea) or the movie theater. I returned every Saturday morning to see what would happen next. Yet, the serial and the theater, as much as the buttered popcorn, had been associated with my nausea. That is, the stimuli had been contiguous.

Let us now consider various factors in classical conditioning.

Review

Classical conditioning is defined as a simple form of (3) _____ing. In classical conditioning, an originally (4) _____al stimulus comes to elicit the response usually brought forth by another stimulus by being paired repeatedly with that stimulus. When Pavlov discovered conditioning, he was attempting to identify neural receptors in the mouth that triggered a response from the (5) _____ary glands. Salivation in response to meat is an unlearned (6) _____ex. Reflexes are elicited by (7) _____li. A stimulus is an (8) _____mental condition that evokes a response from an organism. Pavlov discovered that reflexes can also be learned, or conditioned, through (9) _____tion. Pavlov called learned reflexes (10) _____nal reflexes. Today conditional reflexes are termed (11) _____ _____s. A response to a US is called an (12) _____ned response (UR), and a response to a CS is termed a (13) _____ned response (CR).

In (14) _____ed conditioning, the CS is presented before the US. In (15) _____neous conditioning the CS is presented at the same time as the US and left on until the response occurs. In trace conditioning the CS is presented and removed (16: Prior to or After?) presentation of the US. In (17) _____ward conditioning the US is presented prior to the CS.

Taste aversions differ from other kinds of classical conditioning in a couple of ways: First, (18: Only one or Several?) association(s) is/are usually required. Second, the US and CS need not be presented (19) _____uously; the US (nausea) can occur hours after the CS (flavor of food). Research in taste aversion suggests that organisms are biologically predisposed to develop aversions that are (20) _____tive in their environmental settings.

SECTION III. FACTORS IN CLASSICAL CONDITIONING

In classical conditioning organisms learn to connect stimuli, such as a bell with food. In the following section we consider various factors in classical conditioning, beginning with what happens when the connection between stimuli is severed.

Extinction and Spontaneous Recovery

Question: What are the roles of extinction and spontaneous recovery in classical conditioning? Extinction and spontaneous recovery are aspects of conditioning that help organisms adapt by updating their expectations or revising their representations of the changing environment. For example, a dog may learn to associate a new scent (a conditioned stimulus, or CS) with the appearance of a dangerous animal. It can then take evasive action when it catches a whiff of that scent. A child may learn to connect hearing a car pull into the driveway (a conditioned stimulus, or CS) with the arrival of his or her parents (an unconditioned stimulus, or US). Thus, the child may begin to squeal with delight (squealing is a conditioned response, or CR) when the car is heard.

But times can change. The once dangerous animal may no longer be a threat. (What a puppy perceives to be a threat may lose its fearsomeness once the dog matures.) After moving to a new house, the child's parents may commute by means of public transportation. The sound of a car in a nearby driveway may signal a neighbor's, not a parent's, homecoming. When conditioned stimuli (such as the scent of a dog or the sound of a car) are no longer followed by unconditioned stimuli (a dangerous animal, a parent's homecoming), they lose their ability to elicit conditioned responses. In this way the organism adapts to a changing environment.

FIGURE 6.4 LEARNING AND EXTINCTION CURVES

ACTUAL DATA FROM PAVLOV (1927) COMPOSE THE JAGGED LINE, AND THE CURVED LINES ARE IDEALIZED. IN THE ACQUISITION PHASE, A DOG SALIVATES (SHOWS A CR) IN RESPONSE TO A BELL (CS) AFTER A FEW TRIALS IN WHICH THE BELL IS PAIRED WITH MEAT POWDER (THE US). AFTERWARD, THE CR IS EXTINGUISHED IN ABOUT 10 TRIALS DURING WHICH THE CS IS NOT FOLLOWED BY THE US. AFTER A REST PERIOD, THE CR RECOVERS SPONTANEOUSLY. A SECOND SERIES OF EXTINCTION TRIALS LEADS TO MORE RAPID EXTINCTION OF THE CR.

EXTINCTION In classical conditioning, **extinction** is the process by which conditioned stimuli (CSs) lose the ability to elicit conditioned responses (CRs) because the conditioned stimuli (CSs) are no longer associated with unconditioned stimuli (USs). From the cognitive perspective, extinction teaches the organism to change its representation of the environment because the learned or conditioned stimulus (CS) no longer allows it to make predictions.

In experiments on the extinction of conditioned responses (CRs), Pavlov found that repeated presentations of the conditioned stimulus (the CS—in this case, the bell) without the unconditioned stimulus (US—in this case, meat powder) led to extinction of the conditioned response (the CR—salivation in response to the bell). Figure 6.4 shows that a dog that had been conditioned began to salivate (show a conditioned response, or CR) in response to a bell (the conditioned stimulus, or CS) after only a couple of pairings—referred to as *acquisition trials*—of the bell with meat powder. Continued pairings of the stimuli led to increased salivation (measured in number of drops of saliva). After seven or eight trials, salivation leveled off at 11 to 12 drops.

In the next series of experiments, salivation in response to the bell was extinguished through several trials—referred to as *extinction trials*—in which the bell was presented without the meat powder. After about 10 extinction trials, the animal no longer salivated. That is, it no longer showed the learned or conditioned response (salivation in response to the bell) when the bell was rung (the bell is the learned or conditioned stimulus).

What would happen if we were to allow a day or two to pass after we had extinguished salivation (the conditioned response, or CR) in a dog and then again rang the bell (the conditioned stimulus, or CS)? Where would you place your bet? Would the dog salivate or not?

If you bet that the dog would again show the conditioned response (the CR—in this case, salivation in response to the bell), you were correct. Organisms tend to show **spontaneous recovery** of extinguished conditioned responses (CRs) merely as a function of the passage of time. For this reason, the term *extinction* may be a bit misleading. When a species of animal becomes extinct, all the members of that species capable of reproducing have died. The species vanishes. But the experimental extinction of conditioned responses (CRs) does not lead to their permanent eradication. Rather, it seems that they *inhibit* the response. The response remains available for future performance under the "right" conditions.

Consider Figure 6.4 again. When spontaneous recovery of the conditioned response (salivation in response to the bell) does occur, its strength as measured by the number of drops of saliva is weaker than it was at the

---

REFLECT

What is the difference between extinction and forgetting?

EXTINCTION An experimental procedure in which stimuli lose their ability to evoke learned responses because the events that had followed the stimuli no longer occur. (The learned responses are said to be *extinguished*.)

SPONTANEOUS RECOVERY The recurrence of an extinguished response as a function of the passage of time.

end of the series of acquisition trials. A second set of extinction trials also extinguishes the conditioned response (salivation) more rapidly than the first series of trials. Although the second time around the conditioned response (salivation) is weaker at first, pairing the conditioned stimulus (the bell) with the unconditioned stimulus (meat powder) again builds response strength rapidly. That is, the animal will make the connection between the bell and the meat powder more easily the second time around.

Spontaneous recovery, like extinction, is adaptive. What would happen if the child heard no car in the driveway for several months? It could be that the next time a car entered the driveway, the child would associate the sounds with a parent's homecoming (rather than with the arrival of a neighbor). This expectation could be appropriate. After all, *something* had changed when no car entered the nearby driveway for so long. In the wild, a waterhole may contain water for only a couple of months during the year. But it is useful for animals to associate the waterhole with the thirst drive from time to time so that they will return to it at the appropriate time.

As time passes and the seasons change, things sometimes follow circular paths and arrive where they were before. Spontaneous recovery seems to provide a mechanism whereby organisms adapt to situations that recur from time to time.

Generalization and Discrimination

No two things are exactly alike. Traffic lights are hung at slightly different heights, and shades of red and green differ a little. The barking of two dogs differs, and the sound of the same animal differs slightly from one bark to the next. Rustling sounds in the undergrowth differ, but rabbits and deer do well to flee when they perceive any one of many possible rustling sounds. Adaptation requires us to respond similarly (or *generalize*) to stimuli that are equivalent in function and to respond differently to (or *discriminate* between) stimuli that are not. Question: What are the roles of generalization and discrimination in classical conditioning?

GENERALIZATION Pavlov noted that responding to different stimuli as though they are functionally equivalent—*generalizing*—is adaptive for

Generalization at the Crossroads. Chances are that you have never seen these particular traffic lights in this particular setting. Because of generalization, however, we can safely bet that you would know what to do if you were to drive up to them.

animals. **Generalization** is the tendency for a conditioned response to be evoked by stimuli that are similar to the stimulus to which the response was conditioned. In a demonstration of generalization, Pavlov first conditioned a dog to salivate when a circle was presented. During each acquisition trial, the dog was shown a circle (a learned or conditioned stimulus—CS) and then given meat powder (an unlearned or unconditioned stimulus—US). After several trials the dog salivated when presented with the circle alone. Pavlov demonstrated that the dog also displayed the learned or conditioned response (the CR—in this case, salivation) in response to closed geometric figures such as ellipses, pentagons, and even squares. The more closely the figure resembled a circle, the greater the *strength* of the response (as measured by drops of saliva).

DISCRIMINATION Organisms must also learn that (1) many stimuli perceived as being similar are functionally different and (2) they must respond adaptively to each. During the first couple of months of life, babies can discriminate their mother's voice from those of other women. They often stop crying when they hear their mother but not when they hear a stranger.

Pavlov showed that a dog conditioned to salivate in response to circles could be trained *not* to salivate in response to ellipses. The type of conditioning that trains an organism to respond to a narrow range of stimuli (in this case, circular rather than elliptical geometric figures) is termed **discrimination training**. Pavlov trained the dog by presenting it with circles and ellipses but associating the meat powder with circles only. After a while, the dog no longer salivated in response to the ellipses. Instead, it showed **discrimination**: It salivated only in response to circles.

Pavlov found that increasing the difficulty of the discrimination task apparently tormented the dog. After the dog was trained to salivate in response to circles but not ellipses, Pavlov showed it a series of progressively rounder ellipses. Eventually the dog could no longer discriminate the ellipses from circles. The animal then put on an infantile show. It urinated, defecated, barked profusely, and snapped at laboratory personnel.

How do we explain the dog's belligerent behavior? In a classic work written more than half a century ago, titled *Frustration and Aggression,* a group of behaviorally oriented psychologists suggested that frustration induces aggression (Dollard et al., 1939). Why is failure to discriminate circles from ellipses frustrating? For one thing, in such experiments, rewards—such as food—are usually contingent on correct discrimination. That is, if the dog errs, it doesn't get fed. Cognitive theorists, however, propose that organisms are motivated to construct realistic mental maps of the world. They fine-tune these maps as needed so that they fit a changing environment (Rescorla, 1988). In Pavlov's experiment, the dog lost the ability to adjust its mental map of the environment as the ellipses grew more circular. Thus it was frustrated.

Daily living requires appropriate generalization and discrimination. No two hotels are alike, but when we travel from one city to another it is adaptive to expect to stay in a hotel. It is encouraging that a green light in Washington has the same meaning as a green light in Paris. But returning home in the evening requires the ability to discriminate between our home and those of others. And if we could not readily discriminate our spouse from others, we might land in divorce court.

Higher-Order Conditioning

Consider children who learn that when they hear a car in the driveway their parents are about to arrive. It may be the case that a certain TV car-

---

GENERALIZATION In conditioning, the tendency for a conditioned response to be evoked by stimuli that are similar to the stimulus to which the response was conditioned.

DISCRIMINATION TRAINING Teaching an organism to show a learned response in the presence of only one of a series of similar stimuli, accomplished by alternating the stimuli but following only the one stimulus with the unconditioned stimulus.

DISCRIMINATION In conditioning, the tendency for an organism to distinguish between a conditioned stimulus and similar stimuli that do not forecast an unconditioned stimulus.

REFLECT

Can you think of examples of generalization and discrimination in your own life?

toon show starts a few minutes before the car enters the driveway. The TV show can come to evoke the expectation that the parents are arriving by being paired repeatedly with the car's entering the driveway. This is an example of higher-order conditioning. Question: What is higher-order conditioning?

In **higher-order conditioning,** a previously neutral stimulus comes to serve as a learned or conditioned stimulus (CS) after being paired repeatedly with a stimulus that has already become a learned or conditioned stimulus (CS). Pavlov demonstrated higher-order conditioning by first conditioning a dog to salivate in response to a bell (a learned or conditioned stimulus—CS). He then repeatedly paired the shining of a light with the sounding of a bell. After several pairings, shining the light (the higher-order conditioned stimulus) came to evoke the response (salivation) that had been elicited by the bell (the first-order conditioned stimulus).

In another example of higher-order conditioning, a boy may burn himself by touching a hot stove. After this experience, the sight of the stove may evoke fear (or, more technically, serve as a CS for eliciting a fear response). And because hearing the word *stove* may evoke a mental image of the stove, just hearing the word may evoke fear.

Review

SECTION III

After a US–CS association has been learned, repeated presentation of the CS (for example, a bell) without the US (meat) will (21) ex_____ the CR (salivation). Extinguished responses often show (22) _____eous recovery as a function of the passage of time. In stimulus (23) _____ation, organisms show a CR in response to a range of stimuli similar to the CS. In stimulus (24) _____ation, organisms learn to show a CR in response to a more limited range of stimuli by pairing only the limited stimulus with the US. In (25) _____-order conditioning, a previously neutral stimulus comes to serve as a CS after being paired repeatedly with a stimulus that has already been established as a CS.

SECTION IV. APPLICATIONS OF CLASSICAL CONDITIONING

Classical conditioning is a major means by which we learn. It is how stimuli come to serve as signals for other stimuli. It is why, for example, we come to expect that someone will be waiting outside when the doorbell is rung or why we expect a certain friend to appear when we hear a characteristic knock at the door. Question: What are some applications of classical conditioning?

The Bell-and-Pad Treatment for Bed-Wetting

By the age of five or six, children normally awaken in response to the sensation of a full bladder. They inhibit the urge to urinate, which is an automatic or reflexive response to bladder tension, and instead go to the bathroom. But bed-wetters tend not to respond to bladder tension while asleep. They remain asleep and frequently wet their beds.

By means of the bell-and-pad method, children are taught to wake up in response to bladder tension. They sleep on a special sheet or pad that has been placed on the bed. When the child starts to urinate, the water content of the urine causes an electrical circuit in the pad to close. The

HIGHER-ORDER CONDITIONING (1) According to behaviorists, a classical conditioning procedure in which a previously neutral stimulus comes to elicit the response brought forth by a *conditioned* stimulus by being paired repeatedly with that conditioned stimulus. (2) According to cognitive psychologists, the learning of relationships among events, none of which evokes an unlearned response.

closing of the circuit triggers a bell or buzzer, and the child is awakened. (Similar buzzer circuits have been built into training pants as an aid to toilet training.) In terms of classical conditioning, the bell is a US that wakes the child (waking up is the UR). By means of repeated pairings, a stimulus that precedes the bell becomes associated with the bell and also gains the capacity to awaken the child. What is that stimulus? The sensation of a full bladder. In this way, bladder tension (the CS) gains the capacity to awaken the child *even though the child is asleep during the classical conditioning procedure.*

The bell-and-pad method is a superb example of why behaviorists prefer to explain the effects of classical conditioning in terms of the pairing of stimuli and not in terms of what the learner knows. The behaviorist may argue that we cannot assume a sleeping child "knows" that wetting the bed will cause the bell to ring. We can only note that by repeatedly pairing bladder tension with the bell, the child eventually *learns* to wake up in response to bladder tension alone. *Learning* is demonstrated by the change in the child's behavior. One can only speculate on what the child *knows* about the learning process.

The Classical Conditioning of Fear

If you happen across a gentleman nearly 80 years old who cringes at the sight of a fur coat, he may not be concerned about animal rights. Perhaps he is "Little Albert," who was conditioned to fear furry objects before he reached his first birthday.

In 1920 John B. Watson and his future wife, Rosalie Rayner, published a report of their demonstration that emotional reactions can be acquired through classical conditioning. The subject of their demonstration was a lad who has become known as "Little Albert." At the age of 11 months, Albert was not given to ready displays of emotion, but he did enjoy playing with a laboratory rat.

Using a method that many psychologists have criticized as unethical, Watson startled Little Albert by clanging steel bars behind his head whenever the infant played with the rat. After repeated pairings, Albert showed fear of the rat even when the clanging was halted. Albert's fear also generalized to objects that were similar in appearance to the rat, such as a rabbit and the fur collar on a woman's coat.

Flooding and Systematic Desensitization

Two behavior therapy methods for reducing specific fears are based on the classical conditioning principle of extinction (Wolpe & Plaud, 1997). In one, called **flooding,** the client is exposed to the fear-evoking stimulus until the fear response is extinguished. Little Albert, for example, might have been placed in close contact with a rat until his fear had become fully extinguished. In extinction, the learned or conditioned stimulus (the CS—in this case, the rat) is presented repeatedly in the absence of the unlearned or unconditioned stimulus (the US—in this case, the clanging of the steel bars) until the learned or conditioned response (the CR—in this case, fear) is no longer evoked.

Although flooding is usually effective, it is unpleasant. (When you are fearful of rats, being placed in a small room with one is no picnic.) For this reason, behavior therapists frequently prefer to use **systematic desensitization** (see the "Methods of Therapy" chapter), in which the client is gradually exposed to fear-evoking stimuli under circumstances in which he or she remains relaxed. For example, while feeling relaxed, Little Albert

---

REFLECT

Do you find it easier to explain the effects of the bell-and-pad method in terms of conditioning or in terms of what the learner "knows"? Explain.

FLOODING A behavioral fear-reduction technique based on principles of classical conditioning. Fear-evoking stimuli (CSs) are presented continuously in the absence of actual harm so that fear responses (CRs) are extinguished.

SYSTEMATIC DESENSITIZATION A behavioral fear-reduction technique in which a hierarchy of fear-evoking stimuli are presented while the person remains relaxed.

REFLECT

Do you consider Watson and Rayner's experiment with "Little Albert" to be ethical? Why or why not?

might have been given an opportunity to look at photos of rats or to see live rats from a distance before they were brought closer to him. Systematic desensitization, like flooding, is highly effective. It takes longer but it is not as unpleasant.

Counterconditioning

Early in the 20th century, John Watson's protégée Mary Cover Jones (1924) reasoned that if fears could be conditioned by painful experiences, she could *countercondition* them by substituting pleasant experiences. In counterconditioning, a pleasant stimulus is repeatedly paired with a fear-evoking object, thereby counteracting the fear response.

Two-year-old Peter had an intense fear of rabbits. Jones arranged for a rabbit to be gradually brought closer to Peter while he engaged in some of his favorite activities, such as munching on candy and cookies. She did not simply plop the rabbit in Peter's lap, as in flooding. Had she done so, the cookies on the plate, not to mention those already eaten, might have decorated the walls. Instead, she first placed the rabbit in a far corner of the room while Peter munched and crunched. Peter, to be sure, cast a wary eye, but he continued to consume the treat. Gradually the animal was brought closer until eventually, Peter ate treats and touched the rabbit at the same time. Jones theorized that the joy of eating was incompatible with fear and thus counterconditioned it.

Can Chocolate Chip Cookies Countercondition Fears?   In the 1920s Mary Cover Jones helped a boy overcome his fear of rabbits by having him munch on cookies as the animal was brought closer.

✓ Truth or Fiction Revisited

It is true that psychologists helped a young boy overcome fear of rabbits by having him eat cookies while a rabbit was brought progressively closer. The method was pioneered by John Watson and Mary Cover Jones.

Through classical conditioning, we learn to associate stimuli so that a simple, usually passive, response made to one stimulus is then made in response to the other. In the case of Little Albert, clanging noises were associated with a rat, so the rat came to elicit the fear response brought forth by the noise. However, classical conditioning is only one kind of learning that occurs in these situations. After Little Albert acquired his fear of the rat, his voluntary behavior changed. He avoided the rat as a way of reducing his fear. Thus, Little Albert engaged in another kind of learning— *operant conditioning.*

After I had acquired my taste aversion, I stayed away from buttered popcorn. My avoidance can also be explained in terms of operant conditioning. In *operant conditioning*, organisms learn to do things—or *not* to do things—because of the consequences of their behavior. I avoided buttered popcorn in order to prevent nausea. But we also seek fluids when we are thirsty, sex when we are aroused, and an ambient temperature of 68° to 70°F when we feel too hot or too cold. *Classical conditioning focuses on how organisms form anticipations about their environments. Operant conditioning focuses on what they* do *about them.*

REFLECT

Were you ever taught to overcome a fear? If so, how?

SECTION IV **Review**

In the (26) bell-and-_____ method for teaching children to stop bed-wetting, a (27) b_____ is sounded when the child urinates in bed, waking the child. Urine is detected by a (28) _____ placed beneath the sheets, and then the bell is sounded. The bell is paired repeatedly with fullness in the child's (29) _____er. In this way, sensations of a full bladder (the CS) gain the capacity to wake the child just as the bell (the [30] _____ned stimulus) did.

In the case of "Little (31) _____," a young boy was taught to fear rats. John (32) W_____ and Rosalie Rayner clanged steel bars behind Albert's head when he played with a rat.

In the fear-reduction method called (33) _____ing, the client is exposed to the fear-evoking stimulus until the fear response is extinguished. In systematic (34) _____tion, the client is gradually exposed to fear-evoking stimuli under circumstances in which he or she remains relaxed. In the method of (35) _____tioning, a pleasant stimulus is paired repeatedly with a fear-evoking object, in this way counteracting the fear response.

SECTION V. OPERANT CONDITIONING

"What did you do in the war, Daddy?" is a question familiar to many who served during America's conflicts. Some stories involve heroism, others involve the unusual. When it comes to unusual war stories, few top that of Harvard University psychologist B. F. Skinner. For one of Skinner's wartime efforts was "Project Pigeon" (Bjork, 1997). Question: What is the contribution of B. F. Skinner to the psychology of learning?

During World War II Skinner proposed that pigeons be trained to guide missiles to their targets. In their training, the pigeons would be **reinforced** with food pellets for pecking at targets projected onto a screen (see Figure 6.5). Once trained, the pigeons would be placed in missiles. Their pecking at similar targets displayed on a screen would correct the missile's flight path, resulting in a "hit" and a sacrificed pigeon. However, plans for building the necessary missile—for some reason called the *Pelican* and not the *Pigeon*—were scrapped. The pigeon equipment was too bulky, and, Skinner lamented, his suggestion was not taken seriously. Apparently the Defense Department concluded that Project Pigeon was for the birds.

REINFORCE To follow a response with a stimulus that increases the frequency of the response.

FIGURE 6.5
PROJECT PIGEON
DURING WORLD WAR II, B. F. SKINNER SUGGESTED USING OPERANT CONDITIONING TO TRAIN PIGEONS TO GUIDE MISSILES TO THEIR TARGETS. THE PIGEONS WOULD FIRST BE REINFORCED FOR PECKING TARGETS PROJECTED ON A SCREEN. AFTERWARD, IN COMBAT, PECKING THE ON-SCREEN TARGET WOULD KEEP THE MISSILE ON COURSE.

It is true that during World War II a psychologist devised a plan for training pigeons to guide missiles to their targets. That psychologist was B. F. Skinner, and his plan employed principles of operant conditioning.

Project Pigeon may have been scrapped, but the principles of learning that Skinner applied to the project have found wide application. Project Pigeon also affords insight into the inventiveness of B. F. Skinner. Not only did Skinner make contributions to the understanding of learning; we will see that he also made technological innovations such as the "Skinner box" and the cumulative recorder. In operant conditioning, an organism learns to *do* something because of the effects or consequences of that behavior.

Skinner taught pigeons and other animals to engage in **operant behavior,** behavior that operates on, or manipulates, the environment. In classical conditioning, involuntary responses such as salivation or eyeblinks are often conditioned. In operant conditioning, *voluntary* responses such as pecking at a target, pressing a lever, or many of the skills required for playing tennis are acquired, or conditioned. Question: What is operant conditioning?

Operant conditioning is defined as a simple form of learning in which an organism learns to engage in certain behavior because of the effects of that behavior. Phoebe taught me that fetching the ball would be followed by pleasant events, leading me to repeat the behavior.

In operant conditioning, organisms (such as your author!) learn to engage in operant behaviors, also known simply as *operants,* that result in presumably desirable consequences such as food, a hug, an A on a test, attention, or social approval. Some children learn to conform their behavior to social rules to earn the attention and approval of their parents and teachers. Other children, ironically, may learn to "misbehave" because misbehavior also gets attention from other people. In particular, children may learn to be "bad" when their "good" behavior is routinely ignored.

Methods of Operant Conditioning

In his most influential work, *The Behavior of Organisms,* Skinner (1938) made many theoretical and technological innovations. Among them was his focus on discrete behaviors such as lever pressing as the *unit,* or type, of behavior to be studied (Glenn et al., 1992). Other psychologists might focus on how organisms think or "feel." Skinner focused on measurable things that they do. Many psychologists have found these kinds of behavior inconsequential, especially when it comes to explaining and predicting human behavior. But Skinner's supporters point out that focusing on discrete behavior creates the potential for helpful changes. For example, in helping people combat depression, one psychologist might focus on their "feelings." A Skinnerian psychologist would focus on cataloguing (and modifying) the types of things that depressed people actually *do.* Directly modifying depressive behavior might also brighten clients' self-reports about their "feelings of depression."

To study operant behavior efficiently, Skinner devised an animal cage (or "operant chamber") that was dubbed the *Skinner box* by another psychologist. (Skinner himself repeatedly requested that his operant chamber *not* be called a Skinner box. History has thus far failed to honor his wishes, however.[1]) Such a box is shown in Figure 6.6. The cage is ideal for laboratory

OPERANT BEHAVIOR Voluntary responses that are reinforced.

OPERANT CONDITIONING A simple form of learning in which an organism learns to engage in behavior because it is reinforced.

---

[1] Of course, my using the term *Skinner box* does not aid Skinner's cause, either.

FIGURE 6.6

THE EFFECTS OF REINFORCEMENT

ONE OF THE CELEBRITIES OF MODERN PSYCHOLOGY, AN ALBINO LABORATORY RAT, EARNS ITS KEEP IN A SKINNER BOX. THE ANIMAL PRESSES A LEVER BECAUSE OF REINFORCEMENT DELIVERED THROUGH THE FEEDER. THE HABIT STRENGTH OF THIS OPERANT IS THE FREQUENCY OF LEVER PRESSING.

experimentation because experimental conditions (treatments) can be carefully introduced and removed, and the effects on laboratory animals (defined as changes in rates of lever pressing) can be carefully observed.

The rat in Figure 6.6 was deprived of food and placed in a Skinner box with a lever at one end. At first it sniffed its way around the cage and engaged in random behavior. When organisms are behaving in a random manner, responses that have favorable consequences tend to occur more frequently. Responses that do not have favorable consequences tend to be performed less frequently.

The rat's first pressing of the lever was inadvertent. However, because of this action, a food pellet dropped into the cage. The arrival of the food pellet increased the probability that the rat would press the lever again. The pellet thus is said to have served as a *reinforcement* for lever pressing.

Skinner further mechanized his laboratory procedure by making use of a turning drum, or *cumulative recorder,* a tool that had previously been used by physiologists (see Figure 6.7). The cumulative recorder provides a precise measure of operant behavior. The experimenter need not even be present to record the number of correct responses. In the example used, the lever in the Skinner box is connected to the recorder so that the recording pen moves upward with each correct response. The paper moves

FIGURE 6.7

THE CUMULATIVE RECORDER

IN THE CUMULATIVE RECORDER, PAPER MOVES TO THE LEFT WHILE A PEN JERKS UP TO RECORD EACH TARGETED RESPONSE. WHEN THE PEN REACHES THE TOP OF THE PAPER, IT IS AUTOMATICALLY RESET TO THE BOTTOM.

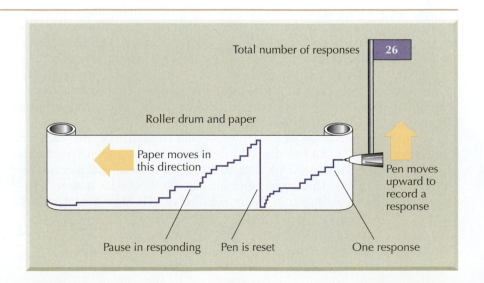

continuously to the left at a slow but regular pace. In the sample record shown in Figure 6.7, lever pressings (which record correct responses) were few and far between at first. But after several reinforced responses, lever pressings became fast and furious. When the rat was no longer hungry, the lever pressing dropped off and then stopped.

THE FIRST "CORRECT" RESPONSE In operant conditioning, it matters little how the first response that is reinforced comes to be made. The organism can happen on it by chance, as in random learning. The organism can also be physically guided to make the response. You may command your dog to "Sit!" and then press its backside down until it is in a sitting position. Finally, you reinforce sitting with food or a pat on the head and a kind word.

Animal trainers use physical guiding or coaxing to bring about the first "correct" response. Can you imagine how long it would take to train your dog if you waited for it to sit or roll over and then seized the opportunity to command it to sit or roll over? Both of you would age significantly in the process.

People, of course, can be verbally guided into desired responses when they are learning tasks such as spelling, adding numbers, or operating a machine. But they need to be informed when they have made the correct response. Knowledge of results often is all the reinforcement people need to learn new skills.

Types of Reinforcers

Any stimulus which increases the probability that responses preceding it will be repeated serves as a reinforcer. Question: What are the various kinds of reinforcers? Reinforcers include food pellets when an organism has been deprived of food, water when it has been deprived of liquid, the opportunity to mate, and the sound of a bell that has previously been associated with eating. Skinner distinguished between positive and negative reinforcers.

POSITIVE AND NEGATIVE REINFORCERS **Positive reinforcers** increase the probability that an operant will occur when they are applied. Food and approval usually serve as positive reinforcers. **Negative reinforcers** increase the probability that an operant will occur when they are *removed* (see Figure 6.8). People often learn to plan ahead so that they need not fear that things will go wrong. In such cases fear acts as a negative reinforcer, because *removal* of fear increases the probability that the behaviors preceding it (such as planning ahead or fleeing a predator) will be repeated.

REFLECT

Have you ever trained an animal like a dog? If so, did you use any principles of conditioning?

POSITIVE REINFORCER A reinforcer that when *presented* increases the frequency of an operant.

NEGATIVE REINFORCER A reinforcer that when *removed* increases the frequency of an operant.

Procedure	Behavior	Consequence	Change in behavior
Use of Positive Reinforcement	Behavior (Studying)	Positive reinforcer (Teacher approval) **is presented** when student studies	Frequency of behavior **increases** (Student studies more)
Use of Negative Reinforcement	Behavior (Studying)	Negative reinforcer (Teacher disapproval) **is removed** when student studies	Frequency of behavior **increases** (Student studies more)

FIGURE 6.8

POSITIVE VERSUS NEGATIVE REINFORCERS

ALL REINFORCERS *INCREASE* THE FREQUENCY OF BEHAVIOR. HOWEVER, NEGATIVE REINFORCERS ARE AVERSIVE STIMULI THAT INCREASE THE FREQUENCY OF BEHAVIOR WHEN THEY ARE *REMOVED*. IN THESE EXAMPLES, TEACHER APPROVAL FUNCTIONS AS A POSITIVE REINFORCER WHEN STUDENTS STUDY HARDER BECAUSE OF IT. TEACHER *DISAPPROVAL* FUNCTIONS AS A NEGATIVE REINFORCER WHEN ITS *REMOVAL* INCREASES THE FREQUENCY OF STUDYING. CAN YOU THINK OF SITUATIONS IN WHICH TEACHER APPROVAL MIGHT FUNCTION AS A NEGATIVE REINFORCER?

Greater reinforcers prompt more rapid learning than do lesser reinforcers. You would probably work much harder for $1,000 than for $10. (If not, get in touch with me—I have some chores that need to be done.) With sufficient reinforcement, operants become *habits*. They have a high probability of recurrence in certain situations.

IMMEDIATE VERSUS DELAYED REINFORCERS Immediate reinforcers are more effective than delayed reinforcers. Therefore, the short-term consequences of behavior often provide more of an incentive than the long-term consequences. Some students socialize when they should be studying because the pleasure of socializing is immediate. Studying may not pay off until the final exam or graduation. (This is why younger students do better with frequent tests.) It is difficult to quit smoking cigarettes because the reinforcement of nicotine is immediate and the health hazards of smoking more distant. Focusing on short-term reinforcement is also connected with careless sexual behavior.

PRIMARY AND SECONDARY REINFORCERS We can also distinguish between primary and secondary, or conditioned, reinforcers. **Primary reinforcers** are effective because of an organism's biological makeup. Food, water, adequate warmth (positive reinforcers), and pain (a negative reinforcer) all serve as primary reinforcers. **Secondary reinforcers** acquire their value through being associated with established reinforcers. For this reason they are also termed **conditioned reinforcers.** We may seek money because we have learned that it may be exchanged for primary reinforcers. Money, attention, social approval—all are conditioned reinforcers in our culture. We may be suspicious of, or not "understand," people who are not interested in money or the approval of others. Part of understanding others lies in being able to predict what they will find reinforcing.

Reinforcers are a key factor in operant conditioning. Let us consider others.

PRIMARY REINFORCER An unlearned reinforcer.

SECONDARY REINFORCER A stimulus that gains reinforcement value through association with established reinforcers.

CONDITIONED REINFORCER Another term for a secondary reinforcer.

Review

SECTION V

B. F. Skinner developed the concept of (36) _____ment as an alternative to the concepts of reward and punishment. Skinner also devised a kind of cage, which has been dubbed the (37) S_____ _____, to study operant behavior in animals. Skinner's use of (38) dis_____ behaviors such as lever pressing and of the (39) _____tive recorder permitted precise measurement of operant behavior, even in the absence of the researcher. A reinforcement is defined as a stimulus that increases the (40) _____cy of an operant.

Positive reinforcers increase the probability that operants will occur when they are (41: Applied or Removed?). Negative reinforcers increase the probability that operants will occur when they are (42: Applied or Removed?). (43) _____ary reinforcers have their value because of the biological makeup of the organism. (44) _____ary reinforcers, such as money and approval, acquire their value through association with established reinforcers. Secondary reinforcers are also referred to as (45) _____ned reinforcers.

SECTION VI. FACTORS IN OPERANT CONDITIONING

Reinforcers are used to strengthen responses. What happens, then, when reinforcement stops? Question: What are the roles of extinction and spontaneous recovery in operant conditioning? In the following sections we consider this question and others.

Extinction and Spontaneous Recovery in Operant Conditioning

In operant conditioning as in classical conditioning, extinction is a process in which stimuli lose the ability to evoke learned responses because the events that followed the stimuli no longer occur. In classical conditioning, however, the "events" that normally follow and confirm the appropriateness of the learned response (that is, the conditioned response) are the unconditioned stimuli. In Pavlov's experiment, for example, the meat powder was the event that followed and confirmed the appropriateness of salivation. In operant conditioning, in contrast, the ensuing events are reinforcers. Thus, in operant conditioning the extinction of learned responses (that is, operants) results from the repeated performance of operant behavior without reinforcement. After a number of trials, the operant behavior is no longer displayed. If you go for a month without mail, you may stop checking the mailbox.

When some time is allowed to pass after the extinction process, an organism usually performs the operant again when placed in a situation in which the operant had been reinforced previously. Such spontaneous recovery of learned responses occurs in operant conditioning as well as in classical conditioning. If the operant is reinforced at this time, it quickly regains its former strength. (Finding a few letters in the mailbox one week may again encourage you to check the mailbox daily.) Spontaneous recovery of extinguished operants suggests they are inhibited or suppressed by the extinction process and not lost permanently.

Reinforcers Versus Rewards and Punishments

Reinforcers are defined as stimuli that increase the frequency of behavior. Question: Why did Skinner make a point of distinguishing between reinforcers on the one hand, and rewards and punishments on the other? Reinforcers are known by their effects, whereas rewards and punishments are known by how they feel. It may be that most reinforcers—food, hugs, having the other person admit to starting the argument, and so on—feel good, or are pleasant events. Yet things that we might assume would feel bad, such as a slap on the hand or disapproval from a teacher, may be reinforcing to some—perhaps because such experiences confirm negative feelings toward teachers.

Rewards, like reinforcers, tend to increase the frequency of behavior, but rewards are defined as pleasant events, things that tend to feel good. Skinner preferred the concept of reinforcement to that of reward because reinforcement does not suggest trying to "get inside the head" of an organism (whether a human or lower animal) to guess what it would find pleasant or unpleasant. A list of reinforcers is arrived at scientifically, *empirically*—that is, by observing what sorts of stimuli increase the frequency of the behavior. However, we should note that some psychologists use the term *reward* synonymously with *positive reinforcement*.

REFLECT

Is extinction within classical conditioning the same as extinction within operant conditioning? Explain.

REWARD A pleasant stimulus that increases the frequency of the behavior it follows.

FIGURE 6.9

NEGATIVE REINFORCERS VERSUS PUNISHMENTS

NEGATIVE REINFORCERS AND PUNISHMENTS BOTH TEND TO BE AVERSIVE STIMULI. HOWEVER, REINFORCERS *INCREASE* THE FREQUENCY OF BEHAVIOR. PUNISHMENTS *DECREASE* THE FREQUENCY OF BEHAVIOR. NEGATIVE REINFORCERS INCREASE THE FREQUENCY OF BEHAVIOR WHEN THEY ARE *REMOVED*. PUNISHMENTS DECREASE OR SUPPRESS THE FREQUENCY OF BEHAVIOR WHEN THEY ARE *APPLIED*. CAN YOU THINK OF SITUATIONS IN WHICH PUNISHING STUDENTS MIGHT HAVE EFFECTS OTHER THAN THOSE DESIRED BY THE TEACHER?

Procedure	Behavior	Consequence	Change in behavior
Use of Negative Reinforcement	Behavior (Studying)	Negative reinforcer (Teacher disapproval) is **removed** when student studies	Frequency of behavior **increases** (Student studies more)
Use of Punishment	Behavior (Talking in class)	Punishment (Detention) is **presented** when student talks in class	Frequency of behavior **decreases** (Student talks less in class)

REFLECT

How does punishment differ from negative reinforcement? Do you believe that parents and teachers should use punishment with children? Explain.

Punishments are defined as aversive events that suppress or decrease the frequency of the behavior they follow (see Figure 6.9). Punishment can rapidly suppress undesirable behavior and may be warranted in "emergencies," such as when a child tries to run into the street.

Question: Why do many psychologists disapprove of punishment? Despite the fact that punishment usually works, many learning theorists agree that punishment often fails to achieve the goals of parents, teachers, and others (Collins, 1995). Consider the following reasons for avoiding the use of punishment:

1. It hurts.

2. Punishment does not in itself suggest an alternative acceptable form of behavior.

3. Punishment tends to suppress undesirable behavior only under circumstances in which its delivery is guaranteed. It does not take children long to learn that they can "get away with murder" with one parent or teacher but not with another.

4. Punished organisms may withdraw from the situation. Severely punished children may run away, cut class, or drop out of school.

5. Punishment can create anger and hostility. Adequate punishment almost always suppresses unwanted behavior—but at what cost? The child may express accumulated feelings of hostility against other children.

6. Punishment may generalize too far. A child who is punished severely for bad table manners may stop eating altogether. Overgeneralization is more likely to occur when children do not know exactly why they are being punished and when they have not been shown alternative acceptable behaviors.

7. Punishment may be modeled as a way of solving problems or coping with stress (Straus & Smith, 1990). We will see that one way children learn is by observing others. Even though children may not immediately perform the behavior they observe, they may perform it later on, even as adults, when their circumstances are similar to those of the model.

8. Finally, children learn responses that are punished. Whether or not children choose to perform punished responses, punishment draws their attention to these responses.

PUNISHMENT An unpleasant stimulus that suppresses the behavior it follows.

It is usually preferable to focus on rewarding children for desirable behavior than on punishing them for unwanted behavior. By ignoring their misbehavior, or by using **time out** from positive reinforcement, we can consistently avoid reinforcing children for misbehavior.

✓ Truth or Fiction Revisited

Actually, punishment does work. Strong punishment generally suppresses the behavior it follows. The issues pertaining to punishment concern its limitations and side effects.

To reward or positively reinforce children for desired behavior takes time and care. It is not enough simply to never use punishment. First, we must pay attention to children when they are behaving well. If we take their desirable behavior for granted and respond to them only when they misbehave, we may be encouraging misbehavior. Second, we must be certain that children are aware of, and capable of performing, desired behavior. It is harmful and fruitless merely to punish children for unwanted behavior. We must also carefully guide them, either physically or verbally, into making the desired responses, and then reward them. We cannot teach children table manners by waiting for them to exhibit proper responses at random and then reinforcing them for their responses. Try holding a reward of ice cream behind your back and waiting for a child to exhibit proper manners. You will have a slippery dining room floor long before the child develops good table manners.

Discriminative Stimuli

B. F. Skinner might not have been able to get his pigeons into the drivers' seats of missiles during the war, but he had no problem training them to respond to traffic lights. Try the following experiment for yourself.

Find a pigeon. Or sit on a park bench, close your eyes, and one will find you. Place it in a Skinner box with a button on the wall. Drop a food pellet into the cage whenever the pigeon pecks the button. (Soon it will learn to peck the button whenever it has not eaten for a while.) Now place a small green light in the cage. Turn it on and off intermittently throughout the day. Reinforce button pecking with food whenever the green light is on, but not when the light is off. It will not take long for this clever city pigeon to learn that it will gain as much by grooming itself or cooing and flapping around as it will by pecking the button when the light is off.

The green light will have become a discriminative stimulus. *Question: What are discriminative stimuli?* **Discriminative stimuli** such as green or red lights act as cues. They provide information about when an operant (in the case of the pigeon, pecking a button) will be reinforced (by a food pellet being dropped into the cage).

Operants that are not reinforced tend to be extinguished. For the pigeon in our experiment, the behavior of pecking the button *when the light is off* is extinguished.

A moment's reflection will suggest many ways in which discriminative stimuli influence our behavior. Isn't it more efficient to answer the telephone when it is ringing? Do you think it is wise to try to get smoochy when your date is blowing smoke in your face or downing a bottle of antacid tablets?

We noted that a pigeon learns to peck a button if food drops into its cage when it does so. What if you want the pigeon to continue to peck the

A Discriminative Stimulus. You might not think that pigeons are very discriminating, yet they readily learn that pecking will not bring food in the presence of a discriminative stimulus such as a red light.

TIME OUT Removal of an organism from a situation in which reinforcement is available when unwanted behavior is shown.

DISCRIMINATIVE STIMULUS In operant conditioning, a stimulus that indicates that reinforcement is available.

button but you're running out of food? Do not despair. (Worse things have happened.) As we see in the following section, you can keep that bird pecking away indefinitely, even as you hold up on most of the food.

Schedules of Reinforcement

In operant conditioning, some responses are maintained by means of **continuous reinforcement.** You probably become warmer every time you put on heavy clothing. You probably become less thirsty every time you drink water. Yet if you have ever watched people throwing money down the maws of slot machines, you know that behavior can also be maintained by means of **partial reinforcement.** Questions: What are the various schedules of reinforcement? How do they affect behavior?

Folklore about gambling is based on solid learning theory. You can hook a person on gambling by fixing the game so as to allow heavy winnings at first. Then you gradually space out the winnings (reinforcements) until gambling is maintained by infrequent winning—or no winning at all. Partial reinforcement schedules can maintain gambling behavior, like other behavior, for a great deal of time, even though it goes unreinforced (Pulley, 1998).

New operants or behaviors are acquired most rapidly through continuous reinforcement or, in some cases, through "one-trial learning" that meets with great reinforcement. People who cannot control their gambling often had big wins at the racetrack or casino or in the lottery in their late teens or early 20s (Greene, 1982). But once the operant has been acquired, it can be maintained by tapering off to a schedule of partial reinforcement.

There are four basic types of reinforcement schedules. They are determined by changing either the *interval* of time that must elapse between correct responses before reinforcement occurs or the *ratio* (number) of responses that must occur before reinforcement is provided. If reinforcement of responses is immediate (zero seconds), the reinforcement schedule is continuous. A larger interval of time, such as 1 or 30 seconds, is one kind of partial-reinforcement schedule. A one-to-one (1:1) ratio of correct responses to reinforcements is also a continuous-reinforcement schedule. A higher ratio such as 2:1 or 5:1 creates another kind of partial-reinforcement schedule.

More specifically, the four basic reinforcement schedules are *fixed-interval, variable-interval, fixed-ratio,* and *variable-ratio* schedules (see Figure 6.10).

CONTINUOUS REINFORCEMENT A schedule of reinforcement in which every correct response is reinforced.

PARTIAL REINFORCEMENT One of several reinforcement schedules in which not every correct response is reinforced.

	Fixed	Variable
Interval	Fixed Interval	Variable Interval
Ratio	Fixed Ratio	Variable Ratio

FIGURE 6.10

SCHEDULES OF REINFORCEMENT   THERE ARE FOUR BASIC REINFORCEMENT SCHEDULES, WHICH ARE CREATED BY CHANGING THE AMOUNT OF TIME THAT ELAPSES BETWEEN PERFORMANCE OF A RESPONSE AND REINFORCEMENT, AND BY CHANGING THE NUMBER OF RESPONSES THAT MUST BE PERFORMED BEFORE REINFORCEMENT IS PROVIDED. THESE ARE FIXED-INTERVAL, VARIABLE-INTERVAL, FIXED-RATIO, AND VARIABLE-RATIO SCHEDULES. WHICH SCHEDULE IS BEST FOR INITIALLY SHAPING A RESPONSE? WHICH SCHEDULE(S) ENABLE RESEARCHERS TO MAINTAIN RESPONSES WITH RELATIVELY LITTLE REINFORCEMENT?

INTERVAL SCHEDULES In a **fixed-interval schedule,** a fixed amount of time—say, a minute—must elapse between the previous and subsequent times when reinforcement for correct responses occurs. With a fixed-interval schedule, an organism's response rate falls off after each reinforcement and then picks up again as the time when reinforcement will occur approaches. For example, in a 1-minute fixed-interval schedule, a rat is reinforced with, say, a food pellet for the first operant—for example, the first pressing of a lever—that occurs after a minute has elapsed. After each reinforcement, the rat's rate of lever pressing slows down, but as the end of the 1-minute interval draws near, lever pressing increases in frequency, as suggested in Figure 6.11. It is as if the rat has learned that it must wait a while before it is reinforced. The resultant record on the cumulative recorder shows a series of characteristic upward-moving waves, or scallops, which are referred to as a *fixed-interval scallop.*

Car dealers use fixed-interval reinforcement schedules when they offer incentives for buying up the remainder of the year's line every summer and fall. In a sense, they are suppressing buying at other times, except for consumers whose current cars are in their death throes or those with little self-control. Similarly, you learn to check your e-mail only at a certain time of day if your correspondent writes at that time each day.

In a **variable-interval schedule,** varying amounts of time are allowed to elapse between occurrences of reinforcement. In a so-called 3-minute variable-interval schedule, a rat would not be reinforced for pressing a lever until an average of 3 minutes had elapsed since the previous reinforcement. However, the intervals could be made to vary, say, from 1 to 5 minutes.

Reinforcement is more unpredictable in a variable-interval schedule. Therefore, the response rate is steadier but lower. If the boss calls us in for a weekly report, we probably work hard to pull things together just before the report is to be given, just as we might cram the night before a weekly quiz. But if we know that the boss might call us in for a report on the progress of a certain project at any time (variable-interval schedule), we are likely to keep things in a state of reasonable readiness at all times. However, our efforts are unlikely to have the intensity they would in a fixed-interval schedule (for example, a weekly report). Similarly, we are less likely to cram for unpredictable pop quizzes than we are to study for regularly scheduled quizzes. But we are likely to do at least some studying on a regular basis. If you receive e-mail from your correspondent at irregular intervals, you are likely to check your e-mail regularly, but with somewhat less eagerness.

RATIO SCHEDULES In a **fixed-ratio schedule,** reinforcement is provided after a fixed number of correct responses have been made. In a **variable-ratio schedule,** reinforcement is provided after a variable number of correct responses have been made. In a 10:1 variable-ratio schedule, the mean number of correct responses that would have to be made before a subsequent correct response would be reinforced is 10, but the ratio of correct responses to reinforcements might be allowed to vary from, say, 1:1 to 20:1 on a random basis.

Fixed- and variable-ratio schedules maintain a high response rate. With a fixed-ratio schedule, it is as if the organism learns that it must make several responses before being reinforced. It then "gets them out of the way" as rapidly as possible. Consider the example of piecework. If

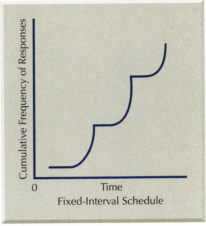

FIGURE 6.11 THE "FIXED-INTERVAL SCALLOP" ORGANISMS WHO ARE REINFORCED ON A FIXED-INTERVAL SCHEDULE TEND TO SLACK OFF RESPONDING AFTER EACH REINFORCEMENT. THE RATE OF RESPONSE PICKS UP AS THEY NEAR THE TIME WHEN REINFORCEMENT WILL BECOME AVAILABLE. THE RESULTS ON THE CUMULATIVE RECORDER LOOK LIKE UPWARD-MOVING WAVES, OR SCALLOPS.

FIXED-INTERVAL SCHEDULE A schedule in which a fixed amount of time must elapse between the previous and subsequent times that reinforcement is available.

VARIABLE-INTERVAL SCHEDULE A schedule in which a variable amount of time must elapse between the previous and subsequent times that reinforcement is available.

FIXED-RATIO SCHEDULE A schedule in which reinforcement is provided after a fixed number of correct responses.

VARIABLE-RATIO SCHEDULE A schedule in which reinforcement is provided after a variable number of correct responses.

a worker must sew five shirts to receive $30, he or she is on a fixed-ratio (5:1) schedule and is likely to sew at a uniformly high rate, although there might be a brief pause after each reinforcement. With a variable-ratio schedule, reinforcement can come at any time. This unpredictability also maintains a high response rate. Slot machines tend to pay off on variable-ratio schedules, and players can be seen popping coins into them and yanking their "arms" with barely a pause. I have seen players who do not even stop to pick up their winnings. Instead, they continue to pop in the coins, whether from their original stack or from the winnings tray.

SHAPING If you are teaching the latest dance craze to people who have never danced, do not wait until they have performed it precisely before telling them they are on the right track. The foxtrot will be back in style before they have learned a thing.

We can teach complex behaviors by **shaping.** Question: How can we use shaping to teach complex behavior patterns? Shaping reinforces progressive steps toward the behavioral goal. At first, for example, it may be wise to smile and say, "Good" when a reluctant newcomer gathers the courage to get out on the dance floor, even if your feet are flattened by his initial clumsiness. If you are teaching someone to drive a car with a standard shift, at first generously reinforce the learner simply for shifting gears without stalling.

But as training proceeds, we come to expect more before we are willing to provide reinforcement. We reinforce **successive approximations** of the goal. If you want to train a rat to climb a ladder, first reinforce it with a food pellet when it turns toward the ladder. Then wait until it approaches the ladder before giving it a pellet. Then do not drop a pellet into the cage until the rat touches the ladder. In this way, the rat will reach the top of the ladder more quickly than if you had waited for the target behavior to occur at random.

✓ Truth or Fiction Revisited

It is true that rats can be trained to climb a ramp, cross a bridge, climb a ladder, pedal a toy car, and do several other tasks—all in sequence. The procedure used to do so is called shaping.

Learning to drive a new standard-shift automobile to a new job also involves a complex sequence of operant behaviors. At first we actively seek out all the discriminative stimuli or landmarks that give us cues for when to turn—signs, buildings, hills, valleys. We also focus on shifting to a lower gear as we slow down so that the car won't stall. After many repetitions, these responses, or chains of behavior, become "habitual" and we need to pay very little attention to them.

Have you ever driven home from school or work and suddenly realized as you got out of your car that you couldn't recall exactly how you had returned home? Your entire trip may seem "lost." Were you in great danger? How could you allow such a thing to happen? Actually, it may be that your responses to the demands of the route and to driving your car had become so habitual that you did not have to focus on them. As you drove, you were able to think about dinner, a problem at work, or the weekend. But if something unusual had occurred on the way, such as hesitation in your engine or a severe rainstorm, you would have devoted as much attention to your driving as was needed to arrive home. Your trip was probably quite safe after all.

REFLECT

A pianist's fingers fly over the keys faster than the player can read notes or even think notes. What kinds of learning are at work in learning to play the piano?

REFLECT

What role does habit play in your life? Do you have "good habits" and "bad habits"? How did they develop?

SHAPING A procedure for teaching complex behaviors that at first reinforces approximations of the target behavior.

SUCCESSIVE APPROXIMATIONS Behaviors that are progressively closer to a target behavior.

Review

SECTION VI

In operant conditioning, repeated performance of a learned response in the absence of reinforcement leads to (46) _____tion of that response. (47) Sp_____ recovery of extinguished responses can occur as a function of the passage of time.

Rewards, like reinforcers, are stimuli that (48: Increase or Decrease?) the frequency of behavior. But rewards differ from reinforcers in that rewards are considered (49) pl_____ stimuli. Punishments are defined as (50) _____sive stimuli that suppress the frequency of behavior. Skinner preferred to use the term *reinforcer* because *reinforcement* is defined in terms of its observable effects on (51) _____ior.

Strong punishment usually (52: Will or Will not?) suppress behavior. However, punishment also has some side effects. One is that punishment (53: Does or Does not?) teach acceptable, alternative behavior. Punishment (54) sup_____ undesired behavior only when its delivery is guaranteed. Punishment also may cause the organism to (55) _____draw from the situation, as in a child's running away from home or cutting classes. Moreover, punishment can create anger and hostility and serve as a (56) m_____ for aggression.

A (57) _____ative stimulus indicates when an operant will be reinforced. A (58) _____-reinforcement schedule leads to the most rapid acquisition of new responses, but operants are maintained most economically through (59) _____tial reinforcement. Partial reinforcement also makes responses more resistant to (60) _____tion.

There are four basic schedules of reinforcement. In a (61) _____-_____ schedule, a specific amount of time must elapse since a previous correct response before reinforcement again becomes available. In a variable-interval schedule, the amount of (62) _____ is allowed to vary. With a (63) _____-interval schedule, an organism's response rate falls off after each reinforcement, then picks up as it nears the time when reinforcement will be dispensed. The resultant record on the cumulative recorder shows a series of upward-moving waves, which are termed (64) fixed-_____ scallops. In a (65) _____-_____ schedule, a fixed number of correct responses must be performed before one is reinforced. In a variable-ratio schedule, the (66) _____ of correct responses that must be performed before reinforcement becomes available is allowed to vary. Payment for piecework is an example of a (67) _____-_____ schedule. The unpredictability of (68: Fixed or Variable?) schedules maintains a high response rate. Slot machines tend to pay off on (69) _____-ratio schedules. In shaping, we reinforce (70) _____sive approximations to the goal.

SECTION VII. APPLICATIONS OF OPERANT CONDITIONING

Operant conditioning, like classical conditioning, is not just an exotic laboratory procedure. We use it every day in our efforts to influence other people. Question: What are some applications of operant conditioning? Parents and peers induce children to acquire so-called gender-appropriate behavior patterns through rewards and punishments. Parents also tend to praise their children for sharing their toys and to punish them for being too aggressive. Peers participate in this **socialization** process by playing with children who are generous and nonaggressive and, often, by avoiding those who are not (Etaugh & Rathus, 1995).

Operant conditioning may also play a role in attitude formation. Parents tend to reward their children for expressing attitudes that coincide with their own and to punish or ignore them for expressing attitudes that deviate. Let us now consider some specific applications of operant conditioning.

Reciting the Pledge. Operant conditioning plays a role in the socialization of children. Parents and teachers usually reward children for expressing attitudes that coincide with their own and punish or ignore them when they express "deviant" attitudes.

SOCIALIZATION Guidance of people into socially desirable behavior by means of verbal messages, the systematic use of rewards and punishments, and other methods of teaching.

Biofeedback Training

Biofeedback training (BFT) is based on principles of operant conditioning. BFT has enabled people and lower animals to learn to control autonomic

REFLECT

Does it seem possible that people can learn to emit particular brain waves? How do learning theorists explain this outcome of learning?

responses in order to attain reinforcement (Miller, 1969). BFT has been an important innovation in the treatment of health-related problems during the past few decades.

Through BFT, organisms can gain control of autonomic functions such as the flow of blood in a finger. They can also learn to improve their control over functions that can be manipulated voluntarily, such as muscle tension. When people receive BFT, reinforcement is given in the form of *information.* Perhaps a sound changes in pitch or frequency of occurrence to signal that they have modified the autonomic function in the desired direction. For example, we can learn to emit alpha waves—the kind of brain wave associated with feelings of relaxation—through feedback from an electroencephalograph (an instrument that measures brain waves). Through the use of other instruments, people have learned to lower their muscle tension, their heart rates, and even their blood pressure.

BFT is also used with people who have lost neuromuscular control of parts of their body as a result of an accident. A "bleep" sound informs them when they have contracted a muscle or sent an impulse down a neural pathway. By concentrating on changing the bleeps, they also gradually regain voluntary control over the damaged function.

Token Economies

Behavior therapists apply operant conditioning in mental hospitals to foster desired responses such as social skills and to extinguish unwanted behaviors such as social withdrawal. In a **token economy,** psychologists give hospital residents or prison inmates tokens such as poker chips as reinforcements for desired behavior. The tokens reinforce the desired behavior because they can be exchanged for time watching television, desserts, and other commodities.

Principles of operant conditioning have also enabled psychologists and educators to develop many beneficial innovations, such as behavior modification in the classroom and programmed learning.

Using Avoidance Learning to Save a Baby's Life

Operant conditioning techniques are sometimes used with children who are too young or distressed to respond to verbal forms of therapy. In one example, reported by Lang and Melamed (1969), a 9-month-old infant vomited regularly within 10 to 15 minutes after eating. Physicians could find no medical basis for the problem, and medical treatments were of no avail. When the case was brought to the attention of Lang and Melamed, the infant weighed only 9 pounds and was in critical condition, being fed by means of a pump.

The psychologists monitored the infant for the first physical indications (local muscle tension) that vomiting was to occur. When the child tensed prior to vomiting, a tone was sounded. The tone was followed by a painful but (presumably) harmless electric shock. After two 1-hour treatment sessions, the infant's muscle tensions ceased in response to the sounding of the tone in the absence of the shock, and vomiting soon ceased altogether. At a 1-year follow-up, the infant was still not vomiting and had gained a reasonable amount of weight.

✓ **Truth or Fiction Revisited**

It is true that psychologists fashioned a method to teach an emaciated 9-month-old infant to stop throwing up. They derived the method from principles of conditioning. Conditioning allowed the psychologists to focus

TOKEN ECONOMY An environmental setting that fosters desired behavior by reinforcing it with tokens (secondary reinforcers) that can be exchanged for other reinforcers.

on what the child actually *did* and not on what the child might know or understand.

How do we use principles of conditioning to explain this remarkable procedure? The psychologists first used classical conditioning. Through repeated pairings, the tone (CS) came to elicit the expectation of electric shock (US). Therefore, the psychologists could use the painful shock sparingly.

Use of punishment explains the infant's halting of vomiting. The electric shock and the tone (which became associated with the shock through classical conditioning) suppressed the local muscle tensions that led to vomiting and, of course, vomiting itself.

This learning occurred at an age long before any sort of verbal intervention could have been understood, and it apparently saved the infant's life. Similar procedures have been used to teach autistic children not to mutilate themselves.

Behavior Modification in the Classroom

Remember that reinforcers are defined as stimuli that increase the frequency of behavior—not as pleasant events. Ironically, adults frequently reinforce undesirable behavior in children by paying attention to them, or punishing them, when they misbehave but ignoring them when they behave in desirable ways. Similarly, teachers who raise their voices when children misbehave may be unintentionally conferring hero status on those pupils in the eyes of their peers (Wentzel, 1994). To the teacher's surprise, some children may go out of their way to earn disapproval.

Teacher preparation and in-service programs show teachers how to use behavior modification to reverse these response patterns. Teachers are taught to pay attention to children when they are behaving appropriately and, when possible, to ignore (that is, avoid reinforcing) misbehavior (Abramowitz & O'Leary, 1991). The younger the child, the more powerful the teacher's attention and approval seem to be.

Among older children and adolescents, peer approval is often a more powerful reinforcer than teacher approval. Peer approval may maintain misbehavior, and ignoring misbehavior may only allow peers to become more disruptive. In such cases it may be necessary to separate troublesome children from less disruptive peers.

Teachers also frequently use time out from positive reinforcement to discourage misbehavior. In this method, children are placed in a drab, restrictive environment for a specified period, usually about 10 minutes, when they behave disruptively. While they are isolated, they cannot earn the attention of peers or teachers, and no reinforcers are present.

Programmed Learning

B. F. Skinner developed an educational method called **programmed learning** that is based on operant conditioning. This method assumes that any complex task involving conceptual learning as well as motor skills can be broken down into a number of small steps. These steps can be shaped individually and then combined in sequence to form the correct behavioral chain.

Programmed learning does not punish errors. Instead, correct responses are reinforced. Every child earns "100," but at her or his own pace. Programmed learning also assumes it is the task of the teacher (or program) to structure the learning experience in such a way that errors will not be made.

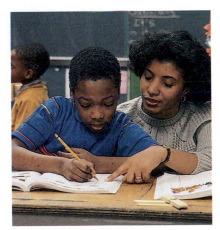

Praise. Praise from the teacher reinforces desirable behavior in most children. Behavior modification in the classroom applies principles of operant conditioning.

PROGRAMMED LEARNING A method of learning in which complex tasks are broken down into simple steps, each of which is reinforced. Errors are not reinforced.

> ✓ **Truth or Fiction Revisited**
>
> *It is not true that we must make mistakes if we are to learn.* The idea that we must make mistakes derives from folklore to the effect that we learn from (bad) experience. However, we also learn from good (positively reinforced) experiences and from the experiences of others.

Review

SECTION VII

Parents and peers socialize children into acquiring (71) "gender-_____iate" behavior patterns through use of rewards and punishments. Parents and peers also tend to (72: Reward or Punish?) children for sharing with others and to (73: Reward or Punish?) them for excessive aggression.

(74) Bio_____ training enables organisms to gain control of autonomic responses in order to attain reinforcement. For example, people can learn to emit alpha waves through feedback from an (75) _____graph. In a (76) _____ economy, psychologists give hospital residents or prison inmates tokens as reinforcements for desired behavior.

Lang and Melamed used (77) _____ance learning to save the life of a baby that repeatedly threw up after eating. When the child tensed prior to vomiting, a tone was sounded and followed by a painful but (presumably) harmless electric shock. Through (78) _____ conditioning, the tone (CS) came to elicit expectation of electric shock (US), so that shock could be used sparingly. Through (79) _____ conditioning the infant learned to suppress the behaviors (muscle tensions) that were followed with aversive stimulation. The aversive stimuli—the shock and the tone—served as (80: Positive or Negative?) reinforcers.

In using behavior (81) _____tion in the classroom, teachers usually reinforce desired behavior and attempt to (82) ex_____ undesired behavior by ignoring it. (83) _____med learning is based on the assumption that learning tasks can be broken down into a number of small steps. Correct performance of each small step is (84) _____ced. Programmed learning (85: Does or Does not?) punish errors.

SECTION VIII. COGNITIVE FACTORS IN LEARNING

Classical and operant conditioning were originally conceived of as relatively simple forms of learning. Much of conditioning's appeal is that it can be said to meet the behaviorist objective of explaining behavior in terms of observable events—in this case, laboratory conditions. Building on this theoretical base, some psychologists have suggested that the most complex human behavior involves the summation of a series of instances of conditioning. However, many psychologists believe that conditioning is too mechanical a process to explain all instances of learned behavior, even in laboratory rats (Weiner, 1991). They turn to cognitive factors to describe and explain additional findings in the psychology of learning. Question: How do we explain what happens during classical conditioning from a cognitive perspective?

In addition to concepts such as *association* and *reinforcement*, cognitive psychologists use concepts such as *mental structures, schemas, templates,* and *information processing.* Cognitive psychologists see people as searching for information, weighing evidence, and making decisions. Let us consider some classic research that points to cognitive factors in learning, as opposed to mechanical associations. These cognitive factors are not necessarily limited to humans—although, of course, people are the only species that can talk about them.

Contingency Theory: What "Really" Happens During Classical Conditioning?

Behaviorists and cognitive psychologists interpret the conditioning process in different ways. Behaviorists explain classical conditioning in terms of the pairing of stimuli. Cognitive psychologists explain classical conditioning in terms of the ways in which stimuli provide information that allows organisms to form and revise mental representations of their environment (Basic Behavioral Science Task Force, 1996).

In classical conditioning experiments with dogs, Robert Rescorla (1967) obtained some results that are difficult to explain without reference to cognitive concepts. Each phase of his work paired a tone (a learned or conditioned stimulus, or CS) with an electric shock (an unlearned or unconditioned stimulus, or US), but in different ways. With one group of animals, the shock was consistently presented after the tone. That is, the unconditioned stimulus followed on the heels of the conditioned stimulus, as in Pavlov's studies. The dogs in this group learned to show a fear response when the tone was presented.

A second group of dogs heard an equal number of tones and received an equal number of electric shocks, but the shock never immediately followed the tone. In other words, the tone and the shock were not paired. Now, from the behaviorist perspective, the dogs should not have learned to associate the tone and the shock because one did not predict the other. Actually, the dogs learned quite a lot: They learned that they had nothing to fear when the tone was sounded! They showed vigilance and fear when the laboratory was quiet—for the shock could apparently come at any time—but they were calm in the presence of the tone.

The third group of dogs also received equal numbers of tones and shocks, but the stimuli were presented at purely random intervals. Occasionally they were paired, but most often they were not. According to Rescorla, behaviorists might argue that intermittent pairing of the tones and shocks should have brought about some learning. Yet it did not. The animals showed no fear in response to the tone. Rescorla suggests that the animals in this group learned nothing because the tones did not allow them to make predictions about electric shock.

Rescorla concluded that contiguity—that is, the co-appearance of two events (the unconditioned stimulus and the conditioned stimulus)—cannot in itself explain classical conditioning. Instead, learning occurs only when the conditioned stimulus (in this case, the tone) provides information about the unconditioned stimulus (in this case, the shock). According to **contingency theory**, learning occurs because a conditioned stimulus indicates that the unconditioned stimulus is likely to follow.

Behaviorists might counter, of course, that for the second group of dogs the *absence* of the tone became the signal for the shock. Shock may be a powerful enough event that the fear response becomes conditioned to the laboratory environment. For the third group of dogs, the shock was as likely to occur in the presence of the neutral stimulus as in its absence. Therefore, many behaviorists would expect no learning to occur.

Latent Learning: Forming Cognitive Maps

I'm all grown up. I know the whole mall.

THE AUTHOR'S DAUGHTER JORDAN AT AGE 7

Many behaviorists argue that organisms acquire only responses, or operants, for which they are reinforced. E. C. Tolman, however, showed that

CONTINGENCY THEORY The view that learning occurs when stimuli provide information about the likelihood of the occurrence of other stimuli.

rats also learn about their environment in the absence of reinforcement. In doing so, he demonstrated that rats must form cognitive maps of their surroundings. Question: What is the evidence that people and lower organisms form cognitive maps of their environments?

Tolman trained some rats to run through mazes for standard food goals. Other rats were permitted to explore the same mazes for several days without food goals or other rewards. After the unrewarded rats had been allowed to explore the mazes for 10 days, food rewards were placed in a box at the far end of the maze. The previously unrewarded rats reached the food box as quickly as the rewarded rats after only one or two reinforced trials (Tolman & Honzik, 1930).

Tolman concluded that rats learned about mazes in which they roamed even when they were unrewarded for doing so. He distinguished between *learning* and *performance*. Rats would acquire a cognitive map of a maze, and even though they would not be motivated to follow an efficient route to the far end, they would learn rapid routes from one end to the other just by roaming about within the maze. Yet this learning might remain hidden, or **latent,** until they were motivated to follow the rapid routes to obtain food goals.

Observational Learning: Monkey See, Monkey May Choose to Do

How many things have you learned from watching other people in real life, in films, and on television? From films and television, you may have gathered vague ideas about how to skydive, ride a surfboard, climb sheer cliffs, run a pattern to catch a touchdown pass in the Super Bowl, and dust for fingerprints, even if you have never tried these activities yourself. Question: How do people learn by observing others?

In his studies of social learning, Albert Bandura and his colleagues have conducted experiments (e.g., Bandura et al., 1963) that show that we can acquire operants by observing the behavior of others. We may need some practice to refine the operants, but we can learn them through observation alone. We may also allow these operants or skills to remain latent. For example, we may not imitate aggressive behavior unless we are provoked and believe that we are more likely to be rewarded than punished for it.

Observational learning may account for most human learning. It occurs when, as children, we watch our parents cook, clean, or repair a broken appliance. Observational learning takes place when we watch teachers solve problems on the blackboard or hear them speak in a foreign language. Observational learning is not mechanically acquired through reinforcement. We can learn through observation without engaging in overt responses at all. It appears sufficient to pay attention to the behavior of others.

In the terminology of observational learning, a person who engages in a response to be imitated is a **model.** When observers see a model being reinforced for displaying an operant, the observers are said to be *vicariously* reinforced. Display of the operant thus becomes more likely for the observer as well as for the model. What happens when the model is *violent?*

The Effects of Media Violence

Much human learning occurs through observation. We learn by observing parents and peers, attending school, reading books, and—in one of the more controversial aspects of modern life—watching media such as TV and films. Nearly all of us have been exposed to television, videotapes, and films in the classroom. Children in day-care centers often watch *Sesame Street.* There are filmed and videotaped versions of great works of literature such as Orson Welles's *Macbeth* or Laurence Olivier's *Hamlet.*

What Are the Effects of Media Violence?   Preschool children in the United States watch TV an average of four hours a day. Schoolchildren spend more hours at the TV set than in the classroom. Is it any wonder that psychologists, educators, and parents express concern about the effects of media violence?

LATENT Hidden or concealed.

OBSERVATIONAL LEARNING The acquisition of knowledge and skills through the observation of others (who are called *models*) rather than by means of direct experience.

MODEL An organism that engages in a response that is then imitated by another organism.

Nearly every school shows films of laboratory experiments. Sometimes we view "canned lectures" by master teachers.

But what about our viewing *outside* the classroom? Television is one of our major sources of informal observational learning. Children are routinely exposed to scenes of murder, beating, and sexual assault—just by turning on the TV set (Huesmann & Miller, 1994; Seppa, 1997). If a child watches 2 to 4 hours of TV a day, she or he will have seen 8,000 murders and another 100,000 acts of violence *by the time she or he has finished elementary school* (DeAngelis, 1993).

Moreover, violence tends to be glamorized on TV. For example, in one cartoon show, superheroes battle villains who are trying to destroy or take over the world. Media violence is often depicted as having only temporary or minimal effects. (How often has Wile E. Coyote fallen from a cliff and been pounded into the ground by a boulder, only to bounce back and pursue the Roadrunner once more?) In the great majority of violent TV shows, there is no remorse, criticism, or penalty for violent behavior (Seppa, 1997). Few TV programs show harmful long-term consequences of aggressive behavior.

Why all this violence? Simple: Violence sells. But does violence do more than sell? Question: What do we know about the effects of media violence? For example, does media violence *cause* real violence? If so, what can parents and educators do to prevent the fictional from spilling over into the real world?

In study after study, children and adults who view violence in the media later show higher levels of aggressive behavior than people who are not exposed to media violence (DeAngelis, 1993). Most psychologists therefore agree that media violence *contributes* to aggression (Huesmann & Miller, 1994; NIMH, 1982).

Consider a number of ways in which depictions of violence make such a contribution:

- *Observational learning.* Children learn from observation (Bandura, 1986). TV violence supplies *models* of aggressive "skills," which children may acquire. In fact, children are more likely to imitate what their parents do than to heed what they say. If adults say they disapprove of aggression but smash furniture or slap each other when frustrated, children are likely to develop the notion that aggression is the way to handle frustration. Classic experiments show that children tend to imitate the aggressive behavior they see in the media (Bandura et al., 1963) (see Figure 6.12). Media violence also provides viewers with aggressive

REFLECT

How much violence have you witnessed on television, in films, and on the streets? How has media violence affected your behavior? How has it affected your attitudes toward violence?

FIGURE 6.12

CLASSIC RESEARCH ON THE IMITATION OF AGGRESSIVE MODELS

ALBERT BANDURA AND HIS COLLEAGUES SHOWED THAT CHILDREN FREQUENTLY IMITATE AGGRESSIVE BEHAVIOR THAT THEY OBSERVE. IN THE TOP ROW, AN ADULT MODEL STRIKES A CLOWN DOLL. THE LOWER ROWS SHOW A BOY AND A GIRL IMITATING THE AGGRESSIVE BEHAVIOR.

FIGURE 6.13

WHAT ARE THE CONNECTIONS BETWEEN MEDIA VIOLENCE AND AGGRESSIVE BEHAVIOR?

DOES MEDIA VIOLENCE LEAD TO AGGRESSION? DOES AGGRESSIVE BEHAVIOR LEAD TO A PREFERENCE FOR VIEWING VIOLENCE? OR DOES A THIRD FACTOR, SUCH AS A PREDISPOSITION TOWARD AGGRESSIVE BEHAVIOR, CONTRIBUTE TO BOTH? MIGHT SUCH A PREDISPOSITION BE IN PART GENETIC?

scripts—that is, ideas about how to behave in situations like those they have observed (Huesmann & Miller, 1994).

- *Disinhibition.* Punishment inhibits behavior. Conversely, media violence may disinhibit aggressive behavior, especially when media characters get away with violence or are rewarded for it.

- *Increased arousal.* Media violence and aggressive video games increase viewers' level of arousal. That is, television "works them up." We are more likely to be aggressive under high levels of arousal.

- *Priming of aggressive thoughts and memories.* Media violence "primes" or arouses aggressive ideas and memories (Berkowitz, 1988).

- *Habituation.* We become "habituated to," or used to, repeated stimuli. Repeated exposure to TV violence may decrease viewers' sensitivity to real violence. If children come to perceive violence as the norm, they may become more tolerant of it and place less value on restraining aggressive urges (Huesmann & Miller, 1994).

✓ **Truth or Fiction Revisited**

Actually, a scientific connection has been established between TV violence and aggression in real life. But does media violence cause aggression? What are the possible relationships between media violence and aggression (see Figure 6.13)?

Although media violence encourages aggression in viewers, it has its greatest impact on the children who are *already* considered the most aggressive by their teachers (Josephson, 1987). There also seems to be a circular relationship between viewing media violence and displaying aggressive behavior (DeAngelis, 1993; Eron, 1982). Yes, TV violence contributes to aggressive behavior, but aggressive children are also more likely to tune in and stay tuned to it.

Aggressive children are frequently rejected by their nonaggressive peers—at least in middle-class culture (Eron, 1982; Patterson, 1993). Aggressive children may watch more television because their peer relationships are less fulfilling and because the high incidence of TV violence tends to confirm their view that aggressive behavior is normal (Eron, 1982). Media violence also interacts with other contributors to violence. For example, parental rejection and use of physical punishment further increase the likelihood of aggression in children (Eron, 1982). A harsh home life may further confirm the TV viewer's vision of the world as a violent place and further encourage reliance on television for companionship.

Cognitive Learning and Diversity: Culture, Ethnicity, and Learning

Do you know where Slovenia is? In at least one respect—how well children learn in school—Slovenia is more "on the map" than the United States.

Learning is essential to competing successfully in the new millennium. The quantity of information that children and adults must absorb is leapfrogging itself every year. According to one psychologist, by the year 2110 it could take half a work-day to catch up on what has happened since one left work the day before (McGuire, 1998). Much of what must be learned is technical—related to math and science. Yet children in the

United States chronically fall behind children in Russia, Japan, and England in most academic subjects. According to the Third International Mathematics and Science Study, 8th-graders in the United States rank 12th in science when compared with children in 41 selected countries (Murray, 1997). Math? Children in the United States rank 14th out of the 15. They lag children in Singapore, the Czech Republic, Slovenia, Hungary, and several other countries. Slovenia thus has more prominence than the United States on the math map.

Why does it matter that Asian and European children learn more about math and science than children in the United States? According to Louis Gerstner, Jr. (1994), the CEO of IBM, one reason is that U.S. businesses are forced to pick up the slack. They spend billions of dollars a year teaching workers to perform tasks and solve problems using skills that they should have learned in school. Many businesses cannot even upgrade their products or streamline their methods because they cannot teach their employees to do the necessary work. As a result, it costs them more money to produce less competitive products. This trend cannot continue if the United States is to maintain its standard of living.

BEYOND THE CLASSROOM According to APA senior scientist Merry Bullock (1997), "Psychological research on learning can provide important input into curriculum development." However, schools have already poured billions of dollars into reworking their curriculums and training their teachers to do a better job. A survey of 20,000 high school students from a variety of ethnic backgrounds suggests that the fault is more likely to lie with parents and teenagers themselves (Steinberg, 1996). Question: What are the roles of parenting, culture, and ethnicity in cognitive learning?

SERIOUSLY DISCONNECTED Consider the factors in learning we have been discussing, for example, reinforcement, punishment, the formation of cognitive maps, and learning by observing others. Some of the most important "others" are parents, especially to young children. Much learning occurs in the home, long before children enter the classroom. Some of this learning is academic—learning about numbers and words and current events. But much of it is attitudinal. Parents can encourage children to learn and reward them for doing so, or they can disconnect themselves from the learning process. According to Steinberg (1996), too many parents have become seriously disconnected from their children's lives. When parents are disconnected from their children's learning, the children often drift.

Consider some of Steinberg's findings:

- Half the high school students surveyed said that it would not upset their parents if they brought home grades of C or worse;

- Forty percent of the students said that their parents never attended school functions;

- One third of the students said that their parents did not know how they were doing in school;

✓ Truth or Fiction Revisited

It is true that one third of high school students in the United States say their parents do not know how well they are doing in school.

- One third said that they spent the day mainly "goofing off" with their friends; and

- Only one third of students said that they even had daily conversations with their parents.

Steinberg and his colleagues (1992, 1996) also looked at the situation from the parents' point of view. Many parents say that they would like to be involved in their children's school and leisure activities but are too busy to do so. By the time the children enter high school, many parents admit that they see education as the school's job, not theirs. In fact, half of the parents surveyed admitted that they do not know who their children's friends are or where their children go (and what they do) after school.

Steinberg makes some recommendations. First and foremost, parents need to be more involved with their teenagers. They should do the following:

- Communicate regularly with their teenagers about school and personal matters;

- Use consistent discipline (as opposed to being dictatorial or too permissive);

- Regularly attend school functions; and

- Consult with their children's teachers and follow through on their suggestions.

REFLECT

Did your peers encourage you to earn good grades in high school? Why or why not?

WHAT ABOUT PEERS? Adolescents' peers also affect how well and how much they learn. Peers provide models who can encourage or discourage learning. In too many schools, it is considered socially wrong for an adolescent to be "too smart." In some schools, peers frown on adolescents doing well at all.

Overall, Steinberg and his colleagues (1996) found that some teenagers encourage others to do well in school. However, by and large, peers have a harmful effect on grades. For example, over half the students surveyed said that they did not talk about schoolwork with their friends. In fact, nearly 1 in 5 said he or she did not do as well as possible for fear of earning the disapproval of peers!

ETHNIC BACKGROUND Of many possible factors, including family income and family structure, Steinberg and his colleagues (1996) conclude that ethnic background is a key factor in teenagers' attitudes toward schooling and grades. For example, consider the following:

- Many White students reported just trying to get by in school;

- African and Hispanic American students recognized the value of good grades and college education, but generally did not fear getting poor grades; and

- Asian American students spent twice as much time doing their homework as students in other ethnic groups and were most fearful of getting poor grades.

Steinberg concludes that schools are likely to continue to fight an uphill battle unless parents become more connected with their children's performance and peers become more supportive of students who do well in school.

SECTION VIII Review

According to contingency theory, the (86) con_____ presentation of stimuli—that is, the co-appearance of the US and the CS—does not explain classical conditioning. Instead, learning occurs only when the CS provides (87) _____tion about the US. According to (88) con_____ theory, learning occurs because a CS indicates that the US stimulus is likely to follow.

E. C. Tolman's work with rats suggests that they develop (89) _____tive maps of the environment. Tolman's work also suggests that operant conditioning works by teaching organisms where (90) rein_____ may be found, not by mechanically increasing the frequency of operants. Tolman refers to learning without necessarily performing as (91) l_____ learning.

Albert (92) B_____ and other social-learning theorists have shown that people can also learn by observing others. In observational learning, it is not necessary that people emit (93) _____nses of their own, nor that their behavior be (94) _____orced, in order for learning to take place. Learners may then choose to (95) p_____ the behaviors they have observed when "the time is ripe"—that is, when they believe that they will be rewarded.

Media violence contributes to violent behavior by supplying (96) _____els for aggressive skills, (97) _____bition of aggressive impulses, priming aggressive thoughts, increasing arousal, and habituating observers to violence.

Steinberg's research finds that about (98) _____ percent of high school students say their parents do not know how well they are doing in school. By and large, peers appear to have a (99: Helpful or Harmful?) effect on grades. Asian Americans make up the ethnic group who are (100: Most or Least?) fearful of getting poor grades.

It would be of little use to discuss how we learn if we were not capable of remembering what we learn from second to second, from day to day, or in many cases for a lifetime. In the next chapter we turn our attention to the subject of memory. And following that, we see how learning is intertwined with thinking and intelligence.

STUDY GUIDE

SUMMARY

1. **What is learning?** Learning is the process by which experience leads to modified representations of the environment and relatively permanent changes in behavior.

2. **What is classical conditioning?** Classical conditioning is a simple form of associative learning in which a previously neutral stimulus (the conditioned stimulus, or CS) comes to elicit the response evoked by a second stimulus (the unconditioned stimulus, or US) as a result of repeatedly being paired with the second stimulus.

3. **What is the contribution of Ivan Pavlov to the psychology of learning?** The Russian physiologist Ivan Pavlov happened upon conditioning by chance, as he was studying salivation in laboratory dogs. Pavlov discovered that reflexes can be learned, or *conditioned*, through association.

4. **What are the various types of classical conditioning?** In delayed conditioning, the CS is presented before the US. In the most efficient delayed conditioning procedure, the CS is presented about 0.5 second before the US. Other classical conditioning procedures include trace conditioning, simultaneous conditioning, and backward conditioning, in which the US is presented first.

5. **What are taste aversions? Why are they of special interest to psychologists?** Taste aversions are examples of classical conditioning in which organisms learn that a food is noxious on the basis of nauseating experience. Taste aversions are of special interest because learning may occur on the basis of a single association and because the unconditioned stimulus (in this case, nausea) can occur hours after the conditioned stimulus (in this case, the flavor of food).

6. **What are the roles of extinction and spontaneous recovery in classical conditioning?** Extinction and spontaneous recovery help organisms adapt to environmental changes. After a US-CS association has been learned, for example, repeated presentation of the CS (for example, a bell) without the US (meat powder) extinguishes the CR (salivation). Extinguished responses may show spontaneous recovery as a function of the time that has elapsed since extinction occurred.

7. **What are the roles of generalization and discrimination in classical conditioning?** Generalization and discrimination are also adaptive. Generalization helps organisms adapt to new events by responding to a range of stimuli similar to the CS. In discrimination, organisms learn to show a CR in response to a more limited range of stimuli by pairing only the limited stimulus with the US.

8. **What is higher-order conditioning?** In higher-order conditioning, a previously neutral stimulus comes to serve as a CS after being paired repeatedly with a stimulus that has already become a CS.

9. **What are some applications of classical conditioning?** Some applications of classical conditioning include the bell-and-pad method for treating bed-wetting, the conditioning of emotional responses (as in the case of "Little Albert"), extinction of fears through methods such as flooding or systematic desensitization, and counterconditioning of fears.

10. **What is the contribution of B. F. Skinner to the psychology of learning?** Skinner developed the concept of reinforcement, encouraged the study of discrete behaviors such as lever pressing by rats, and innovated many techniques for studying operant conditioning such as the "Skinner box" and the cumulative recorder.

11. **What is operant conditioning?** Operant conditioning is a simple form of learning in which organisms learn to engage in behavior that is reinforced. Reinforced responses occur with greater frequency.

12. **What are the various kinds of reinforcers?** These include positive, negative, primary, and secondary reinforcers. Positive reinforcers increase the probability that operants will occur when they are applied. Negative reinforcers increase the probability that operants will occur when they are removed. Primary reinforcers have their value because of the organism's biological makeup. Secondary reinforcers such as money and approval acquire their value through association with established reinforcers.

13. **What are the roles of extinction and spontaneous recovery in operant conditioning?** Extinction and spontaneous recovery are also adaptive in operant conditioning. In operant conditioning, learned responses are extinguished as a result of repeated performance in the absence of reinforcement. (Why continue to engage in a response that goes unreinforced?) And as in classical conditioning, spontaneous recovery occurs as a function of the passage of time, which is adaptive because things may return to the way they were.

14. **Why did Skinner make a point of distinguishing between reinforcers on the one hand, and rewards and punishments on the other?** Rewards and punishments are defined, respectively, as pleasant and aversive events that affect behavior. Skinner preferred the concept of *reinforcement* because its definition does not rely on getting inside the head of the organism. Instead, lists of reinforcers are obtained empirically, by observing their effects on behavior.

15. **Why do many psychologists disapprove of punishment?** Many psychologists recommend not using punishment because it hurts, it does not suggest acceptable behavior, it may create feelings of hostility, it may only suppress behavior in the specific situation in which it is used, it may generalize to the suppression of wide varieties of behavior, and it may suggest that recipients punish others as a way of coping with stress.

16. **What are discriminative stimuli?** Discriminative stimuli (such as a green light) indicate when operants (such as pecking a button) will be reinforced (as with food).

17. **What are the various schedules of reinforcement? How do they affect behavior?** Continuous reinforcement leads to the most rapid acquisition of new responses, but operants are maintained most economically through partial reinforcement. There are four basic schedules of reinforcement. In a fixed-interval schedule, a specific amount of time must elapse after a previous correct response before reinforcement again becomes available. In a variable-interval schedule, the amount of time is allowed to vary. In a fixed-ratio schedule, a fixed number of correct responses must be performed before one is reinforced. In a variable-ratio schedule, this number is allowed to vary. Ratio schedules maintain high response rates.

18. **How can we use shaping to teach complex behavior patterns?** In shaping, successive approximations of the target response are reinforced, leading to the performance of a complex sequence of behaviors.

19. **What are some applications of operant conditioning?** Applications of operant conditioning include socialization, biofeedback training, the token economy, avoidance learning, behavior modification, and programmed learning.

20. **How do we explain what happens during classical conditioning from a cognitive perspective?** According to contingency theory, organisms learn associations between stimuli only when stimuli provide new information about each other. From this perspective, classical conditioning does not occur mechanically but because it provides information.

21. **What is the evidence that people and lower organisms form cognitive maps of their environments?** Some evidence is derived from Tolman's research on latent learning. He demonstrated that rats can learn—that is, they can modify their cognitive map of the environment—in the absence of reinforcement.

22. **How do people learn by observing others?** Bandura has shown that people can learn to do things simply by observing others; it is not necessary that they emit responses that are reinforced in order to learn. Learners may then choose to perform the behaviors they have observed "when the time is ripe"—that is, when they believe that the learned behavior is appropriate or is likely to be rewarded.

23. **What do we know about the effects of media violence?** Media violence can contribute to violent behavior by providing violent models, disinhibiting aggressive impulses, increasing the viewer's level of arousal, priming aggressive thoughts and memories, and habituating the viewer to violence.

24. **What are the roles of parenting, culture, and ethnicity in cognitive learning?** Parents who are highly involved in their children's schooling encourage learning. Peers often have negative effects on high school learning, either by not encouraging good grades or by actively discouraging them. There are cultural and ethnic differences in study habits and in fear of obtaining poor grades.

EXERCISE

CLASSICAL VERSUS OPERANT CONDITIONING

Following are a number of terms that are used in discussions of conditioning. Some terms apply to classical conditioning, some to operant conditioning, and some to both. For each term, place a checkmark in the appropriate blank space, or spaces, to show the type(s) of learning to which it applies.

CLASSICAL CONDITIONING	OPERANT CONDITIONING	TERM
_____	_____	1. Discriminative stimulus
_____	_____	2. Unconditioned stimulus
_____	_____	3. Conditioned response
_____	_____	4. Extinction
_____	_____	5. Reinforcer
_____	_____	6. Backward conditioning
_____	_____	7. Generalization
_____	_____	8. Biofeedback training
_____	_____	9. Bell-and-pad method
_____	_____	10. Contingency theory
_____	_____	11. Delayed conditioning
_____	_____	12. Stimulus
_____	_____	13. Neutral stimulus
_____	_____	14. Skinner box
_____	_____	15. Operant
_____	_____	16. Spontaneous recovery
_____	_____	17. Shaping
_____	_____	18. Cumulative recorder
_____	_____	19. Conditional reflex
_____	_____	20. Variable-ratio schedule
_____	_____	21. Response
_____	_____	22. Higher-order conditioning
_____	_____	23. Successive approximations
_____	_____	24. Programmed learning
_____	_____	25. Rewards and punishments
_____	_____	26. Trace conditioning
_____	_____	27. Simultaneous conditioning

B R I D G I N G   T H E   G A P

LANGUAGE AND CULTURE

ambient (277)   *in circulation, moving around, surrounding*

to arrive at an idea (283)   *to deduce*

aversion (263)   *hatred, dislike*

to be back in style (288)   *to become popular again*

to be on the right track (288)   *to be doing the right thing to accomplish the goal*

bloated (269)   *filled up as with water or food*

by chance (281)   *accidentally*

my business (270)   *my concern*

canned lectures (295)   *lessons by a professor that have been prepared, practiced, and often recorded on video*

cause (279)   *(here) purpose, what was desired by the person*

chamber (279)   *room, enclosed space*

chore (282)   *small task*

circular relationship (296)   *causal relationship (one thing causes the other to happen)*

to clang (266)   *to make a sound like a bell*

to clink (266)   *to make a light metallic sound*

commodity (290)   *merchandise, consumer goods*

contiguous (270)   *connected, happening one after the other*

crossroads (273)   *place where two roads from different directions meet (here, a mind-set of having to make decisions of which direction to go)*

to crunch (277)   *to eat a dry, crisp food and make noise in the eating*

dance craze (288)   *newly popular dance*

in its death throes (287)   *nearly at the end of its usefulness*

discrete (279)   *individual, separate*

to down (liquid) (285)   *to drink fast*

drab (291)   *colorless, bleak*

driver's seat (285)   *position of control*

drum (280)   *(see the picture on p. 280)*

to dust for fingerprints (294)   *(for police) to use a special powder to find the fingerprints of a thief*

emaciated (263)   *very thin, because of starvation*

ensuing (283)   *following*

eradication (272)   *disappearance*

to err (274)   *to make a mistake*

evasive action (271)   *action designed to avoid*

to evoke (275)   *to call out, to elicit*

to face something (270)   *to tolerate*

to fine-tune (274)   *to change to make better*

to fix a game (286)   *to arrange for a specific outcome*

folklore (286)   *popular belief*

to be for the birds (278)   *to be useless*

foxtrot (288)   *a kind of dance step that was popular in the 1930s and 1940s*

to frown on (298)   *to disapprove*

a full bladder (276)   *needing to urinate*

to get away with murder (284)   *to do whatever they want without punishment*

to get inside (someone's) head (283)   *to understand the thought processes or motivations (of someone)*

to be given to (276)   *to be likely to*

to goof off (298)   *to be silly, to waste time and resources being silly*

to guide missiles (278)   *to steer a bomb in a specific direction*

to happen across someone (276)   *to chance to meet someone*

to happen on something (281)   *to meet accidentally*

to hatch (265)   *to emerge (as animals) from an egg*

my head spun (269)   *I felt dizzy*

heavy winnings (286)   *large amounts of money won*

to heed (265)   *to listen to advice*

hindrance (267)   *obstruction, blockage*

to hold up on (286)   *to withhold*

to hook someone on (286)   *to cause someone to become addicted to*

hoopla (263)   *loud publicity*

a hug (279)   *(here) a reward*

inconsequential (279)   *not important*

jagged (272)   *rough and uneven*

to jerk (280)   *to pull or snap in movement*

key factor (282)   *information that guides one to the truth of a topic*

to land (in a divorce court) (274)   *to end up in a situation that would result in a permanent break-up*

to leapfrog itself (296)   *(here) to increase by itself*

to linger (269)   *to stay a long time*

maturation (265)   *process of growing up*

maws (286)   *open mouths, opening*

to munch on (277)   *to snack on, to eat informally*

myriad (265)   *countless, a great number*

nauseating (263)   *sickening*

no picnic (276)   *(an) unpleasant experience*

organisms (265)   *living creatures*

orienting reflex (268)   *tendency to look toward the source of a sound*

passage (272)   *passing*

peer (289)   *someone of the same age group*

peril (265)   *danger*

to pick up the slack (297)   *to compensate for others' deficiency*

a pop quiz (287)   *a surprise test in a class*

to pull things together (287)   *to assemble the parts as a final stage*

to put on a thinking cap (267)   *to concentrate one's thoughts on a specific topic*

to register (265)   *to record in memory*

in retrospect (270)   *in review of the time that it happened*

to rise to the challenge (269)   *to gather one's strength for a difficult task, to accept a dare*

to roam (265)   *to move without specific direction, to travel*

scent (271)   *smell, odor*

to scrap plans (278)   *to stop working on plans, to throw plans away*

to sever (271)   *to cut*

to shape (a behavior or response) (286)   *to train, to teach*

to get smoochy (285)   *to attempt to kiss*

to snap at someone (274)   *to make an action as if to bite*

to space out the winnings (286)   *to make a greater interval between winnings*

to stick to the straight and narrow (265)   *to follow the rules exactly*

to streamline (297)   *to make more efficient*

to surf the Net (265)   *to search on the Internet*

to taper off (286)   *to decease gradually*

targeted (268)   *focuses on, those under scrutiny*

the thirst drive (273)   *instinct to get a drink for survival*

to throw up (263)   *to vomit*

to torment (274)   *to tease, to cause suffering*

touchdown pass (294)   *a throw of the football that leads to a score*

twigs (270)   *tiny branches on a tree*

a two-way mirror (267)   *A mirror that one can see through from behind it*

uncalled for (267)   *unexpected*

undergrowth (273)   *weeds and grass below taller plants like trees*

to upgrade (297)   *to improve the quality*

an uphill battle (298)   *a great challenge, a difficult thing to do*

to warrant (284)   *to require, to need*

waterhole (273)   *pool, source of water*

whiff (271)   *smell, a trace of a smell*

1. Ivan Pavlov is known for his contribution to the understanding of
   - (a) biofeedback training,
   - (b) observational learning,
   - (c) classical conditioning,
   - (d) contingency theory.

2. Which school of psychologists would define learning as a change in behavior that results from experience?
   - (a) Behaviorists,
   - (b) Cognitive psychologists,
   - (c) Gestalt psychologists,
   - (d) Psychoanalysts.

3. In Pavlov's experiments, salivation in response to meat was a(n)
   - (a) conditioned response,
   - (b) conditioned stimulus,
   - (c) unconditioned response,
   - (d) unconditioned stimulus.

4. In using the bell-and-pad method for overcoming bed-wetting, the sensations of a full bladder are the
   - (a) conditioned response,
   - (b) conditioned stimulus,
   - (c) unconditioned response,
   - (d) unconditioned stimulus.

5. Extinction in classical conditioning occurs because of repeated presentation of the
   - (a) conditioned response in the absence of the conditioned stimulus,
   - (b) unconditioned response in the absence of the unconditioned stimulus,
   - (c) conditioned stimulus in the absence of the unconditioned stimulus,
   - (d) unconditioned stimulus in the absence of the conditioned stimulus.

6. In higher-order conditioning, a previously neutral stimulus comes to serve as a conditioned stimulus after being paired with a(n)
   - (a) conditioned response,
   - (b) conditioned stimulus,
   - (c) unconditioned response,
   - (d) unconditioned stimulus.

7. Little Albert learned to fear rats as a result of
   - (a) the clanging of steel bars in the presence of a rat,
   - (b) observing a rat attack another animal,
   - (c) being informed that rats carry certain harmful diseases,
   - (d) being bitten by a rat.

8. Who originated the use of the cumulative recorder?
   - (a) Ivan Pavlov,
   - (b) John Watson,
   - (c) B. F. Skinner,
   - (d) Robert Rescorla.

9. People have learned how to emit alpha waves by means of
   - (a) biofeedback training,
   - (b) the token economy,
   - (c) flooding,
   - (d) counterconditioning.

10. Pain is an example of a
    - (a) primary positive reinforcer,
    - (b) primary negative reinforcer,
    - (c) secondary positive reinforcer,
    - (d) secondary negative reinforcer.

11. Which of the following statements about punishment is *false*?
    - (a) Children learn responses that are punished,
    - (b) Punishment usually increases the frequency of undesired behavior,
    - (c) Punished children may withdraw from the situation,
    - (d) Punishment may be modeled as a way of solving problems.

12. With a _____-_____ schedule, an organism's response rate falls off after each reinforcement.
    - (a) fixed-interval,
    - (b) fixed-ratio,
    - (c) variable-interval,
    - (d) variable-ratio.

13. According to the text, the best way for teachers to use behavior modification in the classroom is to
    - (a) pay attention to children when they are misbehaving,
    - (b) pay attention to children when they are behaving correctly,
    - (c) punish children when they are misbehaving,
    - (d) reward children when they are misbehaving.

14. Project Pigeon relied on principles of
    - (a) classical conditioning,
    - (b) observational learning,
    - (c) operant conditioning,
    - (d) latent learning.

15. For observational learning to take place,
    (a) stimuli must be paired repeatedly,
    (b) a stimulus must elicit a response,
    (c) an organism must be reinforced,
    (d) an organism must observe events.

16. The text defines a stimulus as
    (a) a change in the environment,
    (b) a condition that evokes a response from an organism,
    (c) any change that is learned,
    (d) an environmental condition that evokes a response from an organism.

17. A parent encourages a reluctant child to enter the water of a swimming pool by hugging and petting the child and murmuring, "It's really nice," and, "You'll love it." This method is most similar to the behavior-therapy technique of
    (a) extinction,
    (b) systematic desensitization,
    (c) counterconditioning,
    (d) flooding.

18. According to contingency theory, learning occurs because
    (a) a conditioned stimulus indicates that the unconditioned stimulus is likely to follow,
    (b) stimuli are presented contiguously,
    (c) of the reinforcement of random behavior,
    (d) organisms observe the outcomes of the behaviors of other organisms and act when they expect that the reinforcement contingencies will be rewarding.

19. Which of the following ethnic groups is most likely to fear getting poor grades in high school?
    (a) African Americans,
    (b) Asian Americans,
    (c) Hispanic Americans,
    (d) European Americans.

20. The learning of taste aversions differs from other kinds of classical conditioning in that
    (a) often only one pairing of the stimuli is required,
    (b) learning rapidly decays,
    (c) taste aversions are arbitrary, whereas other kinds of conditioning are adaptive,
    (d) there is no reward for learning.

1. What is learning?

2. What is classical conditioning?

3. What is the contribution of Ivan Pavlov to the psychology of learning?

4. What are the various types of classical conditioning?

5. What are taste aversions? Why are they of special interest to psychologists?

6. What are the roles of extinction and spontaneous recovery in classical conditioning?

7. What are the roles of generalization and discrimination in classical conditioning?

8. What is higher-order conditioning?

9. What are some applications of classical conditioning?

10. What is the contribution of B. F. Skinner to the psychology of learning?

11. What is operant conditioning?

_____
_____
_____
_____
_____

12. What are the various kinds of reinforcers?

_____
_____
_____
_____
_____

13. What are the roles of extinction and spontaneous recovery in operant conditioning?

_____
_____
_____
_____
_____

14. Why did Skinner make a point of distinguishing between reinforcers on the one hand, and rewards and punishments on the other?

_____
_____
_____
_____

15. Why do many psychologists disapprove of punishment?

_____
_____
_____
_____
_____

16. What are discriminative stimuli?

_____
_____
_____
_____
_____

17. What are the various schedules of reinforcement? How do they affect behavior?

_____
_____
_____
_____
_____

18. How can we use shaping to teach complex behavior patterns?

_____
_____
_____
_____

19. What are some applications of operant conditioning?

_____
_____
_____
_____
_____

20. How do we explain what happens during classical conditioning from a cognitive perspective?

_____
_____
_____
_____

21. What is the evidence that people and lower organisms form cognitive maps of their environments?

_____
_____
_____
_____
_____

22. How do people learn by observing others?

_____
_____
_____
_____
_____

23. What do we know about the effects of media violence?

_____
_____
_____
_____

24. What are the roles of parenting, culture, and ethnicity in cognitive learning?

_____
_____
_____
_____

ANSWERS TO SECTION REVIEWS

1. Behavior
2. Represent
3. Learning
4. Neutral
5. Salivary
6. Reflex
7. Stimuli
8. Environmental
9. Association
10. Conditional
11. Conditioned responses
12. Unconditioned
13. Conditioned
14. Delayed
15. Simultaneous
16. Prior to
17. Backward
18. Only one
19. Contiguously
20. Adaptive
21. Extinguish
22. Spontaneous
23. Generalization
24. Discrimination
25. Higher

26. Pad
27. Bell
28. Pad
29. Bladder
30. Unconditioned
31. Albert
32. Watson
33. Flooding
34. Desensitization
35. Counter-conditioning
36. Reinforcement
37. Skinner box
38. Discrete
39. Cumulative
40. Frequency
41. Applied
42. Removed
43. Primary
44. Secondary
45. Conditioned
46. Extinction
47. Spontaneous
48. Increase
49. Pleasant
50. Aversive

51. Behavior
52. Will
53. Does not
54. Suppresses
55. Withdraw
56. Model
57. Discriminative
58. Continuous
59. Partial
60. Extinction
61. Fixed-interval
62. Time
63. Fixed
64. Interval
65. Fixed-ratio
66. Number
67. Fixed-ratio
68. Variable
69. Variable
70. Successive
71. Appropriate
72. Reward
73. Punish
74. Biofeedback
75. Electroencephalograph

76. Token
77. Avoidance
78. Classical
79. Operant
80. Negative
81. Modification
82. Extinguish
83. Programmed
84. Reinforced
85. Does not
86. Contiguous
87. Information
88. Contingency
89. Cognitive
90. Reinforcement or Reinforcers
91. Latent
92. Bandura
93. Responses
94. Reinforced
95. Perform
96. Models
97. Disinhibition
98. 33
99. Harmful
100. Most

ANSWERS TO EXERCISE

1. O	8. O	15. O	22. C
2. C	9. C	16. C, O	23. O
3. C	10. C	17. O	24. O
4. C, O	11. C	18. O	25. O
5. O	12. C, O	19. C	26. C
6. C	13. C	20. O	27. C
7. C, O	14. O	21. C, O	

ANSWERS TO QUIZ

1. C	6. B	11. B	16. D
2. A	7. A	12. A	17. C
3. C	8. C	13. B	18. A
4. B	9. A	14. C	19. B
5. C	10. B	15. D	20. A

MEMORY

7

TRUTH OR FICTION?

T F ✓✓✓✓✓✓✓✓✓✓✓✓✓

☐ ☐ Everyone who can see has a photographic memory.

☐ ☐ It may be easier for you to recall the name of your first-grade teacher than the name of someone you just met at a party.

☐ ☐ All of our experiences are permanently imprinted on the brain, so the proper stimulus can cause us to remember them exactly.

☐ ☐ There is no practical limit to the amount of information you can store in your memory.

☐ ☐ Learning must be meaningful if we are to remember it.

☐ ☐ We can remember the important events that take place during the first two years of life.

☐ ☐ You can use tricks to improve your memory.

This chapter, "Memory," covers the following:

My oldest daughter Jill was talking about how she had run into a friend from elementary school and they had had a splendid time recalling the goofy things they did during their school years. Her sister Allyn, age 6 at the time, was not to be outdone. "I can remember when I was born," she put in.

The family's ears perked up. Being a psychologist, I knew exactly what to say. "You can remember when you were born?" I said.

"Oh, yes," she insisted. "Mommy was there."

So far she could not be faulted. I cheered her on, and she related a remarkably detailed account of how it had been snowing in the wee hours of a bitter December morning when Mommy had to go to the hospital. You see, she said, her memory was so good that she could also summon up what it had been like *before* she was born. She wove a wonderful patchwork quilt, integrating details we had given her with her own recollections of the events surrounding the delivery of her younger sister, Jordan. All in all, she seemed quite satisfied that she had pieced together a faithful portrait of her arrival on the world stage.

Later in the chapter, we will see that children usually cannot recall events that occurred in their first two years, much less those of their first hours. But Allyn's tale dramatized the way we "remember" many of the things that have happened to us. When it comes to long-term memories, truth can take a back seat to drama and embellishment. Very often, our memories are like the bride's apparel—there's something old, something new, something borrowed, and from time to time something blue.

Memory is what this chapter is about. Without memory, there is no past. Without memory, experience is trivial and learning is lost. Shortly we will see what psychologists have learned about the ways in which we remember things. First, try to meet the following challenges to your memory.

FIVE CHALLENGES TO MEMORY

Before we go any further, let's test your memory. If you want to participate, find four sheets of blank paper and number them 1 through 4. Then follow these directions:

1. Following are 10 letters. Look at them for 15 seconds. Later in the chapter, I will ask you if you can write them on sheet number 1. (No cheating! Don't do it now.)

THUNSTOFAM

2. Look at these nine figures for 30 seconds. Then try to draw them in the proper sequence on sheet number 2. (Yes, right after you've finished looking at them. We'll talk about your drawings later.)

3. Okay, here's another list of letters, 17 this time. Look at the list for 60 seconds and then see whether you can reproduce it on sheet number 3. (I'm being generous this time—a full minute.)

GMC-BSI-BMA-TTC-IAF-BI

4. Which of these pennies is an accurate reproduction of the Lincoln penny you see every day? This time there's nothing to draw on another sheet; just circle or put a checkmark by the penny that you think resembles the ones you throw in the back of the drawer.

5. Examine the following drawings for 1 minute. Then copy the names of the figures on sheet number 4. When you're finished, just keep reading. Soon I'll be asking you to draw those figures.

eyeglasses   hourglass   seven   gun

EPISODIC MEMORY Personal memories of specific events.

SEMANTIC MEMORY General knowledge as opposed to episodic memory.

PROCEDURAL MEMORY Knowledge of ways of doing things; skill memory.

SECTION I. THREE KINDS OF MEMORY: THE "ESP" OF MEMORY

There are different kinds of memories. Endel Tulving (1985, 1991) classifies memories according to the kind of information they hold: episodic, semantic, and procedural. Return to Allyn's "recollection." Of course Allyn could not really remember her own birth. That is, she could not recall the particular event or *episode* in which she had participated. As we see in our discussion of types of memory, she was reporting more her general knowledge than an actual episode.

Episodic Memory

Question: What is meant by episodic memory? **Episodic memories** are memories of the events that happen to a person or take place in his or her presence (Wheeler et al., 1997). Your memories of what you ate for breakfast and of what your professor said in class this afternoon are examples of episodic memory.

What Allyn did recount is more accurately characterized as generalized knowledge than as an episodic memory of her birth. From listening to her parents and from her experience with the events of her sister Jordan's birth, she had learned much about what happens during childbirth. She erroneously thought that this knowledge represented her own birth.

Semantic Memory

Question: What is meant by semantic memory? General knowledge is referred to as **semantic memory.** *Semantics* concerns meanings. Allyn was reporting her understanding of the meaning of childbirth rather than an episode in her own life. You can "remember" that the United States has 50 states without visiting them and personally adding them up. You "remember" who authored *Hamlet*, although you were not looking over Shakespeare's shoulder as he did so. These, too, are examples of semantic memory.

Your future recollection that there are three kinds of memory is more likely to be semantic than episodic. In other words, you are more likely to "know" there are three types of memory than to recall the date on which you learned about them, where you were and how you were sitting, and whether you were also thinking about dinner at the time. We tend to use the phrase "I remember . . ." when we are referring to episodic memories, as in "I *remember* the blizzard of 1998." But we are more likely to say, "I know . . ." in reference to semantic memories, as in "I *know* about—" (or, "I heard about—") "—the blizzard of 1898." Put it another way: You may *remember* that you wrote your mother, but you *know* that Shakespeare wrote *Hamlet*.

Procedural Memory

The third type of memory is **procedural memory,** also referred to as *skill memory.* Question: What is meant by procedural memory? Procedural memory means knowing how to do things. You have learned and now "remember" how to ride a bicycle, how to swim or swing a bat, how to type, how to turn on the lights, and how to drive a car. Procedural memories tend to persist even when we have not used them for many years.

REFLECT

What are the earliest episodes you can remember? Is your memory for them accurate? Can you be sure?

REFLECT

You remember that classes have professors, and you remember your professor's name (I hope). Which of these is an episodic memory? Which is a semantic memory? Can you explain the difference between the two?

REFLECT

You remember how to walk or use a pen, but do you remember *how* or *when* you learned these things? Will you ever forget how to walk, ride a bicycle, or use a pen or pencil? What kinds of "memories" are these?

Do you think it would help for a person to have ESP (which usually stands for "extrasensory perception") to remember the three types of memory? That is, E = episodic, S = semantic, and P = procedural. As we proceed, we will see that a good deal of information about memory comes in threes. We will also learn more about **mnemonic devices,** or tricks for retaining memories, such as ESP. By the way, is your use of ESP to help remember the kinds of memory an instance of episodic, semantic, or procedural memory?

Before proceeding to the next section, why don't you turn to the piece of paper on which you wrote the names of the four figures—that is, sheet number 4—and draw them from memory as exactly as you can. Do not look back at the drawings in the book. Now hold on to your drawings. We'll talk about them a bit later.

Review

SECTION I

Memories of the events that happen to a person or take place in the person's presence are referred to as (1) _____dic memory. Generalized knowledge is referred to as (2) _____tic memory. We tend to use the phrase "I remember . . ." when we are referring to (3) _____dic memories, but we are more likely to say, "I know . . ." in reference to (4) _____tic memories. (5) Pro_____ memory involves knowledge of how to do things. Procedural memory is also referred to as (6) _____ memory.

SECTION II. THREE PROCESSES OF MEMORY: MEMORY AS INFORMATION PROCESSING

Both psychologists and computer scientists speak of processing information. Think of using a computer to write a term paper. Once the system is up and operating, you begin to enter information. You place information in the computer's memory by typing letters and numbers on a keyboard. If you were to do some major surgery on your computer (which I am often tempted to do) and open up its memory, however, you would not find these letters inside it. This is because the computer is programmed to *change* the letters—that is, the information you have typed—into a form that can be placed in its electronic memory. Similarly, when we perceive information, we must convert it into a form that can be remembered if we are to place it in our memory.

Encoding

Information about the outside world reaches our senses in the form of physical and chemical stimuli. The first stage of information processing is changing information so that we can place it in memory: **encoding.** Question: What is the role of encoding in memory? When we encode information, we convert it into psychological formats that can be represented mentally. To do so, we commonly use visual, auditory, and semantic codes.

Let us illustrate the uses of coding by referring to the list of letters you first saw in the section on challenges to memory. Try to write the letters on sheet number 1. Go on, take a minute and then come back.

REFLECT

What procedural memories do you have? Do you remember how to type on a keyboard or how to drive a car? Can you provide other examples?

Procedural Memory. Memories of how to ride a bicycle, how to type, how to turn the lights on and off, and how to drive a car are procedural memories. Procedural memories tend to persist even when we do not use them for many years. Here Jean Piaget, the cognitive-developmental theorist, demonstrates that we may never forget how to ride a bicycle.

MNEMONIC DEVICES Systems for remembering in which items are related to easily recalled sets of symbols such as acronyms, phrases, or jingles.

ENCODING Modifying information so that it can be placed in memory. The first stage of information processing.

Okay, now: If you had used a **visual code** to try to remember the list, you would have mentally represented it as a picture. That is, you would have maintained—or attempted to maintain—a mental image of the letters. Some artists and art historians seem to maintain marvelous visual mental representations of works of art. This enables them to quickly recognize whether a work is authentic.

You may also have decided to read the list of letters to yourself—that is, to silently say them in sequence: "t," "h," "u," and so on. By so doing, you would have been using an **acoustic code,** or representing the stimuli as a sequence of sounds. You may also have read the list as a three-syllable word, "thun-sto-fam." This is an acoustic code, but it also involves the "meaning" of the letters, in the sense that you are interpreting the list as a word. This approach has elements of a semantic code.

Semantic codes represent stimuli in terms of their meaning. Our 10 letters were meaningless in and of themselves. However, they can also serve as an acronym—a term made up of the first letters of a phrase—for the familiar phrase "THe UNited STates OF AMerica." This observation lends them meaning.

Storage

The second memory process is **storage.** Question: What is the role of storage in memory? Storage means maintaining information over time. If you were given the task of storing the list of letters—that is, told to remember it—how would you attempt to place it in storage? One way would be by **maintenance rehearsal**—by mentally repeating the list, or saying it to yourself. Our awareness of the functioning of our memory, referred to by psychologists as **metamemory,** becomes more sophisticated as we develop.

You could also have condensed the amount of information you were rehearsing by reading the list as a three-syllable word; that is, you could have rehearsed three syllables (said "thun-sto-fam" over and over again) rather than 10 letters. In either case, repetition would have been the key to memory. (We talk more about such condensing, or "chunking," very soon.)

However, you could also encode the list of letters by relating it to something that you already know. This kind of coding is referred to as **elaborative rehearsal.** That is, you are elaborating or extending the semantic meaning of the letters you are trying to remember. For example, did you recognize that the list of 10 letters is an acronym for "The United States of America"? (That is, you take the first two letters of each of the words in the phrase and string them together to make up the 10 letters of THUNSTOFAM.) If you had recognized this, storage of the list of letters might have been almost instantaneous, and it would probably have been permanent.

Retrieval

The third memory process is **retrieval.** Question: What is the role of retrieval in memory? The retrieval of stored information means locating it and returning it to consciousness. With well-known information such as our names and occupations, retrieval is effortless and, for all practical purposes, immediate. But when we are trying to remember massive quantities of information, or information that is not perfectly understood, retrieval can be tedious and not always successful. It is easiest to retrieve information stored in a computer by using the name of the file. Similarly, retrieval of information from our memories requires knowledge of the proper cues.

VISUAL CODE Mental representation of information as a picture.

ACOUSTIC CODE Mental representation of information as a sequence of sounds.

SEMANTIC CODE Mental representation of information according to its meaning.

STORAGE Maintenance of information over time. The second stage of information processing.

MAINTENANCE REHEARSAL Mental repetition of information in order to keep it in memory.

METAMEMORY Self-awareness of the ways in which memory functions, allowing the person to encode, store, and retrieve information effectively.

ELABORATIVE REHEARSAL A method for increasing retention of new information by relating it to information that is well known.

RETRIEVAL The location of stored information and its return to consciousness. The third stage of information processing.

If you had encoded THUNSTOFAM as a three-syllable word, your retrieval strategy would involve recollection of the word and rules for decoding. In other words, you would say the "word" *thun-sto-fam* and then decode it by spelling it out. You might err in that "thun" sounds like "thumb" and "sto" could also be spelled "stow." However, using the semantic code, or recognition of the acronym for "The United States of America," could lead to flawless recollection.

I stuck out my neck by predicting that you would quickly and perhaps permanently store the list of letters if you recognized them as an acronym. Here, too, there would be recollection (of the name of our country) and rules for decoding. That is, to "remember" the 10 letters, you would have to envision the phrase ("The United States of America") and read off the first two letters of each word. Because using this semantic code is more complex than simply seeing the entire list (using a visual code), it may take a while to recall (actually, to reconstruct) the list of 10 letters. But by using the phrase, you are likely to remember the list of letters permanently.

Now, what if you were not able to remember the list of 10 letters? What would have gone wrong? In terms of the three processes of memory, it could be that you had (1) not encoded the list in a useful way, (2) not entered the encoded information into storage, or (3) stored the information but lacked the proper cues for remembering it—such as the phrase "The United States of America" or the rule for decoding the phrase.

By now you may have noticed that I have discussed three kinds of memory and three processes of memory, but I have not yet *defined* memory. No apologies—we were not ready for a definition yet. Now that we have explored some basic concepts, let us give it a try: **Memory** is the processes by which information is encoded, stored, and retrieved.

Review

SECTION II

Changing information so that we can place it in memory is called (7) _____ding. Encoding is the first stage of (8) _____tion processing. When we (9) en_____ information, we convert it into psychological formats that can be mentally represented. To do so, we commonly use (10) _____ual, (11) _____ory, and (12) _____tic codes. A visual code mentally (13) _____sents information as a picture. An acoustic code represents information as a sequence of (14) _____nds. Semantic codes represent stimuli in terms of their (15) _____ing.

The second process of memory is (16) s_____, or the maintaining of information over time. One way of storing information is by (17) _____nance rehearsal, or by mentally repeating it ("saying it to yourself"). Another is by (18) _____tive rehearsal, in which we relate new information to things we already know.

The third memory process is (19) _____val, or locating stored information and returning it to consciousness. Retrieval of information from memory requires knowledge of the proper (20) _____s. We can define memory as the processes by which information is encoded, stored, and (21) _____ved.

MEMORY The processes by which information is encoded, stored, and retrieved.

SECTION III. THREE STAGES OF MEMORY: MAKING *SENSE* OF THE *SHORT* AND THE *LONG* OF IT

William James (1890) was intrigued by the fact that some memories are unreliable, "going in one ear and out the other," whereas others could be recalled for a lifetime. He wrote:

> The stream of thought flows on, but most of its elements fall into the bottomless pit of oblivion. Of some, no element survives the instant of their passage. Of others, it is confined to a few moments, hours, or days. Others, again, leave vestiges which are indestructible, and by means of which they may be recalled as long as life endures.

Yes, the world is a constant display of sights and sounds and other sources of sensory stimulation, but only some of these things are remembered. James was correct in observing that we remember various "elements" of thought for different lengths of time, and many we do not remember at all. Psychologists Richard Atkinson and Richard Shiffrin (1968) suggested a model for how some stimuli are lost immediately, others held briefly, and still others for a lifetime. Question: What is the Atkinson-Shiffrin model of memory? Atkinson and Shiffrin proposed that there are three stages of memory and suggested that the progress of information through these stages determines whether (and how long) it is retained (see Figure 7.1). These stages are *sensory memory, short-term memory (STM),* and *long-term memory (LTM).*

There is a saying that when you cover a topic completely, you are talking about "the long and short of it." In the case of the stages of memory, we could say that we are trying to "make *sense* of the *short* and the *long* of it."

FIGURE 7.1

THREE STAGES OF MEMORY THE ATKINSON-SHIFFRIN MODEL PROPOSES THAT THERE ARE THREE DISTINCT STAGES OF MEMORY. SENSORY INFORMATION IMPACTS UPON THE REGISTERS OF SENSORY MEMORY, WHERE MEMORY TRACES ARE HELD BRIEFLY BEFORE DECAYING. IF WE ATTEND TO THE INFORMATION, MUCH OF IT IS TRANSFERRED TO SHORT-TERM MEMORY (STM). INFORMATION IN STM MAY DECAY OR BE DISPLACED IF IT IS NOT TRANSFERRED TO LONG-TERM MEMORY (LTM). WE CAN USE REHEARSAL OR ELABORATIVE STRATEGIES TO TRANSFER MEMORIES TO LTM. IF INFORMATION IN LTM IS ORGANIZED POORLY, OR IF WE CANNOT FIND CUES TO RETRIEVE IT, IT MAY BE LOST.

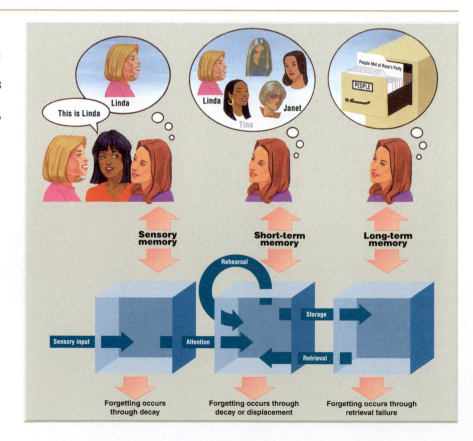

Sensory Memory

William James also wrote about the stream of thought, or consciousness:

> Consciousness . . . does not appear to itself chopped up in bits. A "river" or a "stream" are the metaphors by which it is most naturally described. In talking of it hereafter, let us call it the stream of thought, of consciousness, or of subjective life.

When we look at a visual stimulus, our impressions may seem fluid enough. Actually, however, they consist of a series of eye fixations referred to as **saccadic eye movements.** These movements jump from one point to another about four times each second. Yet the visual sensations seem continuous, or streamlike, because of **sensory memory.** Sensory memory is the type or stage of memory that is first encountered by a stimulus. Although sensory memory holds impressions briefly, it is long enough so that a series of perceptions seem to be connected. Question: How does sensory memory function?

To explain the functioning of sensory memory, let us return to our list of letters: THUNSTOFAM. If the list were flashed on a screen for a fraction of a second, the visual impression, or **memory trace,** of the stimulus would also last for only a fraction of a second afterward. Psychologists speak of the memory trace of the list as being held in a visual **sensory register.**

If the letters had been flashed on a screen for, say, 1/10 of a second, your ability to remember them on the basis of sensory memory alone would be limited. Your memory would be based on a single eye fixation, and the trace of the image would vanish before a single second had passed. At the turn of the century, psychologist William McDougall (1904) engaged in research in which he showed people 1 to 12 letters arranged in rows—just long enough to allow a single eye fixation. Under these conditions, people could typically remember only 4 or 5 letters. Thus recollection of THUNSTOFAM, a list of 10 letters arranged in a single row, would probably depend on whether one had encoded it so that it could be processed further.

George Sperling (1960) modified McDougall's experimental method and showed that there is a difference between what people can see and what they can report. McDougall had used a *whole-report procedure,* in which people were asked to report every letter they saw in the array. Sperling used a modified *partial-report procedure,* in which people were asked to report the contents of one of three rows of letters. In a typical procedure, Sperling flashed three rows of letters like the following on a screen for 50 milliseconds (1/20 of a second):

$$\begin{matrix} A & G & R & E \\ V & L & S & B \\ N & K & B & T \end{matrix}$$

Using the whole-report procedure, people could report an average of 4 letters from the entire display (one out of three). But if immediately after presenting the display Sperling pointed an arrow at a row he wanted viewers to report, they usually reported most of the letters in the row successfully.

If Sperling presented six letters arrayed in two rows, people could usually report either row without error. If people were flashed three rows of 4 letters each—a total of 12—they reported correctly an average of 3 of 4 letters in the designated row, suggesting that about 9 of the 12 letters had been perceived.

SACCADIC EYE MOVEMENT The rapid jumps made by a person's eyes as they fixate on different points.

SENSORY MEMORY The type or stage of memory first encountered by a stimulus. Sensory memory holds impressions briefly, but long enough so that series of perceptions are psychologically continuous.

MEMORY TRACE An assumed change in the nervous system that reflects the impression made by a stimulus. Memory traces are said to be "held" in sensory registers.

SENSORY REGISTER A system of memory that holds information briefly, but long enough so that it can be processed further. There may be a sensory register for every sense.

Sperling found that the amount of time that elapsed before indicating the row to be reported was crucial. If he delayed pointing the arrow for a few fractions of a second after presenting the letters, people were much less successful in reporting the letters in the target row. If he allowed a full second to elapse, the arrow did not aid recall at all. From these data, Sperling concluded that the memory trace of visual stimuli *decays* within a second in the visual sensory register (see Figure 7.1). With a single eye fixation, people can *see* most of a display of 12 letters clearly, as shown by their ability to immediately read off most of the letters in a designated row. Yet as the fractions of a single second are elapsing, the memory trace of the letters is fading. By the time a second has elapsed, the trace has vanished.

ICONIC MEMORY Psychologists believe we possess a sensory register for each one of our senses. The mental representations of visual stimuli are referred to as **icons**. The sensory register that holds icons is labeled **iconic memory**. Iconic memory is one kind of sensory memory. Iconic memories are accurate, photographic memories. So those of us who mentally represent visual stimuli have "photographic memories." However, iconic memories are very brief. What most of us normally think of as a photographic memory—the ability to retain exact mental representations of visual stimuli over long periods of time—is technically referred to as *eidetic imagery*.

EIDETIC IMAGERY A few individuals retain visual stimuli, or icons, in their sensory memories for remarkably long periods of time. About 5% of children can look at a detailed picture, turn away, and several minutes later recall the particulars of the picture with exceptional clarity—as if they were still seeing it. This extraordinary visual sensory memory is referred to as **eidetic imagery** (Haber, 1980). This ability declines with age, however, all but disappearing by adolescence.

Figure 7.2 provides an example of a test of eidetic imagery. Children are asked to look at the first drawing in the series for 20 to 30 seconds, after which it is removed. The children then continue to gaze at a neutral background. Several minutes later the drawing in the center is placed on the backdrop. When asked what they see, many report "a face." A face would be seen only if the children had retained a clear image of the first picture and fused it with the second so that they are, in effect, perceiving the third picture in Figure 7.2 (Haber, 1980).

Eidetic imagery appears remarkably clear and detailed. It seems to be essentially a perceptual phenomenon in which encoding or rehearsal is

ICON A mental representation of a visual stimulus that is held briefly in sensory memory.

ICONIC MEMORY The sensory register that briefly holds mental representations of visual stimuli.

EIDETIC IMAGERY The maintenance of detailed visual memories over several minutes.

FIGURE 7.2
A RESEARCH STRATEGY FOR ASSESSING EIDETIC IMAGERY CHILDREN LOOK AT THE FIRST DRAWING FOR 20 TO 30 SECONDS, AFTER WHICH IT IS REMOVED. NEXT, THE CHILDREN LOOK AT A NEUTRAL BACKGROUND FOR SEVERAL MINUTES. THEY ARE THEN SHOWN THE SECOND DRAWING. WHEN ASKED WHAT THEY SEE, CHILDREN WITH THE CAPACITY FOR EIDETIC IMAGERY REPORT A FACE. THE FACE IS SEEN ONLY BY CHILDREN WHO RETAIN THE FIRST IMAGE AND FUSE IT WITH THE SECOND, THUS PERCEIVING THE THIRD IMAGE.

not necessary to continue to "see" a visual stimulus. Although eidetic imagery is rare, iconic memory, as we see in the following section, universally transforms visual perceptions into smoothly unfolding impressions of the world.

✓ Truth or Fiction Revisited

It is true that everyone who can see has a photographic memory. People who can see have an *iconic* memory, which is what is meant technically by a photographic memory. However, only a few people have *eidetic imagery,* which refers to the ability to continue to "see" the memory trace of a visual stimulus in the visual sensory register long after the trace would have decayed in most people.

ICONIC MEMORY AND SACCADIC EYE MOVEMENTS Iconic memory smooths out the bumps in the visual ride. Saccadic eye movements occur about four times every second. Iconic memory, however, holds icons for up to a second. As a consequence, the flow of visual information seems smooth and continuous. Your impression that the words you are reading flow across the page, rather than jumping across in spurts, is a product of your iconic memory. Similarly, motion pictures present 16 to 22 separate frames, or still images, each second. Iconic memory allows you to perceive the imagery in the film as being seamless (G. R. Loftus, 1983).

ECHOIC MEMORY Mental representations of sounds, or auditory stimuli, are called **echoes.** The sensory register that holds echoes is referred to as **echoic memory.**

The memory traces of auditory stimuli (that is, echoes) can last for several seconds, many times longer than the traces of visual stimuli (icons). The difference in the duration of traces is probably based on biological differences between the eye and the ear. This difference is one of the reasons that acoustic codes aid in the retention of information that has been presented visually—or why saying the letters or syllables of THUNSTOFAM makes the list easier to remember.

Yet echoes, like icons, fade with time. If they are to be retained, we must pay attention to them. By selectively attending to certain stimuli, we sort them out from the background noise. For example, in studies on the development of patterns of processing information, young children have been shown photographs of rooms full of toys and then been asked to recall as many of the toys as they can. One such study found that 2-year-old boys are more likely to attend to and remember toys such as cars, puzzles, and trains. Two-year-old girls are more likely to attend to and remember dolls, dishes, and teddy bears (Renninger & Wozniak, 1985). Even by this early age, the things that children attend to frequently fall into stereotypical patterns.

Short-Term Memory

If you focus on a stimulus in the sensory register, you tend to retain it in **short-term memory**—also referred to as **working memory**—for a minute or so after the trace of the stimulus decays (Baddeley, 1994). Question: How does short-term memory function? As one researcher describes it, "Working memory is the mental glue that links a thought through time from its beginning to its end" (Goldman-Rakic, 1995). When you are given a phone number by directory assistance and write it down or immediately dial the number, you are retaining the number in your short-term

ECHO A mental representation of an auditory stimulus (sound) that is held briefly in sensory memory.

ECHOIC MEMORY The sensory register that briefly holds mental representations of auditory stimuli.

SHORT-TERM MEMORY The type or stage of memory that can hold information for up to a minute or so after the trace of the stimulus decays. Also called *working memory.*

WORKING MEMORY Same as *short-term memory.*

Echoic Memory. The mental representations of auditory stimuli are called echoes, and the sensory register that holds echoes is referred to as echoic memory. By encoding visual information as echoes and rehearsing the echoes, we commit them to memory.

REFLECT

Why are girls more likely than boys to remember the dolls and teddy bears they see in a picture?

REFLECT

What do you do to try to remember names and telephone numbers? What could you do to improve your memory of them?

memory. When you are told the name of someone at a party and then use that name immediately in addressing that person, you are retaining the name in short-term memory. In short-term memory, the image tends to fade significantly after 10 to 12 seconds if it is not repeated or rehearsed. It is possible to focus on maintaining a visual image in the short-term memory, but it is more common to encode visual stimuli as sounds, or auditory stimuli. Then the sounds can be rehearsed, or repeated.

Most of us know that one way of retaining information in short-term memory—and possibly storing it permanently—is to rehearse it repeatedly. When directory assistance tells me a phone number, I usually rehearse it continuously while I am dialing it or running around frantically searching for a pencil and a scrap of paper. The more times we rehearse information, the more likely we are to remember it.

KEEPING THUNSTOFAM IN SHORT-TERM MEMORY Let us now return to the task of remembering the first list of letters in the challenges to memory at the beginning of the chapter. If you had encoded the letters as the three-syllable word THUN-STO-FAM, you would probably have recalled them by mentally rehearsing (saying to yourself) the three-syllable "word" and then spelling it out from the sounds. A few minutes later, if someone asked whether the letters had been uppercase (THUNSTOFAM) or lowercase (thunstofam), you might not have been able to answer with confidence. You used an acoustic code to help recall the list, and uppercase and lowercase letters sound alike.

Because it can be pronounced, THUNSTOFAM is not too difficult to retain in short-term memory. But what if the list of letters had been TBXLFNTSDK? This list of letters cannot be pronounced as it is. You would have to find a complex acronym to code these letters, and do so within a fraction of a second—most likely an impossible task. To aid recall, you would probably choose to try to repeat the letters rapidly—to read each one as many times as possible before the memory trace fades. You might visualize each letter as you say it and try to get back to it (that is, to run through the entire list) before it decays.

Let us assume that you encoded the letters as sounds and then rehearsed the sounds. When asked to report the list, you might mistakenly say T-V-X-L-F-N-T-S-T-K. This would be an understandable error because the incorrect *V* and *T* sounds are similar, respectively, to the correct *B* and *D* sounds.

THE SERIAL-POSITION EFFECT If asked to recall the list of letters TBXLFNTSDK, you would also be likely to recall the first and last letters in the series, *T* and *K*, more accurately than the others. Question: Why are we most likely to remember the first and last items in a list? The tendency to recall the first and last items in a series is known as the **serial-position effect**. This effect may occur because we pay more attention to the first and last stimuli in a series. They serve as the visual or auditory boundaries for the other stimuli. It may also be that the first items are likely to be rehearsed more frequently (repeated more times) than other items. The last items are likely to have been rehearsed most recently and hence are most likely to be retained in short-term memory.

According to cognitive psychologists, the tendency to recall the initial items in a list is referred to as the **primacy effect**. Social psychologists have also noted a powerful primacy effect in our formation of impressions of other people. In other words, first impressions tend to last. The tendency to recall the last items in a list is referred to as the **recency effect**. If

SERIAL-POSITION EFFECT The tendency to recall more accurately the first and last items in a series.

PRIMACY EFFECT The tendency to recall the initial items in a series of items.

RECENCY EFFECT The tendency to recall the last items in a series of items.

we are asked to recall the last items in a list soon after we have been shown the list, they may still be in short-term memory. As a result, they can be "read off." Earlier items, in contrast, may have to be retrieved from long-term memory.

CHUNKING Rapidly rehearsing 10 meaningless letters is not an easy task. With TBXLFNTSDK there are 10 discrete elements, or **chunks,** of information that must be kept in short-term memory. When we encode THUNSTOFAM as three syllables, there are only three chunks to swallow at once—a memory task that is much easier on the digestion.

George Miller (1956) wryly noted that the average person is comfortable with digesting about seven integers at a time, the number of integers in a telephone number: "My problem is that I have been persecuted by an integer [the number *seven*]. For seven years this number has followed me around, has intruded in my most private data, and has assaulted me from the pages of our most public journals" (1956). Question: Is seven a magic number, or did the phone company get lucky?

It may sound as if Miller was being paranoid or magical, but he was actually talking about research findings. Research shows that most people have little trouble recalling five chunks of information, as in a zip code. Some can remember nine, which is, for all but a few, an upper limit. So seven chunks, plus or minus one or two, is a "magic" number in the sense that the typical person can manage to remember that many chunks of information and not a great deal more.

So how, you ask, do we manage to include area codes in our recollections of telephone numbers, hence making them 10 digits long? The truth of the matter is that we usually don't. We tend to recall the area code as a single chunk of information derived from our general knowledge of where a person lives. So we are more likely to remember (or "know") the 10-digit numbers of acquaintances who reside in locales with area codes that we use frequently.

Businesses pay the phone company hefty premiums so that they can attain numbers with two or three zeroes—for example, 592-2000 or 614-3300. These numbers include fewer chunks of information and hence are easier to remember. Customer recollection of business phone numbers increases sales. One financial services company uses the toll-free number CALL-IRA, which reduces the task to two chunks of information that also happen to be meaningfully related (semantically coded) to the nature of the business. Similarly, a clinic that helps people quit smoking arranged for a telephone number that can be reached by dialing the letters NO SMOKE.

Return to the third challenge to memory presented earlier. Were you able to remember the six groups of letters? Would your task have been simpler if you had grouped them differently? How about moving the dashes forward by a letter, so that they read GM-CBS-IBM-ATT-CIA-FBI? If we do this, we have the same list of letters, but we also have six chunks of information that can be coded semantically (according to what they mean). You may have also been able to generate the list by remembering a rule, such as "big corporations and government agencies."

If we can recall seven or perhaps nine chunks of information, how do children remember the alphabet? The alphabet contains 26 discrete pieces of information. How do children learn to encode the letters of the alphabet, which are visual symbols, as spoken sounds? There is nothing about the shape of an *A* that suggests its sound. Nor does the visual stimulus *B* sound "B-ish." One way is for children to simply learn to associate letters with their spoken names by **rote.** It is mechanical associative learning that

CHUNK A stimulus or group of stimuli that are perceived as a discrete piece of information.

ROTE Mechanical associative learning that is based on repetition.

REFLECT

Are you trying to learn anything by rote in the courses you are taking now? Would another strategy also be of help?

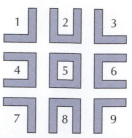

FIGURE 7.3

A Familiar Grid The nine drawings in the second challenge to memory form this familiar tic-tac-toe grid when the numbers are placed inside them and they are arranged in order. This method for recalling the shapes collapses nine chunks of information into two. One is the tic-tac-toe grid. The second is the rule for decoding the drawings from the grid.

takes time and repetition. Use of the alphabet song helps by allowing some chunking. That is, children can group letters and connect them with notes that rise and fall. In the alphabet song, children sing the group AB, then go up a note and sing CD, then go up again and sing EF, then come down a note, sing G, and pause. Later the group LMNO is sung rapidly with the same note. If you think that learning the alphabet by rote, or even with the aid of a little chunking, is a simple task, try learning the Russian alphabet.

If you had recognized THUNSTOFAM as an acronym for the first two letters of each word in the phrase "THe UNited STates OF AMerica," you would also have reduced the number of chunks of information that had to be recalled. You could have considered the phrase to be a single chunk of information. The rule that you must use the first two letters of each word of the phrase would be another chunk.

Reconsider the second challenge to memory presented earlier. You were asked to remember nine chunks of visual information. Perhaps you could have used the acoustic codes "L" and "Square" for chunks 3 and 5, but no obvious codes are available for the seven other chunks. Now look at Figure 7.3. If you had recognized that the elements in the challenge could be arranged as the familiar tic-tac-toe grid, remembering the nine elements might have required two chunks of information. The first would have been the mental image of the grid, and the second would have been the rule for decoding: Each element corresponds to the shape of a section of the grid if read like words on a page (from upper left to lower right). The number sequence 1 through 9 would not in itself present a problem, because you learned this series by rote many years ago and have rehearsed it in countless calculations since then.

INTERFERENCE IN SHORT-TERM MEMORY I mentioned that I often find myself running around looking for a pencil and a scrap of paper to write down a telephone number that has been given to me. If I keep on rehearsing the number while I'm looking, I'm okay. But I have also often cursed myself for failing to keep a pad and pencil by the telephone, and sometimes this has interfered with my recollection of the number. (The moral of the story? Avoid self-reproach.) It has also happened that I have actually looked up a phone number and been about to dial it when someone has asked me for the time or where I said we were going to dinner. Unless I say, "Hold on a minute!" and manage to jot down the number on something, it's back to the phone book. Attending to distracting information, even briefly, prevents me from rehearsing the number, so it falls through the cracks of my short-term memory.

In an experiment with college students, Lloyd and Margaret Peterson (1959) demonstrated how prevention of rehearsal can wreak havoc with short-term memory. They asked students to remember three-letter combinations such as HGB—normally, three easy chunks of information. They then had the students count backward from an arbitrary number, such as 181, by threes (that is, 181, 178, 175, 172, and so on). The students were told to stop counting and to report the letter sequence after the intervals of time shown in Figure 7.4. The percentage of letter combinations that were recalled correctly fell precipitously within seconds. After 18 seconds of interference, counting had dislodged the letter sequences in almost all of these bright young students' memories.

Psychologists say that the appearance of new information in short-term memory **displaces** the old information. Remember: Only a few bits of information can be retained in short-term memory at the same time. Think

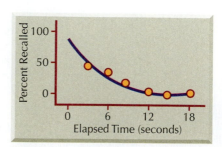

FIGURE 7.4

The Effect of Interference on Short-Term Memory In this experiment, college students were asked to remember a series of three letters while they counted backward by threes. After just three seconds, retention was cut by half. Ability to recall the words was almost completely lost by 15 seconds.

DISPLACE In memory theory, to cause information to be lost from short-term memory by adding new information.

of short-term memory as a shelf or workbench. Once it is full, some things fall off it when new items are shoved onto it. Here we have another possible explanation for the recency effect: The most recently learned bit of information is least likely to be displaced by additional information.

Displacement occurs at cocktail parties, and I'm not referring to jostling by the crowd. The point is this: When you meet Jennifer or Jonathan at the party, you should have little trouble remembering the name. But then you may meet Tamara or Timothy and, still later, Stephanie or Steven. By that time you may have a hard time dredging up Jennifer or Jonathan's name—unless, of course, you were very, very attracted to one of them. A passionate response would set a person apart and inspire a good deal of selective attention. According to signal-detection theory, if you were enamored enough, we may predict that you would "detect" the person's name (sensory signals) with a vengeance, and all the ensuing names would dissolve into background noise.

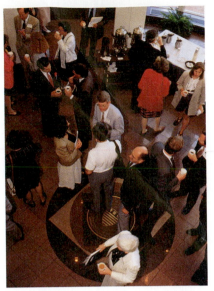

Displacement. Information can be lost to short-term memory through displacement. We may have little trouble remembering the names of the first or second person we meet at a gathering. But as introductions continue, new names may displace the old ones and we may forget the names of people we met only a few minutes earlier.

✓ Truth or Fiction Revisited

It is true that it may be easier for you to recall the name of your first-grade teacher than of someone you just met at a party. Your first-grade teacher's name is stored in long-term memory. However, you may be juggling a new acquaintance's name with many others in short-term memory.

Long-Term Memory

Long-term memory is the third stage of information processing. Think of your long-term memory as a vast storehouse of information containing names, dates, places, what Johnny did to you in second grade, and what Susan said about you when you were 12. Question: How does long-term memory function?

Some psychologists (Freud was one) used to believe that nearly all of our perceptions and ideas are stored permanently. We might not be able to retrieve all of them because some memories might be "lost" because of lack of proper cues, or they might be kept unconscious by the forces of **repression.** Adherents to this view often pointed to the work of neurosurgeon Wilder Penfield (1969). When parts of their brains were electrically stimulated, many of Penfield's patients reported the appearance of images that had something of the feel of memories.

Today most psychologists view this notion as exaggerated. Memory researcher Elizabeth Loftus, for example, notes that the "memories" stimulated by Penfield's probes lacked detail and were sometimes incorrect (Loftus & Loftus, 1980). Now let us consider some other questions about long-term memory.

✓ Truth or Fiction Revisited

It is not true that all of our experiences are permanently imprinted on the brain so that proper stimulation can cause us to remember them exactly. We appear to be more likely to store incidents that have a greater impact on us—events that have more personal meaning.

HOW ACCURATE ARE LONG-TERM MEMORIES? Elizabeth Loftus notes that memories are distorted by our **schemas**—that is, by the ways in which we conceptualize our worlds. Sometimes our schemas are simply our concepts or words for things. Sometimes our schemas reflect our biases and our needs.

LONG-TERM MEMORY The type or stage of memory capable of relatively permanent storage.

REPRESSION In Freud's psychodynamic theory, the ejection of anxiety-evoking ideas from conscious awareness.

SCHEMA A way of mentally representing the world, such as a belief or an expectation, that can influence perception of persons, objects, and situations.

FIGURE 7.5

MEMORY AS RECONSTRUCTIVE IN THEIR CLASSIC EXPERIMENT, CARMICHAEL, HOGAN, AND WALTER (1932) SHOWED PEOPLE THE FIGURES IN THE LEFT-HAND BOX AND MADE REMARKS AS SUGGESTED IN THE OTHER BOXES. FOR EXAMPLE, THE EXPERIMENTER MIGHT SAY, "THIS DRAWING LOOKS LIKE EYEGLASSES [OR A DUMBBELL]." WHEN PEOPLE LATER RECONSTRUCTED THE DRAWINGS, THEY WERE INFLUENCED BY THE LABELS.

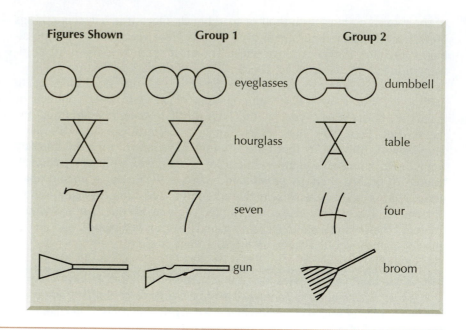

REFLECT

Were you ever convinced that you were remembering something accurately, only to discover, later, that your memory was incorrect? How do you account for the distorted memory? Why were you convinced it was accurate at the time?

Let me give you an example. "Retrieve" the fourth sheet of paper you prepared according to the instructions for the challenges to memory. The labels you wrote on the sheet will remind you of the figures. Take a minute or two to draw them now. Then continue reading.

Now that you have made your drawings, turn to Figure 7.5. Are your drawings closer in form to those in group 1 or to those in group 2? I wouldn't be surprised if they were more like those in group 1—if, for example, your first drawing looked more like eyeglasses than a dumbbell. After all, they were labeled like the drawings in group 1. The labels serve as *schemas* for the drawings—ways of organizing your knowledge of them—and these schemas may have influenced your recollections.

Consider another example of the power of schemas in processing information. Loftus and Palmer (1973) showed people a film of a car crash and then asked them to fill out questionnaires that included a question about how fast the cars were going at the time. The language of the question varied in subtle ways, however. Some people were asked to estimate how fast the cars were going when they "hit" each other. Others were asked to estimate the cars' speed when they "smashed into" each other. On average, people who reconstructed the scene on the basis of the cue "hit" estimated a speed of 34 mph. People who watched the same film but reconstructed the scene on the basis of the cue "smashed" estimated a speed of 41 mph! In other words, the use of the word *hit* or *smashed* caused people to organize their knowledge about the crash in different ways. That is, the words served as diverse schemas that fostered the development of very different ways of processing information about the crash.

How Fast Were These Cars Going When They Collided? Our schemas influence our processing of information. When shown pictures such as these, people who were asked how fast the cars were going when they *smashed* into each other offer higher estimates than people who were told that the cars *hit* each other.

Subjects in the same study were questioned again a week later: "Did you see any broken glass?" Because there was no broken glass shown in the film, an answer of "yes" would be wrong. Of those who had earlier been encouraged to process information about the accident in terms of one car "hitting" the other, 14% incorrectly answered yes. But 32% of the subjects who had processed information about the crash in terms of one car "smashing into" the other reported, incorrectly, that they had seen broken glass. Findings such as these have implications for eyewitness testimony, as we see in the following section. It shows how a particular kind of schema—prejudice—can affect our memories of events.

LONG-TERM MEMORY AND HUMAN DIVERSITY: THE ROLE OF PREJUDICE IN THE RECONSTRUCTION OF MEMORIES You might like to think that memories, especially clear memories, are as fresh as the driven snow. Yet psychological research suggests that memories, even powerful memories, are often distorted by our *schemas*. And our schemas are sometimes prejudices.

To understand how schemas can distort memories, consider the problems of travelers who met up with Procrustes, the legendary hijacker of ancient Greece. Procrustes had a quirk. He was interested not only in travelers' pocketbooks but also in their height. He had a concept—a schema—of how tall people should be, and when people did not fit his schema, they were in trouble. You see, Procrustes also had a bed, the famous "Procrustean bed." He made his victims lie down in the bed, and if they were too short for it, he stretched them to make them fit. If they were too long for the bed, he practiced surgery on their legs.

Although the myth of Procrustes may sound absurd, it reflects a quirky truth about people. People carry their cognitive Procrustean beds around with them—that is, their prejudiced schemas—and they try to make things and other people fit them. Prejudices are ways of processing social information. It is easier for people to remember instances of behavior that are consistent with their prejudices than it is to change their schemas (Devine, 1989; Fiske, 1993).

But prejudices also distort memories. That is, people tend to reconstruct their experiences according to their prejudices, as found in an experiment reported by Elizabeth Loftus (1979). Subjects in the study were shown a picture that contained an African American man who was holding a hat and a White man who was holding a razor. Later, when they were asked what they had seen, many subjects erroneously recalled the razor as being in the hands of the African American. These subjects "chopped off the legs" of their memories; they recalled information that was consistent with their schemas. But it was wrong.

Are your own memories biased by such schemas? Are you sure?

LONG-TERM MEMORY AND EYEWITNESS TESTIMONY Jean Piaget, the investigator of children's cognitive development, distinctly remembered an attempt to kidnap him from his baby carriage as he was being wheeled along the Champs Élysées. He recalled the excited throng, the abrasions on the face of the nurse who rescued him, the police officer's white baton, and the flight of the assailant. Although they were graphic, Piaget's memories were false. Years later, the nurse admitted that she had made up the tale.

Legal professionals are concerned about the accuracy of our memories as reflected in eyewitness testimony. Misidentifications of suspects "create a double horror: The wrong person is devastated by this personal tragedy, and the real criminal is still out on the streets" (Loftus, 1993b, p. 550). Is there reason to believe that the statements of eyewitnesses are any more factual than Piaget's?

There is cause for concern. The words chosen by an experimenter—and those chosen by a lawyer interrogating a witness—have been shown to influence the reconstruction of memories (Loftus & Palmer, 1973). For example, as in the experiment described earlier, an attorney for the plaintiff might ask the witness, "How fast was the defendant's car going when it *smashed into* the plaintiff's car?" In such a case, the car might be reported as going faster than if the question had been: "How fast was the defendant's car going when the accident occurred?" Could the attorney for the defendant claim that use of the word *smashed* biased the witness?

REFLECT

How do attorneys use leading questions to confuse the memories of eyewitnesses? How can attorneys and police help eyewitnesses remember what they have seen more clearly?

Eyewitness Testimony? How trust-worthy is eyewitness testimony? Memories are reconstructive rather than photographic. The wording of questions also influences the content of the memory. Attorneys therefore are sometimes instructed not to phrase questions in such a way that they "lead" the witness.

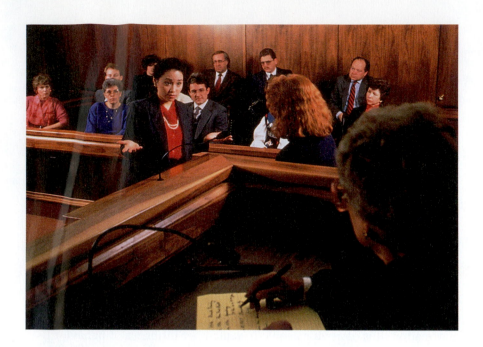

What about jurors who heard the word *smashed?* Would they be biased toward assuming that the driver had been reckless?

Children tend to be more suggestible witnesses than adults, and preschoolers are more suggestible than older children (Ceci & Bruck, 1993). But when questioned properly, even young children may be able to provide accurate and useful testimony (Ceci & Bruck, 1993).

There are cases in which the memories of eyewitnesses have been "refreshed" by hypnosis. Sad to say, hypnosis does more than amplify memories; it can also distort them (Loftus, 1994). One problem is that witnesses may accept and embellish suggestions made by the hypnotist. Another is that hypnotized people may report fantasized occurrences as compellingly as if they were real (Loftus, 1994).

There are also problems in the identification of criminals by eyewitnesses. For one thing, witnesses may pay more attention to the suspect's clothing than to more meaningful characteristics such as facial features, height, and weight. In one experiment, viewers of a videotaped crime incorrectly identified a man as the criminal because he wore the eyeglasses and T-shirt that had been worn by the perpetrator on the tape. The man who had actually committed the crime was identified less often (Sanders, 1984).

Other problems with eyewitness testimony include the following:

- Identification of suspects is less accurate when suspects belong to ethnic or racial groups that differ from that of the witness (Egeth, 1993).

- Identification of suspects is confused when interrogators make misleading suggestions (Loftus, 1997).

- Witnesses are seen as more credible when they claim to be certain in their testimony, but there is little evidence that claims of certainty are accurate (Wells, 1993).

There are thus many problems with eyewitness testimony. Yet even Elizabeth Loftus (1993b), who has extensively studied the accuracy of eyewitness testimony, agrees that it is a valuable tool in the courtroom. After all, identifications made by eyewitnesses are frequently correct, and what, Loftus asks, would be the alternative to the use of eyewitnesses? If we were to prevent eyewitnesses from testifying, how many criminals would go free?

HOW MUCH INFORMATION *CAN* BE STORED IN LONG-TERM MEMORY? How many gigabytes of storage are there in your most personal computer—your brain? Unlike a computer, the human ability to store information is practically unlimited (Goldman-Rakic, 1995). New information may replace older information in short-term memory, but no evidence indicates that long-term memories are lost by displacement. Long-term memories may endure for a lifetime. Now and then it may seem that we have forgotten, or "lost," a long-term memory such as the names of our elementary or high school classmates. Yet it may be that we cannot find the proper cues to help us retrieve them. If long-term memories are lost, they may be lost in the same way a misplaced object is lost. It is "lost," but we sense that it is still somewhere in the room. In other words, it is lost but not destroyed.

✓ Truth or Fiction Revisited

It is true that there is no practical limit to the amount of information you can store in your memory. At least, no limit has been discovered.

TRANSFERRING INFORMATION FROM SHORT-TERM TO LONG-TERM MEMORY How can you transfer information from short-term to long-term memory? By and large, the more often chunks of information are rehearsed, the more likely they are to be transferred to long-term memory. We have seen that repeating information over and over to prevent it from decaying or being displaced is termed *maintenance rehearsal.* But maintenance rehearsal does not give meaning to information by linking it to past learning. Thus it is not considered the best way to permanently store information (Craik & Watkins, 1973).

A more effective method is to make information more meaningful—to purposefully relate new information to things that are already well known (Woloshyn et al., 1994). For example, to better remember the components of levers, physics students might use seesaws, wheelbarrows, and oars as examples (Scruggs & Mastropieri, 1992). The nine chunks of information in our second challenge to memory were made easier to reconstruct once they were associated with the familiar tic-tac-toe grid in Figure 7.3. We saw that relating new material to well-known material is known as *elaborative rehearsal.* For example, have you seen this word before?

FUNTHOSTAM

Say it aloud. Do you know it? If you had used an acoustic code alone to memorize THUNSTOFAM, the list of letters you first saw on page 313, it might not have been easy to recognize FUNTHOSTAM as an incorrect spelling. Let us assume, however, that by now you have used elaborative rehearsal and encoded THUNSTOFAM semantically (according to its "meaning") as an acronym for "The United States of America." Then you would have been able to scan the spelling of the words in the phrase "The United States of America" to determine that FUNTHOSTAM is an incorrect spelling.

Rote repetition of a meaningless group of syllables, such as *thun-sto-fam,* relies on maintenance rehearsal for permanent storage. The process might be tedious (continued rehearsal) and unreliable. Elaborative

REFLECT

Is there any limit to the amount of information you can learn or remember?

rehearsal—tying THUNSTOFAM to the name of a country—might make storage almost instantaneous and retrieval foolproof.

✓ Truth or Fiction Revisited

It is not true that learning must be meaningful if we are to remember it. Nevertheless, elaborative rehearsal, which is based on the meanings of events or subject matter, is more efficient than maintenance rehearsal, which is based on rote repetition (Simpson et al., 1994).

LEVELS OF PROCESSING INFORMATION People who use elaborative rehearsal to remember things are *processing information at a deeper level* than people who use maintenance rehearsal. Question: What is the levels-of-processing model of memory? Fergus Craik and Robert Lockhart (1972) pioneered the levels-of-processing model of memory, which holds that memories tend to endure when information is processed *deeply*— when it is attended to, encoded carefully, pondered, and related to things we already know. Craik and Lockhart believe that remembering relies on how *deeply* people process information, not on whether memories are transferred from one *stage* of memory to another.

Evidence for the importance of levels of processing information is found in an experiment with three groups of college students, all of whom were asked to study a picture of a living room for one minute (Bransford et al., 1977). The groups' examination of the picture entailed different approaches. Two groups were informed that small *x*'s were imbedded in the picture. The first of these groups was asked to find the *x*'s by scanning the picture horizontally and vertically. The second group was informed that the *x*'s could be found in the edges of the objects in the room and was asked to look for them there. The third group was asked, instead, to think about how it would use the objects pictured in the room. As a result of the divergent sets of instructions, the first two groups (the *x* hunters) processed information about the objects in the picture superficially. But the third group rehearsed the objects elaboratively—that is, members of this group thought about the objects in terms of their meanings and uses. It should not be surprising that the third group remembered many times more objects than the first two groups.

In another experiment, researchers asked subjects to indicate whether they recognized photos of faces they had been shown under one of three conditions: (1) being asked to recall the gender of the person in the photo, (2) being asked to recall the width of the person's nose, or (3) being asked to judge whether the person is honest (Sporer, 1991). Subjects asked to form judgments about the persons' honesty recognized more faces. It is likely that asking people to judge other people's honesty stimulates deeper processing of the features of the faces (Bloom & Mudd, 1991). That is, subjects study each face in detail, and they attempt to relate what they see to their ideas about human nature.

Language arts teachers encourage students to use new vocabulary words in sentences to process them more deeply. Each new usage is an instance of elaborative rehearsal. Usage helps build semantic codes that make it easier to retrieve the meanings of words in the future. When I was in high school, teachers of foreign languages told us that learning classical languages "exercises the mind" so that we would understand English better. Not exactly. The mind is not analogous to a muscle that responds to exercise. However, the meanings of many English words are based on foreign ones. A person who recognizes that *retrieve* stems from roots meaning "again" (*re-*) and "find" (*trouver* in French) is less likely to forget that *retrieval* means "finding again" or "bringing back."

Think, too, of all the algebra and geometry problems we were asked to solve in high school. Each problem is an application of a procedure and, perhaps, of certain formulas and theorems. By repeatedly applying the procedures, formulas, and theorems in different contexts, we rehearse them elaboratively. As a consequence, we are more likely to remember them. Knowledge of the ways in which a formula or an equation is used helps us remember the formula. Also, by building one geometry theorem on another, we relate new theorems to ones that we already understand. As a result, we process information about them more deeply and remember them better.

Before proceeding to the next section, cover the preceding paragraph with your hand. Which of the following words is spelled correctly: *retrieval* or *retreival*? The spellings sound alike, so an acoustic code for reconstructing the correct spelling would fail. Yet a semantic code, such as the spelling rule "*i* before *e* except after *c*," would allow you to reconstruct the correct spelling: retr*ie*val.

REFLECT

Do you have difficulty spelling "receive" or "retrieve"? How do you remember how to spell "receive"?

FLASHBULB MEMORIES

You will always remember where you were at 8:18 Central Time on September 8, 1998.

> THE ST. LOUIS SPORTSCASTER, UPON MARK MCGWIRE'S SLAMMING
> HIS 62ND HOME RUN OF THE SEASON, SURPASSING ROGER MARIS'S
> RECORD OF 61.

The attention which we lend to an experience is proportional to its vivid or interesting character; and it is a notorious fact that what interests us most vividly at the time is, other things equal, what we remember best. An impression may be so exciting emotionally as almost to leave a scar upon the cerebral tissues.

WILLIAM JAMES

Do you remember the first time you were in love? Can you remember how the streets and the trees looked transformed? The vibrancy in your step? How generous you felt? How all of life's problems seemed suddenly solved?

Many of us will never forget where we were or what we were doing when we learned that John F. Kennedy, Jr.'s airplane had crashed into the ocean in 1999, or when Britain's Princess Diana died in an automobile accident in 1997. Many of us recall where we were when we learned that O. J. Simpson was acquitted of murder charges in 1995, or where we were at 8:18 Central Time on September 8, 1998 when Mark McGwire slammed his 62nd home run of the season, surpassing Roger Maris's record of 61. We may also have a detailed memory of what we were doing when we learned of a relative's death.

Question: Why is it that some events, like the death of Princess Diana, can be etched in memory for a lifetime? It appears that we tend to remember events that occur under unusual, emotionally arousing circumstances more clearly. Such events can create "flashbulb memories," which preserve experiences in detail (Brown & Kulik, 1977; Thompson & Cowan, 1986). Why is the memory etched when the "flashbulb" goes off? One factor is the distinctness of the memory. It is easier to discriminate stimuli that stand out. Such events are striking in themselves. The feelings caused by them are also special. It is thus relatively easy to pick

REFLECT

Are there some things that you feel certain you will never forget? What is special about these memories?

Flashbulb Memories. Where were you and what were you doing in 1999 when you learned that John F. Kennedy, Jr.'s airplane was missing over the ocean? Major events can illuminate everything about them so that we recall everything that was happening at the time.

FIGURE 7.6

THE HIERARCHICAL STRUCTURE OF LONG-TERM MEMORY WHERE ARE WHALES FILED IN THE HIERARCHICAL CABINETS OF YOUR MEMORY? YOUR CLASSIFICATION OF WHALES MAY INFLUENCE YOUR ANSWERS TO THESE QUESTIONS: DO WHALES BREATHE UNDERWATER? ARE THEY WARM-BLOODED? DO THEY NURSE THEIR YOUNG?

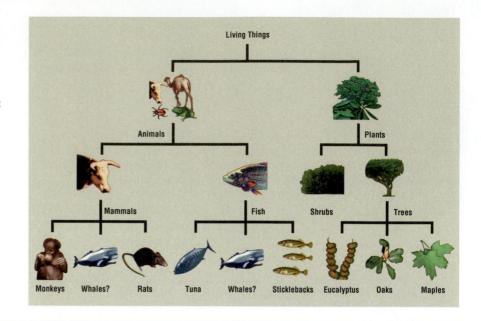

them out from the storehouse of memories. Major events such as the assassination of a president or the loss of a close relative also tend to have important effects on our lives. We are likely to dwell on them and form networks of associations. That is, we are likely to rehearse them elaboratively. Our rehearsal may include great expectations, or deep fears, for the future.

ORGANIZATION IN LONG-TERM MEMORY The storehouse of long-term memory is usually well organized. Items are not just piled on the floor or thrown into closets. Question: How is knowledge organized in long-term memory? We tend to gather information about rats and cats into a certain section of the storehouse, perhaps the animal or mammal section. We put information about oaks, maples, and eucalyptus into the tree section. Such categorization of stimuli is a basic cognitive function. It allows us to make predictions about specific instances and to store information efficiently (Corter & Gluck, 1992).

We tend to organize information according to a *hierarchical structure*, as shown in Figure 7.6. A *hierarchy* is an arrangement of items (or chunks of information) into groups or classes according to common or distinct features. As we work our way up the hierarchy shown in Figure 7.6, we find more encompassing, or *superordinate*, classes to which the items below them belong. For example, all mammals are animals, but there are many types of animals other than mammals.[1]

When items are correctly organized in long-term memory, you are more likely to recall—or know—accurate information about them (Hasselhorn, 1992; Schneider & Bjorklund, 1992). For instance, do you remember whether whales breathe underwater? If you did not know that whales are mammals (or, in Figure 7.6, *subordinate* to mammals), or if you knew nothing about mammals, a correct answer might depend on

[1] A note to biological purists: Figure 7.6 is not intended to represent phyla, classes, orders, and so on accurately. Rather, it shows how an individual's classification scheme might be organized.

some remote instance of rote learning. That is, you might be depending on chancy episodic memory rather than on reliable semantic memory. For example, you might recall some details from a public television documentary on whales. If you *did* know that whales are mammals, however, you would also know—or remember—that whales do not breathe underwater. How? You would reconstruct information about whales from knowledge about mammals, the group to which whales are subordinate. Similarly, you would know, or remember, that because they are mammals, whales are warm-blooded, nurse their young, and are a good deal more intelligent than, say, tunas and sharks, which are fish. Had you incorrectly classified whales as fish, you might have searched your memory and constructed the incorrect answer that they do breathe underwater.

THE TIP-OF-THE-TONGUE PHENOMENON Having something on "the tip of your tongue" can be a frustrating experience. It is like reeling in a fish but having it drop off the line just before it breaks the surface of the water. Psychologists term this experience the **tip-of-the- tongue (TOT) phenomenon,** or the **feeling-of-knowing experience.** Question: Why do we sometimes feel that the answer to a question is on the tip of our tongue?

Research provides insight into the TOT phenomenon. In one experiment, Brown and McNeill (1966) defined some rather unusual words for students, such as *sampan,* a small riverboat used in China and Japan. The students were then asked to recall the words they had learned. Some of the students often had the right word "on the tip of their tongue" but reported words with similar meanings such as *junk, barge,* or *houseboat.* Still other students reported words that sounded similar, such as *Saipan, Siam, sarong,* and *sanching.* Why?

To begin with, the words were unfamiliar, so elaborative rehearsal did not take place. The students, that is, did not have an opportunity to relate the words to other things they knew. Brown and McNeill also suggested that our storage systems are indexed according to cues that include both the sounds and the meanings of words—that is, according to both acoustic and semantic codes. By scanning words similar in sound and meaning to the word on the tip of the tongue, we sometimes find a useful cue and retrieve the word for which we are searching.

The feeling-of-knowing experience also seems to reflect incomplete or imperfect learning. In such cases, our answers may be "in the ballpark" if not on the mark. In some feeling-of-knowing experiments, people are often asked trivia questions. When they do not recall an answer, they are then asked to guess how likely it is that they will recognize the right answer if it is among a group of possibilities. People turn out to be very accurate in their estimations about whether or not they will recognize the answer. Similarly, Brown and McNeill found that the students in their TOT experiment proved to be very good at estimating the number of syllables in words they could not recall. The students often correctly guessed the initial sounds of the words. They sometimes recognized words that rhymed with them.

Are the three kinds of memory on the tip of your tongue now? Can you use the acronym *ESP* to recall them?

Sometimes an answer seems to be on the tip of our tongue because our knowledge of the topic is incomplete. We may not know the exact answer, but we know something. (As a matter of fact, if we have good writing skills, we may present our incomplete knowledge so forcefully that we

TIP-OF-THE-TONGUE (TOT) PHENOMENON The feeling that information is stored in memory although it cannot be readily retrieved. Also called the *feeling-of-knowing experience.*

FEELING-OF-KNOWING EXPERIENCE Same as *tip-of-the-tongue phenomenon.*

earn a good grade on an essay question on the topic!) At such times, the problem lies not in retrieval but in the original encoding and storage.

CONTEXT-DEPENDENT MEMORY: BEEN THERE, DONE THAT?

It's déjà vu *all over again.*

YOGI BERRA

The context in which we acquire information can also play a role in retrieval. I remember walking down the halls of the apartment building where I had lived as a child. I was suddenly assaulted by images of playing under the staircase, of falling against a radiator, of the shrill voice of a former neighbor calling for her child at dinnertime. Have you ever walked the halls of an old school building and been assaulted by memories of faces and names that you would have guessed had been lost forever?

These are examples of **context-dependent memory.** Question: Why may it be useful to study in the room in which we will be tested? One answer is that being in the proper context—for example, studying in the exam room—can dramatically enhance recall (Estes, 1972). One fascinating experiment in context-dependent memory included a number of people who were "all wet." Members of a university swimming club were asked to learn lists of words either while they were submerged or while they were literally high and dry (Godden & Baddeley, 1975). Students who learned the list underwater showed superior recall of the list when immersed. Similarly, those who had rehearsed the list ashore showed better retrieval on terra firma.

Other studies have found that students do better on tests when they study in the room where the test is to be given (Smith et al., 1978). When police are interviewing witnesses to crimes, they ask the witnesses to paint the scene verbally as vividly as possible, or they visit the scene of the crime with the witnesses. People who mentally place themselves back in the context in which they encoded and stored information frequently retrieve it more accurately.

One of the more eerie psychological experiences is *déjà vu* (French for "already seen"). Sometimes we meet someone new or find ourselves in a strange place, yet we have the feeling that we know this person or have been there before. The *déjà vu* experience seems to occur when we are in a context similar to one we have been in before—or when we meet someone who has a way of talking or moving similar to that of someone we know or once knew. Familiarity with the context leads us to think, "I've been here before." Some people might even wonder whether they had experienced the situation in a former life, or whether their experience is something supernatural. Although your feelings and ideas are flooding in because of the similarity of the context, the sense that you have been there before, or done this thing before, can be so strong that you just stand back and wonder.

STATE-DEPENDENT MEMORY

State-dependent memory is an extension of context-dependent memory. It sometimes happens that we retrieve information better when we are in a physiological or emotional state similar to the one in which we encoded and stored the information. Feeling the rush of love may trigger images of other times when we fell in love. The grip of anger may prompt memories of incidents of frustration and rage.

REFLECT

Did you ever have a *déjà vu* experience? For example, did you ever walk through your old neighborhood and recall people's faces or aromas of cooking that were so real that you actually salivated? How do you explain such experiences?

CONTEXT-DEPENDENT MEMORY Information that is better retrieved in the context in which it was encoded and stored, or learned.

DÉJÀ VU A French phrase meaning "already seen," and referring to the experience of having been in a new situation before, apparently because contextual cues trigger the retrieval of images and feelings from the past.

STATE-DEPENDENT MEMORY Information that is better retrieved in the physiological or emotional state in which it was encoded and stored, or learned.

TABLE 7.1	THREE "THREES" OF MEMORY	
CONCEPT	**WHAT IT MEANS**	**EXAMPLE**
THREE KINDS OF MEMORY		
Episodic Memory	Memories of events experienced or personally witnessed by a person	Remembering what you ate for dinner last night
Semantic Memory	General knowledge (as opposed to remembering personal episodes)	Remembering the capital cities of the 50 states
Procedural Memory	Knowledge of ways of doing things; also termed *skill memory*	Remembering how to ride a bicycle, click a mouse, or write with a pencil
THREE PROCESSES OF MEMORY		
Encoding	Modifying information so that it can be placed in memory, sometimes from one sensory modality (e.g., vision) to another (hearing)	Mental representation of the words in this table as a sequence of sounds (an acoustic code)
Storage	Maintenance of information over time	Mental repetition (maintenance rehearsal) of the information in this table in order to keep it in memory
Retrieval	Finding of stored information and bringing it into conscious awareness	Recall of the information in this table; using a mnemonic device such as Roy G. Biv to recall the colors of the visible spectrum
THREE STAGES OF MEMORY		
Sensory Memory	Type or stage of memory that is first encountered by a stimulus and briefly holds impressions of it	Continuing briefly to "see" a visual stimulus after it has been removed
Short-Term Memory	Type or stage of memory that can hold information for up to a minute or so after the trace of the stimulus decays; also termed *working memory*	Repeating someone's name in order to remember it, or relating something new to things that are already known
Long-Term Memory	Type or stage of memory that is capable of relatively permanent storage	The "file cabinets" of memory, where you store items like the names of your primary school teachers and your memories of holidays when you were little

Gordon Bower (1981) ran experiments in which happy or sad moods were induced by hypnotic suggestion. The subjects then learned lists of words. People who learned a list while in a happy mood showed better recall when a happy state was induced again. But people who had learned the list while in a sad mood showed superior recall when they were saddened again.

Psychologists suggest that in day-to-day life a happy mood influences us to focus on positive events (Eich, 1995; Matt et al., 1992). As a result, we have better recall of these events in the future. A sad mood, unfortunately, leads us to focus on and recall the negative. Happiness may feed on happiness, but under extreme circumstances, sadness can develop into a vicious cycle and lead to depression.

Table 7.1 summarizes the "three threes of memory." It includes the three kinds of memory (episodic, semantic, and procedural), the three processes of memory (encoding, storage, and retrieval), and the three stages of memory (sensory memory, short-term memory, and long-term memory). Now that we have explored the nature of remembering, let us consider its opposite—forgetting.

SECTION III   `Review`

The three stages of memory proposed by Atkinson and Shiffrin are (22) _____sory memory, (23) _____-_____ memory (STM), and (24) _____-_____ memory (LTM). A stimulus first encounters (25) _____ memory. Sensory memory holds impressions briefly, but long enough so that series of (26) _____tions seem connected. The memory (27) t_____ of a stimulus lasts for only a fraction of a second. Memory traces are "held" in sensory (28) _____ters. Sensory memory consists of (29) _____ters that can briefly hold information that is entered by the senses.

McDougall used a (30) _____-report procedure and found that people could remember 4 or 5 of 12 letters they viewed with a single eye fixation. Under these conditions, people could typically remember only 4 or 5 letters. Sperling used a (31) _____-report procedure to show that there is a difference between what people can see and what they can report in the visual sensory register. Sperling concluded that the memory trace of visual stimuli (32) d_____ within a second in the visual sensory register.

The mental representations of visual stimuli are referred to as (33) _____s. The sensory register that holds icons is labeled (34) _____ _____ory. Iconic memories are accurate (35) _____phic memories. The ability to retain exact mental representations of visual stimuli over long amounts of time is termed (36) _____tic imagery. The mental representations of (37) _____ory stimuli are called *echoes*. The memory (38) _____ces of echoes can last for several seconds, much longer than the traces of icons.

By focusing attention on a stimulus in the sensory register, you will retain it in (39) _____-_____ memory for a minute or so after the trace of the stimulus decays. Short-term memory is also referred to as (40) _____ing memory. One way of retaining information in short-term memory—and possibly storing it permanently—is to (41) re_____ it. Rote repetition is referred to as (42) _____ance rehearsal.

According to the (43) _____-position effect, we are most likely to recall the first and last items in a series. First items are likely to be rehearsed (44: More or Less?) frequently than other items. Last items are likely to have been rehearsed (45: Most or Least?) recently. The tendency to recall the initial items in a list

is referred to as the (46) _____ effect. The tendency to recall the last items in a list is referred to as the (47) _____ effect.

Miller noted that the average person can maintain about (48: How many?) chunks of information in short-term memory at a time. Children learn the alphabet by (49) r_____—that is, by mechanical associative learning. Rote learning requires time and (50) re_____. The Petersons showed that information can be displaced from short-term memory by means of (51) _____ence. Long-term memory is the third stage of processing of (52) _____tion.

Sigmund (53) F_____ believed that nearly all of our perceptions and ideas were stored permanently, but memories are not complete. Moreover, Elizabeth Loftus and other psychologists have shown that our memories are distorted by our (54) _____as, or ways of conceptualizing our worlds. That is, we (55) re_____ our recollections according to our schemas.

There (56: Is or Is not?) evidence for a limit to the amount of information that can be stored in long-term memory. New information may displace older information in (57: Long or Short?)-term memory, but there is no evidence that memories in long-term memory are lost by displacement. However, we need the proper (58) _____s to help us retrieve information in long-term memory.

Craik and Lockhart view our ability to remember in terms of a single stage or dimension—the degree to which we (59) pr_____ information. Put another way: According to the (60) _____-of-processing model, memories tend to endure when information is processed deeply—when it is attended to, encoded carefully, reflected upon, and rehearsed elaboratively or related to things we already know well.

Psychologists have learned that we tend better to remember the events that occur under (61: Usual or Unusual?) and emotional circumstances. We retain such detailed memories of events like these that they are referred to as (62) "fl_____ memories." One explanation for flashbulb memory is the (63) dis_____ of the memory. But major events, such as the death of a president, have important impacts on our lives so that we are likely to form networks of associations to other pieces of information—that is, to rehearse them (64) _____tively.

We tend to organize information in long-term memory according to a (65) _____cal structure.

The (66) _____-of-the- (67) _____ phenomenon—also referred to as the *feeling-of-knowing experience*—seems to reflect incomplete or imperfect learning. The classic "TOT" experiment by Brown and McNeill also suggests that our storage systems are indexed according to cues that include both the

sounds and the meanings of words—that is, according to both (68) _____tic and (69) _____tic codes.

(70) C_____-dependent memory refers to information that is better retrieved under the circumstances in which it was encoded and stored, or learned. State-dependent memory is an extension of (71) _____-dependent memory and refers to the finding that we sometimes retrieve information better when we are in a (72) phys_____ or emotional state that is similar to the one in which we encoded and stored the information.

SECTION IV. FORGETTING

What do DAL, RIK, BOF, and ZEX have in common? They are all **nonsense syllables.** Nonsense syllables are meaningless sets of two consonants with a vowel sandwiched in between. They were first used by Hermann Ebbinghaus to study memory and forgetting. Because nonsense syllables are intended to be meaningless, remembering them should depend on simple acoustic coding and maintenance rehearsal rather than on elaborative rehearsal, semantic coding, or other ways of making learning meaningful. They are thus well-suited for use in the measurement of forgetting. Question: What types of memory tasks are used in measuring forgetting?

Memory Tasks Used in Measuring Forgetting

Three basic memory tasks have been used by psychologists to measure forgetting: recognition, recall, and relearning. Nonsense syllables have been used in studying each of them. The study of these memory tasks has led to several conclusions about the nature of forgetting. Let us consider them task by task.

RECOGNITION One aspect of forgetting is failure to recognize something we have experienced. There are many ways of measuring **recognition.** In many studies, psychologists ask subjects to read a list of nonsense syllables. The subjects then read a second list of nonsense syllables and indicate whether they recognize any of the syllables as having appeared on the first list. Forgetting is defined as failure to recognize a syllable that has been read before.

In another kind of recognition study, Harry Bahrick and his colleagues (1975) studied high school graduates who had been out of school for various lengths of time. They interspersed photos of the graduates' classmates with four times as many photos of strangers. Recent graduates correctly recognized former classmates 90% of the time. Those who had been out of school for 40 years recognized former classmates 75% of the time. A chance level of recognition would have been only 20% (1 photo in 5 was of an actual classmate). Thus even older people showed rather solid long-term recognition ability.

REFLECT

Are multiple-choice test questions easier for you than fill-in-the-blanks? If so, why?

NONSENSE SYLLABLES Meaningless sets of two consonants, with a vowel sandwiched in between, that are used to study memory.

RECOGNITION In information processing, the easiest memory task, involving identification of objects or events encountered before.

FIGURE 7.7

PAIRED ASSOCIATES PSYCHOLOGISTS OFTEN USE PAIRED ASSOCIATES TO MEASURE RECALL. RETRIEVING CEG IN RESPONSE TO THE CUE WOM IS MADE EASIER BY AN IMAGE OF A WOMAN SMOKING A "CEG-ARETTE."

Recognition is the easiest type of memory task. This is why multiple-choice tests are easier than fill-in-the-blank or essay tests. We can recognize correct answers more easily than we can recall them unaided.

RECALL In his own studies of **recall,** another kind of memory task, Ebbinghaus would read lists of nonsense syllables aloud to the beat of a metronome and then see how many he could produce from memory. After reading through a list once, he usually would be able to recall seven syllables—the typical limit for short-term memory.

Psychologists also often use lists of pairs of nonsense syllables, called **paired associates,** to measure recall. A list of paired associates is shown in Figure 7.7. Subjects read through the lists pair by pair. Later they are shown the first member of each pair and asked to recall the second. Recall is more difficult than recognition. In a recognition task, one simply indicates whether an item has been seen before or which of a number of items is paired with a stimulus (as in a multiple-choice test). In a recall task, the person must retrieve a syllable, with another syllable serving as a cue.

Retrieval is made easier if the two syllables can be meaningfully linked—that is, encoded semantically—even if the "meaning" is stretched a bit. Consider the first pair of nonsense syllables in Figure 7.7. The image of a WOMan smoking a CEG-arette may make CEG easier to retrieve when the person is presented with the cue WOM.

RELEARNING: IS LEARNING EASIER THE SECOND TIME AROUND? **Relearning** is a third method of measuring retention. Do you remember having to learn all of the state capitals in grade school? What were the capitals of Wyoming and Delaware? Even when we cannot recall or recognize material that had once been learned, such as Cheyenne for Wyoming and Dover for Delaware, we can relearn it more rapidly the second time. Similarly, as we go through our 30s and 40s we may forget a good deal of our high school French or geometry. Yet the second time around we could learn much more rapidly what previously took months or years.

To study the efficiency of relearning, Ebbinghaus (1885/1913) devised the **method of savings.** First he recorded the number of repetitions required to learn a list of nonsense syllables or words. Then he recorded the number of repetitions required to relearn the list after a certain amount of time had elapsed. Next he computed the difference in the number of repetitions to determine the **savings.** If a list had to be repeated 20 times before it was learned, and 20 times again after a year had passed, there was no savings. Relearning, that is, was as tedious as the initial learning. However, if the list could be learned with only 10 repetitions after a year had elapsed, half the number of repetitions required for learning had been saved.

Figure 7.8 shows Ebbinghaus's classic curve of forgetting. As you can see, there was no loss of memory as measured by savings immediately after a list had been learned. However, recollection dropped quite a bit, by half, during the first hour after learning a list. Losses of learning then became more gradual. It took a month (31 days) for retention to be cut in half again. In other words, forgetting occurred most rapidly right after material was learned. We continue to forget material as time elapses, but at a relatively slower rate.

Before leaving this section, I have one question for you: What are the capitals of Wyoming and Delaware?

RECALL Retrieval or reconstruction of learned material.

PAIRED ASSOCIATES Nonsense syllables presented in pairs in experiments that measure recall.

RELEARNING A measure of retention. Material is usually relearned more quickly than it is learned initially.

METHOD OF SAVINGS A measure of retention in which the difference between the number of repetitions originally required to learn a list and the number of repetitions required to relearn the list after a certain amount of time has elapsed is calculated.

SAVINGS The difference between the number of repetitions originally required to learn a list and the number of repetitions required to relearn the list after a certain amount of time has elapsed.

FIGURE 7.8

EBBINGHAUS'S CLASSIC CURVE OF FORGETTING

RECOLLECTION OF LISTS OF WORDS DROPS PRECIPITOUSLY DURING THE FIRST HOUR AFTER LEARNING. LOSSES OF LEARNING THEN BECOME MORE GRADUAL. RETENTION DROPS BY HALF WITHIN THE FIRST HOUR. HOWEVER, IT TAKES A MONTH (31 DAYS) FOR RETENTION TO BE CUT IN HALF AGAIN.

Interference Theory

When we do not attend to, encode, and rehearse sensory input, we may forget it through decay of the trace of the image. Material in short-term memory, like material in sensory memory, can be lost through decay. It can also be lost through displacement, as may happen when we try to remember several new names at a party.

Question: Why can learning Spanish make it harder to remember French? The answer may be found in **interference theory.** According to this view, we also forget material in short-term and long-term memory because newly learned material interferes with it. The two basic types of interference are retroactive interference (also called *retroactive inhibition*) and proactive interference (also called *proactive inhibition*).

RETROACTIVE INTERFERENCE In **retroactive interference,** new learning interferes with the retrieval of old learning. For example, a medical student may memorize the names of the bones in the leg through rote repetition. Later he or she may find that learning the names of the bones in the arm makes it more difficult to retrieve the names of the leg bones, especially if the names are similar in sound or in relative location on each limb.

PROACTIVE INTERFERENCE In **proactive interference,** older learning interferes with the capacity to retrieve more recently learned material. High school Spanish may pop in when you are trying to retrieve college French or Italian words. All three are Romance languages, with similar roots and spellings. Previously learned Japanese words probably would not interfere with your ability to retrieve more recently learned French or Italian because the roots and sounds of Japanese differ considerably from those of the Romance languages.

Consider motor skills. You may learn to drive a standard shift on a car with three forward speeds and a clutch that must be let up slowly after shifting. Later you may learn to drive a car with five forward speeds and a clutch that must be released rapidly. For a while, you may make errors on the five-speed car because of proactive interference. (Old learning interferes with new learning.) If you return to the three-speed car after driving the five-speed car has become natural, you may stall it a few times. This is because of retroactive interference (new learning interfering with the old).

Repression

According to Sigmund Freud, we are motivated to forget painful memories and unacceptable ideas because they produce anxiety, fear, guilt, and

Interference. In retroactive interference, new learning interferes with the retrieval of old learning. In proactive interference, older learning interferes with the capacity to retrieve material learned more recently. For example, high school French vocabulary may "pop in" when you are trying to retrieve words you have learned for a Spanish test in college.

INTERFERENCE THEORY The view that we may forget stored material because other learning interferes with it.

RETROACTIVE INTERFERENCE The interference of new learning with the ability to retrieve material learned previously.

PROACTIVE INTERFERENCE The interference of old learning with the ability to retrieve material learned recently.

shame. Question: What is the Freudian concept of repression? Repression, according to Freud, is the automatic ejection of painful memories and unacceptable urges from conscious awareness. Repression is theorized to occur automatically, without our knowing that it is happening. It is motivated by the desire to avoid facing painful memories and emotions. (In terms of operant conditioning, anxiety, guilt, and shame serve as negative reinforcers. We learn to behave in ways that lead to the removal of these reinforcers—that is, we learn *not* to think about certain events and ideas.) Psychoanalysts believe that repression is at the heart of disorders such as **dissociative amnesia.**

REPRESSION OF MEMORIES OF CHILDHOOD SEXUAL ABUSE?

The popular media have recently been filled with stories of people in therapy who have recovered repressed memories of childhood sexual abuse (Pope, 1996). Symptoms such as the following have been presented as evidence of the presence of such memories: poor grades in school, difficulty concentrating, fear of new experiences, problems recollecting parts of childhood, low self-esteem, depression, sexual dysfunctions, and indecision (Hergenhahn, 1997; Loftus & Ketcham, 1994).

Loftus (1993a) does not deny that childhood sexual abuse is a serious problem, but she argues that most such recovered repressed memories are false. Consider that many people enter therapy without such memories but leave therapy with them. Because of the way in which these memories are "acquired," Loftus suspects that some therapists may suggest the presence of such memories to clients (Hergenhahn, 1997). Once more: Loftus is *not* arguing that memories of childhood sexual abuse are false or unimportant. She *is* suspicious of the accuracy of "repressed" memories of abuse that are "recovered" in therapy.

Infantile Amnesia

Question: Can children remember events from the first couple of years of life? When he interviewed people about their early experiences, Freud discovered that they could not recall episodes that had happened prior to the age of 3 or so, and that recall was cloudy through the age of 5. This phenomenon is referred to as **infantile amnesia.**

Infantile amnesia has nothing to do with the fact that the episodes occurred in the distant past. Middle-aged and older people have vivid memories from the ages of 6 and 10, yet the events happened many decades ago. But 18-year-olds show steep declines in memory when they try to recall episodes that occurred earlier than the age of 6, even though they happened less than 18 years earlier (Wetzler & Sweeney, 1986).

Freud believed that young children have aggressive impulses and perverse lusts toward their parents. He attributed infantile amnesia to repression of these impulses (Bauer, 1996). However, the episodes lost to infantile amnesia are not weighted in the direction of such "primitive" impulses.

Infantile amnesia probably reflects the interaction of physiological and cognitive factors. For example, a structure of the limbic system (the **hippocampus**) that is involved in the storage of memories does not become mature until we are about 2 years old (Squire, 1993, 1996). Also, myelination of brain pathways is incomplete for the first few years, contributing to the inefficiency of information processing and memory formation. There are also cognitive reasons for infantile amnesia:

DISSOCIATIVE AMNESIA Amnesia thought to stem from psychological conflict or trauma.

INFANTILE AMNESIA Inability to recall events that occur prior to the age of 2 or 3. Also termed *childhood amnesia.*

HIPPOCAMPUS A structure in the limbic system that plays an important role in the formation of new memories.

REFLECT

Do children really remember nothing from the first two years of life? Don't they remember (recognize) their caregivers? Don't they remember language? Don't they remember how to crawl and sit up and walk? To what kinds of memories, then, does the concept of infantile amnesia apply?

1. Infants are not particularly interested in remembering the past (Goleman, 1993).

2. Infants, in contrast to older children, tend not to weave episodes together into meaningful stories of their own lives. (Freud also recognized the second possibility [Bauer, 1996]). Information about specific episodes thus tends to be lost.

3. Infants do not make reliable use of language to symbolize or classify events. Their ability to *encode* sensory input—that is, to apply the auditory and semantic codes that facilitate memory formation—is therefore limited.

✓ Truth or Fiction Revisited

It is not true that we can remember the important events that take place during the first two years of life. (Really, Allyn, believe me.) Early childhood memories that seem so clear today are probably reconstructed and mostly inaccurate. Or they may be memories of events that occurred when we were older than we think we were.

Anterograde and Retrograde Amnesia

Question: Why do people frequently have trouble recalling being in accidents? In so-called **anterograde amnesia,** there are memory lapses for the period following a trauma such as a blow to the head, an electric shock, or an operation. In some cases the trauma seems to interfere with all the processes of memory. The ability to pay attention, the encoding of sensory input, and rehearsal are all impaired. A number of investigators have linked certain kinds of brain damage—such as damage to the hippocampus—to amnesia (Squire, 1993).

Consider the classic case of a man with the initials H. M. Parts of the brain are sometimes lesioned to help people with epilepsy. In H. M.'s case, a section of the hippocampus was removed (Milner, 1966). Right after the operation, the man's mental functioning appeared to be normal. As time went on, however, it became quite clear that he had severe problems in processing information. For example, two years after the operation, H. M. believed he was 27—his age at the time of the operation. When his family moved to a new address, H. M. could not find his new home or remember the new address. He responded with appropriate grief to the death of his uncle, yet he then began to ask about his uncle and why he did not visit. Each time he was informed of his uncle's passing, he grieved as he had when he first heard of it. All in all, it seems that H. M.'s operation prevented him from transferring information from short-term to long-term memory.

In **retrograde amnesia,** the source of trauma prevents people from remembering events that took place before the accident. A football player who is knocked unconscious or a person in an auto accident may be unable to recall events that occurred for several minutes prior to the trauma. The football player may not recall taking the field. The person in the accident may not recall entering the car. It also sometimes happens that the individual cannot remember events that occurred for several years prior to the traumatic incident.

In one well-known case of retrograde amnesia, a man received a head injury in a motorcycle accident (Baddeley, 1982). When he regained consciousness, he had lost memory for all events that had occurred after the age of 11. In fact, he appeared to believe that he was still 11 years old. During the next few months he gradually recovered more knowledge of

ANTEROGRADE AMNESIA Failure to remember events that occur after physical trauma because of the effects of the trauma.

RETROGRADE AMNESIA Failure to remember events that occur prior to physical trauma because of the effects of the trauma.

his past. He moved toward the present year by year, up until the critical motorcycle ride. But he never did recover the events just prior to the accident. The accident had apparently prevented the information that was rapidly unfolding before him from being transferred to long-term memory. In terms of stages of memory, it may be that our perceptions and ideas need to consolidate, or rest undisturbed for a while, if they are to be transferred to long-term memory.

Review

SECTION IV

German psychologist Hermann (73) _____aus originated the use of nonsense syllables in the study of memory and forgetting. Nonsense syllables are intended to be (74: Meaningful or Meaningless?). Thus their retention is based on (75) ac_____ coding and maintenance (76) _____sal.

The three memory tasks listed in the text are (77) _____ition, (78) _____ll, and relearning. (79) Re_____ is the easiest type of memory task. In his own studies of recall, Ebbinghaus would read lists of (80) _____ _____bles aloud to the beat of a metronome and then see how many he could produce from memory. Psychologists also often use lists of pairs of nonsense syllables, called (81) _____ed _____ates, to measure recall.

Ebbinghaus devised the method of (82) _____ings to study the efficiency of relearning. First he would record the number of repetitions required to learn a list of (83) n_____ syllables or words. Then he would record the number of repetitions required to (84) re_____ the list after a certain amount of time had elapsed. He would compute the difference between the numbers of (85) _____tions required to arrive at the savings. According to Ebbinghaus's classic curve of (86) _____ting, there is no loss of memory as measured by savings immediately after a list has been learned. Recollection drops (87: Gradually or Precipitously?) during the first hour after learning a list. Losses of learning then become more (88: Gradual or Precipitous?).

According to (89) _____ence theory, we forget material in short-term and long-term memory because newly learned material interferes with it. In (90) _____tive interference, new learning interferes with the retrieval of old learning. In (91) _____tive interference, older learning interferes with the capacity to retrieve more recently learned material.

According to Sigmund Freud, we repress many painful memories and unacceptable ideas because they produce (92) an_____, guilt, and shame. Psychoanalysts believe that repression is at the heart of disorders such as (93) _____tive amnesia.

Freud found that we usually cannot remember events that took place prior to the age of (94) _____. Freud labeled this phenomenon infantile (95) am_____ and attributed it to (96) re_____. However, the text suggests that infantile amnesia probably reflects the interaction of physiological and (97) _____tive factors. For example, the (98) hip_____, which is involved in memory formation, does not mature until about the age of 2. Moreover, infants' lack of language impairs their ability to (99) en_____ information.

In (100) _____rade amnesia there are memory lapses for the period following a traumatic event, such as a blow to the head, electric shock, or an operation. In (101) _____rade amnesia the source of trauma prevents people from remembering events that took place beforehand.

SECTION V. METHODS OF IMPROVING MEMORY: USING THE PSYCHOLOGY OF MEMORY TO IMPROVE YOUR MEMORY

Humans have survived the Ice Age, the Stone Age, the Iron Age, and, a bit more recently, the Industrial Revolution. Now we are trying to cope with the so-called Age of Information, in which there has been an explosion of information. Computers have been developed to process it. Humans, too, process information, and there is more of it to process than ever before. We can always add more memory to our computers, but—Question: How can people improve their memory? Fortunately, psychologists have helped devise methods for improving human memory. Let us consider some of them.

Drill and Practice

Repetition (rote maintenance rehearsal) helps transfer information from short-term to long-term memory. Does maintenance rehearsal seem too mechanical for you as a college student? If so, don't forget that this is how you learned the alphabet and how to count! Schoolchildren write spelling words over and over to remember them. Athletes repeat motions so that they will become part of their procedural memory. When you have memorized formulas, during a test you can use your time to think about when to apply them, rather than using up valuable time trying to recall them.

Some students use flash cards to help them remember facts. For example, they might write "The originator of modern behaviorism is _____" on one side of the card and "John Broadus Watson" on the flip side.

In his book *Super Memory,* Douglas Herrmann (1991) recommends the following methods for remembering a person's name:

1. Say the name out loud.
2. Ask the person a question, using her or his name.
3. Use the person's name as many times as you can during your conversation.
4. Write down the name when the conversation has ended.

Relate New Information to What Is Already Known

Relating new information to what is already known is a form of elaborative rehearsal that helps us to remember it (Willoughby et al., 1994). Herrmann (1991) also suggests that you can better remember the name of a new acquaintance by thinking of a rhyme for it. Now you have done some active thinking about the name, and you also have two tags for the person, not one. If you are trying to retrieve the spelling of the word *retrieve,* do so by retrieving the rule "*i* before *e* except after *c*." There are exceptions, of course: Remember that "weird" doesn't follow the rule because it's a "weird" word.

We normally expand our knowledge base by relating new items to things already known. Children learn that a cello is like a violin, only bigger. A bass fiddle is also like a violin, but bigger yet. We remember information about whales by relating whales to other mammals. Similarly, we are better able to recall information about porpoises and dolphins if we think of them as small whales (not as bright fish).

The media are filled with stories about people who exhibit psychological disorders of one kind or another. To help remember the disorders discussed in Chapter 13, think of film or TV characters with those disorders. How were the characters' behaviors consistent (or inconsistent) with the descriptions in the text (and those offered by your

REFLECT

How are drill and practice related to the PQ4R method of learning?

REFLECT

Can you explain how various "Reflect" items throughout the text, including this one, help you relate new information to things you already know?

professor)? You will remember the subject matter better *and* become a good critic of media portrayals of psychological problems if you use this technique.

Form Unusual, Exaggerated Associations

Psychologist Charles L. Brewer uses an interesting method to teach psychology students the fundamentals of shaping:

> In a recent class, Dr. Brewer first danced on his desk, then bleated like a sheep and finally got down on "all fours and oinked like a pig," he said. His antics were in response to a session he teaches on "successive approximation"—shaping behavior into a desired response.
>
> To get students to "shape" him, he told them he would try to figure out what they wanted him to do. If he guessed wrong, they'd "boo and hiss," while if he did what they wanted, they'd applaud him—which is why he eventually acted like a pig. "I'll do anything to get them to learn," he said. (DeAngelis, 1994, p. 40)

It is easier to recall stimuli that stand out from the crowd. We pay more attention to them. Sometimes, therefore, we are better able to remember information when we create unusual, exaggerated associations.

Assume that you are trying to remember the geography of the cerebral cortex, as shown in Figure 2.13 on page 71. Why not think of what you look like in right profile? (Use your left profile if it is better.) Then imagine a new imaging technique in which we can see through your skull and find four brightly colored lobes in the right hemisphere of your cerebral cortex. Not only that, but there are little people (let's call them "homunculi") who are flapping about in the sensory and motor areas (see Figure 2.13 again). In fact, imagine that you're in a crowded line and someone steps on your toe. As a result, the homunculus[2] (a "homunculus" is a single member of the homunculi clan) in the sensory cortex has a throbbing toe. This is communicated to the association areas of the cortex, where you decide that you are annoyed. The language areas of the cortex think up some choice words that are relayed to the throat and mouth of the homunculus in the motor cortex. Then they are sent into your throat and mouth. You also send some messages through the motor cortex that ready your muscles to attack.

Then you see that the perpetrator of the crime is a very attractive and apologetic stranger! What part of the occipital lobe is flashing the wonderful images?

Use the Method of Loci

Another way to form unusual associations is the *method of loci* (pronounced LOW-sigh). Select a series of related images such as the parts of your body or the furniture in your home. Then imagine an item from your shopping list, or another list you want to remember, as being attached to

REFLECT

What is your opinion of Dr. Brewer's method for helping students understand the concept of shaping? Helpful? Too unsophisticated for your class? What do you think? Why?

REFLECT

Can you remember what to buy at the supermarket without a list? How do you do so?

---

[2] I will give extra credit to students who research (and find) the meaning and origin of the word *homunculus*. My generosity does not obligate your professor, of course.

each image. Consider this meaty application: Remember your shopping list by imagining meatloaf in your navel and a strip of bacon draped over your nose.

By placing meatloaf or a favorite complete dinner in your navel, rather than a single item such as ground beef, you can combine several items into one chunk of information. At the supermarket, you recall the ingredients for meatloaf and consider whether you need each one.

Use Mediation

The method of mediation also relies on forming associations: You link two items with a third one that ties them together.

What if you are having difficulty remembering that John's wife's name is Tillie? You can mediate between John and Tillie as follows. Reflect that *john* is a slang term for bathroom. Bathrooms often have ceramic *tiles*. *Tiles*, of course, sounds like *Tillie*. So it goes: John → bathroom tiles → Tillie.

I used a combination of mediation and formation of unusual associations to help me remember foreign vocabulary words in high school. For example, the Spanish word *mujer* (pronounced moo-hair [almost]), means "woman" in English. Women have mo' hair than I do. Woman → mo' hair → mujer. This particular example would no longer work for me because now most men also have more hair than I, but the association was so outlandish that it has stuck with me.

Use Mnemonic Devices

Broadly speaking, methods for jogging memory can all be termed *mnemonics,* or systems for remembering information. But so-called "mnemonic devices" usually combine chunks of information into a format such as an acronym, jingle, or phrase.[3] For example, recalling the phrase "Every Good Boy Does Fine" has helped many people remember the musical keys E, G, B, D, F. In Chapter 2, we saw that the acronym *SAME* serves as a mnemonic device for distinguishing between afferent and efferent neurons. In Chapter 4, we noted that most psychology students use the acronym *Roy G. Biv* to remember the colors of the rainbow, even though your "backward" author chose to use the "word" *vibgyor.*

Acronyms have found applications in many disciplines. Consider geography. The acronym *HOMES* stands for the Great Lakes: *Huron, Ontario, Michigan, Erie,* and *Superior.* In astronomy, the phrase "*Mercury's very eager mother just served us nine potatoes*" helps students recall the order of the planets Mercury, Venus, Earth, Mars, Jupiter, Saturn, Uranus, Neptune, and Pluto. Table 7.2 lists some of my favorite mnemonic devices.

What about biology? You can remember that Dromedary camels have one hump while Bactrian camels have two by turning the letters *D* and *B* on their sides.

REFLECT

Do you use any mnemonic devices? What are they? How do they help you?

---

[3] By the way, the word *mnemonic* is derived from Mnemosyne, the Greek goddess of memory. Her name is pronounced *Nee-MOS-uh-nee.* How can you remember the pronunciation? Why not think of the goddess getting down on her two knees (*nee-nee*) to worship? End of commercial for mnemonic devices.

TABLE 7.2	MNEMONIC DEVICES
MNEMONIC DEVICE	**ENCODED INFORMATION**
HOMES	The names of the Great Lakes: Huron, Ontario, Michigan, Erie, and Superior
No Plan Like Yours to Study History Wisely.	The royal houses of England: Norman, Plantagenet, Lancaster, York, Tudor, Stuart, Hanover, Windsor.
X shall stand for playmates Ten. V for Five stalwart men. I for One, D for Five. M for a Thousand soldiers true. And L for Fifty, I'll tell you.	The value of the Roman numerals. "D for Five" means D = 500.
Mary Eats Peanut Butter.	The first four hydrocarbons of the Alkane class: Methane, Ethane, Propane, and Butane, in ascending order of the number of carbon atoms in their chains.
These Ten Valuable Amino Acids Have Long Preserved Life in Man	Ten vital amino acids: Threonine, Tryptophan, Valine, Arginine, Histidine, Lysine, Phenylalanine, Leucine, Isoleucine, Methionine.
All Hairy Men Will Buy Razors.	Constituents of soil: Air, Humus, Mineral salts, Water, Bacteria, Rock particles.
Soak Her Toe.	Translates into SOHCAHTOA, or: Sine = Opposite/Hypotenuse Cosine = Adjacent/Hypotenuse Tangent = Opposite/Adjacent
Krakatoa Positively Casts Off Fumes; Generally Sulfurous Vapors.	Biological classifications in descending order: Kingdom, Phylum, Class, Order, Family, Genus, Species, Variety.
Never Lower Tillie's Pants; Mother Might Come Home.	The eight bones of the wrist: Navicular, Lunate, Triangular, Pisiform, Multangular greater, Multangular lesser, Capitate, Hamate.
Roy G. Biv	The colors of the spectrum: red, orange, yellow, green, blue, indigo, violet
Lazy French Tarts Sit Naked In Anticipation.	The nerves that pass through the superior orbital fissure of the skull: Lachrymal, Frontal, Trochlear, Superior, Nasal, Inferior, Abducent.

And how can you math students ever be expected to remember the reciprocal of pi (that is, 1 divided by 3.14)? Simple: Just remember the question "Can I remember the reciprocal?" and count the number of letters in each word. The reciprocal of pi, it turns out, is 0.318310. (Remember the last two digits as 10, not as 1 and 0.)

Finally, how can you remember how to spell *mnemonics*? Easy—be willing to grant "a*MN*esty" to those who cannot.

✓ **Truth or Fiction Revisited**

It is true that you can use tricks to improve your memory. The "tricks" all involve ways of forming associations.

Review

SECTION V

One way to improve memory is by rote (102) _____-ance rehearsal, otherwise referred to as (103) dr_____ and practice. A method based on the concept of elaborative rehearsal is to (104) r_____ new information to that which is already known. It is also helpful to form unusual, exaggerated (105) _____tions. So-called (106) _____ic devices combine chunks of information into formats such as acronyms or phrases.

SECTION VI. THE BIOLOGY OF MEMORY: FROM ENGRAMS TO ADRENALINE

Psychologists assume that mental processes such as the encoding, storage, and retrieval of information—that is, memory—are accompanied by changes in the brain. Early in the century, many psychologists used the concept of the **engram** in their study of memory. Engrams were viewed as electrical circuits in the brain that corresponded to memory traces—neurological processes that paralleled experiences. Yet biological psychologists such as Karl Lashley (1950) spent many fruitless years searching for such circuits or for the structures of the brain in which they might be housed. Much contemporary research on the biology of memory focuses on the roles of neurons, neurotransmitters, and hormones.

Changes at the Neural Level

Question: What biological changes are connected with memory at the neural level? Rats who are reared in richly stimulating environments provide some answers. The animals develop more dendrites and synapses in the cerebral cortex than rats reared in relatively impoverished environments (Neisser, 1997). It also has been shown that the level of visual stimulation rats receive is associated with the number of synapses they develop in the visual cortex (Turner & Greenough, 1985). In sum, there is reason to believe that the storage of experience requires the number of avenues of communication among brain cells to be increased.

Visual experience makes changes in the visual cortex. Auditory experience makes changes in the auditory cortex. Information received through the other senses is likely to lead to corresponding changes in the cortical regions that represent them. Experiences perceived by several senses are also stored in numerous areas of the brain (Hilts, 1995). The recollection of experiences, as in the production of visual images, apparently involves neural activity in the appropriate regions of the brain (Kosslyn, 1994).

Research with sea snails has offered insight into the events that take place at existing synapses when learning occurs. One kind of snail, for example, has only about 20,000 neurons compared with humans' *billions*. As a result, researchers have actually been able to study how experience is reflected at the synapses of specific neurons. When sea snails are conditioned, more of the neurotransmitter serotonin is released at certain synapses. As a consequence, transmission at these synapses becomes more efficient as trials (learning) progress (Kandel & Hawkins, 1992). Transmission occurs at synapses because of naturally occurring chemical substances, such as the following:

ENGRAM (1) An assumed electrical circuit in the brain that corresponds to a memory trace. (2) An assumed chemical change in the brain that accompanies learning.

- Serotonin. This neurotransmitter increases the efficiency of conditioning (Kandel & Hawkins, 1992).
- Acetylcholine (ACh). This neurotransmitter is vital in memory formation; low levels of ACh are connected with Alzheimer's disease.
- Adrenaline. This hormone strengthens memory when it is released into the bloodstream following learning (LeDoux, 1997).
- Vasopressin. When people sniff synthetic vasopressin (antidiuretic hormone) in the form of a nasal spray, they show significant improvement in memory. Today, excess vasopressin can have serious side effects, but future versions may target specific receptors without causing these effects.

Other research has focused on the potential of substances as diverse as estrogen and nicotine to aid in the formation of memories and to delay the advance of Alzheimer's disease. As with vasopressin, future versions may target specific receptors without causing side effects.

Changes at the Structural Level

Question: What biological changes are connected with memory at the structural level? The case of H. M. provides some insight. Consider the problems that beset him after his operation. Certain parts of the brain such as the hippocampus also appear to be involved in the formation of new memories—or the transfer of information from short-term to long-term memory. The hippocampus does not comprise the "storage bins" for memories themselves because H. M.'s memories prior to the operation were not destroyed. Rather, it is involved in relaying incoming sensory information to parts of the cortex. Therefore, it appears to be vital to the storage of new information even if old information can be retrieved without it (Squire, 1996).

Where are the storage bins? The brain stores parts of memories in the appropriate areas of the sensory cortex (Goleman, 1994). Sights are stored in the visual cortex, sounds in the auditory cortex, and so on (Hilts, 1995). The limbic system is largely responsible for integrating these pieces of information when we recall an event.

A specific part of the limbic system, the hippocampus, is much involved in the where and when of things. The hippocampus does not become mature until we are about 2 years old, and immaturity of the hippocampus may be connected with infantile amnesia. Adults with hippocampal damage may be able to form new procedural memories, even though they cannot form new episodic ("where and when") memories. For example, they can acquire the skill of reading words backward even though they cannot recall individual practice sessions (Squire, 1996).

The thalamus is involved in verbal memories. Part of the thalamus of an Air Force cadet known as N. A. was damaged in a freak fencing accident. After the episode, N. A. could no longer form verbal memories, such as the names of things. However, his ability to form visual memories was not impaired (Squire, 1996).

The encoding, storage, and retrieval of information thus involve biological activity on several levels. As we learn, new synapses are developed, and changes occur at existing synapses. Various parts and structures of the brain are also involved in the formation of different kinds of memories. In the next chapter, we see how people manipulate the information they have stored to adapt to the environment or create new environments.

Review

SECTION VI

The storage of experience apparently requires that the number of avenues of communication among brain cells be increased by means of development of (107) _____ites and (108) _____pses. Research with sea snails has shown that more of the (109) _____mitter serotonin is released at certain synapses when they are conditioned. As a result, transmission at these synapses becomes (110: More or Less?) efficient as there are more and more trials.

The hormone (111) _____line generally stimulates bodily arousal and activity. Adrenaline and (112) vaso_____ strengthen memory when they are released following learning.

The hippocampus is involved in relaying incoming sensory information to parts of the (113) cor_____. Therefore, it appears vital to the storage of (114: New or Old?) information, even if (115: New or Old?) information can be retrieved without it. Persons with hippocampal damage can form new (116) _____ral memories, even though they cannot form new (117) _____ic memories. The (118) _____mus seems to be involved in the formation of verbal memories.

STUDY GUIDE

SUMMARY

1. **What is meant by episodic memory?** An episodic memory is a memory of a specific event that one has observed or participated in.

2. **What is meant by semantic memory?** Semantic memory is general knowledge, as in remembering that the United States has 50 states or that Shakespeare wrote *Hamlet*.

3. **What is meant by procedural memory?** Procedural memory means knowing how to do things like write with a pencil or ride a bicycle. It is also called *skill memory*.

4. **What is the role of encoding in memory?** Encoding information means changing it so that we can place it in memory. We commonly use visual, auditory, and semantic codes to convert physical and chemical stimulation into psychological formats that can be remembered.

5. **What is the role of storage in memory?** Storage means the maintenance of information over time. The main methods of storing information are maintenance rehearsal (rote repetition) and elaborative rehearsal (relating it to things we already know).

6. **What is the role of retrieval in memory?** Retrieval means locating stored information and bringing it back into consciousness. Retrieval requires use of the proper cues (just as to retrieve information stored on a hard drive, we need to know the filename.) Memory is defined as the processes by which information is encoded, stored, and retrieved.

7. **What is the Atkinson-Shiffrin model of memory?** Atkinson and Shiffrin propose that there are three stages of memory—sensory memory, short-term memory, and long-term memory—and that the progress of information through these stages determines whether and how long it is remembered.

8. **How does sensory memory function?** Each sense is believed to have a sensory register that briefly holds the *memory traces* of stimuli in sensory memory. The traces then *decay*. Visual sensory memory makes discrete visual sensations—produced by saccadic eye movements—seem continuous. McDougall used the whole-report procedure to demonstrate that visual stimuli are maintained in sensory memory for only a fraction of a second.

Sperling used the partial-report procedure to show that we can see more objects than we can report afterward. Icons are mental representations of visual stimuli. Some people, usually children, can maintain icons over long periods of time and are said to have eidetic imagery. Echoes are representations of auditory stimuli (sounds). Echoes can be held in sensory memory for several seconds.

9. **How does short-term memory function?** Focusing on a stimulus allows us to maintain it in short-term memory—also called *working memory*—for a minute or so after the trace decays. Rehearsal allows us to maintain information indefinitely. Miller showed that we can hold seven chunks of information (plus or minus two) in short-term memory. The appearance of new information in short-term memory *displaces* the old information.

10. **Why are we most likely to remember the first and last items in a list?** This phenomenon is referred to as the serial-position effect. We tend to remember the initial items in a list because they are rehearsed most often (the primacy effect). We tend to remember the final items in a list because they are least likely to have been displaced by new information (the recency effect).

11. **Is seven a magic number, or did the phone company get lucky?** Seven may not be a magic number, but it seems that the typical person can remember about seven chunks of information (juggle that many pieces of information in short-term memory).

12. **How does long-term memory function?** There is no known limit to the amount of information that can be stored in long-term memory, and memories can be stored for a lifetime. However, long-term memories have not been shown to be perfectly accurate. They are frequently biased because they are reconstructed according to our schemas—that is, our ways of mentally organizing our experiences. The memories of eyewitnesses can also be distorted by leading questions. Information is usually transferred from short-term to long-term memory by one of two paths: maintenance rehearsal (rote repetition) and elaborative rehearsal (relating information to things that are already known).

13. **What is the levels-of-processing model of memory?** This model views memory in terms of a single dimension—not three stages. It is hypothesized that we encode, store, and retrieve information more efficiently when we have processed it more deeply.

14. **Why is it that some events, like the death of Princess Diana, can be etched in memory for a lifetime?** So-called *flashbulb memories,* as of the death of a public figure like Princess Diana or JFK, Jr., tend to occur within a web of unusual and emotionally arousing circumstances. We may elaborate them extensively—that is, relate them to many things.

15. **How is knowledge organized in long-term memory?** We tend to organize information according to a hierarchical structure. That is, we classify or arrange chunks of information into groups or classes according to common features.

16. **Why do we sometimes feel that the answer to a question is on the tip of our tongue?** Research suggests that the tip-of-the-tongue phenomenon often reflects incomplete learning.

17. **Why may it be useful to study in the room in which we will be tested?** This is because memories are frequently dependent on the context in which they were formed. That is, context dependence refers to the finding that we often retrieve information more efficiently when we are in the same context we were in when we acquired it. State dependence refers to the finding that we often retrieve information better when we are in the same state of consciousness or mood we were in when we learned it.

18. **What types of memory tasks are used in measuring forgetting?** Nonsense syllables were developed by Ebbinghaus in the 19th century as a way of measuring the functions of memory. (How he would use them.) Retention is often tested through three types of memory tasks: recognition, recall, and relearning.

19. **Why can learning Spanish make it harder to remember French?** This is an example of retroactive interference, in which new learning interferes with old learning. In proactive interference, on the other hand, old learning interferes with new learning. According to interference theory, people can forget because learning can cause cues (such as English words) to be connected with the wrong information (perhaps a Spanish word when a French word is sought).

20. **What is repression?** Repression refers to Freud's concept of motivated forgetting. Freud suggested that we are motivated to forget threatening or unacceptable material.

21. **Can children remember events from the first couple of years of life?** Probably not. This phenomenon is referred to as infantile amnesia. Freud believed that infantile amnesia is due to repression, but modern psychologists believe that infantile amnesia reflects factors such as immaturity of the hippocampus and failure to use acoustic and semantic codes to help remember information.

22. **Why do people frequently have trouble recalling being in accidents?** This is because the physical trauma can interfere with memory formation. Two kinds of amnesia are caused by physical trauma. In anterograde amnesia, a traumatic event such as damage to the hippocampus prevents the formation of new memories. In retrograde amnesia, shock or other trauma prevents previously known information from being retrieved.

23. **How can people improve their memory?** People can improve their memory through use of maintenance rehearsal, as in drill and practice, or elaborative rehearsal, as in relating new information to what is already known, forming unusual and exaggerated associations, using the method of loci, using mediation, or using menmonic devices.

24. **What biological changes are connected with memory at the neural level?** Learning is apparently connected with the proliferation of dendrites and synapses in the brain. Learning and memory are also connected with the release of the neurotransmitters serotonin and acetylcholine and the hormones adrenaline and vasopressin.

25. **What biological changes are connected with memory at the structural level?** The hippocampus relays sensory information to the cortex and is therefore vital in formation of new memories. Visual memories appear to be stored in the visual cortex, auditory memories in the auditory cortex, and so on. The thalamus is connected with the formation of visual memories.

E X E R C I S E 1

NAMES TO REMEMBER

In the column to the left are a number of concepts in the psychology of memory. In the column to the right are the names of individuals who have had an impact on the psychology of memory. Write the name(s) of the proper persons in the blank spaces to the left of the concepts.

____ 1. Curve of forgetting	A. Atkinson and Shiffrin
____ 2. Sensory memory	B. Brown and McNeill
____ 3. Nonsense syllables	C. Craik and Lockhart
____ 4. Repression	D. Ebbinghaus
____ 5. Method of savings	E. Freud
____ 6. Levels-of-processing theory	F. Loftus
____ 7. Eyewitness testimony	G. McDougall
____ 8. Stages of memory	H. Penfield
____ 9. Neurosurgery	I. The Petersons
____10. Tip-of-the-tongue phenomenon	J. Sperling
____11. Childhood amnesia	
____12. Interference	
____13. Partial-report procedure	
____14. Psychogenic amnesia	
____15. Whole-report procedure	

EXERCISE 2

THE THREE THREES OF MEMORY

Fill in the blanks in the table.

CONCEPT	WHAT IT MEANS	EXAMPLE
THREE KINDS OF MEMORY		
(1) _____ Memory	Memories of events experienced or witnessed by the individual	Remembering what you ate for dinner last night
(2) _____ Memory	General knowledge (as opposed to remembering personal episodes)	Remembering the capital cities of the 50 states and the author of *Tom Sawyer*
Procedural Memory	Knowledge of ways of doing things; also termed (3) _____ *memory*	Remembering how to ride a bicycle, click a mouse, or write with a pencil
THREE PROCESSES OF MEMORY		
(4) _____ing	Modifying information so that it can be placed in memory, sometimes from one sensory modality (e.g., vision) to another (hearing)	Mental representation of the words in this table as a sequence of sounds, which is an example of an (5) _____tic code
Storage	Maintenance of information over time	Rote repetition—also known as (6) _____ance rehearsal—of the data in this table to keep it in memory
Retrieval	Finding of stored information and bringing it into conscious awareness	Recall of the information in this table; using a (7) _____ device such as Roy G. Biv to recall the colors of the spectrum
THREE STAGES OF MEMORY		
(8) _____ Memory	Type or stage of memory that is first encountered by a stimulus and briefly holds impressions of it	Continuing to "see" the memory trace of a visual stimulus that has been removed
Short-Term Memory	Type or stage of memory that can hold information for up to a minute or so after the trace of the stimulus decays; also termed (9) _____*ing memory*	Repeating someone's name in order to remember it, or relating something new to things that are already known
(10) _____-Term Memory	Type or stage of memory that is capable of relatively permanent storage	The "file cabinets" of memory, where you store the names of primary school teachers and memories of holidays of long ago

BRIDGING THE GAP

LANGUAGE AND CULTURE

to acquit (331)   *to judge innocent, to free someone on trial*

adherent (325)   *believer, follower of a theory*

all fours (344)   *hands and knees*

to be all wet (334)   *(here, a pun) to be unknowing*

amnesia (340)   *mental disorder involving loss of memory*

to be ashore (334)   *(here, a pun) to be on the land (and not in the water)*

assailant (327)   *attacker*

avenue (347)   *road, way*

background noise (325)   *normal distractions in a situation*

in the ballpark (333)   *within the estimate, close enough*

backward (345)   *(pun) slow learning, and also reversing (the letters)*

barge (333)   *motorless boat used to carry freight*

baton (327)   *stick, symbol of authority*

to beset (348)   *to bother, to occur to*

bitter (312)   *(here) very cold*

to bleat (344)   *to make a sound like a lamb*

blizzard (314)   *snow storm of great magnitude*

to boo and hiss (344)   *to express dislike or disapproval with sounds, to jeer*

bottomless pit (318)   *hole, abyss (that which can hold an unlimited number or amount)*

to break the surface of the water (333)   *to emerge (used metaphorically here, to mean "to become obvious or known")*

chance level (337)   *ordinary level, unaffected level*

bright (343)   *intelligent*

chancy (333)   *accidental, not reliable*

commercial (345)   *advertising announcement*

dash (323)   *(here) hyphen (-)*

discipline (345)   *area of study (like biology, literature, mathematics)*

to dislodge (324)   *to pry loose, to cause to disconnect and disappear, to remove*

to dredge up (325)   *to recover as if from the bottom (of a river)*

elaborative (343)   *elaborate, complex, grand*

dysfunction (340)   *inability (to function)*

to be embedded (330)   *to be hidden within*

to enhance (334)   *to add to, to improve*

to entail (330)   *to involve*

eyewitness testimony (326)   *evidence given by someone who saw the event*

fencing (348)   *sport played with swords, masks, and body protectors*

flapping about (344)   *moving around, acting like birds*

freak (338)   *rare, abnormal, totally unexpected*

goofy (312)   *silly*

in a former life (334)   *reference to the belief that people have lived many times, that their souls assume new bodies and return to earth after one body dies*

fresh as the driven snow (327)   *pure, unblemished, unchanged*

to fall through the cracks (324)   *to be lost because attention is elsewhere*

to be faulted (312)   *to be criticized*

foolproof (330)   *simple, well-designed so that a person won't make a mistake*

to go in one ear and out the other (318)   *to be experienced and immediately forgotten*

from time to time (313)   *occasionally, but not regularly*

at the heart of (340)   *the cause of*

hefty (323)   *large, big*

to be high and dry (334)   *(here, a pun) to be unknowing, to be unaware*

hijacker (327)   *thief*

to be housed (347)   *to be situated within*

to intersperse (337)   *to add something at intervals*

to intrude (323)   *to butt in, to encroach, to bother*

jingle (345)   *musical advertising piece*

to jostle (325)   *to push, to bump against*

junk (333)   *large river boat used in the Orient*

Krakatoa (346)   *famous volcano*

Lincoln penny (313)   *small coin with a portrait of Abraham Lincoln on it*

loci (344)   *places, locations*

to make sense of the long and short of it (318)   *(this is a mnemonic device and also an idiom) to understand all aspects of it (the expression is to help people remember that there are three stages of memory:* sensory, long-term, *and* short-term *memory)* to oink (344)   *to make a pig's sounds*

on the mark (333)   *precisely right, exact*

massive (316)   *huge*

meaty (344)   *significant (pun on meatloaf and bacon in the example)*

patchwork quilt (312)   *(here) a theory that is a mixture of unrelated ideas*

perceptual phenomenon (320)   *something unusual that is sensed (not seen)*

to piece together (312)   *to compose*

to practice surgery (327)   *(here) to amputate, to remove with a knife, to cut off*

precipitously (324)   *early, prematurely (here it is a pun, as a* precipice *is a cliff, over which one could fall!)*

premium (323)   *(here) payment of money*

profile (344)   *side view*

quirk (327)   *unusual personality aspect*

oblivion (318)   *nothingness*

to be outdone (312)   *to be surpassed, to have someone else do it better*

to be out on the streets (327)   *to be free, not to be in jail*

outlandish (345)   *unusual, bizarre*

retrieval (339)   *recovery*

sarong (333)   *woman's dress made of a piece of cloth wrapped around the body*

seamless (321)   *made of a single piece*

self-reproach (324)   *blaming oneself*

to shove (325)   *to push*

to slam a home run (331)   *(here) to hit the baseball out of the playing field and score a point*

to stand out from a crowd (344)   *to be unique in a group*

to stick out one's neck (317)   *to risk*

stream of thought (319)   *continuous sequence of ideas*

striking (331)   *unusual, worthy of note*

subordinate (333)   *low in the order or hierarchy*

superordinate (332)   *high in a hierarchy*

to take the field (341)   *to return to the field of play*

tedious (338)   *difficult and boring*

terra firma (334)   *firm land, solid ground*

throng (327)   *crowd*

tic-tac-toe (324)   *cross hatch (#) used for a children's pencil-and-paper game*

trivia (333)   *unimportant*

trivial (313)   *insignificant*

urge (340)   *drive, craving, impulse*

with a vengeance (325)   *with strength and great feeling*

vestige (318)   *trace, remainder*

vibrancy (331)   *liveliness, energy*

a vicious cycle (335)   *periodic cause-and-effect repetition*

to wreak havoc with (324)   *to ruin, to damage*

1. Tim remembers that Shakespeare wrote *Hamlet.* This type of memory is referred to as a(n)
   (a) episodic memory,
   (b) visual memory,
   (c) procedural memory,
   (d) semantic memory.

2. George Sperling used the _____ method in his studies of sensory memory.
   (a) partial-report,
   (b) savings,
   (c) paired-associates,
   (d) whole-report.

3. Visual impressions last for _____ in the sensory memory.
   (a) a fraction of a second,
   (b) about 2–5 seconds,
   (c) about half a minute,
   (d) several minutes or longer.

4. Only about 5% of children show
   (a) metamemory,
   (b) iconic memory,
   (c) photographic memory,
   (d) eidetic imagery.

5. Echoic memory is defined as
   (a) an acoustic code,
   (b) the pathways between the thalamus and the auditory cortex,
   (c) the sensory register that holds auditory stimuli,
   (d) a type of procedural memory.

6. *Working memory* is another term for
   (a) iconic memory,
   (b) semantic memory,
   (c) elaborative rehearsal,
   (d) short-term memory.

7. You are given the task of remembering the written phrase "Every good boy does fine." You "say" the phrase "mentally," or "to yourself," and then you repeat it to yourself 10 times. Which of the following methods have you employed?
   (a) Visual encoding and elaborative rehearsal,
   (b) Acoustic encoding and maintenance rehearsal,
   (c) Semantic encoding and maintenance rehearsal,
   (d) Episodic memory and procedural memory.

8. You are asked to memorize this list of letters: TBJKZMGXTR. You repeat the list several times. Which letters are you most likely to recall?
   (a) The sequence *JKZ,*
   (b) The sequence *ZM,*
   (c) The *Z* and the *X,*
   (d) The first *T* and the *R.*

9. A student studies for a test in the room in which the test will be administered. The student is apparently hoping that performance will be facilitated by
   (a) context-dependent memory,
   (b) state-dependent memory,
   (c) photographic memory,
   (d) iconic memory.

10. Information is *least* likely to be lost through decay in
    (a) iconic memory,
    (b) echoic memory,
    (c) short-term memory,
    (d) long-term memory.

11. Which of the following has been compared with a shelf or workbench so that once it is full, some things fall off when new items are shoved on?
    (a) Episodic memory,
    (b) Sensory memory,
    (c) Short-term memory,
    (d) Long-term memory.

12. Which of the following is most likely to remain firmly "embedded" in your memory over the decades?
    (a) The name of your second-grade teacher,
    (b) A sonnet you memorized in high school,
    (c) How you celebrated your 11th birthday,
    (d) How to ride a bicycle.

13. John forgets a dental appointment about which he had been extremely anxious. Freud would probably attribute his forgetting to
    (a) repression,
    (b) anterograde amnesia,
    (c) proactive interference,
    (d) decay of the memory trace.

14. Loftus and Palmer showed people a film of a car crash and then asked them to fill out questionnaires that included a question about how fast the cars were going at the time. People who reported that the car was going fastest had been asked to estimate how fast the cars were going when they _____ one another.

(a) "hit,"
(b) "smashed,"
(c) "bumped,"
(d) "touched."

15. Which of the following does the text state is the most effective way of transferring information from STM into LTM?
    (a) Eidetic imagery,
    (b) Maintenance rehearsal,
    (c) Elaborative rehearsal,
    (d) Becoming emotionally aroused.

16. According to the text, the feeling-of-knowing experience seems to reflect
    (a) lack of visual retrieval cues,
    (b) incomplete or imperfect learning,
    (c) skill memory rather than semantic memory,
    (d) STM displacement by anxiety-evoking information.

17. A parent knows that you are taking a psychology course and asks how he can teach his young child the alphabet. You note that children usually learn the alphabet by

(a) rote repetition,
(b) use of elaborative rehearsal,
(c) semantic coding,
(d) chunking.

18. Information in short-term memory tends to be forgotten by means of
    (a) psychogenic amnesia,
    (b) failure to use appropriate retrieval cues,
    (c) displacement,
    (d) retrograde amnesia.

19. The easiest type of memory task is
    (a) recall,
    (b) recognition,
    (c) relearning,
    (d) savings.

20. When sea snails are conditioned, more of the neurotransmitter _____ is released at certain synapses. As a result, transmission at these synapses becomes more efficient as trials (learning) progress.
    (a) acetylcholine,
    (b) dopamine,
    (c) noradrenaline,
    (d) serotonin.

1. What is meant by episodic memory?

2. What is meant by semantic memory?

3. What is meant by procedural memory?

4. What is the role of encoding in memory?

5. What is the role of storage in memory?

6. What is the role of retrieval in memory?

7. What is the Atkinson-Shiffrin model of memory?

8. How does sensory memory function?

9. How does short-term memory function?

10. Why are we most likely to remember the first and last items in a list?

11. Is seven a magic number, or did the phone company get lucky?

12. How does long-term memory function?

13. What is the levels-of-processing model of memory?

14. Why is it that some events, like the death of Princess Diana, can be etched in memory for a lifetime?

15. How is knowledge organized in long-term memory?

16. Why do we sometimes feel that the answer to a question is on the tip of our tongue?

17. Why may it be useful to study in the room in which we will be tested?

18. What types of memory tasks are used in measuring forgetting?

19. Why can learning Spanish make it harder to remember French?

20. What is repression?

21. Can children remember events from the first couple of years of life?

22. Why do people frequently have trouble recalling being in accidents?

_____
_____
_____
_____
_____

23. How can people improve their memory?

_____
_____
_____
_____
_____
_____

24. What biological changes are connected with memory at the neural level?

_____
_____
_____
_____
_____
_____

25. What biological changes are connected with memory at the structural level?

_____
_____
_____
_____
_____
_____
_____

ANSWERS TO SECTION REVIEWS

1. Episodic
2. Semantic
3. Episodic
4. Semantic
5. Procedural
6. Skill
7. Encoding
8. Information
9. Encode
10. Visual
11. Auditory
12. Semantic
13. Represents
14. Sounds
15. Meaning
16. Storage
17. Maintenance
18. Elaborative
19. Retrieval
20. Cues
21. Retrieved
22. Sensory
23. Short-term
24. Long-term
25. Sensory
26. Perceptions
27. Trace
28. Registers
29. Registers
30. Whole

31. Partial
32. Decays
33. Icons
34. Iconic memory
35. Photographic
36. Eidetic
37. Auditory
38. Traces
39. Short-term
40. Working
41. Rehearse (or repeat)
42. Maintenance
43. Serial
44. More
45. Most
46. Primacy
47. Recency
48. Seven
49. Rote
50. Repetition
51. Interference
52. Information
53. Freud
54. Schemas
55. Reconstruct
56. Is not
57. Short
58. Cues
59. Process
60. Levels

61. Unusual
62. Flashbulb
63. Distinctness
64. Elaboratively
65. Hierarchical
66. Tip
67. Tongue
68. Acoustic
69. Semantic
70. Context
71. Context
72. Physiological
73. Ebbinghaus
74. Meaningless
75. Acoustic
76. Rehearsal
77. Recognition
78. Recall
79. Recognition
80. Nonsense syllables
81. Paired associates
82. Savings
83. Nonsense
84. Relearn
85. Repetitions
86. Forgetting
87. Precipitously
88. Gradual
89. Interference
90. Retroactive

91. Proactive
92. Anxiety
93. Dissociative
94. Three
95. Amnesia
96. Repression
97. Cognitive
98. Hippocampus
99. Encode
100. Anterograde
101. Retrograde
102. Maintenance
103. Drill
104. Relate
105. Associations
106. Mnemonic
107. Dendrites
108. Synapses
109. Neurotransmitter
110. More
111. Adrenaline
112. Vasopressin
113. Cortex
114. New
115. Old
116. Procedural
117. Episodic
118. Thalamus

ANSWERS TO EXERCISE 1

1. D
2. I, J
3. D
4. E

5. D
6. C
7. F
8. A

9. H
10. B
11. E
12. I

13. J
14. E
15. G

ANSWERS TO EXERCISE 2

1. Episodic
2. Semantic
3. Skill

4. Encoding
5. Acoustic
6. Maintenance

7. Mnemonic
8. Sensory

9. Working
10. Long

ANSWERS TO QUIZ

1. D
2. A
3. A
4. D
5. C

6. D
7. B
8. D
9. A
10. D

11. C
12. D
13. A
14. B
15. C

16. B
17. A
18. C
19. B
20. D

TRUTH OR FICTION?

T F ✓✓✓✓✓✓✓✓✓✓✓✓✓

☐ ☐ Using a "tried and true" formula is the most efficient way to solve a problem.

☐ ☐ Only humans can solve problems by means of insight.

☐ ☐ The best way to solve a frustrating problem is to keep plugging away at it.

☐ ☐ People with great academic ability are also creative.

☐ ☐ If a couple has five sons, the sixth child is likely to be a daughter.

☐ ☐ People change their opinions when they are shown to be wrong.

☐ ☐ "Street smarts" are a kind of intelligence.

☐ ☐ The terms *intelligence* and *IQ* mean the same thing.

☐ ☐ Two children can answer exactly the same items on an intelligence test correctly, yet one child can be above average and the other below average in IQ.

☐ ☐ Early administrators of intelligence tests gave them in English to immigrants who did not understand the language.

☐ ☐ Head Start programs have raised children's IQs.

This chapter, "Thinking and Intelligence," covers the following:

SECTION I. THINKING
Defines *thinking*

SECTION II. CONCEPTS: BUILDING BLOCKS OF THOUGHT
Explains how concepts function as building blocks of thought

SECTION III. PROBLEM SOLVING
Describes various approaches to problem solving

Describes how people sometimes jump to (correct) conclusions rather than use tried and true formulas

Discusses factors that affect effectiveness at solving problems

SECTION IV. CREATIVITY
Discusses the relationships among problem solving, creativity, and intelligence

Discusses factors other than intelligence that affect creativity

SECTION V. REASONING
Discusses various types of reasoning

SECTION VI. JUDGMENT AND DECISION MAKING
Explains how people go about making judgments and decisions

Discusses ways of framing arguments to get your way

Discusses why people tend to be convinced that they are right, even when they are dead wrong

SECTION VII. THINKING AND LINGUISTIC RELATIVITY
Discusses the relationships between thinking and language

SECTION VIII. INTELLIGENCE
Defines *intelligence*

Discusses factor theories of intelligence

Discusses Gardner's theory of multiple intelligences

Discusses Sternberg's triarchic theory of intelligence

Discusses the theory of emotional intelligence

SECTION IX. THE MEASUREMENT OF INTELLIGENCE
Describes the Stanford-Binet Intelligence Scale

Describes the Wechsler Scales

SECTION X. INTELLIGENCE AND DIVERSITY: SOCIOECONOMIC AND ETHNIC DIFFERENCES IN INTELLIGENCE
Discusses socioeconomic and ethnic differences in intelligence

SECTION XI. THE TESTING CONTROVERSY: JUST WHAT DO INTELLIGENCE TESTS MEASURE?
Discusses the issue of whether intelligence tests contain cultural biases against ethnic minority groups and immigrants

SECTION XII. DETERMINANTS OF INTELLIGENCE: WHERE DOES INTELLIGENCE COME FROM?
Discusses research concerning genetic influences on intelligence

Discusses research concerning environmental influences on intelligence

When she was 9, my daughter Jordan stumped me with a problem about a bus driver that she had heard in school. Because I firmly believe in exposing students to the kinds of torture I have undergone, see what you can do with her problem:

> You're driving a bus that's leaving from Pennsylvania. To start off with, there were 32 people on the bus. At the next bus stop, 11 people got off and 9 people got on. At the next bus stop, 2 people got off and 2 people got on. At the next bus stop, 12 people got on and 16 people got off. At the next bus stop, 5 people got on and 3 people got off. What color are the bus driver's eyes?

I was not about to be fooled when I was listening to this problem. Although it seemed clear that I should be keeping track of how many people were on the bus, I had an inkling that a trick was involved. Therefore, I told myself to remember that the bus was leaving from Pennsylvania. Being clever, I also kept track of the number of stops rather than the number of people getting on and off the bus. When I was finally hit with the question about the bus driver's eyes, I was at a loss. I protested that Jordan had said nothing about the bus driver's eyes, but she insisted that she had given me enough information to answer the question.

One of the requirements of problem solving is paying attention to relevant information (de Jong & Das-Smaal, 1995). To do that, you need some familiarity with the type of problem you are dealing with. I immediately classified the bus driver problem as a trick question and paid attention to information that apparently was superfluous. But I wasn't good enough.

SECTION I. THINKING

The Greek philosopher Aristotle pointed out that people differ from lower organisms in their capacity for rational thinking. Thinking enables us to build skyscrapers, create computers, and scan the interior of the body without surgery. Some people even manage to keep track of their children and balance their checkbooks.

Question: What is thinking? **Thinking** may be defined as the mental activity involved in understanding, processing, and communicating information. Thinking entails attending to information, representing it mentally, reasoning about it, and making judgments and decisions about it. The term *thinking* generally refers to conscious, planned attempts to make sense of our world.

In this chapter we explore thinking and the related topic of intelligence. We begin with concepts, which provide the building blocks of thought. But before we proceed, I have one question for you: What color were the bus driver's eyes?

REFLECT

What strategy did you use to try to solve the bus driver problem? Did it work? Why or why not?

Review

SECTION I

Thinking is defined as the mental activity involved in (1) _____ding, (2) _____sing, and communicating information. The bus driver problem illustrates that one of the requirements of problem solving is paying attention to relevant (3) _____tion.

THINKING Mental activity involved in understanding, manipulating, and communicating about information. Thinking entails paying attention to information, mentally representing it, reasoning about it, and making decisions about it.

SECTION II. CONCEPTS: BUILDING BLOCKS OF THOUGHT

I began the chapter with Jordan's problem. Let me proceed with an oral riddle from my own childhood: "What's black and white and read all over?" Because this riddle was spoken, not written, and involved the colors black and white, you would probably assume that "read" meant "red." Thus, in seeking an answer, you might scan your memory for an object that was red although it also somehow managed to be black and white. The answer to the riddle, "newspaper," was usually met with a groan.

The word *newspaper* is a **concept.** *Red, black,* and *white* are also concepts—color concepts. Concepts are mental categories used to group together objects, relations, events, abstractions, or qualities that have common properties.

Question: How do concepts function as building blocks of thought? Concepts are crucial to thinking. Concepts can represent objects, events, and activities—and visions of things that never were. Much thinking has to do with categorizing new concepts and manipulating relationships among concepts.

We tend to organize concepts in *hierarchies.* The newspaper category includes objects such as your school paper and the *Los Angeles Times.* Newspapers, college textbooks, novels, and merchandise catalogs can be combined into higher-order categories such as *printed matter* or *printed devices that store information.* If you add CD-ROMs and floppy disks, you can create a still higher category, *objects that store information.* Now consider a question that requires categorical thinking: How are a newspaper and a CD-ROM alike? Answers to such questions entail supplying the category that includes both objects. In this case, we can say that both objects store information. That is, their functions are similar, even if their technologies differ.

Prototypes are examples that best match the essential features of categories. In less technical terms, prototypes are good examples. When new stimuli closely match people's prototypes of concepts, they are readily recognized as examples (Sloman, 1996). Which animal seems more birdlike to you, a robin or an ostrich? Why? Which of the following better fits the prototype of a fish, a sea horse or a shark? Both self-love and maternal love may be forms of love, but more people readily agree that maternal love is a kind of love. Apparently maternal love better fits their prototype of love (Fehr & Russell, 1991).

Many simple prototypes, such as *dog* and *red,* are taught by means of **exemplars.** We point to a dog and say, "dog" or, "This is a dog" to a child. Dogs represent *positive instances* of the dog concept. *Negative instances*—that is, things that are not dogs—are then shown to the child while we say, "This is *not* a dog." Negative instances of one concept may be positive instances of another. So in teaching a child we may be more likely to say, "This is not a dog—it's a cat" than simply, "This is not a dog."

Children may at first include horses and other four-legged animals within the dog schema or concept until the differences between dogs and horses are pointed out. (To them, the initial category could be more appropriately labeled "fuzzy-wuzzies.") In language development, such overinclusion of instances in a category (reference to horses as dogs) is labeled *overextension.* Children's prototypes become refined after children are shown positive and negative instances and given explanations. Abstract concepts such as *bachelor* or *square root* tend to be formed through verbal explanations that involve more basic concepts.

CONCEPT A mental category used to class together objects, relations, events, abstractions, or qualities that have common properties.

PROTOTYPE A concept of a category of objects or events that serves as a good example of the category.

EXEMPLAR A specific example.

A Goat or a Dog? Yes, yes, you know the answer, but little children may at first include goats, horses, and other four-legged animals within the dog concept until they understand the differences among the animals.

Review

SECTION II

Concepts are mental (4) _____ries used to class objects, relations, or events with common properties. Much of thinking has to do with (5) _____rizing new objects and events and with (6) _____lating the relationships among concepts.

We tend to organize concepts in (7) _____chies. Examples that best match the key features of categories are termed (8) _____types. Simple concepts such as *dog* and *red* are taught by (9) _____plars. Dogs are (10) _____tive instances of the dog concept. Cats are (11) _____tive instances of the dog concept. Abstract concepts such as uncle are often taught through (12) _____nation. In language development, the overinclusion of instances in a category (reference to horses as dogs) is labeled (13) over_____.

SECTION III. PROBLEM SOLVING

Now I would like to share something personal with you. One of the pleasures I derived from my own introductory psychology course lay in showing friends the textbook and getting them involved in the problems in the section on problem solving. First, of course, I struggled with them myself. Now it's your turn. Get some scrap paper, take a breath, and have a go at them. The answers are discussed in the following pages, but don't peek. *Try* the problems first.

1. Provide the next two letters in the series for each of the following:
   a. ABABABAB??
   b. ABDEBCEF??
   c. OTTFFSSE??

2. Draw straight lines through all the points in part A of Figure 8.1, using only *four* lines. Do not lift your pencil from the paper or retrace your steps. (See Figure 8.4 for answer.)

3. Move three matches in part B of Figure 8.1 to make four squares of the same size. You must use *all* the matches. (See Figure 8.4 for answer.)

4. You have three jars—A, B, and C—which hold the amounts of water, in ounces, shown in Table 8.1. For each of the seven problems in Table 8.1, use the jars in any way you wish in order to arrive at the indicated amount of water. Fill or empty any jar as often as you wish. How do you obtain the desired amount of water in each problem? (The solutions are discussed on p. 373.)

Approaches to Problem Solving:
Getting From Here to There

Question: How do people go about solving problems? To answer this question, begin by considering the steps you used to try to solve parts a and b of problem 1. Did you first make sure you understood the problem by rereading the instructions? Or did you dive right in as soon as you saw them on the page? Perhaps the solutions to 1a and 1b came easily, but I'm sure you studied 1c very carefully.

FIGURE 8.1

TWO PROBLEMS   DRAW STRAIGHT LINES THROUGH ALL THE POINTS IN PART A, USING ONLY FOUR LINES. DO NOT LIFT YOUR PENCIL OR RETRACE YOUR STEPS. MOVE THREE MATCHES IN PART B TO MAKE FOUR SQUARES EQUAL IN SIZE. USE ALL THE MATCHES.

TABLE 8.1	WATER-JAR PROBLEMS			
THREE JARS ARE PRESENT WITH THE LISTED CAPACITY (IN OUNCES)				
Problem	Jar A	Jar B	Jar C	Goal
1	21	127	3	100
2	14	163	25	99
3	18	43	10	5
4	9	42	6	21
5	20	59	4	31
6	23	49	3	20
7	10	36	7	3

For each problem, how can you use some combination of the three jars given, and a tap, to obtain precisely the amount of water shown?
SOURCE: Adapted from *Rigidity of Behavior* (p. 109), by Abraham S. Luchins and Edith H. Luchins, 1959, Eugene: University of Oregon Press.

After you believed you understood what was required in each problem, you probably tried to discover the structure of the cycles in each series. Series 1a has repeated cycles of two letters: *AB, AB,* and so on. Series 1b may be seen as having four cycles of two consecutive letters: *AB, DE, BC,* and so on.

Again, did you solve 1a and 1b in a flash of insight, or did you try to find rules that govern each series? In series 1a, the rule is simply to repeat the cycle. Series 1b is more complicated, and different sets of rules can be used to describe it. One correct set of rules is that odd-numbered cycles (*1* and *3,* or *AB* and *BC*) simply repeat the last letter of the previous cycle (in this case, *B*) and then advance by one letter in the alphabet. The same rule applies to even-numbered cycles (*2* and *4,* or *DE* and *EF*).

If you found rules for problems 1a and 1b, you used them to produce the next letters in the series: *AB* in series 1a and *CD* in series 1b. Perhaps you then evaluated the effectiveness of your rules by checking your answers against the solutions in the preceding paragraphs.

REFLECT

How did you go about solving (or trying to solve) the problems presented at the beginning of the section? Why?

UNDERSTANDING THE PROBLEM Let us begin our discussion of understanding problems by considering a bus driver problem very similar to the one Jordan gave me. This one, however, appeared in the psychological literature:

> Suppose you are a bus driver. On the first stop, you pick up 6 men and 2 women. At the second stop, 2 men leave and 1 woman boards the bus. At the third stop, 1 man leaves and 2 women enter the bus. At the fourth stop, 3 men get on and 3 women get off. At the fifth stop, 2 men get off, 3 men get on, 1 woman gets off and 2 women get on. What is the bus driver's name? (Halpern, 1989, p. 392)

Both versions of the bus driver problem demonstrate that a key to understanding a problem is focusing on the right information. If we assume it is crucial to keep track of the numbers of people getting on and off the bus, we focus on information that turns out to be unessential. In fact, it distracts us from the important information.

When we are faced with a novel problem, how can we know which information is relevant and which is not? Background knowledge helps. If you are given a chemistry problem, it helps if you have taken courses in chemistry. If Jordan gives you a problem, it is helpful to expect the unexpected. (In case you still haven't gotten it, the critical information you need to solve both bus driver problems is provided in the first sentence.)

Successful understanding of a problem generally requires three features:

1. *The parts or elements of our mental representation of the problem relate to one another in a meaningful way.* If we are trying to solve a problem in geometry, our mental triangles should have angles that total 180 degrees, not 360 degrees.

2. *The elements of our mental representation of the problem correspond to the elements of the problem in the outer world.* If we are neutralizing an acid in order to produce water and a salt, our mental representation of water should be H_2O, not OH. The elements of our mental representations must include the key elements for solving the problem, such as the information in the first sentence of the bus driver problem. We prepare ourselves to solve a problem by familiarizing ourselves with its elements and defining our goals.

3. *We have a storehouse of background knowledge that we can apply to the problem.* We have taken the necessary courses to solve problems in algebra and chemistry. When given a geometry problem involving a triangle, for example, we may think, "Is this problem similar to problems I've solved by using the quadratic equation?"

ALGORITHMS An **algorithm** is a specific procedure for solving a type of problem. An algorithm invariably leads to the solution—if it is used properly, that is. Mathematical formulas like the Pythagorean theorem are examples of algorithms. They yield correct answers to problems *as long as the right formula is used*. Finding the right formula to solve a problem may require scanning one's memory for all formulas that contain variables that represent one or more of the elements in the problem. The Pythagorean theorem, for example, concerns triangles with right angles. Therefore, it is appropriate to consider using this formula for problems concerning right angles, but not for others.

Consider anagram problems, in which we try to reorganize groups of letters into words. Some anagram problems require us to use every letter from the pool of letters; others allow us to use only some of the letters. How many words can you make from the pool of letters *DWARG*? If you were to use the **systematic random search** algorithm, you would list every possible letter combination, using from one to all five letters. You could use a dictionary or a spell-checking program to see whether each result is, in fact, a word. Such a method might be time-consuming, but it would work.

HEURISTICS Question: Is it best to use a tried and true formula to solve a problem? Not necessarily. Sometimes people use shortcuts that enable them to jump to conclusions—including the correct conclusion. Such shortcuts are called heuristics, or heuristic devices. **Heuristics** are rules of thumb that help us simplify and solve problems. In contrast to algorithms, heuristics do not guarantee a correct solution to a problem. But when they work, they allow for more rapid solutions. A heuristic device for solving the anagram problem would be to look for familiar letter combinations found in words and then check the remaining letters for words that include these combinations. In *DWARG,* for example, we can find the familiar combinations *dr* and *gr*. We may then quickly find *draw, drag,* and *grad*. The drawback to this method, however, is that we might miss some words.

ALGORITHM A systematic procedure for solving a problem that works invariably when it is correctly applied.

SYSTEMATIC RANDOM SEARCH An algorithm for solving problems in which each possible solution is tested according to a particular set of rules.

HEURISTICS Rules of thumb that help us simplify and solve problems.

It is not true that using a "tried and true" formula is the most efficient way to solve a problem. Using a tried and true formula—that is, an algorithm—may be less efficient than using a heuristic device.

One type of heuristic device is the **means–end analysis.** In using this heuristic device, we assess the difference between our current situation and our goals and then do what we can to reduce this discrepancy. Let's say that you are out in your car and have gotten lost. One heuristic device based on analysis of what you need to do to get to where you want to go might be to ask for directions. This approach requires no "sense of direction." An algorithm might be more complicated and require some geographical knowledge. Let us say that you know your destination is west of your current location and on the other side of the railroad tracks. You might, therefore, drive toward the setting sun (west) and, at the same time, watch for railroad tracks. If the road comes to an end and you must turn left or right, you can scan in both directions for tracks. If you don't see any, turn right or left, but at the next major intersection turn toward the setting sun. Eventually you may get there. If not, you can always ask for directions.

ANALOGIES An *analogy* is a partial similarity among things that are different in other ways. During the Cold War, some people in the United States believed in the so-called domino theory. Seeing the nations of Southeast Asia as analogous to dominoes, they argued that if one nation were allowed to fall to communism, its neighbor would be likely to follow. In the late 1980s, a sort of reverse domino effect actually occurred as communism collapsed in the nations of Eastern Europe. When communism collapsed in one nation, it became more likely to collapse in neighboring nations as well.

The analogy heuristic applies the solution of an earlier problem to the solution of a new one. We use the analogy heuristic whenever we try to solve a new problem by referring to a previous problem (Halpern et al., 1990). Consider the water jar problems in Table 8.1. Problem 2 is analogous to problem 1. Therefore, the approach to solving problem 1 works with problem 2. (Later we consider what happens when the analogy heuristic fails.)

Let us see whether you can use the analogy heuristic to your advantage in the following number series problem: To solve problems 1a, 1b, and 1c on page 367, you had to figure out the rules that govern the order of the letters. Scan the following series of numbers and find the rule that governs their order:

8, 5, 4, 9, 1, 7, 6, 3, 2, 0

Hint: The problem is somewhat analogous to problem 1c.[1]

Factors That Affect Problem Solving

The way you approach a problem is central to how effective you are at solving it. Other factors also influence your effectiveness at problem solving. Question: What factors affect effectiveness at solving problems? Three such factors—your level of expertise, whether you fall prey to a mental

---

REFLECT

Have you ever gotten lost and asked for directions? Is asking for directions an algorithm or a heuristic device? (And why are so many men reluctant to ask for directions?!)

REFLECT

Why do math textbooks have all those problems at the end of each chapter? How is solving them of help to you?

MEANS–END ANALYSIS A heuristic device in which we try to solve a problem by evaluating the difference between the current situation and the goal.

---

[1] The analogous element is that there is a correspondence between these numbers and the first letter in the English word that spells them out.

set, and whether you develop insight into the problem—reside within you. A couple of characteristics of problems also affect your ability to solve them effectively: the extent to which the elements of the problem are fixed in function, and the way the problem is defined.

EXPERTISE To appreciate the role of expertise in problem solving, unscramble the following anagrams, taken from Novick and Coté (1992). In each case use all of the letters to form an actual English word:

> D N S U O
> R C W D O
> I A S Y D

How long did it take you to unscramble each anagram? Would a person whose native language is English—that is, an "expert"—unscramble each anagram more efficiently than a bilingual person who spoke another language in the home? Why or why not?

Experts solve problems more efficiently and rapidly than novices do. Generally speaking, people who are experts at solving a certain kind of problem share the following characteristics:

- They know the particular area well,
- have a good memory for the elements in the problems,
- form mental images or representations that facilitate problem solving (Clement, 1991),
- relate the problem to similar problems, and
- have efficient methods for problem solving (Hershey et al., 1990).

These factors are interrelated. Art historians, for example, acquire a database that permits them to understand the intricacies of paintings. As a result, their memory for paintings—and who painted them—expands vastly.

Novick and Coté (1992) found that the solutions to the anagram problems seemed to "pop out" in under 2 seconds among experts. The experts apparently used more efficient methods than the novices. Experts seemed to use *parallel processing*. That is, they dealt simultaneously with two or more elements of the problems. In the case of DNSUO, for example, they may have played with the order of the vowels (*UO* or *OU*) at the same time that they tested which consonant (D, N, or S) was likely to precede them, arriving quickly at *sou* and *sound*. Novices were more likely to engage in *serial processing*—that is, to handle one element of the problem at a time.

MENTAL SETS Jordan hit me with another question: "A farmer had 17 sheep. All but 9 died. How many sheep did he have left?" Being a victim of a mental set, I assumed that this was a subtraction problem and gave the answer 8. She gleefully informed me that she hadn't said "9 died." She had said *"all but* 9 died." Therefore, the correct answer was 9. (Get it?) Put it another way: I had not *understood* the problem. My mental representation of the problem did not correspond to the actual elements of the problem.

Return to problem 1, part c (page 367). To try to solve this problem, did you seek a pattern of letters that involved cycles and the alphabet? If so, it may be because this approach worked in solving parts a and b.

The tendency to respond to a new problem with the same approach that helped solve similar problems is termed a **mental set.** Mental sets

MENTAL SET The tendency to respond to a new problem with an approach that was used successfully with similar problems.

REFLECT

Are you an expert at solving math problems? Social problems? Automobile problems? Musical problems? How did you get to be an expert?

Jordan. The author's daughter Jordan posed this problem: "A farmer had 17 sheep. All but 9 died. How many sheep were left?" What is the answer?

usually make our work easier, but they can mislead us when the similarity between problems is illusory, as in part c of problem 1. Here is a clue: Part c is not an alphabet series. Each of the letters in the series *stands for* something. If you can discover what they stand for (that is, if you can discover the rule), you will be able to generate the 9th and 10th letters. (See Figure 8.4 for the answer.)

INSIGHT: AHA! To gain insight into the role of insight in problem solving, consider the following problem, posed by Janet Metcalfe (1986):

> A stranger approached a museum curator and offered him an ancient bronze coin. The coin had an authentic appearance and was marked with the date 544 B.C. The curator had happily made acquisitions from suspicious sources before, but this time he promptly called the police and had the stranger arrested. Why? (p. 624)

I'm not going to give you the answer to this problem. Instead, I'll make a guarantee. When you arrive at the solution, it will hit you all at once. You'll think "Aha!" or "Of course!" (or something less polite). It will seem as though the pieces of information in the problem have suddenly been reorganized so that the solution leaps out at you—in a flash.

Bismarck, one of University of Michigan psychologist N. R. F. Maier's rats, provided evidence of insight in laboratory rats (Maier & Schneirla, 1935). Bismarck had been trained to climb a ladder to a tabletop where food was placed. On one occasion Maier used a mesh barrier to prevent the rat from reaching his goal. But, as shown in Figure 8.2, a second ladder was provided and was clearly visible to the animal. At first Bismarck sniffed and scratched and made every effort to find a path through the mesh barrier. Then he spent some time washing his face, an activity that apparently signals frustration in rats. Suddenly he jumped into the air, turned, ran down the familiar ladder and around to the new ladder, ran up the new ladder, and claimed his just desserts. It seems that Bismarck suddenly perceived the relationships between the elements of his problem so that the solution occurred by insight. He seems to have had what Gestalt psychologists have termed an "Aha! experience."

FIGURE 8.2
BISMARCK USES A COGNITIVE MAP TO CLAIM HIS JUST DESSERTS BISMARCK HAS LEARNED TO REACH DINNER BY CLIMBING LADDER *A*. BUT NOW THE FOOD GOAL (*F*) IS BLOCKED BY A WIRE MESH BARRIER *B*. BISMARCK WASHES HIS FACE FOR A WHILE, BUT THEN, IN AN APPARENT FLASH OF INSIGHT, HE RUNS BACK DOWN LADDER *A* AND UP NEW LADDER *N* TO REACH THE GOAL.

✓ **Truth or Fiction Revisited**

It is not true that only humans can solve problems by means of insight. Classic research evidence shows that lower animals, even rats, are also capable of **insight** (a sudden reorganization of the perceptual field).

INCUBATION Let us return to the problems at the beginning of the section. How did you do with problem 1, part c, and problems 2 and 3? Students tend to fiddle around with them for a while. The solutions, when they come, appear to arrive in a flash. Students set the stage for the flash of insight by studying the elements in the problems carefully, repeating the rules to themselves, and trying to imagine what a solution might look like. If you tried out solutions that did not meet the goals, you may have become frustrated and thought, "The heck with it! I'll come back to it later." Standing back from the problem may allow for the **incubation** of insight. An incubator warms chicken eggs for a while so that they will hatch. Incubation in problem solving refers to standing back from the problem for a while as some mysterious process within us continues to work on it. Later, the answer may occur to us in a flash of

INSIGHT In Gestalt psychology, a sudden perception of relationships among elements of the "perceptual field," permitting the solution of a problem.

INCUBATION In problem solving, a hypothetical process that sometimes occurs when we stand back from a frustrating problem for a while and the solution "suddenly" appears.

insight. When standing back from the problem is helpful, it may be because it distances us from unprofitable but persistent mental sets (Azar, 1995).

✓ Truth or Fiction Revisited

It is not true that the best way to solve a frustrating problem is to keep plugging away at it. It may be better to distance oneself from the problem for a while and allow it to "incubate." Eventually you may solve the problem in what seems to be a flash of insight.

Have another look at the role of incubation in helping us overcome mental sets. Consider the seventh water jar problem in Table 8.1. What if we had tried several solutions involving the three water jars and none had worked? We could distance ourselves from the problem for a day or two. At some point we might recall a 10, a 7, and a 3—three elements of the problem—and suddenly realize that we can arrive at the correct answer by using only two water jars!

FIGURE 8.3
THE DUNCKER CANDLE PROBLEM   CAN YOU USE THE OBJECTS SHOWN ON THE TABLE TO ATTACH THE CANDLE TO THE WALL OF THE ROOM SO THAT IT WILL BURN PROPERLY?

FUNCTIONAL FIXEDNESS **Functional fixedness** may also hinder problem solving. For example, first ask yourself what a pair of pliers is. Is it a tool for grasping, a paperweight, or a weapon? A pair of pliers could function as any of these, but your tendency to think of it as a grasping tool is fostered by your experience with it. You have probably used pliers only for grasping things. Functional fixedness is the tendency to think of an object in terms of its name or its familiar function. It can be similar to a mental set in that it makes it difficult to use familiar objects to solve problems in novel ways.

Now that you know what functional fixedness is, let's see whether you can overcome it by solving the Duncker candle problem. You enter a room that has the following objects on a table: a candle, a box of matches, and some thumbtacks (see Figure 8.3). Your task is to use the objects on the table to attach the candle to the wall of the room so that it will burn properly. (See Figure 8.4 for the answer.)

FUNCTIONAL FIXEDNESS The tendency to view an object in terms of its name or familiar usage.

SECTION III

Problem solving begins with trying to (14) un_____ the problem. Understanding a problem requires focusing on information and constructing a coherent (15) _____tal _____tation of the problem. Successful understanding of a problem requires three features: First, the parts of the problem should (16) re_____ to one another in a meaningful way. Second, the elements of the mental (17) rep_____tion of the problem should correspond to the elements of the problem in the outer world. Third, a storehouse of background (18) _____ edge is required to apply to the problem.

An (19) _____ithm is a specific procedure for solving a type of problem. In solving anagrams, the algorithm of the (20) sys_____ random search involves listing every possible letter combination, using from one to all letters.

(21) _____tic devices are rules of thumb that help us simplify and solve problems. Heuristics are (22) _____cuts that allow for more rapid solutions. In the heuristic device called the (23) means−_____ analysis, we assess the difference between our current situation and our goals and then do what we can to reduce this discrepancy.

An (24) _____ogy is a partial similarity among things that are different in other ways. We use the analogy heuristic when we solve a new problem by referring to a (25) _____ious problem.

Experts at solving a kind of problem have a more extensive (26) _____edge base in the area, have better memories for the elements in the problems, and (27) re_____ the problem to similar problems.

Review

SECTION III CONTINUED

A (28) _____ set is the tendency to respond to a new problem with the same approach that helped solve earlier, similar-looking problems. Some problems are solved by rapid "perception of relationships" among the elements of the problem, which is called (29) in_____. Standing back from a difficult problem for a while sometimes allows insight to (30) in_____.

(31) _____ fixedness is the tendency to think of an object in terms of its name or its familiar usage. Functional fixedness can be similar to a (32) _____ set in that it can make it difficult to use familiar objects to solve problems in novel ways.

SECTION IV. CREATIVITY

Creativity is the ability to do things that are novel and useful (Sternberg & Lubart, 1996). Creative people can solve problems to which there are no preexisting solutions, no tried and tested formulas. Creative people share several characteristics (Sternberg & Lubart, 1995, 1996):

- They take chances.
- They refuse to accept limitations and try to do the impossible.
- They appreciate art and music.
- They use the materials around them to make unique things.
- They challenge social norms.
- They take unpopular stands.
- They probe ideas.

A professor of mine once remarked that there is nothing new under the sun, only new combinations of existing elements. Many psychologists agree. They see creativity as the ability to make unusual, sometimes remote, associations to the elements of a problem to generate new combinations. An essential aspect of a creative response is the leap from the

REFLECT

Do you consider yourself to be creative? Why or why not?

CREATIVITY The ability to generate novel and useful solutions to problems.

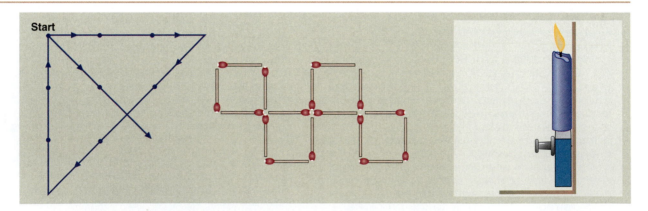

FIGURE 8.4

ANSWERS TO PROBLEMS ON PAGES 367 AND 373   FOR PROBLEM 1C, NOTE THAT EACH OF THE LETTERS IS THE FIRST LETTER OF THE NUMBERS 1 THROUGH 8. THEREFORE, THE TWO MISSING LETTERS ARE *NT*, FOR *N*INE AND *T*EN. THE SOLUTIONS TO PROBLEMS 2 AND 3 ARE SHOWN IN THIS ILLUSTRATION. TO SOLVE THE DUNCKER CANDLE PROBLEM, USE THE THUMBTACK TO PIN THE MATCHBOX TO THE WALL. THEN SET THE CANDLE ON TOP OF THE BOX. FUNCTIONAL FIXEDNESS PREVENTS MANY PEOPLE FROM CONCEPTUALIZING THE MATCHBOX AS ANYTHING MORE THAN A DEVICE TO HOLD MATCHES. COMMONLY GIVEN *WRONG* ANSWERS INCLUDE TRYING TO AFFIX THE BOTTOM OF THE CANDLE TO THE WALL WITH MELTED WAX OR TRYING TO TACK THE CANDLE TO THE WALL.

elements of the problem to the novel solution. A predictable solution is not creative, even if it is hard to reach.

Question: What are the relationships among creativity, problem solving, and intelligence? Creative problem solving demands divergent rather than convergent thinking. In **convergent thinking,** thought is limited to present facts; the problem solver narrows his or her thinking to find the best solution. (You use convergent thinking to arrive at the right answer to a multiple-choice question.) In **divergent thinking,** the problem solver associates freely to the elements of the problem, allowing "leads" to run a nearly limitless course. (You may use divergent thinking when you are trying to generate ideas to answer an essay question on a test.) Problem solving can involve both kinds of thinking. At first divergent thinking helps generate many possible solutions. Convergent thinking is then used to select likely solutions and reject others.

Creativity and Academic Ability

It might seem that a creative person would also have high academic ability of the sort measured on intelligence tests. However, the relationship between intelligence test scores and creativity is only moderate (Sternberg & Williams, 1997). Intelligence test questions usually require analytical, convergent thinking to focus on the one right answer. Tests of creativity determine how flexible a person's thinking is. Here, for example, is an item from a test used by Getzels and Jackson (1962) to measure associative ability, a factor in creativity: "Write as many meanings as you can for each of the following words: (a) duck; (b) sack; (c) pitch; (d) fair." Those who write several meanings for each word, rather than only one, are rated as potentially more creative.

Another measure of creativity might ask people to produce as many words as possible that begin with T and end with N within a minute. Still another item might give people a minute to classify a list of names in as many ways as possible. How many ways can you classify the following group of names?

MARTHA　　PAUL　　JEFFRY　　SALLY　　PABLO　　JOAN

> ### ✓ Truth or Fiction Revisited
>
> *It is not necessarily true that people with academic ability are creative.* Bright people are more likely to be creative than duller people, but many bright people are uncreative.

Factors That Affect Creativity

There is only a modest connection between creativity and other aspects of intelligence. Question: What factors other than intelligence are connected with creativity? Some factors reside within the person and some involve the social setting.

PERSONAL FACTORS Creative people show flexibility, fluency (in generating words and ideas), and originality. They spend time alone, thinking about who they are and exploring new ideas (McIntosh, 1996). Getzels and Jackson (1962) found that creative schoolchildren tend to express, rather than inhibit, their feelings and to be playful and independent. Creative children are often at odds with their teachers because of their independence. Faced with the chore of managing 30 or more pupils, teachers too often label quiet and submissive children as "good" and less inhibited children as "bad."

Pablo Picasso at Work. We know that the great artist was creative, but what about his academic ability? Academic ability and creativity often go hand in hand, but academic ability is no guarantee of imagination or of specific talents.

CONVERGENT THINKING A thought process that attempts to narrow in on the single best solution to a problem.

DIVERGENT THINKING A thought process that attempts to generate multiple solutions to problems.

SOCIAL EVALUATION Research evidence shows that concern about evaluation by other people reduces creativity. In one experiment college students were asked to write poems under two very different sets of expectations (Amabile, 1990). Half the students were informed that the experimenter intended only to examine their handwriting—not the aesthetic value of the poetry. The remaining students were informed that judges, who were poets, would supply them with written evaluations of their poetry's content and form. The students who expected to be evaluated according to the form and content of their work turned in significantly less creative poems.

The literature is mixed as to whether people are more creative when they are rewarded for being creative. It has been argued that rewards reduce inner interest in problem solving and thereby undermine creativity. Yet the research shows that rewarding people for being creative on one task can actually enhance creativity on other tasks (Eisenberger & Cameron, 1996).

BRAINSTORMING **Brainstorming** is a group process that is intended to encourage creativity. The group leader stimulates group members to generate a great number of ideas—even wild ideas. In order to avoid inhibiting group members, judgment is suspended until a great many ideas are on the table.

Psychologists have become somewhat skeptical of the brainstorming concept, however (Matlin, 1997). For one thing, research evidence suggests that people working alone are often more creative than people working in groups. (Consider the saying, "A camel is a horse made by a committee.") Moreover, the ideas produced by brainstorming are often lower in quality than those produced by people working alone.

Review

SECTION IV

(33) _____ is the ability to do things that are novel and useful. Creative people are (34: Willing or Unwilling?) to take chances, unaccepting of limitations, appreciative of art and music, and (35: Challenging or Accepting?) of social norms and assumptions. Creativity demands (36) _____gent thinking rather than convergent thinking. Creative people (37: Do or Do not?) tend to be intelligent. High intelligence (38: Is or Is not?) a guarantee of creativity. The research literature is mixed as to whether people are more creative when they are rewarded for being creative, and on the effects of (39) _____storming on creativity.

SECTION V. REASONING

We are not finished. I have more puzzles to solve, more weighty things to consider. Ponder this proposition:

If some A are B, and some B are C, then some A are C.

Is it true or false? What say you?

I confess that on first seeing this proposition, I believed it was true. It seemed that we were logically progressing to higher-order categories at each step along the way (see Figure 8.5, part A). For example, if apples (A) are fruit (B), and fruit (B) are food (C), then apples (A) are food (C). But I was bamboozled by the "some." My example with the apples omitted the word. Consider another example of this proposition, one that uses "some": If *some* circles (A) are shapes (B), and *some* shapes (B) are squares (C), then *some* circles (A) are squares (C). Not so! By using the qualifying term "some," we can move both up, to a higher-order category

BRAINSTORMING A group process that encourages creativity by stimulating a large number of ideas and suspending judgment until the process is completed.

(from circles to shapes), and back down, to a lower-order category (from shapes to squares) (see Figure 8.5, part B).

Types of Reasoning

We have been toying with an example of reasoning. **Reasoning** is the transformation of information in order to reach conclusions. Question: How do people reason? Let us consider two kinds of reasoning: deductive and inductive.

Deductive reasoning is a form of reasoning in which the conclusion must be true if the premises are true. Consider this classic three-sentence argument:

1. All persons are mortal.

2. Socrates is a person.

3. Therefore, Socrates is mortal.

Sentences 1 and 2 in this argument are the *premises*. Premises provide the assumptions or basic information that allow people to draw conclusions. Sentence 3 is the conclusion. In this example, sentence 1 makes a statement about a category (persons). Sentence 2 assigns an individual (Socrates) to the category (persons). Sentence 3 concludes that what is true of the category (persons) is true for the member of the category (Socrates). The conclusion, sentence 3, is said to be *deduced* from the premises. The conclusion about Socrates is true if the premises are true.

In **inductive reasoning**, we reason from individual cases or particular facts to a general conclusion. Consider this transformation of the previous example:

1. Socrates is a person.

2. Socrates is mortal.

3. Therefore, persons are mortal.

The conclusion happens to be correct, but it is illogical. The fact that one person is mortal does not guarantee that all people are mortal.

Inductive reasoning, then, does not permit us to draw absolute conclusions (Sloman, 1996). Yet inductive reasoning is used all the time. We conclude that a certain type of food will or will not make us feel sick because of our experiences on earlier occasions. ("Buttered popcorn made me nauseous. This is buttered popcorn. Therefore, this will make me nauseous.") We assume that a cheerful smile and "Hello!" will break the ice with a new acquaintance because it has worked before. Although none of these conclusions is as logical as a deductive conclusion, inductive conclusions are correct often enough so that we can get on with our daily lives with some degree of confidence.

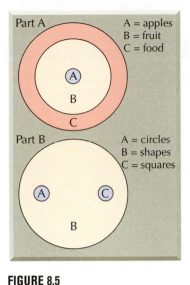

FIGURE 8.5

WHEN ARE A ALSO C? IN PART A OF THIS FIGURE, A (APPLES) ARE ALSO C (FOOD) BECAUSE FOOD REPRESENTS A HIGHER-ORDER CATEGORY THAT CONTAINS ALL APPLES. IN PART B, HOWEVER, C (SQUARES) IS NOT HIGHER ORDER THAN A (CIRCLES). THEREFORE, C DOES NOT CONTAIN A. B (SHAPES), HOWEVER, IS HIGHER ORDER THAN BOTH A AND C AND CONTAINS BOTH.

REFLECT

Can you provide examples of deductive reasoning and inductive reasoning that are connected with your own life?

Review

SECTION V

The text defines reasoning as the (40) _____ming of information to reach conclusions. The (41) _____ses of an argument provide the assumptions or basic information that allow people to draw conclusions. In (42) _____tive reasoning, the conclusion must be true if the premises are true. In (43) _____tive reasoning, we reason from individual cases or particular facts to a general conclusion. Inductive reasoning (44: Does or Does not?) permit us to draw absolute conclusions.

REASONING The transforming of information to reach conclusions.

DEDUCTIVE REASONING A form of reasoning about arguments in which conclusions are deduced from premises. The conclusions are true if the premises are true.

INDUCTIVE REASONING A form of reasoning in which we reason from individual cases or particular facts to a general conclusion.

REFLECT

Do you have trouble making decisions? What kinds of decisions? What is the difficulty?

REFLECT

Do you sometimes make decisions without all the information you need? Why?

REPRESENTATIVENESS HEURISTIC *A decision-making heuristic in which people make judgments about samples according to the populations they appear to represent.*

SECTION VI. JUDGMENT AND DECISION MAKING

Decisions, decisions. Should you go to breakfast before classes begin or catch a few extra winks? Should you get married or remain single? Should you take a job or go on for advanced training when you complete your college program? If you opt for the job, cash will soon be jingling in your pockets. Yet later you may wonder whether you have enough education to reach your full potential. By furthering your education, you may have to delay independence and gratification, but you may find a more fulfilling position later on. Ah, decisions, decisions.

Other kinds of decisions are judgments about the nature of the world. We make judgments about which route to school or work will be the least crowded. We make judgments about where it will be safe and convenient to live. We make judgments about what political candidates to vote for and which brand of ice cream to buy.

Question: How do people go about making judgments and decisions? You might like to think that people are so rational that they carefully weigh all the pros and cons when they make judgments or decisions. Or you might think that they insist on finding and examining all the relevant information. Actually, people make most of their decisions on the basis of limited information. They take shortcuts. They use heuristic devices—rules of thumb—in their judgments and decision making, just as they do in problem solving. For example, they may let a financial adviser select stocks for them rather than research the companies themselves. Or they may see a doctor recommended by a friend rather than examine the doctor's credentials. In this section we consider various factors in judgment and decision making.

Heuristics in Decision Making: If It Works, Must It Be Logical?

Let us begin by asking you to imagine that you flip a coin six times. In the following three possible outcomes, H stands for head and T for tail. Circle the most likely sequence:

H H H H H H
H H H T T T
T H H T H T

Did you select T H H T H T as the most likely sequence of events? Most people do. Why? There are two reasons. First, people recognize that the sequence of six heads in a row is unlikely. (The probability of achieving it is $\frac{1}{2} \times \frac{1}{2} \times \frac{1}{2} \times \frac{1}{2} \times \frac{1}{2} \times \frac{1}{2}$, or $\frac{1}{64}$.) Three heads and three tails are more likely than six heads (or six tails). Second, people recognize that the sequence of heads and tails ought to appear random. T H H T H T has a random look to it, whereas H H H T T T does not.

People tend to select T H H T H T because of the **representativeness heuristic.** According to this decision-making heuristic, people make judgments about events (samples) according to the populations of events that they appear to represent (Kosonen & Winne, 1995). In this case, the sample of events is six coin tosses. The "population" is an infinite number of random coin tosses. But guess what? *Each* of the sequences is equally likely (or unlikely). If the question had been whether six heads or three heads and three tails had been more likely, the correct answer would have been three and three. If the question had been whether heads and tails would be more likely to be consecutive or in random order, the correct answer would have been random order.

But each of the three sequences shown is a *specific* sequence. What is the probability of attaining the specific sequence T H H T H T? The probability that the first coin toss will result in a tail is $\frac{1}{2}$. The probability that the second will result in a head is $\frac{1}{2}$, and so on. Thus, the probability of attaining the exact sequence T H H T H T is identical to that of achieving any other specific sequence: $\frac{1}{2} \times \frac{1}{2} \times \frac{1}{2} \times \frac{1}{2} \times \frac{1}{2} \times \frac{1}{2} = \frac{1}{64}$. (Don't just sit there. Try this out on a friend.)

Or consider this question: If a couple has five children, all of whom are boys, is their sixth child more likely to be a boy or a girl? Use of the representativeness heuristic might lead us to imagine that the couple is due for a girl. That is, five boys and one girl is closer to the assumed random distribution that accounts for roughly equal numbers of boys and girls in the world. But people with some knowledge of reproductive biology might predict that another boy is actually more likely because five boys in a row may be too many to be a random biological event. If the couple's conception of a boy or girl were truly random, however, what would be the probability of conceiving another boy? Answer: $\frac{1}{2}$.

✓ Truth or Fiction Revisited

It is not true that if a couple has five sons, the sixth child is likely to be a daughter.

Another heuristic device used in decision making is the **availability heuristic.** According to this heuristic, our estimates of frequency or probability are based on how easy it is to find examples of relevant events. Let me ask you whether there are more art majors or sociology majors at your college. Unless you are familiar with the enrollment statistics, you will probably answer on the basis of the numbers of art majors and sociology majors that you know personally.

The **anchoring and adjustment heuristic** suggests that there can be a good deal of inertia in our judgments. In forming opinions or making estimates, we have an initial view, or presumption. This is the anchor. As we receive additional information, we make adjustments, sometimes grudgingly. That is, if you grow up believing that one religion or one political party is the "right" one, that belief serves as a cognitive anchor. When inconsistencies show up in your religion or political party, you may adjust your views of them, but perhaps not very willingly.

Let us illustrate further by means of a math problem. Write each of the following multiplication problems on a separate piece of paper:

A. $8 \times 7 \times 6 \times 5 \times 4 \times 3 \times 2 \times 1$

B. $1 \times 2 \times 3 \times 4 \times 5 \times 6 \times 7 \times 8$

Show problem A to a few friends. Give them each 5 seconds to estimate the answer. Show problem B to some other friends and give them 5 seconds to estimate the answer.

The answers to the multiplication problems are the same because the order of the quantities being multiplied does not change the outcome. However, when Tversky and Kahneman (1982) showed these problems to high school students, the average estimate given by students who were shown version A was significantly higher than that given by students who were shown version B. Students who saw 8 in the first position offered an average estimate of 2,250. Students who saw 1 in the first position gave an average estimate of 512. That is, the estimate was larger when 8 served as the anchor. By the way, what is the correct answer to the multiplication

AVAILABILITY HEURISTIC A decision-making heuristic in which our estimates of frequency or probability of events are based on how easy it is to find examples.

ANCHORING AND ADJUSTMENT HEURISTIC A decision-making heuristic in which a presumption or first estimate serves as a cognitive anchor. As we receive additional information, we make adjustments but tend to remain in the proximity of the anchor.

problems? Can you use the anchoring and adjustment heuristic to explain why both groups of students were so far off?

The Framing Effect: Say That Again?

If you were on a low-fat diet, would you be more likely to choose an ice cream that is 97% fat free or one whose fat content makes up 10% of its calorie content? On one shopping excursion I was impressed with an ice cream package's claims that the product was 97% fat free. Yet when I read the label closely, I noticed that a 4-ounce serving had 160 calories, 27 of which were contributed by fat. Fat, then, accounted for 27/160ths, or about 17%, of the ice cream's calorie content. But fat accounted only for 3% of the ice cream's *weight*. The packagers of the ice cream knew all about the *framing effect*. They understood that labeling the ice cream as "97% fat free" would make it sound more healthful than "Only 17% of calories from fat."

Question: How do people frame information in order to persuade others? The **framing effect** refers to the way in which wording, or the context in which information is presented, can influence decision making. Political groups are as aware as advertisers of the role of the framing effect and choose their words accordingly. For example, proponents of legalized abortion refer to themselves as "pro-choice" and opponents refer to themselves as "pro-life." Thus each group frames itself in a way that is positive ("pro" something) and refers to a value (freedom, life) with which it would be difficult to argue.

Parents are also aware of the framing effect. My 3-year-old, Taylor, was invited to a play date at Abigail's house. I asked Taylor, "Would you like to play with Abigail at her house?" The question met with a resounding no. I thought things over and reframed the question: "Would you like to play at Abigail's house and have a real fun time? She has lots of toys and games, and I'll pick you up real soon." This time Taylor's decision was yes.

Overconfidence: Is Your Hindsight 20–20?

Whether our decisions are correct or incorrect, most of us tend to be overconfident about them (Lundeberg et al., 1994). Overconfidence applies to judgments as wide-ranging as whether one will be infected by the virus that causes AIDS (Goldman & Harlow, 1993), predicting the outcome of elections (Hawkins & Hastie, 1990), asserting that one's answers to test items are correct (Lundeberg et al., 1994), and selecting stocks. Many people refuse to alter their judgments even in the face of statistical evidence that shows them to be flawed. (Have you ever known someone to maintain unrealistic confidence in a candidate who was far behind in the polls?)

We also tend to view our situations with 20–20 hindsight. When we are proven wrong, we frequently find a way to show that we "knew it all along." We also become overconfident that we would have known the actual outcome if we had had access to the information that became available after the event (Hawkins & Hastie, 1990). For example, if we had known that a key player would pull a hamstring muscle, we would have predicted a different outcome for the football game. If we had known that it would be blustery on Election Day, we would have predicted a smaller voter turnout and a different outcome.

Question: Why do people tend to be convinced that they are right, even when they are dead wrong? There are several reasons for overconfidence, even when our judgments are wrong. Here are some of them:

FRAMING EFFECT The influence of wording, or the context in which information is presented, on decision making.

- We tend to be unaware of how flimsy our assumptions may be.

- We tend to focus on examples that confirm our judgments and ignore those that do not.

- Because our working memories have limited space, we tend to forget information that runs counter to our judgments.

- We work to bring about the events we believe in, so they sometimes become self-fulfilling prophecies.

- Even when people are told that they tend to be overconfident in their decisions, they usually ignore this information (Gigerenzer et al., 1991).

✓ Truth or Fiction Revisited

It is not necessarily true that people change their opinions when they are shown to be wrong. In some cases they may, but the statement is too general to be true.

Review

SECTION VI

People make most run-of-the-mill, daily decisions on the basis of (45: Complete or Limited?) information. People use rules of thumb called (46) _____tic devices in their judgments and decision making, just as they do in problem solving.

According to the (47) _____tiveness heuristic, people make judgments about events (samples) according to the populations of events that they appear to represent. According to the (48) _____lity heuristic, their estimates of frequency or probability are based on how easy it is to find examples of relevant events. The anchoring and (49) _____ment heuristic suggests that

there can be a good deal of inertia to our judgments. In forming opinions or making estimates, we have an initial view, or presumption, that serves as the (50) a_____. As we receive additional (51) _____mation, we make adjustments.

The (52) _____ming effect refers to the fact that wording, or the context in which information is presented, can influence decision making. People tend (53: To be or Not to be?[2]) confident in their decisions because they are unaware of the flimsiness of their premises and tend to focus on examples that confirm their judgments and to ignore events that do not.

SECTION VII. THINKING AND LINGUISTIC RELATIVITY

Question: What is the effect of language on thinking? Different languages have different words for the same concepts, and concepts do not necessarily overlap. Can we be certain that English speakers can truly share or understand the ideas of people who speak other languages? This question brings us to the linguistic-relativity hypothesis.

The **linguistic-relativity hypothesis** was proposed by Benjamin Whorf (1956). Whorf believed that language structures the way we perceive the world. That is, the categories and relationships we use to understand the world are derived from our language. Therefore, speakers of various languages conceptualize the world in different ways.

Thus most English speakers' ability to think about snow may be limited compared with that of the Inuit (Eskimos). We have only a few words for snow. The Inuit have many words. They differ according to whether the snow is hard-packed, falling, melting, covered by ice, and so on. When we

---

[2] Sound familiar?

LINGUISTIC-RELATIVITY HYPOTHESIS The view that language structures the way in which we view the world.

Inuit Man in an Igloo. The Inuit of Alaska and the Canadian Northwestern Territories have many more words for snow than most of us do. They spend most of their lives in snow, and the subtle differences among various kinds of snow are meaningful to them.

think about snow, we have fewer words to choose from and have to search for descriptive adjectives. The Inuit, however, can readily find a single word that describes a complex weather condition. It might therefore be easier for them to think about this variety of snow in relation to other aspects of their world. Similarly, the Hanunoo people of the Philippines use 92 words for rice, depending on whether the rice is husked or unhusked and on how it is prepared. And whereas we have one word for camel, Arabs have more than 250.

In English, we have hundreds of words to describe different colors, but people who speak Shona use only three words for colors. People who speak Bassa use only two words for colors; these correspond to light and dark. The Hopi culture had two words for flying objects, one for birds and an all-inclusive word for anything else that might be found traveling through the air.

Does this mean that the Hopi were limited in their ability to think about bumblebees and airplanes? Are English speakers limited in their ability to think about skiing conditions? Are people who speak Shona and Bassa "color-blind" for practical purposes? Probably not. People who use only a few words to distinguish among colors seem to perceive the same color variations as people with dozens of words. For example, the Dani of New Guinea, like the Bassa, have just two words for colors: one that refers to yellows and reds, and one that refers to greens and blues. Yet performance on matching and memory tasks shows that the Dani can discriminate the many colors of the spectrum when they are motivated to do so. English-speaking skiers who are concerned about different skiing conditions have developed a comprehensive vocabulary about snow, including the terms *powder, slush, ice, hard packed,* and *corn snow,* that allows them to communicate and think about snow with the facility of the Inuit. When a need to expand a language's vocabulary arises, the speakers of that language apparently have little difficulty meeting the need.

Modern cognitive scientists generally do not accept the linguistic-relativity hypothesis (Pinker, 1990). For one thing, adults use images and abstract logical propositions, as well as words, as units of thought

(Larson, 1990; Miller, 1990). Infants, moreover, display considerable intelligence before they have learned to speak. Another criticism is that a language's vocabulary suggests the range of concepts that the speakers of the language have traditionally found important, not their cognitive limits. For example, people who were magically lifted from the 19th century and placed inside an airplane probably would not think they were flying inside a bird or a large insect, even if their language lacked a word for airplane.

Before leaving the section on thinking, I have a final problem for you:

> You're driving a bus that's leaving from Pennsylvania. To start off with, there were 32 people on the bus. At the next bus stop, 11 people got off and 9 people got on. At the next bus stop, 2 people got off and 2 people got on. At the next bus stop, 12 people got on and 16 people got off. At the next bus stop, 5 people got on and 3 people got off. How many people are now on the bus?

Review

SECTION VII

According to the (54) _____-relativity hypothesis, language structures (and limits) the way in which we perceive the world. Critics of the linguistic-relativity hypothesis argue that the (55) _____lary of a language may suggest the concepts deemed important by its users, but does not necessarily prevent thinking about concepts for which there are no words.

SECTION VIII. INTELLIGENCE

What form of life is so adaptive that it can survive in desert temperatures of 120° F or Arctic climes of −40° F? What form of life can run, walk, climb, swim, live underwater for months on end, and fly to the moon and back?

I won't keep you in suspense any longer. We are that form of life. Yet our unclad bodies do not allow us to adapt to these extremes of temperature. Brute strength does not allow us to live underwater or travel to the moon. Rather, it is our **intelligence** that permits us to adapt to these conditions and to challenge our physical limitations.

Question: Just what is intelligence? Intelligence is closely related to thinking. Whereas *thinking* involves understanding, manipulating, and communicating about information, *intelligence* is somewhat more broadly thought of as the underlying ability to understand the world and cope with its challenges.

Although these concepts overlap, psychologists tend to be concerned with *how* we think, but laypeople and psychologists are often concerned with *how much* intelligence we have. At an early age, we gain impressions of how intelligent or bright we are compared with other people.

Intelligence provides the cognitive basis for academic achievements. It allows us to profit from experiences such as educational experiences. Intelligence allows people to think—to understand complex ideas, reason, and solve problems—and to learn from experience and adapt effectively to the environment (Neisser et al., 1996). As we see in architecture, in the creation of mechanisms for heating and cooling, and in travel through space and under water, intelligence even permits people to create new environments. Although intelligence, like thinking, cannot be directly seen or

INTELLIGENCE A complex and controversial concept. According to David Wechsler (1975), the "capacity . . . to understand the world [and] resourcefulness to cope with its challenges."

REFLECT

When did you form an impression of how intelligent you are? Has this impression helped you or hurt you? Explain.

Going for a "Walk."   Human intelligence permits us to live underwater for months on end or to fly to the moon and back. We are weaker than many other organisms, but intelligence enables us to adapt to the environment, to create new environments, even to go for leisurely "spacewalks." Who can say what wonders human intelligence will devise in the new millennium?

g Spearman's symbol for general intelligence, which he believed underlay more specific abilities.

s Spearman's symbol for specific factors, or s factors, which he believed accounted for individual abilities.

FACTOR ANALYSIS A statistical technique that allows researchers to determine the relationships among a large number of items such as test items.

PRIMARY MENTAL ABILITIES According to Thurstone, the basic abilities that make up intelligence.

touched, psychologists tie the concept to predictors such as school performance and occupational status (Wagner, 1997).

We now discuss theories about the nature of intelligence. We see how intelligence is measured and discuss group differences in intelligence. Finally, we examine the determinants of intelligence: heredity and the environment.

Factor Theories of Intelligence

Many investigators have viewed intelligence as consisting of one or more *factors*. Question: What are factor theories of intelligence? Factor theories argue that intelligence is made up of a number of mental abilities, ranging from one to hundreds.

In 1904, British psychologist Charles Spearman suggested that the behaviors we consider intelligent have a common underlying factor. He labeled this factor *g*, for "general intelligence" or broad reasoning and problem-solving abilities. Spearman supported his view by noting that people rarely score very high in one area (such as knowledge of the meaning of words) and very low in another (such as the ability to compute numbers). People who excel in one area are also likely to excel in others. But he also noted that even the most capable people are relatively superior in some areas—such as music or business or poetry. For this reason, he suggested that specific, or *s,* factors account for specific abilities.

To test his views, Spearman developed **factor analysis.** Factor analysis is a statistical technique that allows researchers to determine which items on tests seem to be measuring the same things. In his research on relationships among scores on tests of verbal, mathematical, and spatial reasoning, Spearman repeatedly found evidence supporting the existence of *s* factors. The evidence for *g* was more limited.

The U.S. psychologist Louis Thurstone (1938) used factor analysis with various tests of specific abilities and also found only limited evidence for the existence of *g*. Thurstone concluded that Spearman had oversimplified the concept of intelligence. Thurstone's data suggested the presence of nine specific factors, which he labeled **primary mental abilities** (see Table 8.2). Thurstone suggested, for example, that we might have high word fluency, enabling us to rapidly develop lists of words that rhyme but not enabling us to solve math problems efficiently.

Over the years, psychologist J. P. Guilford (1988) expanded the numbers of factors found in intellectual functioning to hundreds.

TABLE 8.2	PRIMARY MENTAL ABILITIES, ACCORDING TO THURSTONE
Ability	**Description**
Visual and spatial abilities	Visualizing forms and spatial relationships
Perceptual speed	Grasping perceptual details rapidly, perceiving similarities and differences between stimuli
Numerical ability	Computing numbers
Verbal meaning	Knowing the meanings of words
Memory	Recalling information (words, sentences, etc.)
Word fluency	Thinking of words quickly (rhyming, doing crossword puzzles, etc.)
Deductive reasoning	Deriving examples from general rules
Inductive reasoning	Deriving general rules from examples

The problem with this approach seems to be that the more factors we generate, the more overlap we find among them. For example, several of his "factors" deal with solving math problems and computing numbers.

The Theory of Multiple Intelligences

Howard Gardner (1983) proposes the existence of several kinds of intelligence. Question: What is meant by multiple intelligences? Gardner refers to each kind of intelligence in his theory as "an intelligence" because they can be so different from one another (see Figure 8.6). He also believes that each kind of intelligence has its neurological base in a different area of the brain. Two of these "intelligences" are familiar ones: language ability and logical-mathematical ability. However, Gardner also refers to bodily-kinesthetic talents (of the sort shown by dancers, mimes, and athletes), musical talent, spatial-relations skills, and two kinds of personal intelligence: awareness of one's own inner feelings and sensitivity to other people's feelings. According to Gardner, one can compose symphonies or advance mathematical theory yet be average in, say, language and personal skills. (Are not some academic "geniuses" foolish in their personal lives?)

Critics of Gardner's view grant that people do function more intelligently in some aspects of life than in others. They also concur that many people have special talents, such as bodily-kinesthetic talents, even if their overall intelligence is quite average. However, they question whether such special talents are "intelligences" per se or whether we should continue to think of them as specific talents (Neisser et al., 1996). Language skills, reasoning ability, and ability to solve math problems seem to be more closely related than musical or gymnastic talent to what most people

Musical

Language

Logical-mathematical

Spatial-relations skills

Intrapersonal skills

Interpersonal skills

Bodily-kinesthetic talent

FIGURE 8.6
GARDNER'S THEORY OF MULTIPLE INTELLIGENCES
ACCORDING TO GARDNER, THERE ARE SEVERAL *INTELLIGENCES*, NOT ONE, EACH BASED IN A DIFFERENT AREA OF THE BRAIN. LANGUAGE ABILITY AND LOGIC ARE FAMILIAR ASPECTS OF INTELLIGENCE. BUT GARDNER ALSO REFERS TO BODILY TALENTS, MUSICAL ABILITY, SPATIAL-RELATIONS SKILLS, AND TWO KINDS OF PERSONAL INTELLIGENCE — SENSITIVITY TO ONE'S OWN FEELINGS (INTRAPERSONAL SENSITIVITY) AND SENSITIVITY TO THE FEELINGS OF OTHERS (INTERPERSONAL SENSITIVITY) — AS *INTELLIGENCES*. GARDNER'S CRITICS QUESTION WHETHER SUCH SPECIAL TALENTS ARE TRULY "INTELLIGENCES" OR MERELY SPECIFIC TALENTS.

Analytical Intelligence
(Academic Ability)
Abilities to solve problems,
compare and contrast, judge,
evaluate, and criticize

Creative Intelligence
(Creativity and Insight)
Abilities to invent, discover,
suppose, or theorize

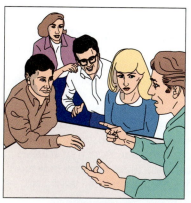

Practical Intelligence
("Street Smarts")
Abilities to adapt to the demands
of one's environment, apply
knowledge in practical situations

FIGURE 8.7
STERNBERG'S THEORY OF INTELLIGENCE
ACCORDING TO ROBERT STERNBERG, THERE ARE THREE TYPES
OF INTELLIGENCE: ANALYTICAL (ACADEMIC ABILITY), CREATIVE,
AND PRACTICAL ("STREET SMARTS").

mean by intelligence. If people have no musical ability, do we really think of them as *unintelligent?*

The Triarchic Theory of Intelligence

Psychologist Robert Sternberg (1985) has constructed a three-pronged, or *triarchic*, theory of intelligence (see Figure 8.7). Question: What is Sternberg's triarchic model of intelligence? The three types are *analytical*, *creative*, and *practical.*

ANALYTICAL INTELLIGENCE Analytical intelligence is what we generally think of as academic ability. It enables us to solve problems and to acquire new knowledge. Problem-solving skills include encoding information, combining and comparing pieces of information, and generating a solution. Consider Sternberg's analogy problem:

Washington is to *1* as *Lincoln* is to (a) 5, (b) 10, (c) 15, (d) 50?

To solve the analogy, we must first correctly *encode* the elements—*Washington, 1,* and *Lincoln*—by identifying them and comparing them with other information. We must first encode *Washington* and *Lincoln* as the names of presidents[3] and then try to combine *Washington* and *1* in a meaningful manner. Two possibilities quickly come to mind. Washington was the first president, and his picture is on the $1 bill. We can then generate two possible solutions and try them out. First, was Lincoln the 5th, 10th, 15th, or 50th president? Second, on what bill is Lincoln's picture found? (Do you need to consult a history book or peek into your wallet at this point?)

Sternberg illustrates academic intelligence through the example of a Yale graduate student. Let's call her Ashley. Ashley scored high on standardized tests such as the Graduate Record Exam (GRE) and had a nearly perfect undergraduate record. But the GRE does not always predict success (Sternberg & Williams, 1997). Ashley did well her first year of graduate school but then dropped in academic standing because of difficulty in generating ideas for research.

CREATIVE INTELLIGENCE Earlier we discussed the connections between creativity and intelligence, but we should note that Sternberg considers creativity to be one of the three key aspects of intelligence. Creative intelligence is defined by the abilities to cope with novel situations and to profit from experience. The ability to quickly relate novel situations to familiar situations (that is, to perceive similarities and differences) fosters adaptation. Moreover, as a result of experience, we also become able to solve problems more rapidly.

"Beth," another of Sternberg's students, had obtained excellent letters of recommendation from undergraduate instructors who found her to be highly creative. However, her undergraduate average and her standardized test scores were relatively low when compared with those of other students applying to Yale. Nevertheless, Beth's analytical skills were adequate and because of her imagination, she surpassed Ashley in performance.

---

[3] There are other possibilities. Both are the names of memorials and cities, for example.

PRACTICAL INTELLIGENCE Practical intelligence, or "street smarts," enables people to adapt to the demands of their environment. For example, keeping a job by adapting one's behavior to the employer's requirements is adaptive. But if the employer is making unreasonable demands, reshaping the environment (by changing the employer's attitudes) or selecting an alternate environment (by finding a more suitable job) is also adaptive (Sternberg, 1997).

A third graduate student of Sternberg's—"Cheryl"—had the greatest practical intelligence of the three. Cheryl's test scores and letters of recommendation fell between those of Ashley and Beth. Cheryl did average-quality graduate work but landed the best job of the three upon graduation—apparently because of her practical intelligence.

REFLECT

Do you know people with "street smarts"? Do street smarts strike you as a kind or form of intelligence? Why or why not?

✓ Truth or Fiction Revisited

According to Sternberg, "street smarts" are a type of intelligence—practical intelligence.

The Theory of Emotional Intelligence

Psychologists Peter Salovey and John Mayer developed the theory of emotional intelligence, which was popularized by The *New York Times* writer Daniel Goleman (1995). The theory holds that social and emotional skills are a form of intelligence, just as academic skills are. Question: Just what is "emotional intelligence"? Emotional intelligence bears more than a little resemblance to two of Gardner's "intelligences"—intrapersonal skills and interpersonal skills.

The theory suggests that self-awareness and social awareness are best learned during childhood. Failure to develop emotional intelligence is connected with childhood depression and aggression. Moreover, childhood experiences may even mold the brain's emotional responses to life's challenges. Therefore, it is useful for schools to teach skills related to emotional intelligence as well as academic ability. "I can foresee a day," wrote Goleman (1995), "when education will routinely include [teaching] essential human competencies such as self-awareness, self-control and empathy, and the arts of listening, resolving conflicts and cooperation."

No one argues that self-awareness, self-control, empathy, and cooperation are unimportant. But critics of the theory of emotional intelligence argue that schools may not have the time (or the competence) to teach these skills, and that emotional intelligence may not really be a kind of intelligence at all.

Should emotional intelligence be taught in the schools? Some psychologists believe that "emotional literacy" is as important as literacy (in reading). However, psychologist Robert McCall (1997) echoes the views of other psychologists when he says that "There are so many hours in a day, and one of the characteristics of American schools is we've saddled them with teaching driver's education, sex education, drug education and other skills, to the point that we don't spend as much time on academics as other countries do. There may be consequences for that."

Is emotional intelligence a form of intelligence? Psychologist Ulric Neisser (1997) says that "The skills that Goleman describes . . . are certainly important for determining life outcomes, but nothing is to be gained by calling them forms of intelligence."

There are thus many views of intelligence—what intelligence is and how many types or kinds of intelligence there may be. We do not yet have the final word on the nature of intelligence, but I would like to share with you David Wechsler's definition of intelligence. Wechsler is the originator of the most widely used series of contemporary intelligence tests, and he defined intelligence as the "capacity of an individual to understand the world [and the] resourcefulness to cope with its challenges" (1975, p. 139). To Wechsler, intelligence involves accurate representation of the world and effective problem solving (adapting to one's environment, profiting from experience, selecting the appropriate formulas and strategies, and so on). His definition leaves room for others to continue to consider the kinds of resourcefulness—academic, practical, emotional, even perhaps bodily—that are considered intelligent.

SECTION VIII Review

(56) _____ence provides the cognitive basis for academic achievement. Intelligence allows people to profit from (57) _____ence. Many investigators view intelligence as consisting of one or more mental abilities that are called (58) _____tors. Charles (59) S_____ suggested that the behaviors we consider to be intelligent have a common underlying factor. Spearman labeled this factor (60) _____, to represent "general intelligence." Spearman also noted that even people are relatively superior in some areas and suggested that (61) s_____, or s, factors account for specific abilities. To test his views, Spearman developed a statistical method called (62) _____ _____sis. Thurstone suggested that there are nine specific factors, which he labeled (63) _____ary mental abilities. The primary mental ability called (64) w_____ fluency enables us to rapidly develop lists of words that rhyme.

Gardner proposes the existence of (65) _____ple intelligences. He believes that each kind of intelligence is based in a different area of the (66) b_____. Gardner's "intelligences" include (67) l_____ ability, logical-mathematical ability,

(68) bodily-_____ talents, musical talent, (69) spatial-_____ skills, awareness of one's own inner feelings, and sensitivity to other people's feelings. Gardner's critics question whether such special talents are equivalent in meaning to what they see as a broader concept of (70) int_____.

Sternberg constructed a three-level, or (71) _____chic, model of intelligence. The kinds of intelligence are analytical (academic), creative, and (72) _____cal ("street smarts").

The theory of emotional intelligence holds that (73) _____al and (74) _____al skills are a form of intelligence, just as academic skills are. Ulric Neisser criticizes the theory of emotional intelligence by writing that "The skills [to which the theory refers] are certainly important for determining life outcomes, but nothing is to be gained by calling them forms of (75) _____ence."

David (76) W_____ described intelligence as the "capacity of an individual to understand the world [and the] resourcefulness to cope with its challenges."

SECTION IX. THE MEASUREMENT OF INTELLIGENCE

Although there are disagreements about the nature of intelligence, laypeople and psychologists are concerned with "how much" intelligence people have, because the question has important implications for their ability to profit from experiences, such as education. Thousands of intelligence tests are administered by psychologists and educators every day. In this section we examine two of the most widely used intelligence tests.

The Stanford-Binet Intelligence Scale

Many of the concepts of psychology have their origins in common sense. The commonsense notion that academic achievement depends on children's intelligence led Alfred Binet and Theodore Simon to invent measures of intelligence.

Question: What is the Stanford-Binet Intelligence Scale? Early in the 20th century, the French public school system was looking for a test that could identify children who were unlikely to benefit from regular classroom instruction. If these children were identified, they could be given special attention. The first version of such a test, the Binet-Simon scale, came into use in 1905. Since that time it has undergone much revision and refinement. The current version is the Stanford-Binet Intelligence Scale (SBIS).

Binet assumed that intelligence increases with age, so older children should get more items right than younger children. Binet therefore included a series of age-graded questions, as in Table 8.3, arranged in order of difficulty.

The Binet-Simon scale yielded a score called a **mental age,** or MA. The MA shows the intellectual level at which a child is functioning. For example, a child with an MA of 6 is functioning intellectually like the average 6-year-old. In taking the test, children earned "months" of credit for each correct answer. Their MA was determined by adding up the years and months of credit they attained.

Louis Terman adapted the Binet-Simon scale for use with children in the United States. The first version of the *Stanford*-Binet Intelligence Scale (SBIS) was published in 1916. (The test is so named because Terman carried

TABLE 8.3	ITEMS SIMILAR TO THOSE ON THE STANFORD-BINET INTELLIGENCE SCALE
Level (Years)	**Item**
2	1. Children show knowledge of basic vocabulary words by identifying parts of a doll, such as the mouth, ears, and hair.
	2. Children show counting and spatial skills along with visual-motor coordination by building a tower of four blocks to match a model.
4	1. Children show word fluency and categorical thinking by filling in the missing words when they are asked questions such as: "Father is a man; mother is a _____?" "Hamburgers are hot; ice cream is _____?"
	2. Children show comprehension by answering correctly when they are asked questions such as: "Why do people have automobiles?" "Why do people have medicine?"
9	1. Children can point out verbal absurdities, as in this question: "In an old cemetery, scientists unearthed a skull which they think was that of George Washington when he was only 5 years of age. What is silly about that?"
	2. Children display fluency with words, as shown by answering these questions: "Can you tell me a number that rhymes with snore?" "Can you tell me a color that rhymes with glue?"
Adult	1. Adults show knowledge of the meanings of words and conceptual thinking by correctly explaining the differences between word pairs like "sickness and misery," "house and home," and "integrity and prestige."
	2. Adults show spatial skills by correctly answering questions like: "If a car turned to the right to head north, in what direction was it heading before it turned?"

MENTAL AGE The accumulated months of credit that a person earns on the Stanford-Binet Intelligence Scale. Abbreviated *MA*.

out his work at Stanford University.) The SBIS included more items than the original test and was used with children aged 2 to 16. The SBIS also yielded an **intelligence quotient (IQ)** rather than an MA. As a result, American educators developed interest in learning the IQs of their pupils. The SBIS is used today with children from the age of 2 upward and with adults.

✓ Truth or Fiction Revisited

The terms intelligence *and* IQ *do not mean the same thing. Intelligence is a hypothetical concept on whose meanings psychologists do not agree. An* IQ *is a score on an intelligence test. Can you see any danger in using the terms as if they meant the same thing?*

The IQ reflects the relationship between a child's mental age and his or her actual or chronological age (CA). Use of this ratio reflects the fact that the same MA score has different implications for children of different ages. That is, an MA of 8 is an above average score for a 6-year-old but below average for a 10-year-old. In 1912 the German psychologist Wilhelm Stern suggested the IQ as a way to deal with this problem. Stern computed IQ using the formula

$$IQ = \frac{\text{Mental Age (MA)}}{\text{Chronological Age (CA)}} \times 100$$

According to this formula, a child with an MA of 6 and a CA of 6 would have an IQ of 100. Children who can handle intellectual problems as well as older children do have IQs above 100. For instance, an 8-year-old who does as well on the SBIS as the average 10-year-old would attain an IQ of 125. Children who do not answer as many items correctly as other children of the same age attain MAs lower than their CAs. Thus, their IQ scores are below 100.

INTELLIGENCE QUOTIENT (IQ) (1) Originally, a ratio obtained by dividing a child's score (or mental age) on an intelligence test by chronological age. (2) Generally, a score on an intelligence test.

TABLE 8.4	SUBTESTS FROM THE WECHSLER ADULT INTELLIGENCE SCALE

Verbal Subtests	**Performance Subtests**
1. *Information:* "What is the capital of the United States?" "Who was Shakespeare?"	7. *Digit Symbol:* Learning and drawing meaningless figures that are associated with numbers.
2. *Comprehension:* "Why do we have ZIP codes?" "What does 'A stitch in time saves 9' mean?"	8. *Picture Completion:* Pointing to the missing part of a picture.
3. *Arithmetic:* "If 3 candy bars cost 25 cents, how much will 18 candy bars cost?"	9. *Block Design:* Copying pictures of geometric designs using multicolored blocks.
4. *Similarities:* "How are good and bad alike?" "How are peanut butter and jelly alike?"	10. *Picture Arrangement:* Arranging cartoon pictures in sequence so that they tell a meaningful story.
5. *Digit Span:* Repeating a series of numbers forward and backward.	11. *Object Assembly:* Putting pieces of a puzzle together so that they form a meaningful object.
6. *Vocabulary:* "What does *canal* mean?"	

Note: Items for verbal subtests 1, 2, 3, 4, and 6 are similar, but not identical, to actual test items on the Wechsler Adult Intelligence Scale.

IQ scores on the SBIS today are derived by comparing their results with those of other people of the same age. People who answer more items correctly than the average for people of the same age attain IQ scores above 100. People who answer fewer items correctly than the average for their age attain scores below 100.

✓ Truth or Fiction Revisited

It is true that two children can answer exactly the same items on an intelligence test correctly, yet one can be above average and the other below average in IQ. This is because the ages of the children may differ. The more intelligent child would be the younger of the two.

The Wechsler Scales

David Wechsler developed a series of scales for use with children and adults. Question: What is different about the Wechsler scales of intelligence? The Wechsler scales group test questions into a number of separate subtests such as those shown in Table 8.4. Each subtest measures a different type of intellectual task. For this reason, the test shows how well a person does on one type of task (such as defining words) as compared with another (such as using blocks to construct geometric designs). In this way, the Wechsler scales highlight children's relative strengths and weaknesses, as well as measure overall intellectual functioning.

As you can see in Table 8.4, Wechsler described some of his scales as measuring *verbal* tasks and others as assessing *performance* tasks. In general, verbal subtests require knowledge of verbal concepts, whereas performance subtests require familiarity with spatial-relations concepts. (Figure 8.8 shows items similar to those found on the performance scales of the Wechsler tests.) But it is not that easy to distinguish between the

Taking the Wechsler. The Wechsler intelligence scales consist of verbal and performance subtests such as the one shown in this photograph.

REFLECT

What types of items do you believe ought to be on intelligence tests? Do the tests discussed in this section include the types of things that you consider important?

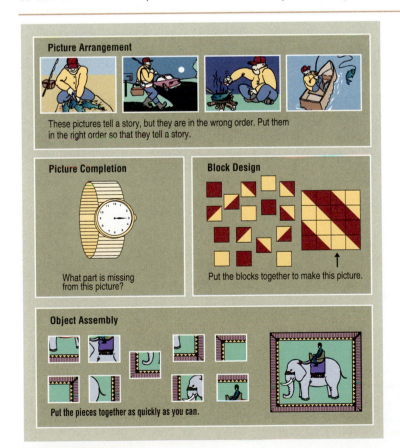

Picture Arrangement

These pictures tell a story, but they are in the wrong order. Put them in the right order so that they tell a story.

Picture Completion

What part is missing from this picture?

Block Design

Put the blocks together to make this picture.

Object Assembly

Put the pieces together as quickly as you can.

FIGURE 8.8
PERFORMANCE ITEMS OF AN INTELLIGENCE TEST
THESE TASKS RESEMBLE THOSE IN THE PERFORMANCE SUBTESTS OF THE WECHSLER ADULT INTELLIGENCE SCALE.

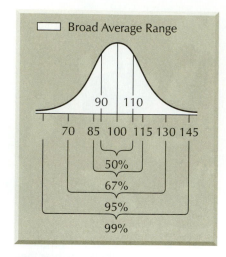

FIGURE 8.9

APPROXIMATE DISTRIBUTION OF IQ SCORES
WECHSLER DEFINED THE DEVIATION IQ SO THAT 50% OF SCORES FALL WITHIN THE BROAD AVERAGE RANGE OF 90–110. THIS BELL-SHAPED CURVE IS REFERRED TO AS A *NORMAL CURVE* BY PSYCHOLOGISTS. IT DESCRIBES THE DISTRIBUTION OF MANY TRAITS, INCLUDING HEIGHT.

TABLE 8.5	VARIATIONS IN IQ SCORES	
Range of Scores	**Percentage of Population**	**Interpretation**
130 and above	2	Very superior
120–129	7	Superior
110–119	16	Above average
100–109	25	High average
90–99	25	Low average
80–89	16	Slow learner
70–79	7	Borderline
Below 70	2	Intellectually deficient

two groupings. For example, associating to the name of the object being pieced together in subtest 11—a sign of word fluency and general knowledge as well as of spatial-relations ability—helps the person construct it more rapidly. In any event, Wechsler's scales permit the computation of verbal and performance IQs. It is not unusual for nontechnically oriented college students to attain higher verbal than performance IQs.

Wechsler also introduced the concept of the deviation IQ. Instead of dividing mental by chronological age to compute an IQ, he based IQ scores on how a person's answers compared with those attained by people in the same age group. The average test result at any age level is defined as an IQ score of 100. Wechsler distributed IQ scores so that the middle 50% of them were defined as the "broad average range" of 90 to 110.

As you can see in Figure 8.9, most IQ scores cluster around the average. Only 4% of the population has IQ scores of above 130 or below 70. Table 8.5 indicates the labels that Wechsler assigned to various IQ scores and the approximate percentages of the population who attain IQ scores at those levels.

Review

SECTION IX

Alfred (77) _____ devised a scale for measuring intelligence to help the French school system identify children who were likely to be in need of special attention. The test was termed the (78) Binet-_____ scale. The Binet-Simon scale yielded a score called a (79) m_____ age, or MA. Louis (80) T_____ adapted the Binet-Simon scale for use in the United States. The resultant version is the (81) _____-Binet Intelligence Scale (SBIS). The SBIS yields a score called an (82) _____ _____ (IQ). The IQ reflects the relationship between a child's mental age and (83) _____ical age (CA). The IQ was first computed by the formula IQ = ([84] M_____ Age/Chronological Age) × 100.

The (85) W_____ scales group test questions into a number of separate subtests. Wechsler described some of his scales as measuring (86) v_____ tasks and others as assessing (87) _____ance tasks. Wechsler introduced the concept of the (88) _____tion IQ. The average test result is defined as an IQ score of (89) _____. Wechsler distributed IQ scores so that the middle 50% of them fall within the "broad (90) _____age range" of 90 to 110.

SECTION X. INTELLIGENCE AND DIVERSITY: SOCIOECONOMIC AND ETHNIC DIFFERENCES IN INTELLIGENCE

There is a body of research suggestive of differences in intelligence among socioeconomic and ethnic groups (Suzuki & Valencia, 1997). Question: What are the socioeconomic and ethnic differences in intelligence? Lower-class U.S. children obtain IQ scores some 10 to 15 points lower than those obtained by middle- and upper-class children. African American children tend to obtain IQ scores some 15 points lower than those obtained by their White age-mates (Neisser et al., 1996). Hispanic American and Native American children also tend to score below the norms for White children (Neisser et al., 1996).

Several studies of IQ have confused the factors of social class and ethnicity because disproportionate numbers of African Americans, Hispanic Americans, and Native Americans are found among the lower socioeconomic classes (Neisser et al., 1996). When we limit our observations to particular ethnic groups, however, we still find an effect for social class. That is, middle-class Whites outscore lower-class Whites. Middle-class African Americans, Hispanic Americans, and Native Americans also outscore lower-class members of their own ethnic groups.

Research has also suggested possible cognitive differences between Asians and White people. Asian Americans, for example, frequently outscore White Americans on the math portion of the Scholastic Aptitude Test. Students in China (Taiwan) and Japan also outscore Americans on standardized achievement tests in math and science (Stevenson et al., 1986). In the United States, moreover, people of Asian Indian, Korean, Japanese, Filipino, and Chinese descent are more likely to graduate from high school and complete four years of college than White Americans, African Americans, and Hispanic Americans are (Sue & Okazaki, 1990). Asian Americans are vastly overrepresented in competitive colleges and universities.

Most psychologists believe that these ethnic differences reflect cultural attitudes toward education rather than differences in intelligence per se

REFLECT

What is your own ethnic background? Are there any stereotypes as to how people from your ethnic background perform in school or on intelligence tests? If so, what is your reaction to these stereotypes? Why?

Who's Smart? Asian children and Asian American children frequently outperform White children on tests of cognitive skills. Sue and Okazaki suggest that Asian Americans place great value on education because they have been discriminated against in careers that do not require advanced education.

(Neisser et al., 1996). That is, the Asian children may be more motivated to work hard in school. Research shows that Chinese and Japanese students and their mothers tend to attribute academic successes to hard work. American mothers, in contrast, are more likely to attribute their children's academic successes to "natural" ability (Basic Behavioral Science Task Force, 1996).

Sue and Okazaki (1990) agree. They note that the achievements of Asian students reflect different values in the home, the school, or the culture at large. They argue that Asian Americans have been discriminated against in careers that do not require advanced education. They therefore place relatively greater emphasis on education. Looking to other environmental factors, Steinberg and his colleagues (1992) claim that parental encouragement and supervision in combination with peer support for academic achievement partially explain the superior performances of White and Asian Americans compared with African and Hispanic Americans. Later we will see that other environmental factors, such as stereotype vulnerability, also contribute to these differences.

Review

SECTION X

Lower-class U.S. children attain IQ scores some 10 to 15 points (91: Higher or Lower?) than those of middle- and upper-class children. African American children tend to attain IQ scores some 15–20 points (92: Higher or Lower?) than their White age-mates. Hispanic American and Native American children score significantly (93: Above or Below?) the norms of White children.

Asian Americans frequently obtain (94: Higher or Lower?) scores on the math portion of the Scholastic Aptitude Test than White Americans. Students in China and Japan obtain (95: Higher or Lower?) scores than Americans on standardized achievement tests in math and science. According to Sue and Okazaki, the higher scores of Asian students may reflect different values in the home, the school, or the culture at large rather than differences in underlying (96) _____ence. They argue that Asian Americans place relatively greater emphasis on the value of (97) _____tion.

SECTION XI. THE TESTING CONTROVERSY: JUST WHAT DO INTELLIGENCE TESTS MEASURE?

It is no secret that during the 1920s intelligence tests were used to prevent many Europeans and others from immigrating to the United States. For example, testing pioneer H. H. Goddard assessed 178 newly arrived immigrants at Ellis Island and claimed that the great majority of Hungarians, Italians, and Russians were "feeble-minded." Apparently it was of little concern to Goddard that these immigrants, by and large, did not understand English—the language in which the tests were administered!

✓ **Truth or Fiction Revisited**

It is true that early users of IQ tests administered them in English to immigrants who did not understand the language.

It is now recognized that intelligence tests cannot be considered valid when they are used with people who do not understand the language. But what of cultural differences? Question: Do intelligence tests contain cultural biases against ethnic minority groups and immigrants? Are the tests valid when used with ethnic minority groups or people who are poorly educated? A survey of psychologists and educational specialists by Mark Snyderman and Stanley Rothman (1987) found that most consider intelligence tests to be **culturally biased** against African Americans and members of the lower classes. Elementary and secondary schools may also place too much emphasis on them in making educational placements.

Intelligence tests measure traits that are required in developed, high-tech societies. The vocabulary and arithmetic subtests on the Wechsler scales, for example, reflect achievements in language skills and computational ability. The broad achievements measured by these tests reflect intelligence, but they also reflect familiarity with the cultural concepts required to answer test questions correctly. In particular, the tests seem to reflect middle-class White culture in the United States.

SECTION XI Review

A survey of psychologists and educational specialists found that most (98: Do or Do not?) consider intelligence tests to be biased against African Americans and members of the lower classes. During the 1920s, intelligence tests were misused to prevent the (99) _____tion of many Europeans and others into the United States. If scoring well on intelligence tests requires a certain type of cultural experience, the tests are said to have a (100) _____ral bias.

SECTION XII. DETERMINANTS OF INTELLIGENCE: WHERE DOES INTELLIGENCE COME FROM?

Let us now discuss the roles of heredity and environmental influences on intelligence more fully. If different ethnic groups tend to score differently on intelligence tests, psychologists—like educators and other people involved in public life—want to know why. This is one debate that can make use of key empirical findings. Psychologists can point with pride to a rich mine of contemporary research on the roles of nature (genetic influences) and nurture (environmental influences) in the development of intelligence.

Genetic Influences on Intelligence

Question: What are the genetic influences on intelligence? Research on the genetic influences on human intelligence has employed several basic strategies. These include kinship studies, twin studies, and adoptee studies (Neisser et al., 1996). Let us consider each of them to see how genes may affect intellectual functioning.

KINSHIP STUDIES We can examine the IQ scores of closely and distantly related people who have been reared together or apart. If heredity is involved in human intelligence, closely related people ought to have more similar IQs than distantly related or unrelated people, even when they are reared separately.

CULTURAL BIAS A factor that provides an advantage for test takers from certain cultural or ethnic backgrounds, such as using test items that are based on middle-class culture in the United States.

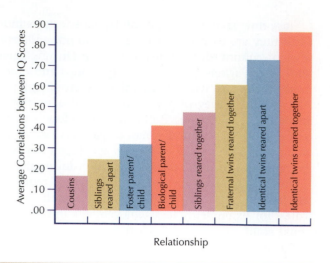

FIGURE 8.10

FINDINGS OF STUDIES OF THE RELATIONSHIP BETWEEN IQ SCORES AND HEREDITY THE DATA ARE A COMPOSITE OF STUDIES SUMMARIZED IN *SCIENCE* MAGAZINE (BOUCHARD ET AL., 1990). BY AND LARGE, CORRELATIONS ARE GREATER BETWEEN PAIRS OF PEOPLE WHO ARE MORE CLOSELY RELATED. YET PEOPLE WHO ARE REARED TOGETHER ALSO HAVE MORE SIMILAR IQ SCORES THAN PEOPLE WHO ARE REARED APART. SUCH FINDINGS SUGGEST THAT BOTH GENETIC AND ENVIRONMENTAL FACTORS CONTRIBUTE TO IQ SCORES.

Figure 8.10 is a composite of the results of more than 100 studies of IQ and heredity in human beings (Bouchard et al., 1990). The IQ scores of identical (monozygotic, or MZ) twins are more alike than scores for any other pairs, even when the twins have been reared apart. There are moderate correlations between the IQ scores of fraternal (dizygotic, or DZ) twins, between those of siblings, and between those of parents and their children. Correlations between the scores of children and their foster parents and between those of cousins are weak.

TWIN STUDIES The results of large-scale twin studies are consistent with the data in Figure 8.10. For instance, a study of 500 pairs of MZ and DZ twins in Louisville, Kentucky (Wilson, 1983), found that the correlations in intelligence between MZ twins were about the same as that for MZ twins in Figure 8.10. The correlations in intelligence between DZ twin pairs was the same as that between other siblings. Research at the University of Minnesota with sets of twins who were reared together and others who were reunited in adulthood has obtained essentially similar results (Bouchard et al., 1990). In the MacArthur Longitudinal Twin Study, Robert Emde (1993) and his colleagues examined the intellectual abilities of 200 primarily White, healthy 14-month-old pairs of twins. They found that identical (MZ) twins were more similar than fraternal (DZ) twins in spatial memory, ability to categorize things, and word comprehension. Emde and his colleagues concluded that genes tend to account for about 40% to 50% of differences in children's cognitive skills.

All in all, studies generally suggest that the **heritability** of intelligence is between 40% and 60% (Bouchard et al., 1990; Neisser et al., 1996). In other words, about half of the variations (the technical term is *variance*) in IQ scores can be accounted for by heredity. This is *not* the same as saying that you inherited about half of your intelligence. The implication of such a statement would be that you "got" the other half of your intelligence somewhere else. It means, rather, that about half of the difference between your IQ score and the IQ scores of other people can be explained in terms of genetic factors.

Note, too, that genetic pairs (such as MZ twins) who were reared together show higher correlations in their IQ scores than similar genetic pairs (such as other MZ twins) who were reared apart. This finding holds for DZ twins, siblings, parents and their children, and unrelated people. Being reared together is therefore related with similarities in IQ. *For this*

HERITABILITY The degree to which the variations in a trait from one person to another can be attributed to, or explained by, genetic factors.

reason, the same group of studies used to demonstrate a role for the heritability of IQ scores also suggests that the environment plays a role in determining IQ scores.

ADOPTEE STUDIES Another strategy for exploring genetic influences on intelligence is to compare the correlations between the IQ scores of adopted children and those of their biological and adoptive parents. When children are separated from their biological parents at an early age, one can argue that strong relationships between their IQs and those of their natural parents reflect genetic influences. Strong relationships between their IQs and those of their adoptive parents might reflect environmental influences.

Several studies with 1- and 2-year-old children in Colorado (Baker et al., 1983), Texas (Horn, 1983), and Minnesota (Scarr & Weinberg, 1983) have found a stronger relationship between the IQ scores of adopted children and those of their biological parents than between the children's scores and those of their adoptive parents. The Scarr and Weinberg report concerns African American children reared by White adoptive parents. We return to its findings in the section on environmental influences on intelligence.

In sum, genetic factors may account for about half of the variation in intelligence test scores among individuals. Environmental factors also affect scores on intelligence tests.

Environmental Influences on Intelligence

Question: What are the environmental influences on intelligence? To answer this question we must consider studies of environmental influences, which also employ a variety of research strategies. These include manipulation of the testing situation, observation of the role of the home environment, and evaluation of the effects of educational programs. We will also see that environmental factors affect intellectual functioning in adulthood—even in late adulthood.

INTELLIGENCE AND DIVERSITY: STEREOTYPE VULNERABILITY
Stereotype vulnerability also affects test scores. Psychologist Claude Steele (1996, 1997) suggests that African American students carry an extra burden in performing scholastic tasks: They believe that they risk confirming their group's negative stereotype by doing poorly on such tasks. This concern creates performance anxiety. Performance anxiety distracts them from the tasks, and as a result they perform more poorly than White students in the same situation.

In an experiment designed to test this view, Steele and Aronson (1995) gave two groups of African American and White Stanford undergraduates the most difficult verbal skills test questions from the GRE. One group was told that the researchers were attempting to learn about the "psychological factors involved in solving verbal problems." The other group was told that the items were "a genuine test of your verbal abilities and limitations." African American students who were given the first message performed as well as White students. African American students who were given the second message—that proof of their abilities was on the line—performed significantly more poorly than the White students. Apparently the second message triggered their stereotype vulnerability, which led them to self-destruct on the test. Steele's findings are further evidence of the limits of intelligence tests as valid indicators of intelligence.

REFLECT

Does performance anxiety affect you on tests? What kinds of thoughts make you anxious? What can you do about it?

STEREOTYPE VULNERABILITY The tendency to focus on a conventional, negative belief about one's group, such that the individual risks behaving in a way that confirms that belief.

HOME ENVIRONMENT AND STYLES OF PARENTING   The home environment and styles of parenting also appear to have an effect on IQ scores (Olson et al., 1992; Steinberg et al., 1992; Suzuki & Valencia, 1997). Children of mothers who are emotionally and verbally responsive, furnish appropriate play materials, are involved with their children, and provide varied daily experiences during the early years obtain higher IQ scores later on (Bradley et al., 1989; Gottfried et al., 1994). Organization and safety in the home have also been linked to higher IQs at later ages and to higher achievement test scores during the first grade (Bradley et al., 1989).

Dozens of other studies support the view that children's early environment is linked to IQ scores and academic achievement. For example, McGowan and Johnson (1984) found that good parent–child relationships and maternal encouragement of independence were both positively linked to Mexican American children's IQ scores by the age of 3. A number of studies have also found that high levels of maternal restrictiveness and punishment of children at 24 months are linked to *lower* IQ scores later on.

EDUCATION   Although intelligence is viewed as permitting people to profit from education, education also apparently contributes to intelligence. For example, government-funded efforts to provide preschoolers with enriched early environments have led to measurable intellectual gains. Head Start programs, for example, enhance the IQ scores, achievement test scores, and academic skills of disadvantaged children (Barnett & Escobar, 1990; Zigler, 1995) by exposing them to materials and activities that middle-class children take for granted. These include letters and words, numbers, books, exercises in drawing, pegs and pegboards, puzzles, toy animals, and dolls.

✓ Truth or Fiction Revisited

It is true that Head Start programs have raised children's IQs.

Preschool intervention programs can have long-term positive effects on children. During the elementary and high school years, graduates of preschool programs are less likely to be left back or placed in classes for

Head Start.   Preschoolers who are placed in Head Start programs have shown dramatic improvements in readiness for elementary school and in IQ scores.

slow learners. They are more likely to graduate from high school, go on to college, and earn higher incomes.

Schooling at later ages also contributes to intelligence test scores. When children of about the same age start school a year apart because of admissions standards related to their date of birth, children who have been in school longer obtain higher IQ scores (Neisser et al., 1996). Moreover, IQ test scores tend to decrease during the summer vacation (Neisser et al., 1996).

ADOPTEE STUDIES The Minnesota adoption studies reported by Scarr and Weinberg suggest a genetic influence on intelligence. But the same studies (Scarr & Weinberg, 1976, 1977) also suggest a role for environmental influences. African American children who were adopted during their first year by White parents with above-average income and education obtained IQ scores some 15 to 25 points higher than those obtained by African American children reared by their natural parents (Scarr & Weinberg, 1976). There are two cautions regarding these findings. One is that the adoptees' average IQ score, about 106, remained below those of their adoptive parents' natural children—117 (Scarr & Weinberg, 1977). The second is that follow-up studies of the adopted children at the age of 17 found that the mean IQ score of the adopted African American children had decreased by 9 points, to 97 (Weinberg et al., 1992). The meaning of the change remains to be unraveled.

ENVIRONMENTAL INFLUENCES IN ADULTHOOD Intellectual functioning is also somewhat plastic in adulthood, even in late adulthood (age 65 and beyond). For example, psychologist Walter Schaie and his colleagues (Schaie, 1994) have been studying the cognitive development of adults for four decades and discovered various factors that contribute to intellectual functioning across the life span:

1. *General health.* People in good health tend to retain higher levels of intellectual functioning into late adulthood. Therefore, paying attention to one's diet, exercising, and having regular medical checkups contribute to intellectual functioning as well as physical health.

2. *Socioeconomic status (SES).* People with high SES tend to maintain intellectual functioning more adequately than people with low SES. High SES is also connected with above-average income and levels of education, a history of stimulating occupational pursuits, maintenance of intact families, and better health.

3. *Stimulating activities.* Cultural events, travel, participation in professional organizations, and extensive reading contribute to intellectual functioning.

4. *Marriage to a spouse with a high level of intellectual functioning.* The spouse whose level of intellectual functioning is lower at the beginning of a marriage tends to increase in intellectual functioning as time goes by. Perhaps that partner is continually challenged by the other.

5. *Openness to new experience.* Being open to new challenges of life apparently helps keep us young—at any age.

Recent research reported in *Nature* suggests that we can add a sixth factor:

6. *Aerobic activity.* Sustained physical activity (such as walking) has been shown to enhance the cognitive abilities of 60–75-year-olds in

REFLECT

Do you know any older people who seem to behave in ways that keep their intelligence "fine-tuned"? Do you know others who do not? What seems to account for the difference?

the areas of planning, scheduling, and memory functioning (Kramer et al., 1999). Physical fitness increases the oxygen supply to the brain and also enhances one's general health.

Perhaps we need not be so concerned with whether we can sort out exactly how much of a person's IQ is due to heredity and how much is due to environmental influences. A majority of psychologists and educators believe that IQ reflects the complex interaction of heredity, early childhood experiences, and sociocultural factors and expectations. Psychology has traditionally supported the dignity of the individual. It might be more appropriate for us to try to identify children, *and adults,* of all ethnic groups whose environments place them at risk for failure and do what we can to enrich their environments.

Review

SECTION XII

Research on the (101) _____tic influences on human intelligence has focused on kinship studies, twin studies, and adoptee studies. Psychologists examine the IQ scores of closely and distantly related people who have been reared together or (102) a_____. If heredity is involved in human intelligence, closely related people ought to have (103: More or Less?) similar IQs than distantly related or unrelated people, even when they are reared separately. The IQ scores of identical (MZ) twins are (104: More or Less?) alike than the scores for any other pairs, even when the twins have been reared apart. When children are separated from their biological parents at early ages, one can argue that strong relationships between their IQs and those of their biological parents reflect (105: Genetic or Environmental?) influences. Studies generally suggest that the (106) _____lity of intelligence is between 40% and 60%. In other words, about half of the variations in IQ scores among people can be accounted for by (107) _____tics.

Studies of (108) _____mental influences on IQ include manipulation of the testing situation, observation of the role of the home environment, and evaluation of the effects of educational programs. Many African Americans perform poorly on intelligence tests due to (109) _____type vulnerability, which is the tendency to focus on a conventional, negative belief about one's group, such that the individual risks behaving in a way that confirms that belief.

The home environment and styles of parenting (110: Do or Do not?) appear to have an effect on IQ. Children of mothers who are emotionally and verbally responsive, who provide appropriate play materials, who are involved with their children, and who provide varied daily experiences during the early years attain (111: Higher or Lower?) IQ scores later on. Good parent−child relationships and maternal encouragement of independence are (112: Positively or Negatively?) linked to Mexican American children's IQ scores. (113) H_____ Start programs enhance the IQ scores and academic skills of poor children by exposing them to materials and activities that middle-class children take for granted. Intellectual functioning (114: Can or Cannot?) be affected by environmental factors in late adulthood.

The largest number of psychologists and educators believe that intellectual functioning reflects the (115) _____action of genetic and environmental factors.

STUDY GUIDE

SUMMARY

1. **What is thinking?** Thinking is cognitive activity involved in understanding, processing, and communicating information. It refers to conscious, planned attempts to make sense of the world.

2. **How do concepts function as building blocks of thought?** Concepts provide mental categories that allow for the grouping together of objects, events, or ideas with common properties. We tend to organize concepts in hierarchies. Prototypes are good examples of particular concepts. Simple prototypes are usually taught by means of exemplars, or positive and negative instances of the concept. Abstract concepts are usually formed through explanations involving more basic concepts.

3. **How do people go about solving problems?** People first attempt to understand the problem. Then they use various strategies for attacking the problem, including algorithms, heuristic devices, and analogies. Algorithms are specific procedures for solving problems (such as formulas) that invariably work as long as they are applied correctly.

4. **Is it best to use a tried and true formula to solve a problem?** Not necessarily. Heuristic devices often help us "jump" to correct conclusions. Heuristics are rules of thumb that help us simplify and solve problems. Heuristics are less reliable than algorithms, but when they are effective, they allow us to solve problems more rapidly. One commonly used heuristic device is means–end analysis, in which we assess the difference between our current situation and our goals and do what we can to reduce the discrepancy. The analogy heuristic applies the solution of an earlier problem to the solution of a new, similar problem.

5. **What factors affect effectiveness at solving problems?** Key factors include one's level of expertise, whether one falls prey to a mental set, whether one develops insight into a problem, incubation, and functional fixedness.

6. **What are the relationships among creativity, problem solving, and intelligence?** Creativity is the ability to make unusual and sometimes remote associations to or among the elements of a problem in order to generate new combinations. There is only a moderate relationship between creativity and academic ability.

7. **What factors other than intelligence are connected with creativity?** Creativity is characterized by divergent thinking. Creative people show traits such as flexibility, fluency, and independence. The pressure of social evaluation appears to reduce creativity, and the effects of brainstorming in fostering creativity are debatable.

8. **How do people reason?** Two types of reasoning used by people are deductive and inductive reasoning. In deductive reasoning, one reaches conclusions about premises that are true so long as the premises are true. In inductive reasoning, we reason from individual cases or particular facts to a general conclusion that is not necessarily true.

9. **How do people go about making judgments and decisions?** People sometimes make decisions by carefully weighing the pluses and minuses, but most make decisions on the basis of limited information. Decision makers frequently use rules of thumb or heuristics, which are shortcuts that are correct (or correct enough) most of the time. According to the representativeness heuristic, people make judgments about events according to the populations of events that they appear to represent. According to the availability heuristic, people's estimates of frequency or probability are based on how easy it is to find examples of relevant events. According to the anchoring and adjustment heuristic, we adjust our initial estimates as we receive additional information—but we often do so unwillingly.

10. **How do people frame information in order to persuade others?** People frequently phrase or frame arguments in ways to persuade others. For example, people on both sides of the abortion issue present themselves as being in favor of an important value—either pro-life or pro-choice.

11. **Why do people tend to be convinced that they are right, even when they are dead wrong?** People tend to retain their convictions, even when proven

false, because they are unaware of the flimsiness of their assumptions, focus on events that confirm their judgments, and work to bring about results consistent with their judgments.

12. **What is the effect of language on thinking?** According to the linguistic-relativity hypothesis, the concepts we use to understand the world are derived from our language. Therefore, speakers of various languages would think about the world in different ways. However, modern cognitive scientists suggest that the vocabulary of a language suggests the range of concepts that the users have traditionally found to be useful, not their cognitive limits.

13. **Just what is intelligence?** Intelligence underlies (provides the cognitive basis for) thinking and academic achievement. It has been defined by Wechsler as the "capacity . . . to understand the world . . . and . . . resourcefulness to cope with its challenges."

14. **What are factor theories of intelligence?** Spearman and Thurstone believed that intelligence is composed of a number of factors. Spearman believed that a common factor, *g*, underlies all intelligent behavior but that people also have specific abilities, or *s* factors. Thurstone suggested that there are several primary mental abilities, including word fluency and numerical ability.

15. **What is meant by multiple intelligences?** Gardner believes that people have several intelligences, not one, and that each is based in a different area of the brain. Two such "intelligences" are language ability and logical-mathematical ability, but Gardner also includes bodily-kinesthetic intelligence and others.

16. **What is Sternberg's triarchic model of intelligence?** Sternberg's triarchic theory proposes three kinds of intelligence: analytical (academic ability), creative, and practical ("street smarts"). Analytical intelligence is not necessarily the best predictor of success.

17. **Just what is "emotional intelligence"?** The theory of emotional intelligence holds that social and emotional skills are a form of intelligence that helps children avert violence and depression. The theory suggests that emotional skills are best learned during childhood.

18. **What is the Stanford-Binet Intelligence Scale?** This is the test originated by Alfred Binet in France and developed by Louis Terman at Stanford University. It includes a series of age-graded questions. The SBIS derives an IQ score by dividing a child's mental age score by the child's chronological age and then multiplying by 100.

19. **What is different about the Wechsler scales of intelligence?** The Wechsler scales use deviation IQs, which are derived by comparing a person's performance with that of age-mates. The Wechsler scales contain verbal and performance subtests that measure general information, comprehension, similarities (conceptual thinking), vocabulary, mathematics, block design (copying designs), and object assembly (piecing puzzles together).

20. **What are the socioeconomic and ethnic differences in intelligence?** Lower-class U.S. children obtain IQ scores some 10 to 15 points lower than those of middle- and upper-class children. African American children tend to obtain IQ scores some 15 to 20 points lower than those of their White age-mates. Asians and Asian Americans usually obtain higher IQ scores than White British or U.S. citizens.

21. **Do intelligence tests contain cultural biases against ethnic minority groups and immigrants?** Intelligence tests were used historically to prevent many Europeans and others from immigrating to the United States. They were administered in English to people who did not know English. Most psychologists and educators believe that intelligence tests are biased against African Americans and people in the lower classes in that they require familiarity with cultural concepts, particularly those that reflect middle-class White culture in the United States.

22. **What are the genetic influences on intelligence?** Research on the genetic influences on human intelligence is generally based on kinship studies, twin studies, and adoptee studies. There appears to be a stronger relationship between the IQ scores of adopted children and those of their biological parents than between the children's scores and those of their adoptive parents. Studies generally suggest that the heritability of intelligence is between 40% and 60%.

23. **What are the environmental influences on intelligence?** Research on environmental influences on intelligence considers factors such as stereotype vulnerability, which leads many African American test-takers to self-destruct; the effects of the home environment, including styles of parenting; the effects of education, including Head Start programs; and, among adults, links to lifestyle, such as engaging in cultural activities; and even exercise. The majority of psychologists and educators believe that intelligence reflects a complex interaction of genetic factors, childhood experiences, and sociocultural factors and expectations.

EXERCISE 1

MATCHING

Items numbered 1–20 consist of concepts concerning the topic of thinking. Items lettered A–T represent examples of these concepts. Match the example to the concept by writing the letter that represents the example in the blank space to the left of the concept.

____ 1. Algorithm
____ 2. Systematic random search
____ 3. Means–end analysis
____ 4. Mental set
____ 5. Insight
____ 6. Convergent thinking
____ 7. Incubation
____ 8. Functional fixedness
____ 9. Creativity
____ 10. Divergent thinking
____ 11. Brainstorming
____ 12. Deductive reasoning
____ 13. Premise
____ 14. Inductive reasoning
____ 15. Representativeness heuristic
____ 16. Availability heuristic
____ 17. Framing effect
____ 18. Prototype
____ 19. Negative exemplar
____ 20. Anchoring and adjustment heuristic

A. Because of sensationalistic newscasts, you assume that New York City is a terrible place to live.

B. You narrow your thinking to find the one correct answer to a question on the SATs or GREs.

C. A Siamese cat is one of these for the concept of *dog*.

D. You generate lists of all the meanings you can think of for the verbs "see" and "pull."

E. You use the formula that helped you solve one problem with problems that seem to be similar.

F. You try to find an address by picturing where you are now and trying to reduce the discrepancy (that is, the distance between locations).

G. The solution to a problem comes to you in a flash.

H. You overcome this to solve the Duncker candle problem.

I. A robin serves as an excellent one of these for the concept of *bird*.

J. An attempt to solve an anagram by trying every possible letter combination.

K. You bring together a group of people to generate as many solutions as they can think of for a particular problem.

L. The statement "People are mortal" serves as this in the syllogism about Socrates.

M. Because a couple already has five daughters, you assume that their sixth child is likely to be a son.

N. You conclude that Socrates is mortal because Socrates is a person and people are mortal.

O. A politician sees that you are unwilling to consider decreasing Social Security benefits and therefore begins to argue with you about the importance of balancing the budget instead.

P. The Pythagorean theorem.

Q. You put aside a difficult problem for a while, hoping that an effective way of approaching it will come to you later on.

R. A person assumes that a greeting that was effective with one person will be effective with another.

S. A psychological concept that involves the ability to make many associations, some of them remote, to a concept.

T. You grow up believing that your political beliefs are correct. When certain beliefs no longer seem to fit the world as it is, you adjust your beliefs somewhat, but not very willingly.

EXERCISE 2

MISSING INFORMATION

What are the names of the subtests in the Wechsler Adult Intelligence Scale?

TABLE 1	SUBTESTS FROM THE WECHSLER ADULT INTELLIGENCE SCALE
Verbal Subtests	**Performance Subtests**
1. (1) In_____: "What is the capital of the United States?" "Who was Shakespeare?"	6. (4) _____: "What does canal mean?"
2. Comprehension: "Why do we have ZIP codes?" "What does 'A stitch in time saves 9' mean?"	7. Digit (5) _____: Learning and drawing meaningless figures that are associated with numbers.
3. Arithmetic: "If 3 candy bars cost 25 cents, how much will 18 candy bars cost?"	8. (6) _____ Completion: Pointing to the missing part of a picture.
4. (2) _____ties: "How are good and bad alike?" "How are peanut butter and jelly alike?"	9. (7) _____ Design: Copying pictures of geometric designs using multicolored blocks.
	10. (8) _____ Arrangement: Arranging cartoon pictures in sequence so that they tell a meaningful story.
5. Digit (3) _____: Repeating a series of numbers forward and backward.	11. (9) _____ Assembly: Putting pieces of a puzzle together so that they form a meaningful object.

Fill in the missing information.

TABLE 2	VARIATIONS IN IQ SCORES	
Range of Scores	**Percentage of Population**	**Interpretation**
130 and above	(10) _____	Very (11) s_____
120–129	(12) _____	Superior
110–119	16	Above (13) a_____
100–109	25	High average
90–99	(14) _____	(15) _____ average
80–89	16	Slow learner
70–79	7	Borderline
Below 70	2	Intellectually deficient

BRIDGING THE GAP

LANGUAGE AND CULTURE

to be at a loss (365)   *to be totally surprised and unable, therefore, to react*

to be at odds with (375)   *to be in mild conflict with*

background knowledge (368)   *supporting information or knowledge*

bachelor (366)   *unmarried man*

bamboozled (376)   *confused*

brute strength (383)   *muscle power (as opposed to brain power)*

building block (365)   *basic element for construction of an idea*

bumblebee (382)   *large fuzzy insect that stings, related to the insect that makes honey*

chronological age (390)   *age in years (not development)*

to cluster (392)   *to form a group or grouping*

curator (372)   *museum official*

database (371)   *bank of information*

deviation IQ (392)   *difference in intelligence measurement compared with the average attained by people in the same age group*

to dive right in (367)   *to begin a project without adequate preparation*

domino effect (370)   *in the game of dominoes, plastic or wooden tiles are arranged so that if one falls, one by one the rest of them will also fall*

duller (375)   *less intelligent*

emotional literacy (387)   *ability to know and recognize how to deal with people's feelings*

empathy (387)   *understanding, ability to feel another's emotions*

to fall prey to (370)   *to become a victim of*

feeble-minded (394)   *well below average in intelligence*

to fiddle around (372)   *to waste time aimlessly thinking about*

a flash of insight (373)   *a sudden understanding*

flimsiness (381)   *inadequate nature*

to flip a coin (378)   *to use a tossed coin to choose whose opinion will be followed*

to foresee (387)   *to predict*

to foster (386)   *to encourage the growth of the ability to*

furthering (378)   *continuing*

fuzzy-wuzzy (366)   *said of creatures that are friendly and have fur (like a teddy bear)*

groan (366)   *sound of exasperation*

grudgingly (379)   *unwillingly, reluctantly*

to have a go at something (367)   *to try to succeed at a task*

"the heck with it" (372)   *I give up on it because it is not worth any effort*

to be hit with something (365)   *to be confronted with suddenly*

illusory (372)   *seen but not real*

inkling (365)   *hint, suspicion*

to jingle in your pocket (378)   *to make the sound of coins in one's pocket*

to jump to conclusions (369)   *to decide on the answer without going through the proper process of figuring it out*

just desserts (372)   *(pun) the proper reward (and also, a dessert is a sweet treat)*

to keep plugging away at something (363, 373)   *to persevere at something, to work on a problem steadily*

to keep track of something (365)   *to watch something for changes*

kinesthetic (385)   *(referring to) body movement or action*

to leap out at a person (372)   *to become obvious in the thought process*

mesh (372)   *wire screen or net*

novice (371)   *newcomer, person who is just learning how*

on the table (376)   *available for inspection and discussion*

opponent (380)   *one who is against*

to outscore (393)   *to score higher than*

outer world (369)   *aspects of the problem that are observable*

overinclusion (366)   *expansion of the category*

pegboard (398)   *board with evenly spaced holes into which hooks (or pegs) for hanging things can be inserted*

plastic (399)   *flexible*

play date (380)   *opportunity to be with other children and play together*

to ponder (376)   *to think about seriously*

to pop out (371)   *to appear without warning*

population (378)   *group of samples with a shared characteristic*

pool (369)   *total collection, source*

preexisting (374)   *already done*

premise (377)   *main topic idea*

to probe (374)   *to investigate, to explore*

proponent of (380)   *supporter of*

pros and cons (378)   *reasons for and against doing something*

prototype (366)   *first model for an invention*

to plug away at (373)   *to work on a problem steadily*

to reason (365)   *to determine by a logical process, to figure out*

remote (374)   *distantly related*

to reside within someone (371)   *to be a natural part of someone*

to retrace (367)   *to return along the same route*

rich mine of contemporary research (395)   *a large and useful collection of current research results*

riddle (366)   *logic puzzle*

sense of direction (370)   *instinctive feeling for which way is which*

to set the stage (372)   *to prepare*

shortcut (369)   *quick way of arriving at a goal or achieving an outcome*

slow learner (399)   *student whose learning abilities are low*

slush (382)   *mixture of melting snow and ice on the ground*

to stand for something (372)   *to mean, to represent something*

stereotype vulnerability (394)   *human propensity to be influenced negatively by becoming anxious about others' expectations*

a stitch in time saves nine (390)   *prudence in action (if you do what you need to do to fix a situation before it is a big problem, then you will save a lot of work)*

street smarts (363)   *knowledge about*

to suspend judgment (376)   *not to criticize immediately, but to wait*

to take a breath (367)   *to pause to prepare*

torture (365)   *distress, great discomfort*

to toy with (377)   *to play with, to figure out a use for*

tried and true (363, 370)   *tested and proven to be authentic or useful*

20–20 hindsight (380)   *(20–20 vision is perfect eyesight) here the reference is to understanding a situation that was not easily understandable when it was happening with perfect insight after the situation is over*

unclad (383)   *naked, not dressed*

to undergo (365)   *to experience*

to unravel (399)   *to solve, to pull apart for investigation*

to unscramble (371)   *to put back into natural order*

vastly (371)   *greatly*

weighty (376)   *important*

wild (376)   *unusual, extraordinary*

QUIZ

1. The bus driver problem indicates the importance of
    - (a) rote repetition of the elements of a problem,
    - (b) prototypes as components of thought,
    - (c) the availability heuristic,
    - (d) paying attention to relevant information.

2. The water-jar problems indicate the role of _____ in problem solving.
    - (a) heuristic devices,
    - (b) functional fixedness,
    - (c) incubation,
    - (d) mental sets.

3. A mathematical formula for solving a problem is an example of a(n)
    - (a) mental set,
    - (b) analogy,
    - (c) algorithm,
    - (d) heuristic device.

4. Means–end analysis is an example of a(n)
    - (a) mental set,
    - (b) analogy,
    - (c) algorithm,
    - (d) heuristic device.

5. All of the following help individuals solve problems, with the exception of
    - (a) insight,
    - (b) incubation,
    - (c) heuristic devices,
    - (d) functional fixedness.

6. In inductive reasoning,
    - (a) we reason from individual cases or particular facts to a general conclusion,
    - (b) the conclusion must be true if the premises are true,
    - (c) thought is limited to present facts,
    - (d) the individual associates fluently and freely to the elements of the problem.

7. Consider the following two multiplication problems:
    - (1) $8 \times 7 \times 6 \times 5 \times 4 \times 3 \times 2 \times 1$
    - (2) $1 \times 2 \times 3 \times 4 \times 5 \times 6 \times 7 \times 8$

    People tend to assume that the answer to number 1 will be greater because of
    - (a) the representativeness heuristic,
    - (b) the anchoring and adjustment heuristic,
    - (c) the availability heuristic,
    - (d) the framing effect.

8. The fact that people often tend to focus on examples that confirm their judgments and ignore events that do not leads to
    - (a) overconfidence,
    - (b) the framing effect,
    - (c) divergent thinking,
    - (d) the availability heuristic.

9. The term *intelligence* is most similar in meaning to
    - (a) academic achievement,
    - (b) musical talent,
    - (c) language ability,
    - (d) underlying competence.

10. Binet's test was developed further in the United States by
    - (a) Sternberg,
    - (b) Stern,
    - (c) Terman,
    - (d) Thurstone.

11. Whose data suggested that intelligence consists of "primary mental abilities"?
    - (a) Wechsler,
    - (b) Thurstone,
    - (c) Spearman,
    - (d) Sternberg.

12. Who suggested that awareness of one's own inner feelings is a kind of intelligence?
    - (a) Wechsler,
    - (b) Binet,
    - (c) Sternberg,
    - (d) Gardner.

13. A child has an MA of 12. From this information we can conclude that she
    - (a) is more intelligent than most of her peers,
    - (b) is less intelligent than most of her peers,
    - (c) has an IQ within the broad average range,
    - (d) is about as intelligent as the typical 12-year-old.

14. The concept of the deviation IQ was introduced by
    - (a) Wechsler,
    - b) Stern,
    - (c) Gardner,
    - (d) Simon.

15. The symbol *g* was used by Spearman to signify
    - (a) general intelligence,
    - (b) primary mental abilities,
    - (c) the ability to do well on intelligence tests,
    - (d) IQ, but not intelligence.

16. Wechsler distributed IQ scores so that
    _____% of them fall within the range
    of 90 to 110.
    (a) 2,
    (b) 16,
    (c) 32,
    (d) 50.

17. Approximately _____% of the popula-
    tion obtain IQ scores on Wechsler scales that are
    suggestive of intellectual deficiency.
    (a) 2,
    (b) 7,
    (c) 16,
    (d) 25.

18. The IQ scores of _____ show the highest
    correlations.
    (a) identical twins reared together,
    (b) fraternal twins reared together,
    (c) identical twins reared apart,
    (d) fraternal twins reared apart.

19. Steele uses the concept of stereotype vulnerabil-
    ity to explain why
    (a) Asian Americans spend more time on
        homework than most other ethnic groups,
    (b) many African Americans self-destruct on
        intelligence tests,
    (c) the environment influences intellectual
        performance only in childhood,
    (d) the heritability of intelligence is about
        40% to 60%.

20. The largest group of psychologists and educa-
    tional specialists express the belief that
    (a) intelligence reflects the interaction of
        heredity and environmental influences,
    (b) only heredity really influences intelli-
        gence,
    (c) only environmental influences really af-
        fect the development of intelligence,
    (d) neither heredity nor the environment has
        a meaningful influence on intelligence.

1. What is thinking?

2. How do concepts function as building blocks of thought?

3. How do people go about solving problems?

4. Is it best to use a tried and true formula to solve a problem?

5. What factors affect effectiveness at solving problems?

6. What are the relationships among creativity, problem solving, and intelligence?

7. What factors other than intelligence are connected with creativity?

8. How do people reason?

9. How do people go about making judgments and decisions?

10. How do people frame information in order to persuade others?

11. Why do people tend to be convinced that they are right, even when they are dead wrong?

12. What is the effect of language on thinking?

13. Just what is intelligence?

14. What are factor theories of intelligence?

15. What is meant by multiple intelligences?

16. What is Sternberg's triarchic model of intelligence?

17. Just what is "emotional intelligence"?

18. What is the Stanford- Binet Intelligence Scale?

19. What is different about the Wechsler scales of intelligence?

20. What are the socioeconomic and ethnic differences in intelligence?

21. Do intelligence tests contain cultural biases against ethnic minority groups and immigrants?

22. What are the genetic influences on intelligence?

_____
_____
_____
_____
_____
_____

23. What are the environmental influences on intelligence?

_____
_____
_____
_____
_____
_____

ANSWERS TO SECTION REVIEWS

1. Understanding
2. Processing
3. Information
4. Categories
5. Categorizing
6. Manipulating
7. Hierarchies
8. Prototypes
9. Exemplars
10. Positive
11. Negative
12. Explanation
13. Overextension
14. Understand
15. Mental representation
16. Relate
17. Representation
18. Knowledge
19. Algorithm
20. Systematic
21. Heuristic
22. Shortcuts
23. Means–end
24. Analogy
25. Previous
26. Knowledge
27. Relate
28. Mental
29. Insight

30. Incubate
31. Functional
32. Mental
33. Creativity
34. Willing
35. Challenging
36. Divergent
37. Do
38. Is not
39. Brainstorming
40. Transforming
41. Premises
42. Deductive
43. Inductive
44. Does not
45. Limited
46. Heuristic
47. Representativeness
48. Availability
49. Adjustment
50. Anchor
51. Information
52. Framing
53. To be
54. Linguistic
55. Vocabulary
56. Intelligence
57. Experience
58. Factors

59. Spearman
60. g
61. Specific
62. Factor analysis
63. Primary
64. Word
65. Multiple
66. Brain
67. Language
68. Kinesthetic
69. Relations
70. Intelligence
71. Triarchic
72. Practical
73. Social or Emotional
74. Emotional or Social
75. Intelligence
76. Wechsler
77. Binet
78. Simon
79. Mental
80. Terman
81. Stanford
82. Intelligence quotient
83. Chronological
84. Mental
85. Wechsler
86. Verbal
87. Performance

88. Deviation
89. 100
90. Average
91. Lower
92. Lower
93. Below
94. Higher
95. Higher
96. Intelligence or Competence
97. Education
98. Do
99. Immigration
100. Cultural
101. Genetic
102. Apart
103. More
104. More
105. Genetic
106. Heritability
107. Genetics
108. Environmental
109. Stereotype
110. Do
111. Higher
112. Positively
113. Head
114. Can
115. Interaction

ANSWERS TO EXERCISE 1

1. P	6. B	11. K	16. A
2. J	7. Q	12. N	17. O
3. F	8. H	13. L	18. I
4. E	9. S (or D)	14. R	19. C
5. G	10. D (or S)	15. M	20. T

ANSWERS TO EXERCISE 2

Table 1
1. Performance
2. Information
3. Similarities
4. Span

5. Digit
6. Picture
7. Block
8. Picture
9. Object

Table 2
10. 2
11. Superior
12. 7

13. Average
14. 25
15. Low

ANSWERS TO QUIZ

1. D	6. A	11. B	16. D
2. D	7. B	12. D	17. A
3. C	8. A	13. D	18. A
4. D	9. D	14. A	19. B
5. D	10. C	15. A	20. A

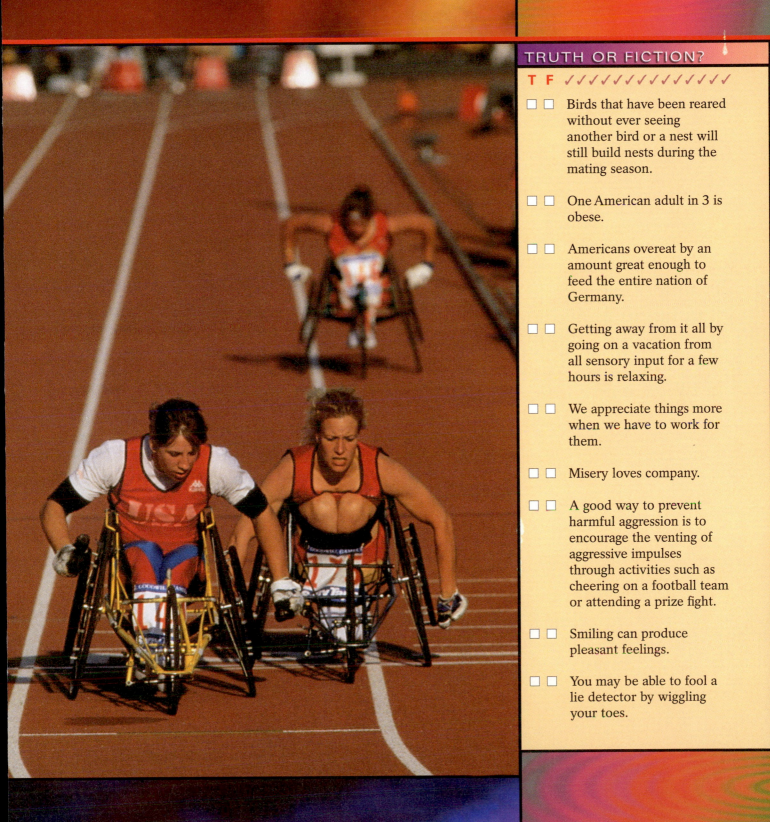

MOTIVATION AND EMOTION

TRUTH OR FICTION?

T F ✓✓✓✓✓✓✓✓✓✓✓✓✓

☐ ☐ Birds that have been reared without ever seeing another bird or a nest will still build nests during the mating season.

☐ ☐ One American adult in 3 is obese.

☐ ☐ Americans overeat by an amount great enough to feed the entire nation of Germany.

☐ ☐ Getting away from it all by going on a vacation from all sensory input for a few hours is relaxing.

☐ ☐ We appreciate things more when we have to work for them.

☐ ☐ Misery loves company.

☐ ☐ A good way to prevent harmful aggression is to encourage the venting of aggressive impulses through activities such as cheering on a football team or attending a prize fight.

☐ ☐ Smiling can produce pleasant feelings.

☐ ☐ You may be able to fool a lie detector by wiggling your toes.

This chapter, "Motivation and Emotion," covers the following:

The Seekers were quite a group. Their brave leader, Marian Keech, dutifully recorded the messages that she believed were sent to her by the Guardians from outer space. One particular message was somewhat disturbing. It specified that the world would come to an end on December 21. A great flood would engulf Lake City, the home of Ms. Keech and many of her faithful followers.

A second message brought good news, however. Ms. Keech received word that the Seekers would be rescued from the flood. You see, Ms. Keech reported that she received messages through "automatic writing." The messengers would communicate through her: She would write down their words, supposedly without awareness. This bit of writing was perfectly clear: The Seekers would be saved by flying saucers at the stroke of midnight on the 21st.

In their classic observational study, Leon Festinger and his colleagues (1956) described how they managed to be present in Ms. Keech's household at the fateful hour by pretending to belong to the group. Their purpose was to observe the behavior of the Seekers during and following (what they assumed would be) the prophecy's failure.

Let us return to the moment of truth. Many Seekers had quit their jobs and gone on spending sprees before the anticipated end. Now they were all gathered together. As midnight approached they fidgeted, awaiting the flying saucers. Midnight came, but no saucers. Anxious glances were exchanged. Silence. Coughs. A few minutes passed, torturously slowly. Watches were checked, more glances exchanged. At 4:00 A.M. a bitter and frantic Ms. Keech complained that she sensed that members of the group were doubting her. At 4:45 A.M., however, she seemed suddenly relieved. A third message was arriving, and Ms. Keech was spelling it out through automatic writing! The Seekers, it turned out, had managed to save the world through their faith. The universal powers had decided to let the world travel on along its sinful way for a while longer. Why? Because of the faith of the Seekers, there was hope!

You guessed it. The faith of most of those present was renewed. They called wire services and newspapers to spread the word. All but three psychologists from the University of Minnesota. They went home, weary but enlightened, and wrote a book entitled *When Prophecy Fails*, which serves as one of the key documents of cognitive-motivational theory.

What about Mr. Keech? He was a tolerant sort. He slept through it all.

SECTION I. THE PSYCHOLOGY OF MOTIVATION: THE *WHYS* OF WHY

Festinger was working on a cognitive theory of motivation called **cognitive-dissonance theory.** The theory suggested that when the prophecy failed, the Seekers would be caught between two key conflicting cognitions: (1) Ms. Keech is a prophet, and (2) Ms. Keech is wrong. Ms. Keech, as it happened, was shown to be wrong. How did the seekers resolve the conflict? One way would have been for the Seekers to lose faith in Ms. Keech—and in their own judgment in following her. But the researchers argued that such a course might be humiliating. (Who likes to admit that he or she has been a fool?) Still, according to cognitive-dissonance theory, the Seekers needed some way to resolve the conflict. Thus they apparently jumped at the "solution" of accepting the "truthfulness" of Ms. Keechs's third message—the message that their faith had saved the world. It is good for the self-esteem to save the world now and then. The Seekers went out to spread the word and find additional converts.

The Seekers were *motivated* to resolve the conflict. They *needed* to maintain their self-esteem. They were *driven* to find a way out. They could not ignore the *incentive* provided by accepting Ms. Keech's third message: It erased the conflict and showed that they, the Seekers, retained the special status.

Questions: What is the psychology of motivation? What are motives, needs, drives, and incentives? The psychology of motivation concerns the *whys* of behavior. Why do people do this or that? Let us begin our journey with some definitions. **Motives** are hypothetical states within an organism that activate behavior and propel the organism toward goals. Why do we say "hypothetical states"? Because motives are not seen and measured directly. Like many other psychological concepts, they are inferred from behavior (Kimble, 1994). Psychologists assume that motives give rise to behavior. Motives may take the form of *needs, drives,* and *incentives.*

Psychologists speak of physiological and psychological **needs.** We must meet physiological needs to survive. Examples include the need for oxygen, food, drink, pain avoidance, proper temperature, and elimination of waste products. Some physiological needs, such as hunger and thirst, are states of physical deprivation. When we have not eaten or drunk for a

COGNITIVE-DISSONANCE THEORY The view that we are motivated to make our cognitions or beliefs consistent.

MOTIVE A hypothetical state within an organism that propels the organism toward a goal. (From the Latin *movere,* meaning "to move.")

NEED A state of deprivation.

while, we develop needs for food and water. The body also has needs for oxygen, vitamins, minerals, and so on.

Examples of psychological needs are the need for achievement, power, self-esteem, social approval, and belonging. Psychological needs differ from physiological needs in two ways. First, psychological needs are not necessarily based on states of deprivation. A person with a need for achievement may already have a history of successful achievements. Second, psychological needs may be acquired through experience, or learned. By contrast, physiological needs reside in the physical makeup of the organism. Because our biological makeups are similar, we all share similar physiological needs. However, we are influenced by our socio-cultural milieu, and our needs may be expressed in diverse ways. All people need food, for example, but some prefer a vegetarian diet whereas others prefer meat. Because learning enters into psychological needs, these needs can differ markedly from one person to the next.

Needs give rise to **drives.** Depletion of food gives rise to the hunger drive, and depletion of liquids gives rise to the thirst drive. **Physiological drives** are the psychological counterparts of physiological needs. When we have gone without food and water, our body may *need* these substances. However, our *experience* of the drives of hunger and thirst is psychological. Drives arouse us to action. Our drive levels tend to be greater the longer we have been deprived. Thus, we are usually more highly aroused by the hunger drive when we have not eaten for several hours than when we have not eaten for, say, 5 minutes.

Psychological needs for approval, achievement, and belonging also give rise to drives. We can be driven to get ahead in the business world just as surely as we can be driven to eat. The drives for achievement and power consume the daily lives of many people.

An **incentive** is an object, person, or situation that is perceived as being capable of satisfying a need or as desirable for its own sake. Money, food, a sexually attractive person, social approval, and attention can all act as incentives that motivate behavior.

In the following section, we explore theories of motivation. We ask: Just what is so motivating about motives?

Review

SECTION I

Motives are hypothetical states within organisms that (1) _____vate behavior and direct organisms toward (2) _____s. Physiological needs generally reflect states of physical (3) _____tion. Psychological needs (4: Are or Are not?) necessarily based on states of deprivation and may be learned, or acquired through (5) ex_____.
Needs give rise to (6) _____s, which are psychological in nature and arouse us to action. An (7) _____tive is an object, person, or situation that is perceived as being capable of satisfying a need.

DRIVE A condition of arousal in an organism that is associated with a need.

PHYSIOLOGICAL DRIVES Unlearned drives with a biological basis, such as hunger, thirst, and avoidance of pain.

INCENTIVE An object, person, or situation perceived as being capable of satisfying a need.

SECTION II. THEORIES OF MOTIVATION: WHICH WHY IS WHICH?

Although psychologists agree that it is important to understand why humans and lower animals do things, they do not agree about the precise nature of motivation. Let us consider four theoretical perspectives on motivation.

The Biological Perspective: "Doing What Comes Naturally"

The biological perspective considers the roles of the nervous system, the endocrine system (hormones), and evolution and heredity in behavior and mental processes. For example, animals tend to be neurally "prewired"—that is, born with preprogrammed tendencies—to respond to certain situations in certain ways. Birds reared in isolation from other birds build nests during the mating season even though they have never observed another bird building a nest or, for that matter, seen a nest. Siamese fighting fish reared in isolation from other fish assume stereotypical threatening stances and attack other males when they are introduced into their tank.

These behaviors are found in particular species. They are *species-specific*. Question: What is meant by species-specific behaviors? Species-specific behaviors do not rely on learning. They are also called **instincts**, or *fixed-action patterns* (FAPs). Spiders spin webs instinctively. Bees "dance" instinctively to communicate the location of food to other bees. All of this activity is inborn. It is genetically transmitted from generation to generation.

A Fixed-Action Pattern. In the presence of another male, Siamese fighting fish assume threatening stances in which they extend their fins and gills and circle each other. If neither male retreats, there will be a conflict.

✓ Truth or Fiction Revisited

It is true that birds that have never seen another bird or a nest will still build nests during the mating season. Nest building is an example of instinctive behavior.

FAPs occur in response to stimuli called *releasers*. For example, male members of many species are sexually aroused by **pheromones** secreted by females. Pheromones thus release the FAP of sexual response. Other pheromones are used to organize food gathering, maintain pecking orders, sound alarms, and mark territories (Azar, 1998).

The question arises whether humans have instincts, and if so, how many. A century ago, psychologists William James (1890) and William McDougall (1908) argued that humans have instincts that foster self-survival and social behavior. James asserted that we have social instincts such as love, sympathy, and modesty. McDougall compiled 12 "basic" instincts, including hunger, sex, and self-assertion. Other psychologists have made longer lists, and still others deny that people have any instincts. The question remains unresolved.

Sigmund Freud also used the term *instincts* to refer to physiological needs in humans. He believed that the instincts of sex and aggression give rise to *psychic energy*, which is perceived as a feeling of tension. Tension motivates us to restore ourselves to a calmer, resting state. The specific behavior patterns we use to reduce the tension—for example, using a weapon or a push when acting aggressively—are largely learned.

THE BIOLOGICAL PERSPECTIVE AND HUMAN SEXUALITY

During prenatal development, genes and sex hormones are responsible for the physical development of female and male sex organs. Sex hormones may also "masculinize" or "feminize" the embryonic brain by creating tendencies to behave in some stereotypical ways (Bailey et al., 2000). For example, testosterone, the male sex hormone, is apparently connected with feelings of self-confidence, high activity levels, and—the negative side—aggressiveness (Pope et al., 2000; Sullivan, 2000). It also appears that deficiencies in testosterone, as found among many older men and men with health problems such as infection with the AIDS virus, are connected with feelings of depression (Barrett-Connor et al., 1999; Sullivan, 2000). Moreover, hormone replacement therapy (that is, injections of

---

REFLECT

Do you believe that humans have instincts? If so, what kinds of instincts? Are your beliefs consistent with evidence presented in this book?

INSTINCT An inherited disposition to activate specific behavior patterns that are designed to reach certain goals.

PHEROMONES Chemical secretions detected by other members of the same species that stimulate stereotypical behaviors.

testosterone) are often helpful in treating depression among these groups (Sullivan, 2000; Yates, 2000). Similarly, low levels of estrogen, as experienced prior to and during menstruation, are frequently connected with depression among women (McGrath et al., 1990).

Sex hormones are also known to affect the sex drive. Research with men who produce little testosterone—due either to age or to health problems—show increased sex drive when they receive testosterone (Sullivan, 2000; Yates, 2000). The most common sexual problem among women is lack of sexual desire or interest. Although men produce 10 to 20 times the testosterone produced by women, women produce androgens ("male" sex hormones) in the adrenal glands, and the sex drive in women is also connected with testosterone levels. And research also shows that the administration of testosterone can heighten the sex drive in women who do not produce enough of the hormone themselves (Tuiten et al., 2000). Therefore, sex hormones have been shown to be connected with sexual motivation and with mood (emotional response) in both women and men.

Drive Reductionism and Homeostasis: "Steady, Steady . . ."

Freud asserted that tension motivates us to behave in ways that restore ourselves to a resting state. His views are similar to those of the **drive-reduction theory** of learning, as set forth by psychologist Clark Hull in the 1930s. Questions: What is drive-reduction theory? How is it related to homeostasis?

According to Hull, **primary drives** such as hunger, thirst, and pain trigger arousal (tension) and activate behavior. We learn to engage in behaviors that reduce the drives. Through association, we also learn **acquired drives.** We may acquire a drive for money because money enables us to obtain food, drink, and homes, which protect us from predators and extremes of temperature. We might acquire drives for social approval and affiliation because other people, and their good will, help us reduce primary drives, especially when we are infants. In all cases, reduction of tension is the goal. Yet some people appear to acquire what could be considered excessive drives for money or affiliation. They gather money apparently for its own sake, long after they have obtained the things that money can buy, and some people find it difficult to be alone, even briefly.

Primary drives like hunger are triggered when we are in a state of deprivation. Sensations of hunger motivate us to act in ways that will restore the bodily balance. This tendency to maintain a steady state is called **homeostasis.** Homeostasis works much like a thermostat. When the temperature in a room drops below the set point, the heating system is triggered. The heat stays on until the set point is reached. Similarly, most animals eat until they are no longer hungry. (The fact that many people eat "recreationally"—for example, when they are presented with an appealing dessert—suggests that there is more to eating than just drive reduction.)

Humanistic Theory: "I've Got to Be Me"

Humanistic psychologists, particularly Abraham Maslow, note that the instinct and drive-reduction theories of motivation are defensive. These theories suggest that human behavior is rather mechanical and aimed toward survival and reduction of tension. Question: How does humanistic theory differ from the instinct and drive-reduction theories of motivation?

As a humanist, Maslow believed that people are also motivated by the conscious desire for personal growth. Humanists note that people tolerate pain, hunger, and many other sources of tension to obtain personal fulfillment.

REFLECT

Do you know people who cannot accumulate enough money? What do you think motivates them?

REFLECT

College students frequently *like* humanistic theory more than they like instinct theory or drive reductionism. Why do you think this is so?

DRIVE-REDUCTION THEORY The view that organisms learn to engage in behaviors that have the effect of reducing drives.

PRIMARY DRIVES Unlearned, or physiological, drives.

ACQUIRED DRIVES Drives acquired through experience, or learned.

HOMEOSTASIS The tendency of the body to maintain a steady state.

Maslow believed that we are separated from lower animals by our capacity for **self-actualization,** or self-initiated striving to become whatever we believe we are capable of being. Maslow considered self-actualization to be as important a need in humans as hunger. It is that need that impels people to strive to become concert pianists or chief executive officers or best-selling authors.

Maslow (1970) organized human needs into a hierarchy. Question: What is Maslow's hierarchy of needs? Maslow's hierarchy ranges from physiological needs such as hunger and thirst, through self-actualization (see Figure 9.1). He believed that we naturally strive to travel up through this hierarchy. Maslow's hierarchy consists of the following sets of needs:

1. *Physiological needs:* hunger, thirst, elimination, warmth, fatigue, pain avoidance, sexual release.

2. *Safety needs:* protection from the environment through housing and clothing; security from crime and financial hardship.

3. *Love and belongingness needs:* love and acceptance through intimate relationships, social groups, and friends. Maslow believed that in a generally well-fed society such as ours, much frustration stems from failure to meet needs at this level.

4. *Esteem needs:* achievement, competence, approval, recognition, prestige, status.

5. *Self-actualization:* fulfillment of our unique potentials. For many individuals, self-actualization involves needs for cognitive understanding (novelty, exploration, knowledge) and aesthetic needs (music, art, poetry, beauty, order).

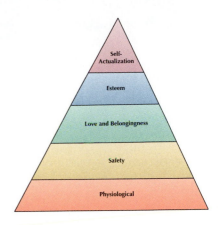

FIGURE 9.1

MASLOW'S HIERARCHY OF NEEDS MASLOW BELIEVED WE PROGRESS TOWARD HIGHER PSYCHOLOGICAL NEEDS ONCE BASIC SURVIVAL NEEDS HAVE BEEN MET. WHERE DO YOU FIT IN THIS PICTURE?

REFLECT

Where would you place yourself in Maslow's hierarchy? Where do you see yourself as being headed? Why?

Cognitive Theory: "I Think, Therefore I Am Consistent"

The brain within its groove
Runs evenly and true . . .

EMILY DICKINSON

"I think, therefore I am," said the French philosopher René Descartes. If he had been a cognitive psychologist, he might have said, "I think, therefore I am *consistent.*"

Cognitive theorists note that people represent their worlds mentally. They hypothesize that people are born scientists who strive to understand the world so that they can predict and control events. Question: Why are people motivated to eliminate inconsistencies in their worldviews? The answer seems to be that people must represent the world accurately in order to predict and control events.

For example, Sandra Bem (1993) argues that children try to create consistency between their own gender and their society's "gender schema"—their society's expectations of what behaviors are appropriate for males and females. As soon as they know whether they are male or female, children imitate the behavior of adults of the same gender. Leon Festinger (1957) believed that people are generally motivated to hold consistent beliefs and to justify their behavior. That is why we are more likely to appreciate what we must work to obtain.

Evaluation of Theories of Motivation

There are thus various perspectives on motivation. Question: How do we make sense of all these different views of motivation? Let us evaluate these views to see which one or ones seem to be most logical and most consistent with the research evidence.

SELF-ACTUALIZATION According to Maslow and other humanistic psychologists, self-initiated striving to become what one is capable of being. The motive for reaching one's full potential, for expressing one's unique capabilities.

There is no question that motivation and emotion are connected with organisms' biology. Many animals are born with preprogrammed tendencies to respond to certain situations in certain ways. Yet instinct theory has been criticized for providing circular explanations of human behavior. In a circular explanation, we say that one thing (A) causes another (B); then, when we see B, we say it is occurring because of A. For example, we might argue a maternal instinct (A) causes mothers to care for their children (B); then we observe a mother caring for her child (B) and accept her behavior as proof of the existence of the maternal instinct (A). We have really just come full circle and explained nothing. As another example, consider William James's notion that sympathy is an instinct. Many people are cruel and cold-hearted; are we to assume that they possess less of this "instinct"? Such an explanation would also be circular.

Then, too, there is the question of how important preprogrammed tendencies are in human beings. Some behaviors, including reflexes and the development of attachment in infants, may be considered instinctive (Ainsworth & Bowlby, 1991). It also appears that sex hormones are connected with the development of behavior patterns and mental processes. They may influence most males and most females in the direction of stereotypical "masculine" or "feminine" behavior patterns. On the other hand, there is so much variation in human behavior and mental processes that it would also appear to be learned, planned, or influenced by cultural values. Still, we should not neglect the roles of sex hormones in problems such as low sex drive (a motivational issue) and feelings of depression (an emotional issue). Ignoring biology in such instances may prevent individuals from obtaining effective treatment.

Drive-reduction theory appears to apply in physiological drives such as hunger and thirst. However, we often eat when we are not hungry! Drive reductionism also runs aground when we consider evidence showing that we often act in ways that *increase,* rather than decrease, the tensions acting on us. When we are hungry, for example, we may take the time to prepare a gourmet meal instead of a snack, even though the snack would satisfy the hunger drive sooner. We drive fast cars, ride roller coasters, and sky dive for sport—all activities that heighten rather than decrease arousal.

People and many lower animals also seek novel stimulation. We may be willing to try a new dish ("just a taste") even when we feel full. We often seek novel ways of doing things—shunning the tried and the true—because of the stimulation provided by novelty. Yet the familiar tried-and-true ways would reduce tension more reliably. In view of examples like these, some psychologists have theorized the existence of stimulus motives that outweigh the motivation to reduce drives.

Critics of Maslow's theory argue that there is too much individual variation for the hierarchy of motives to apply to everyone. Some people whose physiological, safety, and love needs are met show little interest in achievement and recognition. Some artists, musicians, and writers devote themselves fully to their art, even if they have to live in an attic or basement to do so. However, people do appear to seek distant, self-actualizing goals, even while exposing themselves to great danger. This behavior is certainly more consistent with a humanistic than a drive-reductionist explanation of human behavior.

Some psychologists criticize cognitive theory for its reliance on unobservable concepts such as mental representations rather than observable behavior. However, cognitive psychologists tie their concepts to observable behavior whenever possible. It also appears to be difficult to explain a child's active efforts to experiment with and understand other people and the world without resorting to cognitive concepts (Meltzoff & Gopnik, 1997).

It seems that each of the theories of motivation has something to offer. Each would appear to apply to certain aspects of behavior. As the chapter progresses, we will describe research that lends some support to each of these theories. Let us first describe research on the hunger drive. Hunger is based on physiological needs, and drive reduction would appear to explain some—although not all—eating behavior.

Review

SECTION II

According to the (8) _____ical perspective, animals are born with preprogrammed tendencies to behave in certain ways in certain situations. Instincts are also known as (9) species-_____ behaviors or (10) _____-action patterns (FAPs). FAPs occur in the presence of stimuli that are called (11) _____sers. Sigmund Freud believed that the instincts of sex and aggression give rise to (12) _____ energy, which is perceived as tension.

According to Clark (13) _____'s drive-reduction theory of motivation, (14) _____ds are pleasant because they reduce drives. As a consequence, we are motivated to engage in (15) be_____ that leads to rewards. Drive-reduction theorists differentiate between (16) pr_____ (innate) drives and (17) _____red (learned) drives. Drives help the body maintain a steady state, a tendency which is called (18) _____stasis.

(19) _____istic psychologists argue that behavior can be growth-oriented. Abraham (20) M_____ hypothesized that people have a hierarchy of needs, including an innate need for self-actualization. Maslow's hierarchy includes physiological needs, safety needs, love and (21) _____ness needs, esteem needs, and, at the top, the need for (22) self-_____ation.

Cognitive psychologists suggest that people strive to (23) pre_____ and control events. Cognitive psychologists such as Sandra Bem and Leon (24) F_____ assert that prediction and control of events requires cognitive consistency.

SECTION III. HUNGER: DO YOU GO BY "TUMMY-TIME"?

I go by tummy-time and I want my dinner.

SIR WINSTON CHURCHILL

We need food to survive, but to many of us food means more than survival. Food is a symbol of family togetherness and caring. We associate food with the nurturance of the parent–child relationship, with visits home during holidays. Friends and relatives offer us food when we enter their homes, and saying no may be viewed as a personal rejection. Bacon and eggs, coffee with cream and sugar, meat and mashed potatoes—all seem to be part of sharing U.S. values and agricultural abundance. Questions: What bodily mechanisms regulate the hunger drive? What psychological processes are at work?

Bodily Mechanisms That Regulate Hunger

In considering the bodily mechanisms that regulate hunger, let us begin with the mouth. This is an appropriate choice because we are discussing eating. Chewing and swallowing provide some sensations of **satiety,** or satisfaction with the amount eaten. If they did not, we might eat for a long time after we had taken in enough food. It takes the digestive tract time to

SATIETY The state of being satisfied; fullness.

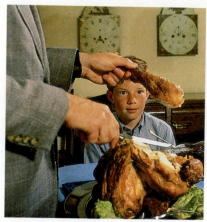

Hunger. How do *you* feel while waiting for someone to carve the meat? Hunger is a physiological drive that motivates us to eat. Why do we feel hungry? Why do we feel satiated? Why do many people continue to eat when they have already supplied their bodies with the needed nutrients?

metabolize food and provide signals of satiety to the brain by way of the bloodstream.

In classic "sham feeding" experiments with dogs, researchers implanted a tube in the animals' throats so that any food swallowed fell out of the dog's body. Even though no food arrived at the stomach, the animals stopped feeding after a brief period (Janowitz & Grossman, 1949). Thus the sensations of chewing and swallowing must provide some feelings of satiety. However, the dogs in the study resumed feeding sooner than animals whose food did reach the stomach. Let us proceed to the stomach, too, as we seek further regulatory factors in hunger.

THE STOMACH An empty stomach leads to stomach contractions, which we call *hunger pangs*. Classic research suggested that stomach contractions are crucial to hunger. A man (A. L. Washburn) swallowed a balloon that was inflated in his stomach. His stomach contractions squeezed the balloon, so the contractions could be recorded by observers. Washburn also pressed a key when he felt hungry, and the researchers found a correspondence between his stomach contractions and his feelings of hunger (Cannon & Washburn, 1912).

But stomach contractions are not as influential as formerly thought. (We apparently go by more than "tummy-time.") Medical observations and classic research also find that people and animals whose stomachs have been removed still regulate food intake so as to maintain their normal weight (Tsang, 1938). (Food is absorbed through their intestines.) This finding led to the discovery of many other mechanisms that regulate hunger, including the hypothalamus, blood sugar level, and even receptors in the liver. When we are deprived of food, the level of sugar in the blood drops. The drop in blood sugar is communicated to the hypothalamus and apparently indicates that we have been burning energy and need to replenish it by eating.

THE HYPOTHALAMUS If you were just reviving from a surgical operation, fighting your way through the fog of the anesthesia, food would probably be the last thing on your mind. But when a researcher uses a probe to destroy the **ventromedial nucleus** (VMN) of a rat's hypothalamus, the rat will grope toward food as soon as its eyes open. Then it eats vast quantities of Purina Rat Chow or whatever else it likes.

The VMN seems to be able to function like a "stop-eating center" in the rat's brain. If the VMN is electrically stimulated—that is, "switched on"—the rat stops eating until the current is turned off. When the VMN is destroyed, the rat becomes **hyperphagic.** It continues to eat until it has about doubled its normal weight (see Figure 9.2). Then it will level off its eating rate and maintain the higher weight. It is as if the set point of the stop-eating center has been raised to a higher level, like turning up the thermostat in a house from 65° F degrees to 70° F. Hyperphagic rats are also more finicky. They eat more fats or sweet-tasting food, but if their food is salty or bitter they actually eat less. Some people develop tumors near the base of the brain, damaging the ventromedial nucleus of the hypothalamus and apparently causing them to overeat and grow obese (Miller, 1995).

The **lateral hypothalamus** may function like a "start-eating center." If you electrically stimulate the lateral hypothalamus, the rat starts to eat (Miller, 1995). If you destroy the lateral hypothalamus, the rat may stop eating altogether—that is, become **aphagic.** If you force-feed an aphagic rat for a while, however, it begins to eat on its own and levels off at a relatively low body weight. It is as if you have lowered the rat's set point. It is like turning down the thermostat from, say, 70° F to 40° F.

Psychological Influences

Although many areas of the body work in concert to regulate the hunger drive, this is only part of the story. In human beings, the hunger drive is more complex. Psychological as well as physiological factors play an important role. How many times have you been made hungry by the sight or aroma of food? How many times have you eaten not because you were hungry but because you were at a relative's home or in a cafeteria? Or because you felt anxious or depressed? Or simply because you were bored? The next section further explores psychological factors that affect eating.

Obesity – A Serious and Pervasive Problem

There is no sincerer love than the love of food.

GEORGE BERNARD SHAW

The two biggest sellers in any bookstore are the cookbooks and the diet books. The cookbooks tell you how to prepare the food and the diet books tell you how not to eat any of it.

ANDY ROONEY

Consider some facts about obesity:

- The prevalence of obesity in the United States has increased by 25% in the past decade (Brownell, 1997).
- One American adult in 3 is obese (Meyer, 1997).

✓ Truth or Fiction Revisited

It is true that 1 adult American in 3 is obese.

- Nearly half of African American women are obese, possibly because they have lower metabolic rates than European American women do (Brody, 1997).
- Americans eat more than a total of 800 billion calories of food each day (200 billion calories more than they need to maintain their weights). The extra calories could feed a nation of 80 million people.

✓ Truth or Fiction Revisited

Yes, Americans do overeat by an amount great enough to feed the entire nation of Germany. The excess calories would feed another 80 million people!

- Within a few years, most dieters regain most of the weight they have lost, even when they have used diet pills "successfully" (Rosenbaum et al., 1997).
- About 300,000 Americans die each year because of excess weight (Brownell, 1997).

American culture idealizes slender heroes and heroines. For those who "more than measure up" to TV and film idols, food may have replaced sex as the central source of guilt. Obese people encounter more than their fair share of illnesses, including heart disease, diabetes, gout, respiratory problems, even certain kinds of cancer. Question: If obesity is connected with

FIGURE 9.2

A HYPERPHAGIC RAT   THIS RODENT WINNER OF THE BASKETBALL LOOK-ALIKE CONTEST WENT ON A BINGE AFTER IT RECEIVED A LESION IN THE VENTROMEDIAL NUCLEUS (VMN) OF THE HYPOTHALAMUS. IT IS AS IF THE LESION PUSHED THE "SET POINT" FOR BODY WEIGHT UP SEVERAL NOTCHES; THE RAT'S WEIGHT IS NOW ABOUT FIVE TIMES NORMAL. BUT NOW IT EATS ONLY ENOUGH TO MAINTAIN ITS PLEASANTLY PLUMP STATURE, SO YOU NEED NOT BE CONCERNED THAT IT WILL EVENTUALLY BURST. IF THE LESION HAD BEEN MADE IN THE LATERAL HYPOTHALAMUS, THE ANIMAL MIGHT HAVE BECOME THE "TWIGGY" OF THE RAT WORLD.

VENTROMEDIAL NUCLEUS A central area on the underside of the hypothalamus that appears to function as a stop-eating center.

HYPERPHAGIC Characterized by excessive eating.

LATERAL HYPOTHALAMUS An area at the side of the hypothalamus that appears to function as a start-eating center.

APHAGIC Characterized by undereating.

health problems and unhappiness with the image in the mirror, why are so many people overweight? Research has contributed to our understanding of obesity and what can be done about it.

BIOLOGICAL FACTORS IN OBESITY Numerous biological factors are involved in obesity, including heredity, adipose tissue (body fat), and the metabolism (the rate at which the individual converts calories to energy).

Obesity runs in families. It was once assumed that obese parents encouraged their children to be overweight by serving fattening foods and setting poor examples. However, a study of Scandinavian adoptees by Stunkard and his colleagues (1990) found that children bear a closer resemblance in weight to their biological parents than to their adoptive parents. Heredity, then, plays a role in obesity (Friedman & Brownell, 1995).

The efforts of obese people to maintain a slender profile may also be sabotaged by microscopic units of life within their own bodies: fat cells. No, fat cells are not overweight cells. They are adipose tissue, or cells that store fat. Hunger might be related to the amount of fat stored in these cells. As time passes after a meal, the blood sugar level drops. Fat is then drawn from these cells to provide further nourishment. At some point, referred to as the *set point,* fat deficiency in these cells is communicated to the hypothalamus, triggering the hunger drive.

People with more adipose tissue than others feel food-deprived earlier, even though they may be equal in weight. This might occur because more signals are being sent to the brain. Obese and *formerly* obese people tend to have more adipose tissue than people of normal weight. Thus many people who have lost weight complain that they are always hungry when they try to maintain normal weight levels.

Fatty tissue also metabolizes (burns) food more slowly than muscle does. For this reason, a person with a high fat-to-muscle ratio metabolizes food more slowly than a person of the same weight with a lower fat-to-muscle ratio. That is, two people who are identical in weight metabolize food at different rates, depending on the distribution of muscle and fat in their bodies. Obese people therefore are doubly handicapped in their efforts to lose weight—not only by their extra weight but by the fact that much of their body is composed of adipose tissue.

In a sense, the normal distribution of fat cells could be considered "sexist." The average man is 40% muscle and 15% fat. The average woman is 23% muscle and 25% fat. If a man and a woman with typical distributions of muscle and fat are of equal weight, therefore, the woman—who has more fat cells—has to eat less to maintain that weight.

Ironically, the very act of dieting can make it progressively more difficult to lose additional weight. This is because people on diets and those who have lost substantial amounts of weight burn fewer calories. That is, their metabolic rates slow down (Schwartz & Seeley, 1997; Wadden et al., 1997). This appears to be a built-in mechanism that helps preserve life in times of famine. However, it also makes it more difficult for dieters to continue to lose weight. The pounds seem to come off more and more reluctantly.

PSYCHOLOGICAL FACTORS IN OBESITY Psychological factors, such as observational learning, stress, and emotional states, also play a role in

REFLECT

Is your weight similar to that of other family members? If so, why?

REFLECT

If you have difficulty controlling your weight, which of the behavior patterns discussed in the text seem to be contributing to the problem? What can you do about it?

obesity (Greeno & Wing, 1994). Our children are exposed to an average of 10,000 food commercials a year. More than 9 of 10 of these commercials are for fast foods (like McDonald's fries), sugared cereals, candy, and soft drinks (Brownell, 1997). Situations also play a role. Family celebrations, watching TV, arguments, and tension at work can all lead to overeating or going off a diet (Drapkin et al., 1995). Efforts to diet also may be impeded by negative emotions like depression and anxiety (Cools et al., 1992).

OBESITY AND DIVERSITY: SOCIOCULTURAL FACTORS IN OBESITY Rates of obesity differ among ethnic groups in our society. Obesity is more prevalent among people of color, especially African Americans, Hispanic Americans, and Native Americans than it is among European Americans. Racial and ethnic differences are most pronounced among women (see Figure 9.3). The question is, why? Many of the answers might be found in socioeconomic factors and acculturation.

Socioeconomic factors play a role in obesity. Obesity is more prevalent among poorer people (Ernst & Harlan, 1991; Stunkard & Sørensen, 1993). People of color are typically of lower socioeconomic status than European Americans, so rates of obesity tend to be higher among African Americans and Hispanic Americans, particularly among women (McMurtrie, 1994).

People on the lower rungs of the socioeconomic ladder appear to have a greater risk of obesity for several reasons. One is that more affluent people have greater access to information about nutrition and health. They have greater access to health care providers. The fitness boom has been largely limited to more affluent people, so that poorer people are more likely to remain sedentary. Wealthier people also have the time and income to participate in organized fitness programs. Many poor people in the inner city also turn to food as a way of coping with the stresses of poverty, discrimination, crowding, and crime.

Results from a study in San Antonio, Texas, provide clear evidence of the link between socioeconomic status and obesity (Hazuda et al., 1991). Obesity is less prevalent among both Mexican Americans and European Americans who live in higher-income neighborhoods than among those living in poorer neighborhoods. In other words, the link between socioeconomic level and obesity holds across ethnic groups.

Acculturation is the process by which immigrant or native groups adopt the cultural values, attitudes, and behaviors of the host or dominant society. Acculturation may help immigrant people to adapt more successfully to their new culture, but it can become a double-edged sword in terms of health if it involves adoption of unhealthful dietary practices of the host culture. For example, Japanese American men living in California and Hawaii eat a higher-fat diet than Japanese men living in Japan do. Not surprisingly, *the prevalence of obesity is two to three times higher among the Japanese American men than among men living in Japan* (Curb & Marcus, 1991).

Acculturation may also contribute to high rates of obesity among Native Americans, who are more likely than European Americans to have diseases linked to obesity, such as cardiovascular disease and diabetes (Broussard et al., 1991; Young & Sevenhuysen, 1989). A study of several hundred Cree and Ojibwa Indians in Canada found that nearly 90% of the women in the 45 to 54 age group were obese. The adoption of a high-fat Western-style diet, the destruction of physically demanding native industries, and chronic unemployment combined with low levels of physical

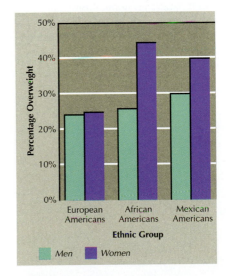

FIGURE 9.3
PREVALENCE OF OVERWEIGHT INDIVIDUALS AMONG EUROPEAN AMERICANS, AFRICAN AMERICANS, AND MEXICAN AMERICANS WHAT FACTORS CONTRIBUTE TO ETHNIC DIFFERENCES IN OBESITY?

activity are cited as factors contributing to obesity among Native Americans in the United States and Canada.

Controlling Your Weight

All right, all right. Many factors—biological, psychological, and sociocultural—contribute to obesity. Question: So what can I do to shed a few pounds?

You can do many things, but first be advised that psychologists warn that not everyone should be trying to slim down. Women in the United States today are under social pressure to conform to an unnaturally slender female ideal (Brownell & Rodin, 1994). As a result, they tend to set unrealistic weight loss goals (Foster et al., 1997). Moreover, many attempts to lose weight are ineffective. For many obese people, however, especially those who are severely obese, shedding excess pounds lowers the risks of health problems such as diabetes and heart disease.

Research on motivation and on methods of therapy has enhanced our knowledge of healthful ways to lose weight. Sound weight control programs do not involve fad diets such as fasting, eliminating carbohydrates, or eating excessive amounts of one particular food. Instead, they involve changes in lifestyle that include improving nutritional knowledge, decreasing calorie intake, exercising, and changing eating habits (see Table 9.1).

Most people in the United States eat too much fat and not enough fruits and vegetables (Kumanyika, 1996). Eating foods low in saturated fats and cholesterol not only is good for the heart but also can contribute to weight loss. Because dietary fat is converted into bodily fat more efficiently than carbohydrates are, a low-fat diet also leads to weight loss. Nutritional knowledge leads to suggestions for taking in fewer calories, which results in lower weight. Taking in fewer calories does not just mean eating smaller portions. It means switching to some lower-calorie foods—relying more on fresh, unsweetened fruits and vegetables (eating apples rather than apple pie), fish and poultry, and skim milk and cheese. It means cutting down on—or eliminating—butter, margarine, oils, and sugar.

The same foods that help control weight also tend to be high in vitamins and fiber and low in fats. Such foods therefore may also reduce the risk of developing heart disease, cancer, and a number of other illnesses.

REFLECT

Do you need to lose weight? (Are you sure?) What standard are you using in making this judgment?

A Sampler of Dietary Methods. At any given time nearly half of the adult American population is on a diet. Dieting has become the "normal" pattern of eating for women. Dozens of diets vie for attention on bookstore shelves. How can we know which ones contain truth and which ones contain fiction?

TABLE 9.1	DIETARY RECOMMENDATIONS OF THE AMERICAN ACADEMY OF SCIENCES

Reduce your total fat intake to 30% or less of your total calorie intake.

Reduce your intake of saturated fats to less than 10% of your total calorie intake.

Reduce your cholesterol intake to less than 300 mg per day.

Eat 5 or more servings of vegetables and fruits each day.

Increase your intake of starches and other complex carbohydrates by eating 6 or more servings of breads, cereals, and legumes each day.

Keep your intake of protein to moderate levels.

Limit your total intake of sodium (salt) to 2,400 mg or less per day.

Maintain adequate intake of calcium.

SOURCE: From Popkin, B. M., Siega-Riz, A. M., & Haines, P. S. (1996). A comparison of dietary trends among racial and socioeconomic groups in the United States. *New England Journal of Medicine, 335,* 716–720.

Dieting plus exercise is more effective than dieting alone for shedding pounds and keeping them off. When we restrict our intake of calories, our metabolic rate compensates by slowing down (Wadden et al., 1997). Exercise burns calories and builds muscle tissue, which metabolizes more calories than fatty tissue does.

Cognitive and behavioral methods have also provided many strategies for losing weight. Among them are the following:

Establish calorie-intake goals and keep track of whether you are meeting them. Get a book that shows how many calories are found in foods. Keep a diary of your calorie intake.

Substitute low-calorie, low-fat foods for high-calorie, high-fat foods. Fill your stomach with celery rather than cheesecake and enchiladas. Eat preplanned low-calorie snacks instead of binge eating a jar of peanuts or a container of ice cream.

Take a 5-minute break between helpings. Ask yourself whether you're still hungry. If not, stop eating.

Avoid temptations that have sidetracked you in the past. Shop at the mall with the Alfalfa Sprout Café, not the Cheesecake Factory. Plan your meal before entering a restaurant. (Avoid ogling that tempting full-color menu.) Attend to your own plate, not to the sumptuous dish at the next table. (Your salad probably looks greener to them, anyhow.) Shop from a list. Walk briskly through the supermarket, preferably after dinner when you're no longer hungry. Don't be sidetracked by pretty packages (fattening things may come in them). Don't linger in the kitchen. Study, watch TV, or write letters elsewhere. Don't bring fattening foods into the house. Prepare only enough food to keep within your calorie goals.

Exercise to burn more calories and increase your metabolic rate. Reach for your mate, not your plate (to coin a phrase). Take a brisk walk instead of eating an unplanned snack. Build exercise routines by adding a few minutes each week.

Reward yourself for meeting calorie goals (but not with food). Imagine how great you'll look in that new swimsuit next summer. Do not go to the latest movie unless you have met your weekly calorie goal. When you meet your weekly calorie goal, put cash in the bank toward a vacation or a new camera.

Use imagery to help yourself lose weight. Tempted by a fattening dish? Imagine that it's rotten, that you would be nauseated by it and have a sick taste in your mouth for the rest of the day.

Mentally walk through solutions to problem situations. Consider what you will do when cake is handed out at the office party. Rehearse your next visit to relatives who tell you how painfully thin you look and try to stuff you with food (Drapkin et al., 1995). Imagine how you will politely (but firmly) refuse seconds and thirds, despite their objections.

Above all, if you slip from your plan for a day, don't blow things out of proportion. Dieters are often tempted to binge, especially when they rigidly see themselves either as perfect successes or as complete failures or when they experience powerful emotions—either positive or negative (Cools et al., 1992). Consider the weekly or monthly trend, not just a single day. Credit yourself for the long-term trend. If you do binge, resume dieting the next day.

Losing weight—and keeping it off—is not easy, but it can be done. Making a commitment to losing weight and establishing a workable plan for doing so are two of the keys.

REFLECT

If you need to shed some pounds, which of the strategies mentioned here are likely to work for you? Why?

SECTION III [Review]

Hunger is regulated by several internal mechanisms, including (25) _____ch contractions, blood (26) s_____ level, receptors in the mouth and liver, and the responses of the hypothalamus. Chewing and swallowing provide some sensations of (27) _____ty. The (28) _____al nucleus (VMN) of the hypothalamus seems to function as a stop-eating center. Damage to this area leads to (29) _____gia in rats, a condition in which the animals grow to several times their normal body weight, but then level off. The (30) _____al hypothalamus apparently functions as a start-eating center.

Obesity (31: Does or Does not?) run in families. A study of Scandinavian adoptees found that children bear a closer resemblance in weight to their (32: Biological or Adoptive?) parents than to their (33: Biological or Adoptive?) parents. Hunger is related to the amount of fat or (34) _____pose tissue in the body. As time passes after a meal, the (35) _____ sugar level drops and fat is drawn from fat cells to provide nourishment. When the (36) _____ point is reached, fat deficiency in these cells is communicated to the (37) hypo_____, triggering the hunger drive. People with more adipose tissue feel food-deprived (38: Earlier or Later?) than others of the same weight, and also metabolize food (39: More or Less?) rapidly. Rates of obesity are highest among (40: Wealthy or Poor?) people in the United States.

Sound weight control programs involve improving (41) _____tional knowledge, (42: Increasing or Decreasing?) calorie intake, exercising, and behavior modification.

SECTION IV. STIMULUS MOTIVES

One day when my daughter Taylor was 5 months old, I was batting her feet. (Why not?) She was sitting back in her mother's lap, and I repeatedly batted her feet up toward her middle with the palms of my hands. After a while, she began to laugh. When I stopped, she pushed a foot toward me, churned her arms back and forth, and blew bubbles as forcefully as she could. So I batted her feet again. She laughed and pushed them toward me again. This went on for a while, and it dawned on me that Taylor was doing what she could to make the stimulation last.

Physical needs give rise to drives like hunger and thirst. In such cases, organisms are motivated to *reduce* the tension or stimulation that impinges on them. Question: Are all motives aimed at the reduction of tension? No, in the case of **stimulus motives,** organisms seek to *increase* stimulation, as Taylor did when she sought to have me bat her feet. Stimulus motives include sensory stimulation, activity, exploration, and manipulation of the environment.

Some stimulus motives provide a clear evolutionary advantage. Humans and lower animals that are motivated to learn about and manipulate their environment are more likely to survive. Learning about the environment increases awareness of resources and of potential dangers, and manipulation permits one to change the environment in beneficial ways. Exploring the environment helps animals locate sources of food and places to hide from predators. Learning and manipulation thus increase the animal's chances of survival until sexual maturity and of transmitting whatever genetic codes may underlie these motives to future generations.

Sensory Stimulation and Activity

When I was a teenager during the 1950s, I was unaware that some lucky students at McGill University in Montreal were being paid $20 a day (which, with inflation, would now be well above $100) for doing ab-

REFLECT

Do you have ways of trying to increase the stimulation impacting on you? What are they? (Hints: How about going to the movies or an amusement park?)

STIMULUS MOTIVES Motives to increase the stimulation impinging upon an organism.

solutely nothing. Would you like to "work" by doing nothing for $100 a day? Don't answer too quickly. According to the results of classic research on sensory deprivation, you might not like it at all. Why?—Questions: Do we need to be active? Do we need to stimulate our senses?

Let us describe the experiment and see what it means for possible needs to be active and stimulate the senses. Student volunteers in the study were placed in quiet cubicles and blindfolded (Bexton et al., 1954). Their arms were bandaged, and they could hear nothing but the dull, continuous hum of air conditioning. With nothing to do, many of the students slept for a while. After a few hours of sensory-deprived wakefulness, most felt bored and irritable. As time went on, many of them grew more uncomfortable, and some reported hallucinations of images of dots and geometric shapes.

Many students quit the experiment during the first day despite the financial incentive. Many of those who remained for a few days found it difficult to concentrate on simple problems for a few days afterward. For many, the experimental conditions did not provide a relaxing vacation. Instead, they produced boredom and disorientation.

FIGURE 9.4

THE ALLURE OF NOVEL STIMULATION PEOPLE AND MANY LOWER ANIMALS ARE MOTIVATED TO EXPLORE THEIR ENVIRONMENT AND TO SEEK NOVEL STIMULATION. THIS MONKEY HAS LEARNED TO UNLOCK A DOOR FOR THE PRIVILEGE OF VIEWING A MODEL TRAIN.

✓ Truth or Fiction Revisited

It is not true that getting away from it all by going on a vacation from all sensory input for a few hours is relaxing. If it is carried out like the experiment at McGill University, such a "vacation" may be highly stressful.

Exploration and Manipulation

Have you ever brought a dog or cat into a new home? At first, it may show excitement. New kittens are also known to hide under a couch or bed for a few hours. But then they begin to explore every corner of their new environment. When placed in novel environments, many animals appear to possess an innate motive to engage in exploratory behavior.

Question: Why do puppies and kittens explore their environments when they are brought into new homes? Both lower animals and humans appear to be motivated to seek novel stimulation. For example, when they have not been deprived of food for a great deal of time, rats often explore unfamiliar arms of mazes rather than head straight for the section of the maze in which they have learned to expect food. Animals that have just copulated and thereby reduced their sex drives often show renewed interest in sexual behavior when presented with a novel sex partner. Monkeys learn how to manipulate gadgets for the incentive of being able to observe novel stimulation through a window (see Figure 9.4). Children spend hour after hour manipulating the controls of video games for the pleasure of zapping video monsters.

The question has arisen of whether people and animals seek to explore and manipulate their environment *because* these activities help them reduce primary drives such as hunger and thirst or whether they engage in these activities for their own sake. Many psychologists believe that such stimulating activities are reinforcing in and of themselves. Monkeys do seem to get a kick out of "monkeying around" with gadgets (see Figure 9.5). They learn how to manipulate hooks and eyes and other mechanical devices without any external incentive whatsoever (Harlow et al., 1950). Young children prolong their play with "busy boxes"—boxes filled with objects that honk, squeak, rattle, and buzz when manipulated in certain ways. They seem to find discovery of the cause-and-effect relationships in these gadgets pleasurable even though they are not rewarded with food, ice cream, or even hugs from their parents.

REFLECT

Can you lie contentedly on the beach for hours, or do you get restless rather soon? Do you have friends or family who differ from you in this regard? What do you think it might mean?

Do you like going out for drives or walks and exploring new neighborhoods or countries? What motivates you?

FIGURE 9.5

MONKEYING AROUND IS THERE SUCH A THING AS A MANIPULATION DRIVE? THESE YOUNG RHESUS MONKEYS APPEAR TO BE MONKEYING AROUND WITH GADGETS JUST FOR THE FUN OF IT. NO EXTERNAL INCENTIVES ARE NEEDED. CHILDREN SIMILARLY ENJOY MANIPULATING GADGETS THAT HONK, SQUEAK, RATTLE, AND BUZZ, EVEN THOUGH THE RESULTANT HONKS AND SQUEAKS DO NOT SATISFY PHYSIOLOGICAL DRIVES SUCH AS HUNGER OR THIRST.

SECTION IV

Stimulus motives (43: Do or Do not?) provide an evolutionary advantage. Physiological needs motivate us to (44: Increase or Reduce?) the stimulation that impinges upon us. Stimulus motives, by contrast, motivate us to (45: Increase or Decrease?) the stimulation impinging upon us. Studies in sensory (46) _____ation show that lack of stimulation is aversive. After a few hours, subjects in these studies become bored and (47) _____table. As time goes on, some of them report visual (48) _____ations of dots and geometric shapes. After a few days, subjects find it difficult to (49) co_____ on problems. Exploring the environment helps animals locate sources of food and places to hide from predators, which (50: Increases or Decreases?) the animal's chances of survival until sexual maturity and of transmitting the genetic codes that may underlie exploring behavior to future generations.

SECTION V. COGNITIVE-DISSONANCE THEORY: MAKING THINGS FIT

Do I contradict myself?
Very well then I contradict myself,
(I am large, I contain multitudes.)

WALT WHITMAN, *SONG OF MYSELF*

Most of us are unlike Walt Whitman, according to cognitive-dissonance theory (Festinger, 1957; Festinger & Carlsmith, 1959). Whitman may not have minded contradicting himself, but most people do not like their attitudes (cognitions) to be inconsistent. Cognitive theorists propose that organisms are motivated to create realistic mental maps of the world. Organisms adjust their representations of the world, as needed, to make things fit. Awareness that two cognitions are dissonant, or that our attitudes are incompatible with our behavior, is unpleasant and motivates us to reduce the discrepancy.

Effort Justification: "If I Did It, It Must Be Important"?

In the first and still one of the best-known studies on cognitive dissonance, one group of participants received $1 (worth $5–$10 today) for telling someone else that a boring task was interesting (Festinger & Carlsmith, 1959). Members of a second group received $20 (worth $100–$200 today) to describe the chore positively. Both groups were paid to engage in **attitude-discrepant behavior**—that is, behavior that ran counter to their cognitions. After "selling" the job to others, the participants were asked to rate their own liking for it. Ironically, those who were paid *less* rated the task as more interesting. Question: Why are people who go unrewarded more likely than those who are rewarded to think or say that what they are doing is worthwhile for its own sake?

According to learning theory, this result would be confusing. Learning theory would say that the more we are reinforced for doing something, the more we should like it. But that is not what happened here. In contrast, cognitive-dissonance theory would predict this "less-leads-to-more

REFLECT

Have you ever changed your opinion of someone when you learned that she or he liked something that you disliked? What happened? Why did it happen?

ATTITUDE-DISCREPANT BEHAVIOR Behavior inconsistent with an attitude that may have the effect of modifying an attitude.

REFLECT

Were you ever subjected to difficult hazing upon joining a sorority, fraternity, or other kind of club? Did the experience affect your feelings about being a member of the group? How? Can you connect your experience to the concept of effort justification?

effect" for the following reason: The cognitions "I was paid very little" and "I told someone that this assignment was interesting" are dissonant. People tend to engage in **effort justification.** The discomfort of cognitive dissonance motivates them to explain their behavior to themselves in such a way that unpleasant undertakings seem worth it. Participants who were paid only $1 may have justified their lie by concluding that they may not have been lying in the first place. Similarly, we appreciate things more when they are more difficult to obtain.

✓ Truth or Fiction Revisited

It is true that we appreciate things more when we have to work for them. This is an example of the principle of effort justification.

   Consider another situation. Many people have very strong political beliefs and fear what might happen if the "wrong" candidate is elected to public office. They tend to see their own candidates as better for their town or state or country, and some even believe that their candidate must win to save the nation from harmful forces. They are therefore strongly motivated to believe that their candidate will be elected. They pin their hopes as well as their ideology on their candidate. Cognitive dissonance would then be created if they were to believe that their candidates were likely to lose and not to win. Research shows that in presidential elections from 1952 to 1980, 4 out of 5 people reduced such dissonance by expressing the belief that their candidate would win (Granberg & Brent, 1983). Nearly half of them were wrong, of course. Yet they often clung to their prediction despite lopsided polls to the contrary. It is the triumph of dissonance reduction, and perhaps of hope, over judgment.

Review

SECTION V

Cognitive theorists propose that awareness that our (51) _____tions are dissonant is unpleasant and motivates us to reduce the discrepancy. Engaging in (52) _____-discrepant behavior may lead us to seek cognitive consistency by changing our attitudes. People tend to explain their behavior to themselves in such a way as to (53) _____fy their efforts. We appreciate things (54: More or Less?) when they are difficult to obtain.

SECTION VI. THE THREE A'S OF MOTIVATION: ACHIEVEMENT, AFFILIATION, AND AGGRESSION

Let us consider some of the powerful motives that bind us together or tear us asunder: achievement, affiliation, and aggression. The Harvard psychologist Henry Murray (1938) hypothesized that each of these "A's" reflects a psychological need. He also referred to them as *social motives,* which he believed differ from primary motives such as hunger in that they are acquired through social learning. However, contemporary researchers believe that hereditary predispositions may also play a role in these behavior patterns. Evolutionary psychologists believe that "genetic whisperings" influence tendencies toward achievement, affiliation, aggression, and many other aspects of personality and social behavior, even if we can also often point to environmental influences (Buss et al., 1998; Plomin et al., 1997; Rose, 1995).

EFFORT JUSTIFICATION In cognitive-dissonance theory, the tendency to seek justification (acceptable reasons) for strenuous efforts.

FIGURE 9.6
TAPPING FANTASIES IN PERSONALITY RESEARCH
THIS PICTURE IS SIMILAR TO A THEMATIC APPERCEPTION TEST CARD USED TO MEASURE THE NEED FOR ACHIEVEMENT. WHAT IS HAPPENING IN THIS PICTURE? WHAT IS THE PERSON THINKING AND FEELING? WHAT IS GOING TO HAPPEN? YOUR ANSWERS TO THESE QUESTIONS REFLECT YOUR OWN NEEDS AS WELL AS THE CONTENT OF THE PICTURE ITSELF.

Achievement: "Just Do It"

Many students persist in studying despite being surrounded by distractions. Many people strive relentlessly to get ahead, to "make it," to earn large sums of money, to invent, to accomplish the impossible. Question: Why do some people strive to get ahead? These people are said to have strong achievement motivation.

Psychologist David McClelland (1958) helped pioneer the assessment of achievement motivation through evaluation of fantasies. One method involves the Thematic Apperception Test (TAT), developed by Henry Murray. The TAT contains cards with pictures and drawings that are subject to various interpretations. Individuals are shown one or more TAT cards and asked to construct stories about the pictured theme: to indicate what led up to it, what the characters are thinking and feeling, and what is likely to happen.

One TAT card is similar to that in Figure 9.6. The meaning of the card is ambiguous—unclear. Is the girl sleeping, thinking about the book, wishing she were out with friends? Consider two stories that could be told about this card:

> Story 1: "She's upset that she's got to read the book because she's behind in her assignments and doesn't particularly like to work. She'd much rather be out with her friends, and she may very well sneak out to do just that."

> Story 2: "She's thinking, 'Someday I'll be a great scholar. I'll write books like this, and everybody will be proud of me.' She reads all the time."

The second story suggests the presence of more achievement motivation than the first. Classic studies find that people with high achievement motivation earn higher grades than people with comparable learning ability but lower achievement motivation. They are more likely to earn high salaries and be promoted than less motivated people with similar opportunities. They perform better at math problems and at unscrambling anagrams, such as decoding RSTA into STAR, TARS, ARTS, or RATS.

McClelland (1965) used the TAT to sort college students into groups—students with high achievement motivation and students with low achievement motivation. He found that 83% of college graduates with high achievement motivation found jobs in occupations characterized by risk, decision making, and the chance for great success, such as business management, sales, or self-employment. Most (70%) of the graduates who chose nonentrepreneurial positions showed low achievement motivation. People with high achievement motivation seem to prefer challenges and are willing to take moderate risks to achieve their goals.

WHAT FLAVOR IS YOUR ACHIEVEMENT MOTIVATION? Do you want to do well in this course? If you do, why? Carol Dweck (1997) finds that achievement motivation can be driven by different forces. Are you motivated mainly by performance goals? That is, is your grade in the course of most importance? If it is, it may be in part because your motives concern tangible rewards such as getting into graduate school, landing a good job, reaping approval from parents or your instructor, or avoiding criticism. Performance goals are usually met through extrinsic rewards such as prestige and income. Parents of children who develop performance goals are likely to respond to good grades with tangible rewards such as toys or money and to respond to poor grades with anger and removal of privileges.

Or do learning goals mainly motivate you to do well? That is, is your central motive the enhancing of your knowledge and skills—your ability to understand and master the subject matter? Learning goals usually lead to intrinsic rewards, such as satisfaction with oneself. Students who develop learning goals often have parents with strong achievement motivation, parents who encourage their children to think and act independently from an early age. They help their children develop learning goals by showing warmth and praising them for their efforts to learn, exposing them to novel and stimulating experiences, and encouraging persistence (Dweck, 1997; Ginsburg & Bronstein, 1993; Gottfried et al., 1994). Children of such parents frequently set high standards for themselves, associate their achievements with self-worth, and attribute their achievements to their own efforts rather than to chance or to the intervention of others.

Of course, many of us strive to meet both performance and learning goals in many subjects, as well as in other areas of life. Grades are important because they are connected with (very) tangible benefits, but learning for its own sake is also of value.

Affiliation: "People Who Need People"

The motive for **affiliation** prompts us to make friends, join groups, and prefer to do things with others rather than alone. Affiliation motivation is part of the social glue that holds families and other groups together. In this sense, it is certainly a positive trait. Yet some people have such a strong need to affiliate that they find it painful to make their own decisions or to be alone.

Question: Why do people need people? There are many reasons. Sometimes we learn that we can accomplish more by doing things with others than we can alone. Certainly infants cannot survive without the support of other people. But the need to affiliate with others may also be instinctive—an inborn aspect of our makeup as social beings. Research by Stanley Schachter suggests that a particularly high need to affiliate may also indicate anxiety, such as when people "huddle together" in fear of an outside force.

In a classic experiment on the effects of anxiety on affiliation, Schachter (1959) manipulated participants' anxiety levels by leading them to believe that they would receive either painful electric shocks (the high-anxiety condition) or mild electric shocks (the low-anxiety condition). Participants were then asked to wait while the shock apparatus was supposedly being set up. They could choose to wait alone or in a room with others. The majority (63%) of those who expected a painful shock chose to wait in a room with other people. Only one third (33%) of those who expected a mild shock chose to wait with others.

Highly anxious participants were placed in two social conditions. In the first, they could choose either to wait alone or with others who would also receive painful shocks. Sixty percent of these people chose to affiliate—that is, to wait with others. In the second condition, highly anxious participants could choose to wait alone or with people they believed were not involved with the study. In this second condition, no one chose to affiliate.

✓ Truth or Fiction Revisited

Schachter found that misery does love company—but only company of a special sort. That is, anxious people preferred to affiliate with other people who were anxious, not with people who seemed to be relaxed.

Why did participants in Schachter's study wish to affiliate only with people who shared their misery? Schachter explained their choice with his

---

REFLECT

Do you seem to be driven mainly by performance goals or learning goals? Explain.

REFLECT

Do you feel a strong need to make friends, join groups, and do things with other people? Why or why not?

REFLECT

Do you feel a greater need to be around other people—or certain specific people—when you are upset about something? If so, why?

AFFILIATION Association or connection with a group.

theory of social comparison. This theory holds that in an ambiguous situation—that is, a situation in which we are not certain about what we should do or how we should feel—we affiliate with people with whom we can compare feelings and behaviors. Schachter's anxious recruits could compare their reactions with those of other "victims," but not with people who had no reason to feel anxious. Anxious participants may also have resented uninvolved people for "getting away free."

Aggression: Some Facts of Life and Death

Consider the following facts:

- After the end of the Cold War and the demise of the Soviet Union, you might have expected the world to become more peaceful. Yet civil wars and other conflicts rage on every continent.

- In the United States, violence has replaced communicable diseases as the leading cause of death among young people. Homicide has become the second leading cause of death among 15- to 24-year-olds (Lore & Schultz, 1993). (Accidents are the leading cause.)

- Aggression is not limited to foreign battlefields or dark streets and alleyways. Each year more than a million U.S. children are brought to the attention of authorities as victims of child abuse. "My sense is that something is deeply wrong with the core unit of our civilization, the family," notes former APA president Ronald Fox (1996). "It's no longer a safe haven for many Americans."

- Domestic violence is a national epidemic. At least 1 woman in 8 is subjected to violence at the hands of her partner each year, and about 2,000 women die from it (Rabasca, 1999). Women are more likely to be raped, injured, or killed by their current or former partners than by other types of assailants (Rabasca, 1999).

- Domestic violence is a greater threat to pregnant women than high blood pressure, diabetes, or any other complication of pregnancy for which women are routinely screened (Rabasca, 1999).

Question: Why do people kill, maim, and injure one another? Let us consider some theories of aggression.

THE BIOLOGICAL PERSPECTIVE Numerous biological structures and chemicals appear to be involved in aggression. In response to certain stimuli, many lower animals show instinctive aggressive reactions. For example, the male robin responds aggressively to the red breast of another robin. The hypothalamus appears to be involved in this inborn reaction pattern: Electrical stimulation of part of the hypothalamus triggers stereotypical aggressive behaviors in many lower animals. However, in humans, whose brains are more complex, other brain structures apparently moderate possible aggressive instincts.

Chemistry is also involved in aggression, especially in the form of the male sex hormone testosterone. Testosterone appears to affect the tendencies to dominate and control other people. Men have higher testosterone levels than women do and are also (usually) more aggressive than women, especially in contacts with male strangers (Pope et al., 2000). Testosterone levels vary somewhat with the occasion, and men's testosterone levels tend to be higher when they are "winning"—whether in athletic competitions such as football or even in chess (Christiansen & Knussman, 1987; Olweus, 1986). It could be that one reason men are more sexually aggressive than women is because of their tendency to dominate others.

THEORY OF SOCIAL COMPARISON The view that people look to others for cues about how to behave when they are in confusing or unfamiliar situations.

The evolutionary view is that aggression is natural. Evolutionary psychologists view much social behavior, including aggressive behavior, as influenced by genetic factors such as brain structures and levels of testosterone. In his theory of evolution, Charles Darwin noted that many more individuals are produced than can find food and survive into adulthood. Therefore, there is a struggle for survival. Individuals who possess characteristics that give them an advantage in this struggle are more likely to mature and contribute their genes to the next generation. In many species, those characteristics include aggressiveness. Because aggressive individuals are more likely to survive and reproduce, whatever genes are linked to aggressive behavior are more likely to be transmitted to new generations.

In the case of humans, intelligence is also a key to survival. The capacity to outwit other species may be more important to human survival than aggressiveness. Now that humans have organized themselves into societies in which aggression is either outlawed or confined to athletic contests, it could be that factors such as intelligence and organizational skills are more important than aggressiveness in having one's genes transmitted to future generations.

THE PSYCHODYNAMIC PERSPECTIVE Sigmund Freud believed that aggressive impulses are inevitable reactions to the frustrations of daily life. Children (and adults) normally desire to vent aggressive impulses on other people, including parents, because even the most attentive parents cannot gratify all of their demands immediately. Yet children also fear punishment and loss of love, so they repress most aggressive impulses and store them in the unconscious recesses of the mind. The Freudian perspective, in a sense, sees humans as "steam engines." By holding in steam rather than venting it, we set the stage for future explosions. Pent-up aggressive impulses demand an outlet. They may be expressed toward parents in roundabout ways, such as destroying furniture; later in life they may be expressed toward strangers.

According to psychodynamic theory, the best way to prevent harmful aggression may be to encourage less harmful aggression. In the steam engine analogy, verbal aggression (through wit, sarcasm, or expression of negative feelings) may vent some of the aggressive steam in a person's unconscious mind. So might cheering on a football team or attending a prize fight. Psychoanalysts refer to the venting of aggressive impulses as **catharsis.** Catharsis thus is viewed as a safety valve. But research findings on the usefulness of catharsis are mixed. Some studies suggest that catharsis leads to pleasant reductions in tension and reduced likelihood of future aggression (e.g., Doob & Wood, 1972). Other studies, however, suggest that "venting" some steam actually encourages more aggression later on (e.g., Bushman et al., 1999). Research evidence has been hard on the psychodynamic perspective, yielding partial support for Freud's views at best.

✓ Truth or Fiction Revisited

Research does not support the value of catharsis as a way to prevent harmful aggression. Research evidence suggests that expressing ("venting") aggressive impulses may encourage additional aggressive behavior.

THE COGNITIVE PERSPECTIVE Cognitive psychologists assert that our behavior is influenced by our values, by how we interpret situations, and by choice. From the cognitive perspective, for example, people who

REFLECT

If violence is "natural," does that mean that society, and we, should not try to contain it? Why or why not?

REFLECT

Do you believe that watching violent sports such as football, boxing, and pro wrestling makes viewers more violent or less violent (or that it has no effect on behavior?) Why?

CATHARSIS In psychodynamic theory, the purging of strong emotions or the relieving of tensions.

believe that aggression is necessary and justified—as during wartime—are likely to act aggressively. People who believe that a particular war or act of aggression is unjust, or who oppose aggression regardless of the circumstances, are less likely to behave aggressively.

One cognitive theory suggests that frustration and discomfort trigger unpleasant feelings (Rule et al., 1987). These feelings, in turn, prompt aggression. Aggression is *not* automatic, however. Cognitive factors intervene (Berkowitz, 1994). People *decide*—sometimes making "split-second decisions"—whether they will strike out or not on the basis of factors such as their previous experiences with aggression and their interpretation of the other person's motives.

Researchers find that many aggressive people distort other people's motives. For example, they assume that other people wish them harm when they actually do not (Akhtar & Bradley, 1991; Dodge et al., 1990). Cognitive therapists note that we are more likely to respond aggressively to a provocation when we magnify the importance of the insult or otherwise stir up feelings of anger (e.g., Lochman & Dodge, 1994). How do you respond when someone bumps into you? If you view it as an intentional insult to your honor, you may respond with aggression. If you view it as an accident, or as a social problem in need of a solution, you are less likely to act aggressively.

LEARNING PERSPECTIVES Two types of learning perspectives are the behavioral perspective and the social-cognitive perspective. From the behavioral perspective, learning is acquired through reinforcement. Organisms reinforced for aggressive behavior are more likely to behave aggressively in similar situations. Environmental consequences make it more likely that strong, agile organisms will be reinforced for aggressive behavior.

From the social-cognitive perspective, aggressive skills are mainly acquired by observation. Social-cognitive theorists do believe that consciousness and choice may play a role, however. In this view, we are not likely to act aggressively unless we believe that aggression is appropriate under the circumstances.

AGGRESSION AND DIVERSITY: THE SOCIOCULTURAL PERSPECTIVE ON AGGRESSION The sociocultural perspective focuses on ways in which ethnicity, gender, and cultural factors may be related to aggression.

The experiences of anthropologist Margaret Mead (1935) on the South Pacific island of New Guinea showed how the sociocultural milieu influences motives such as aggressiveness and nurturance. Among the Mundugumor, a tribe of headhunters and cannibals, both women and men were warlike and aggressive. The women felt that motherhood sidetracked them from more important activities, such as butchering inhabitants of neighboring villages. In contrast, both women and men of the Arapesh tribe were gentle and nurturant of children. Then there were the Tchambuli. In that tribe the women earned a living while the men spent most of their time nurturing the children, primping, and gossiping.

Sociocultural theorists note that U.S. culture has a way of breeding violence. In Thailand and Jamaica, for example, aggression in children is discouraged and politeness and deference are encouraged (Tharp, 1991). Children in the United States are more likely to be argumentative, disobedient, and belligerent (Tharp, 1991). Competitiveness and independence are encouraged in the United States, especially among males. The lessons learned in competitive sports may particularly dispose males to violence

REFLECT

Consider people whom you would label "violent people." Do you believe that they simply explode or that they decide to behave violently? Explain.

REFLECT

What are your feelings about the "lessons" males learn in competitive sports? Explain.

(Levy, 1991). Coaches often urge boys to win at all costs. Boys are encouraged to dominate and vanquish their opponents, even if winning requires injuring or "taking out" the opposition. This philosophy may be carried from the playing field into social relationships. Some athletes distinguish between sports and social relationships, but others do not.

SECTION VI Review

Psychologist David (55) Mc_____ pioneered the assessment of achievement motivation through fantasy. In doing so, McClelland used Murray's Thematic (56) _____tion Test. People with high achievement motivation attain (57: Higher or Lower?) grades and earn (58: More or Less?) money than people of comparable ability with lower achievement motivation. Students with (59) _____ goals are mainly motivated by factors such as good grades, rewards from parents, and the prospect of landing a good job. Students with (60) _____ goals are usually more motivated by intrinsic rewards, such as self-satisfaction. Students who develop (61: Performance or Learning?) goals often have parents who encourage them to think and act independently.

The need for (62) _____ation prompts us to join groups and make friends. Stanley Schachter found that anxiety tends to (63: Increase or Decrease?) the need for affiliation. When anxious, we prefer to affiliate with people who (64: Share or Do not share?) our predicaments. Schachter explains this preference through the theory of social (65) _____ison. This theory holds that when we are in (66) _____guous situations, we seek to affiliate with people with whom we can compare feelings and behaviors.

Electrical stimulation of part of the (67) _____lamus triggers stereotypical aggressive behaviors in many lower animals. The hormone (68) _____one seems to be connected with social dominance and aggression in humans. (69) _____ary psychologists view much social behavior, including aggressive behavior, as genetically determined and natural. Because aggressive individuals are more likely to (70) _____duce, genes linked to aggressive behavior are more likely to be transmitted to subsequent generations. Sigmund Freud believed that aggressive impulses are (71: Common or Rare?) reactions to the frustrations of daily life. Psychodynamic theorists view (72) _____sis as a safety valve for the venting of aggressive impulses, but research does not support this theory. From the (73) c_____ perspective, people who believe that aggression is necessary and justified—as during wartime—are likely to act aggressively. Cognitive theorists (74: Do or Do not?) see aggression as an automatic response to frustration. From the behavioral perspective, the acquisition of aggressive skills is accomplished through (75) _____ment. The (76) socio_____ perspective focuses on ways in which ethnicity, gender, and culture are related to aggression. Social critics suggest that the lessons learned in (77) _____s contribute to aggression.

SECTION VII. EMOTION: ADDING COLOR TO LIFE

Emotions color our lives. We are green with envy, red with anger, blue with sorrow. Poets paint a thoughtful mood as a "brown study." Positive emotions such as love and desire can fill our days with pleasure. Negative emotions such as fear, depression, and anger can fill us with dread and make each day a chore. Question: Just what is an emotion?

An emotion can be a response to a situation, in the way that fear is a response to a threat. An emotion can motivate behavior (e.g., anger can motivate us to act aggressively). An emotion can also be a goal in itself. We may behave in ways that will lead us to experience joy or feelings of love.

Emotions are feeling states with physiological, cognitive, and behavioral components (Carlson & Hatfield, 1992). In terms of physiology, strong emotions arouse the autonomic nervous system (LeDoux, 1997). The greater the arousal, the more intense the emotion. It also appears that the type of arousal affects the emotion being experienced. Although the

EMOTION A state of feeling that has cognitive, physiological, and behavioral components.

REFLECT

Do you consider yourself to be "an emotional person"? Why or why not? Do you see "being emotional" in a positive or negative light? Explain.

TABLE 9.2	COMPONENTS OF EMOTIONS		
Emotion	**Physiological**	**Cognitive**	**Behavioral**
Fear	Sympathetic arousal	Belief that one is in danger	Avoidance tendencies
Anger	Sympathetic and parasympathetic arousal	Frustration or belief that one is being mistreated	Attack tendencies
Depression	Parasympathetic arousal	Thoughts of helplessness, hopelessness, worthlessness	Inactivity, possible self-destructive tendencies

word *emotion* might seem to be about feeling and not about thinking, cognitions—particularly interpretations of the meanings of events—are important aspects of emotions. *Fear,* which usually occurs in response to a threat, involves cognitions that one is in danger as well as arousal of the **sympathetic nervous system** (rapid heartbeat and breathing, sweating, muscle tension). Emotions also involve behavioral tendencies. The emotion of fear is connected with behavioral tendencies to avoid or escape from the situation (see Table 9.2). As a response to a social provocation, *anger* involves cognitions that the provocateur should be paid back, arousal of both the sympathetic and **parasympathetic nervous systems,** and tendencies to attack. *Depression* usually involves cognitions of helplessness and hopelessness, parasympathetic arousal, and tendencies toward inactivity—or, sometimes—self-destruction. *Joy, grief, jealousy, disgust, embarrassment, liking*—all have cognitive, physiological, and behavioral components.

Just how many emotions are there and what are they? The ancient Chinese believed in four basic or instinctive emotions—happiness, anger, sorrow, and fear. They arise, respectively, in the heart, liver, lungs, and kidneys (Carlson & Hatfield, 1992). (No, there is no evidence for this view.) The behaviorist psychologist John B. Watson (1924) believed that there are three basic or inborn emotions: fear, rage, and love. Others, such as Paul Ekman (1980) and Robert Plutchik (1984), have argued for larger numbers of basic emotions. The question remains unresolved (Fischer et al., 1990).

The Expression of Emotions

Joy and sadness are found in all cultures, but Question: How can we tell when other people are happy or despondent? It turns out that the expression of many emotions may be universal (Rinn, 1991). Smiling is apparently a universal sign of friendliness and approval. Baring the teeth, as noted by Charles Darwin (1872) in the 19th century, may be a universal sign of anger. As the originator of the theory of evolution, Darwin believed that the universal recognition of facial expressions would have survival value. For example, in the absence of language, facial expressions could signal the approach of enemies (or friends).

Most investigators (e.g., Buss, 1992; Ekman, 1994; Izard, 1994) concur that certain facial expressions suggest the same emotions in all people. Moreover, people in diverse cultures recognize the emotions manifested by certain facial expressions. In a classic study, Paul Ekman (1980) took photographs of people exhibiting anger, disgust, fear, happiness, sadness,

SYMPATHETIC NERVOUS SYSTEM The branch of the autonomic nervous system that is most active during processes that spend body energy from stored reserves, such as in a fight-or-flight reaction to a predator or when you are anxious about a big test. When people experience fear, the sympathetic nervous system accelerates the heart rate, raises the blood pressure, tenses muscles, and so on.

PARASYMPATHETIC NERVOUS SYSTEM The branch of the autonomic nervous system that is most active during processes that restore reserves of energy to the body, such as relaxing and eating. When people relax, the parasympathetic nervous system decelerates the heart rate, normalizes the blood pressure, relaxes muscles, and so on. The parasympathetic division also stimulates digestion.

FIGURE 9.7

PHOTOGRAPHS USED IN RESEARCH BY PAUL EKMAN   EKMAN'S RESEARCH SUGGESTS THAT THE FACIAL EXPRESSIONS CONNECTED WITH SEVERAL IMPORTANT EMOTIONS SUCH AS HAPPINESS, ANGER, SURPRISE, AND FEAR ARE UNIVERSALLY RECOGNIZED.

and surprise (see Figure 9.7.) He then asked people around the world to indicate what emotions were being depicted. Those queried ranged from European college students to members of the Fore, a tribe that dwells in the New Guinea highlands. All groups, including the Fore, who had almost no contact with Western culture, agreed on the emotions being portrayed. The Fore also displayed familiar facial expressions when asked how they would respond if they were the characters in stories that called for basic emotional responses. Ekman and his colleagues (1987) obtained similar results in a study of 10 cultures. In that study, participants were allowed to identify more than one emotion in facial expressions. The participants generally agreed on which two emotions were being shown and which emotion was more intense.

The Facial-Feedback Hypothesis

We generally recognize that facial expressions reflect emotional states. In fact, various emotional states give rise to certain patterns of electrical activity in the facial muscles and in the brain (Cacioppo et al., 1988). But can it work the other way around? The **facial-feedback hypothesis** argues that facial expressions can also affect our emotional state, that the causal relationship between emotions and facial expressions can work in the opposite direction. Questions: Can smiling give rise to feelings of good will? Can frowning produce anger? Perhaps they can.

Psychological research has yielded some interesting findings concerning the facial-feedback hypothesis (Ekman, 1993). Inducing people to smile, for example, leads them to report more positive feelings (Basic Behavioral Science Task Force, 1996) and to rate cartoons as more humorous. When induced to frown, they rate cartoons as more aggressive. When they exhibit pain through facial expressions, they rate electric shocks as more painful.

What are the possible links between facial feedback and emotion? One link is arousal. Intense contraction of facial muscles such as those used in signifying fear heightens arousal, which, in turn, boosts emotional response. Feedback from the contraction of facial muscles may also induce feeling states. Ekman (1993) has found that engaging in the so-called Duchenne smile, characterized by "crow's feet wrinkles around the eyes

FACIAL-FEEDBACK HYPOTHESIS The view that stereotypical facial expressions can contribute to stereotypical emotions.

and a subtle drop in the eye cover fold so that the skin above the eye moves down slightly toward the eyeball," can induce pleasant feelings.

REFLECT

Have you tried to "keep a stiff upper lip" when you were under stress, or have you preferred to "let it all hang out"? What do the facial-feedback hypothesis and various theories of emotional expression suggest about the effects of one approach or the other?

✓ **Truth or Fiction Revisited**

It is true that smiling can produce pleasant feelings. Research has shown that the Duchenne smile can indeed give rise to pleasant feelings.

You may have heard the British expression "Keep a stiff upper lip" as a recommendation for handling stress. It might be that a "stiff" lip suppresses emotional response—as long as the lip is relaxed rather than quivering with fear or tension. But when the lip is stiffened through strong muscle tension, facial feedback may heighten emotional response.

Theories of Emotion: "How Do You *Feel?*"

David, 32, is not sleeping well. He wakes before dawn and cannot get back to sleep. His appetite is off, his energy level is low, he has started smoking again. He has a couple of drinks at lunch and muses that it's lucky that any more alcohol makes him sick to his stomach—otherwise, he'd probably be drinking too much, too. Then he thinks, "So what difference would it make?" Sometimes he is sexually frustrated; at other times he wonders whether he has any sex drive left. Although he's awake, each day it's getting harder to drag himself out of bed in the morning. This week he missed one day of work and was late twice. His supervisor has suggested in a nonthreatening way that he "do something about it." David knows that her next warning will not be unthreatening. It's been going downhill since Sue walked out. Suicide has even crossed David's mind. He wonder's if he's going crazy. (Rathus & Nevid, 1999, p. 3)

David is experiencing the emotion of depression, seriously so. Depression is to be expected following a loss, such as the end of a relationship, but David's feelings have lingered. His friends tell him that he should get out and do things, but David is so down that he hasn't the motivation to do much of anything at all. After much prompting by family and friends, David consults a psychologist who, ironically, also pushes him to get out and do things—the things he used to enjoy. The psychologist also shows David that part of his problem is that sees himself as a failure who cannot make meaningful changes.

Question: How do the physiological, situational, and cognitive components of emotions interact to produce feelings and behavior? Some psychologists argue that physiological arousal is a more basic component of emotional response than cognition and that the type of arousal we experience strongly influences our cognitive appraisal and our labeling of the emotion (e.g., Izard, 1984). For these psychologists, the body takes precedence over the mind. Do David's bodily reactions—for example, his loss of appetite and energy—take precedence over his cognitions? Other psychologists argue that cognitive appraisal and physiological arousal are so strongly intertwined that cognitive processes may determine the emotional response. Are David's ideas that he is helpless to make meaningful changes more at the heart of his feelings of depression?

The "commonsense theory" of emotions is that something happens (a situation) that is cognitively appraised (interpreted) by the person, and the feeling state (a combination of arousal and thoughts) follows. For example, you meet someone new, appraise that person as delightful, and feelings of attraction follow. Or, as in the case of David, a social relationship comes to an end, you recognize your loss, feel powerless to do anything to change it, and feel down in the dumps.

However, both historic and contemporary theories of how the components of emotions interact are at variance with this commonsense view. Let us consider a number of theories and see whether we can arrive at some useful conclusions.

THE JAMES-LANGE THEORY A century ago, William James suggested that our emotions follow, rather than cause, our behavioral responses to events. At about the same time this view was also proposed by the Danish physiologist Karl G. Lange. It is therefore termed the James-Lange theory of emotion.

According to James and Lange, certain external stimuli instinctively trigger specific patterns of arousal and action, such as fighting or fleeing (see Figure 9.8, part A). We then become angry *because* we are acting aggressively or become afraid *because* we are running away. Emotions are simply the cognitive representations (or by-products) of automatic physiological and behavioral responses.

The James-Lange theory is consistent with the facial-feedback hypothesis. That is, smiling apparently can induce pleasant feelings, even if the effect may not be strong enough to overcome feelings of sadness (Ekman,

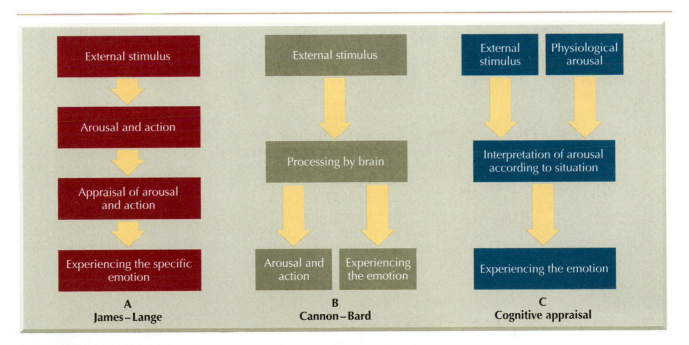

FIGURE 9.8

WHAT THEORIES OF EMOTION ARE THERE? SEVERAL THEORIES OF EMOTION HAVE BEEN ADVANCED, EACH OF WHICH PROPOSES A DIFFERENT ROLE FOR THE COMPONENTS OF EMOTIONAL RESPONSE. ACCORDING TO THE JAMES-LANGE THEORY (PART A), EVENTS TRIGGER SPECIFIC AROUSAL PATTERNS AND ACTIONS. EMOTIONS RESULT FROM OUR APPRAISAL OF OUR BODY RESPONSES. ACCORDING TO THE CANNON-BARD THEORY (PART B), EVENTS ARE FIRST PROCESSED BY THE BRAIN. BODY PATTERNS OF AROUSAL, ACTION, AND OUR EMOTIONAL RESPONSES ARE THEN TRIGGERED SIMULTANEOUSLY. ACCORDING TO THE THEORY OF COGNITIVE APPRAISAL (PART C), EVENTS AND AROUSAL ARE APPRAISED BY THE INDIVIDUAL. THE EMOTIONAL RESPONSE STEMS FROM THE PERSON'S APPRAISAL OF THE SITUATION AND HIS OR HER LEVEL OF AROUSAL.

1993). The theory also suggests that we may be able to change our feelings by changing our behavior. Changing one's behavior to change one's feelings is one aspect of behavior therapy. When David's psychologist urges him to get out and do things, she is assuming that by changing his behavior, David can have a positive effect on the way he feels.

Walter Cannon (1927) criticized the James-Lange assertion that each emotion has distinct physiological correlates. He argued that the physiological arousal associated with emotion A is not as distinct from the arousal associated with emotion B as the theory asserts. Note that the James-Lange view downplays the importance of human cognition; it denies the roles of cognitive appraisal, personal values, and personal choice in our behavioral and emotional responses to events.

THE CANNON-BARD THEORY Cannon (1927) was not content to criticize the James-Lange theory. Along with Philip Bard (1934), he suggested that an event might *simultaneously* trigger bodily responses (arousal and action) and the experience of an emotion. As shown in Figure 9.8 (part B), when an event is perceived (processed by the brain), the brain stimulates autonomic and muscular activity (arousal and action) *and* cognitive activity (experience of the emotion). Thus, according to the Cannon-Bard theory, emotions *accompany* bodily responses. They are not *produced by* bodily changes, as in the James-Lange theory.

The central criticism of the Cannon-Bard theory focuses on whether bodily responses (arousal and action) and emotions are actually stimulated simultaneously. For example, pain or the perception of danger may trigger arousal before we begin to feel distress or fear. Also, many of us have had the experience of having a "narrow escape" and becoming aroused and shaky afterward, when we have had time to consider the damage that might have occurred. What is needed is a theory that allows for an ongoing interaction of external events, physiological changes (such as autonomic arousal and muscular activity), and cognitive activities.

THE THEORY OF COGNITIVE APPRAISAL More recent theoretical approaches to emotion have stressed cognitive factors. Among those who argue that thinking comes first are Gordon Bower, Richard Lazarus, Stanley Schachter, and Robert Zajonc.

Stanley Schachter asserts that emotions are associated with similar patterns of bodily arousal that may be weaker or stronger, depending on the level of arousal. The label we give to an emotion depends largely on our cognitive appraisal of the situation. Cognitive appraisal is based on many factors, including our perception of external events and the ways in which other people seem to respond to those events (see Figure 9.8, part C). Given the presence of other people, we engage in social comparison to arrive at an appropriate response.

In a classic experiment, Schachter and Singer (1962) showed that arousal can be labeled quite differently, depending on the situation. The investigators told participants that they wanted to determine the effects of a vitamin on vision. Half of the participants received an injection of adrenaline, a hormone that increases the arousal of the sympathetic branch of the autonomic nervous system. A control group received an injection of an inactive solution. Those who had been given adrenaline then received one of three "cognitive manipulations," as shown in Table 9.3. Group 1 was told nothing about possible emotional effects of the "vitamin." Group 2 was deliberately misinformed; members of this group were

Group	Substance	Cognitive Manipulation
TABLE 9.3		INJECTED SUBSTANCES AND COGNITIVE MANIPULATIONS IN THE SCHACHTER-SINGER STUDY
1	Adrenaline	No information given about effects
2	Adrenaline	Misinformation given: itching, numbness, etc.
3	Adrenaline	Accurate information given: physiological arousal
4	Inactive	None

SOURCE: From Schachter & Singer (1962).

led to expect itching, numbness, or other irrelevant symptoms. Group 3 was informed accurately about the increased arousal they would experience. Group 4 was a control group injected with an inactive substance and given no information about its effects.

After receiving injections and cognitive manipulations, the participants were asked to wait in pairs while the experimental apparatus was being set up. The participants did not know that the person with whom they were waiting was a confederate of the experimenter. The confederate's purpose was to exhibit a response that the individual would believe was caused by the injection.

Some of those who took part in the experiment waited with a confederate who acted in a happy-go-lucky manner. He flew paper airplanes about the room and tossed paper balls into a wastebasket. Other participants waited with a confederate who acted angry. He complained about the experiment, tore up a questionnaire, and left the waiting room in a huff. As the confederates worked for their Oscar awards, the real participants were observed through a one-way mirror.

The people in groups 1 and 2 were likely to imitate the behavior of the confederate. Those who were exposed to the happy-go-lucky confederate acted jovial and content. Those who were exposed to the angry confederate imitated that person's complaining, aggressive behavior. But those in groups 3 and 4 were less influenced by the confederate's behavior.

Schachter and Singer concluded that participants in groups 1 and 2 were in an ambiguous situation. Members of these groups felt arousal from the adrenaline injection but couldn't label their arousal as any specific emotion. Social comparison with a confederate led them to attribute their arousal either to happiness or to anger. Members of group 3 expected arousal from the injection, with no particular emotional consequences. These participants did not imitate the confederate's display of happiness or anger because they were not in an ambiguous situation; they knew they felt arousal because of the shot of adrenaline. Members of group 4 had no physiological arousal for which they needed an attribution, except perhaps for some arousal induced by observing the confederate. They also did not imitate the behavior of the confederate.

Now, happiness and anger are quite different emotions. Happiness is a positive emotion, whereas anger, for most of us, is a negative emotion. Yet Schachter and Singer suggest that any physiological differences between these two emotions are so slight that different views of the situation can lead one person to label arousal as happiness and another person to label it as anger. The Schachter-Singer view could not be further removed from the James-Lange theory, which holds that each emotion is associated with specific and readily recognized body sensations.

The truth, it happens, may lie somewhere in between.

In science, it must be possible to replicate experiments and attain identical or similar results; otherwise, a theory cannot be considered valid. The Schachter and Singer study has been replicated, but with *different* results (Ekman, 1993). For instance, a number of studies found that participants were less likely to imitate the behavior of the confederate and were likely to perceive unexplained arousal in negative terms, attributing it to nervousness, anger, even jealousy (Zimbardo et al., 1993).

EVALUATION What can we make of all this? Research by Paul Ekman and his colleagues (1993) suggests that the patterns of arousal connected with various emotions are more specific than suggested by Schachter and Singer—although less so than suggested by James and Lange. Research with the PET scan suggests that different emotions, such as happiness and sadness, involve different structures within the brain (Goleman, 1995). Moreover, lack of control over our emotions and lack of understanding of what is happening to us are disturbing experiences (Zimbardo et al., 1993). Thus our cognitive appraisals of situations apparently do affect our emotional responses, even if not quite in the way envisioned by Schachter.

The fact that emotions are accompanied by bodily arousal has led to the development of so-called lie detectors, as we see in the following section.

Arousal, Emotions, and Lie Detection

The connection between autonomic arousal and emotions has led to the development of many kinds of lie detectors. Such instruments detect something, but do they detect specific emotional responses that signify lies? Let us take a closer look at the problem of lying.

Lying—for better or worse—is a part of life (Saxe, 1991). Political leaders lie to get elected. Some students lie about why they have not completed assignments (Saxe, 1991). ('Fess up!) The great majority of people lie to their lovers—most often about other relationships (Saxe, 1991). (Is it really true that you never kissed anyone else before?) People also lie about their qualifications to obtain jobs, and, of course, some people lie in denying guilt for crimes. Although we are unlikely to subject political leaders, students, and lovers to lie detector tests, such tests are frequently used in hiring and in police investigations.

Facial expressions often offer clues to deceit, but some people can lie with a straight face—or a smile. As Shakespeare pointed out in *Hamlet,* "One may smile, and smile, and be a villain." The use of devices to detect lies has a long, if not laudable, history:

> The Bedouins of Arabia . . . until quite recently required conflicting witnesses to lick a hot iron; the one whose tongue was burned was thought to be lying. The Chinese, it is said, had a similar method for detecting lying: Suspects were forced to chew rice powder and spit it out; if the powder was dry, the suspect was guilty. A variation of this test was used during the Inquisition. The suspect had to swallow a "trial slice" of bread and cheese; if it stuck to the suspect's palate or throat he or she was not telling the truth. (Kleinmuntz & Szucko, 1984, pp. 766–767)

REFLECT

Can you tell when people are lying to you? What cues or clues do you focus on?

These methods may sound primitive, even bizarre, but they are broadly consistent with modern psychological knowledge. Anxiety about being caught in a lie is linked to arousal of the sympathetic division of the autonomic nervous system. One sign of sympathetic arousal is lack of saliva, or dryness in the mouth. The emotions of fear and guilt are also linked to sympathetic arousal and, hence, to dryness in the mouth.

Questions: How do lie detectors work? How reliable are they? Modern lie detectors, or polygraphs (see Figure 9.9), monitor indicators of sympathetic arousal while a witness or suspect is being examined. These indicators include heart rate, blood pressure, respiration rate, and electrodermal response (sweating). Questions have been raised about the validity of assessing truth or fiction in this way, however (Sleek, 1998).

The American Polygraph Association claims that use of the polygraph is 85% to 95% accurate. Critics find polygraph testing to be less accurate and claim that it is sensitive to more than lies (Bashore & Rapp, 1993; Saxe, 1998). Studies have found that factors such as tense muscles, drugs, and previous experience with polygraph tests can significantly reduce their accuracy rate (Steinbrook, 1992). In one experiment, people were able to reduce the accuracy of polygraph-based judgments to about 50% by biting their tongue (to produce pain) or by pressing their toes against the floor (to tense muscles) while being interviewed (Honts et al., 1985).

FIGURE 9.9
WHAT DO "LIE DETECTORS" DETECT?
THE POLYGRAPH MONITORS HEART RATE, BLOOD PRESSURE, RESPIRATION RATE, AND SWEAT IN THE PALMS OF THE HANDS. IS THE POLYGRAPH SENSITIVE TO LYING ONLY? IS IT FOOLPROOF? BECAUSE OF THE CONTROVERSY SURROUNDING THESE QUESTIONS, MANY COURTS NO LONGER ADMIT POLYGRAPH EVIDENCE.

✓ **Truth or Fiction Revisited**

It is true that you may be able to fool a lie detector by wiggling your toes. This creates patterns of autonomic arousal that may be misread in interpreting the polygraph.

In a review of the literature on this subject, the government Office of Technology Assessment found little valid research on the use of the polygraph in preemployment screening, "dragnet" investigations (attempts to distinguish a guilty person from other suspects), or determining who should be given access to classified information (U.S. Congress, 1983). The government also looked into studies involving investigations of specific indictments. The studies' conclusions varied widely. In 28 studies judged to have employed adequate methodology, accurate detections of guilt ranged from 35% to 100%. Accurate judgments of innocence ranged from 12.5% to 94%.

In sum, no identifiable pattern of bodily responses pinpoints lying (Bashore & Rapp, 1993; Steinbrook, 1992). Because of validity problems, results of polygraph examinations are no longer admitted as evidence in many courts. Polygraph interviews are still often conducted in criminal investigations and job interviews, but this practice is also being questioned.

In sum, various components of an experience—cognitive, physiological, and behavioral—contribute to our emotional responses. Physiological arousal is a part of emotional response, but people appraise their situations when they feel aroused such that arousal does not appear to directly cause one emotion or another. Humans are thinking beings who gather information from all three sources in determining their behavioral responses and labeling their emotional responses. The fact that none of the theories of emotion we have discussed applies to all people in all situations is comforting. Apparently our emotions are not quite as easily understood, manipulated, or—as in the case of the polygraph—even detected as some theorists have suggested.

An emotion is a (78) _____ing state. Emotions have physiological, cognitive, and (79) _____ components. Emotions motivate behavior, but can also serve as (80) _____nses to situations and as goals in themselves. The emotion of anxiety predominantly involves arousal of the (81) _____ nervous system. Depression involves arousal of the (82) _____ nervous system, cognitions of hopelessness, and tendencies toward (83: Activity or Inactivity?).

Ekman found that the expression of many emotions, including anger, disgust, fear, happiness, sadness, and surprise, appears to be (84: Culture-specific or Universal?). (85) _____ing appears to be a universal sign of friendliness and approval. Charles (86) _____ believed that the universal recognition of facial expressions had survival value.

According to the (87) _____-feedback hypothesis, intense facial expressions can heighten emotional response. Inducing (88) _____ing leads subjects to report more positive feelings. Subjects who are induced to frown rate cartoons as more (89) _____sive.

Psychologists do not agree as to the relative importance of physiological arousal and (90) co_____ appraisal in activating particular emotions. According to the James-Lange theory, emotions have specific patterns of (91) _____sal and (92) _____tion that are triggered by certain external events. Emotions follow, rather than cause, behavioral (93) _____ses to events. The Cannon-Bard theory proposes that processing of events by the brain gives rise simultaneously to (94) _____nomic activity (arousal), action, and cognitive activity (the mental experiencing of the emotion). According to the theory of cognitive appraisal, emotions have largely similar patterns of bodily (95) _____sal. The emotion a person will experience in response to an external stimulus reflects that person's (96) _____sal of the meaning of the stimulus. Research suggests that patterns of arousal are more specific than suggested by the theory of (97) _____tive appraisal, but that cognitive appraisal plays a role in determining responses to events.

Lie detectors are known technically as (98) _____aphs. Polygraphs assess four aspects of sympathetic arousal: heart rate; blood (99) _____e; respiration rate; and electrodermal response (sweating). Research suggests that the accuracy of polygraphs is (100: Perfect or Questionable?).

STUDY GUIDE

SUMMARY

1. **What is the psychology of motivation?** The psychology of motivation concerns why people do certain things. *Motives* are hypothetical states within an organism that activate behavior and propel the organism toward goals. Psychologists also speak of physiological *needs,* such as those for oxygen and food, and of psychological needs, such as those for achievement and self-esteem. Needs give rise to *drives;* for example, depletion of food gives rise to the hunger drive. An *incentive* is an object, person, or situation that can satisfy a need or is desirable for its own sake.

2. **What is meant by species-specific behaviors?** According to instinct theory, organisms are born with preprogrammed tendencies—called *instincts* or *species-specific behaviors* or *fixed-action patterns* (FAPs)—to behave in certain ways in certain situations. FAPs occur in the presence of stimuli called *releasers.* Male members of many species are sexually aroused by pheromones secreted by females. Psychologists debate whether humans have instincts, and if so, what they are.

3. **What is drive-reduction theory? How is it related to homeostasis?** According to drive-reduction theory, we are motivated to engage in behavior that reduces drives. *Primary drives* such as hunger and pain are based on the biological makeup of the organism. *Acquired drives* such as the drive for money are learned. Drives trigger arousal and activate behavior. We learn to do what reduces drives. The body has a tendency called *homeostasis* to maintain a steady state; therefore, food deprivation leads to the hunger drive and eating, which reduces the hunger drive.

4. **How does humanistic theory differ from the instinct and drive-reduction theories of motivation?** Whereas instincts and drives are mainly defensive, aimed at survival and reproduction, humanistic psychologists argue that people are self-aware and that behavior can be growth-oriented; people are motivated to strive for self-actualization.

5. **What is Maslow's hierarchy of needs?** Maslow hypothesized that people have a hierarchy of needs. Once lower-level needs such as physiological and safety needs are satisfied, people strive to meet higher-level needs such as those for love, esteem, and self-actualization.

6. **Why are people motivated to eliminate inconsistencies in their worldviews?** According to cognitive theory, people are motivated to understand and predict events. People must represent the world accurately in order to accomplish these goals, and therefore their cognitions need to be harmonious or consistent with one another.

7. **How do we make sense of all these different views of motivation?** There is no question that many animals are born with instincts; the question remains as to what instincts people have and how compelling they are. Drive-reduction theory appears to apply to physiological drives such as hunger and thirst, but people often act to increase rather than decrease the tension they experience. Although humanistic theory has been criticized as unscientific, many psychologists make room for conscious striving in their views of humans. Cognition appears to be a fact of human life, although psychologists debate ways of dealing scientifically with cognition.

8. **What bodily mechanisms regulate the hunger drive? What psychological processes are at work?** Hunger is regulated by several internal mechanisms, including stomach contractions, blood sugar level, receptors in the mouth and liver, and the responses of the hypothalamus. Stomach contractions correspond with hunger but do not fully regulate it. The *ventromedial nucleus* (VMN)of the hypothalamus functions as a stop-eating center. Damage to this area leads to *hyperphagia* in rats; that is, the animals grow to several times their normal body weight. The *lateral hypothalamus* may function as a start-eating center. External stimuli such as the aroma of food can also trigger hunger. Chewing and swallowing provide some satiety.

9. **If obesity is connected with health problems and unhappiness with the image in the mirror, why are so many people overweight?** Biological factors in obesity include heredity, adipose tissue (body fat), and the metabolic rate (the rate at which the individual converts calories to energy). Psychological factors such as stress can also contribute to overeating. Obesity is more prevalent among poorer people. Since people of color are typically of lower socioeconomic status than White Americans, rates of obesity tend to be higher among African and Hispanic Americans.

10. **So what can I do to shed a few pounds?** Sound weight control programs involve improving nutritional knowledge (e.g., eating more fruits and vegetable and fewer fatty foods), decreasing calorie intake, exercising, and changing eating habits. Behavior modification helps people construct healthful diets and cope with temptations.

11. **Are all motives aimed at the reduction of tension?** Apparently not. Stimulus motives, like physiological motives, are innate, but they involve motives to increase rather than decrease "tension" or the amount of stimulation acting on the organism.

12. **Do we need to be active? Do we need to stimulate our senses?** Sensory-deprivation studies suggest that inactivity and lack of stimulation are aversive in humans. People and many lower animals have needs for stimulation and activity.

13. **Why do puppies and kittens explore their environments when they are brought into new homes?** People and many lower animals have needs for exploration and manipulation. Many psychologists believe that exploration is reinforcing in and of itself.

14. **Why are people who go unrewarded more likely than those who are rewarded to think or say that what they are doing is worthwhile for its own sake?** Cognitive-dissonance theory hypothesizes that people dislike situations in which their attitudes and behavior are inconsistent. Such situations apparently induce cognitive dissonance, which people can reduce by changing their attitudes. For example, people engage in effort justification; that is, they tend to justify boring or fruitless behavior to themselves by concluding that their efforts are worthwhile, even when they go unrewarded.

15. **Why do some people strive to get ahead?** One reason may be that they have more achievement motivation than other people. Achievement motivation is the need to accomplish things. McClelland studied achievement motivation by means of people's responses to TAT cards. People with high achievement motivation attain higher grades and earn more money than people of comparable ability with lower achievement motivation. People may be motivated to achieve in school by performance or learning goals. Performance goals are tangible rewards, such as money or getting into graduate school. Learning goals involve the enhancement of knowledge or skills.

16. **Why do people need people?** People may have an inborn (instinctive) need to affiliate with other people. Anxiety tends to increase the need for affiliation, especially with people who share one's predicament.

17. **Why do people kill, maim, and injure one another?** Certainly people engage in warfare and other kinds of combat as members of groups. However, psychological theories also address the problem of aggression. Biological theory views aggression as instinctive and linked to brain structures, hormone levels, and the Darwinian concept of the "survival of the fittest." Psychodynamic theory views aggression as stemming from inevitable frustrations. Cognitive perspectives predict that people may be aggressive when they see aggression as being appropriate for them, or when they interpret other people's behavior as insults to their honor. Learning theories view aggression as stemming from experience and reinforcement of aggressive skills. The sociocultural perspective examines the effects of culture—such as the culture of athletic competition—on aggression.

18. **Just what is an emotion?** An emotion is a state of feeling with physiological, cognitive, and behavioral components. Emotions motivate behavior and also serve as goals. Fear, for example, is connected with arousal of the *sympathetic nervous system*, cognitions that one is in danger, and behavioral tendencies to escape.

19. **How can we tell when other people are happy or despondent?** Facial expressions are one factor in the expression of emotion. According to Ekman, there are several basic emotions whose expression is recognized in cultures around the world. Darwin believed that the universal recognition of facial expressions had survival value.

20. **Can smiling give rise to feelings of good will? Can frowning produce anger?** It does appear that facial expressions can influence one's experience of emotion. The contraction of facial muscles may be influential.

21. **How do the physiological, situational, and cognitive components of emotions interact to produce feelings and behavior?** According to the James-Lange theory, emotions are associated with specific patterns of arousal and action that are triggered by certain external events. The emotion follows the behavioral response. The Cannon-Bard theory proposes that processing of events by the brain gives rise simultaneously to feelings and bodily responses. According to this view, feelings accompany bodily responses. According to Schachter and Singer's theory of cognitive appraisal, emotions are associated with similar patterns of arousal, but the level of arousal can differ. The emotion a person experiences in response to an external stimulus reflects that person's appraisal of the stimulus. Research evidence suggests that patterns of arousal are more specific than suggested by the theory of

cognitive appraisal, but that cognitive appraisal also plays a role in determining our responses to events.

22. **How do lie detectors work? How reliable are they?** Lie detectors—also called polygraphs—monitor indicators of sympathetic arousal, including heart rate, blood pressure, respiration rate, and electrodermal response (sweating) while a witness or suspect in a crime is being examined. These responses are presumed to indicate the presence of emotions—anxiety and/or guilt—that might be induced by lying. Critics find polygraph testing to be unreliable and argue that it is sensitive to more emotions than those that might be connected with lying.

EXERCISE 1

MATCHING SCIENTISTS AND CONCEPTS

In the left-hand column are a number of statements that express various concepts or positions that concern the psychology of motivation and emotion. In the right-hand column are the names of a number of psychologists and other scientists discussed in Chapter 9. Write the number of the statement to the left of the name of the appropriate scientist. (More than one statement may apply to an individual.)

____ 1. Certain facial expressions suggest the same emotions in people in diverse cultures.

____ 2. People have 12 basic instincts, including hunger, sex, and self-assertion.

____ 3. Once people have met their lower-level needs, they naturally try to find personal fulfillment by actualizing their unique potentials.

____ 4. When people are in an ambiguous situation, they tend to look to other people in the same situation for information as to how they ought to behave.

____ 5. The reason that people and lower animals find rewards to be pleasant is that rewards have the effect of reducing primary or acquired drives.

____ 6. Awareness that two cognitions are dissonant, or that our attitudes are incompatible with our behavior, is unpleasant and motivates us to reduce the discrepancy.

____ 7. External events trigger instinctive patterns of arousal and action such as fighting or fleeing. We then become angry *because* we fight; we become afraid *because* we run away.

____ 8. The instincts of hunger, sex, and aggression give rise to psychic energy, which is perceived as tension. This tension motivates us to find ways to restore ourselves to a calmer, resting state.

____ 9. Individuals who possess characteristics such as aggressiveness that give them an advantage in the struggle for survival are more likely to mature and reproduce.

____ 10. Achievement motivation can be driven by different forces, including performance goals and learning goals.

A. Charles Darwin
B. Sigmund Freud
C. Clark Hull
D. William James
E. Paul Ekman
F. Abraham Maslow
G. William McDougall
H. Leon Festinger
I. Stanley Schachter
J. Carol Dweck

EXERCISE 2

COMPONENTS OF EMOTIONS

Emotions are defined as feeling states with physiological, cognitive, and behavioral components. The following table lists three key emotions and their components. Fill in the missing information.

Emotion	Physiological	Cognitive	Behavioral
Fear	(1) _____tic arousal	Belief that one is in danger	(2) _____ance tendencies
(3) _____	Sympathetic and parasympathetic arousal	Frustration or belief that one is being mistreated	Attack tendencies
Depression	(4) _____tic arousal hopelessness, worthlessness	Thoughts of helplessness, possible self-destructive tendencies	(5: Activity or Inactivity?),

BRIDGING THE GAP

LANGUAGE AND CULTURE

acculturation (425)   *adaptation to a new set of circumstances or social values*

argumentative (436)   *not obeying but arguing, quarrelsome*

to bare the teeth (438)   *to pull back the lips so that the teeth show, a universal sign of anger (opposite meaning of smile)*

basketball look-alike (422)   *resembling a basketball, round (here, a pun) extremely fat*

to bat (428)   *(here) to push on with some force*

belligerent (436)   *quarrelsome, warlike*

to be at variance with (441)   *to disagree, to contrast*

blindfolded (429)   *with eyes covered to prevent seeing*

to butcher (436)   *to cut up as if it were meat*

to cheer someone on (435)   *to encourage*

to churn (428)   *to make a circular motion*

confederate (443)   *accomplice, person who is a friend or helper*

to copulate (429)   *to mate, to unite sexually*

a core unit (434)   *heart, center*

counterpart (416)   *equivalent, balancing part*

to cross one's mind (440)   *for one to think about, to have an idea about, to consider*

crow's feet wrinkles around the eyes (439)   *creases in the skin around the eyes that show age*

cubicle (429)   *small enclosure, tiny room*

to dawn on someone (428)   *for someone to realize or understand*

deference (436)   *politeness, respect*

demise (434)   *death*

deprivation (416)   *hardship caused by not having what is needed for survival*

to dispose someone to (436)   *to change one's tendency toward an action or attitude*

disorientation (429)   *loss of sense of direction and location*

to drag oneself out of bed (440)   *to experience difficulty in arising in the morning*

dread (437)   *fear*

enlightened (415)   *having learned important information*

extrinsic rewards (432)   *rewards that come from outside, from others' approval*

the fateful hour (414)   *the appointed time for a great predicted change*

to 'fess up (444)   *to confess, to acknowledge*

to fidget (415)   *to be restless, to move around restlessly*

finicky (422)   *very particular about what they will eat*

flying saucer (414)   *space vehicle*

gadget (430)   *device for doing a particular task (like a can opener)*

genetic whispering (431)   *subtle information that a person gets from within his or her own self that give direction to the person, inherited directions for growth*

to get away from it all (413)   *to escape responsibilities, to go on vacation*

to get a kick out of (429)   *to enjoy*

to go on a binge (422)   *to eat to excess*

in a groove (419)   *in its natural functioning state*

to grope (422)   *to find with a sense of touch, to reach out for in darkness*

the Guardians (414)   *outer space creatures of great power*

to huddle (433)   *to gather in a close circle for defense or consultation*

humiliating (415)   *being made to feel foolish*

to be intertwined (440)   *to be closely associated*

to jump at (415)   *to accept quickly in changing one's mind*

to keep a stiff upper lip (440)   *to maintain control over one's emotions*

to lie with a straight face (444)   *to act innocent, to tell an untruth but without any indication of guilt*

to linger (440)   *to remain, to stay*

to look greener (427)   *(reference to the grass looks greener on the other side of the fence) to be more appealing*

lopsided (431)   *uneven, out of balance*

on the lower rungs of the socioeconomic ladder (425)   *poor people*

to maim (434)   *to cause disfiguring injury, to cripple*

to make it (432)   *to succeed*

mating season (413)   *time of the year when male and female animals seek to initiate reproduction rituals*

to mark one's territory (417)   *to define the limits of one's personal space*

markedly (416)   *significantly*

misery loves company (413)   *(aphorism or saying) sad people tend to find other sad people (so that they can talk about how unhappy they are)*

to monkey around (429)   *to manipulate objects without purpose*

monogamous (420)   *having only one mate*

more than measure up (423)   *(pun on size) to measure up means to be equal to; those who more than measure up are overweight*

to muse (440)   *to say, to reflect, to guess*

nurturance (421)   *taking care of, feeling of satisfaction and security*

Oscar Award (443)   *an award given once a year in recognition of excellence in film acting*

part of the story (423)   *an incomplete explanation*

to pay back (438)   *to retaliate, to fight back and punish*

pecking order (417)   *hierarchy in animal society*

pent-up (435)   *stored but needing to be released*

to pin one's hopes on (431)   *to expect a positive outcome from*

preemployment screening (445)   *interviewing a prospective worker, checking the person's records*

to primp (436)   *to groom oneself in a feminine way*

provocateur (438)   *person who causes trouble*

provocation (436)   *negative stimulus*

to push someone (440)   *to encourage with some force*

to reap (432)   *to gather, to collect*

the recesses of the mind (435)   *the deepest part of the memory*

to revive (422)   *to regain consciousness, to return to life*

to be removed from (443)   *to be different from and not associated with*

to replicate (444)   *to copy, to do again and get the same results*

roundabout (435)   *indirect*

a routine (427)   *scheduled and outlined series of actions*

the Seekers (414)   *those who were members of a group who considered themselves to be searching for something; searchers*

sham (422)   *phony, false*

to shed (426)   *to lose*

to shun (420)   *to avoid (a person)*

to sidetrack (427)   *to stop progress*

to stress (442)   *to emphasize*

spending spree (414)   *a shopping trip in which a person spends everything he or she has*

to take precedence (440)   *to be more important and therefore come first*

to tear us asunder (431)   *to separate us violently*

togetherness (421)   *shared lives and experiences*

torturously slowly (415)   *with painful slowness*

tummy time (421)   *time measured by when a person gets hungry*

Twiggy (422)   *a famous and very thin fashion model*

to vanquish (437)   *to overcome, to conquer*

to vent (413)   *to discharge, to speak out or act out one's true feelings of anger*

to wiggle one's toes (413)   *to move the toes on one's foot causing muscle action*

wit (435)   *cleverness of verbal expression*

to zap (429)   *to shoot at, to destroy*

Q U I Z

1. Physiological _____ are the psychological counterparts of physiological needs.
   (a) drives,
   (b) incentives,
   (c) responses,
   (d) behaviors.

2. Inherited dispositions that activate behavior patterns designed to reach specific goals are referred to as
   (a) motives,
   (b) drives,
   (c) instincts,
   (d) releasers.

3. A reward of $1,000 for returning a wallet would serve as a(n)
   (a) need,
   (b) incentive,
   (c) drive,
   (d) social motive.

4. Drive-reduction theory has the greatest difficulty explaining
   (a) stimulus motives,
   (b) the thirst drive,
   (c) the hunger drive,
   (d) avoidance of extremes in temperature.

5. When the ventromedial nucleus of a rat's hypothalamus is destroyed, the animal becomes
   (a) hyperglycemic,
   (b) hyperphagic,
   (c) hypoglycemic,
   (d) aphagic.

6. According to the text, _____ theory argues that people are motivated by the conscious desire for personal growth.
   (a) instinct,
   (b) evolutionary,
   (c) cognitive,
   (d) humanistic.

7. People who value the acquiring of skills and knowledge for their own sake are said to be motivated by _____ goals.
   (a) intellectual,
   (b) performance,
   (c) academic,
   (d) learning.

8. _____ psychologists view aggression as natural.
   (a) Evolutionary,
   (b) Sociocultural,
   (c) Cognitive,
   (d) Behavioral.

9. Participants in sensory-deprivation experiments are reported to have experienced all of the following *except* for
   (a) boredom,
   (b) irritability,
   (d) hallucinations,
   (d) ulcers.

10. Who of the following asserts that people are motivated to achieve cognitive consistency?
    (a) Clark Hull,
    (b) Leon Festinger,
    (c) William McDougall,
    (d) Charles Darwin.

11. The polygraph is used to try to detect
    (a) attitude-discrepant behavior,
    (b) effort justification,
    (c) pangs of hunger,
    (d) lies.

12. David McClelland assessed achievement motivation by using the
    (a) MMPI,
    (b) Rorschach inkblot test,
    (c) TAT,
    (d) interview.

13. Who believed that we become angry *because* we fight, and that we become afraid *because* we run away from threats?
    (a) Karl Lange,
    (b) Stanley Schachter,
    (c) Robert Zajonc,
    (d) Jerome Singer.

14. Stanley Schachter explains the findings of his research into anxiety and affiliation by means of
    (a) James-Lange theory,
    (b) cognitive-dissonance theory,
    (c) the theory of social comparison,
    (d) drive reductionism.

15. According to the text, the emotion of _____ involves predominantly sympathetic arousal.
    (a) depression,
    (b) anger,
    (c) happiness,
    (d) fear.

16. Which of the following is true of the catharsis hypothesis?
    (a) It is a valuable part of humanistic theory,
    (b) It explains why athletes tend to be aggressive,
    (c) Research does not support its accuracy,
    (d) It explains the effects of media violence.

17. The advice to "keep a stiff upper lip" would seem to be most consistent with
    (a) the catharsis hypothesis,

    (b) the facial-feedback hypothesis,
    (c) cognitive-dissonance theory,
    (d) evolutionary psychology.

18. Who of the following noted that baring the teeth may be a universal sign of anger?
    (a) Charles Darwin,
    (b) Robert Zajonc,
    (c) Stanley Schachter,
    (d) William James.

19. A person tries to get herself out of a state of depression by engaging in behaviors that were once enjoyable. This approach to overcoming depression is most consistent with a theory proposed by
    (a) William James,
    (b) Walter Cannon,
    (c) Henry Murray,
    (d) Stanley Schachter.

20. Which of the following statements contradicts the theory of emotion proposed by Schachter and Singer?
    (a) Strong arousal is associated with stronger emotions,
    (b) Situations influence the experience of emotions,
    (c) In ambiguous situations, we may try to determine how we should feel by observing others in the same situation,
    (d) There are some reasonably distinct patterns of arousal that are not exchangeable.

Recite Recite Recite Recite Recite

1. What is the psychology of motivation?

2. What is meant by species-specific behaviors?

3. What is drive-reduction theory? How is it related to homeostasis?

4. How does humanistic theory differ from the instinct and drive-reduction theories of motivation?

5. What is Maslow's hierarchy of needs?

6. Why are people motivated to eliminate inconsistencies in their worldviews?

7. How do we make sense of all these different views of motivation?

8. What bodily mechanisms regulate the hunger drive? What psychological processes are at work?

9. If obesity is connected with health problems and un-happiness with the image in the mirror, why are so many people overweight?

10. So what can I do to shed a few pounds?

11. Are all motives aimed at the reduction of tension?

12. Do we need to be active? Do we need to stimulate our senses?

13. Why do puppies and kittens explore their environments when they are brought into new homes?

14. Why are people who go unrewarded more likely than those who are rewarded to think or say that what they are doing is worthwhile for its own sake?

15. Why do some people strive to get ahead?

16. Why do people need people?

17. Why do people kill, maim, and injure one another?

18. Just what is an emotion?

19. How can we tell when other people are happy or despondent?

20. Can smiling give rise to feelings of good will? Can frowning produce anger?

21. How do the physiological, situational, and cognitive components of emotions interact to produce feelings and behavior?

_____
_____
_____
_____
_____

22. How do lie detectors work? How reliable are they?

_____
_____
_____
_____
_____

ANSWERS TO SECTION REVIEWS

1. Motivate
2. Goals
3. Deprivation
4. Are not
5. Experience
6. Drives
7. Incentive
8. Biological
9. Species-specific
10. Fixed-action
11. Releasers
12. Psychic
13. Hull
14. Rewards
15. Behavior
16. Primary
17. Acquired
18. Homeostasis
19. Humanistic
20. Maslow
21. Belongingness
22. Self-actualization
23. Predict
24. Festinger
25. Stomach

26. Sugar
27. Satiety
28. Ventromedial
29. Hyperphasia
30. Lateral
31. Does
32. Biological
33. Adoptive
34. Adipose
35. Blood
36. Set
37. Hypothalamus
38. Earlier
39. Less
40. Poor
41. Nutritional
42. Decreasing
43. Do
44. Increase
45. Decrease
46. Deprivation
47. Irritable
48. Hallucinations
49. Concentrate
50. Increases

51. Cognitions
52. Attitude
53. Justify
54. More
55. McClelland
56. Apperception
57. Higher
58. More
59. Performance
60. Learning
61. Learning
62. Affiliation
63. Increase
64. Share
65. Comparison
66. Ambiguous
67. Hypothalamus
68. Testosterone
69. Evolutionary
70. Reproduce
71. Common
72. Catharsis
73. Cognitive
74. Do not
75. Reinforcement

76. Sociocultural
77. Sports
78. Feeling
79. Behavioral
80. Responses
81. Sympathetic
82. Parasympathetic
83. Inactivity
84. Universal
85. Smiling
86. Darwin
87. Facial
88. Smiling
89. Aggressive
90. Cognitive
91. Arousal
92. Action
93. Responses
94. Autonomic
95. Arousal
96. Appraisal
97. Cognitive
98. Polygraphs
99. Pressure
100. Questionable

ANSWERS TO EXERCISE 1

A. 1 or 9
B. 8
C. 5

D. 7
E. 1
F. 3

G. 2
H. 6

I. 4
J. 10

ANSWERS TO EXERCISE 2

1. Sympathetic
2. Avoidance

3. Anger

4. Parasympathetic

5. Inactivity

ANSWERS TO QUIZ

1. A	6. D	11. D	16. C
2. C	7. D	12. C	17. B
3. B	8. A	13. A	18. A
4. A	9. D	14. C	19. A
5. B	10. B	15. D	20. D

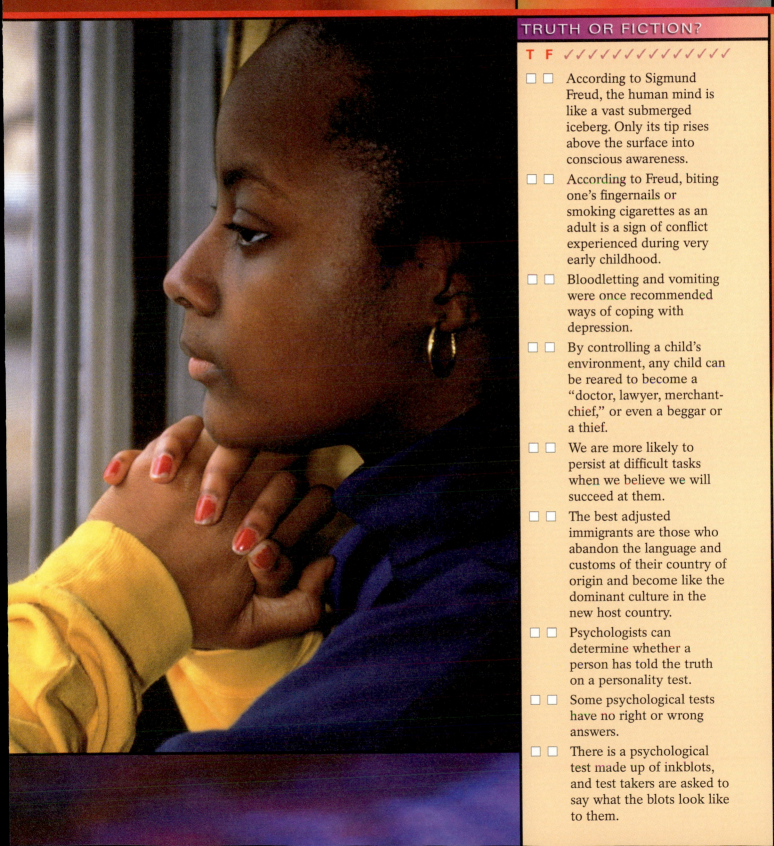

TRUTH OR FICTION?

T F ✓✓✓✓✓✓✓✓✓✓✓✓✓

☐ ☐ According to Sigmund Freud, the human mind is like a vast submerged iceberg. Only its tip rises above the surface into conscious awareness.

☐ ☐ According to Freud, biting one's fingernails or smoking cigarettes as an adult is a sign of conflict experienced during very early childhood.

☐ ☐ Bloodletting and vomiting were once recommended ways of coping with depression.

☐ ☐ By controlling a child's environment, any child can be reared to become a "doctor, lawyer, merchant-chief," or even a beggar or a thief.

☐ ☐ We are more likely to persist at difficult tasks when we believe we will succeed at them.

☐ ☐ The best adjusted immigrants are those who abandon the language and customs of their country of origin and become like the dominant culture in the new host country.

☐ ☐ Psychologists can determine whether a person has told the truth on a personality test.

☐ ☐ Some psychological tests have no right or wrong answers.

☐ ☐ There is a psychological test made up of inkblots, and test takers are asked to say what the blots look like to them.

I was reading Dr. Seuss's *One Fish, Two Fish, Red Fish, Blue Fish* to my daughter Taylor when she was 2 years old. The sneaky author had set up a trap for fathers. A part of the book reads that "Some [fish] are sad. And some are glad. And some are very, very bad. Why are they sad and glad and bad? I do not know. Go ask your dad."

Thanks, Dr. Seuss.

For many months I had just recited this section and then moved on. One day, however, Taylor's cognitive development had apparently flowered, and she would not let me get away with glossing over this. Why, indeed, she wanted to know, were some fish sad whereas others were glad and bad? I paused and then, being a typical American dad, I gave the answer I'm sure has been given by thousands of other fathers:

"Uh, some fish are sad and others are glad or bad because of, uh, the interaction of nature and nurture—I mean, you know, heredity and environmental factors."

At which Taylor laughed and replied, "Not!"

SECTION I. INTRODUCTION TO PERSONALITY: "WHY ARE THEY SAD AND GLAD AND BAD?"

I'm still not certain whether Taylor thought my words came out silly or that my psychological theorizing was simplistic or off base. When applied to people—that is, why are people sad or glad or bad—this is the kind of question that is of interest to psychologists who study personality.

Question: Just what *is* personality? People do not necessarily agree on what the word *personality* means. Many equate personality with liveliness, as in "She's got a lot of personality." Others characterize a person's personality as consisting of his or her most striking traits, as in a "shy personality" or a "happy-go-lucky personality." Psychologists define personality as the reasonably stable patterns of emotions, motives, and behavior that distinguish one person from another.

Psychologists also seek to explain how personality develops—that is, why some (people) are sad or glad or bad—and to predict how people with certain personality traits respond to life's demands. In this chapter we explore five perspectives on personality: the psychodynamic, trait, learning, humanistic–existential, and sociocultural perspectives. Then we discuss personality tests—the methods used to measure whether people are sad, glad, bad, and lots of other things.

SECTION I Review

Psychologists define *personality* as the reasonably stable patterns of (1) _____ions, motives, and (2) b_____ that distinguish people from one another.

PSYCHODYNAMIC THEORY Sigmund Freud's perspective, which emphasizes the importance of unconscious motives and conflicts as forces that determine behavior. *Dynamic* refers to the concept of (psychological) forces being in motion.

SECTION II. THE PSYCHODYNAMIC PERSPECTIVE

There are several **psychodynamic theories** of personality, each of which owes its origin to the thinking of Sigmund Freud. These theories have a number of features in common. Each teaches that personality is characterized by conflict—by a dynamic struggle. At first the conflict is external: Drives like sex, aggression, and the need for superiority come into conflict with laws, social rules, and moral codes. But at some point laws and social rules are brought inward, or *internalized*. After that the conflict is between opposing *inner* forces. At any given moment our behavior, thoughts, and emotions represent the outcome of these inner contests. Question: What is Freud's theory of psychosexual development?

Sigmund Freud's Theory of Psychosexual Development

Sigmund Freud (1856–1939) was a mass of contradictions. He has been praised as the greatest thinker of the 20th century, the most profound of psychologists. He has been criticized as overrated, even a "false and faithless prophet." He preached liberal views on sexuality but was himself a model of sexual restraint. He invented a popular form of psychotherapy but experienced lifelong psychologically related problems such as migraine headaches, bowel problems, fainting under stress, hatred of the telephone, and an addiction to cigars. He smoked 20 cigars a day and could not or would not break the habit even after he developed cancer of the jaw.

Sigmund Freud

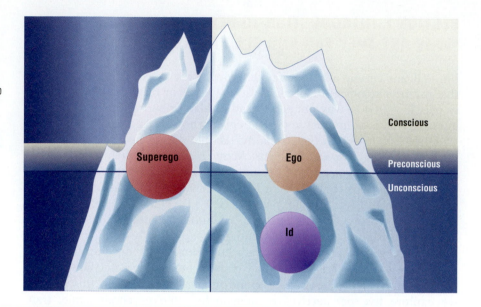

FIGURE 10.1
THE HUMAN ICEBERG ACCORDING TO FREUD
ACCORDING TO PSYCHODYNAMIC THEORY, ONLY THE TIP OF HUMAN PERSONALITY RISES ABOVE THE SURFACE OF THE MIND INTO CONSCIOUS AWARENESS. MATERIAL IN THE PRECONSCIOUS CAN BECOME CONSCIOUS IF WE DIRECT OUR ATTENTION TO IT. UNCONSCIOUS MATERIAL TENDS TO REMAIN SHROUDED IN MYSTERY.

Sigmund Freud was trained as a physician. Early in his practice he was astounded to find that some people apparently experienced loss of feeling in a hand or paralysis of the legs in the absence of any medical disorder. These odd symptoms often disappeared once the person recalled and discussed stressful events and feelings of guilt or anxiety that seemed to be related to the symptoms. For a long time, these events and feelings hid beneath the surface of awareness. Even so, they had the capacity to influence behavior.

From this sort of clinical evidence, Freud concluded that the human mind is like an iceberg. Only the tip of an iceberg rises above the surface of the water; the great mass of it is hidden in the depths (see Figure 10.1). Freud came to believe that people, similarly, are aware of only a small portion of the ideas and impulses that dwell within their minds. He argued that a much greater portion of the mind—our deepest images, thoughts, fears, and urges—remains beneath the surface of conscious awareness, where little light shines.

PRECONSCIOUS Capable of being brought into awareness by the focusing of attention.

UNCONSCIOUS In psychodynamic theory, not available to awareness by simple focusing of attention.

REPRESSION A defense mechanism that protects the person from anxiety by ejecting anxiety-evoking ideas and impulses from awareness.

REFLECT

Do you think that people have unconscious minds? If so, what would be in your unconscious mind? Explain.

✓ Truth or Fiction Revisited

According to Freud, it is true that the human mind is like a vast submerged iceberg. Only the top rises above the surface into conscious awareness. Most personality theorists place more emphasis on conscious thought than Freud did.

Freud labeled the region that pokes through into the light of awareness the *conscious* part of the mind. He called the regions below the surface the *preconscious* and the *unconscious*. The **preconscious** mind contains elements of experience that are out of awareness but can be made conscious simply by focusing on them. The **unconscious** mind is shrouded in mystery. It contains biological instincts such as sex and aggression. Some unconscious urges cannot be experienced consciously because mental images and words could not portray them in all their color and fury. Other unconscious urges may be kept below the surface through repression.

Repression is the automatic ejection of anxiety-evoking ideas from awareness. Research evidence suggests that many people repress bad childhood experiences (Myers & Brewin, 1994). Perhaps "something shocking happens, and the mind pushes it into some inaccessible corner of the unconscious" (Loftus, 1993). Repression is also theorized to protect us from awareness of morally unacceptable impulses within ourselves.

In the unconscious mind, primitive drives seek expression while internalized values try to keep them in check. The resulting conflict can arouse emotional outbursts and psychological problems.

To explore the unconscious mind, Freud engaged in a form of mental detective work called **psychoanalysis.** For this reason, his theory of personality is also referred to as *psychoanalytic theory.* In psychoanalysis, people are prodded to talk about anything that pops into their mind while they remain comfortable and relaxed. They may gain self-insight by pursuing some of the thoughts that pop into awareness. But they are also motivated to evade threatening subjects. The same repression that ejects unacceptable thoughts from awareness prompts *resistance,* or the desire to avoid thinking about or discussing those thoughts. Repression and resistance can make psychoanalysis a tedious process that lasts for years, or even decades.

THE STRUCTURE OF PERSONALITY Freud spoke of mental or **psychic structures** to describe the clashing forces of personality. Psychic structures cannot be seen or measured directly, but their presence is suggested by behavior, expressed thoughts, and emotions. Freud believed that there are three psychic structures: the id, the ego, and the superego.

The **id** is present at birth. It represents physiological drives and is entirely unconscious. Freud described the id as "a chaos, a cauldron of seething excitations" (1927/1964, p. 73). The conscious mind might find it inconsistent to love and hate the same person, but Freud believed that conflicting emotions could dwell side by side in the id. In the id, one can feel hatred for one's mother for failing to gratify immediately all of one's needs while also feeling love for her.

The id follows what Freud termed the *pleasure principle.* It demands instant gratification of instincts without consideration of law, social custom, or the needs of others.

The **ego** begins to develop during the first year of life, largely because a child's demands for gratification cannot all be met immediately. The ego stands for reason and good sense, for rational ways of coping with frustration. It curbs the appetites of the id and makes plans compatible with social convention. Thus a person can find gratification yet avoid social disapproval. The id lets you know you are hungry, but it is the ego that decides to microwave some enchiladas.

The ego is guided by the *reality principle.* It takes into account what is practical along with what is urged by the id. The ego also provides the person's conscious sense of self.

Although most of the ego is conscious, some of its business is carried out unconsciously. For instance, the ego also acts as a censor that screens the impulses of the id. When the ego senses that improper impulses are rising into awareness, it may use psychological defenses to prevent them from surfacing. Repression is one such psychological defense, or **defense mechanism.** Defense mechanisms operate unconsciously; that is, people are unaware of them. They do not solve people's problems; instead, they temporarily protect the ego by keeping impulses under wraps or distorting them so that they cannot be recognized for what they are. Several defense mechanisms are described in Table 10.1.

PSYCHOANALYSIS In this usage, Freud's method of exploring human personality.

PSYCHIC STRUCTURE In psychodynamic theory, a hypothesized mental structure that helps explain different aspects of behavior.

ID The psychic structure, present at birth, that represents physiological drives and is fully unconscious.

EGO The second psychic structure to develop, characterized by self-awareness, planning, and delay of gratification.

DEFENSE MECHANISM In psychodynamic theory, an unconscious function of the ego that protects it from anxiety-evoking material by preventing accurate recognition of this material.

TABLE 10.1	DEFENSE MECHANISMS	
DEFENSE MECHANISM	**DEFINITION**	**EXAMPLES**
Repression	Ejection of anxiety-evoking ideas from awareness.	• A student forgets that a difficult term paper is due. • A person in therapy forgets an appointment when anxiety-evoking material is to be discussed.
Regression	The return, under stress, to a form of behavior characteristic of an earlier stage of development.	• An adolescent cries when forbidden to use the family car. • An adult becomes highly dependent on his parents after the breakup of his marriage.
Rationalization	The use of self-deceiving justifications for unacceptable behavior.	• A student blames her cheating on her teacher's leaving the room during a test. • A man explains his cheating on his income tax by saying "Everyone does it."
Displacement	The transfer of ideas and impulses from threatening or unsuitable objects to less threatening objects.	• A worker picks a fight with her spouse after being sharply criticized by her supervisor.
Projection	The thrusting of one's own unacceptable impulses onto others so that others are assumed to have those impulses.	• A hostile person perceives the world as a dangerous place. • A sexually frustrated person interprets innocent gestures as sexual advances.
Reaction formation	Engaging in behavior that opposes one's genuine impulses in order to keep those impulses repressed.	• A person who is angry with a relative behaves in a "sickly sweet" manner toward that relative. • A sadistic individual becomes a physician.
Denial	The refusal to face the true nature of a threat.	• Belief that one will not contract cancer or heart disease even though one smokes heavily. • "It can't happen to me."
Sublimation	The channeling of primitive impulses into positive, constructive efforts.	• A person paints nudes for the sake of "beauty" and "art." • A hostile person becomes a tennis star.

SUPEREGO The third psychic structure, which functions as a moral guardian and sets forth high standards for behavior.

IDENTIFICATION In psychodynamic theory, the unconscious assumption of the behavior of another person.

REFLECT

Do you have a conscience? How do you think it developed? Is your conscience what Freud meant by a *superego?* Explain.

The **superego** develops throughout early childhood, usually incorporating the moral standards and values of parents and important members of the community through **identification**. The superego functions according to the *moral principle*. The superego holds forth shining examples of an ideal self and also acts like the conscience, an internal moral guardian. Throughout life, the superego monitors the intentions of the ego and hands out judgments of right and wrong. It floods the ego with feelings of guilt and shame when the verdict is negative.

The ego does not have an easy time of it. It stands between the id and the superego, striving to satisfy the demands of the id and the moral sense of the superego. From the Freudian perspective, a healthy personality has found ways to gratify most of the id's demands without seriously offending the superego. Most of the id's remaining demands are contained or repressed. If the ego is not a good problem solver or if the superego is too stern, the ego has a hard time of it.

STAGES OF PSYCHOSEXUAL DEVELOPMENT Freud stirred controversy by arguing that sexual impulses are a central factor in personality development, even among children. Freud believed that sexual feelings are closely linked to children's basic ways of relating to the world, such as sucking on their mother's breasts and moving their bowels.

Freud believed that a major instinct, which he termed **eros,** is aimed at preserving and perpetuating life. Eros is fueled by psychological, or psychic, energy, which Freud labeled **libido.** Libidinal energy involves sexual impulses, so Freud considered it *psychosexual.* As the child develops, libidinal energy is expressed through sexual feelings in different parts of the body, or **erogenous zones.** To Freud, human development involves the transfer of libidinal energy from one erogenous zone to another. He hypothesized that there are five periods of **psychosexual development:** oral, anal, phallic, latency, and genital.

During the first year of life a child experiences much of its world through the mouth. If it fits, into the mouth it goes. This is the **oral stage.** Freud argued that oral activities such as sucking and biting give the child sexual gratification as well as nourishment.

Freud believed that children encounter conflict during each stage of psychosexual development. During the oral stage, conflict centers on the nature and extent of oral gratification. Early weaning (cessation of breast feeding) could lead to frustration. Excessive gratification, on the other hand, could lead an infant to expect that it will routinely be given anything it wants. Insufficient or excessive gratification in any stage could lead to **fixation** in that stage and to the development of traits characteristic of that stage. Oral traits include dependency, gullibility, and excessive optimism or pessimism (depending on the child's experiences with gratification).

Freud theorized that adults with an *oral fixation* could experience exaggerated desires for "oral activities," such as smoking, overeating, alcohol abuse, and nail biting. Like the infant whose very survival depends on the mercy of an adult, adults with oral fixations may be disposed toward clinging, dependent relationships.

✓ Truth or Fiction Revisited

According to Freud, it is true that biting one's fingernails or smoking cigarettes as an adult is a sign of conflict during very early childhood. Freud believed that adult problems tend to have their origins in childhood conflicts that have long been lost to conscious awareness.

During the **anal stage** sexual gratification is attained through contraction and relaxation of the muscles that control elimination of waste products from the body. Elimination, which was controlled reflexively during most of the first year of life, comes under voluntary muscular control, even if such control is not reliable at first. (Complete control is usually not attained before the age of 2½.) The anal stage is said to begin in the second year of life.

During the anal stage children learn to delay the gratification that comes from eliminating as soon as they feel the urge. The general issue of self-control may become a source of conflict between parent and child. *Anal fixations* may stem from this conflict and lead to two sets of traits in adulthood. So-called *anal-retentive* traits involve excessive use of self-control. They include perfectionism, a strong need for order, and exaggerated

The Oral Stage? According to Sigmund Freud, during the first year the child is in the oral stage of development. If it fits, into the mouth it goes. What, according to Freud, are the effects of insufficient or excessive gratification during the oral stage? Is there evidence to support his views?

REFLECT

If you were fixated in a stage of psychosocial development, which stage would it be? Explain.

EROS In psychodynamic theory, the basic instinct to preserve and perpetuate life.

LIBIDO (1) In psychodynamic theory, the energy of Eros; the sexual instinct. (2) Generally, sexual interest or drive.

EROGENOUS ZONE An area of the body that is sensitive to sexual sensations.

PSYCHOSEXUAL DEVELOPMENT In psychodynamic theory, the process by which libidinal energy is expressed through different erogenous zones during different stages of development.

ORAL STAGE The first stage of psychosexual development, during which gratification is hypothesized to be attained primarily through oral activities.

FIXATION In psychodynamic theory, arrested development. Attachment to objects of an earlier stage.

ANAL STAGE The second stage of psychosexual development, when gratification is attained through anal activities.

REFLECT

Have you ever heard anyone referred to as "anal"? What did the term mean? How does the usage relate to Freudian theory?

REFLECT

At what age do you believe children should be toilet-trained? Why?

PHALLIC STAGE The third stage of psychosexual development, characterized by a shift of libido to the phallic region. (From the Greek *phallos*, referring to an image of the penis. However, Freud used the term *phallic* to refer both to boys and girls.)

CLITORIS An external female sex organ that is highly sensitive to sexual stimulation.

OEDIPUS COMPLEX A conflict of the phallic stage in which the boy wishes to possess his mother sexually and perceives his father as a rival in love.

ELECTRA COMPLEX A conflict of the phallic stage in which the girl longs for her father and resents her mother.

CASTRATION ANXIETY Within Freudian theory, fear that one's genital organs will be cut off. Castration anxiety is a normal feature of the Oedipus complex that motivates boys to forego their rivalry with their fathers over possession of their mothers.

DISPLACED Transferred.

LATENCY A phase of psychosexual development characterized by repression of sexual impulses.

GENITAL STAGE The mature stage of psychosexual development, characterized by preferred expression of libido through intercourse with an adult of the other gender.

REFLECT

Were you familiar with any Freudian ideas before you read this book? Which ones? Are they consistent with what you read here?

neatness and cleanliness. *Anal-expulsive* traits, on the other hand, "let it all hang out." They include carelessness, messiness, even sadism.

Children enter the **phallic stage** during the third year of life. During this stage the major erogenous zone is the phallic region (the penis in boys and the **clitoris** in girls). Parent–child conflict is likely to develop over masturbation, to which parents may respond with threats or punishment. During the phallic stage children may develop strong sexual attachments to the parent of the other gender and begin to view the parent of the same gender as a rival for the other parent's affections. Thus boys may want to marry Mommy and girls may want to marry Daddy.

Children have difficulty dealing with feelings of lust and jealousy. Home life would be tense indeed if they were aware of them. These feelings, therefore, remain unconscious, but their influence is felt through fantasies about marriage with the parent of the other gender and hostility toward the parent of the same gender. In boys, this conflict is labeled the **Oedipus complex,** after the legendary Greek king who unwittingly killed his father and married his mother. Similar feelings in girls give rise to the **Electra complex.** According to Greek legend, Electra was the daughter of the king Agamemnon. She longed for him after his death and sought revenge against his slayers—her mother and her mother's lover.

The case of "Little Hans" illustrates some of the Oedipus complex. Hans was a 5-year-old Viennese boy who came to Freud's attention in 1908. Hans's distraught father wrote to Freud that Hans would not leave the house because he had become convinced that horses were biting people in the streets. Freud psychoanalyzed Hans's fear of horses *by mail.* Freud concluded that the horses were symbols. They represented Hans's father. Being bitten symbolized being castrated. In other words, Hans unconsciously feared that his father would castrate him. Why? Because Hans was his father's rival in his affection for his mother. **Castration anxiety,** according to Freud, was a normal part of the Oedipus complex, and it motivated boys to surrender their mothers as love objects.

The Oedipus and Electra complexes are resolved by about the ages of 5 or 6. Children then repress their hostilities toward the parent of the same gender and begin to identify with her or him. Identification leads them to play the social and gender roles of that parent and to internalize his or her values. Sexual feelings toward the parent of the other gender are repressed for a number of years. When the feelings emerge again during adolescence, they are **displaced,** or transferred, to socially appropriate members of the other gender.

Freud believed that by the age of 5 or 6, children have been in conflict with their parents over sexual feelings for several years. The pressures of the Oedipus and Electra complexes cause them to repress all sexual urges. In so doing, they enter a period of **latency** during which their sexual feelings remain unconscious. During the latency phase it is not uncommon for children to prefer playmates of their own gender.

Freud believed that we enter the final stage of psychosexual development, the **genital stage**, at puberty. Adolescent males again experience sexual urges toward their mother and adolescent females experience such urges toward their father. However, the incest taboo causes them to repress these impulses and displace them onto other adults or adolescents of the other gender. Boys might seek girls "just like the girl that married dear old Dad," as the song goes. Girls might be attracted to boys who resemble their fathers.

People in the genital stage prefer, by definition, to find sexual gratification through intercourse with a member of the other gender. In Freud's view, oral or anal stimulation, masturbation, and sexual activity with people of the same gender all represent *pregenital* fixations and immature forms of sexual conduct. They are not consistent with the life instinct, eros.

Other Psychodynamic Theorists

Several personality theorists are among Freud's intellectual heirs. Their theories, like his, include dynamic movement of psychological forces, conflict, and defensive responses to anxiety that involve repression and cognitive distortion of reality. In other respects, however, their theories differ considerably. Questions: Who are some other psychodynamic theorists? What are their views on personality?

CARL JUNG Carl Jung (1875–1961) was a Swiss psychiatrist who had been a member of Freud's inner circle. He fell into disfavor with Freud when he developed his own psychodynamic theory. In contrast to Freud (for whom, he said, "the brain is viewed as an appendage of the genital organs"), Jung downplayed the importance of the sexual instinct. He saw it as just one of several important instincts.

Jung, like Freud, was intrigued by unconscious processes. He believed we not only have a *personal* unconscious that contains repressed memories and impulses but also an inherited **collective unconscious.** The collective unconscious contains primitive images, or **archetypes,** that reflect the history of our species. Examples of archetypes are the all-powerful God, the young hero, the fertile and nurturing mother, the wise old man, the hostile brother—even fairy godmothers, wicked witches, and themes of rebirth or resurrection. Archetypes themselves remain unconscious, but Jung declared that they influence our thoughts and emotions and cause us to respond to cultural themes in stories and films.

ALFRED ADLER Alfred Adler (1870–1937), another follower of Freud, also felt that Freud had placed too much emphasis on sexual impulses. Adler believed that people are basically motivated by an **inferiority complex.** In some people, feelings of inferiority may be based on physical problems and the need to compensate for them. Adler believed, however, that all of us encounter some feelings of inferiority because of our small size as children, and that these feelings give rise to a **drive for superiority.** For instance, the English poet Lord Byron, who had a crippled leg, became a champion swimmer. As a child Adler was crippled by rickets and suffered from pneumonia, and it may be that his theory developed in part from his own childhood striving to overcome repeated bouts of illness.

Adler believed that self-awareness plays a major role in the formation of personality. He spoke of a **creative self,** a self-aware aspect of personality that strives to overcome obstacles and develop the individual's potential.

KAREN HORNEY Karen Horney (1885–1952) agreed with Freud that childhood experiences play a major role in the development of adult personality. But she believed that sexual and aggressive impulses take a back seat in importance to social relationships. She agreed with Freud that parent–child relationships are paramount in importance. Small children are completely dependent. When parents treat them with indifference or harshness, they develop feelings of insecurity and anxiety. Children also resent neglectful parents, so anxious children are also often hostile. Like Freud, Horney thought that children repress rather than express feelings of hostility toward their parents because of fear of reprisal and, just as important, fear of driving them away. But in contrast to Freud, she also

COLLECTIVE UNCONSCIOUS Jung's hypothesized store of vague racial memories.

ARCHETYPES Basic, primitive images or concepts hypothesized by Jung to reside in the collective unconscious.

INFERIORITY COMPLEX Feelings of inferiority hypothesized by Adler to serve as a central motivating force.

DRIVE FOR SUPERIORITY Adler's term for the desire to compensate for feelings of inferiority.

CREATIVE SELF According to Adler, the self-aware aspect of personality that strives to achieve its full potential.

Karen Horney

Erik Erikson

believed that genuine and consistent love could soften the effects of the most traumatic childhood (Quinn, 1987).

ERIK ERIKSON   Erik Erikson (1902–1994) also believed that Freud had placed undue emphasis on sexual instincts. He asserted that social relationships are more crucial determinants of personality than sexual urges. To Erikson, the nature of the mother–infant relationship is more important than the details of the feeding process or the sexual feelings that might be stirred by contact with the mother. Erikson also argued that to a large extent we are the conscious architects of our own personalities. His view grants more powers to the ego than Freud did. In Erikson's theory, it is possible for us to make real choices. In Freud's theory, we may think we are making choices but may actually be merely rationalizing the compromises forced on us by internal conflicts.

Erikson, like Freud, is known for devising a comprehensive theory of personality development. But whereas Freud proposed stages of psycho-*sexual* development, Erikson proposed stages of psycho*social* development. Rather than label stages for various erogenous zones, Erikson labeled them for the traits that might be developed within them. Each stage is named according to its possible outcomes. For example, the first stage of **psychosocial development** is labeled the stage of *trust versus mistrust* because of its two possible outcomes: (1) A warm, loving relationship with the mother (and others) during infancy might lead to a sense of basic trust in people and the world. (2) Or a cold, ungratifying relationship might generate a pervasive sense of mistrust. Erikson believed that most people would wind up with some blend of trust and mistrust—hopefully more trust than mistrust. A basic sense of mistrust could interfere with the formation of relationships unless it was recognized and challenged.

For Erikson, the goal of adolescence is the attainment of **ego identity**, not genital sexuality. The focus is on who we see ourselves as being and what we stand for, not on sexual interests.

Evaluation of the Psychodynamic Perspective

Psychodynamic theories have tremendous appeal. They involve many concepts and explain many varieties of human behavior and traits. Question: What are the strengths and weaknesses of the psychodynamic perspective?

Although today concepts such as "the id" and "libido" strike many psychologists as unscientific, Freud fought for the idea that human personality and behavior are subject to scientific analysis. He developed his theories at a time when many people still viewed psychological problems as signs of possession by the devil or evil spirits, as they had during the Middle Ages. Freud argued that psychological disorders stem from problems within the individual—not evil spirits. His thinking contributed to the development of compassion for people with psychological disorders and methods for helping them.

Psychodynamic theory has also focused attention on the far-reaching effects of childhood events. Freud and other psychodynamic theorists are to be credited for suggesting that personality and behavior *develop* and that it is important for parents to be aware of the emotional needs of their children.

Freud helped us recognize that sexual and aggressive urges are commonplace and that there is a difference between acknowledging these urges and acting on them. As W. Bertram Wolfe put it, "Freud found sex an outcast in the outhouse, and left it in the living room an honored guest."

Freud also noted that people have defensive ways of looking at the world. His list of defense mechanisms has become part of everyday speech. Whether or not we attribute these cognitive distortions to uncon-

PSYCHOSOCIAL DEVELOPMENT Erikson's theory of personality and development, which emphasizes social relationships and eight stages of growth.

EGO IDENTITY A firm sense of who one is and what one stands for.

scious ego functioning, our thinking may be distorted by our efforts to avert anxiety and guilt. If these concepts no longer strike us as innovative, it is largely because of Freud's influence. Psychodynamic theorists also developed many methods of therapy.

Critics note that "psychic structures" such as the id, ego, and superego are too vague to measure scientifically (Hergenhahn, 1997). Nor can they be used to predict behavior with precision. They are little more than useful fictions—poetic ways to express inner conflict. Freud's critics thus have the right to write other "poems"—that is, to use other descriptive terms.

Nor have the stages of psychosexual development escaped criticism. Children begin to masturbate as early as the first year, not in the phallic stage. As parents know from discovering their children playing "doctor," the latency stage is not as sexually latent as Freud believed. Much of Freud's thinking about the Oedipus and Electra complexes remains little more than speculation. The evidence for some of Erikson's developmental views seems somewhat sturdier. For example, people who fail to develop ego identity in adolescence seem to encounter problems developing intimate relationships later on.

Freud's method of gathering evidence from clinical sessions is also suspect (Hergenhahn, 1997). In subtle ways, therapists may influence clients to produce memories and feelings they expect to find. Therapists may also fail to separate what they are told from their own interpretations. Also, Freud and many other psychodynamic theorists restricted their evidence gathering to case studies with individuals who sought help for psychological problems. Their clients were also mostly White and from the middle and upper classes. People who seek therapy are likely to have more problems than the general population.

REFLECT

If Freud's theory has so many scientific problems, why do you think it remains popular in the general population?

Review

SECTION II

Each psychodynamic theory owes its thinking to Sigmund (3) _____. Psychodynamic theories of personality teach that personality is characterized by (4) c_____ between primitive drives on the one hand, and laws, social rules, and moral codes on the other.

Freud believed that the mind had conscious, preconscious, and (5) _____scious parts. Freud labeled the clashing forces of personality (6) _____ic structures. He hypothesized the existence of (7: How many?) psychic structures. The unconscious (8) _____ is the psychic structure present at birth. The id represents psychological drives and operates according to the (9) pl_____ principle, seeking instant gratification. The structure called the (10) _____ is the sense of self, or "I." The ego develops through experience and operates according to the (11) re_____ principle. The ego uses (12) _____ mechanisms such as repression to protect itself from anxiety. The (13) _____ego is the moral sense. It develops by internalizing the standards of parents and others by means of (14) _____fication. The superego operates according to the (15) _____ principle.

People undergo (16: How many?) _____ stages of psychosexual development, during which psychosexual energy, called (17) l_____, is transferred from one (18) _____nous zone to another during childhood. The stages of psychosexual development include the oral, (19) _____, phallic, (20) _____, and genital stages.

(21) _____tion in a stage may lead to the development of traits associated with that stage. Fixation in the oral stage may lead to oral traits such as (22) dep_____ and (23) gull_____. Anal fixation may result in extremes of (24) cl_____ness versus messiness, or of (25) per_____ism versus carelessness.

The Oedipus and Electra complexes are conflicts of the (26) _____ic stage. In these conflicts, children long to possess the parent of the (27: Same or Other?) gender and resent the parent of the (28: Same or Other?) gender. These complexes are theorized to be resolved by identifying with the parent of the (29: Same or Other?) gender.

Carl Jung's psychodynamic theory is called (30) _____cal psychology. Jung believed that in addition to a personal unconscious mind, we also have a (31) _____tive unconscious. Alfred Adler's psychodynamic theory is called (32) _____ual psychology. Adler believed that people are motivated by an (33) _____ity complex and a compensating drive for superiority. Karen (34) H_____, like Freud, saw parent–child relationships as paramount in importance. When parents treat children indifferently or harshly, the children develop feelings of insecurity that Horney labeled basic (35) _____ty. Erik Erikson's psychodynamic theory is called the theory of (36) psycho_____ development. Erikson extended Freud's five developmental stages to (37: How many?) _____ and named them according to their possible outcomes. His first stage is the stage of (38) _____ versus mistrust, and his adolescent stage is that of (39) _____ _____ versus role diffusion.

SECTION III. THE TRAIT PERSPECTIVE

The notion of **traits** is very familiar. If I asked you to describe yourself, you would probably do so in terms of traits such as bright, sophisticated, and witty. (That is you, is it not?) We also describe other people in terms of traits.

Question: What are traits? Traits are reasonably stable elements of personality that are inferred from behavior. If you describe a friend as "shy," it may be because you have observed social anxiety or withdrawal in that person's encounters with others. Traits are assumed to account for consistent behavior in diverse situations. You probably expect your "shy" friend to be retiring in most social confrontations—"all across the board," as the saying goes. The concept of traits is also found in other approaches to personality. Recall that Freud linked the development of certain traits to children's experiences in each stage of psychosexual development.

REFLECT

How would you describe yourself in terms of traits? What is the evidence for your list of traits?

From Hippocrates to the Present

Question: What is the history of the trait perspective? The trait approach dates back to the Greek physician Hippocrates (c. 460–377 B.C.E.) and could be even older (Maher & Maher, 1994). It has generally been assumed that traits are embedded in people's bodies, but *how?* Hippocrates believed that traits are embedded in bodily fluids, which give rise to certain types of personalities. In his view, an individual's personality depends on the balance of four basic fluids, or "humors," in the body. Yellow bile is associated with a choleric (quick-tempered) disposition; blood with a sanguine (warm, cheerful) one; phlegm with a phlegmatic (sluggish, calm, cool) disposition; and black bile with a melancholic (gloomy, pensive) temperament. Disease was believed to reflect an imbalance among the humors. Methods such as bloodletting and vomiting were recommended to restore the balance (Maher & Maher, 1994). Although Hippocrates' theory was pure speculation, the terms *choleric, sanguine,* and so on are still used in descriptions of personality.

✓ Truth or Fiction Revisited

It is true that bloodletting and vomiting were once recommended ways of coping with depression. Hippocrates and others believed that depression was caused by an excess of black bile, and bloodletting and vomiting were thought to be ways of restoring a proper balance of bodily fluids.

TRAIT A relatively stable aspect of personality that is inferred from behavior and assumed to give rise to consistent behavior.

More enduring trait theories assume that traits are heritable and embedded in the nervous system. They rely on the mathematical technique of factor analysis in attempting to determine basic human traits.

Sir Francis Galton was among the first scientists to suggest that many of the world's languages use single words to describe fundamental differences in personality. More than 50 years ago, Gordon Allport and a colleague (Allport & Oddbert, 1936) catalogued some 18,000 human traits from a search through word lists like dictionaries. Some were physical traits such as *short, black,* and *brunette.* Others were behavioral traits such as *shy* and *emotional.* Still others were moral traits such as *honest.* This exhaustive list has served as the basis for personality research by many other psychologists. Question: How have contemporary researchers used factor analysis to reduce the universe of traits to smaller lists of traits that show common features?

Hans Eysenck

One contemporary researcher, British psychologist Hans J. Eysenck (Eysenck & Eysenck, 1985), used factor analysis to reduce the universe of traits to two key dimensions: **introversion–extraversion** and emotional stability–instability. (Emotional *in*stability is also known as **neuroticism.**) Carl Jung was the first to distinguish between introverts and extraverts. Eysenck added the dimension of emotional stability–instability to introversion–extraversion. He has catalogued various personality traits according to where they are situated along these dimensions or factors (see Figure 10.2). For instance, an anxious person would be high in both introversion and neuroticism—that is, preoccupied with his or her own thoughts and emotionally unstable.

INTROVERSION A trait characterized by intense imagination and the tendency to inhibit impulses.
EXTRAVERSION A trait characterized by tendencies to be socially outgoing and to express feelings and impulses freely.

NEUROTICISM Eysenck's term for emotional instability.

REFLECT

Where would you place athletes and artists in terms of the dimensions of introversion–extraversion and emotional stability? Where would you place yourself?

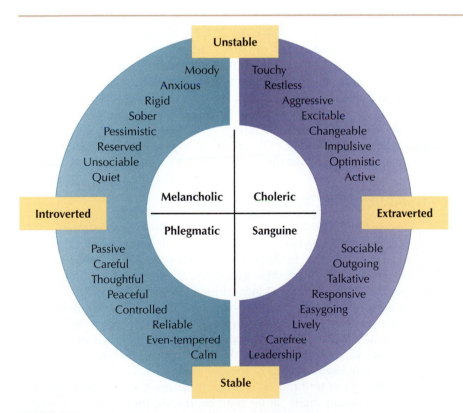

FIGURE 10.2
EYSENCK'S PERSONALITY DIMENSIONS AND HIPPOCRATES' PERSONALITY TYPES VARIOUS PERSONALITY TRAITS SHOWN IN THE OUTER RING FALL WITHIN THE TWO MAJOR DIMENSIONS OF PERSONALITY SUGGESTED BY HANS EYSENCK. THE INNER CIRCLE SHOWS HOW HIPPOCRATES' FOUR MAJOR PERSONALITY TYPES—CHOLERIC, SANGUINE, PHLEGMATIC, AND MELANCHOLIC—FIT WITHIN EYSENCK'S DIMENSIONS.

TABLE 10.2	THE FIVE-FACTOR MODEL	
FACTOR	**NAME**	**TRAITS**
I	Extraversion	Contrasts talkativeness, assertiveness, and activity with silence, passivity, and reserve
II	Agreeableness	Contrasts kindness, trust, and warmth with hostility, selfishness, and distrust
III	Conscientiousness	Contrasts organization, thoroughness, and reliability with carelessness, negligence, and unreliability
IV	Neuroticism	Contrasts traits such as nervousness, moodiness, and sensitivity to negative stimuli with coping ability
V	Openness to Experience	Contrasts imagination, curiosity, and creativity with shallowness and lack of perceptiveness

Eysenck notes that his scheme is reminiscent of that suggested by Hippocrates. According to Eysenck's dimensions, the choleric type would be extraverted and unstable; the sanguine type, extraverted and stable; the phlegmatic type, introverted and stable; and the melancholic type, introverted and unstable.

The Five-Factor Model

More recent research suggests that there are five basic personality factors (McCrae, 1996). These include the two found by Eysenck—extraversion and neuroticism—along with conscientiousness, agreeableness, and openness to new experience (see Table 10.2). Many personality theorists, especially Louis Thurstone, Donald Fiske, Robert McCrae, and Paul T. Costa, Jr., have played a role in the development of the five-factor model. The five-factor model has found applications in areas such as personnel selection and classification, and in the study of psychological disorders (Clark et al., 1994; Widiger & Costa, 1994). Moreover, cross-cultural research has found that these five factors appear to define the personality structure of American, German, Portuguese, Hebrew, Chinese, Korean, and Japanese people (McCrae & Costa, 1997). Yet many psychologists still disagree on the number of basic personality factors (Block, 1995; Zuckerman, 1992).

Evaluation of the Trait Perspective

Trait theories, like psychodynamic theories, have both strengths and weaknesses. Question: What are the strengths and weaknesses of trait theory? Trait theorists have focused much attention on the development of personality tests. They have also given rise to theories about the fit between personality and certain kinds of jobs (Holland, 1996). The qualities that suit a person for various kinds of work can be expressed in terms of abilities, personality traits, and interests. By using interviews and tests to learn about an individual's abilities and traits, testing and counseling centers can make valuable suggestions about that person's chances of success and fulfillment in various kinds of jobs.

One limitation of trait theory is that it is descriptive, not explanatory. It focuses on describing traits rather than on tracing their origins or finding out how they may be modified. Moreover, the "explanations" provided by trait theory are often criticized as being *circular*. That is, they restate what is observed and do not explain it. Saying that John failed to ask Marsha on a date *because* of shyness is an example of a circular explanation: We have merely restated John's (shy) behavior as a trait (shyness).

REFLECT

Are you conscientious? Are you open to new experience? Is there such a thing as being *too* conscientious? As being *too* open to new experience? Explain.

Review

SECTION III

Traits are personality elements that are inferred from
(40) _____ior. Traits are said to endure and to account
for behavioral (41) _____ency. Hippocrates believed
that there were (42: How many?) _____ basic traits
and that each was based on the presence of a bodily fluid
(humor). Allport and Odbert catalogued 18,000 human traits
from a search through word lists of the sort found in
(43) _____aries.

Hans (44) E_____ has used mathematical techniques
to reduce the universe of traits to two basic traits: introversion–extraversion and emotional (45) _____ity (also
called *neuroticism*). More recent research suggests that
there may be five basic personality factors: introversion–
extraversion, emotional stability, (46) con_____, agreeableness, and (47) _____ness to new experience.

SECTION IV. LEARNING-THEORY PERSPECTIVES

Learning theory not only contributes to our understanding of the acquisition of behavior. It also contributes to our understanding of personality.
Question: What does learning theory have to contribute to our understanding of personality? In this section we focus on the contributions of
two learning-theory approaches to personality: behaviorism and social-
cognitive theory.

Behaviorism

You have freedom when you're easy in your harness.

ROBERT FROST

In 1924, at Johns Hopkins University, John B. Watson raised the battle cry
of the behaviorist movement:

> Give me a dozen healthy infants, well-formed, and my own speci-
> fied world to bring them up in and I'll guarantee to take any one at
> random and train him to become any type of specialist I might sug-
> gest—doctor, lawyer, merchant-chief and, yes, even beggar-man
> and thief, regardless of his talents, penchants, tendencies, abilities,
> vocations, and the race of his ancestors. (p. 82)

Question: What is Watson's contribution to personality theory?
Watson's view is extreme and inconsistent with the thrust of evidence
concerning the heritability of various personality traits. But his proclama-
tion underscores the behaviorist view that personality is plastic—that situational variables or environmental influences, not internal, individual
variables, are the key shapers of human preferences and behaviors. In contrast to the psychoanalysts and structuralists of his day, Watson argued
that unseen, undetectable mental structures must be rejected in favor of
that which can be seen and measured.

✓ **Truth or Fiction Revisited**

*Although the environment has effects, it is not true that by environmental
control alone a child can be reared to be a "doctor, lawyer, merchant-chief,"*

or a beggar or a thief. Genetic factors are also involved in personality development, and it does not appear that everyone inherits traits that enable him or her to succeed in any and every walk of life.

In the 1930s Watson's battle cry was taken up by B. F. Skinner, who agreed that psychologists should avoid trying to see into the "black box" of the organism and instead emphasized the effects of reinforcement on behavior.

The views of Watson and Skinner largely ignored the notions of personal freedom, choice, and self-direction. Most of us assume that our wants originate within. But Skinner suggested that environmental influences such as parental approval and social custom shape us into *wanting* certain things and *not wanting* others.

Question: How did Skinner develop Watson's views? In his novel *Walden Two*, Skinner (1948) described a utopian society in which people are happy and content because they are allowed to do as they please. However, from early childhood, they have been trained or conditioned to be cooperative. Because of their reinforcement histories, they *want* to behave in decent, kind, and unselfish ways. They see themselves as free because society makes no effort to force them to behave in particular ways.

Some object to behaviorist notions because they play down the importance of consciousness and choice. Others argue that humans are not blindly ruled by pleasure and pain. In some circumstances people have rebelled against the so-called necessity of survival by choosing pain and hardship over pleasure, or death over life. Many people have sacrificed their own lives to save those of others.

The behaviorist defense might be that the apparent choice of pain or death is forced on altruistic individuals just as conformity to social custom is forced on others. The altruist is also shaped by external influences, even if those influences differ from those that affect many other people.

Social-Cognitive Theory

Social-cognitive theory[1] is a contemporary view of learning developed by Albert Bandura (1986) and other psychologists (e.g., Mischel & Shoda, 1995). It focuses on the importance of learning by observation and on the cognitive processes that underlie individual differences. Question: How does social-cognitive theory differ from the behaviorist view? Social-cognitive theorists differ from behaviorists in that they see people as influencing their environment just as their environment influences them. Bandura terms this mutual pattern of influence **reciprocal determinism.** Social-cognitive theorists agree with behaviorists and other empirical psychologists that discussions of human nature should be tied to observable experiences and behaviors. They assert, however, that variables within people—which they call **person variables**—must also be considered if we are to understand them.

One goal of psychological theories is the prediction of behavior. We cannot predict behavior from situational variables alone. Whether a person will behave in a certain way also depends on the person's **expectancies** about the outcomes of that behavior and the perceived or **subjective values** of those outcomes.

To social-cognitive theorists, people are not simply at the mercy of the environment. Instead, they are self-aware and purposefully engage in

---

REFLECT

Given cultural and social conditioning, is true freedom possible? To behaviorists, even our telling ourselves that we have free will is determined by the environment. Is free will merely an illusion? What is the evidence for your belief?

SOCIAL-COGNITIVE THEORY A cognitively oriented learning theory in which observational learning and person variables such as values and expectancies play major roles in individual differences. Also referred to as *social-learning theory.*

RECIPROCAL DETERMINISM Bandura's term for the social-cognitive view that people influence their environment just as their environment influences them.

PERSON VARIABLES Factors within the person, such as expectancies and competencies, that influence behavior.

EXPECTANCIES Personal predictions about the outcomes of potential behaviors.

SUBJECTIVE VALUE The desirability of an object or event.

MODEL In social-cognitive theory, an organism that exhibits behaviors that others will imitate or acquire through observational learning.

COMPETENCIES Knowledge and skills.

---

[1] The name of this theory remains unsettled. It was formerly referred to as social-learning theory. Today it is also sometimes referred to as *cognitive social theory.*

learning. They seek to learn about their environment and to alter it in order to make reinforcers available.

OBSERVATIONAL LEARNING Observational learning (also termed **modeling** or *cognitive learning*) refers to acquiring knowledge by observing others. Observing others extends to reading about them or seeing what they do and what happens to them in books, TV, radio, and film.

Our expectations stem from our observations of what happens to ourselves and other people. For example, teachers are more likely to call on males and more accepting of "calling out" in class by males than by females (Sadker & Sadker, 1994). As a result, many males expect to be rewarded for calling out. Females, however, may learn that they will be reprimanded for behaving in what some might term an "unladylike" manner.

Social-cognitive theorists believe that behavior reflects person variables and situational variables. Person variables include competencies, encoding strategies, expectancies, emotions, and self-regulatory systems and plans (Mischel & Shoda, 1995; see Figure 10.3).

COMPETENCIES: WHAT CAN YOU DO? **Competencies** include knowledge of rules that guide conduct, concepts about ourselves and other people, and skills. Our ability to use information to make plans depends on our competencies. Knowledge of the physical world and of cultural codes of conduct are important competencies. So are academic skills such as reading and writing, athletic skills such as swimming and tossing a football, social skills such as knowing how to ask someone out on a date, and

How Do Competencies Contribute to Performance? What factors contribute to this girl's performance on the balance beam? Individual differences in competencies stem from variations in genetic endowment, nutrition, and learning opportunities.

REFLECT

What competencies do you have? How did they develop?

FIGURE 10.3

PERSON VARIABLES AND SITUATIONAL VARIABLES IN SOCIAL-COGNITIVE THEORY ACCORDING TO SOCIAL-COGNITIVE THEORY, PERSON VARIABLES AND SITUATIONAL VARIABLES INTERACT TO INFLUENCE BEHAVIOR.

many others. Individual differences in competencies reflect genetic variation, learning opportunities, and other environmental factors.

ENCODING STRATEGIES: HOW DO YOU SEE IT? Different people **encode** (symbolize or represent) the same stimuli in different ways. Their encoding strategies are an important factor in their behavior. One person might encode a tennis game as a chance to bat the ball back and forth and have some fun. Another person might encode the game as a demand to perfect his or her serve. One person might encode a date that doesn't work out as a sign of personal or social incompetence. Another person might encode the date as reflecting the fact that people are not always "made for each other."

Some people make themselves miserable by encoding events in self-defeating ways. A linebacker may encode an average day on the field as a failure because he did not make any sacks. Cognitive therapists foster adjustment by challenging people to view life in more optimistic ways.

REFLECT

Do you expect that you will succeed? Do you believe in your abilities? How do your attitudes toward yourself affect your self-esteem and your behavior?

EXPECTANCIES: WHAT WILL HAPPEN? There are various kinds of expectancies. Some are predictions about what will follow various stimuli or signs. For example, some people predict other people's behavior on the basis of signs such as "tight lips" or "shifty eyes." Other expectancies involve what will happen if we engage in certain behaviors. **Self-efficacy expectations** are beliefs that we can accomplish certain things, such as speaking before a group, doing a backflip into a swimming pool, or solving math problems (Pajares & Miller, 1994).

Competencies influence expectancies. Expectancies, in turn, influence motivation to perform. People with positive self-efficacy expectations are more likely to try difficult tasks than people who do not believe they can master those tasks. One way that psychotherapy helps people is by changing their self-efficacy expectations from "I can't" to "I can" (Bandura, 1986). As a result, people are motivated to try new things.

✓ Truth or Fiction Revisited

It is true that we are more likely to persist at difficult tasks when we believe we will succeed. Positive self-efficacy expectations motivate us to persevere.

ENCODE Interpret; transform.

SELF-EFFICACY EXPECTATIONS Beliefs to the effect that one can handle a task.

EMOTIONS: HOW DOES IT FEEL? Because of our different learning histories, similar situations can arouse different feelings in us—anxiety, depression, fear, hopelessness, and anger. What frightens one person may entice another. What bores one person may excite another. From the social-cognitive perspective, in contrast to the behaviorist perspective, we are not controlled by stimuli. Instead, stimuli arouse feelings in us, and feelings influence our behavior. Hearing Chopin may make one person weep and another person switch to a rock 'n' roll station.

REFLECT

How do you regulate your own behavior to help achieve your goals?

SELF-REGULATORY SYSTEMS AND PLANS: HOW CAN YOU ACHIEVE IT? We tend to regulate our own behavior, even in the absence of observers and external constraints. We set our own goals and standards. We make plans to achieve them. We congratulate or criticize ourselves, depending on whether or not we achieve them (Bandura, 1986).

Self-regulation helps us influence our environments. We can select the situations to which we expose ourselves and the arenas in which we will compete. Depending on our expectancies, we may choose to enter the academic or athletic worlds. We may choose marriage or the single life. And when we cannot readily select our environment, we can to some degree select our responses within an environment—even an aversive one. For example, if we are undergoing an uncomfortable medical procedure, we may try to reduce the stress by focusing on something else—an inner fantasy or an environmental feature such as the cracks in the tiles on the ceiling. This is one of the techniques used in prepared or "natural" childbirth.

Evaluation of Learning-Theory Perspectives

Learning theorists have made monumental contributions to the scientific understanding of behavior, but they have left some psychologists dissatisfied. Question: What are the strengths and weaknesses of learning theories as they apply to personality?

Psychodynamic theorists and trait theorists propose the existence of psychological structures that cannot be seen and measured directly. Learning theorists—particularly behaviorists—have dramatized the importance of referring to publicly observable variables, or behaviors, if psychology is to be accepted as a science.

Similarly, psychodynamic theorists and trait theorists focus on internal variables such as unconscious conflict and traits to explain and predict behavior. Learning theorists emphasize the importance of environmental conditions, or situational variables, as determinants of behavior. They have also elaborated on the conditions that foster learning—even automatic kinds of learning. They have shown that we can learn to do things because of reinforcements and that many behavior patterns are acquired by observing others.

On the other hand, behaviorism is limited in its ability to explain personality. It does not describe, explain, or even suggest the richness of inner human experience. We experience thoughts and feelings and browse through our complex inner maps of the world, but behaviorism does not deal with these. To be fair, however, the so-called limitations of behaviorism are self-imposed. Personality theorists have traditionally dealt with thoughts, feelings, and behavior, whereas behaviorism deals with behavior alone.

Critics of social-cognitive theory cannot accuse its supporters of denying the importance of cognitive activity and feelings. But they often contend that social-cognitive theory has not come up with satisfying statements about the development of traits or accounted for self-awareness. Also, social-cognitive theory—like its intellectual predecessor, behaviorism—may not pay enough attention to genetic variation in explaining individual differences in behavior. Learning theories have done very little to account for the development of traits or personality types.

Review

SECTION IV

The behaviorists John B. Watson and B. F. (48) _____ discarded notions of personal freedom and argued that environmental contingencies can shape people into wanting to do the things that the physical environment and society requires of them. Social-cognitive theory, in contrast to behaviorism, has a strong (49) cog_____ orientation and focuses on the importance of learning by (50) _____tion.

Social-cognitive theorists believe that we must consider both situational variables and (51) _____ variables to predict behavior. Person variables include the following: (52) co_____cies, which refers to knowledge and skill; (53) en_____ing strategies, which refers to our interpretation of events; expectancies, which refers to our "if-then" cognitions; emotions, or our feelings about events and possible outcomes; and (54) self-_____tory systems and plans. Bandura refers to beliefs that one can handle a task as (55) self-_____ expectations. We are (56: More or Less?) likely to persist at difficult tasks when we have positive self-efficacy expectations.

SECTION V. THE HUMANISTIC-EXISTENTIAL PERSPECTIVE

You are unique, and if that is not fulfilled, then something has been lost.

MARTHA GRAHAM

Humanists and existentialists dwell on the meaning of life. Self-awareness is the hub of the humanistic-existential search for meaning. Questions: What is humanism? What is existentialism?

The term **humanism** has a long history and many meanings. It became a third force in American psychology in the 1950s and 1960s, partly in response to the predominant psychodynamic and behavioral models. Humanism puts people and self-awareness at the center of consideration and argues that they are capable of free choice, self-fulfillment, and ethical behavior. Humanism also represented a reaction to the "rat race" spawned by industrialization and automation. Humanists felt that work on assembly lines produced "alienation" from inner sources of meaning. The humanistic views of Abraham Maslow and Carl Rogers emerged from these concerns.

Existentialism in part reflects the horrors of mass destruction of human life through war and genocide, frequent events in the 20th century. The European existentialist philosophers Jean-Paul Sartre and Martin Heidegger saw human life as trivial in the grand scheme of things. But psychiatrists like Viktor Frankl, Ludwig Binswanger, and Medard Boss argued that seeing human existence as meaningless could give rise to withdrawal and apathy—even suicide. Psychological salvation therefore requires giving personal meaning to things and making personal choices. Yes, there is pain in life, and yes, sooner or later life ends, but people can see the world for what it is and make genuine choices.

Freud argued that defense mechanisms prevent us from seeing the world as it is. Therefore, the concept of free choice is meaningless. Behaviorists view freedom as an illusion determined by social forces. To existentialists, we are really and painfully free to do what we choose with our lives. Moreover, the meaning of our lives is the meaning that we give to our lives.

Abraham Maslow and the Challenge of Self-Actualization

Humanists see Freud as preoccupied with the "basement" of the human condition. Freud wrote that people are basically motivated to gratify bio-

REFLECT

Do you know anyone who seems to be alienated? How is the person alienated? What do you think led to feelings of alienation?

REFLECT

Is your life meaningful? If not, what can you do to make it meaningful?

HUMANISM The view that people are capable of free choice, self-fulfillment, and ethical behavior.

EXISTENTIALISM The view that people are completely free and responsible for their own behavior.

logical drives and that their perceptions are distorted by their psychological needs. Question: How do humanistic psychologists differ from psychodynamic theorists? The humanistic psychologist Abraham Maslow argued that people also have a conscious need for **self-actualization**—to become all that they can be—and that people can see the world as it is. Because people are unique, they must follow unique paths to self-actualization. People are not at the mercy of unconscious, primitive impulses. Rather, one of the main threats to individual personality development is control by other people. We must each be free to get in touch with and actualize our selves. But self-actualization requires taking risks. Many people prefer to adhere to the tried and . . . what may be untrue for them. But people who adhere to the "tried and true" may find their lives degenerating into monotony and predictability.

Carl Rogers's Self Theory

The humanistic psychologist Carl Rogers (1902–1987) wrote that people shape themselves—their selves—through free choice and action. Questions: Just what is your *self*? What is self theory?

   Rogers defined the *self* as the center of experience. Your self is your ongoing sense of who and what you are, your sense of how and why you react to the environment and how you choose to act on the environment. Your choices are made on the basis of your values, and your values are also part of your self. Rogers's self theory focuses on the nature of the self and the conditions that allow the self to develop freely. Two of his major concerns are the self-concept and self-esteem.

THE SELF-CONCEPT AND FRAMES OF REFERENCE Our self-concepts consist of our impressions of ourselves and our evaluations of our adequacy. It may be helpful to think of us as rating ourselves according to various scales or dimensions such as good–bad, intelligent–unintelligent, strong–weak, and tall–short.

   Rogers believed that we all have unique ways of looking at ourselves and the world—that is, unique **frames of reference**. It may be that we each use a different set of dimensions in defining ourselves and that we judge ourselves according to different sets of values. To one person, achievement–failure may be the most important dimension. To another person, the most important dimension may be decency–indecency. A third person may not even think in terms of decency.

SELF-ESTEEM AND POSITIVE REGARD Rogers assumed that we all develop a need for self-regard, or self-esteem, as we develop and become aware of ourselves. At first, self-esteem reflects the esteem in which others hold us. Parents help children develop self-esteem when they show them **unconditional positive regard**—that is, when they accept them as having merit regardless of their behavior at the moment. But when parents show children **conditional positive regard**—that is, when they accept them only when they behave in a desired manner—children may develop **conditions of worth**. That is, they may come to think they have merit only if they behave as their parents wish them to behave.

   Because each individual is thought to have a unique potential, children who develop conditions of worth must be somewhat disappointed in themselves. We cannot fully live up to the wishes of others and remain true to ourselves. This does not mean that the expression of the self

Unique.   According to humanistic psychologists like Carl Rogers, each of us views the world from a unique frame of reference. What matters to one person may mean little to another.

SELF-ACTUALIZATION In humanistic theory, the innate tendency to strive to realize one's potential.

FRAME OF REFERENCE One's unique patterning of perceptions and attitudes according to which one evaluates events.

UNCONDITIONAL POSITIVE REGARD A persistent expression of esteem for the value of a person, but not necessarily an unqualified acceptance of all of the person's behaviors.

CONDITIONAL POSITIVE REGARD Judgment of another person's value on the basis of the acceptability of that person's behaviors.

CONDITIONS OF WORTH Standards by which the value of a person is judged.

inevitably leads to conflict. Rogers was optimistic about human nature. He believed that we hurt others or act in antisocial ways only when we are frustrated in our efforts to develop our potential. But when parents and others are loving and tolerant of our differentness, we, too, are loving—even if some of our preferences, abilities, and values differ from those of our parents.

However, children in some families learn that it is bad to have ideas of their own, especially about sexual, political, or religious matters. When they perceive their caretakers' disapproval, they may come to see themselves as rebels and label their feelings as selfish, wrong, or evil. If they wish to retain a consistent self-concept and self-esteem, they may have to deny many of their feelings or disown aspects of themselves. In this way the self-concept becomes distorted. According to Rogers, anxiety often stems from recognition that people have feelings and desires that are inconsistent with their distorted self-concept. Because anxiety is unpleasant, people may deny the existence of their genuine feelings and desires.

According to Rogers, the path to self-actualization requires getting in touch with our genuine feelings, accepting them, and acting on them. This is the goal of Rogers's method of psychotherapy, *client-centered therapy*.

Rogers also believed that we have mental images of what we are capable of becoming. These are termed **self-ideals.** We are motivated to reduce the discrepancy between our self-concepts and our self-ideals.

Evaluation of the Humanistic-Existential Perspective

Question: What are the strengths and weaknesses of humanistic-existential theory? Humanistic-existential theories have tremendous appeal for college students because of their focus on the importance of personal experience. We tend to treasure our conscious experiences (our "selves") and those of the people we care about. For lower organisms, to be alive is to move, to process food, to exchange oxygen and carbon dioxide, and to reproduce. But for human beings, an essential aspect of life is conscious experience—the sense of oneself as progressing through space and time.

Psychodynamic theories see individuals largely as victims of their childhood. Learning theories, to some degree, see people as "victims of circumstances"—or at least as victims of situational variables. But humanistic-existential theorists see humans as free to make choices. Psychodynamic theorists and learning theorists wonder whether our sense of freedom is merely an illusion. Humanistic-existential theorists, in contrast, begin by assuming personal freedom.

Ironically, the primary strength of the humanistic-existential approaches—their focus on conscious experience—is also their main weakness. Conscious experience is private and subjective. Therefore, the validity of formulating theories in terms of consciousness has been questioned. On the other hand, some psychologists (e.g., Bevan & Kessel, 1994) believe that the science of psychology can afford to loosen its methods somewhat if this will help it address the richness of human experience.

Humanistic-existential theories, like learning theories, have little to say about the development of traits and personality types. They assume that we are all unique, but they do not predict the sorts of traits, abilities, and interests we will develop.

SELF-IDEAL A mental image of what we believe we ought to be.

Review

SECTION V

The humanistic view argues that people (57: Are or Are not?) capable of free choice and self-fulfillment. (58) _____tialists assert that our lives have whatever meaning we give to them. Abraham (59) M_____ argued that people have growth-oriented needs for self-actulization. Carl Rogers's theory begins with the assumption of the existence of the (60) s_____, which is an organized way in which a person perceives his or her "I" to relate to the world.

The self is innate and will attempt to become actualized (develop its unique potential) when the person receives (61) _____ional positive regard. We all have needs for self-esteem and see the world through unique frames of (62) _____nce. Conditions of (63) _____ distort the self-concept and lead us to disown parts of the self.

SECTION VI. PERSONALITY AND DIVERSITY: THE SOCIOCULTURAL PERSPECTIVE

Thirteen-year-old Hannah brought her lunch tray to the table in the cafeteria. Her mother, Julie, eyed with horror the french fries, the plate of mashed potatoes in gravy, the bag of potato chips, and the large paper cup brimming with soda. "You can't eat that!" she said. "It's garbage!"

"Oh, come on, Mom! Chill, okay?" Hannah rejoined before taking her tray to sit with some friends rather than with us.

I used to spend Saturdays with my children at the Manhattan School of Music. Not only did they study voice and piano. They—and I—widened our cultural perspective by relating to families and students from all parts of the world.

Julie and Hannah are Korean Americans. Flustered, Julie shook her head and said, "I've now been in the United States longer than I was in Korea, and I still can't get used to the way children act here." Alexandra, a Polish American parent, chimed in. "I never would have spoken to my parents the way Thomas speaks to me. I would have been . . . whipped or beaten."

"I try to tell Hannah she is part of the family," Julie continued. "She should think of other people. When she talks that way, it's embarrassing."

"Over here children are not part of the family," said Ken, an African American parent. "They are either part of their own crowd or they are 'individuals.'"

"Being an individual does not mean you have to talk back to your mother," Julie said. "What do you think, Spencer? You're the psychologist."

I think I made some unhelpful comments about the ketchup on the french fries having antioxidants and some slightly helpful comments about what is typical of teenagers in the United States. But I'm not sure, because I was thinking deeply about Hannah at the time. Not about her lunch, but about the formation of her personality and the influences on her behavior.

Question: Why is the sociocultural perspective important to the understanding of personality? As I thought about Hannah, I realized that in our multicultural society, personality cannot be understood without reference to the **sociocultural perspective.** Moreover, trends in immigration are making the population an even richer mix. Different cultural groups within the United States have different attitudes, beliefs, norms, self-definitions, and values (Basic Behavioral Science Task Force, 1996; Triandis, 1996).

Back to Hannah. Perhaps there were some unconscious psychodynamic influences operating on her. Her traits included exceptional academic ability and musical talent, which were at least partly determined by her heredity. Clearly, she was consciously striving to become a great violinist. But one could not fully understand her personality without also considering the sociocultural influences acting on her.

Here was a youngster who was strongly influenced by her peers—she was completely at home with blue jeans and french fries. She was also a daughter in an Asian American immigrant group that views education as the key to success in our culture (Gibson & Ogbu, 1991). Belonging to this ethnic group had certainly contributed to her ambition. But being a Korean American had not prevented her from becoming an outspoken American teenager. (Would she have been outspoken if she had been reared in Korea? I wondered. Of course, this question cannot be answered with certainty.) Predictably, her outspoken behavior had struck her mother as sassy (Lopez & Hernandez, 1986). Julie was deeply offended by behavior that I consider acceptable in my own children. She reeled off the things that were "wrong" with Hannah from her Korean American perspective. I listed some things that were very right with Hannah and encouraged Julie to worry less.

Let us consider how sociocultural factors can affect personality.

Individualism Versus Collectivism

One could say that Julie's complaint was that Hannah saw herself as an individual and an artist to a greater extent than as a family member and a Korean girl. Questions: What does it mean to be individualistic? What is meant by individualism and collectivism? Cross-cultural research reveals that people in the United States and many northern European nations tend to be individualistic. **Individualists** tend to define themselves in terms of their personal identities and to give priority to their personal goals (Triandis, 1995). When asked to complete the statement "I am . . . ," they are likely to respond in terms of their personality traits ("I am outgoing," "I am artistic") or their occupations ("I am a nurse," "I am a systems analyst") (Triandis, 1990). In contrast, many people from cultures in Africa, Asia, and Central and South America tend to be collectivistic (Basic Behavioral Science Task Force, 1996). **Collectivists** tend to define themselves in terms of the groups to which they belong and to give priority to the group's goals (Triandis, 1995). They feel complete in terms of their relationships with others (Markus & Kitayama, 1991; see Figure 10.4). They are more likely than individualists to conform to group norms and judgments (Bond & Smith, 1996; Okazaki, 1997). When asked to complete the statement "I am. . . ," they are more likely to respond in terms of their families, gender, or nation ("I am a father," "I am a Buddhist," "I am Japanese") (Triandis, 1990).

The seeds of individualism and collectivism are found in the culture in which a person grows up. The capitalist system fosters individualism to some degree. It assumes that individuals are entitled to accumulate personal fortunes and that the process of doing so creates jobs and wealth for large numbers of people. The individualist perspective is found in the self-reliant heroes and antiheroes of Western literature and mass media—from Homer's Odysseus to Clint Eastwood's gritty cowboys and Walt Disney's Pocahontas or Mulan. The traditional writings of the East have exalted

SOCIOCULTURAL PERSPECTIVE The view that focuses on the roles of ethnicity, gender, culture, and socioeconomic status in personality formation, behavior, and mental processes.

INDIVIDUALIST A person who defines the self in terms of personal traits and gives priority to personal goals.

COLLECTIVIST A person who defines the self in terms of relationships to other people and groups and gives priority to group goals.

REFLECT

Do you see yourself as individualistic or collectivistic? Has your view of yourself led to conflict with others? Explain.

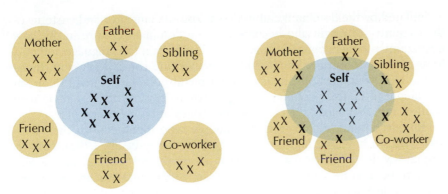

A. Independent View of Self   B. Interdependent View of Self

FIGURE 10.4
THE SELF IN RELATION TO OTHERS FROM THE INDIVIDUALIST AND COLLECTIVIST PERSPECTIVES
TO AN INDIVIDUALIST, THE SELF IS SEPARATE FROM OTHER PEOPLE (PART A). TO A COLLECTIVIST, THE SELF IS COMPLETE ONLY IN TERMS OF RELATIONSHIPS TO OTHER PEOPLE (PART B).
Source: Based on Markus & Kitayama, 1991.

people who resisted personal temptations in order to do their duty and promote the welfare of the group.

Sociocultural Factors and the Self

Carl Rogers noted that our self-concepts tend to reflect how other people see us. Question: How do sociocultural factors affect the self-concept and self-esteem? It turns out that members of the dominant culture in the United States are likely to have a positive sense of self because they share in the expectations of personal achievement and respect that are accorded to those who rise to power. Similarly, members of ethnic groups that have been subjected to discrimination and poverty may have poorer self-concepts and lower self-esteem than members of the dominant culture (Greene, 1993, 1994; Lewis-Fernández & Kleinman, 1994).

Despite the persistence of racial prejudices, a survey by the American Association of University Women (1992) found that African American girls are likely to be happier with their appearance than European American girls are. Sixty-five percent of African American elementary schoolgirls said they were happy with the way they were, compared with 55% of European American girls. By high school age, 58% of African American girls remained happy with the way they were, compared with a surprisingly low 22% of White girls. Why the discrepancy? It appears that the parents of African American girls teach them that nothing is wrong with them if they do not match the ideals of the dominant culture. The world mistreats them because of prejudice, not because of who they are as individuals or what they do (Williams, 1992). The White girls are more likely to blame themselves for not attaining the unreachable ideal.

ACCULTURATION The process of adaptation in which immigrants and native groups identify with a new, dominant culture by learning about that culture and making behavioral and attitudinal changes.

Acculturation and Self-Esteem

Should Hindu women who emigrate to the United States surrender the sari in favor of California Casuals? Should Russian immigrants try to teach their children English at home? Should African American children be acquainted with the music and art of African peoples or those of Europe? Such activities are examples of **acculturation,** in which immigrants become acclimated to the customs and behavior patterns of their new host culture. Question: How does acculturation affect the psychological well-being of immigrants and their families?

Self-esteem is connected with patterns of acculturation among immigrants. Those patterns take various forms. Some immigrants are completely

REFLECT

How did you, your parents, or your ancestors become acculturated to life in the United States? How did acculturation affect your—or their—self-esteem?

This Hispanic American Woman Is Highly Acculturated to Life in the United States. Some immigrants are completely assimilated by the dominant culture and abandon the language and customs of their country of origin. Others retain the language and customs of their country of origin and never become comfortable with those of their new country. Still others become bicultural. They become fluent in both languages and blend the customs and values of both cultures.

assimilated by the dominant culture. They lose the language and customs of their country of origin and become like the dominant culture in the new host country. Others maintain separation. They retain the language and customs of their country of origin and never become comfortable with those of the new country. Still others become bicultural. They remain fluent in the language of their country of origin while learning that of their new country, and they blend the customs and values of both cultures.

Research evidence suggests that people who identify with the bicultural pattern have the highest self-esteem (Phinney et al., 1992). For example, Mexican Americans who are more proficient in English are less likely to be anxious and depressed than less proficient Mexican Americans (Salgado de Snyder et al., 1990). The ability to adapt to the ways of the new society, combined with a supportive cultural tradition and a sense of ethnic identity, apparently helps people adjust.

✓ Truth or Fiction Revisited

It is not true that the best adjusted immigrants are those who abandon the language and customs of their country of origin and become like the dominant culture in the new host country. Research shows that immigrants who identify with a bicultural pattern have the highest self-esteem.

In sum, the sociocultural perspective provides valuable insights into the roles of ethnicity, gender, culture, and socioeconomic status in personality formation. When we ignore sociocultural factors, we deal only with the core of the human being—the potentials that allow the person to adapt to external forces. Sociocultural factors are external forces that are internalized. They run through us deeply, touching many aspects of our cognitions, motives, emotions, and behavior. Without reference to sociocultural factors, we may be able to understand generalities about behavior and cognitive processes. However, we will not be able to understand how individuals think, behave, and feel about themselves within a given cultural setting. The sociocultural perspective enhances our sensitivity to cultural differences and expectations and allows us to appreciate the richness of human behavior and mental processes.

Review

SECTION VI

The (57) _____ cultural perspective considers the influences of factors such as ethnicity, gender, and socioeconomic status on personality. People in the United States tend to be (58) _____ istic in that they define themselves in terms of their personal identities and to give priority to their personal goals. (59) _____ ists tend to define themselves in terms of the groups to which they belong and to give priority to the goals of their group.

Members of minority ethnic groups who have been subjected to discrimination and poverty tend to have (60: Higher or Lower?) self-esteem than members of the dominant culture. Nevertheless, African American girls are likely to be (61: More or Less?) happy with their appearance than European American girls are. Immigrants who identify with the bicultural pattern of assimilation have the (62: Highest or Lowest?) self-esteem. Mexican Americans who are proficient in English are (63: More or Less?) likely to be anxious and depressed than other Mexican Americans.

SECTION VII. MEASUREMENT OF PERSONALITY

Methods of personality assessment take a sample of behavior to predict future behavior. Standardized interviews are often used. Some psychologists use computers to conduct routine interviews. **Behavior-rating scales** assess behavior in settings such as classrooms or mental hospitals. With behavior-rating scales, trained observers check off each occurrence of a behavior within a certain time frame—say, 15 minutes. However, standardized objective and projective tests are used more frequently, and we focus on them in this section.

Question: How are personality measures used? Measures of personality are used to make important decisions, such as whether a person is suited for a certain type of work, a particular class in school, or a drug to reduce agitation. As part of their admissions process, graduate schools often ask professors to rate prospective students on scales that assess traits such as intelligence, emotional stability, and cooperation. Students may take tests to measure their aptitudes and interests to gain insight into whether they are suited for certain occupations. It is assumed that students who share the aptitudes and interests of people who function well in certain positions are also likely to function well in those positions.

There are two major categories of personality tests: objective tests and projective tests.

Objective Tests

Question: What are objective personality tests? **Objective tests** present a **standardized** group of test items in the form of a questionnaire. Respondents are limited to a specific range of answers. One test might ask test takers to indicate whether items are true or false for them. Another might ask them to select the preferred activity from groups of three.

Some tests have a **forced-choice format,** in which respondents are asked to indicate which of two statements is more true for them or which of several activities they prefer. The respondents are not usually given the option of answering "none of the above." Forced-choice formats are frequently used in interest inventories, which help predict whether the person would function well in a certain occupation. The following item is similar to those found in occupational interest inventories:

I would rather

    a. be a forest ranger.

    b. work in a busy office.

    c. play a musical instrument.

The Minnesota Multiphasic Personality Inventory (MMPI) contains hundreds of items presented in a true–false format. The MMPI is designed to be used by clinical and counseling psychologists to help diagnose psychological disorders. Accurate measurement of an individual's problems should point to appropriate treatment. The MMPI is the most widely used psychological test in clinical work (Watkins et al., 1995). It is also the most widely used instrument for personality measurement in psychological research.

Psychologists can score tests by hand, send them to computerized scoring services, or have them scored by on-site computers. Computers

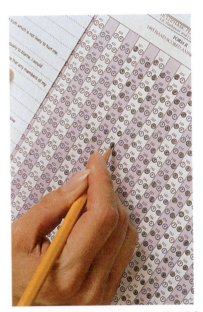

Is This Test Taker Telling the Truth? How can psychologists determine whether or not people answer test items honestly? What are the validity scales of the MMPI?

BEHAVIOR-RATING SCALE A systematic means for recording the frequency with which target behaviors occur.

OBJECTIVE TESTS Tests whose items must be answered in a specified, limited manner. Tests whose items have concrete answers that are considered correct.

STANDARDIZED TEST A test given to a large number of respondents so that data concerning the typical responses can be accumulated and analyzed.

FORCED-CHOICE FORMAT A method of presenting test questions that requires a respondent to select one of a number of possible answers.

TABLE 10.3	MINNESOTA MULTIPHASIC PERSONALITY INVENTORY (MMPI) SCALES	
SCALE	**ABBREVIATION**	**POSSIBLE INTERPRETATIONS**
VALIDITY SCALES		
Question	?	Corresponds to number of items left unanswered
Lie	L	Lies or is highly conventional
Frequency	F	Exaggerates complaints or answers items haphazardly; may have bizarre ideas
Correction	K	Denies problems
CLINICAL SCALES		
Hypochondriasis	Hs	Has bodily concerns and complaints
Depression	D	Is depressed; has feelings of guilt and helplessness
Hysteria	Hy	Reacts to stress by developing physical symptoms; lacks insight
Psychopathic deviate	Pd	Is immoral, in conflict with the law; has stormy relationships
Masculinity/Femininity	Mf	High scores suggest interests and behavior considered stereotypical of the other gender
Paranoia	Pa	Is suspicious and resentful, highly cynical about human nature
Psychasthenia	Pt	Is anxious, worried, high-strung
Schizophrenia	Sc	Is confused, disorganized, disoriented; has bizarre ideas
Hypomania	Ma	Is energetic, restless, active, easily bored
Social introversion	Si	Is introverted, timid, shy; lacks self-confidence

generate reports by interpreting the test record according to certain rules or by comparing it with records in memory.

The MMPI is usually scored for the 4 **validity scales** and 10 **clinical scales** described in Table 10.3. The validity scales suggest whether answers actually represent the person's thoughts, emotions, and behaviors. However, they cannot guarantee that deception will be disclosed.

✓ Truth or Fiction Revisited

Psychologists cannot necessarily determine whether a person has told the truth on a personality test. However, validity scales allow them to make educated guesses.

The validity scales in Table 10.3 assess different **response sets,** or biases, in answering the questions. People with high L scores, for example, may be attempting to present themselves as excessively moral and well-behaved individuals. People with high F scores may be trying to seem bizarre or are answering haphazardly. Many personality measures have some kind of validity scale. The clinical scales of the MMPI assess the problems shown in Table 10.3, as well as stereotypical masculine or feminine interests and introversion.

The MMPI scales were constructed *empirically*—that is, on the basis of actual clinical data rather than on the basis of psychological theory. A

VALIDITY SCALES Groups of test items that indicate whether a person's responses accurately reflect that individual's traits.

CLINICAL SCALES Groups of test items that measure the presence of various abnormal behavior patterns.

RESPONSE SET A tendency to answer test items according to a bias — for instance, to make oneself seem perfect or bizarre.

test-item bank of several hundred items was derived from questions that are often asked in clinical interviews. Here are some examples of the kinds of items that were used:

My father was a good man.	T	F
I am very seldom troubled by headaches.	T	F
My hands and feet are usually warm enough.	T	F
I have never done anything dangerous for the thrill of it.	T	F
I work under a great deal of tension.	T	F

The items were administered to people with previously identified symptoms, such as depressive or schizophrenic symptoms. Items that successfully set these people apart were included on scales named for these conditions. Confidence in the MMPI has developed because of its extensive use.

Now that we have defined objective tests and surveyed the MMPI, we may ask— Questions: How do projective tests differ from objective tests? What are some of the more widely used projective tests?

Projective Tests

In **projective tests** there are no clear, specified answers. People are shown ambiguous stimuli such as inkblots or ambiguous drawings and asked to say what these stimuli look like to them or to tell stories about them. There is no one correct response. It is assumed that people *project* their own personalities into their responses. The meanings they attribute to these stimuli are assumed to reflect their personalities as well as the drawings or blots themselves.

✓ Truth or Fiction Revisited

It is true that there are no right or wrong answers on some psychological tests—these are mainly personality tests.

THE RORSCHACH INKBLOT TEST You may have heard of a personality test that asks people what a drawing or inkblot looks like and that people commonly answer "a bat." There are a number of such tests, the best known of which is the Rorschach inkblot test, named after its originator, the Swiss psychiatrist Hermann Rorschach (1884–1922). During his last two years in the equivalent of high school, Hermann was given the nickname "Klex" by his fraternity brothers. The proper spelling of the word in German is *Klecks*, which translates as "inkblot" in English. Hermann was preoccupied with the child's game of *klecksographie*—dropping ink onto paper and arranging and folding the paper to cause the ink to take on an appealing shape (Figure 10.5).

Rorschach believed that people's responses to inkblots revealed something about their personalities. He tried out dozens of inkblots with patients at a sanitarium and concluded that 15 of them helped diagnose their problems. There are only 10 Rorschach inkblots today. Why? There was not enough money to print all of the plates in Rorschach's research report.

People are given the inkblots, one by one, and are asked what they look like or what they could be. A response that reflects the shape of the blot is considered a sign of adequate **reality testing.** A response that richly

FIGURE 10.5
A RORSCHACH INKBLOT
THE RORSCHACH IS THE MOST WIDELY USED PROJECTIVE PERSONALITY TEST. WHAT DOES THIS LOOK LIKE TO YOU? WHAT COULD IT BE?

PROJECTIVE TEST A psychological test that presents ambiguous stimuli onto which the test taker projects his or her own personality in making a response.

REALITY TESTING The capacity to perceive one's environment and oneself according to accurate sensory impressions.

FIGURE 10.6

A DRAWING SIMILAR TO A TAT CARD   CAN YOU MAKE UP A STORY ABOUT THIS DRAWING? WHAT ARE THE CHARACTERS THINKING AND FEELING? WHAT WILL HAPPEN NEXT? WHAT DOES YOUR STORY REVEAL ABOUT YOURSELF?

integrates several features of the blot is considered a sign of high intellectual functioning. The Rorschach test is thought to provide insight into a person's intelligence, interests, cultural background, degree of introversion or extraversion, level of anxiety, reality testing, and many other variables.

✓ **Truth or Fiction Revisited**

It is true that there is a psychological test made up of inkblots, and test takers are asked to say what the blots look like to them. It is the Rorschach inkblot test.

THE THEMATIC APPERCEPTION TEST   The Thematic Apperception Test (TAT) was developed in the 1930s by Henry Murray and Christiana Morgan. It consists of drawings, like the one shown in Figure 10.6, that are open to a variety of interpretations. Individuals are given the cards one at a time and asked to make up stories about them.

The TAT is widely used in research on motivation and in clinical practice (Watkins et al., 1995). The notion is that we are likely to project our own needs into our responses to ambiguous situations, even if we are unaware of them or reluctant to talk about them. The TAT is also widely used to assess attitudes toward other people, especially parents, lovers, and spouses.

Although personality tests have their uses, most psychologists consider them just one source of information about people. They are best used to enrich the understanding of an individual's personality; they are not a substitute for personal contact with the individual.

In this chapter, we have laid some broad foundations for the understanding of human personality. In Chapter 11 we examine the relationships between personality, stress, and adjustment. And in Chapter 12 we consider connections between personality and psychological disorders.

Review

SECTION VII

In personality measurement, psychologists take a sample of (64) b_____ in order to predict future behavior. (65) _____ive tests present test takers with a standardized set of test items in the form of questionnaires. Projective tests present (66) _____uous stimuli and permit the respondent a broad range of answers.

The (67) _____ _____ Personality Inventory (MMPI) is the most widely used psychological test in the clinical setting. The MMPI is an (68) _____ive personality test that uses a true–false format to assess psychological disorders. The MMPI contains scales that assess the accuracy of answers—that is, (69) _____ity scales—as well as clinical scales.

The foremost projective technique is the (70) R_____ inkblot test, in which test takers are asked to report what inkblots look like or could be. People who take the (71) _____ _____ Test (TAT) interpret ambiguous drawings.

STUDY GUIDE

To help you better understand the content of this chapter, you may go to the student Web site (http://www.harcourtcollege.com/psych/intro.html) to take more quizzes, get more information about the content, and see additional Web sites related to the content. You can also practice using the concepts in this chapter with the PowerPsych CD-ROM, which gives you interactive activities and experiments along with even more quizzes. And, of course, the printed study guide is a reliable way to practice all parts of PQ4R. Your college bookstore can order the PowerPsych CD-ROM for you.

SUMMARY

1. **Just what *is* personality?** Personality is defined as the reasonably stable patterns of behavior, including thoughts and emotions, that distinguish one person from another.

2. **What is Freud's theory of psychosexual development?** Freud's theory is termed psycho*dynamic* because it assumes that we are driven largely by unconscious motives and by the movement of unconscious forces within our minds. People experience conflict as basic instincts of hunger, sex, and aggression come up against social pressures to follow laws, rules, and moral codes. At first this conflict is external, but as we develop, it is internalized. The unconscious id represents psychological drives and seeks instant gratification. The ego, or the sense of self or "I," develops through experience and takes into account what is practical and possible in gratifying the impulses of the id. Defense mechanisms such as repression protect the ego from anxiety by repressing unacceptable ideas or distorting reality. The superego is the conscience and develops largely through the Oedipus complex and identification with others. People undergo psychosexual development as psychosexual energy, or libido, is transferred from one erogenous zone to another during childhood. There are five stages of development: oral, anal, phallic, latency, and genital.

3. **Who are some other psychodynamic theorists? What are their views on personality?** Carl Jung's theory, analytical psychology, features a collective unconscious and numerous archetypes, both of which reflect the history of our species. Alfred Adler's theory, individual psychology, features the inferiority complex and the compensating drive for superiority. Karen Horney's theory focuses on parent–child relationships and the possible development of feelings of anxiety and hostility. Erik Erikson's theory of psychosocial development highlights the importance of early social relationships rather than the gratification of childhood sexual impulses. Erikson extended Freud's five developmental stages to eight, including stages that occur in adulthood.

4. **What are the strengths and weaknesses of the psychodynamic perspective?** Freud fought for the idea that personality is subject to scientific analysis at a time when many people still viewed psychological problems as signs of possession. He also focused attention on the importance of sexuality, the effects of child rearing, and the fact that people distort perceptions according to their needs. On the other hand, there is no evidence for the existence of psychic structures, and his theory is fraught with inaccuracies about child development.

5. **What are traits?** Traits are personality elements that are inferred from behavior and that account for behavioral consistency. Trait theory adopts a descriptive approach to personality.

6. **What is the history of the trait perspective?** Hippocrates, the ancient Greek physician, believed that personality reflects the balance of liquids ("humors") in the body. Galton in the 19th century and Allport in the 20th century surveyed traits by studying words that referred to them in dictionaries.

7. **How have contemporary researchers used factor analysis to reduce the universe of traits to smaller lists of traits that show common features?** Hans Eysenck used factor analysis to arrive at two broad, independent personality dimensions: introversion–extraversion and emotional stability–instability (neuroticism). More recent mathematical analyses point to the existence of five key factors: extraversion, agreeableness, conscientiousness, emotional stability, and openness to experience.

8. **What are the strengths and weaknesses of trait theory?** Trait theorists have helped develop personality tests and used them to predict adjustment in various lines of work. Critics argue that trait theory is descriptive, not explanatory.

9. **What does learning theory have to contribute to our understanding of personality?** Behaviorists believe that we should focus on observable behavior rather than hypothesized unconscious forces, and that we should emphasize the situational determinants of behavior.

10. **What is Watson's contribution to personality theory?** John B. Watson, the "father" of modern behaviorism, rejected notions of mind and personality altogether. He also argued that he could train any child to develop into a professional or a criminal by controlling the child's environment.

11. **How did Skinner develop Watson's views?** B. F. Skinner, like Watson, opposed the idea of personal freedom. In *Walden Two,* Skinner argued that environmental contingencies can shape people into wanting to do the things that society and the physical environment require of them.

12. **How does social-cognitive theory differ from the behaviorist view?** Social-cognitive theory has a cognitive orientation and focuses on learning by observation. To predict behavior, social-cognitive theorists consider situational variables (rewards and punishments) and person variables (competencies, encoding strategies, expectancies, emotions, and self-regulatory systems and plans).

13. **What are the strengths and weaknesses of learning theories as they apply to personality?** Learning theorists have highlighted the importance of referring to publicly observable behaviors in theorizing. However, behaviorism does not describe, explain, or suggest the richness of inner human experience. Critics of social-cognitive theory note that it does not address self-awareness or adequately account for the development of traits. It may also not pay enough attention to genetic variation in explaining individual differences in behavior.

14. **What is humanism? What is existentialism?** Humanism argues that we are capable of free choice, self-fulfillment, and ethical behavior. Existentialists argue that our lives have meaning when we give them meaning.

15. **How do humanistic psychologists differ from psychodynamic theorists?** Whereas Freud wrote that people are motivated to gratify unconscious drives, humanistic psychologists believe that people have a conscious need for self-actualization.

16. **Just what is your *self*? What is self theory?** According to Rogers, the self is an organized and consistent way in which a person perceives his or her "I" in relation to others. Self theory begins by assuming the existence of the self and each person's unique frame of reference. The self attempts to actualize (develop its unique potential) and best does so when the person receives unconditional positive regard. Conditions of worth may lead to a distorted self-concept, to disowning of parts of the self, and to anxiety.

17. **What are the strengths and weaknesses of humanistic-existential theory?** Humanistic-existential theory is appealing because of its focus on self-awareness and freedom of choice, but critics argue that concepts such as conscious experience and self-actualization are unscientific.

18. **Why is the sociocultural perspective important to the understanding of personality?** One cannot fully understand the personality of an individual without understanding the cultural beliefs and socioeconomic conditions that have affected that individual. The sociocultural perspective encourages us to consider the roles of ethnicity, gender, culture, and socioeconomic status in personality formation, behavior, and mental processes.

19. **What does it mean to be individualistic? What is meant by individualism and collectivism?** Individualists define themselves in terms of their personal identities and to give priority to their personal goals. Collectivists define themselves in terms of the groups to which they belong and to give priority to the group's goals. Many Western societies are individualistic and foster individualism in personality. Many Eastern societies are collectivist and foster collectivism in personality.

20. **How do sociocultural factors affect the self-concept and self-esteem?** Members of the dominant culture in the United States are likely to have positive self-concepts because they share expectations of achievement and respect. Members of ethnic groups that have been subjected to discrimination and poverty tend to have poorer self-concepts and lower self-esteem.

21. **How does acculturation affect the psychological well-being of immigrants and their families?** Immigrants who retain the customs and values of their country of origin but who also learn those of their new host country, and blend the two, tend to have higher self-esteem than immigrants who either become completely assimilated or who maintain complete separation from the new dominant culture.

22. **How are personality measures used?** Personality measures are used in many ways, including assessing psychological disorders, predicting the likelihood of adjustment in various lines of work, measuring aptitudes, and determining academic placement.

23. **What are objective personality tests?** Objective tests present test takers with a standardized set of test items to which they must respond in specific, limited ways (as in multiple-choice or true–false tests). A forced-choice format asks respondents to indicate which of two or more statements is true for them or which of several activities they prefer. The Minnesota Multiphasic Personality Inventory (MMPI) is widely used in the assessment of psychological disorders.

24. **How do projective tests differ from objective tests? What are some of the more widely used projective tests?** Projective tests do not have specific correct answers. They present ambiguous stimuli and allow the test taker to give a range of responses that reflect individual differences. Examples include the Rorschach inkblot test and the Thematic Apperception Test.

EXERCISE 1

DEFENSE MECHANISMS

Name each of the defense mechanisms described in the table.

DESCRIPTION OF DEFENSE MECHANISM	NAME OF DEFENSE MECHANISM
Ejection of anxiety-evoking ideas from awareness	(1) _____
The return, under stress, to a form of behavior characteristic of an earlier stage of development	(2) _____
The use of self-deceiving justifications for unacceptable behavior	(3) _____
The transfer of ideas and impulses from threatening or unsuitable objects to less threatening objects	(4) _____
The thrusting of one's own unacceptable impulses onto others so that others are assumed to have those impulses	(5) _____
Engaging in behavior that opposes one's genuine impulses in order to keep those impulses repressed	(6) _____
The refusal to face the true nature of a threat	(7) _____
The channeling of primitive impulses into positive, constructive efforts	(8) _____

EXERCISE 2

THE FIVE-FACTOR MODEL

Name each of the factors described in the table.

FACTOR	NAME	TRAITS
I	(9) _____sion	Contrasts talkativeness, assertiveness, and activity with silence, passivity, and reserve
II	(10) _____ness	Contrasts kindness, trust, and warmth with hostility, selfishness, and distrust
III	(11) _____ness	Contrasts organization, thoroughness, and reliability with carelessness, negligence, and unreliability
IV	(12) _____ism	Contrasts traits such as nervousness, moodiness, and sensitivity to negative stimuli with coping ability
V	(13) _____ness to experience	Contrasts imagination, curiosity, and creativity with shallowness and lack of perceptiveness

EXERCISE 3

PERSPECTIVES ON PERSONALITY

Provide the missing information.

PERSPECTIVE	FOCUS	KEY POINTS
Psychodynamic	The focus is on (14) _____scious conflict. Drives such as sex, aggression, and the need for superiority come into conflict with laws, social rules, and moral codes.	Freud hypothesized (15: How many?) structures of personality (the id, ego, and superego) and (16: How many?) stages of psychosexual development. The stages are the (17) _____, anal, (18) _____lic, latency, and genital stages.
Trait	The focus is on the use of mathematical techniques to catalogue and organize basic human personality traits.	Hippocrates hypothesized the existence of (19: How many?) basic traits. Eysenck updated these traits in terms of two personality dimensions: (20) _____–extraversion and emotional (21) _____. Contemporary researchers find five basic traits, as expressed in the (22) five-_____ model.
Learning Theory	The focus is on the factors that determine observable (23) _____ior.	(24) _____ists see personality as plastic and determined by external, situational variables. (25) Social-_____ theorists also look for variables within the person. Person variables include competencies, (26) en_____ strategies, expectancies, emotions, and self-regulatory systems.
Humanistic-Existential	The experiences of being human and developing one's unique potential within an often hostile environment	People have inborn drives to become what they are capable of being. (27) _____tional positive regard leads to self-esteem, which facilitates individual growth and development.
Sociocultural	The roles of (28) _____city, gender, culture, and socioeconomic status in personality formation	Development differs in individualistic and (29) _____vist societies. Discrimination, poverty, and (30) accul_____ affect the self-concept and self-esteem.

LANGUAGE AND CULTURE

altruistic (474)—*idealistic, describing one who does good for good's sake and not for personal reward*

appendage (467)—*added, hanging on part*

to be off base (461)—*to be incorrect in interpretation*

to bite one's fingernails (459)—*to be nervous (about something)*

bloodletting (459)—*opening a vein to release blood (ancient practice believed to return a person to good humor)*

to browse (477)—*to skim, to observe casually, to be aware of small things that are passing through one's mind*

cauldron (463)—*huge cooking utensil, kettle, pot*

chaos (463)—*disorder*

to compensate (467)—*to make up for, to offset, to balance a negative with a positive*

to be embedded (470)—*to become an integral part or to be inside of*

a false and faithless prophet (461)—*a person who is not worthy of others' trust*

to flower (460)—*to develop and become important*

to fuel (465)—*to power, to cause to work*

to gloss over (460)—*to give little attention to, to ignore for the most part, to answer insufficiently*

gritty cowboys (482)—*people who work outside with animals and are very down-to-earth, masculine men*

gullibility (465)—*result of naivete, state of being easily tricked*

to have a hard time of (it) (464)—*to experience difficulty in dealing with (it)*

hub (478)—*center of activity*

inkblot (459)—*Rorschach test*

to keep under wraps (463)—*to maintain in secrecy, to hide*

to let it all hang out (466)—*to speak openly about one's problems*

to make (any) sacks (476)—*to tackle a quarterback—the player who is carrying the ball behind the line of play*

medical procedure (477)—*clinical test or operation done by a doctor*

outburst (463)—*display of emotion (such as great joy or anger)*

rat race (478)—*intense competitive struggle*

to be reprimanded (475)—*to be scolded officially, to be warned of inappropriate behavior*

retiring (470)—*shy*

to seethe (463)—*to boil and froth with bubbles (used metaphorically to mean filled with many negative and disturbing violent feelings)*

sickly sweet (464)—*unnaturally kind and considerate*

structuralist (473)—*psychologist who believes that personality traits are related to brain structures*

submerged (459)—*under water*

to vomit (459)—*to empty one's stomach through a convulsive action*

1. Freud labeled the clashing forces of personality
   (a) repression and resistance,
   (b) conscious and unconscious,
   (c) defense mechanisms,
   (d) psychic structures.

2. According to Freud, the _____ follows the reality principle.
   (a) id,
   (b) ego,
   (c) superego,
   (d) libido.

3. According to psychodynamic theory, the superego usually incorporates the standards of parents through
   (a) identification,
   (b) self-actualization,
   (c) unconditional positive regard,
   (d) classical and operant conditioning.

4. John throws his clothing and books all over the floor, leaves his hair unkempt, and rarely cleans his room. According to psychodynamic theory, John's behavior is suggestive of conflict during the _____ stage of psychosexual development.
   (a) genital,
   (b) oral,
   (c) phallic,
   (d) anal.

5. Alfred Adler believed that people are basically motivated by
   (a) the collective unconscious,
   (b) hostility,
   (c) biological and safety needs,
   (d) an inferiority complex.

6. Karen Horney agreed with Freud that
   (a) a woman's place is in the home,
   (b) there are eight stages of psychosocial development,
   (c) parent–child relationships are very important,
   (d) sexual impulses are more important than social relationships.

7. According to the text, which of the following theorists believed that a basic element of personality was the self?
   (a) John B. Watson,
   (b) Carl Rogers,
   (c) Sigmund Freud,
   (d) Hans J. Eysenck.

8. Which of the following catalogued some 18,000 human traits?
   (a) Paul T. Costa, Jr.,
   (b) Sir Francis Galton,
   (c) Hans J. Eysenck,
   (d) Gordon Allport.

9. Which of the following traits is *not* a basic trait, according to the five-factor model?
   (a) Emotional stability–instability,
   (b) Self-awareness,
   (c) Openness to new experience,
   (d) Conscientiousness.

10. The outlooks of John B. Watson and B. F. Skinner discarded all of the following notions, with the exception of
    (a) self-direction,
    (b) personal freedom,
    (c) learning,
    (d) free choice.

11. _____ has argued for the inclusion of cognitive points of view within learning theory.
    (a) Carl Rogers,
    (b) Albert Bandura,
    (c) John B. Watson,
    (d) B. F. Skinner.

12. Which of the following is a situational variable?
    (a) A self-efficacy expectation,
    (b) The subjective value of a reward,
    (c) Competencies,
    (d) A reward.

13. According to Rogers, the sense of self
    (a) is an archetype,
    (b) develops as a result of conditions of worth,
    (c) is innate,
    (d) develops once biological and safety needs have been met.

14. A mother and father tell you that their most important goal for their new child is that she develop a strong sense of self-esteem. According to self theory, parents are likely to help their children develop self-esteem when they show them
    (a) conditional positive regard,
    (b) conditions of worth,
    (c) unconditional positive regard,
    (d) psychological congruence.

15. Which theorist has focused on the relationships between introversion–extraversion and neuroticism?

(a) Carl Jung,

(b) Hans J. Eysenck,

(c) Hippocrates,

(d) Karen Horney.

16. According to the text, _____ tend to define themselves in terms of their personal identities and to give priority to their personal goals

    (a) sociocultural theorists,

    (b) existentialists,

    (c) self-actualizers,

    (d) individualists.

17. Research suggests that immigrants to the United States are best adjusted when they

    (a) become completely assimilated by the dominant culture of the new host nation,

    (b) remain isolated from the dominant culture of the new host nation,

    (c) blend the dominant culture of the new host nation with the traditions of their country of origin,

    (d) become individualists.

18. Which of the following theorists would be most likely to agree that people are capable of recognizing and understanding their own feelings?

    (a) B. F. Skinner,

    (b) John Watson,

    (c) Abraham Maslow,

    (d) Sigmund Freud.

19. Objective personality tests

    (a) show test takers ambiguous figures,

    (b) are shorter than projective tests,

    (c) limit respondents to a specific range of answers,

    (d) are less valid than projective tests.

20. The name *Rorschach* is connected with

    (a) a projective testing method,

    (b) the five-factor model,

    (c) social-cognitive theory,

    (d) individual psychology.

Recite Recite Recite Recite **Recite**

1. Just what *is* personality? _____
_____
_____
_____
_____

2. What is Freud's theory of psychosexual development? _____
_____
_____
_____
_____

3. Who are some other psycho-dynamic theorists? What are their views on personality? _____
_____
_____
_____

4. What are the strengths and weaknesses of the psycho-dynamic perspective? _____
_____
_____
_____

5. What are traits? _____
_____
_____
_____
_____

6. What is the history of the trait perspective? _____
_____
_____
_____
_____

7. How have contemporary re-searchers used factor analysis to reduce the universe of traits to smaller lists of traits that show common features? _____
_____
_____
_____

8. What are the strengths and weaknesses of trait theory? _____
_____
_____
_____

9. What does learning theory have to contribute to our understanding of personality? _____
_____
_____
_____

10. What is Watson's contribution to personality theory? _____
_____
_____

11. How did Skinner develop Watson's views?

_____
_____
_____
_____
_____

12. How does social-cognitive theory differ from the behaviorist view?

_____
_____
_____
_____
_____

13. What are the strengths and weaknesses of learning theories as they apply to personality?

_____
_____
_____
_____
_____

14. What is humanism? What is existentialism?

_____
_____
_____
_____
_____
_____

15. How do humanistic psychologists differ from psychodynamic theorists?

_____
_____
_____
_____
_____

16. Just what is your *self?* What is self theory?

_____
_____
_____
_____
_____
_____

17. What are the strengths and weaknesses of humanistic-existential theory?

_____
_____
_____
_____
_____

18. Why is the sociocultural perspective important to the understanding of personality?

_____
_____
_____
_____
_____

19. What does it mean to be individualistic? What is meant by individualism and collectivism?

_____
_____
_____
_____
_____

20. How do sociocultural factors affect the self-concept and self-esteem?

_____
_____
_____
_____
_____

21. How does acculturation affect the psychological well-being of immigrants and their families?

_____

_____

_____

_____

_____

_____

22. How are personality measures used?

_____

_____

_____

_____

_____

_____

23. What are objective personality tests?

_____

_____

_____

_____

_____

24. How do projective tests differ from objective tests? What are some of the more widely used projective tests?

_____

_____

_____

_____

_____

ANSWERS TO SECTION REVIEWS

1. Emotions
2. Behavior
3. Freud
4. Conflict
5. Unconscious
6. Psychic
7. Three
8. Id
9. Pleasure
10. Ego
11. Reality
12. Defense
13. Superego
14. Identification
15. Moral
16. Five
17. Libido
18. Erogenous
19. Anal

20. Latency
21. Fixation
22. Dependence (or Depression)
23. Gullibility
24. Cleanliness
25. Perfectionism
26. Phallic
27. Other
28. Same
29. Same
30. Analytical
31. Collective
32. Individual
33. Inferiority
34. Horney
35. Anxiety
36. Psychosocial
37. Eight

38. Trust
39. Ego identity
40. Behavior
41. Consistency
42. Four
43. Dictionaries
44. Eysenck
45. Stability (or Instability)
46. Conscientiousness
47. Openness
48. Skinner
49. Cognitive
50. Observation (or Imitation)
51. Person
52. Competencies
53. Encoding
54. Self-regulatory

55. Self-efficacy
56. More
57. Sociocultural
58. Individualistic
59. Collectivists
60. Lower
61. More
62. Highest
63. Less
64. Behavior
65. Objective
66. Ambiguous
67. Minnesota Multiphasic
68. Objective
69. Validity
70. Rorschach
71. Thematic Apperception

ANSWERS TO EXERCISES

1. Repression
2. Regression
3. Rationalization
4. Displacement
5. Projection
6. Reaction formation
7. Denial
8. Sublimation
9. Introversion (or Extraversion)
10. Agreeableness
11. Conscientiousness
12. Neuroticism
13. Openness
14. Unconscious
15. Three
16. Five
17. Oral
18. Phallic
19. Four
20. Introversion
21. Stability
22. Five-factor
23. Behavior
24. Behaviorists
25. Social-cognitive
26. Encoding
27. Unconditional
28. Ethnicity
29. Collectivist
30. Acculturation

ANSWERS TO QUIZ

1. D
2. B
3. A
4. D
5. D
6. C
7. B
8. D
9. B
10. C
11. B
12. D
13. C
14. C
15. B
16. D
17. C
18. C
19. C
20. A

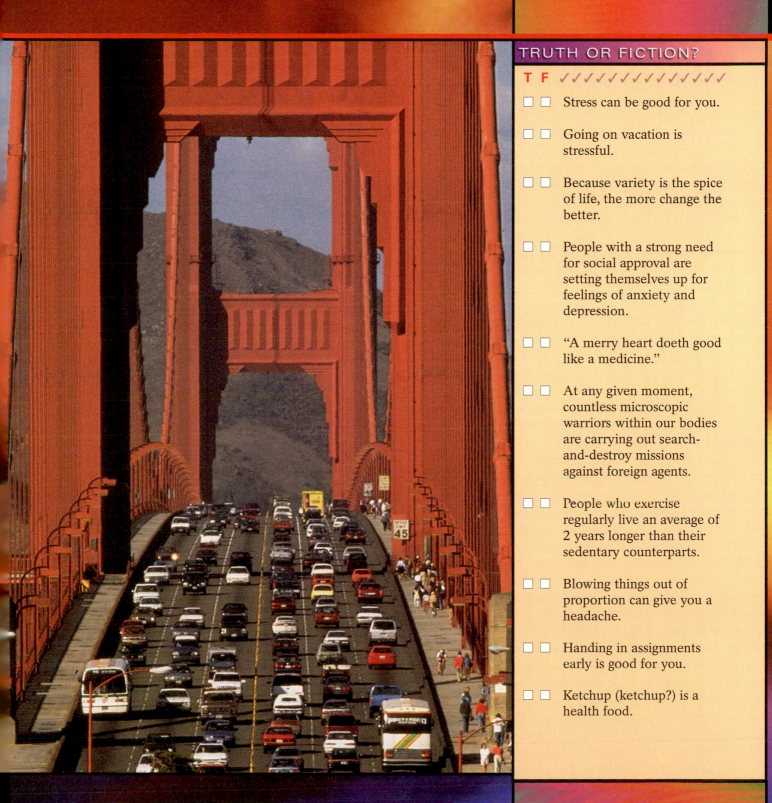

STRESS AND HEALTH

11

This chapter, "Stress and Health," covers the following:

SECTION. I. HEALTH PSYCHOLOGY

Defines health psychology

SECTION II. STRESS: PRESSES, PUSHES, AND PULLS

Defines stress

SECTION III. SOURCES OF STRESS: DON'T HASSLE ME? (RIGHT)

Explains why daily hassles are . . . hassles
Explains why too much of a good thing can turn out to be a bad thing
Defines conflict
Explains how strong needs for social approval and getting things exactly right can make one miserable
Defines Type A behavior

SECTION IV. PSYCHOLOGICAL MODERATORS OF STRESS

Explains how belief in oneself can help one cope with stress
Defines psychological hardiness and how it helps one cope with stress
Reports evidence that "A merry heart doeth good like a medicine"
Explains why predictability and control can reduce the effects of stress
Reports evidence that social support can help one cope with stress

SECTION V. STRESS AND THE BODY

Describes the general adaptation syndrome
Explains how the immune system works
Explains how stress affects the functioning of the immune system

SECTION VI. COPING WITH STRESS

Explains how we can change those nagging irrational thoughts (yes, you can)
Explains how we can lower our levels of arousal and turn down the inner alarm system
Explains how exercise helps people cope with stress

SECTION VII. A MULTIFACTORIAL APPROACH TO HEALTH AND ILLNESS

Defines the multifactorial approach to health and illness
Describes the relationships between ethnicity, gender, and socioeconomic status on the one hand and health on the other

SECTION VIII. HEALTH PROBLEMS AND PSYCHOLOGY

Describes the contributions of psychology to the understanding and treatment of headaches
Describes the contributions of psychology to the understanding and treatment of coronary heart disease
Describes the contributions of psychology to the understanding and treatment of cancer

Sirens. Ambulances. Stretchers. The emergency room at Dallas's public Parkland Memorial Hospital is a busy place. Sirens wail endlessly as ambulances pull up to the doors and discharge people who need prompt attention. Because of the volume of patients, beds line the halls, and people who do not require immediate care cram the waiting room. Many hours may pass before they are seen by a doctor. It is not unusual for people who are not considered in danger to wait 10 to 12 hours.

All this may sound rather foreboding, but good things are happening at Parkland as well. One of them is the attention physicians are devoting to patients' psychological needs as well as to their physical needs. For example, influenced both by his own clinical experience and by Native American wisdom about the healing process, Dr. Ron Anderson teaches his medical students that caring about patients is not an outdated ideal. Rather, it is a powerful weapon against disease.

TV journalist Bill Moyers describes Anderson on his medical rounds with students:

I listen as he stops at the bedside of an elderly woman suffering from chronic asthma. He asks the usual questions: "How did you sleep last night?" "Is the breathing getting any easier?" His next questions surprise the medical students: "Is your son still looking for work?" "Is he still drinking?" "Tell us what happened right before the asthma attack." He explains to his puzzled students. "We know that anxiety aggravates many illnesses, especially chronic conditions like asthma. So we have to find out what may be causing her episodes of stress and help her find some way of coping with it. Otherwise she will land in here again, and next time we might not be able to save her. We cannot just prescribe medication and walk away. That is medical neglect. We have to take the time to get to know her, how she lives, her values, what her social supports are. If we don't know that her son is her sole support and that he's out of work, we will be much less effective in dealing with her asthma." (Moyers, 1993, p. 2)

SECTION I. HEALTH PSYCHOLOGY

Note some key concepts from the slice of hospital life reported by Moyers: "Anxiety aggravates many illnesses." "We have to find out what may be causing . . . stress and . . . find some way of coping with it." "We cannot just prescribe medication and walk away." "We have to take the time to get to know [patients]"—how they live, their values, what their social supports are.

Anderson and Moyers have given us a fine introduction to the field of **health psychology.** Question: What is health psychology? Health psychology is the field of psychology that studies the relationships between psychological factors and the prevention and treatment of physical health problems (Taylor, 1990). The case of the woman with asthma is a useful springboard for discussion because health psychologists study the ways in which

- psychological factors such as stress, behavior patterns, and attitudes can lead to or aggravate illness
- people can cope with stress
- stress and **pathogens** (disease-causing organisms such as bacteria and viruses) interact to influence the immune system
- people decide whether or not to seek health care
- psychological forms of intervention such as health education (e.g., concerning nutrition, smoking, and exercise) and behavior modification can contribute to physical health

In this chapter we consider a number of issues in health psychology: sources of stress, factors that moderate the impact of stress, and the body's response to stress.

SECTION I **Review**

The field of health psychology studies the relationships between (1) _____ical factors and the prevention and treatment of physical health problems. Health psychologists study the ways in which stress and (2) _____gens (disease-causing organisms) interact to influence the immune system.

HEALTH PSYCHOLOGY The field of psychology that studies the relationships between psychological factors (e.g., attitudes, beliefs, situational influences, and behavior patterns) and the prevention and treatment of physical illness.

PATHOGEN A microscopic organism (e.g., bacterium or virus) that can cause disease.

SECTION II. STRESS: PRESSES, PUSHES, AND PULLS

Americans will put up with anything provided it doesn't block traffic.

DAN RATHER

Question: What is stress? In physics, stress is defined as a pressure or force exerted on a body. Tons of rock pressing on the earth, one car smashing into another, a rubber band stretching—all are types of physical stress. Psychological forces, or stresses, also press, push, or pull. We may feel "crushed" by the weight of a big decision, "smashed" by adversity, or "stretched" to the point of snapping.

In psychology, **stress** is the demand made on an organism to adapt, cope, or adjust. Some stress is healthful and necessary to keep us alert and occupied. Stress researcher Hans Selye (1980) referred to such healthful stress as **eustress** (pronounced YOU-STRESS). But intense or prolonged stress can overtax our adjustive capacity, affect our moods, impair our ability to experience pleasure, and harm the body (Berenbaum & Connelly, 1993; Cohen et al., 1993).

✓ Truth or Fiction Revisited

It is true that stress can be good for you. So-called eustress keeps us alert and occupied. However, too much stress is connected with psychological and physical health problems.

SECTION II Review

(3) S_____ is defined as the demand made on an organism to adjust. Healthful (4) eu_____ keeps us alert and occupied.

SECTION III. SOURCES OF STRESS: DON'T HASSLE ME? (RIGHT)

There are many sources of stress. In this section we consider daily hassles, life changes, conflict, irrational beliefs, and Type A behavior.

Daily Hassles

Which straw will break the camel's back? The *last* straw, according to the saying. Similarly, stresses can pile up until we can no longer cope with them. Some of these stresses are **daily hassles.** Question: What are daily hassles? Daily hassles are regularly occurring conditions and experiences that can threaten or harm our well-being. Others are life changes. Lazarus and his colleagues (1985) analyzed a scale that measures daily hassles and their opposites—termed **uplifts**—and found that hassles could be grouped as follows:

1. *Household hassles:* preparing meals, shopping, and home maintenance

2. *Health hassles:* physical illness, concern about medical treatment, and side effects of medication

3. *Time-pressure hassles:* having too many things to do, too many responsibilities, and not enough time

STRESS The demand made on an organism to adapt.

EUSTRESS Stress that is healthful.

DAILY HASSLES Notable daily conditions and experiences that are threatening or harmful to a person's well-being.

UPLIFTS Notable pleasant daily conditions and experiences.

A Daily Hassle. Daily hassles are notable daily conditions and experiences that are threatening or harmful to a person's well-being. The hassles shown in this photograph center on commuting. What are some of the daily hassles in your life?

4. *Inner concern hassles:* being lonely and fearful of confrontation
5. *Environmental hassles:* crime, neighborhood deterioration, and traffic noise
6. *Financial responsibility hassles:* concern about owing money such as mortgage payments and loan installments
7. *Work hassles:* job dissatisfaction, not liking one's duties at work, and problems with co-workers
8. *Future security hassles:* concerns about job security, taxes, property investments, stock market swings, and retirement.

These hassles are linked to psychological variables such as nervousness, worrying, inability to get started, feelings of sadness, and feelings of loneliness. For example, 83% of people in the United States will be victimized by a violent crime at some time, and victimization is connected with problems such as anxiety, physical complaints, hostility, and depression (Norris & Kaniasty, 1994).

Life Changes

You might think that marrying Mr. or Ms. Right, finding a good job, and moving to a better neighborhood all in the same year would propel you into a state of bliss. It might. But too much of a good thing may also make you ill. Question: How is it that too much of a good thing can make you ill? It is because all of these events are life changes. As pleasant as they may be, they require adjustment. Coming one after another, life changes, even positive ones, can lead to headaches, high blood pressure, and other health problems.

Life changes differ from daily hassles in two key ways:

1. Many life changes are positive and desirable. Hassles, by definition, are negative.
2. Hassles occur regularly. Life changes occur at irregular intervals.

Peggy Blake and her colleagues (1984) constructed a scale to measure the impact of life changes among college students. Surveys with students

Life Changes. Life changes differ from daily hassles in that they tend to be more episodic. Also, life changes can be positive as well as negative. What is the relationship between life changes and illness? Is the relationship causal?

revealed that death of a spouse or parent were considered the most stressful life changes (94 and 88 life-change units, respectively; see Table 11.1). Academic failure (77 units) and graduation from college (68 units) were also considered highly stressful, even though graduation from college is a positive event—considering the alternative. Positive life changes such as an outstanding personal achievement (49 units) and going on vacation (30 units) also made the list.

✓ Truth or Fiction Revisited

It is true that going on vacation is stressful. A vacation is a life change, and change requires adjustment. Note that an improvement in one's health is also stressful, but here is some stress that we should welcome!

HASSLES, LIFE CHANGES, AND HEALTH PROBLEMS Hassles and life changes—especially negative life changes—affect us psychologically. They can cause us to worry and affect our moods. But stressors such as hassles and life changes are also connected with health problems such as heart disease and cancer, even athletic injuries (Smith et al., 1990). Holmes and Rahe (1967) found that people who "earned" a high number of life-change units within a year, according to their own scale, were at greater risk for health problems. Eight of 10 developed health problems, compared with only 1 of 3 people whose totals of life-change units for the year were at a low level.

✓ Truth or Fiction Revisited

Although variety may be the spice of life, psychologists have not *found that more change is better.* Changes, even changes for the better, are sources of stress that require adjustment.

Moreover, people who remain married to the same person live longer than people who experience marital breakups and remarry (Tucker et al.,

TABLE 11.1	LIFE-CHANGE UNITS CONNECTED WITH VARIOUS EVENTS

Event	Life-Change Units
1. Death of a spouse, lover, or child	94
2. Death of a parent or sibling	88
3. Beginning formal higher education	84
4. Jail sentence	82
5. Divorce or marital separation	82
6. Unwanted pregnancy of self, spouse, or lover	80
7. Abortion of unwanted pregnancy of self, spouse, or lover	80
8. Academic failure	77
9. Marrying or living with lover against parents' wishes	75
10. Change in love relationship or important friendship	74
11. Change in marital status of parents	73
12. Hospitalization of a parent or sibling	70
13. Graduation from college	68
14. Major personal injury or illness	68
15. Wanted pregnancy of self, spouse, or lover	67
16. Preparing for an important exam or writing a major paper	65
17. Major financial difficulties	65
18. Change in academic status	64
19. Change in relationship with members of your immediate family	62
20. Hospitalization of yourself or a close relative	61
21. Change in course of study, major field, vocational goals, or work status	60
22. Change in own financial status	59
23. Beginning or ceasing service in the armed forces	57
24. Change in living arrangements, conditions, or environment	55
25. Change in frequency or nature of sexual experiences	55
26. Change in degree of interest in college or attitudes toward education	55
27. Academic success	54
28. Change to a new college or university	54
29. Change in number or type of arguments with roommate	52
30. Change in responsibility at work	50
31. Change in amount or nature of social activities	50
32. Change in routine at college or work	49
33. Change in amount of leisure time	49
34. Outstanding personal achievement	49
35. Improvement of own health	47
36. Change in study habits	46
37. Change in religious affiliation	44
38. Change in address or residence	43
39. Change in weight or eating habits	39
40. Vacation or travel	30

SOURCE: Adapted from *Self-Assessment and Behavior Change Manual* (pp. 43-47), by Peggy Blake, Robert Fry, and Michael Pesjack, 1984, New York: Random House. Reprinted by permission of Random House, Inc.

1996). Apparently the life changes of divorce and remarriage—or the instability associated with them—can be harmful to health.

EVALUATION Although the links among daily hassles, life changes, and illness seem to have been supported by a good deal of research, a careful evaluation reveals a number of limitations:

1. *Correlational evidence.* The links uncovered among hassles, life changes, and physical health problems are correlational rather than

FIGURE 11.1

WHAT ARE THE RELATIONSHIPS AMONG DAILY HASSLES, LIFE CHANGES, AND PHYSICAL ILLNESS? THERE ARE POSITIVE CORRELATIONS BETWEEN DAILY HASSLES AND LIFE EVENTS, ON THE ONE HAND, AND ILLNESS ON THE OTHER. IT MAY SEEM LOGICAL THAT HASSLES AND LIFE CHANGES CAUSE ILLNESS, BUT RESEARCH INTO THE ISSUE IS CORRELATIONAL AND NOT EXPERIMENTAL. THE RESULTS ARE THEREFORE SUBJECT TO RIVAL INTERPRETATIONS. ONE IS THAT PEOPLE WHO ARE PREDISPOSED TOWARD MEDICAL OR PSYCHOLOGICAL PROBLEMS ENCOUNTER OR GENERATE MORE HASSLES AND AMASS MORE LIFE-CHANGE UNITS.

experimental. It may seem logical that the hassles and life changes caused the disorders, but these variables were not manipulated experimentally. Other explanations of the data are possible (Figure 11.1). One possible explanation is that people who are predisposed toward medical or psychological problems encounter more hassles and amass more life-change units. For example, undiagnosed medical disorders may contribute to sexual problems, arguments with spouses or in-laws, changes in living conditions and personal habits, and changes in sleeping habits. People may also make certain changes in their lives that lead to physical and psychological disorders (Simons et al., 1993).

2. *Positive versus negative life changes.* Other aspects of the research on the relationship between life changes and illness have also been challenged. For instance, positive life changes may be less disturbing than hassles and negative life changes, even though the number of life-change units assigned to them is high (Lefcourt et al., 1981).

3. *Personality differences.* People with different kinds of personalities respond to life stresses in different ways (Vaillant, 1994). For example, people who are easygoing or psychologically hardy are less likely to become ill under the impact of stress.

4. *Cognitive appraisal.* The stress of an event reflects the meaning of the event to the individual (Whitehead, 1994). Pregnancy, for example, can be a positive or negative life change, depending on whether one wants and is prepared to have a child. We appraise the hassles, traumatic experiences, and life changes that we encounter (Creamer et al., 1992; Kiecolt-Glaser, 1993). In responding to them, we take into account their perceived danger, our values and goals, our beliefs in our coping ability, our social support, and so on. The same event is less taxing to someone with greater coping ability and support than to someone who lacks these advantages.

Despite these research problems, hassles and life changes require adjustment. It seems wise to be aware of hassles and life changes and how they may affect us.

Conflict

Should you eat dessert or try to stick to your diet? Should you live on campus, which is more convenient, or should you rent an apartment, where you may have more independence? Choices like these can place us in **conflict**. Question: What is conflict? In psychology, conflict is the feeling of being pulled in two or more directions by opposing motives. Conflict is frustrating and stressful. Psychologists often classify conflicts into four types: approach–approach, avoidance–avoidance, approach–avoidance, and multiple approach–avoidance.

Approach–approach conflict (Figure 11.2, part A) is the least stressful type. Here, each of two goals is desirable, and both are within reach. You may not be able to decide between pizza or tacos, Tom or Dick, or a trip to Nassau or Hawaii. Such conflicts are usually resolved by making a decision. People who experience this type of conflict may vacillate until they make a decision.

Avoidance–avoidance conflict (Figure 11.2, part B) is more stressful because you are motivated to avoid each of two negative goals. However, avoiding one of them requires approaching the other. You may be fearful of visiting the dentist but also afraid that your teeth will decay if you do not make an appointment and go. You may not want to contribute to the Association for the Advancement of Lost Causes, but you fear that your

CONFLICT Being torn in different directions by opposing motives. Feelings produced by being in conflict.

APPROACH–APPROACH CONFLICT A type of conflict in which the goals that produce opposing motives are positive and within reach.

AVOIDANCE–AVOIDANCE CONFLICT A type of conflict in which the goals are negative, but avoidance of one requires approaching the other.

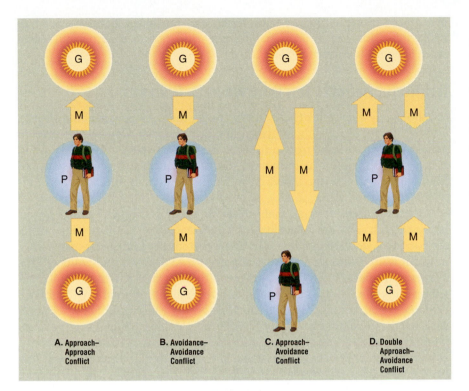

FIGURE 11.2
MODELS FOR CONFLICT   PART A SHOWS AN APPROACH – APPROACH CONFLICT, IN WHICH A PERSON (P) HAS MOTIVES (M) TO REACH TWO GOALS (G) THAT ARE DESIRABLE, BUT APPROACH OF ONE REQUIRES EXCLUSION OF THE OTHER. PART B SHOWS AN AVOIDANCE – AVOIDANCE CONFLICT, IN WHICH BOTH GOALS ARE NEGATIVE, BUT AVOIDING ONE REQUIRES APPROACHING THE OTHER. PART C SHOWS AN APPROACH – AVOIDANCE CONFLICT, IN WHICH THE SAME GOAL HAS DESIRABLE AND UNDESIRABLE PROPERTIES. PART D SHOWS A DOUBLE APPROACH – AVOIDANCE CONFLICT, WHICH IS THE SIMPLEST KIND OF *MULTIPLE* APPROACH – AVOIDANCE CONFLICT. IN A MULTIPLE APPROACH – AVOIDANCE CONFLICT, TWO OR MORE GOALS HAVE MIXED PROPERTIES.

A. Approach–Approach Conflict

B. Avoidance–Avoidance Conflict

C. Approach–Avoidance Conflict

D. Double Approach–Avoidance Conflict

friends will consider you cheap or uncommitted if you do not. Each goal in an avoidance–avoidance conflict is negative. When an avoidance–avoidance conflict is highly stressful and no resolution is in sight, some people withdraw from the conflict by focusing on other matters or doing nothing. Highly conflicted people have been known to refuse to get up in the morning and start the day.

When the same goal produces both approach and avoidance motives, we have an **approach–avoidance conflict** (Figure 11.2, part C). People and things have their pluses and minuses, their good points and their bad points. Cream cheese pie may be delicious, but oh, the calories! Goals that produce mixed motives may seem more attractive from a distance but undesirable from up close. Many couples repeatedly break up and then reunite. When they are apart and lonely, they may recall each other fondly and swear that they could make the relationship work if they got together again. But after they spend time together again, they may find themselves thinking, "How could I ever have believed that this so-and-so would change?"

The most complex form of conflict is the **multiple approach–avoidance conflict,** in which each of several alternative courses of action has pluses and minuses. An example with two goals is shown in Figure 11.2, part D. This sort of conflict might arise on the eve of an examination, when you are faced with the choice of studying or, say, going to a film. Each alternative has both positive and negative aspects: "Studying's a bore, but I won't have to worry about flunking. I'd love to see the movie, but I'd just be worrying about how I'll do tomorrow."

All forms of conflict entail motives that aim in opposite directions. When one motive is much stronger than the other—such as when you feel "starved" and are only slightly concerned about your weight—it will probably not be too stressful to act in accordance with the powerful motive—in this case, to eat. When each conflicting motive is powerful, however, you may experience high levels of stress and confusion about the

APPROACH–AVOIDANCE CONFLICT A type of conflict in which the same goal produces approach and avoidance motives.

MULTIPLE APPROACH–AVOIDANCE CONFLICT A type of conflict in which each of a number of goals produces approach and avoidance motives.

proper course of action. At such times you are faced with the need to make a decision. Yet decision making can also be stressful, especially when there is no clear correct choice.

Irrational Beliefs: Ten Doorways to Distress

Psychologist Albert Ellis (1977, 1993) notes that our beliefs about events, as well as the events themselves, can be stressors. Consider a case in which a person is fired from a job and is anxious and depressed about it. It may seem logical that losing the job is responsible for the misery, but Ellis points out how the individual's beliefs about the loss compound his or her misery.

Question: How do irrational beliefs create or compound stress? Let us examine this situation according to Ellis's A → B → C approach: Losing the job is an *activating event* (A). The eventual outcome, or *consequence* (C), is misery. Between the activating event (A) and the consequence (C), however, lie *beliefs* (B), such as these: "This job was the most important thing in my life," "What a no-good failure I am," "My family will starve," "I'll never find a job as good," "There's nothing I can do about it." Beliefs such as these compound misery, foster helplessness, and divert us from planning and deciding what to do next. The belief that "There's nothing I can do about it" fosters helplessness. The belief that "I am a no-good failure" internalizes the blame and may be an exaggeration. The belief that "My family will starve" may also be an exaggeration.

We can diagram the situation like this:

Activating events → Beliefs → Consequences

or A → B → C

Anxieties about the future and depression over a loss are normal and to be expected. However, the beliefs of the person who lost the job tend to **catastrophize** the extent of the loss and contribute to anxiety and depression. By heightening the individual's emotional reaction to the loss and fostering feelings of helplessness, these beliefs also impair coping ability. They lower the person's self-efficacy expectations.

Ellis proposes that many of us carry with us the irrational beliefs shown in Table 11.2. They are our personal doorways to distress. In fact, they can give rise to problems in themselves. When problems assault us from other sources, these beliefs can magnify their effect.

Ellis finds it understandable that we would want the approval of others but irrational to believe we cannot survive without it. It would be nice to be competent in everything we do, but it's unreasonable to *expect* it. Sure, it would be great to be able to serve and volley like a tennis pro, but most of us do not have the time or natural ability to perfect the game. Demanding perfection prevents us from going out on the court on weekends and batting the ball back and forth just for fun. Belief number 5 is a prescription for perpetual emotional upheaval. Beliefs numbers 7 and 9 lead to feelings of helplessness and demoralization. Sure, Ellis might say, childhood experiences can explain the origins of irrational beliefs, but it is our own cognitive appraisal—here and now—that makes us miserable.

Research findings support the connections between irrational beliefs (e.g., excessive dependence on social approval and perfectionism) and feelings of anxiety and depression (Blatt, 1995). Perfectionists are also more likely than other people to commit suicide when they are depressed (Pilkonis, 1996).

REFLECT

How many of Albert Ellis's irrational beliefs do you harbor? (Are you sure?) What is their effect on your life?

CATASTROPHIZE To interpret negative events as being disastrous; to "blow out of proportion."

TABLE 11.2	IRRATIONAL BELIEFS

Irrational Belief 1: You must have sincere love and approval almost all the time from the people who are important to you.

Irrational Belief 2: You must prove yourself to be thoroughly competent, adequate, and achieving at something important.

Irrational Belief 3: Things must go the way you want them to go. Life is awful when you don't get your first choice in everything.

Irrational Belief 4: Other people must treat everyone fairly and justly. When people act unfairly or unethically, they are rotten.

Irrational Belief 5: When there is danger or fear in your world, you must be preoccupied with and upset by it.

Irrational Belief 6: People and things should turn out better than they do. It's awful and horrible when you don't find quick solutions to life's hassles.

Irrational Belief 7: Your emotional misery stems from external pressures that you have little or no ability to control. Unless these external pressures change, you must remain miserable.

Irrational Belief 8: It is easier to evade life's responsibilities and problems than to face them and undertake more rewarding forms of self-discipline.

Irrational Belief 9: Your past influenced you immensely and must therefore continue to determine your feelings and behavior today.

Irrational Belief 10: You can achieve happiness by inertia and inaction or by just enjoying yourself from day to day.

✓ Truth or Fiction Revisited

People with a strong need for social approval do appear to be setting themselves up for feelings of anxiety and depression. They are anxious about whether or not they will receive social approval, and they are depressed when they do not receive enough of it.

The Type A Behavior Pattern

Some people create stress for themselves through the **Type A behavior** pattern. Question: What is Type A behavior? Type A people are highly driven, competitive, impatient, and aggressive (Thoresen & Powell, 1992). They feel "time urgency"; that is, they are rushed and under pressure and keep one eye firmly glued to the clock. They are not only prompt for appointments but often early. They eat, walk, and talk rapidly and become restless when others work slowly. They attempt to dominate group discussions. Type A people find it difficult to give up control or share power. They are often reluctant to delegate authority in the workplace, and because of this they increase their own workloads. Type A people criticize themselves mercilessly when they fail at a task (Moser & Dyck, 1989). They even seek out negative information about themselves in order to improve themselves (Cooney & Zeichner, 1985).

Type A people find it difficult just to go out on the tennis court and bat the ball back and forth. They watch their form, perfect their strokes, and demand continual self-improvement. They hold to the irrational belief that they must be perfectly competent and achieving in everything they undertake.

TYPE A BEHAVIOR Behavior characterized by a sense of time urgency, competitiveness, and hostility.

REFLECT

Are you Type A? How do you know? If the answer is yes, do you want to change? Explain.

Type A Behavior. The Type A behavior pattern is characterized by a sense of time urgency, competitiveness, and hostility.

Type B people, in contrast, relax more readily and focus more on the quality of life. They are less ambitious and less impatient, and they pace themselves. Type A people earn higher grades and more money than Type B people of equal intelligence. Type A people also seek greater challenges (Ortega & Pipal, 1984).

Review

SECTION III

Daily (5) _____s are regularly occurring conditions and experiences that threaten or harm our well-being. (6) _____ts are the opposite of hassles. Life changes, even pleasant ones, are stressful because they require (7) _____ment. Life changes differ from daily hassles in that many life changes are (8: Positive or Negative?). Life changes occur (9: More or Less?) regularly than daily hassles. Hassles and life changes (10: Are or Are not?) connected with life-threatening health problems such as heart disease and cancer. The links among hassles, life changes, and physical health problems are (11) _____tional rather than experimental.

(12) Con_____ is the feeling of being pulled in two or more directions by opposing motives. The least stressful type of conflict is the (13) approach – _____ conflict. In the multiple (14) _____ – _____ conflict, each of several alternatives has both pluses and minuses.
Albert (15) _____ notes that our beliefs about events, as well as the events themselves, can be stressors. Many people (16) _____phize unfortunate events; that is, they blow them out of proportion. Ellis's first two irrational beliefs are an excessive need for social (17) _____val and the need to be thoroughly competent, adequate, and achieving. Type A behavior is characterized by a sense of time (18) _____cy, competitiveness, and (19) ag_____ness. Type B people, by contrast, relax (20: Less or More?) readily and focus (21: Less or More?) on the quality of life.

SECTION IV. PSYCHOLOGICAL MODERATORS OF STRESS

There is no one-to-one relationship between the amount of stress we undergo and the physical illnesses or psychological distress we experience. Physical factors account for some of the variability in our responses: Some people inherit predispositions toward specific disorders. Psychological factors also play a role, however (Holahan & Moos, 1990). They can influence, or *moderate*, the effects of stress. In this section we discuss several psychological moderators of stress: self-efficacy expectations, psychological hardiness, a sense of humor, predictability, and social support.

Self-Efficacy Expectations: "The Little Engine That Could"

Our **self-efficacy expectations** affect our ability to withstand stress (Basic Behavioral Science Task Force, 1996). Question: How do our self-efficacy expectations affect our ability to withstand stress? For example, when we are faced with fear-inducing objects, high self-efficacy expectations are accompanied by relatively *lower* levels of adrenaline and noradrenaline in the bloodstream (Bandura et al., 1985). Adrenaline is secreted when we are under stress. It arouses the body in several ways, such as accelerating the heart rate and releasing glucose from the liver. As a result, we may have "butterflies in the stomach" and feel nervous. Excessive arousal can impair our ability to manage stress by boosting our motivation beyond optimal levels and by distracting us from the tasks at hand. People with higher self-efficacy expectations thus have biological as well as psychological reasons for remaining calmer.

People who are self-confident are less prone to be disturbed by adverse events (Benight et al., 1997; Holahan & Moos, 1991). People with higher self-efficacy expectations are more likely to lose weight or quit smoking and less likely to relapse afterward (DiClemente et al., 1991). They are better able to function in spite of pain (Lackner et al., 1996).

People are more likely to comply with medical advice when they believe that it will work. Women, for example, are more likely to engage in breast self-examination when they believe that they will really be able to detect abnormal growths (Miller et al., 1996). People with diabetes are more likely to use insulin when they believe that it will help control their blood-sugar level (Brownlee-Duffeck et al., 1987). People are more likely to try to quit smoking when they believe that they can do so successfully (Mischel & Shoda, 1995).

Psychological Hardiness

Psychological hardiness also helps people resist stress. Our understanding of this phenomenon is derived largely from the pioneering work of Suzanne Kobasa and her colleagues (1994). They studied business executives who seemed able to resist illness despite stress. In one phase of the research, executives completed a battery of psychological tests. Kobasa (1990) found that the psychologically hardy executives had three important characteristics. Question: What characteristics are connected with psychological hardiness? The characteristics include commitment, challenge, and control.

1. Kobasa found that psychologically hardy executives were high in *commitment*. They tended to involve themselves in, rather than feel alienated from, whatever they were doing or encountering.

Do you believe in yourself? How does your belief—or lack of belief—in yourself affect your life?

Self-Efficacy Expectations and Performance. Outstanding athletes like figure skater Michelle Kwan tend to have high self-efficacy expectations. That is, they believe in themselves. These expectations moderate the amount of stress that affects us.

SELF-EFFICACY EXPECTATIONS Our beliefs that we can bring about desired changes through our own efforts.

PSYCHOLOGICAL HARDINESS A cluster of traits that buffer stress and are characterized by commitment, challenge, and control.

REFLECT

Are you committed to your undertakings—including college? Do you seek or avoid challenges? Are you in control of your life? What do your answers suggest about your psychological hardiness?

2. They were also high in *challenge*. They believed that change, rather than stability, is normal in life. They appraised change as an interesting incentive to personal growth, not as a threat to security.

3. Finally, they were high in perceived *control* over their lives. They felt and behaved as though they were influential, rather than helpless, in facing the various rewards and punishments of life. Psychologically hardy people tend to have what Julian B. Rotter (1990) terms an internal **locus of control.**

Hardy people are more resistant to stress because they *choose* to face it (Kobasa, 1990). They also interpret stress as making life more interesting. For example, they see a conference with a supervisor as an opportunity to persuade the supervisor rather than as a risk to their position.

Sense of Humor: "A Merry Heart Doeth Good Like a Medicine"

The idea that humor lightens the burdens of life and helps people cope with stress has been with us for millennia (Lefcourt & Martin, 1986). Consider the biblical maxim "A merry heart doeth good like a medicine" (Proverbs 17:22).

Question: Is there any evidence that "A merry heart doeth good like a medicine"? Yes, both anecdotes and controlled research support this ancient maxim. In *Anatomy of an Illness,* writer Norman Cousins (1979) reported on his bout with a painful collagen illness that is similar to arthritis. He found that 10 minutes of belly laughter of the sort he experienced while watching Marx Brothers movies relieved much of his pain. Laughter allowed him to sleep. It may also have reduced the inflammation he suffered. This is consistent with some findings that emotional responses such as happiness and anger may have beneficial effects on the immune system (Kemeny, 1993).

Controlled research has also shown that humor can moderate the effects of stress. In one study, students completed a checklist of negative life events and a measure of mood disturbance (Martin & Lefcourt, 1983). The measure of mood disturbance also yielded a stress score. The students also rated their sense of humor. Behavioral assessments were made of their ability to produce humor under stress. Overall, there was a significant relationship between negative life events and stress scores: High accumulations of negative life events predicted higher levels of stress. However, students who had a greater sense of humor and produced humor in difficult situations were less affected by negative life events than other students. In other studies, Lefcourt (1997) found that watching humorous videotapes raised the level of immunoglobin A (a measure of the functioning of the immune system) in students' saliva.

REFLECT

Do you have a sense of humor? Has it ever helped you get through hard times?

✓ Truth or Fiction Revisited

It appears to be true that "A merry heart doeth good like a medicine." For example, a sense of humor can moderate the impact of stress. In an experiment run by Martin and Lefcourt, humor was shown to serve as a buffer against stress.

How does humor help people cope with stress? We are uncertain, but there has been speculation. One possibility, which would apply to the case of Norman Cousins, is that laughter stimulates the output of endorphins, which could benefit the functioning of the immune system. Another is more psychological: that the benefits of humor may be explained in terms

LOCUS OF CONTROL The place (locus) to which an individual attributes control over the receiving of reinforcers — either inside or outside the self.

of the sudden cognitive shifts they entail and the emotional changes that accompany them.

Predictability and Control

The ability to predict a stressor apparently moderates its impact. Question: How do predictability and control help us cope with stress? Predictability allows us to brace ourselves for the inevitable and, in many cases, plan ways of coping with it. There is also a relationship between the desire to assume control over one's situation and the usefulness of information about impending stressors (Lazarus & Folkman, 1984). Predictability is of greater benefit to **"internals"**—that is, to people who wish to exercise control over their situations—than to **"externals."** People who want information about medical procedures and what they will experience cope better with pain when they undergo those procedures (Ludwick-Rosenthal & Neufeld, 1993).

Social Support

People are social beings, and social support also seems to act as a buffer against the effects of stress (Burman & Margolin, 1992; Uchino et al., 1996).

Sources of social support include the following:

1. *Expression of emotional concern*—listening to people's problems and expressing feelings of sympathy, caring, understanding, and reassurance.

2. *Instrumental aid*—the material supports and services that facilitate adaptive behavior. For example, after a disaster the government may arrange for low-interest loans so that survivors can rebuild. Relief organizations may provide foodstuffs, medicines, and temporary living quarters.

3. *Information*—guidance and advice that enhances people's ability to cope.

4. *Appraisal*—feedback from others about how one is doing. This kind of support involves helping people interpret, or "make sense of," what has happened to them.

5. *Socializing*—simple conversation, recreation, even going shopping with another person. Socializing has beneficial effects, even when it is not oriented specifically toward solving problems.

Question: Is there evidence that social support helps people cope with stress? Yes, research does support the value of social support. Introverts, people who lack social skills, and people who live by themselves seem more prone to developing infectious diseases such as colds when they are under stress (Cohen & Williamson, 1991; Gilbert, 1997). Social support helps people cope with the stresses of cancer and other health problems (Azar, 1996a; Wilcox et al., 1994). People find caring for persons with Alzheimer's disease less stressful when they have social support (Haley et al., 1996). People who have buddies who help them start exercising or quit drinking or smoking are more likely to succeed (Gruder et al., 1993; Nides et al., 1995). Social support helped children cope with the stresses of Hurricane Andrew (Vernberg et al., 1996). It appears to protect people from feelings of depression and to aid in recovery from depression (Holahan et al., 1995; Lewinsohn et al., 1994b). Stress is also less likely to lead to high blood pressure or alcohol abuse in people who have social support (Linden et al., 1993).

REFLECT

Are you an "internal" or an "external"? Are you satisfied with the situation? If not, what are *you* going to do about it?

REFLECT

Do you find social support to be important in your own life? Explain. Do you have a network of social support? If not, how can you find it?

Review

SECTION IV

Our (22) self-_____ expectations are our perceptions of our capacities to bring about change. People with (23: Higher or Lower?) self-efficacy expectations tend to cope better with stress. High self-efficacy expectations (24: Raise or Lessen?) levels of adrenaline in the bloodstream. Kobasa and her colleagues have found that psychologically hardy executives are high in (25) _____ment (they involve themselves in, rather than experience alienation from, what they are doing). Hardy individuals are also high in challenge and in (26) con_____. Being able to predict and control the onset of a stressor (27: Increases or Decreases?) its impact upon us. Research shows that students who produce humor in stressful situations are (28: More or Less?) affected by negative life events than other students. Watching humorous videotapes raises the level of (29) immuno_____ A in students' saliva. Social support (30: Does or Does Not?) buffer the effects of stress.

"INTERNALS" People who perceive the ability to attain reinforcements as being largely within themselves.

"EXTERNALS" People who perceive the ability to attain reinforcements as being largely outside themselves.

GENERAL ADAPTATION SYNDROME Selye's term for a hypothesized three-stage response to stress. Abbreviated *GAS*.

ALARM REACTION The first stage of the GAS, which is triggered by the impact of a stressor and characterized by sympathetic activity.

FIGHT-OR-FLIGHT REACTION An innate adaptive response to the perception of danger.

Are Their Alarm Systems Going Off as They Take Out a Loan? The alarm reaction of the general adaptation syndrome can be triggered by daily hassles and life changes—such as taking out a large loan—as well as by physical threats. When the stressor persists, diseases of adaptation may develop.

REFLECT

What do you experience happening in your body when you are under stress? How do those sensations fit the description of the general adaptation syndrome?

SECTION V. STRESS AND THE BODY

Stress is more than a psychological event. It is more than "knowing" it is there; it is more than "feeling" pushed and pulled. Stress also has very definite effects on the body. Stress researcher Hans Selye outlined a number of them in his concept of the *general adaptation syndrome.*

The General Adaptation Syndrome

How can stress make us ill? Selye (1976) suggested that under stress the body is like a clock with an alarm system that does not shut off until its energy has been depleted. He observed that the body's response to various kinds of stressors shows certain similarities whether the stressor is a bacterial invasion, perceived danger, or a major life change. For this reason, he labeled this response the **general adaptation syndrome** (GAS). Question: What is the general adaptation syndrome? The GAS is a cluster of bodily changes that occur in three stages: an alarm reaction, a resistance stage, and an exhaustion stage.

THE ALARM REACTION The **alarm reaction** is triggered by perception of a stressor. This reaction mobilizes or arouses the body in preparation for defense. Early in the 20th century, physiologist Walter Cannon termed this alarm system the **fight-or-flight reaction.** The alarm reaction involves a number of body changes that are initiated by the brain and further regulated by the endocrine system and the sympathetic division of the autonomic nervous system (ANS). Let us consider the roles of these systems.

Stress has a domino effect on the endocrine system (Figure 11.3). The hypothalamus secretes corticotrophin-releasing hormone (CRH). CRH causes the pituitary gland to secrete adrenocorticotrophic hormone (ACTH). ACTH then causes the adrenal cortex to secrete cortisol and other corticosteroids (steroidal hormones produced by the adrenal cortex). Corticosteroids help protect the body by combating allergic reactions (such as difficulty breathing) and producing inflammation. Inflammation increases circulation to parts of the body that are injured. It ferries in hordes of white blood cells to fend off invading pathogens.

FIGURE 11.3
STRESS AND THE ENDOCRINE SYSTEM STRESS HAS
A DOMINO EFFECT ON THE ENDOCRINE SYSTEM, LEADING TO THE
RELEASE OF CORTICOSTEROIDS AND A MIXTURE OF ADRENALINE
AND NORADRENALINE. CORTICOSTEROIDS COMBAT ALLERGIC RE-
ACTIONS (SUCH AS DIFFICULTY IN BREATHING) AND CAUSE IN-
FLAMMATION. ADRENALINE AND NORADRENALINE AROUSE THE
BODY TO COPE BY ACCELERATING THE HEART RATE AND PROVID-
ING ENERGY FOR THE FIGHT-OR-FLIGHT REACTION.

In the figure:

- Hypothalamus
- Pituitary
- Adrenal cortex
- Adrenal medulla

The Hypothalamus secretes corticotrophin-releasing hormone (CRH)

CRH causes the Pituitary Gland to secrete adrenocorticotrophic hormone (ACTH)

Stressor

ACTH then causes the Adrenal Cortex to secrete corticosteroids

The Adrenal Medulla releases a mixture of adrenaline and noradrenaline

Two other hormones that play a major role in the alarm reaction are secreted by the adrenal medulla. The sympathetic division of the ANS activates the adrenal medulla, causing it to release a mixture of adrenaline and noradrenaline. This mixture arouses the body by accelerating the heart rate and causing the liver to release glucose (sugar). This provides the energy that fuels the fight-or-flight reaction, which activates the body so that it is prepared to fight or flee from a predator.

The fight-or-flight reaction stems from a period in human prehistory when many stressors were life-threatening. It was triggered by the sight of a predator at the edge of a thicket or by a sudden rustling in the undergrowth. Today it may be aroused when you are caught in stop-and-go traffic or learn that your mortgage payments are going to increase. Once the threat is removed, the body returns to a lower state of arousal. Many of the bodily changes that occur in the alarm reaction are outlined in Table 11.3.

THE RESISTANCE STAGE If the alarm reaction mobilizes the body and the stressor is not removed, we enter the adaptation or **resistance stage** of the GAS. Levels of endocrine and sympathetic activity are lower than in the alarm reaction but still higher than normal. In this stage the body attempts to restore lost energy and repair bodily damage.

TABLE 11.3	COMPONENTS OF THE ALARM REACTION
Corticosteroids are secreted	Muscles tense
Adrenaline is secreted	Blood shifts from internal organs to the
Noradrenaline is secreted	skeletal musculature
Respiration rate increases	Digestion is inhibited
Heart rate increases	Sugar is released from the liver
Blood pressure increases	Blood coagulability increases

The alarm reaction is triggered by various types of stressors. It is defined by the release of corticosteroids and adrenaline and by activity of the sympathetic branch of the autonomic nervous system. It prepares the body to fight or flee from a source of danger.

RESISTANCE STAGE The second stage of the GAS, characterized by prolonged sympathetic activity in an effort to restore lost energy and repair damage. Also called the *adaptation stage*.

THE EXHAUSTION STAGE If the stressor is still not dealt with adequately, we may enter the **exhaustion stage** of the GAS. Individual capacities for resisting stress vary, but anyone will eventually become exhausted when stress continues indefinitely. The muscles become fatigued. The body is depleted of the resources required for combating stress. With exhaustion, the parasympathetic division of the ANS may predominate. As a result, our heartbeat and respiration rate slow down and many aspects of sympathetic activity are reversed. It might sound as if we would profit from the respite, but remember that we are still under stress—possibly an external threat. Continued stress in the exhaustion stage may lead to what Selye terms "diseases of adaptation." These are connected with constriction of blood vessels and alternation of the heart rhythm and can range from allergies and hives to ulcers and coronary heart disease—and, ultimately, death.

Let us now consider the effects of stress on the body's immune system. Our discussion will pave the way for understanding the links between various psychological factors and physical illnesses.

Effects of Stress on the Immune System

Research shows that stress suppresses the **immune system** (Delahanty et al., 1996; O'Leary, 1990). Psychological factors such as feelings of control and social support moderate these effects (Gilbert, 1997).

HOW THE IMMUNE SYSTEM WORKS Given the complexity of the human body and the fast pace of scientific change, we often feel we must depend on trained professionals to cope with illness. Yet we actually do most of this coping by ourselves, by means of the immune system. Question: How does the immune system work?

The immune system has several functions that combat disease. One of these is the production of white blood cells, which engulf and kill pathogens such as bacteria, fungi, and viruses as well as worn-out body cells and even cancerous cells. The technical term for white blood cells is **leukocytes** (Figure 11.4). Leukocytes carry on microscopic warfare. They

EXHAUSTION STAGE The third stage of the GAS, characterized by weakened resistance and possible deterioration.

IMMUNE SYSTEM The system of the body that recognizes and destroys foreign agents (antigens) that invade the body.

LEUKOCYTES White blood cells.

FIGURE 11.4
MICROSCOPIC WARFARE   THE IMMUNE SYSTEM HELPS US COMBAT DISEASE. IT PRODUCES WHITE BLOOD CELLS (LEUKOCYTES), SHOWN HERE, WHICH ROUTINELY ENGULF AND KILL PATHOGENS LIKE BACTERIA AND VIRUSES.

carry out search-and-destroy missions in which they "recognize" and eradicate foreign agents and unhealthy cells.

Leukocytes recognize foreign substances by their shapes. These foreign substances are also termed **antigens** because the body reacts to them by generating specialized proteins, or **antibodies.** Antibodies attach themselves to the foreign substances, deactivating them and marking them for destruction. The immune system "remembers" how to battle antigens by maintaining their antibodies in the bloodstream, often for years.

Inflammation is another function of the immune system. When injury occurs, blood vessels in the area first contract (to stem bleeding) and then dilate. Dilation increases the flow of blood to the damaged area, causing the redness and warmth that characterize inflammation. The increased blood supply also floods the region with white blood cells to combat invading microscopic life-forms such as bacteria, which otherwise might use the local damage as a port of entry into the body.

✓ Truth or Fiction Revisited

It is true that countless microscopic warriors within our bodies are carrying out search-and-destroy missions against foreign agents at any given moment. The warriors are the white blood cells of the immune system.

STRESS AND THE IMMUNE SYSTEM Psychologists, biologists, and medical researchers have combined their efforts in a field of study that addresses the relationships among psychological factors, the nervous system, the endocrine system, the immune system, and disease. This field is called **psychoneuroimmunology** (Maier et al., 1994). One of its major concerns is the effect of stress on the immune system. Question: How does stress affect the functioning of the immune system?

One of the reasons that stress eventually exhausts us is that it stimulates the production of steroids. Steroids suppress the functioning of the immune system. Suppression has negligible effects when steroids are secreted intermittently. However, persistent secretion of steroids decreases inflammation and interferes with the formation of antibodies. As a consequence, we become more vulnerable to various illnesses, including the common cold (Cohen et al., 1993).

In one study, dental students showed lower immune system functioning, as measured by lower levels of antibodies in their saliva, during stressful periods of the school year than immediately following vacations (Jemmott et al., 1983). In contrast, social support buffers the effects of stress and enhances the functioning of the immune system (Gilbert, 1997; Uchino et al., 1996). In the Jemmott study, students who had many friends showed less suppression of immune system functioning than students with few friends.

Other studies have shown that the stress of exams depresses the immune system's response to the Epstein-Barr virus, which causes fatigue and other problems (Glaser et al., 1991, 1993). Here, too, students who were lonely showed greater suppression of the immune system than students who had more social support. A study of older people found that a combination of relaxation training, which decreases sympathetic nervous system activity, and training in coping skills *improves* the functioning of the immune system (Glaser et al., 1991). Moreover, psychological methods that reduce stress and anxiety in cancer patients may prolong their survival by boosting the functioning of their immune system (Azar, 1996b).

REFLECT

Do you have the feeling that stress affects your health? Explain.

ANTIGEN A substance that stimulates the body to mount an immune system response to it (the contraction for *anti*body *gen*erator).

ANTIBODIES Substances formed by white blood cells that recognize and destroy antigens.

INFLAMMATION Increased blood flow to an injured area of the body, resulting in redness, warmth, and an increased supply of white blood cells.

PSYCHONEUROIMMUNOLOGY The field that studies the relationships between psychological factors (e.g., attitudes and overt behavior patterns) and the functioning of the immune system.

The general adaptation syndrome (GAS) consists of (31: How many?) _____ stages. These stages are the (32) _____ reaction, the resistance stage, and the (33) _____tion stage. The alarm reaction (34) _____lizes, or arouses, the body for defense. Cannon had earlier termed this alarm system the (35) _____-or-_____ reaction.

The alarm reaction involves a number of body changes that are initiated by the brain and further regulated by the (36) _____rine system and the (37) _____ division of the autonomic nervous system. Under stress, the pituitary gland secretes (38) _____. ACTH causes the adrenal cortex to release (39) _____roids that help the body respond to stress by fighting (40) _____mation and allergic reactions. Two hormones that play a major role in the alarm reaction are secreted by the adrenal medulla: (41) ad_____ and (42) nor_____.

When stress persists we eventually reach the (43) _____tion stage. During the exhaustion stage, the (44) _____tic division of the ANS predominates.

The immune system produces (45) _____ blood cells that routinely engulf and kill pathogens. White blood cells are technically termed (46) _____ytes. Pathogens that are recognized and destroyed by leucocytes are called (47) _____ens. Some leucocytes produce (48) _____dies, or specialized proteins that bind to their antigens and mark them for destruction. One reason that stress eventually exhausts us is that it stimulates us to produce (49) _____ds. Steroids (50: Enhance or Suppress?) the functioning of the immune system. Dental students in one study showed (51: Stronger or Weaker?) immune-system functioning during stressful school periods than immediately following vacations.

SECTION VI. COPING WITH STRESS

What do these strategies have in common: (1) telling yourself you can live with another person's disappointment, (2) taking a deep breath and telling yourself to relax, (3) taking the scenic route to work, and (4) jogging for half an hour? These are all methods suggested by psychologists to help people cope with the stresses of modern life.

Stress takes many forms and can harm our psychological well-being and physical health. Here we highlight ways of coping with stress: controlling irrational thoughts, lowering arousal, and exercising.

Controlling Irrational Thoughts

People often feel pressure from their own thoughts. Consider the following experiences:

1. You have difficulty with the first item on a test and become convinced that you will flunk.

2. You want to express your genuine feelings but think that if you do so you might make another person angry or upset.

3. You haven't been able to get to sleep for 15 minutes and assume that you will lie awake all night and feel "wrecked" in the morning.

4. You're not sure what decision to make, so you try to put the problem out of your mind by going out, playing cards, or watching TV.

5. You decide not to play tennis because your form isn't perfect and you're in less than perfect condition.

If you have had these or similar experiences, it may be because you harbor some of the irrational beliefs identified by Albert Ellis (see Table 11.4).

REFLECT

Have you had anything like these five experiences in your own life? How did you handle them? Can the advice in this chapter help you to handle them better? Explain.

TABLE 11.4	CONTROLLING IRRATIONAL BELIEFS AND THOUGHTS
Irrational (Upsetting) Thoughts	**Incompatible (Calming) Thoughts**
"Oh, my God, I'm going to completely lose control!"	"This is painful and upsetting, but I don't have to go to pieces over it."
"This will never end."	"This will end even if it's hard to see the end right now."
"It'll be awful if Mom gives me that look again."	"It's more pleasant when Mom's happy with me, but I can live with it if she isn't."
"How can I go out there? I'll look like a fool."	"So you're not perfect. That doesn't mean that you're going to look stupid. And so what if someone thinks you look stupid? You can live with that, too. Just stop worrying and have some fun."
"My heart's going to leap out of my chest! How much can I stand?"	"Easy—hearts don't leap out of chests. Stop and think! Distract yourself. Breathe slowly, in and out."
"What can I do? There's nothing I can do!"	"Easy—stop and think. Just because you can't think of a solution right now doesn't mean there's nothing you can do. Take it a minute at a time. Breathe easy."

Do irrational beliefs or catastrophizing thoughts compound your feelings of anxiety and tension? Cognitive psychologists suggest that you can cope with stress by becoming aware of your irrational, upsetting thoughts and replacing them with rational, calming thoughts.

These beliefs may make you overly concerned about the approval of others (item 2 in the preceding list) or perfectionistic (item 5). They may lead you to think that you can solve problems by pretending they do not exist (item 4) or that a minor setback will invariably lead to greater problems (items 1 and 3).

Question: How, then, do we change the irrational thoughts that create and compound stress? The answer is deceptively simple: We just change them. However, this may require work. Moreover, before we can change our thoughts we must become aware of them.

THREE STEPS FOR CONTROLLING IRRATIONAL THOUGHTS

Meichenbaum and Jaremko (1983) suggest a three-step procedure for controlling the irrational or catastrophizing thoughts that often accompany feelings of anxiety, conflict, or tension:

1. Develop awareness of these thoughts through careful self-examination. Study the examples at the beginning of this section or in Tables 11.2 or 11.4 to see whether they apply to you. When you encounter anxiety or frustration, pay close attention to your thoughts. Are they guiding you toward a solution, or are they compounding your problems?

2. Prepare thoughts that are incompatible with the irrational or catastrophizing thoughts and practice saying them firmly to yourself. (If nobody is nearby, why not say them firmly aloud?)

3. Reward yourself with a mental pat on the back for making effective changes in your beliefs and thought patterns.

Lowering Arousal: Turning Down the Inner Alarm

Stress tends to trigger intense activity in the sympathetic branch of the autonomic nervous system—in other words, arousal. Arousal is a sign that something may be wrong. It is a message telling us to survey the situation and take appropriate action. But once we are aware that a stressor is acting on us and have developed a plan to cope with it, it is no longer helpful to have blood pounding fiercely through our arteries. Question: How can we lower our levels of arousal? How can we turn down the inner alarm? Psychologists and other scientists have developed many methods for teaching people to reduce arousal. These include meditation (see the chapter on consciousness), biofeedback (see the chapter on learning), and progressive relaxation.

PROGRESSIVE RELAXATION In progressive relaxation, people purposefully tense a particular muscle group before relaxing it. This sequence allows them to develop awareness of their muscle tensions and also to differentiate between feelings of tension and relaxation.

Progressive relaxation lowers the arousal produced by the alarm reaction. It has been found useful for stress-related illnesses ranging from headaches (Blanchard et al., 1990a) to hypertension (Agras et al., 1983). You can experience muscle relaxation in the arms by doing the exercise described next:

Settle down in a reclining chair, dim the lights, and loosen any tight clothing. Use the instructions given here. They can be memorized (slight variations from the text are all right), recorded and played back, or read aloud by a friend. For instructions about relaxation of the entire body, consult a psychologist or other helping professional who is familiar with the technique.

> Settle back as comfortably as you can. Let yourself relax to the best of your ability. . . . Now, as you relax like that, clench your right fist, just clench your fist tighter and tighter, and study the tension as you do so. Keep it clenched and feel the tension in your right fist, hand, forearm . . . and now relax. Let the fingers of your right hand become loose, and observe the contrast in your feelings. . . . Now, let yourself go and try to become more relaxed all over. . . . Once more, clench your right fist really tight . . . hold it, and notice the tension again. . . . Now let go, relax; your fingers straighten out, and you notice the difference once more. . . . Now repeat that with your left fist. Clench your left fist while the rest of your body relaxes; clench that fist tighter and feel the tension . . . and now relax. Again enjoy the contrast. . . . Repeat that once more, clench the left fist, tight and tense. . . . Now do the opposite of tension—relax and feel the difference. Continue relaxing like that for a while. . . . Clench both fists tighter and together, both fists tense, forearms tense, study the sensations . . . and relax; straighten out your fingers and feel that relaxation. Continue relaxing your hands and forearms more and more. . . . Now bend your elbows and tense your biceps, tense them harder and study the tension feelings . . . all right, straighten out your arms, let them relax and feel that difference again. Let the relaxation develop. . . . Once more, tense your biceps; hold the tension and observe it carefully. . . . Straighten the arms and relax; relax to the best of your ability. . . . Each time, pay close attention to your feelings when you tense up and when you relax. Now

REFLECT

How do you know when your level of arousal is too high? What do you do about it? Can the advice in this chapter help you to handle it better? Explain.

straighten your arms, straighten them so that you feel most tension in the triceps muscles along the back of your arms; stretch your arms and feel that tension. . . . And now relax. Get your arms back into a comfortable position. Let the relaxation proceed on its own. The arms should feel comfortably heavy as you allow them to relax. . . . Straighten the arms once more so that you feel the tension in the triceps muscles; straighten them. Feel that tension . . . and relax. Now let's concentrate on pure relaxation in the arms without any tension. Get your arms comfortable and let them relax further and further. Continue relaxing your arms even further. Even when your arms seem fully relaxed, try to go that extra bit further; try to achieve deeper and deeper levels of relaxation. (Wolpe & Lazarus, 1966, p. 177)

Together, controlling irrational thoughts and reducing arousal lessen the impact of the stressor. These methods give you a chance to develop a plan for effective action. When effective action is not possible, controlling your thoughts and your level of arousal can enhance your capacity to tolerate discomfort.

Exercising: Run for Your Life?

I like long walks, especially when they are taken by people who annoy me.

FRED ALLEN

Exercise, particularly aerobic exercise, not only fosters physical health but can also enhance our psychological well-being and help in coping with stress (Hays, 1995). *Aerobic exercise* refers to exercise that requires a sustained increase in consumption of oxygen. Aerobic exercise promotes cardiovascular fitness. Aerobic exercises include, but are not limited to, running and jogging, running in place, walking (at more than a leisurely pace), aerobic dancing, jumping rope, swimming, bicycle riding, basketball, racquetball, and cross-country skiing.

Anaerobic exercises, in contrast, involve short bursts of muscle activity. Examples of anaerobic exercises are weight training, calisthenics (which usually allow rest periods between exercises), and sports such as baseball, in which there are infrequent bursts of strenuous activity. Anaerobic exercises can strengthen muscles and improve flexibility.

Question: How does exercise help people cope with stress? Exercise helps people cope by enhancing their physical fitness, or "condition." Fitness includes muscle strength; muscle endurance; suppleness or flexibility; cardiorespiratory, or aerobic, fitness; and a higher ratio of muscle to fat (usually due to both building muscle and reducing fat). Cardiovascular fitness, or "condition," means that the body can use more oxygen during vigorous activity, or when it is under stress, and pump more blood with each heartbeat. Because conditioned athletes' hearts pump more blood with each beat, they usually have a slower pulse rate—that is, fewer heartbeats per minute. However, during aerobic exercise they may double or triple their resting heart rate for minutes at a time. Stress can also elevate the heart rate, and conditioned people can sustain elevated heart rates with less wear and tear on the body.

Sustained physical activity does more than promote fitness. It also increases longevity by reducing the risk of heart attacks and other health problems (Curfman, 1993a). In one research program, Paffenbarger and his colleagues (1986, 1993) have been tracking some 17,000 Harvard

FIGURE 11.5

HEART ATTACKS AND PHYSICAL ACTIVITY

PAFFENBARGER AND HIS COLLEAGUES HAVE CORRELATED THE INCIDENCE OF HEART ATTACKS WITH LEVEL OF PHYSICAL ACTIVITY AMONG 17,000 HARVARD ALUMNI. THE INCIDENCE OF HEART ATTACKS DECLINES AS THE ACTIVITY LEVEL RISES TO BURNING ABOUT 2,000 CALORIES A WEEK BY MEANS OF PHYSICAL ACTIVITY. ABOVE 2,000 CALORIES A WEEK, HOWEVER, THE INCIDENCE OF HEART ATTACKS BEGINS TO CLIMB GRADUALLY AGAIN, ALTHOUGH NOT STEEPLY.

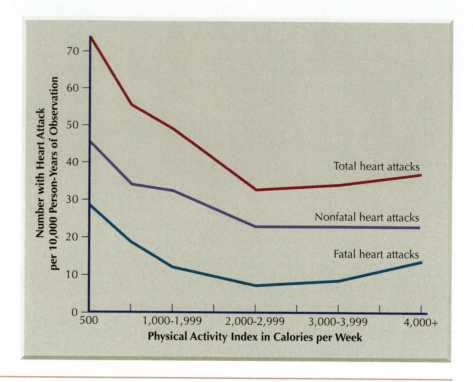

University alumni by means of university records and questionnaires. They have correlated the incidence of heart attacks in this group with their levels of physical activity. As shown in Figure 11.5, the incidence of heart attacks declines as physical activity rises to a level at which about 2,000 calories are used per week—the equivalent of jogging about 20 miles a week. Inactive alumni have the highest risk of heart attacks. Alumni who burn at least 2,000 calories a week through exercise live 2 years longer, on the average, than their less active counterparts.

Like jogging, long daily walks appear to cut the mortality rate. Amy Hakim of the University of Virginia School of Medicine and her colleagues (1998) reviewed 12 years of data on 707 retired men from the Honolulu Heart Program and found that 43.1% of the men who walked less than a mile per day died during that period, compared with 27.7% of those who walked from 1 to 2 miles a day and 21.5% of those who walked at least 2 miles daily (see Figure 11.6). Additional findings: 6.6% of the men who walked less than a mile a day died from coronary heart disease or strokes, compared with only 2.1% of those who walked upwards of 2 miles (see Figure 11.7). Moreover, 13.4% of men who walked less than a mile died from cancer, compared with 5.3% of men who walked more than 2 miles a day.

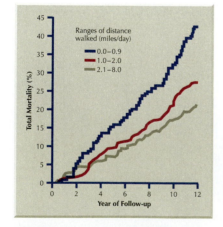

FIGURE 11.6

CUMULATIVE MORTALITY ACCORDING TO YEAR OF FOLLOW-UP AND DISTANCE WALKED PER DAY AMONG PARTICIPANTS IN THE HONOLULU HEART PROGRAM

AFTER 12 YEARS OF FOLLOW-UPS, RETIRED MEN WHO WALKED MORE THAN 2 MILES A DAY HAD LOWER MORTALITY RATES THAN MEN WHO WALKED SHORTER DISTANCES (HAKIM ET AL., 1998).

✓ Truth or Fiction Revisited

It is true that people who exercise regularly live an average of 2 years longer than their sedentary counterparts.

There is an important limitation to these studies: They are correlational and not experimental. It is possible that people who are in better health *choose* to engage in higher levels of physical activity. If such is the case, then their lower mortality rates due to heart attacks and cancer would be attributable to their initial superior health, not to their physical activity. Hakim and her colleagues recognized this problem and got around it partly by using data only on nonsmokers who were physically able to walk a few miles.

Aerobic exercise raises blood levels of high-density lipoproteins (HDL, or "good cholesterol") (Curfman, 1993b). HDL lowers the amount of low-density lipoproteins (LDL, or "bad cholesterol") in the blood. This is another way in which exercise may reduce the risk of heart attacks.

Psychologists are also interested in the effects of exercise on psychological variables. Articles have appeared on exercise as "therapy"—for example, "running therapy."

Consider depression. Depression is characterized by inactivity and feelings of helplessness. Exercise is, in a sense, the opposite of inactivity. Exercise might also help alleviate feelings of helplessness. In one experiment, McCann and Holmes (1984) randomly assigned mildly depressed college women to aerobic exercise, progressive relaxation, and a no-treatment control group. The relaxation group showed some improvement, but aerobic exercise dramatically reduced students' depression. Other experiments also find that exercise alleviates feelings of depression, at least among mildly and moderately depressed individuals (Buffone, 1984; Greist, 1984; Norvell & Belles, 1993). Exercise has also been shown to decrease anxiety and hostility and to boost self-esteem (Norvell & Belles, 1993).

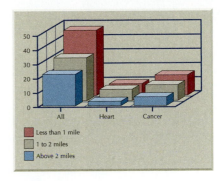

FIGURE 11.7

CAUSES OF DEATH AND DISTANCE WALKED IN MILES PER DAY AMONG PARTICIPANTS IN THE HONOLULU HEART PROGRAM   MEN WHO WALKED MORE THAN 2 MILES A DAY HAD A LOWER MORTALITY RATE THAN MEN WHO WALKED BETWEEN 1 AND 2 MILES A DAY AND MEN WHO WALKED LESS THAN A MILE A DAY. MEN WHO TOOK LONG WALKS WERE LESS LIKELY TO DIE FROM CANCER AND HEART DISEASE (HAKIM ET AL., 1998).

Review

SECTION VI

This section discusses three ways of coping with stress: controlling (52) _____tional thoughts, (53: Raising or Lowering?) arousal, and exercising. Meichenbaum and Jaremko suggest a three-step procedure for controlling irrational thoughts that accompany stress: First, develop awareness of the thoughts. Second, prepare and practice (54) in_____ thoughts. Third, reward yourself for changing. Methods for lowering bodily arousal include meditation, biofeedback, and (55) pro_____ relaxation. In progressive relaxation, people (56) _____ a particular muscle group and then relax it. Exercise helps people cope with stress by enhancing their physical (57) _____ness, or "condition." (58) _____bic exercise requires a sustained increase in consumption of oxygen. Sustained exercise (59: Increases or Decreases?) longevity by reducing the risk of heart attacks and other health problems. Exercise appears to (60: Increase or Alleviate?) feelings of depression.

REFLECT

What role does exercise play in your life? Should you, or can you, make exercise a greater part of your life? What kind of exercise is right for you?

SECTION VII. A MULTIFACTORIAL APPROACH TO HEALTH AND ILLNESS

Why do people become ill? Why do some people develop cancer? Why do others have heart attacks? Why do still others seem to be immune to these illnesses? Why do some of us seem to come down with everything that is going around, whereas others ride out the roughest winters without a sniffle? Question: What is the multifactorial approach to health and illness? The multifactorial approach recognizes that there is no single, simple answer to these questions. The likelihood of contracting an illness—be it a case of the flu or a kind of cancer—can reflect the interaction of many factors (Coie et al., 1993; Stokols, 1992).

TABLE 11.5	ANNUAL PREVENTABLE DEATHS IN THE UNITED STATES

- Elimination of tobacco use could prevent 400,000 deaths each year from cancer, heart and lung diseases, and stroke.

- Improved diet and exercise could prevent 300,000 deaths from conditions like heart disease, stroke, diabetes, and cancer.

- Control of underage and excess drinking of alcohol could prevent 100,000 deaths from motor vehicle accidents, falls, drownings, and other alcohol-related injuries.

- Immunizations for infectious diseases could prevent up to 100,000 deaths.

- Safer sex or sexual abstinence could prevent 30,000 deaths from sexually transmitted infections.

Other measures for preventing needless deaths include improved worker training and safety to prevent accidents in the workplace, wider screening for breast and cervical cancer, and control of high blood pressure and elevated blood cholesterol levels.

REFLECT

Do you seem to be prone to illness? What factors seem to be connected with illness in you?

Biological factors such as pathogens, inoculations, injuries, age, gender, and a family history of disease may strike us as the most obvious causes of illness. Genetics, in particular, tempts some people to assume there is little they can do about their health. But genes only create *predispositions* toward illness. As *The New York Times* health columnist Jane Brody (1995) notes, predispositions "need a conducive environment in which to express themselves. A bad family medical history should not be considered a portent of doom. Rather, it should be welcomed as an opportunity to keep those nasty genes from expressing themselves."

As shown in Figure 11.8, psychological and other factors also play key roles in health and illness (Ader, 1993; Mischel & Shoda, 1995). As shown in Table 11.5, nearly 1 million deaths each year in the United States are preventable (National Center for Health Statistics, 1996). Stopping smoking, eating properly, exercising, and controlling alcohol use would prevent nearly 80% of these. Psychological states such as anxiety and depression can impair the functioning of the immune system, rendering us more vulnerable to health problems (Esterling et al., 1993; Herbert & Cohen, 1993; Kemeny et al., 1994).

Sociocultural factors are also connected with health and illness.

Factors in Health and Diversity: The Roles of Ethnicity, Gender, and Socioeconomic Status

Today we know more about the connections among mental processes, behavior, and health than ever before. The United States also has the resources to provide the most advanced health care in the world. But not all Americans take advantage of contemporary knowledge. Nor do all profit equally from the health-care system. Health psychologists note, therefore, that from the perspective of health and health care we are many nations and not just one. Many factors influence whether people engage in good health practices or let themselves go. Many factors affect whether they act to prevent illness or succumb to it. Question: What are the relationships among ethnicity, gender, socioeconomic status, and health?

Biological Factors

Family history of illness
Exposure to infectious organisms
(e.g., bacteria and viruses)
Functioning of the immune system
Inoculations
Medication history
Congenital disabilities, birth complications
Physiological conditions (e.g., hypertension,
serum cholesterol level)
Reactivity of the cardiovascular system to stress
(e.g., "hot reactor")
Pain and discomfort
Age
Gender
Ethnicity (e.g., genetic vulnerability to
Tay-Sachs disease or sickle-cell anemia)

Sociocultural Factors

Socioeconomic status
Family circumstances (social class, family size, family conflict, family disorganization)
Access to health care (e.g., adequacy of available health care, availability of health
insurance, availability of transportation to health care facilities)
Prejudice and discrimination
Health-related cultural and religious beliefs and practices
Health promotion in the workplace or community
Health-related legislation

Environmental Factors

Vehicular safety
Architectural features (e.g., crowding,
injury-resistant design, nontoxic
construction materials, aesthetic
design, air quality, noise insulation)
Aesthetics of residential, workplace,
and communal architecture and
landscape architecture
Water quality
Solid waste treatment and sanitation
Pollution
Radiation
Global warming
Ozone depletion
Natural disasters (earthquakes, blizzards,
floods, hurricanes, drought, extremes
of temperature, tornadoes)

Personality

Seeking (or avoiding) information about
health risks and stressors
Self-efficacy expectations
Psychological hardiness
Psychological conflict (approach-approach,
avoidance-avoidance, approach-avoidance)
Optimism or pessimism
Attributional style (how one explains one's
failures and health problems to oneself)
Health locus of control (belief that one is or
is not in charge of one's own health)
Introversion/extroversion
Coronary-prone (Type A) personality
Tendencies to express or hold in feelings of
anger and frustration
Depression/anxiety
Hostility/suspiciousness

Behavior

Diet (intake of calories, fats, fiber, vitamins, etc.)
Consumption of alcohol
Cigarette smoking
Level of physical activity
Sleep patterns
Safety practices (e.g., using seat belts; careful driving; practice
of sexual abstinence, monogamy, or "safer sex"; adequate
prenatal care)
Having (or not having) regular medical and dental checkups
Compliance with medical and dental advice
Interpersonal/social skills

Stressors

Daily hassles (e.g., preparing meals, illness, time pressure,
loneliness, crime, financial insecurity, problems with co-workers,
day care)
Major life changes such as divorce, death of a spouse,
taking out a mortgage, losing a job
Frustration
Pain and discomfort
Availability and use of social support vs. peer rejection or isolation
Climate in the workplace (e.g., job overload, sexual harassment)

FIGURE 11.8

FACTORS IN HEALTH AND ILLNESS VARIOUS FACTORS FIGURE INTO A PERSON'S STATE OF HEALTH OR ILLNESS. WHICH OF THE FACTORS IN THIS FIGURE ARE YOU CAPABLE OF CONTROLLING? WHICH ARE BEYOND YOUR CONTROL?

ETHNICITY AND HEALTH The life expectancy of African Americans is 7 years shorter than that of European Americans (Flack et al., 1995). It is unclear whether this difference is connected with ethnicity per se or with factors such as income and level of education (Angell, 1993; Guralnik et al., 1993).

Because of lower socioeconomic status, African Americans have less access to health care than European Americans do (Flack et al., 1995; Penn et al., 1995). They are also more likely to live in unhealthful neighborhoods, eat high-fat diets, and smoke (Pappas et al., 1993).

African Americans also experience different treatment by medical practitioners. Even when they have the same medical conditions as European Americans, African Americans are less likely to receive treatments such as coronary artery bypass surgery, hip and knee replacements, kidney transplants, mammography, and flu shots (Geiger, 1996). Why? Various explanations have been offered, including cultural differences, patient preferences, and lack of information about health care. Another possible explanation, of course, is racism (Geiger, 1996).

Disproportionate numbers of deaths from AIDS occur within ethnic minority groups in the United States, predominantly among African Americans and Hispanic Americans (Centers for Disease Control, 2000). Only 13% of the U.S. population is African American (Schmid, 2000), but African American men account for 31% of people with AIDS. African American women account for 55% of women with AIDS. Only 12% of the population is Hispanic American, but Hispanic American men account for 17% of the men with AIDS. Hispanic American women account for 20% of women with AIDS.

African Americans are five to seven times more likely than European Americans to have hypertension (Leary, 1991). However, African Americans are also more likely to suffer from hypertension than Black Africans are. Many health professionals thus infer that environmental factors found among many African Americans—such as stress, diet, and smoking—contribute to high blood pressure in people who are genetically vulnerable to it (Betancourt & López, 1993; Leary, 1991).

African Americans are more likely than European Americans to have heart attacks and to die from them (Becker et al., 1993). Early diagnosis and treatment might help decrease the racial gap (Ayanian, 1993). African Americans with heart disease are less likely than European Americans to obtain procedures such as bypass surgery, even when it appears that they would benefit equally from the procedure (Peterson et al., 1997).

African Americans are also more likely than European Americans to contract most forms of cancer. Possibly because of genetic factors, the incidences of colon cancer and lung cancer are significantly higher among African Americans than European Americans (Blakeslee, 1994). Once they contract cancer, African Americans are more likely than European Americans to die from it (Bal, 1992). The results for African Americans are connected with their lower socioeconomic status (Baquet et al., 1991).

Also consider some cultural differences in health. Death rates from cancer are higher in nations like the Netherlands, Denmark, England, Canada, and—yes—the United States, where average rates of daily fat intake are high (Cohen, 1987). Death rates from cancer are much lower in such nations as Thailand, the Philippines, and Japan, where average daily fat intake is much lower. Don't assume that the difference is racial just because Thailand, the Philippines, and Japan are Asian nations! The diets of Japanese Americans are similar in fat content to those of other Americans—and so are their rates of death from cancer.

REFLECT

Are people from your ethnic group prone to particular kinds of health problems? What are they? Are you gathering information about them? If not, why not?

There are health-care "overusers" and "underusers" among cultural groups. For example, Hispanic Americans visit physicians less often than African Americans and non-Hispanic European Americans do because of lack of health insurance, difficulty speaking English, misgivings about medical technology, and—for illegal immigrants—fear of deportation (Ziv & Lo, 1995).

GENDER AND HEALTH Also consider a few gender differences. Men are more likely than women to have coronary heart disease. Women are apparently "protected" by high levels of estrogen until menopause. After menopause, women are dramatically more likely to incur heart disease, although this tendency can be counteracted by estrogen replacement therapy (Brody, 1997).

The gender of the physician can also make a difference. According to a study of more than 90,000 women, those whose internists or family practitioners are women are more likely to have screening for cancer (mammograms and Pap smears) than those whose internists or family practitioners are men (Lurie et al., 1993). It is unclear from this study, however, whether female physicians are more likely than their male counterparts to encourage women to seek preventive care, or whether women who choose female physicians are also more likely to seek preventive care. Other research shows that female physicians are more likely than male physicians to conduct breast examinations properly (Hall et al., 1990).

Men's life expectancy is 7 years shorter, on the average, than women's. Surveys of physicians ("Doctors Tie Male Mentality," 1995) and of the general population (Brody, 1998) suggest that this difference is due, at least in part, to women's greater willingness to seek health care. Men often let symptoms go until a problem that could have been prevented or readily treated becomes serious or life-threatening.

HEALTH AND SOCIOECONOMIC STATUS: THE RICH GET RICHER AND THE POOR GET . . . SICKER? **Socioeconomic status** (SES) and health are intimately connected. Generally speaking, people with higher SES enjoy better health and lead longer lives (Goode, 1999). The question is *why*.

Consider three possibilities (Adler et al., 1994). One is that there is no causal connection between health and SES. Perhaps both SES and health reflect genetic factors. For example, "good genes" might lead both to good health and to high social standing. Second, poor health might lead to socioeconomic "drift" (that is, loss of social standing). Third, SES might affect biological functions that, in turn, influence health.

How might SES influence health? SES is defined in part in terms of education. That is, people who attain low levels of education are also likely to have low SES. Less well educated people are more likely to smoke (Winkleby et al., 1991), and smoking has been linked to many physical illnesses. People with lower SES are also less likely to exercise and more likely to be obese—both of which, again, are linked to poor health outcomes (Ford et al., 1991).

Anorexia and bulimia nervosa are uncommon among poor people, but obesity is most prevalent among poor people. The incidence of obesity is also greater in cultures that associate obesity with happiness and health—as is true of some Haitian and Puerto Rican groups. People living in poor urban neighborhoods are more likely to be obese because junk food is heavily promoted in those neighborhoods and many residents tend to eat as a way of coping with stress (Johnson et al., 1995).

REFLECT

Are you reluctant to seek medical advice when something is wrong? Do you tend to "tough it out"? If so, why? Do you intend to change your health-related behavior?

SOCIOECONOMIC STATUS One's social and financial level, as indicated by measures such as income, level of education, and occupational status. Abbreviated *SES*.

✓ **Truth or Fiction Revisited**

It is not true that poor people in the United States eat less than more affluent people. Obesity is actually most prevalent among the lowest socioeconomic groups. (This is not to deny the fact that some poor people in the United States cannot afford food.)

Let us also not forget that poorer people also have less access to health care (Goode, 1999). The problem is compounded by the fact that people with low SES are less likely to be educated about the benefits of regular health checkups and early medical intervention when symptoms arise.

Review

SECTION VII

The likelihood of developing health problems reflects the interaction of many factors. Biological factors such as family history, (61) _____gens, inoculations, injuries, gender, and age play a role. Many health problems are influenced by (62) _____cal factors, such as our attitudes and behavior patterns. Psychological states such as anxiety and depression impair the functioning of the (63) _____ system, rendering us more vulnerable to health problems. Nearly (64: How many?) deaths in the United States are preventable each year.

The life expectancy of African Americans is about 7 years (65: Longer or Shorter?) than that of European Americans. African Americans have (66: More or Less?) access to health care than European Americans do. African Americans and Hispanic Americans are (67: More or Less?) likely to develop AIDS than European Americans. (68) _____ Americans are five to seven times more likely than European Americans to have hypertension, possibly because of genetic factors. African Americans are (69: More or Less?) likely than European Americans to have heart attacks and contract most forms of cancer. Death rates from cancer are higher in nations where the population has a (70: High or Low?) daily fat intake.

Men's life expectancies are 7 years (71: Longer or Shorter?) than women's. The difference is due, at least in part, to women's (72: Greater or Lesser?) willingness to seek health care.

People with (73: Higher or Lower?) socioeconomic status enjoy better health and lead longer lives. Anorexia and bulimia nervosa are (74: Common or Uncommon?) among poor people. Obesity is (75: Most or Least?) common among poor people.

SECTION VIII. HEALTH PROBLEMS AND PSYCHOLOGY

Let us now consider the health problems of headaches, heart disease, and cancer. In each case we consider the interplay of biological, psychological, social, technological, and environmental factors. Although these are medical problems, they have very real psychological consequences. Moreover, psychologists have made important contributions to their treatment.

Headaches

Headaches are among the most common stress-related physical ailments. Nearly 20% of people in the United States suffer from severe headaches. Question: How has psychology contributed to the understanding and treatment of headaches? To answer this question, let us consider the common muscle-tension headache and the more severe migraine headache.

MUSCLE TENSION HEADACHE The single most frequent kind of headache is the muscle tension headache. Psychologists have found that

REFLECT

Do you suffer from headaches? What kind? What are you doing about them?

muscle tension is a product of stress. During the first two stages of the GAS we are likely to contract muscles in the shoulders, neck, forehead, and scalp. Persistent stress can lead to persistent contraction of these muscles, giving rise to muscle tension headaches. Psychological factors, such as the tendency to catastrophize negative events—that is, blow them out of proportion—can bring on a tension headache (Ukestad & Wittrock, 1996). Tension headaches usually come on gradually. They are most often characterized by dull, steady pain on both sides of the head and feelings of tightness or pressure.

✓ Truth or Fiction Revisited

It is true that blowing things out of proportion (and tensing up) can give you a headache. Catastrophizing is a psychological event, but it has effects on the body, such as leading us to tense muscles in the neck, shoulders, and forehead.

MIGRAINE HEADACHE Most other headaches, including severe **migraine headaches,** are vascular in nature. That is, they stem from changes in the blood supply to the head (Welch, 1993). These involve the dilation and consequent expansion of blood vessels in the head, which then place pressure against nerve endings. There is often a warning aura that may include vision problems and perception of unusual odors. The attacks themselves are often accompanied by sensitivity to light, loss of appetite, nausea, vomiting, sensory and motor disturbances such as loss of balance, and changes in mood. The so-called common migraine headache is identified by sudden onset and throbbing on one side of the head. The so-called classic migraine is characterized by sensory and motor disturbances that precede the pain.

The origins of migraine headaches are not clearly understood. It is believed, however, that they can be induced by barometric pressure; pollen; certain drugs; monosodium glutamate (MSG), a chemical often used to enhance flavor; chocolate; aged cheese; beer, champagne, and red wine; and the hormonal changes connected with menstruation. Migraines are also connected with stress, as has been shown to be the case with Type A behavior. In one study, 53% of people who had migraine headaches showed the Type A behavior pattern, compared with 23% of people who had muscle tension headaches (Rappaport et al., 1988).

Regardless of the source of the headache, we can unwittingly propel ourselves into a vicious cycle. Headache pain is a stressor that can lead us to increase, rather than relax, muscle tension in the neck, shoulders, scalp, and face.

TREATMENT Aspirin and ibuprofen are frequently used to decrease pain, including headache pain. They inhibit the production of the prostaglandins that help initiate transmission of pain messages to the brain. Drugs that affect the blood flow in the brain help many people with migraine (Welch, 1993). Many of these medications include the drug caffeine, which occurs naturally in foods such as coffee, tea, colas, and chocolate, and which functions as a *vasoconstrictor.* This means that caffeine acts to constrict blood vessels in the head, counteracting their dilation. (Yes, a cup of coffee can help some people with a migraine headache, but caffeine is a stimulant and might intensify muscle tension headaches.)

Psychologists have shown that behavioral methods also help in the treatment of headaches. Progressive relaxation focuses on decreasing

MIGRAINE HEADACHES Throbbing headaches that are connected with changes in the supply of blood to the head.

muscle tension and has been shown to be highly effective in relieving muscle tension headaches (Blanchard et al., 1990a). Biofeedback training that alters the flow of blood to the head has helped many people with migraine headaches (Blanchard et al., 1990b). People who are sensitive to MSG or red wine can request meals without MSG and switch to white wine.

Coronary Heart Disease

Coronary heart disease (CHD) is the leading cause of death in the United States, most often from heart attacks (National Center for Health Statistics, 1996). Question: How has psychology contributed to the understanding and treatment of coronary heart disease? Let us begin by considering the risk factors for CHD:

1. *Family history.* People with a family history of CHD are more likely to develop the disease themselves (Marenberg et al., 1994).
2. *Physiological conditions.* Obesity, high **serum cholesterol** levels (Stampfer et al., 1991), and **hypertension** are risk factors for CHD.
    Today at least one U.S. adult in three is obese. About 1 American in 5 has hypertension, or abnormally high blood pressure (Leary, 1991). When high blood pressure has no identifiable cause, it is referred to as *essential hypertension.* This condition appears to have a genetic component (Caulfield et al., 1994). However, psychologists have found that blood pressure also rises when we inhibit the expression of strong feelings or are angry or on guard against threats (Jorgensen et al., 1996; Suls et al., 1995). When we are under stress, we may believe that we can feel our blood pressure "pounding through the roof," but this notion is usually false. Most people cannot recognize hypertension. Therefore, it is important to have one's blood pressure checked regularly.
3. *Patterns of consumption.* Problematic behavior patterns include heavy drinking, smoking, overeating, and eating food high in cholesterol, like saturated fats (Jeffery, 1991).
4. *The Type A behavior pattern.* Most studies suggest that there is at least a modest relationship between Type A behavior and CHD (Thoresen & Powell, 1992). It also seems that alleviating Type A behavior may reduce the risk of *recurrent* heart attacks (Friedman & Ulmer, 1984).

SERUM CHOLESTEROL Cholesterol found in the blood.

HYPERTENSION High blood pressure.

Coping With the Type A Sense of Time Urgency. The San Francisco Recurrent Coronary Prevention Project has helped Type A heart attack victims modify their behavior so as to avert future attacks. Type A individuals are taught to alleviate their sense of time urgency and their hostility.

It is not necessarily true that handing in assignments early is good for you. Type A people tend to be early because of the time urgency they experience, and the Type A behavior pattern appears to be related—at least modestly—to coronary heart disease.

5. *Hostility and holding in feelings of anger* (Miller et al., 1996; Powch & Houston, 1996). Hostility taxes the heart.

6. *Job strain.* Overtime work, assembly-line labor, and exposure to conflicting demands can all contribute to CHD. High-strain work, which makes heavy demands on workers but gives them little personal control, puts workers at the highest risk (Karasek et al., 1982; Krantz et al., 1988). As shown in Figure 11.9, the work of many waiters and waitresses fits this description.

7. *Chronic fatigue and chronic emotional strain.*

8. *Sudden stressors.* For example, after the 1994 Los Angeles earthquake, there was an increased incidence of death from heart attacks in people with heart disease (Leor et al., 1996).

9. *A physically inactive lifestyle* (Dubbert, 1992; Lakka et al., 1994).

REDUCING THE RISK OF CHD THROUGH BEHAVIOR MODIFICATION Once CHD has been diagnosed, a number of medical treatments, including surgery and medication, are available. However, people who have not had CHD (as well as those who have) can profit from behavior

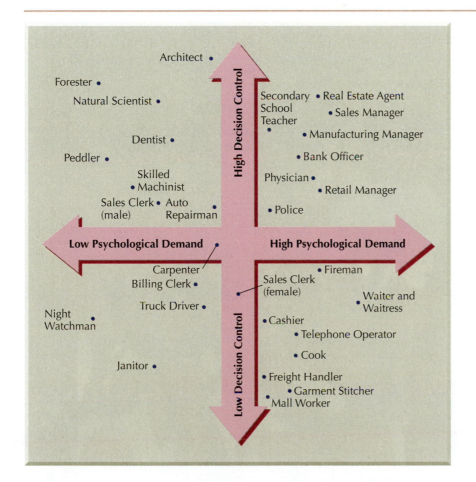

FIGURE 11.9

THE JOB-STRAIN MODEL   THIS MODEL HIGHLIGHTS THE PSYCHOLOGICAL DEMANDS MADE BY VARIOUS OCCUPATIONS AND THE AMOUNT OF PERSONAL (DECISION) CONTROL THEY ALLOW. OCCUPATIONS CHARACTERIZED BY HIGH DEMAND AND LOW DECISION CONTROL PLACE WORKERS AT GREATEST RISK FOR HEART DISEASE.

modification and other techniques designed to reduce the risk factors. These methods are outlined in Table 11.6.

Cancer

Cancer is the number one killer of women in the United States and the number two killer of men (Andersen, 1996). Cancer is characterized by the development of abnormal, or mutant, cells that may take root anywhere in the body: in the blood, bones, digestive tract, lungs, and genital organs. If their spread is not controlled early, the cancerous cells may *metastasize*—that is, establish colonies elsewhere in the body. It appears that our bodies develop cancerous cells frequently. However, these are normally destroyed by the immune system. People whose immune systems are damaged by physical or psychological factors are more likely to develop tumors (Azar, 1996b).

How has psychology contributed to the understanding and treatment of cancer? Health psychologists have participated in research concerning the origins and treatment of cancer.

RISK FACTORS As with many other disorders, people can inherit a disposition toward cancer (Lerman et al., 1997). Carcinogenic genes may remove the brakes from cell division, allowing cells to multiply wildly. Or they may allow mutations to accumulate unchecked. However, many behavior patterns markedly heighten the risk for cancer. These include smoking, drinking alcohol (especially in women), eating animal fats, and sunbathing (which may cause skin cancer due to exposure to ultraviolet light). Agents in cigarette smoke, such as benzopyrene, may damage a gene that would otherwise block the development of many tumors, including lung cancer ("Damaged Gene," 1996). Prolonged psychological conditions such as depression or stress may also heighten the risk of cancer because they, too, suppress the functioning of the immune system (Azar, 1996b).

STRESS AND CANCER Researchers have uncovered links between stress and cancer (Azar, 1996b). One study revealed that a significant

How Have Health Psychologists Helped This Youngster Cope With Cancer?   Cancer is a medical disorder, but psychologists have contributed to the treatment of people with cancer. For example, psychologists help people with cancer remain in charge of their lives, combat feelings of hopelessness, manage stress, and cope with the side effects of chemotherapy.

TABLE 11.6	METHODS SUGGESTED BY HEALTH PSYCHOLOGISTS AND OTHER HEALTH PROFESSIONALS FOR REDUCING THE RISK OF CORONARY HEART DISEASE

Method	About . . .
Stopping smoking	Psychologists suggest methods such as the following: • Tell family and friends that you're quitting. Make a public commitment. • Think of specific things to tell yourself when you feel the urge to smoke: how you'll be stronger, free of fear of cancer, ready for the marathon, etc. • Tell yourself that the first few days are the hardest—after that, withdrawal symptoms weaken dramatically. • Avoid cues for smoking by going on a smoke-ending vacation to get away from places and situations in which you're used to smoking. • Sit in nonsmokers' sections of restaurants and trains. • Fill your days with novel activities—things that won't remind you of smoking. • Use sugar-free mints or gum as substitutes for cigarettes. (Don't light them!) • Interpret withdrawal symptoms as a sign that you're winning and getting healthier. After all, you wouldn't have withdrawal symptoms if you were smoking. • Check with a pharmacist about nicotine replacement therapy in the form of a nicotine gum or skin patch. These methods help avert withdrawal symptoms. Once the smoking habit is interrupted, many ex-smokers wean themselves from the patches or gum.
Controlling weight	See suggestions for controlling weight in the chapter on motivation and emotion.
Reducing hypertension	There are drugs for reducing hypertension, but behavioral changes such as the following often do the trick: relaxation training (Agras et al., 1983), meditation (Benson et al., 1973), aerobic exercise (Danforth et al., 1990), and eating more fruits and vegetables but less fat (Appel et al., 1997).
Lowering LDL	Major methods involve exercise, medication, and cutting down on foods that are high in cholesterol and saturated fats (Shepherd et al., 1995). Read labels.
Changing Type A behavior	Psychologists suggest that people can alleviate the Type A behavior pattern in ways such as the following: • Engage in more social activities with family and friends. • Read books for fun—literature, drama, politics, biographies, science, nature, science fiction. • Visit museums and art galleries; go to the movies, ballet, and theater. • Write letters to family and friends. • Remind yourself daily that life is by nature unfinished and you do not need to have all your projects finished on a given date. • Drive more slowly. Find a scenic route. This saves energy, lives, and traffic citations. It's also less stressful than racing the clock. • Get up earlier to sit and relax, watch the morning news with a cup of tea, or meditate. This may mean going to bed earlier. • Don't try to do two things at once. Space out chores. Avoid scheduling too many classes or appointments back to back. • Set aside some time for yourself: for music, a hot bath, exercise, relaxation.
Reducing feelings of hostility and anger	Feelings of hostility and anger not only threaten to break loose into violence. They also tax the heart. Psychologists suggest coping with these feelings in ways such as the following: • Tell someone that you really appreciate or love him or her. • Don't get into heated arguments; avoid raising topics on which you know that you and the other person have opposing opinions. • When other people do things that fall short of your expectations, don't assume that they intend to upset you. (Sometimes they do, of course; but sometimes we interpret innocent behavior as intentional.) • Give yourself time for that drive so that you won't be cutting people off and cursing at people who drive slowly. • Say "Good morning" in a cheerful manner. Smile. (Yes, you.) • Look at your face in the mirror throughout the day. Search for signs of aggravation and ask yourself whether you need to look like that.
Exercising (getting into the swim—or the jog?—of things)	Sustained physical activity protects people from CHD (Curfman, 1993b). Consider these suggestions for getting going: • Unless you have recently exercised, consult a health professional. If you smoke, have a family history of CHD, are overweight, or over 40, get a stress test. • Consider joining a beginner's aerobics class. You'll be among other beginners and derive the benefits of social support. • Get the proper equipment (such as good-quality walking or running shoes) to facilitate performance and avert injury. • Read up on the activity you are considering. Books and articles can help you get started and make progress. • Try to select activities that you can sustain for a lifetime. Don't worry about building yourself up rapidly. Enjoy yourself. • If you feel severe pain, don't try to exercise "through" it. Soreness is to be expected for beginners (and for old-timers now and then), but sharp pain is a sign that something is wrong. • Have fun! (Exercise can feel good. Enjoy it!)

percentage of children with cancer had encountered severe life changes within a year of the diagnosis (Jacobs & Charles, 1980). These often involved the death of a loved one or the loss of a close relationship.

Experimental research that could not be conducted with humans has been carried out using rats and other animals. In one type of study, animals are injected with cancerous cells or with viruses that cause cancer and then exposed to various conditions. In this way researchers can determine which conditions influence the likelihood that the animals' immune systems will be able to fend off the disease. Such experiments suggest that once cancer has developed, stress can influence its course. In one study, for example, rats were implanted with small numbers of cancer cells so that their own immune systems would have a chance to combat them (Visintainer et al., 1982). Some of the rats were then exposed to inescapable shocks. Others were exposed to escapable shocks or to no shock. The rats exposed to the most stressful condition—the inescapable shock—were half as likely as the other rats to reject the cancer and twice as likely to die from it.

In sum, cancer is frightening, and in many cases, little can be done about its eventual outcome. However, we are not helpless in the face of cancer. Cure rates have been improving, and we can take preventive measures like the following:

1. Limit exposure to behavioral risk factors for cancer. For example, don't smoke.
2. Modify diet by reducing intake of fats and increasing intake of fruits and vegetables (Mevkens, 1990). Tomatoes (especially cooked tomatoes, such as we find in tomato sauce and ketchup—yes, ketchup!), broccoli, cauliflower, cabbage, carrots, grapes, and berries appear to be especially helpful. (Yes, Grandma was right about veggies.)

✓ Truth or Fiction Revisited

It is true that ketchup is a health food. It is derived from one of the fruits and vegetables that have a preventive effect on the development of cancer. It is healthful to remain aware of new developments in dietary recommendations.

3. Have regular medical checkups so that cancer will be detected early. Cancer is most responsive to treatment when it is caught early.
4. Regulate exposure to stress.
5. If we are struck by cancer, we can fight it energetically rather than become passive victims.

We conclude this chapter with good news for readers of this book: *Better educated* people—that means *you*—are more likely to modify health-impairing behavior and reap the benefits of change (Angell, 1993; Guralnik et al., 1993; Pappas et al., 1993).

Review

SECTION VIII

The most common kind of headache is the (76) _____-_____ headache. Most other headaches, including the migraine, are connected with changes in the (77) b_____ supply to the head. (78) _____ headaches have preheadache phases during which there is decreased blood supply to the head, and headache phases, during which the (79) _____ries are dilated, increasing the flow of blood. Migraines (80: Are or Are not?) connected with stress.

There are several risk factors for coronary heart disease: family history; (81) _____gical conditions such as obesity, hypertension, and high levels of serum (82) _____erol; patterns of consumption, such as heavy drinking and smoking; the Type (83) _____ behavior pattern; and job strain.

People (84: Can or Cannot?) inherit dispositions toward developing cancer, but many behavior patterns, such as smoking, drinking, and eating animal fats, heighten the risk for cancer. Experimental research with animals shows that once cancer has affected the individual, stress can (85: Accelerate or Retard?) its course.

STUDY GUIDE

To help you better understand the content of this chapter, you may go to the student Web site (http://www.harcourtcollege.com/psych/intro.html) to take more quizzes, get more information about the content, and see additional Web sites related to the content. You can also practice using the concepts in this chapter with the PowerPsych CD-ROM, which gives you interactive activities and experiments along with even more quizzes. And, of course, the printed study guide is a reliable way to practice all parts of PQ4R. Your college bookstore can order the PowerPsych CD-ROM for you.

SUMMARY

1. **What is health psychology?** Health psychology studies the relationships between psychological factors and the prevention and treatment of physical health problems.

2. **What is stress?** Stress is the demand made on an organism to adjust. Whereas some stress—called eustress—is desirable to keep us alert and occupied, too much stress can tax our adjustive capacities and contribute to physical health problems.

3. **What are daily hassles?** Daily hassles are regularly occurring experiences that threaten or harm our well-being. There are several kinds of hassles, including household, health, time-pressure, inner concern, environmental, financial responsibility, work, and future security hassles.

4. **How is it that too much of a good thing can make you ill?** Too many positive life changes can affect one's health because life changes require adjustment, whether they are positive or negative. In contrast to daily hassles, life changes occur irregularly. Research shows that hassles and life changes are connected with health problems such as heart disease and cancer. However, the demonstrated connection between life changes and health is correlational; thus causality remains clouded.

5. **What is conflict?** Conflict is the stressful feeling of being pulled in two or more directions by opposing motives. There are four kinds of conflict: approach–approach, avoidance–avoidance, approach–avoidance (in the case of a single goal), and multiple approach–avoidance, when each alternative has its pluses and minuses.

6. **How do irrational beliefs create or compound stress?** Albert Ellis shows that negative activating events (A) can be made more aversive (C) when irrational beliefs (B) compound their effects. People often catastrophize negative events. Two common irrational beliefs are excessive needs for social approval and perfectionism. Both set the stage for disappointment and increased stress.

7. **What is the Type A behavior pattern?** Type A behavior is connected with a sense of time urgency and characterized by competitiveness, impatience, and aggressiveness. Type B people relax more readily.

8. **How do our self-efficacy expectations affect our ability to withstand stress?** Self-efficacy expectations encourage us to persist in difficult tasks and to endure discomfort. Self-efficacy expectations are also connected with *lower* levels of adrenaline and noradrenaline, thus having a braking effect on bodily arousal.

9. **What characteristics are connected with psychological hardiness?** Kobasa found that psychological hardiness among business executives is characterized by commitment, challenge, and control.

10. **Is there any evidence that "A merry heart doeth good like a medicine"?** Yes. Research evidence shows that students who produce humor under adversity experience less stress. Moreover, watching humorous videos apparently enhances the functioning of the immune system.

11. **How do predictability and control help us cope with stress?** Predictability allows us to brace ourselves, and control permits us to plan ways of coping with it.

12. **Is there evidence that social support helps people cope with stress?** Social support has been shown to help people resist infectious diseases such as colds. It also helps people cope with the stress of cancer and other health problems. Kinds of social support include expression of emotional concern, instrumental aid, information, appraisal, and simple socializing.

13. **What is the general adaptation syndrome?** The GAS is a cluster of bodily changes triggered by stressors. The GAS consists of three stages: alarm, resistance, and exhaustion. Corticosteroids help resist stress by fighting inflammation and allergic reactions. Adrenaline arouses the body by activating the sympathetic nervous system, which is highly active during the alarm and resistance stages of the GAS. Sympathetic activity is characterized by rapid heartbeat and respiration rate, release of stores of sugar, muscle tension, and other responses that deplete the body's supply of energy. The parasympathetic division of the ANS predominates during the exhaustion stage of the GAS and is connected with depression and inactivity. Prolonged stress is dangerous.

14. **How does the immune system work?** Leukocytes (white blood cells) engulf and kill pathogens, worn-out body cells, and cancerous cells. The immune system also "remembers" how to battle antigens by maintaining their antibodies in the bloodstream. The immune system also facilitates inflammation, which increases the number of white blood cells that are transported to a damaged area.

15. **How does stress affect the functioning of the immune system?** Stress depresses the functioning of the immune system by stimulating the release of corticosteroids. Steroids counter inflammation and interfere with the formation of antibodies.

16. **How do we change the irrational thoughts that create and compound stress?** A three-step process for doing so involves becoming aware of the thoughts, preparing and practicing incompatible thoughts, and rewarding oneself for changing.

17. **How can we lower our levels of arousal? How can we turn down the inner alarm?** There are many methods, including meditation, biofeedback training, and progressive relaxation. In progressive relaxation, people purposefully tense and then relax muscle groups to develop awareness of muscle tensions and learn how to let the tensions go.

18. **How does exercise help people cope with stress?** Exercise enhances our psychological well-being and also strengthens the cardiovascular system (our fitness or "condition") so that we can better resist the bodily effects of stress.

19. **What is the multifactorial approach to health and illness?** This view recognizes that many factors, including biological, psychological, sociocultural, and environmental factors, affect our health. Nearly 1 million preventable deaths occur each year in the United States. Measures such as quitting smoking, eating properly, exercising, and controlling alcohol intake would prevent nearly 80% of them.

20. **What are the relationships among ethnicity, gender, socioeconomic status, and health?** African Americans live about 7 years less than European Americans, largely because of sociocultural and economic factors that are connected with less access to health care and greater likelihood of eating high-fat diets, smoking, and living in unhealthful neighborhoods. African Americans and Hispanic Americans are more likely than European Americans to be infected with HIV and die from AIDS. Women are less likely than men to have heart attacks in early and middle adulthood due to the protective effects of estrogen. Women are more likely to consult health professionals about health problems than men are.

21. **How has psychology contributed to our understanding of the origins and treatment of headaches?** Psychologists participate in research concerning the origins of headaches, including stress and tension. Psychologists help people alleviate headaches by reducing tension. They have also developed biofeedback training methods for helping people cope with migraines.

22. **How has psychology contributed to our understanding of origins and treatment of coronary heart disease?** Psychologists have participated in research that shows that the risk factors for coronary heart disease include family history; physiological conditions such as hypertension and high levels of serum cholesterol; behavior patterns such as heavy drinking, smoking, eating fatty foods, and Type A behavior; work overload; chronic tension and fatigue; and physical inactivity. They help people achieve healthier cardiovascular systems by stopping smoking, controlling weight, reducing hypertension, lowering LDL levels, changing Type A behavior, reducing hostility, and exercising.

23. **How has psychology contributed to our understanding of the origins and treatment of cancer?** Psychologists have participated in research that shows that the risk factors for cancer include family history, smoking, drinking alcohol, eating animal fats, sunbathing, and stress. The following measures can be helpful in preventing and treating cancer: controlling exposure to behavioral risk factors for cancer, having regular medical checkups, regulating exposure to stress, and vigorously fighting cancer if it develops.

THE ALARM REACTION

The alarm reaction is triggered by stress. The bodily events that make up the alarm reaction include responses of the endocrine system and of the sympathetic branch of the autonomic nervous system. The alarm reaction was termed the "fight-or-flight" reaction by Walter Cannon because it prepares the body to fight or flee from a source of danger.

Following is a list of the bodily changes that make up the alarm reaction. Provide the missing information.

1. Cortico_____s are secreted.
2. Adren_____ is secreted.
3. Nor_____line is secreted.
4. Respiration rate (Increases or Decreases?).
5. Heart rate (Increases or Decreases?).
6. Blood pressure (Increases or Decreases?).
7. Muscles (Tense or Relax?).
8. Blood shifts (From the skeletal musculature to the internal organs, or From the internal organs to the skeletal musculature?).
9. Digestion is (Facilitated or Inhibited?).
10. S_____ is released from the liver.
11. Blood coagulability (Increases or Decreases?).

BIOLOGICAL CONCEPTS RELATED TO STRESS AND HEALTH

Indicate the definition of each of the following concepts related to stress and health (1–24) by writing the letter of the proper definition (A–W) in the blank space to the left of the concept.

_____ 1. Adaptation stage
_____ 2. Adrenaline
_____ 3. Adrenocorticotrophic hormone (ACTH)
_____ 4. Alarm reaction
_____ 5. Antibody
_____ 6. Antigen
_____ 7. Corticotrophin-releasing hormone (CRH)
_____ 8. Corticosteroid
_____ 9. Endocrine system
_____10. Exhaustion stage
_____11. Fight-or-flight reaction
_____12. General adaptation syndrome (GAS)
_____13. High-density lipoprotein (HDL)
_____14. Hypertension
_____15. Immune system
_____16. Inflammation
_____17. Leukocyte
_____18. Low-density lipoprotein (LDL)
_____19. Noradrenaline
_____20. Pathogen
_____21. Parasympathetic nervous system
_____22. Resistance stage
_____23. Serum cholesterol
_____24. Sympathetic nervous system

A. The first stage of the GAS, which is triggered by the impact of a stressor and characterized by sympathetic activity
B. A hormone produced by the adrenal cortex that helps protect the body from stress by combating allergic reactions (such as difficulty breathing) and by producing inflammation
C. The "good" kind of cholesterol, which lowers the amount of bad cholesterol in the blood
D. A microscopic organism (e.g., bacterium or virus) that can cause disease
E. The second stage of the GAS, characterized by prolonged sympathetic activity in an effort to restore lost energy and repair damage
F. High blood pressure
G. The third stage of the GAS, characterized by weakened resistance and possible deterioration
H. A substance that stimulates the body to mount an immune system response to it (the word is actually a contraction of the phrase *antibody generator*)
I. The body's system of ductless glands, which secrete hormones directly into the bloodstream
J. Increased blood flow to an injured area of the body, resulting in redness, warmth, and an increased supply of white blood cells
K. Cholesterol in the bloodstream
L. The branch of the autonomic nervous system that is most active during the exhaustion stage of the GAS
M. The branch of the autonomic nervous system that is most active during the alarm reaction
N. Another name for the resistance stage of the GAS
O. A substance formed by white blood cells that recognizes and destroys antigens
P. Hans Selye's term for a hypothesized three-stage response to stress
Q. The system of the body that recognizes and destroys foreign agents (antigens) that invade the body
R. The "bad" kind of cholesterol
S. A hormone secreted by the adrenal medulla—part of a "cocktail" of hormones that accelerate the heart rate and cause the liver to release glucose (sugar)
T. A hormone secreted by the hypothalamus that causes the pituitary gland to secrete adrenocorticotrophic hormone
U. Walter Cannon's term for the activation of the body that occurs in response to a threat and prepares the body to fight or flee from a predator
V. White blood cell
W. A hormone secreted by the pituitary gland that causes the adrenal cortex to secrete cortisol and other corticosteroids

BRIDGING THE GAP

LANGUAGE AND CULTURE

to amass (508)   *to gather, to collect*

to appraise (508)   *to assess*

to avert (534)   *to avoid*

to bat the ball (510)   *to play tennis, but not competitively*

to brace oneself (515)   *to prepare for*

to blow something out of proportion (501)   *to exaggerate*

to break up (509)   *to separate*

buffer (515)   *cushion, free space*

cluster (516)   *a grouping*

to comply (513)   *to follow*

to compound (510)   *to multiply, to double*

depleted (518)   *empty*

to engulf (520)   *to surround*

to entail (509)   *to involve*

to fend off (516)   *to fight*

to ferry in hordes (516)   *to carry in large numbers*

foreboding (502)   *feeling of fear of the unknown*

hardiness (513)   *strength*

hardy (508)   *strong*

incompatible (521)   *not congruent with, foreign to*

junk food (529)   *fast food, candy, snacks*

to keep one's eye firmly glued to the clock (511)   *to remain aware of the time*

The Little Engine that Could (513)   *children's story that teaches persistence and keeping up one's courage*

a pat on the back (521)   *praise*

the pluses and minuses (509)   *the positives and negatives*

to propel (531)   *to push*

predisposed (508)   *likely to develop*

to ride out (525)   *to endure*

rustling (517)   *sound of something moving in the grass*

search and destroy mission (519)   *like an army mission in which soldiers find the enemies and destroy them*

sedentary (501)   *inactive, not active*

sniffle (525)   *runny nose*

so-and-so (509)   *nameless person of little ability*

the straw that breaks the camel's back (504)   *the last of a series of difficult events that finally exceeds a person's ability to handle them all*

to strike us (527)   *to seem to us to be*

to take root (535)   *to attach*

to be taxing to (508)   *to be wearing on, to be tiring*

thicket (517)   *group of trees*

to get into the swim of things (534)   *to join, to become actively involved*

unwittingly (531)   *without intention*

withdrawal (534)   *the effect of reduction*

1. Which is the most accurate statement about stress?
   (a) Stress is the painful price we must pay for living,
   (b) The most stressed people are usually unaware of stress,
   (c) Some stress is necessary to keep us alert and occupied,
   (d) All stress is harmful to the body.

2. Hassles differ from life changes in that
   (a) hassles require adaptation,
   (b) hassles are a source of stress,
   (c) life changes occur more frequently,
   (d) life changes can be positive as well as negative.

3. Type A people are characterized by
   (a) need for affiliation,
   (b) secretion of excessive ACTH,
   (c) competitiveness and impatience,
   (d) a predisposition toward alcoholism.

4. Compared with Type B people, Type A people
   (a) perceive time as passing more rapidly,
   (b) earn less money,
   (c) smoke less frequently,
   (d) are better adjusted in their marriages.

5. Psychologically hardy individuals are characterized by all of the following, *with the exception of*
   (a) conditioning,
   (b) commitment,
   (c) control,
   (d) challenge.

6. Nancy has just had a frightening experience in which she thought her car was going off the road. Which of the following is likely to be happening inside her?
   (a) Her respiration rate is decreasing,
   (b) Her blood pressure is decreasing,
   (c) Her digestive processes are speeding up,
   (d) Her blood flow is shifting away from her skeletal musculature toward her internal organs.

7. Unrelieved stress during the _____ may lead to diseases of adaptation and death.
   (a) fight-or-flight reaction,
   (b) exhaustion stage,
   (c) resistance stage,
   (d) alarm reaction.

8. Which of the following noted that people create much of their own stress through irrational beliefs?
   (a) Hans Selye,
   (b) Albert Ellis,
   (c) Amy Hakim,
   (d) Walter Cannon.

9. According to the text, _____ are five to seven times as likely as European Americans to have hypertension.
   (a) Asian Americans,
   (b) Native Americans,
   (c) Hispanic Americans,
   (d) African Americans.

10. A vascular headache is caused by
    (a) muscle tension,
    (b) change in blood supply to the head,
    (c) injury,
    (d) chronic stress.

11. Which of the following is *not* a risk factor for heart disease?
    (a) Low serum cholesterol,
    (b) Family history of heart disease,
    (c) Hypertension,
    (d) Physical inactivity.

12. The so-called common migraine headache is identified by
    (a) muscle tension in the shoulders and back of the neck,
    (b) hypertension,
    (c) sudden onset and throbbing on one side of the head,
    (d) sensory and motor disturbances that precede the pain.

13. Which of the following is a component of the alarm reaction?
    (a) Muscles relax,
    (b) Adrenaline is secreted,
    (c) Blood coagulability decreases,
    (d) Heart rate decreases.

14. Which of the following is *least* likely to be found among poor people?
    (a) Anorexia nervosa,
    (b) Coronary heart disease,
    (c) Cancer,
    (d) Obesity.

15. Bacteria and viruses are examples of
    (a) antigens,
    (b) antibodies,
    (c) leucocytes,
    (d) pathogens.

16. The immune system has all of the following functions, *with the exception of*
    - (a) producing white blood cells,
    - (b) producing red blood cells,
    - (c) causing inflammation,
    - (d) recognizing pathogens.

17. Which of the following suppresses the functioning of the immune system?
    - (a) Leucocytes,
    - (b) Vaccination,
    - (c) Steroids,
    - (d) Relaxation.

18. The *least* stressful kind of conflict is the _____ conflict.
    - (a) approach–avoidance,
    - (b) avoidance–avoidance,
    - (c) approach–approach,
    - (d) multiple approach–avoidance.

19. Which of the following life changes is most stressful?
    - (a) Transferring to a new college or university,
    - (b) Changing one's religious affiliation,
    - (c) Moving to a new address,
    - (d) Death of a spouse.

20. The causal connections among hassles, life changes, and health problems in people remain open to question because research on this issue has
    - (a) been correlational rather than experimental,
    - (b) been conducted only with lower animals,
    - (c) been conducted with men only,
    - (d) never been undertaken.

1. What is health psychology?

2. What is stress?

3. What are daily hassles?

4. How is it that too much of a good thing can make you ill?

5. What is conflict?

6. How do irrational beliefs create or compound stress?

7. What is the Type A behavior pattern?

8. How do our self-efficacy expectations affect our ability to withstand stress?

9. What characteristics are connected with psychological hardiness?

10. Is there any evidence that "A merry heart doeth good like a medicine"?

11. How do predictability and control help us cope with stress?

_____
_____
_____
_____
_____
_____

12. Is there evidence that social support helps people cope with stress?

_____
_____
_____
_____
_____

13. What is the general adaptation syndrome?

_____
_____
_____
_____
_____

14. How does the immune system work?

_____
_____
_____
_____
_____

15. How does stress affect the functioning of the immune system?

_____
_____
_____
_____
_____

16. How do we change the irrational thoughts that create and compound stress?

_____
_____
_____
_____
_____

17. How can we lower our levels of arousal? How can we turn down the inner alarm?

_____
_____
_____
_____
_____

18. How does exercise help people cope with stress?

_____
_____
_____
_____
_____

19. What is the multifactorial approach to health and illness?

_____
_____
_____
_____

20. What are the relationships among ethnicity, gender, socioeconomic status, and health?

_____
_____
_____
_____

21. How has psychology contributed to our understanding of the origins and treatment of headaches?

_____
_____
_____

22. How has psychology contributed to our understanding of the origins and treatment of coronary heart disease?

_____
_____
_____
_____
_____
_____

23. How has psychology contributed to our understanding of the origins and treatment of cancer?

_____
_____
_____
_____
_____

ANSWERS TO SECTION REVIEWS

1. Psychological
2. Pathogens
3. Stress
4. Eustress
5. Hassles
6. Uplifts
7. Adjustment
8. Positive
9. Less
10. Are
11. Correlational
12. Conflict
13. Approach–approach
14. Approach–avoidance
15. Ellis
16. Catastrophize
17. Approval
18. Urgency
19. Aggressiveness
20. More
21. More
22. Self-efficacy

23. Higher
24. Lessen
25. Commitment
26. Control
27. Decreases
28. Less
29. Immunoglobin
30. Does
31. Three
32. Alarm
33. Exhaustion
34. Mobilizes
35. Fight-or-flight
36. Endocrine
37. Sympathetic
38. ACTH
39. Corticosteroids
40. Inflammation
41. Adrenaline
42. Noradrenaline (or Norepinephrine)
43. Exhaustion

44. Parasympathetic
45. White
46. Leucocytes
47. Antigens
48. Antibodies
49. Steroids
50. Suppress
51. Weaker
52. Irrational
53. Lowering
54. Incompatible
55. Progressive
56. Tense (or Contract, etc.)
57. Fitness
58. Aerobic
59. Increases
60. Alleviate
61. Pathogens
62. Psychological
63. Immune
64. 1 million

65. Shorter
66. Less
67. More
68. African
69. More
70. High
71. Shorter
72. Greater
73. Higher
74. Uncommon
75. Most
76. Muscle-tension
77. Blood
78. Migraine
79. Arteries
80. Are
81. Physiological
82. Cholesterol
83. A
84. Can
85. Accelerate

ANSWERS TO EXERCISE 1

1. Corticosteroids
2. Adrenaline
3. Noradrenaline
4. Increases
5. Increases
6. Increases
7. Tense
8. From the internal organs to the skeletal musculature
9. Inhibited
10. Sugar
11. Increases

ANSWERS TO EXERCISE 2

1. N	7. T	13. C	19. S
2. S	8. B	14. F	20. D
3. W	9. I	15. Q	21. L
4. A	10. G	16. J	22. E
5. O	11. U	17. V	23. K
6. H	12. P	18. R	24. M

ANSWERS TO QUIZ

1. C	6. D	11. A	16. B
2. D	7. B	12. C	17. C
3. C	8. B	13. B	18. C
4. A	9. D	14. A	19. D
5. A	10. B	15. D	20. A

This chapter, "Psychological Disorders," covers the following:

During one long fall semester, the Ohio State campus lived in terror. Four college women were abducted, forced to cash checks or obtain money from automatic teller machines, and then raped. A mysterious phone call led to the arrest of a 23-year-old drifter, William, who had been dismissed from the navy.

William was not the boy next door.

Psychologists and psychiatrists who interviewed William concluded that 10 personalities—8 male and 2 female—resided within him (Scott, 1994). His personality had been fractured as a result of an abusive childhood. His personalities had distinct facial expressions, speech patterns, and memories. They even obtained different scores on psychological tests.

Arthur, the most rational personality, spoke with a British accent. Danny and Christopher were quiet adolescents. Christine was a 3-year-old girl. Tommy, a 16-year-old, had enlisted in the navy. Allen was 18 and smoked. Adelena, a 19-year-old lesbian personality, had committed the rapes. Who had made the mysterious phone call? Probably David, 9, an anxious child.

The defense claimed that William's behavior was caused by a psychological disorder termed *dissociative identity disorder* (also referred to as *multiple personality disorder*). Several distinct identities or personalities dwelled within him. Some knew of the others. Some believed they were unique. Billy, the core identity, had learned to sleep as a child in order to avoid his father's abuse. A psychiatrist asserted that Billy had also been "asleep," or in a "psychological coma," during the abductions. Billy should therefore be found not guilty by reason of insanity.

William was found not guilty. He was committed to a psychiatric institution and released six years later.

In 1982, John Hinckley was also found not guilty of the assassination attempt on President Reagan. Expert witnesses testified that he should be diagnosed with *schizophrenia*—a severe disorder characterized by loss of control of thought processes and inappropriate emotional responses. Hinckley, too, was committed to a psychiatric institution.

✓ Truth or Fiction Revisited

It is true that a man shot the president of the United States in front of millions of television witnesses and was found not guilty by a court of law. His name is John Hinckley, and he was found not guilty by reason of insanity.

SECTION I. HISTORIC VIEWS OF PSYCHOLOGICAL DISORDERS: "THE DEVIL MADE ME DO IT"?

Dissociative identity disorder and schizophrenia are two **psychological disorders.** Question: How have people historically explained psychological disorders? If William and Hinckley had lived in Salem, Massachusetts, in 1692, just 200 years after Columbus set foot in the New World, they might have been hanged or burned as witches. At that time, most people assumed that psychological disorders were caused by possession by the devil. A score of people were executed in Salem that year for allegedly practicing the arts of Satan.

Throughout history people have attributed unusual behavior and psychological disorders to demons. The ancient Greeks believed that the gods punish humans by causing confusion and madness. An exception was the physician Hippocrates, who made the radical suggestion that psychological disorders are caused by an abnormality of the brain. His notion that biology could affect thoughts, feelings, and behavior was to lie dormant for about 2,000 years.

During the Middle Ages in Europe, as well as during the early period of European colonization of Massachusetts, it was generally believed that psychological disorders were signs of possession by the devil. Possession could stem from retribution, in which God caused the devil to possess a person's soul as punishment for committing certain kinds of sins. Agitation and confusion were ascribed to retribution. Possession was also believed to result from deals with the devil, in which people traded their souls for earthly gains. Such individuals were called witches. Witches were held responsible for unfortunate events ranging from a neighbor's infertility to a poor harvest. In Europe, hundreds of thousands of accused witches were killed. The goings-on at Salem were trivial by comparison.

A document authorized by Pope Innocent VIII, *The Hammer of Witches*, proposed ingenious "diagnostic" tests to identify those who were possessed. The water-float test was based on the principle that pure metals

PSYCHOLOGICAL DISORDERS Patterns of behavior or mental processes that are connected with emotional distress or significant impairment in functioning.

sink to the bottom during smelting. Impurities float to the surface. Suspects were thus placed in deep water. Those who sank to the bottom and drowned were judged pure. Those who managed to keep their heads above water were assumed "impure" and in league with the devil. Then they were in real trouble. This ordeal is the origin of the phrase, "Damned if you do and damned if you don't."

✓ Truth or Fiction Revisited

It is true that innocent people were drowned in the Middle Ages to prove they were not possessed by the devil. This method was based on a water-float test designed to determine whether metals are pure.

Few people in the United States today would argue that unusual or un-acceptable behavior is caused by demons. But we continue to use phrases that are suggestive of demonology. How many times have you heard the expressions "Something got into me" or "The devil made me do it"?

Let us now define and look into the origins of psychological disorders.

> ### REFLECT
>
> Have you ever heard anyone say, "Something got into me" or, "The devil made me do it"? What were the circumstances? Was the person trying to evade responsibility for wrongdoing?

Review

SECTION I

Since the Middle Ages, Europeans have explained psychological disorders largely in terms of (1) _____sion by the devil. The ancient Greeks believed that the (2) _____s punish humans by causing confusion and madness. However, the physician (3) _____crates suggested that psychological disorders are caused by an abnormality of the brain. The document called *The* (4) _____ *of Witches* proposed tests to identify people who were thought to be possessed.

SECTION II. WHAT ARE PSYCHOLOGICAL DISORDERS?

Psychology is the study of behavior and mental processes. Question: How, then, do we define psychological disorders? Psychological *disorders* are thus defined as behaviors or mental processes connected with various kinds of distress or disability. However, they are not predictable responses to specific events.

For example, some psychological disorders are characterized by anxiety, but many people are anxious now and then without being considered disordered. It is appropriate to be anxious before an important date or on the eve of a midterm exam. When, then, are feelings like anxiety deemed to be abnormal or signs of a psychological disorder? First, anxiety may suggest a disorder when it is not appropriate to the situation. Anxiety is inappropriate when one is entering an elevator or looking out of a fourth-story window. The magnitude of the problem may also suggest disorder. Some anxiety is common before a job interview. But feeling that your heart is pounding so intensely that it might leap out of your chest—and then avoiding the interview—are not.

> ### REFLECT
>
> Have you ever felt anxious? Did your anxiety strike you as being normal under the circumstances? Why or why not?

✓ Truth or Fiction Revisited

It may not be abnormal to feel anxious. It is normal to feel anxious when one is in a stressful or fearful situation.

Behavior or mental processes are suggestive of psychological disorders when they meet some combination of the following criteria:

Hallucinations. Hallucinations are a feature of schizophrenia. They are perceptions that occur in the absence of external stimulation, as in "hearing voices" or "seeing things." Hallucinations cannot be distinguished from real perceptions. Are the cats in this Sandy Skoglund photograph real or hallucinatory?

1. *They are unusual.* Although people with psychological disorders are a minority, uncommon behavior or mental processes are not abnormal in themselves. Only one person holds the record for running or swimming the fastest mile. That person is different from you and me but is not abnormal. Only a few people qualify as geniuses in mathematics, but mathematical genius is not a sign of a psychological disorder.

   Rarity or statistical deviance may not be sufficient for behavior or mental processes to be labeled abnormal, but it helps. Most people do not see or hear things that are not there, and "seeing things" and "hearing things" are considered abnormal. We must also consider the situation. Although many of us feel "panicked" when we realize that a term paper or report is due the next day, most of us do not have panic attacks out of nowhere. Unpredictable panic attacks thus are suggestive of psychological disorder.

2. *They suggest faulty perception or interpretation of reality.* Our society considers it normal to hear people when they are talking to you, but abnormal to hear people when they are not there. "Hearing voices" and "seeing things" are considered **hallucinations.** Similarly, **ideas of persecution,** such as believing that the Mafia or the FBI is "out to get you," are considered signs of disorder. (Unless, of course, they *are* out to get you.)

3. *They suggest severe personal distress.* Anxiety, exaggerated fears, and other psychological states cause personal distress, and severe personal distress may be considered abnormal. Anxiety may also be an appropriate response to a situation, however, as in the case of a threat.

4. *They are self-defeating.* Behavior or mental processes that cause misery rather than happiness and fulfillment may suggest psychological disorder. Chronic drinking that impairs work and family life or cigarette smoking that impairs health may therefore be deemed abnormal.

HALLUCINATION A perception in the absence of sensory stimulation that is confused with reality.

IDEAS OF PERSECUTION Erroneous beliefs that one is being victimized or persecuted.

5. *They are dangerous.* Behavior or mental processes hazardous to the self or others may be considered suggestive of psychological disorders. People who threaten or attempt suicide may be considered abnormal, as may people who threaten or attack others. Yet criminal behavior or aggressive behavior need not imply a psychological disorder.

6. *The individual's behavior is socially unacceptable.* The cultural context of behavior also affects whether or not it is considered normal. In the United States, it is deemed normal for males to be aggressive in sports and in combat. In other situations warmth and tenderness are valued. Many Americans admire women who are self-assertive, but "traditionalists" may consider outspoken women to be disrespectful.

REFLECT

Do any family members or friends have psychological disorders? Do their behaviors or mental processes correspond to the criteria discussed in the chapter? Are the disorders being treated? If so, how?

Review

SECTION II

Behavior tends to be labeled abnormal when it is unusual or (5) _____cally deviant, when it is socially (6: Acceptable or Unacceptable?), when it involves faulty (7) _____tion of reality (as with hallucinations or delusions), when it is dangerous, when it is self-defeating, or when it is personally distressing.

SECTION III. CLASSIFYING PSYCHOLOGICAL DISORDERS

Toss some people, apes, seaweed, fish, and sponges into a room—preferably a well-ventilated one. Stir slightly. What do you have? It depends on how you classify this hodgepodge of organisms.

Classify them as plants versus animals and you lump the people, chimpanzees, fish, and, yes, sponges together. Classify them as stuff that carries on its business on land or underwater, and we throw in our lot with the chimps and none of the others. How about those that swim and those that do not? Then the chimps, the fish, and some of us are grouped together.

Classification is at the heart of science (Barlow, 1991). Without classifying psychological disorders, investigators would not be able to communicate with one another and scientific progress would come to a standstill. The most widely used classification scheme for psychological disorders is the *Diagnostic and Statistical Manual (DSM)* of the American Psychiatric Association. Question: How are psychological disorders grouped or classified?

The current edition of the *DSM* groups disorders on the basis of observable features or symptoms. However, early editions of the *DSM*, which was first published in 1952, grouped many disorders on the basis of assumptions about their causes. Because Freud's psychodynamic theory was widely accepted at the time, one major diagnostic category contained so-called neuroses. From the psychodynamic perspective, all neuroses—no matter how differently people with various neuroses might behave—were caused by unconscious neurotic conflict. Each neurosis was thought to reflect a way of coping with the unconscious fear that primitive impulses might break loose. As a result, sleepwalking was included as a neurosis (psychoanalysts assumed that sleepwalking reduced this unconscious fear by permitting the partial expression of impulses during the night).

TABLE 12.1	THE MULTIAXIAL CLASSIFICATION SYSTEM OF THE *DSM*	
Axis	**Type of Information**	**About . . .**
Axis I	Clinical syndromes	Includes psychological disorders that impair functioning and are stressful to the individual (a wide range of diagnostic classes, such as substance-related disorders, anxiety disorders, mood disorders, schizophrenia, somatoform disorders, and dissociative disorders)
Axis II	Personality disorders	Includes deeply ingrained, maladaptive ways of perceiving others and behaviors that are stressful to the individual or to persons who relate to that individual
Axis III	General medical conditions	Includes chronic and acute illnesses, injuries, allergies, and so on, that affect functioning and treatment
Axis IV	Psychosocial and environmental problems	Enumerates stressors that occurred during the past year that may have contributed to the development of a new mental disorder or the recurrence of a prior disorder, or that may have exacerbated an existing disorder
Axis V	Global assessment of functioning	An overall judgment of the current functioning and the highest level of functioning in the past year according to psychological, social, and occupational criteria

Now that the focus is on observable behaviors, sleepwalking is classified as a sleep disorder, not as a neurosis.

The *DSM* uses a "multiaxial" system (see Table 12.1) of assessment that provides information about a person's overall functioning, not just a diagnosis. People may receive Axis I or Axis II diagnoses or a combination of the two. Axis III, general medical conditions, lists physical disorders or problems that may affect people's functioning or their response to therapy. Axis IV, psychosocial and environmental problems, includes difficulties that may affect the diagnosis, treatment, or outcome of a psychological disorder. Axis V, global assessment of functioning, allows the clinician to rate the client's current level of functioning and her or his highest level of functioning prior to the onset of the psychological disorder. It helps determine what kinds of psychological functioning are to be restored through therapy.

Some professionals, such as psychiatrist Thomas Szasz, believe that the categories described in the *DSM* are really "problems in living" rather than "disorders." At least, they are not disorders in the sense that high blood pressure, cancer, and the flu are disorders. Szasz argues that labeling people with problems in living as "sick" degrades them and encourages them to evade their personal and social responsibilities. Because sick people are encouraged to obey doctors' orders, Szasz (1984) also contends that labeling people as "sick" accords too much power to health professionals. Instead, he believes, troubled people need to be encouraged to take greater responsibility for solving their own problems.

Let us now consider the various kinds of psychological disorders. Some of them, like anxiety disorders, are very common; others, like dissociative identity disorder, are quite rare.

REFLECT

Do you see any problems in using the word *sick* to describe people who have psychological disorders? Explain. (Hint: Consider how sick people are expected to behave.)

Review

SECTION III

The *DSM* employs a (8) multi_____, or multidimensional, system of assessment. It has (9: How many?) axes. The *DSM* was written by the American (10) _____ Association, and it groups disorders on the basis of observable features or (11) _____toms. Thomas (12) _____ argues that labeling people with problems in living as "sick" degrades them and encourages them to evade responsibility.

SECTION IV. ANXIETY DISORDERS

Anxiety has subjective and physical features (Zinbarg & Barlow, 1996). Subjective features include worrying, fear of the worst things happening, fear of losing control, nervousness, and inability to relax. Physical features reflect arousal of the sympathetic branch of the autonomic nervous system. They include trembling, sweating, a pounding or racing heart, elevated blood pressure (a flushed face), and faintness. Anxiety is an appropriate response to a real threat. It can be abnormal, however, when it is excessive or when it comes out of nowhere—that is, when events do not seem to warrant it. Question: What kinds of anxiety disorders are there? There are different kinds of anxiety disorders, but all of them are characterized by excessive or unwarranted anxiety.

Types of Anxiety Disorders

The anxiety disorders include phobias, panic disorder, generalized anxiety, obsessive-compulsive disorder, and stress disorders.

PHOBIAS   There are several types of phobias, including specific phobias, social phobia, and agoraphobia. **Specific phobias** are excessive, irrational fears of specific objects or situations, such as snakes or heights. One specific phobia is fear of elevators. Some people will not enter elevators despite the hardships they incur as a result (such as walking up six flights of steps). Yes, the cable *could* break. The ventilation *could* fail. One *could* be stuck in midair waiting for repairs. These problems are uncommon, however, and it does not make sense for most people to walk up and down several flights of stairs to elude them. Similarly, some people with a specific phobia for hypodermic needles will not have injections, even to treat profound illness. Injections can be painful, but most people with a phobia for needles would gladly suffer an even more painful pinch if it would help them fight illness. Other specific phobias include **claustrophobia** (fear of tight or enclosed places), **acrophobia** (fear of heights), and fear of mice, snakes, and other creepy-crawlies. Fears of animals and imaginary creatures are common among children.

   Social phobias are persistent fears of scrutiny by others or of doing something that will be humiliating or embarrassing. Fear of public speaking is a common social phobia.

   Agoraphobia is also widespread among adults. Agoraphobia is derived from the Greek words meaning "fear of the marketplace," or fear of being out in open, busy areas. Persons with agoraphobia fear being in places from which it might be difficult to escape or in which help might not be available if they get upset. In practice, people who receive this

SPECIFIC PHOBIA Persistent fear of a specific object or situation.

CLAUSTROPHOBIA Fear of tight, small places.

ACROPHOBIA Fear of high places.

SOCIAL PHOBIA An irrational, excessive fear of public scrutiny.

AGORAPHOBIA Fear of open, crowded places.

REFLECT

Do you know anyone with a phobia? What kind of phobia? Does the phobia seriously interfere with his or her life? How so?

diagnosis often refuse to venture out of their homes, especially by themselves. They find it difficult to hold a job or to maintain an ordinary social life.

Phobias can seriously disrupt a person's life. The person may know that the phobia is irrational yet still experience acute anxiety and avoid the phobic article or circumstance.

PANIC DISORDER

My heart would start pounding so hard I was sure I was having a heart attack. I used to go to the emergency room. Sometimes I felt dizzy, like I was going to pass out. I was sure I was about to die.

KIM WEINER

Panic disorder is an abrupt attack of acute anxiety that is not triggered by a specific object or situation. People with panic disorder have strong physical symptoms such as shortness of breath, heavy sweating, tremors, and pounding of the heart. Like Kim Weiner (1992), they are particularly aware of cardiac sensations (Schmidt et al., 1997). It is not unusual for them to think they are having a heart attack (Clark et al., 1997). Many fear suffocation (McNally & Eke, 1996). People with the disorder may also experience choking sensations; nausea; numbness or tingling; flushes or chills; and fear of going crazy or losing control. Panic attacks may last minutes or hours. Afterward, the person usually feels drained.

Many people panic now and then. The diagnosis of panic disorder is reserved for those who undergo a series of attacks or live in fear of attacks.

Panic attacks seem to come from nowhere. Thus some people who have had them stay home for fear of having an attack in public. They are diagnosed as having panic disorder with agoraphobia.

GENERALIZED ANXIETY DISORDER The central feature of **generalized anxiety disorder** is persistent anxiety. As with panic disorder, the anxiety cannot be attributed to a phobic object, situation, or activity. Rather, it seems to be free floating. Features of this disorder may include motor tension (shakiness, inability to relax, furrowed brow, fidgeting); autonomic overarousal (sweating, dry mouth, racing heart, lightheadedness, frequent urinating, diarrhea); feelings of dread and foreboding; and excessive vigilance, as shown by irritability, insomnia, and a tendency to be easily distracted.

OBSESSIVE-COMPULSIVE DISORDER **Obsessions** are recurrent, anxiety-provoking thoughts or images that seem irrational and beyond control. They are so compelling and recurrent that they disrupt daily life. They may include doubts about whether one has locked the doors and shut the windows, or images such as one mother's repeated fantasy that her children had been run over on the way home from school. One woman became obsessed with the idea that she had contaminated her hands with the cleaner Sani-Flush and that the chemicals were spreading to everything she touched. A 16-year-old boy found "numbers in his head" when he was about to study or take a test.

Compulsions are thoughts or behaviors that tend to reduce the anxiety connected with obsessions. They are seemingly irresistible urges to engage in specific acts, often repeatedly, such as elaborate washing after using the bathroom. The impulse is recurrent and forceful, interfering with daily life. The woman who felt contaminated by Sani-Flush spent 3 to 4 hours at the sink each day and complained, "My hands look like lobster claws."

PANIC DISORDER The recurrent experiencing of attacks of extreme anxiety in the absence of external stimuli that usually elicit anxiety.

GENERALIZED ANXIETY DISORDER Feelings of dread and foreboding and sympathetic arousal of at least 6 months' duration.

OBSESSION A recurring thought or image that seems beyond control.

COMPULSION An apparently irresistible urge to repeat an act or engage in ritualistic behavior such as hand washing.

REFLECT

Do you ever find yourself "in a panic"? Under what circumstances? What is the difference between "being in a panic" and having a panic disorder?

REFLECT

Do you know people who repeatedly check that the doors are locked or the gas jets are turned off before they leave home? Or people who refuse to step on the cracks in the sidewalk? Does their behavior seem to fit the definition of obsessive-compulsive disorder?

A Traumatic Experience. Traumatic experiences like the destruction of one's home can lead to posttraumatic stress disorder (PTSD). PTSD is characterized by intrusive memories of the experience, recurrent dreams about it, and the sudden feeling that it is, in fact, recurring (as in "flashbacks").

POSTTRAUMATIC STRESS DISORDER A disorder that follows a distressing event outside the range of normal human experience; characterized by features such as intense fear, avoidance of stimuli associated with the event, and reliving of the event. Abbreviated *PTSD*.

ACUTE STRESS DISORDER A disorder, like PTSD, characterized by feelings of anxiety and helplessness and caused by a traumatic event. Unlike PTSD, acute stress disorder occurs within a month of the event and lasts from 2 days to 4 weeks.

REFLECT

Have you ever heard anyone described as being "anal"? How does the description relate to the psychodynamic explanation of obsessive-compulsive disorder?

POSTTRAUMATIC STRESS DISORDER Fires, stabbings, shootings, suicides, medical emergencies, accidents, bombs, and hazardous material explosions—these are just some of the traumatic experiences firefighters confront on a fairly regular basis. Because of such experiences, one study found that the prevalence of **posttraumatic stress disorder** (PTSD) among firefighters is 16.5%. This rate is 1% higher than the rate among Vietnam veterans and far above that for the general population, which is 1% to 3% (DeAngelis, 1995).

PTSD is characterized by a rapid heart rate and feelings of anxiety and helplessness caused by a traumatic experience. Such experiences may include a threat or assault, destruction of one's community, or witnessing a death. PTSD may occur months or years after the event. It frequently occurs among combat veterans, people whose homes and communities have been swept away by natural disasters like Hurricane Floyd, which swept the Atlantic coast in 1999, people who have been subjected to toxic hazards, and survivors of childhood sexual abuse (Baum & Fleming, 1993; Rodriguez et al., 1997). A study of victims of Hurricane Andrew, which devastated South Florida in 1992, found that 1 man in 4 and about 1 woman in 3 (36%) had developed PTSD (Ironson, 1993). A national study of more than 4,000 women found that about 1 woman in 4 who had been victimized by crime experienced PTSD (Resnick et al., 1993; see Figure 12.1).

The traumatic event is revisited in the form of intrusive memories, recurrent dreams, and flashbacks—the sudden feeling that the event is recurring. People with PTSD typically try to avoid thoughts and activities connected to the traumatic event. They may also have sleep problems, irritable outbursts, difficulty concentrating, extreme vigilance, and an intensified "startle" response.

ACUTE STRESS DISORDER **Acute stress disorder**, like PTSD, is characterized by feelings of anxiety and helplessness caused by a traumatic event. However, PTSD can occur 6 months or more after the traumatic event and tends to persist. Acute stress disorder occurs within a month of the event and lasts from 2 days to 4 weeks. Women who have been raped, for example, experience acute distress that tends to peak in severity about 3 weeks after the assault (Davidson & Foa, 1991; Rothbaum et al., 1992).

Theoretical Views

There are thus several kinds of anxiety disorders. Question: What is known about the origins of anxiety disorders?

PSYCHOLOGICAL VIEWS According to the psychodynamic perspective, phobias symbolize conflicts originating in childhood. Psychodynamic theory explains generalized anxiety as persistent difficulty in repressing primitive impulses. Obsessions are explained as leakage of unconscious impulses, and compulsions are seen as acts that allow people to keep such impulses partly repressed. For example, fixation in the anal stage is theorized to be connected with development of traits such as excessive neatness of the sort that could explain some cases of obsessive-compulsive disorder.

Some learning theorists—particularly behaviorists—consider phobias to be conditioned fears that were acquired in early childhood. Therefore, their origins are beyond memory. Avoidance of feared stimuli is reinforced by the reduction of anxiety.

Other learning theorists—social-cognitive theorists—note that observational learning plays a role in the acquisition of fears (Basic Behavioral Science Task Force, 1996). If parents squirm, grimace, and shudder at the sight of mice, blood, or dirt on the kitchen floor, children may assume that these stimuli are awful and imitate their parents' behavior.

Cognitive theorists suggest that anxiety is maintained by thinking that one is in a terrible situation and helpless to change it. People with anxiety disorders may be cognitively biased toward paying more attention to threats than other people do (Foa et al., 1996; Mineka, 1991). Cognitive theorists note that people's appraisals of the magnitude of threats help determine whether they are traumatic and can lead to PTSD (Creamer et al., 1992). People with panic attacks tend to catastrophize bodily cues (Meichenbaum, 1993). Obsessions and compulsions may serve to divert attention from more frightening issues, such as "What am I going to do with my life?" When anxieties are acquired at a young age, we may later interpret them as enduring traits and label ourselves as "people who fear _____" (you fill it in). We then live up to the labels. We also entertain thoughts that heighten and perpetuate anxiety such as "I've got to get out of here" or "My heart is going to leap out of my chest." Such ideas intensify physical signs of anxiety, disrupt planning, make stimuli seem worse than they really are, motivate avoidance, and decrease self-efficacy expectations. Believing that we will not be able to handle a threat heightens anxiety. Believing that we are in control reduces anxiety (Bandura et al., 1985).

BIOLOGICAL VIEWS Biological factors play a role in anxiety disorders. Genetic factors are implicated in most psychological disorders, including anxiety disorders (Carey & DiLalla, 1994). For one thing, anxiety disorders tend to run in families (Michels & Marzuk, 1993b). Twin studies also find a higher rate of agreement for anxiety disorders among identical twins than among fraternal twins (Torgersen, 1983). Studies of adoptees who are anxious similarly show that the biological parent places the child at risk for anxiety and related traits (Pedersen et al., 1988).

Susan Mineka (1991) suggests that humans (and nonhuman primates) are genetically predisposed to respond with fear to stimuli that may have once posed a threat to their ancestors. Evolutionary forces would have favored the survival of individuals who were predisposed toward acquiring fears of large animals, spiders, snakes, heights, entrapment, sharp objects, and strangers.

Perhaps a predisposition toward anxiety—in the form of a highly reactive autonomic nervous system—can be inherited. What might make a nervous system "highly reactive"? In the case of panic disorder, faulty regulation of levels of serotonin and norepinephrine may be involved. In other anxiety disorders, receptor sites in the brain may not be sensitive enough to *gamma-aminobutyric acid* (GABA). GABA helps calm anxiety reactions. The *benzodiazepines,* a group of drugs that reduce anxiety, may work by increasing the sensitivity of receptor sites to GABA. However, it is unlikely that GABA levels fully explain anxiety disorders (Michels & Marzuk, 1993a).

In many cases anxiety disorders may reflect the interaction of biological and psychological factors. In panic disorder, biological imbalances may initially trigger attacks. However, subsequent fear of attacks—and of the bodily cues that signal their onset—may heighten discomfort and give one the idea there is nothing one can do about them (Meichenbaum, 1993). Feelings of helplessness increase fear. People with panic disorder therefore can be helped by psychological methods that provide ways of reducing physical discomfort—including regular breathing—and show them that there are, after all, things they can do to cope with attacks (Klosko et al., 1990).

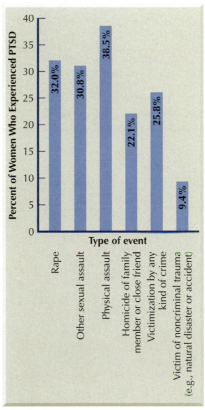

FIGURE 12.1

POSTTRAUMATIC STRESS DISORDER AMONG FEMALE VICTIMS OF CRIME AND AMONG OTHER WOMEN ACCORDING TO RESNICK AND HER COLLEAGUES (1993), ABOUT 1 WOMAN IN 4 (25.8%) WHO WAS VICTIMIZED BY CRIME COULD BE DIAGNOSED WITH PTSD AT SOME POINT FOLLOWING THE CRIME. BY CONTRAST, FEWER THAN 1 WOMAN IN 10 (9.4%) WHO WAS NOT VICTIMIZED BY CRIME EXPERIENCED PTSD.

The anxiety disorders include irrational fears, or (13) _____ias; panic disorder, which is characterized by sudden attacks in which people typically fear that they may be losing (14) con_____ or going crazy; generalized anxiety; (15) obsessive-_____ disorder, in which people are troubled by intrusive thoughts or impulses to repeat some activity; and (16) post_____ and acute stress disorders.

(17) _____phobia is fear of being out in open, busy areas. Stage fright and speech anxiety are examples of (18) _____al phobias, in which people have excessive fear of public scrutiny. Panic disorder differs from other anxiety disorders in part because there is a stronger bodily component to the anxiety, including heavy (19) sw_____ing and pounding of the (20) h_____. An (21) _____ion is a recurring thought or image that seems irrational and beyond control. A (22) _____ion is a seemingly irresistible urge to engage in an act, often repeatedly. Posttraumatic (23) _____ disorder (PTSD) involves intense and persistent feelings of anxiety and helplessness that are caused by a traumatic experience. The precipitating event is reexperienced in the form of intrusive memories, recurrent dreams, and (24) _____cks, or feeling that the event is recurring.

Psychodynamic theory explains generalized anxiety as persistent difficulty in maintaining (25) _____ion of primitive impulses. According to psychodynamic theory, phobias symbolize (26) _____cious conflicts. From the behaviorist perspective, phobias are (27) _____ned fears. Susan (28) M_____ suggests that people are genetically predisposed to fear stimuli that may have once posed a threat to their ancestors. Given the apparent independence of panic attacks from (29: Internal or External?) events, researchers are investigating possible organic causes for panic disorder. Psychoanalysts and learning theorists agree that compulsive behavior may be maintained because it reduces (30) _____ty.

Anxiety disorders (31: Do or Do Not?) tend to run in families. Some people may have a biological predisposition to anxiety in that their receptors to (32) gamma-_____ric acid (GABA) may not be sensitive enough. GABA is a (33) _____mitter that may help quell anxiety reactions.

SECTION V. DISSOCIATIVE DISORDERS

William's disorder, described at the beginning of the chapter, was a dissociative disorder. In the **dissociative disorders** there is a separation of mental processes such as thoughts, emotions, identity, memory, or consciousness—the processes that make the person feel whole. Question: What kinds of dissociative disorders are there?

Types of Dissociative Disorders

The *DSM* lists several dissociative disorders. Among them are dissociative amnesia, dissociative fugue, dissociative identity disorder, and depersonalization.

DISSOCIATIVE AMNESIA In **dissociative amnesia** the person is suddenly unable to recall important personal information. The loss of memory cannot be attributed to organic problems such as a blow to the head or alcoholic intoxication. It is thus a psychological dissociative disorder and not an organic one. In the most common example, the person cannot recall events for a number of hours after a stressful incident, as in warfare or in the case of an uninjured survivor of an accident. In generalized amnesia, people forget their entire lives. Amnesia may last for hours or years.

DISSOCIATIVE FUGUE In **dissociative fugue,** the person abruptly leaves his or her home or place of work and travels to another place, having lost all memory of his or her past life. While at the new location the person either does not think about the past or reports a past filled with invented memories. The new personality is often more outgoing and less inhibited than the "real" identity. Following recovery, the events that occurred during the fugue are not recalled.

DISSOCIATIVE IDENTITY DISORDER **Dissociative identity disorder** (formerly termed *multiple personality disorder*) is the name given to William's disorder. In dissociative identity disorder, two or more identities or personalities, each with distinct traits and memories, "occupy" the same person. Each identity may or may not be aware of the others.

The identities of people with dissociative identity disorder can be very different from one another. They might even have different eyeglass prescriptions (Braun, 1988). Braun reports cases in which assorted identities showed different allergic responses. In one person, an identity named Timmy was not sensitive to orange juice. But when other identities gained control over him and drank orange juice, he would break out with hives. Hives would also erupt if another identity emerged while the juice was being digested. If Timmy reappeared when the allergic reaction was present, the itching of the hives would cease and the blisters would start to subside. In other cases reported by Braun, different identities within a person might show various responses to the same medicine. Or one identity might exhibit color blindness while others have normal color vision.

> ### ✓ Truth or Fiction Revisited
>
> *It is true that some people have more than one identity, and the identities may have different allergies and eyeglass prescriptions.*

A few celebrated cases of this disorder have been portrayed in the popular media. One of them became the subject of the film *The Three Faces of Eve.* A timid housewife named Eve White harbored two other identities. One was Eve Black, a sexually aggressive, antisocial personality. The third was Jane, an emerging identity who was able to accept the existence of her primitive impulses yet engage in socially appropriate behavior. Finally the three faces merged into one—Jane. Ironically, later on, Jane (Chris Sizemore in real life) reportedly split into 22 identities.

DISSOCIATIVE DISORDERS Disorders in which there are sudden, temporary changes in consciousness or self-identity.

DISSOCIATIVE AMNESIA A dissociative disorder marked by loss of memory or self-identity; skills and general knowledge are usually retained. Previously termed *psychogenic amnesia.*

DISSOCIATIVE FUGUE A dissociative disorder in which one experiences amnesia and then flees to a new location. Previously termed *psychogenic fugue.*

DISSOCIATIVE IDENTITY DISORDER A disorder in which a person appears to have two or more distinct identities or personalities that may alternately emerge. Previously termed *multiple personality.*

Dissociative Identity Disorder. In the film *The Three Faces of Eve,* Joanne Woodward played three personalities in the same woman: the shy, inhibited Eve White (lying on couch); the flirtatious, promiscuous Eve Black (in dark dress); and a third personality (Jane) who could accept her sexual and aggressive impulses and still maintain her sense of identity.

Another well-publicized case is that of Sybil, a woman with 16 identities who was portrayed by Sally Field in the film *Sybil*.

DEPERSONALIZATION DISORDER Depersonalization disorder is characterized by persistent or recurrent feelings that one is detached from one's own body, as if one is observing one's thought processes from the outside. For this reason, it is sometimes referred to as an "out-of-body experience." One may also feel as though he or she is functioning on automatic pilot or as if in a dream. The case of Richie illustrates a transient episode of depersonalization:

> We went to Orlando with the children after school let out. I had also been driving myself hard, and it was time to let go. We spent three days "doing" Disneyworld, and it got to the point where we were all wearing shirts with mice and ducks on them and singing Disney songs like "Yo ho, yo ho, a pirate's life for me." On the third day I began to feel unreal and ill at ease while we were watching these middle-American Ivory-soap teenagers singing and dancing in front of Cinderella's Castle. The day was finally cooling down, but I broke into a sweat. I became shaky and dizzy and sat down on the cement next to the 4-year-old's stroller without giving [my wife] an explanation. There were strollers and kids and [adults'] legs all around me, and for some strange reason I became fixated on the pieces of popcorn strewn on the ground. All of a sudden it was like the people around me were all silly mechanical creatures, like the dolls in the "It's a Small World" [exhibit] or the animals on the "Jungle Cruise." Things sort of seemed to slow down, the way they do when you've smoked marijuana, and there was this invisible wall of cotton between me and everyone else.
>
> Then the concert was over and my wife was like "What's the matter?" and did I want to stay for the Electrical Parade and the fireworks or was I sick? Now I was beginning to wonder if I was going crazy and I said I was sick, that my wife would have to take me by the hand and drive us back to the [motel]. Somehow we got back to the monorail and turned in the strollers. I waited in the herd [of people] at the station like a dead person, my eyes glazed over, looking out over kids with Mickey Mouse ears and Mickey Mouse balloons. The mechanical voice on the monorail almost did me in and I got really shaky.
>
> I refused to go back to the Magic Kingdom. I went with the family to Sea World, and on another day I dropped [my wife] and the kids off at the Magic Kingdom and picked them up that night. My wife thought I was goldbricking or something, and we had a helluva fight about it, but we had a life to get back to and my sanity had to come first. (Author's files)

Theoretical Views

The dissociative disorders are some of the odder psychological disorders. Question: What is known about the origins of dissociative disorders?

Before discussing psychological theories of the dissociative disorders, we should note that there is a good deal of skepticism about their existence. For example, there were about 50 known cases of dissociative identity disorder before the public learned about "Sybil." By the 1990s, however, this number had mushroomed to more than 20,000 ("Tapes raise new doubts," 1998). Moreover, psychologists who have listened carefully to tapes of Sybil's therapy have raised the possibility that some of her psychiatrists may have "coached" her into reporting the symptoms. Sybil

---

REFLECT

Have you ever felt removed from the world—as though the things around you could not be really happening? Why do you believe that you felt this way?

DEPERSONALIZATION DISORDER A dissociative disorder in which one experiences persistent or recurrent feelings that one is not real or is detached from one's own experiences or body.

herself is reported to have vacillated as to whether or not her story was true ("Tapes raise new doubts," 1998). It is possible that many or even most people who are diagnosed with dissociative amnesia or dissociative identity disorder are faking. The technical term for faking in order to obtain some benefit—such as being excused from responsibility for a crime or for family obligations—is *malingering*.

In any event, psychologists of different theoretical persuasions have offered hypotheses about the origins of dissociative identity disorder and other dissociative disorders. According to psychodynamic theory, for example, people with dissociative disorders use massive repression to prevent them from recognizing improper impulses or remembering ugly events (Vaillant, 1994). In dissociative amnesia and fugue, the person forgets a profoundly disturbing event or impulse. In dissociative identity disorder, the person expresses unacceptable impulses through alternate identities. In depersonalization, the person stands outside—removed from the turmoil within.

According to learning theorists, people with dissociative disorders have learned *not to think* about bad memories or disturbing impulses in order to avoid feelings of anxiety, guilt, and shame. Technically speaking, *not thinking about these matters* is reinforced by *removal* of the aversive stimulus of anxiety, guilt, or shame.

Both psychodynamic and learning theories suggest that dissociative disorders help people keep disturbing memories or ideas out of mind. Of what could such memories be? Research suggests that many—perhaps most—cases involve memories of sexual or physical abuse during childhood, usually by a relative or caretaker (Weaver & Clum, 1995). Surveys find that the great majority of people diagnosed with dissociative identity disorder report sexual abuse in childhood (Putnam et al., 1986). Many report both physical and sexual abuse.

Perhaps all of us are capable of dividing our awareness so that we become unaware, at least temporarily, of events that we usually focus more attention on. The dissociative disorders raise fascinating questions about the nature of human self-identity and memory. Perhaps it is no surprise that attention can be divided. Perhaps the surprising thing is that human consciousness normally integrates an often chaotic set of experiences into a meaningful whole.

REFLECT

Have you seen a film or a TV show in which a character was supposed to have dissociative identity disorder (perhaps it was called "multiple personality")? What kind of behavior did the character display? Does the behavior seem consistent with the description of the disorder in the text? In the film or TV show, what were the supposed origins of the disorder?

Review

SECTION V

Dissociative disorders are characterized by a sudden temporary change in (34) con_____ness or self-identity. The dissociative disorders include (35) dissociative _____ (motivated forgetting); fugue (forgetting plus fleeing and adopting a new identity); dissociative (36) _____ disorder, in which a person behaves as if distinct personalities occupy the body; and (37) _____tion disorder, in which people feel as if they are not themselves. Dissociative identity disorder is also known as (38) _____ple personality disorder.

According to psychodynamic theory, dissociative disorders involve massive use of (39) _____sion. According to learning theory, dissociative disorders are conditions in which people learn not to (40) t_____ about disturbing acts or impulses in order to avoid feelings of guilt and shame. Many people with dissociative disorders have a history of physical and sexual (41) _____. Cognitive theorists explain dissociative disorders in terms of where we focus our (42) _____tion at a given time.

SECTION VI. SOMATOFORM DISORDERS

People with **somatoform disorders** complain of physical problems such as paralysis, pain, or a persistent belief that they have a serious disease. Yet no evidence of a physical abnormality can be found. Question: What kinds of somatoform disorders are there? In this section we discuss two somatoform disorders: conversion disorder and hypochondriasis.

Conversion disorder is characterized by a major change in, or loss of, physical functioning, although no medical findings can explain the loss of functioning. The behaviors are not intentionally produced. That is, the person is not faking. Conversion disorder is so named because it appears to "convert" a source of stress into a physical difficulty.

If you lost the ability to see at night, or if your legs became paralyzed, you would understandably show concern. But some people with conversion disorder show indifference to their symptoms, a remarkable feature referred to as **la belle indifférence.**

During World War II, some bomber pilots developed night blindness. They could not carry out their nighttime missions, although no damage to the optic nerves was found. In rare cases, women with large families have been reported to become paralyzed in the legs, again with no medical findings. More recently, a Cambodian woman who had witnessed atrocities became blind as a result.

Another more common type of somatoform disorder is **hypochondriasis** (also called *hypochondria*). People with this disorder insist that they are suffering from a serious physical illness, even though no medical evidence of illness can be found. They become preoccupied with minor physical sensations and continue to believe that they are ill despite the reassurance of physicians that they are healthy. They may run from doctor to doctor, seeking the one who will find the causes of the sensations. Fear of illness may disrupt their work or home life.

Question: What is known about the origins of somatoform disorders?

Theoretical Views

We are afforded insight into a prominent psychological explanation of the somatoform disorders when we view the history of their name. Consistent with psychodynamic theory, early versions of the *DSM* labeled what are now referred to as somatoform disorders as "hysterical neuroses." "Hysterical" derives from the word *hystera*, the Greek word for uterus or womb. Like many other Greeks, Hippocrates believed that hysteria was a sort of female trouble caused by a wandering uterus. It was erroneously thought that the uterus could roam through the body—that it was not anchored in place! As the uterus meandered, it could cause pains and odd sensations almost anywhere. The Greeks also believed that pregnancy anchored the uterus and ended hysterical complaints. What do you think Greek physicians prescribed to end monthly aches and pains? Good guess.

Even in the earlier years of the 20th century, it was suggested that strange sensations and medically unfounded complaints were largely the province of women. However, the case of the bomber pilots demonstrates that these disorders are also found among men.

Viewing these disorders as neuroses suggested that they stemmed from unconscious childhood conflicts. The psychodynamic view of conversion disorders is that the symptoms protect the individual from feelings of guilt or shame, or from another source of stress. Conversion disorders, like dissociative disorders, do often seem to serve a purpose. For example, the

---

REFLECT

What kinds of problems do you think are involved in trying to determine whether someone has a true physical health problem or a conversion disorder?

REFLECT

Have you heard someone called a *hypochondriac?* Was the term used accurately or simply as an insult? Explain.

REFLECT

Have you heard someone referred to as "hysterical"? What did the word mean? How do you feel about its usage? Explain.

SOMATOFORM DISORDERS Disorders in which people complain of physical (somatic) problems even though no physical abnormality can be found.

CONVERSION DISORDER A disorder in which anxiety or unconscious conflicts are "converted" into physical symptoms that often have the effect of helping the person cope with anxiety or conflict.

LA BELLE INDIFFÉRENCE (lah bell an-DEEF-fay-rants). A French term that describes the lack of concern sometimes shown by people with conversion disorders.

HYPOCHONDRIASIS Persistent belief that one has a medical disorder despite lack of medical findings.

"blindness" of the World War II pilots may have enabled them to avoid feelings of fear of being literally shot down or of guilt for killing civilians. But learning and cognitive theories would suggest that we need not look solely to unconscious conflicts of childhood origin for an explanation. More simply, focusing on physical symptoms—real or imagined—may be less painful than facing current fears and conflicts.

SECTION VI [Review]

In (43) so_____ disorders, people show or complain of physical problems, such as paralysis, pain, or the persistent belief that they have a serious disease. Evidence of a medical problem (44: Can or Cannot?) be found.

The somatoform disorders include (45) con_____ disorder and (46) _____iasis. In a conversion disorder, there is a major change in or loss of (47) p_____ functioning with no organic basis. Some victims of conversion disorder show a remarkable lack of concern over their loss of function, a symptom known as la (48) _____ indifférence. The (49) _____mic view of conversion disorders is that the symptoms produced by the victim protect the victim from guilt or another source of stress.

SECTION VII. MOOD DISORDERS

Mood disorders are characterized by disturbance in expressed emotions. The disruption generally involves sadness or elation. Most instances of sadness are normal, or "run-of-the-mill." If you have failed an important test, if you have lost money in a business venture, or if your closest friend becomes ill, it is understandable and fitting for you to be sad about it. It would be odd, in fact, if you were *not* affected by adversity.

Types of Mood Disorders

Question: What kinds of mood disorders are there? In this section we discuss two mood disorders: major depression and bipolar disorder.

MAJOR DEPRESSION Depression is the "common cold" of psychological problems, affecting upward of 10% of adults at any given time (Alloy et al., 1990). People with run-of-the-mill depression may feel sad, blue, or "down in the dumps." They may complain of lack of energy, loss of self-esteem, difficulty concentrating, loss of interest in activities and other people, pessimism, crying, and thoughts of suicide.

These feelings are more intense in people with **major depression.** People with this disorder may also show poor appetite, serious weight loss, and agitation or great lethargy. They may be unable to concentrate and make decisions. They may say that they "don't care" anymore and in some cases attempt suicide. They may also display faulty perception of reality—so-called psychotic behaviors. These include delusions of unworthiness, guilt for imagined wrongdoings, even the notion that one is rotting from disease. There may also be delusions (e.g., of the devil administering deserved punishment), or hallucinations (e.g., of strange bodily sensations).

REFLECT

Do you think that you would find it easy or difficult to admit to having feelings of depression? Explain.

MAJOR DEPRESSION A severe depressive disorder in which the person may show loss of appetite and impaired reality testing.

MOOD DISORDERS AND DIVERSITY: THE CASE OF WOMEN AND DEPRESSION It is widely known among psychologists that women are about twice as likely as men to be diagnosed with depression (Culbertson, 1997). Question: Why are women more likely than men to be depressed?

The more or less "standard" explanation for the greater incidence of depression among women has been biologically oriented: That is, the hormonal changes during the menstrual cycle and childbirth have been seen as the key contributors to depression among women (McGrath et al., 1990). However, a panel convened by the American Psychological Association attributed most of the difference to the greater stresses placed on women (McGrath et al., 1990). Women are more likely to experience physical and sexual abuse, poverty, single parenthood, and sexism. Women are also more likely than men to help other people who are under stress. Supporting other people heaps additional caregiving burdens on themselves. One panel member, Bonnie Strickland, expressed surprise that even more women are not depressed, given that they are often treated as second-class citizens.

Social inequality creates many of the problems that lead people to seek therapy (Belle, 1990). This is particularly true among members of oppressed groups, such as women (Brown, 1992). Women—especially single mothers—have lower socioeconomic status than men, and depression and other psychological disorders are more common among poor people (Hobfoll et al., 1995).

REFLECT

How would you distinguish between "normal" depression or "normal" enthusiasm and a mood disorder?

BIPOLAR DISORDER In **bipolar disorder,** formerly known as *manic-depressive disorder,* the person undergoes wide mood swings, from ecstatic elation to deep depression. These cycles seem to be unrelated to external events. In the elated, or manic phase, the person may show excessive excitement or silliness, carrying jokes too far. The manic person may be argumentative. He or she may show poor judgment, destroying property, making huge contributions to charity, or giving away expensive possessions. People may avoid manic individuals, finding them abrasive. Manic people often speak rapidly ("pressured speech") and jump from topic to topic, showing **rapid flight of ideas.** It is hard to get a word in edgewise. The manic individual may also be unable to sit still or sleep restfully.

Depression is the other side of the coin. People with bipolar depression often sleep more than usual and are lethargic. People with major (or unipolar) depression are more likely to have insomnia and agitation. Those with bipolar depression also exhibit social withdrawal and irritability.

Some people with bipolar disorder attempt suicide when the mood shifts from the elated phase toward depression. They will do almost anything to escape the depths of depression that lie ahead.

Theoretical Views

Question: What is known about the origins of mood disorders? Although the mood disorders are connected with processes within the individual, let us begin by noting that many kinds of situations are also connected with depression. For example, depression may be a reaction to losses and unpleasant events. Problems such as marital discord, physical discomfort, incompetence, and failure or pressure at work all contribute to feelings of depression. We tend to be more depressed by things we bring on ourselves, such as academic problems, financial problems, unwanted pregnancy, conflict with the law, arguments, and fights (Simons et al., 1993).

BIPOLAR DISORDER A disorder in which the mood alternates between two extreme poles (elation and depression). Also referred to as *manic-depression.*

RAPID FLIGHT OF IDEAS Rapid speech and topic changes, characteristic of manic behavior.

However, we should also note that some people recover from depression less readily than others. For example, people who remain depressed have lower self-esteem (Andrews & Brown, 1993), are less likely to be able to solve social problems (Marx et al., 1992), and have less social support. Let us now see how psychological and biological theories account for the mood disorders.

PSYCHOLOGICAL VIEWS Psychodynamic theorists suggest various explanations for depression. In one, people are at risk for depression because they are overly concerned about hurting other people's feelings or losing their approval. As a result, they hold in feelings of anger rather than expressing them. Anger is turned inward and experienced as misery and self-hatred. From the psychodynamic perspective, bipolar disorder may be seen as alternating states in which the personality is first dominated by the superego and then by the ego. In the depressive phase of the disorder, the superego dominates, producing exaggerated ideas of wrongdoing and associated feelings of guilt and worthlessness. After a while the ego asserts supremacy, producing the elation and self-confidence often seen in the manic phase. Later, in response to the excessive display of ego, feelings of guilt return and plunge the person into depression once again.

Many learning theorists suggest that depressed people behave as though they cannot obtain reinforcement. For example, they appear to be inactive and apathetic. Moreover, social-cognitive theorists point out that many people with depressive disorders have an external locus of control. That is, they do not believe they can control events so as to achieve reinforcements (Weisz et al., 1993). Research conducted by learning theorists has also found links between depression and **learned helplessness.** In classic research, psychologist Martin Seligman taught dogs that they were helpless to escape an electric shock. The dogs were prevented from leaving a cage in which they received repeated shocks. Later, a barrier to a safe compartment was removed, offering the animals a way out. When they were shocked again, however, the dogs made no effort to escape. They had apparently learned that they were helpless. Seligman's dogs were also, in a sense, reinforced for doing nothing. That is, the shock *eventually* stopped when the dogs were showing helpless behavior—inactivity and withdrawal. "Reinforcement" might have increased the likelihood of repeating the "successful behavior"—that is, doing nothing—in a similar situation. This helpless behavior resembles that of people who are depressed.

The concept of learned helplessness bridges the learning and cognitive approaches in that it is an attitude, a broad expectation. Other cognitive factors also contribute to depression. For example, perfectionists set themselves up for depression by making irrational demands on themselves. They are likely to fall short of their (unrealistic) expectations and to feel depressed as a result (Hewitt et al., 1996).

Cognitive theorists also note that people who ruminate about feelings of depression are more likely to prolong them (Just & Alloy, 1997). Women are more likely than men to ruminate about feelings of depression (Nolen-Hoeksema et al., 1993). Men seem more likely to try to fight off negative feelings by distracting themselves. Men are also more likely to distract themselves by turning to alcohol (Nolen-Hoeksema et al., 1993). They thus expose themselves and their families to further problems.

Still other cognitions involve the ways in which people explain their failures and shortcomings to themselves. Seligman (1996) suggests that when things go wrong we may think of the causes of failure as either *internal* or *external, stable* or *unstable, global* or *specific*. These kinds of

---

REFLECT

Did you ever feel that there was nothing you could do to improve your situation or to solve a personal problem? If so, how did the feeling that you could do nothing affect your mood?

LEARNED HELPLESSNESS A model for the acquisition of depressive behavior, based on findings that organisms in aversive situations learn to show inactivity when their operants go unreinforced.

REFLECT

Do you ever feel depressed? What kinds of experiences lead you to feel depressed? When you fall short of your goals, do you tend to be merciless in your self-criticism or to blame other people or "circumstances"? Do your views of your shortcomings tend to worsen or to ease your feelings of depression?

Why Did He Miss That Tackle? This football player is compounding his feelings of depression by attributing his shortcomings on the field to factors that he cannot change. For example, he tells himself that he missed the tackle out of stupidity and lack of athletic ability. He ignores the facts that his coaching was poor and his teammates failed to support him.

cognitions represent different **attributional styles.** Different attributional styles can be illustrated using the example of a date that does not work out. An internal attribution involves self-blame (e.g., "I really loused it up"). An external attribution places the blame elsewhere ("Some couples just don't take to each other" or "She was the wrong sign for me"). A stable attribution ("It's my personality") suggests a problem that cannot be changed. An unstable attribution ("It was because I had a head cold") suggests a temporary condition. A global attribution of failure ("I have no idea what to do when I'm with other people") suggests that the problem is quite large. A specific attribution ("I have problems making small talk at the beginning of a relationship") chops the problem down to a manageable size.

Research has shown that people who are depressed are more likely to attribute the causes of their failures to internal, stable, and global factors—factors that they are relatively powerless to change (Kinderman & Bentall, 1997; Simons et al., 1993). Such attributions can give rise to feelings of hopelessness.

BIOLOGICAL FACTORS Researchers are also searching for biological factors in mood disorders. Depression, for example, is often associated with the trait of *neuroticism,* which is heritable (Clark et al., 1994). Anxiety is also connected with neuroticism, and mood and anxiety disorders are frequently found in the same person (Clark et al., 1994).

Genetic factors appear to be involved in bipolar disorder. Mood swings tend to run in families (Wachtel, 1994). There is also a higher rate of agreement for bipolar disorder among identical twins than among fraternal twins (Goodwin & Jamison, 1990). Bipolar disorder may be associated with imbalances in the neurotransmitter *glutamate.* Research with mice suggests that too little glutamate may be linked with depression, and too much, with mania (Hokin et al., 1998).

Research into depression focuses on deficiency in the level of the neurotransmitter serotonin in the brain (Cooper et al., 1991; Michels & Marzuk, 1993b). People with severe depression often respond to antidepressant drugs that heighten the action of serotonin.

Relationships between mood disorders and biological factors are complex and under intense study. Even if people are biologically predisposed toward depression, self-efficacy expectations and attitudes—particularly attitudes about whether one can change things for the better—may also play a role.

Suicide

About 30,000 people each year take their lives in the United States (Michels & Marzuk, 1993a). Most suicides are linked to feelings of depression and hopelessness (Beck et al., 1990). Other factors in suicide include anxiety, drug abuse, problems in school or at work, and social problems (Howard-Pitney et al., 1992). Exposure to other people who are committing suicide can increase the risk that an adolescent will attempt suicide (Centers for Disease Control, 1995). Copycat suicides contribute to a so-called cluster effect among adolescents. Question: Why do people commit suicide?

Many of the triggers of suicide appear to be situational. For instance, suicide attempts are more common after stressful events, especially events that entail loss of social support—as in the loss of a spouse, friend, or rel-

ATTRIBUTIONAL STYLE One's tendency to attribute one's behavior to internal or external factors, stable or unstable factors, and so on.

REFLECT

Did you or anyone you know ever feel like committing suicide? What would you advise someone with such feelings to do about them? Explain.

ative. But situational factors do not act in isolation. For example, people under stress who consider suicide have been found less capable of solving problems—particularly interpersonal problems—than nonsuicidal people (Sadowski & Kelley, 1993). Suicidal people thus are less likely to find other ways out of a stressful situation.

Suicide, like so many other psychological problems, tends to run in families. Nearly 1 in 4 people who attempt suicide reports that a family member has committed suicide (Sorensen & Rutter, 1991). Psychological disorders among family members may also be a factor. The causal connections are unclear, however. Do people who attempt suicide inherit disorders that can lead to suicide? Does the family environment subject family members to feelings of hopelessness? Does the suicide of a family member give a person the idea of committing suicide or create the impression that he or she is somehow fated to commit suicide? What do you think?

SUICIDE AND DIVERSITY: WHO COMMITS SUICIDE? Suicide is connected not only with feelings of depression and stressful events, but also with educational status, gender, ethnicity, and age. Question: What sociocultural factors are connected with suicide? Consider some facts about suicide:

- Suicide is more common among college students than among people of the same age who do not attend college. Each year about 10,000 college students attempt suicide.

- Three times as many women as men attempt suicide, but about four times as many men succeed in killing themselves (see Figure 12.2; Rich et al., 1988).

- Among people who attempt suicide, men prefer to use guns or hang themselves; women prefer to use sleeping pills. Males, that is, tend to use quicker and more lethal means (Gelman, 1994).

- Although African Americans are more likely than European Americans to live in poverty and experience the effects of discrimination, the suicide rate is about twice as high among European Americans (Figure 12.2).

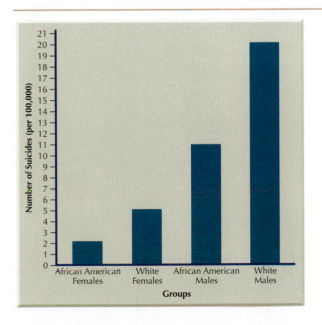

FIGURE 12.2

SUICIDE RATES ACCORDING TO GENDER AND ETHNICITY   MEN ARE MORE LIKELY THAN WOMEN TO COMMIT SUICIDE. WOMEN, HOWEVER, MAKE MORE SUICIDE ATTEMPTS. HOW CAN WE ACCOUNT FOR THIS DISCREPANCY? EUROPEAN AMERICANS ARE ALSO MORE LIKELY TO COMMIT SUICIDE THAN AFRICAN AMERICANS.

FIGURE 12.3

SUICIDE RATES ACCORDING TO AGE   OLDER PEOPLE (AGED 65 AND ABOVE) ARE MORE LIKELY TO COMMIT SUICIDE THAN THE YOUNG AND THE MIDDLE-AGED, YET SUICIDE IS THE SECOND LEADING CAUSE OF DEATH AMONG COLLEGE STUDENTS.

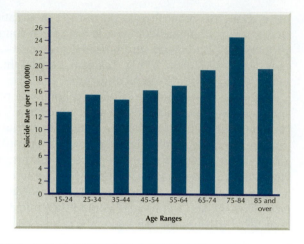

- One in 4 Native American teenagers has attempted suicide—a rate four times higher than that for other U.S. teenagers (Gelman, 1994; Resnick et al., 1992). Among Zuni adolescents of New Mexico, the rate of completed suicides is more than twice the national rate (Howard-Pitney et al., 1992).

- Teenage suicides loom large in the media spotlight, but older people are actually much more likely to commit suicide (Richman, 1993; Figure 12.3). The suicide rate among older people is nearly twice the national rate.

MYTHS ABOUT SUICIDE You may have heard that individuals who threaten suicide are only seeking attention. Those who are serious just "do it." Question: What are some of the myths and realities about suicide?

✓ **Truth or Fiction Revisited**

Actually, it is not true that people who threaten suicide are only seeking attention. Most people who commit suicide give warnings about their intentions (Brody, 1992). In fact, some people who commit suicide state their intentions repeatedly.

Some believe that those who fail at suicide attempts are only seeking attention. But many people who commit suicide have made prior attempts (Lewinsohn et al., 1994). Contrary to widespread belief, discussing suicide with a person who is depressed does not prompt the person to attempt suicide (Centers for Disease Control, 1995). Extracting a promise not to commit suicide before calling or visiting a helping professional seems to prevent some suicides.

Some believe that only "insane" people (meaning people who are out of touch with reality) would take their own lives. However, suicidal thinking is not necessarily a sign of psychosis, neurosis, or personality disorder. Instead, contemplation of suicide can reflect a narrowing of the range of options that people believe are available to them (Schotte et al., 1990).

REFLECT

Do you believe that a person would have to be "insane" to want to take his or her own life? Explain.

Review

SECTION VII

Mood disorders are characterized by disturbance in expressed (50) _____ions. The two mood disorders discussed in the text are major (51) _____ and (52) bi_____ disorder. Bipolar disorder is also known as (53) _____-_____sive disorder.

Depression is characterized by sadness, lack of (54) _____gy, loss of self-esteem, difficulty in concentrating, withdrawal, (55: Optimism or Pessimism?), crying, and, sometimes, thoughts of suicide. (56) M_____ depression can reach psychotic proportions, with grossly impaired reality testing. In bipolar disorder there are mood swings from (57) _____ion to depression and back. Manic people may show pressured speech, have grand, delusional schemes, and jump from topic to topic, a symptom called rapid (58) _____ of ideas.

Depression is a(n) (59: Normal or Abnormal?) reaction to a loss or to exposure to unpleasant events. According to psychodynamic theory, prolonged depression may reflect feelings of (60) _____ that are turned inward rather than expressed. Learning theorists have noted similarities between depressed people and animals who are not (61) _____ced for instrumental behavior. People and animals both show (62) in_____ty and loss of interest when they have repeatedly failed to receive reinforcement. Seligman and his colleagues have explored links between depression and learned (63) _____ness. Depressed people are more likely than nondepressed people to make (64: Internal or External), stable, and (65: Specific or Global?) attributions for failures. Research suggests that deficiencies in the neurotransmitter (66) _____in may create a predisposition toward depression. Bipolar disorder may be associated with inappropriate levels of the neurotransmitter (67) _____mate.

Suicide is more common among (68: College students or Nonstudents?). Three times as many (69: Men as women or Women as men?) attempt suicide. European Americans are (70: More or Less?) likely to commit suicide than African Americans. Suicide is most often linked to feelings of (71) de_____ and hopelessness. People who threaten suicide are (72: More or Less?) likely to carry out the threat than people who do not.

SECTION VIII. SCHIZOPHRENIA

Joyce was 19. Her husband Ron brought her into the emergency room because she had slit her wrists. When she was interviewed, her attention wandered. She seemed distracted by things in the air, or something she might be hearing. It was as if she had an invisible earphone.

She explained that she had cut her wrists because the "hellsmen" had told her to. Then she seemed frightened. Later she said that the hellsmen had warned her not to reveal their existence. She had been afraid that they would punish her for talking about them.

Ron and Joyce had been married for about a year. At first they had been together in a small apartment in town. But Joyce did not want to be near other people and had convinced him to rent a bungalow in the country. There she would make fantastic drawings of goblins and monsters during the days. Now and then she would become agitated and act as if invisible things were giving her instructions.

"I'm bad," Joyce would mutter. "I'm bad." She would begin to jumble her words. Ron would then try to convince her to go to the hospital, but she would refuse. Then the wrist-cutting would begin. Ron thought he had made the cottage safe by removing knives and blades. But Joyce would always find something.

Then Joyce would be brought to the hospital, have stitches put in, be kept under observation for a while, and medicated. She would explain that she cut herself because the hellsmen had told her that she was bad and must die. After a few days she would deny hearing the hellsmen, and she would insist on leaving the hospital.

Ron would take her home. The pattern continued. (Author's files)

When the emergency room staff examined Joyce's wrists and heard that she believed she had been following the orders of "hellsmen," they suspected that she could be diagnosed with **schizophrenia.** Question: What is schizophrenia? Schizophrenia is a severe psychological disorder that touches every aspect of a person's life. It is characterized by disturbances in thought and language, perception and attention, motor activity, mood, and withdrawal and absorption in daydreams or fantasy.

Schizophrenia has been referred to as the worst disorder affecting human beings (Carpenter & Buchanan, 1994). It afflicts nearly 1% of the population worldwide. Its onset occurs relatively early in life, and its adverse effects tend to endure.

People with schizophrenia have problems in memory, attention, and communication (Docherty et al., 1996). Their thought processes unravel. Unless we are allowing our thoughts to wander, our thinking is normally tightly knit. We start at a certain point, and thoughts that come to mind (the associations) tend to be logically connected. But people with schizophrenia often think illogically. Their speech may be jumbled. They may combine parts of words into new words or make meaningless rhymes. They may jump from topic to topic, conveying little useful information. They usually do not recognize that their thoughts and behavior are abnormal.

Many people with schizophrenia have **delusions**—for example, delusions of grandeur, persecution, or reference. In the case of delusions of grandeur, a person may believe that he is a famous historical figure such as Jesus, or a person on a special mission. He may have grand, illogical plans for saving the world. Delusions tend to be unshakable even in the face of evidence that they are not true. People with delusions of persecution may believe that they are sought by the Mafia, CIA, FBI, or some other group. A woman with delusions of reference said that news stories contained coded information about her. A man with such delusions complained that neighbors had "bugged" his walls with "radios." Other people with schizophrenia have had delusions that they have committed unpardonable sins, that they were rotting away from disease, or that they or the world did not exist.

The perceptions of people with schizophrenia often include hallucinations—imagery in the absence of external stimulation that the person cannot distinguish from reality. In Shakespeare's *Macbeth,* for example, after killing King Duncan, Macbeth apparently experiences a hallucination:

Is this a dagger which I see before me,
The handle toward my hand? Come, let me clutch thee:
I have thee not, and yet I see thee still.
Art thou not, fatal vision, sensible
To feeling as to sight? or art thou but
A dagger of the mind, a false creation,
Proceeding from the heat-oppressed brain?

Joyce apparently hallucinated the voices of "hellsmen." Other people who experience hallucinations may see colors or even obscene words spelled out in midair. Auditory hallucinations are the most common type.

In individuals with schizophrenia, motor activity may become wild or become so slow the person is said to be in a stupor. There may be strange

REFLECT

We all get confused now and then. (Don't we?) Where does run-of-the-mill confusion end and something like schizophrenia begin?

REFLECT

People with schizophrenia may experience delusions and hallucinations. Can you think of other reasons for delusions or hallucinations?

SCHIZOPHRENIA A psychotic disorder characterized by loss of control of thought processes and inappropriate emotional responses.

DELUSIONS False, persistent beliefs unsubstantiated by sensory or objective evidence.

PARANOID SCHIZOPHRENIA A type of schizophrenia characterized primarily by delusions — commonly of persecution — and by vivid hallucinations.

DISORGANIZED SCHIZOPHRENIA A type of schizophrenia characterized by disorganized delusions and vivid hallucinations.

CATATONIC SCHIZOPHRENIA A type of schizophrenia characterized by striking impairment in motor activity.

WAXY FLEXIBILITY A feature of catatonic schizophrenia in which persons maintain postures into which they are placed.

MUTISM Refusal to talk.

gestures and facial expressions. The person's emotional responses may be flat or blunted, or inappropriate—as in giggling upon hearing bad news. People with schizophrenia tend to withdraw from social contacts and become wrapped up in their own thoughts and fantasies. Question: What kinds of schizophrenia are there?

Types of Schizophrenia

There are three major types of schizophrenia: paranoid, disorganized, and catatonic.

PARANOID TYPE People with **paranoid schizophrenia** have systematized delusions and, frequently, related auditory hallucinations. They usually have delusions of grandeur and persecution, but they may also have delusions of jealousy, in which they believe that a spouse or lover has been unfaithful. They may show agitation, confusion, and fear, and may experience vivid hallucinations consistent with their delusions. People with paranoid schizophrenia often construct complex or systematized delusions involving themes of wrongdoing or persecution.

DISORGANIZED TYPE People with **disorganized schizophrenia** show incoherence, loosening of associations, disorganized behavior, disorganized delusions, fragmentary delusions or hallucinations, and flat or highly inappropriate emotional responses. Extreme social impairment is common. People with this type of schizophrenia may also exhibit silliness and giddiness of mood, giggling, and nonsensical speech. They may neglect their appearance and personal hygiene and lose control of their bladder and bowels.

CATATONIC TYPE People with **catatonic schizophrenia** show striking impairment in motor activity. It is characterized by a slowing of activity into a stupor that may suddenly change into an agitated phase. Catatonic individuals may maintain unusual, even difficult postures for hours, even as their limbs grow swollen or stiff. A striking feature of this condition is **waxy flexibility,** in which the person maintains positions into which he or she has been manipulated by others. Catatonic individuals may also show **mutism,** but afterward they usually report that they heard what others were saying at the time.

Schizophrenia is thus characterized by extremely unusual behavior. Question: What is known about the origins of schizophrenia?

Theoretical Views

Psychologists have investigated various factors that may contribute to schizophrenia. They include psychological and biological factors.

PSYCHOLOGICAL VIEWS According to the psychodynamic perspective, schizophrenia occurs because the ego is overwhelmed by sexual or aggressive impulses from the id. The impulses threaten the ego and cause intense inner conflict. Under this threat, the person regresses to an early phase of the oral stage in which the infant has not yet learned that it and the world are separate. Fantasies become confused with reality, giving rise to hallucinations and delusions. Yet critics point out that schizophrenic behavior is not the same as infantile behavior.

Paranoid Schizophrenia. People with paranoid schizophrenia have systematized delusions, often involving the idea that they are being persecuted or are on a special mission. Although they cannot be argued out of their delusions, their cognitive functioning is relatively intact compared with that of disorganized and catatonic schizophrenics.

Most learning theorists explain schizophrenia in terms of conditioning and observational learning. From this perspective, people engage in schizophrenic behavior when it is more likely to be reinforced than normal behavior. This may occur when a person is reared in a socially unrewarding or punitive situation. Inner fantasies then become more reinforcing than social realities.

Patients in a psychiatric hospital may learn what is "expected" by observing others. Hospital staff may reinforce schizophrenic behavior by paying more attention to patients who behave bizarrely. This view is consistent with folklore that the child who disrupts the class attracts more attention from the teacher than the "good" child.

Although quality of parenting is connected with the development of schizophrenia (Michels & Marzuk, 1993a; Venables, 1996), critics note that many people who are reared in socially punitive settings are apparently immune to the extinction of socially appropriate behavior. Other people develop schizophrenic behavior without having had opportunities to observe other people with schizophrenia.

Many investigators have considered whether and how social and cultural factors such as poverty, discrimination, and overcrowding contribute to schizophrenia—especially among people who are genetically vulnerable to the disorder. A classic study in New Haven, Connecticut, showed that the rate of schizophrenia was twice as high in the lowest socioeconomic class as in the next-higher class on the socioeconomic ladder (Hollingshead & Redlich, 1958). Some sociocultural theorists therefore suggest that treatment of schizophrenia requires reforming society so as to alleviate poverty and other social ills, rather than trying to change people whose behavior is deviant.

Critics of this view suggest that low socioeconomic status may be a result, rather than a cause, of schizophrenia. People with schizophrenia may drift toward low social status because they lack the social skills and cognitive abilities to function at higher social-class levels. Thus, they may wind up in poor neighborhoods in disproportionately high numbers.

Evidence for the hypothesis that people with schizophrenia drift downward to lower socioeconomic status is mixed. Many people with schizophrenia do drift downward occupationally in comparison with their fathers' occupations. Many others, however, were reared in families in which the father came from the lowest socioeconomic class. Because the stresses of poverty may play a role in the development of schizophrenia, many researchers are interested in the possible interactions between psychosocial stressors and biological factors (Carpenter & Buchanan, 1994).

BIOLOGICAL VIEWS   Research evidence suggests that there are three biological risk factors for schizophrenia: heredity, complications during pregnancy and birth, and birth during winter (Carpenter & Buchanan, 1994).

Schizophrenia, like many other psychological disorders, runs in families. People with schizophrenia constitute about 1% of the population. However, children with one parent who has been diagnosed as schizophrenic have about a 10% chance of being diagnosed as schizophrenic themselves. Children with two such parents have about a 35% to 40% chance (Gottesman, 1991). Twin studies also find about a 40% to 50% rate of agreement for the diagnosis among pairs of identical (MZ) twins, whose genetic codes are the same, compared with about a 10% rate among pairs of fraternal (DZ) twins (Gottesman, 1991). Moreover, adoptee studies find that the biological parent typically places the child at greater risk for schizophrenia than the adoptive parent—even though the child has been reared by the adoptive parent (Carpenter & Buchanan,

REFLECT

There is evidence for a genetic role in schizophrenia. What would you tell the son or daughter of a person with schizophrenia about the likelihood of his or her developing schizophrenia? Explain.

1994; Gottesman, 1991). Sharing genes with relatives who have schizophrenia apparently places a person at risk of developing the disorder.

There seems to be strong evidence for a genetic role in schizophrenia. However, heredity cannot be the sole factor. If it were, we would expect a 100% rate of agreement between identical twins, as opposed to the 40% to 50% rate found by researchers (Carpenter & Buchanan, 1994). It also turns out that many people with schizophrenia have undergone complications during pregnancy and birth. For example, the mothers of many people with schizophrenia had influenza during the sixth or seventh month of pregnancy (Barr et al., 1990). Inadequate maternal nutrition has also been implicated (Susser & Lin, 1992). Individuals with schizophrenia are also somewhat more likely to have been born during winter than would be predicted by chance (Carpenter & Buchanan, 1994). Considered together, these three biological risk factors suggest that schizophrenia involves atypical development of the central nervous system. Problems in the nervous system may involve neurotransmitters as well as the development of brain structures, and research on these problems has led to the dopamine theory of schizophrenia.

Much research has been conducted on the chemistry of schizophrenia. Numerous chemical substances have been suspected of playing a role. Much recent research has focused on the neurotransmitter dopamine (Carpenter & Buchanan, 1994). According to the dopamine theory of schizophrenia, people with schizophrenia *use* more dopamine than other people do, although they may not *produce* more of it. Why? They may have more dopamine receptors in the brain than other people, or their dopamine receptors may be hyperactive. Postmortem studies of the brains of people with schizophrenia have yielded evidence consistent with both possibilities (Davis et al., 1991). Many researchers agree that dopamine plays a role in schizophrenia but argue that other neurotransmitters are also involved. Supportive evidence is found in the fact that drugs acting on dopamine alone are not always effective in the treatment of schizophrenia (Carpenter & Buchanan, 1994).

Because so many psychological and biological factors have been implicated in schizophrenia, most investigators today favor a *multifactorial* model. According to this model, genetic factors create a predisposition toward schizophrenia (see Figure 12.4). Genetic vulnerability to the disorder interacts with other factors, such as stress, complications during pregnancy and birth, and quality of parenting, to cause the disorder to develop (Michels & Marzuk, 1993a; Venables, 1996).

REFLECT

Have you ever heard the expression "split personality"? Does the expression seem to apply more to dissociative identity disorder or schizophrenia? Explain.

FIGURE 12.4

A MULTIFACTORIAL MODEL OF SCHIZOPHRENIA

ACCORDING TO THE MULTIFACTORIAL MODEL OF SCHIZOPHRENIA, PEOPLE WITH A GENETIC VULNERABILITY TO THE DISORDER EXPERIENCE INCREASED RISK FOR SCHIZOPHRENIA WHEN THEY ENCOUNTER PROBLEMS SUCH AS VIRAL INFECTIONS, BIRTH COMPLICATIONS, STRESS, AND POOR PARENTING. PEOPLE WITHOUT THE GENETIC VULNERABILITY WOULD NOT DEVELOP SCHIZOPHRENIA DESPITE SUCH PROBLEMS.

Review

SECTION VIII

Schizophrenic disorders are characterized by disturbances in (73) th_____ and language (as found in the loosening of associations and in delusions); in (74) per_____ and attention (as found in hallucinations); in (75) m_____ activity (as found in a stupor); in mood (as found in flat and inappropriate emotional responses); and by withdrawal and autism.

Major types of schizophrenia include paranoid schizophrenia, (76) dis_____ schizophrenia, and catatonic schizophrenia. Paranoid schizophrenia is characterized by paranoid (77) _____ions. Disorganized schizophrenia is characterized by disorganized delusions and vivid, abundant (78) _____nations. Catatonic schizophrenia is characterized by impaired motor activity, as in a catatonic (79) _____or, and by (80) _____ flexibility.

According to psychodynamic theory, schizophrenic behavior occurs when impulses of the (81: Id, Ego, or Superego?) overwhelm the (82: Id, Ego, or Superego?). Schizophrenia (83: Does or Does not?) tend to run in families. Children with two schizophrenic parents have about a (84) _____% chance of becoming schizophrenic. People with schizophrenia may use more of the neurotransmitter (85) _____ine than other people do. Many people with schizophrenia have undergone complications during pregnancy and birth. For example, the mothers of many people with schizophrenia had (86) _____ during the sixth or seventh month of pregnancy. Individuals with schizophrenia are (87: More or Less?) likely to have been born during the winter than would be predicted by chance.

SECTION IX. PERSONALITY DISORDERS

Personality disorders, like personality traits, are characterized by enduring patterns of behavior. But personality disorders are inflexible and maladaptive. They impair personal or social functioning and are a source of distress to the individual or to other people. Question: What kinds of personality disorders are there?

Types of Personality Disorders

There are a number of personality disorders, including the paranoid, schizotypal, schizoid, antisocial, and avoidant personality types. The defining trait of the *paranoid personality disorder* is a tendency to interpret other people's behavior as threatening or demeaning. People with the disorder do not show the grossly disorganized thinking of paranoid schizophrenia. However, they are mistrustful of others, and their social relationships suffer as a result. They may be suspicious of co-workers and supervisors, but they can generally hold a job.

Schizotypal personality disorder is characterized by peculiarities of thought, perception, or behavior, such as excessive fantasy and suspiciousness, feelings of being unreal, or odd usage of words. The bizarre behaviors characterizing schizophrenia are absent, so this disorder is schizo*typal,* not schizophrenic.

The *schizoid personality* is defined by indifference to relationships and flat emotional response. People with this disorder are loners. They do not develop warm, tender feelings for others. They have few friends and rarely get married. Some people with schizoid personality disorder do very well on the job provided that continuous social interaction is not required. They do not have hallucinations or delusions.

People with *antisocial personality disorder* persistently violate the rights of others and are often in conflict with the law (see Table 12.2). They often show a superficial charm and are at least average in intelli-

REFLECT

Do you know some people whom you consider to have "bad personalities"? How does the term *bad personality* differ from the diagnosis of personality disorder?

PERSONALITY DISORDERS Enduring patterns of maladaptive behavior that are sources of distress to the individual or others.

TABLE 12.2	CHARACTERISTICS OF PEOPLE DIAGNOSED WITH ANTISOCIAL PERSONALITY DISORDER	
Key Characteristics	**Other Common Characteristics**	
History of delinquency and truancy	Lack of loyalty or of formation of enduring relationships	
Persistent violation of the rights of others	Failure to maintain good job performance over the years	
Impulsiveness	Failure to develop or adhere to a life plan	
Poor self-control	Sexual promiscuity	
Lack of remorse for misdeeds	Substance abuse	
Lack of empathy	Inability to tolerate boredom	
Deceitfulness and manipulativeness	Low tolerance for frustration	
Irresponsibility	Irritability	
Glibness; superficial charm		
Exaggerated sense of self worth		

SOURCES: Harris et al., 1994; White et al., 1994; Widiger et al., 1996.

gence. Striking features are their lack of guilt or anxiety about their misdeeds and their failure to learn from punishment or to form meaningful bonds with other people (Widiger et al., 1996). Although they are often heavily punished by their parents and rejected by peers, they continue in their impulsive, careless styles of life (Patterson, 1993). Women are more likely than men to have anxiety and depressive disorders. Men are more likely to have antisocial personality disorder (Sutker, 1994).

People with *avoidant personality disorder* are generally unwilling to enter a relationship without some assurance of acceptance because they fear rejection and criticism. As a result, they may have few close relationships outside their immediate families. Unlike people with schizoid personality disorder, however, they have some interest in, and feelings of warmth toward, other people. Question: What is known about the origins of personality disorders?

Theoretical Views

PSYCHOLOGICAL VIEWS Many of the theoretical explanations of personality disorders are derived from the psychodynamic model. Traditional Freudian theory focuses on Oedipal problems as the source of many psychological disorders, including personality disorders. Faulty resolution of the Oedipus complex might lead to antisocial personality disorder because the moral conscience, or superego, is believed to depend on proper resolution of the Oedipus complex. Research evidence supports the theory that lack of guilt, a frequent characteristic of people with antisocial personality disorder, is more likely to develop among children who are rejected and punished by their parents rather than given warmth and affection (Baumeister et al., 1994; Zahn-Waxler & Kochanska, 1990). Psychodynamic theory proposed that men are more likely than women to experience feelings of guilt because men are subjected to the throes of the Oedipus complex. However, empirical research shows that *women* are actually more likely to feel guilty about moral transgressions (Baumeister et al., 1994). Men are more likely to fear being caught.

Learning theorists suggest that childhood experiences can contribute to maladaptive ways of relating to others in adulthood—that is, can lead

REFLECT

Sick people may be excused from school or work. If some criminals are "sick" in the sense of being diagnosed with antisocial personality disorder, does the disorder relieve them of responsibility for criminal behavior? Explain.

to personality disorders. Cognitive psychologists find that antisocial adolescents encode social information in ways that bolster their misdeeds. For example, they tend to interpret other people's behavior as threatening, even when it is not (Crick & Dodge, 1994; Lochman, 1992). Cognitive therapists have encouraged some antisocial adolescents to view social provocations as problems to be solved rather than as threats to their "manhood," with some favorable initial results (Lochman, 1992).

BIOLOGICAL VIEWS Genetic factors are apparently involved in some personality disorders (Rutter, 1997). For example, antisocial personality disorder tends to run in families. Adoptee studies reveal higher incidences of antisocial behavior among the biological parents than among the adoptive relatives of individuals with the disorder (DiLalla & Gottesman, 1991). Yet genetic influences seem to be moderate at most (Plomin et al., 1997).

Genetic factors in antisocial personality disorder may influence the level of arousal of the nervous system. People with the disorder are unlikely to show guilt for their misdeeds or to be deterred by punishment. Low levels of guilt and anxiety may reflect lower-than-normal levels of arousal, which, in turn, may be partially genetically based (Lykken, 1982).

Why are people with antisocial personality disorder undeterred by punishment? Experiments show that people with antisocial personality disorder do not learn as rapidly as other people who are equal in intelligence when the payoff is ability to stop a threatened electric shock. But when their levels of arousal are increased by injections of adrenaline, they learn to avoid punishment as rapidly as others (Chesno & Kilmann, 1975; Schachter & Latané, 1964).

Genetic factors such as a lower-than-normal level of arousal would not by themselves cause the development of an antisocial personality (Rutter, 1997). Perhaps a person must also be reared under conditions that do not foster the self-concept of a law-abiding citizen. Punishment for deviant behavior would then be unlikely to induce feelings of guilt and shame. Such an individual might well be "undeterred" by punishment.

Review

SECTION IX

Personality disorders, like personality traits, are characterized by enduring patterns of (88) be_____. Personality disorders are inflexible, (89) mal_____ive behavior patterns that impair personal or social functioning and are a source of (90) dis_____ to the individual or to others.

The defining trait of the (91) _____ personality is suspiciousness. Persons with (92) _____typal personality disorders show oddities of thought, perception, and behavior. However, schizotypal personalities do not show bizarre (93) _____tic behavior. Social (94) _____wal is the major characteristic of the schizoid personality. Persons with (95) _____oid personality disorder prefer to be by themselves and do not develop warm, tender feelings for others.

Persons with (96) _____ personality disorders persistently violate the rights of others. They show little or no (97) g_____ or shame over their misdeeds and are largely undeterred by (98) _____ment.

Various factors seem to contribute to antisocial behavior. One is parental (99) re_____ion during childhood. Second is inconsistent (100) _____line. Third is a biological factor. Research suggests that persons with antisocial personalities have (101: Higher or Lower?)-than-normal levels of arousal, which might explain why they are undeterred by most forms of punishment. Cognitive psychologists find that antisocial adolescents tend to interpret other people's behavior as (102) _____ning, even when it is not.

SECTION X. EATING DISORDERS

Most of us either deprive ourselves or consume vast quantities of food now and then. This is normal. The **eating disorders** listed in the *DSM* are characterized by persistent, gross disturbances in eating patterns. Question: What kinds of eating disorders are there?

Types of Eating Disorders

The major eating disorders are anorexia nervosa and bulimia nervosa.

ANOREXIA NERVOSA There is a saying that you can never be too rich or too thin. Excess money may be pleasant enough, but, as in the case of Karen, one can certainly be too thin.

> Karen was the 22-year-old daughter of a renowned English professor. She had begun her college career full of promise at the age of 17. But two years ago, after "social problems" occurred, she had returned to live at home and taken progressively lighter course loads at a local college. Karen had never been overweight, but about a year ago her mother noticed that she seemed to be gradually "turning into a skeleton."
>
> Karen spent hours every day shopping at the supermarket, butcher, and bakeries; and in conjuring up gourmet treats for her parents and younger siblings. Arguments over her lifestyle and eating habits had divided the family into two camps. The camp led by her father called for patience. That headed by her mother demanded confrontation. Her mother feared that Karen's father would "protect her right into her grave" and wanted Karen placed in residential treatment "for her own good." The parents finally compromised on an outpatient evaluation.
>
> At an even 5 feet, Karen looked like a prepubescent 11-year-old. Her nose and cheekbones protruded crisply, like those of an elegant young fashion model. Her lips were full, but the redness of the lipstick was unnatural, as if too much paint had been dabbed on a corpse for the funeral. Karen weighed only 78 pounds, but she had dressed in a stylish silk blouse, scarf, and baggy pants so that not one inch of her body was revealed. More striking than her mouth was the redness of her rouged cheeks. It was unclear whether she had used too much makeup or whether minimal makeup had caused the stark contrast between the parts of her face that were covered and those that were not.
>
> Karen vehemently denied that she had a problem. Her figure was "just about where I want it to be" and she engaged in aerobic exercise daily. A deal was struck in which outpatient treatment would be tried as long as Karen lost no more weight and showed steady gains back to at least 90 pounds. Treatment included a day hospital with group therapy and two meals a day. But word came back that Karen was artfully toying with her food—cutting it, licking it, and moving it about her plate—rather than eating it. After three weeks Karen had lost another pound. At that point her parents were able to persuade her to enter a residential treatment program where her eating could be carefully monitored. (Author's files)

Karen was diagnosed with **anorexia nervosa,** a life-threatening disorder characterized by refusal to maintain a healthful body weight, intense

EATING DISORDERS Psychological disorders characterized by distortion of the body image and gross disturbances in eating patterns.

ANOREXIA NERVOSA A life-threatening eating disorder characterized by refusal to maintain a healthful body weight, intense fear of being overweight, a distorted body image, and, in females, suspension of menstruation.

fear of being overweight, a distorted body image, and, in women, lack of menstruation (amenorrhea). People with anorexia usually weigh less than 85% of what would be considered a healthy weight.

By and large, eating disorders afflict women during adolescence and young adulthood (Heatherton et al., 1997). The typical person with anorexia or bulimia is a young White female of higher socioeconomic status. Women with anorexia may lose 25% or more of their body weight in a year. Severe weight loss stops ovulation. Their overall health declines.

✓

The statement that "You can never be too rich or too thin" is false. I won't pass judgment on whether or not you can be too rich. You can clearly be too thin, however. About 4% of women with anorexia die from related problems such as weakness or imbalances in body chemistry (Herzog et al., 1988).

In the typical pattern, a girl notices some weight gain after menarche and decides that it must come off. However, dieting—and, often, exercise—continue at a fever pitch. They persist even after the girl reaches an average weight, and even after family members and others have told her that she is losing too much. Girls with anorexia almost always adamantly deny that they are wasting away. They may point to their fierce exercise regimens as proof. Their body image is distorted (Williamson et al., 1993). Other people perceive women with anorexia as "skin and bones." The women themselves frequently sit before the mirror and see themselves as heavy.

Many people with anorexia become obsessed with food. They engross themselves in cookbooks, take on the family shopping chores, and prepare elaborate dinners—for others.

BULIMIA NERVOSA The case of Nicole is a vivid account of a young woman who was diagnosed with bulimia nervosa:

Nicole awakens in her cold dark room and already wishes it was time to go back to bed. She dreads the thought of going through this day, which will be like so many others in her recent past. She asks herself the question every morning, "Will I be able to make it through the day without being totally obsessed by thoughts of food, or will I blow it again and spend the day [binge eating]"? She tells herself that today she will begin a new life, today she will start to live like a normal human being. However, she is not at all convinced that the choice is hers (Boskind-White & White, 1983, p. 29).

It turns out that this day Nicole begins by eating eggs and toast. Then she binges on cookies; doughnuts; bagels smothered with butter, cream cheese, and jelly; granola; candy bars; and bowls of cereal and milk—all within 45 minutes. When she cannot take in any more food, she turns her attention to purging. She goes to the bathroom, ties back her hair, turns on the shower to mask any noise she will make, drinks a glass of water, and makes herself vomit. Afterward she vows, "Starting tomorrow, I'm going to change." But she knows that tomorrow she will probably do the same thing.

✓ **Truth or Fiction Revisited**

It is true that some college women control their weight by going on cycles of binge eating followed by self-induced vomiting. Many other women do so as well. People who behave in this way are diagnosed with bulimia nervosa.

REFLECT

Are you happy with your body shape? Do you feel pressure to be thinner (or heavier) than you are? Explain.

Bulimia nervosa is characterized by recurrent cycles of binge eating followed by dramatic measures to purge the food. Binge eating frequently follows food deprivation—for example, severe dieting. Purging includes self-induced vomiting, fasting or strict dieting, use of laxatives, and vigorous exercise. People with bulimia are often perfectionistic about body shape and weight (Joiner et al., 1997). Like anorexia, bulimia afflicts many more women than men.

Question: What is known about the origins of eating disorders?

Theoretical Views

Numerous explanations of anorexia nervosa and bulimia nervosa have been proposed. Some psychoanalysts suggest that anorexia represents an unconscious effort by the girl to cope with sexual fears, particularly the prospect of pregnancy. Because anorexia is connected with amenorrhea, some psychodynamic theorists suggest that anorexia represents an effort by the girl to revert to a prepubescent stage. Anorexia allows the girl to avoid growing up, separating from her family, and taking on adult responsibilities. Because of the loss of fatty deposits, her breasts and hips flatten. In her fantasies, perhaps, a woman with anorexia remains a child, sexually undifferentiated.

There is great social pressure in the United States for women to be slender. Fashion models, who represent the female ideal, are 9% taller and 16% slimmer than the average woman (Williams, 1992). As the cultural ideal grows slimmer, women with average or heavier-than-average figures come under more pressure to control their weight.

REFLECT

Consider your sociocultural background. Are women from this background traditionally expected to be well-rounded or slender? What attitudes are connected with weight and body shape within your traditions?

SECTION X **Review**

The eating disorders include (103) an_____ nervosa and bulimia (104) _____. Anorexia is characterized by refusal to maintain a healthful body weight, intense fear of being overweight, a distorted (105) _____ image, and, in females, lack of ovulation. Anorexia is more likely to afflict young (106: Men or Women?). Bulimia nervosa is defined as recurrent cycles of (107) b_____ eating and the taking of dramatic measures to (108) p_____ the food, such as self-induced vomiting. Both disorders tend to begin in (109) _____ence.

Psychodynamic theorists suggest that anorexia may represent an unconscious effort by the girl to remain (110) pre_____. However, other psychologists point to the current cultural (111) _____zation of the slender female as a motivating force.

Although the causes of many psychological disorders remain in dispute, a variety of methods of therapy have been devised to deal with them. They are described in the chapter "Methods of Therapy."

BULIMIA NERVOSA An eating disorder characterized by recurrent cycles of binge eating followed by dramatic measures to purge the food.

STUDY GUIDE

SUMMARY

1. **How have people historically explained psychological disorders?** People throughout history have mainly attributed psychological disorders to some sort of spiritual intervention. The ancient Greeks believed that people with such disorders were being punished by the gods. Since the Middle Ages, Europeans mainly attributed these disorders to possession by the devil.

2. **How do we define psychological disorders?** Psychological disorders are characterized by unusual behavior, socially unacceptable behavior, faulty perception of reality, personal distress, dangerous behavior, or self-defeating behavior.

3. **How are psychological disorders grouped or classified?** The most widely used classification scheme is found in the *Diagnostic and Statistical Manual (DSM)* of the American Psychiatric Association. The current edition of the *DSM* groups disorders on the basis of observable symptoms and no longer uses the category of neuroses.

4. **What kinds of anxiety disorders are there?** Anxiety disorders are characterized by motor tension, feelings of dread, and overarousal of the sympathetic branch of the autonomic nervous system. These disorders include irrational, excessive fears, or phobias; panic disorder, characterized by sudden attacks in which people typically fear that they may be losing control or going crazy; generalized or pervasive anxiety; obsessive-compulsive disorder, in which people are troubled by intrusive thoughts or impulses to repeat some activity; and stress disorders, in which a stressful event is followed by persistent fears and intrusive thoughts about the event. Posttraumatic stress disorder can occur 6 months or more after the event, whereas acute stress disorder occurs within a month.

5. **What is known about the origins of anxiety disorders?** The psychodynamic perspective tends to view anxiety disorders as representing difficulty in repressing primitive impulses. Many learning theorists view phobias as conditioned fears. Cognitive theorists focus on ways in which people interpret threats. Some people may also be genetically predisposed to acquire certain kinds of fears. Anxiety disorders tend to run in families. Some psychologists suggest that biochemical factors—which could be inherited—may create a predisposition toward anxiety disorders. One such factor is faulty regulation of neurotransmitters.

6. **What kinds of dissociative disorders are there?** Dissociative disorders are characterized by sudden, temporary changes in consciousness or self-identity. They include dissociative amnesia; dissociative fugue, which involves forgetting plus fleeing and adopting a new identity; dissociative identity disorder (multiple personality), in which a person behaves as if more than one personality occupies his or her body; and depersonalization, characterized by feelings that one is not real or that one is standing outside oneself.

7. **What is known about the origins of dissociative disorders?** Many psychologists suggest that dissociative disorders help people keep disturbing memories or ideas out of mind. These memories may involve episodes of sexual or physical abuse during childhood. However, a number of cases may involve malingering.

8. **What kinds of somatoform disorders are there?** People with somatoform disorders exhibit or complain of physical problems, although no medical evidence of such problems can be found. The somatoform disorders include conversion disorder and hypochondria.

9. **What is known about the origins of somatoform disorders?** These disorders were once called "hysterical neuroses" and expected to be found more often among women. However, they are also found among men and may reflect the relative benefits of focusing on physical symptoms rather than fears and conflicts.

10. **What kinds of mood disorders are there?** Mood disorders involve disturbances in expressed emotions. Major depression is characterized by persistent feelings of sadness, loss of interest, feelings of worthlessness or guilt, inability to concentrate, and physical symptoms that may include disturbances in regulation of eating and sleeping. Feelings of unworthiness and guilt may be so excessive that they are considered delusional. Bipolar disorder is characterized by dramatic swings in mood between elation and depression.

11. **Why are women more likely than men to be depressed?** Part of the gender difference may reflect hormonal factors, but women also experience greater stresses than men in our culture—including the stresses that accompany second-class citizenship.

12. **What is known about the origins of mood disorders?** Research emphasizes possible roles for learned helplessness, attributional styles, and serotonin deficiency in depression. People who are depressed are more likely than other people to make internal, stable, and global attributions for failures. Genetic factors involving regulation of neurotransmitters may also be involved in mood disorders. For example, bipolar disorder has been linked to inappropriate levels of the neurotransmitter glutamate. Moreover, people with severe depression often respond to antidepressant drugs that heighten the action of serotonin.

13. **Why do people commit suicide?** Suicide is connected with stressful events, and especially events that involve loss of social support. Suicide tends to run in families, but it is unclear whether the reasons are genetic or environmental.

14. **What sociocultural factors are connected with suicide?** More women attempt suicide, but more men "succeed" because they use more lethal means. European Americans are twice as likely as African Americans to commit suicide. Native Americans are at the greatest risk.

15. **What are some of the myths and realities about suicide?** It is mythical that people who truly intend to kill themselves do it without warning, and that those who fail at the attempt are just seeking attention. Many people who commit suicide had issued warnings, and many had made prior attempts.

16. **What is schizophrenia?** Schizophrenia is a most severe psychological disorder that is characterized by disturbances in thought and language, such as loosening of associations and delusions; in perception and attention, as found in hallucinations; in motor activity, as shown by a stupor or by excited behavior; in mood, as in flat or inappropriate emotional responses; and in social interaction, as in social withdrawal and absorption in daydreams or fantasy.

17. **What kinds of schizophrenia are there?** The major types of schizophrenia are paranoid, disorganized, and catatonic. Paranoid schizophrenia is characterized largely by systematized delusions; disorganized schizophrenia by incoherence; and catatonic schizophrenia by motor impairment.

18. **What is known about the origins of schizophrenia?** According to the multifactorial model, genetic vulnerability to schizophrenia may interact with other factors, such as stress, complications during pregnancy and childbirth, and quality of parenting, to cause the disorder to develop. According to the dopamine theory of schizophrenia, people with schizophrenia *use* more dopamine than other people do, perhaps because they have more dopamine receptors in the brain than other people, or perhaps because their dopamine receptors are hyperactive.

19. **What kinds of personality disorders are there?** Personality disorders are inflexible, maladaptive behavior patterns that impair personal or social functioning and cause distress for the individual or others. The defining trait of paranoid personality disorder is suspiciousness. People with schizotypal personality disorders show oddities of thought, perception, and behavior. Social withdrawal is the major characteristic of schizoid personality disorder. People with antisocial personality disorders persistently violate the rights of others and are in conflict with the law. They show little or no guilt or shame over their misdeeds and are largely undeterred by punishment. People with avoidant personality disorder tend to avoid entering relationships for fear of rejection and criticism.

20. **What is known about the origins of personality disorders?** Psychodynamic theory connected many personality disorders with hypothesized Oedipal problems. Genetic factors may be involved in some personality disorders. Antisocial personality disorder may develop from some combination of genetic vulnerability (which may provide lower-than-normal levels of arousal), inconsistent discipline, and cynical processing of social information.

21. **What kinds of eating disorders are there?** The eating disorders include anorexia nervosa and bulimia nervosa. Anorexia is characterized by refusal to eat and extreme thinness. Bulimia is characterized by cycles of binge eating and purging. Women are more likely than men to develop these disorders.

22. **What is known about the origins of eating disorders?** The major psychodynamic explanation of the eating disorders is that a conflicted female is attempting to remain prepubescent. However, most psychologists look to cultural idealization of the slender female—and the pressure that such idealization places on young women—as the major contributor.

E X E R C I S E 1

PSYCHOLOGICAL DISORDERS – SYMPTOMS

In the first column are symptoms of psychological disorders. The second column lists disorders. Write the letter of the type of disorder in the appropriate blank space. More than one type of disorder may apply. Answers are given below.

____ 1. Waxy flexibility	A. Phobic disorder
____ 2. Flashbacks	B. Panic disorder
____ 3. Binge eating	C. Generalized anxiety disorder
____ 4. Nervousness	D. Obsessive-compulsive disorder
____ 5. Weight loss	E. Posttraumatic stress disorder
____ 6. Free-floating anxiety	F. Dissociative amnesia
____ 7. Loss of a sense of one's personal identity	G. Dissociative identity disorder
	H. Depersonalization disorder
____ 8. Pressured speech	I. Conversion disorder
____ 9. Vivid, abundant hallucinations	J. Hypochondriasis
____10. Delusions of persecution	K. Anorexia nervosa
____11. Delusions of unworthiness	L. Bulimia nervosa
____12. Self-induced vomiting	M. Major depression
____13. Sudden anxiety attacks in the absence of threatening stimuli	N. Bipolar disorder
	O. Disorganized schizophrenia
____14. Lack of guilt over misdeeds	P. Catatonic schizophrenia
____15. Elation	Q. Paranoid schizophrenia
____16. Hallucinations	R. Paranoid personality
____17. Lack of energy	S. Schizoid personality
____18. Suspiciousness	T. Antisocial personality
____19. La belle indifférence	
____20. Compulsive behavior	
____21. Social withdrawal	
____22. Fear of public scrutiny	
____23. Physical complaints	
____24. Loose associations	
____25. Giddiness	

E X E R C I S E   2

PSYCHOLOGICAL DISORDERS—CLASSES, DESCRIPTION, SUBTYPES

Following is a summary chart of the types and subtypes of psychological disorders. Fill in the missing information.

Class	Description	Major Subtypes
(1) _____ disorders	Generally characterized by worrying, fear of the worst happening, fear of losing control, nervousness, and inability to relax	Phobic, panic, generalized anxiety, (2) obsessive-_____, and stress disorders
(3) _____ disorders	Generally characterized by separation of mental processes such as thoughts, emotions, identity, memory, or consciousness	Dissociative (4) am_____, dissociative fugue, dissociative identity disorder, and (5) _____zation
(6) _____form disorders	Generally characterized by complaints of (7) _____ problems such as paralysis or pain, or the persistent belief that one has a serious disease in the absence of medical findings	(8) Con_____ disorder and (9) _____driasis
Mood disorders	Generally characterized by disturbance in expressed emotions	Major (10) _____ and (11) bi_____ disorder
(12) _____phrenia	Generally characterized by disturbances in language and thought (e.g., delusions, loose associations), attention and perception (e.g., hallucinations), motor activity, and mood, and by withdrawal and absorption in daydreams or fantasy	(13) Par_____, disorganized, and (14) _____tonic
Personality disorders	Generally characterized by inflexible and (15) mal_____ patterns of behavior that impair personal or (16) so_____ functioning and are a source of distress to oneself or others	Paranoid, schizotypal, schizoid, (17) anti_____, and avoidant personality disorders
Eating disorders	Generally characterized by persistent, gross disturbances in eating patterns	(18) _____ nervosa and bulimia nervosa

B R I D G I N G   T H E   G A P

LANGUAGE AND CULTURE

abrupt (557) *sudden*

apathetic (567) *without feeling*

atrocity (564) *act of inhuman degree*

atypical (575) *unusual*

to binge (549) *to eat without control until it is all gone*

blade (571) *knife*

blunted (573) *dulled*

to bolster (578) *to strengthen*

to break into a sweat (562) *to become nervous suddenly and to perspire profusely*

to bug (572) *to install a listening device*

bungalow (571) *small house*

burden (566) *heavy weight to carry*

cottage (571) *small house*

delusional (571) *not based on reality, dreamlike*

demeaning (576) *inferior, treating as if inferior*

down in the dumps (565) *depressed, sad*

dread (557) *fear*

to drift downward (574) *to descend slowly*

to enlist (550) *to join the army voluntarily*

entrapment (559) *fear of being caught in small places*

to feel drained (557) *to experience fatigue, to be empty of energy*

to fake (563) *to pretend*

to be fated to (569) *to feel unavoidably compelled to*

at a fever pitch (580) *working fast*

to become fixated (562) *to become obsessed with*

flat (573) *colorless, weak*

foreboding (557) *feeling of fear of the unknown*

fractured (550) *broken up*

to get a word in edgewise (566) *to be able to contribute by breaking into another's flow of words*

giddiness (573) *silliness*

to giggle (573) *to laugh*

glibness (577) *shallow, meaningless expression*

goblin (571) *ghostlike creature*

goings-on (551) *happenings, events, especially when regarded with disapproval*

to goldbrick (562) *to be lazy, to avoid work*

grimace (559) *facial distortion*

to harbor (561) *to hold within*

helluva (562) *(here) big*

herd (562) *group*

hives (561) *skin welts, allergic reaction*

hodgepodge (554) *mixture*

to jumble (571) *to mix up*

lethargy (565) *state of low energy*

to loom large (570) *to appear as if important*

to meander (564) *to wander*

maladaptive (555) *not easily assimilated, useless, doesn't fit*

to mushroom (562) *to grow rapidly*

posture (573) *a way of standing up straight, a particular way of placing the arms or legs*

to be reared (578) *to be raised by parents or caretakers*

remorse (577) *sorrow*

to rot (565) *to decay*

to run in families (574) *to be common among relatives*

run-of-the-mill (565) *ordinary*

to shudder (559) *to shake involuntarily*

to slit one's wrists (571) *to make a cut into one's wrist-veins in an attempt to kill oneself*

to squirm (559) *to wiggle uncomfortably*

to startle (558) *to frighten*

stupor (572) *trance, daze, as if drugged*

syndrome (555) *series of symptoms*

tightly knit (572) *close*

a trigger (568) *a cause*

vehemently (579) *strongly, forcefully, loudly*

to venture (557) *to go out*

to be wasting away (580) *to be dying*

to be wrapped up in (573) *to be strongly involved with*

1. Throughout history, people have attributed unusual behavior and psychological disorders to
    (a) poverty,
    (b) unconscious urges,
    (c) demons,
    (d) observational learning.

2. The most widely used system of classification of psychological disorders in the United States is written by the
    (a) American Psychiatric Association,
    (b) American Psychological Association,
    (c) American Medical Association,
    (d) World Health Organization.

3. Fear of high places is known as
    (a) speech anxiety,
    (b) claustrophobia,
    (c) agoraphobia,
    (d) acrophobia.

4. Dan has a problem in which he encounters heavy sweating and a pounding heart—both for no apparent reason. Dan would probably be diagnosed as having a(n)
    (a) phobic disorder,
    (b) panic disorder,
    (c) generalized anxiety disorder,
    (d) obsessive-compulsive disorder.

5. A difference between a phobic disorder and a fear is that the phobic response
    (a) is out of proportion to the actual danger,
    (b) involves cognitive as well as behavioral reactions,
    (c) is characterized by rapid heart rate,
    (d) is characterized by avoidance of the feared object or situation.

6. By definition, all dissociative disorders involve
    (a) massive repression of unacceptable impulses,
    (b) a sudden change in consciousness or identity,
    (c) the presence of at least two conflicting personalities,
    (d) malingering.

7. In which of the following does the individual feel unreal and separated from his or her body?
    (a) Depersonalization disorder,
    (b) Schizotypal personality disorder,
    (c) Dissociative identity disorder,
    (d) Schizoid personality disorder.

8. Mary believes that she is suffering from a serious stomach or intestinal disease because she has difficulty keeping down food and has unusual sensations in these regions of the body. However, repeated visits to physicians have not uncovered evidence of any medical disorder. Mary is most likely to be diagnosed with
    (a) conversion disorder,
    (b) malingering,
    (c) anorexia nervosa,
    (d) hypochondriasis.

9. Mood disorders are primarily characterized by disturbance in
    (a) thought processes,
    (b) biological processes,
    (c) expressed emotions,
    (d) motor responses.

10. The symptom that differentiates bipolar disorder from other disorders is
    (a) suicide attempts,
    (b) severe bouts of depression,
    (c) delusional thinking,
    (d) rapid flight of ideas.

11. Imbalances in _____ are most likely to be connected with both types of mood disorders discussed in the chapter.
    (a) GABA,
    (b) glutamate,
    (c) neurotransmitters,
    (d) dopamine.

12. Schizophrenic disorders are known primarily by disturbances in
    (a) motor responses,
    (b) thought,
    (c) expressed emotions,
    (d) physical functioning.

13. A person with _____ is most likely to show confused, jumbled thinking.
    (a) schizotypal personality disorder,
    (b) paranoid schizophrenia,
    (c) paranoid personality disorder,
    (d) schizoid personality disorder.

14. Evidence seems clearest that people with schizophrenia
    (a) produce more dopamine than other people do,
    (b) have a greater number of dopamine receptors in the brain than other people do,

(c) are more sensitive to dopamine than other people are,

(d) utilize more dopamine than other people do.

15. The defining trait of the paranoid personality disorder is
    (a) social withdrawal,
    (b) oddities of thought,
    (c) suspiciousness,
    (d) self-absorption.

16. According to Susan Nolen-Hoeksema, people who respond to feelings of depression by focusing on their symptoms and the possible causes and effects of their symptoms tend to
    (a) develop insight into the origins of their problems,
    (b) prolong depressive episodes,
    (c) increase the amount of noradrenaline available to the brain,
    (d) utilize lower-than-normal levels of dopamine.

17. According to the chapter, evidence suggests that there is a role for genetic factors in each of the following disorders, *with the exception of*
    (a) anxiety disorders,
    (b) schizophrenia,
    (c) bipolar disorder,
    (d) dissociative fugue.

18. Which of the following statements about suicide is true?
    (a) Women are more likely than men to commit suicide,
    (b) Teenagers are more likely than older people to commit suicide,
    (c) Men are more likely than women to attempt suicide by using pills,
    (d) African Americans are more likely than European Americans to commit suicide.

19. Emotional response tends to be flat or blunted in _____ disorders.
    (a) personality,
    (b) anxiety,
    (c) mood,
    (d) schizophrenic.

20. According to the chapter, adoptee studies show that the biological parent typically places the child at greater risk than the adoptive parent for _____, even when the child has been reared by the adoptive parent.
    (a) anxiety disorders,
    (b) somatoform disorders,
    (c) schizophrenic disorders,
    (d) dissociative disorders.

1. How have people historically
   explained psychological
   disorders?

2. How do we define psychological disorders?

3. How are psychological disorders grouped or classified?

4. What kinds of anxiety disorders are there?

5. What is known about the
   origins of anxiety disorders?

6. What kinds of dissociative
   disorders are there?

7. What is known about the
   origins of dissociative
   disorders?

8. What kinds of somatoform
   disorders are there?

9. What is known about the
   origins of somatoform
   disorders?

10. What kinds of mood dis-
    orders are there?

11. Why are women more likely than men to be depressed?

12. What is known about the origins of mood disorders?

13. Why do people commit suicide?

14. What sociocultural factors are connected with suicide?

15. What are some of the myths and realities about suicide?

16. What is schizophrenia?

17. What kinds of schizophrenia are there?

18. What is known about the origins of schizophrenia?

19. What kinds of personality disorders are there?

20. What is known about the origins of personality disorders?

21. What kinds of eating disorders are there?

22. What is known about the origins of eating disorders?

_____

_____

_____

_____

_____

ANSWERS TO SECTION REVIEWS

1. Possession
2. Gods
3. Hippocrates
4. Hammer
5. Statistically
6. Unacceptable
7. Perception
8. Multiaxial
9. Five
10. Psychiatric
11. Symptoms
12. Szasz
13. Phobias
14. Control
15. Obsessive-compulsive
16. Posttraumatic
17. Agoraphobia
18. Social
19. Sweating
20. Heart
21. Obsession
22. Compulsion
23. Stress
24. Flashbacks
25. Repression
26. Unconscious
27. Conditioned
28. Mineka
29. External
30. Anxiety
31. Do
32. Gamma-aminobutyric
33. Neurotransmitter
34. Consciousness
35. Amnesia
36. Identity
37. Depersonalization
38. Multiple
39. Repression
40. Think
41. Abuse
42. Attention
43. Somatoform
44. Cannot
45. Conversion
46. Hypochondriasis
47. Physical
48. Belle
49. Psychodynamic
50. Emotions
51. Depression
52. Bipolar
53. Manic-depressive
54. Energy
55. Pessimism
56. Major
57. Elation
58. Flight
59. Normal
60. Anger
61. Reinforced
62. Inactivity
63. Helplessness
64. Internal
65. Global
66. Serotonin
67. Glutamate
68. College students
69. Women as men
70. More
71. Depression (or Despair, etc.)
72. More
73. Thought (or Thinking, etc.)
74. Perception
75. Motor
76. Disorganized
77. Delusions
78. Hallucinations
79. Stupor
80. Waxy
81. Id
82. Ego
83. Does
84. 35% to 40%
85. Dopamine
86. Influenza
87. More
88. Behavior
89. Maladaptive
90. Distress (or Discomfort, etc.)
91. Paranoid
92. Schizotypal
93. Psychotic
94. Withdrawal
95. Schizoid
96. Antisocial
97. Guilt
98. Punishment
99. Rejection
100. Discipline
101. Lower-than-normal
102. Threatening (or Insulting, etc.)
103. Anorexia
104. Nervosa
105. Body
106. Women
107. Binge
108. Purge
109. Adolescence
110. Prepubescent
111. Idealization

ANSWERS TO EXERCISE 1

1. P
2. E
3. L
4. A, B, C, etc.
5. K, M
6. C
7. F, H
8. N
9. O
10. Q
11. M
12. L
13. B
14. T
15. N
16. O, P, Q
17. M
18. Q, R
19. I
20. D, W
21. M, S
22. A
23. J
24. O, P, Q
25. O

ANSWERS TO EXERCISE 2

1. Anxiety
2. Obsessive-compulsive
3. Dissociative
4. Amnesia
5. Depersonalization

6. Somatoform
7. Physical (or Bodily, etc.)
8. Conversion
9. Hypochondriasis

10. Depression
11. Bipolar
12. Schizophrenia
13. Paranoid
14. Catatonic

15. Maladaptive
16. Social
17. Antisocial
18. Anorexia

ANSWERS TO QUIZ

1. C
2. A
3. D
4. B
5. A

6. B
7. A
8. D
9. C
10. D

11. C
12. B
13. B
14. D
15. C

16. B
17. D
18. A
19. D
20. C

METHODS OF THERAPY

13

Jasmine is a 19-year-old college sophomore. She has been crying almost without letup for several days. She feels that her life is falling apart. Her college dreams are in a shambles. She has brought shame upon her family. Thoughts of suicide have crossed her mind. She can barely drag herself out of bed in the morning. She is avoiding her friends. She can pinpoint some sources of stress in her life: a couple of poor grades, an argument with a boyfriend, friction with roommates. Still, her misery seemed to descend on her out of nowhere.

Jasmine is depressed—so depressed that her family and friends have finally prevailed on her to seek professional help. Had she broken her leg, her treatment by a qualified professional would have followed a fairly standard course. Yet treatment of psychological problems and disorders like depression may be approached from very different perspectives. Depending on the therapist Jasmine sees, she may be doing the following:

- Lying on a couch talking about anything that pops into her awareness and exploring the possible meaning of a recurrent dream

- Sitting face to face with a warm, gentle therapist who accepts Jasmine as she is and expresses faith in Jasmine's ability to make the right decisions for herself

- Listening to a frank, straightforward therapist assert that Jasmine is depressing herself with her self-defeating attitudes and perfectionistic beliefs
- Taking antidepressant medication
- Participating in some combination of these approaches

These methods, although different, all represent methods of therapy. In this chapter we explore various methods of psychotherapy and biological therapy. Question: What is psychotherapy?

SECTION I. WHAT IS THERAPY? THE SEARCH FOR A "SWEET OBLIVIOUS ANTIDOTE"[1]

There are many kinds of psychotherapy, but they all have certain common characteristics. **Psychotherapy** is a systematic interaction between a therapist and a client that applies psychological principles to affect the client's thoughts, feelings, or behavior in order to help the client overcome psychological disorders, adjust to problems in living, or develop as an individual. Quite a mouthful? True. But note the essentials:

1. *Systematic interaction.* Psychotherapy is a systematic interaction between a client and a therapist. The therapist's theoretical point of view interacts with the client's to determine how the therapist and client relate to each other.

2. *Psychological principles.* Psychotherapy is based on psychological theory and research in areas such as personality, learning, motivation, and emotion.

3. *Thoughts, feelings, and behavior.* Psychotherapy influences clients' thoughts, feelings, and behavior. It can be aimed at any or all of these aspects of human psychology.

4. *Psychological disorders, adjustment problems, and personal growth.* Psychotherapy is often used with people who have psychological disorders. Other people seek help in adjusting to problems such as shyness, weight problems, or loss of a spouse. Still other clients want to learn more about themselves and to reach their full potential as individuals, parents, or creative artists.

The History of Therapies

Historically speaking, "treatments" of psychological disorders often reflected demonological thinking. Question: How, then, have people with psychological problems and disorders been treated throughout the ages? Because of this belief, treatment tended to involve cruel practices such as exorcism and death by hanging or burning. Some people who could not meet the demands of everyday life were tossed into prisons. Others begged in the streets, stole food, or became prostitutes. A few found their way to monasteries or other retreats that offered a kind word and some support. Generally speaking, they died early.

ASYLUMS Asylums originated in European monasteries. They were the first institutions meant primarily for people with psychological disorders. But their function was warehousing, not treatment. Their inmate populations

---

[1] The phrase is from Shakespeare's *Macbeth*.

REFLECT

Before you get deeply into the chapter, consider what you think happens in psychotherapy. Then ask yourself whether your ideas fit what happens in the type of therapy you are reading about.

PSYCHOTHERAPY A systematic interaction between a therapist and a client that brings psychological principles to bear on influencing the client's thoughts, feelings, or behavior to help that client overcome abnormal behavior or adjust to problems in living.

REFLECT

Had you heard the words *asylum* or *bedlam*? What did you think they meant? Were you correct?

The Unchaining of the Patients at La Bicêtre. Philippe Pinel sparked the humanitarian reform movement by unchaining the patients at this asylum in Paris.

mushroomed until the stresses created by noise, overcrowding, and disease aggravated the problems they were meant to ease. Inmates were frequently chained and beaten.

The word *bedlam* derives from St. Mary's of *Bethlehem*, the London asylum that opened its gates in 1547. Here unfortunate people with psychological disorders were chained, whipped, and allowed to lie in their own waste. And here the ladies and gentlemen of the British upper class might stroll on a lazy afternoon to be amused by the inmates' antics. The price of admission was one penny.

✓ Truth or Fiction Revisited

It is true that residents of London used to visit the insane asylum for amusement.

Humanitarian reform movements began in the 18th century. In Paris, the physician Philippe Pinel unchained the patients at La Bicêtre. Rather than running amok, most patients profited from kindness and freedom. Many could eventually reenter society. Later movements to reform institutions were led by the Quaker William Tuke in England and by Dorothea Dix in America.

MENTAL HOSPITALS In the United States mental hospitals gradually replaced asylums. In the mid-1950s more than a million people resided in state, county, Veterans Administration, or private facilities. The mental hospital's function is treatment, not warehousing. Still, because of high patient populations and understaffing, many patients received little attention. Even today, with somewhat improved conditions, one psychiatrist may be responsible for the welfare of several hundred residents on a weekend when other staff members are absent.

THE COMMUNITY MENTAL HEALTH MOVEMENT Since the 1960s, efforts have been made to maintain people with serious psychological disorders in their communities. Community mental health centers attempt to maintain new patients as outpatients and to serve patients who have been released from mental hospitals. Today most people with chronic psychological disorders live in the community, not the hospital.

Critics note that many people who had resided in hospitals for decades were suddenly discharged to "home" communities that seemed foreign and forbidding to them. Many do not receive adequate follow-up care (Bernstein, 1999). Many join the ranks of the homeless.

SECTION I | Review

Psychotherapy is a systematic interaction between a therapist and a client that brings (1) _____ical principles to bear on influencing clients' thoughts, feelings, or behavior. Psychotherapy helps clients overcome psychological (2) _____rs or adjust to problems in living. Historic treatments of psychological disorders were based on the demonological model and included the (3) ex_____ of evil spirits. The first institutions intended primarily for the mentally ill were called (4) _____ms. St. Mary's of (5) _____ is the name of a well-known London asylum.

Humanitarian reform movements began in the (6) _____ century. Philippe (7) _____ unchained the patients at the asylum called La Bicêtre. Mental (8) _____tals replaced asylums in the United States.

SECTION II. PSYCHODYNAMIC THERAPIES

Psychodynamic therapies are based on the thinking of Sigmund Freud, the founder of psychodynamic theory. They assume that psychological problems reflect early childhood experiences and internal conflicts. According to Freud, these conflicts involve the shifting of psychic, or libidinal, energy among the three psychic structures—the id, ego, and superego. These shifts of psychic energy determine our behavior. When primitive urges threaten to break through from the id or when the superego floods us with excessive guilt, defenses are established and distress is created. Freud's psychodynamic therapy method—psychoanalysis— aims to modify the flow of energy among these structures, largely to bulwark the ego against the torrents of energy loosed by the id and the superego. With impulses and feelings of guilt and shame placed under greater control, clients are freer to develop adaptive behavior. Question: How, then, do psychoanalysts conduct a traditional Freudian psychoanalysis?

Traditional Psychoanalysis: "Where Id Was, There Shall Ego Be"

Canst thou not minister to a mind diseas'd,
Pluck out from the memory a rooted sorrow,
Raze out the written troubles of the brain,
And with some sweet oblivious antidote
Cleanse the stuff'd bosom of that perilous stuff
Which weighs upon the heart?

SHAKESPEARE, *Macbeth*

In the passage just quoted, Macbeth asks a physician to minister to Lady Macbeth after she has gone mad. In the play, her madness is caused partly by events—namely, her role in murders designed to seat her husband on the throne of Scotland. There are also hints of mysterious, deeply rooted problems, such as conflicts about infertility.

If Lady Macbeth's physician had been a traditional psychoanalyst, he might have asked her to lie on a couch in a slightly darkened room. He would have sat behind her and encouraged her to talk about anything that came to mind, no matter how trivial, no matter how personal. To avoid interfering with her self-exploration, he might have said little or nothing for session after session. That would have been par for the course. A traditional **psychoanalysis** can extend for months or even years.

Psychoanalysis is the clinical method devised by Freud for plucking "from the memory a rooted sorrow," for razing "out the written troubles of the brain." It aims to provide *insight* into the conflicts that are presumed to lie at the roots of a person's problems. Insight means many things, including knowledge of the experiences that lead to conflicts and maladaptive behavior, recognition of unconscious feelings and conflicts, and conscious evaluation of one's thoughts, feelings, and behavior.

Psychoanalysis also aims to help the client express feelings and urges that have been repressed. By so doing, Freud believed that the client spilled forth the psychic energy that had been repressed by conflicts and guilt. He called this spilling forth **catharsis.** Catharsis would provide relief by alleviating some of the forces assaulting the ego.

Freud was also fond of saying, "Where id was, there shall ego be." In part, he meant that psychoanalysis could shed light on the inner workings of the mind. He also sought to replace impulsive and defensive behavior with coping behavior. In this way, for example, a man with a phobia for knives might discover that he had been repressing the urge to harm someone who had taken advantage of him. He might also find ways to confront the person verbally.

FREE ASSOCIATION Early in his career as a therapist, Freud found that hypnosis allowed his clients to focus on repressed conflicts and talk about them. The relaxed "trance state" provided by hypnosis seemed to allow clients to "break through" to topics of which they would otherwise be unaware. Freud also found, however, that many clients denied the accuracy of this material once they were out of the trance. Other clients found

PSYCHOANALYSIS Freud's method of psychotherapy.

CATHARSIS In psychoanalysis, the expression of repressed feelings and impulses to allow the release of the psychic energy associated with them.

A View of Freud's Consulting Room. Freud would sit in a chair by the head of the couch while a client free-associated. The basic rule of free association is that no thought is censored.

them to be premature and painful. Freud therefore turned to **free association,** a more gradual method of breaking through the walls of defense that block a client's insight into unconscious processes.

In free association, the client is made comfortable—for example, lying on a couch—and asked to talk about any topic that comes to mind. No thought is to be censored—that is the basic rule. Psychoanalysts ask their clients to wander "freely" from topic to topic, but they do not believe that the process occurring *within* the client is fully free. Repressed impulses clamor for release.

The ego persists in trying to repress unacceptable impulses and threatening conflicts. As a result, clients might show **resistance** to recalling and discussing threatening ideas. A client about to entertain such thoughts might claim, "My mind is blank." The client might accuse the analyst of being demanding or inconsiderate. He or she might "forget" the next appointment when threatening material is about to surface.

The therapist observes the dynamic struggle between the compulsion to utter certain thoughts and the client's resistance to uttering them. Through discreet remarks, the analyst subtly tips the balance in favor of utterance. A gradual process of self-discovery and self-insight ensues. Now and then the analyst offers an **interpretation** of an utterance, showing how it suggests resistance or deep-seated feelings and conflicts.

TRANSFERENCE Freud believed that clients not only responded to him as an individual but also in ways that reflected their attitudes and feelings toward other people in their lives. He labeled this process **transference.** For example, a young woman client might respond to him as a father figure and displace her feelings toward her father onto Freud, perhaps seeking affection and wisdom. A young man could also see Freud as a father figure, but rather than wanting affection from Freud, he might view Freud as a rival, responding to Freud in terms of his own unresolved Oedipal complex.

Analyzing and working through transference has been considered a key aspect of psychoanalysis. Freud believed that clients reenact their childhood conflicts with their parents when they are in therapy. Clients might thus transfer the feelings of anger, love, or jealousy they felt toward their own parents onto the analyst. Childhood conflicts often involve unresolved feelings of love, anger, or rejection. A client may interpret a suggestion by the therapist as a criticism and see it as a devastating blow, transferring feelings of self-hatred that he had repressed because his parents had rejected him in childhood. Transference can also distort clients' relationships with other people here and now, such as relationships with spouses or employers. The following therapeutic dialogue illustrates the way in which an analyst may interpret a client's inability to communicate his needs to his wife as a function of transference. The purpose is to provide his client, a Mr. Arianes, with insight into how his relationship with his wife has been colored by his childhood relationship with his mother:

> Arianes: I think you've got it there, Doc. We weren't communicating. I
>   wouldn't tell [my wife] what was wrong or what I wanted from her.
>   Maybe I expected her to understand me without saying anything.
> Therapist: Like the expectations a child has of its mother.
> Arianes: Not my mother!
> Therapist: Oh?
> Arianes: No, I always thought she had too many troubles of her
>   own to pay attention to mine. I remember once I got hurt on my
>   bike and came to her all bloodied up. When she saw me she got
>   mad and yelled at me for making more trouble for her when she
>   already had her hands full with my father.

FREE ASSOCIATION In psychoanalysis, the uncensored uttering of all thoughts that come to mind.

RESISTANCE The tendency to block the free expression of impulses and primitive ideas — a reflection of the defense mechanism of repression.

INTERPRETATION An explanation of a client's utterance according to psychoanalytic theory.

TRANSFERENCE Responding to one person (such as a spouse or the psychoanalyst) in a way that is similar to the way one responded to another person (such as a parent) in childhood.

Therapist: Do you remember how you felt then?

Arianes: I can't remember, but I know that after that I never brought my troubles to her again.

Therapist: How old were you?

Arianes: Nine, I know that because I got that bike for my ninth birthday. It was a little too big for me still, that's why I got hurt on it.

Therapist: Perhaps you carried this attitude into your marriage.

Arianes: What attitude?

Therapist: The feeling that your wife, like your mother, would be unsympathetic to your difficulties. That there was no point in telling her about your experiences because she was too preoccupied or too busy to care.

Arianes: But she's so different from my mother. I come first with her.

Therapist: On one level you know that. On another, deeper level there may well be the fear that people—or maybe only women, or maybe only women you're close to—are all the same, and you can't take a chance at being rejected again in your need.

Arianes: Maybe you're right, Doc, but all that was so long ago, and I should be over that by now.

Therapist: That's not the way the mind works. If a shock, or a disappointment is strong enough it can permanently freeze our picture of ourselves and our expectations of the world. The rest of us grows up—that is, we let ourselves learn about life from experience and from what we see, hear, or read of the experiences of others, but that one area where we really got hurt stays unchanged. So what I mean when I say you might be carrying that attitude into your relationship with your wife is that when it comes to your hopes of being understood and catered to when you feel hurt or abused by life, you still feel very much like that nine-year-old boy who was rebuffed in his need and gave up hope that anyone would or could respond to him. (Basch, 1980, pp. 29–30)

DREAM ANALYSIS Freud often asked clients to jot down their dreams upon waking so that they could discuss them in therapy. Freud considered dreams the "royal road to the unconscious." He believed that the content of dreams is determined by unconscious processes as well as by the events of the day. Unconscious impulses tend to be expressed in dreams as a form of **wish fulfillment.**

But unacceptable sexual and aggressive impulses are likely to be displaced onto objects and situations that reflect the client's era and culture. These objects become symbols of unconscious wishes. For example, long, narrow dream objects might be **phallic symbols,** but whether the symbol takes the form of a spear, rifle, stick shift, or spacecraft partially reflects the dreamer's cultural background.

In psychodynamic theory, the perceived content of a dream is referred to as its shown, or **manifest content.** Its presumed hidden or symbolic content is its **latent content.** Suppose a man dreams that he is flying. Flying is the manifest content of the dream. Freud usually interpreted flying as symbolic of erection, so issues concerning sexual potency might make up the latent content of such a dream.

WISH FULFILLMENT A primitive method used by the id to attempt to gratify basic instincts.

PHALLIC SYMBOL A sign that represents the penis.

MANIFEST CONTENT In psychodynamic theory, the reported content of dreams.

LATENT CONTENT In psychodynamic theory, the symbolized or underlying content of dreams.

✔ Truth or Fiction Revisited

It is true that some psychotherapists interpret clients' dreams. Psychoanalysis is a case in point.

Modern Psychodynamic Approaches

Some psychoanalysts adhere faithfully to Freud's techniques. They engage in protracted therapy that continues to rely heavily on free association, interpretation of dreams, and other traditional methods. In recent years, however, more modern forms of psychodynamic therapy have been devised. Question: How do modern psychodynamic approaches differ from traditional psychoanalysis? Modern psychodynamic therapy is briefer and less intense, and makes treatment available to clients who do not have the time or money for long-term therapy. Many modern psychodynamic therapists do not believe that prolonged therapy is needed or justifiable in terms of the ratio of cost to benefits.

✓ Truth or Fiction Revisited

It is not true that psychotherapy must continue for months, perhaps years, to be effective. There are many effective brief forms of psychotherapy.

Some modern psychodynamic therapies continue to focus on revealing unconscious material and breaking through psychological defenses. Nevertheless, they differ from traditional psychoanalysis in several ways (Prochaska & Norcross, 1999). One is that the client and therapist usually sit face to face (the client does not lie on a couch). The therapist is usually directive. That is, modern therapists often suggest helpful behavior instead of focusing on insight alone. Finally, there is usually more focus on the ego as the "executive" of personality and less emphasis on the id. For this reason, many modern psychodynamic therapists are considered **ego analysts.**

Many of Freud's followers, the "second generation" of psychoanalysts—from Jung and Adler to Horney and Erikson—believed that Freud had placed too much emphasis on sexual and aggressive impulses and underestimated the role of the ego. For example, Freud aimed to establish conditions under which clients could spill forth psychic energy and eventually shore up the ego. Erikson, in contrast, spoke to clients directly about their values and concerns, encouraging them to develop desired traits and behavior patterns. Even Freud's daughter, the psychoanalyst Anna Freud (1895–1982), was more concerned with the ego than with unconscious forces and conflicts.

EGO ANALYST A psychodynamically oriented therapist who focuses on the conscious, coping behavior of the ego instead of the hypothesized, unconscious functioning of the id.

Review

SECTION II

Psychodynamic therapies are based on the thinking of Sigmund (9) _____. Freud's method of psychoanalysis attempts to shed light on (10) _____cious conflicts that are presumed to lie at the roots of clients' problems and transferences. Freud sought to replace impulsive and defensive behavior with (11) _____ng behavior. Freud also believed that psychoanalysis would allow clients to engage in (12) _____sis—that is, the spilling forth of repressed psychic energy.

The chief psychoanalytic method is (13) _____ association. The cardinal rule of free association is that no thought is to be (14) _____ed. In this way, material that has been (15) _____sed should eventually come to the surface of awareness.

Freud considered (16) _____s to be the "royal road to the unconscious." The perceived content of a dream is termed its (17) _____ content. The presumed symbolic content of a dream is termed its hidden or (18) _____ content.

Contemporary psychodynamic approaches tend to be (19: Longer or Briefer?) and (20: More or Less?) intense than Freud's. Modern psychodynamic therapists focus more on the (21) _____ as the "executive" of personality.

SECTION III. HUMANISTIC-EXISTENTIAL THERAPIES

Psychodynamic therapies focus on internal conflicts and unconscious processes. Humanistic-existential therapies focus on the quality of the client's subjective, conscious experience. Traditional psychoanalysis focuses on early childhood experiences. Humanistic-existential therapies usually focus on what clients are experiencing "here and now."

These differences, however, are mainly a matter of emphasis. The past has a way of influencing current thoughts, feelings, and behavior. Carl Rogers, the originator of client-centered therapy, believed that childhood experiences gave rise to the conditions of worth that troubled his clients here and now. He and Fritz Perls, the originator of Gestalt therapy, recognized that early incorporation of other people's values often leads clients to "disown" parts of their own personalities.

Client-Centered Therapy: Removing Roadblocks to Self-Actualization

Carl Rogers (1902–1987) spent his early years in a wealthy Chicago suburb, where he attended school with Ernest Hemingway and Frank Lloyd Wright's children. His family, with its six children, was religious and close-knit. Rogers's father viewed such activities as smoking, drinking, playing cards, and going to the movies as questionable. It was all right to be tolerant of them, but relationships with those who engaged in them were discouraged. When Rogers was 12, his family moved to a farm farther from the city to protect the children from such unwholesome influences.

Rogers took refuge in books and developed an interest in science. His first college major was agriculture. During a student visit to Peking, he was exposed for the first time to people from different ethnic backgrounds. He wrote his parents to proclaim his independence from their conservative views. Shortly thereafter he developed an ulcer and had to be hospitalized.

Rogers then attended New York's Union Theological Seminary with the goal of becoming a minister. At the same time he took courses in psychology and education across the street at Columbia University. After a couple of years he came to believe that psychology might be a better way of helping people, so he transferred to Columbia. Perhaps in response to his parents' efforts to "protect" him from other ways of thinking, Rogers developed a form of therapy that encourages individuals to rely on their own values and frames of references. He called his approach **client-centered therapy.** Question: What is Carl Rogers's method of client-centered therapy? His method is intended to help people get in touch with their genuine feelings and pursue their own interests, regardless of other people's wishes.

Rogers believed that we are free to make choices and control our destinies, despite the burdens of the past. He also believed that we have natural tendencies toward health, growth, and fulfillment. Psychological problems arise from roadblocks placed in the path of **self-actualization**—that is, what Rogers believed was an inborn tendency to strive to realize one's potential. If, when we are young, other people approve of us only when we are doing what they want us to do—as did Rogers's father—we may learn to disown the parts of ourselves to which they object. We may learn to be seen but not heard—not even by ourselves. As a result, we may experience stress and discomfort and the feeling that we—or the world—are not real.

Client-centered therapy aims to provide insight into the parts of us we have disowned so that we can feel whole. It creates a warm, therapeutic

REFLECT

Do you think that it is important to know about a friend's experiences from early childhood if you are to give him or her advice today?

CLIENT-CENTERED THERAPY Carl Rogers's method of psychotherapy, which emphasizes the creation of a warm, therapeutic atmosphere that frees clients to engage in self-exploration and self-expression.

SELF-ACTUALIZATION In humanistic theory, the inborn tendency to strive to realize one's potential.

REFLECT

Do you think you can separate your "real self" from your sociocultural experiences and religious training? What would you be like if you had been reared by other people in another place?

REFLECT

Do you think that your experiences have pressured you to disown parts of yourself? Could you find out if this has happened?

atmosphere that encourages self-exploration and self-expression. The therapist's acceptance of the client is thought to foster self-acceptance and self-esteem. Self-acceptance frees the client to make choices that develop his or her unique potential.

Client-centered therapy is nondirective. The client takes the lead, stating and exploring problems.

✓ Truth or Fiction Revisited

It is true that some psychotherapists encourage their clients to take the lead in the therapy session. Client-centered therapists are an example.

An effective client-centered therapist has several qualities:

- **Unconditional positive regard:** respect for clients as human beings with unique values and goals.
- **Empathic understanding:** recognition of the client's experiences and feelings. Therapists view the world through the client's **frame of reference** by setting aside their own values and listening closely.
- **Genuineness:** Openness and honesty in responding to the client. Client-centered therapists must be able to tolerate differentness because they believe that every client is different in important ways.

The following excerpt from a therapy session shows how Carl Rogers uses empathetic understanding and paraphrases a client's (Jill's) feelings. His goal is to help her recognize feelings that she has partially disowned:

> Jill: I'm having a lot of problems dealing with my daughter. She's 20 years old; she's in college; I'm having a lot of trouble letting her go. . . . And I have a lot of guilt feelings about her; I have a real need to hang on to her.
>
> C.R.: A need to hang on so you can kind of make up for the things you feel guilty about. Is that part of it?
>
> Jill: There's a lot of that. . . . Also, she's been a real friend to me, and filled my life. . . . And it's very hard. . . . a lot of empty places now that she's not with me.
>
> C.R.: The old vacuum, sort of, when she's not there.
>
> Jill: Yes. Yes. I also would like to be the kind of mother that could be strong and say, you know, "Go and have a good life," and this is really hard for me, to do that.

UNCONDITIONAL POSITIVE REGARD Acceptance of the value of another person, although not necessarily acceptance of everything the person does.

EMPATHIC UNDERSTANDING Ability to perceive a client's feelings from the client's frame of reference.

FRAME OF REFERENCE One's unique perceptions and attitudes, according to which one evaluates events.

GENUINENESS Recognition and open expression of the therapist's own feelings.

Client-Centered Therapy. By showing the qualities of unconditional positive regard, empathic understanding, and genuineness, client-centered therapists create an atmosphere in which clients can explore their feelings.

C.R.: It's very hard to give up something that's been so precious in your life, but also something that I guess has caused you pain when you mentioned guilt.

Jill: Yeah. And I'm aware that I have some anger toward her that I don't always get what I want. I have needs that are not met. And, uh, I don't feel I have a right to those needs. You know. . . . she's a daughter; she's not my mother. Though sometimes I feel as if I'd like her to mother me . . . it's very difficult for me to ask for that and have a right to it.

C.R.: So, it may be unreasonable, but still, when she doesn't meet your needs, it makes you mad.

Jill: Yeah I get very angry, very angry with her.

C.R.: (*Pauses*) You're also feeling a little tension at this point, I guess.

Jill: Yeah. Yeah. A lot of conflict. . . .   (C.R.: M-hm.) A lot of pain.

C.R.: A lot of pain. Can you say anything more about what that's about? (Farber, et al., 1996, pp. 74–75)

Client-centered therapy is practiced widely in college and university counseling centers, not just to help students experiencing, say, anxieties or depression but also to help them make decisions. Many college students have not yet made career choices or wonder whether they should become involved with particular people or in sexual activity. Client-centered therapists do not tell clients what to do. Instead, they help clients arrive at their own decisions.

Gestalt Therapy: Getting It Together

REFLECT

Do you feel that parts of your personality pull you in different directions? Explain.

Gestalt therapy was originated by Fritz Perls (1893–1970). Question: What is Fritz Perls's method of Gestalt therapy? Like client-centered therapy, Gestalt therapy assumes that people disown parts of themselves that might meet with social disapproval or rejection. People also don social masks, pretending to be things that they are not. Therapy aims to help individuals integrate conflicting parts of their personality. Perls used the term *Gestalt* to signify his interest in giving the conflicting parts of the personality an integrated form or shape. He aimed to have his clients become aware of inner conflict, accept the reality of conflict rather than deny it or keep it repressed, and make productive choices despite misgivings and fears. People in conflict frequently find it difficult to make choices, and Perls sought to encourage—*compel* might be a better word—them to do so.

Although Perls's ideas about conflicting personality elements owe much to psychodynamic theory, his form of therapy, unlike psychoanalysis, focuses on the here and now. In Gestalt therapy, clients perform exercises to heighten their awareness of their current feelings and behavior, rather than exploring the past. Perls also believed, along with Rogers, that people are free to make choices and to direct their personal growth. But the charismatic and forceful Perls was unlike the gentle and accepting Rogers in temperament (Prochaska & Norcross, 1999). Thus, unlike client-centered therapy, Gestalt therapy is highly directive. The therapist leads the client through planned experiences.

There are a number of Gestalt exercises and games, including the following:

1. *The dialogue.* In this game, the client undertakes verbal confrontations between opposing wishes and ideas to heighten awareness of internal conflict. An example of these clashing personality elements is "top dog" and "underdog." One's top dog might conservatively suggest, "Don't take chances. Stick with what you have or you might lose it all." One's frustrated underdog might then rise up and assert,

GESTALT THERAPY Fritz Perls's form of psychotherapy, which attempts to integrate conflicting parts of the personality through directive methods designed to help clients perceive their whole selves.

"You never try anything. How will you ever get out of this rut if you don't take on new challenges?" Heightened awareness of the elements of conflict can clear the path toward resolution, perhaps through a compromise of some kind.

2. *I take responsibility*. Clients end statements about themselves by adding, "and I take responsibility for it."

3. *Playing the projection*. Clients role-play people with whom they are in conflict, expressing, for example, the ideas of their parents.

Body language also provides insight into conflicting feelings. Clients might be instructed to attend to the ways in which they furrow their eyebrows and tense their facial muscles when they express certain ideas. In this way, they often find that their body language asserts feelings they have been denying in their spoken statements.

The following excerpt from a therapy session with a client named Max shows how Perls would make clients take responsibility for what they experience. One of his techniques is to show how clients are treating something they are doing (a "verb") like something that is just out there and beyond their control (a "noun"):

Max: I feel the tenseness in my stomach and in my hands.
Perls: *The* tenseness. Here we've got a noun. Now *the* tenseness is a noun. Now change the noun, the thing, into a verb.
Max: I am tense. My hands are tense.
Perls: Your hands are tense. They have nothing to do with you.
Max: I am tense.
Perls: You are tense. How are you tense? What are you doing?
Max: I am tensing myself.
Perls: That's it. (Perls, 1969, p. 115)

Once Max understands that he is tensing himself and takes responsibility for it, he can choose to stop tensing himself. The tenseness is no longer something out there that is victimizing him; it is something he is doing to himself.

Psychodynamic theory views dreams as the "royal road to the unconscious." Perls saw the content of dreams as representing disowned parts of the personality. Perls would often ask clients to role-play elements of their dreams in order to get in touch with these parts of their personality.

REFLECT

Have you heard the expression "getting it together"? How might it relate to Gestalt therapy?

Review

SECTION III

Humanistic-existential therapies focus on the quality of clients' (22) _____tive, conscious experience. Client-centered therapy was originated by (23) _____ _____. Client-centered therapy is a (24: Directive or Nondirective?) method that provides clients with a warm, accepting atmosphere that enables them to explore and overcome roadblocks to self-actualization. The characteristics shown by the client-centered therapist include (25: Conditional or Unconditional?) positive regard, (26) em_____ understanding, and (27) gen_____. Client-centered therapy is practiced widely in college (28) _____ling centers.

Gestalt therapy was originated by (29) _____ _____. Gestalt therapy provides (30: Directive or Nondirective?) methods that are designed to help clients integrate conflicting parts of the (31) _____ity.

SECTION IV. BEHAVIOR THERAPY: ADJUSTMENT IS WHAT YOU DO

Psychodynamic and humanistic-existential forms of therapy tend to focus on what people think and feel. Behavior therapists tend to focus on what people *do.* Question: What is behavior therapy? **Behavior therapy**—also called *behavior modification*—applies principles of learning to directly promote desired behavioral changes (Wolpe & Plaud, 1997). Behavior therapists rely heavily on principles of conditioning and observational learning. They help clients discontinue self-defeating behavior patterns such as overeating, smoking, and phobic avoidance of harmless stimuli. They also help clients acquire adaptive behavior patterns such as the social skills required to start social relationships or say no to insistent salespeople.

Behavior therapists may help clients gain "insight" into maladaptive behavior in the sense of fostering awareness of the circumstances in which it occurs. They do not foster insight in the psychoanalytic sense of unearthing the childhood origins of problems and the symbolic meanings of maladaptive behavior. Behavior therapists, like other therapists, may also build warm, therapeutic relationships with clients, but they see the efficacy of behavior therapy as deriving from specific, learning-based procedures (Wolpe, 1990). They insist that their methods be established by experimentation and that therapeutic outcomes be assessed in terms of observable, measurable behavior. In this section we consider some frequently used behavior-therapy techniques.

Fear-Reduction Methods

Many people seek therapy because of fears and phobias that interfere with their functioning. This is one of the areas in which behavior therapy has made great inroads. Question: What are some behavior-therapy methods for reducing fears? These include flooding, systematic desensitization, and modeling.

FLOODING In **flooding,** the client is exposed to a fear-evoking stimulus until fear is extinguished (Turner et al., 1994). Aaron Beck, the originator of a key approach to cognitive therapy, used flooding on himself before he became a psychiatrist. One of the reasons he went into medicine was to confront his own fear of blood. He had had a series of operations as a child, and from then on the sight of blood had made him feel faint. During his first year of medical school, he forced himself to watch operations. In his second year, he became a surgical assistant. Soon the sight of blood became normal to him. His fear of blood became extinguished because it was not connected with any real consequence, such as pain.

Flooding is an unpleasant sink-or-swim method for overcoming fears. Most behavior therapists prefer to use systematic desensitization.

SYSTEMATIC DESENSITIZATION Adam has a phobia for receiving injections. His behavior therapist treats him as he reclines in a comfortable padded chair. In a state of deep muscle relaxation, Adam observes slides projected on a screen. A slide of a nurse holding a needle has just been shown three times, 30 seconds at a time. Each time Adam has shown no anxiety. So now a slightly more discomforting slide is shown: one of the nurse aiming the needle toward someone's bare arm. After 15 seconds,

BEHAVIOR THERAPY Systematic application of the principles of learning to the direct modification of a client's problem behaviors.

FLOODING Exposing a person to a fear-evoking stimulus without aversive consequences until fear is extinguished.

Overcoming a Phobia. One way behavior therapists help clients overcome phobias is by having them gradually approach the feared object or situation while they remain relaxed.

our armchair adventurer notices twinges of discomfort and raises a finger as a signal (speaking might disturb his relaxation). The projector operator turns off the light, and Adam spends 2 minutes imagining his "safe scene"—lying on a beach beneath the tropical sun. Then the slide is shown again. This time Adam views it for 30 seconds before feeling anxiety.

Adam is undergoing **systematic desensitization,** a method originated by psychiatrist Joseph Wolpe (1990) for reducing phobic responses. Systematic desensitization is a gradual process in which the client learns to handle increasingly disturbing stimuli while anxiety to each one is being counterconditioned. About 10 to 20 stimuli are arranged in a sequence, or hierarchy, according to their capacity to elicit anxiety. In imagination or by being shown photos, the client travels gradually up through this hierarchy, approaching the target behavior. In Adam's case, the target behavior was the ability to receive an injection without undue anxiety.

Wolpe developed systematic desensitization on the assumption that anxiety responses, like other behaviors, are learned or conditioned. He reasoned that they can be unlearned by means of counterconditioning or extinction. In counterconditioning, a response incompatible with anxiety is made to appear under conditions that usually elicit anxiety. Muscle relaxation is incompatible with anxiety. For this reason, Adam's therapist is teaching him to relax in the presence of (usually) anxiety-evoking slides of needles. (Muscle relaxation is usually achieved by means of *progressive relaxation,* a method for lowering the arousal created by anxiety reactions.)

Remaining in the presence of phobic imagery, rather than running away from it, is also likely to enhance self-efficacy expectations (Galassi, 1988). Self-efficacy expectations are negatively correlated with levels of adrenaline in the bloodstream (Bandura et al., 1985). Raising clients' self-efficacy expectations thus may help lower their adrenaline levels and reduce their feelings of nervousness.

✓ Truth or Fiction Revisited

It is true that lying in a reclining chair and fantasizing can be an effective way of confronting fears. This is what happens in the method of systematic desensitization.

SYSTEMATIC DESENSITIZATION Wolpe's method for reducing fears by associating a hierarchy of images of fear-evoking stimuli with muscle relaxation.

MODELING Modeling relies on observational learning. In this method clients observe, and then imitate, people who approach and cope with the objects or situations that the clients fear. Bandura and his colleagues (1969) found that modeling worked as well as systematic desensitization—and more rapidly—in reducing fear of snakes. Like systematic desensitization, modeling is likely to increase self-efficacy expectations in coping with feared stimuli.

Aversive Conditioning

Many people also seek behavior therapy because they want to break bad habits, such as smoking, excessive drinking, nail biting, and the like. One behavior-therapy approach to helping people do so is aversive conditioning. **Question: How do behavior therapists use aversive conditioning to help people break bad habits?** **Aversive conditioning** is a controversial procedure in which painful or aversive stimuli are paired with unwanted impulses, such as desire for a cigarette or desire to engage in antisocial behavior, in order to make the impulse less appealing. For example, to help people control alcohol intake, tastes of different alcoholic beverages can be paired with drug-induced nausea and vomiting or with electric shock.

Aversive conditioning has been used with problems as diverse as cigarette smoking, sexual abuse (Rice et al., 1991), and retarded children's self-injurious behavior. *Rapid smoking* is an aversive-conditioning method designed to help smokers quit. In this method, the would-be quitter inhales every 6 seconds. In another method the hose of a hair dryer is hooked up to a chamber containing several lit cigarettes. Smoke is blown into the quitter's face as he or she also smokes a cigarette. A third method uses branching pipes so that the smoker draws in smoke from several cigarettes at the same time. In all of these methods overexposure causes once-desirable cigarette smoke to become aversive. The quitter becomes motivated to avoid, rather than seek, cigarettes. Many reports have shown a quit rate of 60% or higher at 6-month follow-ups. Yet interest in these methods for quitting smoking has waned because of side effects such as raising blood pressure and the availability of nicotine-replacement techniques.

Aversive Conditioning. In aversive conditioning, unwanted behaviors take on a noxious quality as a result of being repeatedly paired with aversive stimuli. Overexposure is making cigarette smoke aversive to this smoker.

✓ Truth or Fiction Revisited

It is true that smoking cigarettes can be an effective treatment for helping people stop smoking cigarettes. The trick is to inhale enough smoke so that it is aversive rather than enjoyable.

In one study of aversive conditioning in the treatment of alcoholism, 63% of the 685 people treated remained abstinent for 1 year afterward, and about a third remained abstinent for at least 3 years (Wiens & Menustik, 1983). It may seem ironic that punitive aversive stimulation is sometimes used to stop children from punishing themselves, but people sometimes hurt themselves in order to obtain sympathy and attention. If self-injury leads to more pain than anticipated and no sympathy, it might be discontinued.

Operant Conditioning Procedures

We usually prefer to relate to people who smile at us rather than ignore us and to take courses in which we do well rather than fail. We tend to repeat behavior that is reinforced. Behavior that is not reinforced tends to become extinguished. Behavior therapists have used these principles of op-

MODELING A behavior-therapy technique in which a client observes and imitates a person who approaches and copes with feared objects or situations.

AVERSIVE CONDITIONING A behavior-therapy technique in which undesired responses are inhibited by pairing repugnant or offensive stimuli with them.

erant conditioning with psychotic patients as well as with clients with milder problems. Question: How do behavior therapists apply principles of operant conditioning in behavior modification?

The staff at one mental hospital was at a loss about how to encourage withdrawn schizophrenic patients to eat regularly. Ayllon and Haughton (1962) observed that staff members were making the problem worse by coaxing patients into the dining room and even feeding them. Staff attention apparently reinforced the patients' lack of cooperation. Some rules were changed. Patients who did not arrive at the dining hall within 30 minutes after serving were locked out. Staff could not interact with patients at mealtime. With uncooperative behavior no longer reinforced, patients quickly changed their eating habits. Then patients were required to pay one penny to enter the dining hall. Pennies were earned by interacting with other patients and showing other socially appropriate behaviors. These target behaviors also became more frequent.

THE TOKEN ECONOMY Many psychiatric wards and hospitals now use *token economies* in which patients must use tokens such as poker chips to purchase TV viewing time, extra visits to the canteen, or a private room. The tokens are reinforcements for productive activities such as making beds, brushing teeth, and socializing. Token economies have not eliminated all features of schizophrenia. However, they have enhanced patient activity and cooperation. Tokens have also been used to modify the behavior of children with conduct disorders. In one program, for example, children received tokens for helpful behaviors such as volunteering and lost tokens for behaviors such as arguing and failing to pay attention (Schneider & Byrne, 1987).

SUCCESSIVE APPROXIMATIONS The operant conditioning method of **successive approximations** is often used to help clients build good habits. Let us use a (not uncommon!) example: You want to study 3 hours each evening but can concentrate for only half an hour. Rather than attempting to increase your study time all at once, you could do so gradually by adding, say, 5 minutes each evening. After every hour or so of studying, you could reinforce yourself with 5 minutes of people-watching in a busy section of the library.

> **REFLECT**
>
> Can you think of a way to use the method of successive approximations to improve your own life?

SOCIAL SKILLS TRAINING In social skills training, behavior therapists decrease social anxiety and build social skills through operant-conditioning procedures that employ self-monitoring, coaching, modeling, role-playing, practice ("behavior rehearsal"), and feedback. Social skills training has been used to help formerly hospitalized mental patients maintain jobs and apartments in the community. For example, a worker can rehearse politely asking a supervisor for assistance or asking a landlord to fix the plumbing in an apartment.

Social skills training is effective in groups. Group members can role-play important people—such as parents, spouses, or potential dates—in the lives of other members.

BIOFEEDBACK TRAINING Through **biofeedback training** (BFT), therapists help clients become more aware of, and gain control over, various bodily functions. Therapists attach clients to devices that measure bodily functions such as heart rate. "Bleeps" or other electronic signals are used to indicate (and thereby reinforce) changes in the desired direction—for

SUCCESSIVE APPROXIMATIONS In operant conditioning, a series of behaviors that gradually become more similar to a target behavior.

BIOFEEDBACK TRAINING The systematic feeding back to an organism of information about a bodily function so that the organism can gain control of that function. Abbreviated *BFT*.

example, a slower heart rate. (Knowledge of results is a powerful reinforcer.) One device, the electromyograph (EMG), monitors muscle tension. It has been used to augment control over muscle tension in the forehead and elsewhere, thereby alleviating anxiety, stress, and headaches.

BFT also helps clients voluntarily regulate functions once thought to be beyond conscious control, such as heart rate and blood pressure. Hypertensive clients use a blood pressure cuff and electronic signals to gain control over their blood pressure. The electroencephalograph (EEG) monitors brain waves and can be used to teach people how to produce alpha waves, which are associated with relaxation. Some people have overcome insomnia by learning to produce the kinds of brain waves associated with sleep.

Self-Control Methods

Do mysterious forces sometimes seem to be at work in your life? Forces that delight in wreaking havoc on New Year's resolutions and other efforts to put an end to your bad habits? Just when you go on a diet, that juicy pizza stares at you from the TV set. Just when you resolve to balance your budget, that sweater goes on sale. Question: How can you— yes, *you*—use behavior therapy to deal with temptation and enhance your self-control?

REFLECT

Do you have any habits you would like to change? Can you use any of the methods of self-control discussed here to help you do so?

FUNCTIONAL ANALYSIS OF BEHAVIOR Behavior therapists usually begin with a **functional analysis** of the problem behavior. In this way, they help determine the stimuli that trigger the behavior and the reinforcers that maintain it. Then clients are taught how to manipulate the antecedents and consequences of their behavior and how to increase the frequency of desired responses and decrease the frequency of undesired responses. You can use a diary to jot down each instance of a problem behavior. Note the time of day, location, your activity at the time (including your thoughts and feelings), and reactions (yours and others'). Functional analysis serves a number of purposes. It makes you more aware of the

TABLE 13.1	**EXCERPTS FROM BRIAN'S DIARY OF NAIL BITING FOR APRIL 14**				
Incident	**Time**	**Location**	**Activity (Thoughts, Feelings)**	**Reactions**
1	7:45 A.M.	Freeway	Driving to work, bored, not thinking	Finger bleeds, pain
2	10:30 A.M.	Office	Writing report	Self-disgust
3	2:25 P.M.	Conference	Listening to dull financial report	Embarrassment
4	6:40 P.M.	Living room	Watching evening news	Self-disgust

Note: A functional analysis of problem behavior like nail biting increases awareness of the environmental context in which it occurs, spurs motivation to change, and, in highly motivated people, might lead to significant behavioral change.

FUNCTIONAL ANALYSIS A systematic study of behavior in which one identifies the stimuli that trigger problem behavior and the reinforcers that maintain it.

environmental context of your behavior and can increase your motivation to change.

✓ Truth or Fiction Revisited

It is true that you might be able to put an end to bad habits merely by keeping a record of where and when you engage in them. The record may help motivate you, make you more aware of the problems, and suggest strategies for behavior change.

Brian used functional analysis to master his nail biting. Table 13.1 shows a few items from his notebook. He discovered that boredom and humdrum activities seemed to serve as triggers for nail biting. He began to watch out for feelings of boredom as signs to practice self-control. He also made some changes in his life so that he would feel bored less often.

There are numerous self-control strategies aimed at the stimuli that trigger behavior, the behaviors themselves, and reinforcers. Table 13.2 describes some of these strategies.

✓ Truth or Fiction Revisited

It is true that some psychotherapists tell their clients precisely what to do. That is, they outline behavioral prescriptions for their clients. Behavior therapists, Gestalt therapists, and some cognitive therapists are examples.

Review

SECTION IV

Behavior therapy is also referred to as behavior (32) _____tion. Behavior therapy is defined as the systematic application of principles of (33) _____ing to bring about desired behavioral changes. Behavior therapists insist that their methods be established by (34) _____tation and that therapeutic outcomes be assessed in terms of (35) ob_____ble, measurable behavior.

Behavior-therapy methods for reducing fears include flooding, in which the client is exposed to a fear-evoking stimulus until fear is (36) _____shed; systematic (37) _____tion, in which a client is gradually exposed to more fear-arousing stimuli; and modeling, in which a client observes and then imitates a model who handles fear-arousing stimuli. In systematic desensitization, clients confront a (38) h_____ of anxiety-evoking stimuli while they remain relaxed.

In the method of aversive conditioning, undesired responses are decreased in frequency by being associated with (39) _____ive stimuli. An example of aversive conditioning is (40) _____ smoking, in which cigarette smoke is made aversive by frequent puffing.

In operant-conditioning methods, desired responses are (41) _____ced and unde-sired responses are (42) _____shed. In social-skills training, behavior therapists decrease social anxiety and build social skills through operant-conditioning procedures that employ (43) _____-monitoring, coaching, modeling, (44) _____ playing, (45) _____ rehearsal, and (46) _____back. Through (47) _____back training (BFT), therapists help clients become more aware of, and gain control over, various bodily functions. "Bleeps" or other electronic signals are used to (48) _____orce bodily changes in the desired direction. The (49) _____ograph (EMG) monitors muscle tension. The (50) _____ograph (EEG) monitors brain waves. The EEG can be used to teach people how to produce (51) _____ waves, which are associated with relaxation.

In self-control methods, clients first engage in a (52) _____nal analysis of their problem behavior. A functional analysis helps them learn what stimuli trigger and (53) _____ain the behavior. Then clients are taught how to manipulate the antecedents and (54) _____nces of their behavior and how to increase the frequency of desired responses and decrease the frequency of undesired responses.

TABLE 13.2	BEHAVIORAL STRATEGIES FOR SELF-CONTROL
Strategy	**About . . .**
STRATEGIES AIMED AT STIMULI THAT TRIGGER BEHAVIOR	
Restriction of the stimulus field	Gradually exclude the problem behavior from more environments. For example, at first make smoking off limits in the car, then in the home.
Avoidance of powerful stimuli that trigger habits	Avoid obvious sources of temptation. People who go window-shopping often wind up buying more than windows. If eating at The Pizza Glutton tempts you to forget your diet, eat at home or at The Celery Stalk instead.
Stimulus control	Place yourself in an environment in which desirable behavior is likely to occur. Maybe it's difficult to lift your mood directly at times, but you can place yourself in the audience of an uplifting concert or film. It might be difficult to force yourself to study, but how about rewarding yourself for spending time in the library?
STRATEGIES AIMED AT BEHAVIOR	
Response prevention	Make unwanted behavior difficult or impossible. Impulse buying is curbed when you shred your credit cards, leave your checkbook home, and carry only a couple of dollars with you. You can't reach for the strawberry cream cheese pie in your refrigerator if you didn't buy it at the supermarket.
Competing responses	Engage in behaviors that are incompatible with the bad habit. It is difficult to drink a glass of water and a fattening milkshake simultaneously. Grasping something firmly is a useful competing response for nail biting or scratching.
Chain breaking	Interfere with unwanted habitual behavior by complicating the process of engaging in it. Break the chain of reaching for a readily available cigarette and placing it in your mouth by wrapping the pack in aluminum foil and placing it on the top shelf of a closet. Rewrap the pack after taking one cigarette. Put your cigarette in the ashtray between puffs, or put your fork down between mouthfuls of dessert. Ask yourself whether you really want more.
Successive approximations	Gradually approach targets through a series of relatively painless steps. Increase studying by only 5 minutes a day. Decrease smoking by pausing for a minute when the cigarette is smoked halfway, or by putting it out a minute before you would wind up eating the filter. Decrease your daily intake of food by 50 to 100 calories every couple of days, or cut out one type of fattening food every few days.
STRATEGIES AIMED AT REINFORCEMENTS	
Reinforcement of desired behavior	Why give yourself something for nothing? Make pleasant activities such as going to films, walking on the beach, or reading a new novel contingent on meeting reasonable daily behavioral goals. Each day you remain within your calorie limit, put a dollar away toward that camera or vacation trip you have been dreaming of.
Response cost	Heighten awareness of the long-term reasons for dieting or cutting down on smoking by punishing yourself for not meeting a daily goal or for engaging in a bad habit. For example, if you bite your nails or inhale that cheesecake, make out a check to a cause you oppose and mail it at once.
"Grandma's method"	How did Grandma persuade children to eat their vegetables? Simple: No veggies, no dessert. In this method, desired behaviors such as studying and brushing your teeth can be increased by insisting that those behaviors be done before you engage in a pleasant or frequently occurring activity. For example, don't watch television unless you have studied first. Don't leave the apartment until you've brushed your teeth. You can also place reminders about new attitudes you're trying to acquire on little cards and read them regularly. For example, in quitting smoking, you might write "Every day it becomes a little easier" on one card and "Your lungs will turn pink again" on another. Place these cards and others in your wallet, and read them each time you leave the house.
Covert sensitization	Create imaginary horror stories about problem behavior. Psychologists have successfully reduced overeating and smoking by having clients imagine that they become acutely nauseated at the thought of fattening foods or that a cigarette is made from vomit. Some horror stories are not so "imaginary." Deliberately focusing on heart strain and diseased lungs every time you overeat or smoke, rather than ignoring these long-term consequences, might also promote self-control.
Covert reinforcement	Create rewarding imagery for desired behavior. When you have achieved a behavioral goal, fantasize about how wonderful you are. Imagine friends and family members patting you on the back.

SECTION V. COGNITIVE THERAPIES

There is nothing either good or bad, but thinking makes it so.

SHAKESPEARE, *Hamlet*

In this line from *Hamlet,* Shakespeare did not mean to suggest that injuries and misfortunes are painless or easy to manage. Rather, he meant that our appraisals of unfortunate events can heighten our discomfort and impair our coping ability. In so doing, Shakespeare was providing a kind of motto for cognitive therapists. Question: What is cognitive therapy?

Cognitive therapists focus on the beliefs, attitudes, and automatic types of thinking that create and compound their clients' problems. Cognitive therapists, like psychodynamic and humanistic-existential therapists, aim to foster self-insight, but they aim to heighten insight into *current cognitions* as well as those of the past. Cognitive therapists also aim to directly *change* maladaptive cognitions in order to reduce negative feelings, provide insight, and help the client solve problems.

You may have noticed that many behavior therapists incorporate cognitive procedures in their methods (Jacobson et al., 1996; Meichenbaum, 1993). For example, techniques such as systematic desensitization, covert sensitization, and covert reinforcement ask clients to focus on visual imagery. Behavioral methods for treating bulimia nervosa focus on clients' irrational attitudes toward their weight and body shape as well as foster healthful eating habits.

Let us look at the approaches and methods of some major cognitive therapists.

Cognitive Therapy: Correcting Cognitive Errors

Aaron Beck used the behavior-therapy method of flooding on himself to overcome fear of blood. However, he also experimented with himself using cognitive methods. For example, he argued himself out of an irrational fear (a phobia) of tunnels. He convinced himself that the tunnels did not cause the fear because the symptoms of faintness and shallow breathing would appear before he entered them.

As a psychiatrist, Beck first practiced psychoanalysis. However, he could not find scientific evidence for psychoanalytic beliefs. Psychoanalytic theory explained depression as anger turned inward, so that it becomes transformed into a need to suffer. Beck's own clinical experiences led him to believe that it is more likely that depressed people experience cognitive distortions such as the **cognitive triad.** That is, they expect the worst of themselves ("I'm no good"), the world at large ("This is an awful place"), and their future ("Nothing good will ever happen"). Question: What is Aaron Beck's method of cognitive therapy?

Beck's cognitive therapy is active. Beck encourages clients to become their own personal scientists and challenge beliefs—such as the cognitive triad—that are not supported by evidence. He questions people in a way that encourages them to see the irrationality of their ways of thinking. For example, depressed people tend to minimize their accomplishments and to assume that the worst will happen. Both distortions heighten feelings of depression. Beck (1991, 1993) notes that cognitive distortions can be fleeting and automatic, difficult to detect. His therapy methods help clients pin down such distortions and challenge them.

Beck notes the pervasive influence of cognitive errors beyond the cognitive triad that contribute to clients' miseries. Consider these examples:

COGNITIVE TRIAD A cluster of depressing attitudes identified by Aaron Beck: expecting the worst of oneself, the world at large, and the future.

REFLECT

Do you ever engage in any of Beck's cognitive errors? For example, do you magnify the importance of negative events? Do these errors give rise to feelings of frustration, anxiety, or depression? What can you do about them?

1. Clients may *selectively perceive* the world as a harmful place and ignore evidence to the contrary.

2. Clients may *overgeneralize* on the basis of a few examples. For example, they may perceive themselves as worthless because they were laid off at work, or as unattractive because they were refused a date.

3. Clients may *magnify,* or blow out of proportion, the importance of negative events. They may catastrophize failing a test by assuming they will flunk out of college, or catastrophize losing a job by believing that they will never find another one and that serious harm will befall their family as a result.

4. Clients may engage in *absolutist thinking,* or looking at the world in black and white rather than in shades of gray. In doing so, a rejection on a date takes on the meaning of a lifetime of loneliness; an uncomfortable illness takes on life-threatening proportions.

The concept of pinpointing and modifying cognitive errors may become clearer from the following excerpt from a case in which a 53-year-old engineer obtained cognitive therapy for depression. The engineer had left his job and become inactive. As reported by Beck and his colleagues, the first goal of treatment was to foster physical activity—even chores like raking leaves and preparing dinner—because activity is incompatible with depression.

> [The engineer's] cognitive distortions were identified by comparing his assessment of each activity with that of his wife. Alternative ways of interpreting his experiences were then considered.
>
> In comparing his wife's résumé of his past experiences, he became aware that he had (1) undervalued his past by failing to mention many previous accomplishments, (2) regarded himself as far more responsible for his "failures" than she did, and (3) concluded that he was worthless since he had not succeeded in attaining certain goals in the past. When the two accounts were contrasted, he could discern many of his cognitive distortions. In subsequent sessions, his wife continued to serve as an "objectifier."
>
> In midtherapy, [he] compiled a list of new attitudes that he had acquired since initiating therapy. These included:
>
> 1. "I am starting at a lower level of functioning at my job, but it will improve if I persist."
>
> 2. "I know that once I get going in the morning, everything will run all right for the rest of the day."
>
> 3. "I can't achieve everything at once."
>
> 4. "I have my periods of ups and downs, but in the long run I feel better."
>
> 5. "My expectations from my job and life should be scaled down to a realistic level."
>
> 6. "Giving in to avoidance [e.g., staying away from work and social interactions] never helps and only leads to further avoidance."
>
> He was instructed to reread this list daily for several weeks even though he already knew the content. (Rush et al., 1975)

The engineer gradually became less depressed and returned to work and an active social life. Along the way, he learned to combat inappropriate self-blame for problems, perfectionistic expectations, magnification of failures, and overgeneralization from failures.

Becoming aware of cognitive errors and modifying catastrophizing thoughts helps us cope with stress. Internal, stable, and global attributions of failure lead to depression and feelings of helplessness. Cognitive therapists also alert clients to cognitive errors such as these so that the clients can change their attitudes and pave the way for more effective overt behavior.

Rational Emotive Behavior Therapy: Overcoming "Musts" and "Shoulds"

Not very modestly, Albert Ellis refers to himself as "the father of REBT [rational emotive behavior therapy] and the grandfather of cognitive-behavioral therapy." Like Aaron Beck, Ellis first practiced psychoanalysis. And, like Beck, he, too, found Freud's methods to be slow and ineffective. He noted that people who were undergoing analysis often *felt* better, at least for a while, because of talking about their problems and getting attention from the therapist. But he did not believe they *got* better. He also was not convinced that it was useful for the therapist to be so passive, so he became more active and began to offer direct advice. Question: What is Albert Ellis's method of rational emotive behavior therapy (REBT)?

In REBT, Ellis and his colleagues (1986, 1996) point out that our beliefs *about* events, not only the events themselves, shape our responses to them. Moreover, many of us harbor a number of irrational beliefs that can

RATIONAL EMOTIVE BEHAVIOR THERAPY Albert Ellis's form of therapy, which encourages clients to challenge and correct irrational expectations and maladaptive behaviors.

REFLECT

Do you believe that you must have the love and approval of people who are important to you? Do you believe that you must prove yourself to be thoroughly competent, adequate, and achieving? Do such beliefs make you miserable? What can you do about them?

TABLE 13.3	METHODS OF PSYCHOTHERAPY AT A GLANCE		
Type of Therapy	**Goals**	**Methods**	**About . . .**
Psychodynamic therapies	To strengthen the ego; to provide self-insight into unconscious conflict	Traditional psychoanalysis is lengthy and nondirective and involves methods such as free association and dream analysis.	Most effective with verbal, "upscale" clients. Modern ego analytic approaches are briefer and more directive.
Humanistic- existential therapies	To help clients get in touch with parts of themselves that they have "disowned" and actualize their unique desires and abilities	Client-centered therapy is nondirective; it provides an atmosphere in which clients can engage in self-exploration without fear. Gestalt therapy is highly directive.	Client-centered therapy is practiced widely in college and university counseling centers to help students make academic and personal decisions.
Behavior therapy	To use principles of learning to help clients engage in adaptive behavior and discontinue maladaptive behavior	Behavior therapy is directive and uses fear-reduction methods (including systematic desensitization), aversive conditioning (to help clients discontinue bad habits), operant conditioning procedures (e.g., social skills training), and self-control methods (beginning with functional analysis of behavior).	Behavior therapists have developed treatments for problems (e.g., smoking, phobias, sexual dysfunctions) for which there previously were no effective treatment methods.
Cognitive therapies	To make clients aware of the beliefs, attitudes, and automatic types of thinking that create and compound their problems; to help them correct these kinds of thinking to reduce negative feelings and solve problems	Beck's cognitive therapy helps people recognize and correct cognitive errors such as selective perception, overgeneralization, magnification of negative events, and absolutist thinking. Rational emotive behavior therapists show clients how irrational beliefs and catastrophizing events make them miserable.	Many theorists consider cognitive therapy to be part of behavior therapy, and some call it "cognitive *behavioral* therapy." In fact, Ellis recently changed the name of his approach to therapy from rational emotive therapy to rational emotive *behavior* therapy.

give rise to problems or magnify their impact. Two of the most important ones are the belief that we must have the love and approval of people who are important to us and the belief that we must prove ourselves as thoroughly competent, adequate, and achieving. When Ellis sees clients behaving according to irrational beliefs, he may refute them by asking questions like "Where is it written that you must . . . ?" or "What evidence do you have that . . . ?"

Ellis's methods are active and directive. He urges clients to seek out their irrational beliefs. Then he shows clients how those beliefs lead to misery and challenges them to change them. According to Ellis, we need less misery and less blaming in our lives, and more action.

Ellis also straddles behavioral and cognitive therapies. In keeping with his broad philosophy, he recently changed the name of rational emotive therapy to rational emotive *behavior* therapy. Table 13.3 summarizes methods of psychotherapy.

Review

SECTION V

Cognitive therapists focus on the (55) be_____s, attitudes, and (56) _____tic types of thinking that create and compound their clients' problems.

Psychiatrist Aaron Beck has focused on ways in which cognitive errors or (57) dis_____s heighten feelings of (58) de_____. Beck notes the pervasive influence of four basic types of cognitive errors that contribute to clients' miseries: selective (59) _____tion of the world as a harmful place; (60) over_____zation on the basis of a few examples; (61) mag_____tion of the significance of negative events; and (62) _____tist thinking, or looking at the world in black and white rather than in shades of gray.

(63) Rational _____ behavior therapy (REBT) is another type of cognitive therapy. It was originated by (64) _____ _____. Rational emotive behavior therapy confronts clients with the ways in which (65) _____nal beliefs contribute to problems such as anxiety, depression, and feelings of hopelessness.

SECTION VI. GROUP THERAPIES

When a psychotherapist has several clients with similar problems—anxiety, depression, adjustment to divorce, lack of social skills—it often makes sense to treat them in a group rather than in individual sessions. The methods and characteristics of the group reflect the needs of the members and the theoretical orientation of the leader. In group psychoanalysis, clients might interpret one another's dreams. In a client-centered group, they might provide an accepting atmosphere for self-exploration. Members of behavior therapy groups might be jointly desensitized to anxiety-evoking stimuli or might practice social skills together. Question: What are the advantages and disadvantages of group therapy?

Group therapy has the following advantages:

1. It is economical (Sleek, 1995). It allows the therapist to work with several clients at once.

Group Therapy. Group therapy has a number of advantages over individual therapy for many clients. It is economical, provides a fund of experience for clients to draw on, elicits group support, and provides an opportunity to relate to other people. Some clients do need individual attention, however.

2. Compared with one-to-one therapy, group therapy provides more information and life experience for clients to draw upon.

3. Appropriate behavior receives group support. Clients usually appreciate an outpouring of peer approval.

4. When we run into troubles, it is easy to imagine that we are different from other people or inferior to them. Affiliating with people with similar problems is reassuring.

5. Group members who show improvement provide hope for other members.

6. Many individuals seek therapy because of problems in relating to other people. People who seek therapy for other reasons also may be socially inhibited. Members of groups have the opportunity to practice social skills in a relatively nonthreatening atmosphere. In a group consisting of men and women of different ages, group members can role-play one another's employers, employees, spouses, parents, children, and friends. Members can role-play asking one another out on dates, saying no (or yes), and so on.

But group therapy is not for everyone. Some clients fare better with individual treatment. Many prefer not to disclose their problems to a group. They may be overly shy or want individual attention. It is the responsibility of the therapist to insist that group disclosures be kept confidential, to establish a supportive atmosphere, and to ensure that group members obtain the attention they need.

Many types of therapy can be conducted either individually or in groups. Encounter groups and family therapy are conducted only in groups.

Encounter Groups

Encounter groups are not appropriate for treating serious psychological problems. Rather, they are intended to promote personal growth by heightening awareness of one's own needs and feelings and those of others. This goal is sought through intense confrontations, or encounters, between strangers. Questions: What are encounter groups? What are their effects?

> **REFLECT**
>
> If you went for therapy, do you think you would prefer being treated on a one-to-one basis or in a group? Explain.

ENCOUNTER GROUP A type of group that fosters self-awareness by focusing on how group members relate to one another in a setting that encourages open expression of feelings.

Like ships in the night, group members come together out of the darkness, touch one another briefly, then sink back into the shadows of one another's lives. But something is gained from the passing.

Encounter groups stress interactions between group members in the here and now. Discussion of the past may be outlawed. Interpretation is out. However, expression of genuine feelings toward others is encouraged. When group members think a person's social mask is phony, they may descend en masse to rip it off.

Encounter groups can be damaging when they urge overly rapid disclosure of intimate matters or when several members attack one member. Responsible leaders do not tolerate these abuses and try to keep the group moving in a growth-enhancing direction.

Family Therapy

Question: What is family therapy? **Family therapy** is a form of group therapy in which one or more families constitute the group. Family therapy may be undertaken from various theoretical viewpoints. One is the "systems approach," in which family interaction is studied and modified to enhance the growth of individual family members and of the family unit as a whole (Prochaska & Norcross, 1999).

Family members with low self-esteem often cannot tolerate different attitudes and behaviors in other family members. Faulty communication within the family also creates problems. In addition, it is not uncommon for the family to present an "identified patient"—that is, the family member who has *the* problem and is *causing* all the trouble. Yet family therapists usually assume that the identified patient is a scapegoat for other problems within and among family members. It is a sort of myth: Change the bad apple—or identified patient—and the barrel—or family—will be functional once more.

The family therapist—often a specialist in this field—attempts to teach the family to communicate more effectively and encourage growth and autonomy in each family member.

Review

SECTION VI

What happens in group therapy reflects the clients' needs and the (66) _____ical orientation of the group leader. Group therapy tends to be (67: More or Less?) economical than individual therapy because it allows several clients to be seen at once. (68) _____ter groups promote personal growth by heightening awareness of people's needs and feelings through intense confrontations between strangers. In the (69) _____s approach to family therapy, family interaction is modified to enhance the growth of family members and the family unit as a whole.

SECTION VII. DOES PSYCHOTHERAPY WORK?

Many of us know people who swear by their therapists, but the evidence is often limited or shaky—for example, "I was a wreck before, but now . . ." or, "I feel so much better now." Anecdotes like these are encouraging, but we do not know what would have happened to these people had they not sought help. Many people feel better about their

FAMILY THERAPY A form of therapy in which the family unit is treated as the client.

problems as time goes on, with or without therapy. Sometimes, happily, problems seem to go away by themselves. Sometimes people find solutions on their own. Then, too, we hear some stories about how therapy was useless and about people who hop fruitlessly from one therapist to another.

Before we report on research dealing with the effectiveness of therapy, let us review some of the problems of this kind of research. Question: What kinds of problems do researchers encounter when they conduct research on psychotherapy?

Problems in Conducting Research on Psychotherapy

As noted by Hans Strupp, "The problem of evaluating outcomes from psychotherapy continues to bedevil the field" (1996, p. 1017).

PROBLEMS IN RUNNING EXPERIMENTS ON PSYCHOTHERAPY

The ideal method for evaluating a treatment—such as a method of therapy—is the experiment (Shadish & Ragsdale, 1996). However, experiments on therapy methods are difficult to arrange and control. The outcomes can be difficult to define and measure.

Consider psychoanalysis. In well-run experiments, people are assigned at random to experimental and control groups. A true experiment on psychoanalysis would require randomly assigning people seeking therapy to psychoanalysis and to a control group or other kinds of therapy for comparison (Luborsky et al., 1993). But a person may have to remain in traditional psychoanalysis for years to attain beneficial results. Could we create control treatments that last as long? Moreover, some people seek psychoanalysis per se, not psychotherapy in general. Would it be ethical to assign them at random to other treatments or to a no-treatment control group? Clearly not.

In an ideal experiment, participants and researchers are "blind" with regard to the treatment the participants receive. Blinds in research designs allow researchers to control for participants' expectations. In an ideal experiment on therapy, individuals would be blind regarding the type of therapy they are obtaining—or whether they are obtaining a placebo (Carroll et al., 1994). However, it is difficult to mask the type of therapy clients are obtaining. Even if we could conceal it from clients, could we hide it from therapists?

DOES THERAPY HELP BECAUSE OF THE METHOD OR BECAUSE OF "NONSPECIFIC FACTORS"?

Sorting out the benefits of therapy per se from other aspects of the therapy situation is a staggering task. These other aspects are termed *nonspecific factors*. They refer to features found in most therapies, such as the client's relationship with the therapist (Prochaska & Norcross, 1999). Most therapists, regardless of theoretical outlook, show warmth and empathy, encourage exploration, and instill hope (Blatt et al., 1996; Burns & Nolen-Hoeksema, 1992). The benefits of therapy thus could stem largely from these behaviors. If so, the method itself might have little more value than a placebo ("sugar pill") does in combating physical health problems.

Analyses of Therapy Effectiveness

Despite these evaluation problems, research on the effectiveness of therapy has been encouraging (Barlow, 1996; Shadish et al., 1997). Some of this research has relied on a technique termed **meta-analysis.** Meta-analysis combines and averages the results of individual studies. Generally speaking, the studies included in the analysis address similar issues in a similar way. Moreover, the analysts judge them to have been conducted in a valid manner. Question: What, then, do we know about the effectiveness of psychotherapy?

In their classic early use of meta-analysis, Mary Lee Smith and Gene Glass (1977) analyzed the results of dozens of outcome studies of various types of therapies. They concluded that people who obtained psychodynamic therapy showed greater well-being, on the average, than 70% to 75% of those who did not obtain treatment. Similarly, nearly 75% of the clients who obtained client-centered therapy were better off than people who did not obtain treatment. Psychodynamic and client-centered therapies appear to be most effective with well-educated, verbal, strongly motivated clients who report problems with anxiety, depression (of light to moderate proportions), and interpersonal relationships. Neither form of therapy appears to be effective with people with psychotic disorders such as major depression, bipolar disorder, and schizophrenia. Smith and Glass (1977) found that people who obtained Gestalt therapy showed greater well-being than about 60% of those who did not obtain treatment. The effectiveness of psychoanalysis and client-centered therapy thus was reasonably comparable. Gestalt therapy fell behind.

Smith and Glass (1977) did not include cognitive therapies in their meta-analysis because at the time of their study many cognitive approaches were relatively new. Because behavior therapists also incorporate many cognitive techniques, it can be difficult to sort out which aspects—cognitive or otherwise—of behavioral treatments are most effective. However, many meta-analyses of cognitive-behavioral therapy have been conducted since the early work of Smith and Glass. Their results are encouraging (Lipsey & Wilson, 1993).

A number of studies of cognitive therapy per se have also been conducted. For example, they show that modifying irrational beliefs of the type described by Albert Ellis helps people with problems such as anxiety and depression (Engels et al., 1993; Haaga & Davison, 1993). Modifying self-defeating beliefs of the sort outlined by Aaron Beck also frequently alleviates anxiety and depression (Robins & Hayes, 1993; Whisman et al., 1991). Cognitive therapy may be helpful for people with severe depression, who had been thought responsive only to biological therapies (Jacobson & Hollon, 1996; Simons et al., 1995). Cognitive therapy has also helped people with personality disorders (Beck & Freeman, 1990).

Behavioral and cognitive therapies have also provided strategies for treating anxiety disorders, social skills deficits, and problems in self-control (Chambless & Hollon, 1998; DeRubeis & Crits-Christoph, 1998). These two kinds of therapies—which are often integrated as *cognitive behavioral therapy*—have also provided empirically supported methods for helping couples and families in distress (Baucom et al., 1998), and for modifying behaviors related to health problems such as headaches (Blanchard, 1992), smoking, chronic pain, and bulimia nervosa (Compas et al., 1998). Cognitive behavioral therapists have also innovated treatments for sexual problems for which there previously were no effective treatments (Rathus et al., 2000). Cognitive therapy has helped many people with schizophrenia (who are also using drug therapy) modify their delusional beliefs (Chadwick & Lowe, 1990). Behavior therapy has helped to coordinate the care of institutionalized patients, including people with schizophrenia and mental retardation (Spreat & Behar, 1994). However, little evidence indicates that psychological therapy alone is effective in

META-ANALYSIS A statistical method for averaging the results of individual studies.

treating the quirks of thought exhibited in people with severe psychotic disorders (Wolpe, 1990).

Thus it is not enough to ask which type of therapy is most effective. We must ask which type is most effective for a particular problem and a particular patient. What are its advantages? Its limitations? Clients may successfully use systematic desensitization to overcome stagefright, as measured by ability to speak to a group of people. If clients also want to know *why* they have stagefright, however, behavior therapy alone will not provide the answer.

Psychotherapy and Diversity: Issues of Ethnicity, Gender, and Sexual Orientation

The United States, they are a-changing. Most of the prescriptions for psychotherapy discussed in the chapter were originated by, and intended for use with, Europeans and European Americans (Hall, 1997)—especially for male heterosexuals. Question: What kinds of issues develop when people from different ethnic groups, women, and gay males and lesbians could profit from psychotherapy?

People from ethnic minority groups are less likely than European Americans to seek therapy (Penn et al., 1995). Reasons for their lower participation rate include the following:

- Unawareness that therapy would help
- Lack of information about the availability of professional services, or inability to pay for them (DeAngelis, 1995)
- Distrust of professionals, particularly European American professionals and (for women) male professionals (Basic Behavioral Science Task Force, 1996)
- Language barriers (American Psychological Association, 1993)
- Reluctance to open up about personal matters to strangers—especially strangers who are not members of one's own ethnic group (LaFramboise, 1994)
- Cultural inclinations toward other approaches to problem solving, such as religious approaches (LaFramboise, 1994)
- Negative experiences with professionals and authority figures

Women and gay males and lesbians have also sometimes found therapy to be insensitive to their particular needs. Let us consider ways in which psychotherapy can be of more use to people from ethnic minority groups, women, and gay males and lesbians.

> **REFLECT**
>
> Consider your part of the country and your sociocultural background. Do people in your area and from your background frequently go for "therapy"? Is psychotherapy considered a normal option for people having problems in your area, or is it stigmatized?

PSYCHOTHERAPY AND ETHNIC MINORITY GROUPS Clinicians need to be sensitive to the cultural heritage, language, and values of the people they see in therapy (American Psychological Association, 1993). Let us consider some of the issues involved in conducting psychotherapy with African Americans, Asian Americans, Hispanic Americans, and Native Americans.

In addition to addressing the psychological problems of African American clients, therapists often need to help them cope with the effects of prejudice and discrimination. Beverly Greene (1993) notes that some African Americans develop low self-esteem because they internalize negative stereotypes.

African Americans often are reluctant to seek psychological help because of cultural assumptions that people should manage their own problems and because they mistrust the therapy process. They tend to assume that people are supposed to solve their own problems. Signs of emotional weakness such as tension, anxiety, and depression are stigmatized (Boyd-Franklin, 1995; Greene, 1993).

Many African Americans are also suspicious of their therapists—especially when the therapist is European American. They may withhold personal information because of the society's history of racial discrimination (Boyd-Franklin, 1995; Greene, 1993).

Asian Americans tend to stigmatize people with psychological disorders. As a result, they may deny problems and refuse to seek help for them (Sue, 1991). Asian Americans, especially recent immigrants, also may not understand or believe in Western approaches to psychotherapy. For example, Western psychotherapy typically encourages people to express their feelings openly. This mode of behavior may conflict with the Asian tradition of restraint in public. Many Asians prefer to receive concrete advice rather than Western-style encouragement to develop their own solutions (Isomura et al., 1987).

Because of a cultural tendency to turn away from painful thoughts, many Asians experience and express psychological complaints as physical symptoms (Zane & Sue, 1991). Rather than thinking of themselves as anxious, they may focus on physical features of anxiety such as a pounding heart and heavy sweating. Rather than thinking of themselves as depressed, they may focus on fatigue and low energy levels.

Therapists need to be aware of potential conflicts between the traditional Hispanic American value of interdependency in the family and the typical European American belief in independence and self-reliance (De la Cancela & Guzman, 1991). Many Hispanic Americans adhere to a patriarchal (male-dominated) family structure and strong kinship ties. Measures like the following may help bridge the gaps between psychotherapists and Hispanic American clients:

1. Interacting with clients in the language requested by them or, if this is not possible, referring them to professionals who can do so.

2. Using methods that are consistent with the client's values and levels of *acculturation*, as suggested by fluency in English and level of education.

3. Developing therapy methods that incorporate clients' cultural values. Malgady and his colleagues (1990), for example, use *cuento therapy* with Puerto Ricans. *Cuento therapy* modifies Hispanic folktales, or *cuentos*, so that the characters serve as models for adaptive behavior.

Many psychological disorders experienced by Native Americans involve the disruption of their traditional culture caused by European colonization (LaFramboise, 1994). Native Americans have also been denied full access to key institutions in Western culture (LaFramboise, 1994). Loss of cultural identity and social disorganization have set the stage for problems such as alcoholism, substance abuse, and depression. Theresa LaFramboise (1994) argues that efforts to prevent such disorders should focus on strengthening Native American cultural identity, pride, and cohesion.

Some therapists use ceremonies that reflect clients' cultural or religious traditions. Purification and cleansing rites are therapeutic for many Native Americans (Lefley, 1990). Such rites are commonly sought by Native Americans who believe that their problems are caused by failure to placate malevolent spirits or perform required rituals (Lefley, 1990).

FEMINIST PSYCHOTHERAPY Feminist psychotherapy is not a particular method of therapy. It is an approach to therapy rooted in feminist political theory and philosophy. Feminism challenges the validity of stereotypical gender-role stereotypes and the tradition of male dominance (Greene, 1993).

Feminist therapy developed as a response to male dominance of health professions and institutions. It suggested that the mental health establishment often worked to maintain inequality between men and women by trying to help women "adjust" to traditional gender roles when they wished to challenge these roles in their own lives. Feminist therapists note that many women experience depression and other psychological problems as a result of being treated as second-class citizens, and they argue that society rather than the individual woman must change if these psychological problems are to be alleviated.

PSYCHOTHERAPY AND SEXUAL ORIENTATION The American Psychiatric Association (1994) does not consider a gay male or a lesbian sexual orientation to be a psychological disorder. The association did list homosexuality as a mental disorder until 1973, however, and many efforts have been made to "help" gay males and lesbians change their sexual orientation. For example, William Masters and Virginia Johnson (1979) adapted methods they had devised for the treatment of sexual dysfunctions and reported that the majority of gays seen in therapy "reversed" their sexual orientations. However, most of these individuals were bisexuals and not exclusively gay. More than half were married, and they all were motivated to change their sexual behavior.

Many critics argue that it is unprofessional to try to help people change their sexual orientations (Sleek, 1997). They note that the great majority of gay males and lesbians are satisfied with their sexual orientations and seek therapy only because of conflicts that arise from social pressure and prejudice. They believe that the purpose of therapy for gay males and lesbians should be to help relieve conflicts caused by prejudice so that they will find life as gay people more gratifying.

In sum, psychotherapy is most effective when therapists attend to and respect people's sociocultural as well as individual differences. Although it is the individual who experiences psychological anguish, the fault often lies in the cultural setting and not the individual.

REFLECT

Would you be more comfortable having therapy with a psychologist of your own gender? Explain.

Review

SECTION VII

It is difficult to run experiments on the effects of psychotherapy because of difficulties in creating control groups and in using experimental blinds. A true experiment on psychoanalysis, for example, would require (70) _____ly assigning people seeking therapy to psychoanalysis and to a control group or other kinds of therapy for comparison. (71) _____s in research designs allow researchers to control for participants' expectations. So-called benefits of therapy may not reflect therapy methods per se, but rather the (72) non_____ factors found in many types of therapy. These nonspecific factors include showing warmth, (73: Encouraging or Discouraging?) exploration, and combating feelings of hopelessness.

Smith and Glass used the method of (74) _____-analysis to analyze the results of dozens of outcome studies of various types of therapies. They found that people who receive psychoanalysis show greater well-being than (75) _____% of those who are left untreated. Psychoanalysis is most effective with clients who are (76: Well or Poorly?) educated, highly verbal, and (77: Highly or Poorly?) motivated. About (78) _____% of clients obtaining client-centered therapy were better off than people left untreated. People receiving (79) G_____ therapy showed greater well-being than about 60% of those who were left untreated. (80) _____ therapy may be helpful for people with severe depression, who had been thought to respond only to biological therapies. Cognitive (81) _____al therapists have innovated effective treatments for sexual problems.

Most of the prescriptions for psychotherapy discussed in the chapter were originated by, and intended for use with, Europeans and (82) _____ Americans. People from ethnic minority groups are (83: More or Less?) likely than European Americans to seek psychotherapy. African Americans often are reluctant to seek psychological help because of cultural assumptions that people (84: Should or Should not?) manage their own problems and because they (85: Trust or Mistrust?) European American professionals. Many Asian Americans prefer (86: Encouragement to develop their own solutions to their problems, or Concrete advice?). There may be

conflict between the traditional Hispanic American value of (87) _____dency in the family and the typical European American belief in independence. Many psychological disorders among (88) _____ Americans involve the disruption of their traditional culture by European colonization.

(89) _____ psychotherapists challenge the validity of stereotypical gender-role stereotypes and the tradition of male dominance. The American Psychiatric Association (90: Does or Does not?) consider a gay male or a lesbian sexual orientation to be a psychological disorder. Many critics argue that it is unprofessional to try to help people change their sexual (91) _____tions because the great majority of gay males and lesbians seek such therapy only because of conflicts that arise from social pressure and prejudice.

An Arsenal of Chemical Therapies. Many drugs have been developed to combat psychological disorders. They include antianxiety drugs, antipsychotic drugs, antidepressants, and lithium.

SECTION VIII. BIOLOGICAL THERAPIES

The kinds of therapy we have discussed so far are psychological in nature—forms of *psycho*therapy. Psychotherapies apply *psychological* principles to treatment, principles based on psychological knowledge of matters such as learning and motivation. People with psychological disorders are also often treated with biological therapies. Biological therapies apply what is known of people's *biological* structures and processes to the amelioration of psychological disorders. For example, they may work by altering events in the nervous system, as by changing the action of neurotransmitters. In this section, we discuss three biological, or medical, approaches to treating people with psychological disorders: drug therapy, electroconvulsive therapy, and psychosurgery. Question: What kinds of drug therapy are available for psychological disorders?

Drug Therapy: In Search of the Magic Pill?

In the 1950s Fats Domino popularized the song "My Blue Heaven." Fats was singing about the sky and happiness. Today "blue heavens" is one of the street names for the 10-milligram dose of the antianxiety drug Valium. Clinicians prescribe Valium and other drugs for people with various psychological disorders.

ANTIANXIETY DRUGS Most antianxiety drugs (also called *minor tranquilizers*) belong to the chemical class known as *benzodiazepines*. Valium (diazepam) is a benzodiazepine. Other benzodiazepines include chlordiazepoxide (for example, Librium), oxazepam (Serax), and alprazolam (Xanax). Antianxiety drugs are usually prescribed for outpatients who complain of generalized anxiety or panic attacks, although many people also use them as sleeping pills. Valium and other antianxiety drugs depress the activity of the central nervous system (CNS). The CNS, in turn, decreases sympathetic activity, reducing the heart rate, respiration rate, and feelings of nervousness and tension.

Many people come to tolerate antianxiety drugs very quickly. When tolerance occurs, dosages must be increased for the drug to remain effective.

Sedation (feelings of being tired or drowsy) is the most common side effect of antianxiety drugs. Problems associated with withdrawal from these drugs include **rebound anxiety.** That is, some people who have been using these drugs regularly report that their anxiety becomes worse than before once they discontinue them. Antianxiety drugs can induce physical dependence, as evidenced by withdrawal symptoms such as tremors, sweating, insomnia, and rapid heartbeat.

ANTIPSYCHOTIC DRUGS People with schizophrenia are often given antipsychotic drugs (also called *major tranquilizers*). In most cases these drugs reduce agitation, delusions, and hallucinations. Many antipsychotic drugs, including phenothiazines (for example, Thorazine) and clozapine (Clozaril) are thought to act by blocking dopamine receptors in the brain (Kane, 1996). Research along these lines supports the theory that schizophrenia is connected with overactivity of the neurotransmitter dopamine.

ANTIDEPRESSANTS People with major depression often take so-called **antidepressant** drugs. These drugs are also helpful for some people with eating disorders, panic disorder, obsessive-compulsive disorder, and social phobia (Abramowitz, 1997; Lydiard et al., 1996; Thase & Kupfer, 1996). Problems in the regulation of serotonin may be involved in panic disorder and eating disorders as well as in depression, and antidepressants are sometimes of use with them. However, cognitive-behavior therapy addresses irrational attitudes concerning weight and body shape, fosters normal eating habits, and helps people resist the urges to binge and purge. Cognitive-behavior therapy, therefore, apparently is more effective with people with bulimia than antidepressants are (Wilson & Fairburn, 1993).

LITHIUM The ancient Greeks and Romans were among the first people to use the metal lithium as a psychoactive drug. They prescribed mineral water for people with bipolar disorder. They had no inkling why this treatment sometimes helped, but it might have been because mineral water contains lithium. A salt of the metal lithium (lithium carbonate), in tablet form, flattens out cycles of manic behavior and depression in most people. It is not known precisely how lithium works, although it affects the functioning of several neurotransmitters, including—perhaps most importantly—glutamate (Hokin et al., 1998).

It might be necessary for people with bipolar disorder to use lithium indefinitely, just as a person with diabetes must continue to use insulin to control the illness. Lithium also has been shown to have side effects such as hand tremors, memory impairment, and excessive thirst and urination.

Electroconvulsive Therapy

Question: What is electroconvulsive therapy (ECT)? **Electroconvulsive therapy** (ECT) is a biological form of therapy for psychological disorders that was introduced by the Italian psychiatrist Ugo Cerletti in 1939. Cerletti had noted that some slaughterhouses used electric shock to render animals unconscious. The shocks also produced convulsions. Along with other European researchers of the period, Cerletti erroneously believed that convulsions were incompatible with schizophrenia and other major psychological disorders.

Electroconvulsive Therapy. In ECT, electrodes are placed on each side of the patient's head and a current is passed between them, inducing a seizure. ECT is used mainly in cases of major depression when antidepressant drugs and psychotherapy fail.

REBOUND ANXIETY Strong anxiety that can attend the suspension of usage of a tranquilizer.

ANTIDEPRESSANT Acting to relieve depression.

ELECTROCONVULSIVE THERAPY Treatment of disorders like major depression by passing an electric current (that causes a convulsion) through the head. Abbreviated *ECT.*

ECT was originally used for a variety of psychological disorders. Because of the advent of antipsychotic drugs, however, it is now used mainly for people with major depression who do not respond to antidepressants (Thase & Kupfer, 1996).

People typically obtain one ECT treatment three times a week for up to 10 sessions. Electrodes are attached to the temples and an electrical current strong enough to produce a convulsion is induced. The shock causes unconsciousness, so the patient does not recall it. Nevertheless, patients are given a **sedative** so that they are asleep during the treatment.

ECT is controversial for many reasons. First, many professionals are distressed by the idea of passing an electric shock through a patient's head and producing convulsions. Second, there are side effects, including memory problems. Third, nobody knows *why* ECT works.

Psychosurgery

REFLECT

Are you disturbed by the thought of ECT or psychosurgery? Explain.

Psychosurgery is more controversial than ECT. Questions: What is psychosurgery? How is it used to treat psychological disorders? The best-known modern technique, **prefrontal lobotomy,** has been used with people with severe disorders. In this method, a picklike instrument severs the nerve pathways that link the prefrontal lobes of the brain to the thalamus. This method was pioneered by the Portuguese neurologist Antonio Egas Moniz and was brought to the United States in the 1930s. As pointed out by Valenstein (1986), the theoretical rationale for the operation was vague and misguided. Moreover, Moniz's reports of success were exaggerated. Nevertheless, by 1950 prefrontal lobotomies were performed on more than a thousand people in an effort to reduce violence and agitation. Anecdotal evidence of the method's unreliable outcomes is found in an ironic footnote to history: One of Dr. Moniz's "failures" shot the doctor, leaving a bullet lodged in his spine and paralyzing his legs.

✓ Truth or Fiction Revisited

It is true that the originator of a surgical technique intended to reduce violence learned that it was not always successful . . . when one of his patients shot him. That technique is prefrontal lobotomy.

Prefrontal lobotomy also has a host of side effects, including hyperactivity and distractibility, impaired learning ability, overeating, apathy and withdrawal, epileptic-type seizures, reduced creativity, and, now and then, death. Because of these side effects, and because of the advent of antipsychotic drugs, this method has been largely discontinued in the United States.

Does Biological Therapy Work?

There are thus a number of biological approaches to the therapy of psychological disorders. Question: What do we know about the effectiveness of biological therapies?

There is little question that drug therapy has helped many people with severe psychological disorders. For example, antipsychotic drugs largely account for the reduced need for the use of restraint and supervision (padded cells, straitjackets, hospitalization, and so on) with people diagnosed with schizophrenia. Antipsychotic drugs have allowed hundreds of thousands of former mental hospital residents to lead largely normal lives in the community, hold jobs, and maintain family lives. Most of the problems related to these drugs concern their side effects.

SEDATIVE A drug that relieves nervousness or agitation, or puts one to sleep.

PSYCHOSURGERY Surgery intended to promote psychological changes or to relieve disordered behavior.

PREFRONTAL LOBOTOMY The severing or destruction of a section of the frontal lobe of the brain.

But many comparisons of psychotherapy (in the form of cognitive therapy) and drug therapy for depression suggest that cognitive therapy may be more effective than antidepressants (Antonuccio, 1995). Cognitive therapy provides coping skills that reduce the risk of recurrence of depression once treatment ends. Perhaps antidepressant medication is most appropriate for people who fail to respond to psychotherapy.

Many psychologists and psychiatrists are comfortable with the short-term use of antianxiety drugs to help clients manage periods of unusual anxiety or tension. However, many people use antianxiety drugs routinely to dull the arousal stemming from anxiety-producing lifestyles or interpersonal problems. Rather than make the often painful decisions required to confront their problems and change their lives, they prefer to take a pill.

Despite the controversies surrounding ECT, it helps many people who do not respond to antidepressant drugs (Thase & Kupfer, 1996). In sum, drug therapy and perhaps ECT seem to be effective for some disorders that do not respond to psychotherapy alone. Yet common sense and research evidence suggest that psychotherapy is preferable for problems such as anxiety, mild depression, and interpersonal conflict. No chemical can show a person how to change an idea or solve an interpersonal problem.

REFLECT

If psychotherapy can be as helpful with depression as antidepressant medication, why do you think so many pills are prescribed for depression?

Review

SECTION VIII

Valium is an example of (92) _____ therapy. (93: Minor or Major?) tranquilizers are usually prescribed for people who complain of anxiety or tension. (94) V_____ and other minor tranquilizers are theorized to depress the activity of the (95) _____ nervous system, which, in turn, decreases sympathetic activity. Many patients who have regularly used minor tranquilizers encounter (96) re_____ anxiety when they discontinue. Major tranquilizers are sometimes referred to as (97) anti_____ drugs. In most cases, major tranquilizers reduce agitation, (98) del_____s, and hallucinations. Major tranquilizers that belong to the chemical class of (99) _____iazines are thought to work by blocking the action of the neurotransmitter (100) _____ine. (101) Anti_____ drugs have relieved many instances of major depression. Antidepressants are believed to work by regulating the neurotransmitter (102) _____nin. Lithium helps flatten out the cycles of (103) m_____ behavior and depression found in (104) _____ar disorder. Lithium affects the levels of many neurotransmitters, including (105) _____mate.

Electroconvulsive therapy (ECT) was introduced by Ugo (106) C_____. ECT uses electric shock to produce (107) _____ions. Since the advent of major tranquilizers, use of ECT has been generally limited to people with (108) _____sion who do not respond to drugs. ECT is controversial because it impairs (109) m_____, and nobody knows why it works.

Psychosurgery was pioneered by Antonio Egas (110) M_____. The best-known technique is called the (111) pre_____ _____omy. The prefrontal lobotomy has been used with severely disturbed patients and severs the nerve pathways that link the prefrontal (112) _____s of the brain to the (113) _____mus. The prefrontal lobotomy has been largely discontinued because of the advent of major tranquilizers and because of (114) s_____ effects.

STUDY GUIDE

To help you better understand the content of this chapter, you may go to the student Web site (http://www.harcourtcollege.com/psych/intro.html) to take more quizzes, get more information about the content, and see additional Web sites related to the content. You can also practice using the concepts in this chapter with the PowerPsych CD-ROM, which gives you interactive activities and experiments along with even more quizzes. And, of course, the printed study guide is a reliable way to practice all parts of PQ4R. Your college bookstore can order the PowerPsych CD-ROM for you.

SUMMARY

1. **What is psychotherapy?** Psychotherapy is a systematic interaction between a therapist and a client that uses psychological principles to help the client overcome psychological disorders or adjust to problems in living.

2. **How have people with psychological problems and disorders been treated throughout the ages?** Mostly badly. It has been generally assumed that psychological disorders represented possession due to witchcraft or divine retribution, and cruel methods such as exorcism were used to try to rid the person of evil spirits. Asylums were the first institutions for people with psychological disorders, and eventually mental hospitals and the community mental health movement came into being.

3. **How do psychoanalysts conduct a traditional Freudian psychoanalysis?** The goals of psychoanalysis are to provide self-insight, encourage the spilling forth (catharsis) of psychic energy, and replace defensive behavior with coping behavior. The main method is free association, but dream analysis and interpretations are used as well. For example, a psychoanalyst may help clients gain insight into the ways in which they are transferring feelings toward their parents onto a spouse or even onto the analyst.

4. **How do modern psychodynamic approaches differ from traditional psychoanalysis?** Modern approaches are briefer and more directive, and the therapist and client usually sit face to face.

5. **What is Carl Rogers's method of client-centered therapy?** The client-centered therapist uses nondirective methods to help clients overcome obstacles to self-actualization. The therapist shows unconditional positive regard, empathic understanding, and genuineness.

6. **What is Fritz Perls's method of Gestalt therapy?** Perls's highly directive method aims to help people integrate conflicting parts of their personality. He aimed to make clients aware of conflict, accept its reality, and make choices despite fear.

7. **What is behavior therapy?** Behavior therapy relies on psychological learning principles (for example, conditioning and observational learning) to help clients develop adaptive behavior patterns and discontinue maladaptive ones.

8. **What are some behavior-therapy methods for reducing fears?** These include flooding, systematic desensitization, and modeling. Flooding exposes a person to fear-evoking stimuli without aversive consequences until fear is extinguished. Systematic desensitization counterconditions fears by gradually exposing clients to a hierarchy of fear-evoking stimuli while they remain deeply relaxed. Modeling encourages clients to imitate another person (the model) in approaching fear-evoking stimuli.

9. **How do behavior therapists use aversive conditioning to help people break bad habits?** This is a behavior-therapy method for discouraging undesirable behaviors by repeatedly pairing clients' self-defeating goals (for example, alcohol, cigarette smoke, deviant sex objects) with aversive stimuli so that the goals become aversive rather than tempting.

10. **How do behavior therapists apply principles of operant conditioning in behavior modification?** These are behavior therapy methods that foster adaptive behavior through principles of reinforcement. Examples include token economies, successive approximation, social skills training, and biofeedback training.

11. **How can you—yes, *you*—use behavior therapy to deal with temptation and enhance your self-control?** Behavior-therapy methods for adopting desirable behavior patterns and breaking bad habits begin with a functional analysis to determine the antecedents and consequences of the problem behavior, along with the details of the behavior itself. They then focus on modifying the antecedents (stimuli that act as triggers) and consequences (reinforcers) of behavior and on modifying the behavior itself.

12. **What is cognitive therapy?** Cognitive therapies aim to give clients insight into irrational beliefs and cognitive distortions and replace these cognitive errors with rational beliefs and accurate perceptions.

13. **What is Aaron Beck's method of cognitive therapy?** Aaron Beck notes that clients develop emotional problems such as depression because of

cognitive errors that lead them to minimize accomplishments and catastrophize failures. He found that depressed people experience cognitive distortions such as the cognitive triad; that is, they expect the worst of themselves, the world at large, and the future. Beck teaches clients how to scientifically dispute cognitive errors.

14. **What is Albert Ellis's method of rational emotive behavior therapy?** Albert Ellis originated rational emotive behavior therapy, which holds that people's beliefs *about* events, not only the events themselves, shape people's responses to them. Ellis points out how irrational beliefs, such as the belief that we must have social approval, can worsen problems. Ellis literally argues clients out of irrational beliefs.

15. **What are the advantages and disadvantages of group therapy?** Group therapy is more economical than individual therapy. Moreover, group members benefit from the social support and experiences of other members. However, some clients cannot disclose their problems in the group setting or risk group disapproval. They need individual attention.

16. **What are encounter groups? What are their effects?** Encounter groups attempt to foster personal growth by heightening awareness of people's needs and feelings through intense confrontations between strangers. Encounter groups can be harmful when they urge too rapid disclosure of personal matters or when several members attack an individual.

17. **What is family therapy?** In family therapy, one or more families make up the group. Family therapy undertaken from the "systems approach" modifies family interactions to enhance the growth of individuals in the family and the family as a whole.

18. **What kinds of problems do researchers encounter when they conduct research on psychotherapy?** It is difficult and perhaps impossible to randomly assign clients to therapy methods such as traditional psychoanalysis. Moreover, clients cannot be kept blind as to the treatment they are receiving. Further, it can be difficult to sort out the effects of nonspecific therapeutic factors such as instillation of hope from the effects of specific methods of therapy.

19. **What do we know about the effectiveness of psychotherapy?** Statistical analyses such as meta-analysis show that people who obtain most forms of psychotherapy fare better than people who do not. Psychodynamic and client-centered approaches are particularly helpful with highly verbal and motivated individuals. Cognitive and behavior therapies are probably most effective. Cognitive therapy appears to be as effective as drug therapy in the treatment of depression.

20. **What kinds of issues develop when people from different ethnic groups, women, and gay males and lesbians could profit from psychotherapy?** People from ethnic minority groups are frequently mistrustful of European American therapists. Therapy methods and goals may also conflict with their cultural values. Feminist therapy heightens awareness of sociocultural issues that contribute to women's problems and challenges the tradition of male dominance. Many professionals believe that psychotherapy should not attempt to change a gay male or lesbian's sexual orientation but should help that person adjust to social and cultural pressures to be heterosexual.

21. **What kinds of drug therapy are available for psychological disorders?** Antipsychotic drugs help many people with schizophrenia by blocking the action of dopamine receptors. Antidepressants often help people with severe depression, apparently by raising levels of serotonin available to the brain. Lithium often helps people with bipolar disorder, apparently by regulating levels of glutamate. The use of antianxiety drugs for daily tensions and anxieties is not recommended because people who use them rapidly build tolerance for the drugs. Also, these drugs do not solve personal or social problems, and people attribute their resultant calmness to the drug and not to self-efficacy.

22. **What is electroconvulsive therapy (ECT)?** In ECT an electrical current is passed through the temples, inducing a seizure and frequently relieving severe depression. ECT is controversial because of side effects such as loss of memory and because nobody knows why it works.

23. **What is psychosurgery? How is it used to treat psychological disorders?** Psychosurgery is a controversial method for alleviating agitation by severing nerve pathways in the brain. The best-known psychosurgery technique, prefrontal lobotomy, has been largely discontinued because of side effects.

24. **What do we know about the effectiveness of biological therapies?** There is controversy as to whether psychotherapy or drug therapy should be used with people with anxiety disorders or depression. Drugs do not teach people how to solve problems and build relationships. Having said that, antidepressants are apparently advisable when psychotherapy does not help people with depression; furthermore, ECT appears to be helpful in some cases in which neither psychotherapy nor drug therapy (antidepressants) is of help. Psychosurgery is all but discontinued because of questions about whether it is effective and because of side effects. Most health professionals agree that antipsychotic drugs are of benefit to large numbers of people with schizophrenia.

EXERCISE 1

THERAPY METHODS AND KINDS OF THERAPY

In the first column are a number of therapy methods. In the second column are types of therapy. Match the method to the type of therapy by placing the letter of the type of therapy in the blank space to the left of the method. Answers are given below. (More than one answer may apply.)

THERAPY METHODS	KINDS OF THERAPY
____ 1. The dialogue	A. Psychoanalysis
____ 2. Genuineness	B. Client-centered therapy
____ 3. Lithium carbonate	C. Gestalt therapy
____ 4. Free association	D. Cognitive therapy
____ 5. Restriction of the stimulus field	E. Behavior therapy
____ 6. Dream analysis	F. Drugs
____ 7. Prefrontal lobotomy	G. Psychosurgery
____ 8. Empathic understanding	
____ 9. Phenothiazines	
____10. Interpretation	
____11. Aversive conditioning	
____12. Token economy	
____13. Challenging irrational beliefs	
____14. Unconditional positive regard	
____15. Systematic desensitization	
____16. Biofeedback training	

EXERCISE 2

THERAPISTS AND METHODS OF THERAPY

In the column to the left are the names of people who have made a contribution to the development of therapy methods. In the column to the right are therapy methods. Match the person to the therapy method by writing the letter that signifies the method in the blank space to the left of the name.

PERSON	METHOD OF THERAPY
____ 1. Aaron Beck	A. Psychoanalysis
____ 2. Carl Rogers	B. Behavior therapy
____ 3. Fritz Perls	C. Cognitive therapy
____ 4. Albert Ellis	D. Family therapy
____ 5. Joseph Wolpe	E. Gestalt therapy
____ 6. Erik Erikson	F. Client-centered therapy
____ 7. Ugo Cerletti	G. Electroconvulsive therapy
____ 8. Anna Freud	H. Psychosurgery
____ 9. Antonio Egas Moniz	I. Rational emotive behavior therapy
____10. Sigmund Freud	

B R I D G I N G   T H E   G A P

LANGUAGE AND CULTURE

to alleviate (623)   *to lessen the intensity*

amelioration (624)   *improvement, lessening*

antecedent (610)   *one who precedes*

to bedevil (619)   *to bother, to trouble*

chronic (597)   *lasting over time*

to confront (606)   *to challenge*

to be counterconditioned (607)   *to be programmed so as not to respond (to disturbing stimuli)*

demonological (595)   *devilish*

to disown (602)   *to take away one's rights of inheritance, to refuse responsibility for*

en masse (618)   *in a group*

exorcism (595)   *act of driving out devils from a person*

to extinguish (606)   *to put out, to kill*

to fare (617)   *to manage*

fruitlessly (619)   *without any positive result*

to furrow (605)   *to plow, to cause lines to form (as on one's brow)*

hierarchy (607)   *list organized in order of importance*

night out on the town (593)   *an evening's entertainment*

outpatient (624)   *person getting treatment at a hospital by coming to the hospital for it*

outpouring (617)   *expression of lots (of peer approval)*

premature (599)   *before its time*

quite a mouthful (595)   *a long name or description*

to rip it off (618)   *to remove*

to run amok (596)   *to get into trouble, to act out violently*

scapegoat (618)   *easy person to blame*

to spill forth (598)   *to allow to escape freely*

unwholesome (602)   *not good for the body*

Q U I Z

1. A leader of the humanitarian reform movement in the United States was
   - (a) Philippe Pinel,
   - (b) Dorothea Dix,
   - (c) Thomas Szasz,
   - (d) William Tuke.

2. Of the following, the form of treatment that seems to be the most helpful with severe depression is
   - (a) cognitive therapy,
   - (b) behavior therapy,
   - (c) traditional psychoanalysis,
   - (d) client-centered therapy.

3. Sigmund Freud remarked, "Where id was, there shall ego be." According to the text, Freud meant that
   - (a) all unconscious ideas should be made conscious,
   - (b) feelings of guilt should be removed,
   - (c) coping behavior should replace impulsive behavior,
   - (d) defense mechanisms should be destroyed.

4. A person has a dream in which she is flying. According to Sigmund Freud, the perceived subject matter of a dream — in this case, flying — is its _____ content.
   - (a) manifest,
   - (b) objective,
   - (c) symbolic,
   - (d) latent.

5. Regulation of glutamate is involved in the treatment of
   - (a) anxiety disorders,
   - (b) schizophrenia,
   - (c) major depression,
   - (d) bipolar disorder.

6. Many critics argue that it is unprofessional to try to help people change their sexual orientations because most gay males and lesbians
   - (a) are suffering from deep-seated psychological disorders and the discontent with their sexual orientations is not the real problem,
   - (b) could decide to change their sexual orientations on their own,

(c) are satisfied with their sexual orientations and seek therapy only because of conflicts that arise from social pressure and prejudice,

(d) there is no evidence that sexual behavior can be changed by means of psychotherapy.

7. According to Albert Ellis, the central factors in our problems are
   (a) genetic factors,
   (b) maladaptive habits,
   (c) unconscious conflicts,
   (d) irrational beliefs.

8. Behavior rehearsal is most similar in meaning to
   (a) practice,
   (b) role-playing,
   (c) modeling,
   (d) imitation.

9. According to the text, the technique of modeling is connected with
   (a) client-centered therapy,
   (b) traditional psychoanalysis,
   (c) social-skills training,
   (d) Gestalt therapy.

10. The technique called _____ is an example of aversive conditioning.
    (a) "Grandma's method,"
    (b) restriction of the stimulus field,
    (c) operant conditioning,
    (d) rapid smoking.

11. Tom cut down on his cigarette intake by simply pausing between puffs. This technique is an example of
    (a) successive approximations,
    (b) chain breaking,
    (c) response prevention,
    (d) avoiding stimuli that trigger unwanted behavior.

12. Which of the following forms of therapy is nondirective?
    (a) Gestalt therapy,
    (b) Behavior therapy,
    (c) Cognitive therapy,
    (d) Client-centered therapy.

13. According to the studies meta-analyzed by Smith and Glass, the *least* effective form of therapy is
    (a) Gestalt therapy,
    (b) psychoanalysis,
    (c) cognitive therapy,
    (d) behavior therapy.

14. Valium and other minor tranquilizers are thought to depress the activity of the _____, which, in turn, decreases sympathetic activity.
    (a) central nervous system,
    (b) parasympathetic nervous system,
    (c) adrenal medulla,
    (d) adrenal cortex.

15. Phenothiazines are thought to work by blocking the action of
    (a) acetylcholine,
    (b) noradrenaline,
    (c) dopamine,
    (d) serotonin.

16. Which of the following is used to treat bipolar disorder?
    (a) ECT,
    (b) the prefrontal lobotomy,
    (c) lithium carbonate,
    (d) major tranquilizers.

17. According to the text, each of the following is a problem in assessing the effectiveness of psychotherapy, except for
    (a) lack of availability of appropriate statistical techniques,
    (b) difficulty in conducting experiments in psychotherapy,
    (c) the role of nonspecific factors in therapy,
    (d) difficulty in defining the outcomes of therapy.

18. According to the text, the person who wrote that many people are depressed because they are pessimistic and tend to minimize their own accomplishments is a
    (a) cognitive therapist,
    (b) traditional psychoanalyst,
    (c) behavior therapist,
    (d) Gestalt therapist.

19. Psychosurgery was pioneered by
    (a) Wolpe,
    (b) Dix,
    (c) Moniz,
    (d) Cerletti.

20. The self-control technique of _____ is a strategy that is aimed at the reinforcements that maintain behavior.
    (a) response prevention,
    (b) stimulus control,
    (c) successive approximations,
    (d) covert sensitization.

1. What is psychotherapy?

2. How have people with psychological problems and disorders been treated throughout the ages?

3. How do psychoanalysts conduct a traditional Freudian psychoanalysis?

4. How do modern psycho-dynamic approaches differ from traditional psychoanalysis?

5. What is Carl Rogers's method of client-centered therapy?

6. What is Fritz Perls's method of Gestalt therapy?

7. What is behavior therapy?

8. What are some behavior-therapy methods for reducing fears?

9. How do behavior therapists use aversive conditioning to help people break bad habits?

10. How do behavior therapists apply principles of operant conditioning in behavior modification?

11. How can you—yes, *you*—
    use behavior therapy to deal
    with temptation and enhance
    your self-control?

    _____
    _____
    _____
    _____
    _____

12. What is cognitive therapy?

    _____
    _____
    _____
    _____
    _____
    _____

13. What is Aaron Beck's
    method of cognitive therapy?

    _____
    _____
    _____
    _____
    _____

14. What is Albert Ellis's method
    of rational emotive behavior
    therapy?

    _____
    _____
    _____
    _____
    _____

15. What are the advantages and
    disadvantages of group
    therapy?

    _____
    _____
    _____
    _____
    _____

16. What are encounter groups?
    What are their effects?

    _____
    _____
    _____
    _____
    _____
    _____

17. What is family therapy?

    _____
    _____
    _____
    _____
    _____
    _____

18. What kinds of problems do
    researchers encounter when
    they conduct research on
    psychotherapy?

    _____
    _____
    _____
    _____

19. What do we know about
    the effectiveness of
    psychotherapy?

    _____
    _____
    _____
    _____

20. What kinds of issues develop
    when people from different
    ethnic groups, women, and
    gay males and lesbians could
    profit from psychotherapy?

    _____
    _____
    _____
    _____

21. What kinds of drug therapy are available for psychological disorders?

_____
_____
_____
_____
_____
_____

22. What is electroconvulsive therapy (ECT)?

_____
_____
_____
_____
_____

23. What is psychosurgery? How is it used to treat psychological disorders?

_____
_____
_____
_____
_____

24. What do we know about the effectiveness of biological therapies?

_____
_____
_____
_____
_____
_____

ANSWERS TO SECTION REVIEWS

1. Psychological
2. Disorders
3. Exorcism
4. Asylums
5. Bethlehem
6. 18th
7. Pinel
8. Hospitals
9. Freud
10. Unconscious
11. Coping
12. Catharsis
13. Free
14. Censored
15. Repressed
16. Dreams
17. Manifest
18. Latent
19. Briefer
20. Less
21. Ego
22. Subjective
23. Carl Rogers
24. Nondirective
25. Unconditional
26. Empathic
27. Genuineness
28. Counseling
29. Fritz Perls
30. Directive
31. Personality
32. Modification
33. Learning
34. Experimentation
35. Observable
36. Extinguished
37. Desensitization
38. Hierarchy
39. Aversive
40. Rapid
41. Reinforced
42. Extinguished
43. Self
44. Role
45. Behavior
46. Feedback
47. Biofeedback
48. Reinforce
49. Electromyograph
50. Electroencephalograph
51. Alpha
52. Functional
53. Maintain
54. Consequences
55. Beliefs
56. Automatic
57. Distortions
58. Depression
59. Perception
60. Overgeneralization
61. Magnification
62. Absolutist
63. Rational emotive
64. Albert Ellis
65. Irrational
66. Theoretical
67. More
68. Encounter
69. Systems
70. Randomly
71. Blinds
72. Nonspecific
73. Encouraging
74. Meta-analysis
75. 70–75
76. Well
77. Highly
78. 75
79. Gestalt
80. Cognitive
81. Behavioral
82. European
83. Less
84. Should
85. Mistrust
86. Concrete advice
87. Interdependency
88. Native
89. Feminist
90. Does not
91. Orientations
92. Drug (or Biological or Chemotherapy)
93. Minor
94. Valium
95. Central
96. Rebound
97. Antipsychotic
98. Delusions
99. Phenothiazines
100. Dopamine
101. Antidepressant
102. Serotonin
103. Manic
104. Bipolar
105. Glutamate
106. Cerletti
107. Convulsions
108. Major depression
109. Memory
110. Moniz
111. Prefrontal lobotomy
112. Lobes
113. Thalamus
114. Side

ANSWERS TO EXERCISE 1

1. C	5. E	9. F	13. D
2. B	6. A, C	10. A, C	14. B
3. F	7. G	11. E	15. E
4. A	8. B	12. E	16. E

ANSWERS TO EXERCISE 2

1. C	4. C, I	7. G	9. H
2. F	5. B	8. A	10. A
3. E	6. A		

ANSWERS TO QUIZ

1. B	6. C	11. B	16. C
2. A	7. D	12. D	17. A
3. C	8. A	13. A	18. A
4. A	9. C	14. A	19. C
5. D	10. D	15. C	20. D

SOCIAL PSYCHOLOGY 14

This chapter, "Social Psychology," covers the following:

Candy and Stretch. A new technique for controlling weight gains? No, these are the names of a couple who have just met at a camera club. Candy and Stretch stand above the crowd—literally. Candy, an attractive woman in her early 30s, is almost 6 feet tall. Stretch is more plain looking, but wholesome, in his late 30s, and 6 feet 5 inches tall.

Stretch has been in the group for some time. Candy is a new member. Let's listen in on them as they make conversation during a coffee break.[1] Note some differences between what they say and what they are thinking:

---

[1] From *Pairing,* by G. R. Bach and R. M. Deutsch, 1970, New York: Peter H. Wyden.

THEY SAY	**THEY THINK**
Stretch: Well, you're certainly a welcome addition to our group.	(Can't I ever say something clever?)
Candy: Thank you. It certainly is friendly and interesting.	(He's cute.)
Stretch: My friends call me Stretch. It's left over from my basketball days. Silly, but I'm used to it.	(It's safer than saying my name is David Stein.)
Candy: My name is Candy.	(At least my nickname is. He doesn't have to hear Hortense O'Brien.)
Stretch: What kind of camera is that?	(Why couldn't a girl named Candy be Jewish? It's only a nickname, isn't it?)
Candy: Just this old German one of my uncle's. I borrowed it from the office.	(He could be Irish. And that camera looks expensive.)
Stretch: May I? (He takes her camera, brushing her hand and then tingling with the touch.) Fine lens. You work for your uncle?	(Now I've done it. Brought up work.)
Candy: Ever since college. It's more than being just a secretary. I get into sales, too.	(So okay, what if I only went for a year. If he asks what I sell, I'll tell him anything except underwear.)
Stretch: Sales? That's funny. I'm in sales, too, but mainly as an executive. I run our department. I started using cameras on trips. Last time I was in the Bahamas. I took—	(Is there a nice way to say used cars? I'd better change the subject.) (Great legs! And the way her hips move . . .)
Candy: Oh! Do you go to the Bahamas, too? I love those islands.	(So I went just once, and it was for the brassiere manufacturers' convention. At least we're off the subject of jobs.)
Stretch:	(She's probably been around. Well, at least we're off the subject of jobs.)
I did a little underwater work there last summer. Fantastic colors. So rich in life.	(And lonelier than hell.)
Candy:	(Look at that build. He must swim like a fish. I should learn.)
I wish I'd had time when I was there. I love the water.	(Well, I do. At the beach, anyway, where I can wade in and not go too deep.)

So begins a relationship. Candy and Stretch have a drink and talk, sharing their likes and dislikes. Amazingly, they seem to agree on everything—from cars to music to politics. The attraction is very strong, and neither is willing to risk turning the other off by disagreeing. They scrupulously avoid one topic: religion. Their religious differences become apparent when they exchange last names. But that doesn't mean they have to talk about it.

They also put off introductions to their parents. The O'Briens and the Steins are narrow-minded about religion. If the truth be known, so are Candy and Stretch.

What happens in this tangled web of deception? After some deliberation, and not without misgivings, they decide to get married. Do they live happily ever after? We can't say. "Ever after" is not here yet.

We do not have all the answers, but we have some questions. Candy and Stretch pretended to share each other's attitudes. What are *attitudes*? Why didn't Candy and Stretch introduce each other to their parents? Did they fear that their parents would want them to *conform* to their own standards? Would their parents try to *persuade* them to limit dating to people of their own religions? Would they *obey*?

SECTION I. SOCIAL PSYCHOLOGY

Attitudes, conformity, persuasion, obedience—these are some of the topics we find in the field of psychology called **social psychology.** Candy and Stretch went to dinner at a restaurant where they served fine wine and soft music swelled in the background. The ways in which their behavior was influenced by this environment are also part of social psychology. Question: What is social psychology? Social psychologists study the nature and causes of behavior and mental processes in social situations. The social psychological topics we discuss in this chapter include attitudes, social perception, social influence, group behavior, and environmental psychology.

> **Review**
>
> **SECTION I**
>
> Social psychology is the study of the nature and causes of our behavior and (1) m_____ processes in (2) _____al situations.

SECTION II. ATTITUDES

How do you feel about abortion, foreign cars, and the Republican party? The only connection I draw among these items is that people have *attitudes* toward them. They each give rise to cognitive evaluations (such as approval or disapproval), feelings (liking, disliking, or something stronger), and behavioral tendencies (such as approach or avoidance). Although I asked you how you "feel," attitudes are not just feelings or emotions. Many psychologists view thinking—or judgment—as primary. Feelings and behavior follow (Eagly & Chaiken, 1993). Question: What are attitudes?

Attitudes are behavioral and cognitive tendencies expressed by evaluating particular people, places, or things with favor or disfavor (Eagly & Chaiken, 1993). Attitudes are learned, and they affect behavior. They can foster love or hate. They can give rise to helping behavior or to mass destruction. They can lead to social conflict or to the resolution of conflicts. Attitudes can change, but not easily. Most people do not change their religion or political affiliation without serious reflection or coercion.

The A-B Problem: Do We Do as We Think?

Our definition of attitude implies that our behavior is consistent with our cognitions—with our beliefs and feelings. Questions: Do people do as they think? (For example, do people really vote their consciences?) When we are free to do as we wish, our behavior is often consistent with our cognitions. But, as indicated by the term **A-B problem,** there are exceptions. In fact, the links between attitudes (A) and behaviors (B) tend to be weak to moderate (Eagly & Chaiken, 1993). For example, research reveals that attitudes toward health-related behaviors such as use of alcohol, smoking, and drunken driving are not consistent predictors of these behaviors (Stacy et al., 1994).

A number of factors influence the likelihood that we can predict behavior from attitudes:

1. *Specificity.* We can better predict specific behavior from specific attitudes than from global attitudes. For example, we can better predict

SOCIAL PSYCHOLOGY The field of psychology that studies the nature and causes of people's thoughts and behavior in social situations.

ATTITUDE An enduring mental representation of a person, place, or thing that evokes an emotional response and related behavior.

A-B PROBLEM The issue of how well we can predict behavior on the basis of attitudes.

church attendance by knowing people's attitudes toward church attendance than by knowing whether they are Christian.

2. *Strength of attitudes.* Strong attitudes are more likely to determine behavior than weak attitudes (Fazio, 1990). A person who believes that the nation's destiny depends on Republicans taking control of Congress is more likely to vote than a person who leans toward the Republican party but does not believe that the outcome of elections makes much difference.

3. *Vested interest.* People are more likely to act on their attitudes when they have a vested interest in the outcome (Johnson & Eagly, 1989). People are more likely to vote for (or against) unionization of their workplace, for example, when they believe that their job security depends on the outcome.

4. *Accessibility.* People are more likely to express their attitudes when they are accessible—that is, when they are brought to mind (Fazio, 1990; Krosnick, 1989). This is why politicians attempt to "get out the vote" by means of media blitzes just prior to an election. It does them little good to have supporters who forget them on Election Day. Attitudes with a strong emotional impact are more accessible (Wu & Shaffer, 1987), which is one reason that politicians strive to get their supporters "worked up" over the issues.

Candy and Stretch avoided discussing matters on which they differed. One motive might have been to avoid heightening the *accessibility* of their clashing attitudes. By keeping them concealed, they might be less likely to act on them and go their separate ways.

Origins of Attitudes

You were not born a Republican or a Democrat. You were not born a Catholic or a Muslim—although your parents may have practiced one of these religions when you came along. Question: Where do attitudes come from? Political, religious, and other attitudes are learned. In this section we describe some of the processes that result in the learning of attitudes.

Conditioning may play a role in acquiring attitudes. Experiments have shown that attitudes toward national groups can be influenced by associating them with positive words (such as *gift* or *happy*) or negative words (such as *ugly* or *failure*) (Lohr & Staats, 1973). Parents often reward children for saying and doing things that agree with their own attitudes. Patriotism is encouraged by showing approval to children when they sing the national anthem or wave the flag.

Attitudes formed through direct experience may be stronger and easier to recall, but we also acquire attitudes by observing others. The approval or disapproval of peers leads adolescents to prefer short or long hair, baggy jeans, or preppy sweaters. The media inform us that body odor, bad breath, and the frizzies are dreaded diseases—and, perhaps, that people who use harsh toilet paper are somehow un-American.

COGNITIVE APPRAISAL Despite what we have said, the learning of attitudes is not so mechanical. Now and then we evaluate information and attitudes on the basis of evidence. We may revise **stereotypes**—fixed, conventional ideas about groups of people or objects—on the basis of new information (Weber & Crocker, 1983). For example, we may believe that a car is more reliable than we had thought if a survey by *Consumer Reports* finds that it has an excellent repair record. Still, our initial attitudes act as

REFLECT

What are your political attitudes? Liberal? Conservative? Middle of the road? How did you develop these attitudes? (Are you sure?)

STEREOTYPE A fixed, conventional idea about a group.

cognitive anchors. We often judge new ideas in terms of how much they deviate from our existing attitudes. Accepting larger deviations requires more information processing—in other words, more intellectual work (Quattrone, 1982). For this reason, perhaps, great deviations—such as changes from liberal to conservative attitudes, or vice versa—are apt to be resisted.

Changing Attitudes Through Persuasion

Let advertisers spend the same amount of money improving their product that they do on advertising and they wouldn't have to advertise it.

WILL ROGERS

Rogers's social comment sounds on the mark, but he was probably wrong. It does little good to have a wonderful product if its existence remains a secret. Question: Can you really change people?—their attitudes and behavior, that is?

The **elaboration likelihood model** describes the ways in which people respond to persuasive messages (Petty et al., 1994). Consider two routes to persuading others to change attitudes. The first, or central, route inspires thoughtful consideration of arguments and evidence. The second, or peripheral, route associates objects with positive or negative cues. When politicians avow, "This bill is supported by Jesse Jackson (or Jesse Helms)," they are seeking predictable, knee-jerk reactions, not careful consideration of a bill's merits. Other cues are rewards (such as a smile or a hug), punishments (such as parental disapproval), and such factors as the trustworthiness and attractiveness of the communicator.

Advertisements, which are a form of persuasive communication, also rely on central and peripheral routes. Some ads focus on the quality of the product (central route). Others attempt to associate the product with appealing images (peripheral route). Ads for Total cereal, which highlight its nutritional benefits, provide information about the quality of the product. So, too, did the "Pepsi Challenge" taste test ads, which claimed that Pepsi tastes better than Coca-Cola. Marlboro cigarette ads that focus on the masculine, rugged image of the "Marlboro man"[2] offer no information about the product itself. Nor do ads that show football players heading for Disney World or choosing a brand of beer.

In this section we look at one central factor in persuasion—the nature of the message—and three peripheral factors: the messenger, the context of the message, and the audience. We also examine the foot-in-the-door technique.

THE PERSUASIVE MESSAGE: SAY WHAT? SAY HOW? SAY HOW OFTEN? How do we respond when TV commercials are repeated until we have memorized every dimple on the actors' faces? Research suggests that familiarity breeds content, not contempt.

You might not be crazy about *zebulons* and *afworbu's* at first, but Robert Zajonc (1968) found that people began to react favorably toward these bogus foreign words on the basis of repeated exposure. In fact, repeated exposure to people and things as diverse as the following enhances their appeal (Baron & Byrne, 1997):

Are you entertained by radio or TV commercials? Which ones? Why? Did these commercials ever convince you to buy a product? Which one? Was the commercial accurate?

ELABORATION LIKELIHOOD MODEL The view that persuasive messages are evaluated (elaborated) on the basis of central and peripheral cues.

---

[2] The rugged actor in the original TV commercials died of lung cancer. Apparently cigarettes were more rugged than he was.

- political candidates (who are seen in repeated TV commercials)
- photographs of African Americans
- photographs of college students
- abstract art
- classical music

The more complex the stimuli, the more likely that frequent exposure will have favorable effects (Smith & Dorfman, 1975). The 100th playing of a Bach fugue may be less tiresome than the 100th performance of a pop tune.

✓ Truth or Fiction Revisited

It is not true that airing a TV commercial repeatedly hurts sales. Repeated exposure frequently leads to liking and acceptance.

When trying to persuade someone, is it helpful or self-defeating to alert them to the arguments presented by the opposition? In two-sided arguments, the communicator recounts the arguments of the opposition in order to refute them. Theologians and politicians sometimes expose their followers to the arguments of the opposition and then refute each one. By doing so, they create a kind of psychological immunity to them in their followers. Two-sided product claims, in which advertisers admit their product's weak points in addition to highlighting its strengths, are the most believable (Bridgwater, 1982). For example, one motel chain admits that it does not offer a swimming pool or room service but points out that the customer therefore saves money.

We would like to think that people are too sophisticated to be persuaded by a **fear appeal**. However, women who are warned of the dire risk they run if they fail to be screened for breast cancer are more likely to obtain mammograms than women who are informed of the *benefits* of mammography (Banks et al., 1995). Interestingly, although sun tanning has been shown to increase the likelihood of skin cancer, warnings against sun tanning were shown to be more effective when students were warned of risks to their *appearance* (premature aging, wrinkling, and scarring of the skin) than when the warning dealt with the risk to their health (Jones & Leary, 1994). That is, students informed of tanning's cosmetic effects were more likely to say they would protect themselves from the sun than

FEAR APPEAL A type of persuasive communication that influences behavior on the basis of arousing fear instead of rational analysis of the issues.

REFLECT

Has anyone ever tried to convince you to change your behavior or your attitudes by means of a fear appeal? What was the appeal? Did it work on you? Explain.

Would You Buy This Product? Advertisers use a combination of central and peripheral cues to sell their products. What factors contribute to the persuasiveness of messages? To the persuasiveness of communicators? Why is Michael Jordan considered an MVE ("Most Valuable Endorser")?

were students informed about the risk of cancer. Fear appeals are most effective when the audience believes that the risks are serious—as in causing wrinkles!—and that the audience members can change their behavior to avert the risks—as in preventing wrinkling (Eagly & Chaiken, 1993).

Audiences also tend to believe arguments that appear to run counter to the vested interests of the communicator (Eagly & Chaiken, 1993). If the president of Ford or General Motors said that Toyotas and Hondas were superior, you can bet we would pay attention.

THE PERSUASIVE COMMUNICATOR: WHOM DO YOU TRUST?

Would you buy a used car from a person who had been convicted of larceny? Would you leaf through fashion magazines featuring homely models? Probably not. Research shows that persuasive communicators are characterized by expertise, trustworthiness, attractiveness, or similarity to their audiences (Mackie et al., 1990; Wilder, 1990). Because of the adoration of their fans, sports superstars such as Michael Jordan are also persuasive as endorsers of products. Fans may consider Jordan to be an MVP, or Most Valuable Player. To advertisers, however, Jordan is an MVE, or Most Valuable Endorser (Goldman, 1993).

TV news anchors enjoy high prestige. One study (Mullen et al., 1987) found that before the 1984 presidential election, Peter Jennings of ABC News had shown significantly more favorable facial expressions when reporting on Ronald Reagan than when reporting on Walter Mondale. Tom Brokaw of NBC and Dan Rather of CBS had not shown favoritism. The researchers also found that viewers of ABC News voted for Reagan in greater proportions than viewers of NBC or CBS News. It is tempting to conclude that Jennings subtly persuaded viewers to vote for Reagan—and maybe this did happen in a number of cases. But viewers do not simply absorb, spongelike, whatever the tube feeds them. Instead, they show **selective avoidance** and **selective exposure** (Sweeney & Gruber, 1984). They often switch channels when the news coverage runs counter to their own attitudes. They also seek communicators whose outlook coincides with their own. Thus it may simply be that Reaganites favored Jennings over Brokaw and Rather.

THE CONTEXT OF THE MESSAGE: "GET 'EM IN A GOOD MOOD"

You are too shrewd to let someone persuade you by buttering you up, but perhaps someone you know would be influenced by a sip of wine, a bite of cheese, and a sincere compliment. Aspects of the immediate environment, such as music, increase the likelihood of persuasion. When we are in a good mood, we apparently are less likely to evaluate the situation carefully (Schwarz et al., 1991).

It is also counterproductive to call your dates fools when they differ with you—even though their ideas are bound to be foolish if they do not agree with yours. Agreement and praise are more effective ways to encourage others to embrace your views. Appear sincere, or else your compliments will look manipulative. (It seems unfair to let out this information.)

THE PERSUADED AUDIENCE Why do some people have sales resistance? Why do others enrich the lives of every door-to-door salesperson? It may be that people with high self-esteem and low social anxiety are more likely to resist social pressure (Santee & Maslach, 1982).

A classic study by Schwartz and Gottman (1976) reveals the cognitive nature of the social anxiety that can make it difficult for some people to refuse requests. The researchers found that people who comply with unreasonable requests are more apt to report thoughts like the following:

REFLECT

In a recent year, there was a dip in the prices of technology stocks after the CEO of Microsoft expressed the view that this group of stocks was overvalued. Why do you think that the public believed him?

REFLECT

Can you think of some celebrities who are being used as pitchmen (or pitchwomen) in ads or commercials? What is the source of their appeal?

SELECTIVE AVOIDANCE Diverting one's attention from information that is inconsistent with one's attitudes.

SELECTIVE EXPOSURE Deliberately seeking and attending to information that is consistent with one's attitudes.

REFLECT

Are you a person who can't say no? If so, why?

- "I was worried about what the other person would think of me if I refused."
- "It is better to help others than to be self-centered."
- "The other person might be hurt or insulted if I refused."

People who refuse unreasonable requests reported thoughts like these:

- "It doesn't matter what the other person thinks of me."
- "I am perfectly free to say no."
- "This request is unreasonable."

THE FOOT-IN-THE-DOOR TECHNIQUE You might suppose that contributing money to door-to-door solicitors for charity will get you off the hook. Perhaps they will take the cash and leave you alone for a while. Actually, the opposite is true. The next time they mount a campaign, they may call on you to go door to door on their behalf! Organizations compile lists of people they can rely on. Because they have gotten their "foot in the door," this is known as the **foot-in-the-door technique.**

Consider a classic experiment by Freedman and Fraser (1966). Groups of women received phone calls from a consumer group requesting that they let a six-person crew come to their home to catalog their household products. The job could take hours. Only 22% of one group acceded to this irksome request. But 53% of another group of women assented to a visit from this wrecking crew. Why was the second group more compliant? They had been phoned a few days earlier and had agreed to answer a few questions about the soap products they used. Thus they had been primed for the second request: The caller had gotten a foot in the door.

Research suggests that people who accede to small requests become more amenable to larger ones because they come to see themselves as the kind of people who help in this way (Eisenberg et al., 1987). Regardless of how the foot-in-the-door technique works, if you want to say no, it may be easier to do so (and stick to your guns) the first time a request is made. Later may be too late.

✔ Truth or Fiction Revisited

Actually, when you give to charity once, you are more, not less, likely to give when the charity calls on you again. The charity has gotten its "foot in the door" with you.

Attitudes and Diversity: The Problem of Prejudice

People have condemned billions of other people. Without ever meeting them. Without ever learning their names. In this section, we discuss some of the reasons for this. We will be dealing with a particularly troubling kind of attitude: prejudice. Questions: What is prejudice? Why are people prejudiced?

Prejudice is an attitude toward a group that leads people to evaluate members of that group negatively—even though they have never met these individuals. On a cognitive level, it is linked to expectations that members of the target group will behave poorly, say, in the workplace, or engage in criminal behavior. On an emotional level, prejudice is associated with negative feelings such as dislike or hatred. In behavioral terms, it is connected with avoidance, aggression, and discrimination. Prejudice is the most troubling kind of attitude. It is connected with the genocide of millions upon millions of people.

FOOT-IN-THE-DOOR TECHNIQUE A method for inducing compliance in which a small request is followed by a larger request.

PREJUDICE The unfounded belief that a person or group — on the basis of assumed racial, ethnic, sexual, or other features — will possess negative characteristics or perform inadequately.

REFLECT

Have you ever been a victim of prejudice? What happened? How did you feel? What did you do about it? Are you content with your response? If not, what can you do if it happens again?

It is true that people have condemned billions of other people without meeting them or learning their names. Such are the effects of prejudice.

DISCRIMINATION One form of negative behavior that results from prejudice is **discrimination.** Many groups in the United States have experienced discrimination—women, gay males and lesbians, older people, and ethnic groups such as African Americans, Asian Americans, Hispanic Americans, Irish Americans, Jewish Americans, and Native Americans. Discrimination takes many forms, including denial of access to jobs, housing, and the voting booth.

STEREOTYPES Are Jewish Americans shrewd and ambitious? Are African Americans superstitious and musical? Are gay men and lesbians unfit for military service? Such ideas are *stereotypes*—prejudices about certain groups that lead people to view members of those groups in a biased fashion.

SOURCES OF PREJUDICE The sources of prejudice are many and varied. Here are some of them:

1. *Dissimilarity.* We are apt to like people who share our attitudes. In forming impressions of others, we are influenced by attitudinal similarity and dissimilarity (Duckitt, 1992). People of different religions and races often have different backgrounds, however, giving rise to dissimilar attitudes. Even when people of different races share values, they may assume that they do not.

2. *Social conflict.* There is a lengthy history of social and economic conflict between people of different races and religions. For example, for many decades southern White people and African Americans have competed for jobs, giving rise to negative attitudes, even lynchings (Green et al., 1998).

3. *Social learning.* Children acquire some attitudes from other people, especially their parents. Children tend to imitate their parents, and parents reinforce their children for doing so (Duckitt, 1992). In this way prejudices can be transmitted from generation to generation.

4. *Information processing.* One cognitive view is that prejudices act as cognitive filters through which we perceive the social world. Prejudice is a way of processing social information. It is easier to attend to, and remember, instances of behavior that are consistent with our prejudices than it is to change our beliefs (Devine, 1989; Fiske, 1993). If you believe Jewish Americans are stingy, it is easier to recall a Jewish American's negotiation of a price than a Jewish American's charitable donation. If you believe Californians are airheads, it may be easier to recall TV images of surfing than of scientific conferences at Caltech and Berkeley.

5. *Social categorization.* A second cognitive perspective focuses on the tendency to divide our social world into "us" and "them." People usually view those who belong to their own groups—the "in-group"—more favorably than those who do not—the "out-group" (Duckitt, 1992; Linville et al., 1989). Moreover, we tend to assume that members of the out-group are more similar in their attitudes and behavior than members of our own groups (Judd & Park, 1988).

REFLECT

Do people hold any stereotypes of your sociocultural group? Are these stereotypes positive or negative? What is their effect?

REFLECT

How do you treat people of different religions or races? Do you treat them as individuals or are your expectations based on stereotypes? Explain.

DISCRIMINATION The denial of privileges to a person or a group on the basis of prejudice.

Stereotyping. How well is this child doing? Research shows that our expectations concerning a child's performance on a test are linked to our awareness of that child's socioeconomic background.

TABLE 14.1	SOURCES OF PREJUDICE
Dissimilarity	People prefer to affiliate with people who have similar attitudes. People of different religions and races often have different backgrounds, which may give rise to *dissimilar* attitudes. People also tend to *assume* that people of different races have different attitudes, even when they do not.
Social conflict	Social and economic conflict give rise to feelings of prejudice. People of different races and religions often compete for jobs, giving rise to feelings of prejudice.
Social learning	Children acquire some attitudes by observing other people, especially their parents. Parents often reinforce their children for behaving in ways that express their attitudes, including prejudices.
Information processing	Prejudices serve as cognitive schemes or anchors, filters through which people perceive the social world. It is easier to remember instances of behavior that are consistent with prejudices than those that might force people to reconstruct their mental categories.
Social categorization	People tend to divide their social world into "us" and "them." People usually view people who belong to their own groups—the "in-group"—more favorably than those who do not—the "out-group."
Victimization by prejudice	People who have been victims of prejudice sometimes attempt to rebuild a sense of pride by asserting superiority over other groups of people.

Our isolation from the out-group makes it easier to maintain our stereotypes.

6. *Victimization by prejudice.* Ironically, people who have been victims of prejudice sometimes attempt to gain a sense of pride by asserting superiority over other socioeconomic or ethnic groups (Van Brunt, 1994). For example, *some* Irish immigrants who had been subjected to prejudice and discrimination by British Americans then discriminated against Polish and Italian Americans. *Some* Polish and Italian Americans then discriminated against African Americans. *Some* African Americans then discriminated against recent waves of Hispanic Americans and Asian Americans. In many cases, of course, experiencing discrimination leads people to *combat* prejudice and discrimination. These sources of prejudice are summarized in Table 14.1.

✓ Truth or Fiction Revisited

It is true that victimization by prejudice can lead people to become prejudiced themselves.

Review

SECTION II

Attitudes are behavioral and (3) _____tive tendencies that are expressed by evaluating particular people, places, or things with favor or (4) dis_____. When we are free to do as we wish, our behavior (5: Is or Is not?) most often consistent with our at-titudes. According to the (6) A_____ problem, the link between attitudes and behavior tends to be weak. However, we are likely to act on attitudes that are (7: Specific or General?) and (8: Weak or Strong?).

Attitudes may be acquired through conditioning, observational learning, and (9) cog_____ appraisal. Attitudes toward national groups can be influenced by (10) _____ing them with positive or negative words. Parents often (11) re_____ children for doing or saying things that are consistent with their own attitudes. Early attitudes tend to serve as cognitive (12) _____ors. We judge subsequent points of view in terms of how much they (13) d_____ from the first set.

Petty and Cacioppo have devised the (14) _____ likelihood model for understanding the processes by which people examine the information in persuasive messages. According to this view, there are central and (15) _____ral routes to persuading others to change attitudes. The (16) _____ral route views attitudinal change as resulting from conscientious consideration of arguments and evidence. The (17) _____ral route associates the objects of attitudes with positive or negative cues.

Repeated messages generally "sell" (18: Better or Worse?) than messages delivered once. In (19) two-_____d arguments, the communicator recounts the arguments of the opposition in order to refute them. People tend to show greater response to (20) _____tional appeals than to purely factual presentations, especially when appeals offer concrete advice for avoiding negative consequences. Audiences also tend to believe arguments that appear to (21: Be in agreement with, or Run counter to?) the personal interests of the communicator.

Persuasive communicators tend to show (22) ex_____, trustworthiness, attractiveness, or (23) _____ity to the audience. People show selective avoidance of and selective (24) ex_____ to communicators. People who are easily persuaded frequently show (25: High or Low?) self-esteem and (26: High or Low?) social anxiety. They also tend (27: To be or Not to be?) highly concerned with what the persuader might think of them if they fail to comply. According to the (28) _____-in-the-door effect, people are more likely to accede to large requests after they have acceded to smaller requests.

Prejudice is an (29) at_____ toward a group. Denial of access to privileges is termed (30) _____nation. A (31) _____ type is a fixed, conventional idea about a group that can lead us to make certain assumptions about group members we have not met.

Sources of prejudice include attitudinal (32: Similarity or Dissimilarity?). We tend to assume that members of out-groups hold attitudes that are (33: Similar or Dissimilar?) to our own. Other sources may include social and (34) ec_____ conflict, social learning from parents, and social (35) _____za-tion, which refers to the tendency to divide the social world into two categories: "us" and "them."

SECTION III. SOCIAL PERCEPTION

An important area of social psychology concerns the ways in which we perceive other people—for example, the importance of the first impressions they make on us. Next we explore some factors that contribute to **social perception:** the primacy and recency effects, attribution theory, and body language.

Primacy and Recency Effects: The Importance of First Impressions

Why do you wear a suit to a job interview? Why do defense attorneys make sure that their clients dress neatly and get their hair cut before they are seen by the jury? Questions: Do first impressions really matter? What are the primacy and recency effects? Apparently first impressions do matter—a great deal. As social psychologist Solomon Asch discovered, first impressions are important and reasonably accurate (Gleitman et al.,

SOCIAL PERCEPTION A subfield of social psychology that studies the ways in which we form and modify impressions of others.

1997). First impressions are an example of the primacy effect. In this section we discuss the primacy and recency effects.

When I was a teenager, a young man was accepted or rejected by his date's parents the first time they were introduced. If he was considerate and made small talk, her parents would allow the couple to stay out past curfew—perhaps even to watch submarine races at the beach during the early morning hours. If he was boorish or uncommunicative, he was seen as a cad forever after. Her parents would object to him, no matter how hard he worked to gain their favor.

My experiences demonstrated to me that first impressions often make or break us. This phenomenon is known as the **primacy effect.** Why are first impressions so important? The answer may be because we infer traits from behavior. If we act considerately at first, we are labeled considerate. The *trait* of consideration is used to explain and predict our future behavior. If, after being labeled considerate, one keeps a date out past curfew, this lapse is likely to be seen as an exception to a rule—excused by circumstances or external causes. If one is first seen as inconsiderate, however, several months of considerate behavior may be perceived as a cynical effort to "make up for it."

Subjects in a classic experiment on the primacy effect read different stories about "Jim" (Luchins, 1957). The stories consisted of one or two paragraphs. The one-paragraph stories portrayed Jim as either friendly or unfriendly. These paragraphs were also used in the two-paragraph stories, but in this case the paragraphs were read in the reverse order. Of those reading only the "friendly" paragraph, 95% rated Jim as friendly. Of those who read just the "unfriendly" paragraph, 3% rated him as friendly. Seventy-eight percent of those who read two-paragraph stories in the "friendly-unfriendly" order labeled Jim as friendly. When they read the paragraphs in the reverse order, only 18% rated Jim as friendly.

First Impressions. Why is it important to make a good first impression? What are some ways of doing so?

REFLECT

Did you ever try to "make a good first impression"? Why? What did you do? Did it work? Explain.

✓ Truth or Fiction Revisited

It is true that you may never get a second chance if you don't make a good first impression. People interpret future events in the light of first impressions.

How can we encourage people to pay more attention to impressions occurring after the first encounter? Abraham Luchins accomplished this by allowing time to elapse between the presentations of the two paragraphs. In this way, fading memories allowed more recent information to take precedence. This is known as the **recency effect.** Luchins found a second way to counter first impressions: He simply asked subjects to avoid making snap judgments and to weigh all the evidence.

Attribution Theory: You're Free, but I'm Caught in the Middle?

At the age of 3, one of my daughters believed a friend's son was a boy because he *wanted* to be a boy. Because she was 3 at the time, this error in my daughter's **attribution** of the boy's gender is understandable. Adults tend to make somewhat similar attribution errors, however. Although they do not believe that people's preferences have much to do with their gender, they do tend to exaggerate the role of choice in their behavior. Questions: What is attribution theory? Why do we assume that other people intend the mischief that they do?

PRIMACY EFFECT The tendency to evaluate others in terms of first impressions.

RECENCY EFFECT The tendency to evaluate others in terms of the most recent impression.

ATTRIBUTION A belief concerning why people behave in a certain way.

ATTRIBUTION PROCESS The process by which people draw inferences about the motives and traits of others.

DISPOSITIONAL ATTRIBUTION An assumption that a person's behavior is determined by internal causes such as personal attitudes or goals.

SITUATIONAL ATTRIBUTION An assumption that a person's behavior is determined by external circumstances such as the social pressure found in a situation.

FUNDAMENTAL ATTRIBUTION ERROR The tendency to assume that others act predominantly on the basis of their dispositions, even when there is evidence suggesting the importance of their situations.

ACTOR-OBSERVER EFFECT The tendency to attribute our own behavior to situational factors but to attribute the behavior of others to dispositional factors.

An attribution is an assumption about why people do things (Jones, 1990). When you assume that one child is mistreating another child because she is "mean," you are making an attribution. The process by which we make inferences about the motives and traits of others through observation of their behavior is the **attribution process.** This section focuses on *attribution theory*, or the processes by which people draw conclusions about the factors that influence one another's behavior. Attribution theory is important because attributions lead us to perceive others either as purposeful actors or as victims of circumstances.

DISPOSITIONAL AND SITUATIONAL ATTRIBUTIONS Social psychologists describe two types of attributions. **Dispositional attributions** ascribe a person's behavior to internal factors such as personality traits and free will. The assumption that one child is mistreating another child because she is mean is a dispositional attribution. **Situational attributions** attribute a person's actions to external factors such as social influence or socialization. If you assume that one child is mistreating the other because her parents have given her certain attitudes toward the other child, you are making a situational attribution.

THE FUNDAMENTAL ATTRIBUTION ERROR In cultures that view the self as independent, such as ours, people tend to attribute other people's behavior primarily to internal factors such as personality, attitudes, and free will (Basic Behavioral Science Task Force, 1996). This bias in the attribution process is known as the **fundamental attribution error.** In individualistic societies, people tend to focus on the behavior of others rather than on the circumstances surrounding their behavior. For example, if a teenager gets into trouble with the law, individualistic societies are more likely to blame the teenager than the social environment in which the teenager lives.

One reason for the fundamental attribution error is that we tend to infer traits from behavior. But in cultures that stress interdependence, such as Asian cultures, people are more likely to attribute other people's behavior to those persons' social roles and obligations (Basic Behavioral Science Task Force, 1996). For example, Japanese people might be more likely to attribute a businessperson's extreme competitiveness to the "the culture of business" rather than to the personality of that individual.

THE ACTOR-OBSERVER EFFECT When we see people (including ourselves) doing things we do not like, we tend to see the others as willful actors but to see ourselves as victims of circumstances (Baron & Byrne, 1997). The tendency to attribute other people's behavior to dispositional factors and our own behavior to situational influences is called the **actor-observer effect.**

Consider an example. Parents and children often argue about the children's choice of friends or dates. When they do, the parents tend to infer traits from behavior and to see the children as stubborn and resistant. The children also infer traits from behavior. Thus they may see their parents as bossy and controlling. Parents and children alike attribute the others' behavior to internal causes. That is, both make dispositional attributions about other people's behavior.

REFLECT

Did you ever try to excuse your behavior by making a situational attribution? Do you make the fundamental attribution error of attributing too much of other people's behavior to choice? Give examples.

REFLECT

Do you ever do anything that is wrong? How do you explain your misdeeds to yourself? Are other people harsher in their judgment of you than you yourself are? If so, why?

How do the parents and children perceive themselves? The parents probably see themselves as being forced into combat by their children's foolishness. If they become insistent, it is in response to the children's stubbornness. The children probably see themselves as responding to peer pressures and, perhaps, to sexual urges that may have come from within but seem like a source of outside pressure. The parents and the children both tend to see their own behavior as motivated by external forces. That is, they make situational attributions for their own behavior.

✓ Truth or Fiction Revisited

It is true that we take others to task for their misdeeds but tend to see ourselves as victims of circumstances when our conduct falls short of our ideals. This bias in the attribution process is referred to as the actor-observer effect.

The actor-observer effect extends to our perceptions of both the in-group (an extension of ourselves) and the out-group. Consider conflicts between nations, for example. Both sides may engage in brutal acts of violence. Each side usually considers the other to be calculating, inflexible, and—not infrequently—sinister. Each side also typically views its own people as victims of circumstances and its own violent actions as justified or dictated by the situation. After all, we may look at the other side as being in the wrong, but can we expect them to agree with us?[3]

THE SELF-SERVING BIAS There is also a **self-serving bias** in the attribution process. We are likely to ascribe our successes to internal, dispositional factors but our failures to external, situational influences (Baumgardner et al., 1986). When we have done well on a test or impressed a date, we are likely to credit our intelligence and charm. But when we fail, we are likely to blame bad luck, an unfair test, or our date's bad mood.

It seems that we extend the self-serving bias to others in our perceptions of why we win or lose when we gamble. If we win a bet on a football game, we tend to attribute our success to the greater ability of the winning team—a dispositional factor (Gilovich, 1983). But when we lose the bet, we tend to ascribe the outcome to a fluke such as an error by a referee.

There are exceptions to the self-serving bias. For example, depressed people are more likely than other people to ascribe their failures to internal factors, even when external forces are mostly to blame.

Another interesting attribution bias is a gender difference in attributions for friendly behavior. Men are more likely than women to interpret a woman's friendliness toward a man as flirting (Abbey, 1987). Perhaps traditional differences in gender roles still lead men to expect that a "decent" woman will be passive.

FACTORS CONTRIBUTING TO THE ATTRIBUTION PROCESS Our attribution of behavior to internal or external causes can apparently be influenced by three factors: *consensus, consistency,* and *distinctiveness*

The Actor-Observer Effect. Who is at fault here? When parents and teenagers argue about the teenagers' choices of friends or dates, the parents tend to perceive the teenagers as stubborn and independent. But the children may perceive their parents as bossy and controlling. Parents and children alike make dispositional attributions for each other's behavior. But the parents and teenagers both tend to see their own behavior as motivated by situational factors. Teenagers often see themselves as caught between peer pressures and parental restrictiveness. Parents, on the other hand, tend to see themselves as forced to act out of love of their impetuous children and fear for what might happen to them.

---

[3] I am not suggesting that all nations are equally blameless (or blameworthy) for their brutality toward other nations. I am pointing out that there is a tendency for the people of a nation to perceive themselves as driven to undesirable behavior. Yet they are also likely to perceive other nations' negative behavior as willful.

SELF-SERVING BIAS The tendency to view one's successes as stemming from internal factors and one's failures as stemming from external factors.

TABLE 14.2	FACTORS LEADING TO INTERNAL OR EXTERNAL ATTRIBUTIONS OF BEHAVIOR	
	INTERNAL ATTRIBUTION	**EXTERNAL ATTRIBUTION**
Consensus	Low: Few people behave this way.	High: Most people behave this way.
Consistency	High: The person behaves this way frequently.	Low: The person does not behave this way frequently
Distinctiveness	Low: The person behaves this way in many situations.	High: The person behaves this way in few situations.

(Kelley & Michela, 1980). When few people act in a certain way—that is, when the **consensus** is low—we are likely to attribute behavior to internal factors. Consistency refers to the degree to which the same person acts in the same way on other occasions. Highly consistent behavior can often be attributed to internal factors. Distinctiveness is the extent to which the person responds differently in different situations. If the person acts similarly in different situations, distinctiveness is low. We therefore are likely to attribute his or her behavior to internal factors.

Let us apply the criteria of consensus, consistency, and distinctiveness to the behavior of a customer in a restaurant. She takes one bite of her blueberry cheesecake and calls the waiter. She tells him that her food is inedible; she demands that it be replaced. The question is whether she complained as a result of internal causes (for example, because she is hard to please) or external causes (that is, because the food really is bad). Under the following circumstances, we are likely to attribute her behavior to internal causes: (1) No one else at the table is complaining, so consensus is low. (2) She has returned her food on other occasions, so consistency is high. (3) She complains in other restaurants also, so distinctiveness is low (see Table 14.2). Given these circumstances, we are likely to believe that the customer is just a complainer.

Under the following circumstances, however, we are likely to attribute the customer's behavior to external causes: (1) Everyone else at the table is also complaining, so consensus is high. (2) She does not usually return food, so consistency is low. (3) She usually does not complain at restaurants, so distinctiveness is high. Given these conditions, we are likely to believe that the blueberry cheesecake really is awful and that the customer is justified in her response.

Body Language

Body language is important in social perception. Question: What is body language? Body language is nonverbal language; it refers to the meanings we infer from the ways in which people carry themselves and the gestures they make. At an early age we learn that the way people carry themselves provides cues about how they feel and are likely to behave (Saarni, 1990). You may have noticed that when people are "uptight" they may also be rigid and straight-backed. People who are relaxed are more likely to "hang loose." Factors such as eye contact, posture, and the distance between two people provide cues to the individuals' moods and their feelings toward their companions. When people face us and lean toward us,

CONSENSUS General agreement.

REFLECT

Look around. Can you tell whether other people are enjoying being with one another or whether they are finding the experience annoying? How can you tell?

we may assume that they like us or are interested in what we are saying. If we overhear a conversation between a couple and observe that the woman is leaning toward the man but the man is sitting back and toying with his hair, we are likely to infer that he is not interested in what she is saying.

TOUCHING: PUT THE ARM ON PEOPLE (LITERALLY) Touching also communicates. Women are more likely than men to touch other people when they are interacting with them (Stier & Hall, 1984). In one "touching"experiment, Kleinke (1977) showed that appeals for help can be more effective when the distressed person makes physical contact with people who are asked for aid. A woman obtained more coins for phone calls when she touched the arm of the person she was asking for money. In another experiment, waitresses obtained higher tips when they touched patrons on the hand or the shoulder while making change (Crusco & Wetzel, 1984).

In these experiments, the touching was noncontroversial. It was usually gentle, brief, and done in familiar settings. However, when touching suggests greater intimacy than desired, it can be seen as negative. A study in a nursing home found that responses to being touched depended on factors such as the status of the staff member, the type of touch, and the part of the body that was touched (Hollinger & Buschmann, 1993). Touching was considered positive when it was appropriate to the situation and did not appear to be condescending. It was seen as negative when it was controlling, unnecessary, or overly intimate.

Body language can also be used to establish and maintain territorial control, as any student who has had to step aside because a football player was walking down the hall knows. Werner and her colleagues (1981) found that players in a game arcade used touching as a way of signaling others to keep their distance. Solo players engaged in more touching than did groups, perhaps because they were surrounded by strangers.

GAZING AND STARING: THE EYES HAVE IT Gazing and staring are important aspects of body language. We usually feel that we can learn much from eye contact. When other people "look us squarely in the eye," we may assume they are being assertive or open with us. Avoidance of eye contact may suggest deception or depression. Gazing is interpreted as a sign of liking or friendliness (Kleinke, 1986). In one penetrating study, men and women were asked to gaze into each other's eyes for 2 minutes (Kellerman et al., 1989). After doing so, they reported having passionate feelings toward one another. (Watch out!)

Of course, a gaze is not the same as a persistent hard stare. A hard stare is interpreted as a provocation or a sign of anger. Adolescent males sometimes engage in staring contests as an assertion of dominance. The male who looks away first loses the contest. In a classic series of field experiments, Phoebe Ellsworth and her colleagues (1972) subjected drivers stopped at red lights to hard stares by riders of motor scooters (see Figure 14.1). When the light changed, people who were stared at crossed the intersection more rapidly than people who were not. People who are stared at show higher levels of anxiety as measured by heart rate, blood pressure, and so on, than people who are not (Strom & Buck, 1979).

FIGURE 14.1
DIAGRAM OF AN EXPERIMENT IN HARD STARING AND AVOIDANCE
IN THE STUDY BY PHOEBE ELLSWORTH AND HER COLLEAGUES, THE CONFEDERATE OF THE EXPERIMENTER STARED AT SOME DRIVERS AND NOT AT OTHERS. RECIPIENTS OF THE STARES DROVE ACROSS THE INTERSECTION MORE RAPIDLY ONCE THE LIGHT TURNED GREEN. WHY?

REFLECT

How do you feel when strangers touch you? Why? How do you feel when a physician or nurse touches you during a physical examination? Why?

REFLECT

Have you ever been made uncomfortable by a stare?

SECTION III **Review**

The psychology of social (36) _____tion concerns our perception of others. We often perceive others in terms of first impressions; this is an example of the (37) _____cy effect. In a classic experiment on the primacy effect, (38) L_____ had subjects read different stories about "Jim." In the (39) _____cy effect, fading memories allow more recent information to take precedence.

Our inference of the motives and traits of others through the observation of their behavior is called the (40) _____tion process. When we make dispositional attributions, we attribute people's behavior to (41: Internal or External?) factors, such as their personality traits and decisions. When we make (42) _____nal attributions, we attribute people's behavior to their circumstances or external forces.

Certain biases operate in the attribution (43) _____ss. The (44) _____tal attribution error is the tendency to attribute too much of other people's behavior to dispositional factors. According to the (45) actor-_____er effect, we tend to attribute the behavior of others to internal, (46) _____nal factors. We tend to attribute our own behavior to external, (47) _____nal factors. According to the (48) self-_____ing bias, we are more likely to ascribe our successes to internal, dispositional factors but our failures to external, situational influences.

At an early age we learn to "read" body language. People who feel (49: Positively or Negatively?) toward one another tend to position themselves close together and to touch. Women are (50: More or Less?) likely than men to touch other people when they are interacting with them. Gazing into another's eyes can be a sign of love, but a (51) h_____ stare is an aversive challenge.

SECTION IV. SOCIAL INFLUENCE

Most people would be reluctant to wear blue jeans to a funeral, walk naked on city streets, or, for that matter, wear clothes at a nudist colony. This is because other people and groups can exert enormous pressure on us to behave according to their norms. **Social influence** is the area of social psychology that studies the ways in which people alter the thoughts, feelings, and behavior of others. We already learned how attitudes can be changed through persuasion. In this section we describe a couple of classic experiments that demonstrate how people influence others to engage in destructive obedience or conform to social norms.

Obedience to Authority: Does Might Make Right?

Throughout history soldiers have followed orders—even when it comes to slaughtering innocent civilians. The Turkish slaughter of Armenians, the Nazi slaughter of Jews, the Serbian slaughter of Albanians and Bosnian Muslims, the mutual slaughter of Hutus and Tutsis in Rwanda—these are all examples of the tragedies that can arise from simply following orders. We may say we are horrified by such crimes and we cannot imagine why people engage in them. But how many of us would refuse to follow orders issued by authority figures? Questions: Why will so many people commit crimes against humanity if they are ordered to do so? (Why don't they just say no?)

THE MILGRAM STUDIES Stanley Milgram also wondered how many people would resist immoral requests made by authority figures. To find out, he ran the series of experiments described in the chapter "Psychology as a Science" (Milgram, 1974). People responded to newspapers ads seeking subjects for an experiment on "the effects of punishment on learning." The experiment required a "teacher" and a "learner." The newspaper recruit was assigned the role of teacher—supposedly by chance.

Figures 1.5 and 1.6 show the bogus shock apparatus employed in the experiment and the layout of the laboratory. "Teachers" were given the task of administering shocks to learners when they made errors. The level of shock was to increase with each consecutive error. Despite the professed purpose of the research, Milgram's sole aim was to determine how many people would deliver high levels of apparently painful electric shock to "learners."

In various phases of Milgram's research, nearly half or the majority of the subjects complied throughout the series, believing they were delivering 450-volt, XXX-rated shocks. These findings held for men from the New Haven community, for male students at Yale, and for women.

Many people obey the commands of others even when they are required to perform immoral tasks. But *why?* Why did Germans just "follow orders" during the Holocaust? Why did "teachers" obey the experimenter in Milgram's study? We do not have all the answers, but we can offer a number of hypotheses:

> **REFLECT**
>
> How do you think you would have behaved if you had been a "teacher" in the Milgram studies? Are you sure?

1. *Socialization.* Despite the expressed American ideal of independence, we are socialized from early childhood to obey authority figures such as parents and teachers. Obedience to immoral demands may be the ugly sibling of socially desirable respect for authority figures.

2. *Lack of social comparison.* In Milgram's experimental settings, experimenters displayed command of the situation. Teachers (subjects), however, were on the experimenter's ground and very much on their own so they did not have the opportunity to compare their ideas and feelings with those of other people in the same situation. They therefore were less likely to have a clear impression of what to do.

3. *Perception of legitimate authority.* One phase of Milgram's research took place within the hallowed halls of Yale University. Subjects might have been overpowered by the reputation and authority of the setting. An experimenter at Yale might have appeared to be a highly legitimate authority figure—as might a government official or a high-ranking officer in the military. Yet further research showed that the university setting contributed to compliance but was not fully responsible for it. The percentage of individuals who complied with the experimenter's demands dropped from 65% to 48% when Milgram (1974) replicated the study in a dingy storefront in a nearby town. At first glance, this finding might seem encouraging. But the main point of the Milgram studies is that most people are willing to engage in morally reprehensible acts at the behest of a legitimate-looking authority figure. Hitler and his henchmen were authority figures in Nazi Germany. "Science" and Yale University legitimized the authority of the experimenters in the Milgram studies.

4. *The foot-in-the-door technique.* The foot-in-the-door technique might also have contributed to the obedience of the teachers. Once they had begun to deliver shocks to learners, they might have found it progressively more difficult to extricate themselves from the situation. Soldiers, similarly, are first taught to obey orders unquestioningly in unimportant matters such as dress and drill. By the time they are ordered to risk their lives, they have been saluting smartly and following commands without question for a long time.

Conformity. In the military, individuals are taught to conform until the group functions in machine-like fashion. What pressures to conform do you experience? Do you surrender to them? Why or why not?

CONFORM To changes one's attitudes or overt behavior to adhere to social norms.

SOCIAL NORMS Explicit and implicit rules that reflect social expectations and influence the ways people behave in social situations.

5. *Inaccessibility of values.* People are more likely to act in accordance with their attitudes when their attitudes are readily available, or accessible. Most people believe that it is wrong to harm innocent people. But strong emotions interfere with clear thinking. As the teachers in the Milgram experiments became more upset, their attitudes might have become less "accessible." As a result, it might have become progressively more difficult for them to behave according to these attitudes.

6. *Buffers.* Several buffers decreased the effect of the learners' pain on the teachers. For example, the "learners" (who were actually confederates of the experimenter) were in another room. When they were in the same room with the teachers—that is, when the teachers had full view of their victims—the compliance rate dropped from 65% to 40%. Moreover, when the teacher held the learner's hand on the shock plate, the compliance rate dropped to 30%. In modern warfare, opposing military forces may be separated by great distances. They may be little more than a blip on a radar screen. It is one thing to press a button to launch a missile or aim a piece of artillery at a distant troop carrier or a faraway mountain ridge. It is quite another to hold a weapon to a victim's throat.

Thus there are many possible explanations for obedience. Milgram's research has alerted us to a real danger—the tendency of many, if not most, people to obey the orders of an authority figure even when they run counter to moral values. It has happened before. It is happening now. What will you do to stop it?

Conformity: Do Many Make Right?

We are said to **conform** when we change our behavior in order to adhere to social norms. **Social norms** are widely accepted expectations concerning social behavior. Explicit social norms are often made into rules and laws such as those that require us to whisper in libraries and to slow down when driving past a school. There are also unspoken or implicit social norms, such as those that cause us to face the front in an elevator or to be "fashionably late" for social gatherings.

The tendency to conform to social norms is often good. Many norms have evolved because they promote comfort and survival. Group pressure can also promote maladaptive behavior, as when people engage in risky behavior because "everyone is doing it." Question: Why do so many people tend to follow the crowd?

To answer this question, let us look at a classic experiment on conformity conducted by Solomon Asch in the early 1950s. We then examine factors that promote conformity.

SEVEN LINE JUDGES CAN'T BE WRONG: THE ASCH STUDY Can you believe what you see with your own eyes? Seeing is believing, isn't it? Not if you were a subject in Asch's (1952) study.

You entered a laboratory room with seven other subjects, supposedly taking part in an experiment on visual discrimination. At the front of the room stood a man holding cards with lines drawn on them.

The eight of you were seated in a series. You were given the seventh seat, a minor fact at the time. The man explained the task. There was a single line on the card on the left. Three lines were drawn on the card at the right (Figure 14.2). One line was the same length as the line on the other card. You and the other subjects were to call out, one at a time, which of

A. Standard Line   **B. Comparison Lines**

FIGURE 14.2
CARDS USED IN THE ASCH STUDY ON CONFORMITY
WHICH LINE ON CARD B—1, 2, OR 3—IS THE SAME LENGTH AS
THE LINE ON CARD A? LINE 2, RIGHT? BUT WOULD YOU SAY
"2" IF YOU WERE A MEMBER OF A GROUP AND SIX PEOPLE AN-
SWERING AHEAD OF YOU ALL SAID "3"? ARE YOU SURE?

the three lines—1, 2, or 3—was the same length as the one on the card on the left. Simple.

The subjects to your right spoke out in order: "3," "3," "3," "3," "3," "3." Now it was your turn. Line 3 was clearly the same length as the line on the first card, so you said, "3." The fellow after you then chimed in: "3." That's all there was to it. Then two other cards were set up at the front of the room. This time line 2 was clearly the same length as the line on the first card. The answers were "2," "2," "2," "2," "2," "2." Again it was your turn. You said, "2," and perhaps your mind began to wander. Your stomach was gurgling a bit. The fellow after you said "2."

Another pair of cards was held up. Line 3 was clearly the correct answer. The six people on your right spoke in turn: "1," "1 . . ." Wait a second! ". . . 1," "1." You forgot about dinner and studied the lines briefly. No, line 1 was too short by a good half inch. But the next two subjects said "1," and suddenly it was your turn. Your hands had become sweaty and there was a lump in your throat. You wanted to say "3," but was it right? There was really no time, and you had already paused noticeably. You said, "1," and so did the last fellow.

Now your attention was riveted on the task. Much of the time you agreed with the other seven judges, but sometimes you did not. And for some reason beyond your understanding, they were in perfect agreement even when they were wrong—assuming you could trust your eyes. The experiment was becoming an uncomfortable experience, and you began to doubt your judgment.

The discomfort in the Asch study was caused by the pressure to conform. Actually, the other seven recruits were confederates of the experimenter. They prearranged a number of incorrect responses. The sole purpose of the study was to see whether you would conform to the erroneous group judgments.

How many people in Asch's study caved in? How many went along with the crowd rather than give what they thought to be the right answer? Seventy-five percent. *Three out of four agreed with the majority's wrong answer at least once.*

✓ Truth or Fiction Revisited

Research evidence reveals that seeing is not necessarily believing—*at least when most people seem to see things differently than we do.*

FACTORS THAT INFLUENCE CONFORMITY Several factors increase the tendency to conform. They include the following:

- belonging to a collectivist rather than an individualistic society (Bond & Smith, 1996),

- the desire to be liked by other members of the group (but valuing being right over being liked *decreases* the tendency to conform),
- low self-esteem,
- social shyness (Santee & Maslach, 1982), and
- lack of familiarity with the task.

Other factors in conformity include group size and social support. The likelihood of conformity, even to incorrect group judgments, increases rapidly as group size grows to five members, then rises more slowly as the group grows to about eight members. At about that point the maximum chance of conformity is reached. Yet finding just one other person who supports your minority opinion apparently is enough to encourage you to stick to your opinions (Morris et al., 1977).

SECTION IV [Review]

Most people (52: Do or Do not?) comply with the demands of authority figures, even when these demands seem immoral, as shown in the studies on obedience run by Stanley (53) M_____. The following factors appear to have contributed to obedience in the Milgram studies: participants' history of socialization, lack of (54) _____al comparison, perception of experimenters as being legitimate (55) _____ity figures, the (56) foot-in-the-_____ technique, (57: Accessibility or Inaccessibility?) of values, and the presence of (58) _____ers that separated "teachers" from their victims.

In Asch's studies of conformity to group pressure, (59) _____% of the participants agreed with an incorrect majority judgment at least once. The following factors contribute to the tendency to conform: belonging to a(n) (60) _____ist society and (61: High or Low?) self-esteem. People experience increasing pressure to conform to group norms and opinions as groups grow to (62: How many?) _____ people. The presence of at least (63: How many?) _____ person(s) who share(s) one's minority view, and familiarity with the tasks at hand, decrease conforming behavior.

SOCIAL FACILITATION The process by which a person's performance is increased when other members of a group engage in similar behavior.

REFLECT

Families, classes, religious groups, political parties, nations, circles of friends, bowling teams, sailing clubs, conversation groups, therapy groups—how many groups do you belong to? How does belonging to groups influence your behavior?

SECTION V. GROUP BEHAVIOR

To be human is to belong to groups. Groups have much to offer us. They help us satisfy our needs for affection, attention, and belonging. They empower us to do things we could not manage by ourselves. But groups can also pressure us into doing things we might not do if we were acting alone, such as taking great risks or attacking other people.

This section considers ways in which people behave differently as group members than they would as individuals. We begin with social facilitation.

Social Facilitation: Monkey See, Monkey Do Faster?

One effect of groups on individual behavior is **social facilitation,** or the effects on performance that result from the presence of others. Question: Do we run faster when we are in a group? Apparently we do. For example, runners and bicycle riders both tend to move faster when they are members of a group. This effect is not limited to people. Dogs and cats eat more rapidly around others. Even roaches—yes, roaches—run more rapidly when other roaches are present (Zajonc, 1980).

According to Robert Zajonc (1980), the presence of other people increases our levels of arousal, or motivation. At high levels of arousal, our performance of simple tasks is facilitated. Our performance of complex responses may be impaired, however. For this reason, a well-rehearsed speech may be delivered more masterfully before a larger audience. An offhand speech or a question-and-answer session may be hampered by a large audience.

Social facilitation may be influenced by **evaluation apprehension** as well as arousal (Sanna & Shotland, 1990). Our performance before a group is affected not only by the presence of others but also by concern that they are evaluating us. When giving a speech, we may "lose our thread" if we are distracted by the audience and focus too much on its apparent reaction. If we believe we have begun to flounder, evaluation apprehension may skyrocket. As a result, our performance may falter even more.

The presence of others can also impair performance—not when we are acting *before* a group but when we are anonymous members *of* a group (Shepperd, 1993). Workers, for example, may "goof off" or engage in *social loafing* on humdrum jobs when they believe they will not be found out and held accountable. Under these conditions there is no evaluation apprehension. There may also be **diffusion of responsibility** in groups. Each person may feel less obligation to help because others are present. Group members may also reduce their efforts if an apparently capable member makes no contribution but "rides free" on the efforts of others.

How would you perform in a tug of war? Would the presence of other people pulling motivate you to pull harder? (If so, we would attribute the result to "social facilitation.") Or would the fact that no one can tell how hard you are pulling encourage you to "loaf"? (If so, we would attribute the result to "diffusion of responsibility.")

Group Decision Making

Organizations use groups such as committees or juries to make decisions in the belief that group decisions are more accurate than individual decisions (Gigone & Hastie, 1997). Question: How do groups make decisions? Social psychologists have discovered a number of "rules," or *social decision schemes*, that govern much of group decision making. Here are some examples:

1. *The majority-wins scheme.* In this commonly used scheme, the group arrives at the decision that was initially supported by the majority. This scheme appears to guide decision making most often when there is no single objectively correct decision. An example would be a decision about what kind of election campaign ads to run when their popularity has not been tested in the court of public opinion.

2. *The truth-wins scheme.* In this scheme, as more information is provided and opinions are discussed, the group comes to recognize that one approach is objectively correct. For example, a group deciding whether to use SAT scores in admitting students to college would profit from information about whether the scores do predict college success.

Social Facilitation. Runners tend to move faster when they are members of a group. Does the presence of other people raise our levels of arousal or produce "evaluation apprehension"?

EVALUATION APPREHENSION Concern that others are evaluating our behavior.

DIFFUSION OF RESPONSIBILITY The spreading or sharing of responsibility for a decision or behavior within a group.

3. *The two-thirds majority scheme.* Juries tend to convict defendants when two-thirds of the jury initially favors conviction.

4. *The first-shift scheme.* In this scheme, the group tends to adopt the decision that reflects the first shift in opinion expressed by any group member. If a car-manufacturing group is divided on whether to produce a convertible, it may opt to do so after one member of the group who initially was opposed to the idea changes her mind. Similarly, if a jury is deadlocked, the members may eventually follow the lead of the first juror to switch his position.

Polarization and the "Risky Shift"

We might think that a group decision would be more conservative than an individual decision. After all, shouldn't there be an effort to compromise, to "split the difference"? We might also expect that a few mature individuals would be able to balance the opinions of daredevils. Questions: Are group decisions more risky or more conservative than those of the individual members of the group? Why?

Groups do not always appear to work as we might expect, however. Consider the **polarization** effect. As an individual, you might recommend that your company risk an investment of $500,000 to develop a new product. Other company executives, polled individually, might risk similar amounts. If you were gathered together to make a group decision, however, you would probably recommend either an amount well above this figure or nothing at all (Burnstein, 1983). This group effect is called *polarization,* or the taking of an extreme position. If you had to gamble on which way the decision would go, however, you would do better to place your money on movement toward the higher sum—that is, to bet on a **risky shift.** Why?

One possibility is that one member of the group may reveal information the others were not aware of. This information may clearly point in one direction or the other. With doubts removed, the group becomes polarized. It moves decisively in the appropriate direction. It is also possible that social facilitation occurs in the group setting and that the resulting greater motivation prompts more extreme decisions.

Why, however, do groups tend to take *greater* risks than those their members would take as individuals? One answer is diffusion of responsibility (Burnstein, 1983). If the venture flops, the blame will not be placed on you alone. Remember the self-serving bias: You can always say (and think) that the failure was the result of a group decision. You thus protect your self-esteem (Larrick, 1993). If the venture pays off, however, you can attribute the outcome to your cool analysis and boast of your influence on the group.

✓ Truth or Fiction Revisited

It is not true that group decisions tend to represent conservative compromises among the opinions of the group's members. Group decisions tend to be riskier than the average decision that would be made by each member of the group acting as an individual—probably because of diffusion of responsibility.

Groupthink

Groupthink is a problem that sometimes arises in group decision making. Question: What is groupthink? In **groupthink,** group members tend to be more influenced by group cohesiveness and a dynamic leader than by the realities of the situation (Janis, 1982). Group problem solving may degenerate into groupthink when a group senses an external threat. The external

POLARIZATION In social psychology, taking an extreme position or attitude on an issue.

RISKY SHIFT The tendency to make riskier decisions as a member of a group than as an individual acting independently.

GROUPTHINK A process in which group members are influenced by cohesiveness and a dynamic leader to ignore external realities as they make decisions.

threat heightens the cohesiveness of the group and is a source of stress. Group members under stress tend not to consider all their options carefully (Keinan, 1987). Flawed decisions are frequently made as a result.

Groupthink has been connected with fiascos such as the Bay of Pigs invasion of Cuba (when President Kennedy supported a misguided invasion of the island of Cuba by Cuban exiles), the Watergate scandal (in which President Nixon helped cover up a robbery of Democratic headquarters), the Iran-Contra affair (in which people high in President Reagan's administration made a deal with Iran that would enable them to illegally send guns to anticommunist rebels in Latin America), and NASA's decision to launch the *Challenger* space shuttle despite engineers' warnings about the dangers created by cold weather (Aldag & Fuller, 1993). Irving Janis notes five characteristics of groupthink that contribute to such flawed group decisions:

1. *Feelings of invulnerability.* Each decision-making group might have believed it was beyond the reach of critics or the law—in some cases, because the groups consisted of powerful people who were close to the president of the United States.

2. *The group's belief in its rightness.* These groups apparently believed in the rightness of what they were doing. In some cases, they were carrying out the president's wishes. In the case of the *Challenger* launch, NASA had a track record of successful launches.

3. *Discrediting of information contrary to the group's decision.* The government group involved in the Iran-Contra affair knowingly broke the law. Its members apparently discredited the law by (1) deciding that it was inconsistent with the best interests of the United States and (2) enlisting private citizens to do the dirty work so that the government was not directly involved.

4. *Pressures on group members to conform.* Group cohesiveness and a dynamic leader pressure group members to conform.

5. *Stereotyping of members of the out-group.* Members of the group that broke the law in the Iran-contra affair reportedly stereotyped people who would oppose them as "communist sympathizers" and "knee-jerk liberals."

Groupthink can be averted if group leaders encourage members to remain skeptical about options and to feel free to ask probing questions and disagree with one another.

Mob Behavior and Deindividuation: The "Beast With Many Heads"

The Frenchman Gustave Le Bon (1895/1960) branded mobs and crowds as irrational, resembling a "beast with many heads." Mob actions such as race riots and lynchings sometimes seem to operate on a psychology of their own. Questions: Do mobs bring out the beast in us? How is it that mild-mannered people commit mayhem when they are part of a mob? In seeking an answer, let us examine a lynching.

THE LYNCHING OF ARTHUR STEVENS In their classic volume *Social Learning and Imitation,* Neal Miller and John Dollard (1941) vividly describe a lynching that occurred in the South in the 1930s. Arthur Stevens, an African American, was accused of murdering his lover, a European American woman, when she wanted to break up with him. Stevens was arrested, and he confessed to the crime. Fearing violence, the sheriff moved Stevens to a town 200 miles away during the night. But his

REFLECT

Have you ever done something as a member of a group that you would not have done as an individual? What was it? What motivated you? How do you feel about it?

An Angry Mob Is Contained by Police. Gustave Le Bon branded mobs as irrational, like a "beast with many heads."

location was discovered. The next day a mob of 100 people stormed the jail and returned Stevens to the scene of the crime.

Outrage spread from one member of the mob to another like a plague bacillus. Laborers, professionals, women, adolescents, and law-enforcement officers alike were infected. Stevens was tortured and murdered. His corpse was dragged through the streets. The mob then went on a rampage, chasing and assaulting other African Americans. The riot ended only when troops were sent in to restore law and order.

Why did the mob engage in behavior that its members might have rejected as individuals acting alone? One possible answer is *deindividuation*.

DEINDIVIDUATION When people act as individuals, fear of consequences and self-evaluation tend to prevent them from engaging in antisocial behavior. But in a mob, they may experience **deindividuation,** a state of reduced self-awareness and lowered concern for social evaluation. Many factors lead to deindividuation. These include anonymity, diffusion of responsibility, arousal due to noise and crowding, and a focus on emerging group norms rather than on one's own values (Baron & Byrne, 1997). Under these circumstances crowd members behave more aggressively than they would as individuals.

Police know that mob actions are best averted early by dispersing small groups that could gather into a crowd. On an individual level, perhaps we can resist deindividuation by instructing ourselves to stop and think whenever we begin to feel highly emotional in a group. If we dissociate ourselves from such groups when they are forming, we are more likely to remain critical and avoid behavior that we might later regret.

Altruism and the Bystander Effect: Some Watch While Others Die

People throughout the nation were shocked by the murder of 28-year-old Kitty Genovese in New York City. Murder was not unheard of in the Big Apple, but Kitty had screamed for help as her killer stalked her for more than half an hour and stabbed her in three separate attacks (Rosenthal, 1994). Thirty-eight neighbors heard the commotion. Twice the assault was interrupted by their voices and bedroom lights. Each time the attacker returned. Yet nobody came to the victim's aid. No one even called the police. Why? Some witnesses said matter-of-factly that they did not want to get involved. One said that he was tired. Still others said, "I don't know." As a nation, are we a callous bunch who would rather watch than help when others are in trouble?

✓ Truth or Fiction Revisited

It is true that nearly 40 people stood by and did nothing while a woman was stabbed to death. Their failure to come to her aid has been termed the bystander effect.

Question: Why do people sometimes sacrifice themselves for others and, at other times, ignore people who are in trouble? Why did 38 bystanders allow Kitty Genovese to die? When do we decide to come to the aid of someone who is in trouble?

DEINDIVIDUATION The process by which group members may discontinue self-evaluation and adopt group norms and attitudes.

THE HELPER: WHO HELPS? Many factors affect helping behavior:

1. Empathic observers who are in good moods are more likely to help. Most psychologists focus on the roles of a helper's mood and personality

traits. By and large, we are more likely to help others when we are in a good mood (Baron & Byrne, 1997). Perhaps good moods impart a sense of personal power. People who are empathic are also more likely to help people in need (Darley, 1993). Empathic people feel the distress of others, feel concern for them, and can imagine what it must be like to be in need. Women are more likely than men to be empathic, and thus more likely to help people in need (Trobst et al., 1994).

2. Bystanders may not help unless they believe an emergency exists (Baron & Byrne, 1997). Perhaps some people who heard Kitty Genovese's calls for help were not certain what was happening. (But remember that others admitted they did not want to get involved.)

3. Observers must assume the responsibility to act (Baron & Byrne, 1997). It may seem logical that a group of people would be more likely to have come to the aid of Kitty Genovese than a lone person. After all, a group could more effectively have overpowered her attacker. Yet research by Darley and Latané (1968) suggests that a lone person may have been more likely to try to help her.

In their classic experiment, male subjects were performing meaningless tasks in cubicles when they heard a (convincing) recording of a person apparently having an epileptic seizure. When the men thought that four other persons were immediately available, only 31% tried to help the victim. When they thought no one else was available, however, 85% of them tried to help. As in other areas of group behavior, it seems that *diffusion of responsibility* inhibits helping behavior in groups or crowds. When we are in a group, we are often willing to let George (or Georgette) do it. When George is not around, we are more willing to help others ourselves. (Perhaps some who heard Kitty Genovese thought, "Why should I get involved? Other people can hear her, too.")

4. Observers must know what to do (Baron & Byrne, 1997). We hear of cases in which people impulsively jump into the water to save a drowning child and then drown themselves. Most of the time, however, people do not try to help unless they know what to do. For example, nurses are more likely than people without medical training to try to help accident victims (Cramer et al., 1988). Observers who are not sure they can take charge of the situation may stay on the sidelines for fear of making a social blunder and being ridiculed. Or they may fear getting hurt themselves. (Perhaps some who heard Kitty Genovese thought, "If I try to intervene, I may get killed or make an idiot of myself.")

5. Observers are more likely to help people they know (Rutkowski et al., 1983). Aren't we also more likely to give to charity when asked directly by a co-worker or supervisor in the socially exposed situation of the office as compared with a letter received in the privacy of our own homes?

Evolutionary psychologists suggest that **altruism** is a natural aspect of human nature (Guisinger & Blatt, 1994). Self-sacrifice sometimes helps close relatives or others who are similar to us to survive. That is, by battling courageously against the enemy—whether a natural predator or another human—we may assure that members of our family survive even if we lose our individual lives. Ironically, self-sacrifice is selfish from an evolutionary point of view. It helps us perpetuate a genetic code similar to our own. This view suggests that we are more likely to be altruistic with our relatives rather than strangers, however. The Kitty Genoveses of the world may remain out of luck unless they are surrounded by kinfolk or friends.

6. Observers are more likely to help people who are similar to themselves. Similarity also seems to promote helping behavior. Poorly dressed people are more likely to succeed in requests for a dime with poorly dressed strangers. Well-dressed people are more likely to get money from well-dressed strangers (Hensley, 1981).

REFLECT

Research concerning altruism and the bystander effect highlight the fact that we are members of a vast, interdependent social fabric. The next time you see a stranger in need, what will you do? Are you sure?

ALTRUISM Unselfish concern for the welfare of others.

THE VICTIM: WHO IS HELPED? Although women are more likely than men to help people in need, it is traditional for men to help women, particularly in the South. Women were more likely than men to receive help, especially from men, when they dropped coins in Atlanta (a southern city) than in Seattle or Columbus (northern cities) (Latané & Dabbs, 1975). Why? The researchers suggest that traditional gender roles persist more strongly in the South.

Women are also more likely than men to be helped when their cars have broken down on the highway or they are hitchhiking. Is this gallantry, or are there sexual overtones to some of this "altruism"? There may be, because attractive and unaccompanied women are most likely to be helped by men (Benson et al., 1976).

Review

SECTION V

Social (64) _____tion refers to the effects on performance that result from the presence of others. According to Zajonc, the presence of others influences us by increasing our levels of (65) _____sal. We may also be concerned that the other people present are evaluating our performance— a phenomenon termed (66) _____ _____sion. However, researchers have found that task performance may decline when we are (67) _____mous members of a group. This phenomenon is referred to as social (68) _____ing.

Social psychologists have discovered a number of rules, or (69) so_____-_____ sion schemes, that seem to govern group decision making. In the (70) _____-wins scheme, the group arrives at the decision that was initially supported by the majority. In the (71) _____-wins scheme, the group comes to recognize that one approach is objectively correct as more information is provided and opinions are discussed. The (72) _____-_____ds majority scheme is frequently adopted by juries, who tend to convict defendants when two-thirds of the jury initially favors conviction. In the (73) _____-shift rule, the group tends to adopt the decision that reflects the first shift in opinion expressed by any group member.

Groups are (74: More or Less?) likely than individuals to take extreme positions. That is, people in a group are likely to experience a (75) _____ shift. The tendency to take extreme positions is termed (76) _____zation.

As members of a group, we may experience (77) _____duation, which is a state of reduced self-awareness and lowered concern for social (78) ev_____tion. Factors that lead to deindividuation include anonymity, (79) _____sion of responsibility, a high level of (80) ar_____ due to noise and crowding, and focusing of individual attention on the group process.

Groupthink is usually (81: Realistic or Unrealistic?) and can lead to flawed decisions. Groupthink is usually instigated by a dynamic group leader. It tends to be fueled by the perception of (82) _____nal threats to the group or to those the group wishes to protect. The perception of external threat heightens group (83) _____siveness and serves as a source of stress. When under stress, group members (84: Tend or Tend not?) to weigh carefully all their options. The following factors contribute to groupthink: feelings of (85: Vulnerability or Invulnerability?), group belief in its rightness, discrediting of (86) _____tion opposed to the group's decision, pressures on group members to conform, and stereotyping of members of the (87) out-_____.

Helping behavior is otherwise termed (88) _____ism. We are more likely to help others when we are in a (89: Good or Bad?) mood. According to the (90) _____der effect, people are less likely to aid others in distress when they are members of crowds. A powerful case in point is the tragedy of Kitty (91) Ge_____, who was stabbed to death while neighbors did nothing to help. One reason for failure to help is that in a crowd there is diffusion of (92) _____ity. People who are (93) _____pathic are more likely to help people in need. We are also more likely to help when we are in a (94: Good or Bad?) mood and when we (95: Know or Do not know?) what to do. We are more likely to help people who are (96: Similar or Dissimilar?) to ourselves.

SECTION VI. ENVIRONMENTAL PSYCHOLOGY: THE BIG PICTURE

What do you picture when you hear the phrase "the environment"? Is it vast acres of wilderness? Is it deep, rolling oceans? Or do you picture seagulls and ducks coated in gunk as a result of an oil spill? Do you think of billowing summer storm clouds and refreshing rain, or do you conjure up visions of crowded sidewalks and acid rain? All this—the beauty and the horror—is the territory of environmental psychology. Question: What is environmental psychology?

Environmental psychologists study the ways in which people and the physical environment influence each other. As people, we have needs that must be met if we are to remain physically and psychologically healthy. Environmental conditions such as temperature and population density affect our capacities to meet these needs. People also affect the environment. We have pushed back forests and driven many species to extinction. In recent years, our impact has mushroomed. So have the controversies over the greenhouse effect, the diminution of the ozone layer, and acid rain. Many of us have an aesthetic interest in the environment and appreciate the remaining pockets of wilderness. Protecting the environment also ultimately means protecting ourselves—for it is in the environment that we flourish or fade away.

In this section, we touch on environmental activism. We then consider some findings of environmental psychologists concerning the effects of atmospheric conditions, noise, heat, and crowding.

Environmental Activism

Because people cause much environmental damage, environmental psychologists try to find ways to persuade people to change their environmental behavior (Stokols, 1992). Most people consider themselves pro-environment. Many think of themselves as "environmentalists." People may not put their behaviors where their mouths are, however, as shown by the fact that many people believe that they are conserving natural resources more than they actually are (Hamilton, 1985). Many people are unaware of the individual impact they have on the environment—for example, how much electricity, natural gas, and water they consume (Kushler, 1989). Research has shown that when people obtain accurate information on the resources they use—and squander—they are more likely to modify their behavior. When homeowners begin to read their meters and check for drafts, they become more likely to weatherize their homes (Aronson, 1990).

Question: Can bottle laws and other recycling laws change people's attitudes? According to **cognitive-dissonance theory,** people find it unpleasant when they hold conflicting views on an issue or when they behave in a way that is inconsistent with their attitudes. People are therefore motivated to behave in ways that are consistent with their beliefs. Research into cognitive-dissonance theory has shown that we may change our attitudes when we are compelled to change our behavior. In that way, we reduce the discrepancy between our attitudes and our behavior. People who must conform to antidiscrimination laws may become less prejudiced. People may similarly grumble when "bottle bills" are passed—laws that require them to pay high deposits on bottled beverages and return the used bottles to regain their money. As time passes, however, their behavior tends to conform and their attitudes tend to grow positive (Kahle &

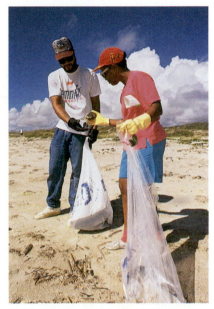

What Is Our Impact on Planet Earth? People's impact on planet Earth has been less than benevolent. Environmental psychologists study the ways in which people and the physical environment influence each other. One concern of environmental psychologists is finding ways to persuade people to change their environmental behavior.

ENVIRONMENTAL PSYCHOLOGY The field of psychology that studies the ways in which people and the environment influence each other.

COGNITIVE-DISSONANCE THEORY The view that we are motivated to make our cognitions or beliefs consistent.

Beatty, 1987). Similar patterns are found when communities legislate the recycling of aluminum cans, newspapers, and bottles.

Noise: Of Muzak, Rock 'n' Roll, and Low-Flying Aircraft

Environmental psychologists apply knowledge of sensation and perception to design environments that produce positive emotional responses and contribute to human performance. They may thus suggest soundproofing certain environments or using pleasant background sounds such as music or recordings of water in natural environments (rain, the beach, brooks, and so on). Noise can be aversive, however—especially loud noise (Staples, 1996). How do you react when chalk is scraped on the blackboard or when a low-flying airplane screeches overhead? Question: What are the effects of noise on behavior and mental processes?

The decibel (dB) is used to express the loudness of noise. The hearing threshold is defined as zero dB. Your school library is probably about 30 to 40 dB. A freeway is about 70 dB. One hundred forty dB is painfully loud, and 150 dB can rupture your eardrums. After 8 hours of exposure to 110 to 120 dB, your hearing may be damaged (rock groups play at this level). High noise levels are stressful and can lead to health problems such as hypertension, neurological and intestinal disorders, and ulcers (Cohen et al., 1986; Staples, 1996).

High noise levels also impair daily functioning. They foster forgetfulness, perceptual errors, even dropping things (Cohen et al., 1986). Children exposed to greater traffic noise on the lower floors of apartment complexes or to loud noise from low-flying airplanes at their schools may experience stress, hearing loss, and impairments in learning and memory. Time to adjust and subsequent noise abatement do not seem to reverse their cognitive and perceptual deficits (Cohen et al., 1986).

Couples may enjoy high noise levels at the disco, but grating noises of 80 dB seem to decrease feelings of attraction. They cause couples to stand farther apart. Loud noise also dampens helping behavior. People are less likely to help pick up a dropped package when the background noise of a construction crew is at 92 dB than when it's at 72 dB (Staples, 1996). They're even less willing to make change for a quarter.

If you and your date have had a fight and are then exposed to a sudden tire blowout, look out. Angered people are more likely to behave aggressively when exposed to a sudden noise of 95 dB than one of 55 dB (Donnerstein & Wilson, 1976).

Temperature: The Perils of Getting Hot Under the Collar

Environmental psychologists also study the ways in which temperature can facilitate or impair behavior and mental processes. Question: What are the effects of extremes in temperature on our bodies and on our behavior and mental processes? Extremes of heat can make excessive demands on our bodies' circulatory systems, leading to dehydration, heat exhaustion, and heat stroke. When it is too cold, the body responds by attempting to generate and retain heat. For example, the metabolism increases and blood vessels in the skin constrict, decreasing flow of blood to the periphery of the body.

Despite their obvious differences, both hot and cold temperatures are aversive events with some similar consequences, the first of which is increased arousal. A number of studies suggest that moderate shifts in temperature are mildly arousing. They may thus facilitate learning and performance, increase feelings of attraction, and have other positive

At the Disco. Couples may enjoy high noise levels (up to 140 dB) at the discotheque. Less desirable noises of only 80 dB, however, can decrease feelings of attraction, put a damper on helping behavior, and contribute to aggressive behavior.

effects. Extreme temperatures cause performance and activity levels to decline, however.

Environmental psychologists point out that small changes in arousal tend to get our attention, motivate us to perform, and facilitate the performance of tasks—whether we are talking about writing a term paper, working on an assembly line, or public speaking. Great increases in arousal, like those that can result from very high or very low temperatures, are uncomfortable and interfere with performing complex tasks. We try to cope with uncomfortable temperatures through clothing, air conditioning, or traveling to areas with milder climes. Extreme temperatures can sap our ability to cope.

Heat apparently makes some people hot under the collar. That is, high temperatures are connected with aggression. The frequency of car honking at traffic lights in Phoenix increases with the temperature (Kenrick & MacFarlane, 1986). In Houston, murders and rapes are most likely to occur when the temperature is in the 90s F (Anderson & DeNeve, 1992). In Raleigh, North Carolina, the incidence of rape and aggravated assault escalates with the average monthly temperature (Cohn, 1990; Simpson & Perry, 1990).

✓ Truth or Fiction Revisited

It is true that heat makes some people hot under the collar—that is, it increases the likelihood of aggression.

Some psychologists (e.g., Anderson & DeNeve, 1992) suggest that the probability of aggressive behavior continues to increase as the temperature soars. Other psychologists (e.g., Bell, 1992) argue that once temperatures become extreme, people tend to avoid aggressive behavior so that they will not be doubly struck by hot temper and hot temperature. The evidence does not absolutely support either view. Thus the issue remains, well, heated.

Of Aromas and Air Pollution: Facilitating, Fussing, and Fuming

Environmental psychologists also investigate the effects of odors ranging from perfumes to auto fumes, industrial smog, cigarette smoke, fireplaces, even burning leaves. Question: What are the effects of air pollution on behavior and mental processes? As an example, the lead in auto fumes may impair children's intellectual functioning in the same way that eating lead paint does.

Carbon monoxide, a colorless, odorless gas found in cigarette smoke, auto fumes, and smog, decreases the capacity of the blood to carry oxygen. Carbon monoxide impairs learning ability and perception of the passage of time. It may also contribute to highway accidents. Residents of Los Angeles, New York, and various other major cities are accustomed to warnings to remain indoors or to be inactive in order to reduce air consumption when atmospheric conditions allow smog to accumulate. In December 1952, high amounts of smog collected in London, causing nearly 4,000 deaths (Schenker, 1993). High levels of air pollution have also been connected with higher mortality rates in U.S. cities (Dockery et al., 1993).

People tend to become psychologically accustomed to air pollution. For example, newcomers to polluted regions such as Southern California are more concerned about the air quality than long-term residents (Evans et al., 1982). Acceptance of pollution backfires when long-term illnesses result.

Unpleasant smelling pollutants, like other forms of aversive stimulation, decrease feelings of attraction and heighten aggression (Baron & Byrne, 1997).

Crowding and Personal Space: "Don't Burst My Bubble, Please"

Psychologists distinguish between "density" and "crowding." *Density* refers to the number of people in an area. *Crowding* suggests an aversive high-density social situation. (In other words, *crowding* is used to mean that we are "too close for comfort.") Questions: When are we too close for comfort? What are the effects of crowding on behavior and mental processes?

First, let us note that all instances of density are not equal. Whether we feel crowded depends on who is thrown in with us and our interpretation of the situation (Baron & Byrne, 1997). (One student of mine reported that she had not at all minded being crowded in by the Dallas Cowboys football players who surrounded her on an airplane ride.) Environmental psychologists apply principles of information processing and social psychology in explaining why.

A fascinating experiment illustrates the importance of cognitive factors—in this case, our interpretations of our arousal—in transforming high density into crowding. Worchel and Brown (1984) showed small groups of people films when the people were spaced comfortably apart or uncomfortably close. There were four different films. Three were arousing (either humorous, sexual, or violent), and one was just plain boring.

As shown in Figure 14.3, viewers who sat more closely together generally felt more crowded than those seated farther apart. Note that those who were seated far enough apart uniformly rated the seating arrangements as uncrowded. Among those who were seated too close for comfort, viewers of the boring (unarousing) film felt most crowded. Viewers of the arousing films felt less crowded. Why? The researchers suggest that viewers who were packed in could explain their arousal in terms of their response to the content of the films. Viewers of the unarousing film could not. They were therefore likely to attribute their arousal to the seating arrangements.

PSYCHOLOGICAL MODERATORS OF THE IMPACT OF HIGH DENSITY A sense of control enhances psychological hardiness. Examples from everyday life suggest that a sense of control—of choice—over the situation also helps us cope with the stress of being packed in. When we are at a concert, a disco, or a sports event, we may encounter higher density than we do in those frustrating ticket lines. But we may be having a wonderful time. Why? We have *chosen* to be at the concert and are focusing on our good time (unless a tall or noisy person sits in front of us). We feel in control.

We tend to moderate the effects of high density in subway cars and other mass-transportation vehicles by ignoring fellow passengers and daydreaming, by reading newspapers and books, and by finding humor in the situation. Some people catch a snooze and wake up just before their stop.

SOME EFFECTS OF CITY LIFE Big-city dwellers are more likely to experience stimulus overload and fear crime than suburbanites and rural folk. Overwhelming crowd stimulation, bright lights, shop windows, and so on cause them to narrow their perceptions to a particular face, destination, or job. The pace of life literally picks up—pedestrians walk faster in bigger cities (Sadalla et al., 1990).

REFLECT

How do you feel when you're crowded into an elevator or a subway car? Is there anything that helps you handle your feelings?

FIGURE 14.3

TYPE OF FILM AND APPRAISAL OF HIGH-DENSITY SEATING

IN A STUDY BY WORCHEL AND BROWN (1984), VIEWERS SEATED INAPPROPRIATELY CLOSE OR AT APPROPRIATE DISTANCES WATCHED FOUR KINDS OF FILMS. OF THE INDIVIDUALS SEATED TOO CLOSELY, THOSE WHO COULD ATTRIBUTE THEIR AROUSAL TO THE FILM WERE LESS LIKELY TO EXPERIENCE CROWDING THAN THOSE WHO COULD NOT.

City dwellers are less willing to shake hands with, make eye contact with, or help strangers (Milgram, 1977; Newman & McCauley, 1977). People who move to the city from more rural areas adjust by becoming more deliberate in their daily activities. They plan ahead to take safety precautions, and they increase their alertness to potential dangers.

Farming, anyone?

PERSONAL SPACE One adverse effect of crowding is the invasion of **personal space,** which is an invisible boundary, sort of a bubble, that surrounds you. You are likely to become anxious and, perhaps, angry when others invade your space. This may happen when someone sits down across from or next to you in an otherwise empty cafeteria or stands too close in an elevator. Personal space appears to serve protective and communicative functions.

People sit and stand closer to people of the same race, similar age, or similar socioeconomic status. Dating couples come closer together as the attraction between them increases.

North Americans and northern Europeans apparently distance themselves from others more so than southern Europeans, Asians, and Middle Easterners do (Baron & Byrne, 1997). A study by Pagan and Aiello (1982) suggests the contribution of cultural experiences. Puerto Ricans tend to interact more closely than Americans of northern European extraction. Pagan and Aiello found that Puerto Ricans reared in New York City required more personal space when interacting with others of the same gender than did Puerto Ricans reared in Puerto Rico.

People in some cultures apparently learn to cope with high density and also share their ways of coping with others (Gillis et al., 1986). Asians in crowded cities such as Tokyo and Hong Kong interact more harmoniously than North Americans and English people, who dwell in less dense cities. The Japanese are used to being packed sardinelike into subway cars by white-gloved pushers employed by the transit system. Imagine the rebellion that would occur at such treatment in American subways! It has been suggested that Asians are accustomed to adapting to the environment, whereas Westerners are more prone to try to change the environment.

Southern Europeans apparently occupy a middle ground between Asians, on the one hand, and northern Europeans, on the other. They are more outgoing and comfortable with less personal space than northern Europeans but not as tolerant of it as Asians are.

PERSONAL SPACE An invisible boundary that surrounds a person and serves protective functions.

Review

SECTION VI

Environmental psychologists study the ways in which people and the (97) _____ environment influence each other. Most people consider themselves (98: Pro- or Anti-?) environment. Research shows that when people obtain accurate information on the resources they use, they are (99: More or Less?) likely to modify their environmental behavior. According to (100) _____-dissonance theory, people find it unpleasant when they behave in a way that is inconsistent with their attitudes. Thus, people may grumble when recycling laws are passed, but as time passes, their behavior tends to conform and their attitudes tend to grow (101: Positive or Negative?).

High noise levels impair learning and memory, (102: Increase or Decrease?) feelings of attraction, (103: Increase or Decrease?) helping behavior, and (104: Increase or Decrease?) aggressive behavior.

Extremes of heat make excessive demands on our bodies' (105) _____tory systems. Both hot and cold temperatures are (106) _____sive events with some similar consequences, the first of which is increased arousal. Moderate shifts in temperature tend to (107: Facilitate or Impair?) learning and performance, and to (108: Increase or Decrease?) feelings of attraction, and have other positive effects. Extreme heat (109: Facilitates or Impairs?) performance and (110: Increases or Decreases?) aggressiveness.

The (111) _____ in auto fumes may impair children's intellectual functioning. Carbon (112) _____ide decreases the capacity of the blood to carry oxygen and impairs learning ability. High levels of air pollution are connected with (113: Higher or Lower?) mortality rates in U.S. cities. Unpleasant odors (114: Increase or Decrease?) feelings of attraction and (115: Increase or Decrease?) aggressive behavior.

Psychologists distinguish between "density" and "crowding." (116) _____ refers to the number of people in an area. (117) _____ suggests an aversive high-density social situation. Whether we feel crowded depends on whom we are with and our (118) _____ tation of the situation. A sense of (119) _____trol helps us cope with the stress of being packed in. Big-city dwellers are more likely to experience stimulus (120) _____ load and fear crime than suburbanites and rural people.

One adverse effect of crowding is the invasion of (121) _____ space, which is an invisible boundary that surrounds and protects you from others. People sit and stand (122: Closer to or Farther from?) people of the same race, similar age, or similar socioeconomic status.

And so we conclude our discussion of the nature and causes of behavior and mental processes in social situations. People do many things in social situations that they would not do as individuals, and sometimes they do nothing—not even come to the aid of a person in danger—when other people are present. People are social beings. We cannot live without other people, and many times people lose their lives because of other people. So it has been; so it would appear to be. How do you behave when you are a member of a group—a family, a class, a crowd of friends, a crowd on a city sidewalk, a religious group, the armed services? Is your behavior the same as it would be if you were acting alone? Why or why not?

STUDY GUIDE

To help you better understand the content of this chapter, you may go to the student Web site (http://www.harcourtcollege.com/psych/intro.html) to take more quizzes, get more information about the content, and see additional Web sites related to the content. You can also practice using the concepts in this chapter with the PowerPsych CD-ROM, which gives you interactive activities and experiments along with even more quizzes. And, of course, the printed study guide is a reliable way to practice all parts of PQ4R. Your college bookstore can order the PowerPsych CD-ROM for you.

SUMMARY

1. **What is social psychology?** Social psychology is the field of psychology that studies the factors that influence our thoughts, feelings, and behaviors in social situations.

2. **What are attitudes?** Attitudes are behavioral and cognitive tendencies expressed by evaluating particular people, places, or things with favor or disfavor.

3. **Do people do as they think? (For example, do people really vote their consciences?)** When we are free to act as we wish, our behavior is often consistent with our beliefs and feelings. But as indicated by the term *A-B problem,* the links between attitudes (A) and behaviors (B) are often weak to moderate. The following strengthen the A-B connection: specificity of attitudes, strength of attitudes, whether people have a vested interest in the outcome of their behavior, and the accessibility of the attitudes.

4. **Where do attitudes come from?** Attitudes are acquired or learned. They can be learned by conditioning, by observation, and by cognitive appraisal (personal evaluation of a situation).

5. **Can you really change people?—their attitudes and behavior, that is?** Changes in attitudes and behavior can be brought about by persuasion. According to the elaboration likelihood model, persuasion occurs through both central and peripheral routes. Change occurs through the central route by means of consideration of arguments and evidence. Peripheral routes involve associating the objects of attitudes with positive or negative cues, such as attractive or unattractive communicators. Repeated messages generally "sell" better than messages delivered only once. People tend to show greater response to fear appeals than to purely factual presentations. This is especially so when the appeals offer concrete advice for avoiding negative outcomes. Persuasive communicators tend to show expertise, trustworthiness, attractiveness, or similarity to the audience. In the foot-in-the-door technique, people are asked to comply with larger requests after they have complied with smaller ones.

6. **What is prejudice? Why are people prejudiced?** Prejudice is an attitude toward a group that leads people to evaluate members of that group negatively. Discrimination is a form of negative behavior that results from prejudice; discrimination takes forms such as denial of access to jobs, housing, and the voting booth. Prejudices are typically based on stereotypes, which are fixed, conventional ideas about groups of people. Sources of prejudice include dissimilarity, social conflict, social learning, ease of stereotypical information processing, social categorization, and victimization by prejudice.

7. **Do first impressions really matter? What are the primacy and recency effects?** First impressions can last (the primacy effect) because we tend to label or describe people in terms of the behavior we see initially. The recency effects appears to be based on the fact that—other things being equal—recently learned information is easier to remember.

8. **What is attribution theory? Why do we assume that other people intend the mischief that they do?** The tendency to infer the motives and traits of others through observation of their behavior is referred to as the attribution process. In dispositional attributions, we attribute people's behavior to internal factors such as their personality traits and decisions. In situational attributions, we attribute people's behavior to their circumstances or external forces. According to the actor-observer effect, we tend to attribute the behavior of others to internal, dispositional factors. However, we tend to attribute our own behavior to external, situational factors. The so-called fundamental attribution error is the tendency to attribute too much of other people's behavior to dispositional factors. The attribution of behavior to internal or external causes is influenced by three factors: consensus, consistency, and distinctiveness. For example, when few people act in a certain way—that is, when the consensus is low—we are likely to attribute behavior to internal factors.

9. **What is body language?** Body language refers to the tendency to infer people's thoughts and feelings from their postures and gestures. For example, people who

feel positively toward one another position themselves closer together and are more likely to touch. Touching results in a negative reaction when it suggests more intimacy than is desired. Gazing into another's eyes can be a sign of love, but a hard stare is an aversive challenge. Women are more likely than men to touch people with whom they are interacting.

10. **Why will so many people commit crimes against humanity if they are ordered to do so?** *(Why don't they just say no?)* The majority of subjects in the Milgram studies complied with the demands of authority figures, even when the demands required that they hurt innocent people by means of electric shock. Factors contributing to obedience include socialization, lack of social comparison, perception of legitimate authority figures, the foot-in-the-door technique, inaccessibility of values, and buffers between the perpetrator and the victim.

11. **Why do so many people tend to follow the crowd?** Asch's research in which subjects judged the lengths of lines suggests that the majority of people will follow the crowd, even when the crowd is wrong. Personal factors such as desire to be liked by group members, low self-esteem, high self-consciousness, and shyness contribute to conformity. Belonging to a collectivist society and group size also contribute to conformity.

12. **Do we run faster when we are in a group?** Apparently we do, because of *social facilitation*. Social facilitation refers to the effects on performance that result from the presence of other people. The presence of others may facilitate performance for reasons such as increased arousal and evaluation apprehension. However, when we are anonymous group members, we may experience diffusion of responsibility and task performance may fall off. This phenomenon is termed *social loafing*.

13. **How do groups make decisions?** Social psychologists have identified several decision-making schemes, including the majority-wins scheme, the truth-wins scheme, the two-thirds majority scheme, and the first-shift rule.

14. **Are group decisions more risky or more conservative than those of the individual members of the group? Why?** Group decisions tend to be more polarized and riskier than individual decisions, largely because groups diffuse responsibility. Group decisions may be highly productive when group members are knowledgeable, there is an explicit procedure for arriving at decisions, and there is a process of give and take.

15. **What is groupthink?** Groupthink is an unrealistic kind of decision making that is fueled by the perception of external threats to the group or to those whom the group wishes to protect. It is facilitated by feelings of invulnerability, the group's belief in its rightness, discrediting of information that contradicts the group's decision, conformity, and stereotyping of members of the out-group.

16. **Do mobs bring out the beast in us? How is it that mild-mannered people commit mayhem when they are part of a mob?** Highly emotional crowds may induce attitude-discrepant behavior through the process of *deindividuation,* which is a state of reduced self-awareness and lowered concern for social evaluation.

17. **Why do people sometimes sacrifice themselves for others and, at other times, ignore people who are in trouble?** A number of factors contribute to altruism (the tendency to help others). Among them are empathy, being in a good mood, feelings of responsibility, knowledge of how to help, and acquaintance with—and similarity to—the person in need of help. According to the bystander effect, we are unlikely to aid people in distress when we are members of crowds. Crowds tend to diffuse responsibility.

18. **What is environmental psychology?** Environmental psychology is the field of psychology that studies the ways in which humans and the physical environment influence each other.

19. **Can bottle laws and other recycling laws change people's attitudes?** Apparently many people come to support laws they initially opposed in order to reduce the cognitive dissonance of behaving in ways that they do not believe in.

20. **What are the effects of noise on behavior and mental processes?** High noise levels are stressful and can lead to health problems such as hearing loss, hypertension, and neurological and intestinal disorders. High noise levels impair learning and memory. Loud noise also dampens helping behavior and heightens aggressiveness.

21. **What are the effects of extremes in temperature on our bodies and on our behavior and mental processes?** Moderate shifts in temperature are mildly arousing and have positive effects such as facilitating learning and performance and increasing feelings of attraction. But extreme temperatures tax the body, are a source of stress, and impair performance. High temperatures are also connected with aggression.

22. **What are the effects of air pollution on behavior and mental processes?** The lead in auto fumes may impair learning and memory. Carbon monoxide decreases the capacity of the blood to carry oxygen and thus impairs learning ability and perception and contributes to accidents. Unpleasant odors decrease feelings of attraction and heighten aggression.

23. **When are we too close for comfort? What are the effects of crowding on behavior and mental processes?** *Density* refers to the number of people in an area. *Crowding* suggests aversive high density. A sense of control or choice—as in choosing to attend a concert or athletic contest—helps us cope with the stress of high density. Perhaps because of crowding, noise, and so on, city dwellers are less likely than people who live in small towns to interact with or help strangers.

EXERCISE 1

FACTORS LEADING TO INTERNAL OR EXTERNAL ATTRIBUTIONS OF BEHAVIOR

Directions: For each of the following, 1–6, indicate whether the answer is "High" or "Low." For example, in item 1, indicate whether people tend to make an internal attribution for behavior when consensus is high or low.

	INTERNAL ATTRIBUTION	EXTERNAL ATTRIBUTION
Consensus	1: High or Low? _____	2: High or Low? _____
Consistency	3: High or Low? _____	4: High or Low? _____
Distinctiveness	5: High or Low? _____	6: High or Low? _____

EXERCISE 2

REASONS FOR FOLLOWING ORDERS IN THE MILGRAM STUDIES

Directions: Fill in the blanks in the reasons for obedience in the following table.

REASON	EXPLANATION
(1) _____tion	People are socialized from early childhood to obey authority figures such as parents and teachers.
Lack of social (2) _____son	Being on their own, subjects ("teachers") did not have the opportunity to compare their feelings with those of other people in the same situation.
Perception of (3) _____ authority	When Milgram's research took place at Yale University, subjects may have been influenced by the reputation and authority of the setting. An experimenter at Yale may have appeared to be a legitimate authority figure.
The (4) _____-in-the-door technique	Once they had begun to deliver shocks to learners, subjects may have found it progressively more difficult to pull out of the situation.
(5) _____lity of values	People are more likely to act in accordance with their attitudes when their attitudes are readily available, or accessible. Most people believe that it is wrong to harm innocent people, but strong emotions interfere with clear thinking. As the subjects in the Milgram experiments became more upset, their attitudes may have become less accessible.
(6) _____fers	Distance between the "teachers" and the "learners" may have decreased the effect of the "learners'" pain on the actual subjects in the study (that is, the "teachers"). For example, the learners were in another room.

EXERCISE 3

MATCHING CONCEPTS AND EXAMPLES

The numbered items represent concepts in social psychology. The lettered items are instances of behavior that serve as examples of these concepts. Match the example with the concept by writing the letter of the example in the blank space to the left of the concept. Answers are given below. We are allowing more than one answer in some cases.

CONCEPTS

_____ 1. Prejudice
_____ 2. Bystander effect
_____ 3. Recency effect
_____ 4. Discrimination
_____ 5. Conformity
_____ 6. Dispositional attribution
_____ 7. Emotional appeal
_____ 8. Foot-in-the-door technique
_____ 9. Actor-observer effect
_____ 10. Primacy effect
_____ 11. Evaluation apprehension
_____ 12. Self-serving bias
_____ 13. Situational attribution
_____ 14. Deindividuation
_____ 15. Diffusion of responsibility
_____ 16. Fundamental attribution error
_____ 17. The first-shift rule
_____ 18. Buffer
_____ 19. Inaccessibility of attitudes
_____ 20. The A-B problem
_____ 21. Groupthink

EXAMPLES

A. A person assumes that someone who bumped into him did so on purpose.

B. We have done well on a test and credit the outcome to our intelligence and charm.

C. A person asks a small favor to prepare someone to grant a larger favor later.

D. A new worker is late and the boss conceptualizes him as "a late person."

E. John blames his mood on the weather.

F. A person does not come to the aid of a crime victim because many people surround the victim.

G. A mob member adopts the norms of the crowd.

H. Parents and their teenagers are arguing about the teenagers' choice of dates, and the parents therefore perceive their children to be stubborn, difficult, and independent.

I. A student wears blue jeans because "everyone" is wearing them.

J. An athlete runs faster because he is concerned that fellow racers are aware of his performance.

K. A man assumes that a woman will not be assertive enough to perform well in the business world.

L. The man in item K, above, chooses not to hire a woman.

M. A dentist shows photos of diseased gums to convince patients to improve their oral hygiene.

N. Fading memories allow recent information to take precedence over first impressions.

O. A group with a dynamic leader ignores the evidence and makes foolish decisions.

P. A person becomes so aroused as a member of a mob that he completely forgets his personal moral values.

Q. A psychologist cannot predict a voter's behavior because the voter's political beliefs are very generalized.

R. A "teacher" in the Milgram study shocks the "learner" because the learner is out of sight, behind a wall.

S. A deadlocked jury votes to convict a defendant after one person who had previously thought the defendant not guilty changes his mind.

LANGUAGE AND CULTURE

the Big Apple (662)   *New York City*

bogus (655)   *phony, fake*

boorish (649)   *ill-mannered*

to "burst my bubble" (668)   *(here) to invade my personal space*

cad (649)   *an ill-mannered person*

to be caught in the middle (649)   *to be between two opposing forces and understand aspects of both sides*

condescending (653)   *superior, scornful*

cynical (649)   *hostile, unsociable*

to extricate oneself from (655)   *to escape difficult circumstances*

to fade away (665)   *to die slowly*

to flounder (659)   *to be awkward, to struggle*

foot-in-the-door technique (642)   *way to get someone's attention and hold it*

genocide (645)   *killing of a whole race of people*

gunk (665)   *mixture of oil, sand, and water that sticks onto animal coats*

to hang loose (652)   *to be easygoing*

heat stroke (666)   *sun sickness*

horror (665)   *bad aspects*

hot under the collar (637, 666)   *angry*

in the wrong (651)   *at fault*

to let George do it (663)   *to sit back and allow another to take the responsibility*

to look someone squarely in the eye (653)   *to appear to be completely honest with someone*

to lose our thread (659)   *to lose concentration*

to make up for (649)   *to compensate for*

media blitz (641)   *heavy television or radio advertising*

morally reprehensible (655)   *blameworthy, of low standards*

mortality rate (667)   *rate of people dying*

Muzak (666)   *canned, prerecorded music; nondescript music, played in elevators and stores*

nudist colony (654)   *fenced place where people do not wear clothing*

to be packed sardinelike (669)   *to be as crowded as a group of fish in a can*

to perpetuate (663)   *to help something continue*

to pick up (speed) (668)   *to increase in pace*

to be prone (669)   *(here) to be likely*

to put the arm on someone (653)   *to touch, to manipulate, to attempt to control*

rigid (652)   *not flexible*

to be riveted (657)   *to be totally focused (as if nailed to it)*

to snooze (668)   *to nap*

straight-backed (652)   *high in morals*

to stand above the crowd (638)   *to be unusual in some quality or trait, (here, a pun) to be unusual in height*

to stick to your guns (645)   *to hold firm on an opinion*

take others to task (637)   *to criticize others*

tangled web of deception (639)   *confusion of lies*

uptight (652)   *ill at ease, nervous*

to watch submarine races (649)   *(a euphemism for engaging in illicit sexual activity for one cannot see submarines racing underwater)*

willful (650)   *intentional, purposeful*

1. Which of the following most nearly expresses the relationship between attitudes and behaviors?
   (a) People always behave in ways that are consistent with their attitudes,
   (b) People always change their attitudes so that they are consistent with their behavior,
   (c) There is no relationship between attitudes and behaviors,
   (d) People are likely to act in accord with strong, specific attitudes.

2. Which of the following is a central cue for persuading people to drink Coke or Pepsi?
   (a) Providing information about the taste of the drink,
   (b) Having a rock star deliver a television commercial,
   (c) Showing attractive, slender people drinking the soda,
   (d) Using a person with a fine voice to sell the product.

3. People tend to be easy to persuade when they
   (a) have high self-esteem,
   (b) focus on the needs and feelings of the persuader,
   (c) have low social anxiety,
   (d) focus on their own needs and feelings.

4. One teacher of religion believes that children are more likely to adhere to their own religion's beliefs when they are also taught opposing beliefs. Another teacher of religion believes that it is dangerous to teach children opposing beliefs. Research concerning persuasion shows that two-sided arguments have the advantage of
   (a) offering peripheral cues for persuasion,
   (b) conditioning the audience,
   (c) appealing to the intellect only, not the emotions,
   (d) showing the audience how to refute the opposition's arguments.

5. When people who do not want to bother to recycle are compelled by the law to do so, they may eventually change their attitudes toward recycling because of
   (a) cognitive dissonance,
   (b) evaluation apprehension,
   (c) diffusion of responsibility,
   (d) deindividuation.

6. When Milgram moved the site of his research on obedience from Yale University to a storefront in a nearby city,

   (a) no one complied with the demands of the authority figure,
   (b) fewer people complied with the demands of the authority figure,
   (c) more people complied with the demands of the authority figure,
   (d) the results were about the same.

7. Which of the following sources of prejudice is reflected in the statement that "It is easier to attend to, and remember, instances of behavior that are consistent with our prejudices than it is to reconstruct our mental categories"?
   (a) Assumptions of dissimilarity,
   (b) Social conflict,
   (c) Authoritarianism,
   (d) Information processing.

8. One form of behavior that results from prejudice is called
   (a) social facilitation,
   (b) deindividuation,
   (c) attitude-discrepant behavior,
   (d) discrimination.

9. Which of the following statements reflects a clear dispositional attribution?
   (a) "Something got the best of him,"
   (b) "He did what he thought was right,"
   (c) "He did it that way because of the weather,"
   (d) "He could not refuse the money."

10. Attributing too much of other people's behavior to dispositional factors is called
    (a) the fundamental attribution error,
    (b) the actor-observer effect,
    (c) internalization,
    (d) evaluation apprehension.

11. Research shows that loud noises are likely to do all of the following, except for
    (a) decreasing feelings of attraction,
    (b) decreasing aggressiveness,
    (c) decreasing helping behavior,
    (d) impairing learning and memory.

12. People are not as likely to be as disturbed by high density at a concert as they are in a commuter train because
    (a) people tend to smell better at the concert,
    (b) they choose to attend the concert,
    (c) the music at the concert is at very loud levels,
    (d) the crowd tends to be yelling and screaming.

13. Important experiments on obedience to authority were carried out by
    (a) Stanley Milgram,
    (b) Solomon Asch,
    (c) Abraham Luchins,
    (d) John Dollard.

14. Mob behavior appears to be characterized by all of the following, with the exception of
    (a) reduced self-awareness,
    (b) focusing of individual attention on the group process,
    (c) arousal due to noise and crowding,
    (d) heightened concern for social evaluation.

15. Conformity is defined as
    (a) obedience to authority,
    (b) deindividuation,
    (c) behavior in accordance with social norms,
    (d) diffusion of responsibility.

16. When we are members of a group, we are most likely to engage in social loafing when
    (a) we experience evaluation apprehension,
    (b) our level of arousal increases,
    (c) we are anonymous,
    (d) the leader is an authority figure.

17. When juries are deadlocked, the members may eventually arrive at a verdict by means of the
    (a) two-thirds rule,
    (b) majority-wins scheme,
    (c) first-shift rule,
    (d) truth-wins scheme.

18. Luchins had subjects read different stories about "Jim" in order to study
    (a) cognitive dissonance,
    (b) the primacy effect,
    (c) diffusion of responsibility,
    (d) factors that contribute to attraction.

19. All of the following appear to lead to deindividuation, with the exception of
    (a) a low level of arousal,
    (b) anonymity,
    (c) diffusion of responsibility,
    (d) focusing of individual attention on the group process.

20. The case of Kitty Genovese illustrates
    (a) cognitive-dissonance theory,
    (b) group decision making,
    (c) the bystander effect,
    (d) the principle of social loafing.

Recite Recite Recite Recite **Recite**

1. What is social psychology? _____
_____
_____
_____
_____

2. What are attitudes? _____
_____
_____
_____
_____

3. Do people do as they think? (For example, do people really vote their consciences?) _____
_____
_____
_____

4. Where do attitudes come from? _____
_____
_____
_____
_____

5. Can you really change people?—their attitudes and behavior, that is? _____
_____
_____
_____

6. What is prejudice? Why are people prejudiced? _____
_____
_____
_____

7. Do first impressions really matter? What are the primacy and recency effects? _____
_____
_____

8. What is attribution theory? Why do we assume that other people intend the mischief that they do? _____
_____
_____
_____

9. What is body language? _____
_____
_____
_____

10. Why will so many people commit crimes against humanity if they are ordered to do so? (Why don't they just say no?) _____
_____
_____
_____

11. Why do so many people tend to follow the crowd?

_____
_____
_____
_____
_____
_____

12. Do we run faster when we are in a group?

_____
_____
_____
_____
_____

13. How do groups make decisions?

_____
_____
_____
_____
_____

14. Are group decisions more risky or more conservative than those of the individual members of the group? Why?

_____
_____
_____
_____
_____

15. What is groupthink?

_____
_____
_____
_____
_____

16. Do mobs bring out the beast in us? How is it that mild-mannered people commit mayhem when they are part of a mob?

_____
_____
_____
_____

17. Why do people sometimes sacrifice themselves for others and, at other times, ignore people who are in trouble?

_____
_____
_____
_____

18. What is environmental psychology?

_____
_____
_____
_____
_____

19. Can bottle laws and other recycling laws change people's attitudes?

_____
_____
_____
_____

20. What are the effects of noise on behavior and mental processes?

_____
_____
_____
_____

21. What are the effects of extremes in temperature on our bodies and on our behavior and mental processes?

_____
_____
_____
_____

22. What are the effects of air pollution on behavior and mental processes?

_____
_____
_____
_____
_____

23. When are we too close for comfort? What are the effects of crowding on behavior and mental processes?

_____
_____
_____
_____
_____

ANSWERS TO SECTION REVIEWS

1. Mental
2. Social
3. Cognitive
4. Disfavor
5. Is
6. A-B
7. Specific
8. Strong
9. Cognitive
10. Associating (or Pairing, etc.)
11. Reward or Reinforce
12. Anchors
13. Deviate
14. Elaboration
15. Peripheral
16. Central
17. Peripheral
18. Better
19. Two-sided
20. Emotional
21. Run counter to
22. Expertise
23. Similarity
24. Exposure
25. Low
26. High
27. To be
28. Foot
29. Attitude
30. Discrimination

31. Stereotype
32. Dissimilarity
33. Dissimilar
34. Economic
35. Categorization
36. Perception
37. Primacy
38. Luchins
39. Recency
40. Attribution
41. Internal
42. External
43. Process
44. Fundamental
45. Actor-observer
46. Dispositional
47. Situational
48. Self-serving
49. Positively
50. More
51. Hard
52. Do
53. Milgram
54. Social
55. Authority
56. Door
57. Inaccessibility
58. Buffers
59. 75
60. Collectivist
61. Low

62. Eight
63. One
64. Facilitation
65. Arousal
66. Evaluation apprehension
67. Anonymous
68. Loafing
69. Social-decision
70. Majority
71. Truth
72. Two-thirds
73. First-shift
74. More
75. Risky
76. Polarization
77. Deindividuation
78. Evaluation
79. Diffusion
80. Arousal
81. Unrealistic
82. External
83. Cohesiveness
84. Tend not
85. Vulnerability
86. Information
87. Out-group
88. Altruism
89. Good
90. Bystander
91. Genovese

92. Responsibility
93. Empathic
94. Good
95. Know
96. Similar
97. Physical
98. Pro-
99. More
100. Cognitive
101. Positive
102. Decrease
103. Decrease
104. Increase
105. Circulatory
106. Aversive
107. Facilitate
108. Increase
109. Impairs
110. Increases
111. Lead
112. Monoxide
113. Higher
114. Decrease
115. Increase
116. Density
117. Crowding
118. Interpretation
119. Control
120. Overload
121. Personal
122. Closer to

ANSWERS TO EXERCISE 1

1. Low
2. High
3. High
4. Low
5. Low
6. High

ANSWERS TO EXERCISE 2

1. Socialization
2. Comparison
3. Legitimate
4. Foot
5. Inaccessibility
6. Buffers

ANSWERS TO EXERCISE 3

1. K
2. F
3. N
4. L
5. G, I
6. A, H
7. M
8. C
9. E, H
10. D
11. J
12. B
13. E
14. G, P
15. F
16. A, H
17. S
18. R
19. P
20. Q
21. O

ANSWERS TO QUIZ

1. D
2. A
3. B
4. D
5. A
6. B
7. D
8. D
9. B
10. A
11. B
12. B
13. A
14. D
15. C
16. C
17. C
18. B
19. A
20. C

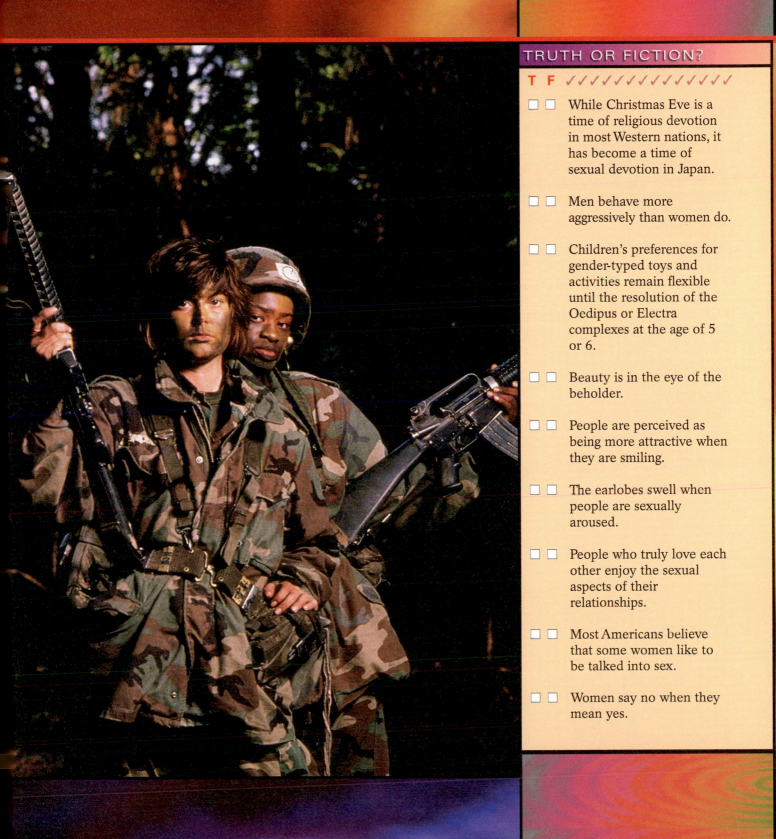

☐ ☐ While Christmas Eve is a time of religious devotion in most Western nations, it has become a time of sexual devotion in Japan.

☐ ☐ Men behave more aggressively than women do.

☐ ☐ Children's preferences for gender-typed toys and activities remain flexible until the resolution of the Oedipus or Electra complexes at the age of 5 or 6.

☐ ☐ Beauty is in the eye of the beholder.

☐ ☐ People are perceived as being more attractive when they are smiling.

☐ ☐ The earlobes swell when people are sexually aroused.

☐ ☐ People who truly love each other enjoy the sexual aspects of their relationships.

☐ ☐ Most Americans believe that some women like to be talked into sex.

☐ ☐ Women say no when they mean yes.

This chapter, "Gender and Sexuality," covers the following:

SECTION I. GENDER POLARIZATION: GENDER STEREOTYPES AND THEIR COSTS

Defines gender roles and stereotypes
Discusses the costs of gender polarization

SECTION II. PSYCHOLOGICAL GENDER DIFFERENCES: VIVE LA DIFFÉRENCE OR VIVE LA SIMILARITÉ?

Discusses gender differences in cognitive abilities
Discusses gender differences in social behavior

SECTION III. GENDER-TYPING: ON BECOMING A WOMAN OR A MAN

Discusses biological influences on gender-typing
Discusses psychological influences on gender-typing

SECTION IV. ATTRACTION: ON LIKING, LOVING, AND RELATIONSHIPS

Describes the factors that contribute to attraction
Takes the bold initiative of defining romantic love!
Defines sexual orientation
Discusses research concerning the origins of sexual orientation

SECTION V. SEXUAL RESPONSE

Describes the sexual response cycle
Describes the various types of sexual dysfunctions
Discusses the origins of sexual dysfunctions
Describes what can be done about sexual dysfunctions

SECTION VI. SEXUAL COERCION

Discusses rape—what it is and why men rape women
Describes ways of preventing rape
Discusses sexual harassment
Describes ways of preventing sexual harassment

Off the misty coast of Ireland lies the small island of Inis Beag. From the air it is a green jewel, warm and inviting. At ground level, life is somewhat different.

For example, the residents of Inis Beag do not believe that women experience orgasm. The woman who chances to find pleasure in sex is considered deviant. Premarital sex is all but unknown. Women engage in sexual relations to conceive children and to appease their husbands' carnal cravings. They need not worry about being called on for frequent performances, however, because the men of Inis Beag believe, erroneously, that sex saps their strength. Sex on Inis Beag is carried out in the dark—both literally and figuratively—and with nightclothes on. The man lies on top in the so-called missionary position. In accordance with local concepts of masculinity, he ejaculates as fast as he can. Then he rolls over and falls asleep.

If Inis Beag does not sound like your cup of tea, you may find the atmosphere of Mangaia more congenial. Mangaia is a Polynesian pearl of an island, lifting languidly from the blue waters of the Pacific. It is on the other side of the world from Inis Beag—in more ways than one.

From an early age, Mangaian children are encouraged to get in touch with their sexuality through masturbation. Mangaian adolescents are expected to engage in sexual intercourse. They may be found on secluded beaches or beneath the swaying fronds of palms, diligently practicing techniques learned from village elders.

Mangaian women are expected to reach orgasm several times before their partners do. Young men want their partners to reach orgasm, and they compete to see who is more effective at bringing young women to multiple orgasms.

REFLECT

In which society would you rather live? Inis Beag or Mangaia? In which society would you rather rear your children? Explain.

On the island of Inis Beag, a woman who has an orgasm is considered deviant. On Mangaia, multiple orgasms are the norm (Rathus et al., 2000). If we take a quick tour of the world of sexual diversity, we also find the following:

- Nearly every society has an incest taboo, but some societies believe that a brother and sister who eat at the same table are engaging in a mildly sexual act. The practice is therefore forbidden.

- What is considered sexually arousing varies enormously among different cultures. Women's breasts and armpits stimulate a sexual response in some cultures, but not in others.

- Kissing is a nearly universal form of petting in the United States but is unpopular in Japan and unknown among some cultures in Africa and South America. Upon seeing European visitors kissing, a member of an African tribe remarked, "Look at them—they eat each other's saliva and dirt."

- Sexual exclusiveness in marriage is valued highly in most parts of the United States, but among the people of Alaska's Aleutian Islands it is considered good manners for a man to offer his wife to a house guest.

- The United States has its romantic Valentine's Day, but Japan has eroticized another day—Christmas Eve. (You read that right: Christmas Eve.) Christmas Eve may be a time of religious devotion in many Western nations, but it has become a time of sexual devotion in Japan. On Christmas Eve every single person must have a date that includes an overnight visit (Reid, 1990). During the weeks prior to Christmas, the media brim with reports on hotels for overnight stays, proper attire, and breakfast ideas for the morning after. Where do Tokyo singles like to go before their overnighter? Tokyo Disneyland.

✓ Truth or Fiction Revisited

It is true that Christmas Eve has become a time of sexual devotion in Japan, although it is a time of religious devotion in most Western nations. There is a good deal of social pressure on single people to have a date that includes an overnight stay.

The residents of Inis Beag and Mangaia have similar anatomical features but vastly different attitudes toward sex. Their sociocultural settings influence their patterns of sexual behavior and the pleasure they gain—or do not gain—from sex. Sex may be a natural function, but few natural functions have been influenced so strongly by religious and moral beliefs, cultural tradition, folklore, and superstition.

This chapter is about gender and sexuality. We begin by exploring gender polarization—the behaviors that make up the stereotypes of "masculinity" and "femininity." We then examine *actual* psychological differences between males and females and consider the development of these differences. Next we turn our attention to sexual orientation; we ask why some people are attracted to people of their own gender, whereas most are attracted to people of the other gender. We describe sexual anatomy and sexual response, and we see that women and men are probably more alike in their sexual response than you may have thought. Then we consider sexual dysfunctions and their treatment. Finally, we turn to the dark side of gender and sexuality: issues in sexual coercion, including rape and sexual harassment.

SECTION I. GENDER POLARIZATION: GENDER STEREOTYPES AND THEIR COSTS

"Why Can't a Woman Be More Like a Man?" You may recognize this song title from the musical *My Fair Lady*. In the song, Henry Higgins laments that women are emotional and fickle, whereas men are logical and dependable.

The excitable woman is a **stereotype.** Question: What is a gender-role stereotype? Stereotypes are fixed, conventional ideas about a group of people that can give rise to prejudice and discrimination. A gender stereotype is a fixed, conventional idea about how men and women ought to behave. The logical man is a **gender**-role stereotype. Higgins's stereotypes reflect cultural beliefs. Cultural beliefs about men and women involve clusters of stereotypes called **gender roles.** Gender-role stereotypes define the ways in which men and women are expected to behave within a given culture.

Sandra Lipsitz Bem (1993) writes that three beliefs about women and men have prevailed throughout the history of Western culture:

1. Women and men have basically different psychological and sexual natures.

2. Men are the superior, dominant gender.

3. Gender differences and male superiority are "natural."

These beliefs have tended to polarize our views of women and men. It is thought that gender differences in power and psychological traits are natural, but what does "natural" mean? Throughout most of history, people viewed naturalness in terms of religion, or God's scheme of things (Bem, 1993). For the past century or so, naturalness has been seen in biological, evolutionary terms—at least by most scientists. But these views ignore cultural influences.

What are perceived as the so-called natural gender roles? In our society, people tend to see the feminine gender role as warm, emotional, dependent, gentle, helpful, mild, patient, submissive, and interested in the arts (Bem, 1993). The typical masculine gender role is perceived as independent, competitive, tough, protective, logical, and competent at business, math, and science. Women are typically expected to care for the kids and cook the meals. Cross-cultural studies confirm that these gender-role stereotypes are widespread (see Table 15.1). For example, in their survey of 30 countries, John Williams and Deborah Best (1994) found that men are more likely to be judged as active, adventurous, aggressive, arrogant, and autocratic (and we have only gotten through the *a*'s). Women are more likely seen as fearful, fickle, foolish, frivolous, and fussy (and these are only a handful of the *f*'s).

Costs of Gender Polarization

Gender polarization is more than tradition, more than a cultural artifact. It can be extremely costly for both genders in terms of education, activities, careers, psychological well-being, and interpersonal relationships. Question: What are the costs of gender polarization?

EDUCATION   Polarization has historically worked to the disadvantage of women. In past centuries, girls were considered unable to learn. Even the great Swiss-French philosopher Jean Jacques Rousseau, who was in the

---

REFLECT

Do you think of males and females as being the "opposite" of one another? If so, in what ways? Why?

REFLECT

Do you see the traditional masculine and feminine gender roles as being "natural"? Explain.

STEREOTYPE A fixed, conventional idea about a group.

GENDER The state of being male or female.

GENDER ROLE A cluster of behaviors that characterizes traditional female or male behaviors within a cultural setting.

TABLE 15.1	GENDER-ROLE STEREOTYPES AROUND THE WORLD		
STEREOTYPES OF MALES		**STEREOTYPES OF FEMALES**	
Active	Opinionated	Affectionate	Nervous
Adventurous	Pleasure-	Appreciative	Patient
Aggressive	seeking	Cautious	Pleasant
Arrogant	Precise	Changeable	Prudish
Autocratic	Quick	Charming	Self-pitying
Capable	Rational	Complaining	Sensitive
Coarse	Realistic	Complicated	Sentimental
Conceited	Reckless	Confused	Sexy
Confident	Resourceful	Dependent	Shy
Courageous	Rigid	Dreamy	Softhearted
Cruel	Robust	Emotional	Sophisticated
Determined	Sharp-witted	Excitable	Submissive
Disorderly	Showoff	Fault-finding	Suggestible
Enterprising	Steady	Fearful	Superstitious
Hardheaded	Stern	Fickle	Talkative
Individualistic	Stingy	Foolish	Timid
Inventive	Stolid	Forgiving	Touchy
Loud	Tough	Frivolous	Unambitious
Obnoxious	Unscrupulous	Fussy	Understanding
		Gentle	Unstable
		Imaginative	Warm
		Kind	Weak
		Mild	Worrying
		Modest	

SOURCE OF DATA: Williams & Best, 1994, p. 193, Table 1.

Psychologists John Williams and Deborah Best (1994) found that people in 30 nations around the world tended to agree on the nature of masculine and feminine gender-role stereotypes. Men are largely seen as more adventurous and hardheaded than women. Women are generally seen as more emotional and dependent.

forefront of a movement toward a more open approach to education, believed that girls are basically irrational and naturally disposed to child rearing and homemaking—certainly not to commerce, science, and industry, pursuits for which education is required.

Intelligence tests show that boys and girls are about equal in overall learning ability. Nevertheless, girls are expected to excel in language arts, and boys in math and science. Such expectations dissuade girls from taking advanced courses in the so-called male domain. Boys take more math courses in high school than girls do (American Association of University Women, 1992). Math courses open doors for them in fields such as natural science, engineering, and economics. There are several reasons why boys are more likely than girls to feel at home with math:

1. Fathers are more likely than mothers to help children with math homework.

2. Advanced math courses are more likely to be taught by men.

3. Teachers often show higher expectations for boys in math courses.

4. Math teachers spend more time working with boys than with girls.

Given these experiences, we should not be surprised that by junior high, boys view themselves as more competent in math than girls do, even when they receive the same grades. Boys are more likely to have positive feelings about math. Girls are more likely to have math anxiety. Even girls

REFLECT

Are you good in math and science? Do you see math and science as being part of the so-called "male domain"? Explain.

who excel in math and science are less likely than boys to choose courses or careers in these fields (American Association of University Women, 1992).

If women are to find their places in professions related to math, science, and engineering, we may need to provide more female role models in these professions. Such models will help shatter the stereotype that these are men's fields. We also need to encourage girls to take more courses in math and science.

REFLECT

Gloria Steinem wrote, "I have yet to hear a man ask for advice on how to combine marriage and a career." Have you ever heard a man express such a concern? Why are women more likely to have this concern?

REFLECT

Have you experienced any inequalities for men and women in school or in the workplace? What did you experience? What did you do about it?

A Female Architectural Engineer. Women remain underrepresented in many kinds of careers. Although women have made marked gains in medicine and law, their numbers remain relatively low in math and engineering. Why?

CAREERS Gender polarization in the United States is linked to the traditional view of men as breadwinners and women as homemakers (Eagly & Steffen, 1984).

As one consequence, women are less likely than men to enter higher-paying careers in math, science, and engineering. They account for perhaps 1 in 6 of the nation's scientists and engineers. Although women are awarded more than half of the bachelor's degrees in the United States, they receive fewer than one third of the degrees in science and engineering. Why? It is partly because math, science, and engineering are perceived as inconsistent with the feminine gender role. Many little girls are dissuaded from thinking about professions such as engineering and architecture because they are given dolls, rather than trucks and blocks. Many boys are likewise deterred from entering child-care and nursing professions because others scorn them when they play with dolls.

There are other inequalities in the workplace that are based on gender polarization. For example, women's wages average only about 72% of men's (Bianchi & Spain, 1997). Women physicians and college professors earn less than men in the same positions (Honan, 1996; "Study Finds," 1996). Women are less likely than men to be promoted into high-level managerial positions (Valian, 1998). Once in managerial positions, women often feel pressured to be "tougher" than men in order to seem just as tough. They feel pressured to be careful about their appearance because co-workers pay more attention to what they wear, how they style their hair, and so forth. If they don't look crisp and tailored every day, others may think they are not in command. But if they dress up too much, they may be denounced as fashion plates rather than serious workers! Female managers who are deliberate and take time making decisions may be seen as weak. What happens when female managers change their minds? They run the risk of being labeled fickle and indecisive rather than flexible.

Women in the workplace are also often expected to make the coffee or clean up after the conference lunch, along with the jobs they were hired to do. Women who work also usually have the responsibility of being the major caretaker for children in the home (Bianchi & Spain, 1997). Yet in the 1990s women's wages averaged 72% of men's, compared with 59% in 1970 (Bianchi & Spain, 1997). Wives share about equally with their husbands in supporting their families (Lewin, 1995).

PSYCHOLOGICAL WELL-BEING AND RELATIONSHIPS Gender polarization also interferes with psychological well-being and relationships. Women who adhere to the traditional feminine gender role are likely to believe that women, like children, should be seen and not heard. They therefore are unlikely to assert themselves to make their needs and wants known. They are likely to feel frustrated as a result.

Men who accept the traditional masculine gender role are less likely to feel comfortable performing the activities involved in caring for children, such as bathing them, dressing them, and feeding them (Bem, 1993). Such men are less likely to ask for help—including medical help—when they need it ("Doctors Tie," 1995). They are also less likely to be sympathetic and tender or express feelings of love in their marital relationships (Coleman & Ganong, 1985).

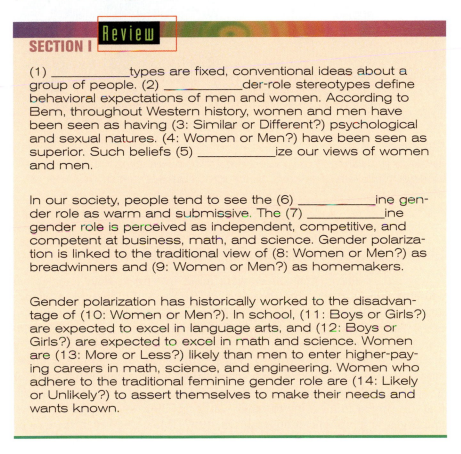

Review

SECTION I

(1) _____ types are fixed, conventional ideas about a group of people. (2) _____ der-role stereotypes define behavioral expectations of men and women. According to Bem, throughout Western history, women and men have been seen as having (3: Similar or Different?) psychological and sexual natures. (4: Women or Men?) have been seen as superior. Such beliefs (5) _____ ize our views of women and men.

In our society, people tend to see the (6) _____ ine gender role as warm and submissive. The (7) _____ ine gender role is perceived as independent, competitive, and competent at business, math, and science. Gender polarization is linked to the traditional view of (8: Women or Men?) as breadwinners and (9: Women or Men?) as homemakers.

Gender polarization has historically worked to the disadvantage of (10: Women or Men?). In school, (11: Boys or Girls?) are expected to excel in language arts, and (12: Boys or Girls?) are expected to excel in math and science. Women are (13: More or Less?) likely than men to enter higher-paying careers in math, science, and engineering. Women who adhere to the traditional feminine gender role are (14: Likely or Unlikely?) to assert themselves to make their needs and wants known.

SECTION II. PSYCHOLOGICAL GENDER DIFFERENCES: VIVE LA DIFFÉRENCE OR VIVE LA SIMILARITÉ?

The French have an expression "Vive la différence," which means "Long live the difference" (between men and women). Yet modern life has challenged our concepts of what it means to be a woman or a man. The obvious anatomical differences between women and men are connected with the biological aspects of reproduction. Biologists therefore have a relatively easy time describing and interpreting the gender differences they study. The task of psychology is more complex and wrapped up with sociocultural and political issues (Eagly, 1995; Marecek, 1995). Psychological gender differences are not as obvious as biological gender differences. In fact, in many ways women and men are more similar than different.

To put it another way: To reproduce, women and men have to be biologically different. Throughout history, it has also been assumed that women and men must be psychologically different in order to fulfill different roles in the family and society (Bem, 1993). But what are the psychological differences between women and men? Let us begin by asking: Question: What are the gender differences in cognitive abilities?

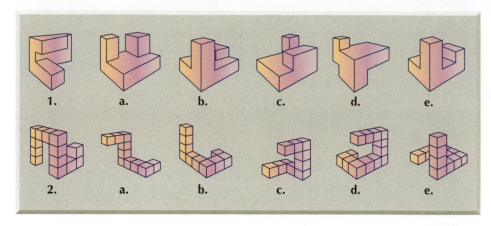

FIGURE 15.1

ROTATING FIGURES IN SPACE   MALES AS A GROUP OUTPERFORM FEMALES ON SPATIAL RELATIONS TASKS, SUCH AS ROTATING FIGURES IN SPACE AND PICTURING THE RESULTS. HOWEVER, FEMALES DO AS WELL AS MALES WHEN THEY RECEIVE TRAINING IN THE TASK.

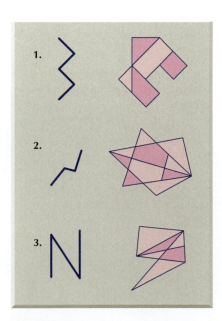

FIGURE 15.2

ITEMS FROM AN EMBEDDED-FIGURES TEST

Gender Differences in Cognitive Abilities

It was once believed that males were more intelligent than females because of their greater knowledge of world affairs and their skill in science and industry. We now know that greater male knowledge and skill did not reflect differences in intelligence. Rather, it reflected the systematic exclusion of females from world affairs, science, and industry. Assessments of intelligence do not show overall gender differences in cognitive abilities. However, reviews of the research suggest that girls are somewhat superior to boys in verbal abilities, such as verbal fluency, ability to generate words that are similar in meaning to other words, spelling, knowledge of foreign languages, and pronunciation (Halpern, 1997). Males, however, seem to be somewhat superior in visual-spatial abilities. Differences in mathematical ability are more complex (Neisser et al., 1996).

Girls seem to acquire language somewhat faster than boys do (Hyde & Linn, 1988). Also, in the United States far more boys than girls have reading problems, ranging from reading below grade level to severe disabilities (Halpern, 1997; Neisser et al., 1996). But the males headed for college seem to catch up in verbal skills.

Males apparently excel in visual-spatial abilities of the sort used in math, science, and even reading a map (Voyer et al., 1995). Tests of spatial ability assess skills such as mentally rotating figures in space (see Figure 15.1) and finding figures embedded within larger designs (see Figure 15.2).

In math, differences at all ages are small and seem to be narrowing (Hyde et al., 1990). Females excel in computational ability in elementary school, however. Males excel in mathematical problem solving in high school and college (Hyde et al., 1990). Boys outperform girls on the math part of the Scholastic Aptitude Test (Byrnes & Takahira, 1993). According to Byrnes and Takahira (1993), boys' superiority in math does not reflect gender per se. Instead, boys do as well as they do because of greater experience in solving math problems.

In any event, psychologists note three factors that should caution us not to attach too much importance to apparent gender differences in cognition:

1. In most cases, gender differences are small (Hyde & Plant, 1995). Differences in verbal, math, and spatial abilities are also narrowing (Hyde et al., 1990; Voyer et al., 1995).

2. These gender differences are *group* differences. There is greater variation in these skills between individuals *within* the groups than between males and females (Maccoby, 1990). That is, there may be a greater difference in, say, verbal skills between two women than between a woman and a man. Millions of females outdistance the "average" male in math and spatial abilities. Men have produced their Shakespeares. Women have produced their Madame Curies.

3. Some differences may largely reflect sociocultural influences. In our culture, spatial and math abilities are stereotyped as masculine. Women who are given just a few hours of training in spatial skills—for example, rotating geometric figures or studying floor plans—perform at least as well as men on tests of these skills (Azar, 1997).

Gender Differences in Social Behavior

There are many other psychological differences between males and females. For example, women exceed men in extraversion, anxiety, trust, and nurturance (Feingold, 1994). Men exceed women in assertiveness and tough-mindedness. Question: What are the gender differences in social behavior? In the arena of social behavior, women seem more likely than men to cooperate with other people and to hold groups, such as families, together (Bjorklund & Kipp, 1996).

Despite the stereotype of women as gossips and chatterboxes, research in communication styles suggests that in many situations men spend more time talking than women do. Men are more likely to introduce new topics and to interrupt (Hall, 1984). Women, in contrast, seem more willing to reveal their feelings and personal experiences (Dindia & Allen, 1992).

Women interact at closer distances than men do. They also seek to keep more space between themselves and strangers of the other gender than men do (Rüstemli, 1986). Men are made more uncomfortable by strangers who sit across from them, whereas women are more likely to feel "invaded" by strangers who sit next to them. In libraries, men tend to pile books protectively in front of them. Women place books and coats in adjacent seats to discourage others from taking them.

There are also gender differences in three major areas of social behavior (Archer, 1996): sex and relationships, mate selection, and aggression. Men are more interested than women in casual sex and in having more than one sex partner (Leitenberg & Henning, 1995). In our society there are constraints on unbridled sexual behavior, so most men are not promiscuous (Archer, 1996). Women are more likely to want to combine sex with a romantic relationship.

Susan Sprecher and her colleagues (1994) surveyed more than 13,000 people in the United States. They asked how willing a person would be to marry someone who was older, younger, of a different religion, unlikely to hold a steady job, not good-looking, and so on. Each item was answered by checking off a 7-point scale in which 1 meant "not at all" and 7 meant "very willing." Women were more willing than men to marry someone who was not good-looking (see Figure 15.3). But they were less willing to marry someone who was unlikely to hold a steady job.

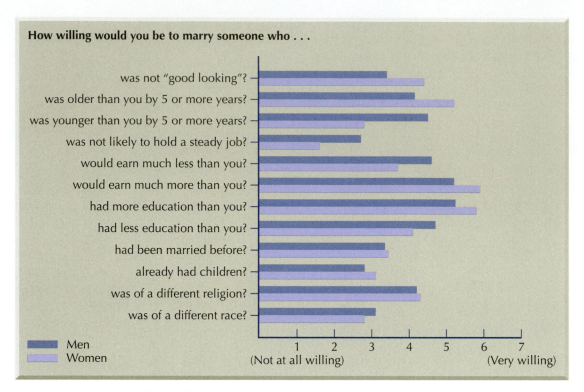

FIGURE 15.3
GENDER DIFFERENCES IN MATE PREFERENCES   SUSAN SPRECHER AND HER COLLEAGUES FOUND THAT MEN ARE MORE WILL-ING THAN WOMEN TO MARRY SOMEONE WHO IS SEVERAL YEARS YOUNGER AND LESS WELL-EDUCATED. WOMEN ARE MORE WILLING THAN MEN TO MARRY SOMEONE WHO IS NOT GOOD-LOOKING AND WHO EARNS MORE MONEY THAN THEY DO.

In most cultures, it is the males who battle for glory in war (and in sneaker commercials on TV). Psychological studies of aggression find that male children and adults behave more aggressively than females do (Archer, 1996).

✓ **Truth or Fiction Revisited**

It is true that men behave more aggressively than women do—at least in most cultures. The issue is whether this gender difference is inborn or reflects sociocultural factors.

In a classic review of 72 studies concerning gender differences in aggression, Ann Frodi and her colleagues (1977) found that females are more likely to act aggressively under some circumstances than others:

1. Females are more likely to feel anxious or guilty about aggression. Such feelings inhibit aggressive behavior.

2. Females behave as aggressively as males when they have the means to do so and believe that aggression is justified.

3. Females are more likely to empathize with the victim—to imagine themselves in the victim's place. Empathy encourages helping behavior, not aggression.

4. Gender differences in aggression decrease when the victim is anonymous. Anonymity may prevent females from empathizing with their victims.

Intelligence tests (15: Do or Do not?) show overall gender differences in cognitive abilities. (16: Girls or Boys?) are somewhat superior in verbal abilities. (17: Girls or Boys?) are somewhat superior in visual-spatial abilities. In math, gender differences at all ages are (18: Large or Small?). (19: Boys or Girls?) excel in computational ability in elementary school. (20: Boys or Girls?) excel in mathematical problem solving in high school and college.

(21: Women or Men?) tend to be more extraverted, anxious, trusting, and nurturant. (22: Women or Men?) tend to be more assertive and tough-minded. In conversations and in classrooms, (23: Women or Men?) are more likely to introduce new topics and to interrupt.

(24: Women or Men?) are more willing to reveal their feelings.

(25: Women or Men?) are more interested in casual sex and multiple sex partners. (26: Women or Men?) are more likely to want to engage in sexual activity within a romantic relationship. Women are (27: More or Less?) willing to marry someone who is not good-looking. Women are (28: More or Less?) willing to marry someone who is unlikely to hold a steady job. Women are (29: More or Less?) aggressive than men. Women are (30: More or Less?) likely to feel anxious or guilty about aggression. Women (31: Do or Do not?) behave as aggressively as males when they have the means to do so and believe that aggression is justified.

SECTION III. GENDER-TYPING: ON BECOMING A WOMAN OR A MAN

There are thus a number of psychological gender differences. They include minor differences in cognitive functioning and differences in personality and social behavior. The process by which these differences develop is termed **gender-typing.** In this section we explore several possible sources of gender-typing, both biological and psychological.

Biological Influences on Gender-Typing

Question: What are some biological views of gender-typing? According to evolutionary psychologists like David Buss (1999), gender differences were fashioned by natural selection in response to problems in adaptation that were repeatedly encountered by humans over thousands of generations. On a biological level, the psychological differences that have evolved between men and women may largely reflect differences in brain organization and sex hormones.

BRAIN ORGANIZATION A number of studies suggest that we can speak of "left brain" versus "right brain" functions (Springer & Deutsch, 1993). Some psychological activities, such as language, seem to be controlled largely by the left side of the brain. Other psychological activities, such as spatial relations and aesthetic and emotional responses, seem to be controlled largely by the right side. Brain-imaging research suggests that the brain hemispheres are more specialized in males than in females (Shaywitz et al., 1995). For example, men with damage to the left hemisphere are more likely to experience difficulties in verbal functioning than women with similar damage. Men with damage to the right hemisphere are more likely to have problems with spatial relations than women with similar injuries.

GENDER-TYPING The process by which people acquire a sense of being female or male and acquire the traits considered typical of females or males within a cultural setting.

REFLECT

Are there possible social problems connected with attributing gender differences in cognitive abilities to organization of the brain?

Gender differences in brain organization might, in part, explain why women exceed men in verbal skills that require some spatial organization, such as reading, spelling, and crisp articulation of speech. Men, however, might be superior at more specialized spatial-relations tasks such as interpreting road maps and visualizing objects in space.

SEX HORMONES Sex hormones are responsible for the prenatal differentiation of sex organs. Prenatal sex hormones may also "masculinize" or "feminize" the brain by creating predispositions consistent with some gender-role stereotypes (Collaer & Hines, 1995; Crews, 1994). Yet John Money (1987) argues that social learning plays a stronger role in the development of **gender identity,** personality traits, and preferences. Money (1987) claims that social learning is powerful enough to counteract many prenatal predispositions.

Some evidence for the possible role of hormonal influences has been obtained from animal studies (Collaer & Hines, 1995; Crews, 1994). For example, male rats are generally superior to females in maze-learning ability, a task that requires spatial skills. Female rats exposed to male sex hormones in the uterus (e.g., because they have several male siblings in the uterus with them) or soon after birth learn maze routes as rapidly as males, however. They also roam over larger distances and mark larger territories than most females do (Vandenbergh, 1993).

Men are more aggressive than women, and aggression in lower animals has been connected with the male sex hormone testosterone (Collaer & Hines, 1995). However, cognitive psychologists argue that boys (and girls) can choose whether or not to act aggressively, regardless of the levels of hormones in their bloodstreams.

Many aspects of human development, including gender-typing, appear to involve both nature and nurture. Biological factors, such as heredity, provide a "natural" explanation of psychological gender differences. Psychological influences would provide an explanation based on the different experiences of males and females. Question: What are some psychological views of gender-typing?

Psychological Influences on Gender-Typing

The two most prominent psychological perspectives on gender-typing today are social-cognitive theory and gender-schema theory. However, we begin with psychodynamic theory because of its historic interest.

PSYCHODYNAMIC THEORY Sigmund Freud explained the acquisition of gender roles in terms of *identification.* He believed that gender identity remains flexible until the Oedipus and Electra complexes are resolved at about the age of five or six. Appropriate gender-typing requires that boys identify with their fathers and give up the wish to possess their mothers. Girls have to give up the wish to have a penis and identify with their mothers.

Boys and girls develop stereotypical preferences for toys and activities much earlier than might be predicted by psychodynamic theory, however. Even within their first year, boys are more explorative and independent. Girls are relatively more quiet, dependent, and restrained (Etaugh & Rathus, 1995). By 18 to 36 months, girls are more likely to prefer soft toys and dolls and to dance. Boys of this age are more likely to prefer blocks and toy cars, trucks and airplanes.

GENDER IDENTITY One's psychological sense of being female or male.

Acquiring Gender Roles. How do people develop gender roles? What contributions are made by biological and psychological factors? Social-cognitive theory focuses on imitation of the behavior of adults of the same gender and reinforcement by parents and peers.

✓ Truth or Fiction Revisited

It is not true that children's preferences for gender-typed toys and activities remain flexible until the resolution of the Oedipus or Electra complexes at the age of 5 or 6. Children's preferences for gender-typed toys and activities become rather fixed by the age of 3.

SOCIAL-COGNITIVE THEORY Social-cognitive theorists explain gender-typing in terms of observational learning, identification, and socialization. Children learn much of what is considered masculine or feminine by observational learning, as suggested by a classic experiment conducted by David Perry and Kay Bussey (1979). In this study, children learned how behaviors are gender-typed by observing the *relative frequencies* with which men and women performed them. The adult role models expressed arbitrary preferences for one item from each of 16 pairs of items—pairs such as oranges versus apples and toy cows versus toy horses—while 8- and 9-year-old boys and girls watched them. The children were then asked to show their own preferences. Boys selected an average of 14 of 16 items that agreed with the "preferences" of the men. Girls selected an average of only 3 of 16 items that agreed with the choices of the men. In other words, boys and girls learned gender-typed preferences even though those preferences were completely arbitrary.

Social-cognitive theorists view **identification** as a continuous learning process in which children are influenced by rewards and punishments to imitate adults of the same gender—particularly the parent of the same gender. In identification, as opposed to imitation, children do not simply imitate a certain behavior pattern. They also try to become similar to the model.

Socialization also plays a role. Parents and other adults—even other children—inform children about how they are expected to behave. They reward children for behavior they consider appropriate for their gender. They punish (or fail to reinforce) children for behavior they consider inappropriate. Girls, for example, are given dolls while they are still sleeping in their cribs. They are encouraged to use the dolls to rehearse caretaking behaviors in preparation for traditional feminine adult roles.

Concerning gender and aggression, Maccoby and Jacklin (1974) note that aggression is more actively discouraged in girls through punishment, withdrawal of affection, or being told that "girls don't act that way." If

IDENTIFICATION The process of becoming broadly like another person.

SOCIALIZATION The guiding of behavior through instruction and rewards and punishments.

REFLECT

What are the implications of the Richardson study for understanding aggressive behavior in women?

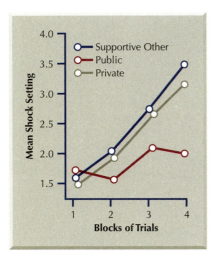

FIGURE 15.4
MEAN SHOCK SETTINGS SELECTED BY WOMEN IN RETALIATION AGAINST MALE OPPONENTS WOMEN IN THE RICHARDSON STUDY CHOSE HIGHER SHOCK LEVELS FOR THEIR OPPONENTS WHEN THEY WERE ALONE OR WHEN ANOTHER PERSON (A "SUPPORTIVE OTHER") URGED THEM ON.

GENDER-SCHEMA THEORY The view that gender identity plus knowledge of the distribution of behavior patterns into feminine and masculine roles motivate and guide the gender-typing of the child.

REFLECT

Is your self-esteem connected with how well you fit the masculine or feminine gender schema in our society? Explain.

girls retaliate when they are insulted or attacked, they usually experience social disapproval. They therefore learn to feel anxious about the possibility of acting aggressively. Boys, in contrast, are usually encouraged to strike back (Frodi et al., 1977).

Classic experiments point to the importance of social learning in female aggressiveness. In one study, for example, college women competed with men to see who could respond to a stimulus more quickly (Richardson et al., 1979). There were four blocks of trials, with six trials in each block. The subjects could not see their opponents. The loser of each trial received an electric shock whose intensity was set by the opponent. Women competed under one of three experimental conditions: public, private, or with a supportive other. In the public condition, another woman observed the subject silently. In the private condition, there was no observer. In the supportive-other condition, another woman urged the subject to retaliate strongly when her opponent selected high shock levels. As shown in Figure 15.4, women in the private and supportive-other conditions selected increasingly higher levels of shock in retaliation. Presumably, the women assumed that an observer, although silent, would frown on aggressive behavior. This assumption is likely to reflect the women's own early socialization experiences. Women who were not observed or who were urged on by another person apparently felt free to violate the gender norm of nonaggressiveness when their situations called for aggressive responses.

Social-cognitive theory outlines ways in which rewards, punishments, and modeling foster "gender-appropriate" behavior. Gender-schema theory suggests that we tend to assume gender-appropriate behavior patterns by blending our self-concept with cultural expectations.

GENDER-SCHEMA THEORY You have probably heard the expression, "looking at the world through rose-colored glasses." According to Sandra Bem (1993), the originator of **gender-schema theory**, people look at the social world through "the lenses of gender." Bem argues that our culture polarizes females and males by organizing social life around mutually exclusive gender roles. Children come to accept the polarizing scripts without realizing it. Unless parents or unusual events encourage them to challenge the validity of gender polarization, children attempt to construct identities that are consistent with the "proper" script. Most children reject behavior—in others and in themselves—that deviates from it. Children's self-esteem soon becomes wrapped up in the ways in which they measure up to the gender schema. For example, boys soon learn to hold a high opinion of themselves if they excel in sports.

Once children understand the labels *boy* and *girl,* they have a basis for blending their self-concepts with the gender schema of their culture. No external pressure is required. Children who have developed a sense of being male or being female, which usually occurs by the age of 3, actively seek information about their gender schema. As in social-cognitive theory, children seek to learn through observation what is considered appropriate for them.

Powerful evidence indicates that the polarized female-male scripts influence cognitive activity (Bowes & Goodnow, 1996). Researchers in one study showed 5- and 6-year-old boys and girls pictures of actors engaged in "gender-consistent" or "gender-inconsistent" activities. The gender-consistent pictures showed boys playing with trains or sawing wood. Girls were shown cooking and cleaning. Gender-inconsistent pictures showed actors of the other gender engaged in these gender-typed activities. Each child was shown a randomized set of pictures that included only one picture of each activity. One week later, the children were asked who had engaged in the activity, a male or a female. Both boys and girls gave wrong answers more often when the picture they had seen showed gender-*inconsistent* activity. In other words, they distorted what they had seen to conform to the gender schema.

In sum, brain organization and sex hormones may contribute to gender-typed behavior and play a role in verbal ability, math skills, and aggression. Yet the effects of social learning may counteract biological influences. Social-cognitive theory outlines the environmental factors that influence children to engage in so-called gender-appropriate behavior. Gender-schema theory focuses on how children blend their self-identities with the gender schema of their culture.

Review

SECTION III

Gender differences develop by the process called (32) _____-_____ing. According to evolutionary psychologists, gender differences were fashioned by means of (33) _____ selection. Research in brain-imaging suggests that the brain hemispheres are more specialized in (34: Males or Females?). Gender differences in brain organization might partially explain why (35: Males or Females?) excel in verbal skills that require some spatial organization, such as reading and spelling. But (36: Males or Females?) might excel at more specialized spatial-relations tasks such as interpreting road maps.

Sex (37) _____ones are responsible for the prenatal differentiation of sex organs. Prenatal sex hormones may (38) _____ize or feminize the brain by creating predispositions consistent with gender-role stereotypes. Female rats exposed to (39: Male or Female?) sex hormones in the uterus or soon after birth learn maze routes as rapidly as males do. Aggression in lower animals has been connected with the male sex hormone (40) _____one.

Freud explained the acquisition of gender roles in terms of (41) _____cation. He believed that gender identity remains flexible until the (42) _____pus and Electra complexes are resolved at about the age of five or six. Children develop gender-typed behavior patterns (43: Earlier or Later?) than would be predicted by psychodynamic theory.

(44) Social-_____ theorists explain gender-typing in terms of observational learning, identification, and socialization. Children learn much of what is considered masculine or feminine by (45) _____tional learning. In using (46) _____tion, parents and other people inform children about how they are expected to behave and use rewards and punishments to encourage them to behave "appropriately." Research shows that girls (47: Do or Do not?) behave aggressively when they are provoked, have the means to do so, and believe that the social environment will not punish them.

Bem argues that our culture (48) _____izes females and males by organizing social life around mutually exclusive gender roles. According to (49) _____-schema theory, children accept polarizing scripts without realizing it. Once children understand the labels *boy* and *girl*, they blend their self-concepts with the gender (50) _____a of their culture. Their (51) self-_____ becomes wrapped up in the ways in which they fit the gender schema.

SECTION IV. ATTRACTION: ON LIKING, LOVING, AND RELATIONSHIPS

Sexual interactions usually take place within relationships. Feelings of attraction can lead to liking and perhaps to love, and to a more lasting relationship. In this section we see that **attraction** to another person is

ATTRACTION In social psychology, an attitude of liking or disliking (negative attraction).

influenced by factors such as physical appearance and attitudes. We will see that most people are *hetero*sexual; that is, they are sexually attracted to people of the other gender. However, some people are *homo*sexual; that is, they are sexually attracted to people of their own gender. Question: What factors contribute to attraction in our culture?

Factors Contributing to Attraction

Among the factors contributing to attraction are physical appearance, similarity, and reciprocity.

PHYSICAL APPEARANCE: HOW IMPORTANT IS LOOKING GOOD?

Physical appearance is a key factor in attraction and in the consideration of partners for dates and marriage. What determines physical allure? Are our standards subjective—that is, "in the eye of the beholder"? Or is there general agreement on what is appealing?

Some aspects of beauty appear to be cross-cultural. For example, a study of people in England and Japan found that both British and Japanese men consider women with large eyes, high cheekbones, and narrow jaws to be most attractive (Perret, 1994). In his research, Perret created computer composites of the faces of 60 women and, as shown in Part A of Figure 15.5, of the 15 women who were rated the most attractive. He then used computer enhancement to exaggerate the differences between the composite of the 60 and the composite of the 15 most attractive women. He arrived at the image shown in Part B of Figure 15.5. Part B, which shows higher cheekbones and a narrower jaw than Part A, was rated as the most attractive image. Similar results were found for the image of a Japanese woman. Works of art suggest that the ancient Greeks and Egyptians favored similar facial features.

In our society, tallness is an asset for men, but tall women are viewed less positively (Sheppard & Strathman, 1989). College women prefer their

FIGURE 15.5

WHAT FEATURES CONTRIBUTE TO FACIAL ATTRACTIVENESS?   IN BOTH ENGLAND AND JAPAN, FEATURES SUCH AS LARGE EYES, HIGH CHEEKBONES, AND NARROW JAWS CONTRIBUTE TO PERCEPTIONS OF THE ATTRACTIVENESS OF WOMEN. LEFT: A COMPOSITE OF THE FACES OF 15 WOMEN RATED AS THE MOST ATTRACTIVE OF A GROUP OF 60. RIGHT: A COMPOSITE IN WHICH THE FEATURES OF THESE 15 WOMEN ARE EXAGGERATED—THAT IS, DEVELOPED FURTHER IN THE DIRECTION THAT SEPARATES THEM FROM THE AVERAGE OF THE ENTIRE 60.

"Looking Good."   Naomi Campbell, Claudia Schiffer, and Christie Turlington are among those who set the standards for beauty in contemporary American culture. How important is physical attractiveness?

dates to be about 6 inches taller than they are. College men tend to favor women who are about 4½ inches shorter than they are (Gillis & Avis, 1980).

Although preferences for facial features may transcend time and culture, preferences for body weight and shape may be more culturally determined. For example, plumpness has been valued in many cultures. Grandmothers who worry that their granddaughters are starving themselves often come from cultures in which stoutness is acceptable or desirable. In contemporary Western society, both genders find slenderness appealing (Franzoi & Herzog, 1987). Women generally favor men with a V-taper—broad shoulders and a narrow waist.

✓ Truth or Fiction Revisited

It is not true that beauty is in the eye of the beholder, despite the familiarity of the adage. It appears that some aspects of physical appeal may be innate or inborn. There are also cultural standards for beauty that influence people who are reared in that culture.

Although both genders perceive overweight people as unappealing, there are fascinating gender differences in perceptions of desirable body shapes. College men tend to consider their current physique similar to the ideal male build and to the one that women find most appealing (Fallon & Rozin, 1985). College women, in contrast, generally see themselves as markedly heavier than the figure that is most appealing to men and heavier still than the ideal (see Figure 15.6). Both mothers and fathers of college students see themselves as heavier than their ideal weight (Rozin & Fallon, 1988). Both genders err in their estimates of the other gender's preferences, however. Men of both generations actually prefer women to be heavier than the women presume. Both college women and their mothers prefer men who are slimmer than the men presume.

FIGURE 15.6

CAN YOU EVER BE TOO THIN? RESEARCH SUGGESTS THAT MOST COLLEGE WOMEN BELIEVE THAT THEY ARE HEAVIER THAN THEY OUGHT TO BE. HOWEVER, MEN ACTUALLY PREFER WOMEN TO BE A BIT HEAVIER THAN WOMEN ASSUME THE MEN WOULD LIKE THEM TO BE.

ATTRACTION AND DIVERSITY: GENDER DIFFERENCES IN THE IMPORTANCE OF PHYSICAL ATTRACTIVENESS

Your Daddy's rich
And your Ma is good lookin',
So hush, little baby,
Don't you cry.

FROM "SUMMERTIME" (FROM THE OPERA *PORGY & BESS*)

How important to you is your partner's physical appearance? Studies on mate selection find that women tend to place greater emphasis than men on traits such as professional status, consideration, dependability, kindness, and fondness for children. Men place relatively greater emphasis on physical allure, cooking ability (can't they turn on the microwave oven themselves?), even thrift (Buss, 1994; Feingold, 1992a).

Evolutionary psychologists believe that evolutionary forces favor the survival of women who desire status in their mates and men who emphasize physical allure because these preferences provide reproductive advantages. Some physical features such as cleanliness, good complexion, clear eyes, strong teeth and healthy hair, firm muscle tone, and a steady gait are found universally appealing to both genders (Buss, 1999; Rathus et al., 2000). Perhaps such traits have value as markers of better reproductive potential in prospective mates. According to the "parental investment model," a woman's appeal is more strongly connected with her age and health, both of which are markers of reproductive capacity. The value of men as reproducers, however, is more intertwined with factors that contribute to a stable environment for child rearing—such as social standing and reliability (Feingold, 1992a). For such reasons, evolutionary psychologists speculate that these qualities may have grown relatively more alluring to women over the millennia (e.g., Buss, 1994).

This theory is largely speculative, however, and not fully consistent with all the evidence. Women, like men, are attracted to physically appealing partners, and women tend to marry men similar to them in physical attractiveness and socioeconomic standing. Aging men are more likely than younger men to die from natural causes. The wealth they accrue may not always be transmitted to their spouses and children, either. Many women may be more able to find reproductive success by mating with a fit, younger male than with an older, higher-status male. Even evolutionary psychologists allow that despite any innate predispositions, many men desire older women.

"PRETTY IS AS PRETTY DOES"? Both men and women are perceived as more attractive when they are smiling (Reis et al., 1990). There is thus ample reason to, as the song goes, "put on a happy face" when you are meeting people or looking for a date.

✓ Truth or Fiction Revisited

It is true that people are perceived as being more attractive when they are smiling. Does this research finding provide a reason to "put on a happy face" early in the development of social relationships?

Other aspects of behavior also affect interpersonal attraction. Women who are shown videotapes of prospective dates prefer men who act outgoing and self-assertive (Riggio & Woll, 1984). College men who exhibit dominance (defined as control over a social interaction with a professor) in a videotape are rated as more attractive by women (Sadalla et al., 1987). However, college men respond negatively to women who show self-assertion and social dominance (Riggio & Wolf, 1984; Sadalla et al., 1987). Despite the liberating trends of recent years, the cultural stereotype of the ideal woman still includes modesty. I am *not* suggesting that self-assertive women should take a back seat in order to make themselves more appealing to traditional men. Assertive women might find nothing but conflict in their interactions with such men in any case.

THE MATCHING HYPOTHESIS: DO "OPPOSITES ATTRACT" OR DO "BIRDS OF A FEATHER FLOCK TOGETHER"? Although we may rate highly attractive people as most desirable, most of us are not left to blend in with the wallpaper. According to the **matching hypothesis,** we tend to date people who are similar to ourselves in physical attractiveness rather than the local Will Smith or Sandra Bullock look-alike. One motive for asking out "matches" seems to be fear of rejection by more attractive people (Bernstein et al., 1983).

The quest for similarity extends beyond physical attractiveness. Our marital and sex partners tend to be similar to us in race/ethnicity, age,

MATCHING HYPOTHESIS The view that people tend to choose persons similar to themselves in attractiveness and attitudes in the formation of interpersonal relationships.

level of education, and religion. Consider some findings of the National Health and Social Life Survey (Michael et al., 1994, pp. 45–47):

- Nearly 94% of single European American men have European American women as their sex partners; 2% are partnered with Latina American women, 2% with Asian American women, and less than 1% with African American women.

- About 82% of African American men have African American women as their sex partners; nearly 8% are partnered with European American women and almost 5% with Latina American women.

- About 83% of the women and men in the study chose partners within five years of their own age and of the same or a similar religion.

- Of nearly 2,000 women in the study, not one with a graduate college degree had a partner who had not finished high school.

Why do most people have partners from the same background as their own? One reason is that marriages are made in the neighborhood and not in heaven (Michael et al., 1994). We tend to live among people who are similar to us in background, and we therefore come into contact with them more often than with people from other backgrounds. Another reason is that we are drawn to people whose attitudes are similar to ours. People from a similar background are more likely to have similar attitudes. Similarity in attitudes and tastes is a key contributor to attraction, friendships, and love relationships (Griffin & Sparks, 1990; Laumann et al., 1994).

REFLECT

Could you maintain a relationship with a partner whose attributes toward religion, politics, education, and child rearing differed significantly from your own? Would you want to?

REFLECT

Has anyone told you how good-looking, brilliant, and mature you are? That your taste is refined? That all in all, you are really something special? If so, have you been impressed by his or her fine judgment? Explain.

How do you know when you are in love? Can you express the feelings in words? Can you think of a way that psychologists can measure them?

RECIPROCITY: IF YOU LIKE ME, YOU MUST HAVE EXCELLENT JUDGMENT **Reciprocity** is a powerful determinant of attraction (Condon & Crano, 1988). We tend to return feelings of admiration. We tend to be more open, warm, and helpful when we are interacting with strangers who seem to like us (Curtis & Miller, 1986).

Feelings of attraction are influenced by factors such as physical appearance and similarity. Let us explore what we mean when we say that feelings of attraction have blossomed into love. Questions: Just what is love? What is romantic love?

Love: Doing What Happens . . . Culturally?

Love—the ideal for which we make great sacrifice. Love—the sentiment that launched a thousand ships in Homer's epic poem the *Iliad*. Through the millennia, poets have sought to capture love in words. Dante, the Italian poet who shed some light on the Dark Ages, wrote of "the love that moves the sun and the other stars." The Scottish poet Robert Burns wrote that his love was like "a red, red rose." Love is beautiful and elusive. Passion and romantic love are also lusty, surging with sexual desire.

THE LOVE TRIANGLE No, this love triangle does not refer to two men wooing the same woman. It refers to Robert Sternberg's **triangular model of love.** Sternberg (1988) believes that love can include combinations of three components: intimacy, passion, and commitment (see Figure 15.7).

Intimacy refers to a couple's closeness, to their mutual concern and sharing of feelings and resources. **Passion** means romance and sexual feelings. Commitment means deciding to enhance and maintain the relationship. Passion is most crucial in short-term relationships. Intimacy and commitment are relatively more important in enduring relationships. The

RECIPROCITY In interpersonal attraction, the tendency to return feelings and attitudes that are expressed about us.

TRIANGULAR MODEL OF LOVE Sternberg's view that love involves combinations of three components: intimacy, passion, and decision/commitment.

INTIMACY Close acquaintance and familiarity; a characteristic of a relationship in which partners share their inmost feelings.

PASSION Strong romantic and sexual feelings.

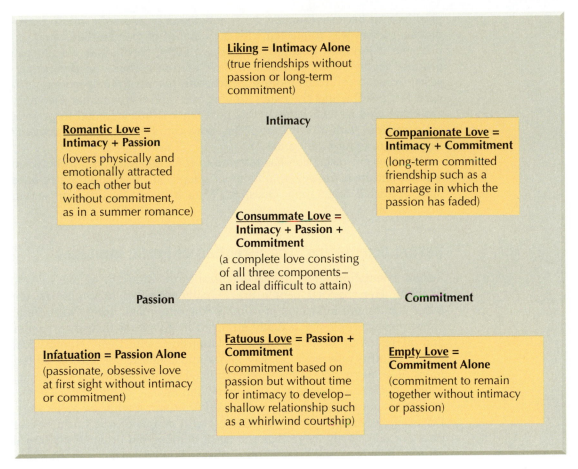

FIGURE 15.7

THE TRIANGULAR MODEL OF LOVE   ACCORDING TO THIS MODEL, LOVE HAS THREE COMPONENTS: INTIMACY, PASSION, AND COMMITMENT. THE IDEAL OF CONSUMMATE LOVE CONSISTS OF ROMANTIC LOVE PLUS COMMITMENT.

ideal form of love, which combines all three, is **consummate love.** Consummate love, in this model, is romantic love plus commitment.

Romantic love is characterized by passion and intimacy. Passion involves fascination (preoccupation with the loved one); sexual craving; and the desire for exclusiveness (a special relationship with the loved one). Intimacy involves caring—championing the interests of the loved one, even if it entails sacrificing one's own. People who are dating, or who expect to be dating each other, are cognitively biased toward evaluating each other positively (Fiske, 1993). They tend to pay attention to information that confirms their romantic interests. In less technical terms, romantic lovers often idealize each other. They magnify each other's positive features and overlook their flaws.

To experience romantic love, in contrast to attachment or sexual arousal, one must be exposed to a culture that idealizes the concept. In Western culture, romantic love blossoms in fairy tales about Sleeping Beauty, Cinderella, Snow White, and all their princes charming. It matures with romantic novels, television tales and films, and the personal accounts of friends and relatives about dates and romances.

Men seem to be somewhat more reluctant than women to make commitments in their romantic relationships (Rathus et al., 2000). Evolutionary psychologists suggest that men may be naturally more

CONSUMMATE LOVE The ideal form of love within Sternberg's model, which combines passion, intimacy, and commitment.

ROMANTIC LOVE An intense, positive emotion that involves sexual attraction, feelings of caring, and the belief that one is in love.

promiscuous because they are the genetic heirs of ancestors whose reproductive success was connected with the number of women they could impregnate (Bjorklund & Kipp, 1996; Buss, 1994, 1999). But women can produce relatively few children in their lifetimes. Thus, the theory suggests, women need to be more selective with respect to their mating partners. Is it possible that the man's "roving eye" and the woman's selectivity are embedded in their genes? (This possibility is *not* intended to provide male readers with the excuse, "But how can I make a commitment? Running around is in my genes.")

Much of our discussion has referred to romantic relationships between women and men. However, millions of people in the United States have another sexual orientation. Question: What is meant by the term *sexual orientation?*

Sexual Orientation: The Direction of Erotic Impulses

Sexual orientation refers to the organization or direction of one's erotic interests. **Heterosexual** people are sexually attracted to people of the other gender and interested in forming romantic relationships with them. **Homosexual** people are sexually attracted to people of their own gender and interested in forming romantic relationships with them. Homosexual males are also referred to as **gay males** and homosexual females as **lesbians**. **Bisexual** people are sexually attracted to, and interested in forming romantic relationships with, both women and men.

Do not confuse the concept of *sexual orientation* with *sexual activity*. For example, engaging in sexual activity with people of one's own gender does not necessarily mean that one has a homosexual orientation. Sexual activity between males sometimes reflects limited sexual opportunities. Adolescent males may manually stimulate one another while fantasizing about girls. Men in prisons may similarly turn to each other as sexual outlets. Young Sambian men in New Guinea engage in sexual practices exclusively with older males because it is believed that they must drink "men's milk" to achieve the fierce manhood of the headhunter (Money, 1987). Once they reach marrying age, however, their sexual activities are limited to female partners.

Surveys find that about 3% of men in the United States identify themselves as gay (e.g., Laumann et al., 1994). About 2% of the U.S. women surveyed say that they have a lesbian sexual orientation (Laumann et al., 1994). The following section describes the experiences of gay people from various ethnic groups.

SEXUAL ORIENTATION AND DIVERSITY: A MATTER OF BELONGING Societal prejudices make it difficult for many young people to come to terms with an emerging homosexual orientation (American Psychological Association, 1998b). You might assume that members of ethnic minority groups in the United States, who themselves have been subjected to prejudice and discrimination, would be more tolerant of a homosexual orientation. However, according to psychologist Beverly Greene (1994), you might be wrong.

Greene (1994) admits that it is difficult to generalize about ethnic groups in the United States. For example, African Americans may find their cultural origins in the tribes of West Africa, but they have also been influenced by Christianity and the local subcultures of North American towns and cities. Native Americans represent hundreds of tribal groups, languages, and cultures. By and large, homosexuality is rejected by ethnic

SEXUAL ORIENTATION The directionality of one's erotic interests — that is, whether one is sexually attracted to and interested in forming romantic relationships with people of the other or the same gender.

HETEROSEXUAL Referring to people who are sexually aroused by and interested in forming romantic relationships with people of the other gender.

HOMOSEXUAL Referring to people who are sexually aroused by and interested in forming romantic relationships with people of the same gender.

GAY MALE A male homosexual.

LESBIAN A female homosexual.

BISEXUAL A person who is sexually aroused by and interested in forming romantic relationships with people of either gender.

REFLECT

What are the attitudes of people from your sociocultural group toward gay males and lesbians? Do you share these attitudes? Why, or why not?

minority groups in the United States. Lesbians and gay males are pressured to keep their sexual orientation a secret or to move to communities where they can express it without condemnation.

In traditional Latino and Latina American culture, the family is the primary social unit. Men are expected to support and defend the family, and women are expected to be submissive, respectful, and deferential (Morales, 1992). Also, Latino and Latina American culture frequently denies the sexuality of women. Thus lesbians are doubly condemned—because of their sexual orientation and because their independence from men threatens the tradition of male dominance (Trujillo, 1991).

Asian American cultures emphasize respect for one's elders, obedience to one's parents, and distinct masculine and feminine gender roles (Chan, 1992). The topic of sex is generally taboo within the family. Asian Americans, like Latino and Latina Americans, tend to assume that sex is unimportant to women. Women are also considered less important than men. Open admission of a homosexual orientation is seen as a rejection of one's traditional cultural roles and a threat to the continuity of the family line (Chan, 1992).

Because many African American men have had difficulty finding jobs, gender roles among African Americans have been more flexible than those found among most other ethnic minority groups and among European Americans (Greene, 1994). Nevertheless, the African American community appears to reject gay men and lesbians strongly, pressuring them to remain secretive about their sexual orientation (Gomez & Smith, 1990; Poussaint, 1990). One factor that influences African Americans to be hostile toward lesbians and gay men is allegiance to Christian beliefs and biblical Scripture (Greene, 1994).

Prior to the European conquest of the Americas, sex was seen as a natural part of life. Native American individuals who incorporated both traditional feminine and masculine styles were generally accepted, even admired. The influence of colonists' religions led to greater rejection of lesbians and gay men and pressure on them to move from reservations to large cities (Greene, 1994). Native American lesbians and gay men thus often feel doubly removed from their families.

If any generalization is possible, it may be that lesbians and gay men find a greater sense of belonging in the gay community than in their ethnic communities.

ORIGINS OF SEXUAL ORIENTATION Sexual orientation, like gender-typing, is an aspect of the development of the individual. And, as with gender-typing, there are psychological and biological theories of its origin, as well as theories that bridge the two. Question: How do researchers explain gay male and lesbian sexual orientations?

As was the case with gender-typing, let us begin our search for the psychological roots of sexual orientation with psychodynamic theory, largely because of its historic importance. Psychodynamic theory ties sexual orientation to identification with male or female figures. Identification, in turn, is related to resolution of the Oedipus and Electra complexes. In men, faulty resolution of the **Oedipus complex** would stem from a "classic pattern" of child rearing in which there is a "close binding" mother and a "detached hostile" father. Boys reared in such a home environment would identify with their mother and not with their father. Psychodynamic theory has been criticized, however, because many gay males have had excellent relationships with both parents (Isay, 1990). Also, the childhoods of many heterosexuals fit the "classic pattern."

OEDIPUS COMPLEX Within psychodynamic theory, a conflict of the phallic stage characterized by romantic feelings toward the parent of the other gender and feelings of rivalry toward the parent of the same gender.

www.planetout.com. The home page for the Web site of Planetout.com. The Web site addresses the interests of gay males and lesbians.

From a learning theory point of view, early reinforcement of sexual behavior (e.g., by orgasm achieved through interaction with people of one's own gender) can influence one's sexual orientation. But most people are aware of their sexual orientation before they have sexual contacts (Bell et al., 1981).

Biologically oriented psychologists look to factors such as heredity in their search for the origins of sexual orientation. For example, they have found evidence for family patterns in sexual orientation (Pillard, 1990; Pillard & Weinrich, 1986). In one study, 22% of the brothers of 51 primarily gay men were either gay or bisexual themselves. This is about four times the percentage found in the general population (Pillard & Weinrich, 1986). Genes connected with sexual orientation might be found on the X sex chromosome and be transmitted from mother to child (Hamer et al., 1993). Moreover, identical (MZ) twins have a higher agreement rate for a gay male sexual orientation than do fraternal (DZ) twins: 52% for MZ twins versus 22% for DZ twins (Bailey & Pillard, 1991). Although genetic factors may partly determine sexual orientation, psychologist John Money, who has specialized in research on sexual behavior, concludes that sexual orientation is "not under the direct governance of chromosomes and genes" (1987, p. 384).

Sex hormones may play a role in sexual orientation. These hormones promote biological sexual differentiation and regulate the menstrual cycle. They also have organizing and activating effects on sexual behavior. They predispose lower animals toward masculine or feminine mating patterns—a directional or **organizing effect** (Crews, 1994). They also affect the sex drive and promote sexual response; these are **activating effects.**

Sexual behavior among many lower animals is almost completely governed by hormones (Crews, 1994). In many species, if the sex organs and brains of fetuses are exposed to large doses of **testosterone** in the uterus (which occurs naturally when they share the uterus with many brothers, or artificially as a result of hormone injections), they become masculine in structure (Crews, 1994). Prenatal testosterone organizes the brains of females in the masculine direction, predisposing them toward masculine behaviors in adulthood. Testosterone in adulthood then apparently activates the masculine behavior patterns.

Because sex hormones predispose lower animals toward masculine or feminine mating patterns, some have asked whether gay males and lesbians might differ from heterosexuals in levels of sex hormones. However, a gay male or lesbian sexual orientation has not been reliably linked to current (adult) levels of male or female sex hormones (Friedman & Downey, 1994). What about the effects of sex hormones on the developing fetus? As just noted, we know that prenatal sex hormones can masculinize or feminize the brains of laboratory animals.

Lee Ellis (1990; Ellis & Ames, 1987) theorizes that sexual orientation is hormonally determined prior to birth and affected by genetic factors, synthetic hormones (such as male sex hormones), and maternal stress. Why maternal stress? Stress causes the release of hormones such as **adrenaline** and **cortisol,** which can masculinize the embryonic brain. Perhaps the brains of some gay males have been feminized and the brains of some lesbians masculinized prior to birth (Collaer & Hines, 1995; Friedman & Downey, 1994).

In sum, the determinants of sexual orientation are mysterious and complex (American Psychological Association, 1998b). Research suggests that they may involve prenatal hormone levels—which can be affected by factors such as heredity, drugs, and maternal stress—and postnatal socialization. But the precise interaction among these influences is not yet understood.

We can note quite seriously that the difficulties in explaining homosexuality are hardly different from the difficulties in explaining heterosexuality. Most people tend to assume that heterosexuality is "natural," but this assumption does not explain how individuals develop to become either heterosexual or homosexual. (People do not simply become heterosexual because of cultural or religious tradition!) We still need to consider the likely interactions of psychological and biological factors in heterosexuality. Until we find the answers, the origins of heterosexuality will also remain mysterious.

In the meantime, Table 15.2 may answer some of your questions about sexual orientation and homosexuality. Regardless of one's sexual orientation, an individual—female or male—responds to sexual stimulation in a more or less predictable way. Let us now turn our attention to sexual response.

ORGANIZING EFFECT The directional effect of sex hormones — for example, along stereotypically masculine or feminine lines.

ACTIVATING EFFECT The arousal-producing effects of sex hormones that increase the likelihood of sexual behavior.

TESTOSTERONE A male sex hormone that promotes development of male sexual characteristics and that has activating effects on sexual arousal.

ADRENALINE A hormone produced by the adrenal glands that generally arouses people and heightens their emotional responsiveness.

CORTISOL A hormone produced by the adrenal glands that increases resistance to stress.

TABLE 15.2	THE AMERICAN PSYCHOLOGICAL ASSOCIATION ANSWERS QUESTIONS ABOUT SEXUAL ORIENTATION AND HOMOSEXUALITY
What Is Sexual Orientation?	Sexual Orientation is an enduring emotional, romantic, sexual, or affectional attraction to another person. It is easily distinguished from other components of sexuality, including biological sex, gender identity (the psychological sense of being male or female), and the social gender role (adherence to cultural norms for feminine and masculine behavior). . . . Sexual orientation is different from sexual behavior because it refers to feelings and self-concept. Persons may or may not express their sexual orientation in their behaviors.
What Causes a Person to Have a Particular Sexual Orientation?	There are numerous theories about the origins of a person's sexual orientation; most scientists today agree that sexual orientation is most likely the result of a complex interaction of environmental, cognitive, and biological factors. In most people, sexual orientation is shaped at an early age. There is also considerable recent evidence to suggest that biology, including genetic or inborn hormonal factors, plays a significant role in a person's sexuality.
Is Sexual Orientation a Choice?	No, human beings cannot choose to be either gay or straight. Sexual orientation emerges for most people in early adolescence without any prior sexual experience. Although we can choose whether to act on our feelings, psychologists do not consider sexual orientation to be a conscious choice that can be voluntarily changed.
Can Therapy Change Sexual Orientation?	No; even though most homosexuals live successful, happy lives, some homosexual or bisexual people may seek to change their sexual orientation through therapy, often coerced by family members or religious groups to try and do so. The reality is that homosexuality is not an illness. It does not require treatment and is not changeable. However, not all gay, lesbian, and bisexual people who seek assistance from a mental health professional want to change their sexual orientation. Gay, lesbian, and bisexual people may seek psychological help with the coming-out process or for strategies to deal with prejudice, but most go into therapy for the same reasons and life issues that bring straight people to mental health professionals.
What About So-Called Conversion Therapies?	Some therapists who undertake so-called conversion therapy report that they have been able to change their clients' sexual orientation from homosexual to heterosexual. Close scrutiny of these reports, however, shows several factors that cast doubt on their claims. For example, many of the claims come from organizations with an ideological perspective that condemns homosexuality. Furthermore, their claims are poorly documented. For example, treatment outcome is not followed and reported over time as would be the standard to test the validity of any mental health intervention.
Is Homosexuality a Mental Illness or Emotional Problem?	No. Psychologists, psychiatrists, and other mental health professionals agree that homosexuality is not an illness, a mental disorder, or an emotional problem. Over 35 years of objective, well-designed scientific research has shown that homosexuality, in and of itself, is not associated with mental disorders or emotional or social problems. Homosexuality was once thought to be a mental illness because mental health professionals and society had biased information.
Can Lesbians, Gay Men, and Bisexuals Be Good Parents?	Yes. Studies comparing groups of children raised by homosexual and by heterosexual parents find no developmental differences between the two groups of children in four critical areas: their intelligence, psychological adjustment, social adjustment, and popularity with friends. It is also important to realize that a parent's sexual orientation does not indicate the children's.
Why Do Some Gay Men, Lesbians, and Bisexuals Tell People About Their Sexual Orientation?	Because sharing that aspect of themselves with others is important to their mental health. In fact, the process of identity development for lesbians, gay men, and bisexuals, called "coming out," has been found to be strongly related to psychological adjustment; the more positive the gay, lesbian, or bisexual identity, the better one's mental health and the higher one's self-esteem.
Why Is the "Coming-Out" Process Difficult for Some Gay, Lesbian, and Bisexual People?	For some gay and bisexual people the coming out process is difficult; for others it is not. Often lesbian, gay, and bisexual people feel afraid, different, and alone when they first realize that their sexual orientation is different from the community norm. This is particularly true for people becoming aware of their gay, lesbian, or bisexual orientation as a child or adolescent, which is not uncommon. And, depending on their families and where they live, they may have to struggle against prejudice and misinformation about homosexuality. . . . Unfortunately, gay, lesbian, and bisexual people are at a higher risk for physical assault and violence than are heterosexuals. Studies done in California in the mid-1990s showed that nearly one-fifth of all lesbians who took part in the study and more than one-fourth of all gay men who participated had been the victim of a hate crime based on their sexual orientation. In another California study of approximately 500 young adults, half of all the young men participating in the study admitted to some form of anti-gay aggression from name calling to physical violence.

Table Continues

TABLE 15.2	THE AMERICAN PSYCHOLOGICAL ASSOCIATION ANSWERS QUESTIONS ABOUT SEXUAL ORIENTATION AND HOMOSEXUALITY (CONTINUED)
What Can Be Done to Overcome the Prejudice and Discrimination the Gay Men, Lesbians, and Bisexuals Experience?	Research has found that the people who have the most positive attitudes toward gay men, lesbians, and bisexuals are those who say they know one or more gay, lesbian, or bisexual person well, often as a friend or co-worker. For this reason, psychologists believe negative attitudes toward gay people as a group are prejudices that are not grounded in actual experiences but are based on stereotypes and prejudice. Furthermore, protection against violence and discrimination are very important, just as they are for any other minority groups. Some states include violence against an individual on the basis of his or her sexual orientation as a "hate crime," and ten U.S. states have laws against discrimination on the basis of sexual orientation.
Why Is It Important for Society to Be Better Educated About Homosexuality?	Educating all people about sexual orientation and homosexuality is likely to diminish anti-gay prejudice. Accurate information about homosexuality is especially important to young people who are first discovering and seeking to understand their sexuality whether homosexual, bisexual, or heterosexual. Fears that access to such information will make more people gay have no validity. Information about homosexuality does not make someone gay or straight.
Are All Gay and Bisexual Men HIV Infected?	No. This is a commonly held myth. In reality, the risk of exposure to HIV is related to a person's behavior, not his or her sexual orientation. What's important to remember about HIV/AIDS is that it is a preventable disease through the use of safe sex practices and by not using drugs.
Where Can I Find More Information About Homosexuality?	National Gay and Lesbian Task Force 2320 17th St. Washington, DC 20009 (202) 332-6483 Email: NGLTF@NGLTF.org Parents, Families and Friends of Lesbians and Gays 1101 14th St. NW, Ste. 1030 Washington, DC (202) 638-4200 Email: Info@PFLAG.org Sexuality Information and Education Council of the United States 130 W 42nd St., Ste. 350 New York, NY 10036 (212) 819-9770 Email: Siecus@APA Public Information Home Page www.apa.org

SOURCE: American Psychological Association (1998, October 4). Answers to your questions about sexual orientation and homosexuality. APA Public Information Home Page; www.apa.org.

Review

SECTION IV

British and Japanese men consider women with (52: Large or Small?) eyes, high cheekbones, and (53: Wide or Narrow?) jaws to be most attractive. In our society, (54: Tallness or Shortness?) is an asset for men. Preferences for body weight and shape appear to be (55: Universal or Culturally determined?). In contemporary Western society, (56: Both genders or Only men?) find slenderness to be appealing. College men tend to see their current physique as (57: Too heavy, Too slender, or Ideal?). College women tend to see their figure as (58: Too heavy, Too slender, or Ideal?).

(59: Men or Women?) tend to place more emphasis on traits such as professional status and kindness. (60: Men or Women?) place relatively more emphasis on physical allure and cooking ability. Evolutionary psycholo-gists believe that evolutionary forces favor the survival of (61: Men or Women?) who desire status in their mates and (62: Men or Women?) who emphasize physical allure because these preferences provide reproductive advantages.

Men and women are perceived as (63: More or Less?) attractive when they are smiling. (64: Men or Women?) prefer partners who act outgoing and self-assertive. According to the (65) _____ing hypothesis, we tend to date people who are similar to ourselves in physical attractiveness. Our marital and sex partners tend to be (66: Like or Unlike?) us in race/ethnicity, age, level of education, and religion. The concept of (67) _____city refers to the finding that we are more attracted to people who like us.

According to Sternberg's (68) _____lar model of love, love can include combinations of three components: intimacy, (69) _____sion, and commitment. (70) Con_____ love is the ideal form of love and combines all three. (71) _____tic love is characterized by passion and intimacy. (72: Men or Women?) seem to be more reluctant to make commitments in their romantic relationships.

Sexual (73) _____tion refers to the organization or direction of one's erotic interests. (74) _____sexual people are sexually attracted to people of the other gender and interested in forming romantic relationships with them. (75) _____-sexual people are sexually attracted to people of their own gender and interested in forming romantic relationships

with them. Members of ethnic minority groups in the United States tend to be (76: More or Less?) tolerant of homosexuality than are European Americans. Psychodynamic theory ties sexual orientation to (77) _____cation with male or female figures. Identification is related to resolution of the (78) _____pus and Electra complexes. According to learning theory, early (79) _____ment of sexual behavior can influence sexual orientation. Biologically ori-ented psychologists (80: Find or Do not find?) evidence for genetic factors in sexual orientation. Sex hormones have (81) _____ing and activating effects. The hormone (82) _____rone appears to organize the brain in the masculine direction. Sexual orientation (83: Has or Has not?) been linked to adult levels of sex hormones. Sex hormones are (84: More or Less?) likely to be influential prior to birth.

SECTION V. SEXUAL RESPONSE

Although we may consider ourselves sophisticated about sex, it is surprising how little we know about sexual biology. How many male readers know that women have different orifices for urination and sexual intercourse? How many readers know that the penis—sometimes referred to by the slang term "boner" when erect—contains no bones? In this section we consider how females and males respond to sexual stimulation—that is, the so-called sexual response cycle.

The Sexual Response Cycle

Although we may be culturally attuned to focus on gender differences rather than similarities, William Masters and Virginia Johnson (1966) found that the biological responses of males and females to sexual stimulation—that is, their sexual response cycles—are quite similar. Question: What is the sexual response cycle? Masters and Johnson use the term **sexual response cycle** to describe the changes that occur in the body as men and women become sexually aroused. Masters and Johnson divide the sexual response cycle into four phases: *excitement, plateau, orgasm,* and *resolution.* Figure 15.8 suggests the levels of sexual arousal associated with each phase.

The sexual response cycle is characterized by vasocongestion and myotonia. **Vasocongestion** is the swelling of the genital tissues with blood. It causes erection of the penis and swelling of the area surrounding the vaginal opening. The testes, the nipples, and even the earlobes swell as blood vessels dilate in these areas.

SEXUAL RESPONSE CYCLE Masters and Johnson's model of sexual response, which consists of four stages or phases.

VASOCONGESTION Engorgement of blood vessels with blood, which swells the genitals and breasts during sexual arousal.

MYOTONIA Muscle tension.

✓ Truth or Fiction Revisited

It is true that the earlobes swell when people become sexually aroused. The swelling is a result of vasocongestion.

Myotonia is muscle tension. It causes facial grimaces, spasms in the hands and feet, and then the spasms of orgasm. In this section we explore these and other bodily changes that make up the sexual response cycle.

FIGURE 15.8

LEVELS OF SEXUAL AROUSAL DURING THE PHASES OF THE SEXUAL RESPONSE CYCLE   MASTERS AND JOHNSON DIVIDE THE SEXUAL RESPONSE CYCLE INTO FOUR PHASES: EXCITEMENT, PLATEAU, ORGASM, AND RESOLUTION. DURING THE RESOLUTION PHASE, THE LEVEL OF SEXUAL AROUSAL RETURNS TO THE PREAROUSED STATE. FOR MEN THERE IS A REFRACTORY PERIOD FOLLOWING ORGASM. AS SHOWN BY THE BROKEN LINE, HOWEVER, MEN CAN BECOME REAROUSED TO ORGASM ONCE THE REFRACTORY PERIOD IS PAST AND THEIR LEVELS OF SEXUAL AROUSAL HAVE RETURNED TO PRE-PLATEAU LEVELS. PATTERN A FOR WOMEN SHOWS A TYPICAL RESPONSE CYCLE, WITH THE BROKEN LINE SUGGESTING MULTIPLE ORGASMS. PATTERN B SHOWS THE CYCLE OF A WOMAN WHO REACHES THE PLATEAU PHASE BUT FOR WHOM AROUSAL IS "RESOLVED" WITHOUT REACHING THE ORGASMIC PHASE. PATTERN C SHOWS THE POSSIBILITY OF ORGASM IN A HIGHLY AROUSED WOMAN WHO PASSES QUICKLY THROUGH THE PLATEAU PHASE.

EXCITEMENT PHASE Vasocongestion during the **excitement phase** can cause erection in young men as soon as 3 to 8 seconds after sexual stimulation begins. The scrotal skin also thickens, becoming less baggy. The testes increase in size and become elevated.

In the female, excitement is characterized by vaginal lubrication, which may start 10 to 30 seconds after sexual stimulation begins. Vasocongestion swells the clitoris and flattens and spreads the vaginal lips. The inner part of the vagina expands. The breasts enlarge, and blood vessels near the surface become more prominent. The nipples may become erect in both men and women. Heart rate and blood pressure also increase.

PLATEAU PHASE The level of sexual arousal remains somewhat stable during the **plateau phase** of the cycle. Because of vasocongestion, men show some increase in the circumference of the head of the penis, which also takes on a purplish hue. The testes are elevated into position for **ejaculation** and may reach one and a half times their unaroused size.

In women, vasocongestion swells the outer part of the vagina, contracting the vaginal opening in preparation for grasping the penis. The inner part of the vagina expands farther. The clitoris withdraws beneath the clitoral hood and shortens. Breathing becomes rapid, like panting. Heart rate may increase to 100 to 160 beats per minute. Blood pressure continues to rise.

ORGASMIC PHASE The orgasmic phase in the male consists of two stages of muscular contractions. In the first stage, **seminal fluid** collects at the base of the penis. The internal sphincter of the urinary bladder prevents urine from mixing with semen. In the second stage, muscle contractions

EXCITEMENT PHASE The first phase of the sexual response cycle, characterized by muscle tension, increases in the heart rate, and erection in the male and vaginal lubrication in the female.

PLATEAU PHASE The second phase of the sexual response cycle, which is characterized by increases in vasocongestion, muscle tension, heart rate, and blood pressure in preparation for orgasm.

EJACULATION The ejection of semen from the penis.

SEMINAL FLUID The fluid produced by the prostate and other glands that carries and nourishes sperm. Also called *semen*.

propel the ejaculate out of the body. Sensations of pleasure tend to be related to the strength of the contractions and the amount of seminal fluid present. The first 3 to 4 contractions are generally most intense and occur at 0.8-second intervals (5 contractions every 4 seconds). Another 2 to 4 contractions occur at a somewhat slower pace. Rates and patterns can vary from one man to another.

Orgasm in the female is manifested by 3 to 15 contractions of the pelvic muscles that surround the vaginal barrel. The contractions first occur at 0.8-second intervals. As in the male, they produce release of sexual tension. Weaker and slower contractions follow.

Erection, vaginal lubrication, and orgasm are all reflexes. That is, they occur automatically in response to adequate sexual stimulation. Of course, the decision to enter a sexual relationship is voluntary, as are the decisions to kiss and pet and so on.

During the orgasmic phase, blood pressure and heart rate reach a peak, with the heart beating up to 180 times per minute. Respiration may increase to 40 breaths per minute.

RESOLUTION PHASE After orgasm the body returns to its unaroused state. This is called the **resolution phase.** After ejaculation, blood is released from engorged areas, so that the erection disappears. The testes return to their normal size.

In women, orgasm also triggers the release of blood from engorged areas. The nipples return to their normal size. The clitoris and vaginal barrel gradually shrink to their unaroused sizes. Blood pressure, heart rate, and breathing also return to their levels before arousal. Both partners may feel relaxed and satisfied.

Unlike women, men enter a **refractory period** during which they cannot experience another orgasm or ejaculate. The refractory period of adolescent males may last only minutes, whereas that of men age 50 and above may last from several minutes to a day. Women do not undergo a refractory period and therefore can become quickly rearoused to the point of repeated (multiple) orgasm if they desire and receive continued sexual stimulation.

We have described common patterns of sexual response, but we should note that not everyone becomes sexually aroused by the same kinds of stimulation. In fact, a number of people experience serious sexual problems or "dysfunctions." Question: What are sexual dysfunctions?

Sexual Dysfunctions and Sex Therapy

Sexual dysfunctions are persistent problems in becoming sexually aroused or reaching orgasm. Many people are troubled by a sexual dysfunction at one time or another. Let's take a look at the main types of sexual dysfunctions and their causes.

TYPES OF SEXUAL DYSFUNCTIONS Sexual dysfunctions include hypoactive sexual desire disorder, female sexual arousal disorder, male erectile disorder, orgasmic disorder, premature ejaculation, dyspareunia, and vaginismus.

In **hypoactive sexual desire disorder,** a person lacks interest in sexual activity and frequently reports a lack of sexual fantasies. This diagnosis exists because it is assumed that sexual fantasies and interests are normal responses that may be blocked by anxiety or other factors.

In women, sexual arousal is characterized by lubrication of the vaginal walls, which facilitates entry by the penis. Sexual arousal in men is characterized by erection. Almost all women sometimes have difficulty becoming

---

ORGASM The height or climax of sexual excitement, involving involuntary muscle contractions, release of sexual tensions, and, usually, subjective feelings of pleasure.

RESOLUTION PHASE The fourth phase of the sexual response cycle, during which the body gradually returns to its prearoused state.

REFRACTORY PERIOD In the sexual response cycle, a period of time following orgasm during which an individual is not responsive to sexual stimulation.

SEXUAL DYSFUNCTION A persistent or recurrent problem in becoming sexually aroused or reaching orgasm.

HYPOACTIVE SEXUAL DESIRE DISORDER A sexual dysfunction in which people lack sexual desire.

REFLECT

Do the changes experienced by women and men during the sexual response cycle seem to be more different or more alike? Explain.

REFLECT

Does it surprise you that hypoactive sexual desire disorder is the most common sexual dysfunction among women, or that premature ejaculation is the most common dysfunction among men? Explain.

or remaining lubricated. Almost all men have occasional difficulty attaining or maintaining an erection through intercourse. When these events are persistent or recurrent, they are considered dysfunctions (**female sexual arousal disorder** and **male erectile disorder**).

In **orgasmic disorder,** the man or woman, although sexually excited, takes a long time to reach orgasm or does not reach it at all. Orgasmic disorder is more common among women than among men. In **premature ejaculation,** the male ejaculates after minimal sexual stimulation, too soon to permit his partner or himself to enjoy sexual relations fully. Other dysfunctions include **dyspareunia** (painful sexual activity) and **vaginismus** (involuntary contraction of the muscles surrounding the vaginal opening, which makes entry painful and/or difficult).

The prevalence of various sexual dysfunctions according to one national survey is shown in Table 15.3. However, it should be noted that many researchers believe that erectile dysfunction may affect half or more of older men (Rathus et al., 2000).

Since not everyone experiences sexual dysfunctions, researchers have sought to determine why some do and some do not. Question: What are the origins of sexual dysfunctions?

ORIGINS OF SEXUAL DYSFUNCTIONS Some sexual dysfunctions reflect biological problems. Lack of desire, for example, can be due to diabetes or to diseases of the heart and lungs. Fatigue can reduce sexual desire and inhibit orgasm. Depressants such as alcohol, narcotics, and tranquilizers can also impair sexual response. Physical factors sometimes interact with psychological factors. For instance, dyspareunia can heighten anxiety, and extremes of anxiety can dampen sexual arousal. The changes of aging can lead to erectile problems in men and orgasmic problems in women.

Physically or psychologically painful sexual experiences, such as rape, can block future sexual response (Koss, 1993). Moreover, a sexual relationship is usually no better than other aspects of a relationship or

---

REFLECT

Erectile disorder is extremely disturbing to many men who experience it. What sorts of attitudes and expectations heighten the stress of this dysfunction?

REFLECT

How do you account for gender differences in the incidence of sexual dysfunctions? Why do you think that women are more likely than men to find sex painful or unenjoyable? Why do you think that men are more likely to be anxious about their performance or to reach orgasm too early? (And how would you define "too early"?)

TABLE 15.3	CURRENT SEXUAL PROBLEMS AND DYSFUNCTIONS ACCORDING TO THE NATIONAL HEALTH AND SOCIAL LIFE SURVEY		
PERCENTAGE OF RESPONDENTS REPORTING THE PROBLEM WITHIN THE PAST YEAR			
		MEN (%)	**WOMEN (%)**
Pain during sex (*dyspareunia*)		3.0	14.4
Sex not pleasurable		8.1	21.2
Unable to reach orgasm (*orgasmic disorder*)		8.3	24.1
Lack of interest in sex (*hypoactive sexual desire*)		15.8	33.4
Anxiety about performance*		17.0	11.5
Reaching climax too early (*premature ejaculation,* in the male)		28.5	10.3
Unable to keep an erection (*male erectile disorder*)		10.4	—
Having trouble lubricating (*female sexual arousal disorder*)		—	18.8

SOURCE: Adapted from Tables 10.8A and 10.8B, pages 370 and 371, in Laumann, E. O., Gagnon, J. H., Michael, R. T., & Michaels, S. (1994). *The social organization of sexuality: Sexual practices in the United States.* Chicago: University of Chicago Press.

* Anxiety about performance is not itself a sexual dysfunction, but it figures in most sexual dysfunctions.

FEMALE SEXUAL AROUSAL DISORDER A sexual dysfunction in which females fail to become adequately sexually aroused to engage in sexual intercourse.

MALE ERECTILE DISORDER A sexual dysfunction in which males fail to obtain or maintain erections that are adequate for sexual intercourse.

ORGASMIC DISORDER A sexual dysfunction in which people have persistent or recurrent problems in reaching orgasm.

PREMATURE EJACULATION Ejaculation that occurs before the couple are satisfied with the duration of sexual relations.

DYSPAREUNIA A sexual dysfunction characterized by persistent or recurrent pain during sexual intercourse. (From roots meaning "badly paired.")

VAGINISMUS A sexual dysfunction characterized by involuntary contraction of the muscles surrounding the vagina, preventing entry by the penis or making entry painful.

marriage. Couples who have difficulty communicating are at a disadvantage in expressing their sexual desires.

Cognitive psychologists point out that irrational beliefs and attitudes can contribute to sexual dysfunctions. If we believe that we need a lover's approval at all times, we may view a disappointing sexual episode as a catastrophe. If we demand that every sexual encounter be perfect, we set ourselves up for failure.

In most cases of sexual dysfunction, the physical and psychological factors we have outlined lead to yet another psychological factor—**performance anxiety,** or fear of not being able to perform sexually. People with performance anxiety may focus on past failures and expectations of another disaster rather than enjoying present erotic sensations and fantasies. Performance anxiety can make it difficult for a man to attain erection, yet also spur him to ejaculate prematurely. It can prevent a woman from lubricating adequately and contribute to vaginismus.

> ✓ **Truth or Fiction Revisited**
>
> *It is not necessarily true that people who truly love each other enjoy the sexual aspects of their relationships.* The statement is too broad to be true. Sexual dysfunctions can occur even in a loving relationship.

Now that we have described a number of sexual dysfunctions, let us ask the following: Question: How are sexual dysfunctions treated?

SEX THERAPY Sexual dysfunctions are generally treated by means of **sex therapy,** which refers to a collection of mainly cognitive and behavior therapy techniques. Sex therapy is largely indebted to the pioneering work of Masters and Johnson (1970), although other therapists have also developed important techniques. Sex therapy generally focuses on:

1. *Reducing performance anxiety.* Therapists frequently prescribe that clients engage in activities such as massage or petting under "nondemand" circumstances for a while to reduce performance anxiety. Nondemand activity means sexual arousal and intercourse are not expected at first. Lessened anxiety allows natural reflexes such as erection, lubrication, and orgasm to occur.

2. *Changing self-defeating attitudes and expectations.* Clients are shown how expectations of failure can raise anxiety levels and become self-fulfilling prophecies.

3. *Teaching sexual skills.* Clients may be taught how to provide each other with adequate sexual stimulation. In the case of premature ejaculation, they may also be shown how to delay ejaculation by means such as the stop-and-go method (pausing when the male becomes too aroused).

4. *Enhancing sexual knowledge.* Some problems are connected with ignorance or misinformation about biological and sexual functioning.

5. *Improving sexual communication.* Partners are taught ways of showing each other what they like and do not like.

Moreover, a number of biological treatments are available for various problems, such as male erectile disorder. Readers interested in learning more about sex therapy are advised to consult a human sexuality textbook, contact their state's psychological association, or ask their professors or college counseling centers for a referral.

Sexual dysfunctions are one category of problems in sexual interaction. Let us now consider a darker side of human interaction: sexual coercion. In sexual dysfunctions, individuals and couples generally wish to remove ob-

PERFORMANCE ANXIETY Anxiety concerning one's ability to perform, especially when performance may be evaluated by other people.

SEX THERAPY A collective term for short-term cognitive-behavioral models for treatment of sexual dysfunctions.

stacles to having a fulfilling sexual relationship. In the case of sexual coercion, individuals—usually women—need effective barriers to prevent other people from damaging their physical and psychological well-being.

Review

SECTION V

Masters and Johnson use the term sexual (85) _____ cycle to describe the bodily changes that occur as people become sexually aroused. They divide the sexual response cycle into four phases: (86) _____ement, plateau, orgasm, and (87) _____tion. The sexual response cycle is characterized by (88) vaso_____ and myotonia. Vasocongestion is the swelling of the genital tissues with (89) _____. (90) _____nia is muscle tension. The excitement phase is characterized by (91) _____tion in the male and vaginal (92) _____tion in the female. Orgasm is characterized by muscle (93) _____tions, and release of sexual tension. The male (94) _____lates seminal fluid. Following orgasm, men enter a (95) _____tory period during which they cannot experience another orgasm or ejaculate.

Sexual (96) _____tions are persistent problems in becoming sexually aroused or reaching orgasm. In (97) _____ sexual desire disorder, a person lacks interest in sexual activity. Women with female sexual (98) _____ disorder have persistent difficulty becoming or remaining lubricated. Men who have persistent difficulty attaining or maintaining an erection are said to have male (99) _____ disorder.

People who take a long time to reach orgasm or who do not reach it at all are said to have (100) _____ disorder. Males who ejaculate too quickly are diagnosed with (101) _____ ejaculation. (102) Dys_____ is characterized by painful sexual activity. (103) Vag_____ is characterized by involuntary contraction of the muscles surrounding the vaginal opening, making entry painful. Sexual dysfunctions are frequently connected with performance (104) _____, which refers to fear of not being able to perform sexually.

Sexual dysfunctions are usually treated by means of (105) _____ therapy. Sex therapy generally focuses on reducing (106) per_____ anxiety, changing self-defeating attitudes and expectations, teaching sexual skills, enhancing sexual knowledge, and improving sexual communication.

SECTION VI. SEXUAL COERCION

Sexual coercion includes rape and other forms of sexual pressure. It also includes *any* sexual activity between an adult and a child. Even when children cooperate, sexual relations with children are coercive because the child is below the legal age of consent. In this section we focus on rape and sexual harassment.

Rape

As many as 1 woman in 4 in the United States has been raped (Koss, 1993). Parents regularly encourage their daughters to be wary of strangers and strange places—places where they could fall prey to rapists. Certainly the threat of rape from strangers is real enough. Yet 4 out of 5 rapes are committed by acquaintances (Laumann et al., 1994).

Date rape is a pressing concern on college campuses, where thousands of women have been victimized and there is much controversy over what exactly constitutes rape. Nine percent of one sample of 6,159 college women reported that they had given in to sexual intercourse as a result of threats or physical force (Koss et al., 1987).

If we add to these statistics instances in which women are subjected to forced kissing and petting, the numbers grow even more alarming. At a major university, 40% of 201 male students surveyed admitted to using force to unfasten a woman's clothing, and 13% reported that they had forced a woman to engage in sexual intercourse (Rapoport & Burkhart, 1984). Forty-four percent of the college women in the Koss study (Koss et al., 1987) reported that they had "given in to sex play" because of a "man's continual arguments and pressure."

Rape is thus common—far too common. Question: Why do men rape women?

WHY DO MEN RAPE WOMEN? Why do men force women into sexual activity? Sex is not the only reason. Many social scientists argue that rape is often a man's way of expressing social dominance over, or anger toward, women (Hall & Barongan, 1997). With some rapists, violence appears to enhance sexual arousal. They therefore seek to combine sex and aggression (Barbaree & Marshall, 1991).

Many social critics contend that American culture socializes men—including the nice young man next door—into becoming rapists (Powell, 1996). This occurs because males are often reinforced for aggressive and competitive behavior (Hall & Barongan, 1997). The date rapist could be said to be asserting culturally expected dominance over women.

College men frequently perceive a date's protests as part of an adversarial sex game. One male undergraduate said, "Hell, no" when asked whether a date had consented to sex. He added, "... But she didn't say no, so she must have wanted it, too. . . . It's the way it works" (Celis, 1991).

MYTHS ABOUT RAPE In the United States there are numerous myths about rape—myths that tend to blame the victim, not the aggressor. For example, a majority of Americans aged 50 and older believe that the woman is partly responsible for being raped if she dresses provocatively (Gibbs, 1991). As a result, they are unlikely to be sympathetic if such a woman complains of being raped. A majority of Americans believe that some women like to be talked into sex.

✓ **Truth or Fiction Revisited**

It is true that most Americans believe that some women like to be talked into sex. A majority of Americans—including a majority of American

Kristine, Amy, and Karen. These college women are among the thousands who have been raped by their dates. The great majority of rapes are committed by dates or acquaintances, not by strangers.

women—share this belief. Does this belief encourage men to pressure their dates into sex?

Other myths include the notions that "women say no when they mean yes," "all women like a man who is pushy and forceful," and "rapists are crazed by sexual desire" (Powell, 1996, p. 139). Still another myth is that deep down inside, women *want* to be raped. All these myths deny the impact of the assault and transfer blame onto the victim. They contribute to a social climate that is too often lenient toward rapists and unsympathetic toward victims.

✓ Truth or Fiction Revisited

It is not *true that women say no when they mean yes.* Myths such as this foster a social climate that encourages rape.

The causes of rape are many and complex. They include the aggressiveness of the individual who commits the rape and societal attitudes that have the effects of encouraging aggressiveness in males and of blaming the victim. Given the prevalence of rape and the multiplicity of causes, Question: How can we prevent rape?

PREVENTING RAPE (SHOUT "FIRE!" NOT "RAPE!") Let us begin this section with a disclaimer. We are going to talk about measures that women can take to reduce their vulnerability to rapists. However, we are *not* implying that the prevention of rape is the responsibility of the victim. Society at large harbors many attitudes that have the effect of supporting rape. For example, large numbers of people believe that a woman loses the right to say no if she has "led on" a man or even goes with him to his apartment. Also, men are reinforced for aggressive behavior in our society. Many people even expect men to exert social dominance over women. These social attitudes and expectations have catastrophic consequences for women and even for men who are uncomfortable with the stereotypes. It is thus the responsibility of any people who can communicate, such as your author, to lay the blame at the proper door and to insist on social change. We are doing precisely that—*now*. For example, many colleges and universities have workshops for new students—male and female— that explain when sexual forwardness becomes rape and how students can prevent criminal sexual aggressiveness.

Social change is a tedious process, however, and it may never come to pass. It may also be that your college or university has not held workshops concerning rape. Even if it has, all students may not change as a result of them. Women can thus profit from being armed with strategies for preventing rape in this less-than-ideal society.

The Boston Women's Health Book Collective (1992) lists a number of such strategies that women can use to lower the likelihood of rape at the hands of strangers:

- Establish signals and arrangements with other women in an apartment building or neighborhood.
- List only first initials in the telephone directory or on the mailbox.
- Use deadbolt locks.
- Keep windows locked and obtain iron grids for first-floor windows.
- Keep entrances and doorways brightly lit.
- Have keys ready for the front door or the car.
- Do not walk alone in the dark.

Gender and Sexuality

Sexual Harassment. Is this behavior acceptable in the workplace? Many women have switched jobs or colleges because of sexual harassment.

- Avoid deserted areas.
- Never allow a strange man into your apartment or home without checking his credentials.
- Drive with the car windows up and the door locked.
- Check the rear seat of the car before entering.
- Avoid living in an unsafe building (if you can).
- Do not pick up hitchhikers (including women).
- Do not talk to strange men in the street.
- Shout "Fire!" not "Rape!" People crowd around fires but avoid scenes of violence.

The following tactics may help prevent *date rape* (Rathus et al., 2000):

- Avoid getting into secluded situations until you know your date very well. But be aware that victims of date rapes have sometimes gotten to know their assailants.
- Be wary when a date attempts to control you in any way, such as frightening you by driving rapidly or taking you someplace you would rather not go.
- Be very assertive and clear concerning your sexual intentions. Some rapists, particularly date rapists, tend to misinterpret women's wishes. If their dates begin to implore them to stop during kissing or petting, they construe pleading as "female game playing." So if kissing or petting is leading where you don't want it to go, speak up.
- When dating a person for the first time, try to date in a group.
- Encourage your college or university to offer educational programs about date rape. The University of Washington, for example, offers students lectures and seminars on date rape and provides women with escorts to get home. Brown University requires all first-year students to attend orientation sessions on rape. Men need to learn that "No" means "No," despite the widespread belief that some women like to be "talked into" sex.
- Talk to your date about his attitudes toward women. If you get the feeling that he believes that men are in a war with women, or that women "play games" with men, you may be better off dating someone else.

Rape is one form of sexual coercion. There are many others. For example, some people—female and male—are exposed to continuous verbal sexual pressure from their dates and acquaintances. Some experience sexual harassment. Question: What is sexual harassment?

Sexual Harassment

Sexual harassment is common on college campuses, in the business world, and in the military (Seppa, 1997). It is sometimes difficult to draw the line between sexual persuasion and attempted rape. It can be even *more* difficult to distinguish between a legitimate (if unwelcome) sexual invitation and sexual harassment. People accused of sexual harassment often claim that the charges are exaggerated. They say that the victim "overreacted" to normal male–female interaction, or "She took me too seriously." However, sexual harassment *is* a serious problem, and most harassers know very well what they are doing (see Table 15.4).

Sexual harassment involves deliberate or repeated unwanted comments, gestures, or physical contact of a sexual nature (Powell, 1996). Consider some examples:

SEXUAL HARASSMENT Deliberate or repeated verbal comments, gestures, or physical contact of a sexual nature that is unwanted by the recipient.

REFLECT

Where does "normal male–female interaction" end and sexual harassment begin? Is it sometimes difficult to discriminate between them? Explain.

TABLE 15.4	SEXUAL HARASSMENT: MYTHS AND REALITIES
MYTHS	**REALITIES**
Sexual harassment is rare.	Sexual harassment is extremely widespread. It touches the lives of 40% to 60% of working women and similar proportions of female students in colleges and universities.
The seriousness of sexual harassment has been exaggerated; most so-called harassment is really trivial and harmless flirtation.	Sexual harassment can be devastating. Studies indicate that most harassment has nothing to do with "flirtation" or sincere sexual or social interest. Rather, it is offensive, often frightening, and insulting to women. Research shows that women are often forced to leave school or jobs to avoid harassment. They may experience serious psychological and health problems.
Many women make up and report stories of sexual harassment to get back at their employers or others who have angered them.	Research shows that less than 1% of complaints are false. Women rarely file complaints even when they are justified in doing so.
Women who are sexually harassed generally provoke harassment by the way they look, dress, and behave.	Harassment does not occur because women dress provocatively or initiate sexual activity in the hope of getting promoted and advancing their careers. Studies have found that victims of sexual harassment vary in physical appearance, type of dress, age, and behavior. The only thing they have in common is that over 99% of them are female.
If you ignore harassment, it will go away.	It will not. Research has shown that simply ignoring the behavior is ineffective; harassers generally do not stop on their own. Ignoring such behavior may even be seen as agreement or encouragement.

SOURCE: American Psychological Association (1998, March 16). Sexual harassment: Myths and realities. APA Public Information Home Page; www.apa.org.

- Verbal abuse,
- Unwelcome sexual overtures or advances,
- Pressure to engage in sexual activity,
- Remarks about a person's body, clothing, or sexual activities,
- Leering at, or ogling, someone,
- Telling unwanted dirty jokes in mixed company,
- Unnecessarily touching, patting, or pinching,
- Whistles and catcalls,
- Brushing up against someone,
- Demands for sex that are accompanied by threats, such as being fired from a job or not getting a promotion.

Your college may publish guidelines about sexual harassment. Check with the dean of students or the president's office.

College students are sexually harassed by other students and sometimes by professors. Professors are sometimes harassed by students. Most often the victims of sexual harassment are women. Some cases are so serious that women switch majors or schools to avoid it. Ironically, as with rape, society often blames the victim of sexual harassment for being provocative or for not saying no firmly enough (Powell, 1996).

RESISTING SEXUAL HARASSMENT Question: What do you do if you are sexually harassed by another student or by a professor? Do you try to ignore it and hope for the best—that it will be mild or that the harasser will come to his or her senses and cut it out? Do you take action? If so, what do you do? Here are some suggestions:

REFLECT

Have you ever heard people blame the victim of sexual harassment or rape? What did they say? How did you feel about it? Why?

1. Impart a professional attitude. Harassment is often stopped cold if you respond to the harasser in a curt, businesslike manner.

2. Discourage harassment and promote the kind of social behavior you want. Speak up. If your professor asks you to come to the office after dinner to review your paper to avoid being disturbed, say that you would rather talk over the paper during office hours. Stick to business. If the harasser does not take this suggestion, be more direct: "Mr. Smith, I'd like to keep our relationship purely student–professor, okay?"

3. Don't get into a situation in which you are alone with the harasser. Have a friend wait outside while you consult the professor in his office. Or see the harasser before or after class, when other people are around.

4. Keep a record of incidents to document them in case you decide to lodge an official complaint.

5. Put the harasser on direct notice that you recognize the harassment for what it is and that you want it to stop.

6. Confide about harassment to reliable friends, school counselors or advisers, or parents or relatives. Harassment is stressful, and social support helps us cope with stress. Other people may also have helpful advice.

7. Many campuses have offices where complaints about sexual harassment are filed and acted on. Check with the dean of students or the president's office.

8. See a lawyer. Sexual harassment is illegal, and you can stop it.

REFLECT

Were you or anyone you know ever sexually harassed? How was it handled? Do you believe it was handled well? Explain.

Review

SECTION VI

As many as one woman in (107) _____ in the United States has been raped. Four out of (108) _____ rapes are committed by people that the victim is acquainted with. Many social scientists argue that rape is often a man's way of expressing social (109) _____nance over, or anger toward, women. Many social critics argue that American culture (110) _____izes men into becoming rapists by reinforcing them for aggressive and competitive behavior.

In the United States rape myths tend to blame the (111) _____tim, not the aggressor. A majority of Americans aged 50 and older believe that the woman (112: Is or Is not?) partly responsible for being raped if she dresses provocatively.

It can be difficult to distinguish between a legitimate (if unwelcome) sexual invitation and sexual (113) _____ment. Sexual harassment (114: Is or Is not?) illegal and students can talk to a lawyer to stop it.

Gender and sexuality may be "the facts of life," but many of the "facts" we have taken for granted may be little more than myth. Some of the more questionable facts have to do with the nature and extent of supposed gender differences, and the burdens that these supposed differences have historically placed on women. Both in terms of personality and sexual response, males and females are apparently more alike than most people have assumed. Nevertheless, we all differ greatly as individuals, and one of the great lessons of research in gender and sexuality is that we need to respect our differences as individuals.

STUDY GUIDE

To help you better understand the content of this chapter, you may go to the student Web site (http://www.harcourtcollege.com/psych/intro.html) to take more quizzes, get more information about the content, and see additional Web sites related to the content. You can also practice using the concepts in this chapter with the PowerPsych CD-ROM, which gives you interactive activities and experiments along with even more quizzes. And, of course, the printed study guide is a reliable way to practice all parts of PQ4R. Your college bookstore can order the PowerPsych CD-ROM for you.

S U M M A R Y

1. **What are gender-role stereotypes?** Cultures have broad expectations of men and women that are termed *gender-role stereotypes*. In our culture women are expected to be gentle, dependent, kind, helpful, patient, and submissive. Men are expected to be tough, competitive, gentlemanly, and protective.

2. **What are the costs of gender polarization?** Polarization has historically worked to the disadvantage of women. For example, women have until recent years been excluded from careers in medicine and law, and math and science courses in the schools are still seen as mainly in the male "domain." Women who adhere to traditional feminine gender roles are likely to take a back seat to men in the workplace and in the home. "Masculine" men may not be able to ask for help when they need it or to express tender feelings.

3. **What are the gender differences in cognitive abilities?** Boys have historically been seen as excelling in math and spatial relations skills, whereas girls have been viewed as excelling in language skills. However, these differences are small and growing narrower.

4. **What are the gender differences in social behavior?** Females are more extraverted and nurturant than males. Males are more tough-minded and aggressive than females. Men are more interested than women in casual sex and in multiple sex partners. Women are more willing than men to marry someone who is not good-looking, but less willing to marry someone who is unlikely to hold a steady job.

5. **What are some biological views of gender-typing?** Biological views of gender-typing focus on the roles of evolution, genetics, and prenatal influences in predisposing men and women to gender-linked behavior patterns. Testosterone in the brains of male fetuses spurs greater growth of the right hemisphere of the brain, which may be connected with the ability to manage spatial relations tasks. Testosterone is also connected with aggressiveness.

6. **What are some psychological views of gender-typing?** Psychologists have attempted to explain gender typing in terms of psychodynamic, social-cognitive, and gender-schema theories. Freud ex-

plained gender-typing in terms of identification with the parent of the same gender through resolution of the Oedipus complex. Social-cognitive theorists explain the development of gender-typed behavior in terms of processes such as observational learning, identification, and socialization. Research shows that women can behave as aggressively as men when they are provoked, have the means, and believe that the social climate will tolerate their aggression. Gender-schema theory proposes that once children learn the gender schema of their culture, their self-esteem becomes tied up in how well they express the traits considered relevant to their gender.

7. **What factors contribute to attraction in our culture?** Men seem to find large eyes and narrows jaws to be attractive in women. In our culture, slenderness is considered attractive in both men and women, and tallness is valued in men. Women tend to see themselves as being heavier than the cultural ideal. We are more attracted to good-looking people. Similarity in attitudes and sociocultural factors (ethnicity, education, and so on), and reciprocity in feelings of admiration, also enhance attraction. According to the matching hypothesis, we tend to seek dates and mates at our own level of attractiveness, largely because of fear of rejection.

8. **Just what is love? What is romantic love?** Sternberg's theory suggests that love has three components: intimacy, passion, and commitment. Different kinds of love combine these components in different ways. Romantic love is characterized by the combination of passion and intimacy. Consummate love has all three factors.

9. **What is meant by the term *sexual orientation?*** Sexual orientation refers to the direction of one's erotic interests. Heterosexual people are sexually attracted to people of the other gender and interested in forming romantic relationships with them. Homosexual people are sexually attracted to people of their own gender and interested in forming romantic relationships with them. Members of ethnic minority groups in the United States appear to be less tolerant of homosexuality than are European Americans.

10. **How do researchers explain gay male and lesbian sexual orientations?** Psychodynamic theory connects sexual orientation with improper resolution of the Oedipus and Electra complexes. Learning theorists focus on the role of reinforcement of early patterns of sexual behavior. Evidence of a genetic contribution to sexual orientation is accumulating. Sex hormones are known to have both organizing and activating effects, but research has failed to connect sexual orientation with differences in adult levels of sex hormones. However, sex hormones may play a role in determining sexual orientation during prenatal development.

11. **What is the sexual response cycle?** The sexual response cycle describes the body's response to sexual stimulation and consists of four phases: excitement, plateau, orgasm, and resolution. Excitement is characterized by erection in the male and lubrication in the female. Orgasm is characterized by muscle contractions and release of sexual tension. Following orgasm, males enter a refractory period during which they are temporarily unresponsive to sexual stimulation.

12. **What are sexual dysfunctions?** Sexual dysfunctions are persistent or recurrent problems in becoming sexually aroused or reaching orgasm. They include hypoactive sexual desire disorder (lack of interest in sex), female sexual arousal disorder and male erectile disorder (characterized by inadequate vasocongestion), orgasmic disorder, premature ejaculation, dyspareunia (pain during sex), and vaginismus (involuntary contraction of the muscles of the vaginal barrel, making intercourse difficult).

13. **What are the origins of sexual dysfunctions?** Sexual dysfunctions may be caused by physical problems, negative attitudes toward sex, lack of sexual knowledge and skills, problems in the relationship, and performance anxiety.

14. **How are sexual dysfunctions treated?** Sexual dysfunctions are treated by sex therapy, which focuses on reducing performance anxiety, changing self-defeating attitudes and expectations, teaching sexual skills, enhancing sexual knowledge, and improving sexual communication. There are also some biological treatments, such as medicine for male erectile disorder.

15. **Why do men rape women?** Social critics argue that men are socialized into sexual aggression by being generally reinforced for aggressiveness and competitiveness. Social attitudes such as gender-role stereotyping, seeing sex as adversarial, and myths that tend to blame the victim all help create a climate that encourages rape.

16. **How can we prevent rape?** Rape can be prevented by social change and by cautionary measures such as avoiding deserted areas and—in dating—by dating in groups and being assertive in expressing one's sexual intentions and limits.

17. **What is sexual harassment?** Sexual harassment consists of gestures, verbal comments, or physical contact of a sexual nature that is unwelcome to the recipient.

18. **What do you do if you are sexually harassed by another student or by a professor?** Sexual harassment is often stopped by means such as imparting a professional attitude, avoiding being alone with the harasser, keeping a record of incidents, notifying the harasser that you recognize the harassment for what it is and that you want it to stop, filing complaints with appropriate campus offices, and consulting a lawyer about the problem.

E X E R C I S E   1

IDENTIFYING GENDER-ROLE STEREOTYPES

This exercise will afford you insight as to whether you can identify various traits as being either stereotypically masculine or stereotypically feminine in the eyes of people from various countries around the world. The exercise does not endorse the polarity of these stereotypes but seeks to see whether you are aware of people's expectations of others. Write an *M* in the blank space to the left of the item if you believe that the trait is part of the masculine gender-role stereotype. Write an *F* in the blank space to the left of the item if you believe that the trait is part of the feminine gender-role stereotype.

M or *F*?

____	1.	Active	____ 21.	Patient
____	2.	Aggressive	____ 22.	Pleasure-seeking
____	3.	Capable	____ 23.	Precise
____	4.	Changeable	____ 24.	Rational
____	5.	Confident	____ 25.	Reckless
____	6.	Courageous	____ 26.	Resourceful
____	7.	Cruel	____ 27.	Rigid
____	8.	Dependent	____ 28.	Sensitive
____	9.	Emotional	____ 29.	Sharp-witted
____	10.	Enterprising	____ 30.	Shy
____	11.	Fearful	____ 31.	Sophisticated
____	12.	Fickle	____ 32.	Stingy
____	13.	Fussy	____ 33.	Submissive
____	14.	Hardheaded	____ 34.	Suggestible
____	15.	Imaginative	____ 35.	Talkative
____	16.	Individualistic	____ 36.	Timid
____	17.	Kind	____ 37.	Touchy
____	18.	Loud	____ 38.	Understanding
____	19.	Modest	____ 39.	Warm
____	20.	Opinionated	____ 40.	Worrying

EXERCISE 2

THEORIES OF GENDER-TYPING

Most psychologists believe that gender-typing involves the interaction of biological and psychological forces. Can you associate various statements about gender-typing with the theory to which they "belong"? Indicate whether each of the following statements is associated with:

Biological theory,
Psychodynamic theory,
Social-cognitive theory, or
Gender-schema theory.

____ 1. Children learn much of what is considered masculine or feminine by observational learning.

____ 2. Gender identity remains flexible until the Oedipus and Electra complexes are resolved.

____ 3. Female rats exposed to male sex hormones in the uterus learn maze routes more rapidly, roam over larger distances, and mark larger territories than other females.

____ 4. Gender differences were fashioned by natural selection in response to problems in adaptation that were repeatedly encountered by humans over thousands of generations.

____ 5. Children naturally try to construct identities that are consistent with the "proper" gender-role stereotypes in their culture.

____ 6. Parents and others socialize children by informing them about how they are expected to behave and rewarding them for behavior they consider appropriate for their gender.

____ 7. Our culture polarizes females and males by organizing social life around mutually exclusive gender roles which children come to accept without realizing it.

____ 8. Aggression is more actively discouraged in girls through punishment, withdrawal of affection, or being told that "girls don't act that way."

____ 9. Prenatal testosterone may "masculinize" the brain by creating predispositions consistent with the masculine gender-role stereotype.

____ 10. Children are more likely to accurately remember information that is consistent with the gender-role stereotypes found in their culture.

____ 11. The hemispheres of the brain are more specialized in males than in females.

____ 12. Appropriate gender-typing requires that boys identify with their fathers and surrender the wish to possess their mothers.

____ 13. Identification is theorized to be a continuous learning process in which children are influenced by rewards and punishments to imitate adults of the same gender.

____ 14. Once children understand the labels *boy* and *girl*, they have a basis for blending their self-concepts with the gender-role stereotypes found in their culture.

____ 15. Research shows that men with damage to the right hemisphere are more likely to have problems with spatial relations than women with similar injuries.

E X E R C I S E   3

THE SEXUAL RESPONSE CYCLE

The sexual response cycle has four phases:

Excitement,

Plateau,

Orgasmic, and

Resolution.

Following are events that occur during the various phases of the cycle. Indicate which phase applies to each event.

____ 1. Seminal fluid collects at the base of the penis.

____ 2. Blood is released from engorged areas.

____ 3. The heart rate may increase to 100 to 160 beats per minute.

____ 4. The blood pressure and heart rate reach a peak, with the heart beating up to 180 times per minute.

____ 5. Vasocongestion causes the head of the penis to take on a purplish hue.

____ 6. The body returns to its unaroused state.

____ 7. The female experiences 3 to 15 contractions of the pelvic muscles that surround the vagi-nal barrel. The contractions first occur at 0.8-second intervals.

____ 8. Vasocongestion causes the clitoris to begin to swell and the vaginal lips to begin to spread.

____ 9. The internal sphincter of the urinary bladder prevents urine from mixing with semen.

____10. Males enter a refractory period during which they cannot experience another orgasm or ejaculate.

____11. Muscle contractions propel the ejaculate out of the body.

____12. Vasocongestion swells the outer part of the vagina.

LANGUAGE AND CULTURE

acquaintance (715)   *person known to another*

adversarial (716)   *characterized by being opponents*

arrogant (686)   *proud, disdainful, unsociable*

breadwinner (688)   *person who earns the money for a family, traditional role for men*

catastrophic (717)   *disastrous, unexpectedly bad*

chatterbox (691)   *talkative person*

to come to pass (717)   *to happen*

coercion (715)   *force (against one's will)*

crisp (688)   *clean and freshly ironed (said of clothes)*

deadbolt lock (717)   *door lock that requires a key, even from the inside*

disclaimer (717)   *statement to clarify attitude toward or position on an issue*

to dissuade (687)   *to convince not to*

earlobe (683)   *the lowest part of the outer ear*

engorged (712)   *filled (as with blood)*

enterprising (687)   *energetic, forceful*

extraversion (691)   *condition of looking outside of oneself*

to be a fashion plate (688)   *a plate is a picture, a photograph; a fashion plate is a woman who dresses in the latest fashions*

figuratively (684)   *metaphorically, not really (pun:* in the dark *means without light and also without knowledge)*

to figure in (713)   *to be a contributor to*

frivolous (686)   *not serious, trivial, extravagant*

forwardness (717)   *sexual aggressiveness*

fussy (686)   *hard to please*

gender (685)   *sex (male or female)*

homemaker (688)   *traditional role for women*

incest taboo (685)   *prohibition against family members becoming intimately involved*

to be indebted to (714)   *to be grateful to, to feel one must repay a favor*

in the eye of the beholder (698)   *according to the view of the person who is receiving the message*

to lead someone on (717)   *to act as though inviting*

to leer (719)   *to stare, usually with sexual interest*

lenient (717)   *free, not strict*

lifting languidly (684)   *rising into view lazily, as if it were lazy*

missionary position (684)   *sexual intercourse position with the man on top, woman under him*

to ogle (719)   *to stare with obvious desire*

orgasm (684)   *sexual climax*

orifice (710)   *opening*

petting (685)   *mild sexual stimulation*

plumpness (699)   *roundness of body*

polarization (685)   *process of defining the extremes, or moving toward the extremes*

provocatively (716)   *with sexual invitation as an underlying meaning*

prudish (687)   *reserved, modest (negatively so)*

robust (687)   *strong and healthy*

to shatter (688)   *to destroy*

to be stopped cold (720)   *to be extinguished*

stoutness (699)   *heaviness*

straight (708)   *(here) not homosexual, i.e., not gay or lesbian*

to transcend (699)   *to rise above, to exceed*

unbridled (691)   *uncontrolled, unchecked*

unfasten (715)   *to unbutton, unzip in removing clothing*

unscrupulous (687)   *without good morals*

vulnerability (717)   *position of disadvantage, open to attack*

QUIZ

1. Which of the following traits is considered to be part of the masculine gender-role stereotype?
   (a) Sensitive,
   (b) Dependent,
   (c) Shy,
   (d) Enterprising.

2. Which of the following traits is considered to be part of the feminine gender-role stereotype?
   (a) Resourceful,
   (b) Sophisticated,
   (c) Cruel,
   (d) Stingy.

3. Which of the following statements about gender and mathematics is true?
   (a) Teachers of math courses often show higher expectations for female students,
   (b) Mothers are more likely than fathers to help children with math homework,
   (c) Boys take more math courses in high school than girls do,
   (d) Boys are more likely than girls to have math anxiety.

4. Women's wages average about _____ percent of men's wages.
   (a) 32,
   (b) 52,
   (c) 72,
   (d) 92.

5. Which of the following statements about gender differences in cognition is true?
   (a) In the United States more girls than boys have reading problems,
   (b) Girls seem to acquire language somewhat faster than boys do,
   (c) Boys are somewhat superior to girls in spelling,
   (d) Girls are superior to boys in visual-spatial skills, such as map reading.

6. Which of the following statements about gender differences in social behavior is true?
   (a) Women are more likely than men to gossip,
   (b) Men are more extraverted than women,
   (c) Men are more trusting than women,
   (d) Women are more willing than men to reveal their feelings and personal experiences.

7. Which of the following statements about gender differences in aggression is true?
   (a) Females behave as aggressively as males when they have the means to do so and believe that aggression is justified,
   (b) Females are less likely than males to feel anxious or guilty about aggression,
   (c) Males are more likely to empathize with the victim of aggression,
   (d) Gender differences in aggression increase when the victim is anonymous.

8. Men with damage to the _____ are more likely to have problems with spatial relations than women with similar injuries.
   (a) hypothalamus,
   (b) sensorimotor area of the cerebral cortex,
   (c) left hemisphere of the brain,
   (d) right hemisphere of the brain.

9. Which of the following conditions needs to be present for gender-typing to occur, according to gender-schema theory?
   (a) Children must understand the labels *boy* and *girl*,
   (b) The Oedipus complex must be resolved,
   (c) Children must be reinforced for gender-appropriate behavior,
   (d) Society must avoid gender polarization.

10. According to psychodynamic theory, a "classic pattern" of child rearing in which there is a "close binding" mother and a "detached hostile" father is connected with
    (a) a gay male sexual orientation,
    (b) male erectile disorder,
    (c) aggressive behavior,
    (d) dysfunction in the left hemisphere of the brain.

11. Research shows that British and Japanese men are attracted to women who
    (a) have small eyes,
    (b) have narrow jaws,
    (c) are tall,
    (d) are socially dominant.

12. In their dating practices, people tend to ask out persons who are similar in attractiveness largely because of
    (a) fairness,
    (b) fear of rejection,
    (c) balance theory,
    (d) evaluation apprehension.

13. In terms of the triangular model of love, romantic love is characterized by
    (a) passion and commitment,
    (b) commitment and intimacy,

(c) passion alone,

(d) passion and intimacy.

14. Why do young Sambian males engage in oral sexual relations with older males?

    (a) They have Dominican Republic syndrome and spend their early years as females,

    (b) They are attempting to achieve the fierce manhood of the headhunter,

    (c) Sexual orientation changes frequently during childhood and adolescence,

    (d) They are paid to do so as part of a religious ritual.

15. Which of the following statements about genetics and twins is most accurate?

    (a) A gay male orientation is not found among MZ and DZ twins,

    (b) The agreement rate for a gay male orientation is equal among MZ and DZ twins,

    (c) The agreement rate for a gay male orientation is higher among MZ twins,

    (d) The agreement rate for a gay male orientation is higher among DZ twins.

16. Female rats that are exposed to _____ in the uterus have better spatial relations skills and seek larger territories than other female rats.

    (a) adrenaline,

    (b) estrogen,

    (c) female siblings,

    (d) testosterone.

17. Erection first occurs during the _____ phase of the sexual response cycle.

    (a) excitement,

    (b) plateau,

    (c) orgasmic,

    (d) resolution.

18. Which of the following is defined as involuntary contraction of the muscles surrounding the vaginal opening?

    (a) Vasocongestion,

    (b) Myotonia,

    (c) Vaginismus,

    (d) The refractory period.

19. Men are more likely than women to

    (a) experience painful sex,

    (b) be unable to reach orgasm,

    (c) lack interest in sex,

    (d) reach orgasm too early.

20. Three of the following four statements about rape are myths. Which one is true?

    (a) Deep down inside, women want to be raped,

    (b) College men often interpret a date's protests as part of an adversarial sex game.

    (c) Some women like to be talked into sex,

    (d) The woman is partly responsible for being raped if she dresses provocatively.

1. What are gender-role stereotypes?

2. What are the costs of gender polarization?

3. What are the gender differences in cognitive abilities?

4. What are the gender differences in social behavior?

5. What are some biological views of gender-typing?

6. What are some psychological views of gender-typing?

7. What factors contribute to attraction in our culture?

8. Just what is love? What is romantic love?

9. What is meant by the term *sexual orientation?*

10. How do researchers explain gay male and lesbian sexual orientations?

11. What is the sexual response
    cycle?

    _____
    _____
    _____
    _____
    _____

12. What are sexual
    dysfunctions?

    _____
    _____
    _____
    _____
    _____

13. What are the origins of
    sexual dysfunctions?

    _____
    _____
    _____
    _____
    _____

14. How are sexual dysfunctions
    treated?

    _____
    _____
    _____
    _____
    _____

15. Why do men rape women?

    _____
    _____
    _____
    _____
    _____

16. How can we prevent rape?

    _____
    _____
    _____
    _____
    _____

17. What is sexual harassment?

    _____
    _____
    _____
    _____

18. What do you do if you are
    sexually harassed by another
    student or by a professor?

    _____
    _____
    _____
    _____

ANSWERS TO SECTION REVIEWS

1. Stereotypes
2. Gender
3. Different
4. Men
5. Polarize
6. Feminine
7. Masculine
8. Men
9. Women
10. Women
11. Girls
12. Boys
13. Less
14. Unlikely
15. Do not
16. Girls
17. Boys
18. Small
19. Girls
20. Boys
21. Women
22. Men
23. Men
24. Women
25. Men
26. Women
27. More
28. Less
29. Less
30. More
31. Do
32. Gender-typing
33. Natural
34. Males
35. Females
36. Males
37. Hormones
38. Masculinize
39. Male
40. Testosterone
41. Identification
42. Oedipus
43. Earlier
44. Cognitive (or Learning)
45. Observational
46. Socialization
47. Do
48. Polarizes
49. Gender-schema
50. Schema
51. Self-esteem
52. Large
53. Narrow
54. Tallness
55. Culturally determined
56. Both genders
57. Ideal
58. Too heavy
59. Women
60. Men
61. Women
62. Men
63. More
64. Women
65. Matching
66. Like
67. Reciprocity
68. Triangular
69. Passion
70. Consummate
71. Romantic
72. Men
73. Orientation
74. Heterosexual
75. Homosexual
76. Less
77. Identification
78. Oedipus
79. Reinforcement
80. Find
81. Organizing
82. Testosterone
83. Has not
84. More
85. Response
86. Excitement
87. Resolution
88. Vasocongestion
89. Blood
90. Myotonia
91. Erection
92. Lubrication
93. Contractions
94. Ejaculates
95. Refractory
96. Dysfunctions
97. Hypoactive
98. Arousal
99. Erectile
100. Orgasmic
101. Premature
102. Dyspareunia
103. Vaginismus
104. Anxiety
105. Sex
106. Performance
107. Four
108. Five
109. Dominance
110. Socializes
111. Victim
112. Is
113. Harassment
114. Is

ANSWERS TO EXERCISE 1

1. M
2. M
3. M
4. F
5. M
6. M
7. M
8. F
9. F
10. M
11. F
12. F
13. F
14. M
15. F
16. M
17. F
18. M
19. F
20. M
21. F
22. M
23. M
24. M
25. M
26. M
27. M
28. F
29. M
30. F
31. F
32. M
33. F
34. F
35. F
36. F
37. F
38. F
39. F
40. F

ANSWERS TO EXERCISE 2

1. Social-cognitive theory or Gender-schema theory
2. Psychodynamic theory
3. Biological theory
4. Biological theory
5. Gender-schema theory
6. Social-cognitive theory
7. Gender-schema theory
8. Social-cognitive theory
9. Biological theory
10. Gender-schema theory
11. Biological theory
12. Psychodynamic theory
13. Social-cognitive theory
14. Gender-schema theory
15. Biological theory

ANSWERS TO EXERCISE 3

1. Orgasmic phase	4. Orgasmic phase	7. Orgasmic phase	10. Resolution phase
2. Resolution phase	5. Plateau phase	8. Excitement phase	11. Orgasmic phase
3. Plateau phase	6. Resolution phase	9. Orgasmic phase	12. Plateau phase

ANSWERS TO QUIZ

1. D	6. D	11. B	16. D
2. B	7. A	12. B	17. A
3. C	8. D	13. D	18. C
4. C	9. A	14. B	19. D
5. B	10. A	15. C	20. B

STATISTICS

This appendix, "Statistics," covers the following:

SECTION I. STATISTICS
Defines statistics
Defines what is meant by samples and populations

SECTION II. DESCRIPTIVE STATISTICS
Defines descriptive statistics (and explains why it isn't always good to be a "10")
Illustrates various kinds of frequency distributions
Describes measures of central tendency (and explains why you never want to try to

walk across a river that is an average of 4 feet deep!)
Describes two measures of variability

SECTION III. THE NORMAL CURVE
Describes the normal curve

SECTION IV. THE CORRELATION COEFFICIENT
Defines the correlation coefficient

SECTION V. INFERENTIAL STATISTICS
Defines inferential statistics
Explains what is meant by statistically significant differences

SECTION I. STATISTICS

Imagine that some visitors from outer space arrive outside Madison Square Garden in New York City. Their goal this dark and numbing winter evening is to learn all they can about planet Earth. They are drawn inside the Garden by lights, shouts, and warmth. The spotlighting inside rivets their attention to a wood-floored arena where the New York Big Apples are hosting the California Quakes in a briskly contested basketball game.

Our visitors use their sophisticated instruments to take some measurements of the players. Some interesting statistics are sent back to their planet of origin: It appears that (1) 100% of Earthlings are male, and (2) the height of Earthlings ranges from 6 feet 1 inch to 7 feet 2 inches.

These measurements are called **statistics.** Question: What is statistics? Statistics is the name given the science concerned with obtaining and organizing numerical information or measurements. Our imagined visitors have sent home statistics about the gender and size of human beings that are at once accurate and misleading. Although they accurately measured the basketball players (we have translated their units of measurement into feet and inches for readers' convenience), their small **sample** of Earth's **population** was, shall we say, distorted.

Question: What are samples and populations? A population is a complete group of people, other animals, or measures from which a sample is drawn. For example, all people on Earth could be defined as the population of interest. So could all women, or all women in the United States. A sample is a group of measures drawn from a population. Fortunately for us Earthlings, about half of the world's population is female. And the **range** of heights observed by the aliens, of 6 feet 1 inch to 7 feet 2 inches, is both restricted and too high—much too high. People vary in height by more than 1 foot and 1 inch. And our **average** height is not between 6 feet 1 inch and 7 feet 2 inches; rather, it is a number of inches below.

Psychologists, like our imagined visitors, are vitally concerned with measuring human as well as animal characteristics and traits—not just physical characteristics like height, but also psychological traits like intelligence, sociability, aggressiveness, neatness, anxiety, and depression. By observing the central tendencies (averages) and variations in measurement from person to person, psychologists can say that some person is average

REFLECT
Why would the observations of the basketball players give the aliens a distorted impression of the traits of Earthlings?

REFLECT
How do psychologists measure psychological characteristics like intelligence and anxiety?

A2

or above average in intelligence, or that someone else is less anxious than, say, 60% of the population.

But psychologists, unlike our aliens, are careful in their attempts to select a sample that accurately represents the entire population. Professional basketball players do not represent the entire human species. They are taller, stronger, and more agile than the rest of us. They also make appreciably higher numbers of commercials for sneakers.

✓ Truth or Fiction Revisited

It is true that basketball players are abnormal—statistically speaking. They are much taller than average and possess better-than-average athletic skills. (Fans consider these abnormalities to be assets, not deficits.)

In this appendix we survey some of the statistical methods used by psychologists to draw conclusions about the measurements they take in research activities. First we discuss *descriptive statistics* and learn what types of statements we can make about height and other human traits. Then we discuss the *normal curve* and learn why basketball players are abnormal—at least in terms of height. We explain *correlation coefficients* and provide you with some less-than-shocking news: As a group, students who study obtain higher grades than students who do not study. Finally we have a look at *inferential statistics* and we see why we can be bold enough to say that the difference in height between basketball players and other people is not a chance fluctuation or fluke. Basketball players are, in fact, *statistically significantly* taller than the general population.

Review

SECTION I

The science that obtains and organizes numerical information or measurements is called (1) _____ics. A (2) _____tion is a complete group of people or other animals or measures. A (3) _____le is a group of measures drawn from a population. The (4) r_____ of heights of the basketball players discussed in this section was restricted and too high to represent the general population. By observing the (5) _____ tendencies (averages) and variations in measurement from person to person, psychologists can say that an individual is average or above average in intelligence, or that someone else is less anxious than a certain percentage of the population.

SECTION II. DESCRIPTIVE STATISTICS

Being told that someone is a "10" may sound great at first. However, it is not very descriptive unless you know something about how the scores on the scale are distributed and how frequently one finds a 10. Fortunately—for 10s, if not for the rest of us—one usually means that the person is a 10 on a scale of 1 to 10 and that 10 is the highest possible score on the scale. If this is not sufficient, one will also be told that 10s are few and far between—rather unusual statistical events. But note that the scale could also vary from 0 to 100, in which case a score of 10 would place one nearer the bottom of the scale and make a score of 50 the center point of the scale. With such a scale, being a 10 would be much less impressive.

STATISTICS Numerical facts assembled in such a manner that they provide useful information about measures or scores. (From the Latin *status*, meaning "standing" or "position.")

SAMPLE Part of a population.

POPULATION A complete group from which a sample is selected.

RANGE A measure of variability defined as the high score in a distribution minus the low score.

AVERAGE The central tendency of a group of measures, expressed either as the mean, median, or mode of a distribution.

DESCRIPTIVE STATISTICS The branch of statistics that is concerned with providing descriptive information about a distribution of scores.

FREQUENCY DISTRIBUTION An ordered set of data that indicates the frequency (how often) with which scores appear.

It is true that being a "10" is not necessarily a good thing. Being a 10 may be good if the scale varies from 1 to 10, but not if the scale varies from, say, 0 to 100.

The idea of the scale from 1 to 10 may not be very scientific, but it does suggest something about **descriptive statistics**. Question: What is descriptive statistics? (Why isn't it always good to be a "10"?) Descriptive statistics is the branch of statistics that provides information about distributions of scores. We can use descriptive statistics to clarify our understanding of a distribution of scores such as heights, test grades, IQs, or even increases or decreases in measures of aggressive behavior following the drinking of alcohol. For example, descriptive statistics can help us determine measures of central tendency (averages) and how much fluctuation or variability there is in the scores. Being a 10 loses much of its charm if the average score is an 11. Being a 10 is more remarkable in a distribution whose scores range from 1 to 10 than it is in a distribution whose scores range from 9 to 11.

Let us now consider some of the concerns of descriptive statistics: the frequency distribution, measures of central tendency (types of averages), and measures of variability.

The Frequency Distribution

Question: What is a frequency distribution? A frequency distribution takes scores or items of raw data, puts them into order, as from the lowest to the highest, and indicates how often a score appears. A frequency distribution groups data according to class intervals, although the class may be a single unit (one), as in Table APP.2. Table APP.1 shows the rosters for a recent basketball game between the California Quakes and the New York Big Apples. The players are listed according to the numbers on their uniforms. Table APP.2 shows a frequency distribution of the heights of the players, with the two teams combined. The class interval in Table APP.2 is 1 inch.

It would also be possible to use other class intervals, such as 3 inches, as shown in Table APP.3. In determining the size of a class interval, the researcher tries to collapse the data into a small enough number of classes

TABLE APP.1	ROSTERS OF QUAKES VERSUS BIG APPLES AT NEW YORK

A glance at the rosters for a recent basketball game in which the New York Big Apples "entertained" the California Quakes shows that the heights of the team members, combined, ranged from 6 feet 1 inch to 7 feet 2 inches. Do the heights of the team members represent those of the general male population? What do you think?

California Quakes		New York Big Apples	
2 Callahan	6'7"	3 Roosevelt	6'1"
5 Daly	6'11"	12 Chaffee	6'5"
6 Chico	6'2"	13 Baldwin	6'9"
12 Capistrano	6'3"	25 Delmar	6'6"
21 Brentwood	6'5"	27 Merrick	6'8"
25 Van Nuys	6'3"	28 Hewlett	6'6"
31 Clemente	6'9"	33 Hollis	6'9"
32 Whittier	6'8"	42 Bedford	6'5"
41 Fernando	7'2"	43 Coram	6'2"
43 Watts	6'9"	45 Hampton	6'10"
53 Huntington	6'6"	53 Ardsley	6'10"

TABLE APP.2	FREQUENCY DISTRIBUTION OF BASKETBALL PLAYERS (QUAKES AND BIG APPLES COMBINED), WITH A 1-INCH CLASS INTERVAL
Class Interval	**Number of Players in Class**
6'1"–6'1.9"	1
6'2"–6'2.9"	2
6'3"–6'3.9"	2
6'4"–6'4.9"	0
6'5"–6.5.9"	3
6'6"–6'6.9"	3
6'7"–6'7.9"	1
6'8"–6'8.9"	2
6'9"–6'9.9"	4
6'10"–6'10.9"	2
6'11"–6'11.9"	1
7'0"–7'0.9"	0
7'1"–7'1.9"	0
7'2"–7'2.9"	1

to ensure that they will be meaningful at a glance. But the researcher also tries to keep a large enough number of categories (classes) to ensure that important differences are not obscured.

Table APP.3 obscures the fact that no players are 6 feet 4 inches tall. If the researcher believes that this information is extremely important, a class interval of 1 inch may be maintained.

✓ Truth or Fiction Revisited

It is true that researchers can often group their data to highlight or to hide their findings. In the example shown in the text, they can highlight the fact that no basketball player they measured was 6'4" tall, which could give the impression that basketball players are not that tall.

Figure APP.1 shows two methods of graphing the information in Table APP.3: the **frequency histogram** and the **frequency polygon**. Students sometimes have difficulty interpreting graphs, but the purpose of graphs is to reveal key information about frequency distributions at a glance. Note that in both kinds of graph, the frequency histogram and the frequency polygon, the class intervals are usually drawn along the horizontal line. The horizontal line is also known as the X-axis. The numbers of cases (scores, persons, or events) in each class interval are shown along the vertical line, which is also known as the Y-axis. In the histogram, the number of scores in each class interval is represented by a bar—a rectangular solid—so that the graph looks like a series of steps. In the polygon, the

FREQUENCY HISTOGRAM A graphic representation of a frequency distribution that uses rectangular solids (bars) to represent the frequency with which scores appear.

FREQUENCY POLYGON A graphic representation of a frequency distribution that connects the points that show the frequencies with which scores appear, thereby creating a multisided geometric figure.

TABLE APP.3	FREQUENCY DISTRIBUTION OF HEIGHTS OF BASKETBALL PLAYERS, USING A 3-INCH CLASS INTERVAL
Class Interval	**Number of Players in Class**
6'1"–6'3.9"	5
6'4"–6'6.9"	6
6'7"–6'9.9"	7
6'10"–7'0.9"	3
7'1"–7'3.9"	1

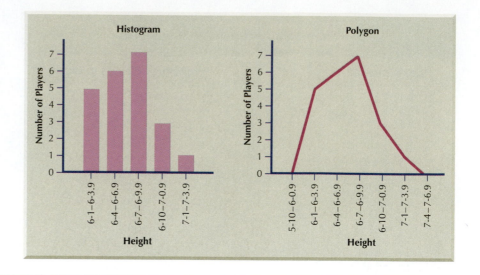

number of scores in each class interval is plotted as a point. The points are connected to form a many-sided geometric figure (polygon). Note that empty class intervals were added at each end of the frequency polygon so that the sides of the figure could be brought down to the X-axis to close the geometric figure.

Measures of Central Tendency

Never try to walk across a river just because it has an average depth of four feet.

MARTIN FRIEDMAN

As you see in the quip by Martin Friedman, a measure of central tendency can sometimes be misleading. Question: What are measures of central tendency? Measures of central tendency are "averages" that show the center or balancing points of a frequency distribution. There are three commonly used types of measures of central tendency: the *mean, median,* and *mode.* Each attempts to describe something about the scores in a frequency distribution through the use of a typical or representative number.

The **mean** is what most people think of as "the average." We obtain the mean of a distribution by adding up the scores and then dividing the sum by the number of scores. In the case of the basketball players, it would be advisable to first convert the heights into a single unit, such as inches (6′1″ becomes 73″, and so on). If we add all the heights in inches and then divide by the number of players (22), we obtain a mean height of 78.73″. If we convert that number back into units of feet and inches, we obtain 6′6.73″.

The **median** is the score of the middle case in a distribution. It is the score beneath which 50% of the cases fall. In a distribution with an even number of cases, such as the distribution of the heights of the 22 basketball players in Table APP.2, we obtain the median by finding the mean of the two middle cases. When we list the 22 cases in ascending order (moving from lowest to highest), the 11th case is 6′6″ and the 12th case is 6′7″. Therefore, the median of the distribution is (6′6″ + 6′7″) ÷ 2, or 6′6½″.

When we analyze the heights of the basketball players, we find that the mean and median are similar. Either one serves as a useful indicator of the central tendency of the data. But suppose we are trying to find the av-

MEAN A type of average that is calculated by adding all the scores and then dividing by the number of scores.

MEDIAN The central score in a frequency distribution; the score beneath which 50% of the cases fall.

erage savings of 30 families living on a suburban block. Let us assume that 29 of the 30 families have savings between $8,000 and $12,000, adding up to $294,000. But the 30th family has savings of $1,400,000! The mean savings for a family on this block would thus be $56,467. The mean can be greatly distorted by one or two extreme scores. An IQ score of 145 would similarly distort the mean of the IQ scores of a class of 20 students, among whom the other 19 IQ scores ranged from 93 to 112. Then, too, if a few basketball players signed up for one of your classes, the mean of the students' heights would be distorted in an upward direction.

✓ Truth or Fiction Revisited

Thus it is true that adding people's incomes and then dividing them by the number of people can be an awful way of showing the average income. A few extremely high incomes, or IQ scores, or heights can distort the average of a group in an upward direction.

When there are a few extreme scores in a distribution, the median is a better indicator of central tendency. The median savings on our hypothetical block would lie between $8,000 and $12,000. Thus it would be more representative of the central tendency of savings. Studies of the incomes of families in the United States usually report median rather than mean incomes just to avoid the distortion of findings that would occur if the incomes of a handful of billionaires were treated in the same way as more common incomes. On the other hand, one could argue that choosing the median as the average obscures or hides the extreme scores, which are just as "real" as the other scores. Perhaps it is best to use the median and a footnote—a rather big footnote.

The **mode** is simply the most frequently occurring score or measure in a distribution. The mode of the data in Table APP.1 is 6′9″ because this height occurs most often among the players on the two teams. The median class interval for the data shown in Table APP.3 is 6′6½″ to 6′9½″. With this particular distribution, the mode is somewhat higher than the mean or median.

In some cases the mode is a more appropriate description of the central tendency of a distribution than the mean or the median. Figure APP.2 shows a **bimodal** distribution—that is, a distribution with two modes. This is a hypothetical distribution of test scores obtained by a class. The mode at the left indicates the most common class interval (45–49) for students who did not study, and the mode to the right shows the most common class interval (65–69) for students who did study. (Don't be alarmed. I'm sure that the professor, who is extremely fair, will be delighted to curve the grades so that the interval of 75–79 is an A+ and the interval of 65–69 is at least a B.) The mean and median test scores would probably

MODE The most frequently occurring number or score in a distribution.

BIMODAL Having two modes.

FIGURE APP.2

A Bimodal Distribution This hypothetical distribution represents students' scores on a test. The mode at the left represents the central tendency of the test scores of students who did not study. The mode at the right represents the mode of the test scores of students who did study. (I'm allowed to be moralistic about studying; I wrote the book.)

Class Interval of Test Scores

lie within the 55–59 class interval, yet use of that interval as the measure of central tendency could obscure rather than reveal the important aspects of this distribution of test scores. It might suggest that the test was too hard, not that a number of students chose not to study. Similarly, one of the distribution's modes might be a bit larger than the other, so one could follow the exact rule for finding the mode and report just one of them. But this approach would also hide the meaning of this particular distribution of scores. All in all, it is clearly best to visualize this distribution of scores as bimodal. Even when the modes are not exactly equal, it is often most accurate to report distributions as bimodal or, when there are three or more modes, as multimodal. One chooses one's measure or measures of central tendency to describe the essential features of a frequency distribution, not to hide them.

Measures of Variability

Our hypothetical class obtained test scores ranging from call intervals of 35–39 to 75–79. That is, the scores *varied* from the lower class interval to the higher class interval. Now, if all the students had obtained scores from 55–59 to 65–69, the scores would not have varied as much; that is, they would have clustered closer to one another and would have had lower variability.

Question: What are measures of variability? The measures of the variability of a distribution inform us about the spread of scores—that is, about the typical distances of scores from the average score. Two commonly used measures of variability are the *range* of scores and the *standard deviation* of scores.

The range of scores in a distribution, as noted earlier, is defined as the difference between the highest score and the lowest score. The range is obtained by subtracting the lowest score from the highest score. The range of heights in Table APP.2 is obtained by subtracting 6′1″ from 7′2″, or 1′1″. It is useful to know the range of temperatures when we move to an area with a different climate so that we may anticipate the weather and dress for it appropriately. A teacher must have some understanding of the range of abilities or skills in a class in order to teach effectively. An understanding of the range of human heights can be used to design doorways, beds, and headroom in automobiles. Even so, the typical doorway is 6′8″ high, and as we saw with the California Quakes and New York Big Apples, some people will have to duck to get through.

The range is an imperfect measure of variability because of the manner in which it is influenced by extreme scores. The range of savings of the 30 families on our suburban block is $1,400,000 minus $8,000, or $1,392,000. This is a large number, and it is certainly true. However, it tells us little about the *typical* variation of savings accounts, which lie within a more restricted range of $8,000 to $12,000.

The **standard deviation** is a statistic that does a better job of showing how the scores in a distribution are distributed (spread) about the mean. It is usually better than the range because it considers every score in the distribution, not just the extreme (highest and lowest) scores. Consider Figure APP.3. Each distribution in the figure has the same number of scores, the same mean, and the same range of scores. However, the scores in the distribution on the right side cluster more closely about the mean. Therefore, the standard deviation of the distribution on the right is smaller. That is, the typical score deviates less from the mean score.

REFLECT

What is the range of test grades in your class? What is the standard deviation? Which measure gives a more accurate impression of the variability of grades? Explain.

STANDARD DEVIATION A measure of the variability of a distribution, obtained by the formula S.D. =

$$\sqrt{\frac{\text{Sum of } d^2}{N}}$$

FIGURE APP.3

HYPOTHETICAL DISTRIBUTIONS OF STUDENT TEST SCORES EACH DISTRIBUTION HAS THE SAME NUMBER OF SCORES, THE SAME MEAN, EVEN THE SAME RANGE, BUT THE STANDARD DEVIATION (A MEASURE OF VARIABILITY) IS GREATER FOR THE DISTRIBUTION ON THE LEFT BECAUSE THE SCORES TEND TO BE FARTHER FROM THE MEAN.

The standard deviation is usually abbreviated as S.D. It is calculated by the formula

$$\text{S.D.} = \sqrt{\frac{\text{Sum of } d^2}{N}}$$

where d equals the deviation of each score from the mean of the distribution, and N equals the number of scores in the distribution.

Let us find the mean and standard deviation of the IQ scores listed in column 1 of Table APP.4. To obtain the mean we add all the scores, attain 1,500, and then divide by the number of scores (15) to obtain a mean of 100. We obtain the deviation score (d) for each IQ score by subtracting the score from 100. The d for an IQ score of 85 equals 100 minus 85, or 15, and so on. Then we square each d and add the squares. The S.D. equals the square root of the sum of squares (1,426) divided by the number of scores (15), or 9.75.

TABLE APP.4	HYPOTHETICAL SCORES OBTAINED FROM AN IQ TESTING	
IQ Score	**d (Deviation Score)**	**d^2 (Deviation Score Squared)**
85	15	225
87	13	169
89	11	121
90	10	100
93	7	49
97	3	9
97	3	9
100	0	0
101	1	1
104	4	16
105	5	25
110	10	100
112	12	144
113	13	169
117	17	289
Sum of IQ scores = 1,500		Sum of d^2 scores = 1,426

$$\text{Mean} = \frac{\text{Sum of Scores}}{\text{Number of scores}} = \frac{1{,}500}{15} = 100$$

$$\text{Standard Deviation (S.D.)} = \sqrt{\frac{\text{Sum of } d^2}{N}} = \sqrt{\frac{1{,}426}{15}} = \sqrt{95.07} = 9.75$$

As an additional exercise, the Study Guide section of this appendix will assign the grades points according to a 4.0 system and then ask you to show that the S.D. of the test scores on the left (in Figure APP.3) is greater than that for the scores on the right. We will let A = 4, B = 3, C = 2, D = 1, and F = 0. If you do your math correctly, you will find that the S.D. for the distribution of scores on the left is larger. The larger S.D. indicates that the scores in that distribution are more variable, or tend to be farther from the mean.

Review

SECTION II

Being told that one is a "10" is not very descriptive unless one knows what the scale is and about the (6) _____tion of scores on that scale. (7) _____ statistics is the branch of statistics that provides information about distributions of scores. Descriptive statistics can help us determine measures of central tendency and how much fluctuation or (8) v_____ there is in the scores. Being a "10" is (9: More or Less?) remarkable in a distribution whose scores range from 1 to 10 than it is in a distribution whose scores range from 9 to 11.

A (10) f_____ distribution takes scores or items of raw data, puts them into order, and indicates how often a score appears. A frequency distribution groups data according to class (11) _____vals.

(12) _____phs are intended to reveal important information about frequency distributions at a glance. In the frequency (13) _____gram and the frequency (14) poly_____, the class intervals are usually drawn along the horizontal line. The horizontal line is also known as the (15: X or Y?) axis. The numbers of cases (scores, persons, or events) in each class interval are shown along the (16: Horizontal or Vertical?) line. The vertical line is also known as the (17: X or Y?) axis. In the (18) his_____, the number of scores in each class interval is represented by a bar. The points of the (19) _____cy polygon are connected to form a many-sided geometric figure.

There are three commonly used averages or measures of central tendency: the

(20) me_____, median, and (21) m_____. We obtain the mean of a distribution by adding up the scores and then dividing the sum by the (22) _____ of scores. The (23) _____ is the score of the middle case in a distribution. The median is the score beneath which (24) _____ percent of the cases fall. When there are a few extreme scores in a distribution, the (25: Mean or Median?) is a better indicator of central tendency. The (26) _____ is the most frequently occurring measure in a distribution. When a distribution is (27) _____modal, reference to the modes provides a more accurate description of the central tendency than the mean or the median.

The measures of the (28) _____bility of a distribution inform us about the spread of scores. Two commonly used measures of variability are the (29) r_____ and the standard (30) _____tion. The range of scores in a distribution is obtained by subtracting the (31) _____est score from the highest score. The range is (32: More or Less?) influenced by extreme scores than the standard deviation. The standard deviation is calculated by the formula

$$S.D. = \sqrt{\frac{\text{Sum of (33)} _____^2}{(34)\ \_\_\_\_\_}}$$

where *d* equals the deviation of each score from the (35) _____ of the distribution and *N* equals the number of scores in the distribution.

SECTION III. THE NORMAL CURVE

NORMAL DISTRIBUTION A symmetrical distribution that is assumed to reflect chance fluctuations; approximately 68% of cases lie within a standard deviation of the mean.

Many human traits and characteristics including height and intelligence seem to be distributed in a pattern known as a normal distribution. Question: What is a normal distribution? In a **normal distribution**, the mean, median, and mode all fall at the same data point or score. Scores

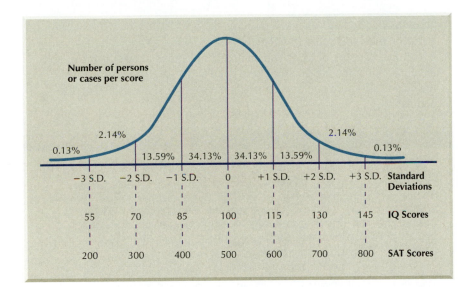

FIGURE APP.4
A Bell-Shaped or Normal Curve In a normal curve, approximately two out of three cases (68%) lie within a standard deviation (S.D.) from the mean. The mean, median, and mode all lie at the same score. IQ tests and the Scholastic Assessment Tests (SATs) are constructed so that their distributions approximate the normal curve.

cluster most heavily about the mean, fall off rapidly in either direction at first (as shown in Figure APP.4), and then taper off more gradually.

The curve in Figure APP.4 is bell-shaped. This type of distribution is also called a **normal curve** or bell-shaped curve. This curve is hypothesized to reflect the distribution of variables in which different scores are determined by chance variation. Height is thought to be largely determined by chance combinations of genetic material. A distribution of the heights of a random sample of the population approximates normal distributions for men and women, with the mean of the distribution for men a few inches higher than the mean for women.

Test developers traditionally assumed that intelligence was also randomly or normally distributed among the population. For that reason, they constructed intelligence tests so that scores would be distributed as close to "normal" as possible. In actuality, IQ scores are also influenced by environmental factors and chromosomal abnormalities, so that the resultant curves are not perfectly normal. The means of most IQ tests are defined as scores of 100 points. The Wechsler scales are constructed to have standard deviations of 15 points, as shown in Figure APP.4. A standard deviation of 15 points causes 50% of the Wechsler scores to fall between 90 and 110, which is called the "broad average" range. About 68% of scores (two out of three) fall between 85 and 115 (within a standard deviation of the mean), and more than 95% fall between 70 and 130—that is, within two standard deviations of the mean.

REFLECT

Do you tend to place yourself on the normal curve according to traits like nurturance, conscientiousness, and openness to new experience? Explain. Do you feel that people should be informed of their IQ scores? Explain.

✓ Truth or Fiction Revisited

It is true that psychologists may express your IQ score in terms of how deviant you are. The more extreme high (and low) IQ scores deviate more from the mean score.

The Scholastic Assessment Tests (SATs) were constructed so that the mean scores would be 500 points and the S.D. would be 100 points. Thus, a score of 600 would equal or excel that of some 84% to 85% of the test takers. Because of the complex interaction of variables that determine SAT scores, their distribution is not exactly normal, either. Moreover, the actual mean scores and standard deviations tend to vary from year to year, and in the case of the SAT IIs, from test to test. The normal curve is an idealized curve.

NORMAL CURVE Graphic presentation of a normal distribution, which shows a characteristic bell shape.

REFLECT

Do you feel that your SAT scores (or SAT II scores, or ACT scores) represent you accurately as a person? Explain.

It is true that an IQ score of 130 may be more impressive than an SAT score of 500. The IQ score of 130 is two standard deviations above the mean and exceeds that of more than 97% of the population. An SAT score of 500 is the mean SAT score and thus equals or excels that of about 50% of the population.

Review

SECTION III

In a (36) _____ distribution, the mean, median, and mode all fall at the same score. Scores cluster most heavily about the (37) _____, then fall off rapidly at first and then taper off more gradually. A normal distribution yields a graph called a normal (38) _____, which has the shape of a (39) _____.

The means of most IQ tests are defined as scores of (40) _____ points. The Wechsler scales have standard deviations of (41) _____ points. About (42) _____ of scores fall within a standard deviation of the mean. The Scholastic Assessment Tests (SATs) were constructed so that the mean scores would be (43) _____ points and the S.D. would be (44) _____ points.

SECTION IV. THE CORRELATION COEFFICIENT

What is the relationship between intelligence and educational achievement? Between cigarette smoking and lung cancer among humans? Between the personality trait of introversion and numbers of dates among college students? We cannot run experiments to determine whether the relationships between these variables are causal because we cannot manipulate the independent variable. That is, we cannot assign high or low intelligence at random. Nor can we (ethically) assign some people to smoke cigarettes and others not to smoke. People must be allowed to make their own decisions, so it is possible that the same factors that lead some people to smoke—or to continue to smoke after they have experimented with cigarettes—also lead to lung cancer. (Even if we were to assign a group of people to a nonsmoking condition, could we monitor them continuously to make sure that they weren't sneaking puffs?) Nor can we designate who will be introverted and who will be extraverted. True, we could encourage people to act as if they are introverted or extraverted, but behavior is not the same thing as a personality trait. We cannot run true experiments to answer any of these questions, but the **correlation coefficient** can be used to reveal whether there is a relationship between intelligence and achievement, a relationship between smoking and cancer, or a relationship between personality and dating.

✓ **Truth or Fiction Revisited**

It is not true that correlational research shows that smoking cigarettes causes cancer. Correlational research shows that smoking and cancer are related but does not reveal cause and effect. (Experimental research with animals does strongly suggest that smoking will cause cancer in humans, however.)

CORRELATION COEFFICIENT A number between −1.00 and +1.00 that indicates the direction (negative or positive) and extent (from none to perfect) of the relationship between two variables.

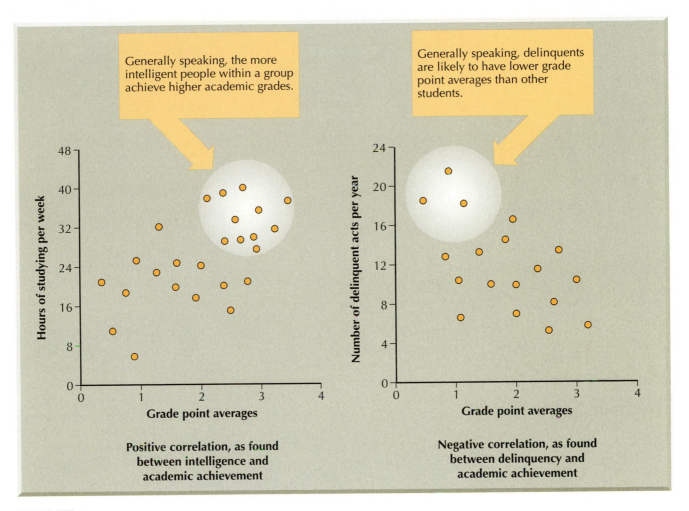

FIGURE APP.5

POSITIVE AND NEGATIVE CORRELATIONS   WHEN THERE IS A POSITIVE CORRELATION BETWEEN VARIABLES, AS THERE IS BETWEEN INTELLIGENCE AND ACHIEVEMENT, ONE INCREASES AS THE OTHER INCREASES. BY AND LARGE, THE MORE TIME STUDENTS SPEND STUDYING, THE BETTER THEIR GRADES ARE LIKELY TO BE, AS SUGGESTED IN THE DIAGRAM TO THE LEFT. (EACH DOT REPRESENTS THE AMOUNT OF TIME A STUDENT SPENDS STUDYING EACH WEEK AND HIS OR HER GRADE POINT AVERAGE.) BUT THERE IS A NEGATIVE CORRELATION BETWEEN GRADES AND JUVENILE DELINQUENCY. AS THE NUMBER OF DELINQUENT ACTS PER YEAR INCREASES, ONE'S GRADE POINT AVERAGE TENDS TO DECLINE. CORRELATIONAL RESEARCH MAY SUGGEST BUT DOES NOT DEMONSTRATE CAUSE AND EFFECT.

Question: What is the correlation coefficient? The correlation coefficient is a statistic that describes the relationship between two variables. A correlation coefficient can vary from +1.00 to −1.00. A correlation coefficient of +1.00 is called a perfect positive correlation, and it describes the relationship between temperatures as measured by the Fahrenheit and centigrade scales. A correlation coefficient of −1.00 is a perfect negative correlation, and a correlation of 0 (zero) reveals no relationship between variables.

As suggested by Figures APP.5 and APP.6, most correlation coefficients in psychological research are less than perfect. The left-hand graph in Figure APP.5 reveals a positive relationship between time spent studying and grade point averages. Since there is a positive correlation between the variables but the relationship is not perfect, the correlation coefficient will lie between 0.00 and +1.00. Perhaps it is about +0.6 or +0.7. However, we cannot absolutely predict what a person's GPA will be if we know the hours per week that he or she spends studying (nor can we predict exactly how much time the person spends studying on the basis of his or her GPA).

REFLECT

How would you explain the correlation between studying and grades? (Have you sketched out the entire picture?)

FIGURE APP.6

CORRELATIONAL RELATIONSHIPS, CAUSE AND EFFECT   CORRELATIONAL RELATIONSHIPS MAY SUGGEST BUT DO NOT DEMONSTRATE CAUSE AND EFFECT. IN PART A, THERE IS A CORRELATION BETWEEN VARIABLES X AND Y. DOES THIS MEAN THAT EITHER VARIABLE X CAUSES VARIABLE Y OR THAT VARIABLE Y CAUSES VARIABLE X? NOT NECESSARILY. OTHER FACTORS COULD AFFECT BOTH VARIABLES X AND Y. CONSIDER THE EXAMPLES OF ACADEMIC GRADES (VARIABLE X) AND TIME SPENT STUDYING (VARIABLE Y) IN PART B. THERE IS A POSITIVE CORRELATION BETWEEN THE TWO. DOES THIS MEAN THAT STUDYING CONTRIBUTES TO GOOD GRADES? PERHAPS. DOES IT MEAN THAT GOOD GRADES ENCOURAGE STUDYING? AGAIN, PERHAPS. BUT THERE COULD ALSO BE OTHER VARIABLES—SUCH AS CULTURAL BELIEF IN THE VALUE OF EDUCATION, ENJOYMENT OF LEARNING, EVEN PARENTAL PRESSURE TO DO WELL—THAT CONTRIBUTE BOTH TO TIME SPENT STUDYING AND GOOD GRADES.

Nevertheless, it would seem advisable to place oneself among those who spend a good deal of time studying if one wishes to achieve a good GPA.

The right-hand drawing in Figure APP.5 reveals a negative relationship between number of delinquent acts committed per year and GPA. The causal connection is less than perfectly clear. Does delinquency interfere with studying and academic achievement? Does poor achievement weaken a student's commitment to trying to get ahead through work? Do feelings of distance from "the system" contribute both to delinquent behavior and a low GPA? The answers are not to be found in Figure APP.5, but the negative correlation between delinquent behavior and GPA does suggest that it is worthwhile to study the issues involved and—for a student—to distance himself or herself from delinquent behavior if he or she wishes to achieve in the academic world.

SECTION IV   Review

The correlation (45) _____ is a statistic that describes the relationship between two variables. Correlational research (46: Does or Does not?) reveal cause and effect. A correlation coefficient can vary from +1.00 to (47) _____. A correlation coefficient of +1.00 is called a (48) per_____ _____tive correlation. A correlation of (49) _____ reveals no relationship between variables.

SECTION V. INFERENTIAL STATISTICS

Head Start programs have apparently raised children's intellectual functioning as reflected in their grades and IQ scores. In one such study, children enrolled in a Head Start program obtained a mean IQ score of 99, whereas children similar in background who were not enrolled in Head Start obtained a mean IQ score of 93 (Palmer, 1976). Is this difference of six points in IQ *significant,* or does it represent a chance fluctuation in scores? In a study reported in Chapter 1, college students were provoked by people in league with the researchers. Some of the students believed they had drunk alcohol (in a cocktail with tonic water); others believed they had drunk tonic water only. The students were then given the opportunity to shock the individuals who had provoked them. Students who believed they had drunk alcohol chose higher levels of shock than students who believed they had drunk tonic water only. Did the mean difference in shock level chosen by the two groups of students represent actual differences between the groups, or might it have been a chance fluctuation? The individuals in the Head Start study were a sample of young children. The individuals in the alcohol study were a sample of college students. Inferential statistics help us determine whether we can conclude that the differences between such samples reflect real differences that are found in the populations that they represent.

Descriptive statistics enable us to provide descriptive information about samples of scores. Question: What are inferential statistics? **Inferential statistics** assist us in determining whether we can generalize differences among samples to the populations that they represent.

Figure APP.7 shows the distribution of heights of 1,000 men and 1,000 women who were selected at random from the general U.S. population. The mean height for men is greater than the mean height for women. Can we conclude, or **infer,** that this difference in height is not just a chance fluctuation but represents an actual difference between the general populations of men and women? Or must we avoid such an inference and summarize our results by stating only that the mean height of the sample of men in the study was greater than the mean height of the sample of women in the study?

If we could not draw inferences about populations from studies of samples, our research findings would be limited indeed. We could speak about only the specific individuals studied. There would be no point to learning about any study in which you did not participate because it would not apply to you! Fortunately, that is not the case. Inferential statistics permits us to extend findings with samples to the populations from which they were drawn.

Statistically Significant Differences

We asked whether the differences in height between our samples of men and women were simply a chance fluctuation or whether they represented actual differences between the heights of men and women. Researchers tend not to talk about "real differences" or "actual differences" between groups, however. Instead, they speak of statistically significant differences. Similarly, researchers asked whether differences in IQ scores between children in Head Start programs and other children from similar backgrounds

INFERENTIAL STATISTICS The branch of statistics that is concerned with confidence with which conclusions drawn about samples can be extended to the populations from which the samples were drawn.

INFER To go from the particular to the general; to draw a conclusion.

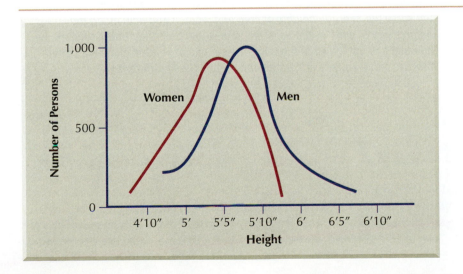

FIGURE APP.7

DISTRIBUTION OF HEIGHTS FOR RANDOM SAMPLES OF MEN AND WOMEN NOTE THAT THE MEAN HEIGHT OF THE MEN IS GREATER THAN THAT OF THE WOMEN. IS THE GROUP MEAN DIFFERENCE IN HEIGHT STATISTICALLY SIGNIFICANT? RESEARCHERS USE A TOOL CALLED INFERENTIAL STATISTICS TO DETERMINE THE ANSWER.

were chance fluctuations or statistically significant differences. Question: What are "statistically significant" differences? Statistically significant differences are differences that are unlikely to be due to chance fluctuation. Psychologists usually do not accept a difference as being statistically significant unless the probability (p) that it is due to chance fluctuation is less than 1 in 20 (i.e., $p < .05$). They are more comfortable labeling a difference as statistically significant when the probability (p) that it is due to chance fluctuation is less than 1 in 100 (i.e., $p < .01$).

Psychologists use formulas involving the means (e.g., mean IQ scores of 93 versus 99) and the standard deviations of sample groups to determine whether differences in means are statistically significant. As you can see in Figure APP.8, the farther apart group means are, the more likely it is that they are statistically significant. In other words, if the men are on the average 5 inches taller than the women, it is more likely that the difference is statistically significant than if the men are only one-quarter of an inch taller on average. Principle 1: Everything else being equal, the greater the difference between means, the greater the probability that the difference is statistically significant. This makes common sense. After all, if you were told that your neighbor's car had gotten one-tenth of a mile more per gallon of gas than your car in the past year, you would probably attribute the difference to chance fluctuation. But if the difference were greater, say, 14 miles per gallon, you would probably assume that the difference reflected an actual difference in driving habits or the efficiency of the automobile.

As you can see in Figure APP.9, the smaller the standard deviations (a measure of variability) of the groups, the more likely it is that the difference between means is statistically significant. Consider the extreme example in which there is *no* variability within each group. That is, imagine that every woman in the randomly selected sample of 1,000 women is exactly 5′5″ tall. Similarly, imagine that every man in the randomly selected sample of 1,000 men is exactly 5′10″ tall. In such a case the heights of the men and women would not overlap at all, and it would appear that the differences were statistically significant. Consider the other extreme—one with unnaturally large variability. Imagine that the heights of the women vary from 2′ to 14′ and that the heights of the men vary from 2′1″ to 14′3″. In such a case we might be more likely to assume that the difference in group means of 5″ was a chance fluctuation. Principle 2: Everything else being equal, the smaller the variability of the distributions of scores, the greater the probability that the difference in group means is statistically significant.

✓ Truth or Fiction Revisited

It is true that we cannot conclude that men are taller than women unless we know the average heights of men and women and how much the heights within each group vary. We must know both the central tendencies (means) and variability of the two distributions of heights in order to infer that the mean heights are statistically significantly different.

FIGURE APP.8

DECREASING AND INCREASING THE MEAN GROUP DIFFERENCE IN HEIGHTS EVERYTHING ELSE BEING EQUAL, THE GREATER THE DIFFERENCE IN GROUP MEANS, THE GREATER THE PROBABILITY THAT THE DIFFERENCE IS STATISTICALLY SIGNIFICANT. THE DISTRIBUTION ON THE RIGHT SHOWS A GREATER DIFFERENCE IN GROUP MEANS; THEREFORE, THERE IS A GREATER PROBABILITY THAT THE DIFFERENCE IS STATISTICALLY SIGNIFICANT.

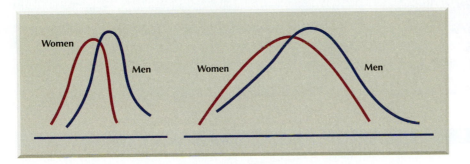

FIGURE APP.9

DECREASING AND INCREASING THE VARIABILITY OF THE DISTRIBUTIONS OF SCORES EVERYTHING ELSE BEING EQUAL, THE SMALLER THE VARIABILITY IN GROUP SCORES, THE GREATER THE PROBABILITY THAT THE DIFFERENCE IN GROUP MEANS IS STATISTICALLY SIGNIFICANT. THE DISTRIBUTION ON THE RIGHT SHOWS A GREATER DIFFERENCE IN THE VARIABILITY OF THE GROUPS; THEREFORE, THERE IS A *LOWER* PROBABILITY THAT THE DIFFERENCE IN GROUP MEANS IS STATISTICALLY SIGNIFICANT.

We have been "eyeballing" the data and making assumptions. We have been relying on what one professor of mine called the "Wow!" effect. As noted, psychologists and other researchers actually use mathematical techniques that take group means and standard deviations into account to determine whether group differences are statistically significant. It is often the case that eyeballing real data does not yield clear results, or even good guesses.

Samples and Populations

Inferential statistics are mathematical tools that psychologists apply to samples of scores to determine whether they can generalize or extend their findings to populations of scores. They must, therefore, be quite certain that the samples involved actually represent the populations from which they were drawn. Sampling techniques are crucial. Random sampling is the best method, and sampling is random only if every member of the target population has an equal chance of being selected.

It matters little how sophisticated our statistical methods are if the samples studied do not represent the target populations. We could use a variety of sophisticated statistical techniques to analyze the heights of the New York Big Apples and the California Quakes, but none of these methods would tell us much about the height of the general population. Or about the height of women. (Or about the height of people who can't pass the ball, shoot, or play defense.)

SECTION V

Descriptive statistics enable us to provide descriptive information about samples of scores. (50) _____ statistics help us decide whether we can generalize differences among samples to their populations. Statistically (51) _____ differences are unlikely to be due to chance fluctuation. Psychologists usually do not accept a difference as being statistically significant unless the probability that it is due to chance fluctuation is less than one in (52) _____.

Psychologists use formulas involving the means and (53) _____ deviations of sample groups to determine whether differences in means are statistically significant. The (54: Larger or Smaller?) the difference between means, the greater the probability that the difference is statistically significant. The (55: Larger or Smaller?) the variability of the distributions of scores, the greater the probability that the difference in group means is statistically significant.

STUDY GUIDE

S U M M A R Y

1. **What is statistics?** Statistics is the science that assembles data in such a way that they provide useful information about measures or scores. Such measures or scores include people's height, weight, and scores on psychological tests such as IQ tests.

2. **What are samples and populations?** A sample is part of a population. A population is a complete group from which a sample is drawn. The example with basketball players shows that a sample must represent its population if it is to provide accurate information about the population.

3. **What is descriptive statistics? (Why isn't it always good to be a "10"?)** Descriptive statistics is the branch of statistics that provides information about distributions of scores.

4. **What is a frequency distribution?** A frequency distribution organizes a set of data, usually from low scores to high scores, and indicates how frequently a score appears. Class intervals may be used on large sets of data to provide a quick impression of how the data tend to cluster. The frequency histogram and frequency polygon are two ways of graphing data to help people visualize the way in which the data are distributed.

5. **What are measures of central tendency?** Measures of central tendency are "averages" that show the center or balancing points of a frequency distribution. The mean—which is what most people consider the average—is obtained by adding the scores in a distribution and dividing by the number of scores. The median is the score of the middle or central case in a distribution. The mode is the most

common score in a distribution. Distributions can be bimodal (having two modes) or multimodal.

6. **What are measures of variability?** Measures of variability provide information about the spread of scores in a distribution. The range is defined as the difference between the highest and lowest scores. The standard deviation is a statistic that shows how scores cluster around the mean. Distributions with higher standard deviations are more spread out.

7. **What is a normal distribution?** The normal or bell-shaped curve is hypothesized to occur when the scores in a distribution occur by chance. The normal curve has one mode, and approximately two of three scores (68%) are found within one standard deviation of the mean. Fewer than 5% of cases are found beyond two standard deviations from the mean.

8. **What is the correlation coefficient?** The correlation coefficient is a statistic that describes how variables such as IQ and grade point averages are related. It varies from +1.00 to −1.00. When correlations between two variables are positive, it means that one (such as school grades) tends to rise as the other (such as IQ) rises.

9. **What are inferential statistics?** Inferential statistics is the branch of statistics that indicates whether researchers can extend their findings with samples to the populations from which they were drawn.

10. **What are "statistically significant" differences?** Statistically significant differences are believed to represent real differences between groups, and not chance fluctuation.

EXERCISE 1

THE STANDARD DEVIATION

Directions: The following table contains the grades for the test-score distributions shown in Figure APP.3. We have already converted the letter grades (A–F) to numbers (4–0). Calculate the mean for each distribution. Then calculate each deviation score and each deviation score squared. Finally, use the following formula to find the standard deviation for each distribution:

$$S.D. = \sqrt{\frac{\text{Sum of } d^2}{N}}$$

DISTRIBUTION AT LEFT			DISTRIBUTION TO THE RIGHT		
Grade	*d*	*d²*	**Grade**	*d*	*d²*
A (4)	2	4	A (4)	___	___
A (4)	___	___	B (3)	___	___
A (4)	___	___	B (3)	___	___
B (3)	___	___	B (3)	___	___
B (3)	___	___	B (3)	___	___
B (3)	___	___	C (2)	___	___
B (3)	___	___	C (2)	___	___
C (2)	___	___	C (2)	___	___
C (2)	___	___	C (2)	___	___
C (2)	___	___	C (2)	___	___
C (2)	___	___	C (2)	___	___
D (1)	___	___	C (2)	___	___
D (1)	___	___	C (2)	___	___
D (1)	___	___	D (1)	___	___
D (1)	___	___	D (1)	___	___
F (0)	___	___	D (1)	___	___
F (0)	___	___	D (1)	___	___
F (0)	___	___	F (0)	___	___

EXERCISE 2

THE NORMAL CURVE

Directions: Refer to the figure of the normal curve as you answer the following questions. You may round off your answers.

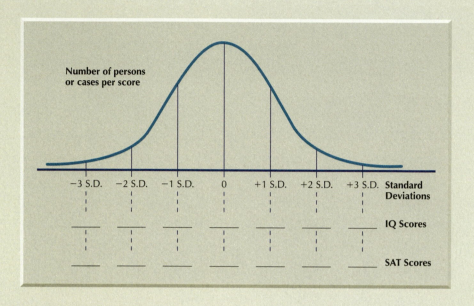

1. What percentage of the population lies between 0 and +1 standard deviations?

2. What IQ score corresponds with a standard deviation of −1?

3. What percentage of the population lies within a standard deviation of the mean?

4. What percentage of the population lies within two standard deviations of the mean?

5. Approximately what percentage of the population obtains IQ scores above 130?

6. Approximately what percentage of test takers obtains SAT scores above 500?

7. Approximately what percentage of test takers obtains SAT scores below 400?

8. Approximately what percentage of the population can be expected to obtain IQ scores between 115 and 130?

1. In a normal distribution, all of the following are at the same data point, with the exception of
   (a) the median,
   (b) the mode,
   (c) the mean,
   (d) the range.

2. The standard deviation is usually preferred to the range as a measure of variability because it
   (a) is derived by means of a sophisticated formula,
   (b) considers every score in a distribution,
   (c) is a smaller number than the range,
   (d) applies to populations as well as samples.

3. Which of the following is used in a frequency histogram to indicate the frequences with which scores appear in a distribution?
   (a) Rectangular solids,
   (b) Letters,
   (c) Frequences as measured by Hz,
   (d) A multisided geometric figure.

4. One group of students in a class studies and gets good grades. Another group in the class does not study and gets poor grades. If we combine all of the class's grades into a single frequency distribution, that distribution will probably be
   (a) normal,
   (b) ideal,
   (c) bimodal,
   (d) skewed.

5. An IQ score of 130 is more impressive than an SAT score of 500 because it
   (a) reflects inborn ability rather than achievement,
   (b) is two standard deviations above the mean, whereas the SAT score is at the mean,
   (c) can be computed only by using standard deviations,
   (d) can be achieved by a young child, whereas the SAT is taken by college applicants.

6. In a normal distribution, approximately _____ percent of the scores lie within a standard deviation of the mean.
   (a) 15,
   (b) 30,
   (c) 68,
   (d) 95.

7. The correlation coefficient that expresses the relationship between temperatures as measured by the Fahrenheit and centigrade scales is
   (a) −1.00,
   (b) 0.00,
   (c) +0.6 to +0.7,
   (d) +1.00.

8. The correlation coefficient that expresses the relationship between the number of miles I drive on a day and the number of minutes you spend watching MTV on the same day is
   (a) −1.00,
   (b) 0.00,
   (c) +0.6 to +0.7,
   (d) +1.00.

9. A difference between group means is said to be statistically significant if it
   (a) is large,
   (b) is small,
   (c) can be represented as a percentage of the variability in a distribution,
   (d) is unlikely to be due to chance fluctuation.

10. In order to conclude that men are taller than women, we must
    (a) know the central tendencies and variability of the two distributions of heights,
    (b) personally observe the differences in height between the two groups,
    (c) sort out the effects of heredity and environmental influences on height,
    (d) "eyeball" the graph that shows how the two distributions of heights overlap.

Recite Recite Recite Recite **Recite**

1. What is statistics?

2. What are samples and populations?

3. What is descriptive statistics? (Why isn't it always good to be a "10"?)

4. What is a frequency distribution?

5. What are measures of central tendency?

6. What are measures of variability?

7. What is a normal distribution?

8. What is the correlation coefficient?

9. What are inferential statistics?

10. What are "statistically significant" differences?

ANSWERS TO SECTION REVIEW

1. Statistics
2. Population
3. Sample
4. Range
5. Central
6. Distribution
7. Descriptive
8. Variability
9. More
10. Frequency
11. Intervals
12. Graphs
13. Histogram
14. Polygon
15. X

16. Vertical
17. Y
18. Histogram
19. Frequency
20. Mean,
21. Mode
22. Number
23. Median
24. Fifty (50)
25. Median
26. Mode
27. Bimodal (or Multimodal)
28. Variability
29. Range

30. Deviation
31. Lowest
32. More
33. d
34. N
35. Mean
36. Normal
37. Mean (Median, or Mode)
38. Curve
39. Bell
40. One hundred (100)
41. Fifteen (15)
42. 68% (or Two-thirds)
43. Five hundred (500)

44. One hundred (100)
45. Coefficient
46. Does not
47. Minus one (-1)
48. Perfect positive
49. Zero
50. Inferential
51. Significant
52. Twenty (20)
53. Standard
54. Larger
55. Smaller

ANSWERS TO EXERCISE 1

Exercise 1 asks you to compute the standard deviations for the test-score distributions in Figure APP.3. The following table will walk you through the computations, step by step.

DISTRIBUTION AT LEFT			DISTRIBUTION TO THE RIGHT		
Grade	**d**	**d^2**	**Grade**	**d**	**d^2**
A (4)	2	4	A (4)	2	4
A (4)	2	4	B (3)	1	1
A (4)	2	4	B (3)	1	1
B (3)	1	1	B (3)	1	1
B (3)	1	1	B (3)	1	1
B (3)	1	1	C (2)	0	0
B (3)	1	1	C (2)	0	0
C (2)	0	0	C (2)	0	0
C (2)	0	0	C (2)	0	0
C (2)	0	0	C (2)	0	0
C (2)	0	0	C (2)	0	0
D (1)	−1	1	C (2)	0	0
D (1)	−1	1	C (2)	0	0
D (1)	−1	1	D (1)	−1	1
D (1)	−1	1	D (1)	−1	1
F (0)	−2	4	D (1)	−1	1
F (0)	−2	4	D (1)	−1	1
F (0)	−2	4	F (0)	−2	4

Sum of grades = 36
Mean grade = 36/18 = 2
Sum of d^2 = 32
S.D. = $\sqrt{32/18}$ = 1.33

Sum of grades = 36
Mean grade = 36/18 = 2
Sum of d^2 = 16
S.D. = $\sqrt{16/18}$ = 0.94

ANSWERS TO EXERCISE 2

1. 34 (or 34.13)   3. 68 (or 68.26)   5. 2 (or 2.27)   7. 16 (or 15.87)
2. 85   4. 95 (or 95.44)   6. .50   8. 14 (or 13.59)

ANSWERS TO QUIZ

1. D   4. C   7. D   9. D
2. B   5. B   8. B   10. A
3. A   6. C

A-B problem The issue of how well we can predict behavior on the basis of attitudes.

Absolute threshold The minimal amount of energy that can produce a sensation.

Abstinence syndrome A characteristic cluster of symptoms that results from sudden decrease in an addictive drug's level of usage.

Accommodation According to Piaget, the modification of schemes so that information inconsistent with existing schemes can be integrated or understood.

Acculturation The process of adaptation in which immigrants and native groups identify with a new, dominant culture by learning about that culture and making behavioral and attitudinal changes.

Acetylcholine A neurotransmitter that controls muscle contractions. Abbreviated *ACh*.

Acoustic code Mental representation of information as a sequence of sounds.

Acquired drives Drives acquired through experience, or learned.

Acrophobia Fear of high places.

Action potential The electrical impulse that provides the basis for the conduction of a neural impulse along an axon of a neuron.

Activating effect The arousal-producing effects of sex hormones that increase the likelihood of sexual behavior.

Activation-synthesis model The view that dreams reflect activation of cognitive activity by the reticular activating system and synthesis of this activity into a pattern by the cerebral cortex.

Actor-observer effect The tendency to attribute our own behavior to situational factors but to attribute the behavior of others to dispositional factors.

Acute stress disorder A disorder, like posttraumatic stress disorder, characterized by feelings of anxiety and helplessness and caused by a traumatic event. Unlike posttraumatic stress disorder, acute stress disorder occurs within a month of the event and lasts from 2 days to 4 weeks.

Adolescence The period of life bounded by puberty and the assumption of adult responsibilities.

Adrenaline A hormone produced by the adrenal medulla that stimulates sympathetic ANS activity and generally arouses people and heightens their emotional responsiveness. Also called *epinephrine*.

Afferent neurons Neurons that transmit messages from sensory receptors to the spinal cord and brain. Also called *sensory neurons*.

Affiliation Association or connection with a group.

Afterimage The lingering visual impression made by a stimulus that has been removed.

Age regression In hypnosis, taking on the role of childhood, commonly accompanied by vivid recollections of one's past.

Age-30 transition Levinson's term for the ages from 28 to 33, which are characterized by reassessment of the goals and values of the 20s.

Agoraphobia Fear of open, crowded places.

Alarm reaction The first stage of the general adaptation syndrome, which is triggered by the impact of a stressor and characterized by sympathetic activity.

Algorithm A systematic procedure for solving a problem that works invariably when it is correctly applied.

All-or-none principle The fact that a neuron fires an impulse of the same strength whenever its action potential is triggered.

Alpha waves Rapid low-amplitude brain waves that have been linked to feelings of relaxation.

Altruism Unselfish concern for the welfare of others.

Amniotic sac A sac within the uterus that contains the embryo or fetus.

Amphetamines Stimulants derived from *alpha-methyl-beta-phenyl-ethyl-amine*, a colorless liquid consisting of carbon, hydrogen, and nitrogen.

Amygdala A part of the limbic system that apparently facilitates stereotypical aggressive responses.

Anal stage The second stage of psychosexual development, when gratification is attained through anal activities.

Anchoring and adjustment heuristic A decision-making heuristic in which a presumption or first estimate serves as a cognitive anchor. As we receive additional information, we make adjustments but tend to remain in the proximity of the anchor.

Androgens Male sex hormones.

Animism The belief that inanimate objects move because of will or spirit.

Anorexia nervosa A life-threatening eating disorder characterized by refusal to maintain a healthful body weight, intense fear of being overweight, a distorted body image, and, in females, suspension of menstruation.

Anterograde amnesia Failure to remember events that occur after physical trauma because of the effects of the trauma.

Antibodies Substances formed by white blood cells that recognize and destroy antigens.

Antidepressant Acting to relieve depression.

Antidiuretic hormone A pituitary hormone that conserves body fluids by increasing reabsorption of urine and is connected with paternal behavior in some mammals. Also called *vasopressin*.

Antigen A substance that stimulates the body to mount an immune system response to it (the contraction for *anti*body *gen*erator).

Aphagic Characterized by undereating.

Aphasia A disruption in the ability to understand or produce language.

Applied research Research conducted in an effort to find solutions to particular problems.

Approach–approach conflict A type of conflict in which the goals that produce opposing motives are positive and within reach.

Approach–avoidance conflict A type of conflict in which the same goal produces approach and avoidance motives.

Archetypes Basic, primitive images or concepts hypothesized by Jung to reside in the collective unconscious.

Artificialism The belief that natural objects have been created by human beings.

Assimilation According to Piaget, the inclusion of a new event into an existing scheme.

Attachment The enduring affectional tie that binds one person to another.

Attachment-in-the-making phase The second phase in forming bonds of attachment, characterized by preference for familiar figures.

Attention-deficit/hyperactivity disorder A disorder that begins in childhood and is characterized by a persistent pattern of lack of attention, with or without hyperactivity and impulsive behavior.

Attitude An enduring mental representation of a person, place, or thing that evokes an emotional response and related behavior.

Attitude-discrepant behavior Behavior inconsistent with an attitude that may have the effect of modifying an attitude.

Attraction In social psychology, an attitude of liking or disliking (negative attraction).

Attribution A belief concerning why people behave in a certain way.

Attributional style One's tendency to attribute one's behavior to internal or external factors, stable or unstable factors, and so on.

Attribution process The process by which people draw inferences about the motives and traits of others.

Auditory nerve The axon bundle that transmits neural impulses from the organ of Corti to the brain.

Authoritarian parents Parents who are rigid in their rules and who demand obedience for the sake of obedience.

Authoritative parents Parents who are strict and warm. Authoritative parents demand mature behavior but use reason rather than force in discipline.

Autonomic nervous system (ANS) The division of the peripheral nervous system that regulates glands and activities such as heartbeat, respiration, digestion, and dilation of the pupils.

Autonomy Self-direction.

Availability heuristic A decision-making heuristic in which our estimates of frequency or probability of events are based on how easy it is to find examples.

Average The central tendency of a group of measures, expressed either as the mean, median, or mode of a distribution.

Aversive conditioning A behavior-therapy technique in which undesired responses are inhibited by pairing repugnant or offensive stimuli with them.

Avoidance–avoidance conflict A type of conflict in which the goals are negative, but avoidance of one requires approaching the other.

Axon A long, thin part of a neuron that transmits impulses to other neurons from branching structures called *terminals*.

Backward conditioning A classical conditioning procedure in which the unconditioned stimulus is presented prior to the conditioned stimulus.

Barbiturate An addictive depressant used to relieve anxiety or induce sleep.

Basilar membrane A membrane that lies coiled within the cochlea.

Behavioral genetics The study of the genetic transmission of structures and traits that give rise to behavior.

Behaviorism The school of psychology that defines psychology as the study of observable behavior and studies relationships between stimuli and responses.

Behavior-rating scale A systematic means for recording the frequency with which target behaviors occur.

Behavior therapy Systematic application of the principles of learning to the direct modification of a client's problem behaviors.

Bimodal Having two modes.

Binocular cues Stimuli suggestive of depth that involve simultaneous perception by both eyes.

Biofeedback training The systematic feeding back to an organism of information about a bodily function so that the organism can gain control of that function. Abbreviated *BFT*.

Bipolar cells Neurons that conduct neural impulses from rods and cones to ganglion cells.

Bipolar disorder A disorder in which the mood alternates between two extreme poles (elation and depression). Also referred to as *manic-depression*.

Bisexual A person who is sexually aroused by and interested in forming romantic relationships with people of either gender.

Blind In experimental terminology, unaware of whether or not one has received a treatment.

Blind spot The area of the retina where axons from ganglion cells meet to form the optic nerve.

Bottom-up processing The organization of the parts of a pattern to recognize, or form an image of, the pattern they compose.

Brainstorming A group process that encourages creativity by stimulating a large number of ideas and suspending judgment until the process is completed.

Brightness constancy The tendency to perceive an object as being just as bright even though lighting conditions change its intensity.

Broca's aphasia A language disorder characterized by slow, laborious speech.

Bulimia nervosa An eating disorder characterized by recurrent cycles of binge eating followed by dramatic measures to purge the food.

Case study A carefully drawn biography that may be obtained through interviews, questionnaires, and psychological tests.

Castration anxiety Within Freudian theory, fear that one's genital organs will be cut off. Castration anxiety is a normal feature of the Oedipus complex that motivates boys to forego their rivalry with their fathers over possession of their mothers.

Catastrophize To interpret negative events as being disastrous; to "blow out of proportion."

Catatonic schizophrenia A type of schizophrenia characterized by striking impairment in motor activity.

Catch 30s Sheehy's term for the fourth decade of life, when many people undergo major reassessments of their accomplishments and goals.

Catharsis In psychodynamic theory, the purging of strong emotions or the relieving of tensions. The expression of repressed feelings and impulses to allow the release of the psychic energy associated with them.

Center   According to Piaget, to focus one's attention.

Central nervous system   The brain and spinal cord.

Cerebellum   A part of the hindbrain involved in muscle coordination and balance.

Cerebral cortex   The wrinkled surface area (gray matter) of the cerebrum.

Cerebrum   The large mass of the forebrain, which consists of two hemispheres.

Chromosomes   Structures consisting of genes that are found in the nuclei of the body's cells.

Chunk   A stimulus or group of stimuli that are perceived as a discrete piece of information.

Circadian rhythm   Referring to cycles that are connected with the 24-hour period of the earth's rotation.

Cirrhosis of the liver   A disease caused by protein deficiency in which connective fibers replace active liver cells, impeding circulation of the blood. Alcohol does not contain protein; therefore, persons who drink excessively may be prone to this disease.

Classical conditioning   A simple form of learning in which an organism comes to associate or anticipate events. A neutral stimulus comes to evoke the response usually evoked by another stimulus by being paired repeatedly with the other stimulus. (Cognitive theorists view classical conditioning as the learning of relationships among events so as to allow an organism to represent its environment.) Also referred to as *respondent conditioning* or *Pavlovian conditioning.*

Claustrophobia   Fear of tight, small places.

Clear-cut-attachment phase   The third phase in forming bonds of attachment, characterized by intensified dependence on the primary caregiver.

Client-centered therapy   Carl Rogers's method of psychotherapy, which emphasizes the creation of a warm, therapeutic atmosphere that frees clients to engage in self-exploration and self-expression.

Clinical scales   Groups of test items that measure the presence of various abnormal behavior patterns.

Clitoris   An external female sex organ that is highly sensitive to sexual stimulation.

Closure   The tendency to perceive a broken figure as being complete or whole.

Cochlea   The inner ear; the bony tube that contains the basilar membrane and the organ of Corti.

Cognitive   Having to do with mental processes such as sensation and perception, memory, intelligence, language, thought, and problem solving.

Cognitive-dissonance theory   The view that we are motivated to make our cognitions or beliefs consistent.

Cognitive triad   A cluster of depressing attitudes identified by Aaron Beck: expecting the worst of oneself, the world at large, and the future.

Collective unconscious   Jung's hypothesized store of vague racial memories.

Collectivist   A person who defines the self in terms of relationships to other people and groups and gives priority to group goals.

Color constancy   The tendency to perceive an object as being the same color even though lighting conditions change its appearance.

Common fate   The tendency to perceive elements that move together as belonging together.

Competencies   Knowledge and skills.

Compulsion   An apparently irresistible urge to repeat an act or engage in ritualistic behavior such as hand washing.

Computerized axial tomography   (AX-ee-al toe-MOG-raf-fee). Formation of a computer-generated image of the anatomical details of the brain by passing a narrow X-ray beam through the head and measuring from different angles the amount of radiation that passes through. Abbreviated *CAT scan.*

Consensus   General agreement.

Concept   A mental category used to class together objects, relations, events, abstractions, or qualities that have common properties.

Concrete-operational stage   Piaget's third stage, characterized by logical thought concerning tangible objects, conservation, and subjective morality.

Conditional positive regard   Judgment of another person's value on the basis of the acceptability of that person's behaviors.

Conditioned reinforcer   Another term for a secondary reinforcer.

Conditioned response (CR)   In classical conditioning, a learned response to a conditioned stimulus.

Conditioned stimulus (CS)   A previously neutral stimulus that elicits a conditioned response because it has been paired repeatedly with a stimulus that already elicited that response.

Conditions of worth   Standards by which the value of a person is judged.

Conductive deafness   The forms of deafness in which there is loss of conduction of sound through the middle ear.

Cones   Cone-shaped photoreceptors that transmit sensations of color.

Conflict   Being torn in different directions by opposing motives. Feelings produced by being in conflict.

Conform   To changes one's attitudes or overt behavior to adhere to social norms.

Conservation   According to Piaget, recognition that basic properties of substances such as weight and mass remain the same when superficial features change.

Consummate love   The ideal form of love within Sternberg's model, which combines passion, intimacy, and commitment.

Contact comfort   A hypothesized primary drive to seek physical comfort through contact with another.

Context-dependent memory   Information that is better retrieved in the context in which it was encoded and stored, or learned.

Contingency theory   The view that learning occurs when stimuli provide information about the likelihood of the occurrence of other stimuli.

Continuity   The tendency to perceive a series of points or lines as having unity.

Continuous reinforcement   A schedule of reinforcement in which every correct response is reinforced.

Control groups   In experiments, groups whose members do not obtain the treatment, while other conditions are held constant.

Conventional level   According to Kohlberg, a period during which moral judgments largely reflect social conventions. A "law and order" approach to morality.

Convergence   A binocular cue for depth based on the inward movement of the eyes as they attempt to focus on an object that is drawing nearer.

Convergent thinking   A thought process that attempts to narrow in on the single best solution to a problem.

Conversion disorder   A disorder in which anxiety or unconscious conflicts are "converted" into physical symptoms that often have the effect of helping the person cope with anxiety or conflict.

Cornea   Transparent tissue forming the outer surface of the eyeball.

Corpus callosum   A thick fiber bundle that connects the hemispheres of the cortex.

Correlation coefficient   A number from +1.00 to –1.00 that expresses the direction (positive or negative) and extent (from none to perfect) of the relationship between two variables.

Corticosteroids   Steroids produced by the adrenal cortex that regulate carbohydrate metabolism and increase resistance to stress by fighting inflammation and allergic reactions. Also called *cortical steroids*.

Cortisol   A hormone produced by the adrenal glands that increases resistance to stress.

Creative self   According to Adler, the self-aware aspect of personality that strives to achieve its full potential.

Creativity   The ability to generate novel and useful solutions to problems.

Critical thinking   An approach to thinking characterized by skepticism and thoughtful analysis of statements and arguments—for example, probing arguments' premises and the definitions of terms.

Critical period   A period of time when an instinctive response can be elicited by a particular stimulus.

Crystallized intelligence   One's lifetime of intellectual achievement, as shown largely through vocabulary and knowledge of world affairs.

Cultural bias   A factor that provides an advantage for test takers from certain cultural or ethnic backgrounds, such as using test items that are based on middle-class culture in the United States.

Daily hassles   Notable daily conditions and experiences that are threaten-

ing or harmful to a person's well-being.

Dark adaptation   The process of adjusting to conditions of lower lighting by increasing the sensitivity of rods and cones.

Debrief   To elicit information about a completed procedure.

Decentration   Simultaneous focusing on more than one dimension of a problem, so that flexible, reversible thought becomes possible.

Decibel   A unit expressing the loudness of a sound. Abbreviated *dB*.

Deductive reasoning   A form of reasoning about arguments in which conclusions are deduced from premises. The conclusions are true if the premises are true.

Defense mechanism   In psychodynamic theory, an unconscious function of the ego that protects it from anxiety-evoking material by preventing accurate recognition of this material.

Deindividuation   The process by which group members may discontinue self-evaluation and adopt group norms and attitudes.

Déjà vu   A French phrase meaning "already seen," and referring to the experience of having been in a new situation before, apparently because contextual cues trigger the retrieval of images and feelings from the past.

Delayed conditioning   A classical conditioning procedure in which the CS is presented before the US and remains in place until the response occurs.

Delirium tremens   A condition characterized by sweating, restlessness, disorientation, and hallucinations. The DTs occurs in some chronic alcohol users when there is a sudden decrease in usage.

Delta waves   Strong, slow brain waves usually emitted during stage 4 sleep.

Delusions   False, persistent beliefs unsubstantiated by sensory or objective evidence.

Dendrites   Rootlike structures, attached to the cell body of a neuron, that receive impulses from other neurons.

Dependent variable   A measure of an assumed effect of an independent variable.

Depersonalization disorder   A dissociative disorder in which one expe-

riences persistent or recurrent feelings that one is not real or is detached from one's own experiences or body.

Depolarize   To reduce the resting potential of a cell membrane from about –70 millivolts toward zero.

Depressant   A drug that lessens activity of the nervous system.

Descriptive statistics   The branch of statistics that is concerned with providing descriptive information about a distribution of scores.

Desensitization   The type of sensory adaptation in which we become less sensitive to constant stimuli. Also called *negative adaptation*.

Dichromat   A person who is insensitive to the colors of red and green and hence partially color blind.

Difference threshold   The minimal difference in intensity required between two sources of energy so that they will be perceived as being different.

Diffusion of responsibility   The spreading or sharing of responsibility for a decision or behavior within a group.

Direct inner awareness   Knowledge of one's own thoughts, feelings, and memories without use of sensory organs.

Discrimination   In conditioning, the tendency for an organism to distinguish between a conditioned stimulus and similar stimuli that do not forecast an unconditioned stimulus. Also, the denial of privileges to a person or a group on the basis of prejudice.

Discrimination training   Teaching an organism to show a learned response in the presence of only one of a series of similar stimuli, accomplished by alternating the stimuli but following only the one stimulus with the unconditioned stimulus.

Discriminative stimulus   In operant conditioning, a stimulus that indicates that reinforcement is available.

Disorganized schizophrenia   A type of schizophrenia characterized by disorganized delusions and vivid hallucinations.

Displace   In memory theory, to cause information to be lost from short-term memory by adding new information.

Displaced Transferred.

Dispositional attribution An assumption that a person's behavior is determined by internal causes such as personal attitudes or goals.

Dissociative amnesia A dissociative disorder marked by loss of memory or self-identity, thought to stem from psychological conflict or trauma; skills and general knowledge are usually retained. Previously termed *psychogenic amnesia.*

Dissociative disorders Disorders in which there are sudden, temporary changes in consciousness or self-identity.

Dissociative fugue A dissociative disorder in which one experiences amnesia and then flees to a new location. Previously termed *psychogenic fugue.*

Dissociative identity disorder A disorder in which a person appears to have two or more distinct identities or personalities that may alternately emerge. Previously termed *multiple personality.*

Divergent thinking A thought process that attempts to generate multiple solutions to problems.

Dizygotic (DZ) twins Fraternal twins. Twins who develop from separate zygotes.

Dopamine A neurotransmitter that is involved in Parkinson's disease and that appears to play a role in schizophrenia.

Double-blind study A study in which neither the subjects nor the observers know who has received the treatment.

Dream Levinson's term for the overriding drive of youth to become someone important, to leave one's mark on history.

Drive A condition of arousal in an organism that is associated with a need.

Drive for superiority Adler's term for the desire to compensate for feelings of inferiority.

Drive-reduction theory The view that organisms learn to engage in behaviors that have the effect of reducing drives.

Dyspareunia A sexual dysfunction characterized by persistent or recurrent pain during sexual intercourse. (From roots meaning "badly paired.")

Eardrum A thin membrane that vibrates in response to sound waves, transmitting the waves to the middle and inner ears.

Eating disorders Psychological disorders characterized by distortion of the body image and gross disturbances in eating patterns.

Echo A mental representation of an auditory stimulus (sound) that is held briefly in sensory memory.

Echoic memory The sensory register that briefly holds mental representations of auditory stimuli.

Efferent neurons Neurons that transmit messages from the brain or spinal cord to muscles and glands. Also called *motor neurons.*

Effort justification In cognitive-dissonance theory, the tendency to seek justification (acceptable reasons) for strenuous efforts.

Egocentrism According to Piaget, assuming that others view the world as one does oneself.

Ego The second psychic structure to develop, characterized by self-awareness, planning, and delay of gratification.

Ego analyst A psychodynamically oriented therapist who focuses on the conscious, coping behavior of the ego instead of the hypothesized, unconscious functioning of the id.

Ego identity Erikson's term for a firm sense of who one is and what one stands for.

Ego integrity versus despair Erikson's term for the crisis of late adulthood, characterized by the task of maintaining one's sense of identity despite physical deterioration.

Eidetic imagery The maintenance of detailed visual memories over several minutes.

Ejaculation The ejection of semen from the penis.

Elaboration likelihood model The view that persuasive messages are evaluated (elaborated) on the basis of central and peripheral cues.

Elaborative rehearsal A method for increasing retention of new information by relating it to information that is well known.

Electra complex A conflict of the phallic stage in which the girl longs for her father and resents her mother.

Electroconvulsive therapy Treatment of disorders like major depression by passing an electric current (that causes a convulsion) through the head. Abbreviated *ECT.*

Electroencephalograph (el-eck-trow-en-SEFF-uh-lo-graf). An instrument that measures electrical activity of the brain. Abbreviated *EEG.* ("Cephalo-" derives from the Greek *kephale,* meaning "head.")

Electromyograph (EMG) An instrument that measures muscle tension.

Embryonic stage The baby from the third through the eighth weeks following conception, during which time the major organ systems undergo rapid differentiation.

Emotion A state of feeling that has cognitive, physiological, and behavioral components.

Empathic understanding Ability to perceive a client's feelings from the client's frame of reference.

Empty-nest syndrome A sense of depression and loss of purpose felt by some parents when the youngest child leaves home.

Encoding Interpreting; transforming; modifying information so that it can be placed in memory. The first stage of information processing.

Encounter group A type of group that fosters self-awareness by focusing on how group members relate to one another in a setting that encourages open expression of feelings.

Endocrine system The body's system of ductless glands that secrete hormones and release them directly into the bloodstream.

Endorphins Neurotransmitters that are composed of amino acids and that are functionally similar to morphine.

Engram (1) An assumed electrical circuit in the brain that corresponds to a memory trace. (2) An assumed chemical change in the brain that accompanies learning.

Environmental psychology The field of psychology that studies the ways in which people and the environment influence each other.

Epilepsy Temporary disturbances of brain functions that involve sudden neural discharges.

Episodic memory Personal memories of specific events.

Erogenous zone An area of the body that is sensitive to sexual sensations.

Eros   In psychodynamic theory, the basic instinct to preserve and perpetuate life.

Estrogen   A generic term for several female sex hormones that promote growth of female sex characteristics and regulate the menstrual cycle.

Ethical   Moral; referring to one's system of deriving standards for determining what is moral.

Ethics review committee   A group found in an institutional setting that helps researchers consider the potential harm of their methods and reviews proposed studies according to ethical guidelines.

Ethnic group   A group characterized by common features such as cultural heritage, history, race, and language.

Eustress   Stress that is healthful.

Evaluation apprehension   Concern that others are evaluating our behavior.

Evolutionary psychology   The field of psychology that studies the ways in which adaptation and natural selection are connected with behavior and mental processes. It is based on the evolutionary principle of natural selection—that only the "fittest" organisms reach maturity and reproduce, thereby transmitting their genes to future generations and enabling their species to evolve in adaptive directions.

Excitement phase   The first phase of the sexual response cycle, characterized by muscle tension, increases in the heart rate, and erection in the male and vaginal lubrication in the female.

Exemplar   A specific example.

Exhaustion stage   The third stage of the general adaptation syndrome, characterized by weakened resistance and possible deterioration.

Existentialism   The view that people are completely free and responsible for their own behavior.

Expectancies   Personal predictions about the outcomes of potential behaviors.

Experiment   A scientific method that seeks to confirm cause-and-effect relationships by introducing independent variables and observing their effects on dependent variables.

Experimental groups   In experiments, groups whose members obtain the treatment.

"Externals"   People who perceive the ability to attain reinforcements as being largely outside themselves.

Extinction   An experimental procedure in which stimuli lose their ability to evoke learned responses because the events that had followed the stimuli no longer occur. (The learned responses are said to be *extinguished*.)

Extraversion   A trait characterized by tendencies to be socially outgoing and to express feelings and impulses freely.

Facial-feedback hypothesis   The view that stereotypical facial expressions can contribute to stereotypical emotions.

Factor analysis   A statistical technique that allows researchers to determine the relationships among large number of items such as test items.

Family therapy   A form of therapy in which the family unit is treated as the client.

Fear appeal   A type of persuasive communication that influences behavior on the basis of arousing fear instead of rational analysis of the issues.

Feature detectors   Neurons in the sensory cortex that fire in response to specific features of sensory information such as lines or edges of objects.

Feeling-of-knowing experience   Same as *tip-of-the-tongue phenomenon*.

Female sexual arousal disorder   A sexual dysfunction in which females fail to become adequately sexually aroused to engage in sexual intercourse.

Fetal stage   The baby from the third month following conception through childbirth, during which time there is maturation of organ systems and dramatic gains in length and weight.

Fight-or-flight reaction   An innate adaptive response to the perception of danger.

Fixation   In psychodynamic theory, arrested development. Attachment to objects of an earlier stage.

Fixation time   The amount of time spent looking at a visual stimulus.

Fixed-interval schedule   A schedule in which a fixed amount of time must elapse between the previous and subsequent times that reinforcement is available.

Fixed-ratio schedule   A schedule in which reinforcement is provided after a fixed number of correct responses.

Flashbacks   Distorted perceptions or hallucinations that occur days or weeks after LSD usage but mimic the LSD experience.

Flooding   A behavioral fear-reduction technique based on principles of classical conditioning. Fear-evoking stimuli (CSs) are presented continuously in the absence of actual harm so that fear responses (CRs) are extinguished.

Fluid intelligence   Mental flexibility as shown in learning rapidly to solve new kinds of problems.

Foot-in-the-door technique   A method for inducing compliance in which a small request is followed by a larger request.

Forced-choice format   A method of presenting test questions that requires a respondent to select one of a number of possible answers.

Formal-operational stage   Piaget's fourth stage, characterized by abstract logical thought; deduction from principles.

Fovea   An area near the center of the retina that is dense with cones and where vision is consequently most acute.

Frame of reference   One's unique patterning of perceptions and attitudes according to which one evaluates events.

Framing effect   The influence of wording, or the context in which information is presented, on decision making.

Free association   In psychoanalysis, the uncensored uttering of all thoughts that come to mind.

Frequency distribution   An ordered set of data that indicates the frequency (how often) with which scores appear.

Frequency histogram   A graphic representation of a frequency distribution that uses rectangular solids (bars) to represent the frequency with which scores appear.

Frequency polygon   A graphic representation of a frequency distribution that connects the points that show the frequencies with which scores appear, thereby creating a multisided geometric figure.

Frequency theory   The theory that the pitch of a sound is reflected in the frequency of the neural impulses that are generated in response to the sound.

Frontal lobe   The lobe of the cerebral cortex that lies to the front of the central fissure.

Functional analysis   A systematic study of behavior in which one identifies the stimuli that trigger problem behavior and the reinforcers that maintain it.

Functional fixedness   The tendency to view an object in terms of its name or familiar usage.

Functionalism   The school of psychology that emphasizes the uses or functions of the mind rather than the elements of experience.

Fundamental attribution error   The tendency to assume that others act predominantly on the basis of their dispositions, even when there is evidence suggesting the importance of their situations.

g   Spearman's symbol for general intelligence, which he believed underlay more specific abilities.

Ganglion cells   Neurons whose axons form the optic nerve.

Gay male   A male homosexual.

Gender   The state of being female or being male.

Gender identity   One's psychological sense of being female or male.

Gender role   A cluster of behaviors that characterizes traditional female or male behaviors within a cultural setting.

Gender-schema theory   The view that gender identity plus knowledge of the distribution of behavior patterns into feminine and masculine roles motivate and guide the gender-typing of the child.

Gender-typing   The process by which people acquire a sense of being female or male and acquire the traits considered typical of females or males within a cultural setting.

General adaptation syndrome   Selye's term for a hypothesized three-stage response to stress. Abbreviated *GAS*.

Generalization   In conditioning, the tendency for a conditioned response to be evoked by stimuli that are similar to the stimulus to which the response was conditioned.

Generalize   To extend from the particular to the general; to apply observations based on a sample to a population.

Generalized anxiety disorder   Feelings of dread and foreboding and sympathetic arousal of at least 6 months' duration.

Generativity versus stagnation   Erikson's term for the crisis of middle adulthood, characterized by the task of being productive and contributing to younger generations.

Genes   The basic building blocks of heredity, which consist of DNA.

Genetics   The branch of biology that studies heredity.

Genital stage   The mature stage of psychosexual development, characterized by preferred expression of libido through intercourse with an adult of the other gender.

Genuineness   Recognition and open expression of the therapist's own feelings.

Germinal stage   The first stage of prenatal development, during which the dividing mass of cells has not become implanted in the uterine wall.

Gestalt psychology   The school of psychology that emphasizes the tendency to organize perceptions into wholes and to integrate separate stimuli into meaningful patterns.

Gestalt therapy   Fritz Perls's form of psychotherapy, which attempts to integrate conflicting parts of the personality through directive methods designed to help clients perceive their whole selves.

Gland   An organ that secretes one or more chemical substances such as hormones, saliva, or milk.

Glial cells   Cells that nourish and insulate neurons, direct their growth, and remove waste products from the nervous system.

Gray matter   In the spinal cord, the grayish neurons and neural segments that are involved in spinal reflexes.

Groupthink   A process in which group members are influenced by cohesiveness and a dynamic leader to ignore external realities as they make decisions.

Growth hormone   A pituitary hormone that regulates growth.

Hallucination   A perception in the absence of sensory stimulation that is confused with reality.

Hallucinogenic   Giving rise to hallucinations.

Hashish   A drug derived from the resin of *Cannabis sativa*. Often called "hash."

Health psychology   The field of psychology that studies the relationships between psychological factors (e.g., attitudes, beliefs, situational influences, and behavior patterns) and the prevention and treatment of physical illness.

Heredity   The transmission of traits from one generation to another through genes.

Heritability   The degree to which the variations in a trait from one person to another can be attributed to, or explained by, genetic factors.

Hertz   A unit expressing the frequency of sound waves. One Hertz, or *1 Hz*, equals one cycle per second.

Heterosexual   Referring to people who are sexually aroused by and interested in forming romantic relationships with people of the other gender.

Heuristics   Rules of thumb that help us simplify and solve problems.

Higher-order conditioning   (1) According to behaviorists, a classical conditioning procedure in which a previously neutral stimulus comes to elicit the response brought forth by a *conditioned* stimulus by being paired repeatedly with that conditioned stimulus. (2) According to cognitive psychologists, the learning of relationships among events, none of which evokes an unlearned response.

Hippocampus   A structure in the limbic system that plays an important role in the formation of new memories.

Holophrase   A single word used to express complex meanings.

Homeostasis   The tendency of the body to maintain a steady state.

Homosexual   Referring to people who are sexually aroused by and interested in forming romantic relationships with people of the same gender.

Hormone   A substance secreted by an endocrine gland that regulates various body functions.

Hue   The color of light, as determined by its wavelength.

Humanism The philosophy and school of psychology that asserts that people are conscious, self-aware, and capable of free choice, self-fulfillment, and ethical behavior.

Hydrocarbons Chemical compounds consisting of hydrogen and carbon.

Hypermnesia Greatly enhanced or heightened memory.

Hyperphagic Characterized by excessive eating.

Hypertension High blood pressure.

Hypnagogic state The drowsy interval between waking and sleeping, characterized by brief, hallucinatory, dreamlike experiences.

Hypnosis A condition in which people appear to be highly suggestible and behave as though they are in a trance.

Hypoactive sexual desire disorder A sexual dysfunction in which people lack sexual desire.

Hypochondriasis Persistent belief that one has a medical disorder despite lack of medical findings.

Hypothalamus A bundle of nuclei below the thalamus involved in body temperature, motivation, and emotion.

Hypothesis In psychology, a specific statement about behavior or mental processes that is tested through research.

Icon A mental representation of a visual stimulus that is held briefly in sensory memory.

Iconic memory The sensory register that briefly holds mental representations of visual stimuli.

Id The psychic structure, present at birth, that represents physiological drives and is fully unconscious.

Ideas of persecution Erroneous beliefs that one is being victimized or persecuted.

Identification The process of becoming broadly like another person. In psychodynamic theory, the unconscious assumption of the behavior of another person.

Illusions Sensations that give rise to misperceptions.

Imaginary audience An aspect of adolescent egocentrism; the belief that other people are as concerned with our thoughts and behaviors as we are.

Immune system The system of the body that recognizes and destroys foreign agents (antigens) that invade the body.

Imprinting A process occurring during a critical period in the development of an organism, in which that organism responds to a stimulus in a manner that will afterward be difficult to modify.

Incentive An object, person, or situation perceived as being capable of satisfying a need.

Incubation In problem solving, a hypothetical process that sometimes occurs when we stand back from a frustrating problem for a while and the solution "suddenly" appears.

Independent variable A condition in a scientific study that is manipulated so that its effects may be observed.

Indiscriminate attachment Showing attachment behaviors toward any person.

Individualist A person who defines the self in terms of personal traits and gives priority to personal goals.

Inductive Reasoning A form of reasoning in which we reason from individual cases or particular facts to a general conclusion.

Infantile amnesia Inability to recall events that occur prior to the age of 2 or 3. Also termed *childhood amnesia*.

Infer To go from the particular to the general; to draw a conclusion.

Inferential statistics The branch of statistics that is concerned with confidence with which conclusions drawn about samples can be extended to the populations from which the samples were drawn.

Inferiority complex Feelings of inferiority hypothesized by Adler to serve as a central motivating force.

Inflammation Increased blood flow to an injured area of the body, resulting in redness, warmth, and an increased supply of white blood cells.

Informed consent The term used by psychologists to indicate that a person has agreed to participate in research after receiving information about the purposes of the study and the nature of the treatments.

Initial-preattachment phase The first phase in forming bonds of attachment, characterized by indiscriminate attachment.

Insight In Gestalt psychology, a sudden perception of relationships among elements of the "perceptual field," permitting the solution of a problem.

Instinct An inherited disposition to activate specific behavior patterns that are designed to reach certain goals.

Instrumental competence Ability to manipulate one's environment to achieve one's goals.

Intelligence A complex and controversial concept. According to David Wechsler (1975), the "capacity . . . to understand the world [and] resourcefulness to cope with its challenges."

Intelligence quotient (IQ) (1) Originally, a ratio obtained by dividing a child's score (or mental age) on an intelligence test by chronological age. (2) Generally, a score on an intelligence test.

Interference theory The view that we may forget stored material because other learning interferes with it.

"Internals" People who perceive the ability to attain reinforcements as being largely within themselves.

Interneuron A neuron that transmits a neural impulse from a sensory neuron to a motor neuron.

Interposition A monocular cue for depth based on the fact that a nearby object obscures a more distant object behind it.

Interpretation An explanation of a client's utterance according to psychoanalytic theory.

Intimacy Close acquaintance and familiarity; a characteristic of a relationship in which partners share their inmost feelings.

Intimacy versus isolation Erikson's life crisis of young adulthood, which is characterized by the task of developing abiding intimate relationships.

Introspection Deliberate looking into one's own mind to examine one's own thoughts and feelings.

Introversion A trait characterized by intense imagination and the tendency to inhibit impulses.

Iris A muscular membrane whose dilation regulates the amount of light that enters the eye.

Just noticeable difference The minimal amount by which a source of energy must be increased or decreased so that a difference in intensity will be perceived.

Kinesthesis The sense that informs us about the positions and motion of parts of our bodies.

Kinship studies Studies that compare the presence of traits and behavior patterns in people who are biologically related or unrelated in order to help determine the role of genetic factors in their occurrence.

La belle indifférence A French term that describes the lack of concern sometimes shown by people with conversion disorders.

Language acquisition device (LAD) In psycholinguistic theory, neural "prewiring" that facilitates the child's learning of grammar.

Latency A phase of psychosexual development characterized by repression of sexual impulses.

Latent Hidden or concealed.

Latent content In psychodynamic theory, the symbolized or underlying content of dreams.

Lateral hypothalamus An area at the side of the hypothalamus that appears to function as a start-eating center.

Learned helplessness A model for the acquisition of depressive behavior, based on findings that organisms in aversive situations learn to show inactivity when their operants go unreinforced.

Learning (1) According to behaviorists, a relatively permanent change in behavior that results from experience. (2) According to cognitive theorists, the process by which organisms make relatively permanent changes in the way they represent the environment because of experience. These changes influence the organism's behavior but do not fully determine it.

Lens A transparent body behind the iris that focuses an image on the retina.

Lesbian A female homosexual.

Lesion (LEE-shun). An injury that results in impaired behavior or loss of a function.

Leukocytes White blood cells.

Libido (1) In psychodynamic theory, the energy of Eros; the sexual instinct. (2) Generally, sexual interest or drive.

Limbic system A group of structures involved in memory, motivation, and emotion that forms a fringe along the inner edge of the cerebrum.

Linguistic-relativity hypothesis The view that language structures the way in which we view the world.

Locus of control The place (locus) to which an individual attributes control over the receiving of reinforcers—either inside or outside the self.

Long-term memory The type or stage of memory capable of relatively permanent storage.

LSD Lysergic acid diethylamide. A hallucinogenic drug.

Magnetic resonance imaging (REZZ-oh-nants). Formation of a computer-generated image of the anatomy of the brain by measuring the signals emitted when the head is placed in a strong magnetic field.

Maintenance rehearsal Mental repetition of information in order to keep it in memory.

Major depression A severe depressive disorder in which the person may show loss of appetite and impaired reality testing.

Male erectile disorder A sexual dysfunction in which males fail to obtain or maintain erections that are adequate for sexual intercourse.

Manifest content In psychodynamic theory, the reported content of dreams.

Marijuana The dried vegetable matter of the *Cannabis sativa* plant.

Matching hypothesis The view that people tend to choose persons similar to themselves in attractiveness and attitudes in the formation of interpersonal relationships.

Maturation The orderly unfolding of traits, as regulated by the genetic code.

Mean A type of average that is calculated by adding all the scores and then dividing by the number of scores.

Means–end analysis A heuristic device in which we try to solve a problem by evaluating the difference between the current situation and the goal.

Median The central score in a frequency distribution; the score beneath which 50% of the cases fall.

Medulla An oblong area of the hindbrain involved in regulation of heartbeat and respiration.

Melatonin A pineal hormone which helps regulate the sleep-wake cycle and may affect the onset of puberty.

Memory The processes by which information is encoded, stored, and retrieved.

Memory trace An assumed change in the nervous system that reflects the impression made by a stimulus. Memory traces are said to be "held" in sensory registers.

Menarche The beginning of menstruation.

Menopause The cessation of menstruation.

Mental age The accumulated months of credit that a person earns on the Stanford-Binet Intelligence Scale. Abbreviated *MA*.

Mental set The tendency to respond to a new problem with an approach that was used successfully with similar problems.

Mescaline A hallucinogenic drug derived from the mescal (peyote) cactus.

Meta-analysis A statistical method for averaging the results of individual studies.

Metamemory Self-awareness of the ways in which memory functions, allowing the person to encode, store, and retrieve information effectively.

Methaqualone An addictive depressant. Often called "ludes."

Method of constant stimuli A psychophysical method for determining thresholds in which the researcher presents stimuli of various magnitudes and asks the person to report detection.

Method of savings A measure of retention in which the difference between the number of repetitions originally required to learn a list and the number of repetitions required to relearn the list after a certain amount of time has elapsed is calculated.

Middlescence Sheehy's term for a stage of life, from 45 to 55, when people seek new identity and are frequently "lost in a buzz of confusion."

Midlife crisis A crisis experienced by many people during the midlife transition when they realize that life may be more than halfway over and reassess their achievements in terms of their dreams.

Midlife transition Levinson's term for the ages from 40 to 45, which are characterized by a shift in psychological perspective from viewing ourselves in terms of years lived to viewing ourselves in terms of the years we have left.

Migraine headaches Throbbing headaches that are connected with changes in the supply of blood to the head.

Mnemonic devices Systems for remembering in which items are related to easily recalled sets of symbols such as acronyms, phrases, or jingles.

Mode The most frequently occurring number or score in a distribution.

Model An organism that engages in a response that is then imitated by another organism; in social-cognitive theory, an organism that exhibits behaviors that others will imitate or acquire through observational learning.

Modeling A behavior-therapy technique in which a client observes and imitates a person who approaches and copes with feared objects or situations.

Monochromat A person who is sensitive to black and white only and hence color blind.

Monocular cues Stimuli suggestive of depth that can be perceived with only one eye.

Monozygotic (MZ) twins Identical twins. Twins who develop from a single zygote, thus carrying the same genetic instructions.

Motion parallax A monocular cue for depth based on the perception that nearby objects appear to move more rapidly in relation to our own motion.

Motive A hypothetical state within an organism that propels the organism toward a goal. (From the Latin *movere,* meaning "to move.")

Motor cortex The section of cortex that lies in the frontal lobe, just across the central fissure from the sensory cortex. Neural impulses in the motor cortex are linked to muscular responses throughout the body.

Multiple approach–avoidance conflict A type of conflict in which each of a number of goals produces approach and avoidance motives.

Mutism Refusal to talk.

Myelin A fatty substance that encases and insulates axons, facilitating transmission of neural impulses.

Myotonia Muscle tension.

Narcotics Drugs used to relieve pain and induce sleep. The term is usually reserved for opiates.

Naturalistic observation A scientific method in which organisms are observed in their natural environments.

Nature In behavior genetics, heredity.

Need A state of deprivation.

Negative correlation A relationship between two variables in which one variable increases as the other decreases.

Negative reinforcer A reinforcer that when *removed* increases the frequency of an operant.

Neodissociation theory A theory of hypnotic events as the splitting of consciousness.

Neonate A newly born child.

Nerve A bundle of axons and dendrites from many neurons.

Neural impulse The electrochemical discharge of a nerve cell, or neuron.

Neuron A nerve cell.

Neuroticism Eysenck's term for emotional instability.

Neurotransmitters Chemical substances involved in the transmission of neural impulses from one neuron to another.

Nonconscious Descriptive of bodily processes such as the growing of hair, of which we cannot become conscious. We may "recognize" that our hair is growing but cannot directly experience the biological process.

Non-rapid-eye-movement sleep Stages of sleep, 1 through 4. Abbreviated *NREM* sleep.

Nonsense syllables Meaningless sets of two consonants, with a vowel sandwiched in between, that are used to study memory.

Noradrenaline A neurotransmitter whose action is similar to that of the hormone adrenaline and that may play a role in depression.

Normal curve Graphic presentation of a normal distribution, which shows a characteristic bell shape.

Normal distribution A symmetrical distribution that is assumed to reflect chance fluctuations; approximately 68% of cases lie within a standard deviation of the mean.

Nurture In behavior genetics, environmental influences on behavior, such as nutrition, culture, socioeconomic status, and learning.

Objective responsibility According to Piaget, the assignment of blame according to the amount of damage done rather than the motives of the actor.

Objective tests Tests whose items must be answered in a specified, limited manner. Tests whose items have concrete answers that are considered correct.

Object permanence Recognition that objects removed from sight still exist, as demonstrated in young children by continued pursuit.

Observational learning The acquisition of knowledge and skills through the observation of others (who are called *models*) rather than by means of direct experience.

Obsession A recurring thought or image that seems beyond control.

Occipital lobe The lobe that lies behind and below the parietal lobe and behind the temporal lobe.

Oedipus complex Within psychodynamic theory, a conflict of the phallic stage characterized by romantic feelings toward the parent of the other gender and feelings of rivalry toward the parent of the same gender.

Olfactory nerve The nerve that transmits information concerning odors from olfactory receptors to the brain.

Operant behavior Voluntary responses that are reinforced.

Operant conditioning A simple form of learning in which an organism learns to engage in behavior because it is reinforced.

Opiates A group of narcotics derived from the opium poppy that provide a euphoric rush and depress the nervous system.

Opioids Chemicals that act on opiate receptors but are not derived from the opium poppy.

Opponent-process theory The theory that color vision is made possible by three types of cones, some of which respond to red or green light, some to blue or yellow light, and some only to the intensity of light.

Optic nerve The nerve that transmits sensory information from the eye to the brain.

Oral stage   The first stage of psychosexual development, during which gratification is hypothesized to be attained primarily through oral activities.

Organizing effect The directional effect of sex hormones—for example, along stereotypically masculine or feminine lines.

Organ of Corti   The receptor for hearing that lies on the basilar membrane in the cochlea.

Orgasm   The height or climax of sexual excitement, involving involuntary muscle contractions, release of sexual tensions, and, usually, subjective feelings of pleasure.

Orgasmic disorder   A sexual dysfunction in which people have persistent or recurrent problems in reaching orgasm.

Overextension   Overgeneralizing the use of words to objects and situations to which they do not apply—a normal characteristic of the speech of young children.

Overregularization   The application of regular grammatical rules for forming inflections (e.g., past tense and plurals) to irregular verbs and nouns.

Oxytocin   A pituitary hormone that stimulates labor and lactation.

Paired associates   Nonsense syllables presented in pairs in experiments that measure recall.

Panic disorder   The recurrent experiencing of attacks of extreme anxiety in the absence of external stimuli that usually elicit anxiety.

Paranoid schizophrenia   A type of schizophrenia characterized primarily by delusions—commonly of persecution—and by vivid hallucinations.

Parasympathetic nervous system   The branch of the autonomic nervous system that is most active during processes that restore reserves of energy to the body, such as relaxing and eating. When people relax, the parasympathetic nervous system decelerates the heart rate, normalizes the blood pressure, relaxes muscles, and so on. The parasympathetic division also stimulates digestion.

Parietal lobe   The lobe that lies just behind the central fissure.

Partial reinforcement   One of several reinforcement schedules in which not every correct response is reinforced.

Passion   Strong romantic and sexual feelings.

Passive smoking   Inhaling of smoke from the tobacco products and exhalations of other people; also called *secondhand smoking*.

Pathogen   A microscopic organism (e.g., bacterium or virus) that can cause disease.

Perception   The process by which sensations are organized into an inner representation of the world.

Performance anxiety   Anxiety concerning one's ability to perform, especially when performance may be evaluated by other people.

Period of the ovum   Another term for the *germinal stage*.

Peripheral nervous system   The part of the nervous system consisting of the somatic nervous system and the autonomic nervous system.

Permissive parents   Parents who impose few, if any, rules and who do not supervise their children closely.

Personal fable   Another aspect of adolescent egocentrism; the belief that our feelings and ideas are special and unique and that we are invulnerable.

Personality disorders   Enduring patterns of maladaptive behavior that are sources of distress to the individual or others.

Personal space   An invisible boundary that surrounds a person and serves protective functions.

Person variables   Factors within the person, such as expectancies and competencies, that influence behavior.

Perspective   A monocular cue for depth based on the convergence (coming together) of parallel lines as they recede into the distance.

Phallic stage   The third stage of psychosexual development, characterized by a shift of libido to the phallic region. (From the Greek *phallos*, referring to an image of the penis. However, Freud used the term *phallic* to refer both to boys and girls.)

Phallic symbol   A sign that represents the penis.

Phencyclidine   Another hallucinogenic drug whose name is an acronym for its chemical structure. Abbreviated *PCP*.

Pheromones   Chemical secretions detected by other members of the same species that stimulate stereotypical behaviors.

Phi phenomenon   The perception of movement as a result of sequential presentation of visual stimuli.

Photoreceptors   Cells that respond to light.

Physiological drives   Unlearned drives with a biological basis, such as hunger, thirst, and avoidance of pain.

Pitch   The highness or lowness of a sound, as determined by the frequency of the sound waves.

Pituitary gland   The gland that secretes growth hormone, prolactin, antidiuretic hormone, and other hormones.

Placebo   A bogus treatment that has the appearance of being genuine.

Placenta   A membrane that permits the exchange of nutrients and waste products between the mother and her developing child but does not allow the maternal and fetal bloodstreams to mix.

Place theory   The theory that the pitch of a sound is determined by the section of the basilar membrane that vibrates in response to the sound.

Plateau phase   The second phase of the sexual response cycle, which is characterized by increases in vasocongestion, muscle tension, heart rate, and blood pressure in preparation for orgasm.

Polarization   In social psychology, taking an extreme position or attitude on an issue.

Polarize   To ready a neuron for firing by creating an internal negative charge in relation to the body fluid outside the cell membrane.

Pons   A structure of the hindbrain involved in respiration, attention, and sleep and dreaming.

Population   A complete group of organisms or events. In statistics, a complete group from which a sample is selected.

Positive correlation   A relationship between variables in which one variable increases as the other also increases.

Positive reinforcer   A reinforcer that when *presented* increases the frequency of an operant.

Positron emission tomography   (POZZ-I-tron). Formation of a computer-generated image of the neural activity of parts of the brain by tracing the amount of glucose used by the various parts. Abbreviated *PET scan.*

Postconventional level According to Kohlberg, a period during which moral judgments are derived from moral principles and people look to themselves to set moral standards.

Posttraumatic stress disorder A disorder that follows a distressing event outside the range of normal human experience; characterized by features such as intense fear, avoidance of stimuli associated with the event, and reliving of the event. Abbreviated *PTSD.*

Preconscious In psychodynamic theory, descriptive of material that is not in awareness but can be brought into awareness by focusing one's attention.

Preconventional level According to Kohlberg, a period during which moral judgments are based largely on expectation of rewards or punishments.

Prefrontal lobotomy The severing or destruction of a section of the frontal lobe of the brain.

Prejudice The unfounded belief that a person or group—on the basis of assumed racial, ethnic, sexual, or other features—will possess negative characteristics or perform inadequately.

Premature ejaculation Ejaculation that occurs before the couple are satisfied with the duration of sexual relations.

Preoperational stage The second of Piaget's stages, characterized by illogical use of words and symbols, spotty logic, and egocentrism.

Presbyopia A condition characterized by brittleness of the lens.

Primacy effect The tendency to recall the initial items in a series of items. The tendency to evaluate others in terms of first impressions.

Primary drives Unlearned, or physiological, drives.

Primary mental abilities According to Thurstone, the basic abilities that make up intelligence.

Primary reinforcer An unlearned reinforcer.

Proactive interference The interference of old learning with the ability to retrieve material learned recently.

Procedural memory Knowledge of ways of doing things; skill memory.

Progesterone A female sex hormone that promotes growth of the sex organs and helps maintain pregnancy.

Programmed learning A method of learning in which complex tasks are broken down into simple steps, each of which is reinforced. Errors are not reinforced.

Programmed senescence The view that aging is determined by a biological clock that ticks at a rate governed by genes.

Projective test A psychological test that presents ambiguous stimuli onto which the test taker projects his or her own personality in making a response.

Prolactin A pituitary hormone that regulates production of milk and, in lower animals, maternal behavior.

Prototype A concept of a category of objects or events that serves as a good example of the category.

Proximity Nearness. The perceptual tendency to group together objects that are near one another.

Psychedelic Causing hallucinations, delusions, or heightened perceptions.

Psychic structure In psychodynamic theory, a hypothesized mental structure that helps explain different aspects of behavior.

Psychoactive substances Drugs that have psychological effects such as stimulation or distortion of perceptions.

Psychoanalysis The school of psychology that emphasizes the importance of unconscious motives and conflicts as determinants of human behavior; Freud's method of exploring human personality.

Psychodynamic Referring to Freud's theory, which proposes that the motion of underlying forces of personality determines our thoughts, feelings, and behavior.

Psychodynamic theory Sigmund Freud's perspective, which emphasizes the importance of unconscious motives and conflicts as forces that determine behavior. *Dynamic* refers to the concept of (psychological) forces being in motion.

Psycholinguistic theory The view that language learning involves an interaction between environmental fac-

tors and an inborn tendency to acquire language.

Psychological disorders Patterns of behavior or mental processes that are connected with emotional distress or significant impairment in functioning.

Psychological hardiness A cluster of traits that buffer stress and are characterized by commitment, challenge, and control.

Psychology The science that studies behavior and mental processes.

Psychoneuroimmunology The field that studies the relationships between psychological factors (e.g., attitudes and overt behavior patterns) and the functioning of the immune system.

Psychophysicist A person who studies the relationships between physical stimuli (such as light or sound) and their perception.

Psychosexual development In psychodynamic theory, the process by which libidinal energy is expressed through different erogenous zones during different stages of development.

Psychosocial development Erikson's theory of personality and development, which emphasizes social relationships and eight stages of growth.

Psychosurgery Surgery intended to promote psychological changes or to relieve disordered behavior.

Psychotherapy A systematic interaction between a therapist and a client that brings psychological principles to bear on influencing the client's thoughts, feelings, or behavior to help that client overcome abnormal behavior or adjust to problems in living.

Puberty The period of physical development during which sexual reproduction first becomes possible.

Punishment An unpleasant stimulus that suppresses the behavior it follows.

Pupil The apparently black opening in the center of the iris, through which light enters the eye.

Pure research Research conducted without concern for immediate applications.

Random sample A sample drawn so that each member of a population has an equal chance of being selected to participate.

Range   A measure of variability defined as the high score in a distribution minus the low score.

Rapid-eye-movement sleep   A stage of sleep characterized by rapid eye movements, which have been linked to dreaming. Abbreviated *REM* sleep.

Rapid flight of ideas   Rapid speech and topic changes, characteristic of manic behavior.

Rational emotive behavior therapy   Albert Ellis's form of therapy, which encourages clients to challenge and correct irrational expectations and maladaptive behaviors.

Reaction time   The amount of time required to respond to a stimulus.

Reality testing   The capacity to perceive one's environment and oneself according to accurate sensory impressions.

Reasoning   The transforming of information to reach conclusions.

Rebound anxiety   Strong anxiety that can attend the suspension of usage of a tranquilizer.

Recall   Retrieval or reconstruction of learned material.

Recency effect   The tendency to recall the last items in a series of items. The tendency to evaluate others in terms of the most recent impression.

Receptor site   A location on a dendrite of a receiving neuron tailored to receive a neurotransmitter.

Reciprocal determinism   Bandura's term for the social-cognitive view that people influence their environment just as their environment influences them.

Reciprocity   In interpersonal attraction, the tendency to return feelings and attitudes that are expressed about us.

Recognition   In information processing, the easiest memory task, involving identification of objects or events encountered before.

Reflex   A simple, unlearned response to a stimulus.

Refractory period   A phase following firing during which a neuron is less sensitive to messages from other neurons and will not fire. In the sexual response cycle, a period of time following orgasm during which an individual is not responsive to sexual stimulation.

Regression   Return to a form of behavior characteristic of an earlier stage of development.

Reinforce   To follow a response with a stimulus that increases the frequency of the response.

Reinforcement   A stimulus that follows a response and increases the frequency of the response.

Relearning   A measure of retention. Material is usually relearned more quickly than it is learned initially.

Replicate   Repeat, reproduce, copy.

Representativeness heuristic   A decision-making heuristic in which people make judgments about samples according to the populations they appear to represent.

Repression   In Freud's psychodynamic theory, the ejection of anxiety-evoking ideas from conscious awareness.

Repression   In psychodynamic theory, the automatic (unconscious) ejection of anxiety-evoking ideas, impulses, or images from awareness; a defense mechanism that protects the person from anxiety by ejecting anxiety-evoking ideas and impulses from awareness.

Resistance   The tendency to block the free expression of impulses and primitive ideas—a reflection of the defense mechanism of repression.

Resistance stage   The second stage of the general adaptation syndrome, characterized by prolonged sympathetic activity in an effort to restore lost energy and repair damage. Also called the *adaptation stage*.

Resolution phase   The fourth phase of the sexual response cycle, during which the body gradually returns to its prearoused state.

Response set   A tendency to answer test items according to a bias—for instance, to make oneself seem perfect or bizarre.

Resting potential   The electrical potential across the neural membrane when it is not responding to other neurons.

Reticular activating system   A part of the brain involved in attention, sleep, and arousal.

Retina   The area of the inner surface of the eye that contains rods and cones.

Retinal disparity   A binocular cue for depth based on the difference in the image cast by an object on the retinas of the eyes as the object moves closer or farther away.

Retrieval   The location of stored information and its return to consciousness. The third stage of information processing.

Retroactive interference   The interference of new learning with the ability to retrieve material learned previously.

Retrograde amnesia   Failure to remember events that occur prior to physical trauma because of the effects of the trauma.

Reversibility   According to Piaget, recognition that processes can be undone, that things can be made as they were.

Reward   A pleasant stimulus that increases the frequency of the behavior it follows.

Risky shift   The tendency to make riskier decisions as a member of a group than as an individual acting independently.

Rods   Rod-shaped photoreceptors that are sensitive only to the intensity of light.

Role diffusion   Erikson's term for lack of clarity in one's life roles (due to failure to develop ego identity).

Role theory   A theory that explains hypnotic events in terms of the person's ability to act *as though* he or she were hypnotized. Role theory differs from faking in that subjects cooperate and focus on hypnotic suggestions instead of pretending to be hypnotized.

Romantic love   An intense, positive emotion that involves sexual attraction, feelings of caring, and the belief that one is in love.

Rooting   The turning of an infant's head toward a touch, such as by the mother's nipple.

Rote   Mechanical associative learning that is based on repetition.

s   Spearman's symbol for *specific* factors, or *s factors,* which he believed accounted for individual abilities.

Saccadic eye movement   The rapid jumps made by a person's eyes as they fixate on different points.

Sample   Part of a population.

Satiety   The state of being satisfied; fullness.

Savings   The difference between the number of repetitions originally required to learn a list and the number of repetitions required to relearn the list after a certain amount of time has elapsed.

Schema A way of mentally representing the world, such as a belief or an expectation, that can influence perception of persons, objects, and situations.

Scheme According to Piaget, a hypothetical mental structure that permits the classification and organization of new information.

Schizophrenia A psychotic disorder characterized by loss of control of thought processes and inappropriate emotional responses.

Secondary reinforcer A stimulus that gains reinforcement value through association with established reinforcers.

Secondary sex characteristics Characteristics that distinguish the sexes, such as distribution of body hair and depth of voice, but that are not directly involved in reproduction.

Sedative A drug that relieves nervousness or agitation, or puts one to sleep.

Selection factor A source of bias that may occur in research findings when subjects are allowed to choose for themselves a certain treatment in a scientific study.

Selective attention The focus of one's consciousness on a particular stimulus.

Selective avoidance Diverting one's attention from information that is inconsistent with one's attitudes.

Selective exposure Deliberately seeking and attending to information that is consistent with one's attitudes.

Self-actualization According to Maslow and other humanistic psychologists, self-initiated, innate striving to become what one is capable of being. The motive for reaching one's full potential, for expressing one's unique capabilities.

Self-efficacy expectations Beliefs to the effect that one can handle a task, that one can bring about desired changes through one's own efforts.

Self-ideal A mental image of what we believe we ought to be.

Self-serving bias The tendency to view one's successes as stemming from internal factors and one's failures as stemming from external factors.

Semantic code Mental representation of information according to its meaning.

Semantic memory General knowledge as opposed to episodic memory.

Seminal fluid The fluid produced by the prostate and other glands that carries and nourishes sperm. Also called *semen*.

Sensation The stimulation of sensory receptors and the transmission of sensory information to the central nervous system.

Sensitization The type of sensory adaptation in which we become more sensitive to stimuli that are low in magnitude. Also called *positive adaptation*.

Sensorimotor stage The first of Piaget's stages of cognitive development, characterized by coordination of sensory information and motor activity, early exploration of the environment, and lack of language.

Sensorineural deafness The forms of deafness that result from damage to hair cells or the auditory nerve.

Sensory adaptation The processes by which organisms become more sensitive to stimuli that are low in magnitude and less sensitive to stimuli that are constant or ongoing in magnitude.

Sensory memory The type or stage of memory first encountered by a stimulus. Sensory memory holds impressions briefly, but long enough so that series of perceptions are psychologically continuous.

Sensory register A system of memory that holds information briefly, but long enough so that it can be processed further. There may be a sensory register for every sense.

Serial-position effect The tendency to recall more accurately the first and last items in a series.

Serotonin A neurotransmitter, deficiencies of which have been linked to affective disorders, anxiety, and insomnia.

Serum cholesterol Cholesterol found in the blood.

Sex chromosomes The 23rd pair of chromosomes, which determine whether the child will be male or female.

Sex therapy A collective term for short-term cognitive-behavioral models for treatment of sexual dysfunctions.

Sexual dysfunction A persistent or recurrent problem in becoming sexually aroused or reaching orgasm.

Sexual harassment Deliberate or repeated verbal comments, gestures, or physical contact of a sexual nature that is unwanted by the recipient.

Sexual orientation The directionality of one's erotic interests—that is, whether one is sexually attracted to and interested in forming romantic relationships with people of the other or the same gender.

Sexual response cycle Masters and Johnson's model of sexual response, which consists of four stages or phases.

Shadowing A monocular cue for depth based on the fact that opaque objects block light and produce shadows.

Shape constancy The tendency to perceive an object as being the same shape although the retinal image varies in shape as it rotates.

Shaping A procedure for teaching complex behaviors that at first reinforces approximations of the target behavior.

Short-term memory The type or stage of memory that can hold information for up to a minute or so after the trace of the stimulus decays. Also called *working memory*.

Signal-detection theory The view that the perception of sensory stimuli involves the interaction of physical, biological, and psychological factors.

Similarity The perceptual tendency to group together objects that are similar in appearance.

Simultaneous conditioning A classical conditioning procedure in which the CS and US are presented at the same time.

Situational attribution An assumption that a person's behavior is determined by external circumstances such as the social pressure found in a situation.

Size constancy The tendency to perceive an object as being the same size even as the size of its retinal image changes according to the object's distance.

Sleep terrors Frightening dreamlike experiences that occur during the deepest stage of NREM sleep. Nightmares, in contrast, occur during REM sleep.

Social-cognitive theory A school of psychology in the behaviorist tradition that includes cognitive factors in the explanation and prediction of behavior; a cognitively oriented learning theory in which observational learning and person variables such as values and expectancies play major roles in individual differences. Formerly termed *social-learning theory.*

Social facilitation   The process by which a person's performance is increased when other members of a group engage in similar behavior.

Social influence   The area of social psychology that studies the ways in which people influence the thoughts, feelings, and behavior of others.

Socialization   Guidance of people into socially desirable behavior by means of verbal messages, the systematic use of rewards and punishments, and other methods of teaching.

Social norms   Explicit and implicit rules that reflect social expectations and influence the ways people behave in social situations.

Social perception   A subfield of social psychology that studies the ways in which we form and modify impressions of others.

Social phobia   An irrational, excessive fear of public scrutiny.

Social psychology   The field of psychology that studies the nature and causes of people's thoughts and behavior in social situations.

Sociocultural perspective   The view that focuses on the roles of ethnicity, gender, culture, and socioeconomic status in personality formation, behavior, and mental processes.

Socioeconomic status   One's social and financial level, as indicated by measures such as income, level of education, and occupational status. Abbreviated *SES.*

Somatic nervous system   The division of the peripheral nervous system that connects the central nervous system with sensory receptors, skeletal muscles, and the surface of the body.

Somatoform disorders   Disorders in which people complain of physical (somatic) problems even though no physical abnormality can be found.

Somatosensory cortex   The section of cortex in which sensory stimulation

is projected. It lies just behind the central fissure in the parietal lobe.

Specific phobia   Persistent fear of a specific object or situation.

Spinal cord   A column of nerves within the spine that transmits messages from sensory receptors to the brain and from the brain to muscles and glands throughout the body.

Spinal reflex   A simple, unlearned response to a stimulus that may involve only two neurons.

Spontaneous recovery   The recurrence of an extinguished response as a function of the passage of time.

Standard deviation   A measure of the variability of a distribution, obtained by the formula

$$S.D. = \sqrt{\frac{Sum\ of\ d^2}{N}}$$

Standardized test   A test given to a large number of respondents so that data concerning the typical responses can be accumulated and analyzed.

State-dependent memory   Information that is better retrieved in the physiological or emotional state in which it was encoded and stored, or learned.

Statistics   Numerical facts assembled in such a manner that they provide useful information about measures or scores. (From the Latin *status,* meaning "standing" or "position.")

Stereotype   A fixed, conventional idea about a group.

Stereotype vulnerability   The tendency to focus on a conventional, negative belief about one's group, such that the individual risks behaving in a way that confirms that belief.

Stimulant   A drug that increases activity of the nervous system.

Stimulus   An environmental condition that elicits a response.

Stimulus motives   Motives to increase the stimulation impinging upon an organism.

Storage   Maintenance of information over time. The second stage of information processing.

Stratified sample   A sample drawn so that identified subgroups in the population are represented proportionately in the sample. How can stratified sampling be carried out to

ensure that a sample represents the ethnic diversity we find in the population at large?

Stress   The demand made on an organism to adapt.

Stroboscopic motion   A visual illusion in which the perception of motion is generated by a series of stationary images that are presented in rapid succession.

Structuralism   The school of psychology that argues that the mind consists of three basic elements—sensations, feelings, and images—which combine to form experience.

Subjective moral judgment   According to Piaget, moral judgments that are based on the motives of the perpetrator.

Subjective value   The desirability of an object or event.

Substance abuse   Persistent use of a substance even though it is causing or compounding problems in meeting the demands of life.

Successive approximations   In operant conditioning, a series of behaviors that gradually become more similar to a target behavior.

Superego   The third psychic structure, which functions as a moral guardian and sets forth high standards for behavior.

Suppression   The deliberate, or conscious, placing of certain ideas, impulses, or images out of awareness.

Survey   A method of scientific investigation in which a large sample of people answer questions about their attitudes or behavior.

Sympathetic nervous system   The branch of the autonomic nervous system that is most active during processes that spend body energy from stored reserves, such as in a fight-or-flight reaction to a predator or when you are anxious about a big test. When people experience fear, the sympathetic nervous system accelerates the heart rate, raises the blood pressure, tenses muscles, and so on.

Synapse   A junction between the axon terminals of one neuron and the dendrites or cell body of another neuron.

Systematic desensitization   Wolpe's behavioral fear-reduction technique in which a hierarchy of fear-evoking stimuli are presented while the person remains relaxed. The fear-evoking stimuli thereby become associated with muscle relaxation.

Systematic random search   An algorithm for solving problems in which each possible solution is tested according to a particular set of rules.

Taste buds   The sensory organs for taste. They contain taste cells and are located on the tongue.

Taste cells   Receptor cells that are sensitive to taste.

Temporal lobe   The lobe that lies below the lateral fissure, near the temples of the head.

Testosterone   A male sex hormone produced by the testes that promotes development of male sexual characteristics and sperm and that has activating effects on sexual arousal.

Texture gradient   A monocular cue for depth based on the perception that closer objects appear to have rougher (more detailed) surfaces.

Thalamus   An area near the center of the brain involved in the relay of sensory information to the cortex and in the functions of sleep and attention.

Theory   A formulation of relationships underlying observed events.

Theory of social comparison   The view that people look to others for cues about how to behave when they are in confusing or unfamiliar situations.

Theta waves   Slow brain waves produced during the hypnagogic state.

Thinking   Mental activity involved in understanding, manipulating, and communicating about information. Thinking entails paying attention to information, mentally representing it, reasoning about it, and making decisions about it.

Thyroxin   The thyroid hormone that increases metabolic rate.

Time out   Removal of an organism from a situation in which reinforcement is available when unwanted behavior is shown.

Tip-of-the-tongue (TOT) phenomenon   The feeling that information is stored in memory although it cannot be readily retrieved. Also called the *feeling-of-knowing experience.*

Token economy   An environmental setting that fosters desired behavior by reinforcing it with tokens (secondary reinforcers) that can be exchanged for other reinforcers.

Tolerance   Habituation to a drug, with the result that increasingly higher doses of the drug are needed to achieve similar effects.

Top-down processing   The use of contextual information or knowledge of a pattern in order to organize parts of the pattern.

Trace conditioning   A classical conditioning procedure in which the CS is presented and then removed before the US is presented.

Trait   A relatively stable aspect of personality that is inferred from behavior and assumed to give rise to consistent behavior.

Transcendental meditation (TM)   The simplified form of meditation brought to the United States by the Maharishi Mahesh Yogi and used as a method for coping with stress.

Transference   Responding to one person (such as a spouse or the psychoanalyst) in a way that is similar to the way one responded to another person (such as a parent) in childhood.

Treatment   In experiments, a condition received by subjects so that its effects may be observed.

Triangular model of love   Sternberg's view that love involves combinations of three components: intimacy, passion, and decision/commitment.

Trichromat   A person with normal color vision.

Trichromatic theory   The theory that color vision is made possible by three types of cones, some of which respond to red light, some to green, and some to blue.

Trust versus mistrust   Erikson's first stage of psychosexual development, during which children do—or do not—come to trust that primary caregivers and the environment will meet their needs.

Trying 20s   Sheehy's term for the third decade of life, when people are frequently occupied with advancement in the career world.

Two-point threshold   The least distance by which two rods touching the skin must be separated before the person will report that there are two rods, not one, on 50% of occasions.

Type A behavior   Behavior characterized by a sense of time urgency, competitiveness, and hostility.

Umbilical cord   A tube between the mother and her developing child through which nutrients and waste products are conducted.

Unconditional positive regard   A persistent expression of esteem for the value of a person, but not necessarily an unqualified acceptance of all of the person's behaviors.

Unconditioned response (UR)   An unlearned response to an unconditioned stimulus.

Unconditioned stimulus (US)   A stimulus that elicits a response from an organism prior to conditioning.

Unconscious   In psychodynamic theory, descriptive of ideas and feelings that are not available to awareness by simple focusing of attention.

Uplifts   Notable pleasant daily conditions and experiences.

Vaginismus   A sexual dysfunction characterized by involuntary contraction of the muscles surrounding the vagina, preventing entry by the penis or making entry painful.

Validity scales   Groups of test items that indicate whether a person's responses accurately reflect that individual's traits.

Variable-interval schedule   A schedule in which a variable amount of time must elapse between the previous and subsequent times that reinforcement is available.

Variable-ratio schedule   A schedule in which reinforcement is provided after a variable number of correct responses.

Vasocongestion   Engorgement of blood vessels with blood, which swells the genitals and breasts during sexual arousal.

Ventromedial nucleus   A central area on the underside of the hypothalamus that appears to function as a stop-eating center.

Vestibular sense   The sense that informs us about our bodies' positions relative to gravity.

Visible light   The part of the electromagnetic spectrum that stimulates the eye and produces visual sensations.

Visual acuity   Sharpness of vision.

Visual code   Mental representation of information as a picture.

Volunteer bias   A source of bias or error in research reflecting the prospect that people who offer to participate in research studies differ systematically from people who do not.

Waxy flexibility A feature of catatonic schizophrenia in which persons maintain postures into which they are placed.

Wear-and-tear theory The view that factors such as pollution, disease, and ultraviolet light contribute to wear and tear on the body, so that the body loses the ability to repair itself.

Weber's constant The fraction of the intensity by which a source of physical energy must be increased or decreased so that a difference in intensity will be perceived.

Wernicke–Korsakoff syndrome A cluster of symptoms associated with chronic alcohol abuse and characterized by confusion, memory impairment, and filling in gaps in memory with false information (confabulation).

Wernicke's aphasia A language disorder characterized by difficulty comprehending the meaning of spoken language.

White matter In the spinal cord, axon bundles that carry messages from and to the brain.

Wish fulfillment A primitive method used by the id to attempt to gratify basic instincts.

Working memory Same as *short-term memory*.

Zygote A fertilized ovum (egg cell).

Abbey, A. (1987). Misperceptions of friendly behavior as sexual interest. *Psychology of Women Quarterly, 11,* 173–194.

Abeles, N. (1997a). Psychology and the aging revolution. *APA Monitor, 28*(4), 2.

Abeles, N. (1997b). Memory problems in later life. *APA Monitor, 28*(6), 2.

Aber, J. L., & Allen, J. P. (1987). Effects of maltreatment of young children on young children's socioemotional development: An attachment theory perspective. *Developmental Psychology, 23,* 406–414.

Abramowitz, A. J., & O'Leary, S. G. (1991). Behavioral interventions for the classroom. *School Psychology Review, 20,* 220–234.

Abramowitz, J. S. (1997). Effectiveness of psychological and pharmacological treatments for obsessive-compulsive disorder. *Journal of Consulting and Clinical Psychology, 65,* 44–52.

Ader, D. N., & Johnson, S. B. (1994). Sample description, reporting, and analysis of sex in psychological research. *American Psychologist, 49,* 216–218.

Ader, R. (1993). Conditioned responses. In B. Moyers (Ed.), *Healing and the mind.* New York: Doubleday.

Adler, N. E., et al. (1994). Socioeconomic status and health. *American Psychologist, 49,* 15–24.

Adler, T. (1993a). Shy, bold temperament? It's mostly in the genes. *APA Monitor, 24*(1), 7, 8.

Adler, T. (1993b). Sleep loss impairs attention–and more. *APA Monitor, 24*(9), 22–23.

Agras, W. S., Southam, M. A., & Taylor, C. B. (1983). Long-term persistence of relaxation-induced blood pressure lowering during the working day. *Journal of Consulting and Clinical Psychology, 51,* 792–794.

Ainsworth, M. D. S., & Bowlby, J. (1991). An ethological approach to personality development. *American Psychologist, 46,* 333–341.

Ainsworth, M. D. S., Blehar, M. C., Waters, E., & Wall, S. (1978). *Patterns of attachment: A psychological study of the strange situation.* Hillsdale, NJ: Erlbaum.

Akhtar, N., & Bradley, E. J. (1991). Social information processing deficits of aggressive children. *Clinical Psychology Review, 11,* 621–644.

Alan Guttmacher Institute. (1998). Cited in Brody, J. E. (1998, September 15). Teen-agers and sex: Younger and more at risk. *The New York Times* online.

Aldag, R. J., & Fuller, S. R. (1993). Beyond fiasco: A reappraisal of the groupthink phenomenon and a new model of group decision processes. *Psychological Bulletin, 113,* 533–552.

Allen, L. (1993, August). Integrating a sociocultural perspective into the psychology curriculum. G. Stanley Hall lecture presented to the American Psychological Association, Toronto, Canada.

Alloy, L. B., Abramson, L. Y., & Dykman, B. M. (1990). Depressive realism and nondepressive optimistic illusions. In R. E. Ingram (Ed.), *Contemporary psychological approaches to depression.* New York: Plenum.

Allport, G. W., & Oddbert, H. S. (1936). Trait names: A psycholexical study. *Psychological Monographs, 47,* 1–36.

Amabile, T. M. (1990). Within you, without you: The social psychology of creativity, and beyond. In M. A. Runco & R. S. Albert (Eds.), *Theories of creativity.* Newbury Park, NY: Sage.

American Association of University Women. (1992). *How schools shortchange women: The A.A.U.W. report.* Washington, DC: AAUW Educational Foundation.

American Psychiatric Association (1994). *Diagnostic and statistical manual of the mental disorders* (4th ed.). Washington, DC: Author.

American Psychological Association (1992a). Ethical principles of psychologists and code of conduct. *American Psychologist, 47,* 1597–1611.

American Psychological Association (1992b). *Guidelines for ethical conduct in the care and use of animals.* Washington, DC: Author.

American Psychological Association. (1993). Guidelines for providers of psychological services to ethnic, linguistic, and culturally diverse populations. *American Psychologist, 48,* 45–48.

American Psychological Association (1998a, March 16). Sexual harassment: Myths and realities. APA Public Information Home Page; www.apa.org.

American Psychological Association (1998b, October 4). Answers to your questions about sexual orientation and homosexuality. APA Public Information Home Page; www.apa.org.

Andersen, B. L. (1996). Psychological and behavioral studies in cancer prevention and control. *Health Psychology, 15,* 411–412.

Anderson, C. A., & DeNeve, K. M. (1992). Temperature, aggression, and the negative affect escape model. *Psychological Bulletin, 111,* 347–351.

Andrews, B., & Brown, G. W. (1993). Self-esteem and vulnerability to depression. *Journal of Abnormal Psychology, 102,* 565–572.

Angell, M. (1993). Privilege and health—What is the connection? *New England Journal of Medicine, 329,* 126–127.

Antonuccio, D. (1995). Psychotherapy for depression: No stronger medicine. *American Psychologist, 50,* 452–454.

APA Monitor (1999). Once behind the scenes, now in the fore. *APA Monitor, 30*(11), 23.

Appel, L. J., et al. (1997). A clinical trial of the effects of dietary patterns on blood pressure. *New England Journal of Medicine, 336,* 1117–1124.

Apter, T. (1995). *Secret paths.* New York: W. W. Norton.

Archer, J. (1996). Sex differences in social behavior. *American Psychologist, 51,* 909–917.

Archer, S. L. (1992). A feminist's approach to identity research. In G. R. Adams, T. P. Gullotta, & R. Montemayor (Eds.), *Adolescent identity formation.* Newbury Park, CA: Sage.

Arnett, J. (1992). Reckless behavior in adolescence: A developmental perspective. *Developmental Review, 12,* 339–373.

Arnold, D. H., Lonigan, C. J., Whitehurst, G. J., & Epstein, J. N. (1994). Accelerating language development through picture book reading. *Journal of Educational Psychology, 86,* 235–243.

Aronson, E. (1990). Applying social psychology to desegregation and energy conservation. *Personality and Social Psychology Bulletin, 16,* 118–132.

Aronson, E., Wilson, T. D., & Akert, R. M. (1998). *Social psychology* (3rd ed.). New York: Addison Wesley Longman.

Asch, S. E. (1952). *Social psychology.* Englewood Cliffs, NJ: Prentice-Hall.

Atkinson, R. C., & Shiffrin, R. M. (1968). Human memory: A proposed system and its control processes. In K. Spence (Ed.), *The psychology of learning and motivation* (Vol. 2). New York: Academic Press.

Ayanian, J. Z. (1993). Heart disease in Black and White. *New England Journal of Medicine, 329,* 656–658.

Ayllon, T., & Haughton, E. (1962). Control of the behavior of schizophrenic patients by food. *Journal of the Experimental Analysis of Behavior, 5,* 343–352.

Azar, B. (1995). Breaking through barriers to creativity. *APA Monitor, 26*(8), 1, 20.

Azar, B. (1996a). Musical studies provide clues to brain functions. *APA Monitor, 27*(4), 1, 24.

Azar, B. (1996b). Scientists examine cancer patients' fears. *APA Monitor, 27*(8), 32.

Azar, B. (1996c). Studies investigate the link between stress and immunity. *APA Monitor, 27*(8), 32.

Azar, B. (1997a). Poor recall mars research and treatment. *APA Monitor, 28*(1), 1, 29.

Azar, B. (1997b). Environment is key to serotonin levels. *APA Monitor, 28*(4), 26, 29.

Azar, B. (1997c). It may cause anxiety, but day care can benefit kids. *APA Monitor, 28*(6), 13.

Azar, B. (1997d). Environment can mitigate differences in spatial ability. *APA Monitor, 28*(6), 28.

Azar, B. (1998). Communicating through pheromones. *APA Monitor, 29*(1), 1, 12.

Azar, B. (1999). New pieces filling in addiction puzzle. *APA Monitor, 30*(1), 1, 15.

Baddeley, A. (1982). *Your memory: A user's guide.* New York: Macmillan.

Baddeley, A. (1994). Working memory. In D. L. Schacter & E. Tulving (Eds.), *Memory systems 1994.* Cambridge, MA: The MIT Press, a Bradford Book.

Bahrick, H. P., Bahrick, P. O., & Wittlinger, R. P. (1975). Fifty years of memory for names and faces. *Journal of Experimental Psychology: General, 104,* 54–75.

Bailey, J. M., & Pillard, R. C. (1991). A genetic study of male sexual orientation. *Archives of General Psychiatry, 48,* 1089–1096.

Baker, L. A., DeFries, J. C., & Fulker, D. W. (1983). Longitudinal stability of cognitive ability in the Colorado adoption project. *Child Development, 54,* 290–297.

Bal, D. G. (1992). Cancer in African Americans. *Ca-A Cancer Journal for Clinicians, 42,* 5–6.

Baltes, P. B. (1997). On the incomplete architecture of human ontogeny: Selection, optimization, and compensation as foundation of developmental theory. *American Psychologist, 52,* 366–380.

Bandura, A. (1986). *Social foundations of thought and action: A social-cognitive theory.* Englewood Cliffs, NJ: Prentice-Hall.

Bandura, A., Blanchard, E. B., & Ritter, B. (1969). The relative efficacy of desensitization and modeling approaches for inducing behavioral, affective, and cognitive changes. *Journal of Personality and Social Psychology, 13,* 173–199.

Bandura, A., & McDonald, F. J. (1963). Influence of social reinforcement and the behavior of models in shaping children's moral judgments. *Journal of Abnormal and Social Psychology, 67,* 274–281.

Bandura, A., Ross, S. A., & Ross, D. (1963). Imitation of film-mediated aggressive models. *Journal of Abnormal and Social Psychology, 66,* 3–11.

Bandura, A., Taylor, C. B., Williams, S. L., Medford, I. N., & Barchas, J. D. (1985). Catecholamine secretion as a function of perceived coping self-efficacy. *Journal of Consulting and Clinical Psychology, 53,* 406–414.

Banks, M. S., & Shannon, E. (1993). Spatial and chromatic visual efficiency in human neonates. In C. E. Granrud (Ed.), *Visual perception and cognition in infancy.* Hillsdale, NJ: Erlbaum.

Banks, S. M., et al. (1995). The effects of message framing on mammography utilization. *Health Psychology, 14,* 178–184.

Baquet, C. R., Horm, J. W., Gibbs, T., & Greenwald, P. (1991). Socioeconomic factors and cancer incidence among Blacks and Whites. *Journal of the National Cancer Institute, 83,* 551–557.

Barbaree, H. E., & Marshall, W. L. (1991). The role of male sexual arousal in rape. *Journal of Consulting and Clinical Psychology, 59,* 621–631.

Bard, P. (1934). The neurohumoral basis of emotional reactions. In C. A. Murchison (Ed.), *Handbook of general experimental psychology.* Worcester, MA: Clark University Press.

Barlow, D. H. (1991). Introduction to the special issue on diagnoses, definitions, and *DSM-IV. Journal of Abnormal Psychology, 100,* 243–244.

Barlow, D. H. (1996). Health care policy, psychotherapy research, and the future of psychotherapy. *American Psychologist, 51,* 1050–1058.

Barnett, W. S., & Escobar, C. M. (1990). Economic costs and benefits of early intervention. In S. J. Meisels & J. P. Shonkoff (Eds.), *Handbook of early childhood intervention.* New York: Cambridge University Press.

Baron, R. A., & Byrne, D. (1997). *Social psychology* (8th ed.). Boston: Allyn & Bacon.

Barr, C. E., Mednick, S. A., & Munk-Jorgensen, P. (1990). Exposure to influenza epidemics during gestation and adult schizophrenia. *Archives of General Psychiatry, 47,* 869–874.

Barringer, F. (1993, April 25). Polling on sexual issues has its drawbacks. *The New York Times,* p. A23.

Bartoshuk, L. M., & Beauchamp, G. K. (1994). Chemical senses. *Annual Review of Psychology, 45,* 419–449.

Basch, M. F. (1980). *Doing psychotherapy.* New York: Basic Books.

Basen-Engquist, K., Edmundson, E. W., & Parcel, G. S. (1996). Structure of health risk behavior among high school students. *Journal of Consulting and Clinical Psychology, 64,* 764–775.

Bashore, T. R., & Rapp, P. E. (1993). Are there alternatives to traditional polygraph procedures? *Psychological Bulletin, 113,* 3–22.

Basic Behavioral Science Task Force of the National Advisory Mental Health Council. (1996a). Basic behavioral science research for mental health: Vulnerability and resilience. *American Psychologist, 51,* 22–28.

Basic Behavioral Science Task Force of the National Advisory Mental Health Council. (1996b). Basic behavioral science research for mental health: Perception, attention, learning, and memory. *American Psychologist, 51,* 133–142.

Basic Behavioral Science Task Force of the National Advisory Mental Health Council. (1996c). Basic behavioral science research for mental health: Sociocultural and environmental practices. *American Psychologist, 51,* 722–731.

Baucom, D. H., Shoham, V., Mueser, K. T., Daiuto, A. D., & Stickle, T. R. (1998). Empirically supported couple and family interventions for marital distress and adult mental health problems. *Journal of Consulting and Clinical Psychology, 66,* 53–88.

Bauer, P. J. (1996). What do infants recall of their lives? Memory for specific events by one- to two-year-olds. *American Psychologist, 51,* 29–41.

Baum, A., & Fleming, I. (1993). Implications of psychological research on stress and technological accidents. *American Psychologist, 48,* 665–672.

Baumeister, R. F., Stillwell, A. M., & Heatherton, T. F. (1994). Guilt. *Psychological Bulletin, 115,* 243–267.

Baumgardner, A. H., Heppner, P. P., & Arkin, R. M. (1986). Role of causal attribution in personal problem solving. *Journal of Personality and Social Psychology, 50,* 636–643.

Baumrind, D. (1973). The development of instrumental competence through socialization. In A. D. Pick (Ed.), *Minnesota Symposia on Child Development, Vol. 7.* Minneapolis: University of Minnesota Press.

Baumrind, D. (1991). Parenting styles and adolescent development. In J. Brooks-Gunn, R. Lerner, & A. C. Petersen (Eds.), *Encyclopedia of Adolescence, II.* New York: Garland.

Beck, A. T. (1991). Cognitive therapy: A 30-year retrospective. *American Psychologist, 46,* 368–375.

Beck, A. T. (1993). Cognitive therapy: Past, present, and future. *Journal of Consulting and Clinical Psychology, 61,* 194–198.

Beck, A. T., Brown, G., Berchick, R. J., Stewart, B. L., & Steer, R. A. (1990). Relationship between hopelessness and ultimate suicide. *American Journal of Psychiatry, 147,* 190–195.

Beck, A. T., & Freeman, A. (1990). *Cognitive therapy of personality disorders.* New York: Guilford.

Becker, L. B., et al. (1993). Racial differences in the incidence of cardiac arrest and subsequent survival. *New England Journal of Medicine, 329,* 600–606.

Bell, A. P., Weinberg, M. S., & Hammersmith, S. K. (1981). *Sexual preference: Its development in men and women.* Bloomington, IN: University of Indiana Press.

Bell, P. A. (1992). In defense of the negative affect escape model of heat and aggression. *Psychological Bulletin, 111,* 342–346.

Belle, D. (1990). Poverty and women's mental health. *American Psychologist, 45,* 385–389.

Belsky, J. (1990). Developmental risks associated with infant day care. I. S. Cherazi (Ed.), *Psychosocial issues in day care* (pp. 37–68). New York: American Psychiatric Press.

Belsky, J. (1993). Etiology of child maltreatment. *Psychological Bulletin, 114,* 413–434.

Belsky, J., Fish, M., & Isabella, R. (1991). Continuity and discontinuity in infant negative and positive emotionality: Family attachments and attachment consequences. *Developmental Psychology, 27,* 421–431.

Bem, D. J., & Honorton, C. (1994). Does Psi exist? Replicable evidence for an anomalous process of information transfer. *Psychological Bulletin, 115,* 4–18.

Bem, S. L. (1993). *The lenses of gender.* New Haven: Yale University Press.

Benight, C. C., et al. (1997). Coping self-efficacy buffers psychological and physiological disturbances in HIV-infected men following a natural disaster. *Health Psychology, 16,* 248–255.

Benson, H. (1975). *The relaxation response.* New York: Morrow.

Benson, H., Manzetta, B. R., & Rosner, B. (1973). Decreased systolic blood pressure in hypertensive subjects who practiced meditation. *Journal of Clinical Investigation, 52,* 8.

Benson, P. L., Karabenick, S. A., & Lerner, R. M. (1976). Pretty pleases: The effects of physical attractiveness, race, and sex on receiving help. *Journal of Experimental Social Psychology, 12,* 409–415.

Berenbaum, H., & Connelly, J. (1993). The effect of stress on hedonic capacity. *Journal of Abnormal Psychology, 102,* 474–481.

Berkowitz, L. (1988). Frustrations, appraisals, and aversively stimulated aggression. *Aggressive Behavior, 14,* 3–11.

Berkowitz, L. (1994). Is something missing? Some observations prompted by the cognitive-neoassociationist view of anger and emotional aggression. In L. R. Huesmann (Ed.), *Aggressive behavior: Current perspectives.* New York: Plenum.

Bernstein, N. (1999, September 13). Back on the streets without a safety net. *The New York Times,* pp. B1, B6.

Bernstein, W. M., Stephenson, B. O., Snyder, M. L., & Wicklund, R. A. (1983). Causal ambiguity and heterosexual affiliation. *Journal of Experimental Social Psychology, 19,* 78–92.

Berquier, A., & Ashton, R. (1992). Characteristics of the frequent nightmare sufferer. *Journal of Abnormal Psychology, 101,* 246–250.

Betancourt, H., & López, S. R. (1993). The study of culture, ethnicity, and race in American psychology. *American Psychologist, 48,* 629–637.

Bevan, W., & Kessel, F. (1994). Plain truths and home cooking. *American Psychologist, 49,* 505–509.

Bexton, W. H., Heron, W., & Scott, T. H. (1954). Effects of decreased variation in the sensory environment. *Canadian Journal of Psychology, 8,* 70–76.

Bianchi, S. M., & Spain, D. (1997). *Women, work and family in America*. Population Reference Bureau.

Bjork, D. W. (1997). *B. F. Skinner: A life*. Washington, DC: American Psychological Association.

Bjorklund, D. F. (1995). *Children's thinking* (2nd ed). Pacific Grove, CA: Brooks/Cole.

Bjorklund, D. F., & Kipp, K. (1996). Parental investment theory and gender differences in the evolution of inhibition mechanisms. *Psychological Bulletin, 120,* 163–188.

Blake, P., Fry, R., & Pesjack, M. (1984). *Self-assessment and behavior change manual* (pp. 43–47). New York: Random House.

Blakeslee, S. (1994, April 13). Black smokers' higher risk of cancer may be genetic. *The New York Times,* p. C14.

Blakeslee, S. (1995, May 16). The mystery of music. *The New York Times,* pp. C1, C10.

Blakeslee, S. (1998, August 4). Re-evaluating significance of baby's bond with mother. *The New York Times,* pp. F1, F2.

Blanchard, E. B. (1992). Psychological treatment of benign headache disorders. *Journal of Consulting and Clinical Psychology, 60,* 537–551.

Blanchard, E. B., et al. (1990a). Placebo-controlled evaluation of abbreviated progressive muscle relaxation and of relaxation combined with cognitive therapy in the treatment of tension headache. *Journal of Consulting and Clinical Psychology, 58,* 210–215.

Blanchard, E. B., et al. (1990b). A controlled evaluation of thermal biofeedback and thermal feedback combined with cognitive therapy in the treatment of vascular headache. *Journal of Consulting and Clinical Psychology, 58,* 216–224.

Blatt, S. J. (1995). The destructiveness of perfectionism: Implications for the treatment of depression. *American Psychologist, 50,* 1003–1020.

Blatt, S. J., Zuroff, D. C., Quinlan, D. M., & Pilkonis, P. A. (1996). Interpersonal factors in brief treatment of depression. *Journal of Consulting and Clinical Psychology, 64,* 162–171.

Block, J. (1995). A contrarian view of the five-factor approach to personality description. *Psychological Bulletin, 117,* 187–215.

Bloom, L., Merkin, S., & Wootten, J. (1982). *Wh*-questions: Linguistic factors that contribute to the sequence of acquisition. *Child Development, 53,* 1084–1092.

Bloom, L., & Mudd, S. A. (1991). Depth of processing approach to face recognition: A test of two theories. *Journal of Experimental Psychology: Learning, Memory, and Cognition, 17,* 556–565.

Blum, D. (1997). *Sex on the brain: The biological differences between men and women*. New York: Viking.

Bogen, J. E. (1969). The other side of the brain II: An appositional mind. *Bulletin of the Los Angeles Neurological Society, 34,* 135–162.

Bond, R., & Smith, P. B. (1996). Culture and conformity. *Psychological Bulletin, 119,* 111–137.

Bootzin, R. R., Epstein, D., & Wood, J. N. (1991). Stimulus control instructions. In P. Hauri (Ed.), *Case studies in insomnia*. New York: Plenum.

Boskind-White, M., & White, W. C. (1983). *Bulimarexia: The binge/purge cycle*. New York: Norton.

Boston Women's Health Book Collective. (1992). *The new our bodies, ourselves*. New York: Simon & Schuster.

Bouchard, T. J., Jr., Lykken, D. T., McGue, M., Segal, N. L., & Tellegen, A. (1990). Sources of human psychological differences: The Minnesota study of twins reared apart. *Science, 250,* 223–228.

Bower, G. H. (1981). Mood and memory. *American Psychologist, 36,* 129–148.

Bowers, K. S., & Woody, E. Z. (1996). Hypnotic amnesia and the paradox of intentional forgetting. *Journal of Abnormal Psychology, 105,* 381–390.

Bowes, J. M., & Goodnow, J. J. (1996). Work for home, school, or labor force. *Psychological Bulletin, 119,* 300–321.

Bowlby, J. (1988). *A secure base*. New York: Basic Books.

Boyatzis, R. E. (1974). The effect of alcohol consumption on the aggressive behavior of men. *Quarterly Journal for the Study of Alcohol, 35,* 959–972.

Boyd-Franklin, N. (1995, August). A multisystems model for treatment interventions with inner-city African American families. Master lecture delivered to the meeting of the American Psychological Association, New York.

Bradley, R. H., et al. (1989). Home environment and cognitive development in the first 3 years of life. *Developmental Psychology, 25,* 217–235.

Bransford, J. D., Nitsch, K. E., & Franks, J. J. (1977). Schooling and the facilitation of knowing. In R. C.

Anderson, R. J. Spiro, & W. E. Montague (Eds.), *Schooling and the acquisition of knowledge.* Hillsdale, NJ: Erlbaum.

Braun, B. G. (1988). *Treatment of multiple personality disorder.* Washington, DC: American Psychiatric Press.

Brewin, C. R., Andrews, B., & Gotlib, I. H. (1993). Psychopathology and early experience. *Psychological Bulletin, 113,* 82–98.

Bridgwater, C. A. (1982). What candor can do. *Psychology Today, 16*(5), 16.

Broberg, A., Hwang, P., Wessels, H., & Lamb, M. (1997). Cited in Azar, B. (1997). It may cause anxiety, but day care can benefit kids. *APA Monitor, 28*(6), 13.

Brody, J. E. (1992, June 17). Psychotherapists warn parents not to dismiss their children's statements about suicide. *The New York Times,* p. B8.

Brody, J. E. (1993, December 1). Liberated at last from the myths about menopause. *The New York Times,* p. C15.

Brody, J. E. (1995). Cited in DeAngelis, T. (1995), Eat well, keep fit, and let go of stress. *APA Monitor, 26*(10), 20.

Brody, J. E. (1996, September 4). Osteoporosis can threaten men as well as women. *The New York Times,* p. C9.

Brody, J. E. (1997, March 26). Race and weight. *The New York Times,* p. C8.

Brody, J. E. (1997, August 20). Estrogen after menopause? A tough dilemma. *The New York Times,* p. C8.

Brody, J. E. (1998, August 4). Personal health: Giving men directions to the road to better health. *The New York Times;* America Online.

Broussard, B. A., et al. (1991). Prevalence of obesity in American Indians and Alaska natives. *American Journal of Clinical Nutrition, 53,* 1535–1542.

Brown, L. S. (1992). A feminist critique of the personality disorders. In L. Brown & M. Balou (Eds.), *Personality and psychopathology: Feminist reappraisals.* New York: Guilford.

Brown, R., & Kulik, J. (1977). Flashbulb memories. *Cognition, 5,* 73–99.

Brown, R., & McNeill, D. (1966). The tip-of-the-tongue phenomenon. *Journal of Verbal Learning and Verbal Behavior, 5,* 325–337.

Brownell, K. D. (1997). We must be more militant about food. *APA Monitor, 28*(3), 48.

Brownell, K. D., & Rodin, J. (1994). The dieting maelstrom. *American Psychologist, 49,* 781–791.

Brownlee-Duffeck, M., et al. (1987). The role of health beliefs in the regimen adherence and metabolic control of adolescents and adults with diabetes mellitus. *Journal of Consulting and Clinical Psychology, 55,* 139–144.

Buchanan, C. M., Eccles, J. S., & Becker, J. B. (1992). Are adolescents the victims of raging hormones? Evidence for activational effects of hormones on moods and behavior at adolescence. *Psychological Bulletin, 111,* 62–107.

Buffone, G. W. (1984). Running and depression. In M. L. Sachs & G. W. Buffone (Eds.), *Running as therapy: An integrated approach.* Lincoln, NE: University of Nebraska Press.

Bullock, M. (1997). Cited in Murray, B. (1997). America still lags behind in mathematics test scores. *APA Monitor, 28*(1), 44.

Burman, B., & Margolin, G. (1992). Analysis of the association between marital relationships and health problems. *Psychological Bulletin, 112,* 39–63.

Burnette, E. (1997). "Father of Ebonics" continues his crusade. *APA Monitor, 28*(4), 12.

Burns, D. D., & Nolen-Hoeksema, S. (1992). Therapeutic empathy and recovery from depression in cognitive-behavioral therapy. *Journal of Consulting and Clinical Psychology, 60,* 441–449.

Burnstein, E. (1983). Persuasion as argument processing. In M. Brandstatter, J. H. Davis, & G. Stocker-Kreichgauer (Eds.), *Group decision processes.* London: Academic Press.

Bushman, B. J., Baumeister, R. F., & Stack, A. D. (1999). Catharsis, aggression, and persuasive influence: Self-fulfilling or self-defeating prophecies? *Journal of Personality and Social Psychology, 76*(3), 367–376.

Buss, D. M. (1992). Is there a universal human nature? *Contemporary Psychology, 37,* 1262–1263.

Buss, D. M. (1994). *The evolution of desire.* New York: Basic Books.

Buss, D. M. (1999, June 1). Evolutionary science ponders: Where is fancy bred? *The New York Times Online.*

Buss, D. M., Haselton, M. G., Shackelford, T. K., Bleske, A. L., & Wakefield, J. C. (1998). Adaptations, exaptations, and spandrels. *American Psychologist, 53,* 533–548.

Butler, R. (1998). Cited in CD-ROM that accompanies Nevid, J. S., Rathus, S. A., & Rubenstein, H.

(1998). *Health in the new millennium*. New York: Worth.

Byrnes, J., & Takahira, S. (1993). Explaining gender differences on SAT-math items. *Developmental Psychology, 29*, 805–810.

Cacioppo, J. T., Martzke, J. S, Petty, R. E., & Tassinary, L. G. (1988). Specific forms of facial EMG response index emotions during an interview. *Journal of Personality and Social Psychology, 54*, 552–604.

Campos, J. J., Hiatt, S., Ramsey, D., Henderson, C., & Svejda, M. (1978). The emergence of fear on the visual cliff. In M. Lewis & L. Rosenblum (Eds.), *The origins of affect*. New York: Plenum.

Cannon, W. B. (1927). The James-Lange theory of emotions: A critical examination and an alternative theory. *American Journal of Psychology, 39*, 106–124.

Cannon, W. B., & Washburn, A. (1912). An explanation of hunger. *American Journal of Physiology, 29*, 441–454.

Carey, G., & DiLalla, D. L. (1994). Personality and psychopathology: Genetic perspectives. *Journal of Abnormal Psychology, 103*, 32–43.

Carlson, J. G., & Hatfield, E. (1992). *Psychology of emotion*. Fort Worth: Harcourt Brace Jovanovich.

Carpenter, W. T., Jr., & Buchanan, R. W. (1994). Schizophrenia. *New England Journal of Medicine, 330*, 681–690.

Carroll, K. M., Rounsaville, B. J., & Nich, C. (1994). Blind man's bluff: Effectiveness and significance of psychotherapy and pharmacotherapy blinding procedures in a clinical trial. *Journal of Consulting and Clinical Psychology, 62*, 276–280.

Carstensen, L. (1997, August 17). The evolution of social goals across the life span. Paper presented to the American Psychological Association, Chicago.

Case, R. (1992). *The mind's staircase*. Hillsdale, NJ: Erlbaum.

Caulfield, M., et al. (1994). Linkage of the angiotensinogen gene to essential hypertension. *New England Journal of Medicine, 330*, 1629–1633.

Cavanaugh, J. C., & Green, E. E. (1990). I believe, therefore I can: Self-efficacy beliefs in memory aging. In E. A. Lovelace (Ed.), *Aging and cognition: Mental processes, self-awareness, and interventions*. North-Holland, Elsevier.

Ceci, S. J., & Bruck, M. (1993). Suggestibility of the child witness. *Psychological Bulletin, 113*, 403–439.

Celis, W. (1991, January 2). Students trying to draw line between sex and an assault. *The New York Times*, pp. 1, B8.

Center for the Study of Social Policy. (1993). *Kids count data book*. Washington, DC: Author.

Centers for Disease Control (1995). *Suicide surveillance: 1980–1990*. Washington, DC: USDHHS.

Chadwick, P. D. J., & Lowe, C. F. (1990). Measurement and modification of delusional beliefs. *Journal of Consulting and Clinical Psychology, 58*, 225–232.

Chambless, D. L., & Hollon, S. D. (1998). Defining empirically supported therapies. *Journal of Consulting and Clinical Psychology, 66*, 7–18.

Chan, C. (1992). Cultural considerations in counseling Asian American lesbians and gay men. In S. Dworkin & F. Gutierrez (Eds.), *Counseling gay men and lesbians*. Alexandria, VA: American Association for Counseling and Development.

Chassin, L., Curran, P. J., Hussong, A. M., & Colder, C. R. (1996). The relation of parent alcoholism to adolescent substance use. *Journal of Abnormal Psychology, 105*, 70–80.

Chesno, F. A., & Kilmann, P. R. (1975). Effects of stimulation intensity on sociopathic avoidance learning. *Journal of Abnormal Psychology, 84*, 144–151.

Chomsky, N. (1980). Rules and representations. *Behavioral and Brain Sciences, 3*, 1–16.

Chomsky, N. (1991). Linguistics and cognitive science. In A. Kasher (Ed.), *The Chomskyan turn*. Cambridge, MA: Blackwell.

Christiansen, K., & Knussman, R. (1987). Androgen levels and components of aggressive behavior in men. *Hormones and Behavior, 21*, 170–180.

Clark, D. M., et al.. (1997). Misinterpretation of body sensations in panic disorder. *Journal of Consulting and Clinical Psychology, 65*, 203–213.

Clark, L. A., Watson, D., & Mineka, S. M. (1994). Temperament, personality, and the mood and anxiety disorders. *Journal of Abnormal Psychology, 103*, 103–116.

Clarke-Stewart, K. A. (1990). The "effects" of infant day care reconsidered. In N. Fox & G. G. Fein (Eds.), *Infant day care* (pp. 61–86). Norwood, NJ: Ablex.

Clarke-Stewart, K. A. (1991). A home is not a school: The effects of child care on children's development. *Journal of Social Issues, 47*, 105–123.

Clay, R. A. (1996). Beating the "biological clock" with zest. *APA Monitor, 27*(2), 37.

Clement, J. (1991). Nonformal reasoning in experts and in science students. In J. Voss, D. Perkins, & J. Siegel (Eds.), *Informal reasoning and education*. Hillsdale, NJ: Erlbaum.

Cohen, L. A. (1987, November). Diet and cancer. *Scientific American*, pp. 42–48, 53–54.

Cohen, S., Evans, G. W., Stokols, D., & Krantz, D. S. (1986). *Behavior, health, and environmental stress*. New York: Plenum.

Cohen, S., Tyrrell, D. A. J., & Smith, A. P. (1993). Negative life events, perceived stress, negative affect, and susceptibility to the common cold. *Journal of Personality and Social Psychology, 64*, 131–140.

Cohen, S., & Williamson, G. M. (1991). Stress and infectious disease in humans. *Psychological Bulletin, 109*, 5–24.

Cohn, E. G. (1990). Weather and violent crime. *Environment and Behavior, 22*, 280–294.

Cohn, L. D., Macfarlane, S., Yanez, C., & Imai, W. K. (1995). Risk-perception: Differences between adolescents and adults. *Health Psychology, 14*, 217–222.

Coie, J. D., et al. (1993). The science of prevention. *American Psychologist, 48*, 1013–1022.

Coleman, M., & Ganong, L. H. (1985). Love and sex role stereotypes. *Journal of Personality and Social Psychology, 49*, 170–176.

Collaer, M. L., & Hines, M. (1995). Human behavioral sex differences: A role for gonadal hormones during early development? *Psychological Bulletin, 118*, 55–107.

Collier, G. (1994). *Social origins of mental ability*. New York: Wiley.

Collins, C. (1995, May 11). Spanking is becoming the new don't. *The New York Times*, p. C8.

Compas, B. E., Haaga, D. A. F., Keefe, F. J., Leitenberg, H., & Williams, D. A. (1998). Sampling of empirically supported psychological treatments from health psychology: Smoking, chronic pain, cancer, and bulimia nervosa. *Journal of Consulting and Clinical Psychology, 66*, 89–112.

Cools, J., Schotte, D. E., & McNally, R. J. (1992). Emotional arousal and overeating in restrained eaters. *Journal of Abnormal Psychology, 101*, 348–351.

Cooney, J. L., & Zeichner, A. (1985). Selective attention to negative feedback in Type A and Type B individuals. *Journal of Abnormal Psychology, 94*, 110–112.

Cooper, J. R., Bloom, F. E., & Roth, R. H. (1991). *The biochemical basis of neuropharmacology*. New York: Oxford University Press.

Cooper, M. L., & Orcutt, H. K. (1997). Drinking and sexual experience on first dates among adolescents. *Journal of Abnormal Psychology, 106*, 191–202.

Corter, J. E., & Gluck, M. A. (1992). Explaining basic categories: Feature predictability and information. *Psychological Bulletin, 111*, 291–303.

Cousins, N. (1979). *Anatomy of an illness as perceived by the patient*. New York: Norton.

Cowley, G. (1996, September 16). Attention: Aging men. *Newsweek*, pp. 68–77.

Cox, M. J., Owen, M. T., Henderson, V. K., & Margand, N. A. (1992). Prediction of infant-father and infant-mother attachment. *Developmental Psychology, 28*, 474–483.

Craik, F. I. M., & Lockhart, R. S. (1972). Levels of processing. *Journal of Verbal Learning and Verbal Behavior, 11*, 671–684.

Craik, F. I. M., & Watkins, M. J. (1973). The role of rehearsal in short-term memory. *Journal of Verbal Learning and Verbal Behavior, 12*, 599–607.

Cramer, R. E., McMaster, M. R., Bartell, P. A., & Dragna, M. (1988). Subject competence and minimization of the bystander effect. *Journal of Applied Social Psychology, 18*, 1133–1148.

Crawford, H. J., Brown, A. M., & Moon, C. E. (1993). Sustained attentional and disattentional abilities: Differences between low and highly hypnotizable persons. *Journal of Abnormal Psychology, 102*, 534–543.

Creamer, M., Burgess, P., & Pattison, P. (1992). Reaction to trauma. *Journal of Abnormal Psychology, 101*, 452–459.

Crews, D. (1994). Animal sexuality. *Scientific American, 270*(1), 108–114.

Crick, F., & Koch, C. (1997). The problem of consciousness. *Scientific American mysteries of the mind, Special Issue Vol. 7*, No. 1, 18–26.

Crick, N. R., & Dodge, K. A. (1994). A review and reformulation of social information-processing mechanisms in children's social adjustment. *Psychological Bulletin, 115*, 74–101.

Crusco, A. H., & Wetzel, C. G. (1984). The Midas touch: The effects of interpersonal touch on restaurant tipping. *Personality and Social Psychology Bulletin, 10*, 512–517.

Culbertson, F. M. (1997). Depression and gender. *American Psychologist, 52*, 25–31.

Curb, J. D., & Marcus, E. B. (1991). Body fat and obesity in Japanese-Americans. *American Journal of Clinical Nutrition, 53*, 1552S–1555S.

Curfman, G. D. (1993a). The health benefits of exercise. *New England Journal of Medicine, 328*, 574–576.

Curfman, G. D. (1993b). Is exercise beneficial—or hazardous—to your heart? *New England Journal of Medicine, 329*, 1730–1731.

Curran, P. J., Stice, E., & Chassin, L. (1997). The relation between adolescent alcohol use and peer alcohol use. *Journal of Consulting and Clinical Psychology, 65*, 130–140.

Damaged gene is linked to lung cancer. (1996, April 6.) *The New York Times*, p. A24.

Danforth, J. S., et al. (1990). Exercise as a treatment for hypertension in low-socioeconomic-status Black children. *Journal of Consulting and Clinical Psychology, 58*, 237–239.

Darley, J. M. (1993). Research on morality. *Psychological Science, 4*, 353–357.

Darley, J. M., & Latané, B. (1968). Bystander intervention in emergencies: Diffusion of responsibility. *Journal of Personality and Social Psychology, 8*, 377–383.

Darwin, C. A. (1872). *The expression of the emotions in man and animals*. London: J. Murray.

Darwin, F. (Ed.). (1958). *The autobiography of Charles Darwin and selected letters* (p. 27). New York: Dover. (Original work published 1892).

Davey, L. F. (1993, March). *Developmental implications of shared and divergent perceptions in the parent–adolescent relationship*. Paper presented at the biennial meeting of the Society for Research in Child Development, New Orleans.

Davidson, J. R., & Foa, E. G. (1991). Diagnostic issues in posttraumatic stress disorder. *Journal of Abnormal Psychology, 100*, 346–355.

Davis, K. L., Kahn, R. S., Ko, G., & Davidson, M. (1991). Dopamine in schizophrenia. *American Journal of Psychiatry, 148*, 1474–1486.

de Jong, P. F., & Das-Smaal, E. A. (1995). Attention and intelligence. *Journal of Educational Psychology, 87*, 80–92.

De La Cancela, V., & Guzman, L. P. (1991). Latino mental health service needs. In H. F. Myers et al. (Eds.), *Ethnic minority perspectives on clinical training and services in psychology* (pp. 59–64). Washington, DC: American Psychological Association.

Deacon, T. W. (1997). *The symbolic species: The co-evolution of language and the brain*. New York: W. W. Norton & Company.

DeAngelis, T. (1993a). Law helps American Indians enter field. *APA Monitor, 24*(3), 26–27.

DeAngelis, T. (1993b). It's baaack: TV violence, concern for kid viewers. *APA Monitor, 24*(8), 16.

DeAngelis, T. (1995a). Firefighters' PTSD at dangerous levels. *APA Monitor, 26*(2), 36–37.

DeAngelis, T. (1995b). Mental health care is elusive for Hispanics. *APA Monitor, 26*(7), 49.

DeAngelis, T. (1997). Abused children have more conflicts with friends. *APA Monitor, 28*(6), 32.

DeCasper, A. J., & Prescott, P. A. (1984). Human newborns' perception of male voices. *Developmental Psychobiology, 17*, 481–491.

DeFries, J. C., Plomin, R., & LaBuda, M. C. (1987). Genetic stability of cognitive development from childhood to adulthood. *Developmental Psychology, 23*, 4–12.

Delahanty, D. L., et al. (1996). Time course of natural killer cell activity and lymphocyte proliferation in response to two acute stressors in healthy men. *Health Psychology, 15*, 48–55.

Delgado, J. M. R. (1969). *Physical control of the mind*. New York: Harper & Row.

Denmark, F. L. (1994). Engendering psychology. *American Psychologist, 49*, 329–334.

DeRubeis, R. J., & Crits-Christoph, P. (1998). Empirically supported individual and group psychological treatments for adult mental disorders. *Journal of Consulting and Clinical Psychology, 66*, 37–52.

DeValois, R. L., & Jacobs, G. H. (1984). Neural mechanisms of color vision. In I. Darian-Smith (Ed.), *Handbook of physiology* (Vol. 3). Bethesda, MD: American Physiological Society.

Devine, P. G. (1989). Stereotypes and prejudice. *Journal of Personality and Social Psychology, 56*, 5–18.

DiClemente, C. C., et al. (1991). The process of smoking cessation. *Journal of Consulting and Clinical Psychology, 59*, 295–304.

DiLalla, D. L., Carey, G., Gottesman, I. I., & Bouchard, T. J., Jr. (1996). Heritability of MMPI personality indicators of psychopathology in twins reared apart. *Journal of Abnormal Psychology, 105,* 491–499.

DiLalla, D. L., & Gottesman, I. I. (1991). Biological and genetic contributors to violence—Widom's untold tale. *Psychological Bulletin, 109,* 125–129.

Dill, C. A., Gilden, E. R., Hill, P. C., & Hanselka, L. L. (1982). Federal human subjects regulations. *Personality and Social Psychology Bulletin, 8,* 417–425.

Dindia, K., & Allen, M. (1992). Sex differences in self-disclosure. *Psychological Bulletin, 112,* 106–124.

Docherty, N. M., et al. (1996). Working memory, attention, and communication disturbances in schizophrenia. *Journal of Abnormal Psychology, 105,* 212–219.

Dockery, D. W., et al. (1993). An association between air pollution and mortality in six U.S. cities. *New England Journal of Medicine, 329,* 1753–1759.

Doctors tie male mentality to shorter life span. (1995, June 14). *The New York Times,* p. C14.

Dodge, K. A., Price, J. M., Bachorowski, J., & Newman, J. P. (1990). Hostile attributional biases in severely aggressive adolescents. *Journal of Abnormal Psychology, 99,* 385–392.

Dollard, J., Doob, L. W., Miller, N. E., Mowrer, O. H., & Sears, R. R. (1939). *Frustration and aggression.* New Haven, CT: Yale University Press.

Donnerstein, E. I., & Wilson, D. W. (1976). Effects of noise and perceived control on ongoing and subsequent aggressive behavior. *Journal of Personality and Social Psychology, 34,* 774–781.

Doob, A. N., & Wood, L. (1972). Catharsis and aggression. *Journal of Personality and Social Psychology, 22,* 236–245.

Dowd, M. (1997, August 9). The brain drain. *The New York Times,* p. 23.

Drapkin, R. G., Wing, R. R., & Shiffman, S. (1995). Responses to hypothetical high risk situations. *Health Psychology, 14,* 427–434.

Dubbert, P. M. (1992). Exercise in behavioral medicine. *Journal of Consulting and Clinical Psychology, 60,* 613–618.

Duckitt, J. (1992). Psychology and prejudice. *American Psychologist, 47,* 1182–1193.

Dweck, C. (1997). Paper presented to the meeting of the Society for Research in Child Development. Cited in Murray, B. (1997). Verbal praise may be the best motivator of all. *APA Monitor, 28*(6), 26.

Eagly, A. H. (1995). The science and politics of comparing women and men. *American Psychologist, 50,* 145–158.

Eagly, A. H., & Chaiken, S. (1993). *The psychology of attitudes.* Fort Worth: Harcourt Brace Jovanovich.

Eagly, A. H., & Steffen, V. J. (1984). Gender stereotypes stem from the distribution of men and women into social roles. *Journal of Personality and Social Psychology, 46,* 735–754.

Ebbinghaus, H. (1913). *Memory: A contribution to experimental psychology.* (H. A. Roger & C. E. Bussenius, Trans.). New York: Columbia University Press. (Original work published 1885)

Egeth, H. E. (1993). What do we *not* know about eyewitness identification? *American Psychologist, 48,* 577–580.

Eich, E. (1995). Searching for mood dependent memory. *Psychological Science, 6,* 67–75.

Eisenberg, N., Cialdini, R. B., McCreath, H., & Shell, R. (1987). Consistency-based compliance: When and why do children become vulnerable? *Journal of Personality and Social Psychology, 52,* 1174–1181.

Eisenberger, R., & Cameron, J. (1996). Detrimental effects of reward: Reality or myth? *American Psychologist, 51,* 1153–1166.

Ekman, P. (1980). *The face of man.* New York: Garland.

Ekman, P. (1993). Facial expression and emotion. *American Psychologist, 48,* 384–392.

Ekman, P. (1994). Strong evidence for universals in facial expression. *Psychological Bulletin, 115,* 268–287.

Ekman, P., et al. (1987). Universals and cultural differences in the judgments of facial expressions of emotion. *Journal of Personality and Social Psychology, 53,* 712–717.

Elkind, D. (1967). Egocentrism in adolescence. *Child Development, 38,* 1025–1034.

Elkind, D. (1985). Egocentrism redux. *Developmental Review, 5,* 218–226.

Elkind, D., & Bowen, R. (1979). Imaginary audience behavior in children and adolescents. *Developmental Psychology, 15,* 38–44.

Ellickson, P. L., Hays, R. D., & Bell, R. M. (1992). Stepping through the drug use sequence. *Journal of Abnormal Psychology, 101,* 441–451.

Ellis, A. (1977). The basic clinical theory of rational-emotive therapy. In A. Ellis & R. Grieger (Eds.),

Handbook of rational-emotive therapy. New York: Springer.

Ellis, A. (1993). Reflections on rational-emotive therapy. *Journal of Consulting and Clinical Psychology, 61,* 199–201.

Ellis, A., & Dryden, W. (1996). The practice of rational emotive behavior therapy. New York: Springer.

Ellis, A., & Grieger, R. (Eds.) (1986). *Handbook of rational-emotive therapy.* New York: Springer.

Ellis, L. (1990). Prenatal stress may affect sex-typical behaviors of a child. *Brown University Child Behavior and Development Letter, 6*(1), 1–3.

Ellis, L., & Ames, M. A. (1987). Neurohormonal functioning and sexual orientation. *Psychological Bulletin, 101,* 233–258.

Ellsworth, P. C., Carlsmith, J. M., & Henson, A. (1972). The stare as a stimulus to flight in human subjects. *Journal of Personality and Social Psychology, 21,* 302–311.

Emde, R. (1993). Cited in Adler, T. (1993). Shy, bold temperament? It's mostly in the genes. *APA Monitor, 24*(1), 7, 8.

Engel, J. (1996). Surgery for seizures. *New England Journal of Medicine, 334,* 647–652.

Engels, G. I., Garnefski, N., & Diekstra, R. F. W. (1993). Efficacy of rational-emotive therapy. *Journal of Consulting and Clinical Psychology, 61,* 1083–1090.

Erikson, E. H. (1963). *Childhood and society.* New York: W. W. Norton.

Ernst, N. D., & Harlan, W. R. (1991). Obesity and cardiovascular disease in minority populations: Executive summary. *American Journal of Clinical Nutrition, 53,* 1507S–1511S.

Eron, L. D. (1982). Parent—child interaction, television violence, and aggression of children. *American Psychologist, 37,* 197–211.

Esterling, B. A., Antoni, M. H., Kumar, M., & Schneiderman, N. (1993). Defensiveness, trait anxiety, and Epstein-Barr viral capsid antigen antibody titers in healthy college students. *Health Psychology, 12,* 132–139.

Estes, W. K. (1972). An associative basis for coding and organization in memory. In A. W. Melton & E. Martin (Eds.), *Coding processes in human memory.* Washington, DC: Winston.

Etaugh, C., & Rathus, S. A. (1995). *The world of children.* Fort Worth: Harcourt Brace.

Evans, G. W., Jacobs, S. V., & Frager, N. B. (1982). Behavioral responses to air pollution. In A. Baum & J. E. Singer (Eds.), *Advances in environmental psychology* (Vol. 4). Hillsdale, NJ: Erlbaum.

Eysenck, H. J., & Eysenck, M. W. (1985). *Personality and individual differences.* New York: Plenum.

Fantz, R. L. (1961). The origin of form perception. *Scientific American, 204*(5), 66–72.

Farber, B. A., Brink, D. C., & Raskin, P. M. (1996). *The psychotherapy of Carl Rogers: Cases and commentary.* New York: The Guilford Press.

Fazio, R. H. (1990). Multiple processes by which attitudes guide behavior. In M. P. Zanna (Ed.), *Advances in experimental social psychology.* San Diego, CA: Academic Press.

Feder, B. J. (1997, April 20). Surge in the teenage smoking rate left the tobacco industry vulnerable. *The New York Times,* pp. A1, A28.

Fehr, B., & Russell, J. A. (1991). The concept of love viewed from a prototype perspective. *Journal of Personality and Social Psychology, 60,* 425–438.

Fein, E. (1998, January 5). A doctor puts herself in the world of abused children. *The New York Times;* America Online.

Feingold, A. (1994). Gender differences in personality: A meta-analysis. *Psychological Bulletin, 116,* 429–456.

Festinger, L. (1957). *A theory of cognitive dissonance.* Evanston, IL: Row, Peterson.

Festinger, L., & Carlsmith, J. M. (1959). Cognitive consequences of forced compliance. *Journal of Abnormal and Social Psychology, 58,* 203–210.

Festinger, L., Riecken, H. W., Jr., & Schachter, S. (1956). *When prophecy fails.* Minneapolis: University of Minnesota Press.

Field, T. M. (1991). Young children's adaptations to repeated separations from their mothers. *Child Development, 62,* 539–547.

Fischer, K. W., Shaver, P. R., & Carochan, P. (1990). How emotions develop and how they organize development. *Cognition and Emotion, 4,* 81–127.

Fisher, C. B., & Fyrberg, D. (1994). Participant partners. *American Psychologist, 49,* 417–427.

Fiske, S. T. (1993). Controlling other people: The impact of power on stereotyping. *American Psychologist, 48,* 621–628.

Flack, J. M., et al. (1995). Panel I: Epidemiology of minority health. *Health Psychology, 14,* 592–600.

Flavell, J. H., Miller, P. H., & Miller, S. A. (1993). *Cognitive development* (3rd ed). Englewood Cliffs, NJ: Prentice-Hall.

Foa, E. B., Franklin, M. E., Perry, K. J., & Herbert, J. D. (1996). Cognitive biases in generalized social phobia. *Journal of Abnormal Psychology, 105,* 433–439.

Ford, E. S., et al. (1991). Physical activity behaviors in lower and higher socioeconomic status populations. *American Journal of Epidemiology, 133,* 1246–1256.

Foster, G. D., Wadden, T. A., Vogt, R. A., & Brewer, G. (1997). What is a reasonable weight loss? Patients' expectations and evaluations of obesity treatment outcomes. *Journal of Consulting and Clinical Psychology, 65,* 79–85.

Fowler, R. D. (1992). Solid support needed for animal research. *APA Monitor, 23*(6), 2.

Fox, R. (1996). Cited in Seppa, N. (1996). APA releases study on family violence. *APA Monitor, 26*(4), 12.

Frankel, K. A., & Bates, J. E. (1990). Mother—toddler problem solving. *Child Development, 61,* 810–819.

Freedman, J. L., & Fraser, S. C. (1966). Compliance without pressure: The foot-in-the-door technique. *Journal of Personality and Social Psychology, 4,* 195–202.

Freeman, M. S., Spence, M. J., & Oliphant, C. M. (1993, June). *Newborns prefer their mothers' low-pass filtered voices over other female filtered voices.* Paper presented at the annual convention of the American Psychological Society, Chicago.

Freud, S. (1927). A religious experience. In *Standard edition of the complete psychological works of Sigmund Freud, Vol. 21.* London: Hogarth Press, 1964.

Friedman, M. A., & Brownell, K. D. (1995). Psychological correlates of obesity. *Psychological Bulletin, 117,* 3–20.

Friedman, M., & Ulmer, D. (1984). *Treating Type A behavior and your heart.* New York: Fawcett Crest.

Friedman, R. C., & Downey, J. I. (1994). Homosexuality. *New England Journal of Medicine, 331,* 923–930.

Frisch, R. (1997). Cited in Angier, N. (1997). Chemical tied to fat control could help trigger puberty. *The New York Times,* pp. C1, C3.

Fritsch, G., & Hitzig, E. (1870). On the electrical excitability of the cerebrum. In G. von Bonin (Ed.), *Some papers on the cerebral cortex.* Springfield, IL: Charles C Thomas. (1960).

Frodi, A. M., Macauley, J., & Thome, P. R. (1977). Are women always less aggressive than men? A review of the experimental literature. *Psychological Bulletin, 84,* 634–660.

Furumoto, L. (1992). Joining separate spheres— Christine Ladd-Franklin, woman-scientist. *American Psychologist, 47,* 175–182.

Galambos, N. L. (1992, October). Parent-adolescent relations. *Current Directions in Psychological Science,* 146–149.

Galambos, N. L., & Almeida, D. M. (1992). Does parent-adolescent conflict increase in early adolescence? *Journal of Marriage and the Family, 54,* 737–747.

Galassi, J. P. (1988). Four cognitive-behavioral approaches. *The Counseling Psychologist, 16*(1), 102–105.

Garcia, J., Brett, L. P., & Rusiniak, K. W. (1989). Limits of Darwinian conditioning. In S. B. Klein & R. R. Mowrer (Eds.), *Contemporary learning theories: Instrumental conditioning theory and the impact of biological constraints on learning.* Hillsdale, NJ: Erlbaum.

Garcia, J., & Koelling, R. A. (1966). Relation of cue to consequences in avoidance learning. *Psychonomic Science 4,* 123–124.

Gardner, H. (1983). *Frames of mind.* New York: Basic Books.

Garfinkel, R. (1995). Cited in Margoshes, P. (1995). For many, old age is the prime of life. *APA Monitor, 26*(5), 36–37.

Garland, A. F., & Zigler, E. (1993). Adolescent suicide prevention. *American Psychologist, 48,* 169–182.

Gaziano, J. M., et al. (1993). Moderate alcohol intake, increased levels of high-density lipoprotein and its subfractions, and decreased risk of myocardial infarction. *New England Journal of Medicine, 329,* 1829–1834.

Gazzaniga, M. S. (1995). Consciousness and the cerebral hemispheres. In M. S. Gazzaniga (Ed.), *The cognitive neurosciences.* Cambridge, MA: MIT Press.

Gazzaniga, M. S. (1997), Cited in Gorman, J. (1997, April 29). Consciousness studies: From stream to flood. *The New York Times,* pp. C1, C5.

Geiger, H. J. (1996). Race and health care. *New England Journal of Medicine, 335,* 815–816.

Gelman, D. (1994, April 18). The mystery of suicide. *Newsweek*, pp. 44–49.

Gentry, J., & Eron, L. D. (1993). American Psychological Association Commission on Violence and Youth. *American Psychologist, 48,* 89.

Gerstner, L. V., Jr. (1994, May 27). Our schools are failing. Do we care? *The New York Times,* p. A27.

Geschwind, N., & Galaburda, A. M. (1987). *Cerebral lateralization: Biological mechanisms, associations, and pathology.* Cambridge, MA: Harvard University Press.

Getzels, J. W., & Jackson, P. W. (1962). *Creativity and intelligence.* New York: Wiley.

Gibbs, J. T. (1992). Negotiating ethnic identity: Issues for Black–White biracial adolescents. In M. P. P. Root (Ed.), *Racially mixed people in America.* Newbury Park, CA: Sage.

Gibbs, N. (1991, June 3). When is it rape? *Time,* pp. 48–54.

Gibson, M., & Ogbu, J. (Eds.) (1991). *Minority status and schooling.* New York: Garland.

Gigerenzer, G., Hoffrage, U., & Kleinbölting, H. (1991). Probabilistic mental models. *Psychological Review, 98,* 506–528.

Gigone, D., & Hastie, R. (1997). Proper analysis of the accuracy of group judgments. *Psychological Bulletin, 121,* 149–167.

Gilbert, S. (1997, June 25). Social ties reduce risk of a cold. *The New York Times,* p. C11.

Gilligan, C. (1982). *In a different voice.* Cambridge, MA: Harvard University Press.

Gilligan, C., Lyons, P., & Hanmer, T. J. (Eds.) (1990). *Making connections.* Cambridge, MA: Harvard University Press.

Gilligan, C., Rogers, A. G., & Tolman, D. L. (Eds.) (1991). *Women, girls, and psychotherapy.* New York: Haworth.

Gilligan, C., Ward, J. V., & Taylor, J. M. (1989). *Mapping the moral domain: A contribution of women's thinking to psychological theory and education.* Cambridge, MA: Harvard University Press.

Gillis, A. R., Richard, M. A., & Hagan, J. (1986). Ethnic susceptibility to crowding. *Environment and Behavior, 18,* 683–706.

Gilovich, T. (1983). Biased evaluation and persistence in gambling. *Journal of Personality and Social Psychology, 44,* 1110–1126.

Ginsburg, G., & Bronstein, P. (1993). Family factors related to children's intrinsic/extrinsic motivational orientation and academic performance. *Child Development, 64,* 1461–1474.

Glaser, R., et al. (1991). Stress-related activation of Epstein-Barr virus. *Brain, Behavior, and Immunity, 5,* 219–232.

Glaser, R., et al. (1993). Stress and the memory T-cell response to the Epstein-Barr virus. *Health Psychology, 12,* 435–442.

Gleason, J. B., & Ratner, N. B. (1993). Language development in children. In J. B. Gleason & N. B. Ratner (Eds.), *Psycholinguistics.* Fort Worth: Harcourt Brace Jovanovich.

Gleitman, H., Rozin, P., & Sabini, J. (1997). Solomon E. Asch (1907–1996). *American Psychologist, 52,* 984–985.

Glenn, S. S., Ellis, J., & Greenspoon, J. (1992). On the revolutionary nature of the operant as a unit of behavioral selection. *American Psychologist, 47,* 1326–1329.

Godden, D. R., & Baddeley, A. D. (1975). Context-dependent memory in two natural environments: On land and underwater. *British Journal of Psychology, 66,* 325–331.

Goldman, J. A., & Harlow, L. L. (1993). Self-perception variables that mediate AIDS-preventive behavior in college students. *Health Psychology, 12,* 489–498.

Goldman, K. (1993, June 1). Jordan & Co. play ball on Madison Avenue. *The Wall Street Journal,* p. B9.

Goldman-Rakic, P. S. (1992). Working memory and the mind. *Scientific American, 267*(3), 110–117.

Goldman-Rakic, P. S. (1995). Cited in Goleman, D. (1995, May 2). Biologists find site of working memory. *The New York Times,* pp. C1, C9.

Goleman, D. J. (1993, April 6). Studying the secrets of childhood memory. *The New York Times,* pp. C1, C11.

Goleman, D. J. (1994, May 31). Miscoding is seen as the root of false memories. *The New York Times,* pp. C1, C8.

Goleman, D. J. (1995a). *Emotional intelligence.* New York: Bantam Books.

Goleman, D. J. (1995b, March 28). The brain manages happiness and sadness in different centers. *The New York Times,* pp. C1, C9.

Goleman, D. J. (1995c, May 2). Biologists find site of working memory. *The New York Times,* pp. C1, C9.

Goleman, D. J. (1996, July 21). A set point for happiness. *The New York Times,* p. E2.

Gomez, J., & Smith, B. (1990). Taking the home out of homophobia: Black lesbian health. In E. C. White (Ed.), *The Black women's health book.* Seattle: Seal Press.

Goode, E. (1999, June 1). For good health, it helps to be rich and important. *The New York Times* online.

Goodwin, F. K., & Jamison, K. R. (1990). *Manic-depressive illness.* New York: Oxford University Press.

Gorman, J. (1997, April 29). Consciousness studies: From stream to flood. *The New York Times,* pp. C1, C5.

Gottesman, I. I. (1991). *Schizophrenia genesis.* New York: Freeman.

Gottfried, A. E., Fleming, J. S., & Gottfried, A. W. (1994). Role of parental motivational practices in children's academic intrinsic motivation and achievement. *Journal of Educational Psychology, 86,* 104–113.

Grady, D. (1997b, May 21). Exercise may not curb depression. *The New York Times,* p. C11.

Graf, P. (1990). Life-span changes in implicit and explicit memory. *Bulletin of the Psychonomic Society, 28,* 353–358.

Granberg, D., & Brent, E. (1983). When prophecy bends. *Journal of Personality and Social Psychology, 45,* 477–491

Green, D. P., Glaser, J., & Rich, A. (1998). From lynching to gay bashing: The elusive connection between economic condition and hate crime. *Journal of Personality and Social Psychology, 75,* 82–92.

Greene, B. (1993). African American women. In L. Comas-Diaz & B. A. Greene (Eds.), *Women of color and mental health.* New York: Guilford.

Greene, B. (1994). Ethnic-minority lesbians and gay men. *Journal of Consulting and Clinical Psychology, 62,* 243–251.

Greene, J. (1982). The gambling trap. *Psychology Today, 16*(9), 50–55.

Greenfield, S. A. (1995). *Journey to the center of the mind.* New York: W. H. Freeman.

Greeno, C. G., & Wing, R. R. (1994). Stress-induced eating. *Psychological Bulletin, 115,* 444–464.

Greist, J. H. (1984). Exercise in the treatment of depression. *Coping with mental stress: The potential and limits of exercise intervention.* Washington, DC: National Institute of Mental Health.

Grodstein, F., et al.. (1997). Postmenopausal hormonal therapy and mortality. *New England Journal of Medicine, 336,* 1769–1775.

Gruder, C. L., et al. (1993). Effects of social support and relapse prevention training as adjuncts to a televised smoking-cessation intervention. *Journal of Consulting and Clinical Psychology, 61,* 113–120.

Guilford, J. P. (1988). Some changes in the structure-of-intellect model. *Educational and Psychological Measurement, 48,* 1–4.

Guisinger, S., & Blatt, S. J. (1994). Individuality and relatedness. *American Psychologist, 49,* 104–111.

Guralnik, J. M., Land, K. C., Blazer, D., Fillenbaum, G. G., & Branch, L. G. (1993). Educational status and active life expectancy among older Blacks and Whites. *New England Journal of Medicine, 329,* 110–116.

Haaf, R. A., Smith, P. H., & Smitley, S. (1983). Infant response to facelike patterns under fixed trial and infant-control procedures. *Child Development, 54,* 172–177.

Haaga, D. A. F., & Davison, G. C. (1993). An appraisal of rational-emotive therapy. *Journal of Consulting and Clinical Psychology, 61,* 215–220.

Haber, R. N. (1980). Eidetic images are not just imaginary. *Psychology Today, 14*(11), 72–82.

Hakim, A. A., et al. (1998). Effects of walking on mortality among nonsmoking retired men. *New England Journal of Medicine, 338,* 94–99.

Haley, W. E., et al. (1996). Appraisal, coping, and social support as mediators of well-being in Black and White caregivers of patients with Alzheimer's disease. *Journal of Consulting and Clinical Psychology, 64,* 121–129.

Hall, C. S. (1984). "A ubiquitous sex difference in dreams" revisited. *Journal of Personality and Social Psychology, 46,* 1109–1117.

Hall, G. C. I. (1997). Cultural malpractice: The growing obsolescence of psychology with the changing U.S. population. *American Psychologist, 52,* 642–651.

Hall, G. C. I., & Barongan, C. (1997). Prevention of sexual aggression. *American Psychologist, 52,* 5–14.

Hall, J. A., et al. (1990). Performance quality, gender, and professional role. *Medical Care, 28,* 489–501.

Halpern, D. F. (1989). *Thought and knowledge* (2nd ed.). Hillsdale, NJ: Erlbaum.

Halpern, D. F. (1997). Sex differences in intelligence: Implications for education. *American Psychologist, 52,* 1091–1102.

Halpern, D. F., Hansen, C., & Riefer, D. (1990). Analogies as an aid to understanding and memory. *Journal of Educational Psychology, 82,* 298–305.

Hamer, D. H., et al. (1993, July 16). A linkage between DNA markers on the X chromosome and male sexual orientation. *Science, 261,* 321–327.

Hamilton, L. C. (1985). Self-reported and actual savings in a water conservation campaign. *Environment and Behavior, 17,* 315–326.

Haney, M., et al. (1994). Cocaine sensitivity in Roman high and low avoidance rats is modulated by sex and gonadal hormone status. *Brain Research, 645*(1–2), 179–185.

Harlow, H. F. (1959). Love in infant monkeys. *Scientific American, 200,* 6–86.

Harlow, H. F., Harlow, M. K., & Meyer, D. R. (1950). Learning motivated by a manipulation drive. *Journal of Experimental Psychology, 40,* 228–234.

Harlow, H. F., & Zimmermann, R. R. (1959). Affectional responses in the infant monkey. *Science, 130,* 421–432.

Harnishfeger, K. K., & Bjorklund, D. F. (1990). Children's strategies. In D. F. Bjorklund (Ed.), *Children's strategies* (pp. 1–184). Hillsdale, NJ: Erlbaum.

Hasselhorn, M. (1992). Task dependency and the role of typicality and metamemory in the development of an organizational strategy. *Child Development, 63,* 202–214.

Hawkins, S. A., & Hastie, R. (1990). Hindsight: Biased judgments of past events after the outcomes are known. *Psychological Bulletin, 107,* 311–327.

Hays, K. F. (1995). Putting sport psychology into (your) practice. *Professional Psychology: Research and Practice, 26,* 33–40.

Hazuda, H. P., et al. (1991). Obesity in Mexican American subgroups: Findings from the San Antonio Heart Study. *American Journal of Clinical Nutrition, 53,* 1529S–1534S.

Heatherton, T. F., Mahamedi, F., Striepe, M., Field, A. E., & Keel, P. (1997). A 10-year longitudinal study of body weight, dieting, and eating disorder symptoms. *Journal of Abnormal Psychology, 106,* 117–125.

Heller, D. A., de Faire, U., Pedersen, N. L., Dahlén, G., & McClearn, G. E. (1993). Genetic and environmental influences on serum lipid levels in twins. *New England Journal of Medicine, 328,* 1150–1156.

Helson, R., & Moane, G. (1987). Personality change in women from college to midlife. *Journal of Personality and Social Psychology, 53,* 176–186.

Hensley, W. E. (1981). The effects of attire, location, and sex on aiding behavior. *Journal of Nonverbal Behavior, 6,* 3–11.

Hepper, P. G., Shahidullah, S., & White, R. (1990, October 4). Origins of fetal handedness. *Nature, 347,* 431.

Herbert, T. B., & Cohen, S. (1993). Depression and immunity. *Psychological Bulletin, 113,* 472–486.

Hergenhahn, B. R. (1997). *An introduction to the history of psychology* (3rd ed.). Pacific Grove, CA: Brooks/Cole.

Hershey, D. A., Walsh, D. A., Read, S. J., & Chulef, A. S. (1990). Relationships between metamemory, memory predictions, and memory task performance in adults. *Psychology and Aging, 5,* 215–227.

Herzog, D. B., Keller, M. B., & Lavori, P. W. (1988). Outcome in anorexia and bulimia nervosa. *The Journal of Nervous and Mental Disease, 176,* 131–143.

Hewitt, P. L., Flett, G. L., & Ediger, E. (1996). Perfectionism and depression. *Journal of Abnormal Psychology, 105,* 276–280.

Hilgard, E. R. (1994). Neodissociation theory. In S. J. Lynn & J. W. Rhue (Eds.), *Dissociation: Clinical, theoretical and research perspectives.* New York: Guilford Press.

Hilts, P. J. (1995, May 30). Brain's memory system comes into focus. *The New York Times,* pp. C1, C3.

Hobfoll, S. E., Ritter, C., Lavin, J., Hulsizer, M. R., & Cameron, R. P. (1995). Depression prevalence and incidence among inner-city pregnant and postpartum women. *Journal of Consulting and Clinical Psychology, 63,* 445–453.

Hobson, J. A., & McCarley, R. W. (1977). The brain as a dream-state generator: An activation-synthesis hypothesis of the dream process. *American Journal of Psychiatry, 134,* 1335–1348.

Hokin, L., et al. (1998). *Proceedings of the National Academy of Sciences, 95*(14), 8363–8368.

Holahan, C. J., & Moos, R. H. (1990). Life stressors, resistance factors, and psychological health. *Journal of Personality and Social Psychology, 58,* 909–917.

Holahan, C. J., & Moos, R. H. (1991). Life stressors, personal and social resources, and depression. *Journal of Abnormal Psychology, 100,* 31–38.

Holahan, C. J., Moos, R. H., Holahan, C. K., & Brennan, P. L. (1995). Social support, coping, and depressive symptoms in a late-middle-aged sample of patients reporting cardiac illness. *Health Psychology, 14,* 152–163.

Holland, J. L. (1996). Exploring careers with a typology. *American Psychologist, 51,* 397–406.

Hollinger, L. M., & Buschmann, M. B. (1993). Factors influencing the perception of touch by elderly nursing home residents and their health caregivers. *International Journal of Nursing Studies, 30,* 445–461.

Hollingshead, A. B., & Redlich, F. C. (1958). *Social class and mental illness.* New York: Wiley.

Holmes, D. S. (1984). Meditation and somatic arousal reduction. *American Psychologist, 39,* 1–10.

Holmes, T. H., & Rahe, R. H. (1967). The social readjustment rating scale. *Journal of Psychosomatic Research, 11,* 213–218.

Honan, W. H. (1996, April 11). Male professors keep 30% lead in pay over women, study says. *The New York Times,* p. B9.

Honorton, C. (1985). Meta-analysis of psi Ganzfeld research. *Journal of Parapsychology, 49,* 51–91.

Honorton, C., et al. (1990). Psi communication in the Ganzfeld. *Journal of Parapsychology, 54,* 99–139.

Honts, C., Hodes, R., & Raskin, D. (1985). *Journal of Applied Psychology, 70*(1).

Hopper, J. L., & Seeman, E. (1994). The bone density of female twins discordant for tobacco use. *New England Journal of Medicine, 330,* 387–392.

Horn, J. M. (1983). The Texas adoption project. *Child Development, 54,* 268–275.

Howard-Pitney, B., LaFramboise, T. D., Basil, M., September, B., & Johnson, M. (1992). Psychological and social indicators of suicide ideation and suicide attempts in Zuni adolescents. *Journal of Consulting and Clinical Psychology, 60,* 473–476.

Hubel, D. H., & Wiesel, T. N. (1979). Brain mechanisms of vision. *Scientific American, 241,* 150–162.

Huesmann, L. R., & Miller, L. S. (1994). Long-term effects of repeated exposure to media violence in childhood. In L. R. Huesmann (Ed.), *Aggressive behavior.* New York: Plenum.

Hyde, J. S., Fennema, E., & Lamon, S. J. (1990). Gender differences in mathematics performance. *Psychological Bulletin, 107,* 139–155.

Hyde, J. S., & Linn, M. C. (1988). Gender differences in verbal ability. *Psychological Bulletin, 104,* 53–69.

Hyde, J. S., & Plant, E. A. (1995). Magnitude of psychological gender differences. *American Psychologist, 50,* 159–161.

Hyman, R. (1994). Anomaly or artifact? Comments on Bem and Honorton. *Psychological Bulletin, 115,* 19–24.

Ironson, G. (1993). Cited in Adler, T. (1993). Men and women affected by stress, but differently. *APA Monitor, 24*(7), 8–9.

Isabella, R. A. (1993). Origins of attachment: Maternal interactive behavior across the first year. *Child Development, 64,* 605–621.

Isay, R. A. (1990). Psychoanalytic theory and the therapy of gay men. In D. P. McWhirter, S. A. Sanders, & J. M. Reinisch (Eds.), *Homosexuality/heterosexuality* (pp. 283–303). New York: Oxford University Press.

Isomura, T., Fine, S., & Lin, T. (1987). Two Japanese families. *Canadian Journal of Psychiatry, 32,* 282–286.

Izard, C. E. (1984). Emotion-cognition relationships and human development. In C. E. Izard, J. Kagan, & R. B. Zajonc (Eds.), *Emotions, cognition, and behavior.* New York: Cambridge University Press.

Izard, C. E. (1994). Basic emotions, relations among emotions, and emotion-cognition relations. *Psychological Bulletin, 115,* 561–565.

Jacob, T., Krahn, G. L., & Leonard, K. (1991). Parent-child interactions in families with alcoholic fathers. *Journal of Consulting and Clinical Psychology, 59,* 176–181.

Jacobs, T. J., & Charles, E. (1980). Life events and the occurrence of cancer in children. *Psychosomatic Medicine, 42,* 11–24.

Jacobson, N. S., & Hollon, S. D. (1996). Cognitive-behavior therapy versus pharmacotherapy. *Journal of Consulting and Clinical Psychology, 64,* 74–80.

Jacobson, N. S., et al. (1996). A component analysis of cognitive-behavioral treatment for depression. *Journal of Consulting and Clinical Psychology, 64,* 295–304.

James, W. (1890). *The principles of psychology.* New York: Henry Holt.

Janis, I. L. (1982). *Groupthink* (2nd ed.). Boston: Houghton Mifflin.

Janowitz, H. D., & Grossman, M. I. (1949). Effects of variations in nutritive density on intake of food in dogs and cats. *American Journal of Physiology, 158,* 184–193.

Jeffery, R. W. (1991). Population perspectives on the prevention and treatment of obesity in minority populations. *American Journal of Clinical Nutrition, 53,* 1621S–1624S.

Jemmott, J. B., et al. (1983). Academic stress, power motivation, and decrease in secretion rate of salivary secretory immunoglobin A. *Lancet, 1,* 1400–1402.

Johnson, B. T., & Eagly, A. H. (1989). Effects of involvement on persuasion. *Psychological Bulletin, 106,* 290–314.

Johnson, K. (1998, August 31). As drugs in sports proliferate, so do ethical questions. *The New York Times,* pp. C1, C4.

Johnson, K. W., et al. (1995). Panel II: Macrosocial and environmental influences on minority health. *Health Psychology, 14,* 601–612.

Johnston, L. D., O'Malley, P. M., & Bachman, J. G. (1996). National survey results on drug use from the Monitoring the Future Study, 1975–1995. National Institute on Drug Abuse, 5600 Fishers Lane, Rockville, MD 20957; USDHHS, Public Health Service, National Institutes of Health.

Joiner, T. E., Heatherton, T. F., Rudd, M. D., & Schmidt, N. B. (1997). Perfectionism, perceived weight status, and bulimic symptoms. *Journal of Abnormal Psychology, 106,* 145–153.

Jones, E. E. (1990). *Interpersonal perception.* New York: Freeman.

Jones, J. L., & Leary, M. R. (1994). Effects of appearance-based admonitions against sun exposure on tanning intentions in young adults. *Health Psychology, 13,* 86–90.

Jones, M. C. (1924). Elimination of children's fears. *Journal of Experimental Psychology, 7,* 381–390.

Jorgensen, R. S., Johnson, B. T., Kolodziej, M. E., & Schreer, G. E. (1996). Elevated blood pressure and personality. *Psychological Bulletin, 120,* 293–320.

Josephson, W. D. (1987). Television violence and children's aggression: Testing the priming, social script, and disinhibition prediction. *Journal of Personality and Social Psychology, 53,* 882–890.

Judd, C. M., & Park, B. (1988). Out-group homogeneity. *Journal of Personality and Social Psychology, 54,* 778–788.

Just, N., & Alloy, L. B. (1997). The response styles theory of depression. *Journal of Abnormal Psychology, 106,* 221–229.

Kail, R. V., & Salthouse, T. A. (1994). Processing speed as a mental capacity. *Acta Psychologica, 86,* 199–225.

Kandel, E. R., & Hawkins, R. D. (1992). The biological basis of learning and individuality. *Scientific American, 267*(3), 78–86.

Kane, J. M. (1996). Schizophrenia. *New England Journal of Medicine, 334,* 34–41.

Kaplan, S. J. (1991). Physical abuse and neglect. In M. Lewis (Ed.), *Child and adolescent psychiatry: A comprehensive textbook* (pp. 1010–1019). Baltimore: Williams & Wilkins.

Karasek, R. A., et al. (1982). Job, psychological factors and coronary heart disease. *Advances in Cardiology, 29,* 62–67.

Karoly, P., & Ruehlman, L. S. (1996). Motivational implications of pain. *Health Psychology, 15,* 383–390.

Kaufman, J., & Zigler, E. (1989). The intergenerational transmission of child abuse. In D. Cicchetti & V. Carlson (Eds.), *Child maltreatment: Theory and research on the causes and consequences of child abuse and neglect* (pp. 129–150). Cambridge: Cambridge University Press.

Kaufman, M., et al. (1998, February 4). Cocaine-induced cerebral vasoconstriction detected in humans with magnetic resonance angiography. *Journal of the American Medical Association, 279*(5).

Kazdin, A. E. (1993). Adolescent mental health. *American Psychologist, 48,* 127–141.

Keinan, G. (1987). Decision making under stress. *Journal of Personality and Social Psychology, 52,* 639–644.

Kellerman, J., Lewis, J., & Laird, J. D. (1989). Looking and loving: The effects of mutual gaze on feelings of romantic love. *Journal of Research in Personality, 23,* 145–161.

Kelley, H. H., & Michela, J. L. (1980). Attribution theory and research. *Annual Review of Psychology, 31,* 457–501.

Kelley, K., & Byrne, D. (1992). *Human sexuality.* Englewood Cliffs, NJ: Prentice Hall.

Kellman, P. J., & von Hofsetn, C. (1992). The world of the moving infant. In C. Rovee-Collier & L. P. Lipsitt (Eds.), *Advances in infancy research* (Vol. 7). Norwood, NJ: Ablex.

Kemeny, M. E. (1993). Emotions and the immune system. In B. Moyers (Ed.), *Healing and the mind.* New York: Doubleday.

Kemeny, M. E., Weiner, H., Taylor, S. E., Schneider, S., Visscher, B., & Fahey, J. L. (1994). Repeated bereavement, depressed mood, and immune parameters in HIV seropositive and seronegative gay men. *Health Psychology, 13,* 14–24.

Kenrick, D. T., & MacFarlane, S. W. (1986). Ambient temperature and horn honking. *Environment and Behavior, 18,* 179–191.

Kessler, D. A. (1995). Nicotine addiction in young people. *New England Journal of Medicine, 333,* 186–189.

Kiecolt-Glaser, J. K. (1993). Cited in Adler, T. (1993). Men and women affected by stress, but differently. *APA Monitor, 24*(7), 8–9.

Kilshaw, D., & Annett, M. (1983). Right- and left-hand skill: Effects of age, sex, and hand preferences showing superior in left-handers. *British Journal of Psychology, 74,* 253–268.

Kimble, D. P. (1992). *Biological psychology,* 2nd ed. Fort Worth: Harcourt Brace Jovanovich.

Kimble, G. A. (1994). A frame of reference for psychology. *American Psychologist, 49,* 510–519.

Kinderman, P., & Bentall, R. P. (1997). Causal attributions in paranoia and depression. *Journal of Abnormal Psychology, 106,* 341–345.

Kinnunen, T., Doherty, K., Militello, F. S., & Garvey, A. J. (1996). Depression and smoking cessation. *Journal of Consulting and Clinical Psychology, 64,* 791–798.

Kinnunen, T., Zamansky, H. S., & Block, M. L. (1994). Is the hypnotized subject lying? *Journal of Abnormal Psychology, 103,* 184–191.

Kinsey, A. C., Pomeroy, W. B., & Martin, C. E. (1948). *Sexual behavior in the human male.* Philadelphia: W. B. Saunders.

Kinsey, A. C., Pomeroy, W. B., Martin, C. E., & Gebhard, P. H. (1953). *Sexual behavior in the human female.* Philadelphia: W. B. Saunders.

Kirsch, I., Montgomery, G., & Sapirstein, G. (1995). Hypnosis as an adjunct to cognitive-behavioral psychotherapy. *Journal of Consulting and Clinical Psychology, 63,* 214–220.

Klein, J. (1993, June 21). Make the daddies pay. *Newsweek,* p. 33.

Kleinke, C. L. (1977). Compliance to requests made by gazing and touching experimenters in field settings. *Journal of Experimental Social Psychology, 13,* 218–223.

Kleinke, C. L. (1986). Gaze and eye contact. *Psychological Review, 100,* 78–100.

Kleinmuntz, B., & Szucko, J. J. (1984). Lie detection in ancient and modern times. *American Psychologist, 39,* 766–776.

Klesges, R. C., et al. (1997). How much weight gain occurs following smoking cessation? *Journal of Consulting and Clinical Psychology, 65,* 286–291.

Klorman, R., Brumaghim, J. T., Fitzpatrick, P. A., Borgstedt, A. D., & Strauss, J. (1994). Clinical and cognitive effects of methylphenidate on children with attention deficit disorder as a function of aggression/oppositionality and age. *Journal of Abnormal Psychology, 103,* 206–221.

Klosko, J. S., Barlow, D. H., Tassinari, R., & Cerny, J. A. (1990). A comparison of alprazolam and behavior therapy in treatment of panic disorder. *Journal of Consulting and Clinical Psychology, 58,* 77–84.

Klüver, H., & Bucy, P. C. (1939). Preliminary analysis of functions of the temporal lobe in monkeys. *Archives of Neurology and Psychiatry, 42,* 979–1000.

Knight, M. (1994). Darwinian functionalism. *The Psychological Record, 44,* 271–287.

Kobasa, S. C. O. (1990). Stress-resistant personality. In R. E. Ornstein & C. Swencionis (Eds.), *The healing brain* (pp. 219–230). New York: The Guilford Press.

Kobasa, S. C. O., Maddi, S. R., Puccetti, M. C., & Zola, M. A. (1994). Effectiveness of hardiness, exercise, and social support as resources against illness. In A. Steptoe & J. Wardle (Eds.), *Psychosocial processes and health* (pp. 247–260). Cambridge: Cambridge University Press.

Kohlberg, L. (1969). *Stages in the development of moral thought and action.* New York: Holt, Rinehart and Winston.

Kohlberg, L. (1981). *The philosophy of moral development.* San Francisco: Harper & Row.

Kolata, G. (1994, February 16). Debate on using marijuana as medicine turns to question of whether it works. *The New York Times,* p. C12.

Kolbe, L. (1998, September 18). Cited in Poll shows decline in sex by high school students. *The New York Times,* p. A26.

Koocher, G. P. (1991). Questionable methods in alcoholism research. *Journal of Consulting and Clinical Psychology, 59,* 246–248.

Kosonen, P., & Winne, P. H. (1995). Effects of teaching statistical laws on reasoning about everyday problems. *Journal of Educational Psychology, 87,* 33–46.

Koss, M. P. (1993). Rape. *American Psychologist, 48,* 1062–1069.

Koss, M. P., Gidycz, C. A., & Wisniewski, N. (1987). The scope of rape. *Journal of Consulting and Clinical Psychology, 55,* 162–170.

Kosslyn, S. M. (1994). *Image and brain.* Cambridge, MA: The MIT Press, a Bradford Book.

Kramer, A. F. (1999). Ageing, fitness, and neurocognitive function. *Nature, 400,* 418–419.

Krantz, D. S., Contrada, R. J., Hill, D. R., & Friedler, E. (1988). Environmental stress and biobehavioral antecedents of coronary heart disease. *Journal of Consulting and Clinical Psychology, 56,* 333–341.

Krosnick, J. A. (1989). Attitude importance and attitude accessibility. *Personality and Social Psychology Bulletin, 15,* 297–308.

Kübler-Ross, E. (1969). *On death and dying.* New York: Macmillan.

Kumanyika, S. (1996). Improving our diet—Still a long way to go. *New England Journal of Medicine, 335,* 738–740.

Kupfer, D. J., & Reynolds, C. F. (1997). Management of insomnia. *New England Journal of Medicine, 336,* 341–346.

Kunstler, M. G. (1989). Use of evaluation to improve energy conservation programs. *Journal of Social Issues, 45,* 153–168.

Lackner, J. M., Carosella, A. M., & Feuerstein, M. (1996). Pain expectancies, pain, and functional self-efficacy expectancies as determinants of disability in patients with chronic low back disorders. *Journal of Consulting and Clinical Psychology, 64,* 212–220.

Lacks, P., & Morin, C. M. (1992). Recent advances in the assessment and treatment of insomnia. *Journal of Consulting and Clinical Psychology, 60,* 586–594.

LaFramboise, T. (1994). Cited in DeAngelis, T. (1994). History, culture affect treatment for Indians. *APA Monitor, 27*(10), 36.

Lakka, T. A., et al. (1994). Relation of leisure-time physical activity and cardiorespiratory fitness to the risk of acute myocardial infarction in men. *New England Journal of Medicine, 330,* 1549–1554.

Lamb, M. E., & Baumrind, D. (1978). Socialization and personality development in the preschool years. In M. E. Lamb (Ed.), *Social and personality development.* New York: Holt, Rinehart and Winston.

Lamb, M. E., Sternberg, K. J., & Prodromidis, M. (1992). Nonmaternal care and the security of infant-mother attachment. *Infant Behavior and Development, 15,* 71–83.

Lang, A. R., Goeckner, D. J., Adesso, V. J., & Marlatt, G. A. (1975). Effects of alcohol on aggression in male social drinkers. *Journal of Abnormal Psychology, 84,* 508–518.

Lang, P. J., & Melamed, B. B. (1969). Case report: Avoidance conditioning therapy of an infant with chronic ruminative vomiting. *Journal of Abnormal Psychology, 74,* 1–8.

Lang, S. S., & Patt, R. B. (1994). *You don't have to suffer.* New York: Oxford University Press.

Langer, E. J., Rodin, J., Beck, P., Weinan, C., & Spitzer, L. (1979). Environmental determinants of memory improvement in late adulthood. *Journal of Personality and Social Psychology, 37,* 2003–2013.

Lapsley, D. K. (1990). Continuity and discontinuity in adolescent social cognitive development. In R. Montemayor, G. R. Adams, & T. P. Guillotta (Eds.), *From childhood to adolescence: A transitional period?* Newbury Park, CA: Sage.

Lapsley, D. K. (1991). Egocentrism theory and the "new look" at the imaginary audience and personal fable in adolescence. In R. M. Lerner, A. C. Petersen, & J. Brooks-Gunn (Eds.), *Encyclopedia of adolescence.* New York: Garland.

Larrick, R. P. (1993). Motivational factors in decision theories. *Psychological Bulletin, 113,* 440–450.

Larson, R. K. (1990). Semantics. In D. N. Osherson & H. Lasnik (Eds.), *An invitation to cognitive science: Language* (Vol. 1). Cambridge, MA: The MIT Press, a Bradford Book.

Larson, R., & Richards, M. H. (1991). Daily companionship in late childhood and early adolescence. *Child Development, 62,* 284–300.

Lashley, K. S. (1950). In search of the engram. In *Symposium of the Society for Experimental Biology* (Vol. 4). New York: Cambridge University Press.

Latané, B., & Dabbs, J. M. (1975). Sex, group size, and helping in three cities. *Sociometry, 38,* 180–194.

Laumann, E. O., Gagnon, J. H., Michael, R. T., & Michaels, S. (1994). *The social organization of sexuality.* Chicago: University of Chicago Press.

Lazarus, R. S., DeLongis, A., Folkman, S., & Gruen, R. (1985). Stress and adaptational outcomes. *American Psychologist, 40,* 770–779.

Lazarus, R. S., & Folkman, S. (1984). *Stress, appraisal, and coping.* New York: Springer.

Le Bon, G. (1960). *The crowd.* New York: Viking. (Original work published 1895).

Leary, W. E. (1991, October 22). Black hypertension may reflect other ills. *The New York Times,* p. C3.

Lederberg, A. R., & Mobley, C. E. (1990). The effect of hearing impairment on the quality of attachment and mother–toddler interaction. *Child Development, 61,* 1596–1604.

LeDoux, J. E. (1997). Emotion, memory, and the brain. *Scientific American Mysteries of the Mind, Special Issue, 7*(1), 68–75.

Lefcourt, H. M. (1997). Cited in Clay, R. A. (1997). Researchers harness the power of humor. *APA Monitor, 28*(9), 1, 18.

Lefcourt, H. M., & Martin, R. A. (1986). *Humor and life stress.* New York: Springer-Verlag.

Lefcourt, H. M., Miller, R. S., Ware, E. E., & Sherk, D. (1981). Locus of control as a modifier of the relationship between stressors and moods. *Journal of Personality and Social Psychology, 41,* 357–369.

Lefley, H. P. (1990). Culture and chronic mental illness. *Hospital and Community Psychiatry, 41,* 277–286.

Leibowitz, H. W. (1996). The symbiosis between basic and applied research. *American Psychologist, 51,* 366–370.

Leigh, B. C. (1993). Alcohol consumption and sexual activity as reported with a diary technique. *Journal of Abnormal Psychology, 102,* 490–493.

Leitenberg, H., & Henning, K. (1995). Sexual fantasy. *Psychological Bulletin, 117,* 469–496.

Leor, J., Poole, K., & Kloner, R. A. (1996). Sudden cardiac death triggered by an earthquake. *New England Journal of Medicine, 334,* 413–419.

Lerman, C., et al. (1997). Incorporating biomarkers of exposure and genetic susceptibility into smoking cessation treatment. *Health Psychology, 16,* 87–99.

Levinson, D. J., Darrow, C. N., Klein, E. B., Levinson, M. H., & McKee, B. (1978). *The seasons of a man's life.* New York: Knopf.

Levy, D. S. (1991, September 16). Why Johnny might grow up violent and sexist. *Time,* pp. 16–19.

Lewin, T. (1995a). Women are becoming equal providers. *The New York Times,* p. A27.

Lewin, T. (1995b, December 7). Parents poll shows higher incidence of child abuse. *The New York Times,* p. B16.

Lewinsohn, P. M., et al. (1994a). Adolescent psychopathology: II. Psychosocial risk factors for depression. *Journal of Abnormal Psychology, 103,* 302–315.

Lewinsohn, P. M., Rohde, P., & Seeley, J. R. (1994b). Psychosocial risk factors for future suicide attempts. *Journal of Consulting and Clinical Psychology, 62,* 297–305.

Lewis, M. (1997). *Altering fate — Why the past does not predict the future.* New York: Guilford Press.

Lewis, M. (1998). Cited in Blakeslee, S. (1998, August 4). Re-evaluating significance of baby's bond with mother. *The New York Times,* pp. F1, F2.

Lewis-Fernández, R., & Kleinman, A. (1994). Culture, personality, and psychopathology. *Journal of Abnormal Psychology, 103,* 67–71.

Lieber, C. S. (1990). Cited in Barroom biology: How alcohol goes to a woman's head (January 14). *The New York Times,* p. E24.

Linden, W., Chambers, L., Maurice, J., & Lenz, J. W. (1993). Sex differences in social support, self-deception, hostility, and ambulatory cardiovascular activity. *Health Psychology, 12,* 376–380.

Lindenberger, U., Mayr, U., & Kliegl, R. (1993). Speed and intelligence in old age. *Psychology and Aging, 8,* 207–220.

Linville, P. W., Fischer, G. W., & Salovey, P. (1989). Perceived distribution of the characteristics of in-group and out-group members. *Journal of Personality and Social Psychology, 57,* 165–188.

Lipsey, M. W., & Wilson, D. B. (1993). The efficacy of psychological, educational, and behavioral treatment. *American Psychologist, 48,* 1181–1209.

Lochman, J. E. (1992). Cognitive-behavioral intervention with aggressive boys. *Journal of Consulting and Clinical Psychology, 60,* 426–432.

Lochman, J. E., & Dodge, K. A. (1994). Social-cognitive processes of severely violent, moderately aggressive, and nonaggressive boys. *Journal of Consulting and Clinical Psychology, 62,* 366–374.

Loftus, E. F. (1979). *Eyewitness testimony.* Cambridge, MA: Harvard University Press.

Loftus, E. F. (1993a). The reality of repressed memories. *American Psychologist, 48,* 518–537.

Loftus, E. F. (1993b). Psychologists in the eyewitness world. *American Psychologist, 48,* 550–552.

Loftus, E. F. (1994). Cited in D. Goleman (1994, May 31). Miscoding is seen as the root of false memories. *The New York Times,* pp. C1, C8.

Loftus, E. F. (1997). Cited in Loftus consulting in Oklahoma City bombing trial. *APA Monitor, 28*(4), 8–9.

Loftus, E. F., & Ketcham, K. (1994). *The myth of repressed memory.* New York: St. Martin's Press.

Loftus, E. F., & Loftus, G. R. (1980). On the permanence of stored information in the brain. *American Psychologist, 35,* 409–420.

Loftus, E. F., & Palmer, J. C. (1973). Reconstruction of automobile destruction. *Journal of Verbal Learning and Verbal Behavior, 13,* 585–589.

Loftus, G. R. (1983). The continuing persistence of the icon. *Behavioral and Brain Sciences, 6,* 28.

Lohr, J. M., & Staats, A. (1973). Attitude conditioning in Sino-Tibetan languages. *Journal of Personality and Social Psychology, 26,* 196–200.

Longer, healthier, better (1997, March 9). *The New York Times Magazine,* pp. 44–45.

Lopez, S., & Hernandez, P. (1986). How culture is considered in evaluations of psychopathology. *Journal of Nervous and Mental Diseases, 176,* 598–606.

Lore, R. K., & Schultz, L. A. (1993). Control of human aggression. *American Psychologist, 48,* 16–25.

Lorenz, K. Z. (1981). *The foundations of ethology.* New York: Springer-Verlag.

Luborsky, L., Barber, J. P., & Beutler, L. (1993). Introduction to special section. *Journal of Consulting and Clinical Psychology, 61,* 539–541.

Luchins, A. S. (1957). Primacy-recency in impression formation. In C. I. Hovland (Ed.), *The order of presentation in persuasion.* New Haven, CT: Yale University Press.

Ludwick-Rosenthal, R., & Neufeld, R. W. J. (1993). Preparation for undergoing an invasive medical procedure. *Journal of Consulting and Clinical Psychology, 61,* 156–164.

Lundeberg, M. A., Fox, P. W., & Puncochar, J. (1994). Highly confident but wrong. *Journal of Educational Psychology, 86,* 114–121.

Lurie, N., et al. (1993). Preventive care for women? *New England Journal of Medicine, 329,* 478–482.

Lydiard, R. B., Brawman, A., Mintzer, O., & Ballenger, J. C. (1996). Recent developments in the psychopharmacology of anxiety disorders. *Journal of Consulting and Clinical Psychology, 64,* 660–668.

Lykken, D. T. (1982). Fearlessness. *Psychology Today, 16*(9), 20–28.

Lykken, D. T., McGue, M., Tellegen, A., & Bouchard, T. J., Jr. (1992). Emergenesis: Genetic traits that may not run in families. *American Psychologist, 47,* 1565–1577.

Lyons-Ruth, K., Alpern, L., & Repacholi, B. (1993). Disorganized infant attachment classification and maternal psychosocial problems as predictors of hostile-aggressive behavior in the preschool classroom. *Child Development, 64,* 572–585.

Maas, J. B. (1998). *Power sleep: Revolutionary strategies that prepare your mind and body for peak performance.* New York: Villard.

Maccoby, E. E. (1990). Gender and relationships. *American Psychologist, 45,* 513–520.

Maccoby, E. E., & Jacklin, C. N. (1974). *The psychology of sex differences.* Stanford, CA: Stanford University Press.

MacDonald, K. (1992). Warmth as a developmental construct. *Child Development, 63,* 753–773.

Macfarlane, J. A. (1975). Olfaction in the development of social preferences in the human neonate. In M. A. Hofer (Ed.), *Parent-infant interaction.* Amsterdam: Elsevier.

Mackie, D. M., Worth, L. T., & Asuncion, A. G. (1990). Processing of persuasive in-group messages. *Journal of Personality and Social Psychology, 58,* 812–822.

Maher, B. A., & Maher, W. B. (1994). Personality and psychopathology. *Journal of Abnormal Psychology, 103,* 72–77.

Maier, N. R. F., & Schneirla, T. C. (1935). *Principles of animal psychology.* New York: McGraw-Hill.

Maier, S. F., Watkins, L. R., & Fleshner, M. (1994). Psychoneuroimmunology: The interface between behavior, brain, and immunity. *American Psychologist, 49,* 1004–1017.

Malgady, R. G., Rogler, L. H., & Costantino, G. (1990). Hero/heroine modeling for Puerto Rican adolescents. *Journal of Consulting and Clinical Psychology, 58,* 469–474.

Malinosky-Rummell, R., & Hansen, D. H. (1993). Long-term consequences of childhood physical abuse. *Psychological Bulletin, 114,* 68–79.

Marecek, J. (1995). Gender, politics, and psychology's ways of knowing. *American Psychologist, 50,* 162–163.

Marenberg, M. E., et al. (1994). Genetic susceptibility to death from coronary heart disease in a study of twins. *New England Journal of Medicine, 330,* 1041–1046.

Margoshes, P. (1995). For many, old age is the prime of life. *APA Monitor, 26*(5), 36–37.

Markstrom-Adams, C. (1992). A consideration of intervening factors in adolescent identity formation. In G. R. Adams, T. P. Gullotta, & R. Montemayor (Eds.), *Adolescent identity formation.* Newbury Park, CA: Sage.

Markus, H., & Kitayama, S. (1991). Culture and the self. *Psychological Review, 98*(2), 224–253.

Martin, R. A., & Lefcourt, H. M. (1983). Sense of humor as a moderator of the relation between stressors and moods. *Journal of Personality and Social Psychology, 45,* 1313–1324.

Marx, E. M., Williams, J. M. G., & Claridge, G. C. (1992). Depression and social problem solving. *Journal of Abnormal Psychology, 101,* 78–86.

Maslow, A. H. (1970). *Motivation and personality* (2nd ed.). New York: Harper & Row.

Masters, W. H., & Johnson, V. E. (1966). *Human sexual response.* Boston: Little, Brown.

Masters, W. H., & Johnson, V. E. (1970). *Human sexual inadequacy.* Boston: Little, Brown.

Masters, W. H., & Johnson, V. E. (1979). *Homosexuality in perspective.* Boston: Little, Brown.

Matefy, R. (1980). Role-playing theory of psychedelic flashbacks. *Journal of Consulting and Clinical Psychology, 48,* 551–553.

Matlin, M. W. (1997). *Cognition* (4th ed.). Fort Worth: Harcourt Brace.

Matlin, M. W., & Foley, H. J. (1995). *Sensation and perception* (4th ed.). Boston: Allyn & Bacon.

Matt, G. E., Vasquez, C., & Campbell, W. K. (1992). Mood-congruent recall of affectively toned stimuli: A meta-analytic review. *Clinical Psychology Review, 12,* 227–255.

Matthews, K. (1994). Cited in Azar, B. (1994). Women are barraged by media on "the change." *APA Monitor, 25*(5), 24–25.

Matthews, K., et al.. (1997). Women's Health Initiative. *American Psychologist, 52,* 101–116.

Matus, I. (1996.) Cited in Clay, R. A. (1996). Beating the "biological clock" with zest. *APA Monitor, 27*(2), 37.

Mazzella, R., & Feingold, A. (1994). The effects of physical attractiveness, race, socioeconomic status, and gender of defendants and victims on judgments of mock jurors. *Journal of Applied Social Psychology, 24*(15), 1315–1344.

McCall, R. (1997). Cited in Sleek, S. (1997). Can "emotional intelligence" be taught in today's schools? *APA Monitor, 28*(6), 25.

McCann, I. L., & Holmes, D. S. (1984). Influence of aerobic exercise on depression. *Journal of Personality and Social Psychology, 46,* 1142–1147.

McCarley, R. W. (1992). Cited in Blakeslee, S. (1992, January 7). Scientists unraveling chemistry of dreams. *The New York Times,* pp. C1, C10.

McClelland, D. C. (1958). Methods of measuring human motivation. In J. W. Atkinson (Ed.), *Motives in fantasy, action, and society.* Princeton, NJ: Van Nostrand.

McClelland, D. C. (1965). Achievement and entrepreneurship. *Journal of Personality and Social Psychology, 1,* 389–392.

McCrae, R. R. (1996). Social consequences of experiential openness. *Psychological Bulletin, 120,* 323–337.

McCrae, R. R., & Costa, P. T., Jr. (1997). Personality trait structure as a human universal. *American Psychologist, 52,* 509–516.

McDougall, W. (1904). The sensations excited by a single momentary stimulation of the eye. *British Journal of Psychology, 1,* 78–113.

McDougall, W. (1908). *An introduction to social psychology.* London: Methuen.

McGovern, T. V. (1989). Task force eyes the making of a major. *APA Monitor, 20*(7), 50.

McGovern, T. V., Furumoto, L., Halpern, D. F., Kimble, G. A., & McKeachie, W. J. (1991). Liberal education, study in depth, and the arts and sciences major—psychology. *American Psychologist, 46,* 598–605.

McGowan, R. J., & Johnson, D. L. (1984). The mother-child relationship and other antecedents of childhood intelligence. *Child Development, 55,* 810–820.

McGrath, E., Keita, G. P., Strickland, B. R., & Russo, N. F. (1990). *Women and depression.* Washington, DC: American Psychological Association.

McGuire, P. A. (1998). Wanted: Workers with flexibility for 21st century jobs. *APA Monitor, 29*(7), 10, 12.

McIntosh, H. (1996). Solitude provides an emotional tune-up. *APA Monitor, 26*(3), 1, 10.

McMurtrie, B. (1994, July 19.) Overweight fatten ranks. *New York Newsday,* p. A26.

McNally, R. J., & Eke, M. (1996). Anxiety sensitivity, suffocation fear, and breath-holding duration as predictors of response to carbon dioxide challenge. *Journal of Abnormal Psychology, 105,* 146–149.

McTiernan, A. (1997). Exercise and breast cancer. *New England Journal of Medicine, 336,* 1311–1312.

Mead, M. (1935). *Sex and temperament in three primitive societies.* New York: Dell.

Meckler, L. (1998, June 26). Teen abortion, pregnancy rates fall. Associated Press online.

Mednick, A. (1993). Domestic abuse is seen as worldwide "epidemic." *APA Monitor, 24*(5), 33.

Meichenbaum, D. (1993). Changing conceptions of cognitive behavior modification. *Journal of Consulting and Clinical Psychology, 61,* 202–204.

Meichenbaum, D., & Jaremko, M. E. (Eds.) (1983). *Stress reduction and prevention.* New York: Plenum.

Meltzoff, A. N. (1997). Cited in Azar, B. (1997). New theory on development could usurp Piagetian beliefs. *APA Monitor, 28*(6), 9.

Meltzoff, A. N., & Gopnik, A. (1997). *Words, thoughts, and theories.* Cambridge, MA: MIT Press.

Melzack, R. (1980). Psychological aspects of pain. In J. J. Bonica (Ed.), *Pain.* New York: Raven Press.

Melzack, R. (1997). Phantom limbs. *Scientific American mysteries of the mind, Special Issue 7*(1), 84–91.

Metcalfe, J. (1986). Premonitions of insight predict impending error. *Journal of Experimental Psychology: Learning, Memory, and Cognition, 12,* 623–634.

Mevkens, F. L. (1990). Coming of age—The chemoprevention of cancer. *New England Journal of Medicine, 323,* 825–827.

Meyer, T. (1997). Americans are getting fatter. Associated Press; America Online.

Meyers, A. W., et al. (1997). Are weight concerns predictive of smoking cessation? *Journal of Consulting and Clinical Psychology, 65,* 448–452.

Michael, R. T., Gagnon, J. H., Laumann, E. O., & Kolata, G. (1994). *Sex in America: A definitive survey.* Boston: Little, Brown.

Michels, R., & Marzuk, P. M. (1993a). Progress in psychiatry (Part 1). *New England Journal of Medicine, 329,* 552–560.

Michels, R., & Marzuk, P. M. (1993b). Progress in psychiatry (Part 2). *New England Journal of Medicine, 329,* 628–638.

Milgram, S. (1963). Behavioral study of obedience. *Journal of Abnormal and Social Psychology, 67,* 371–378.

Milgram, S. (1974). *Obedience to authority.* New York: Harper & Row.

Milgram, S. (1977). *The individual in a social world.* Reading, MA: Addison-Wesley.

Miller, G. A. (1956). The magical number seven, plus or minus two: Some limits on our capacity for processing information. *Psychological Review, 63,* 81–97.

Miller, J. L. (1990). Speech perception. In D. N. Osherson & H. Lasnik (Eds.), *An invitation to cognitive science: Language* (Vol. 1). Cambridge, MA: The MIT Press, a Bradford Book.

Miller, J. L. (1992). Trouble in mind. *Scientific American, 267*(3), 180.

Miller, M. E., & Bowers, K. S. (1993). Hypnotic analgesia. *Journal of Abnormal Psychology, 102,* 29–38.

Miller, M. F., Barabasz, A. F., & Barabasz, M. (1991). Effects of active alert and relaxation hypnotic inductions on cold pressor pain. *Journal of Abnormal Psychology, 100,* 223–226.

Miller, N. B., Cowan, P. A., Cowan, C. P., Hetherington, E. M., & Clingempeel, W. G. (1993). Externalizing in preschoolers and early adolescents. *Developmental Psychology, 29,* 3–18.

Miller, N. E. (1969). Learning of visceral and glandular responses. *Science, 163,* 434–445.

Miller, N. E. (1995). Clinical-experimental interactions in the development of neuroscience. *American Psychologist, 50,* 901–911.

Miller, N. E., & Dollard, J. (1941). *Social learning and imitation.* New Haven, CT: Yale University Press.

Miller, S. M., Shoda, Y., & Hurley, K. (1996). Applying cognitive-social theory to health-protective behavior: Breast self-examination in cancer screening. *Psychological Bulletin, 199,* 70–94.

Miller, T. Q., Smith, T. W., Turner, C. W., Guijarro, M. L., & Hallet, A. J. (1996). A meta-analytic review of research on hostility and physical health. *Psychological Bulletin, 119,* 322–348.

Milner, B. R. (1966). Amnesia following operation on temporal lobes. In C. W. M. Whitty & O. L. Zangwill (Eds.), *Amnesia.* London: Butterworth.

Milstead, M., Lapsley, D., & Hale, C. (1993, March). *A new look at imaginary audience and personal fable.* Paper presented at the meeting of the Society for Research in Child Development, New Orleans, LA.

Mindell, J. A. (1993). Sleep disorders in children. *Health Psychology, 12,* 151–162.

Mineka, S. (1991, August). Paper presented to the annual meeting of the American Psychological Association, San Francisco. Cited in Turkington, C. (1991). Evolutionary memories may have phobia role. *APA Monitor, 22*(11), 14.

Mischel, W., & Shoda, Y. (1995). A cognitive-affective system theory of personality. *Psychological Review, 102,* 246–268.

Moliterno, D. J., et al. (1994). Coronary-artery vasoconstriction induced by cocaine, cigarette smoking, or both. *New England Journal of Medicine, 330,* 454–459.

Money, J. (1987). Sin, sickness, or status? Homosexual gender identity and psychoneuroendocrinology. *American Psychologist, 42,* 384–399.

Montemayor, R., & Flannery, D. J. (1991). Parent-adolescent relations in middle and late adolescence. In R. M. Lerner, A. C. Petersen, & J. Brooks-Gunn (Eds.), *Encyclopedia of adolescence.* New York: Garland.

Moore, R. Y. (1995). Vision without sight. *New England Journal of Medicine, 332,* 54–55.

Morales, E. (1992). Latino gays and Latina lesbians. In S. Dworkin & F. Gutierrez (Eds.), *Counseling gay men and lesbians.* Alexandria, VA: American Association for Counseling and Development.

More research needed on medical use of marijuana. (1997). *APA Monitor, 28*(4), 9.

Morris, W. N., Miller, R. S., & Spangenberg, S. (1977). The effects of dissenter position and task difficulty on conformity and response conflict. *Journal of Personality, 45,* 251–256.

Morrison, E. S., et al. (1980). *Growing up sexual.* New York: Van Nostrand Reinhold.

Moruzzi, G., & Magoun, H. W. (1949). Brain stem reticular formation and activation of the EEG. *Electroencephalography and Clinical Neurophysiology, 1,* 455–473.

Moser, C. G., & Dyck, D. G. (1989). Type A behavior, uncontrollability, and the activation of hostile self-schema responding. *Journal of Research in Personality, 23,* 248–267.

Moyers, B. (1993). *Healing and the mind.* New York: Doubleday.

Mullen, B., et al. (1987). Newscasters' facial expressions and voting behavior of viewers. *Journal of Personality and Social Psychology, 53.*

Murray, B. (1997). America still lags behind in mathematics test scores. *APA Monitor, 28*(1), 44.

Murray, H. A. (1938). *Explorations in personality.* New York: Oxford University Press.

Muslim Women Bridging Culture Gap. (1993, November 8). *The New York Times,* p. B9.

Myers, L. B., & Brewin, C. R. (1994). Recall of early experience and the repressive coping style. *Journal of Abnormal Psychology, 103,* 288–292.

Nadol, J. B., Jr. (1993). Hearing loss. *New England Journal of Medicine, 329,* 1092–1102.

National Center for Health Statistics (1996, March). News Releases and Fact Sheets. *Monitoring Health Care in America: Quarterly Fact Sheet.*

National Highway Traffic Safety Administration. (1998). Cited in Brody, J. E. (1998, March 31). Facing up to the realities of sleep deprivation. *The New York Times,* p. F7.

National Sleep Foundation. (1998). Cited in Brody, J. E. (1998, March 31). Facing up to the realities of sleep deprivation. *The New York Times,* p. F7.

National Sleep Foundation. (1999). Cited in Hellmich, N. (1999, March 23). Boomers' lifestyles lead to insomnia. *USA Today.*

Neisser, U. (1997). Cited in Sleek, S. (1997). Can "emotional intelligence" be taught in today's schools? *APA Monitor, 28*(6), 25.

Neisser, U., Boodoo, G., Bouchard, T. J., Jr., Boykin, A. W., Brody, N., Ceci, S. J., Halpern, D. F., Loehlin, J.

C., Perloff, R., Sternberg, R. J., & Urbina, S. (1996). Intelligence: Knowns and unknowns. *American Psychologist, 51,* 77–101.

Nelson, K. (1973). Structure and strategy in learning to talk. *Monographs for the Society for Research in Child Development, 38* (Whole No. 149).

Nelson, K., Hampson, J., & Shaw, L. K. (1993). Nouns in early lexicons: Evidence, explanations, and implications. *Journal of Child Language, 20,* 228.

Newman, J., & McCauley, C. (1977). Eye contact with strangers in city, suburb, and small town. *Environment and Behavior, 9,* 547–558.

Newport, E. L. (1994). Cited in Senior, J. (1994, January 3). Language of the deaf evolves to reflect new sensibilities. *The New York Times,* pp. A1, A12.

Newport, E. L. (1998). Cited in Azar, B. (1998). Acquiring sign language may be more innate than learned. *APA Monitor, 29*(4), 12.

Nides, M. A., et al. (1995). Predictors of initial smoking cessation and relapse through the first 2 years of the lung health study. *Journal of Consulting and Clinical Psychology, 63,* 60–69.

NIMH (National Institute of Mental Health). (1982). *Television and behavior: Ten years of scientific progress and implications for the eighties.* Washington, DC: NIMH.

Nolen-Hoeksema, S., Morrow, J., & Fredrickson, B. L. (1993). Response styles and the duration of depressed mood. *Journal of Abnormal Psychology, 102,* 20–28.

Norris, F. H., & Kaniasty, K. (1994). Psychological distress following criminal victimization in the general population: Cross-sectional, longitudinal, and prospective analyses. *Journal of Consulting and Clinical Psychology, 62,* 111–123.

Norvell, N., & Belles, D. (1993). Psychological and physical benefits of circuit weight training in law enforcement personnel. *Journal of Consulting and Clinical Psychology, 61,* 520–527.

Novick, L. R., & Coté, N. (1992). The nature of expertise in anagram solution. In *Proceedings of the Fourteenth Annual Conference of the Cognitive Science Society.* Hillsdale, NJ: Erlbaum.

O'Brien, C. P. (1996). Recent developments in the pharmacotherapy of substance abuse. *Journal of Consulting and Clinical Psychology, 64,* 677–686.

O'Leary, A. (1990). Stress, emotion, and human immune function. *Psychological Bulletin, 108,* 363–382.

ODEER (Office of Demographic, Employment, and Educational Research). (1994). *Summary report on doctorate recipients from United States universities.* Washington, DC: American Psychological Association.

Okazaki, S. (1997). Sources of ethnic differences between Asian American and White American college students on measures of depression and social anxiety. *Journal of Abnormal Psychology, 106,* 52–60.

Olds, J. (1969). The central nervous system and the reinforcement of behavior. *American Psychologist, 24,* 114–132.

Olds, J., & Milner, P. (1954). Positive reinforcement produced by electrical stimulation of the septal area and other regions of the rat brain. *Journal of Comparative and Physiological Psychology, 47,* 419–427.

Olson, S. L., Bates, J. E., & Bayles, K. (1990). Early antecedents of childhood impulsivity: The role of parent–child interaction, cognitive competence, and temperament. *Journal of Abnormal Child Psychology, 18,* 317–334.

Olson, S. L., Bates, J. E., & Kaskie, B. (1992). Caregiver-infant interaction antecedents of children's school-age cognitive ability. *Merrill-Palmer Quarterly, 38,* 309–330.

Olweus, D. (1986). Aggression and hormones: Behavioral relationship with testosterone and adrenaline. In D. Olweus, J. Block, & M. Rade-Yarrows (Eds.), *Development of antisocial and prosocial behavior* (pp. 51–72). New York: Academic Press.

Ortega, D. F., & Pipal, J. E. (1984). Challenge seeking and the Type A coronary-prone behavior pattern. *Journal of Personality and Social Psychology, 46,* 1328–1334.

Ouimette, P. C., Finney, J. W., & Moos, R. H. (1997). Twelve-step and cognitive-behavioral treatment for substance abuse. *Journal of Consulting and Clinical Psychology, 65,* 230–240.

Paffenbarger, R. S., Jr., et al. (1986). Physical activity, all-cause mortality, and longevity of college alumni. *New England Journal of Medicine, 314,* 605–613.

Paffenbarger, R. S., Jr., et al. (1993). The association of changes in physical-activity level and other lifestyle characteristics with mortality among men. *New England Journal of Medicine, 328,* 538–545.

Pagan, G., & Aiello, J. R. (1982). Development of personal space among Puerto Ricans. *Journal of Nonverbal Behavior, 7,* 59–68.

Paikoff, R. L., & Collins, A. C. (1991). Editor's notes: Shared views in the family during adolescence. In R. L. Paikoff & A. C. Collins (Eds.), *New Directions for Child Development* (Vol. 51). San Francisco: Jossey-Bass.

Pajares, F., & Miller, M. D. (1994). Role of self-efficacy and self-concept beliefs in mathematical problem solving. *Journal of Educational Psychology, 86,* 193–203.

Palmer, F. H. (1976). The effects of minimal early intervention on subsequent IQ scores and reading achievement. Report to the Education Commission of the States, contract 13-76-06846, State University of New York at Stony Brook.

Papini, D. R., & Roggman, L. A. (1992). Adolescent perceived attachment to parents in relation to competence, depression, and anxiety. *Journal of Early Adolescence, 12,* 420–440.

Pappas, G., Queen, S., Hadden, W., & Fisher, G. (1993). The increasing disparity of mortality between socioeconomic groups in the United States, 1960 and 1986. *New England Journal of Medicine, 329,* 103–109.

Parker, J. G., & Herrera, C. (1996). Interpersonal processes in friendship: A comparison of abused and nonabused children's experience. *Developmental Psychology, 32,* 1025–1038.

Patterson, G. R. (1993). Orderly change in a stable world: The antisocial trait as a chimera. *Journal of Consulting and Clinical Psychology, 61,* 911–919.

Patterson, S. J., Sochting, I., & Marcia, J. E. (1992). The inner space and beyond: Women and identity. In G. R. Adama, T. P. Gullotta, & R. Montemayor (Eds.), *Adolescent identity formation.* Newbury Park, CA: Sage.

Pavlov, I. (1927). *Conditioned reflexes.* London: Oxford University Press.

Pedersen, N. L., Plomin, R., McClearn, G. E., & Friberg, L. (1988). Neuroticism, extraversion, and related traits in adult twins reared apart and reared together. *Journal of Personality and Social Psychology, 55,* 950–957.

Penfield, W. (1969). Consciousness, memory, and man's conditioned reflexes. In K. H. Pribram (Ed.), *On the biology of learning.* New York: Harcourt Brace Jovanovich.

Penn, N. E., Kar, S., Kramer, J., Skinner, J., & Zambrana, R. E. (1995). Panel VI. Ethnic minorities, health care systems, and behavior. *Health Psychology, 14,* 641–648.

Penton-Voak, I. S., et al. (1999, June). Menstrual cycle alters face preference. *Nature, 399,* 741–742.

Perls, F. (1969). *Gestalt therapy verbatim.* Lafayette, CA: Real People Press.

Perrett, D. I. (1994). *Nature.* Cited in Brody, J. E. (1994, March 21). Notions of beauty transcend culture, new study suggests. *The New York Times,* p. A14.

Perry, D. G., & Bussey, K. (1979). The social learning theory of sex differences. *Journal of Personality and Social Psychology, 37,* 1699–1712.

Peterson, E. D., et al. (1997). Racial variation in the use of coronary-revascularization procedures. *New England Journal of Medicine, 336,* 480–486.

Peterson, L. R., & Peterson, M. J. (1959). Short-term retention of individual verbal items. *Journal of Experimental Psychology, 58,* 193–198.

Petraitis, J., Flay, B. R., & Miller, T. Q. (1995). Reviewing theories of adolescent substance use. *Psychological Bulletin, 1995,* 67–86.

Petty, R. E., Cacioppo, J. T., Strathman, A. J., & Priester, J. R. (1994). To think or not to think: Exploring two routes to persuasion. In S. Shavitt & T. C. Brock (Eds.), *Persuasion* (pp. 113–147). Boston: Allyn & Bacon.

Phinney, J. S. (1996). When we talk about American ethnic groups, what do we mean? *American Psychologist, 51,* 918–927.

Phinney, J. S., Chavira, V., & Williamson, L. (1992). Acculturation attitudes and self-esteem among high school and college students. *Youth and Society, 23*(3), 299–312.

Phinney, J. S., & Rosenthal, D. A. (1992). Ethnic identity in adolescence: Process, context, and outcome. In G. R. Adams, T. P. Gullotta, & R. Montemayor (Eds.), *Adolescent identity formation.* Newbury Park, CA: Sage.

Piaget, J. (1963). *The origins of intelligence in children.* New York: W. W. Norton.

Piaget. J. (1997). *The moral judgment of the child.* New York: Free Press Paperbacks.

Pihl, R. O., Peterson, J. B., & Finn, P. (1990). Inherited predisposition to alcoholism. *Journal of Abnormal Psychology, 99,* 291–301.

Pilkonis, P. (1996). Cited in Goleman, D. J. (1996, May 1). Higher suicide risk for perfectionists. *The New York Times,* p. C12.

Pillard, R. C. (1990). The Kinsey Scale: Is it familial? In D. P. McWhirter, S. A. Sanders, & J. M. Reinisch

(Eds.), *Homosexuality/heterosexuality: Concepts of sexual orientation* (pp. 88–100). New York: Oxford University Press.

Pillard, R. C., & Weinrich, J. D. (1986). Evidence of familial nature of male homosexuality. *Archives of Sexual Behavior, 43,* 808–812.

Pinker, S. (1990). Language acquisition. In D. N. Osherson & H. Lasnik (Eds.), *An invitation to cognitive science: Language* (Vol. 1). Cambridge, MA: The MIT Press, a Bradford Book.

Pinker, S. (1994). *The language instinct.* New York: William Morrow.

Pinpointing chess moves in the brain. (1994, May 24). *The New York Times,* p. C14.

Pion, G. M., Mednick, M. T., Astin, H. S., Hall, C. C. I., Kenkel, M. B., Keita, G. P., Kohout, J. L., & Kelleher, J. C. (1996). The shifting gender composition of psychology. *American Psychologist, 51,* 509–528.

Plomin, R., DeFries, J. C., McClearn, G., & Rutter, M. (1997). *Behavioral genetics* (3rd ed.). New York: Freeman.

Plous, S. (1996). Attitudes toward the use of animals in psychological research and education. *American Psychologist, 51,* 1167–1180.

Plutchik, R. (1984). A general psychoevolutionary theory. In K. Scherer & P. Ekman (Eds.), *Approaches to emotion.* Hillsdale, NJ: Erlbaum.

Pomerleau, O. F., Collins, A. C., Shiffman, S., & Pomerleau, C. S. (1993). Why some people smoke and others do not. *Journal of Consulting and Clinical Psychology, 61,* 723–731.

Pope, K. S. (1996). Memory, abuse, and science: Questioning claims about the false memory syndrome epidemic. *American Psychologist, 51,* 957–974.

Porter, R. H., Makin, J. W., Davis, L. B., & Christensen, K. M. (1992). Breast-fed infants respond to olfactory cues from their own mother and unfamiliar lactating females. *Infant Behavior and Development, 15,* 85–93.

Posner, M. I., & Raichle, M. E. (1994). *Images of mind.* New York: W. H. Freeman.

Poussaint, A. (1990, September). An honest look at Black gays and lesbians. *Ebony,* pp. 124, 126, 130–131.

Powch, I. G., & Houston, B. K. (1996). Hostility, anger-in, and cardiovascular reactivity in White women. *Health Psychology, 15,* 200–208.

Powell, E. (1996). *Sex on your terms.* Boston: Allyn & Bacon.

Prochaska, J. O., & Norcross, J. C. (1999). *Systems of psychotherapy* (4th ed.). Pacific Grove, CA: Brooks/Cole.

Pulley, B. (1998, June 16). Those seductive snake eyes: Tales of growing up gambling. *The New York Times,* A1, A28.

Putallaz, M., & Heflin, A. H. (1990). Parent-child interaction. In S. R. Asher & J. D. Coie (Eds.), *Peer rejection in childhood.* New York: Cambridge University Press.

Putnam, F. W., Guroff, J. J., Silberman, E. K., Barban, L., & Post, R. M. (1986). The clinical phenomenology of multiple personality disorder. *Journal of Clinical Psychiatry, 47,* 285–293.

Quattrone, G. A. (1982). Overattribution and unit formation. *Journal of Personality and Social Psychology, 42,* 593–607.

Quinn, S. (1987). *A mind of her own: The life of Karen Horney.* New York: Summit Books.

Rabasca, L. (1999). More research is needed on violence and reproduction. *APA Monitor, 30*(8), 26.

Raichle, M. E. (1994). Visualizing the mind. *Scientific American, 270*(4), 58–64.

Rakowski, W. (1995). Cited in Margoshes, P. (1995). For many, old age is the prime of life. *APA Monitor, 26*(5), 36–37.

Rapoport, K., & Burkhart, B. R. (1984). Personality and attitudinal characteristics of sexually coercive college males. *Journal of Abnormal Psychology, 93,* 216–221.

Rappaport, N. B., McAnulty, D. P., & Brantley, P. J. (1988). Exploration of the Type A behavior pattern in chronic headache sufferers. *Journal of Consulting and Clinical Psychology, 56,* 621–623.

Rathus, S. A., & Nevid, J. S. (1999). *Adjustment and growth: The challenges of life* (7th ed.). Fort Worth: Harcourt Brace.

Rathus, S. A., Nevid, J. S., & Fichner-Rathus, L. (2000). *Human sexuality in a world of diversity* (4th ed.). Boston: Allyn & Bacon.

Reid, P. T. (1994). The real problem in the study of culture. *American Psychologist, 49,* 524–525.

Reid, T. R. (1990, December 24). Snug in their beds for Christmas Eve: In Japan, December 24th has become the hottest night of the year. *The Washington Post.*

Reinke, B. J., Holmes, D. S., & Harris, R. L. (1985). The timing of psychosocial changes in women's lives. *Journal of Personality and Social Psychology, 48,* 1353–1364.

Reis, H. T., et al. (1990). What is smiling is beautiful and good. *European Journal of Social Psychology, 20,* 259–267.

Reiser, M. (1992). *Memory and mind and brain.* New York: Basic Books.

Renninger, K. A., & Wozniak, R. H. (1985). Effect of interest on attentional shift, recognition, and recall in young children. *Developmental Psychology, 21,* 624–632.

Rescorla, R. A. (1967). Pavlovian conditioning and its proper control procedures. *Psychological Review, 74,* 71–80.

Rescorla, R. A. (1988). Pavlovian conditioning: It's not what you think it is. *American Psychologist, 43,* 151–160.

Resnick, H. S., Kilpatrick, D. G., Dansky, B. S., Saunders, B. E., & Best, C. L. (1993). Prevalence of civilian trauma and posttraumatic stress disorder in a representative national sample of women. *Journal of Consulting and Clinical Psychology, 61,* 984–991.

Resnick, M., et al. (1992, March 24). *Journal of the American Medical Association.* Cited in Young Indians prone to suicide, study finds. (1992, March 25). *The New York Times,* p. D24.

Rest, J. R. (1983). Morality. In P. H. Mussen, J. Flavell, & E. Markman (Eds.), *Handbook of child psychology: Vol. 3. Cognitive development.* New York: Wiley.

Rice, M. E., Quinsey, V. L., & Harris, G. T. (1991). Sexual recidivism among child molesters released from a maximum security psychiatric institution. *Journal of Consulting and Clinical Psychology, 59,* 381–386.

Rich, C. L., Ricketts, J. E., Thaler, R. C., & Young, D. (1988). Some differences between men and women who commit suicide. *American Journal of Psychiatry, 145,* 718–722.

Richardson, D. C., Bernstein, S., & Taylor, S. P. (1979). The effect of situational contingencies on female retaliative behavior. *Journal of Personality and Social Psychology, 37,* 2044–2048.

Richardson, P. H., & Vincent, C. A. (1986). Acupuncture for the treatment of pain. *Pain, 24,* 15–40.

Richman, J. (1993). *Preventing elderly suicide.* New York: Springer.

Riggio, R. E., & Woll, S. B. (1984). The role of nonverbal cues and physical attractiveness in the selection of dating partners. *Journal of Social and Personal Relationships, 1,* 347–357.

Rinn, W. E. (1991). Neuropsychology of facial expression. In R. S. Feldman & B. Rime (Eds.), *Fundamentals of nonverbal behavior.* Cambridge, England: Cambridge University Press.

Robbins, C., & Ehri, L. C. (1994). Reading storybooks to kindergartners helps them learn new vocabulary words. *Journal of Educational Psychology, 86,* 54–64.

Robins, C. J., & Hayes, A. M. (1993). An appraisal of cognitive therapy. *Journal of Consulting and Clinical Psychology, 61,* 205–214.

Rodriguez, N., Ryan, S. W., Kemp, H. V., & Foy, D. W. (1997). Posttraumatic stress disorder in adult female survivors of childhood sexual abuse. *Journal of Consulting and Clinical Psychology, 65,* 53–59.

Rose, J. S., Chassin, L., Presson, C. C., & Sherman, S. J. (1996). Prospective predictors of quit attempts and smoking cessation in young adults. *Health Psychology, 15,* 261–268.

Rose, R. J. (1995). Genes and human behavior. *Annual Review of Psychology, 46,* 625–654.

Rosenbaum, M., Leibel, R. L., & Hirsch, J. (1997). Obesity. *New England Journal of Medicine, 337,* 396–407.

Rosenblatt, R. (1994, March 20). How do tobacco executives live with themselves? *The New York Times Magazine,* pp. 34–41, 55, 73–76.

Rosenthal, A. M. (1994, March 15). The way she died. *The New York Times,* p. A23.

Rosenthal, E. (1993, March 28). Patients in pain find relief, not addiction, in narcotics. *The New York Times,* pp. A1, A24.

Rothbart, M. K., & Ahadi, S. A. (1994). Temperament and the development of personality. *Journal of Abnormal Psychology, 103,* 55–66.

Rothbaum, B. O., Foa, E. B., Riggs, D. S., Murdock, T., & Walsh, W. (1992). A prospective examination of post-traumatic stress disorder in rape victims. *Journal of Traumatic Stress, 5,* 455–475.

Rotter, J. B. (1990). Internal versus external control of reinforcement. *American Psychologist, 45,* 489–493.

Rule, B. G., Taylor, B. R., & Dobbs, A. R. (1987). Priming effects of heat on aggressive thoughts. *Social Cognition, 5,* 131–143.

Rush, A. J., Khatami, M., & Beck, A. T. (1975). Cognitive and behavior therapy in chronic depression. *Behavior Therapy, 6,* 398–404.

Rüstemli, A. (1986). Male and female personal space needs and escape reactions under intrusion: A Turkish sample. *International Journal of Psychology.*

Rutkowski, G. K., Gruder, C. L., & Romer, D. (1983). Group cohesiveness, social norms, and bystander intervention. *Journal of Personality and Social Psychology, 44,* 545–552.

Rutter, M. (1997). Nature-nurture integration. *American Psychologist, 52,* 390–398.

Rychlak, J. F. (1997). *In defense of human consciousness.* Washington, DC: American Psychological Association.

Saarni, C. (1990). Emotional competence. In R. Thompson (Ed.), *Nebraska Symposium on Motivation: Vol. 36. Socioemotional development.* Lincoln: University of Nebraska Press.

Sadalla, E. K., Sheets, V., & McCreath, H. (1990). The cognition of urban tempo. *Environment and Behavior, 22,* 230–254.

Sadker, M., & Sadker, D. (1994). *How America's schools cheat girls.* New York: Scribners.

Sadowski, C., & Kelley, M. L. (1993). Social problem solving in suicidal adolescents. *Journal of Consulting and Clinical Psychology, 61,* 121–127.

Salgado de Snyder, V. N., Cervantes, R. C., & Padilla, A. M. (1990). Gender and ethnic differences in psychosocial stress and generalized distress among Hispanics. *Sex Roles, 22,* 441–453.

Sanders, G. S. (1984). Effects of context cues on eyewitness identification responses. *Journal of Applied Social Psychology, 14,* 386–397.

Sandman, C., & Crinella, F. (1995) Cited in Margoshes, P. (1995). For many, old age is the prime of life. *APA Monitor, 26*(5), 36–37.

Sanna, L. J., & Shotland, R. L. (1990). Valence of anticipated evaluation and social facilitation. *Journal of Experimental Social Psychology, 26,* 82–92.

Santee, R. T., & Maslach, C. (1982). To agree or not to agree: Personal dissent amid social pressure to conform. *Journal of Personality and Social Psychology, 42,* 690–700.

Sarbin, T. R., & Coe, W. C. (1972). *Hypnosis.* New York: Holt, Rinehart and Winston.

Sarter, M., Berntson, G. G., & Cacioppo, J. T. (1996). Brain imaging and cognitive neuroscience. *American Psychologist, 51,* 13–21.

Saxe, L. (1991). Lying. *American Psychologist, 46,* 409–415.

Saxe, L. (1998). Cited in Sleek, S. (1998). Psychologists debate merits of the polygraph. *APA Monitor, 29*(6).

Scarr, S., & Kidd, K. K. (1983). Developmental behavior genetics. In M. Haith & J. J. Campos (Eds.), *Handbook of child psychology.* New York: Wiley.

Scarr, S., & Weinberg, R. A. (1976). IQ test performance of Black children adopted by White families. *American Psychologist, 31,* 726–739.

Scarr, S., & Weinberg, R. A. (1977). Intellectual similarities within families of both adopted and biological children. *Intelligence, 1,* 170–191.

Scarr, S., & Weinberg, R. A. (1983). The Minnesota adoption studies: Genetic differences and malleability. *Child Development, 54,* 260–267.

Schachter, S. (1959). *The psychology of affiliation.* Stanford, CA: Stanford University Press.

Schachter, S., & Latané, B. (1964). Crime, cognition, and the autonomic nervous system. In D. Levine (Ed.), *Nebraska Symposium on Motivation.* Lincoln: University of Nebraska Press.

Schachter, S., & Singer, J. E. (1962). Cognitive, social, and physiological determinants of emotional state. *Psychological Review, 69,* 379–399.

Schaie, K. W. (1994). The course of adult intellectual development. *American Psychologist, 49,* 304–313.

Schmidt, N. B., Lerew, D. R., & Trakowski, J. H. (1997). Body vigilance in panic disorder. *Journal of Consulting and Clinical Psychology, 65,* 214–220.

Schneider, B. H., & Byrne, B. M. (1987). Individualizing social skills training for behavior-disordered children. *Journal of Consulting and Clinical Psychology, 55,* 444–445.

Schneider, W., & Bjorklund, D. (1992). Expertise, aptitude, and strategic remembering. *Child Development, 63,* 461–473.

Schotte, D. E., Cools, J., & Payvar, S. (1990). Problem-solving deficits in suicidal patients. *Journal of Consulting and Clinical Psychology, 58,* 562–564.

Schuckit, M. A. (1996). Recent developments in the pharmacotherapy of alcohol dependence. *Journal of Consulting and Clinical Psychology, 64,* 669–676.

Schulz, R., & Heckhausen, J. (1996). A life span model of successful aging. *American Psychologist, 51,* 702–714.

Schwartz, M. W., & Seeley, R. J. (1997). Neuroendocrine responses to starvation and weight loss. *New England Journal of Medicine, 336,* 1802–1811.

Schwartz, R. M., & Gottman, J. M. (1976). Toward a task analysis of assertive behavior. *Journal of Consulting and Clinical Psychology, 44,* 910–920.

Schwarz, N., Bless, H., & Bohner, G. (1991). Mood and persuasion. In M. Zanna (Ed.), *Advances in experimental social psychology* (Vol. 24). New York: Academic Press.

Scott, J. (1994, May 9). Multiple personality cases perplex legal system. *The New York Times,* pp. A1, B10, B11.

Scruggs, T. E., & Mastropieri, M. A. (1992). Remembering the forgotten art of memory. *American Educator, 16*(4), 31–37.

Seligman, M. E. P. (1996, August). Predicting and preventing depression. Master lecture presented to the meeting of the American Psychological Association, Toronto.

Selye, H. (1976). *The stress of life* (rev. ed.). New York: McGraw-Hill.

Selye, H. (1980). The stress concept today. In I. L. Kutash et al. (Eds.), *Handbook on stress and anxiety.* San Francisco: Jossey-Bass.

Seppa, N. (1997a). Sexual harassment in the military lingers on. *APA Monitor, 28*(5), 40–41.

Seppa, N. (1997b). Children's TV remains steeped in violence. *APA Monitor, 28*(6), 36.

Shadish, W. R., & Ragsdale, K. (1996). Random versus nonrandom assignment in controlled experiments. *Journal of Consulting and Clinical Psychology, 64,* 1290–1305.

Shadish, W. R., et al. (1997). Evidence that therapy works in clinically representative conditions. *Journal of Consulting and Clinical Psychology, 65,* 355–365.

Shalala, D. (1998). Cited in Meckler, L. (1998, June 26). Teen abortion, pregnancy rates fall. Associated Press; America Online.

Shaywitz, B. A., et al. (1995). Sex differences in the functional organization of the brain for language. *Nature, 373,* 607–609.

Shaywitz, S. E. (1998). Dyslexia. *New England Journal of Medicine,* 338, 307–312.

Sheehy, G. (1976). *Passages.* New York: Dutton.

Sheehy, G. (1995). *New passages: Mapping your life across time.* New York: Random House.

Sheehy, G. (1998a). *Menopause—The silent passage.* New York: Random House.

Sheehy, G. (1998b). *Understanding men's passages.* New York: Random House.

Shepherd, J., et al. (1995). Prevention of coronary heart disease with pravastatin in men with hypercholesterolemia. *New England Journal of Medicine, 333,* 1301–1307.

Shepperd, J. A. (1993). Productivity loss in performance groups. *Psychological Bulletin, 113,* 67–81.

Sher, K. J., Wood, M. D., Wood, P. K., & Raskin, G. (1996). Alcohol outcome expectancies and alcohol use. *Journal of Abnormal Psychology, 105,* 561–574.

Sherman, R. A. (1997). *Phantom pain.* New York: Plenum.

Shiffman, S., et al.. (1997). A day at a time: Predicting smoking lapse from daily urge. *Journal of Abnormal Psychology, 106,* 104–116.

Simons, A. D., Angell, K. L., Monroe, S. M., & Thase, M. E. (1993). Cognition and life stress in depression. *Journal of Abnormal Psychology, 102,* 584–591.

Simons, A. D., Gordon, J. S., Monroe, S. M., & Thase, M. E. (1995). Toward an integration of psychologic, social, and biologic factors in depression. *Journal of Consulting and Clinical Psychology, 63,* 369–377.

Simons, R. L., Whitbeck, L. B., Conger, R. D., & Chyi-In, W. (1991). Intergenerational transmission of harsh parenting. *Developmental Psychology, 27,* 159–171.

Simpson, M. L., Olejnik, S., Tam, A. Y., & Supattathum, S. (1994). Elaborative verbal rehearsals and college students' cognitive performance. *Journal of Educational Psychology, 86,* 267–278.

Simpson, M. L., & Perry, J. D. (1990). Crime and climate. *Environment and Behavior, 22,* 295–300.

Skinner, B. F. (1938). *The behavior of organisms: An experimental analysis.* New York: Appleton.

Skinner, B. F. (1948). *Walden two.* New York: Macmillan.

Skinner, B. F. (1983). Intellectual self-management in old age. *American Psychologist, 38,* 239–244.

Sleek, S. (1995). Group therapy. *APA Monitor, 26*(7), 1, 38–39.

Sleek, S. (1997). Resolution raises concerns about conversion therapy. *APA Monitor, 28*(10), 15.

Sleek, S. (1998). Psychologists debate merits of the polygraph. *APA Monitor, 29*(6).

Slobin, D. I. (1983). Crosslinguistic evidence for basic child grammar. Paper presented to the biennial meeting of the Society for Research in Child Development, Detroit.

Sloman, S. A. (1996). The empirical case for two systems of reasoning. *Psychological Bulletin, 119,* 3–22.

Smetana, J. G., Yau, J., Restrepo, A., & Braeges, J. L. (1991). Conflict and adaptation in adolescence. In M. E. Colten & S. Gore (Eds.), *Adolescent stress: Causes and consequences.* New York: Aldine deGruyter.

Smith, G. F., & Dorfman, D. (1975). The effect of stimulus uncertainty on the relationship between frequency of exposure and liking. *Journal of Personality and Social Psychology, 31,* 150–155.

Smith, M. L., & Glass, G. V. (1977). Meta-analysis of psychotherapy outcome studies. *American Psychologist, 32,* 752–760.

Smith, R. E., Smoll, F. L., & Ptacek, J. T. (1990). Conjunctive moderator variables in vulnerability and resiliency research. *Journal of Personality and Social Psychology, 58,* 360–370.

Smith, S. M., Glenberg, A. M., & Bjork, R. A. (1978). Environmental context and human memory. *Memory and Cognition, 6,* 342–355.

Snarey, J. R. (1985). Cross-cultural universality of social-moral development: A critical review of Kohlbergian research. *Psychological Bulletin 97,* 202–232.

Snyderman, M., & Rothman, S. (1987). Survey of expert opinion on intelligence and aptitude testing. *American Psychologist, 42,* 137–144.

Sorenson, S. B., & Rutter, C. M. (1991). Transgenerational patterns of suicide attempt. *Journal of Consulting and Clinical Psychology, 59,* 861–866.

Sperling, G. (1960). The information available in brief visual presentations. *Psychological Monographs, 74,* 1–29.

Sperry, R. W. (1993). The impact and promise of the cognitive revolution. *American Psychologist, 48,* 878–885.

Sporer, S. L. (1991). Deep—deeper—deepest? Encoding strategies and the recognition of human faces. *Journal of Experimental Psychology: Learning, Memory, and Cognition, 17,* 323–333.

Spreat, S., & Behar, D. (1994). Trends in the residential (inpatient) treatment of individuals with a dual diagnosis. *Journal of Consulting and Clinical Psychology, 61,* 43–48.

Sprecher, S., Sullivan, Q., & Hatfield, E. (1994). Mate selection preferences. *Journal of Personality and Social Psychology, 66*(6), 1074–1080.

Springer, S. P., & Deutsch, G. (1993) *Left brain, right brain* (4th ed.). New York: Freeman.

Squire, L. R. (1993). Memory and the hippocampus. *Psychological Review, 99,* 195–231.

Squire, L. R. (1996, August). Memory systems of the brain. Master lecture presented to the meeting of the American Psychological Association, Toronto.

Sroufe, A. (1998). Cited in Blakeslee, S. (1998, August 4). Re-evaluating significance of baby's bond with mother. *The New York Times,* pp. F1, F2.

Stacy, A. W., Bentler, P. M., & Flay, B. R. (1994). Attitudes and health behavior in diverse populations. *Health Psychology, 13,* 73–85.

Stacy, A. W., Newcomb, M. D., & Bentler, P. M. (1991). Cognitive motivation and drug use. *Journal of Abnormal Psychology, 100,* 502–515.

Stampfer, M. J., et al. (1991). A prospective study of cholesterol, apolipoproteins, and the risk of myocardial infarction. *New England Journal of Medicine, 325,* 373–381.

Staples, S. I. (1996). Human responses to environmental noise. *American Psychologist, 51,* 143–150.

Steele, C. M. (1996, August). The role of stereotypes in shaping intellectual identity. Master lecture presented to the meeting of the American Psychological Association, Toronto.

Steele, C. M. (1997). A threat in the air: How stereotypes shape intellectual identity and performance. *American Psychologist, 52,* 613–629.

Steele, C. M., & Aronson, J. (1995). Stereotype threat and the intellectual test performance of African Americans. *Journal of Personality and Social Psychology, 69,* 797–811.

Steele, C. M., & Josephs, R. A. (1990). Alcohol myopia. *American Psychologist, 45,* 921–933.

Steinberg, L. (1996). *Beyond the classroom.* New York: Simon & Schuster.

Steinberg, L., Brown, B. B., & Dornbusch, S. M. (1996). Ethnicity and adolescent achievement. *American Educator, 20*(2), 28–35.

Steinberg, L., Lamborn, S. D., Dornbusch, S. M., & Darling, N. (1992). Impact of parenting practices on adolescent achievement: Authoritative parenting, school involvement, and encouragement to succeed. *Child Development, 63,* 1266–1281.

Steinbrook, R. (1992). The polygraph test—A flawed diagnostic method. *New England Journal of Medicine, 327,* 122–123.

Sternberg, R. J. (1985). *Beyond IQ: A triarchic theory of human intelligence.* New York: Cambridge University Press.

Sternberg, R. J. (1997). The concept of intelligence and its role in lifelong learning and success. *American Psychologist, 52,* 1030–1037.

Sternberg, R. J., & Lubart, T. I. (1995). *Defying the crowd: Cultivating creativity in a culture of conformity.* New York: Free Press.

Sternberg, R. J., & Lubart, T. I. (1996). Investing in creativity. *American Psychologist, 51,* 677–688.

Sternberg, R. J., Wagner, R. K., Williams, W. M., & Horvath, J. A. (1995). Testing common sense. *American Psychologist, 50,* 912–927.

Sternberg, R. J., & Williams, W. M. (1997). Does the Graduate Record Examination predict meaningful success in the graduate training of psychologists? *American Psychologist, 52,* 630–641.

Stevenson, H. W., Lee, S. Y., & Stigler, J. W. (1986). Mathematics achievement of Chinese, Japanese, and American children. *Science, 231,* 693–699.

Stier, D. S., & Hall, J. A. (1984). Gender differences in touch. *Journal of Personality and Social Psychology, 47,* 440–459.

Stokols, D. (1992). Establishing and maintaining healthy environments. *American Psychologist, 47,* 6–22.

Strauss, M. A. (1995). Cited in Collins, C. (1995, May 11). Spanking is becoming the new don't. *The New York Times,* p. C8.

Strauss, M. A., & Smith, C. (1990). Family patterns and child abuse. In M. A. Straus & R. J. Gelles (Eds.), *Physical violence in American families.* New Brunswick, NJ: Transaction.

Strom, J. C., & Buck, R. W. (1979). Staring and participants' sex. *Personality and Social Psychology Bulletin, 5,* 114–117.

Strupp, H. H. (1996). The tripartite model and the *Consumer Reports* study. *American Psychologist, 51,* 1017–1024.

Study finds smaller pay gap for male and female doctors. (1996, April 11). *The New York Times,* p. B9.

Stunkard, A. J., Harris, J. R., Pedersen, N. L., & McLearn, G. E. (1990). A separated twin study of the body mass index. *New England Journal of Medicine, 322,* 1483–1487.

Stunkard, A. J., & Sørensen, T. I. A. (1993). Obesity and socioeconomic status—A complex relation. *New England Journal of Medicine, 329,* 1036–1037.

Sue, S. (1991). In J. D. Goodchilds (Ed.), *Psychological perspectives on human diversity in America.* Washington, DC: American Psychological Association.

Sue, S., & Okazaki, S. (1990). Asian-American educational achievements. *American Psychologist, 45,* 913–920.

Suls, J., Wan, C. K., & Costa, P. T., Jr. (1995). Relationship of trait anger to resting blood pressure. *Health Psychology, 14,* 444–456.

Susser, E. S., & Lin, S. P. (1992). Schizophrenia after prenatal exposure to the Dutch Hunger Winter of 1944–1945. *Archives of General Psychiatry, 49,* 983–988.

Sutker, P. B. (1994). Psychopathy: Traditional and clinical antisocial concepts. In D. C. Fowles, P. B. Sutker, & S. H. Goodman (Eds.), *Progress in experimental personality and psychopathology research* (pp. 73–120). New York: Springer.

Suzuki, L. A., & Valencia, R. R. (1997). Race-ethnicity and measured intelligence: Educational implications. *American Psychologist, 52,* 1103–1114.

Sweeney, P. D., & Gruber, K. L. (1984). Selective exposure. *Journal of Personality and Social Psychology, 46,* 1208–1221.

Szasz, T. S. (1984). *The therapeutic state.* Buffalo, NY: Prometheus.

Tailoring treatments for alcoholics is not the answer. (1997). *APA Monitor, 28*(2), 6–7.

Tang, A. (1999, September 21). Cocaine's grip on the blood and the brain. *The New York Times,* p. F8.

Tapes raise new doubts about "Sybil" personalities. (1998, August 19). *The New York Times* online.

Tavris, C. (1998, January 2). Call us unpredictable. *The New York Times,* p. A17.

Taylor, S. E. (1990). Health psychology: The science and the field. *American Psychologist, 45,* 40–50.

Teller, D. Y., & Lindsey, D. T. (1993). Motion nulling techniques and infant color vision. In C. E.

Granrud (Ed.), *Visual perception and cognition in infancy.* Hillsdale, NJ: Erlbaum.

Tharp, R. G. (1991). Cultural diversity and treatment of children. *Journal of Consulting and Clinical Psychology, 59,* 799–812.

Thase, M. E., & Kupfer, D. J. (1996). Recent developments in the pharmacotherapy of mood disorders. *Journal of Consulting and Clinical Psychology, 64,* 646–659.

Thompson, C. P., & Cowan, T. (1986). The neurobiology of learning and memory. *Science, 233,* 941–947.

Thompson, R. A. (1991a). Attachment theory and research. In M. Lewis (Ed.), *Child and adolescent psychiatry.* Baltimore: Williams & Wilkins.

Thompson, R. A. (1991b). Infant daycare. In J. V. Lerner & N. L. Galambos (Eds.), *Employed mothers and their children* (pp. 9–36). New York: Garland.

Thoresen, C., & Powell, L. H. (1992). Type A behavior pattern. *Journal of Consulting and Clinical Psychology, 60,* 595–604.

Thurstone, L. L. (1938). Primary mental abilities. *Psychometric Monographs, 1.*

Tolman, E. C., & Honzik, C. H. (1930). Introduction and removal of reward, and maze performance in rats. *University of California Publications in Psychology, 4,* 257–275.

Tomes, H. (1993). It's in the nation's interest to break abuse cycle. *APA Monitor, 24*(3), 28.

Torgersen, S. (1983). Genetic factors in anxiety disorders. *Archives of General Psychiatry, 40,* 1085–1089.

Triandis, H. C. (1990). Cross-cultural studies of individualism and collectivism. In J. J. Berman (Ed.), *Nebraska Symposium on Motivation, 1989. Cross-cultural perspectives.* Lincoln: University of Nebraska Press.

Triandis, H. C. (1995). *Individualism and collectivism.* Boulder, CO: Westview Press.

Triandis, H. C. (1996). The psychological measurement of cultural syndromes. *American Psychologist, 51,* 407–415.

Trickett, P. K., Aber, J. L., Carlson, V., & Cicchetti, D. (1991). Relationship of socioeconomic status to the etiology and developmental sequelae of physical child abuse. *Developmental Psychology, 27,* 148–158.

Trobst, K. K., Collins, R. L., & Embree, J. M. (1994). The role of emotion in social support provision. *Journal of Social and Personal Relationships, 11,* 45–62.

Trujillo, C. (Ed.) (1991). *Chicana lesbians: The girls our mothers warned us about.* Berkeley, CA: Third Woman Press.

Tsang, Y. C. (1938). Hunger motivation in gastrectomized rats. *Journal of Comparative Psychology, 26,* 1–17.

Tucker, J. S., Friedman, H. S., Wingard, D. L., & Schwartz, J. E. (1996). Marital history at midlife as a predictor of longevity. *Health Psychology, 15,* 94–101.

Tulving, E. (1985). How many memory systems are there? *American Psychologist, 40,* 385–398.

Tulving, E. (1991). Memory research is not a zero-sum game. *American Psychologist, 46,* 41–42.

Turner, A. M., & Greenough, W. T. (1985). Differential rearing effects on rat visual cortex synapses: I. Synaptic and neuronal density and synapses per neuron. *Brain Research, 329,* 195–203.

Turner, S. M., Beidel, D. C., & Jacob, R. G. (1994). Social phobia: A comparison of behavior therapy and atenolol. *Journal of Consulting and Clinical Psychology, 62,* 350–358.

Tversky, A., & Kahneman, D. (1982). Judgment under uncertainty. In D. Kahneman, P. Slovic, & A. Tversky (Eds.), *Judgment under uncertainty: Heuristics and biases.* New York: Cambridge University Press.

Uchino, B. N., Cacioppo, J. T., & Kiecolt-Glaser, J. K. (1996). The relationship between social support and physiological processes. *Psychological Bulletin, 119,* 488–531.

Ukestad, L. K., & Wittrock, D. A. (1996). Pain perception and coping in female tension headache sufferers and headache-free controls. *Health Psychology, 15,* 65–68.

United States Bureau of the Census (1998). *Statistical abstract of the United States* (118th ed.). Washington, DC: U.S. Government Printing Office.

United States Congress (1983, November). *Scientific validity of polygraph testing* (OTA-TM-H-15). Washington, DC: Office of Technology Assessment.

Vaillant, G. E. (1994). Ego mechanisms of defense and personality psychopathology. *Journal of Abnormal Psychology, 103,* 44–50.

Valenstein, E. S. (1986). *Great and desperate cures.* New York: Basic Books.

Valian, V. (1998). *Why so slow? The advancement of women*. Cambridge, MA: MIT Press.

Van Brunt, L. (1994, March 27). About men: Whites without money. *The New York Times Magazine*, p. 38.

Vandell, D. L., & Corasaniti, M. A. (1990). Child care and the family. In K. McCartney (Ed.), *New Directions for Child Development* (Vol. 49, pp. 23–37). San Francisco: Jossey-Bass.

Vandenbergh, J. G. (1993). Cited in Angier, N. (1993, August 24). Female gerbil born with males is found to be begetter of sons. *The New York Times*, p. C4.

Venables, P. H. (1996). Schizotypy and maternal exposure to influenza and to cold temperature. *Journal of Abnormal Psychology, 105*, 53–60.

Vernberg, E. M., La Greca, A. M., Silverman, W. K., & Prinstein, M. J. (1996). Prediction of posttraumatic stress symptoms in children after Hurricane Andrew. *Journal of Abnormal Psychology, 105*, 237–248.

Visintainer, M. A., Volpicelli, J. R., & Seligman, M. E. P. (1982). Tumor rejection in rats after inescapable or escapable shock. *Science, 216*(23), 437–439.

Von Békésy, G. (1957, August). The ear. *Scientific American*, pp. 66–78.

Voyer, D., Voyer, S., & Bryden, M. P. (1995). Magnitude of sex differences in spatial abilities. *Psychological Bulletin, 117*, 250–270.

Wachtel, P. L. (1994). Cyclical processes in personality and psychopathology. *Journal of Abnormal Psychology, 103*, 51–54.

Wadden, T. A., et al. (1997). Exercise in the treatment of obesity. *Journal of Consulting and Clinical Psychology, 65*, 269–277.

Wade, N. (1998, January 6). Was Freud Wrong? Are Dreams the Brain's Start-Up Test? *The New York Times*.

Wagner, R. K. (1997). Intelligence, training, and employment. (1997). *American Psychologist, 52*, 1059–1069.

Walk, R. D., & Gibson, E. J. (1961). A comparative and analytical study of visual depth perception. *Psychological Monographs, 75*(15).

Watkins, C. E., Jr., Campbell, V. L., Nieberding, R., & Hallmark, R. (1995). Contemporary practice of psychological assessment by clinical psychologists. *Professional Psychology: Research and Practice, 26*, 54–60.

Watson, J. B. (1913). Psychology as the behaviorist views it. *Psychological Review, 20*, 158–177.

Watson, J. B. (1924). *Behaviorism*. New York: Norton.

Watson, J. B., & Rayner, R. (1920). Conditioned emotional reactions. *Journal of Experimental Psychology, 3*, 1–14.

Weaver, T. L., & Clum, G. A. (1995). Psychological distress associated with interpersonal violence. *Clinical Psychology Review, 15*, 115–140.

Webb, W. (1993). Cited in Adler, T. (1993). Sleep loss impairs attention—and more. *APA Monitor, 24*(9), 22–23.

Weber, R., & Crocker, J. (1983). Cognitive processes in the revision of stereotypic beliefs. *Journal of Personality and Social Psychology, 45*, 961–977.

Wechsler, D. (1975). Intelligence defined and undefined. *American Psychologist, 30*, 135–139.

Weekes, J. R., Lynn, S. J., Green, J. P., & Brentar, J. T. (1992). Pseudomemory in hypnotized and task-motivated subjects. *Journal of Abnormal Psychology, 101*, 356–360.

Weinberg, R. A., Scarr, S., & Waldman, I. D. (1992). The Minnesota Transracial Adoption Study: A follow-up of IQ test performance at adolescence. *Intelligence, 16*, 117–135.

Weiner, B. (1991). Metaphors in motivation and attribution. *American Psychologist, 46*, 921–930.

Weiner, K. (1992). Cited in Goleman, D. J. (1992, January 8). Heart seizure or panic attack? *The New York Times*, p. C12.

Weisz, J. R., Sweeney, L., Proffitt, V., & Carr, T. (1993). Control-related beliefs and self-reported depressive symptoms in late childhood. *Journal of Abnormal Psychology, 102*, 411–418.

Welch, K. M. A. (1993). Drug therapy of migraine. *New England Journal of Medicine, 329*, 1476–1483.

Wells, G. L. (1993). What do we know about eyewitness identification? *American Psychologist, 48*, 553–571.

Wentzel, K. R. (1994). Relations of social goal pursuit to social acceptance, classroom behavior, and perceived social support. *Journal of Educational Psychology, 86*, 173–182.

Werner, C. M., Brown, B. B., & Damron, G. (1981). Territorial marking in a game arcade. *Journal of Personality and Social Psychology, 41*, 1094–1104.

Westerman, M. A. (1990). Coordination of maternal directives with preschoolers' behavior in compliance-problem and healthy dyads. *Developmental Psychology, 26,* 621–630.

Wetzler, S. E., & Sweeney, J. A. (1986). Childhood amnesia. In D. C. Rubin (Ed.), *Autobiographical memory.* New York: Cambridge University Press.

Wheeler, M. A., Stuss, D. T., & Tulving, E. (1997). Toward a theory of episodic memory: The frontal lobes and autonoetic consciousness. *Psychological Bulletin, 121,* 331–354.

Whisman, M. A., Miller, I. W., Norman, W. H., & Keitner, G. I. (1991). Cognitive therapy with depressed inpatients. *Journal of Consulting and Clinical Psychology, 59,* 282–288.

White, J. L., & Nicassio, P. M. (1990, November). The relationship between daily stress, pre-sleep arousal and sleep disturbance in good and poor sleepers. Paper presented at the annual meeting of the Association for the Advancement of Behavior Therapy, San Francisco.

Whitehead, W. E. (1994). Assessing the effects of stress on physical symptoms. *Health Psychology, 13,* 99–102.

Whorf, B. (1956). *Language, thought, and reality.* New York: Wiley.

Widiger, T. A., & Costa, P. T., Jr. (1994). Personality and personality disorders. *Journal of Abnormal Psychology, 103,* 78–91.

Widiger, T. A., et al. (1996). DSM-IV antisocial personality disorder field trial. *Journal of Abnormal Psychology, 105,* 3–16.

Wiens, A. N., & Menustik, C. E. (1983). Treatment outcome and patient characteristics in an aversion therapy program for alcoholism. *American Psychologist, 38,* 1089–1096.

Wilcox, V. L., Kasl, S. V., & Berkman, L. F. (1994). Social support and physical disability in older people after hospitalization. *Health Psychology, 13,* 170–179.

Wilder, D. A. (1990). Some determinants of the persuasive power of in-groups and out-groups. *Journal of Personality and Social Psychology, 59,* 1202–1213.

Williams, J. E., & Best, D. L. (1994). Cross-cultural views of women and men. In W. J. Lonner & R. Malpass (Eds.), *Psychology and culture.* Boston: Allyn & Bacon.

Williams, L. (1992, February 6). Woman's image in a mirror: Who defines what she sees? *The New York Times,* pp. A1, B7.

Williamson, D. A., Cubic, B. A., & Gleaves, D. H. (1993). Equivalence of body image disturbances in anorexia and bulimia nervosa. *Journal of Abnormal Psychology, 102,* 177–180.

Wills, T. A., McNamara, G., Vaccaro, D., & Hirky, A. E. (1996). Escalated substance abuse. *Journal of Abnormal Psychology, 195,* 166–180.

Wilson, G. T., & Fairburn, C. G. (1993). Cognitive treatments for eating disorders. *Journal of Consulting and Clinical Psychology, 61,* 261–269.

Wilson, R. S. (1983). The Louisville twin study: Developmental synchronies in behavior. *Child Development, 54,* 298–316.

Winkleby, M., Fortmann, S., & Barrett, D. (1991). Social class disparities in risk factors for disease. *Preventive Medicine, 19,* 1–12.

Witelson, S. F., Kigar, D. L., & Harvey, T. (1999). The exceptional brain of Albert Einstein. *Lancet, 353,* 2149–2153.

Woloshyn, V. E., Paivio, A., & Pressley, M. (1994). Use of elaborative interrogation to help students acquire information consistent with prior knowledge and information inconsistent with prior knowledge. *Journal of Educational Psychology, 86,* 79–89.

Wolpe, J. (1990). *The practice of behavior therapy* (4th ed.). New York: Pergamon.

Wolpe, J., & Lazarus, A. A. (1966). *Behavior therapy techniques.* New York: Pergamon Press.

Wolpe, J., & Plaud, J. J. (1997). Pavlov's contributions to behavior therapy: The obvious and the not so obvious. *American Psychologist, 52,* 966–972.

Wood, J. M., & Bootzin, R. R. (1990). The prevalence of nightmares and their independence from anxiety. *Journal of Abnormal Psychology, 99,* 64–68.

Wood, J. M., Bootzin, R. R., Rosenhan, D., Nolen-Hoeksema, S., & Jourden, F. (1992). Effects of the 1989 San Francisco earthquake on frequency and content of nightmares. *Journal of Abnormal Psychology, 101,* 219–224.

Worchel, S., & Brown, E. H. (1984). The role of plausibility in influencing environmental attributions. *Journal of Experimental Social Psychology, 20,* 86–96.

Wu, C., & Shaffer, C. R. (1987). Susceptibility to persuasive appeals as a function of source credibility and prior experience with the attitude object. *Journal of Personality and Social Psychology, 52,* 677–688.

Young, T. K., & Sevenhuysen, G. (1989). Obesity in Northern Canadian Indians: Patterns, determinants, and consequences. *American Journal of Clinical Nutrition, 49,* 786–793.

Youngblade, L. M., & Belsky, J. (1992). Parent-child antecedents of 5-year-olds' close friendships: A longitudinal analysis. *Developmental Psychology, 28,* 700–713.

Zahn-Waxler, C., & Kochanska, G. (1990). The origins of guilt. In R. A. Thompson (Ed.), *Nebraska Symposium on Motivation: Vol. 38. Socioemotional development.* Lincoln: University of Nebraska Press.

Zajonc, R. B. (1968). Attitudinal effects of mere exposure. *Journal of Personality and Social Psychology, Monograph Supplement 2(9),* 1–27.

Zajonc, R. B. (1980). Compresence. In P. Paulus (Ed.), *The psychology of group influence.* Hillsdale, NJ: Erlbaum.

Zane, N., & Sue, S. (1991). Culturally responsive mental health services for Asian Americans. In H. F. Myers et al. (Eds.), *Ethnic minority perspectives on clinical training and services in psychology* (pp. 49–58). Washington, DC: American Psychological Association.

Zheng, C., Heintz, H., & Hatten, M. E. (1996). CNS gene encoding astrotacin. Which supports neural migration along glial fibers. *Science, 272,* 417–421.

Zigler, E. (1995, August). Modernizing early childhood intervention to better serve children and families in poverty. Master Lecture delivered to the meeting of the American Psychological Association, New York.

Zimbardo, P. G., LaBerge, S., & Butler, L. D. (1993). Psychophysiological consequences of unexplained arousal. *Journal of Abnormal Psychology, 102,* 466–473.

Zinbarg, R. E., & Barlow, D. H. (1996). Structure of anxiety and anxiety disorders. *Journal of Abnormal Psychology, 105,* 181–193.

Ziv, T. A., & Lo, B. (1995). Denial of care to illegal immigrants. *New England Journal of Medicine, 332,* 1095–1098.

Zuckerman, M. (1992). What is a basic factor and which factors are basic? Tumbles all the way down. *Personality and Individual Differences, 13,* 675–681.

Zuger, A. (1997, August 19). Removing half of brain improves young epileptics' lives. *The New York Times,* p. C4.